HUMAN
PROBLEM SOLVING

HUMAN
PROBLEM SOLVING

ALLEN NEWELL
University Professor
Carnegie-Mellon University

HERBERT A. SIMON
Professor of Computer Science and Psychology
Carnegie-Mellon University

PRENTICE-HALL, INC., Englewood Cliffs, New Jersey

13–445403–0

Library of Congress Catalog Card Number: 79–15252

Printed in the United States of America

Current printing (last digit):
10 9 8 7 6 5 4 3

PRENTICE-HALL INTERNATIONAL, INC., *London*
PRENTICE-HALL OF AUSTRALIA, PTY. LTD., *Sydney*
PRENTICE-HALL OF CANADA, LTD., *Toronto*
PRENTICE-HALL OF INDIA PRIVATE LIMITED, *New Delhi*
PRENTICE-HALL OF JAPAN, INC., *Tokyo*

TO CLIFF

*. . . who helped us
start all this*

PREFACE

The problem solving that went into this volume on human problem solving extends over a seventeen-year period—the actual writing of it over more than a decade: one of us claims to remember a portion of a draft dated 1956 and both remember a draft dated 1959. Since our aims and intentions for the book are spelled out in the introduction and we do not think that we should further delay giving the reader the results of our deliberations, we will limit this preface to acknowledgments.

An alarming number of debts to colleagues can be incurred during seventeen years. Our more general intellectual obligations are sketched in the historical addendum with which the book closes, but we should like to mention by name some of those with whom we have worked most closely, and from whom we have borrowed most specifically, in the preparation of this volume.

There is first of all Cliff Shaw who, as the dedication states, "helped us start all this." He participated as a full member of the triumvirate from the beginning of the project, in 1955, until about 1959, when his own interests and activities gradually took him off in other directions. His grasp of the basic principles of information processing was profound and original, providing indispensable ingredients for our approach.

For the most part the others who participated directly in the work reported in this book were our doctoral students: David Bree, Andrew Chenzoff, and Peter Houts, who collected most of the logic and cryptarithmetic protocols; Arnold Winikoff, who carried out the eye-movement studies; George Baylor, who programmed MATER II and gathered several chess protocols; and Michael Barenfeld, who did much of the programming for the chess perception system reported in Chapter 13.

But there are many others—students and faculty colleagues—whose contributions were less direct, but certainly not less appreciated. We have worked in close association on related projects with Lee Gregg and Walter Reitman, and more recently with William Chase and Donald Waterman. We have enjoyed continuing communication and interchange of ideas with Adriaan de Groot of the University of Amsterdam. We have learned much from our doctoral students working on topics in psychology and artificial intelligence outside the area of problem solving: Geoffrey Clarkson, Stephen Coles, Donald Dansereau, George Ernst, Edward Feigenbaum, Julian Feldman, Kenneth Laughery, Robert Lindsay, James Moore, Laurent Siklóssy, Frederick Tonge, Donald Williams, Thomas Williams, and Richard Young.

Several organizations and agencies have provided generous financial support for our research. During the first years of work, the largest part of the support came from the RAND Corporation, on whose computers, JOHNNIAC and its successors, most of the simulation was then done. At Carnegie-Mellon University we had initially been granted a substantial research allowance from the Carnegie Corporation. Since the middle sixties, the principal support has come from the National Institute of Mental Health (Project MH-07722), and from the Advanced Research Projects Agency of the Office of the Secretary of Defense (F44620-67-C-0058). We are grateful to all of these organizations for the confidence they have placed in us, and the broad terms upon which they have offered their support. Throughout the period of our investigations, we have been in the ideal but embarrassing position for researchers: the rate at which we could progress has been determined by the rate of generating research ideas, rather than by limits on the magnitude of the financial resources available to us.

Most of the empirical data analyzed in detail here comes from our own laboratory. However, in Chapter 7, we have made some use of protocols published by Professor F. C. Bartlett in his book, *Thinking*; and in Chapter 13, some of Adriaan de Groot's chess protocols. In Chapters 9 and 10, we present analyses of data provided to us by O. K. Moore and Scarvia Anderson, gathered in the course of problem-solving studies carried out at Yale University. Our debt to them is acknowledged more specifically in the chapters themselves.

We would be embarrassed to count up the number of drafts that have passed through the typewriters and editorial hands of our secretaries, Evelyn Adams and Mildred Sisko. They have been most patient and helpful through this whole long process. Finally, we want to thank the members of the editorial and production staffs of Prentice-Hall, who showed great skill in interpreting our intentions—some of them all too implicitly indicated in our manuscript.

Some portions of our data and analysis have been published previously, but most of this work has been extensively revised for the present volume. The last half of Chapter 4 is based on Newell, Shaw, and Simon, 1957; Chapter 6 on Newell, 1967c and 1968b; Chapter 8, with much revision, on Newell, Shaw, and Simon, 1960a; parts of Chapter 9 on Newell and Simon, 1961a; Chapter 11 on Newell, Shaw, and Simon, 1958c—again with much modification; Chapter 12 on Newell and Simon, 1965b; and parts of Chapter 13 on Baylor, 1965, Baylor and Simon, 1966, and Simon and Barenfeld, 1969.

CONTENTS

5

THE THEORY 785

14

THE THEORY
OF
HUMAN PROBLEM SOLVING

HUMAN
PROBLEM SOLVING

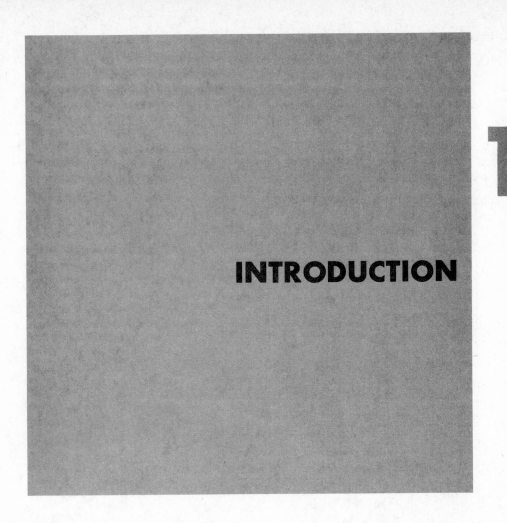

INTRODUCTION

The aim of this book is to advance our understanding of how humans think. It seeks to do so by putting forth a theory of human problem solving, along with a body of empirical evidence that permits assessment of the theory.

No single work advances understanding very far. The aims of a scientific work are limited by the formal character of the theory, by the phenomena it encompasses, by the experimental situations it uses, by the types of subjects it studies, and by the data it gathers. Of course, a theory may speak beyond its initial base—all scientists hope for just that. But science is a series of successive approximations. Not all things can be done at once, and even if one aspires to go far, he must start somewhere. If one aims at covering all of human thinking in a single work, the work will necessarily be superficial. If one aims at probing in depth, then many aspects of the subject, however important, will be left untouched.

THE SCOPE OF THE BOOK

Our first task, then, is to indicate the scope of this work—what it includes and what it deliberately excludes. The boundaries need not be carefully marked; but the central focus should be made clear.

Figure 1.1 attempts to compress in one diagram many of the dimensions

FIGURE 1.1

dimensions of variation of the human system

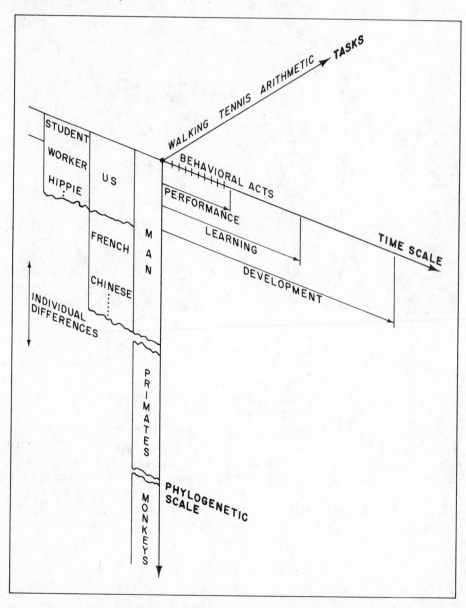

along which the total human system can vary. Its purpose is to demark the particular portions included in the present work, not to provide a new or total view. The focus of the diagram is the individual human being. He is a system consisting of parts: sensory subsystems, memory, effectors, arousal subsystems, and so on. It makes little difference for immediate purposes that we are unsure just what is the most appropriate way to enumerate the subsystems. We can limit study— and we will—to one or a few parts.

Task Dimension.   A human behaves in a number of different classes of situations, which we will come to call *task environments*. In the figure, we have represented these in a single dimension, but clearly a whole geography is intended: a human does mathematics, he walks, he interacts with his fellow man, he drives cars, he makes love, he argues, he buys food, he dies.

Performance-Learning-Development Dimension.   Holding the task environment constant, we usually distinguish a human who is *performing* a task from one who is *learning* to perform a task, or one who is *developing* with respect to a task. Within the first group, those who are performing, we can focus on successively smaller acts, so that we need not even be concerned with an entire performance. It is not important that the distinctions are imperfect. (For example, it is often impossible to distinguish with confidence between learning and maturation.) The distinctions among these three kinds of activities are to some extent correlated with time scale, and we have so depicted them.

Individual-Difference Dimension.   A single man may be viewed as a member of various *populations*. Each man differs—both in systematic ways and simply by virtue of his unique genetic endowment and historical fate—from all other men. Differences dependent on age are strongly related to development and are indicated along the temporal axis. But cultures also differ, and within a culture various demographic variables, such as socioeconomic status, isolate distinct populations. More broadly, of course, Man is only one among innumerable species, and so the vertical axis extends to other organisms.

The Book's Focus

From the many directions of variation expressed or implied in Figure 1.1 limited regions can be carved out for attention: the development of intelligence as a function of organismic level (in the evolutionary sense); the learning of personal roles in social groups of college students; and so on. Each region provides a starting point for investigation and description; each leaves out most of the human phenomena.

The present study is concerned with the performance of intelligent adults in our own culture. The tasks discussed are short (half-hour), moderately difficult problems of a symbolic nature. The three main tasks we use—chess, symbolic logic, and algebra-like puzzles (called cryptarithmetic puzzles)—typify this class of problems. The study is concerned with the integrated activities that constitute problem solving. It is not centrally concerned with perception, motor skill, or what are called personality variables. The study is concerned primarily with performance, only a little with learning, and not at all with development or differences related to age. Finally, it is concerned with integrated activities, hence deemphasizes the details of processing on the time scale of elementary reactions (that is, half a second or less). Similarly, long-term integrated activities extending over periods of days or years receive no attention.

These restrictions on the scope of our study delineate a central focus, not a set of boundaries. Thus, the possibility that learning is taking place cannot be excluded in complex tasks that last tens of minutes. Likewise, it is an empirical question, not a matter of definition or fiat, to what extent perceptual mechanisms are important in problem solving—although limiting our investigation to symbolic tasks helps to restrict the importance of perception. Again, how the basic mechanisms of immediate memory and immediate processing affect integrated behavior at the next higher level is an open question. One recent author on cognitive processes (Neisser, 1967) has taken the description of the immediate processing mechanisms as the important first task, devoting only a last chapter of his book to the integrated level of behavior that is central to this volume.

Information Processing Theory

The reasons for our choices are various and largely opportunistic (although with an opportunism that has lasted twenty years and thus may constitute philosophic conviction). For several decades psychology, responding to different opportunities and convictions, focused on learning, lower organisms, and tasks that are simple from an adult human viewpoint. Within the last dozen years a general change in scientific outlook has occurred, consonant with the point of view represented here. One can date the change roughly from 1956: in psychology, by the appearance of Bruner, Goodnow, and Austin's *Study of Thinking* and George Miller's "The magical number seven"; in linguistics, by Noam Chomsky's "Three models of language"; and in computer science, by our own paper on the Logic Theory Machine.

As these titles show, the common new emphasis was not the investigation of problem solving, but rather the exploration of complex processes and the acceptance of the need to be explicit about internal, symbolic mechanisms. Nor do all four of these works stem from a specific common lineage, unless it be the whole of applied mathematics and technology: control theory, information theory, operational mathematics including game theory and decision theory, computers and programming. These topics emerged in World War II and ramified through the late forties and early fifties in many directions, the new approach to the study of man being only one.

We ourselves, through the forties and early fifties, were largely concerned with human organizational behavior and were influenced strongly by the growing technologies just mentioned. But the specific opportunity that has set the course of the present work is the development of a science of information processing (now generally termed computer science). Thus, this study is concerned with thinking—or that subspecies of it called problem solving—but it approaches the subject in a definite way. It asserts specifically that thinking can be explained by means of an information processing theory. This assertion requires some explanation.

The present theory views a human as a processor of information. Both of these notions—*information* and *processing*—are long-established, highly general concepts. Thus, the label could be thought vacuous unless the phrase *information processing* took on additional technical meaning.

One may try to provide this meaning by saying that a computer is an instance of an information processor. This would suggest that the phrase is a metaphor: that man is to be modeled as a digital computer. Metaphors have their own good place in science, though there is neither terminology nor metatheory of science to explicate the roles of metaphors, analogs, models, theories and descriptions, or the passage from one category to another (Simon and Newell, 1956). Something ceases to be metaphor when detailed calculations can be made from it; it remains metaphor when it is rich in features in its own right, whose relevance to the object of comparison is problematic. Thus a computer can indeed be a metaphor for man; then it becomes relevant to discover whether man is all bits on the inside.

But an alternative to metaphor is at hand. An abstract concept of an information processing system has emerged with the development of the digital computer. In fact, a whole array of different abstract concepts has developed, as scientists have sought to capture the essence of the new technology in different ways (Minsky, 1967). The various features that make the digital computer seem machinelike—its fast arithmetic, its simply ordered memory, its construction by means of binary elements—all have faded in the search for the essential. Thus, in this book we will introduce a suitable abstract information processing system to describe how man processes task-oriented symbolic information. This is not the most abstract possible way to describe an information processing system, but it is tailored to our scientific needs.

An information processing theory is not restricted to stating generalities about Man. With a model of an information processing system, it becomes meaningful to try to represent in some detail a particular man at work on a particular task. Such a representation is no metaphor, but a precise symbolic model on the basis of which pertinent specific aspects of the man's problem solving behavior can be calculated. This model of symbol manipulation remains very much an approximation, of course, hypothesizing in an extreme form the neatness of discrete symbols and a small set of elementary processes, each with precisely defined and limited behavior. This abstraction, though possibly severe, does provide a grip on symbolic behavior that was not available heretofore. It does, equally, steer away from physiological models, with their concern for fidelity to continuous physiological mechanisms, either electrical, chemical, or hormonal. Perhaps the nonphysiological nature of the theory is not as disadvantageous as one might first believe, for the collection of mechanisms that are at present somewhat understood in neuropsychology is not at all adequate to the tasks dealt with in this book. We could not have proceeded to construct theories of human behavior in these tasks had we restricted ourselves to mechanisms that can today be provided with physiological bases.

The Choice of Scope

We have brought out the general grounding of our work in computer science to explain the limitation of our aims—asserting that this limitation is really an opportunity, since information processing systems provide our first precise notion of what symbols and symbol manipulation could mean. However, once we have chosen to study symbolic systems in a technical and precise way, many alternative paths still remain open along both the task dimension and the performance-learning-development dimension. Something needs to be said of our choices here.

Relation to Artificial Intelligence.   The most important influence upon our choice of tasks such as chess and symbolic logic is the development of the field of artificial intelligence. This is the part of computer science devoted to getting computers (or other devices) to perform tasks requiring intelligence. As will become clear, a theory of the psychology of problem solving requires not only good task analyses but also an inventory of possible problem solving mechanisms from which one can surmise what actual mechanisms are being used by humans. Thus, one must work with task environments in which artificial intelligence has provided the requisite array of plausible mechanisms. The task areas represented in this book satisfy these conditions: game players, theorem provers, and puzzle solvers constitute a large fraction of the existing artificial intelligence systems. Many other task areas that are attractive on other grounds have not yet been studied extensively from the standpoint of artificial intelligence, hence are less useful for our purposes than those mentioned above.

On two counts the previous paragraph is insufficient to explain our choice of tasks. First, it assumes that artificial intelligence moves independently of psychology. This is demonstrably not the case. Much of the work in artificial intelligence started from psychological concerns. Second, and more important, the explanation simply raises the new question of why artificial intelligence research should take up the types of tasks represented in this book and not others.

A partial answer is that many other tasks have in fact been worked on. Language processing is an example. But while there has been a great deal of work in linguistics, almost all of it has focused on grammatical analysis (*competence*), rather than on the use of language (*performance*). Programs dealing with semantics and pragmatics are fewer, more recent, and somewhat less developed than the problem solving programs represented here. Thus, we will have little to say about language processing behavior as such. However, we shall see that our theory of problem solving has strong implications for what the linguist calls the deep structure of language.

Pattern recognition is another area in which there has been much work, both theoretical and empirical, even more extensive than the body of work upon which we draw. We make little use of this research here, because sequential, integrated behavior is at the heart of most thinking, while most artificial intelligence pattern recognition machines are built around the single act of recognition. While many of the schemes do involve some sequential processing, none of them is adequate for modeling general sequential behavior.

There are many kinds of thinking that one might like to study: designing a house, discovering a new scientific law, preparing a law case, arguing over political parties, creating new music, daydreaming while watching the clouds, preparing a five-year economic plan, and so on. Detailed theories of these and many other kinds of thinking are largely beyond the current state of the art. Of course, there have been investigations into some of these areas, many of them still in midstream. Only their incomplete state and our limits of space and energy have inhibited us from including some of them in this work, since they are in fact part of the same story we wish to tell.

Emphasis on Performance. Turning to the performance-learning-development dimension, our emphasis on performance again represents a scientific bet. We recognize that what sort of information processing system a human becomes depends intimately on the way he develops. The kernel from which development starts—say, the neonate—already contains a genetically determined set of mechanisms of immense complexity. How complex they are is easily appreciated by anyone who follows the acts of self organization that take place in the embryo as it progresses to the neonatal starting position. Still, by common scientific assent, the emerging system is remarkably content-free, and without the powers of integrated action shown by the normal adult. Many constraints on the nature of the fully developed system arise from the requirement of self organization—help from the external environment (say via language) can only be used after the system has developed itself to a point where it is capable of such assimilation. Yet, acknowledging this, it still seems to us that we have too imperfect a view of the system's final nature to be able to make predictions from the development process to the characteristics of the structures it produces.

Similar remarks apply to learning. Humans learn continuously, and much that they do involves using in obvious ways information gathered for a specific purpose, rather than solving difficult problems like those studied in this book. One enters a department store: "Where do I find men's suits?" "Third floor, down the center aisle and to your right"; "Thank you"; and off one goes, following directions. Several phenomena here are closely allied to the interests of this book: language production and reception; deciding to ask for information to solve a problem; following directions, once assimilated; perhaps (if the directions were imperfect) solving some smallish subproblems along the way. Certainly this is the behavior of an information processing system. But the task in this case is carefully contrived to permit simple learning to substitute for most of the work of problem solving.

Learning is a second-order effect. That is, it transforms a system capable of certain performances into a system capable of additional ones (usually better ones; usually accomplished without losing much of the preexisting performance capability; and usually integrated with existing capability so they can be evoked on appropriate occasions). The study of learning, if carried out with theoretical precision, must start with a model of a performing organism, so that one can represent, as learning, the changes in the model.[1] The mathematization of learning theory in the last decade shows this very well (Atkinson, Bower, and Crothers, 1965). In the prototype version of mathematical learning theories, the organism is represented by a set of probabilities of occurrence of a fixed set of responses; learning involves changes in these probabilities under the impact of experience.

The study of learning takes its cue, then, from the nature of the performance system. If performance is not well understood, it is somewhat premature to study learning. Nevertheless, we pay a price for the omission of learning, for we might otherwise draw inferences about the performance system from the fact that the system must be capable of modification through learning. It is our judgment that in the present state of the art, the study of performance must be given precedence, even if the strategy is not costless. Both learning and development must then be incorporated in integral ways in the more complete and successful theory of human information processing that will emerge at a later stage in the development of our science.

Other Omissions.   The omission of both sensory and motor skills, and many aspects of perception, from our study is perhaps plausible on the surface: we are concerned with central symbolic activities. Nevertheless, at least one scientist, Bartlett, in *Thinking* (1958), made motor skills the key metaphor for attempting to understand thinking. And a whole school, the Gestaltists, have used perception as the touchstone of central activity (Wertheimer, 1945). On the perceptual side, a basis for our choice has already been indicated: our concern with sequential behavior. However, as even this book will reveal, the boundary between perceptual and symbolic behavior may not be maintainable for long, especially if work pushes in the direction of better models of the immediate processor.

On the motor side the situation is peculiar. Bartlett chose to compare thinking with motor skills precisely because he felt sequential behavior was central both in thinking and in motor skills, where it had been studied intensively. Our own feeling is that, while there has been much experimental investigation, motor skills have not yet found a mechanistic representation having anything like the power of the information processing representation exploited here. Furthermore, motor skills seem in considerable part to be nonsymbolic—and that makes them a poor model for a system where symbols are central.

Our final choice is to exclude motivational and personality variables—what Abelson (1963) covered in part by the term "hot cognition." We omit them by reason of convictions, not about the importance or unimportance of the phenomena, but about the order in which theory should develop. Many motivational and emotional phenomena operate through the lens of the cognitive system, as the work of Schachter and Singer (1962) and others has indicated. A plausible scientific strategy is to put our cognitive models in order before moving to these other phenomena. Our one exploratory foray in the direction of motivation and emotion was precisely in this vein (Simon, 1967a).

---

[1] For empirical purposes, of course, one can always get by for a while by talking in the language of experimental protocols—simply describing the changed behavior in the experimental situation.

With this general explication of the scope of this study, we can now turn to a brief overview of the type of theory we will be presenting and the types of problems that are central to it.

THE SHAPE OF THE THEORY

The theory proclaims man to be an information processing system, at least when he is solving problems. What that means, and how it can be brought to terms with the real world, are questions to consider in extenso. However, the theory has a certain gross shape that can be characterized briefly. We say of Newtonian mechanics that it is axiomatic and deductive; of classical astronomy, that it is empirical, but not experimental; of biochemistry, that it consists in part of a large catalog of mechanisms; of intelligence testing, that it deals with the human as a static collection of traits or factors; of a part of sociology, that it deals with humans as ideal types. Such statements do not convey the content of a theory, nor how successful it is; they give an overall framework within which the pieces of the theory fit as it is assembled sequentially. The statements also suggest, sometimes, what issues will be important—what problems the theory will have to contend with repeatedly. Let us try now to provide such a picture of the shape of the present theory.

A Process Theory

The theory posits a set of processes or mechanisms that produce the behavior of the thinking human. Thus, the theory is reductionistic; it does not simply provide a set of relations or laws about behavior from which one can often conclude what behavior must be. (The elementary processes and their organization, of course, are not explained: reduction is always relative.) Thus, the theory purports to explain behavior—and not just to describe it, however parsimoniously (Newell, 1969a). (We are aware that some would dispute such a distinction, viewing all causal explanations as simply descriptions.)

The processes posited by the theory presumably exist in the central nervous system; they are internal to the organism. Nothing in *our* theory says they are in the central nervous system, but massive physiological evidence indicates that is clearly where they belong. We do not speculate on the physiological correspondences of mechanisms presented in this book. Because of the gap that still exists between physiological and behavioral science, nothing would be served by such speculation. There do not yet exist plausible physiological localizations (even in mechanism, much less in physical space) for immediate memory, the symbol (that is, the engram), or the act of adding two plus two. Without these, nothing much of physiological interest can be said about the material in this book. Furthermore, the search for such physiological mechanisms needs no motivation from the present theory (John, 1967).

As far as the great debates about the empty organism, behaviorism, intervening variables, and hypothetical constructs are concerned, we take these simply as a phase in the historical development of psychology. Our theory posits internal mechanisms of great extent and complexity, and endeavors to make contact between them and the visible evidences of problem solving. That is all there is to it.

A Theory of the Individual

The technical apparatus for conceptualizing information processing systems leads first of all to constructing particular programs that accomplish particular tasks. When applied to psychology, this procedure leads naturally to constructing information processing systems that model the behavior of a single individual in a single task situation. Full particularity is the rule, not the exception. Thus, it becomes a problem to get back from this particularity to theories that describe a class of humans, or to processes and mechanisms that are general to all humans.

This situation is just the reverse of the one faced in earlier psychological theorizing. Indeed, a terminological line is usually drawn just to distinguish clinical efforts that deal with the individual in all his uniqueness (*idiographic*) from efforts of experimental psychology to deal with an individual only as an intersection of statistically defined populations (*nomothetic*).

The reversal of the usual emphasis gives the present theory a quite distinct flavor. Thus, individual differences is not a topic that is tacked on to the main body of our theory. On the contrary, we never use grouped data to test the theory if we can help it. The models describe individuals, so that the hard part is to say with precision what is common to all human information processors. With this approach it does not seem natural to assume that human behavior is fundamentally stochastic, its regularities showing up only with averaging (as in statistical learning theory); rather, Freud's dictum that all behavior is caused seems the natural one, and only reluctantly do we assign some aspects of behavior to probabilistic generators.

This aspect of the theory, highly visible against the contrasting background of experimental psychology, is really just a consequence of viewing the human as a complex mechanism (of whatever kind) whose parts and connections can ultimately be deciphered. This point of view is accepted in most of science outside psychology without question or comment.[2]

A Content-Oriented Theory

In 1955 McClelland wrote an article decrying psychology's abstraction from content. The opposition then was between content and process: by attempting only to describe basic universal processes used by humans (say, in learning), psychology was ignoring a major part of its domain.

The present theory is oriented strongly to content. This is dramatized in the peculiarity that the theory performs the tasks it explains. That is, a good informa-

---

[2] Cf. the relation of the general theory of geological processes to the specific hypothesis of continental drift, or to the character of the Moon's surface.

tion processing theory of a good human chess player can play good chess; a good theory of how humans create novels will create novels; a good theory of how children read will likewise read and understand. There is nothing mysterious in this. The theories explain behavior in a task by describing the manipulation of information down to a level where a simple interpreter (such as a digital computer) can turn the description into an effective process for performing the task. Not all versions of the theory are carried so far, of course. Nevertheless, in general, the theory can deal with the full content of a task.

The attention paid to content in information processing theories should not be contrasted with concern for process, which is how the matter appeared to Mc-Clelland. The contrast fails because it is of the nature of information processes to deal with content. It is almost tautological that one can talk of something as content only if processes exist that treat it as information—that is, discriminate on the basis of it.

Of course, there is no compelling evidence that the kinds of content that information processing theories demonstrably handle typify the entire range of content handled by humans. No information processing systems now exist that understand, say, a poem—that is, that can fully assimilate its content. Faith that this might be done goes well beyond the evidence presented in this book and elsewhere in the artificial intelligence literature. Each reader must make his own extrapolation of the evidence.

The importance of the orientation toward content is twofold. On the one hand, it removes a barrier toward extension of the theory. On the other hand, if content is a substantial determinant of human behavior—if in fact the message is a lot more message than medium—then information processing theories have opportunities for describing human behavior veridically that are foreclosed to theories unable to cope with content.

A Dynamically Oriented Theory

An information processing theory is dynamic, not in the sense in which that term is used in depth psychology, but in the sense of describing the change in a system through time. Such a theory describes the time course of behavior, characterizing each new act as a function of the immediately preceding state of the organism and of its environment.

The natural formalism of the theory is the program, which plays a role directly analogous to systems of differential equations in theories with continuous state spaces (for example, classical physics). In information processing systems the state is a collection of symbolic structures in a memory, rather than the set of values of position and momentum of a physical system in some coordinate system. Furthermore, a program generally specifies a discrete change in a single component of the state (that is, in just one symbol structure) at a moment in time, whereas a differential equation system specifies infinitesimal changes in all coordinates simultaneously. But these are details of the formalism, dictated by the underlying nature of the system under study.

All dynamic theories pose problems of similar sorts for the theorist. Fundamentally, he wants to infer the behavior of the system over long periods of time, given only the differential laws of motion. Several strategies of analysis are used, more or less, in the scientific work on dynamic theory. The most basic is taking a completely specific initial state and tracing out the time course of the system by applying iteratively the given laws that say what happens in the next instant of time. This is often, but not always, called simulation, and is one of the chief uses of computers throughout engineering and science. It is also a mainstay of the present work.

A second strategy is to solve the differential laws to yield an expression describing the state of the system at each point in time as a function of the initial state, represented symbolically. This is the classical act of integrating the laws of motion. It is only rarely successful for systems of any complexity—even for differential equation systems, where analytic techniques are most developed. It cannot be used as yet with theories like those in this book.

Complete detailed solutions are not always necessary (or even illuminating). The theorist of dynamic theories often spends his time trying to circumvent solving the system explicitly. One standard approach is to explore the steady state solutions of the system—the places where the laws of motion say that nothing changes. Another is to explore the asymptotic behavior—what happens in the long run. A more general tack is to prove that some property of the system is invariant over time—that it holds despite variation in other aspects of the system. In the systems of classical physics, conservation of energy, momentum, and angular momentum provide examples of such invariants.

All the above strategies show up in the study of information processing systems. Limitations on mathematical technique keep most of the analyses informal and heavily empirical,[3] but the underlying motivation is dictated by the basic dynamic character of the theory.

An Empirical, Not Experimental, Theory

There is no lack of orientation towards the data of human behavior in the theory presented in this book. Yet we employ little experimental design using control groups of the sort so familiar in psychology. Because of the strong history-dependence of the phenomena under study, the focus on the individual, and the fact that much goes on within a single problem solving encounter, experiments of the classical sort are only rarely useful. Instead, it becomes essential to get enough data about each individual subject to identify what information he has and how he is processing it. This method leads, in conjunction with the content orientation, to emphasizing the use of verbal behavior as data, because of its high output rate. Thus, the analysis of verbal protocols is a typical technique for verifying the theory, and in fact has become a sort of hallmark of the information processing approach. The nature of the theory leads also to a continuing search for new

---

[3] But see, for example, Ernst, 1969; King, 1969; Minsky and Papert, 1969; Pohl, 1969; and Robinson, 1965, for a few indications that formal analysis can be applied successfully to the kinds of IPS's considered in this book.

sources of data that can be conjoined to existing data to ease the problem of identification. The use of data on gross eye movements, briefly reported in Chapter 7, is a case in point.

A Nonstatistical Theory

It is difficult to test theories of dynamic, history-dependent systems. The saturation with content—with diverse meaningful symbolic structures—only makes matters worse. There is not even a well-behaved Euclidean space of numerical measurements in which to plot and compare human behavior with theory. Thus, this book makes very little use of the standard statistical apparatus. Theory and data are compared, and some attempts are made to measure and tabulate such comparisons. But our data analysis techniques resemble those of the biochemist or archaeologist more than those of the agricultural experimenter.

Sufficiency Analysis

The theory tends to put a high premium on discovering and describing systems of mechanisms that are *sufficient* to perform the cognitive task under study. Producing a system capable of performing provides a first approximation, taking into account, of course, gross limitations on the human's ability to process information—processing rate, immediate memory, and so on. If an information processing system meeting these constraints can be devised that does the task, one then attempts to develop a revised system that has higher fidelity to specific data on human processing.

The emphasis on sufficiency is still rather foreign to psychology. Almost never has it been asked of a psychological theory whether it could explain why man was capable of performing the behaviors in question. Concern with sufficiency arises, of course, not just in the present theory, but within the whole development of which this theory is a part. Thus, it is a current lively question in psycholinguistics whether the mechanisms of classical S-R learning theory are sufficient to account for the child's learning of language (it being concluded, not surprisingly, that they are not).

To take sufficiency as a first requirement of a theory is simply to adopt a particular approximating sequence in science's progress (a choice not without consequences, however). Since not all things can be done first, a particular theoretical orientation gets some of its flavor from what it puts first.

These characteristics of the theory, although neither systematically nor completely described, should help the reader assimilate the development of the theory through the book without being too surprised at the emergence of certain features and the (otherwise curious) absence of others. It remains to provide a plan of the book before beginning in earnest.

The book is divided into five parts. The first lays the technical groundwork for the remainder. Each of the subsequent three parts takes up a different task environment: first a type of puzzle called cryptarithmetic, then a form of elementary symbolic logic, and finally chess. The fifth and last part states the theory in comprehensive form.

Chapter 2, the first of the preparatory chapters, defines an information processing system (IPS). This is done in a somewhat axiomatic way in order to make clear what concepts are involved.

Chapter 3 considers the nature of the task environment and its role in a psychological theory. It takes up the major issue of whether a theory of problem solving (or thinking, or learning) is really a theory about human beings or a theory about the nature of the task environment. Of course, the total system always includes both environment and organism. But in a highly adaptive and intelligent organism the boundary becomes obscured. Most of the chapter is devoted to clarifying this question. A part of the chapter deals with more detailed questions of how task environments and problems are represented in information processing terms.

Chapter 4 discusses that species of information processing system that solves problems, especially problems stated in the representations introduced in Chapter 3. The notions of generate-and-test, of selective search, and of heuristics (devices that aid discovery) are introduced. We consider the assessment of task difficulty and introduce various tasks as concrete examples. A substantial fraction of the chapter is devoted to a detailed examination of the Logic Theorist (LT), a venerable program that was the first theorem-proving program. LT incorporates many of the lessons we wish to draw, and serves to consolidate the notions of the three chapters of Part I by providing a specific example of an information processing system operating in a task environment to solve problems.

Chapter 5 starts Part II, on cryptarithmetic, with an analysis of the task. It exhibits various representations of the task and analyzes the behavior of various problem solvers.

Chapter 6 provides the first analysis of human problem solving. A particular subject, S3, tackles a single cryptarithmetic problem, DONALD + GERALD = ROBERT. From a protocol of his verbal behavior we make an extensive analysis; then we describe a method for plotting his search behavior (the Problem Behavior Graph), and a way of representing his program as a production system (a kind of information processing system to be defined in Chapter 2). Since this is the first chapter that deals with protocol data, it contains a good deal of methodological discussion.

Chapter 7 continues the analysis of human behavior in the cryptarithmetic task. We examine the behavior of four other subjects, and to do so we introduce another tool of analysis: the episode. As a final piece of evidence for the theory, we study yet one more subject, for whom we have eye movement data as well as verbal data.

Chapters 8, 9, and 10, comprising Part III, deal with a particular task in elementary symbolic logic in the same manner as Part II dealt with cryptarithmetic. Chapter 8 discusses the task environment, including a program called the General Problem Solver (GPS) that has long figured in work on simulation. Chapter 9 discusses attempts at simulating with GPS two fragments of protocols. Chapter 10 moves back to a broader base, giving analyses of various subjects working on various logic tasks, and examining a number of aspects of their behavior.

Chapters 11, 12, and 13, comprising Part IV, deal with chess. As in the two previous empirical parts, the first chapter (11) provides a task analysis; the second chapter (12) concentrates on the empirical analysis of an individual protocol; and the third chapter (13) provides a broader view of human problem solving in chess.

Chapter 14 constitutes the whole of Part V. It attempts to state a theory of human problem solving that encompasses the phenomena that have emerged in the three separate task areas. Although the investigations in the book have been strictly limited to the areas of cryptarithmetic, logic, and chess, the theory has a more substantial scope.

We have made no attempt in the body of this book to provide the historical context for our work beyond references to research on which we have drawn directly. Instead we have recorded in an historical appendix our picture of the relation of the work reported here to the broader trend of events during this century in psychology and other relevant disciplines.

This, then, is the plan we shall follow: first, technical apparatus for analyzing problem solving behavior; next, application of the apparatus to three task environments and to empirical data of human problem solving behavior in each; finally, a comprehensive statement of the theory of human problem solving.

1

PRELIMINARIES

2

INFORMATION
PROCESSING SYSTEMS

This chapter undertakes two related tasks. First, it describes the organization and functions of an information processing system (IPS). Second, it introduces various notations that will be used throughout the book for describing the structure and behavior of IPS's.

Our theory of human thinking and problem solving postulates that the human operates as an information processing system. An important function of this chapter is to discuss the meaning of that postulate. The explication does not, of course, justify the postulate, but simply clarifies its meaning. Empirical verification is the task of later chapters.

In particular, we cannot reliably test the postulate by judging its intrinsic plausibility. Many people will find it highly implausible, others, quite plausible. The plausibility of a fundamental hypothesis about the world is almost always time-dependent. Hypotheses are seldom thought plausible when they are new and have not yet been widely accepted. If empirical evidence supports an hypothesis increasingly, and if the hypothesis succeeds in providing explanations for a significant range of phenomena, it becomes more and more plausible. If it survives empirical tests for several generations, it is likely to be regarded not merely as plausible but as self-evident.

Thus, there is little point in trying to judge directly whether a postulate is plausible. That judgment will be made more easily after the empirical evidence has been marshaled. In this chapter we shall be concerned only with explaining what is meant by saying that something operates as an information processing system.

Definition of an IPS

Figure 2.1 shows the general characteristics of an IPS. An IPS is a system consisting of a memory containing symbol structures, a processor, effectors, and receptors. As we indicated in the introduction, we are abstracting from the complications of sensory and motor processing; hence we will not treat these aspects in detail. With respect to the central aspects, we can lay down a number of inter-related definitions and postulates:

1. There is a set of elements, called *symbols*.
2. A *symbol structure* consists of a set of *tokens* (equivalently, *instances* or *occurrences*) of symbols connected by a set of *relations*.
3. A *memory* is a component of an IPS capable of storing and retaining symbol structures.
4. An *information process* is a process that has symbol structures for (some of) its inputs or outputs.
5. A *processor* is a component of an IPS consisting of:
   (a) a (fixed) set of *elementary information processes* (eip's);
   (b) a *short-term memory* (STM) that holds the input and output symbol structures of the eip's;
   (c) an *interpreter* that determines the sequence of eip's to be executed by the IPS as a function of the symbol structures in STM.

FIGURE 2.1

general structure of an information processing system

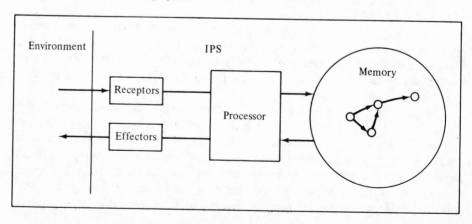

6. A symbol structure *designates* (equivalently, *references* or *points to*) an object if there exist information processes that admit the symbol structure as input and either:
   (a) affect the object; or
   (b) produce, as output, symbol structures that depend on the object.

7. A symbol structure is a *program* if (a) the object it designates is an information process and (b) the interpreter, if given the program, can execute the designated process. (Literally this should read, "if given an input that designates the program.")

8. A symbol is *primitive* if its designation (or its creation) is fixed by the elementary information processes or by the external environment of the IPS.

What Is an Object?

The indefinite term *object* is used in the definitions above to encompass at least three sorts of things:

1. symbol structures stored in one or another of the IPS's memories, which are often usefully classified into (a) data structures, and (b) programs (see item 7 in the list above);

2. processes that the IPS is capable of executing;

3. an external environment of sensible (readable) stimuli. *Reading* consists in creating in memory internal symbol structures that designate external stimuli; *writing* is the inverse operation of creating responses in the external environment that are designated by internal symbol structures.

The relation between a designating symbol and the object it points to can have any degree of directness or indirectness. Thus, a symbol structure can point to a program; but a symbol structure can also point to a symbol structure that points to a symbol structure that points to . . . a program. Because this book focuses on central processes, we will frequently be concerned with symbol structures that designate other structures in memory, and with structures that designate programs. We will be concerned less frequently with symbol structures that designate external stimuli or responses, for at the time we deal with them, stimuli and responses in the external environment will already be encoded internally—designated by symbol structures. Hence, we will almost always deal with these designations rather than with the external objects designated.

An Example of an IPS

Before we enter into a detailed discussion of these assumptions, a simple example may help make their meaning more concrete. Consider an IPS for sending and receiving Morse code. The system would have to be able to perceive the basic external stimuli of the Morse alphabet: short (dot) and long (dash) signals; short (letter space) and long (word space) intervals. These features of the external world would evoke, as their designating internal symbols, tokens of four primitive symbol types inside the STM (short-term memory). Sequences of the stimuli would need to be represented as symbol structures. These structures could be lists of the primitive tokens, composed with the relation *next*. Thus, one could have the symbol structure (–, –, –) for a sequence of three dashes, where we have used the sequential order on the page to represent a structure consisting of the token designating a dash next to another dash token next to another dash token. There would also be symbol types designating the letters of the Roman alphabet (the latter being external objects).

A program for reading would designate a process that, taking as its input a symbol structure designating an external stimulus location, would create in STM the symbol structure designating the stimulus at that location. Thus, if three dashes were at a given external location, the read process would store in STM the list (–, –, –). If the letter S were at that location, the process would store "S". A program for writing would designate the inverse process, producing in the environment the object designated by an internal structure—three dashes if the designator were (–, –, –), and S if the designator were "S".

Encoding and decoding processes could also exist that, when given a symbol token for "S", for example, would produce in STM the list (–, –, –), or vice versa. Other processes could combine lists (designating letters, say) into higher-order lists (designating words, say). Thus, the word "was" could be designated by the list (W, A, S), where each member of the list designates the appropriate symbol token— or, alternatively, the appropriate list of Morse code.

Among the elementary information processes would be one to find the member of a list that is next to a given member. Thus, given the symbol token "A" on the list (W, A, S), this process would find the symbol token "S". Another elementary process would test whether two symbol tokens are identical—whether, for example, the second symbol token of (W, A, S) is identical with or different from, the second symbol token of (H, A, S) (i.e., whether they are instances of the same symbol type). The elementary processes would be combined to effect larger processes. For example, the process for testing symbol identity could be combined with the process for finding the next symbol on a list to test whether two lists are identical, as shown in Figure 2.2 (for simplicity, we have not shown the added steps to find the first symbol token on the list).

To execute this composite process, the IPS could use an interpretive process. There would be a symbol structure—the program—that would designate the sequence of elementary processes to be executed, much as we have done in the figure. The interpreter would keep track of the current elementary process being executed, and after execution would find the next process to be executed.

Finally, additional information could be associated with the symbol structures. With the list (W, A, S) might be associated the descriptors: (part-of-speech: verb) and (tense: past), the two pairs constituting a description of the list, each pair consisting of an attribute followed by its value for that list. There would then be additional processes to obtain the descriptions, given the list.

Notice that our postulates for an IPS characterize the memory, elementary information processes, symbol structures, and interpretive process abstractly.

They make no assertions about how these structures and processes are realized, physically or biologically. That systems of this kind *can* be realized by a determinate mechanism is amply demonstrated by the existence and behavior of digital computers, which can be programmed to fit the postulates—hence to simulate the system we are defining. The fact that there are computer realizations of an IPS does not prove, of course, that humans are well modeled by such a system. That question must be considered later.[1]

FIGURE 2.2

process for finding whether two lists are identical

---

1. find next symbol-token in list-1,
    if fail go to 4;
2. find next symbol-token in list-2,
    if fail stop and report not identical;
3. test if symbol-token-1 = symbol-token-2,
    if false stop and report not identical,
    if true go to 1;
4. find next symbol-token in list-2,
    if find stop and report not identical,
    if fail stop and report identical.

SYMBOLS AND SYMBOL STRUCTURES

(Assumptions 1, 2, 6, and 8)

Symbol tokens are patterns that can be compared by the IPS and judged equal or different. A class of all tokens that are judged to be identical is called a *symbol type*. Thus, tokens of the same symbol type differ from each other only in being distinct occurrences or instances. The term *symbol* is used to refer to either the token or the type, context making clear which is meant.

Symbol structures are built up from symbol tokens and relations. There may be only a single relation, such as *next*, used in the prior example. With this relation, one can build sequences of symbols. There must also be information processes that can manipulate and access the symbols in such a structure, else the IPS would not be able to make use of the structure in any real way—i.e., would not "have" it. Alternatively, there may be several relations. For example, in writing normal

---

[1] At some level, biological realizations do exist, since a human can simulate anything a computer can, albeit somewhat slowly. However, the behavior of a human simulating a computer that is simulating a human solving a problem is observably different from the behavior of the human solving the problem, even if the behavior of the computer is not. Hence, the ability of the human to simulate the computer proves nothing about the adequacy of the computer's simulation of the human.

mathematical notation—e.g., $3x^2 + A_{i,j}$—one uses not only the relation *next*, but also *above* and *below*, to represent exponentiation and subscripting.

The importance of distinguishing symbol types from symbol tokens becomes obvious if we consider symbol structures such as (–, –, –), in which several tokens of the same type appear. The question, "How many symbols appear in (–, –, –)?" is ambiguous until one knows whether types or tokens are meant.

Designation

What makes symbols symbolic is their ability to *designate*—i.e., to have a referent. This means that an information process can take a symbol (more precisely, a symbol token) as input and gain access to the referenced object to affect it or be affected by it in some way—to read it, modify it, build a new structure with it, and so on. Actually, designation applies to symbol structures, not just symbols, although it is easier to think of it in terms of single symbols. If an information process takes as input the symbol structure (color, house) and produces the symbol white, then the symbol structure (color, house) designates white and hence, indirectly, designates the color of the house in question.

In discussing linguistic matters one normally takes as prototypic of designation the relation between a proper name and the object named—e.g., George Washington and a particular man who was once President of the United States. One then attempts to pass from that relation to others more difficult to envision: e.g., the relation between house and any of a certain class of sheltering structures; between running and any of certain activities, and on to truth, beauty, and justice. In our theory of information processing systems, the prototypic designatory relationship is between a symbol and a symbol structure. Thus, X2 is the name of (i.e., designates) the list (A, B, C); so that given a symbol token of X2 one can obtain access to the list—for example, obtain its first element, which is A. Given this designatory ability, almost all others follow, since symbol structures can be used to encode information about any conceivable thing (including an external object), hence can act as a surrogate for it. As we have seen, one essential use of designating is to reference elementary information processes by programs so that the processes can be executed.

In discussing the basic characteristics of symbols and symbol structures we always assume the existence of information processes that behave in certain ways. This is typical in definitions of abstract systems: each of the parts remains essentially undefined except when taken in conjunction with the other parts. In the discussion that follows, we will not always be explicit in postulating the underlying information processes, but the reader can supply the continuing qualification.

Many, if not most, of the concepts we have introduced apply to arbitrary information processes and not just to elementary information processes. For instance, designation applies to symbol structures and not just to symbols; the processes that interpret indirect designations need not be elementary processes, but can be built up out of other processes. Presently, we will see an example of this kind of composition in discussing recognition systems. Of course, there will usually be some elementary designatory processes, but they may be very simple (and in the limit can be absent altogether). We will not often use the circumlocution that is needed to emphasize that a given notion is applicable at all levels; this augment can be supplied by the reader. As examples of IPS's multiply throughout the book, the full generality of the concepts will become apparent.

Primitive Symbols

Some symbols have their meaning fixed by the existence of elementary information processes that treat them in fixed ways. The most important examples are:

1. Symbols that designate specific events or structures in the external environment of the IPS. Such symbols may be evoked within the IPS by the occurrence of the events or structures externally (the result of a receptor process), or they may cause the IPS to create such events or structures externally (the input to an effector process).
2. Symbols that designate elementary information processes, so that these eip's can be executed by means of these symbols.

What collection of symbols is primitive for a specific IPS will vary with the particular application. For example, to describe sensory and perceptual processes in visual pattern recognition, the primitive symbols might be set up to correspond, more or less approximately, to the elementary discriminations of which the retina is capable. Thus, in information processing theories of visual pattern recognition it is usual to describe the sensory input as a two-dimensional array of zeros and ones (more generally, intensities). Similarly, an information processing theory of speech recognition might take as primitive symbols the elementary characteristics (features) into which phonemes are assumed to be analyzed by the auditory perceptual apparatus.

In applications where sensory discrimination is not the central concern, it may be more convenient to omit pattern recognition at this elementary level, and to take encodings of familiar configurations of sensory objects as the alphabet of primitive symbols. Thus, in the theory of problem solving set forth in this book, we shall not be concerned with the information processing involved in determining that a particular visual pattern represents a token of the letter c. We will simply take the letters of the English alphabet, the digits, punctuation marks, and a few special symbols (for example, the implication sign, $\supset$, used in logic) as primitive symbols designating these external stimuli.

All instances of the letter c, then, will be treated as belonging to the same type. This is equivalent, from the standpoint of psychology, to assuming that the subject whose behavior is under study does not, under the conditions of the experiment, discriminate between two tokens each of which is classifiable as a c. Whether this is a suitable assumption will depend on the experimental setting, and can be settled, in the last instance, only empirically. For example, by inducing the subject to assume the psychological set of a proofreader, he can be made to discriminate between a c that is clearly printed and one that is broken or printed unevenly. Under these conditions, not all tokens of c belong to the same type.

In taking the letters of the alphabet as primitive symbols in our analysis of problem solving, we divorce the problem solving theory from detailed concern with the sensory mechanisms. If we are wrong in doing so in particular applications, the error will be revealed by the inability of the theory to account for the observed behavior of subjects.

An important consequence of taking letters as primitive symbols is that we cannot then speak of one pair of letters as more closely resembling each other than another pair. We cannot say that s resembles z more closely than it resembles t. Letters, as primitive symbols, can only be tokens of the *same* type or tokens of *different* types. There is no notion of degree of difference among primitive symbols. (There is, of course, a notion of ordering within the alphabet, but again, this is primitively defined.) To introduce degrees of difference and similarity among letters, we would have to represent the letters not as primitives, but as organizations of simpler elementary characteristics. For example, each (printed) letter might be represented by a description: whether it contains a closed loop, an intersection of lines, a curved line, and so on. Then we could say that a t contains an intersection of lines, while both s and z contain a single zigzag curve. The EPAM theory of verbal learning, to be mentioned later, proceeds in just this way, hence permits predictions to be made about the behavioral consequences of similarity among letters.

Representing Symbol Structures

A simple example has already been provided to show how primitive symbols are combined into lists and descriptions. A couple of additional examples will illustrate the wide range of representations that can be accommodated. One of the problem solving situations we shall consider later involves choosing a move in the game of chess. In storing information about the chessmen in memory, the men are designated by symbols that have descriptions—sets of attribute-value pairs—associated with them. The attributes of a chessman include his type (king, queen, rook, bishop, knight, pawn), his color (White, Black), and his position (the name of the square on which he stands). Thus, a described symbol can represent the black rook on the king's bishop's third square. Squares are also represented as described symbols. A position is a symbol structure that associates with each square the man occupying that square, if there is any, and the names of the adjacent squares in various directions.

In another problem solving situation, the subjects are dealing with expressions from symbolic logic, for example: $(P \lor Q) \cdot (Q \supset R)$. This expression can be represented in memory as the *list* of its primitive symbols: $(, P, \lor, Q,), \cdot, (, Q, \supset, R,)$, where the parentheses are symbol tokens in the list. Alternatively, if the parentheses are interpreted in their usual role as delimiters of subgroups of symbols, the string can be represented as a *list structure* in memory, with the parentheses omitted: $(\cdot, A, B)$, where A is a symbol that designates the list $(\lor, P, Q)$ and B designates $(\supset, Q, R)$. Again, if one had relations *left* and *right* (to be interpreted as *left subexpression* and *right subexpression*, respectively), the same logic expression could be represented as a *tree structure* (Figure 2.3).

FIGURE 2.3

tree structure for (P ∨ Q)·(Q ⊃ R)

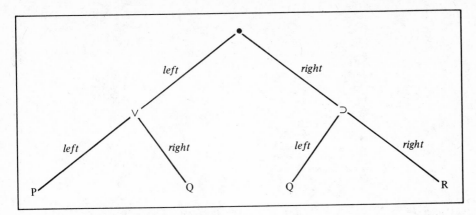

Yet another representation of the same information can be achieved by means of descriptions. Suppose symbols have descriptive associations, as with the chessmen described above. That is, a pair of symbols (one taken as *attribute*, the other as the base symbol having the association) designate a third symbol (the *value* of the attribute). Take as attributes *term, connective, left,* and *right;* and as the base symbols a number of nodes, x1, x2, ... Then the logic expression above could be represented by the following associations:

$$\begin{aligned}
&\text{connective}(x1) = \cdot &&\text{left}(x1) = x2 &&\text{right}(x1) = x3 \\
&\text{connective}(x2) = \vee &&\text{left}(x2) = x4 &&\text{right}(x2) = x5 \\
&\text{connective}(x3) = \supset &&\text{left}(x3) = x6 &&\text{right}(x3) = x7 \\
&\text{term}(x4) = P \\
&\text{term}(x5) = Q \\
&\text{term}(x6) = Q \\
&\text{term}(x7) = R
\end{aligned}$$

These associations can be represented pictorially in a graph (Figure 2.4).

All of these representations are very closely related. The algebraic representation uses the parentheses to encode the structure of the expression. Both the list representation and the tree representation use the organization of symbol structures to encode the structure of the expression. The list representation uses the first, second, and third positions on the list to encode the expression's connective, its left side, and its right side, respectively (more precisely, to encode the symbols naming the sides). The tree provides separate primitive relations to represent these distinctions. The attribute-value representation encodes both structure and content in a uniform way; it involves no symbol structure at all, but only a pattern of namings.

That there are many ways of representing something should not be surprising. We could give still others; e.g., Polish prefix notation encodes our logic expression as ·∨PQ⊃QR, using each connective to specify the exact number of operands that should follow to its right. All that is needed for a representation is some scheme of associations, together with a set of information processes that can extract the

FIGURE 2.4
association structure for (P $\vee$ Q)·(Q $\supset$ R)

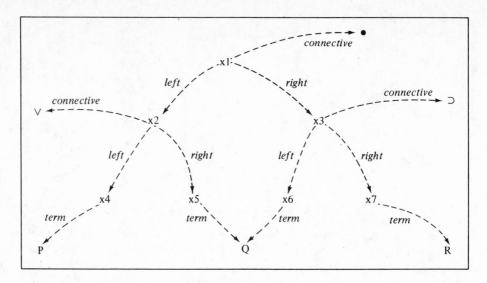

appropriate information about the connections. It is not always possible to tell from its output what internal representation is being used by an IPS, especially when alternate representations are as isomorphic as those presented here. However, in other cases, especially in representing problems, the choice of representations may have striking observable consequences for external behavior.

The IPS postulates listed above indicate nothing about what sorts of symbol structures and designations are available. The variety of possibilities precludes any simple statement. However, if too limited a repertory of structures and designations is provided, the encoding of complex varieties of information can become an exercise in virtuosity that yields little benefit of any other kind. It appears that the essential structures to provide appropriate direct representation of most things of interest to this book are:

1. *List structures.* Lists are symbol structures constructed from the single relation, *next* (with sometimes the inverse relation, *prior*), linking one symbol token with the next. Since symbols can designate lists, hierarchical structures of lists may be built up, in which some lists contain symbols that name other lists.
2. *Attribute-value associations.* These structures comprise sets of attributes and values, which are both symbols. The attribute designates a unique value in each such association.

Both list structures and attribute-value associations have been illustrated several times already. Other symbol structures and designations are needed occasionally, but these two types of structures are the core of the representational capability we shall use; all the rest can be introduced as representations for special purposes.

(Assumptions 3, 4, and 5)

The assumptions state that an IPS possesses a number of *elementary information processes* that operate upon symbol structures. The entire behavior of the IPS is compounded out of sequences of these elementary processes. *Elementary* means that they are not further analyzed in the theory into still simpler processes. As in the case of the primitive symbols, what they shall be depends on the purposes of the particular application. However, reasons for the variation are quite different in this case. In the case of the primitive symbols, choices were being made about how the external world would be symbolized. The nature of the symbols, qua internal entities, remains the same no matter what the choice—that is, the mechanics of processing are determined by the nature of the processor and not by what the primitive symbols designate in the external world.

As for the elementary processes, however, there must be a sufficiently general and powerful collection of operations to compose out of them all the macroscopic performances of the IPS. Furthermore, it is essential that these elementary processes be well defined—i.e., realizable by known mechanisms. Otherwise, there is no point to taking them as primitives. For example, there is no point in taking solve-problem as an eip. A system with such a primitive would tell us nothing about how problem solving is actually accomplished.

It might be thought that the possible variation in elementary processes (and how to compose them, a matter to which we will turn in the next section) would still be essentially unlimited, dependent entirely on the nature of the tasks the IPS was intended to perform. This proves not to be the case. It is one of the major foundation stones of computer science that a relatively small set of elementary processes suffices to produce the full generality of information processing. The general-purpose flexibility of the digital computer rests firmly on this foundation stone. On the other hand, there turns out to be no *unique* basis. Rather, there are many ways in which adequate sets of elementary processes can be chosen (in conjunction with corresponding schemes of composition). However, all of these ways do incorporate certain fundamental types of operations, even though the manner of incorporation may vary sufficiently so that it is not possible to cast them all into a single form of well-defined eip's with specified inputs and outputs. It is easy to list and illustrate the fundamental types of eip's that constitute a sufficient basic set. (Proof of their sufficiency, and the question of what such a proof could mean, is somewhat more involved.)

1. *Discrimination.* It must be possible for the system to behave in alternative ways depending on what symbol structures are in its STM. Furthermore, the behavior needs to be *arbitrarily* alterable; i.e., transfer of control to an independent program must be possible.
2. *Tests and comparisons.* It must be possible to determine that two symbol tokens do or do not belong to the same symbol type. Often comparisons

29

are directly coupled with conditional behavior, but they may equally well lead to the production of a conventional symbol (e.g., *true* or *false*) that can later be discriminated.

3. *Symbol creation.* It must be possible to create new symbols and set them to designate specified symbol structures. Again, this process must be performable arbitrarily; i.e., whenever a new symbol is desired it can be created, and it carries no meaning other than that it designates the desired symbol structure. Whether the system must also be able to destroy symbols depends primarily on whether memory capacity is limited.

4. *Writing symbol structures.* It must be possible to create a new symbol structure, copy an existing symbol structure, and modify an existing symbol structure, either by changing or deleting symbol tokens belonging to the structure or by appending new tokens with specified relations to the structure. Many variations are possible, as long as they permit building up arbitrary structures.

5. *Reading and writing externally.* It must be possible to designate stimuli received from the external environment by means of internal symbols or symbol structures, and to produce external responses as a function of internal symbol structures that designate these responses.

6. *Designating symbol structures.* It must be possible to designate various parts of any given symbol structure, and to obtain designations of other parts, as a function of given parts and relations. Again, this can be achieved in many ways but it must be always possible; i.e., there must not be any parts of symbol structures that are in principle inaccessible.

7. *Storing symbol structures.* It must be possible to remember a symbol structure for later use, by storing it in the memory and retrieving it at any arbitrary time via a symbol structure that designates it. How much memory is available, of course, conditions strongly how complex the totality of stored structures may be. The memory must be highly reliable over time.

PROGRAMS AND THE INTERPRETIVE PROCESS

(Assumption 7)

The behavior of an IPS consists in executing sequences of elementary information processes of the sorts we have been describing. Out of these sequences more macroscopic processes may be composed, until the integrated behavior called problem solving emerges.

The processor has three parts: the elementary processes, the short-term memory (STM) to hold their inputs and outputs, and the *interpreter*, to provide the integration. We make the final assumption that the interpreter bases its determination of sequential behavior solely on the information that is stored in the STM.

Since the contents of the STM change with almost every eip that is executed, this constraint imposes no essential limitation on behavior in the long run, although it does localize the immediate stimulus on which behavior depends in the short run.

The interpreter is at the heart of our theoretical proposals. Two distinct problems arise in describing it.

First, observing an IPS in operation, we must hypothesize a set of rules and regularities that describe the sequences of eip's it executes as a function of the informational context it is in. Such a set of rules is usually called a *program* for the IPS's behavior. As inductive scientists, we must discover this program in order to describe a human solving a problem.

Second, we must discover to what extent the IPS itself runs according to a program stored in its own memory. The subpart of the processor that we have labeled the interpreter need not contain the whole of the process specification, but only enough mechanism to interpret a program stored in memory. Let us delay consideration of this second problem for a moment and consider the first one—how we, as external observers, might describe the behavior of an IPS.

Program Representation

Programming Language. As an example, we might write a description of a house thermostat in a *programming language* as shown in Figure 2.5. The elementary processes in the example are *tests* that determine the current temperature and *actions* that turn the furnace off and on. (Because of the simplicity of the situation, all these eip's either affect or detect something external to the IPS itself.) The program is a structure of processes. For each list in the structure, each component designates either an elementary process or a subprogram—that is, a sublist (e.g., turning the furnace on could be a complex operation). A program is executed, recursively, by executing in turn each of its successive components.

FIGURE 2.5

program for thermostat

```
thermostat:
1.  observe-temperature,
            if < 70° go to 2,
            if > 72° go to 4,
            otherwise go to 1;
2.  test if furnace-on,
            if true go to 1;
3.  turn-furnace-on,
            go to 1;
4.  test if furnace-on,
            if false go to 1;
5.  turn-furnace-off,
            go to 1.
```

In this program, discriminations are made by carrying out a test or comparison and then branching to the step of the program indicated by the immediately following *control statements*. If none of these control statements is satisfied, then the program proceeds in the order in which the steps are written down. For example, at line 1 the control statements cover all possible results of the process observe-temperature. But at line 2 the control statement covers only the case of the test being true; if the test were false, then line 3 would be executed next. The program also contains *loops*, in which a cycle of program steps is repeated over and over. In the thermostat example, the program has a single loop and simply stays in it forever. More generally, programs have many loops, and loops within loops. Then, each loop must contain at least one conditional branch process so that, when the condition is finally satisfied, the program can branch out of the loop and the action can terminate.

Flow Diagram. As a second simple example we might describe a man driving a nail into a board by the *flow diagram* shown in Figure 2.6. Here the elementary processes are (1) lifting the hammer, (2) striking with it, and (3) observing the nail. The execution sequence is indicated by the arrows.

FIGURE 2.6
simple flow diagram

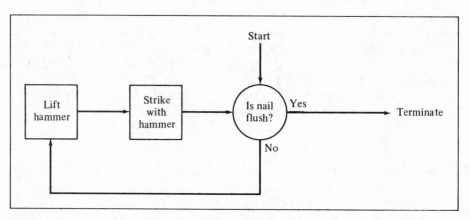

Production System. As yet a third simple example, consider a man walking down a block and crossing a street. We can describe his behavior by taking as elementary processes such acts as: step-with-left-foot, step-with-right-foot, observe-color-of-traffic-light, and so on. We can then write a program that describes how he steps alternately with left and right foot until he reaches the end of a block, then observes the traffic light, stops if it is red, steps left and right to cross the street if it is green. We might define a programming scheme for this as shown in Figure 2.7. We have written a series of four conditional statements, each expressing what to do under specified conditions. The act of executing the various tests is implicit. The system is assumed to perform the processes to the right of an arrow ($\rightarrow$), if the condition to the left of the same arrow becomes true. In case more than one condition is true, the one higher in the list takes priority; thus, no movement will occur if the traffic light is red (condition in first statement satisfied) even though both of the bottom conditions are satisfied (the system is in the move state). A system of this kind is called a *production system* and each of the conditional statements is called a *production*.

FIGURE 2.7
simple production system

traffic-light red ⟶ stop.
traffic-light green ⟶ move.
move and left-foot-on-pavement ⟶ step-with-right-foot.
move and right-foot-on-pavement ⟶ step-with-left-foot.

Interpretive Processes

As we have been describing it, a program is purely external to the IPS—it is *our* way, as outside observers, of describing the system. Our use of a different scheme for each of the three examples was meant (in part) to emphasize this conventional character of the description. There may be nothing inside the system itself that corresponds to the program, but only a mechanism that *behaves* in the manner described by the program. Thus, there may be in the thermostat a bimetallic strip that bends on heating so that it opens an electrical circuit and shuts off the furnace when it becomes warmer than 72°, and that straightens on cooling so that it closes the circuit and starts the furnace when it becomes cooler than 70°. The system does not follow a program; it simply behaves according to physical laws in the manner determined by its geometry and construction.

In other instances, the IPS may possess an internal representation of the program, and this internal representation may control the behavior of the system—the system may execute processes in accordance with, or under the *control* of, the program. A simple example of such a system (for those who can remember it) is an old-fashioned player piano. Here the program is symbolized by a pattern of holes in a roll of paper that is inserted in the piano. This roll, during operation of the instrument, passes over a mechanism that senses the locations of the holes in a lateral band across the roll and activates, by air pressure, particular piano keys corresponding to the locations of the holes.

The player piano is no less a physical device than the thermostat; it operates under no less definite physical laws. What differentiates the two from our present viewpoint is that the piano, but not the thermostat, contains a specialized subpart that records (in a pattern of holes) the scheme of its behavior, and another specialized subpart (tubes pressing against the player roll and connected with valves) that interprets this record and causes the mechanism to act in obedience to it. The first of these specialized parts is a memory that contains the piano's program, the second is the program interpreter.

In analyzing the behavior of an information processing system, it is not always possible to draw a sharp boundary between the part of the system that is to be regarded as simply a mechanism and the part that is best viewed as governed by an interpreted program. Suppose, for example, that the system is capable of finding the first occurrence of a particular symbol (say S) on a list (say L): find-the-first S in L. On the one hand, the system might simply possess a mechanism for carrying out this *find* operation. On the other hand, the find operation might be performed by executing the program of Figure 2.8, under control of an interpreter. Unless we had some means for examining the microstructure of the system, it would be impossible to distinguish between these two ways of carrying out the find operation.

FIGURE 2.8

process for finding symbol in list

```
1.  find first symbol in list L,
        if fail stop and report false;
2.  test if symbol = S,
        if true stop and report true;
3.  find next symbol in L,
        if find go to 2,
        if fail stop and report false.
```

Example of a Recognition Process

A more elaborate example of the two alternative possibilities is provided by mechanisms for discriminating, or recognizing. Since such mechanisms will play an important role in our psychological theories, we will pursue the example here briefly.

Consider a process that is capable of recognizing English words. By *recognizing* we mean: when a word is input to the process, outputting to STM the designation of a symbol structure that contains various aspects of the meaning of the word—e.g., its spelling, pronunciation, synonyms, visual representations of its referent, and so on. Thus a recognition process makes the word into a symbol, since it provides a designatory mechanism for it—i.e., a way to gain access to an appropriate symbol structure, given the word. This process is often called *discrimination*, and the mechanism we will be immediately describing, a *discrimination net*—even though the result of the process is not to select different behaviors, but rather to identify a symbol structure on which to base subsequent differential behavior. We continue to use the common descriptive name here, even though it clashes somewhat with our terminology.

Discrimination might be accomplished by a unitary process that is simply executed when an English word is input, providing thereupon the desired output. Alternatively, discrimination might be accomplished by an interpretive system. We describe it here primarily as an illustration of interpretation. In fact this scheme forms the basis of an information processing theory of verbal learning (called EPAM, see Feigenbaum, 1961; Simon and Feigenbaum, 1964), but the psychological phenomena it covers lie outside the scope of the present work.

In memory is stored a set of symbol structures, or *nodes*, of two types: *test nodes* and *terminal nodes*. Associated with each test node is a *test* and a set of other nodes, corresponding to the various possible test outcomes. Associated with each terminal node is a symbol structure that provides the meaning of input words sorted to that node. Figure 2.9 shows a fragment of such a structure.

FIGURE 2.9

fragment of discrimination net

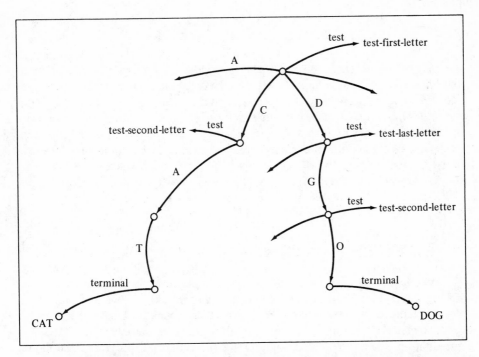

There is a process, called the net-interpreter (Figure 2.10), which takes the input word and applies the test associated with the first test node. In the net of Figure 2.9, for instance, the test is test-first-letter. If the input word were DOG, the test-result would be D. Next, the program associates along the test-result (i.e., along D) to find the next node—which could be another test node or a terminal node.

In the figure the node associated along D from the top node is a test node with the test: test-last-letter. Now the test-result would be G, and the net-interpreter would be led to a new node, and so on, until a terminal node was reached. The output of this process would be the designator of the symbol structure for the word DOG.

The important characteristic of an interpreter is that it replaces a large amount of mechanism by a small amount (the interpreter proper), plus a large amount of

FIGURE 2.10
net-interpreter

```
net-interpreter (word):
1.  find first node,
        if fail stop and report not recognized;
2.  find test of node,
        if fail stop and report not recognized;
3.  apply test to word (⇒ test-result);
4.  find node of test-result (⇒ new-node),
        if fail stop and report not recognized;
5.  find terminal of new-node,
        if fail go to 2 (new-node ⇒ node),
        if succeed stop and report recognized word.
```

symbolic structure. Then, in spite of the simplicity of its interpreter, the behavior that an IPS can exhibit is limited only by the complexity of the symbol structures that can be built up. But since the whole orientation of an IPS is to provide a set of tools (the eip's) with which to construct and read symbol structures, the complexity of behavior is quite unlimited. Stated otherwise, the limitations of behavior all reside in the content of the programs stored in the IPS, and are not inherent features of the IPS itself. There are, of course, limits on the speed at which the IPS can accomplish complex endeavors, for these may require very long sequences of eip's, and there may be no way of speeding up the elementary processes.

The Interpretive Sequence

We have called the specifying component of the processor the interpreter, since it is convenient to think of it as interpreting programs, and in our descriptions, IPS's will always be presented as programs. Often it makes no difference whether the interpreter is a complete mechanism that produces the effective behavior in question, or whether it is a true interpreter that follows a program. The matter becomes important only if the IPS wishes to do something with a program other than to execute it. If it wishes also to analyze, construct or modify a program, then it must deal with the program as a symbol structure, and hence must operate in a truly interpretive mode.

If the interpreter is simply a mechanism that produces a sequence of behaviors, then of course we have no way of describing its internal structure in information processing terms. If it is a true interpreter, then we can describe its operation. Our description will depend intimately on the nature of the programming language we use. Indeed the interpreter is just a process-oriented view of the conventions of the language, since the interpreter must unravel the program statements to determine what sequence of elementary processes it is to execute.

As an example, consider a simplified form of the sequential programming language that we have been using in this chapter. Each symbol on the program list is either an eip or the name of another program list:

P1: $(eip_1, eip_2, P2, P3, eip_3)$;
P2: (eip_4, eip_5);
P3: $(eip_6, P4, eip_7)$;
P4: $(P2, P2, eip_8)$.

Here we have abstracted from the use of English phrases and (more important) from the specification of operands for the various processes.

The interpreter for this language is described in Figure 2.11. The reader can verify for himself that it would execute the eip's of the simple four-statement program above in the sequence: $eip_1, eip_2, eip_4, eip_5, eip_6, eip_4, eip_5, eip_4, eip_5, eip_8,$ eip_7, eip_3. The elementary processes that this interpreter requires are the ability to tell if a symbol in the program designates an elementary process and, if so, the ability to execute it. The interpreter must also have the ability to read the program as a symbol structure—i.e., to get the next symbol and to detect the end of a program list. In addition it must have the ability to create and modify a symbol structure that keeps its place in the program. We have called this structure a *stack*—a list that can have a new symbol added to its front end (called *pushing* the stack), and can have a symbol removed from its front end (called *popping* the stack). The stack and its associated processes provide the essentials for keeping track of a hierarchically organized structure: when a subprogram is to be executed, its name is pushed on the stack; and when execution is complete, popping the stack returns the prior symbol to the top and lets the system proceed to the next step.

FIGURE 2.11

basic interpreter for sequential programming language

Interpreter:
1. find next symbol in current-program-list,
   if fail go to 4;
2. test if symbol designates eip,
   if true go to 5;
3. push symbol onto stack,
   go to 1;
4. pop top-symbol from stack,
   if fail stop and report end of program,
   if succeed go to 1;
5. execute process of symbol,
   go to 1.

The stack is not the only kind of symbol structure that can be used for the place-keeping function, especially if indefinitely deep hierarchies do not occur, but it is a convenient and powerful device. The fact that we have described the interpreter as a program does not mean that there is yet another interpreter that interprets it. At some level the interpreter must just be a mechanism that accomplishes directly the actions described.

THE RELATION OF AN IPS TO LANGUAGE

It should be evident from the discussion of symbols, symbol structures, the designation relation, and programs that an information processing system of the sort we have described in this chapter is, in some fundamental sense, a language processor. As a matter of historical fact, the basic concepts that have entered into our description of an IPS have almost the same origins as the concepts that underlie the formalized transformational grammars that linguists have developed over the past fifteen years (Chomsky, 1957). What is the relation, then, of language and the concepts of modern linguistics to our concept of an information processing system?

In modern linguistics, a language is a formal system containing a set of elements (cf. our "symbols") that can be arranged in linear strings (cf. our "lists"). A set of rules, or grammar, determines which strings, from among all possible concatenations of elements, are to be regarded as admissible in the language. The admissible strings are called "well-formed" or "grammatical."

A linguistic system also associates with each string one or more other symbol structures that constitute grammatical analyses of the string. Thus, the *surface structure* of a string—usually represented as a symbolic tree structure—is obtained by "parsing" the string to reveal its underlying phrase structure. In some well-known modern linguistic theories (e.g., Chomsky, 1965), the surface structure is transformed, in turn, to reveal a symbolic *deep structure*, whose exact form has never been fully characterized in these theories. The deep structure is generally portrayed as closely related to the semantics or meaning that underlies the original string. The system for extracting the deep structure contains, as one of its components, a lexicon where certain information about the symbols is stored.

These concepts from modern linguistics can be applied directly to an IPS of the kind we have been describing. The symbol structures stored in the IPS, which its programs manipulate, function as linguistic structures. In general, they are not strings, hence cannot be interpreted directly as sentences in a natural language. The further discussion of these symbol structures in the next chapter will make clear that they play the role assigned to the deep structures that are postulated by contemporary linguists. They are the representations of "meanings," with the aid of which the IPS represents problems and solves them.

Thus, although we shall have very little to say, explicitly, about linguistics in this volume, our theory of problem solving can properly be viewed as also a partial theory of linguistics—specifically, a theory of the nature of the deep structures used by the human IPS in the course of its problem solving activities.

NOTATION FOR INFORMATION PROCESSING SYSTEMS

We have now defined information processing systems and discussed their several parts and aspects. We have done so without formalizing our language, depending on the simplicity of the examples to make clear what is intended. Since we will be defining and discussing many IPS's in this book, we now need to be somewhat more systematic in our notation.

Notation has four related uses in this book:

1. *To define programs:* The substantive psychological theories of an individual's behavior to be developed here.
2. *To define task environments:* The external situations that define tasks for the programs. Since we are not concerned with receptors or effectors, task environments can be described in symbolic terms.
3. *To describe traces:* The step-by-step accounts of the sequences of processes and symbol structures that occur when a particular program is executed in a particular task environment.
4. *To encode protocols:* The records of behavior of the human subjects used to test the theories, including the subjects' English language verbalizations and written expressions produced throughout the task. Protocols can often be rendered directly by the same kinds of symbol structures as are used to define the task environment.

We could define a completely formal language for expressing programs and symbol structures. In fact, if we wish to simulate an information processing system on a computer, we *must* define such a formal language, together with an interpreter or compiler that will translate processes from that language into the language of the computer's machine instructions. Formal languages and associated interpreters have been constructed that fit the description of an information processing system given in this chapter. One of these languages, Information Processing Language V (IPL-V) (Newell, Tonge, Feigenbaum, Green, Kelly, and Mealy, 1964) has been used to carry out most of the computer simulations that are discussed in this volume.

Formal languages have drawbacks, however. They tend to be unreadable by humans; and in a book intended for human (as opposed to computer) consumption, this sin is nearly unpardonable. Furthermore, we wish to use several different representations of processes and symbol structures, adapting our language to the needs of the occasion. The programs discussed in this book were individually conceived and created at different times and with varying intents. Although some recasting is appropriate to bring out the relations among the programs, a certain fidelity to the original formulations is also required. It is entirely infeasible to go back and reprogram these systems in a uniform programming language.

We will adopt, then, a set of notational conventions for describing information processing systems and their behavior that attempts to preserve comprehensibility, while still providing a reasonable guarantee that the notation could be formalized, say by creating a programming language. In Appendix 2.1 of this chapter we provide a formal definition for the notation, for those who are interested. We adhere to the conventions given in the appendix throughout the book. But since the programs and behavior to be presented in the book are to be read, rather than written, the syntactic details of the notation are of secondary importance. Thus, we will define the notation here informally by means of examples.

We will first state some general conventions for symbols, symbol structures, and the designation of processes. Then we will state the conventions for sequential processes, followed by the conventions for production systems. We will not state any special conventions for flow diagrams, but will treat these entirely informally. To have something specific to talk about, we show in Figure 2.12 one version of the top level of the Logic Theorist (LT) program that will be discussed in Chapter 4.

General Conventions

We will use ordinary English words as the identifiers for symbols, symbol structures, and processes, augmented by letters, indexed words (e.g., x4, list13), and special characters (e.g., $\vee$, $\supset$). We often hyphenate a series of words into a single identifier, so there will be no ambiguity as to what constitutes a simple identifier (i.e., one with no implied composition or processing). Thus, in Figure 2.12, untried-problems is the name of a list, effort-used is the name of a process, and effort-limit is the name of a number. Since these are arbitrary identifiers, we could have used xyz, pq, and x3 instead, except that the latter give no mnemonic help to the reader.

In both text and figures we have kept the typography as simple as possible. Important terms are sometimes printed in italics in the text when they are first

FIGURE 2.12

sequential process for the Logic Theorist

Logic Theorist (problem):
1. insert problem on untried-problems at end;
2. generate untried-problems ($\Rightarrow$ current-problem):
3.   find utility of current-problem,
          if low continue generation;
4.   find status of current-problem,
          if proved go to 10,
          if too-complex continue generation;
5.   effort-used(problem),
          if effort-used $>$ effort-limit stop Logic Theorist
          and report unable to find proof;
6.   generate methods:
7.   apply method to current-problem
            ($\Rightarrow$ new-problem),
             if fail continue generation;
8.   test-if-theorem (new-problem),
            if true go to 10;
9.   insert new-problem on untried-problems
            at end.;
10.   reconstruct-proof(current-problem),
          stop Logic Theorist and report result.,
      stop and report no proof and nothing more to do.

introduced. We have used italics or quotation marks to note that a term is mentioned, not used, only when failure to do so would cause serious ambiguity.

With these exceptions, we have departed from Roman type only in occasional moments of desperation when some typographical signal for a distinction seemed unavoidable. For example, the algebraic symbol a is italicized to distinguish it from the word "a" (and the latter placed in quotes in the present context because it really seems awkward here not to note that it is mentioned, not used). However, digits and other algebraic symbols in the text—c, x, and so on—that cannot be confused with words are not usually italicized.

We believe that this artless attitude toward typography will not seriously inconvenience readers who like formal rigor, yet will make the book more readable for those who prefer English.

The program in Figure 2.12 does not show any symbol structures, but only their identifiers. We will use the standard notations for expressions of various kinds (logical or algebraic expressions). We will represent lists by parenthesized sequences, e.g., (theorem1 theorem2 theorem3). We will not use commas in these sequences, although we used them earlier in the chapter to emphasize that (W A S) was a list of three elements.

We will use a colon to indicate the assignment of an identifier to a process or a symbol structure. In the figure, the top line gives an identifier for a process and follows this with a colon; Logic-Theorist thus becomes the identifier for the process structure that follows in lines 1–10.

The operands to be used with a process can be indicated either by standard functional notation, as in line 5, or by phrases in which prepositions are used as separators, as in line 1. The choice of notation is determined at the time of definition of the process. Thus, the operand of the Logic-Theorist (called problem) is given in parentheses. (Infix operations may also be defined, which take operands on both sides of the operation identifier.)

Although no example occurs in Figure 2.12, it is sometimes convenient to parametrize processes, and to think of the parameters as distinct from the operands. Thus, in Chapter 4 we will define the operation of substitution as:

$$\text{Substitute[expression for variable](expression)}$$

The parameters are given in the square brackets, and the operand in parentheses. Again, as with the operands, the parameters can be shown either as a list (as in normal functional notation) or as a phrase with prepositional separators.

Conventions for Sequential Processes

A sequential process consists (naturally enough) of a sequence of processes. In Figure 2.12 there are actually three such sequences: lines 1 and 2; lines 3, 4, 5, 6, and 10; and lines 7, 8, and 9. The indentations on the page show that the latter two sequences are subordinate (actually, subprocesses for the two generate processes).

Normally three things happen in connection with a bit of processing. (1) Something is done—e.g., an observation is made, a new symbol structure is constructed, or whatever. (2) This new result is given an identifier so that it can be referred to by some subsequent process. (3) Control is passed to the next process to be executed. In common programming languages, such as FORTRAN and ALGOL, the name assignment is given linguistic priority and the control actions are on the same linguistic level as all other actions. Thus, expressions such as the following are typical in those languages:

$$\text{new-problem} \leftarrow \text{apply(method, current-problem)}$$
$$\text{if effort-used(problem)} > \text{effort-limit then stop}$$

Neither of these ways of expressing processes is inappropriate, but they do seem to hide some of what is going on from an IPS point of view. The convention we shall use instead is always to give first place to defining the process (calculation or observation), and then to associate with this process definition, subordinately, indications of whether a name change is required and where control is to pass. In line 7 of the figure, for instance, the main process that occurs is the application of the method. Then it is noted parenthetically that a new identifier, new-problem, is to be assigned. The double arrow ($\Rightarrow$) can be read "and produces" or "producing." It can be followed by any description of the output symbol structure—in this case, a new identifier. Following the name assignment (which can be absent, of course) there may be subordinate clauses to tell what happens to control. In line 7, if the method fails, then control is to stop the process and return to the generator (line 6). *fail* is one of several possible products from *apply*, and it is understood that the discrimination (as indicated by the *if*) is made on the immediately produced result.

Almost every line in Figure 2.12 has a control action, although line 1 is an exception, since control is always to pass to line 2. There may be more than one control action, as in line 4. Also, the control action need not be conditional—e.g., in line 10, where the action is to stop the Logic Theorist (Note: not just stop the immediately superordinate process) and then *report* a result.

Control actions depend on sensing the nature of the result just produced. Thus, they are limited to simple discriminations. For example, in line 4 status is an attribute of the current-problem whose value is one of the symbols: proved, too-complex, unproved, and so on. Having obtained this symbol by the find process, the control action can discriminate which symbol was obtained. However, the following is asking too much of the control action:

$$\text{select first from untried-problems,}$$
$$\text{if too-complex stop.}$$

The result of *select* is the problem, not all the descriptive information associated with that problem, hence the test, too-complex, cannot be applied for control without first finding the status of the problem. All processes produce signals to indicate their result—e.g., succeed or fail, true or false—which may be sensed by the control action. These may be general signals, as succeed or fail, or they may be uniquely defined for the process, as generation-stopped and generation-completed, used with the generate process.

As we noted, standard programming languages provide two ways to refer to symbol structures produced elsewhere in a program: *assignment*, which makes use of an unused identifier; and *embedding*, in which the expression for the result is located in the place where its result is to be used [e.g., F(a + b) instead of x ← a + b; F(x)]. The embedding technique helps reduce the need for temporary identifiers, which are a major contributor to the obscurity of programs. We wish to avoid embedding (composition of functions), since it obscures the sequential control flow; but we substitute three other conventions to keep down the number of temporary names. The first, placing the control actions in the context of the processing on which they depend, has already been noted. The second is to use the name of a process to identify its result. In line 5 we have deliberately done this in the control action, where we use "effort-used" to stand for the result of the process, effort-used. The third is to use the special term *result* to indicate the most recently obtained result. The only example of this in Figure 2.12 occurs in line 10 in a control action in the line in which the result was obtained. But result can be used in lines subsequent to the one that defines it—e.g.,

> sum(3, 5);
> divide result by 2;
> subtract 1 from result,
>   if result = 3 stop and report ok.

The three occurrences of result above are all different, having values of 8, 4, and 3, respectively.

A number of generalized basic processes occur in Figure 2.12. The functions of most of them will be apparent from the discussions in the first part of the chapter, and the most important are defined in the appendix. *apply* simply causes a process to be executed on the specified operands. *find* attempts to find the value of a relation (e.g., next, first) from a given position in a symbol structure. It also attempts to find the symbol structure designated by an association (e.g., find the color of apple). *report* simply outputs (for the reader's benefit, mostly) the text following it.

The process *test* (or, equivalently *test if*) does not appear in Figure 2.12. It is followed by a condition, which can be composed of basic Boolean connectives and some basic relations. Thus, one can write:

> test if A and (B or not C),
>   if true go to 3,
>   otherwise go to 7.

However, deep nesting will never occur in our examples, even though it is permitted by the conventions.

The *generate* process figures prominently in almost all programs, since it is used for all repetitive operations. Two generates occur nested in Figure 2.12, at lines 2 and 6. A generate takes as operand a set, and produces in sequence the elements of the set, giving each element as operand to a subprocess (which is therefore technically another operand of generate). The term *element* can be used in the subprocess to refer to the element produced by the generator, but sometimes it is more convenient to assign a distinct identifier to the element. This is done in the generate at line 2, where each element is named *current-problem* and can be referred to by that name within the body of the subprocess (lines 3 to 10). We usually also allow an element to be named by its set name. Thus the generate at line 6 has the set of methods as its operand, so we use method as the identifier of the element without further definition.

Elementary processes are often used without further definition (e.g., *insert* on line 1), since their action is usually clear. However, sometimes a bit of ambiguity remains. For instance, the insert on line 1 is unambiguous, but an insert may be used without specifying exactly where on the list the insertion is to take place. This is done either when the place of insertion makes no substantial difference to the discussion at hand, or when the place is still an open parameter to be determined by some other process.

Production Systems

Figure 2.13 shows a slightly elaborated thermostat, written as a production system to illustrate the notation. Just as with any other process, the identifier, thermostat, is assigned to designate the entire production system consisting of the four productions. Each production has a condition and an action-sequence. An action can be some operator, such as call-repairman (again, written as a single long identifier, to indicate that no internal structure at all has been assigned to that operator, but only an identifier). Operators can be parameterized, as with turn-on[furnace] and turn-on[electric-heater]. A condition can be a single discrimination, as in the second production of Figure 2.13, or it can be a conjunction of several, as in the others. However, a condition is an operation involving only matching and detection, so that only simple discriminations can be made, just as in the control action of the sequential processes [e.g., just as (test if $(a + b) > (c - d)$ is not permitted].

As noted earlier, control starts at the top of the list of productions and proceeds sequentially down until the first true condition is encountered; then the corresponding action sequence is executed and control starts over at the top of the list. The only other control action is stop, as shown in the first production, which simply terminates the entire execution. No directed control, as with a go to, is possible in a production system.

Patterns and BNF. The Thermostat of Figure 2.13 is highly special in its conditions, which are simply discriminations on predefined variables (temperature and

FIGURE 2.13
production system for thermostat

Thermostat:
    temperature $> 70°$ and temperature $< 72° \longrightarrow$ stop.
    temperature $< 32° \longrightarrow$ call-repair-man; turn-on [electric-heater].
    temperature $< 70°$ and furnace-state $=$ off $\longrightarrow$ turn-on [furnace].
    temperature $> 72°$ and furnace-state $=$ on $\longrightarrow$ turn-off [furnace].

furnace-state). More generally, the conditions can be *patterns* of symbol structures. To specify these patterns we need a language for talking about classes of symbol expressions. *Backus-Normal-Form* (BNF), a standard metanotation used to describe the grammars of programming languages, provides a suitable tool.

BNF is built around five simple notions (to which we will add one other). First we wish to designate classes of expressions. We will do this by enclosing identifiers in angular brackets (e.g., ⟨letter⟩ will be a class of expressions, say, the class of letters). Second, we wish to compose expressions out of linear sequences of subexpressions (e.g., WARD is a sequence of four letters). We will do this by concatenating class names and characters. For example,

$$\langle \text{letter} \rangle \; A \; \langle \text{letter} \rangle \; D$$

is any string of characters consisting of a letter, the letter A, a letter, and the letter D, e.g., WARD, BARD, BAAD, ZAPD. Third, we wish to define classes that are arbitrary disjunctions. We do this by using the bar (|) as a metaconnective so that A | B means: either A or B. For example,

$$\langle \text{letter} \rangle \; | \; \langle \text{letter} \rangle \; \langle \text{letter} \rangle$$

is the class of all strings containing either one or two letters. Fourth, we wish to be able to assign new identifiers to classes of expressions built up with the above rules. We do this by a meta-assignment symbol: (:: =). Thus,

$$\langle \text{small-word} \rangle :: = \langle \text{letter} \rangle \; | \; \langle \text{letter} \rangle \; \langle \text{letter} \rangle$$

gives a name to the class of all one- or two-letter words. The class name can then be used in further constructions, e.g.,

$$\langle \text{bigger-word} \rangle :: = \langle \text{small-word} \rangle \; | \; \langle \text{letter} \rangle \; \langle \text{small-word} \rangle$$

The fifth and last notion is to admit recursive definition, thus expanding the definitional capabilities of the system to infinite classes (of simple, but useful, structure). Thus, if ⟨digit⟩ names the class of digits, then

$$\langle \text{integer} \rangle :: = \langle \text{digit} \rangle \; | \; \langle \text{digit} \rangle \; \langle \text{integer} \rangle$$

defines the class ⟨integer⟩ as all strings of digits. (That is, 3 is a ⟨digit⟩, 4 is a ⟨digit⟩, hence an ⟨integer⟩, hence 3 followed by 4—i.e., 34—is an ⟨integer⟩, hence 334, hence 4334, hence ....) Similarly,

$$\langle \text{list} \rangle :: = (\langle \text{symbol-sequence} \rangle)$$
$$\langle \text{symbol-sequence} \rangle :: = \langle \text{symbol} \rangle \; | \; \langle \text{symbol} \rangle \; \langle \text{symbol-sequence} \rangle$$

identifies as lists all sequences of symbols enclosed in a single pair of parentheses. As a final example,

$$\langle \text{constant} \rangle :: = P \; | \; Q \; | \; R \; | \; S$$
$$\langle \text{connective} \rangle :: = \vee \; | \; \cdot \; | \; \supset$$
$$\langle \text{expression} \rangle :: = \langle \text{constant} \rangle \; | \sim \langle \text{expression} \rangle \; | \; (\langle \text{expression} \rangle$$
$$\langle \text{connective} \rangle \; \langle \text{expression} \rangle)$$

defines all well-formed logic expressions containing P, Q, R, and S as the terminal letters.

To apply these conventions to our situation we need to view a BNF expression as describing a class of symbol structures. We need not be overly concerned with the underlying representation, since almost all the information needed to process the symbol structures is given by the BNF grammar. Each of the concatenations represents a distinct relation in a symbol structure. The relation of the tilde ($\sim$) to its ⟨expression⟩ is one such relation, the one shown by ⟨expression⟩ ⟨connective⟩ is another (i.e., the relation of left-hand subexpression), the one shown by ⟨connective⟩ ⟨expression⟩ is yet another (i.e., right-hand subexpression). These relations could all be encoded into a single list or string (with the single relation *next*), but then some of the logic relations would be encoded as distant relations in the structure of the string (see the discussion earlier in the chapter of the various representations for logic expressions).

One additional notion is required so that a part of a symbol structure, identified by a pattern in the condition of a production, can be designated in the action sequence of the production. For example, suppose we want to program the expansive side of the distributive law $(A \lor (B \cdot C) = (A \lor B) \cdot (A \lor C))$ in a production:

$$\langle \text{expression} \rangle \ \lor \ (\langle \text{expression} \rangle \cdot \langle \text{expression} \rangle) \longrightarrow \text{expand}$$

The condition part correctly recognizes an expression to which the expansion process applies. But how can expand refer to the specific expression that must be copied in order to create the expanded expression? BNF only identifies class membership; it does not automatically provide designations for variables. If there is only one class of a given type, then the identifier itself can designate an occurrence of a class member, just as we used the name of a process to identify its product. This device can be extended by indexing distinct occurrences of the class names to distinguish the several class members under consideration. Thus, we can write the expand process:

$$\langle \text{expression.1} \rangle \ \lor \ (\langle \text{expression.2} \rangle \cdot \langle \text{expression.3} \rangle) \longrightarrow$$
$$(\text{expression.1} \ \lor \ \text{expression.2}) \cdot (\text{expression.1} \ \lor \ \text{expression.3})$$

We have dispensed with the expand operator and have represented the newly constructed symbol structure directly in terms of the variables: expression. 1, expression. 2, and expression. 3. These obtain their values according to the pattern in the condition.

With this extension of BNF we now have a pattern language suitable for the needs of this book. BNF admits a quite restricted set of patterns, but these correspond generally to the kinds of patterns that can be recognized directly—i.e., by match and detection processes. We do not wish to endow the condition side of the productions with too elaborate a pattern-matching capability.

The primary use of patterns is as the conditions of productions, but they are useful wherever classes of symbol structures need to be described. We can use them to describe the output of a process; e.g., FC ($\Rightarrow$ ⟨column⟩), which asserts that the output of the process FC is a symbol structure of the class ⟨column⟩.

In this chapter we have carried out the first steps toward specifying the basic hypothesis proposed and tested in this volume: that human beings, in their thinking and problem solving activities, operate as information processing systems. We have described, by means of eight postulates, the basic characteristics of the hypothesized information processing system, and in the first four sections of the chapter we have spelled out in some detail the meaning of these postulates.

In the final section of the chapter we set forth the system of notation we shall use in the remainder of the book whenever we have occasion to talk formally about information processing systems or behaviors. This notation will be used to define theories of individual behavior as programs, to define task environments, to describe the step-by-step traces produced by programs when they are exercised in specific task environments, and to encode protocols of human behavior in task environments for comparison with the theory.

In the next chapter, also introductory, we will make a careful analysis of the concept of task environment. Then we will be ready, in Chapter 4, to propose a general framework for the study of problem solving behavior.

APPENDIX 2.1

Formal Definitions of Language for Describing IPS's

The definition makes use of standard BNF notation for defining syntax, but also uses quotation marks. The notation is illustrated in the following example:

$$\langle X \rangle ::= A \mid B\,C \mid D\,\langle E \rangle \mid F\,\langle X \rangle\,G \mid H\,``|"\,G$$

This example defines a class of expressions named $\langle X \rangle$. All names of expressions will be formed with angular brackets. The class $\langle X \rangle$ comprises all the expressions indicated on the right of the ($::=$). There are five alternative possiblities here, each separated by the *vertical-bar* (|). The first alternative is simply the expression consisting of the letter A. The second is the expression consisting of the letter B followed by the letter C. The third is the letter D followed by any member of the class $\langle E \rangle$. Thus, if $\langle E \rangle$ were defined by

$$\langle E \rangle ::= K \mid K\,K$$

then the subclass $D\langle E \rangle$ would contain two expressions: D K and D K K. The fourth subclass is any expression starting with the letter F followed by any expression of class $\langle X \rangle$ itself followed by (and ending with) the letter G. This is a recursive definition that includes infinitely many expressions. For instance, F A G, F F A G G, F F F A G G G, ... are all members of this subclass. The fifth subclass is simply the expression H | G, it being necessary to put the vertical-bar between quotes to show that it is not to be interpreted as the metasymbol *vertical-bar*.

Chapter 2 has been devoted to introducing and discussing the various concepts indicated by the following syntax, and we will not define here the semantics of the language. We will comment on some of the reasons for particular definitions, to help tie the syntax to the prior discussion.

The language has three parts. The first introduces symbols, symbol structures, and ways of naming processes. This part underlies all the definitions in this book. The remaining definitions split into two groups, one defining sequential processes and the other defining production systems.

The definitions are given from the bottom up; i.e., classes of expressions are defined before they are used. However, the definitions come in clumps; the definition of a class of some conceptual importance heads a clump, followed by auxiliary definitions, which play a role only in the definition of the main class.

[The reader need not concern himself with the conventions for spacing between words. However, the following rules do, in fact, determine the spacing. If two classes occur together without space in a BNF expression, then their instances must occur without spaces in an instance-expression. If any space occurs in the BNF expression, then one or more corresponding spaces should occur in the instance-expression, with the following exception: if one of the constituents is a ⟨mark⟩ (see below), then the space may be eliminated.]

⟨identifier⟩ :: = ⟨word⟩ | ⟨word⟩ - ⟨identifier⟩
⟨word⟩ :: = ⟨letter⟩ | ⟨letter⟩ ⟨word⟩ | ⟨word⟩ ⟨index⟩
⟨letter⟩ :: = ⟨small-letter⟩ | ⟨capital-letter⟩
⟨small-letter⟩ :: = a | b | c | d | e | f | g | h | i | j | k | l | m
                n | o | p | q | r | s | t | u | v | w | x | y | z
⟨capital-letter⟩ :: = A | B | C | D | E | F | G | H | I | J | K | L | M
                N | O | P | Q | R | S | T | U | V | W | X | Y | Z
⟨index⟩ :: = ⟨integer⟩
⟨integer⟩ :: = ⟨digit⟩ | ⟨digit⟩ ⟨integer⟩
⟨digit⟩ :: = 0 | 1 | 2 | 3 | 4 | 5 | 6 | 7 | 8 | 9
⟨mark⟩ :: = . | , | ; | = | − | + | : | (|) | [|] | ′ | " < " | " > " | " | " | / | *

The set of definitions above determines all the identifiers that can be used in the language. Almost every construct will have a special class of identifiers that may be any ⟨identifier⟩, with the sole restriction that all the identifiers in the language must be distinct.

⟨symbol-structure⟩ :: = ⟨symbol⟩ | ⟨list⟩ | ⟨symbol-structure-identifier⟩ |
    ⟨symbol-structure⟩ ⟨relation⟩ ⟨symbol-structure⟩ | (⟨symbol-structure-set⟩)
⟨symbol-structure-set⟩ :: = ⟨symbol-structure⟩ | ⟨location⟩. ⟨symbol⟩ |
    ⟨symbol-structure⟩, symbol-structure-set⟩
⟨symbol-structure-identifier⟩ :: = ⟨identifier⟩
⟨symbol⟩ :: = ⟨symbol-identifier⟩ | ⟨relation⟩(⟨symbol⟩)
⟨relation⟩ :: = next | prior | left | right | first | last | symbol
⟨location⟩ :: = ⟨integer⟩
⟨symbol-identifier⟩ :: = ⟨identifier⟩
⟨list⟩ :: = ⟨list-identifier⟩ | (⟨symbol-sequence⟩)
⟨symbol-sequence⟩ :: = ⟨symbol⟩ | ⟨symbol⟩ ⟨symbol-sequence⟩
⟨list-identifier⟩ :: = ⟨identifier⟩
⟨association-structure⟩ :: = ⟨symbol⟩ [⟨association-sequence⟩]
⟨association-sequence⟩ :: = ⟨association⟩ | ⟨association⟩ ⟨association-sequence⟩
⟨association⟩ :: = ⟨attribute⟩: ⟨symbol-structure⟩
⟨attribute⟩ :: = ⟨symbol⟩
⟨associate⟩ :: = ⟨attribute⟩ of ⟨result-identifier⟩ | ⟨attribute⟩ of ⟨associate⟩

The above set of definitions determines the basic kinds of symbol structures. Symbols are defined by their identifiers or by being designated relatively to some other symbol in a structure. Thus, ⟨symbol⟩ defined above is really a symbol token. Association structures are defined independently of symbol structures, since they are taken to describe designational associations. The association gives the attribute and the value to be associated to the symbol that heads the structure. Attributes have been defined to include only symbols, though symbol structures may also be capable of functioning similarly (recall the discussion on page 24). The associate, a symbol-structure, is the value of the attribute of the symbol that follows the *of* in its definition. The ⟨result-identifier⟩ will be defined below.

⟨pattern-definition⟩ :: = ⟨pattern-identifier⟩ ":: = " ⟨pattern⟩.
⟨pattern⟩ :: = ⟨symbol-structure⟩ | ⟨symbol-form⟩ | ⟨pattern⟩ |
   ⟨pattern⟩ ⟨pattern⟩ | ⟨pattern⟩ " | " ⟨pattern⟩
⟨pattern-identifier⟩ :: = "⟨"⟨identifier⟩"⟩" | "⟨"⟨identifier⟩·⟨index⟩"⟩"
⟨symbol-form⟩ :: = ⟨extended-symbol⟩ | ⟨list-form⟩ | ⟨symbol-form-identifier⟩ |
   ⟨symbol-form⟩ ⟨relation⟩ ⟨symbol-form⟩ | (⟨symbol-form-set⟩)
⟨symbol-form-set⟩ :: = ⟨symbol-form⟩ | ⟨location⟩. ⟨extended-symbol⟩ |
   ⟨symbol-form⟩, ⟨symbol-form-set⟩
⟨extended-symbol⟩ :: = ⟨symbol⟩ | ⟨pattern⟩ | ⟨variable⟩ | ⟨result-identifier⟩
⟨symbol-form-identifier⟩ :: = ⟨identifier⟩
⟨variable⟩ :: = ⟨identifier⟩
⟨variable-definition⟩ :: = variable: ⟨variable-list⟩.
⟨variable-list⟩ :: = ⟨variable⟩ | ⟨variable⟩, ⟨variable-list⟩

Besides symbol structures, the language needs classes of symbol structures, i.e., patterns. The pattern language is just BNF itself; thus we need to use the quotes to define it. The class of symbol-forms is identical with that of symbol-structures, except that everywhere we allowed ⟨symbol⟩ in defining ⟨symbol-structure⟩ we now allow ⟨extended-symbol⟩—i.e., variables and patterns.

⟨process-definition⟩ :: = ⟨process⟩: ⟨process-structure⟩.
⟨process-structure⟩ :: = ⟨sequential-process⟩ | ⟨production-system⟩
⟨process⟩ :: = ⟨process-designation⟩ | ⟨process-designation⟩ ⟨operand-statement⟩ |
   ⟨operand-statement⟩ ⟨process-designation⟩ ⟨operand-statement⟩ |
   ⟨special-syntax-process⟩ | ⟨process⟩ (⟨result-identification-list⟩)
⟨process-designation⟩ :: = ⟨process-identifier⟩ |
   ⟨process-identifier⟩ [⟨parameter-statement⟩]
⟨process-identifier⟩ :: = ⟨identifier⟩ | ⟨process⟩
⟨parameter-statement⟩ :: = ⟨parameter-list⟩ | ⟨parameter-phrase⟩
⟨parameter-list⟩ :: = ⟨parameter⟩ | ⟨parameter⟩, ⟨parameter-list⟩
⟨parameter-phrase⟩ :: = ⟨parameter⟩ | ⟨preposition⟩ ⟨parameter-phrase⟩ |
   ⟨parameter⟩ ⟨preposition⟩ ⟨parameter-phrase⟩
⟨parameter⟩ :: = ⟨symbol-structure⟩ | ⟨variable⟩ | ⟨association⟩
⟨operand-statement⟩ :: = (⟨operand-list⟩) | ⟨operand-phrase⟩
⟨operand-list⟩ :: = ⟨operand⟩ | ⟨operand⟩, ⟨operand-list⟩
⟨operand-phrase⟩ :: = ⟨operand⟩ | ⟨preposition⟩ ⟨operand-phrase⟩ |
   ⟨operand⟩ ⟨preposition⟩ ⟨operand-phrase⟩
⟨operand⟩ :: = ⟨symbol-structure⟩ | ⟨variable⟩ | ⟨association⟩
⟨preposition⟩ :: = after | at | by | before | for | from | in | into | on | onto | the | to | until |
   while | with
⟨result-identification-list ⟩:: = ⟨result-identification⟩ |
   ⟨result-identification⟩, ⟨result-identification-list⟩
⟨result-identification⟩ :: = ⇒ ⟨result-identifier⟩ |
   ⟨result-identifier⟩ ⇒ ⟨result-identifier⟩
⟨result-identifier⟩ :: = result | element | ⟨process-designation⟩ |
   ⟨attribute⟩ | ⟨symbol-structure-identifier⟩ | ⟨pattern⟩

The set of definitions above determines how processes may be designated. The second line, defining ⟨process-structure⟩, indicates the division into two separate languages: sequential processes and production systems. The remainder gives common ways of naming processes by combining identifiers and operands. ⟨process⟩ and ⟨process-designation⟩ define the basic possibilities. We permit both prefixed [e.g., P(x, y)] and infixed (e.g., x R y) process identifiers. We permit both functional notation [e.g., P(x, y)] and prepositional phrasing (e.g., P to x with y). In giving operands by means of a phrase, the prepositions operate solely as separators and identifiers of their respective operands [e.g., in (insert x on y) the proposition *on* has no function other than to identify y]. We permit operands [e.g., P(x, y)] to be distinguished from parameters [e.g., P[x](y)].

Besides the possibilities just discussed for ⟨process⟩, there is ⟨special-syntax-process⟩, which will be defined below, and a provision for adding a list of result identifications. This latter provides a way to specify the name of the output of the process. It also provides a way of describing the output, by using a ⟨pattern⟩ for the *result-identifier* rather than just an *identifier*.

⟨sequential-process⟩ :: = ⟨process⟩ | ⟨process⟩; ⟨sequential-process⟩ |
    ⟨process⟩, ⟨control-sequence⟩; ⟨sequential-process⟩ |
    ⟨location⟩. ⟨sequential-process⟩
⟨control-sequence⟩ :: = ⟨control-statement⟩ | ⟨control-statement⟩, ⟨control-sequence⟩
⟨control-statement⟩ :: = if ⟨value⟩ ⟨sequential-control-action⟩ |
    if not ⟨value⟩ ⟨sequential-control-action⟩ |
    otherwise ⟨sequential-control-action⟩ | ⟨sequential-control-action⟩
⟨sequential-control-action⟩ :: = stop | stop ⟨process-designation⟩ | continue generation |
    go to ⟨location⟩ | ⟨sequential-control-action⟩ and ⟨report-process⟩ |
    ⟨sequential-control-action⟩ (⟨result-identification-list⟩)
⟨value⟩ :: = ⟨symbol-structure⟩ | ⟨discrimination-relation⟩ ⟨symbol-structure⟩ |
    ⟨result-identifier⟩ ⟨discrimination-relation⟩ ⟨symbol-structure⟩ |
    from ⟨symbol-structure⟩ to ⟨symbol-structure⟩
⟨discrimination-relation⟩ :: = = | ≠ | < | > | ≤ | ≥

The set of definitions above determines the basic way of writing sequential processes. It incorporates the notion of giving the process first and following it by an associated control action to determine what process is to occur next in the sequence. A limited set of relations (discrimination-relations) can be detected directly for the purposes of control; more complex relations require processing for their detection. The control statement also includes assignment of identifiers for later reference. Finally, output can be reported simultaneously with the performance of processes, rather than in a separate step of the sequence.

⟨special-syntax-process⟩ :: = ⟨test-process⟩ | ⟨find-process⟩ | ⟨generate-process⟩ |
    ⟨report-process⟩

⟨test-process⟩ :: = test ⟨test-condition⟩ | test if ⟨test-condition⟩
⟨test-condition⟩ :: = ⟨symbol-structure⟩ ⟨relation⟩ ⟨symbol-structure⟩ |
    ⟨test-condition⟩ and ⟨test-condition⟩ | ⟨test-condition⟩ or ⟨test-condition⟩ |
    not ⟨test-condition⟩ | true | false | (⟨test-condition⟩)

⟨generate-process⟩ :: = generate ⟨set⟩; ⟨subprocess⟩. |
    generate ⟨set⟩ (⟨result-identification⟩): ⟨subprocess⟩.
⟨subprocess⟩ :: = ⟨sequential-process⟩ | ⟨process⟩
⟨set⟩ :: = ⟨set-identifier⟩ | ⟨associate⟩

⟨find-process⟩ :: = find ⟨find-condition⟩
⟨find-condition⟩ :: = ⟨relation⟩ (⟨symbol⟩) | ⟨associate⟩ | ⟨pattern⟩ in ⟨pattern⟩

⟨report-process⟩ :: = report ⟨text⟩
⟨text⟩ :: = ⟨output-word⟩ | ⟨output-word⟩ ⟨text⟩
⟨output-word⟩ :: = ⟨word⟩ | ⟨identifier⟩ | ⟨result-identifier⟩

These four classes of processes—test-processes, generate-processes, find-processes, and report-processes—are distinguished from other processes, as defined by the syntax earlier, in having a special syntax for giving their operands, instead of the ⟨operand-statement⟩ that is otherwise used.

⟨production-system⟩ :: = ⟨production⟩. | ⟨production⟩. ⟨production-system⟩
⟨production⟩ :: = ⟨condition⟩ ⟶ ⟨action-sequence⟩ |
    ⟨production-identifier⟩: ⟨production⟩
⟨production-identifier⟩ :: = ⟨identifier⟩
⟨action-sequence⟩ :: = ⟨action⟩ | ⟨action⟩; ⟨action-sequence⟩
⟨action⟩ :: = ⟨operator⟩ | ⟨symbol-structure⟩ | ⟨production-control-action⟩

⟨production-control-action⟩ :: = stop | stop ⟨process⟩ |
    ⟨production-control-action⟩ and ⟨report-process⟩
⟨operator⟩ :: = ⟨process-designation⟩ |
    ⟨process-designation⟩ (⟨result-identification-list⟩)
⟨condition⟩ :: = ⟨elementary-condition⟩ | ⟨elementary-condition⟩ and ⟨condition⟩ |
    ⟨condition⟩ (⟨result-identification-list⟩)
⟨elementary-condition⟩ :: = ⟨pattern⟩ | ⟨value⟩ | not ⟨pattern⟩ | not ⟨value⟩ |
    ⟨elementary-condition⟩ " | " ⟨elementary-condition⟩ | (⟨elementary-condition⟩)

The set of definitions above determines the basic way of writing production systems. Although there are similarities between sequential processes and production systems, e.g., control actions, each requires separate definition. Note in particular that the condition part cannot be an arbitrarily complex test condition. Only a single level of conjunction is permitted and a single level of negation. Result identification is permitted not only after an operator, but after a condition as well. The latter option is necessary, since only a pattern name may be written down, and some item within that pattern may need to be identified for use on the action side of the production.

3

TASK
ENVIRONMENTS

The behaviors commonly elicited when people (or animals) are placed in problem solving situations (and are motivated toward a goal) are called *adaptive*, or *rational*. These terms denote that the behavior is appropriate to the goal in the light of the problem environment; it is the behavior demanded by the situation.

Now if there is such a thing as behavior demanded by a situation, and if a subject exhibits it, then his behavior tells more about the task environment than about him. We learn about the subject only that he is in fact motivated toward the goal, and that he is in fact capable of discovering and executing the behavior called for by the situation. If we put him in a different situation, he would behave differently.

Problem solving situations in which motivation is not in question and emotion is not aroused would therefore seem austere surroundings in which to study psychology. They would appear rather more suitable for investigating the structure of task environments than the nature of behaving organisms. Indeed, one modern social science, economics, has erected an impressive structure for predicting certain human behavior on the foundation of a single psychological postulate. By assuming that economic man is always motivated to maximize his utility (or, in some applications, his profit), and that he is always able to discover and execute the maximizing behavior, we can infer the actions of economic man from the structure of the choices with which he is confronted.

By this stratagem, economics is able to avoid a concern with the psychology of decision making, and to turn, instead, to an analysis of the environment of choice—markets, cost functions, and the like. Likewise, economics finesses questions of value and preference by placing the economic actor's utility function among the given data of the problem, rather than among the behavior variables to be explained and predicted.

Now consider a standard paradigm for an experiment in concept attainment. A sequence of stimuli is presented to a subject, who is asked to classify each as an instance, or noninstance, of a concept (as yet unknown to him). He is informed whether each reply is right or wrong. The conditions of the experiment are carefully arranged so that the subject will be motivated to perform the task well—say, to guess the concept from as few stimuli as possible. If the conditions of the experiment do not achieve appropriate motivation—if the subject refuses to try the task, is obviously inattentive, or undertakes to spoof the experimenter—we would not regard it as an experiment in concept attainment. We would also reclassify the experiment if it turned out that the subject could not discriminate among the stimuli because the light was too dim or because his eyes could not resolve the differences among them. In these cases, we would call it an experiment in visual sensation or, possibly, in perception.

For the properly motivated subject, however, there presumably exists an optimal strategy—a strategy that will disclose the concept in the minimum expected number of trials. (We presuppose that a set of possible concepts is given—this is usually defined by the experimental instructions and the situation.) If the situation is not too complicated, the optimal strategy can sometimes be deduced by means of principles drawn from information theory (Hovland, 1952). It would be perfectly possible for the psychologist to follow the route of the economist: to construct a theory of concept formation that depended on no characteristic of the subject other than his being adequtely motivated to perform well. It would be a theory of how perfectly rational man would behave in that task environment—hence, not a psychological theory but a theory of the structure of the task environment.

In a few cases psychology has in fact begun to explore this route. The applications of statistical decision theory to experiments on choice under uncertainty fit precisely into the mold of formal economic thinking (Edwards, Lindman, and Phillips, 1965). In psychology, however, the deductions from premises of rationality about how rational man *would* behave are almost always accompanied by experiments on how laboratory man *does* behave. The discrepancies between behavior and predictions from the rational model are often large; they tend to vanish only when the rational behavior is transparently obvious, and not always even then. (We may well ask, "Obvious to whom?" If the subject does not behave rationally, we may take this fact as the definition of the rational behavior's not being obvious to him!)

It is precisely when we begin to ask *why* the properly motivated subject does not behave in the manner predicted by the rational model that we recross the boundary again from a theory of the task environment to a psychological theory of human rationality. The explanation must lie inside the subject: in limits of his ability to determine what the optimal behavior is, or to execute it if he can determine it. In simple concept attainment experiments, for example, the most important mechanism that prevents the subject from adopting an efficient strategy is usually the limit on the number of symbols he can retain and manipulate in short-term memory. To the extent that this is true, such experiments are experiments to reveal the structure of human short-term memory, and it is for this reason that *cognitive strain* plays such a central role in the Bruner-Goodnow-Austin (1956) explanation of concept attainment phenomena.

In summary, then, when we study a properly motivated subject confronted with an intellective task, we are observing *intendedly rational behavior* or behavior of *limited rationality* (Simon, 1947). Our examination of such behavior will lead to two kinds of knowledge:

1. To the extent that the behavior is precisely what is called for by the situation, it will give us information about the task environment. By observing the behavior of a grandmaster over a chessboard, we gain information about the structure of the problem space associated with the game of chess.
2. To the extent that the behavior departs from perfect rationality, we gain information about the psychology of the subject, about the nature of the internal mechanisms that are limiting his performance.

Just as a scissors cannot cut paper without two blades, a theory of thinking and problem solving cannot predict behavior unless it encompasses both an analysis of the structure of task environments and an analysis of the limits of rational adaptation to task requirements. We shall attempt such a two-bladed theory here, but we shall have to place bounds on the undertaking. A complete theory of task environments would have to cover all of human knowledge—natural science, practical arts, games, fine arts, and what not. We have no stomach (yet) for such a quixotic undertaking. Nevertheless, we will devote much more attention throughout the book to the analysis of the task environment than is customary in psychological works.

The term *task environment*, as we shall use it, refers to an environment coupled with a goal, problem, or task—the one for which the motivation of the subject is assumed.[1] It is the task that defines a point of view about an environment, and that, in fact, allows an environment to be delimited. Also, throughout the book, we shall often distinguish the two aspects of the theory of problem solving as (1) demands of the task environment and (2) psychology of the subject. These shorthand expressions should never seduce the reader into thinking that as a psychologist he should be interested only in the psychology of the subject. The two aspects are in fact like figure and ground—although which is which depends on the momentary viewpoint.

---

[1] There could of course be several such goals; the complication can be ignored here.

Because the task environment plays such a large role in the theory of problem solving, this chapter examines in detail a number of issues relating to it. The first section discusses how the external environment is to be represented. The second section considers how the subject represents a problem internally, and introduces the concept of a problem space, which we will use throughout the book. These two sections, then, focus on very general issues of the relations between experimenter and environment (i.e., the task environment) and the subject (i.e., his problem space).

The chapter's third and fourth sections carry further the treatment of problems and problem spaces. The third section draws upon the description of an information processing system provided in Chapter 2 to show, by example and in some detail, how a problem space is to be represented in an IPS, and how the processes of the IPS operate on such a representation to solve problems. The fourth section moves from the detail of the examples to a more general characterization of problem spaces, introducing two very broad classes of problem representations: set representations and search representations. This classification will provide the foundation for a discussion, in the next chapter, of the dependence of the structure of problem solving methods upon the structure of the problem space.

The chapter's fifth, and final, section returns from viewing internal representations—problem spaces—to considering again what it means for a task environment to impose demands upon a problem solver. The conclusions from this discussion will be important in justifying the techniques we use in later chapters to abstract from detail when we describe task environments and when we compare subjects' behavior with the behavior demanded by the environment.

REPRESENTATION OF THE EXTERNAL ENVIRONMENT

In talking about the task environment we must maintain clear distinctions among the environment itself (the Kantian *Ding an sich*, as it were), the internal representation of the task environment used by the subject (the problem space), and the theorist's "objective" description of that environment. This is the classical problem in psychology of defining the effective stimulus.

Consider a typical demonstration in perception—the Necker cube. A two-dimensional geometric figure drawn on a sheet of paper (Figure 3.1) is shown to the

FIGURE 3.1
Necker cube

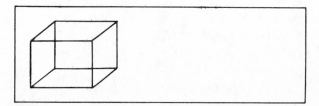

subject, and he is asked, essentially, to interpret it in three dimensions (translate: to construct an internal representation of the stimulus as three-dimensional). For almost all subjects, two such representations are possible—there are two ways of interpreting the stimulus on the retina as if it were produced by a three-dimensional object "out there in the real world." In fact, of course, neither interpretation is veridical, for the experimenter knows (as does the subject) that the geometric object producing the retinal stimulation is "really" two-dimensional. Now the distinction we wish to maintain is the distinction between the way or ways the subject interprets the Necker cube, and the actual stimulus provided by the experimenter.[2]

In the case at hand, and many like it, there is no serious difficulty in describing the stimulus itself as it impinges on the sense organs of the subject. In the case of the Necker cube, all that is required is to describe (or better, to exhibit) the two-dimensional figure, to state (or exhibit) the conditions under which it is presented to the subject (size, distance, illumination, and so on), and to quote (or exhibit) the verbal instructions that are given to the subject.

Even in this instance, the amount and fineness of detail required for veridicality can in the last analysis only be determined empirically. For example, small imperfections in the figure—slight departures from linearity, or nonuniform color of the surface—might, under some circumstances, turn out to be important. The experimenter's intonations in reading the instructions to the subject could sometimes be relevant. Any description of the stimulus—short of exhibiting the actual experimental setup—involves abstraction, hence the possibility of omitting detail that affects the subject's behavior. (Even total exhibition involves abstraction—it just pushes the responsibility off on the observer.) Of course this difficulty, while present in principle, is not always of practical importance. In practice, the Necker cube stimulus can easily be described without leaving out aspects of the situation that will turn out to affect significantly the responses of the subject.[3]

If the stimulus had been, say, a van Gogh painting instead of a Necker cube, no veridical verbal description would have been possible. Here, exhibiting the actual stimulus, under the actual lighting and other conditions of the experiment, would be the only way of guaranteeing that it was properly characterized. For purposes of some experiments a good color photographic reproduction of the painting might suffice, but it is easy to conceive of experiments where such a reproduction would be a wholly different stimulus from the painting itself. And even if the color photograph were the actual stimulus, we would still have no satisfactory way of describing the stimulus except by reproducing it accurately. It could not be described in words.

It is instructive to try to explain *why* we can describe some stimuli verbally, but not others—why we can describe the Necker cube, but not a van Gogh painting

[2] We are using the Necker cube in the service of a methodological discussion. There is also a large literature on the psychology of the Necker cube, some of which contributes directly to the points made here (e.g., Gregory, 1966; Simon, 1967b).

[3] We can use this criterion as the basic test for the veridicality of the description of a stimulus: it is veridical if a stimulus built from the description (by one skilled in the art) produces the same behavior in subjects as the original stimulus did.

or even a reproduction of one. A necessary condition for a stimulus to be describable is that it can and will be encoded in highly simplified form by any subject exposed to it. If we know the language that will be used in the encoding, then we also have sufficient conditions for a description, for we can describe the stimulus in that same language. But if different subjects encode the stimulus in different languages, we cannot construct a single description that is guaranteed to be veridical for all; for a stimulus reconstructed from the description may alter properties of the original stimulus that are ignored by the language of the description but are not ignored by other encoding languages subjects may use.

In the case of the Necker cube, for example, we can describe the stimulus adequately on the assumption that each subject will handle the figure as an arrangement of line segments and plane figures bounded by line segments. We must assume that if there are very slight irregularities in the heaviness or directions of the lines, he will ignore them, retaining and using only the information that a certain distribution of ink is a straight line joining points A and B.

The vast body of experience—in the laboratory and in everyday life—with subjects' interpretations of line drawings gives the experimenter assurance that his descriptions of such stimuli (i.e., describing them as line drawings) are veridical. If he were to experiment with subjects from other species than his own (or perhaps even from other cultures), he would have less reason for assurance. If the subject were a frog, for instance, the experimenter would be rash to describe the stimulus in terms of lines (Lettvin, Maturana, McCulloch, and Pitts, 1959). All sorts of alternative encodings are conceivable. The difficulties that have been encountered in designing pattern-recognizing devices for two-dimensional stimuli provide concrete evidence that representation of the stimuli in terms of lines requires a nontrivial encoding scheme. Only a subject whose inborn physiological mechanisms provide such a scheme, or who has acquired one by learning, will perceive a Necker cube as made up of a few line segments.

What we have said about visual stimuli applies equally well to verbal stimuli, including experimental instructions. A printed report of verbal instructions will be a veridical description of the stimulus only if the sound waves striking the subjects' ears when the instructions are read to them will be encoded as words in the language of the printed description. (Of course, veridicality requires more than this—in particular, that inflections and intonations omitted from the printed version do not affect the subjects' behaviors significantly.)

To say, then, that the stimulus can be described adequately means that we can predict the vocabulary of elements and relations the subject will use in his initial encoding of it. The description no longer refers exclusively to the stimulus; it postulates something also about the first stages of processing that the stimulus will undergo as it is perceived by the subject. This does not mean, of course, that the subjects' encodings are verbal—that the word "line" appears in a subject's encoding of the Necker cube. It does mean that the subject's initial encoding of the Necker cube stimulus must be composed of elements, however represented, that correspond to the lines in the drawing.

It need not be assumed, however, that the initial encoding of the stimulus will bear any close relation to the way in which it is represented internally in the subject's processing of it at some later stage. The stimulus may—and usually will—be subjected to further transformations as the subject seeks a convenient internal representation—one that he can process relatively easily. (E.g., the subject transforms the Necker cube internally into a representation of a 3-dimensional object.) Our next section will examine these further transformations into the problem space, the way in which the subject represents the problem internally once he has perceived the stimulus.

INTERNAL REPRESENTATIONS: THE PROBLEM SPACE

Even more difficult than describing the stimulus is finding a neutral and objective way of talking about the responses of the subject, including his internal thinking responses, as he goes about dealing with the stimulus situation. Our description of his behavior will necessarily be molar rather than molecular—we will not be tempted to refer to the space-time coordinates of his body parts and the sound waves emanating from his mouth. But that is not the main source of difficulty. We shall find it necessary to describe not only his actual behaviors, but the set of possible behaviors from which these are drawn; and not only his overt behaviors, but also the behaviors he considers in his thinking that don't correspond to possible overt behaviors. In sum, we need to describe the space in which his problem solving activities take place. We will call it the *problem space.*

This is not a space that can yet be pointed to and described as an objective fact for a human subject. An attempt at describing it amounts, again, to constructing a representation of the task environment—the subject's representation in this case. The subject in an experiment is presented with a set of instructions and a sequence of stimuli. He must encode these problem components—defining goals, rules, and other aspects of the situation—in some kind of space that represents the initial situation presented to him, the desired goal situation, various intermediate states, imagined or experienced, as well as any concepts he uses to describe these situations to himself.

Example of an Internal Representation

A specific example will help delineate the exact nature of the difficulty, and will provide a starting point for our discussion of how to obviate it. We consider, as our problem situation, a two-person game (*number scrabble*) having the following rules: A set of nine cardboard squares (pieces), like those used in the game of Scrabble, is placed, face-up, between the two players. Each piece bears a different integer, from 1 to 9, so that all nine digits are represented. The players draw pieces alternately from the set. The first player who holds any subset of exactly *three* pieces, from among those he has drawn, with digits summing to 15, wins. If all the pieces are drawn from the set without either player obtaining three whose digits sum to 15, the game is a draw. Thus, if the alternate draws are 2, 7; 5, 8; 4, 6; 9, the first player wins, since $2 + 4 + 9 = 15$. If the alternate draws are 5, 2; 8, 6; 7, 3; 1, 9; 4, neither player wins, since no combination of three digits selected from the set (5, 8, 7, 1, 4) sums to 15, nor does any combination of three selected from the set (2, 6, 3, 9).

The description, just given, of number scrabble constitutes a description of the stimulus confronting each player that is adequate for all practical purposes. It is objective in the sense that it simply (if only grossly) describes the visual and aural stimuli actually presented to the subjects when the game is explained to them. But the subject's task environment contains more than just this stimulus. It contains also the various possibilities that exist for playing the game—that is, for changing the stimulus. How can we represent these possibilities objectively?

One possible representation is provided by the game tree. Every possible play of the number scrabble game can be represented by a permutation of the nine digits. We can represent the set of permutations as a tree, arranged according to the first digit selected; then, among those branches having the same first digit, arranged according to the second digit; and so on. The tree contains a total of 9!—352,880—terminal branches. A few initial branches are shown in Figure 3.2. (Some of these branches are inessential, in cases where the game would end before the ninth move.) Since the game is a game of perfect information with a finite (large but not enormous) game tree, an optimal strategy can in fact be devised with only a finite number of calculations. The strategy is based on the well-known minimax principle of game theory. The player simply examines all the branches of the game tree, and assigns to each terminal the value, to him—win, draw, or lose. He then works backward, assigning to each branch the best of the outcomes (win, draw, or lose) for the subbranches at nodes where it is his turn to move, and the worst of the outcomes for the subbranches at nodes where it is his opponent's turn to move.

But in examining internal representations are we safe in limiting ourselves to the alternatives contained in the game tree? Consider the following situation. The players have made the initial moves 3, 5; 9, 7. The first player now calculates what his next move shall be. He has already drawn the digits 3 and 9, which together total 12. A winning strategy would be to draw the number which, when added to this total, yields 15. The appropriate move for this strategy is readily calculated: it is $15 - 12 = 3$. So the first player wishes to consider the winning sequence 3, 5; 9, 7; 3.

It will be objected immediately (and correctly) that 3 is not a legal move here, because a 3 has been drawn previously, and each digit appears on only one piece. Presumably the player will check for the legality of his move, and will discover that 3 is not available. (If actual physical pieces are used, he will discover it, if in no other way, from his failure to find 3 among the pieces remaining in the center.) Nevertheless, we must not exclude the possibility that the player will actually carry through the calculation of subtracting 12 from 15, get 3 as his result, and only then discover that the move 3 is not available. If we are to construct a theory of the subject's thought processes, and to refer in that theory to the set of behaviors he *considers*, we must include in that set even behaviors that, though considered, prove infeasible, illegal, or in some other way impossible. We must, so to speak, represent the subject's wishes and dreams as well as his more realistic thoughts. There is no essential reason, of course, why such considerations should remain covert. If, in our example, the player said, "Oh, there is no 3," we would thereby have concrete evidence of his having gone outside the game tree.

FIGURE 3.2

game tree for number scrabble

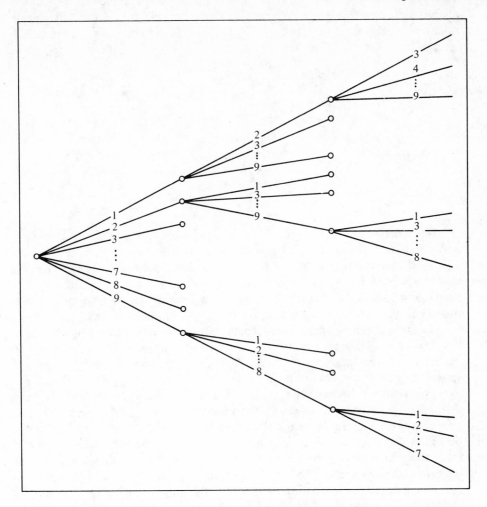

Recoding of Representations

The situation where the subject considers alternatives beyond those included in the game tree or other representation of the genuine behavior possibilities is not the only one that makes it difficult to describe the task environment objectively. Another whole set of difficulties arises out of the fact that the subject may recode the situation completely.

Consider the familiar game of tic-tac-toe. There is a three-by-three array of blank squares. Players occupy squares alternately, marking the square occupied by a ○ or ×, respectively. The first player who attains a horizontal, vertical, or diagonal sequence of three of his symbols wins. If the whole array is filled without either player's attaining such a sequence, the game is a draw.

Now it is true, although not obvious, that the game of tic-tac-toe is formally

61

equivalent to the game of number scrabble that we described earlier. (We wonder how many readers, almost all of whom have surely played tic-tac-toe, were aware of this equivalence before we mentioned it.) To see this, we construct the magic square whose rows, columns, and diagonals each sum to 15, as shown in Figure 3.3.

FIGURE 3.3
magic square for tic-tac-toe

2	7	6
9	5	1
4	3	8

If we played tic-tac-toe on this magic square, whenever a player attained a horizontal, vertical, or diagonal row, he would possess a set of three numbers adding to 15. The construction of the magic square assures this. The converse is also true, as can be verified by enumeration: any player occupying three squares that add to 15 will find that these squares lie in a horizontal, vertical, or diagonal row. Thus, the formal equivalence of the two games has been proved.

To say that the two games are formally equivalent does not say that a person who knew a good strategy for playing one of them would be capable of transferring the strategy immediately to the other. Tic-tac-toe experts will readily persuade themselves that this is not at all easy.

The following is generally regarded as a good strategy for the first player in tic-tac-toe. Since the game is a draw when viewed from a game-theoretic standpoint, *good* means here a strategy that will guarantee a draw and that will give the opponent as many opportunities as possible of making a losing mistake. We outline the strategy as a production system (Figure 3.4). We do not show details of the patterns to be detected on the board, which are familiar to all tic-tac-toe players. ⟨own-winning-pattern⟩ is a line with two of the player's marks and one blank. ⟨opponent-winning-pattern⟩ is the same, but with the opponent's marks rather

FIGURE 3.4
production system for playing tic-tac-toe

tic-tac-toe-strategy:
1. side-to-move = opponent ⟶ stop.
2. ⟨own-winning-pattern⟩ (⇒ blank-square) ⟶ play (blank-square).
3. ⟨opponent-winning-pattern⟩ (⇒ blank-square) ⟶ play (blank-square).
4. ⟨own-forking-pattern⟩ (⇒ intersection-square) ⟶ play (intersection-square).
5. center = blank ⟶ play (center).
6. ⟨opponent-on-side⟩ ⟶ find corner = blank; play (corner).
7. ⟨opponent-on-corner⟩ ⟶ find opposite of corner; play (opposite).

than the player's. ⟨own-forking-pattern⟩ contains two lines, each with one of player's mark and two blanks, intersecting in a single blank square. Playing in the intersecting square creates two ⟨own-winning-pattern⟩'s, thus forking the opponent.

How would a player, knowing this tic-tac-toe strategy, play number scrabble? We assume the players are not allowed pencil and paper to assist their memories. If the player is gifted with a certain amount of visual imagery, he can proceed as follows. He memorizes the array of numbers in the magic square. Then as he, or his opponent, draws a numbered piece in the number scrabble game, he visualizes the corresponding ◯ or × on the square. In this way, he can detect two-in-a-row situations, and can distinguish center, side, and corner locations as required in order to apply the strategy. We have verified that this is a feasible method for at least some subjects.

An alternative method would be to translate the tic-tac-toe strategy into the language of the number scrabble game, and learn to apply the new strategy directly in that game. The translation of the strategy is fairly straightforward. *Winning move* is redefined as *triplet adding to 15, blocking* as *taking the number needed by the opponent to complete such a triplet, forking move* as *move creating two pairs each of which belongs to a triplet still completable.* For *center square*, we read 5; for *corner square, even number;* for *side square, odd number other than 5.* Finally, we translate *square opposite* as *ten's complement of*—i.e., the number, x, such that square + x = 10. Strategy for tic-tac-toe can be translated word-for-word into the equivalent strategy for number scrabble. For example: "If the opponent then occupies a corner square, occupy the opposite corner" becomes "If the opponent then takes an even number, take its ten's complement." We leave the rest of the translation as an exercise for the reader.

Finding an Objective Representation

The games of number scrabble and tic-tac-toe provide us with an example of a very simple problem situation where subjects can (and occasionally do) represent the task internally in quite different ways. How shall the experimenter talk about the task? Since the two games are formally equivalent, it is not clear which, if either, of the descriptions we have presented should be chosen to represent the problem space. Any player could use either representation (or some other) when playing either game. He could use a combination of them—for example, representing number scrabble as tic-tac-toe on a magic square, as we outlined earlier. And, as we have also seen, he can use a representation that permits him to consider moves that are not legal moves in the actual game. It would seem that the experimenter's description of the task environment, whatever representation he uses for that description, would be no less subjective than the player's. No particular description appears to have claim to complete or exclusive veridicality.

Rather than try to untie this Gordian knot, we might ask whether we can cut it. Perhaps it is not necessary, in constructing and testing a theory of problem solving, for the experimenter to use an explicit representation of the task environment. What are some of the other possibilities?

One possibility is to omit a description of the objective problem space, but to incorporate in the theory hypotheses about the internal representation the subject will himself use for the problem space. This possibility exists because the behavior of the subject cannot depend on what the problem really is—neither he nor we know that—but only on what the stimulus is. Hence it is the stimulus, including the feedback the subject receives from the environment as a result of his behavior in the problem situation, not the real problem, that should enter as an independent variable if we wish to predict the representation. Even in situations where we wish to predict how differences in problem statements affect ability to solve the problem, we need not describe the external task environment, but only the stimulus and feedback rules.

A somewhat different possibility, a pragmatic one in this case, is to construct a hypothetical problem space that is objective only in the sense that all of the representations that human subjects in fact use for handling the problem can be imbedded as specializations in this larger space. This solution operates as follows: Consider a large number of subjects placed in a task environment and allowed to study and analyze that environment over a long period of time. Presumably, they will devise a number of representations for characterizing the environment, and the representations they use will change over time. If we allow enough time, the rate at which they generate new representations will gradually decrease, and presently additional ones will appear rarely if at all. We shall equate the real environment with the whole set of representations generated up to the time when this asymptote is reached, together with the mappings that define the relations of each of the representations to the others. With this strategy the experimenter knows, for all practical purposes, this entire set of representations and mappings.[4]

What does this latter requirement amount to from a practical standpoint? First, it is important only in situations where subjects do, in fact, employ a number of internal representations, and where the theory is concerned with which representation they employ, or how they acquire a representation. Of course, most situations that are interesting for a theory of thinking and problem solving have these characteristics.

Second, the requirement can be satisfied approximately by studying situations where the complexity is great relative to the time available to subjects for analyzing it. Then the experimenter, even if he is no more intelligent than his subjects, can meet the requirement by devoting much more time to the analysis of the situation than is available to any subject (or alternatively, by withholding from them some of the information that is available to him about the structure of the environment).

In the studies in this book, we conform reasonably with this strategy for two of our tasks, cryptarithmetic and elementary logic, but fall short with the third, chess. We are, in fact, somewhat handicapped in studying the behavior of masters and grandmasters in chess, since we cannot attain a better understanding of the task environment than such subjects.

---

[4] It is conceivable that for a formally given IPS one could develop a formal theory of *all* representations of a given task. However, no such theory has yet come forth for any interesting task environment.

Since the theories that will be discussed in this book include in their structure explicit descriptions of the central processes and memory contents of the subjects, these theories, in effect, assert what the subjects' representations will be. To the extent that different problem spaces would lead to different behavior in the face of the experimental task, these assertions are empirically testable.

Let us consider a simple example from the number scrabble game. Suppose we were to hypothesize that a particular subject was using the magic square representation in choosing his moves—that is, that he visualized his choices, and his opponent's, as lying in rows and columns in the square. Now suppose that the subject, having already drawn the numbers 9 and 3, said something like: "That makes 12. I need 3 to make 15," and then searched for a 3 among the pieces remaining to be chosen. This behavior would provide rather conclusive evidence that the hypothesis was wrong—that the subject was not using the magic square representation, but some kind of arithmetic problem space. For 9 and 3 do not lie on a row, column, or central diagonal of the magic square; hence a subject using that representation would not treat those numbers as a possible basis for a winning triad.

In later chapters of this book we shall present various examples of inferences that predict the behavior of the subject from his (hypothesized) representation, and then test the prediction by comparing it with the actual behavior. Hypotheses about internal representations will, in fact, be a major source of the predictive power and parsimony of our theories. For the assumption that a particular problem space is being used generally has many consequences for behavior, hence permits many predictions. Moreover, if we are willing to assume (1) that the number of representations available to human subjects is not enormous—is, in fact, quite modest—and (2) that the same representations are used in performing a considerable range of tasks, then the parsimony of the theories is greatly enhanced.

Representations and Linguistic Deep Structure

We are now in a position to see more clearly the meaning of the assertion in the previous chapter that the internal representations employed by the IPS are to be regarded as the deep structures postulated by modern structural linguists. Language is usually discussed in a context of interpersonal symbol processing—speaking (writing) and listening (reading). But there has also been much inconclusive discussion in psychology about the role of language in internal symbol processing—in thinking. John Dewey (1910, p. 170) has described the alternative views as well as anyone:

> Three typical views have been maintained regarding the relation of thought and language: first, that they are identical; second, that words are the garb or clothing of thought, necessary not for thought but only for conveying it; and third . . . that while language is not thought it is necessary for thinking as well as for its communication. When it is said, however, that

thinking is impossible without language, we must recall that language includes much more than oral and written speech. Gestures, pictures, monuments, visual images, finger movements—anything consciously employed as a *sign* is, logically, language.

The difficulties, we submit, in choosing among these views, stem from ambiguity of the term "language." The position implicit in the analysis of this book can be summed up as follows:

1. The generation or processing of symbol structures that are isomorphic with the strings of natural language or with their surface structures (in the linguist's meaning of that phrase) is inessential to human problem solving of the kinds we examine.
2. The internal symbol structures that represent problems and information about problems are synonymous with the linguist's deep structure. If "language" means deep structure, then language is essential to thinking and problem solving.

In sum, paraphrasing Dewey: (1) The surface structure of language, and language strings, are the garb or clothing of thought, necessary not for thought but only for conveying it. (2) While linguistic deep structure is not thought, it is necessary for thinking.

To the extent that the problem representations we shall postulate do, in fact, explain the problem solving behavior of human beings, the claim that the structures embodying these representations are linguistic deep structures gains strong support. For if this were not so, *and* if language is implicated in thinking, then we would have to postulate a distinct set of deep structures, holding the meanings of the surface structures, carried along by the IPS in parallel with the "nonlinguistic" problem representations. But this is an unnecessary and unparsimonious multiplication of hypothetical entities that has no evidential support. We prefer the simpler course that identifies deep structures closely with semantics, hence with the internal symbol structures that are the media of thought.

The theories of deep structure that have been sketched by linguists (up to the present time no more than sketches are available) generally associate individual deep structures with individual sentences of the surface strings. In contrast, the internal structures we shall postulate for problem solving situations generally constitute large, complex, interrelated contexts that do not factor in any simple way into components that are isomorphic with single sentences. These complex internal structures, extending far beyond sentence boundaries, provide a promising route toward explaining how context can determine the meanings of otherwise ambiguous natural language strings. The exploration of this route, however tempting, cannot be undertaken in this book. The early work by Lindsay (1961, 1963) gives some general indication of what we mean by this brief allusion, and provides the reader with a starting point if he wishes to undertake the exploration himself.

In developing our tic-tac-toe and number scrabble examples of possible problem spaces, we have already been drawing implicitly on the assumption that the subjects in our experiments behave like information processing systems of the sort that we described in Chapter 2. We need now to consider in more detail how an IPS can store and process problem space representations. The game of number scrabble again provides a simple example of how this can be done.

Our concern at present is not with hypothesizing specifically how human subjects in fact represent this problem, but with providing a concrete illustration of how an IPS can represent it—how it can encode the elements of the problem space into symbol structures, and how it can operate on these structures to accomplish the processing required to play the game.

Objects will be represented by symbols; *sets of objects* will be represented by lists. The *relations* between various objects and sets of objects will be represented by associations. *Moves* will be represented by processes, which modify the internal symbol structures in correspondence with the way the moves would modify the external sets of objects or their relations. In addition, for the IPS to play, other processes are needed to test the representation for certain features and to embody various strategies of play.

Figure 3.5 gives the details of the representation. The basic objects are players (two) and pieces (nine). There are three sets: unmoved-pieces, pieces-of-player-1, and pieces-of-player-2. Each player has an association (attribute: own-pieces) to the set of his pieces. Each piece has an association (attribute: integer) to the name of the integer (from 1 to 9) on that piece.

Thus, at the beginning of the game, the sets of pieces-of-player-1 and pieces-of-player-2 are empty, while the set of unmoved-pieces contains all nine of the pieces. A move is a process that removes one piece from the list of unmoved-pieces and adds it to the list of own-pieces of the player who is moving. Besides the basic process for moving, some processes are needed for manipulating integers: *sum*, which adds up two integers to produce a third (their sum); and *complement*, which takes an integer as input and produces the difference between it and 15 as output (thus, more accurately, *15's-complement*).

The three processes listed in Figure 3.5 are taken as primitive, but they can also be expressed as programs in terms of still more primitive processes for manipulating and testing lists and associations. In Figure 3.6 we give programs for all three. The arithmetic is of the "counting fingers" variety, since we do not wish to introduce a full array of arithmetic processes; still, it gets the job done. The processes used in Figure 3.6 are truly primitive, in that we have not introduced any other representation in terms of which we could discuss how they are realized.

With this representation of number scrabble we can express how a player could discover, for example, whether he had an immediately winning move. Figure 3.7 shows the program. We have used a generator of all pairs from a set. This produces, as element, a list of two symbols. Again, we could take this as primitive (as we have taken generate as primitive). However, Figure 3.8 does show a process for realizing *generate-pairs*.

FIGURE 3.5

symbol structures and primitive processes for tic-tac-toe

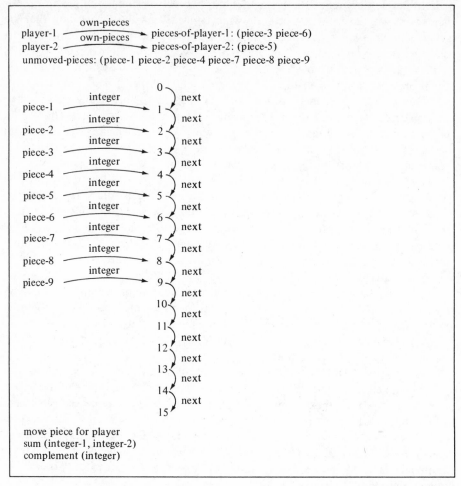

In Figure 3.7 it might appear costly, in terms of processing time, to have to repeat the subprocess (lines 2–6) for each pair on the list of own-pieces. However, this list would never have more than three members (if the player has already made four moves, his fifth move is forced); hence, there would never be more than six such pairs. Actually, a more efficient process would consider only pairs that contain the most recently moved piece, since the others would already have been considered on a previous move. With this added refinement, three pairs, at most, would have to be examined.

On the other hand, with this representation, somewhat more processing is required to determine if the player has a forking move—i.e., a move that sets up two possible winning moves for the next round, hence cannot be countered by the opponent. Figure 3.9 gives the program. The processing cost for finding forking moves in this way may be large. Three generators are nested: the first generates pairs of pieces from the list of own-pieces, the second and third generate pieces from

FIGURE 3.6

basic processes for number scrabble

move piece for player:
1. delete piece from unmoved-pieces,
      if fail stop move and report illegal;
2. find own-pieces of player;
3. insert piece on result.

sum (integer-1, integer-2):
1. initialize count to be 0;
2. initialize total to be integer-1;
3. test if count = integer-2,
      if true stop and report total;
4. find next of count ($\Rightarrow$ count);
5. find next of total ($\Rightarrow$ total),
      go to 3.

complement (integer):
1. initialize count to be 0;
2. initialize total to be integer;
3. test if total = 15,
      if true stop and report count;
4. find next of count ($\Rightarrow$ count);
5. find next of total ($\Rightarrow$ total),
      go to 3.

FIGURE 3.7

program for finding winning move

make-winning-move for player:
1.   generate-pairs own-pieces of player ($\Rightarrow$ (first second)):
2.   sum (integer of first, integer of second);
3.   complement (sum);
4.   generate unmoved-pieces:
5.   test if integer of unmoved-piece = complement,
                  if false continue generation;
6.   move unmoved-piece for player,
                  stop process.,
      stop and report no move.

the list of unmoved-pieces. On the first player's fourth move, for example, the three nested generators involve consideration of a maximum of $6 \times 3 \times 3 = 54$ cases, and if the branch is reached, yet another generator is called into operation.

   Consider, on the other hand, how the forking moves could be discovered with the tic-tac-toe representation. We could associate with each piece the rows, columns, and diagonals (i.e., the lists of three pieces, or triads) to which it belongs.

69

FIGURE 3.8
program for generate-pairs

```
generate-pairs list: subprocess:
1.      generate list (⇒ first-element):
2.          generate remainder-list of first-element (⇒ second-element):
3.              construct (first-element second-element);
4.              apply subprocess to result,
                    if stop-generate stop process and report stopped..,
            stop and report completed.
```

FIGURE 3.9
program for finding forking moves

```
make-forking-move for player:
1.      generate-pairs own-pieces of player (⇒ (first second)):
2.          generate unmoved-pieces (⇒ potential-fork):
3.              sum (integer of first, integer of potential-fork);
4.              complement (sum);
5.              generate unmoved-pieces:
6.                  test if unmoved-piece = potential-fork,
                        if true stop;
7.                  test if integer of unmoved-piece = complement,
                        if true stop generation.,
                    if completed stop;
8.              sum (integer of second, integer of potential-fork);
9.              complement (sum);
10.             generate unmoved-pieces:
11.                 test if unmoved-piece = potential-fork,
                        if true continue generation;
12.                 test if integer of unmoved-piece = complement,
                        if true stop generation.,
                    if completed stop;
13.             move potential-fork for player,
                    stop process..,
            stop and report no move.
```

For each piece on the unmoved-piece list, we look for those rows, columns, and diagonals for which one of the remaining pieces is on the unmoved-piece list, the other on the player's own-pieces list. If there are two such triads, the piece gives a forking move. (In addition, triads already blocked could be marked, further cheapening the search.) This is clearly a much simpler process than the one previously described.

Now there is nothing that prevents us, in the number scrabble representation, from storing in memory the lists of triads associated with each move, and hence making it possible to use essentially the same process for finding forking moves as we used in the tic-tac-toe representation. But the presence or absence of this information, in readily accessible form, is precisely the crux of the difference in representations. For the human being playing number scrabble, these lists are not in fact available, unless he explicitly goes to the trouble of writing them down or memorizing them. In tic-tac-toe, the lists are directly available in the visual diagram, which can be scanned rapidly along rows, columns, and diagonals.

In summary, let us return to a point made earlier about the requisite level of detail in describing information processing. As long as the processes being discussed are quite definite and elementary, it can often simply be assumed that there exists some encoding of the objects into symbol structures and some straightforward programs adapted to that encoding that will accomplish the processing and produce the indicated information as output (in an appropriate encoding). When the existence of such an encoding and such programs can be postulated, it is not necessary to specify the details of either encoding or programs.

We have given an explicit specification here for number scrabble to illustrate exactly what is involved in such a description of structure and processes. We will also provide such specifications at several other places throughout the book, where the specific encoding of objects or operations becomes important. But generally we will float above this level of detail. The fact that running computer programs exist for various tasks provides a continuing guarantee that the lower, more detailed levels of specification have been made explicit in many cases and could be in others.

The ability to abstract from detail partly reflects the simple hierarchical structure of information processing. However, it also reflects the power of lists and associations as general-purpose representations for encoding information. If, perchance, we had started with a linearly addressed memory, such as is found in a standard computer, we would have faced questions about how particular task environments could be encoded. The representation in terms of list structures and associations is particularly convenient in making it possible to add additional information to memory without destroying the information already encoded into the representation. It thereby greatly simplifies the representation task.

SOME CLASSES OF PROBLEM SPACES

So far we have proceeded almost entirely by example in characterizing representations of problem spaces and problems. It is time now to view matters more broadly and, abstracting from the detailed structure of either the IPS or its specific problem representations, characterize problem solving tasks in more general terms. Taking this broader view will give us a better picture of the whole area. It will also provide essential vantage points for the treatment of problem solving in the next chapter. Let us indicate briefly the nature of the connection.

In our illustrations of problem spaces we have already introduced important abstractions. Implicitly, the problem spaces have all been defined in relation to task goals, and the representations have been restricted to aspects of the total environment that were task-relevant. For example, we did not specify the physical dimensions of the pieces used in number scrabble, or their color. Reader and authors automatically assumed that such properties were irrelevant to the goal.

However, since the relation of problem space to goal has thus far been left implicit, we have not had to state explicitly what a problem is, and what the interdependence is between task environment and goal. This interdependence is crucial —as we have already seen—for separating the task-relevant from the task-irrelevant components of the task environment, so that only the former need be incorporated in the problem space. The interdependence is crucial, also, in enabling the processes that the IPS has available—which must, after all, be provided to it in advance of its meeting a *specific* problem—to be brought to bear upon the tasks posed by these specific task environments. By introducing a general typology of problem spaces, we take the first step toward showing how general methods, associated with these types, can be used to solve specific problems. The demonstration will be continued in Chapter 4.

What Is a Problem?

A person is confronted with a *problem* when he wants something and does not know immediately what series of actions he can perform to get it. The desired object may be very tangible (an apple to eat) or abstract (an elegant proof for a theorem). It may be specific (that particular apple over there) or quite general (something to appease hunger). It may be a physical object (an apple) or a set of symbols (the proof of a theorem). The actions involved in obtaining desired objects include physical actions (walking, reaching, writing), perceptual activities (looking, listening), and purely mental activities (judging the similarity of two symbols, remembering a scene, and so on).

In this book, the objects we shall mainly be concerned with are systems of symbols—for example, proofs of theorems or English sentences. The actions we shall examine are mainly manipulations of symbol structures. Restricting the discussion to symbolic entities and processes does not severely limit our analysis of problem solving, except at its physiological boundaries (e.g., the physiological aspects of sensory and motor skills, especially those requiring real-time action and coordination). For the crucial activities, at least in human problem solving of any complexity, are symbol-manipulating activities that take place centrally. This is true even when the desired object and the required activity are physical—e.g., going to the orchard to pick an apple.

Consider the problem of finding a proof for a theorem—say, a theorem in elementary symbolic logic. The objects in this problem, theorems and other logic expressions, are composed of symbols. We represent them internally as list structures, like those we introduced in the last chapter. A proof is a sequence of axioms and theorems, terminating in the theorem to be proved. Hence, a proof may be represented as a list of list structures—which is itself a list structure. The task of finding a proof for a theorem is, then, a task of finding a list structure with appropriate characteristics.

Instead of defining directly what it means most generally for a human to have a problem (or for any organism or device to have one), let us try the following strategy. To have a problem implies (at least) that certain information is given to the problem solver: information about what is desired, under what conditions, by means of what tools and operations, starting with what initial information, and with access to what resources. The problem solver has an interpretation of this information—exactly that interpretation which lets us label some part of it as *goal*, another part as *side conditions*, and so on. Consequently, if we provide a representation for this information (in symbol structures), and assume that the interpretation of these structures is implicit in the program of the problem solving IPS, then we have defined a problem. Thus, we say with any textbook on Euclidean plane geometry:

> Given: A general triangle, ABC.
> Prove: The three lines bisecting its angles
> intersect in a common point.

This is a problem, provided that the problem solver has (implicit) not only information defining triangle, bisecting, and so on, but also appropriate interpretations of Given and Prove. In the appropriate context (e.g., a homework assignment) the problem solver will come to "have" the problem stated above—and will be found diligently at work on it some time before the next class period (assuming he is appropriately motivated).

We need not make special provision for a separate representation for each particular problem. Instead, we can define representations that cover large classes of problems. Likewise, we need not assume that the problem is presented by means of English language statements. This would imply capabilities of understanding natural language that are beside the main issue. Instead, we can define our general representations directly in terms of the essential symbol structures (deep structures). We will introduce two such general representations: the *set representation* and the *search representation*. We have no guarantee that all problems can be represented in one of these two forms. It is always possible that some important classes of problems have not yet been represented.

Set Representation of a Problem

A problem proposed to an information processing system is *well defined* if a test exists, performable by the system, that will determine whether an object proposed as a solution is in fact a solution.[5] By *performable* we mean, more specifically, performable with a relatively small amount of processing effort.

Consider the problem of constructing a symbolic expression having the characteristics $p_1, p_2, \ldots, p_n$. If the system has a set of relatively simple tests for determining whether any expression does or does not have each of the characteristics, p_i, this is a well-defined problem.

In most cases it is possible to define a set of objects—the set of possible solutions—that contains the solution or solutions. Where the solution is a symbolic expression, we can take as this set the set of "all possible" symbolic expressions.

---

[5] The notion of a *well-defined problem* was proposed by McCarthy (1956).

When we need to be more precise, we may define it as the set generated by a certain enumerative procedure from an alphabet of elementary expressions. Hence, in set-theoretical terms, a problem may be characterized as follows:

Given a set U, to find a member of a subset of U having
specified properties (called the goal-set, G).

We will call this the *set representation* of a problem, although either of the longer terms *set-theoretic representation* or *set-predicate representation* would have been equally appropriate. We have already commented on the phrase *having specified properties*. In the sections that follow we shall have more to say about what is meant by *given* and *find*.

Three reasons (not the only ones) why problems are problems are that: (1) the original set, U, of possible solutions given to the problem solver can be very large (it is often immense[6]), (2) the actual solutions, G, can be dispersed very widely and rarely throughout it, and (3) the cost of obtaining each new element and testing it can be very high (e.g., the search for the Northwest Passage). Thus the problem solver is not really given the set of possible solutions; instead he is given some process for generating elements of that set (all or some of them) in some order. Such a generator has properties of its own, not usually specified in stating the problem—e.g., there is associated with it a certain cost per element produced, it may or may not be possible to change the order in which it produces the elements, and so on. The test that a given element has the desired properties also has costs and times associated with it. The problem can be solved if all of these costs are not too large relative to the time and computing power available for solution.

In some cases, a problem that is characterized set-theoretically can be decomposed into a number of subproblems, each of which can be characterized in the same way. Consider how we might represent the problem of solving a crossword puzzle. Take as U all possible arrays of letters of the English alphabet that will fill the white squares of the puzzle. The subset G comprises those arrays in which all consecutive linear horizontal and vertical sequences of letters form words that satisfy the specified definitions.

Decomposed into subproblems, the crossword puzzle may be described thus: There are n problems, $i = 1, \ldots, n$. Take as U_i the set of all English words. The subset G_i comprises those words that (1) satisfy definition d_i, (2) are of length k_i, and (3) at each intersection with a word belonging to one of the other subproblems (say, at square s_{ij}) have the same English letter as that other word. The last-mentioned condition on the subset G_i, of course, introduces an interdependency among the solution sets for the different subproblems.

The respective responsibilities of generators and tests in obtaining and verifying solutions could be divided in different ways. For example, it might be possible to devise a generator that produced only words satisfying conditions (1) and (2),

---

[6] The term *immense* was proposed by Elsasser (1958) to stand for numbers so large that their logarithms were themselves very large [e.g., N is immense if log (N) = 10^{40}]. The numbers we deal with (e.g., 10^{120}) are not so large, but do satisfy the same functional criterion: that no revision of the number from more detailed investigations and assumptions can affect the argument at hand.

and then simply to test for satisfaction of (3). As expert crossword-puzzle solvers know, this is not the only—nor usually the best—procedure. An alternative is to find a generator that produces only words that satisfy (1) and (3), then test for satisfaction of (2).

In continuing our discussion of factorization it is time to introduce another class of problem representations where the role of factorization into subproblems is even more prominent. We turn now to the search representation.

Search Representation of a Problem

The set representation of a problem, while it is relatively general, is not always the most convenient characterization. As a first step toward constructing an alternative, let us describe in detail, in the set-theoretic framework, the problem of finding a proof for a theorem in Euclidean geometry or elementary symbolic logic. As in the crossword puzzle example, we will exploit the factorability of the problem into subproblems.

Discovering the Proof of a Theorem. A proof of a theorem, t, is a symbolic expression that consists of a sequence of subexpressions (the proof steps). Hence, the set U is the set of such sequences. A sequence, u, belongs to G, the set of proofs of t, if it has properties p_1 and p_2, where p_1 means that each subexpression in u either is an axiom or is derivable by certain allowable transformations (the rules of inference) from previous subexpressions in u, and p_2 means that the final subexpression in u is t.

Consider the tests that determine whether p_1 and p_2 are satisfied. The tests can be factored into parts, each of which is concerned with characteristics of only a portion of u. (1) The test for p_2 concerns only the characteristics of the final subexpression. (2) Let u_i be the object comprised of the first i subexpressions of the sequence u. Then the test for p_1 can be factored into tests p_{11}, p_{12}, and so on, where p_{1i} is a test on the final subexpression, $last(u_i)$, in the sequence u_i.

Moreover, these latter tests are relational—they are satisfied if $last(u_i)$ stands in a certain relation to one or two prior subexpressions in u_i, the subexpressions from which it is directly derived. We can regard the sequence u_i as having been generated from the sequence u_{i-1} by the application of an operator, Q_i, to the latter sequence. We can then write:

$$u_t = Q_t(Q_{t-1}(\ldots Q_1(u_0))\ldots) \tag{1}$$

where $u_i = Q_i(u_{i-1})$ means the expression (sequence) obtained from u_{i-1} by applying to it the operator Q_i, and where u_0 is the sequence of axioms and theorems given initially.

Thus, we can designate the theorem, t, in several ways. It is the final subexpression in the sequence u_t. From the right-hand side of equation (1) we see that it is also the subexpression $last(u_t)$, generated by applying the sequence of operators, Q_i, to u_0. In order to talk about these different ways of referring to objects, it is convenient to introduce the terms *state language* and *process language*. Symbols that designate expressions, elements of expressions, characteristics of expressions, or differences between expressions belong to the state language for the problem. Symbols that designate operators for transforming expressions, sequences of operators, or characteristics of operators belong to the process langugge.

A proof is most simply characterized by using both state and process language. Thus, u_t is a proof of t if $last(u_t) = t$, and if it can be represented in the form of equation (1), where all the Q_i are *admissible* operators—i.e., operators corresponding to the rules of inference—and where the subexpressions of u_0 are axioms and previously proved theorems.

State Space and Action Space. This dual aspect of problem situations is not peculiar to theorem proving. Problem solutions in most domains are defined by (1) characteristics of a terminal state, (2) an initial state, (3) conditions on the admissible transformations from one state into another, and sometimes (4) characteristics of the intermediate states. The state-process distinction is fundamental to understanding the behavior of an organism when it seeks a goal object. The internal representation of the goal object symbolizes it in the state language. What is required is a series of signals (or symbols) in the process language that will transmit the proper instructions through the motor system to the effectors in order to enable the organism to attain the goal (i.e., to change the state to the desired one). Hence, the state language is related to the operation of the afferent system, the process language to the operation of the efferent system. The problem is solved by an appropriate translation of afferent stimuli into efferent responses; and tests of the solution are applied to new stimuli received through the afferent channels.

In everyday language, the term *solution* is used in several different ways. Sometimes (e.g., in theorem proving) we call the sequence of expressions, u_t, the solution. Sometimes (e.g., in the organism's attempt to reach a goal object), we call the sequence of operators, $Q_1, \ldots, Q_t$, the solution. Sometimes (e.g., in a crossword puzzle) we call the terminal state, $last(u_t)$, the solution. Where it is necessary to distinguish them, we may call these the *solution-path*, *solution-action-sequence*, and *solution-object* (or *goal-object*), respectively. When we use the term solution without qualification, it will be clear from the context which one of these is intended.

In the course of solving a problem, more than one potential solution path is sometimes generated. In working forward, for example, more than one admissible operator may be applicable to u_0. Applying each, we obtain paths u_{01}, u_{02}, and so on. Again, in general, more than one admissible operator may be applicable to each of these, giving $u_{011}, u_{012}, \ldots, u_{021}, u_{022}$, and so on. In this way a branching tree of paths (*search tree* or *discovery tree*) is obtained, and the terminal branches are compared with the conditions on $last(u_t)$ until one is found that satisfies these conditions. The path that leads to this branch is a solution path.

Alternative Spaces for Search. In our description of the search representation, the nodes of the search space have been realizable states of affairs, and the links between nodes have been the actions that changed one state into another. But in problem solving the actual search for a solution need not, and usually does not, take place in the external environment. Accordingly, the states represented by nodes of the search space need not correspond with realizable states of the outside world, but can be imaginable states—literally so, since they are internal to the problem solver. These states may be generated, in turn, by operators that do not satisfy all the conditions of admissibility. For example, operators may be employed in the problem space that generate plausible sequences of states, and those sequences that do not satisfy the admissibility tests may be modified or rejected at later stages of the problem solving process.

Putting the matter in different terms, the tree of solution action sequences is only one of a number of trees that may be associated with transformations on a problem space. The structure of the search space that is used is not a property solely of the task environment—its states and admissible actions—but depends also on the problem space and program the problem solver employs. He may, for example, work backward from the desired state, applying operators that are, roughly, the inverses of the admissible actions, in order to see whether he can discover a path that leads back to the initial state.

Operators that are not admissible in the external environment may take the form of conjectures of intermediate states of affairs which, if they could be attained, would be likely steps toward the final goal. Thus, a chess player might conceive through search a specific mating configuration, then initiate a new search to find a sequence of moves to attain this particular checkmate.

Moreover, the solution to the problem of a chess player making a move is not to discover a whole sequence of future moves, but simply to discover a good *next* move. The search tree of subsequent moves that he explores is not a part of a solution action sequence, but is simply a structure he creates to predict future consequences, and to evaluate, thereby, the move directly before him.

Still another possibility—search in a planning space—is illustrated by the crossword puzzle example. At each step of solving a crossword puzzle, a skillful problem solver may first pose the subproblem of finding a good next problem to attack. For example, he may look for a particular word, j, whose initial letter or letters are already known, using this information to simplify the task of the generator seeking to produce a word satisfying the definition, d_j. Thus, at each stage in constructing the solution object, a subsidiary search is evolved to determine which generator is to be activated.

In spite of these qualifications and complications, it is true that in many classes of problems the solution is defined by (1) properties of a solution object, conjoined with (2) the requirement that the solution object be reached by a path that can be generated by application of a sequence of operators drawn from a set of admissible operators (legal moves). In these cases, an elementary problem solving program might generate possible solution paths, using the admissible operators to produce sequences of one kind or another. But we must keep in mind that the problem solver may also make searches in which the states and operators of the problem space do not correspond with the states and admissible operators of the external environment.

Further Examples of Problems

To be a bit more concrete about both set representation and search representation, let us characterize some other common problems in the terms we have been using:

Finding the Combination of a Safe. Take as U all possible settings of the dials of the safe, and as G those particular settings that open the safe. As safes are usually constructed, G consists of a single element. If the safe has several dials, a particular search tree might be produced by trying, for each setting of the first dial, all possible settings of the others, and so on. As in the crossword puzzle example, different problem solving techniques might define vastly different search spaces.

Designing a Machine. Take as U the set of all possible parameter values for a machine design; take as G the subset of parameter values that: (1) satisfy the design specifications, and (2) meet certain criteria of cost minimization. For cases of practical interest, the set U will be immense and hence will have to be explored in somewhat systematic fashion. In early stages of the search, for example, particular design variables may be bounded, or even fixed, prior to establishing limits on the other variables. If the priorities are fairly definite, then the search tree will have hierarchic properties—the branchings at different stages referring to different classes of design variables.

Programming a Computer to Invert a Matrix. Take as U the set of all possible sequences of computer instructions, and as G a particular sequence that will perform the specified matrix inversion. The branching tree of sequences in U also defines a search tree.

Translating a German Article into English. Take as U the set of all possible sequences of English words; take as G the subset of sequences that: (1) satisfy certain criteria of English syntax and style, and (2) have the same meaning as the German original. Again, the interpretation in terms of the search representation can be carried a step further by identifying the elements of the sequences mentioned with the successive segments of the maze that constitutes a path. However, in all these examples, the formulation in terms of the sets, U and G, is more general, in the sense that there are often numerous alternative ways of representing the problem, so stated, by a maze.

ANALYSIS OF THE TASK ENVIRONMENT

What does it mean to analyze a task environment? The topics so far discussed in this chapter and the presentation of an IPS in the prior chapter show what it means to present a theory of a specific segment of human behavior. A representation of the problem space is given, comprised of a representation of the environment and one of the problem. (If needed, a representation of the actual environment, independent of the subject's perception of it in his problem space, may also be given—say, if the situation involves feedback from the actual environment during the process of solution.) Then the IPS is specified. It incorporates the problem space, not in the sense of spanning its whole extent, but in possessing symbol structures and programs that provide access to that space via the system's processes for generation, testing, and so on. In addition, the IPS incorporates the goal or task, either explicitly in a symbol structure (with an appropriate interpreter) or implicitly in the behavior of some of its programs, as we saw earlier in the chapter. The IPS, when set in the environment and given the goal, becomes a determinate system that produces a stream of behavior. This is the theoretical behavior to be compared with the human's actual behavior.

All the above is familiar in outline, and we understand generally in what sense such a theory would explain the empirical events (or would fail to, if the IPS or task environment were incorrectly posited). But there is an alternative route to explaining the behavior. Remembering that a problem solver is an adaptive system, we might postulate that the human problem solver produced the behavior that he did because he had to—because the behavior was demanded by the task environment. This is also an explanation of the behavior. There is no necessary conflict between the two explanations, assuming that the IPS did in fact solve the problem. Then the various symbol manipulations that occurred under the control of the program constituted an effective means for responding to the demands of the task environment, with the production of appropriate behavior.

It is a premise of the second kind of explanation—that the behavior corresponds to the demands of the situation—not only that the goal was held by the problem solver and that he was adequately motivated, but also that he was able to attain the goal. It might seem, then, that this form of explanation would make few predictions in cases where the problem solver was *unable* to solve the problem— unable to meet the demands of the situation. But this is not entirely so, for one may explain (or predict) behavior by observing what are the "obvious" things to do to attain the goal (even though they may be insufficient), and therefore what are the things that the problem solver, being a bear of little brain, *will* do.

It is a cautionary note to (rather than a premise of) the classical kind of process explanation that the program and symbol structures that are inferred to produce the problem solving behavior may themselves be idiosyncratic to the task and ephemeral, being simply what is demanded by the task environment. Thus, quite different structures and programs would be generated by different tasks. In that case, the process explanation would show only that indeed the problem solver could adapt sufficiently to the situation.

We will employ both kinds of explanation in this book. Indeed, as we observed earlier, one of our main tasks will be to understand what is demanded by the task environment, so that we can understand—by elimination—what aspects of behavior are determined by the psychology of the problem solver. The purpose of this section is to be sure we understand what it means to analyze a task environment in order to reveal its demands.

It is easy to give an essentially correct definition of a demand of the task environment: it is a constraint on the behavior of the problem solver that must be satisfied in order that the goal be attained. Thus, the environment per se does not make demands: rather the problem or goal makes them via the problem solver's commitment to attain it. The features of the environment that give rise to these demands constitute the relevant structure or texture of the environment (Tolman and Brunswick, 1935).

Difficulties arise with this definition from the question of the independence of the demands and task structures from the nature of the problem solver. The whole point of viewing the environment as making demands is to provide a framework outside the problem solver to which his behavior can then be related. If this can be done, it seems natural to make an analysis of the task environment before looking at behavior. We have organized each of the main empirical parts of this book in exactly this fashion. Each main task starts with a chapter on task analysis, followed by chapters on behavior.

But if something's being a demand is only *apparently* independent of the problem solver, and *in fact* depends on intimate features of his program, then the factorization into task environment and problem solver is a mirage. The possibility of such interaction arises from two sources: first, that the problem solver has a goal; second, and most important, that a bond of necessity underlies the constraints upon modes of goal attainment.

With respect to the first, the goal, we have eliminated the difficulty by fiat—by conditioning the concept of demand both on the goal's being held and on the problem solver's being adequately motivated. Both of these side conditions clearly do depend on the nature of the problem solver, but in the experiments reported throughout the book they are always satisfied. Furthermore, it is often easy to know that they are satisfied, for in our culture (at least) people are willing to declare publicly (either verbally or behaviorally) many of their goals.

Thus the remaining difficulty is to clarify what it means for behavior to be necessary for a goal. This will require some discussion. We start with an extreme case where the issues are clear, and then move to the complexities.

Task Invariants

We are given three things: an environment, a problem solver, and a goal or task. Suppose it is possible to demonstrate that *all* paths in the environment that lead to attainment of the goal have a certain property. For instance, any way of winning tic-tac-toe involves having three-in-a-row. Or, all proofs of a given theorem from a set of axioms involve the use of a specific axiom. Clearly the behaviors corresponding to these features—making three-in-a-row or using the specified axiom—are demands of the task environment. These elements cannot depend on the nature of the problem solver, because the demands are invariants of the situation. Their invariance is quite independent of the amount of analysis that is required to reveal them. In the case of tic-tac-toe the invariance is obvious; in the case of the theorem it may require a difficult proof to establish it. For example, the classic problems of squaring a circle, duplicating a cube, and trisecting an angle are all impossible in a given task environment (when the only operators admitted are constructions with straight-edge and compass), but proof of their impossibility took many centuries.

These examples raise the issue of whether the set of admissible operators—and consequently the tree of reachable states in the problem space—can always be regarded as a property of the task environment, independent of the properties of the problem solving IPS. Consider the task of crossing a deep chasm with only a single bridge across it. Going over the bridge would seem to be a demand that the environment places on any problem solver. But suppose a problem solver arrives who is provided with a chartered airplane, or who is equipped with wings, is capable of teleportation, or whatever. For such a problem solver, the environment no longer demands going over the bridge. In the original statement of the problem, we have smuggled in, it would seem, some assumptions about the nature of the problem solvers—that they lack wings, chartered planes, or the capacity for teleportation.

In the case of a mathematical proof this difficulty does not arise, because the set of admissible operators is defined formally, and the definition is accepted by both experimenter and subject. In problems involving actions upon the real world, possibility and the admissibility of operators are empirical, not definitional matters. Pragmatically, however, we can usually take care of the difficulty by drawing the boundary between IPS and environment a little closer to the center of the IPS, so that capabilities for actually altering the external environment are treated as properties of that environment and not of the problem solver. Then it becomes part of the specification of the task environment whether the problem solver has an airplane, or whether he can acquire one by an action sequence that is open to him.

We must exercise caution, however, in shifting the boundary between problem solver and environment. If we remove particular operators and classify them with the task environment, there is a danger that the problem solver will disappear entirely, and that there will be no room at all for a theory of him. For example, how shall we treat the problem solver's capabilities (and inabilities) for doing arithmetic? Is it a description of the problem solver that he can do mental multiplications at a certain speed in solving the problem? Or is this a specification of the environment (as we might want to regard it if there were a question of the availability of paper and pencil or desk calculators)? And how shall we treat the problem solver's capacity for attempting goals? If we follow the path of assigning all means to the environment, there will be nothing left of the problem solver: he will do what he does because all that he is—being means—is specified by the environment.

These examples suggest that a suitable way to fix the boundary is to regard possibilities of actual physical actions as part of the description of the environment, but to regard the information processing activities of the problem solver—the processes for searching through his internal problem space—as describing him. We must now consider more carefully whether such a strategy provides at least a usable and pragmatically tenable boundary between IPS and environment.

Adaptivity and Task Demands

The success that an information processing system will experience with problems of a certain kind can be used to construct a measure of its adaptivity or intelligence in environments resembling those in which the test problems were set. Such a measure will be highly predictive of performance in a very similar environment, less predictive of performance in environments with different characteristics.

To the extent that such a measure is predictive at all over diverse environments, we might want to call it a measure of general intelligence, but such a measure is not needed for our purposes. We can be content with measures that are specific to certain classes of environments; and that consequently permit us to predict performance in tasks in the appropriate environment, to scale such tasks according to difficulty, and to scale IPS's according to adaptivity, ability, or intelligence in performing these tasks. All of this corresponds to the common practice in psychometrics.

Now the demands that a particular environment places on an IPS may depend on intelligence. In our example of the chasm to be crossed, going over the bridge may be a demand on an IPS of ordinary intelligence. A very much more intelligent IPS might solve the problem by inventing the airplane (or, less dramatically, by thinking of the still unusual possibility of chartering one). For him, there is no demand that he cross the bridge. If, as we proposed earlier, we include *all* external action possibilities as part of the description of the environment, then crossing the bridge is not a demand on either problem solver. If we include only thinkable external actions in the description of the environment, then the environments are not the same for the two problem solvers.

A pragmatic solution to the dilemma, which preserves for all practical purposes the concept of demands of the environment, is to assume that all the problem solvers whose behavior is to be studied are drawn from a reasonably narrow range on the scale of intelligence. If two populations of widely differing intelligence are to be studied, then the environment (for the same task) must be described differently for them. In the description of the environment for any given, relatively homogeneous, group of problem solvers, only external actions that are thinkable by them need be included.

In the search representation of a problem, the task environment can be identified with the whole space of search paths that are accessible to IPS's of a specified level of intelligence. To the extent that intelligence in the problem domain is scalable along a single dimension, the search space describing the task environment of a highly intelligent problem solver can be assumed to include, as a subpart, the smaller and sparser space describing the environment of a less intelligent problem solver. (Thus, the space for the airplane inventor of the previous example would contain branches leading to the invention of that alternative; while these branches would be missing from the search spaces of noninventive problem solvers.)

Once a search space of this kind—a network of possible wanderings, so to speak—has been specified, the demands of the environment simply become properties of the space that are invariant over all paths that lead to a problem solution. It is easy to see that an analogous notion of demands of the environment can be introduced into the set-theoretical representation of a problem. For present purposes, we can restrict our discussion to the search representation.

It is worth noting that the ability measures that are relevant here reflect the problem solver's knowledge of the problem domain in addition to whatever problem solving aptitudes he may possess. Consider the game of chess, for example. Although there are no hard data to prove it, there probably is some correlation between skill in chess—for those who play the game at all—and standard measures of intelligence. There is undoubtedly a much *higher* correlation between skill in chess and chess knowledge (which, in turn, is correlated to some degree with amount of experience). Chess skill is sufficiently unidimensional so that official chess organizations assign to players scalar numerical rankings. In the American system, for example, a class A player has a rating between 1800 and 2000, an expert between 2000 and 2200, a master between 2200 and 2400, and a senior master over 2400. In a game between two players whose ratings differ by, say, 300 points, the outcome is predictable to a high degree: the stronger player would probably not lose more than one game in twenty or more, and not draw more than one in five.

Players of about the same strength see roughly the same things in a given game situation. Hence the task environment can be described in about the same way for them, and the demands of the situation can be inferred. Indeed, the idea that a move is demanded by the situation is a standard part of the chess culture. At master and grandmaster levels, it is also taken for granted that if enough time is allowed for the analysis of a position (in difficult cases this may mean hours or days of analysis), the move that is demanded by the situation can be detected more or less unequivocally. (We will have more to say about these matters as they apply specifically to chess in later chapters.)

We can now summarize our account of what comprises an analysis of the task environment. An analysis of the task environment produces a descripion of the constraints on behavior that must be satisfied to attain the problem goal at a specified level of intelligence or adaptivity. For a given level of intelligence, certain paths in the task environment are not available as paths to the goal—they are too difficult. Removing these paths, one can then search for the invariant features of the remaining paths that do lead to the goal.

Simplification of the Problem Space

Our approach to task description provides us with at least one valuable byproduct—a technique for vastly simplifying the description of search paths through the problem space. We consider, again, a task environment described as a search space, relative to an IPS of a given level of intelligence. As we shall see in the next chapter, we can measure the difficulty of search through such a space, for an IPS of given intelligence, by the expected size of his search tree. We can measure in this same way not only the difficulty for the IPS of an entire search path, but also the difficulty of any segment.

An IPS, let us suppose, solves a problem by finding a path from A to G, via B, C, D, E, and F. We can speak of the difficulty of getting from A to G, but also the difficulty of getting from C to D. Perhaps getting from C to D was easy, but getting from D to E was very hard. With any particular node, say C, in such a search space, we can associate all the nearby nodes whose attainment is *obvious*, once they have reached C, to problem solvers of the specified level of intelligence. How they traverse these obvious subsegments is often of little interest in explaining their overall problem solving behavior. Hence, in describing a task domain, we need not include the detail of the links connecting a set of nodes that are all obviously reachable from each other. Instead, each such set can be treated as a single node and detail retained only for the interesting and difficult passageways that separate one such cluster from another.

In terms of a different metaphor, in describing the terrain of the problem environment, the detailed topography of flat or slightly rolling plains will have little import. What will be interesting and significant is the location and detailed configuration of the mountain passes. In our later discussions, we will be assuming, for instance, that our (adult) subjects can simply follow rules at the level of executing chess moves or carrying out simple arithmetic processes. We will not consider how these component acts are done—they amount to moving in a plain. If our subjects had been young children, such assumptions would not have been viable. Making a legal move in chess can be a problem for a child or for any person just learning the game; but for our subjects it is not problematic but obvious. We incorporate such assumptions of obviousness by declaring the legal moves to be processes that are immediately available to the IPS without calling on its problem solving apparatus.

Thus, we will eliminate the obvious in describing our subjects' behavior and focus on the difficult and uncertain aspects of their behavior—their progress over the high passes and ridges. We will often describe the behavior as a sequence of *episodes*, each of which is a succinctly describable segment of behavior associated with attaining a goal. If the goal is sufficiently easy to attain (or to identify as not attainable), then we need not be concerned with the detailed behavior of the problem solver in getting to it. We can treat each episode as a unit, paying attention primarily to what determines which episodes are initiated and how they are terminated.

Specificity of Environments and Adaptability

This approach to defining the demands of the task environment, while committing us to specifying the intelligence of the problem solver, does not commit us to the assumption that intelligence is generalizable over different task domains. Its generality remains an empirical question, to be settled by evidence, not definition. We are thus free to restrict and normalize the domains that we wish to analyze in any given instance.

Perhaps the most important restriction that we can impose is to choose a series of problems for a definite class of task environments. Then we only assume a unidimensional ability for, say chess or cryptarithmetic or elementary logic. In contrast with the task domains covered by intelligence test batteries, these are extremely homogeneous. Indeed, all three domains put together are still a relatively homogeneous area. Yet, we will not need even to postulate that the ordering of problem solvers in chess ability agrees with that in, say, logic. We also use a restricted class of subjects—subjects who are intelligent enough to understand and accept the tasks, yet not so smart or knowledgeable that the tasks are trivial for them.

A second important restriction we can accept is to adapt our analysis to the subject's internal representation of the task. Much of the variation—especially the extreme variation—of response to a task by different problem solvers comes about from differences among the representations they use. Our analysis of a task will assume that the problem solvers are using a problem space of a specific character. If two subjects use radically different problem spaces, we would expect to make two separate analyses of the task, and perhaps then arrive at correspondingly different measures of difficulty and different invariant features of the task environment. Our theory of problem solving will in fact give us a good deal of basis for understanding the nature of intelligence and its relation to the structure of the problem space.

A third restriction, already noted, is to treat some of the informational resources as aspects of the task environment instead of aspects of the problem solvers. For example, in analyzing the cryptarithmetic task, we may assume that all subjects know that a number of the form $B = A + A$ is an even number; hence, we may regard this fact as a feature of the task environment rather than a property of the subject. This again reduces the variance among the problem solvers. In the tasks we shall examine, our most important technique for reducing intersubject variance in representation of the task environment is to select subjects who are naive in certain dimensions—e.g., who have not previously seen the particular problems we give them, or the specific kind of task we ask them to perform. (In the chapters on chess we clearly relax this latter requirement of naiveté, though not the former one. The subjects must be chess players, but the positions given them must be new to them.)

With these restrictions, as well as the fact that we only need approximate validity, the assumption of scalable intelligence becomes tenable. The final demonstration of this, of course, comes from the analyses that we undertake in later chapters of the book. All we have done here is to establish the methodological basis for those analyses.

SUMMARY

This chapter has focused on some major issues that arise in defining a task environment for a human problem solver, viewed as an IPS. The first question is how to represent the external environment. We, as experimenters, have no privileged access to the real world that constitutes the external environment for another human. Even when we create a laboratory situation, we still must describe the aspects of that environment that are relevant for our subjects' behavior. We saw, in effect, that our choice of representation amounts to a set of hypotheses about what encoding will be provided by the subject IPS.

The second question is how the subject will represent the environment internally. Here we introduced the key concept of the problem space, which not only represents the current situation, but also the possibilities for change and transformation of that situation. We noted especially that one must not assume automatically that the subject's problem space will lie inside a legal problem space as understood by the experimenter.

We made these two issues concrete by detailing an explicit representation in an IPS for both the external environment and the problem space of tic-tac-toe.

The third question is how to represent problems and their goals. We provided representations for two large classes of problems: the set-predicate representation and the search representation. In each representation, the problem solver is viewed as having certain information, and the definition of the desired solution may be viewed as a request for specified additional information. Although these two representations—the set-predicate and the search—cover a vast territory, we left open the possibility that there are other problem representations that cannot usefully be subsumed under either of these paradigms.

The final question (returning to the one that opened the chapter) concerns the relation of task environment to problem solver, and the extent to which either can be analyzed separately. We posed the issue by observing that the behavior of an adaptive organism can often be explained as behavior demanded by the task environment, rather than behavior that flows from the operation of mechanisms internal to the organism (i.e., from the program of the IPS). At the core of this environment-centric view is the notion of invariants of the environment—aspects of behavior that are constant along all paths that lead to a goal, hence are necessarily exhibited by all problem solvers that are successful. We found that this environment-centric mode of analysis could be extended considerably if a measure of adaptivity or intelligence could be assumed to exist, even approximately. We showed how such an assumption was in fact implicit in the concept of problem space.

We also introduced the concept of episode, defined as a segment of behavior devoted to attainment of a goal. If the goal is easy enough (relative to the power of the problem solver), then the episodes can be derived from analysis of the task environment and treated as units.

In general, this chapter has had to be content with raising issues, introducing the concepts appropriate to understanding the issues (e.g., problem space, task invariants), and illustrating these concepts by brief examples. For full understanding, task environments must be dealt with in their particularity, and to make any of these general concepts fully operational requires an analysis of an environment in detail. We used simple examples and metaphors, precisely because illustrating the concepts with a real task environment would obscure the broad issues in the technical particulars of that environment. In three later parts of the book, where we deal respectively with cryptarithmetic, elementary logic, and chess, the concepts and issues introduced here will provide the framework for analysis.

However, there is still one more preliminary chapter. Chapters 2 and 3 have set the stage for a general description of the problem solving activity itself. We have described the two principal components—the information processing system in Chapter 2, the task environment in the present chapter. The goal, accepted by the problem solver, and to be attained in the given task environment, provides the interface between the two components. In the next chapter, Chapter 4, we consider in general terms how an IPS goes about solving a problem, then illustrate the general discussion by an extensive analysis of the behavior of one of the first problem solving systems that was programmed for a digital computer—the Logic Theorist.

PROBLEM
SOLVING

We now have before us the essential components of a problem solving situation: the task environment and the IPS. The next step, to complete the picture, is to consider how an IPS can actually solve problems in a given task environment. In this chapter we must answer two questions:

1. How can a problem be solved?
2. What makes a problem difficult?

The answers to these questions constitute a theory of problem solving, one that should be applicable to man, beast, and machine alike, insofar as they can be represented as information processing systems of the type posited in Chapter 2.

Our purpose in this first part of the book is to supply the tools with which to undertake an analysis of *human* problem solving. Hence, we wish to carry the general theory no further than is appropriate for this undertaking. In the following three parts of the book we will be analyzing three specific problem solving tasks

87

in great detail. Consequently, in the present chapter, we need not demonstrate the breadth of the theory. We can start with an overview of our theory of problem solving, using only a few simple examples to illustrate its various aspects. Then we take up a single problem solving program, the Logic Theorist, to explore the theory in depth. Not only does the Logic Theorist have a certain historical interest, being one of the first heuristic problem solving programs, but it also provides good illustrations for many of the basic ideas of the problem solving theory.

OVERVIEW

The problem space and the problem formulation already impose an overall organization on the problem solving process. This organization is sketched in Figure 4.1.

1. An initial process, here called the *input translation*, produces inside the problem solver an internal *representation* of the external environment, at the same time selecting a problem space. The problem solving then proceeds in the framework of the internal representation thus produced—a representation that may render problem solutions obvious, obscure, or perhaps unattainable.

2. Once a problem is represented internally, the system responds by selecting a particular problem solving *method*. A method is a process that bears some rational relation to attaining a problem solution, as formulated and seen in terms of the internal representation.

3. The selected method is applied: which is to say, it comes to control the behavior, both internal and external, of the problem solver. At any moment, as the outcome either of processes incorporated in the method itself or of more general processes that monitor its application, the execution of the method may be halted.

4. When a method is terminated, three options are open to the problem solver: (a) another method may be attempted, (b) a different internal representation may be selected and the problem reformulated, or (c) the attempt to solve the problem may be abandoned.

5. During its operation, a method may produce new problems—i.e., sub-goals—and the problem solver may elect to attempt one of these. The problem solver may also have the option of setting aside a new subgoal, continuing instead with another branch of the original method.[1]

The implementation of a problem solver organized in this way calls for an IPS of the general sort described in Chapter 2. For only such a system can manipulate symbols, switch methods and representations, and make decisions as the scheme

---

[1] To complete this list of options, we should add that the continuous influx of new information from the external environment may offer new solution possibilities or demands that cause the problem solver to interrupt its current activities to try different ones.

requires. As described, the IPS is fundamentally serial in its operation: it is a processor that evokes and activates one method at a time. At a more detailed perceptual level—its scanning of task environment or internal representation—it may have some parallel processing capabilities. The problem solver may *see* many things at once; it only *does* one thing at a time about them.

FIGURE 4.1

general organization of problem solver

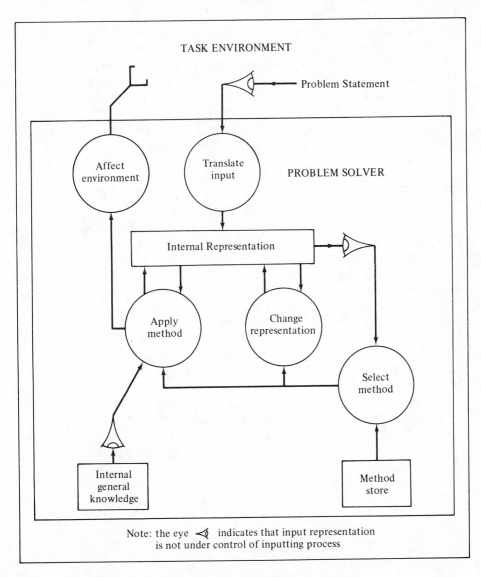

Note: the eye ◁ indicates that input representation is not under control of inputting process

Several characteristics of the problem solver's behavior can also be inferred from Figure 4.1. The behavior will be segmented, under the control now of this method, now of that. Each method, representing as it does a rational organization of processes, will be ordered within itself; but there will be discontinuities as activity shifts from one method to another. Since a goal may be attacked by a whole sequence of methods, a single segment of behavior addressed entirely to a single goal may encompass several sharply divergent sequences of behavior.

The system's behavior will be iterative in character, consisting of repeated loops around a circuit: select a goal $\rightarrow$ select a method $\rightarrow$ evaluate the results $\rightarrow$ select a goal again. The existence of useful methods that generate subgoals and make use of the results of pursuing these subgoals implies that behavior can also be recursive: pending goals may be held in abeyance while new goals are attended to; then the prior goals may be re-evoked when the new goals are reached. This recursiveness causes dependencies between behaviors that are remote from each other in time. It requires an apparatus for goal control and storage.[2]

These general characteristics of the system have implications for the structure of the theory of problem solving as well as for the system's behavior. One part of the theory will deal with possible representations, their selection and installation. The other principal part of the theory will deal with problem solving within a given representation. This second part of the theory will define a set of methods, together with executive organizations for selecting and evaluating them.

Representation

Most of the progress that has been made to date in developing a theory of problem solving has focused on the second component of the theory. Much less has been learned about the nature of representations, and their selection and modification. However, since some of the representations that have been studied have very wide applicability, this limitation may not be too damaging. The theory to be presented in this book has much more to say about methods and executive organizations than about creating new representations or shifting from one representation to another. This emphasis turns out to be consonant with the kinds of problem solving we have studied, where our human subjects do not in fact change or modify their representations appreciably during the course of their problem solving activity.

However, some problems do exist in which the whole difficulty of solution resides in finding the right representation. Once that representation has been discovered, solving the problem becomes a trivial matter. A familiar example of this is the Nine Dot Problem. The subject is presented with a square array of nine dots:

$$\cdot \quad \cdot \quad \cdot$$

$$\cdot \quad \cdot \quad \cdot$$

$$\cdot \quad \cdot \quad \cdot$$

---

[2] In computer parlance we can say that goals are pushed down and then, later, popped up—a terminology that derives from the pushdown list or stack. See the discussion of the interpreter in Chapter 2 (Figure 2.11), where stacks are used with programming languages for essentially the same purposes.

He is directed to draw four straight lines, without raising his pencil from the paper, that pass through all nine dots. Most subjects adopt a representation that assumes the straight lines must all terminate on the dots and cannot continue outside the boundaries of the square. With this restriction—imposed by the representation and not by the problem statement—the problem is unsolvable. If the subject at any moment considers the possibility of generating lines that extend outside the square, he finds a solution very quickly.

The Nine Dot Problem is perhaps rather untypical—at least untypical of the problems that have been imported into the psychological laboratory. In any event, the first part of the theory, the theory of how representations are selected, has not received much attention as yet.

Methods

Thus the theory focuses on the method: a collection of information processes that combine a series of means to attain an end, or at least to attempt to attain an end. The means that are usable by a problem solving system are dictated by the nature of the internal representation, for specifying a problem space determines the various ways in which the initial situation can be changed to reach the goal situation. Ends arise out of the formulation of goals or subgoals. As we observed earlier, a goal may be represented explicitly as a symbol structure or it may be implicit in the structure of the method itself. In either event, a method can be understood only in reference to its goal.

As a consequence, the theory falls naturally into a number of parts, each part concerned with the methods associated with a particular problem formulation. Several methods may exist for a single problem formulation, representing alternative ways to attain the goal. However, in general there turns out to be only a single method associated with each of the more basic types of problem formulations. In particular, we shall see that we can associate a single, particular method with each of the two formulations introduced in Chapter 3: With the set-predicate formulation of problem solving, we can associate a generate-and-test method; with the search formulation, a heuristic search method.

A method, then, is tied closely to its associated problem formulation. The method resides in the problem solver prior to its evocation to deal with any individual task. Thus the method must be fashioned without specific knowledge of the particular problem situations it will be called upon to handle. Consequently, mechanisms must exist in the problem solver for bringing the problem solving method into effective correspondence with each individual problem situation, so that the method can actually discover something about the situation and act on it. If we regard the method as a very general characterization of a whole set of potential problem situations, then the process of fitting a particular situation to the method is a process of *interpretation*, in the sense in which logicians use that term.

In any given instance, interpretation may be easy or hard, simple or complex. There must, however, be something in the structure of the method that permits the interpretation—that is, some interface between method and problem. One very general scheme for interpretation—though we have no reason to suppose that it is the only possible scheme—imbeds in the method symbol structures that represent in abstracted form the various potential situations with which the method will have to deal. The method is so constructed as to be capable of manipulating these symbol structures. Then, when a specific problem situation is presented, interpretation matches the various parts of these symbol structures (their *variables*, in a broad sense) with corresponding elements of the internally symbolized problem.[3]

Once it is interpreted, the symbol structure belonging to the method becomes a particularized problem formulation. It communicates to the method what information is known about the specific problem situation, and thus provides the *givens* that the method requires in order to execute its processes. Thus, a method is inextricably interwoven with its problem formulation. The problem as presented must be capable of interpretation in terms of the method's symbol structures, both to guarantee that the information required by the method will be provided, and to set limits to the information that will be available.

The problem formulation must be coupled with the problem space as well as with the method. The problem space defines the internal representation in which the current situation is cast. Out of the information and transformations available in the problem space it must be possible to generate the kinds of information guaranteed to the method by the problem formulation. Of course, a problem space can contain more information than the minimum required by a problem formulation and its method, since information need not be utilized simply because it is there. Thus, in an information-rich problem space, many methods may become applicable as one makes use of less and less of the total information available. In an information-poor problem space, there are likely to be only one or two weak methods that are usable at all—methods that are still able to proceed, though inefficiently (Newell, 1969a).

Difficulty

What makes a problem difficult? Difficulty can be measured in many ways: whether a solution is attained or not; the time required to find a solution; the quality of the solution; and so on. All of these measures are related, though imperfectly. None is applicable uniformly, nor free from all conceptual difficulties.

But no matter what measures are used, problem difficulty will be determined by the interaction between the task environment and the program of the IPS. As just described, this program is a set of methods together with an executive structure for selecting and applying them.

---

[3] This same technique of interpretation is exhibited, in a simple form, in the standard procedures for handling subroutines in computer programs. The problem is to write a routine for computing, say sin (x) and to do so in such a way that the routine can be applied to a particular angle—say, 30°—in order to compute sin (30). The technique is to write the routine in terms of a cell designated by a variable name, say x; then to include in the programming language a special process that obtains the particular value 30, and stores it in the cell called x. The execution of this process is called *parameter passing*.

We should like to go beneath global measures of problem difficulty and attribute particular aspects of difficulty to the operation of particular components of the methods in application to corresponding parts of the problem. A measure of the total time required to solve a problem could then be dissected into measures of the time required by individual methods, or even by the component processes of which the measures are composed.

Each part of the problem solving program contributes an increment of time to the solution of a problem. In constructing a theory of problem difficulty we should like to identify those aspects of the task environment and the problem solver that are major determinants of difficulty—whether measured by solution time or any of the alternative measures. But we should not expect to isolate all determinants of difficulty unless we are prepared to examine the entire program and problem structure down to the last detail.

The basic structure of a problem solver is disjunctive: it selects one method; if it suceeds, it is done; if not, it selects another method; and so on. Each method has a chance of solving the problem. Thus we might write:

$$\text{probability-of-solution} = 1 - [1 - \text{probability(method)}]^N$$
$$\text{time-to-solution} = \text{setup-time} + N(\text{selection-time} + \text{execution-time})$$

where N is the number of methods tried. These formulae are exceedingly approximate. Associated with each method is an execution time and chance of success, both assumed to be constant. It is not clear in general what the "probability" of a solution can mean: in many tasks either a method will solve the problem or it won't. Finally, the formula assumes that the chance of success of different methods is mutually independent. But methods need not be independent of each other. The failure of one method may give diagnostic information about which method to select next. A method may fail to solve the problem, but still produce a symbol structure that turns out to be useful later. In spite of these limitations, the formulae written above express the essence of what is going on in problem solving: that the problem solver must keep trying one method after another until it solves the problem (or quits) and that for each method it pays a price in time (and possibly effort). Unfortunately, the formulae do not reflect qualitative differences among solutions at all.

To apply these formulae in practice requires individual study of each particular method. If there were a large number of methods, then we might be satisfied with an estimated average time per method. However, the subjects in our experiments employ only a few methods—often only one or two. Consequently, it becomes essential to consider the structure of individual methods in assessing difficulty.

The size of the problem space provides one key to the estimation of problem difficulty. The problem space defines the set of possibilities for the solution, as seen by the problem solver. (It also defines the various ways for obtaining different elements of that space and for describing elements, but these aspects are not relevant at the moment.) Basically, methods consider elements of the problem space, one by one. For the most elementary methods conceivable, which involve searching through the entire space, time to solution will be roughly proportional to the total size of the space. The effect of more sophisticated methods can often be described as cutting down effectively the part of the space that must be explored in order to find a solution.

A somewhat olympian way of viewing the situation is this: The problem solver starts with a problem space that imbeds the initial situation and the final goal in the most directly "obvious" space available to him. He can be mistaken, of course, and select a space that contains no way of getting to the solution—as in the Nine Dots Problem. Thus the initial space in which the solver encodes the problem already provides some measure of how big a world he has to consider. Then, with each piece of relevant information that he is able to apply (either information contained in the problem specification or information already stored in his memory), the problem solver cuts down the size of the problem space by limiting himself to a more relevant subspace.

The olympian aspect of this way of describing the matter is our implicit assumption that *having* information is sufficient for *using* that information to make the reduction. In fact, the problem solver may not know how to use information to reduce the space. In any event, after whatever reduction he achieves, he is left with a subspace that he cannot reduce further because he has no more relevant information. At this point, the problem solver must adopt a method that involves, essentially, examining all the elements of the remaining subspace. We will see later, in detail, how this whole reduction process works.

In the terms of our discussion of the task environment in Chapter 3, two problem solvers at about the same level of intelligence and ability will detect and use about the same information in going from the space in which they formulate the problem initially to the subspace in which they actually apply their problem solving methods. Hence, the demands of the situation—defined by this subspace—will be essentially the same for both. Problem solvers at widely different levels of intelligence and ability may achieve quite different reductions, hence be faced with quite different problem demands. In the latter case, separate analyses may be required for the problem solving behavior of the two of them; in the former case, we would predict highly similar behaviors. Hence, if we can determine by observation in which problem space a subject is operating, we can use this information to predict subsequent behavior.

The Recognition Method

Before we turn to an examination of specific problem formulations and their methods, we need to look at the one universal method of solving problems—by recognizing the answer. If one is asked "What is the value of pi?" and immediately answers "3.1416," it is probable that the answer to the question was *recognized*: i.e., was already in memory and was simply evoked by the act of understanding the question. One might object that this is hardly an example of a problem. In terms of difficulty, of course, the objection is correct. But the situation fits strictly the set-predicate definition of problem (given the set of real numbers, find the one that equals pi). Thus the triviality of the problem must owe something to the problem solver's repertoire of methods. The problem is not easy for all solvers.

If a problem solver knows only the definition of pi as the ratio of the circumference to the diameter of a circle, he might have to solve the problem by circumscribing a polygon about the circle—not at all a recognition process.

Recognition processes are important for solving problems, but not because they can be used directly for hard problems (although occasionally a subject will solve one in this way because he has seen it before). They are important because problem solving often proceeds by reduction: a hard problem is solved by replacing it with ostensibly easier problems. Eventually, if this reduction process is to succeed, some subproblems must actually be solved and not just reduced further. Recognition is very often the way this last step is accomplished. We say "he reduced the problem to something he already knew."

There are many program structures within an IPS that can perform recognition. We will mention three explicitly. The standard way of constructing small recognition schemes in sequential program languages is by means of a series of *conditional branch statements*. Such a series of statements forms an implicit tree of tests, which can also be converted into a *discrimination net*, like those we discussed in Chapter 2. Alternatively, the *production system* provides a recognition scheme:

$$\text{problem-statement}_1 \longrightarrow \text{solution}_1.$$
$$\text{problem-statement}_2 \longrightarrow \text{solution}_2.$$

$$\cdot$$
$$\cdot$$
$$\cdot$$

$$\text{problem-statement}_n \longrightarrow \text{solution}_n.$$

If no limits are placed on the size of such a production system, then any problem statement that is recognized leads immediately to its solution. The wide array of pattern recognition programs that can be found in the literature (e.g., Kanal, 1968; Nilsson, 1965) provide a number of additional schemes on which recognition methods can be based. Most of these, unfortunately for our purposes, operate with continuous signal spaces or with two-dimensional spaces holding geometric figures of various sorts (e.g., characters), so that they do not all lead immediately to recognizers of problem statements. But for present purposes we wish only to emphasize the diversity of known program structures that can provide direct recognition methods for problem solving.

Recognition is applicable to all problem formulations because it is not sensitive to the details of the formulation. By the same token, when a problem is solved by recognition the usual measures of problem difficulty do not apply, for the result is immediate.

The Generate and Test Method

We turn now to the first and most general of our two ways of stating a problem: the set-predicate formulation. Recall that to be given a problem in this formulation means to be given, somehow, a set, U, and the goal of finding, producing, or determining a member of a subset G of that set—this latter identified most generally by a test that can be performed on the elements of U. We wish now to consider methods that can solve (or attempt to solve) specific problems when they are formulated in this way. We are severely limited in creating such methods, for they can make use of no other information than that which is implied by the formulation: First, we are guaranteed that the set U exists for the problem solver. Thus, there must be some way to obtain the members of this set, the specific way depending on the particular problem space in question. Second, we are guaranteed some way of determining the elements of G—not, however, by generating elements of G directly, since that would solve the problem instantly.

FIGURE 4.2

generate-and-test method

```
generate U:
        test if element in G,
            if true stop generation and report solution is element.,
    stop and report no solution.
```

We will consider a single method that is applicable to this formulation, called *generate-and-test*. The method makes use of the information available in the problem formulation, as described above, in the obvious way (in fact, in the only sensible way). First, a process generates potential solutions from the set U. Then, as each is generated, it is tested to see if it is also a member of the set G. Figure 4.2 shows a program for this method. Variants of the method are conceivable, but they do not change its essential character. For instance, several or all solutions may be wanted, not just the first one found. In this case, the generator must continue to operate, and the solutions must be stored in some memory as they are found. Alternatively, the main generator may provide a number of solution candidates at once—it may not be able to produce them one at a time. These candidates must be listed temporarily, and another generator must then go through the list so that the test process can be applied to each element on it. Clearly these two generators, taken together, are equivalent to a single overall generator of candidates.

From the program in Figure 4.2 we can see that the solution will always be found if the conditions of the problem formulation hold and the generator is allowed to run long enough. In this case, the interesting measure of problem difficulty is the amount of time it takes to find the first solution. This solution time will be determined by four things: (1) the average effort required to generate each element of the problem space; (2) the average effort required to test whether a candidate actually satisfies the solution conditions; (3) the size of the problem space that must be searched; and (4) the relative position of the solution in the sequence in which the generator produces new elements. In particular cases, any of these components (or some combination) may be the sources of problem difficulty. Let us consider some examples.

1. An extra chair is needed from the living room to seat an additional guest at dinner. Here the set U is small (say four chairs) and accessible (simply step into the living room and look at each chair in turn); furthermore the test is rapid (reject large stuffed chairs, reject tacky chairs, any others will do). Generate-and-test is an excellent method for solving the problem.

2. Consider the problem of opening a safe, mentioned earlier. Here, both generating and testing are very cheap, but the size of the space is very large. If a safe has ten independent dials, each with numbers running from 00 to 99, then there are $100^{10} = 10^{20}$ or one hundred billion billion possible settings. Furthermore, only one combination will unlock the safe, and that combination is situated at random in the sequence for any generator available to a would-be safecracker who does not know the combination (i.e., who has no recognition process available). This is a difficult problem, then, because it would take on the average 50 billion billion trials to open the safe; and the difficulty lies entirely in the size of the space.

3. Now consider applying the method of generate-and-test to the problem of choosing a move in chess. On the average a chess player has some twenty to thirty legal alternatives when he is on move. Hence, there is no difficulty in generating possible moves, or even (with a little care) generating all of them. The great difficulty lies in determining whether a particular legal move is a good move. The problem lies in the verifier, not in the generator. A principal procedure for evaluating each move is by considering the consequences it can lead to if various subsequent moves are taken by the player and his opponent. If we undertake to look ahead only five moves, with 30 legal alternatives at each step, we must consider some 10^{15} positions in order to evaluate a single move. This only shows, of course, that a problem formulation that is more sensitive than this one to the structure of chess must be adopted if the problem solver is to find good moves.

4. Suppose in a crossword puzzle one is asked to find a word with three g's, and one sees from his progress so far that the word's fourth letter is z. One might choose to solve this problem by using a generate-and-test process, with the generator producing words with three g's and the test determining whether the fourth letter is z. Here the space is probably quite small, and the test is certainly cheap. However, the generator is likely to be very expensive. One could of course try to construct such a generator out of yet another generator and test: the generator producing the words in the dictionary sequentially and the test a count of three g's. These two processes, packaged together, make a generator of three-g words. Now both generating and testing are cheap and the difficulty has again become localized in the size of the space (the dictionary).

While all these examples are superficial, they serve to illustrate the generate-and-test method and to show how problem difficulty can be localized in the various parts of the method.

We now take up the second formulation of a problem: as a search for a path from an initial element in the problem space to a desired element (or elements). The problem space itself is assumed to be characterized by a set of operators that can be used at any point in the space to generate the neighboring points, although not all operators need be applicable at each point.

Let us first observe that any problem in this formulation can be recast in the set-predicate formulation, and the generate-and-test method can then be applied to it. Thus, in the search formulation there must exist a test of whether an element of the space is a desired element, hence whether the solution has been reached. Take this to be the test of the generate-and-test method. Then the operators can be organized in any of a number of ways to generate one element of the space after another with an assurance that all elements of the space will eventually be generated. In this way one can attempt to solve the problem by the generate-and-test method.

Note that there is a subtle shift of task in doing this. We have replaced the problem of finding a path with the problem of finding the final element of the path. Thus, if we are to solve the original problem we must retain a record of the successful path.

If gains over random search are to be attainable from a search method, then these gains must come from exploiting the additional information available—namely, from controlling the search at each step of the way in the light of what has been discovered and what remains to be done. The generality (and weakness) of the generate-and-test scheme lies precisely in the fact that the generation process and the test process are completely independent. Each has only to fulfill certain minimal conditions of its own. Conversely, the power (and specificity) of a method for the search formulation must lie in the dependence of the search process upon the nature of the object being sought and the progress being made toward it.

Consider as a simple example the combination safe that we looked at earlier. With 10 independent dials having 100 different settings each, so that the set U contains 10^{20} elements, random search for the correct combination is impractical. It would not require a very elaborate heuristic generator, however, to change this very large number into a quite small one. If the safe were defective, so that a faint click could be heard each time any dial was turned to its correct setting, it would take an average of only 50 trials to find the correct setting of any one dial, or 500 trials to open the safe. The ten successive clicks that told the problem solver when he was getting warmer would make all the difference to the safecracker between an impossible task and a trivial one.

Thus, information that tells us which solutions to try first, and in particular, information that allows us to factor one large problem into several small ones—and to know when we have successfully solved each of the small ones—reduces the search task tremendously.

Let us consider a somewhat more complex example: solving a simple equation in elementary algebra. We are given as the initial object, in state language, an algebraic equation, say:

and we are to solve this equation for x. That is, we are to obtain a new equation that has only the symbol x on the left-hand side of the equality sign and a constant on the right-hand side; and this new equation is to be derivable from the initial one by a sequence of applications of the admissible algebraic processes for manipulating equations. A solution action sequence, representable by a sequence of admissible operators, $Q = Q_1 Q_2 \cdots Q_n$, is to connect the initial object, A1, and the solution object.

Let us look more closely at the nature of these operators, Q_i. The admissible operations in algebra are:

Add[k]   adding the same number to both sides of an equation
Sub[k]   subtracting the same number from both sides
Mult[k]   multiplying both sides by the same number
Div[k]   dividing both sides by the same number[4]

Each operator contains a parameter, k, that can assume an infinity of values. There are four *types* of operators, but an infinity of operators of each type. Hence there is an infinity of possible solution action sequences of any finite length, n. Expressed in this way, the task of finding an actual solution sounds formidable.

Anyone familiar with elementary algebra can construct immediately a solution action sequence corresponding to the problem of equation (1). One such sequence is:

$$Q = \text{Sub}[cx]\text{Sub}[b]\text{Div}[a - c]$$

That is: subtract cx from both sides, then subtract b from both sides, and then divide both sides by (a − c). Now this sequence can be discovered easily as follows: We note that the desired object has only a term in x on the left side and only a constant term on the right side. Hence, we eliminate the term in x from the right side, and the constant term from the left side by subtracting appropriate quantities; then we eliminate the coefficient of x by dividing both sides by that coefficient.

The point is that we do not have to guess at or search for the appropriate arguments, k, because this information is provided by the initial problem expression and the subsequent expressions obtained from it along the solution path. In the first subtraction we set k = cx, because cx is precisely the term in x on the right side; we set k = b in the second subtraction for the analogous reason. The object that results from these two operations (after regrouping) is

$$\text{A2:} \quad (a - c)x = (d - b)$$

which informs us that we must now set k = (a − c) in the division operation.

The information extracted from the problem expression in the algebra example

---

[4] To simplify the illustration, we assume that rearrangement and regrouping of terms on either side of the equation is handled automatically. Nothing essential is lost by the simplification.

performs the same function that was performed by the clicks in the example of the safe. It provides information about the subset, among the set of all solution paths, within which a solution lies. Hence, only a very small part of the set of possible solution paths needs to be examined before a correct solution is found. The algebra example illustrates, as a matter of fact, the limiting case: trial-and-error search is eliminated entirely, and the first path generated is a solution path.

The safe and algebra examples illustrate, respectively, two types of search-reducing devices. In the safe-opening process, many alternative paths (settings) are explored for each dial, but information (the click) is obtained immediately as to which is the right one. Hence, exploration (investigating the next dial) is continued only along the correct path; the others are terminated. The click is a *test* that discriminates correct from incorrect paths. It produces an exploration tree like that shown in Figure 4.3. The process for solving the algebraic equation *generates* directly the correct values of k, copying them from the problem expression in state language. Hence, it explores only a single, unbranching path.

FIGURE 4.3

exploration tree for safe-opening task

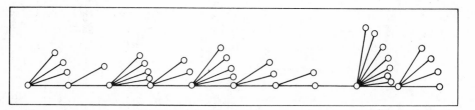

In both the safe and the algebra problem we note that the order in which operators are tried is related to the order of operators in the solution action sequence. This is a common characteristic of problem solving processes, but not a logically necessary one. It would be perfectly admissible to construct various disconnected segments of the final action sequence, and subsequently connect these together. In fact we shall discuss later some problem solving methods that operate in this way.

Most often, however, the search for a solution path operates either by working forward from the initial object toward the desired object, or by working backward from the desired object toward the initial object. In this way, each operator successively tried is applied to a known object to produce a new known object, and the information regarding the characteristics of these objects is available immediately to help in the selection of subsequent operators. We can view these as two methods for the search formulation. With either working-backward or working-forward methods, the search for a solution path (and the corresponding action sequence) can be represented by a tree, like the one just depicted, of the paths actually explored. This representation says nothing, of course, about the order in which various branches are added to the tree. In terms of this representation, the task of a problem solving procedure is to grow a tree of operator sequences that will not branch too luxuriantly, and will include at least one solution path.

We have illustrated some ways in which a problem solver might exploit the information in a task environment, using the search formulation of a problem. It is not difficult to identify the possible opportunities for the application of information. We can show these in the form of a program, as in Figure 4.4, which we can

FIGURE 4.4
heuristic-search method

Heuristic-search-method(initial-element, goals):
1. insert initial-element on untried-problems;
2. select-element from untried-problems ($\Longrightarrow$ current-element),
        if fail stop and report fail: nothing more to do;
3. select-operator(current-element) ($\Longrightarrow$ operator),
        if fail go to 2;
4. apply operator to current-element ($\Longrightarrow$ new-element),
        if fail go to 3;
5. test-for-solution(new-element, goals),
        if true go to 9;
6. evaluate(new-element),
        if reject go to 8;
7. insert new-element on untried-problems;
8. decide-next-step,
        if continue go to 3,
        if advance go to 3 (new-element $\Longrightarrow$ current-element),
        if backup go to 2;
9. reconstruct-path from initial-element to new-element,
        stop and report result: succeed.

take as our basic method for the search formulation. In Figure 4.5 we give a flow diagram of the method, which corresponds exactly to the program of Figure 4.4, with one minor exception. In the flow diagram an extra box is used to assign the name, current-element, to new-element, whereas the assignment can be made in passing in the program (line 8). This method has come to be called *heuristic search*.[5]

The basic cycle involves selecting an element in the problem space from which to work next, selecting an operator, attempting to produce a new element of the space, and testing whether it is a solution to the problem. If this test is successful, the problem is solved. Normally, however, there follows an evaluation of the new element, resulting in a decision to accept it, hence remember it for later use (on

[5] The name *heuristic search* has been used for both the problem formulation and the method of Figure 4.4, since these two are essentially in one-one correspondence. The situation is similar to the relation between the set-predicate formulation and the generate-and-test method (Newell and Ernst, 1965).

FIGURE 4.5

flow diagram of heuristic-search-method

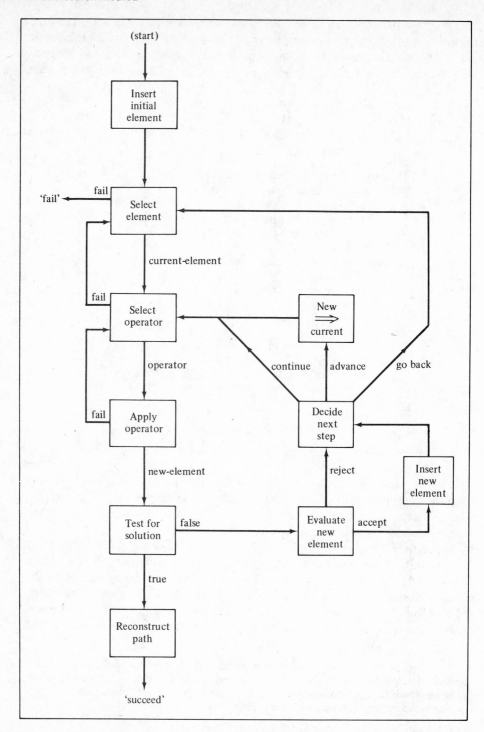

untried-problems), or to reject it. This evaluation can also associate with the element information to be used for later selection. The basic cycle completes itself with a three-way choice: to continue applying operators to the current element; to replace the current element by the new element (hence advance in the search); or to abandon the path defined by the current and new elements and go back to untried-problems. This latter choice allows further search to be initiated from any of the elements of the space that have previously been remembered. The basic cycle can terminate either by finding a new element that is a solution, which leads to reconstructing the solution path, or by exhausting untried-problems. Although not shown in the program, there could also be an additional exit from decide-next-step to terminate on external criteria, such as time or space limits.

We have presented the program of Figure 4.4 as *the* heuristic search method. Actually, it is more appropriate to view it as an encompassing scheme from which more specific methods can be derived. Many heuristic search programs have been constructed in the field of artificial intelligence; almost without exception any one of them has incorporated only some of the mechanisms implicit in the program shown in the figure. There are two reasons for this. First, there has been a gradual process of discovery of the full generality of heuristic search, so that some of the earlier programs are simply underdeveloped. Second, and more important, particular task environments permit the use of some of the mechanisms of the program, but not of others. If various mechanisms in the general program are inapplicable to some set of problems, one can generally write a more direct executive structure for solving those problems incorporating only the heuristic mechanisms that are actually used.

The method, as described in Figure 4.4, has four undefined processes: select-element, select-operator, evaluate(new-element), and decide-next-step. In Table 4.1 we list some of the ways these processes have been specified in existing heuristic search programs reported in the literature. The table lists only key notions; it can hardly give complete specifications of the processes. In particular, it does not indicate whether a heuristic mechanism is to select on a particular value of a characteristic, reject on a value, or order all candidates according to their values on that characteristic. For example, the table lists ease of applicability as a consideration for selecting operators for feasibility. Operators that are too easy to apply could be rejected (since they add too many unprofitable branches to the search); operators that are difficult to apply in general could be selected if they seem to apply to current-element (since whenever they can be applied they should be); or all operators could be ordered according to ease of applicability and generated in that order. Programs exist that reject and/or select on ease of application, though we know of none that order on this measure. Similar possibilities exist, for example, using measures of the complexity (equivalently, simplicity) of new elements.

We will not discuss these various heuristics in Table 4.1 in detail here, but the figure can be used as a check list with which to compare various programs and partial programs as they are developed throughout the book. In particular, this guide provides an appropriate backdrop as we go through the detailed example in the next section. A similar table, with references to the literature, is given in Newell and Ernst (1965).

TABLE 4.1
heuristics for heuristic-search method

Select-element
    fixed strategy
        last-in-first-out (depth-first search)
        first-in-first-out (breadth-first search)
    on evaluation (see below)
Select-operator
    on necessary and/or sufficient conditions
        must lie on solution path through current-element
        cannot lie on solution path through current-element
    for feasibility
        ease of applicability (a priori)
        specialize operator type to apply to current-element
    for desirability
        functional description (a priori)
        relevance to difference between current-element and goals
        specialize operator type to produce goal-like element
        success experience on past problems
        success experience in other parts of the problem space
    for diversity
        systematic generation
        random generation
        specified distribution a/c some operator classification
Evaluate(new-element)
    source of information
        current problem space
        model of problem space
        experience on past problems
    type of information
        duplication (identity)
        necessary and sufficient conditions
            features that must be true for all elements on solution path
            features that cannot hold for any element on solution path
        complexity-simplicity
        weighted sum of features to approximate goals or distance to goals
        comparison with goals (differences)
        comparison with current-element
        expected success
        expected effort
        growth rate of search
    source of criteria
        absolute limits
        adapted limits from experience with past problems
        upper and lower bounds from tried-problems
            alpha-beta procedure
            branch and bound
Decide-next-step
    fixed strategy
        always advance (depth-first search)
        always continue (one-level breadth-first search)
        always go back (search and scan)

```
limits
        number of operators (width)
        depth of search
        effort and/or space
    on evaluation of new-element (see above)
```

THE LOGIC THEORIST: AN EXAMPLE

Let us now consider a single problem solver in some depth. Though not illustrating all the heuristic mechanisms in Table 4.1, it provides explicit examples of a substantial number of them. We start by describing the task environment. To provide a feeling for its structure, we will first construct a generate-and-test scheme for solving problems in this task environment. Then, we will describe both the behavior and the internal structure of the Logic Theorist (LT) and investigate its problem solving abilities and their locus in the program.

The Task

The task is to discover proofs for theorems in elementary symbolic logic, or more precisely, in the propositional calculus.[6] The propositional calculus is a formalized system of mathematics, consisting of expressions built from combinations of basic symbols. In the particular system we shall use here, five of these expressions are taken as axioms, and there are rules of inference for generating new theorems from the axioms and from other theorems. In flavor and form, elementary symbolic logic is much like abstract algebra. Normally the variables of the system are interpreted as sentences, and the axioms and rules of inference as formalizations of logical operations, e.g., deduction. However, we shall deal with the system as a purely formal mathematics, and will have no further need of the interpretation. We do need to introduce a smattering of the propositional calculus.

There is postulated a set of *constants* P, Q, R, . . . , and *variables* A, B, C, . . . , with which the calculus deals. These terms can be combined into expressions by means of *connectives*. Given any variable P, we can form the expression $\sim$P (not-P). Given any two variables P and Q, we can form the expression (P $\vee$ Q), P or Q, or the expression (P $\supset$ Q), P implies Q, where or ($\vee$) and implies ($\supset$) are the connectives. There are other connectives, for example $\wedge$ (and), but we shall not need them here.

Simple expressions can be formed into more complex ones:

$$(P \supset \sim P) \supset \sim P$$

In Chapter 2 we considered at length a number of ways in which expressions in the logical calculus could be represented in an IPS. In fact, different versions of LT have represented expressions in different ways. In the earliest version, each

---

[6] The reader should not be misled by the words "proofs" and "logic." *Discovering* proofs is not a deductive process. Moreover, the fact that the task is one in symbolic logic does not make the problem solving process any more "logical" than if some other task—e.g., writing this book—were involved.

expression was represented as a linear list with each term and connective tagged by its location in the expression hierarchy. This is still another representation, different from all those we discussed in Chapter 2. An example is shown in Figure 4.6. In the second version each expression was a list-structure, in which the connective was the first symbol and the names of the subexpressions were the second and third symbols (Figure 2.4, page 28). However, we will have no further need to refer to actual representations, since all of the processes we will discuss are well defined for any adequate representation of logic expressions.

FIGURE 4.6

first representation of logic expression used in LT

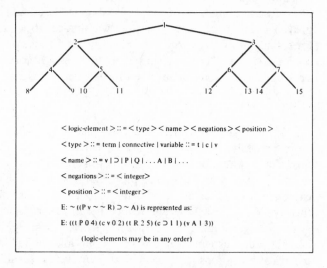

< logic-element > :: = < type > < name > < negations > < position >

< type > :: = term | connective | variable :: = t | c | v

< name > :: = v | ⊃ | P | Q | . . . A | B | . . .

< negations > :: = < integer>

< position > :: = < integer >

E: ~ ((P v ~ ~ R) ⊃ ~ A) is represented as:

E: ((t P 0 4) (c v 0 2) (t R 2 5) (c ⊃ 1 1) (v A 1 3))

(logic-elements may be in any order)

There is also a given list of expressions that are axioms. These are interpreted as the universally true expressions from which theorems are to be derived by means of various rules of inference. For the sake of definiteness, we employ the system of axioms, definitions, and rules of the *Principia Mathematica* of Whitehead and Russell (1935). *Principia* lists five axioms:[7]

$$(A \lor A) \supset A \tag{1.2}$$
$$A \supset (B \lor A) \tag{1.3}$$
$$(A \lor B) \supset (B \lor A) \tag{1.4}$$
$$A \lor (B \lor C) \supset B \lor (A \lor C) \tag{1.5}$$
$$(A \supset B) \supset (C \lor A) \supset (C \lor B) \tag{1.6}$$

Given some true theorems one can derive new theorems by means of three rules of inference: *substitution*, *replacement*, and *detachment;* and by a fourth, derived rule, *chaining*. Applying a rule to one expression produces a new one. Hence rules may be interpreted as operators and expressions as objects, in the process language and state language, respectively, of the problem domain.

[7] For easy reference the axioms and theorems are numbered to correspond with their numbers in the *Principia*.

1. By the rule of *substitution*, any expression may be substituted for any variable in any theorem, provided the substitution is made throughout the theorem wherever that variable appears. For example, by substitution of $(P \lor Q)$ for A, in the second axiom (1.3) we get the new theorem:

$$(P \lor Q) \supset B \lor (P \lor Q)$$

2. By the rule of *replacement*, a connective can be replaced by its definition, and vice versa, in any of its occurrences. By definition $(P \supset Q)$ is equivalent to $(\sim P \lor Q)$. Hence the former expression can always be replaced by the latter and vice versa. For example, from Axiom 1.3, by replacing $\supset$ with $\lor$ we get the new theorem:

$$\sim A \lor (B \lor A)$$

3. By the rule of *detachment*, if A and $A \supset B$ are theorems, then B is a theorem. For example, from

$$(P \lor P) \supset P \quad \text{and} \quad [(P \lor P) \supset P] \supset (P \supset P)$$

we get the new theorem:

$$(P \supset P)$$

4. By the rule of *chaining*, if $(A \supset B)$ and $(B \supset C)$ are theorems, then $(A \supset C)$ is a theorem. For example, from

$$P \supset (Q \lor P) \quad \text{and} \quad (Q \lor P) \supset (P \lor Q)$$

we get the new theorem:

$$P \supset (P \lor Q)$$

Whitehead and Russell did not assume chaining (which they called syllogism) as a separate rule of inference, but, rather, derived it by two successive applications of detachment to Axiom 1.6.

Given an expression to prove, one starts from the set of axioms and theorems already proved, applying the various rules successively until the desired expression is produced. The proof (solution path) is the list of expressions, each one validly derived from the previous ones, that leads from the axioms and known theorems to the desired expression.

Let us first pose the task in the set-predicate formulation. We shall take as the element of the set U—i.e., a possible proof—an arbitrary list of symbolic logic expressions. If we impose no limits on the length or other characteristics of such sequences, their number, obviously, is infinite. Hence, we must suppose at the outset that we are not concerned with the whole set of possible proofs, but with some subset comprising, say, the "simpler" elements of that set. We might restrict U, for example, to lists consisting of not more than 20 logic expressions, with each expression not more than 23 symbols in length and involving only the variables P, Q, R, S, and T and the connectives $\sim$, $\lor$, and $\supset$. The number of possible proofs meeting these restrictions is about 10^{235}—one followed by 235 zeros.

The task is also not trivial of verifying that a particular element of the set U, as we have just defined it, is a proof of a particular problem in logic; for it is necessary to determine whether each expression in the sequence is an axiom or follows from some of the expressions preceding it by the rules of deductive inference. In addition, of course, the expression to be proved has to be contained in the sequence.

Clearly, selecting possible proofs by *sheer* trial and error and testing whether each element selected is actually the desired proof is not a feasible method for proving logic theorems—for either humans or machines. The set to be searched is too large and the testing of the elements selected is too costly. How can a problem solver bring this task down to manageable proportions?

British Museum Algorithm

The size of the space just computed—10^{235}—is not only exceedingly large but also arbitrary, for it depends entirely on the restrictions of simplicity we impose on U. Nothing in this generator reflects the demands of the task, except in the weakest possible sense of generating elements of the problem space (as opposed, say, to mixing in letters from other alphabets, such as numerals, Greek letters, and so on). Let us construct a more meaningful generator, that takes into account some of the conditions that have to be met by a solution.

Let us generate elements of U according to the following simple scheme (which we call the British Museum Algorithm in honor of the primates who are credited with employing it):

1. We consider only lists of logic expressions that are valid proofs—that is, whose initial expressions are axioms, and each of whose expressions is derived from prior ones by valid rules of inference. By generating only sequences that are proofs (of something), we eliminate the major part of the task of verification.

2. We generate first those proofs that consist of a single expression (the axioms themselves), then proofs two expressions long, and so on, limiting the alphabet of symbols as before. Given all the proofs of length k, we generate those of length (k + 1) by applying the rules of inference in all permissible ways to the former to generate new derived expressions that can be added to the sequences. That is, we generate a tree, each choice point of which represents a proof, with the branches leading from the choice point representing the legitimate ways of deriving new expressions as immediate consequences of the expressions contained in the proof.[8]

Figure 4.7 shows how the set of n-step proofs generated by the algorithm increases with n at the very start of the proof-generating process. This enumeration

---

[8] A number of fussy but not fundamental points must be taken care of in constructing the algorithm. The phrase "all permissible ways" needs to be qualified, for there is an infinity of substitutions. Care must be taken not to duplicate expressions that differ only in the names of their variables. We will not go into details here; the difficulties can be removed. The essential feature in constructing the algorithm is to allow only one thing to happen in generating each new expression—i.e., one replacement, substitution of $\sim P$ for P, and so on.

only extends to replacements of ∨ with ⊃, ⊃ with ∨, and substitution of negated variables (e.g., ∼P for P). No detachments and no complex substitutions [e.g., (Q ∨ R) for P] are included. No specializations have been made (e.g., substitution of P for Q in P ∨ Q). If we include the specializations, which take three more steps, the algorithm will generate an (estimated) additional 600 theorems, thus providing a set of proofs, all of 11 steps or less, containing almost 1000 theorems, none of them duplicates.

FIGURE 4.7

number of proofs generated by first few steps of British Museum algorithm

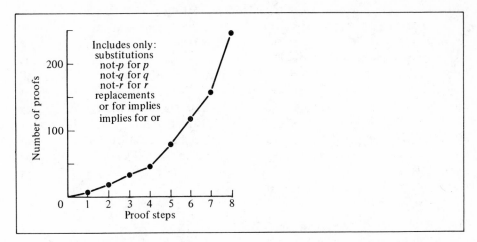

Note what has happened to the verifier with the construction of this more elaborate generator. It now has to verify only that the desired theorem occurs somewhere in the sequence of expressions produced by the generator. This is quite a simple process compared to the original one of checking the validity of the deductions.

What does the algorithm do with the sixty-odd theorems of Chapter 2 of *Principia*? One theorem (2.01) is obtained in step 4 of the generation, hence is among the first 42 theorems proved. Three more (2.02, 2.03, and 2.04) are obtained in step 6, hence among the first 115. One more (2.05) is obtained in step 8, hence in the first 246. Only one more theorem is included in the first 1000 (2.07). The proofs of all the remainder require either complex substitutions or detachment.

We have no easy way to estimate how many proofs must be generated to include proofs of all theorems of Chapter 2 of *Principia*. It is almost certainly more than 10^{1000}. Moreover, apart from the six theorems listed, there is no reason to suppose that the proofs of the *Principia* theorems would occur early in the list. It would take eons of eons of computation for the British Museum Algorithm to generate proofs for the theorems in Chapter 2 of *Principia*. By this measure, the set U is still immense, and something more effective than the British Museum Algorithm is needed in order for a man or machine to solve problems in symbolic logic in a reasonable time.

It is worth observing that, in spite of its spectacular inefficiency, the generating process of the British Museum Algorithm is far from random. In adding to subsequences of expressions, it applies only admissible operators; hence all the sequences it generates are valid proofs (of something). The algorithm does not explore the space of possible sequences of expressions, but only the space of proofs. Even in this space, it proceeds in an orderly way from short to long proofs.

We have now examined two ways of formulating this theorem-proving task in set-predicate terms. Although one was almost incomparably better than the other, both are impossible ways of solving the problem. Why should one take the trouble to study such formulations at all? For one, they provide information about the structure of the task environment. They do so by revealing just how difficult the problems will be for weak problem solvers. Thus, they provide a standard with which more powerful formulations, if they can be found, can be compared.

A second reason for exploring the set-predicate formulation and the generate-and-test method is the role they play in all problem solving as a method of last resort. Almost always, no matter how else a problem is formulated, it can also be formulated so that generate-and-test becomes a possible method. Thus, when all else fails, this method can be tried. Furthermore, as we observed in the example of the chairs in the living room, if a problem is small, generate-and-test may be the best way to solve it, in that the selection or construction of a more efficient (but elaborate) method is more costly than simply generating possible solutions and testing them. If it were not for the existence of some weak but general-purpose methods such as this one, the basic strategy of reducing a single hard problem to a myriad of small subproblems might not be feasible.

The Performance of the Logic Theorist

Let us start the description of LT with an external view, considering how it operates and performs on various theorems. We supply LT the list of five axioms, instructing it that these are theorems it can assume to be true. (It translates these to its list-structure internal representation.) LT already has stored the rules of inference and the definitions—the processes that substitute, replace, detach, and chain. Next we give LT a single expression, say Theorem 2.01, and ask LT to find a proof for it. LT works for about ten seconds,[9] then prints out the following proof:

SOLUTION PATH	SOLUTION ACTION SEQUENCE
$(P \supset \sim P) \supset \sim P$	(THEOREM 2.01, TO BE PROVED)
1. $(A \vee A) \supset A$	P1. (copy Axiom 1.2)
2. $(\sim A \vee \sim A) \supset \sim A$	P2. (subs. $\sim A$ for A in 1)
3. $(A \supset \sim A) \supset \sim A$	P3. (replace $\vee$ with $\supset$ in 2)
4. $(P \supset \sim P) \supset \sim P$	P4. (subs. P for A in 3; QED)

[9] Absolute times are deceptive measures of the performance of programs, since they depend on the particular computer on which the program was run. LT was run on JOHNNIAC, a first-generation machine of the mid-fifties no longer in service, whose addition time was 50 microseconds. All times quoted are JOHNNIAC times. To give some rough comparison, the 10-second JOHNNIAC time would correspond to .1 second on an IBM 360/65 (about 100 times faster).

Next we ask LT to prove a fairly advanced theorem in Chapter 2 of *Principia*, Theorem 2.45, allowing it to use all 38 theorems proved prior to 2.45. After about 12 minutes (7 360/65 seconds), LT produces the following proof:

$$\sim (P \lor Q) \supset \sim P \qquad \text{(THEOREM 2.45, TO BE PROVED)}$$

1.	$A \supset (A \lor B)$	(copy Theorem 2.2)
2.	$P \supset (P \lor Q)$	(subs. P for A, Q for B in 1)
3.	$(A \supset B) \supset (\sim B \supset \sim A)$	(copy Theorem 2.16)
4.	$(P \supset (P \lor Q)) \supset (\sim (P \lor Q) \supset \sim P)$	(subs. P for A, $(P \lor Q)$ for B in 3)
5.	$\sim (P \lor Q) \supset \sim P$	(detach right side of 4, using 2; QED)

Finally, all the theorems prior to 2.31 are given to LT (a total of 28); and then LT is asked to prove:

$$P \lor (Q \lor R) \supset (P \lor Q) \lor R \qquad (2.31)$$

LT works for about 23 minutes (14 360/65 seconds), but then reports that it cannot prove 2.31 and has exhausted its resources.

Let us summarize the behavior of LT when it was presented with three series of problem solving tasks.

1. As the initial task, we stored the axioms of *Principia Mathematica*, together with the program, in the memory of LT, and then presented to the machine the first 52 theorems in Chapter 2 of *Principia* in the sequence in which they appear there. LT's program specified that regardless of whether a theorem was proved it was stored in memory (on the list with the axioms) and was available along with the axioms as material for the construction of proofs of subsequent theorems. With this program and this order of presentation of problems, LT succeeded in proving 38 (73 percent) of the 52 theorems. About half of the proofs were accomplished in less than a minute each (half a 360/65 second); most of the remainder took from one to five minutes (up to 3 360/65 seconds). A few theorems were proved in times ranging from 15 minutes to 45 minutes (10 to 30 360/65 seconds). There was a strong relation between the times and the lengths of the proofs—the time increasing sharply (perhaps exponentially) with each additional proof step.

2. The initial conditions were now restored by removing from LT's memory the theorems it had proved. (Translate: A new subject was obtained who knew how to solve problems in logic but was unfamiliar with the particular problems to be used in the experiment.) When one of the later theorems of Chapter 2—Theorem 2.12—was presented to LT, it was not able to find a proof, although when it had held the prior theorems in memory, it had done so in about ten seconds (.1 360/65 seconds).

3. Next, an experiment was performed intermediate between the first two. The axioms and Theorem 2.03 were stored in memory, but not the other

theorems prior to Theorem 2.12, and LT was again given the task of proving the latter. Now, using Theorem 2.03 as one of its resources, the machine succeeded—in fifteen minutes (10 360/65 seconds)—where it had failed in the second experiment. The proof required three steps. In the first experiment, with all prior theorems available, the proof required only one step.

Thus, LT does in fact succeed in finding proofs for a large number of theorems. It represents a problem solver, effective on human scales of difficulty, as contrasted with prior schemes—i.e., the British Museum Algorithm—which were completely ineffective in human terms. The next step is to describe the internal structure of LT.

LT's Structure

The representation in terms of a tree of possible solution paths is a natural one for a theorem-proving program. If we take as the desired object the theorem to be proved, then the condition for a problem solution is that this object be obtained by a sequence of admissible operations on the axioms and previously proved theorems, taken as the initial objects.

In the state language, we are concerned with logic expressions (L), and sets and sequences (s) of logic expressions (some of the latter being proofs). In the process language, we are concerned with operators (Q) that construct sets or trees of logic expressions. Each elementary operator adds to a set of logic expressions one additional such expression. When the members of a set obtained by the application of a sequence, $Q = Q_1 \ldots Q_n$, of elementary operators to an initial set are listed in the order in which they were generated, we call this list, $s = (s_0, L_1, \ldots, L_n)$, the *sequence generated by Q from s_0*.

There are some problems to be overcome before the search formulation can be applied to symbolic logic. The elementary operators available in the task environment are substitution, replacement, detachment, and chaining. If the element in the problem space is a single logic expression, then all but one of these operators requires additional inputs to produce a new element—that is, a new logic expression. Replacement is simple: it transforms a logic expression into a logic expression (assuming that we know the connective to be replaced). But substitution requires that we know the new expressions that are to be substituted (assuming, as well, that we know the variables involved). And both detachment and chaining require that a second theorem be given—e.g., A and A $\supset$ B to produce B. Also it must be decided whether the search will be forward from the axioms in search of the desired theorem (as we have been tacitly assuming) or backward from the theorem in search of axioms. In the latter case, it must be decided how to handle the reversal of the elementary operators. Substitution now replaces sets of identical subexpressions with a variable; and detachment and chaining take a single logic expression as input but produce as output a pair of logic expressions, both of which must be shown to be true—e.g., to prove B prove both A and A $\supset$ B.

The choices made in LT are the following: First, the element of the problem space is the single logic expression. Second, LT works backward. Thus, the initially given element in the space is the theorem to be proved, and the search will proceed backwards in the direction of the axioms and assumed theorems. Third, the operators of the problem space are formed from the detachment and chaining operations by insisting that a theorem or axiom always enter into the operation as one of the inputs, so as to create one-input-one-output operators. Fourth, the other two elementary operations, replacement and substitution, are used as components of all the operators of the space, and in performing a test for whether a solution has actually been found.

Let us be more specific. *Theorems* is the set of axioms and previously proved theorems. Then the operators of the problem space are formed from the basic rules of inferences with a member of theorems as a parameter—e.g., as Q[T], where T is in theorems. The situation is exactly analogous to the parametrized operators we defined earlier in the chapter for the illustrative problem of solving algebraic equations—e.g., Add[k]. Thus, at the ith step in an exploration along a path, we can write $s_i = (Q_i[T_i], s_{i-1})$. The initial sequence, s_0, consists of the theorem to be proved.

The goal set, G, is the set, theorems, so that a proof has been found when s_i finally contains some T in theorems. Thus LT works backward, but with theorems entering as parameters into each specific operator, so that members of theorems enter the proof in two different roles. (Actually, this account has left out the role of substitution and replacement, which will become clear presently.)

The test, which for historical reasons we will call the Substitution Test,[10] and the three operators are constructed as follows:

The Substitution Test (SB).   This test takes as inputs two logic expressions, say X and T. It seeks, by a series of substitutions for variables and replacements of connectives, to transform T into X, SB(T) = X. When we wish to make the parameters explicit we write SB[a for A, b for B](T) to designate the operation of substituting a for A and b for B in expression T. (Replacements are always clear without being stated.) Thus,

$$SB[P \lor Q \text{ for } A, Q \text{ for } B](A \supset B) = ((P \lor Q) \supset Q)$$

The Detachment Operator (DT).   This operator takes as input an expression X, and has as a parameter a member, T, of theorems, where the latter has the form $T = (A \supset B)$. It seeks, by substitution and replacement, to transform B into X, SB(B) = X. If it succeeds, it produces the expression, SB(A), obtained by making in A the same substitutions as were made in B. Thus, if we call the detachment operator DT, then DT[A $\supset$ B](X) = SB(A), if SB(B) = X and (A $\supset$ B) belongs to theorems.

---

[10] In the original version of LT (Newell, Shaw, and Simon, 1957) what are here called *submethods* were called *methods*, and all were treated as having a similar function —namely, to make a contribution to the solution. Only later did it become clear that the fundamental units were the three operators and the test, and that the submethods were simply a way of packaging the application of operators. We use *submethod* simply as a way of retaining contact with the original terminology, consistently with our current use of *method* as a complete organization that has a chance to solve the problem.

The Forward Chaining Operator (CF). Chaining forward takes as its input an expression X, having the form $X = (A \supset C)$, and as a parameter a member of theorems having the form $T = (D \supset B)$. It seeks, by substitution and replacement, to transform D into A, $SB(D) = A$. If it succeeds, it produces the expression $SB(B) \supset C$, where $SB(B)$ is the expression obtained from B by making the same substitutions as were made in D. If we designate the operator by CF, then $CF[A \supset C](D \supset B) = SB(B) \supset C$, if $SB(D) = A$ and $(D \supset B)$ belongs to theorems.

The Backward Chaining Operator (CB). Chaining backward works analogously to chaining forward: given $X = (A \supset C)$ and $T = (B \supset D)$ it seeks to transform D into C, $SB(D) = C$. If it succeeds, it produces the expression $A \supset SB(B)$. Thus $CB[B \supset D](A \supset C) = A \supset SB(B)$, if $SB(D) = C$.

Figure 4.8 shows the executive structure of LT. It is a particular variant of the heuristic search method, shown in Figure 4.4, in the problem space of operators just defined. It differs somewhat from the LT executive shown in Chapter 2 (Figure 2.12, p. 40), partly in eliminating (for clarity) several of the terminating tests, and partly in incorporating a series of specialized subroutines, called submethods,[11] which organize the application of the three operators and the substitution test. Each submethod is devoted to one of the operators (DT, CF, CB) or to the test (SB). Each systematically tries its operator for all theorems in the list, theorems, taking these in the order in which they are listed.

The *substitution-submethod* is effectively the test of whether there is any theorem or axiom that can be reached directly from the input, X. If this submethod succeeds in transforming a theorem T, from theorems, into X, it announces that X has been proved. It prints out X together with all expressions, $X_1, \ldots, X_m$, from which X was obtained by a succession of detachments and chainings.

The *detachment-submethod* takes as its input an expression, X, and applies the detachment operator to X paired with each member of theorems in turn. For each *new-problem* produced, it tests (by means of the substitution-submethod) whether a solution has been found to the original problem. If not, it adds new-problem to the list, *untried-problems*. In due course, new-problem will become the *current-problem* for another cycle of search (via the generator in line 3 of the LT executive). The *chaining-forward-submethod* and the *chaining-backward-submethod* operate in exactly the same way. Thus, each submethod is an independent unit that can add a number of branches to a given sequence (at most, one branch for each member of theorems).

Let us illustrate the operation of LT with the proof of Theorem 2.45 given earlier. When all 38 theorems that precede 2.45 in *Principia* were included in theorems, along with the axioms, the program achieved a two-step proof, with the tree of sequences (and the corresponding tree of expressions) shown in Figure 4.9. The top node in the tree corresponds to the problem input to LT. Let us consider just the sequence that achieved the proof. The detachment operator, applied to 2.45 and Theorem 2.16, added to untried-problems the expression:

$$L2: \quad P \supset (P \lor Q)$$

---

[11] See footnote 10.

FIGURE 4.8

LT executive program with submethods

LT(problem, theorems):
1. Substitution-submethod(problem),
        if succeed stop and report immediate proof.
2. insert problem on untried-problems at end;
3. generate untried-problems ($\Longrightarrow$ current-problem):
4.   Detachment-submethod(current-problem);
5.   Chaining-forward-submethod(current-problem);
6.   Chaining-backward-submethod(current-problem).,
        stop and report no proof and nothing more to do.

Substitution-submethod(problem):
1. generate theorems:
2.   apply SB(theorem, problem),
            if fail continue generation;
3.   reconstruct-proof from problem,
            stop LT and report result. .

Detachment-submethod(problem):
1. generate theorems:
2.   test if theorem of form A $\supset$ B,
            if false continue generation;
3.   apply DT[theorem](problem) ($\Longrightarrow$ new-problem),
            if fail continue generation;
4.   apply Substitution-submethod(new-problem),
            if succeed stop process;
5.   insert new-problem on untried-problems at end..

Chaining-forward-submethod(problem):
1. test if problem of form A $\supset$ B,
        if false stop;
2. generate theorems:
3.   test if theorem of form A $\supset$ B,
            if false continue generation;
4.   apply CF[theorem](problem) ($\Longrightarrow$ new-problem),
            if fail continue generation;
5.   apply Substitution-submethod(new-problem),
            if succeed stop process;
6.   insert new-problem on untried-problems at end..

Chaining-backward-submethod(problem):
1. test if problem of form A $\supset$ B,
        if false stop;
2. generate theorems:
3.   test if theorem of form A $\supset$ B,
            if false continue generation;
4.   apply CB[theorem](problem) ($\Longrightarrow$ new-problem),
            if fail continue generation;
5.   apply Substitution-submethod(new-problem),
            if succeed stop process;
6.   insert new-problem on untried-problems at end..

Then the substitution operator, applied to L2 and Theorem 2.2, determined that the latter could be made equal to the former by substitution. Prior to the production of L2, the detachment operator had added seven other expressions to untried-problems that did not figure in the proof finally discovered.

FIGURE 4.9

exploration tree for proof of Theorem 2.45 (all previous theorems available)

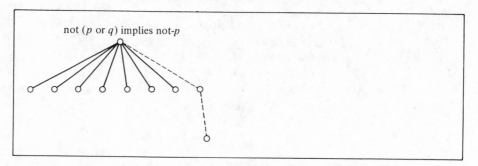

Heuristic Character of the Method. The method used by LT gives no guarantee that it will work. There is no guarantee that a suitable theorem can be found on the theorem list to carry out a proof by the substitution-submethod, or a theorem that will produce a subproblem by any of the other three submethods. Since the system works backward from the desired theorem, if a subproblem is generated, there is no guarantee that it is part of the desired proof sequence, or even that it is part of any proof sequence (e.g., it can be false). On the other hand, the operators do guarantee that any subproblem generated is part of a sequence of expressions that ends in the desired theorem (this is one of the conditions that a sequence be a proof). The operators also guarantee that each expression of the sequence is derived by the rules of inference from the preceding ones (a second condition of proof). What is not guaranteed is that the sequence can be connected with the axioms and previously proved theorems (i.e., with the list, theorems).

There is also no guarantee that the combination of the four methods, used in any fashion whatsoever and with unlimited computing effort, comprises a sufficient set of methods to prove all theorems. For example, LT cannot prove Theorem 2.13, $P \lor \sim \sim \sim P$. All the new members of untried-problems generated for 2.13 after a certain point are false expressions, and therefore cannot lead to a proof (i.e., cannot be derived from the list, theorems).

If we examine the proof that Whitehead and Russell give for this theorem, we can see the reason for LT's failure—and why, more generally, LT's program is not a complete algorithm for all problems of this class. To simplify our discussion of the Whitehead and Russell proof, we shall leave out of account the substitutions that have to be made and shall assume that they are accomplished automatically. We shall be concerned, in fact, only with detachment.

In their proof, Whitehead and Russell use Axiom 1.06 and two previously proved theorems, 2.11 and 2.12. Let us call Theorem 2.11, A; Theorem 2.12, B; and Theorem 2.13, the theorem to be proved, C. Axiom 1.06 of *Principia* (leaving substitutions out of account) is of the form:

$$B \supset (A \supset C)$$

Thus, by the rule of detachment, from B, which is a theorem, and $B \supset (A \supset C)$, which is an axiom, they obtain $(A \supset C)$. Again by the rule of detachment, from $(A \supset C)$, and from A, which is a theorem, they obtain C, completing the proof.

Why cannot LT discover this proof by two applications of the rule of detachment, working backward? Because, given C, the theorem to be proved, the detachment method searches for an already proved theorem or axiom of the form $(X \supset C)$. But, $(A \supset C)$ not having yet been proved, there is no such theorem in memory, and therefore the submethod fails. The detachment-submethod does not treat the two premises A and $A \supset C$ symmetrically. If LT had previously been given the problem of proving $(A \supset C)$, it would have found that proof by detachment. If it were then given the problem of proving C, with $(A \supset C)$ already listed in memory as a theorem, it would have succeeded, for the detachment-submethod would have discovered $(A \supset C)$. Hence, there is a very large class of branched proofs that LT will not discover unless it is given some of the intermediate expressions in an appropriate sequence as subproblems.

Selectivity of the Method. Let us look more closely at the guarantee that the method does provide: that any logic expression generated by an operator belongs to a sequence of admissible inferences leading to the desired theorem. LT is searching for a proof of a theorem, X, in the space of all sets of logic expressions. The operators generate only sequences of expressions that belong to the class of sequences ending in X. Moreover, each expression in a sequence is derivable from its successor in the sequence, so that if one of these sequences leads back to an axiom or previously proved theorem, then it also belongs to the set of proof sequences. Hence, such a sequence also is automatically guaranteed to be a proof of X. The British Museum Algorithm possesses similar guarantees—it generates only proof sequences; and we saw in the previous section that this single selective property reduced the size of the space of possibilities in which it searches from something of the order of 10^{235} to something of the order of 10^7.

The solution generators of these programs have, then, a great deal of built-in selectivity. Many irrelevant parts of the space of possible solutions are excluded from the search. Since this is a basic property of an important class of problem solving heuristics, we shall restate the matter more generally. Many problems have the following form: G, the set of solutions, consists of all elements with property p1, and property p2, and property p3. No generator is available that will generate elements having all these properties; but there are generators for generating elements having any two of the properties. Thus there are three possible schemes: (1) to generate elements with properties p1 and p2 until one is found that also has p3; (2) to generate elements with p1 and p3 until one is found with property p2; (3) to generate elements with p2 and p3 until one is found with property p1. Which generator should be chosen depends on which constraints are the more difficult to satisfy, and on the relative costs of generation. If there are lots of elements satisfying p1, then generating elements with p2 and p3 is reasonable, since a p1 can be expected to show up soon. If p1's are rare, it is better to generate elements that already have property p1.

Thus, a proof is a list of logic expressions satisfying the following properties:

p1. The beginning of the list consists of known theorems (any number of them).

p2. All other expressions on the list are direct and valid consequences of prior expressions on the list.

p3. The last expression on the list is the expression to be proved.

Now, although there is no generator that will turn out sequences satisfying all three of these conditions, there are generators that satisfy any two of them. It is easy to write down lists that start with theorems and end with the known expression. The difficult condition, however, is p2: that the list must consist of valid inference steps. Hence, it would obviously be foolish to choose a generator that automatically satisfied p1 and p3, and simply wait until it generated a list that also satisfied p2.

It is also possible to construct a generator satisfying p1 and p2—one that produces lists that are proofs of something. This generator could find a proof by producing such lists until one appeared containing the desired expression—condition p3. The British Museum Algorithm is a generator of this kind. Finally, one can build a generator that satisfies conditions p2 and p3. Fixing the last expression to be the desired one, lists are produced that consist only of valid inference steps leading to the last expression. Then the problem is solved when a list is generated that satisfies condition p1, so that the expressions on the front of the list are all theorems. With this kind of generator the list is constructed backwards from the desired result toward the given theorems. This is the way LT actually goes about discovering proofs.

Information Content of the Method. From the analysis thus far it is clear that if a generator is to be other than a generate-and-test process it must have access to information in the situation that allows it to construct the required objects directly. To see where this information comes from, consider the detachment-submethod (Figure 4.8). It does not add new expressions in an arbitrary way, but only when certain very special conditions are satisfied—and these conditions determine what expression is to be added. These special conditions incorporate the guarantees that the set, theorems, will always possess property p1 of a proof, and that the set, untried-problems, will always possess properties p2 and p3. Thus the detachment-submethod uses in its search of the set, theorems, the information that the particular proof sequence it is attempting to construct contains the expression X. It also uses the information that only a theorem of the form $A \supset X$ in theorems is of interest. If a theorem of this form is found, the operator has immediately at hand the information that A is an expression that can be added to untried-problems.

While the detachment and chaining submethods, taken jointly, generate only a highly selective subset of possible proof sequences, they do not usually generate a unique sequence. Nor do they guarantee that the sequences they generate possess all the properties of a proof. Hence, the need for a test process, the substitution-submethod. The substitution-submethod needs merely to check each partial sequence against the members of theorems to determine whether the remaining requirement is satisfied—whether the partial sequence is now a complete proof, or can be made into one by substitution in a theorem. Thus, the substitution-submethod, like the other submethods, takes positive action only when special conditions are satisfied, and these conditions determine the action.

In these respects there is no fundamental difference between the British Museum Algorithm and LT. Both incorporate highly selective generators; the generators construct trees of possible solutions; a relatively simple test determines whether any of these possibilities is a solution. The superiority of LT as a problem solver arises from the fact that its generator is more selective than the generator in the British Museum Algorithm.

We can make these considerations more specific. First, let us see how the selective power of a generator can be evaluated quantitatively. Consider the problem space taking the form of a tree, with m alternatives at each branch point and a length of k branch points. If there were a single correct path to the goal, finding that path by random search would require on the order of m^k trials. If a generator were available that produced only half of the alternatives at each branch point, then a random search with this heuristic would require only on the order of $(m/2)^k$ trials. This is a reduction in search by a ratio of 2^k, which if the search were only seven steps in length would amount to a factor of 128, and if the search were ten steps in length, to a factor of just over one thousand. (The information provided by the heuristics in this case is one bit per step.)

In LT, we have initially a set, U, consisting of a single member (the theorem to be proved), and a set, T, consisting of the axioms and theorems previously proved. Let us consider the way U grows with the depth, n, of the search, U[n]. We will use the names of the sets also to denote the number of elements in the set. Thus, U[0] = 1, and T has T members. The generator that consists of applying the detachment and chaining operators, in turn, to the member of U[0] and each of the members of T, will create aT new expressions to be added to U[0], where a is the probability that application of the operators to any given member of T will be successful; this gives U[1]. Next, the generator is applied to each pair, obtained by taking each new member of U[1], with each member of T, in turn. Since we have now seen that U[1] $\sim$ aT, this will produce approximately $(aT)^2$ additional members of U. Thus, on each round of application of the generator, the size of U, and hence of the subproblem tree, is multiplied by the factor aT. Hence, the number U[n], of branches of length n or less will be of the order of $(aT)^n$. The tree will grow exponentially, like the search we discussed above.

The tree produced by the British Museum Algorithm will branch more rapidly, because the generator is constructed in a slightly different fashion. The differences in efficiency stem from differences in the application of the substitution test, on the one hand, and the detachment and chaining operators, on the other. For the moment, let us consider only the latter, leaving a discussion of the differences in substitution to the next section. In order to abstract from the differences in substitution, we consider, instead of the British Museum Algorithm, a more selective working-forward algorithm that can be compared directly with LT. It incorporates submethods corresponding to the detachment and chaining submethods of LT, but works forward from the axioms and previously proved theorems, instead of backward from the expression to be proved.

The operators in this working-forward algorithm corresponding to the detachment and chaining operators in LT take a pair of members of T, and attempt to construct a new expression to be added to T. The number of new members added after one round of generation will be of the order of $T[1] = aT^2$. On the second round, $T[2] = a(aT^2)^2$ new members will be added to T, and so on. If aT^2 is large relative to T, the number $T[n]$, of branches of length n or less will be of the order of $(aT)^{2^n}$. This number grows, of course, very much more rapidly with n than does $(aT)^n$. Hence, if the problem solution is an n-step proof, LT should be expected to find it, on the average, much more rapidly than the working-forward algorithm. In Table 4.2 we show the estimates, based on these approximations, of sizes of the trees, for $1 < n < 6$, generated by LT and the working-forward algorithm, respectively, for the hypothetical case where $a = .3$ and $T[0] = 6$.

TABLE 4.2

estimated number of proofs of n steps generated by LT and BMA, respectively, a = .3, T[0] = 6

NUMBER OF STEPS (n)	LT	BMA
1	2	11
2	3	45
3	6	1.2×10^3
4	10	4.3×10^5
5	19	5.6×10^{10}
6	34	9.3×10^{20}

Summary: The Submethods. The submethods of LT and the corresponding generators of the working-forward algorithm and the British Museum Algorithm illustrate a very important class of problem solving heuristics: generators that produce a selective tree of possible solution action sequences and paths. The selectivity of such generators is based on two main characteristics they usually possess:

1. They usually generate only sequences that satisfy certain criteria of admissibility—criteria that may also be required for an action sequence or path to be a solution.
2. They use information extracted from the partial sequences and paths already generated to select the specific directions in which these sequences and paths should be continued. The generators are more or less selective in producing new continuations as they use more or less information from the expressions already generated.

Since the problem spaces that describe the task environments are generally immense, it is hard to exaggerate the amount of selectivity exercised even by apparently blind-trial-and-error generators like the working-forward algorithm and the British Museum Algorithm. For the same reason, apparently small differences between heuristics may make very large differences in their selectivity, and hence in their problem solving efficacy. In the next section we shall see the point illustrated in connection with matching and substitution processes.

The Matching Process

In our analysis of the methods of LT, we have generally ignored the process whereby substitutions of variables and replacements of connectives are made. We shall now show that the matching process in LT, which carries out substitutions and replacements, introduces important additional elements of selectivity into the generators, and makes LT even more selective than we have indicated so far. We shall return to the British Museum Algorithm for comparison.

Example of a Proof by Substitution. First of all, we can show that even when only substitution is employed, and not also the detachment and chaining sub-methods, the times required to generate proofs for even the simplest theorems by the British Museum Algorithm are larger than the times required by LT by factors ranging from five (for one particular theorem) to a hundred and upwards. Let us consider as an example one of the theorems that the British Museum Algorithm would prove rather early in its generation of proofs. Theorem 2.02 of *Principia*, P ⊃ (Q ⊃ P), was proved by LT in about 10 seconds (.1 360/65 seconds), using the method of substitution. It would be the seventy-ninth theorem generated by the British Museum Algorithm, and, assuming comparable machine speeds, might be proved in about 158 seconds (1.6 360/65 seconds) by a sequence of substitutions and replacements. The reason for the difference becomes apparent if we focus attention on Axiom 1.3, A ⊃ (B ∨ A), from which the theorem is derived by either program.

Figure 4.10 shows the tree of proofs of the first twelve theorems obtained from 1.3 by the British Museum Algorithm. Theorem 2.02 is node (9) on the tree and

FIGURE 4.10

tree for proofs of first 12 theorems produced by British Museum algorithm

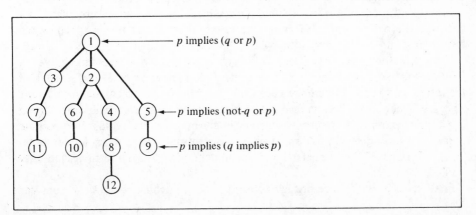

is obtained by substituting $\sim Q$ for Q in Axiom 1.3 to reach node (5), and then by replacing the $(\sim Q \vee P)$ by $(Q \supset P)$ in (5) to get (9). The ninth theorem generated from Axiom 1.3 is the seventy-ninth generated from the five axioms considered together.

This proof is obtained directly by LT with the substitution method using the following matching procedure. We compare the axiom with (9), the expression to be proved:

$$A \supset (B \vee A) \tag{1.3}$$
$$P \supset (Q \supset P) \tag{9}$$

First, by a direct comparison, the matching process determines that the main connectives are identical. Second, it determines that the terms to the left of the main connective differ, one being the variable A, the other the constant P. It substitutes P for A throughout the expression, thus making the left-hand terms identical. Third, it determines that the connectives within parentheses on the right-hand sides are different. It is necessary to replace the $\vee$ with $\supset$, but in order to do this (in accordance with the definition of $\supset$) there must be a $\sim$ before the variable that precedes the $\vee$. Hence, the matching process first replaces the B on the right-hand side with $\sim B$ to get the required $\sim$, obtaining the expression (5). Now the matching process can change the $\vee$ to $\supset$. Fourth, it determines that the terms on the left side of the right-hand subexpressions differ, one being the variable B and the other the constant Q. It substitutes Q for B, thus making these terms identical. Finally, it determines that the terms on the far right are identical (both P), so that the resulting expression is identical with (9).

The matching process allowed LT to proceed directly down the branch from (1) through (5) to (9) without even exploring the other branches. Quantitatively, it looked at only two expressions instead of eight, thus reducing the work of comparison by a factor of four. Actually, the saving is even greater, since the matching procedure does not deal with whole expressions, but with a single pair of elements at a time.

Efficacy of the Matching Process. The matching process derives its efficiency from two sources. First, it generates the correct substitutions, rather than searching for them. (It resembles the algorithm for algebraic equations in this respect, rather than the algorithm for the clicking safe.) By comparing the symbols in a given expression with the symbols in a desired expression, it determines exactly what substitution will (partially) transform the former into the latter. It avoids search simply by copying information provided by the desired expression.

Second, the matching process proceeds componentwise (resembling the algorithm for the clicking safe in this respect), obtaining at each step a feedback of the results of a substitution or replacement that can be used to guide the next step. This feedback keeps the search on the correct path, and, even when the correct substitution cannot be determined immediately by copying, avoids the necessity of a search through the whole space of possible substitutions for various combinations of variables. This characteristic of the matching process is a form of factorization.

To see the significance of factorization in the matching process, we consider again the proof of Theorem 2.02, P ⊃ (Q ⊃ P). In our previous discussion of this theorem we assumed that LT would immediately select 1.3 as the appropriate axiom in which to make substitutions and replacements. In actual fact, the substitution-submethod begins by matching with each axiom in turn, abandoning it for the next one if the matching proves impossible. For example, in the attempt to match Theorem 2.02 against Axiom 1.2, the matching process determines almost immediately (on the second test) that (R ∨ P) cannot be made into P by substitution, and it eliminates 1.2 as a possibility. Thus, the matching process permits LT to abandon unprofitable lines of search as well as guiding it to correct substitutions and replacements.

Matching in the Substitution-Submethod. The matching process is an essential part of the substitution-submethod. Without it, the substitution-submethod is just that part of the British Museum Algorithm that uses only replacements and substitutions. With it, LT is able, either directly or in combination with the other methods, to prove many theorems with reasonable effort.

We have mentioned that LT found proofs for 38 of the first 52 theorems in *Principia Mathematica*. These proofs were obtained by various combinations of methods, but the substitution-submethod was an essential component of all of them. Seventeen of the proofs—almost half—were accomplished by the substitution-submethod alone. Subjectively evaluated, these seventeen theorems have the appearance of corollaries of the theorems they are derived from; they occur fairly close to them in the chapter. These theorems generally required three or fewer attempts at matching per theorem proved (54 attempts for 17 theorem).

The performance of the substitution-submethod on new subproblems is somewhat different, owing, we think, to the kind of selectivity implicit in the order of theorems in *Principia*. In 338 attempts at solving subproblems by substitution, there were 21 successes (6.2 percent). Thus, there was about one chance in three of proving an original problem directly by the substitution-submethod, but only about one chance in sixteen of so proving a subproblem generated from the original problem.

Matching in Detachment and Chaining. We have been considering the matching process as a part of the substitution-submethod, but we have seen earlier that it is also an essential component of the other three submethods. In detachment, for example, a theorem of form (A ⊃ B) is sought, where B is identical with the expression to be proved. The chances of finding such a theorem are negligible unless we allow some modification of B to make it match the theorem to be proved. Hence, once a theorem is selected from the theorem list, its right-hand subexpression is matched against the expression to be proved. An analogous procedure is used in the chaining methods.

We can evaluate the performance of the detachment and chaining submethods with the same sample of problems used for evaluating the substitution-submethod. However, a successful match with the former three methods generates a subproblem and does not directly prove the theorem. With the detachment-submethod, an average of 3 new subproblems were generated for each application of the method: with forward chaining the average was 2.7; and with backward chaining the average was 2.2. For all submethods, this represents about one subproblem per 7.5 theorems tested (the number of theorems available varied slightly).

As in the case of substitution, when these three submethods were applied to the original problem, the chances of success were higher than when they were applied to subproblems. When applied to the original problem, the number of subproblems generated averaged 8 to 9; when applied to subproblems derived from the original, the number of subproblems generated fell to an average of 2 or 3.

In handling the first 52 problems in Chapter 2 of *Principia*, seventeen theorems were proved in one step—that is, in one application of substitution. Nineteen theorems were proved in two steps—twelve by detachment followed by substitution, and seven by chaining forward followed by substitution. Two others were proved in three steps. Hence, 38 theorems were proved in all. There are no two-step proofs by backward chaining, since—for two-step proofs only—if there exists a proof by backward chaining, there is also one by forward chaining. In 14 cases LT failed to find a proof. Most of these unsuccessful attempts were terminated by time or space limitations. One of these 14 theorems we know LT cannot prove, and one other we believe it cannot prove. Most of the remaining twelve can be proved by LT if it has sufficient time and memory (see the section on subproblems, however).

Search Heuristics

In LT the four submethods are organized by the executive routine, shown in Figure 4.8. We see that the executive builds the search tree by exploring in breadth—first for one-step proofs, then two-step proofs, and so on. As Figure 4.8 shows, if all the submethods have been tried on a given problem and no proof has been produced, the executive routine selects the next untried subproblem from the list of untried-problems, and makes the same sequence of attempts with it.

Subproblem Trees. In the three examples cited earlier, the proof of 2.01, $(P \supset {\sim}P) \supset {\sim}P$, was obtained by the substitution-submethod directly, hence did not involve the use of the subproblem list.

The proof of 2.45, ${\sim}(P \lor Q) \supset {\sim}P$, was achieved by an application of the detachment-submethod followed by a substitution. This proof required LT to create a subproblem and to use the substitution-submethod on it. It did not require LT ever to select any subproblem from the subproblem list, since the substitution was successful.

LT did not prove Theorem 2.31 also mentioned earlier, giving as its reason that it could think of nothing more to do. This means that LT had considered, unsuccessfully, all subproblems on untried-problems (there were six in this case) and had no new subproblems to work on. In none of the examples mentioned here did LT terminate because of time or space limitations; however, this is the most common result in the cases where LT does not find a proof. Only rarely does LT run out of things to do.

Subproblem Selection. The executive routine as we have described it is not in itself a selective process, but a means for organizing a systematic search in breadth along the possible solution paths that can be generated by the submethods. By trying the submethods in rotation on each of the subproblems that is generated with each of the available axioms and theorems, it builds out the tree of potential proofs. However, it is possible by some elaboration of the executive routine to make it contribute also to the selectivity of the entire system, as we shall now see.

In Figure 4.11 two searches are shown, derived from two attempts under slightly different conditions, to prove Theorem 2.45 from the same list of known theorems. In Figure 4.9 we depicted the exploration tree for the proof of the same theorem when all previous theorems were available on the theorem list. For the searches shown in Figure 4.11, a smaller list of theorems was used—omitting one of those that had been employed in the earlier proof. Thus, the new search trees are deeper than the previous one.

In each search, the desired theorem, 2.45, is represented by the top node; and each node below corresponds to a new expression generated (as a subproblem) from

FIGURE 4.11

exploration trees for two proofs of Theorem 2.45 (the heavy line is the proof—dotted lines show additional branches eliminated by selective heuristics already in the first program)

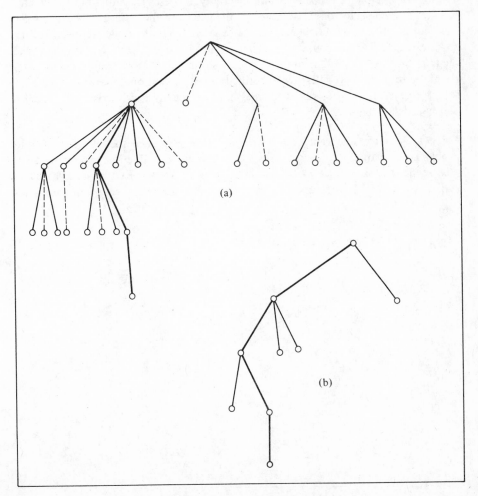

(a)

(b)

the node immediately above it. In both cases LT found the same proof, which is designated in each maze by the heavy line. When it was generating the lower search, LT had available two selective heuristics it did not have during the run that generated the upper search. One of these heuristics weeded out new expressions that appeared unprovable on the basis of certain plausible criteria; the other heuristic weeded out expressions that seemed too complicated, in the sense of having too many negation signs ($\sim$'s). These two heuristics reduced the amount of search required to find the solution by a factor of 24/9 or 2.7. When the cost of the additional testing is taken into account, the net saving in total problem solving effort was a factor of 2.3. Neither of these two heuristics is foolproof. Both eliminate some paths that lead to solutions. They can even eliminate all paths to solutions.

These selective procedures are illustrative of a class of heuristics that may be called *stop rules*. The costliness in pursuing the wrong paths in the problem solving tree arises from the exponentially branching character of that tree. If we generate ten branches at a node, only one of which leads to a solution path, effort has been multiplied by ten. But worse than that, if each of the nine false branches itself has a tenfold branch, and so on, the lack of selectivity increases the effort not by a factor of ten, but by a factor of 10^n, where n is the length of the paths. Hence, even if it were not possible to avoid generating the false branches at a node, almost all of the consequent inefficiency could be avoided if a test were available that discriminated the false branches from the correct branch (like the click in the safe-opening algorithm, or the two stop rules just described) after generation. (See Figure 4.3.) We shall see other applications of stop rules in our discussion of heuristics for a chess player in later chapters.

Using a Selective Theorem List. Another way to reduce the number of subproblems generated is to limit the lists of theorems available for generating them (i.e., reduce the size of set T). That this approach may be effective is suggested by statistics of LT's performance, which show that the number of subproblems

FIGURE 4.12

exploration tree for Theorem 2.17 (all previous theorems available)

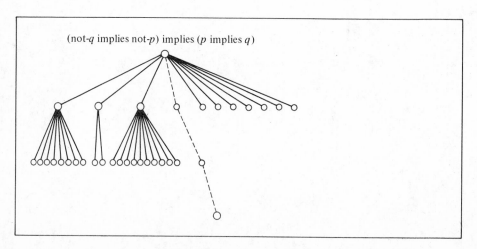

generated by a submethod per theorem examined is relatively constant (about one subproblem per seven theorems).

An impression of how the number of available theorems affects the generation of subproblems may be gained by comparing the proof trees of Theorems 2.17 (Figure 4.12) and 2.27 (Figure 4.13). The broad tree for 2.17 was produced with a list of twenty theorems, while the deep tree for 2.27 was produced with a list of only five theorems. The smaller theorem list in the latter case generated fewer subproblems at each application of one of the submethods.

FIGURE 4.13

exploration tree for Theorem 2.27 (using the axioms)

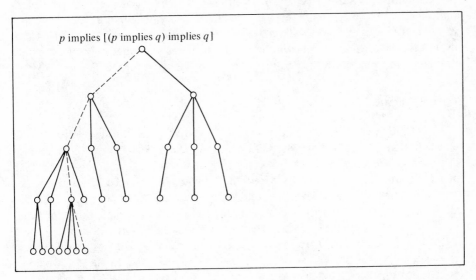

p implies $[(p$ implies $q)$ implies $q]$

Another example of the same point is provided by two proofs of Theorem 2.48 obtained with different lists of available theorems. In the one case 2.48 was proved starting with all prior theorems on the theorem list; in the other case it was proved starting only with the axioms and Theorem 2.16. We had conjectured that the proof would be more difficult to obtain under the latter conditions, since a longer proof chain would have to be constructed than under the former. We were wrong: with the longer theorem list, LT proved Theorem 2.48 in two steps; with the shorter list, LT proved the theorem in three steps, but in about one-third the time that was required in the former case. Examination of the first proof shows that the many irrelevant theorems on the list took a great deal of processing effort. The comparison shows dramatically that a problem solver may be encumbered by too much information, just as he may be handicapped by too little—if the additional information reduces the selectivity of his search.

Evaluating Theorems on the Untried-Problems List. Since all the expressions LT has produced up to any particular point in its work on a problem are available to it on untried-problems, it is not condemned to searching in breadth—it need not take up these problems in the order in which they are placed on untried-problems.

Instead, each expression can be assigned a *value* when it is placed on the list, the value representing an estimate of the likelihood that that expression lies on a short path to a proof. Expressions can then be taken from untried-problems, in continuation of the search, according to their values, the expression with highest value first.

In one version of LT, a primitive form of such an evaluation function was used. It consisted merely in assigning to each expression a measure of simplicity, so that simpler expressions would be taken ahead of more complex expressions. This heuristic produced only a small average improvement in the performance of LT (though it changed considerably the ranking of proofs by difficulty), but it has been used in subsequent problem solving programs, employing more sophisticated evaluation functions, to powerful effect.

Selecting new subproblems from untried-problems on the basis of an evaluation function is sometimes called the *scan-search* heuristic. First, untried-problems is scanned for its most promising member, then a burst of search is carried out, using that member as the starting point. New nodes generated by the search are evaluated and placed on untried-problems, and the cycle repeats.

Abstraction in LT: Similarity and Descriptions

Matching permeates all of the operators, and without it none of them would be useful within practical amounts of computing effort. However, a large amount of search is still used in the submethods to find the correct theorems with which matching works. We have mentioned that the overall chances of a particular matching being successful are .3 percent for substitution, 13.4 percent for detachment, 13.8 percent for forward chaining, and 9.4 percent for backward chaining.

The amount of search through the theorem list can be reduced by interposing a screening process that will reject any theorem for matching that has low likelihood of success. LT has such a screening device, called the *similarity test*. Two logic expressions are here defined to be *similar* if both their left-hand and right-hand sides are equal, with respect to (1) the maximum number of *levels* from the main connective to any variable; (2) the number of *distinct variables;* and (3) the number of *variable places*. Speaking intuitively, two logic expressions are similar if they look alike, and look alike if they are similar. Consider for example:

$$(P \lor Q) \supset (Q \lor P) \qquad (1)$$
$$P \supset (Q \lor P) \qquad (2)$$
$$R \supset (M \supset R) \qquad (3)$$

By the definition of similarity, (2) and (3) are similar, but (1) is not similar to either (2) or (3).

The similarity test involves a simple use of abstraction. Instead of matching expressions in detail, it matches only certain descriptive characteristics. Less processing is required to handle these descriptions than the complete expressions, and this reduction in processing effort makes the abstraction potentially useful.

In all of the submethods, LT applies the similarity tests to all expressions to be matched, and applies the matching process only if the expressions are similar; otherwise, it passes on to the next theorem in the theorem list. The similarity test reduces substantially the number of matchings attempted, as the numbers in Table 4.3 show, and correspondingly raises the probability of attaining a match if the matching is attempted. The effect is particularly strong in substitution, where the similarity test reduces the matchings attempted by a factor of ten, and increases the probability of a successful match by the same factor.

TABLE 4.3ª

statistics of similarity tests and matching

METHOD	THEOREMS CONSIDERED	PASSED SIMILARITY TEST	MATCHED	PERCENT SIMILAR OF CONSIDERED	PERCENT MATCHED OF SIMILAR
Substitution	11,298	993	37	8.8	3.7
Detachment	1,591	406	210	25.5	51.7
Chaining Forward	869	200	120	23.0	60.0
Chaining Backward	693	146	63	21.7	43.2

These figures reveal a gross, but not necessarily a net, gain in performance through the use of the similarity test. There are two reasons why the entire gross gain may not be realized. First, the similarity test is only a heuristic. It offers no guarantee that it will let through only expressions that will subsequently match. The similarity test also offers no guarantee that it will not reject expressions that would match if attempted. The similarity test does not often commit this type of error (corresponding to a type II statistical error), as will be shown later. However, even rare occurrences of such errors can be costly. One example occurs in the proof of Theorem 2.07:

$$P \supset (P \lor P) \qquad (2.07)$$

This theorem can be proved simply by substituting P for Q in Axiom 1.3:

$$P \supset (Q \lor P) \qquad (1.3)$$

However, the similarity test, since it demands equality in the number of distinct variables on the right-hand side, calls 2.07 and 1.3 dissimilar because 2.07 contains only P while 1.3 contains P and Q. LT discovers the proof through chaining forward, where it checks for a direct match before creating the new subproblem, but the proof is about five times as expensive as when the similarity test is omitted.

The second reason why the gross gain will not all be realized is that the similarity test is not costless. In fact for those theorems that pass the test the cost of the similarity test must be paid in addition to the cost of the matching. We will examine these costs in the next section when we consider the effort LT expends.

Experiments have been carried out with a weaker similarity test, which compares only the number of variable places on both sides of the expression. This test will not commit the particular type II error cited above, and 2.07 is proved by a substitution using it. Apart from this, the modification had remarkably little effect on performance. On a sample of ten problems it admitted only 10 percent more similar theorems and about 10 percent more subproblems. The reason why the two tests do not differ more radically is that there is a high correlation among the descriptive measures.

Processing Effort in the Logic Theorist

So far we have focused on the selectivity of the heuristics in LT and have not given much attention to the time required by generators, tests, and processing filters for their operation. However, it is clear that each additional test, search, description, and the like, has its costs in processing effort as well as its gains in performance. The costs must always be balanced against the performance gains, since there are always alternative heuristics that could be added to the system in place of those being used. In this section we will analyze the processing effort used by LT. The memory space used by the various processes also constitutes a cost, but one that will not be discussed.

Measuring Effort. LT is written in an information processing language. It is defined in terms of a set of elementary processes, which in turn are defined for computer realization by subroutines in JOHNNIAC machine language. Since these elementary processes provide a convenient unit of effort, all effort measurements will be stated in terms of total number of elementary information processes (eip's) executed. Because the relative frequencies of the different eip's are reasonably constant, the total number of eip's is an adequate index of effort. In the JOHNNIAC realization the average time per eip is quite constant at about 30 milliseconds.[12]

Processing Effort and Performance. On a priori grounds we would expect the amount of processing effort required to solve a logic problem to be roughly proportional to the total number of theorems examined (i.e., tested for similarity, if there is a similarity routine; or tested for matching, if there is not) by the various methods in the course of solving the problem. In fact, this turns out to be a reasonably good predictor of effort; but the fit to the data is much improved if we assign a greater weight to theorems considered for chaining and detachment than to those considered for substitution.

Actual and predicted efforts are compared in Table 4.4 (with the full similarity test included, and excluding theorems proved by substitution) on the assumption that the number of eip's per theorem considered is twice as great for chaining as for substitution, and three times as great for detachment. About 45 eip's are executed per theorem considered with the substitution-submethod (hence 135 with detachment and 90 with chaining). As the table shows, the estimates are generally accurate within a few percent, except for Theorem 2.06 for which the estimate is too low.

There is an additional source of variation in the machine realization not shown in theorems selected for Table 4.4. The descriptions used in the similarity

[12] The corresponding time on the IBM 360/65 is about 300 microseconds.

test must be computed from the logic expressions. Since the descriptions of the theorems are used over and over again, LT computes these at the start of a problem and stores the values with the theorems, so they do not have to be computed again. However, as the number of theorems increases, the space devoted to storing the precomputed descriptions becomes prohibitive, and LT switches to recomputing them each time it needs them. With recomputation, the problem effort is still roughly proportional to the total number of theorems considered, but now the number of eip's per theorem is around 70 for the substitution method, 210 for detachment, and 140 for chaining.

Our analysis of the effort statistics shows, then, that in first approximation the effort required to prove a theorem is proportional to the number of theorems that have to be considered before a proof is found—the number of theorems considered is an effort measure for evaluating a heuristic. A good heuristic, by securing the consideration of the right theorems early in the proof, reduces the expected number of theorems to be considered before a proof is found.

TABLE 4.4

effort statistics for LT

	(Total eip's in thousands)	
THEOREM	ACTUAL	ESTIMATE
2.06	3.2	0.8
2.07	4.3	4.4
2.08	3.5	3.3
2.11	2.2	2.2
2.13	24.5	24.6
2.14	3.3	3.2
2.15	15.8	13.6
2.18	34.1	35.8
2.25	11.1	11.5

Evaluation of the Similarity Test. As we noted in the previous section, to evaluate an improved heuristic, account must be taken of any additional processing that the improvement introduces. The net advantage may be less than the gross advantage— or the extra processing effort may actually cancel out the gross gain in selectivity. We are now in a position to evaluate the similarity tests as preselectors of theorems for matching.

A number of theorems were run, first with the full similarity tests, then with the modified similarity test (which tests only the number of variable places), and finally with no similarity test at all. We also made some comparisons with both precomputed and recomputed descriptions.

When descriptions are precomputed, the processing effort is less with the full similarity test than without it—the factor of saving ranging from 10 percent to 60 percent (e.g., 3534/5206 for Theorem 2.08). However, if LT must recompute the descriptions every time, the full similarity test is actually about 15 percent more expensive than no similarity test at all (e.g., 26,739/22,914 for Theorem 2.45).

The modified similarity test fares somewhat better. For example, in proving Theorem 2.45 it requires only 18,035 eip's compared to the 22,914 for no similarity test (see paragraph above). These comparisons involve recomputed descriptions; we have no figures for precomputed descriptions, but the additional saving appears small, since there is much less to process with the abridged than with the full test.

Thus the similarity test is rather marginal, and does not provide anything like the factors of improvement achieved by the matching process, although we have seen that the performance figures (Table 4.3) seem to indicate much more substantial gains. The reason for the discrepancy is not difficult to find. In a sense, the matching process consists of two parts. One is a testing part that locates the differences between elements and diagnoses the corrective action to be taken. The other part comprises the processes of substituting and replacing. The latter part is the major expense in a matching that works, but most of this effort is saved when the matching fails. Thus matching turns out to be inexpensive for precisely those expressions that the similarity test excludes. The similarity test trims off the problem tree only stubs that would be pruned off rapidly in any case by the matching process.

Subproblems. LT can prove a great many theorems in symbolic logic. However, there are numerous theorems that LT cannot prove, and we may describe LT as having reached a plateau in its problem solving ability.

FIGURE 4.14

distribution of LT's proofs by effort—data include all proofs from attempts on the first 52 theorems in chap. 2 of *Principia*

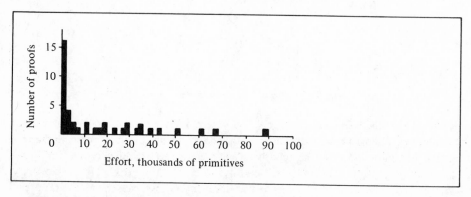

Figure 4.14 shows the amount of effort required for the problems LT solved out of the sample of 52. Almost all the proofs that LT found took less than 30,000 eip's of effort. Among the numerous attempts at proofs that went beyond this effort limit, only a few succeeded, and these required a total effort that was very much greater.

The predominance of short proofs is even more striking than the approximate upper limit of 30,000 eip's suggests. The proofs by substitution—almost half of the total—required about 1000 eip's or less each. The effort required for the longest proof—89,000 eip's—is some 250 times the effort required for the shortest proofs. We estimate that to prove the 12 additional theorems that we believe LT can prove requires the effort limit to be extended to about a million eip's.

From the data we infer that LT's power as a problem solver is largely restricted to problems of a certain class. While it is logically possible for LT to solve others by large expenditures of effort, major adjustments are needed in the program to extend LT's powers to essentially new classes of problems. We believe that this situation is typical: good heuristics produce differences in performance of large orders of magnitude, but invariably a plateau is reached that can be surpassed only with quite different heuristics. These new heuristics will again make differences of orders of magnitude. In this section we shall analyze LT's difficulties with those theorems it cannot prove, with a view to indicating the general type of heuristic that might extend its range of effectiveness.

The Subproblem Tree.   Let us examine the proof of Theorem 2.17 when all the preceding theorems are available. This is the proof that cost LT 89,000 eip's (see Figure 4.12). The proof is reproduced below:

$(\sim Q \supset \sim P) \supset (P \supset Q)$	(THEOREM 2.17 TO BE PROVED)
1. $A \supset \sim\sim A$	(Theorem 2.12)
2. $P \supset \sim\sim P$	(subs. P for A in 1)
3. $(A \supset B) \supset (B \supset C) \supset (A \supset C)$	(Theorem 2.06)
4. $(P \supset \sim\sim P) \supset (\sim\sim P \supset Q) \supset (P \supset Q)$	(subs. P for A, $\sim\sim P$ for B, Q for C in 3)
5. $(\sim\sim P \supset Q) \supset (P \supset Q)$	(detach 4 from 3)
6. $(\sim A \supset B) \supset (\sim B \supset A)$	(Theorem 2.15)
7. $(\sim Q \supset \sim P) \supset (\sim\sim P \supset Q)$	(subs. Q for A, $\sim P$ for B)
8. $(\sim Q \supset \sim P) \supset (P \supset Q)$	(chain 7 and 5)

The proof is longer than either of the two given at the beginning of this section. In terms of LT's operators it takes three steps instead of two or one: a forward chaining, a detachment, and a substitution. This leads to the not surprising notion—given human experience—that length of proof is an important variable in determining total effort: short proofs will be easy and long proofs difficult, and difficulty will increase more than proportionately with length of proof. Indeed, all the one-step proofs require 500 to 1500 eip's, while the number of eip's for two-step proofs ranges from 3000 to 50,000. Further, LT has obtained only six proofs longer than two steps, and those require from 10,000 to 90,000 eip's.

The significance of length of proof can be seen by comparing Figure 4.12, which gives the proof tree for 2.17, with Figure 4.9, which gives the proof tree for 2.45, a two-step proof. In going one step deeper in the case of 2.17, LT had to generate and examine many more subproblems. A comparison of the various statistics of the proofs confirms this statement: the problems are roughly similar in other respects (e.g., in effort per theorem considered), hence the difference in total effort can be attributed largely to the differences in number of subproblems generated.

Let us examine some more evidence for this conclusion. Figure 4.13 shows the subproblem tree for the proof of 2.27 from the axioms, which is the only four-step proof LT achieved. The tree reveals immediately why LT was able to find the proof. Instead of branching widely at each point, multiplying rapidly the number of subproblems to be looked at, LT in this case only generates a few subproblems at each point, and thus manages to penetrate to a depth of four steps with a reasonable amount of effort (38,367 eip's). If this tree had branched as the other two did, LT would have had to process about 250 subproblems before arriving at a proof, and the total effort would have been at least 250,000 eip's. The statistics quoted earlier on the effectiveness of subproblem generation support the general hypothesis that the number of subproblems to be examined increases more or less exponentially with the depth of the proof.

The difficulty is that LT uses a systematic unselective procedure to govern its generation of subproblems. (Recall our earlier analysis of the executive program.) Apart from a few subproblems excluded by the type II errors of the similarity test, the procedure guarantees that all subproblems that can be generated by detachment and chaining will in fact be obtained (duplicates are eliminated). LT also uses an algorithm to determine the order in which it will try to solve subproblems. The subproblems are considered in order of generation (search in breadth) so that a proof will not be missed through failure to consider a subproblem that has been generated.

Because of these systematic principles incorporated in the executive program, and because the methods, applied to a theorem list averaging thirty expressions in length, generate a large number of subproblems, LT must find a rare sequence that leads to a proof by searching through a very large set of such sequences. For proofs of one step, this is no problem at all; for proofs of two steps, the set to be examined is still of reasonable size in relation to the computing power available. For proofs of three steps, the size of the search already presses LT against its computing limits; and if one or two additional steps are added, the amount of search required to find a proof exceeds any amount of computing power that could practically be made available.

Learning: The Heuristic Use of Experience

LT is an effective problem solver to the extent that its structure reflects information about the nature of the task. Understanding LT has involved discovering the nature of this information and how the structure of LT can contain it in operational terms. All of the heuristics mentioned so far are simply built into LT by design.

But LT's experience in problem solving also contains information on the nature of its task. Incorporating that information into LT's structure can lead to further gains in performance. For this to happen requires three things: (1) some aspect of LT's performance must be variable; (2) some information from LT's experience must be gathered; and (3) this information must be used to affect the (variable) behavior.

Perhaps the simplest learning method is to make the list, theorems, variable, modifying LT so as to put onto theorems any new theorem it proves. Then, in proving a sequence of theorems, LT would gradually become more capable. Indeed, if the sequence were right, it could become capable of proving 2.13 (P $\lor$ $\sim$ $\sim$ $\sim$ P), the theorem we discussed on page II to illustrate that LT was not complete. As we actually experimented with LT, the sequences of problems that it tried were dictated to it by the external environment (i.e., its designers). However, LT could be modified so as to pose problems for itself (Pitrat, 1966).[13]

A more complex method for incorporating experience is to make variable the theorems used by the operator submethods (detachment, forward and backward chaining). As they are given in Figure 4.8, the submethods systematically try all members of theorems. By the general breadth-first strategy of search used in LT, little good would come simply from ordering the theorems by some measure of past usefulness—they will all be generated anyway. On the other hand, theorems cannot simply be removed from the list, theorems, just because they were not used in some prior proof. They may be needed for a current problem. A possible scheme is to provide each submethod with its own list of theorems—in fact, with *two* lists of theorems: those that, in past experience, have participated in proofs with the appropriate operator (detachment, forward chaining, backward chaining, respectively) (*valuable theorems*), and those that have not participated in a proof. The submethods will work exclusively from their respective lists of valuable theorems. The secondary lists are used as backup, in case the valuable theorem lists prove insufficient.[14] If experience shows that certain methods and operators characteristically go together, then this scheme should allow LT to profit from that experience.

To study the effects of introducing this scheme, we performed the following experiment. As a pretest, we instructed LT to attempt in sequence the first 52 theorems in Chapter 2 of *Principia Mathematica*, using all prior theorems (whether it had succeeded in proving them or not). Then, we erased the results of this experience from memory, and as a test of the scheme, instructed LT to attempt the same 52 theorems, this time using the separate valuable theorem lists and the associated strategy.

The main result of the experiment can be seen by comparing the times required by the program to obtain proofs for the twenty theorems that were proved

[13] There is an interesting difference in working forward and working backward (as LT does) with respect to accumulating new theorems. In working forward, all generated elements of the problem space are theorems, hence candidates for addition to theorems for future use. In working backward, none of the elements of the space generated are known to be theorems. Hence for LT (but not for the British Museum Algorithm) to gain this kind of experience automatically requires that it have an active process for problem posing, not just a process for recognizing that an expression might be worth keeping.

[14] Such a scheme complicates the executive structure of LT. For example, not all branches are extended from a node when it is selected, and additional branches can be added later. We do not describe these modifications here.

in both pretest and test and whose proofs were not trivial. (We disregard 18 additional theorems proved on both runs, but proved in one step by substitution.)

The abscissa of each point in Figure 4.15 shows the time required to prove a theorem in the pretest; the ordinate of that point, the time to prove the same theorem in the test run. The remarkable fact about this scatter diagram is that it consists of two straight lines, each containing about half of the points. For the points on the upper line, almost twice as much time was required to discover a proof on the test run as on the pretest; for the points on the lower line, less than half as long was required on the test as on the pretest.

FIGURE 4.15

effect of special methods learning on performance of LT

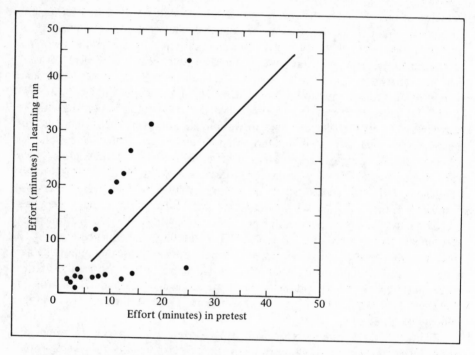

Closer examination of LT's protocols provides a simple explanation. In the test run, the program tried valuable theorems first. Only when these failed—i.e., when the problem was of a new type that did not yield to any methods that had worked on previous problems—did the program fall back on its full store of available theorems. The additional time required in the test run for these problems was the time spent in the futile attempt to use the valuable theorems lists it had learned. On the other hand, where a problem yielded to proof by a method that had worked on a previous problem, this was soon discovered in the test run with a corresponding large improvement in performance. This is just what one would expect: past experience can help in tasks that are similar to the past; it can hinder when novel tasks come along.

The two examples we have considered in this section are clearly instances where LT learns. It changes its structure in apparently adaptive ways as a function of experience with similar tasks. We will deal hardly at all with learning phenomena in this book. Yet the approach to learning from the direction just illustrated, where we have the internal structure of the performing program laid out before us, shows clearly (1) that experience is simply one more source of information that can be exploited to attain adaptive performance and (2) that to affect performance experience must find some variable aspect of the performance program's structure that it can specify.

CONCLUSION

We have now examined problem solving within a framework that views the process as selecting from a large set of possibilities an element having certain properties, or as traversing a large space to find one of a rare set of paths with preferred properties. The problem solver is given a description of the solution in a language called the state language, and is required to find an alternative process description that will specify how to generate it. Problem difficulty arises usually from the size of the set of possibilities—which, we have seen, is immense even in relatively simple problem situations.

We used an example of an IPS that is capable of solving problems—the Logic Theorist—to illustrate some of the main kinds of selective principles that enable solutions frequently to be found after examining only a relatively tiny subset of the set of possibilities. One such principle—illustrated by the methods in the Logic Theorist—is to generate only elements of the set that are already guaranteed to possess at least some of the properties that define a solution. Another principle—illustrated by the matching process in LT—is to make use of information obtained sequentially in the course of generating possible solutions in order to guide the continuing search. A third principle—illustrated by the use of similarity tests in LT—is to abstract from the detail of the problem expressions and to work in terms of the simpler abstractions.

The processes of LT were built up from elementary units like those we described in Chapter 2 in our characterization of information processing systems. We saw that the number of executions of elementary processes required to find solutions was closely correlated with the amount of search in the problem tree. Hence, major reductions in problem solving effort were generally associated with heuristics that increased the selectivity of the system. In some cases, however (e.g., in the description processes) the increased selectivity was almost balanced by the increased processing effort required to produce it. Our description of the behavior of LT in these terms provides us with a general approach to the study of the heuristic power and information processing efficiency of problem solving programs.

To the extent that efficiency in a system like LT can be equated with selectivity in exploring the problem space, the system's behavior casts more light on the nature of the task environment in which it operates than on its own detailed characteristics as an information processing system. Its important property is that it requires a more or less constant amount of processing effort per subproblem generated, or, what amounts to the same thing, per branch added to the search tree. The search trees it has generated, even for problems like 2.17, are of modest size—about 33 branches in that instance.

The absolute time required by the system to solve any particular problem depends, of course, on the speed of the computer on which it is implemented. It can solve problems about 100 times as fast on an IBM 360/65 as on the JOHNNIAC, where the runs were actually made. But the increases in problem solving power that are attainable through conceivable increases in basic processing speed—increases much greater than 100/1—are miniscule compared with the increases obtained by incorporating effective sets of selective heuristics in the program. No conceivable increase in the speed of a processor incorporating the British Museum Algorithm or the more selective working-forward algorithm would allow them to compete even with the relatively weak and simple heuristics of LT. LT, in turn, reaches a plateau of problem solving power from which we can lift it only by devising and incorporating new heuristics in it.

LT, constructed in 1956, was one of the first problem solving programs. Many heuristic programs have been written since. A few of them will enter into our description of other task environments, especially chess in Part 4, but most will not.[15] A large number of heuristic mechanisms have been explored, beyond those that LT illustrates. We indicated in Table 4.1 the range of mechanisms that fit into the heuristic search method.

But there have been numerous other advances as well in problem solving programs. For example, to make the working-backward operators yield only a single output expression, LT's operators took a theorem as a parameter. We saw how this constrained LT, making it impossible, for example, to prove P $\lor$ $\sim \sim \sim$ P. It was not long after the work on LT that a theorem-proving program was constructed with the appropriate structure to solve this problem (Gelernter, 1959). The multiple outputs of an operator are simply accepted, and the goal is created of proving them all. For instance, the detachment operator would become $DT(X)$ ($\Rightarrow$ (A and $A \supset X$). The necessary additional executive structures are added to the problem solver so that it knows—after it has proved one of the expressions—that it still has to prove the other. This kind of a tree structure has become known as an *AND-OR tree*. Some nodes of such a tree give a set of subproblems, all of which have to be solved; others give a set of subproblems, only *one* of which has to be solved.

Experiences comparable to those we have described with LT have been reported for the other problem solving systems that have been programmed. Gelernter, Hansen, and Loveland (1960), for example, have experimented with changes in heuristics in a program for proving theorems in plane geometry. Adding or subtracting one or two heuristic elements of the program often produced 2/1 or 3/1

---

[15] For those who would like to examine current work, two collections cover the programs completed up to about 1965 (Feigenbaum and Feldman, 1963; Minsky, 1968). Feigenbaum (1968) gives a recent review with many references. In addition, see the series of annual volumes entitled *Machine Intelligence* (Collins and Michie, 1967; Dale and Michie, 1968; Michie, 1968; Meltzer and Michie, 1969). Finally, a new journal, *Artificial Intelligence*, contains descriptions of heuristic programs (e.g., Fikes, 1970; Waterman, 1970).

differences in the time required to solve simple problems. In other cases, the effect was much more dramatic. Gelernter's basic program checked the subgoals it generated against a diagram for the problem. If the property postulated by the subgoal was not valid in the diagram, the subgoal was rejected. They report (page 155):

> As an experiment, a number of attempts were made to prove extremely simple theorems with the latter heuristic "disconnected" from the system. . . . In each case, the computer's entire stock of available storage space was quickly exhausted by the initial several hundreds of first level subgoals generated, and, in fact, the machine never finished generating a complete set of first level subgoals. We estimate conservatively on the average, a number of the order of 1000 subgoals are generated per stage by the decoupled system. If one compares the latter figure with the average of 5 subgoals per stage accepted when the diagram is consulted by the machine, it is easy to see that the use of a diagram is crucial for our system.

Here we have a factor of selectivity of 200/1 *per step in the proof* from a single, albeit powerful, heuristic.

Since the effectiveness of particular heuristics is a function of the structure of the problem space, these results, for the Logic Theorist or the Geometry Theory Machine, do not depend on specific properties of the information processing system that carries out the search. Such generalizations belong to the theory of problem environments rather than to psychology—that is, they are independent of any very specific characteristics of human cognitive processes.

In discussing the heuristics of LT, we made no special effort to examine their generality—that is, to distinguish between those that are effective because of the special nature of the problem space and those that might have value when transferred to quite different problem spaces. But Gelernter's geometry theorem prover incorporates many of the same heuristics as LT (although Gelernter's powerful diagram-using heuristic has no close analog in LT).

Both LT and the Geometry Theorem Machine work backward. They both have available a powerful matching heuristic for determining which substitutions to make for the variables in the axioms. Both programs generate subproblems that are placed on a list where they can be examined to determine which subproblem should be attempted next. In both programs the subproblems generated provide guarantees that a path (or, in some cases, a conjunction of paths) from the axioms to the final goal will be a valid proof. These heuristics are not only common to these two programs, but they are applicable to any realm of mathematics where proofs involve some kind of substitution of appropriate constants for variables. We will encounter the same heuristics again in other contexts.

In more general terms, our illustrations have provided specific examples of both the set-predicate and search formulations of problem solving, and have shown how generate-and-test methods can be used to solve problems formulated in the former way, while heuristic search methods can be used to solve problems formulated in the latter way. We have seen that, as problem formulation and method are specified, the notion of demands of the task is transformed into a description of the problem space that will be explored by generators or search operators, and into estimates of the size of this space. In this way we arrive at techniques for predicting problem difficulty and, more specifically, for making many predictions about the specific paths that problem solution will take. We are now ready to use this general theory to understand human problem solving in the task environments of cryptarithmetic, logic, and chess.

2

CRYPTARITHMETIC

5

CRYPTARITHMETIC:
Task Analysis

Consider the following problem:

$$\begin{array}{r} \text{DONALD} \\ + \text{GERALD} \\ \hline \text{ROBERT} \end{array} \qquad \text{D} \longleftarrow 5$$

Here each letter represents a digit (0, 1, . . . , 9). For example, you know that D is 5. Each letter is a distinct digit. For example, no letter other than D may equal 5. What digits should be assigned to the letters such that, when the letters are replaced by their corresponding digits, the sum above is satisfied?

There are many such puzzles, called cryptarithmetic tasks by one collector (Brooke, 1963), all involving the assignment of distinct digits to distinct letters to represent some arithmetic problem. The most familiar one (in the United States, at any rate), seems to be SEND+MORE=MONEY. The DONALD+GERALD =ROBERT task was taken from a study by Bartlett (1958), whose work is apparently the only other psychological investigation using cryptarithmetic. This particular problem has a unique solution, even when D ← 5 is not provided as given information.

In this part of our book (Chapters 5 through 7) we examine how humans behave in solving cryptarithmetic tasks. The present chapter is devoted to analyzing the task, using the concepts and techniques we have introduced. We turn in the next chapter to a detailed examination of a single human problem solving attempt, and follow that up in Chapter 7 with an examination of the behavior of a number of subjects on the task.

The initial requirement for analyzing the task is to provide a problem space and a task formulation in which the problem solving methods we have already examined can be used. The first candidate is the set-predicate formulation. We observe that there are in the problem 10 digits and 10 letters, which may be assigned to each other arbitrarily. Thus there are 10! possible combinations of assignments, each of which is a potential solution for the problem. In fact D is already assigned the digit 5, so that the actual number of possible assignments remaining is 9! = 362,480. The condition to be satisfied by the solution in this formulation could be checked by a straightforward addition test. Thus, one could proceed by the *generate-and-test* method. The number of cases to be presented and tested is sizable, though not overwhelming for a computer. Notice that even in this primitive formulation we have constructed a generator that makes use of the problem constraint that any given digit can be assigned to only a single letter. Without this constraint, 9^9 (i.e., 300 million) assignments would have to be considered instead of a third of a million.

As an alternative to the set-predicate formulation, we consider next a search formulation. The latter fares considerably better than the former, as it usually does whenever there is enough structure to apply it. To formulate this as a search problem we require a set of positions (or nodes) that correspond to the information that has been accumulated at a given point in the problem solving, and a set of operators that can modify this information. The initial state of information—namely, knowing no assignments (or only D ← 5)—must be expressible, as must the final state—namely, a complete, successful assignment of digits to all the letters.

There can of course be many such problem spaces, as we emphasized in Chapters 3 and 4. Each is defined by specifying the class of expressions that can represent possible states of information, and then defining the set of admissible operators in terms of these expressions. We will define and examine three different problem spaces to which the search formulation is applicable. We will call these the *basic*, *augmented*, and *algebraic* problem spaces, respectively. They are arranged according to how much information they use to limit search.

BASIC PROBLEM SPACE

We can define initially a simple problem space for the DONALD+GERALD task. Figure 5.1 gives the definition, using BNF (defined in Chapter 2, pages 44–51). To review: the angular-bracketed identifiers designate symbol structures that satisfy certain patterns. Thus, ⟨digit⟩ is any digit and ⟨letter⟩ is any letter in the task. Both patterns are defined by enumerating the alternative symbols that are acceptable as instances (thus, the vertical bar is read as *or*). ⟨expression⟩ is any symbol structure consisting of a letter followed by the assignment arrow (←) followed by a digit.

The actual representation of a symbol structure is not completely determined by the pattern. An expression could be encoded as a simple list of three symbols, in which case *followed by* is represented by the relation *next*. But it could also be represented by associations: one attribute to give the letter, another attribute to give the arrow, and a third attribute to give the digit. These details of encoding need not concern us here. We assume the IPS has processes for finding the letter in an expression as well as the digit. The availability of these processes shields us from the lower level of encoding.

Given these basic symbol structures, the problem space, U, is defined as the set of *knowledge-states*, where a knowledge-state is a list of one or more expressions (recall the way BNF is used recursively to define sequences). A knowledge-state is the knowledge that all the assignments indicated by the member expressions hold. Duplicate expressions in a knowledge-state are, therefore, redundant and we will eliminate them (actually, the operators avoid duplication).

FIGURE 5.1

basic problem space

⟨letter⟩ :: = A | B | D | E | G | L | N | O | R | T
⟨digit⟩ :: = 0 | 1 | 2 | 3 | 4 | 5 | 6 | 7 | 8 | 9
⟨expression⟩ :: = ⟨letter⟩ ← ⟨digit⟩
⟨knowledge-state⟩ :: = Ø | ⟨expression⟩ |
　　　　⟨expression⟩, ⟨knowledge-state⟩
U: set (⟨knowledge-state⟩)
⟨operator⟩ :: = Add [⟨expression⟩]
Q: set (⟨operator⟩)

Next, in Figure 5.1, we define Q, the set of operators for the problem space, to be the processes for making all possible new assignments. We express these with a single process, *Add*, parametrized by *expression*—i.e., by an assignment. Add operates on an element of the problem space to produce a new element:

$$\text{Add}[A \longleftarrow 2](D \longleftarrow 5) \Longrightarrow (A \longleftarrow 2, D \longleftarrow 5)$$

If the assignment is redundant, *Add* does nothing:

$$\text{Add}[A \longleftarrow 2](A \longleftarrow 2, D \longleftarrow 5) \Longrightarrow (A \longleftarrow 2, D \longleftarrow 5)$$

We call the problem space just defined the *basic problem space*, since the type of knowledge it admits is limited to the basic elements that are explicit in the problem statement, namely, specific assignments. This space is the simplest one in which the total problem can be defined. Simplicity refers here to the directness and ease with which such a problem space could be constructed from the explicit problem instructions.

Figure 5.2 states the instructions for the DONALD+GERALD problem in this space: i.e., it specifies the initial-state and the test-for-solution. The *initial-state* is D ← 5. The set of goal states, G, is not given explicitly, but is defined by a test process (recall the heuristic-search-method in Figure 4.4, page 101). Alternatively, it would be possible to define a problem space in which an expression could be written for the goal set, but such a space would be considerably more elaborate.

FIGURE 5.2

instructions for DONALD+GERALD in basic problem space

initial-state: (D ← 5)

test-for-solution(state):
1. test if (D ← 5) in state,
    if false stop and report fail;
2. test-letter-assignments(state),
    if multiple stop and report fail;
3. test-digit-assignments(state),
    if multiple stop and report fail;
4. test-addition(state),
    if fail stop and report fail,
    if incomplete stop and report incomplete,
    if succeed stop and report succeed.

The *test-for-solution* has four separate parts. The first checks that 5 is still assigned to D. The second checks that no multiple assignments of digits to letters have been made. The third checks that no digit has been assigned to more than one letter. The fourth checks the addition, i.e., that DONALD+GERALD = ROBERT. The *test-addition* also verifies completeness—i.e., that all letters have been assigned a digit.

The program of Figure 5.2 is sufficiently explicit for discussing problem solving. However, just for the curious, Figure 5.3 provides definitions of the three nonelementary processes: test-letter-assignments, test-digit-assignments, and test-addition. We have written these processes to distinguish *succeed, fail,* and *incomplete,* not just succeed and fail. Thus, test-for-solution can notice that a partial assignment has failed the addition test, and can then provide a partial, though weak, evaluation—namely, "incomplete but not yet fail." A variant of these processes could have tested for completeness immediately in test-letter-assignments and test-digit-assignments. If they had done so, and quit immediately if the assignments were incomplete, then errors of addition would have been masked.

Within this problem space we can consider various problem-solving programs —that is, various ways of starting at the initial-state and searching for a member of the goal set. Figure 5.4, for example, shows a simple program for a depth-first

FIGURE 5.3

subprocesses for test-for-solution

test-letter-assignments(state):
1. generate letters:
2.   find (letter ⟵ ⟨digit⟩) in state,
          if fail stop process and report incomplete,
          if find many stop process and report fail.,
    if completed stop and report succeed.

test-digit-assignments(state):
1. generate digits:
2.   find (⟨letter⟩ ⟵ digit) in state,
          if fail stop process and report incomplete,
          if find many stop process and report fail.,
    if completed stop and report succeed.

test-addition(state):
1. initialize carry = 0;
2. generate columns (⟹ (top middle bottom));
3.   find (top ⟵ ⟨digit⟩) in state (⟹ top-digit),
          if fail stop process and report incomplete;
4.   find (middle ⟵ ⟨digit⟩) in state (⟹ middle-digit),
          If fail stop process and report incomplete;
5.   find (bottom ⟵ ⟨digit⟩) in state (⟹ bottom-digit),
          if fail stop process and report incomplete;
6.   sum (top-digit, middle-digit);
7.   sum (result, carry);
8.   find units-digit(sum),
          if ≠ bottom-digit stop process and report fail;
9.   find tens-digit(sum) (⟹ carry).,
    if completed stop and report succeed.

search strategy.[1] It uses the test-for-solution to terminate a branch of the search when a state is reached that cannot possibly lead to a solution: one that assigns two different digits to the same letter, assigns the same digit to two letters, or yields a false column sum, working from right to left. Search continues by a recursive use of the process whenever test-for-solution indicates an incomplete but consistent state. Of course, if test-for-solution reports *succeed*, then the task is done and a solution has been found.

We have also provided in Figure 5.4 a program for generating the operators. It produces them in the order of their occurrence in the DONALD+GERALD display, right to left in the columns, top to bottom within each column. It must record when a letter is used, so that it does not generate it a second time. This is done by marking it with a property, *used*. Again, we need not be concerned about details, as long as we know we can mark a letter used and test for it later.

[1] We could have used the general heuristic search method, but it was simpler to show the specialization directly.

FIGURE 5.4
depth-first search program

Depth-first-search(state):
1. generate-operators(state):
2.   apply operator to state ($\Longrightarrow$ new-state),
      if fail continue generation;
3.   test-for-solution(new-state),
      if fail continue generation,
      if succeed stop process and
      report problem solved;
4.   Depth-first-search(new-state),
      if fail continue generation.

generate-operators(state): subprocess:
1. generate columns:
2.   generate column ($\Longrightarrow$ letter):
3.   test if letter in state,
        if true continue generation;
4.   generate digits:
5.   construct (letter $\longleftarrow$ digit);
6.   apply subprocess to result,
          if stop-generate stop process
          and report stopped.
    stop and report completed.

The search tree generated by the program of Figure 5.4 is shown in Figure 5.5. We do not show the final assignment that produces each contradiction. The tree of Figure 5.5 contains 252 branches, taking into account the final branches just mentioned, but not depicted.[2] The threefold increase in size over the tree depicted (which has only 87 terminals) comes from using the arithmetic sum of each column as a test only, and not as a generator of assignments. Thus all values for T, from 0 to 9, are generated, but only $T = 0$ is retained after testing the last column sum. Actually, test-for-solution is even more inefficient than it need be, for this simple way of searching. It restarts its addition check each time from the far right, whereas by the way the assignments are generated, only the currently active column need be checked.

In spite of its primitive character, the procedure is highly selective. If it did not check for failure until all assignments were made, then the tree would have had 9! terminals—the same as for the generate-and-test method. The advantage of the heuristic search method is that failure shows up early, and each failure eliminates an entire subtree. With both methods the actual number of alternatives searched to find the first solution is less than the full number of possibilities for the method (see Figure 5.5). Usually, the actual number is estimated at one-half of the total on the assumption that the order of generation is random relative to the location of

[2] The tree would have had 1263 terminals if D $\longleftarrow$ 5 were not given.

FIGURE 5.5

search tree from depth-first search

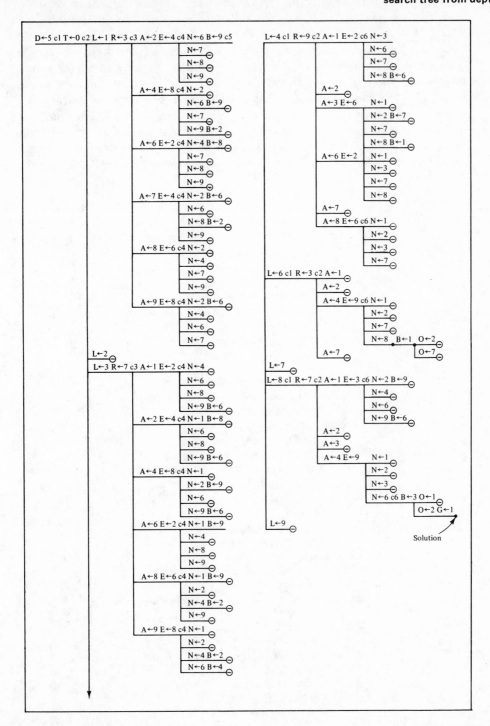

Solution

a solution. In fact, for the depth-first case of Figure 5.5 we see that the actual amount of search to the first (and only) solution is 99 percent of the total possible, since the last unexplored branch (L ← 9) terminates immediately by implying R = 9.

As we know from the analysis of Chapter 4, we can advance from such simple search schemes to others in which various heuristics are applied to cut the search still further. These usually require more processing for each node, but compensate by reducing the number of nodes that must be examined. We listed in Table 4.1 (page 104) the major types of heuristics that are possible. Several different problem solvers can be formed from the heuristics shown in that table. One obvious technique is to realize the tree actually presented in Figure 5.5 by using the column sum to generate the value of letters in the bottom row of a column whenever the

FIGURE 5.6

heuristics for basic problem space

generate-operators(state): subprocess:
1. generate columns (⟹ column):
2.   find-unique-unassigned-letter(column) (⟹ letter),
          if fail continue generation,
          if succeed stop generation.,
        if stopped go to 5;
3. generate columns (⟹ column):
4.   find-unassigned-letter(column) (⟹ letter),
          if fail continue generation,
          if succeed stop generation.,
        if completed stop process and report finished;
5. find-digit(letter, column, state) (⟹ digit),
        if fail stop process and report fail;
6. construct (letter ← digit);
7. apply subprocess to result,
        if stop-generation stop process and report stopped.

find-digit(letter, column, state) (⟹ digit):
1. find carry of prior(column) in state,
        if fail go to 4;
2. compute-value(letter, column, carry, state) (⟹ digit),
        if fail stop and report fail;
3. test-if-unassigned(digit, state),
        if true stop and report succeed,
        if false stop and report fail;
4. compute-value(letter, column, 0, state) (⟹ digit),
        if fail go to 6;
5. test-if-unassigned(digit, state),
        if true stop and report succeed;
6. compute-value(letter, column, 1, state) (⟹ digit),
        if fail stop and report fail;
7. test-if-unassigned(digit, state),
        if true stop and report succeed,
        if false stop and report fail.

operands in the two top rows have been assigned. Another technique is to free up the order in which assignments are made, rather than working rigidly from right to left in the problem array. This requires the ability to detect contradictions in a column, even though not all its components (carries as well as letters) are known. Inferences of this kind can be of various degrees of sophistication, of course. Likewise the process that actually selects the next letter to be assigned can have various degrees of sophistication. Figure 5.6 gives one program that incorporates these notions. The process in the figure replaces the generate-operators process in the basic depth-first search of Figure 5.4. It attempts to select a letter that occurs alone in a column; only if this attempt fails does it proceed from right to left in the manner of the original generator. Once it has selected a column and letter, it finds digits to assign that are permitted in that column. Either it computes the assignment directly, if the carry is known, or it assigns the carry (first 0, then 1) in order to

FIGURE 5.7

search tree from modified depth-first search

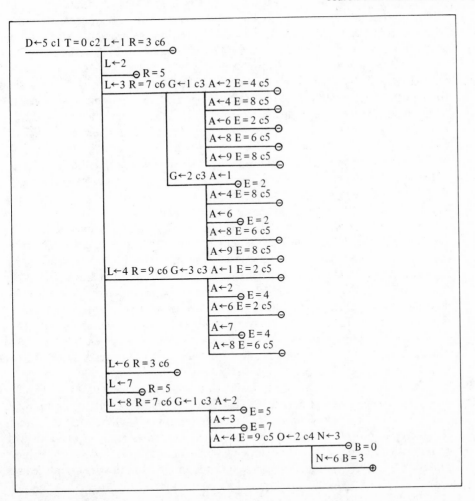

compute a permissible value. If, for any reason, it is unable to compute a digit, then it fails, thus terminating the search in that particular line of assignments. Two basic subroutines, compute-value and test-if-unassigned, are not defined explicitly in Figure 5.6; both are straightforward.

Figure 5.7 shows the search tree that results if the program of Figure 5.6 is used. We indicate on the figure not only the letter that was selected for assignment, but also the column. As the figure shows, the search has now come down to 23 nodes.

Rather than define and discuss additional variants of this scheme, let us consider what other problem spaces might be used instead of the basic space.

AUGMENTED PROBLEM SPACE

The main feature of the basic problem space is that specific assignments are the only form of information expressible in it. Hence, partial information (i.e., the information obtained en route to a solution) is limited to assignments of subsets of the letters. It is possible to enrich the expressions in the problem space and thus hold other kinds of partial information. We call this enriched space the *augmented problem space*. It is shown in Figure 5.8.

Along the way, it can often be inferred that a letter must be assigned a digit from among a restricted subset of digits. This partial information can take various forms: the assignment must satisfy an inequality (e.g., $R > 5$); it must have the property of being even (or odd) (e.g., R odd); it must be one of an enumerated disjunction (e.g., $R = 7 \lor 9$); or certain assignments must be excluded (e.g., $E \neq 0$). Adding expressions for these relations to the basic set enlarges the total set of states of knowledge that can be specified. There is redundancy among these relations, but from a processing viewpoint, knowing that $E \neq 6$ or that $E = 0 \lor 1 \lor 2 \lor 3 \lor 4 \lor 5 \lor 7 \lor 8 \lor 9$, respectively, may be quite different.

Besides this extension from single specific assignments to various descriptions of classes of possible assignments, the set of variables in the problem space can be augmented to include carries. It is a peculiarity of cryptarithmetic problems that they introduce some of the variables (the letters) explicitly, but leave others (the carries) implicit. As we saw in the basic problem space, there are ways of solving cryptarithmetic problems that never express the carries as separate variables, but only use a single temporary carry variable to evaluate column sums. However, carries can be included among the variables whose values can be expressed in the states of knowledge. Carries and letters together are called variables (see Figure 5.8). All types of expressions admit carries.

Generalizing the means of expression in a problem space is of no use without providing corresponding operators. The various inferences that produce the assignments to classes of digits derive from inferences made on the various columns of the cryptarithmetic sum. Thus, we must augment the assignment operator with a column processor, capable of drawing such inferences. Introducing a column processor is still not enough, since class information must be not only produced but used. The most obvious use is to generate the individual digits that belong to these classes. For example, from the information: (G even) and $(G < 5)$, the system must be able to generate 0, 2, 4—the three digits that satisfy both relations. In addition, the process for making inferences on the columns must be capable of using such information about classes. If it is known that $c6 = 0$ (there is no carry into the leftmost column), that $D = 5$, and that R is odd, then the system must be able to infer that G is even.

FIGURE 5.8

knowledge state for augmented problem space

$\langle\text{digit}\rangle :: = 0\,|\,1\,|\,2\,|\,3\,|\,4\,|\,5\,|\,6\,|\,7\,|\,8\,|\,9$
$\langle\text{letter}\rangle :: = A\,|\,B\,|\,D\,|\,E\,|\,G\,|\,L\,|\,N\,|\,O\,|\,R\,|\,T$
$\langle\text{carry}\rangle :: = c1\,|\,c2\,|\,c3\,|\,c4\,|\,c5\,|\,c6$
$\langle\text{variable}\rangle :: = \langle\text{letter}\rangle\,|\,\langle\text{carry}\rangle$
$\langle\text{expression}\rangle :: = \langle\text{variable}\rangle\,\langle\text{digit}\rangle\,|\,\langle\text{variable}\rangle\,\langle\text{relation}\rangle\,\langle\text{digit}\rangle\,|$
    $\langle\text{variable}\rangle\,\langle\text{parity}\rangle\,|\,\langle\text{variable}\rangle = \langle\text{digit-set}\rangle$
$\langle\text{relation}\rangle :: = =\,|\,\neq\,|\,>\,|\,<\,|\,\leq\,|\,\geq$
$\langle\text{parity}\rangle :: = \text{even}\,|\,\text{odd}$
$\langle\text{digit-set}\rangle :: = \langle\text{digit}\rangle\,|\,\langle\text{digit}\rangle \vee \langle\text{digit-set}\rangle$
$\langle\text{knowledge-state}\rangle :: = \varnothing\,|\,\langle\text{expression}\rangle\,|\,\langle\text{expression}\rangle, \langle\text{knowledge-state}\rangle$

In the basic problem space the test for a solution was a substantial process, involving the tests that all digit assignments were distinct, and requiring evaluation of the problem sum. The effect of introducing the augmented problem space is to replace much of this testing by generating. What is left is a test to determine whether a digit is admissible—i.e., has not already been assigned to some other letter, and is within the set of digits still compatible with known conditions on the particular letter. Whereas in the basic problem space digits were generated in a way that assured their being disjoint, this is no longer possible in the present situation. Instead their disjointness must be determined by a test.

These considerations may be summarized by saying that at least four types of operators must be used in the augmented problem space:

    Assign-value (AV)
    Process-column (PC)
    Generate-numbers (GN)
    Test-if-digits-admissible (TD)

There can still be substantial variation in the details of these operators, most especially in the power of the column processor (PC). We will see some of this variation in the human behavior to follow in the next two chapters. Hence, rather than provide examples now, let us consider yet a third problem space.

ALGEBRAIC PROBLEM SPACE

Instead of taking the states of knowledge to be information about the individual assignments of digits to letters, let us symbolize the constraints themselves and manipulate them directly. The DONALD+GERALD=ROBERT condition is equivalent to the following algebraic equations:

$$2D = T + 10c_2 \tag{1}$$
$$c_2 + 2L = R + 10c_3 \tag{2}$$
$$c_3 + 2A = E + 10c_4 \tag{3}$$
$$c_4 + N + R = B + 10c_5 \tag{4}$$
$$c_5 + O + E = O + 10c_6 \tag{5}$$
$$c_6 + D + G = R \tag{6}$$

These equations augmented by the conditions that each letter is to be assigned a distinct digit, and that carries are to be assigned 0 or 1, independently, constitute a complete statement of the problem.

The six equations can be viewed as the initial element in a problem space. Various algebraic and logical manipulations permit the derivation of new algebraic expressions, which then augment the existing set of equations (or replace specific expressions) to form a new element of the space—i.e., a new *set* of equations. A completed assignment is indicated in this space either by a derived equation, such as $(R = 7)$, or by a stipulated assignment $(D \leftarrow 5)$. A set of equations that includes such assignment equations for all the letters constitutes a final desired state. We can call this space the *algebraic problem space*. We will not bother to formalize its definition; it can be done along exactly the same lines as the other spaces (a good exercise for the reader!).

Let us see how problem solving would be carried out in this space, using the simple production system of Figure 5.9 as a problem solver. These two productions simply oscillate between inferring consequences from previous assignments or inferences and substituting in the equations any new assignments that are made or derived either for letters or carries. The mark-used process that follows the substitutions simply marks the assignment equation so that it will not be matched again, thus avoiding repetition of the substitution. We can ignore the details of how this is done. For instance, a tag could be added to the equation, such as $(R = 7$ *used*).

Since substitution involves only straightforward processing of the equations, it need not be discussed further. The process of inferring consequences is less well

FIGURE 5.9

production system for algebraic problem space

P1 : $\langle$variable$\rangle$ = $\langle$digit$\rangle$ | $\langle$variable$\rangle$ $\longleftarrow$ $\langle$digit$\rangle$ $\longrightarrow$
      substitute digit for variable; mark-used.
P2 : otherwise $\longrightarrow$ infer-consequences.

defined. We take infer-consequences to mean a process for deducing as many new algebraic and arithmetic consequences as possible from the given set of equations. Let us consider by illustration how this might be done.

In the problem at hand, the condition for production P1 is satisfied; hence, since $D \leftarrow 5$ is given, production P1 is applied (D is replaced by 5 throughout), yielding equations (1') and (6'):

$$10 = T + 10c2 \tag{1'}$$
$$c6 + 5 + G = R \tag{6'}$$

The other equations remain unaltered. Thus, the second node in the problem space is the set of six equations (1', 2, 3, 4, 5, 6') plus $(D \leftarrow 5)$. Applying infer-consequences, from equation (1') we obtain: $T = 0$, $c2 = 1$; from equation (6') we obtain: $(G = 1 \lor 2 \lor 3 \lor 4)$ (since $T = 0$, $G \neq 0$), and $R > 5$.

Since values were obtained for T and c2, we apply production P1 twice, obtaining:

$$1 + 2L = R + 10c3 \tag{2'}$$

From (2') it is inferred that R is odd. Since it was found previously that $R > 5$, we now have: $(R = 7 \lor 9)$. No new assignments are obtained, however, so infer-consequences is executed a second time. Subtracting O from both sides of (5), we obtain

$$c5 + E = 10c6 \tag{5'}$$

Therefore, $(E = 9 \lor 0)$. But $T = 0$; therefore, $E = 9$, $c5 = 1$, $c6 = 1$. Since we had previously $(R = 7 \lor 9)$, it follows that $R = 7$. Applying P1 once more, we now get

$$2L = 6 + 10c3 \tag{2''}$$
$$c3 + 2A = 9 + 10c4 \tag{3''}$$
$$c4 + N = B + 3 \tag{4''}$$
$$5 + G = 6 \tag{6''}$$

Equations (1) and (5) have dropped out, since they no longer impose conditions on the remaining variables.

Applying infer-consequences again, we deduce: $A = 4$, $c3 = 1$, $c4 = 0$, $G = 1$. Substituting these values, we get

$$2L = 16 \tag{2'''}$$
$$N = B + 3 \tag{4'''}$$

From this, infer-consequences obtains $L = 8$, $N > 3$.

The program takes us no further, but there remain only 2, 3, and 6 to assign to N, B, and O. Since $N > B$, there are only two trial values for N: 6 and 3. We readily find that $N = 6$, hence $B = 3$ and $O = 2$.

In outlining the solution, we have not provided the details of the infer-consequences process. It is not unlike the process for solving algebraic equations described in Chapter 4. The main difference is that we are here concerned with fixed sets of nonnegative integer values for the variables,[3] and this limitation permits logical inferences that reduce the set of possible values for a variable. Instead of considering alternative paths in the space of possible assignments, the solution process deduces enough information about some one of the assignments (first for T, then for E) that a definite assignment can be made, rather than an "iffy" one. Thus, the information that $(R = 7 \lor 9)$ is not used to make a tentative assignment until one of the alternatives can be eliminated conclusively by the knowledge that $E = 9$, so that R can be assigned the definite value 7. Thus, the program discovers the solution path:

$$(D \longleftarrow 5) \longrightarrow (T = 0) \longrightarrow (E = 9) \longrightarrow (R = 7) \longrightarrow (A = 4) \longrightarrow (G = 1)$$
$$\longrightarrow (L = 8) \longrightarrow (N \longleftarrow 6) \longrightarrow (B = 3) \longrightarrow (0 = 2).$$

The almost complete elimination of trial and error in this way is not posssible in all cryptarithmetic problems. Indeed, if we had not been given $D \longleftarrow 5$, the inference process would have stopped almost immediately. The process could have inferred that $(E = 0 \lor 9)$, T is even, and $R > D$; then that $(A = 4 \lor 5)$. It would then have stopped. Of course, once a tentative assignment was made (e.g., $E \longleftarrow 0$), then $c5 = 0$, $c6 = 0$, $A = 5$, $c3 = 0$, $c4 = 1$, and $L < 5$ would have been deduced in quick succession. However, further inferences would not have been forthcoming, so that a new tentative assignment would again have been necessary. [Actually, by careful argument one can obtain that $3 \leq R \leq 7$ and hence $(L = 2 \lor 3)$, but even so one must then assign a tentative value for L.]

OTHER PROBLEM SPACES

The problem spaces we have described so far seem to cover most of the ways in which a problem solver might represent the cryptarithmetic task. It would not be easy to provide formal demonstrations of the completeness of such a list. Indeed, in the present case there are other spaces that might be considered. Some depend on special features of a cryptarithmetic task that are not present in DONALD+ GERALD=ROBERT. For example, in

$$
\begin{array}{r}
AA \\
+BB \\
\hline
CBC
\end{array}
$$

it is natural to work with the multiples of 11, so that one sees immediately that CBC must be a multiple of 11, and in fact equal to $11 \times 11 = 121$, so that BB must be 22 and AA = 99.

---

[3] Equations in variables that take only integer values are called Diophantine equations, and there is a body of theory devoted to their solution. However, the peculiar additional conditions—that some variables have only 0 or 1 as possible values, that others are in a different, fixed range and are all disjoint, make classical Diophantine theory largely inapplicable here. (Uspensky and Heaslet, 1939, pp. 55, 388–428.)

Still other representations depend on taking a more global view—e.g., that one is looking for a correspondence between letters and digits, and should search in the space of such correspondences. For example: map the letters on the digits according to their numerical positions in the alphabet: $A = 1$, $B = 2$, ... [This is not far-fetched, for one of Bartlett's (1958) subjects used precisely this representation.]

Problem spaces can be characterized either by the types of information that can be expressed at an element, or by the operators that can produce and react to such information. Neither characterization is more basic than the other, since they depend mutually on each other. Let us characterize the spaces we have introduced by the types of expressions that comprise elements or, to say the same thing, by the entities they admit (letters, digits, carries) and the relations they admit among these entities. Then we can write:

basic space:	(letter digit ⟵——)
augmented space:	(letter digit carry ⟵—— ∨ inequality parity)
algebraic space:	(letter digit carry ⟵—— ∨ inequality parity arithmetic)

Thus, in the basic problem space, the only entities are the letters and the digits, and the assignment relation between them. The augmented problem space adds to these carries and the relations of disjunction, inequality, and parity. The algebraic problem space adds the arithmetic operations, $+$, $-$, $\times$, and $/$.

This notation suggests that we might be able to generate other interesting problem spaces by ringing changes on subsets of these entities. It is easy enough to produce minor variants by excluding one or more of the relations from the algebraic space. But what about more radical alternatives—e.g., the space: (letter carry ⟵—)? This space admits information that assignments have been made to certain letters and carries, but it does not permit indicating what specific digits have been assigned in each case. This is the kind of information one uses with systems of equations to count equations and variables, in order to determine how many unknowns there are in relation to the number of equations, and which equations might conveniently be solved first.

In the present problem, this information does not carry the solution very far. From the fact that the assignment has been made to D, it follows that T and c2 are determined, and some restriction is placed on R and G (one variable can be eliminated from the equation connecting them). But this information is insufficient to suggest a good order for considering the columns in the problem. Still, the inadequacy of this space to guide solution efforts cannot be known until it has been tried. In other cases it might be more useful—e.g., to suggest the order of solving the simultaneous equations: $3x + 2y + z = 27$, $x = 2$, $x + 3y = 11$.

Another interesting variant is the space defined by

$$\text{(letter carry} \longleftarrow \text{parity high-low)}$$

In this space, specific digits cannot be expressed, but a particular digit can be described as being odd or even and as being low (< 5) or high (> 5). This information permits certain kinds of inferences to be made. For example, the sum of two even digits is even; and the sum of two high digits gives an odd carry (i.e., a carry of 1). The tree of Figure 5.10 shows a search for the solution to DONALD+ GERALD=ROBERT in this abstracted problem space. The element of the problem space, representing the problem solver's state of knowledge, is depicted as a box, with entries (a) for the four specific values that can be expressed in the abstract space (low-even = le, low-odd = lo, high-even = he, high-odd = ho), and (b) for the marginals—where it is known, for example, only that a letter is high, but not whether it is odd or even. From the initial assignment, $D \leftarrow 5$, it can be inferred that $T = le$ (not merely that $T = e$, which is all that can be inferred from $D \leftarrow ho$). A carry into the second column can also be inferred, so that $c_2 = o$. (We actually know that c_2 is 1, but in the abstract space retain only the fact that it is odd.)

In Figure 5.10, the reader can trace through the inferences that can be drawn. The relation $N \sim B$ means that N and B must be the same on the high-low dimension, either both high or both low; similarly $N \nsim B$ means that they must have opposite values on that dimension. The constraint that no two assignments may be identical is translated, in the abstract space, into specification of the number of letters that can occupy each cell of the box:

	low	high	
even	× × ×	× ×	
odd	× ×	× × ×	

The solution of DONALD+GERALD in the abstract space is represented by the particular box:

	low	high	
even	TAO	NL	
odd	GB	DRE	

It will be observed that, given $D \leftarrow 5$, there are $6 \times 2 \times 2 \times 2 = 48$ possible assignments of letters in the basic problem space that are consistent with the assignment in the abstract space depicted above. But the ambiguity that would result from trying to solve the problem in the abstract space is even greater than this calculation suggests. The search tree in Figure 5.10 shows that examination of all consistent assignments in the abstract space leads to a disjunction of five admissible boxes. Each of these is consistent with at least 48 possible assignments in the basic problem space, and three of them are consistent with even more, because they do not provide full information about the assignment of all the letters, even in the abstract space. For example, the box labeled "5" in Figure 5.10 corresponds to the

FIGURE 5.10

search tree in abstract space

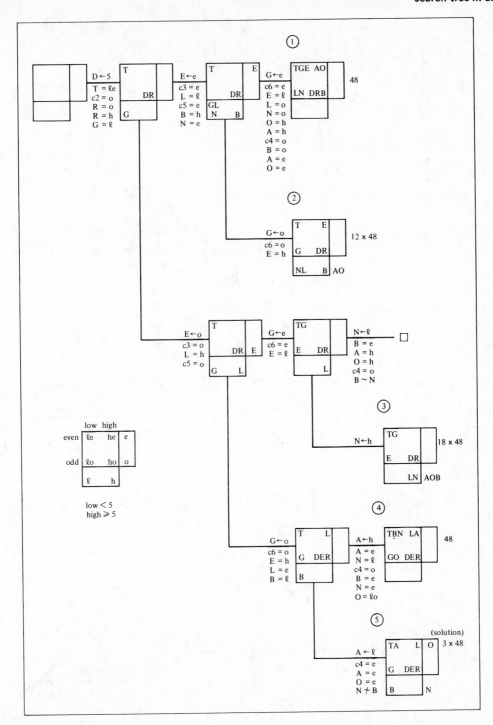

159

FIGURE 5.11

search trees in basic space from solutions in abstract space

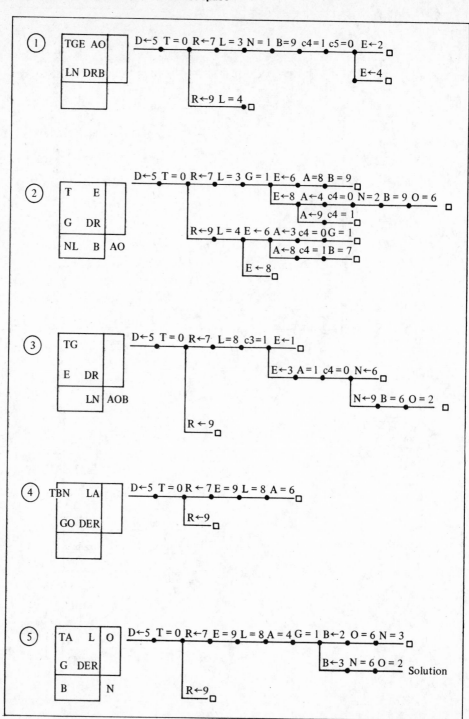

actual solution of the problem in the basic problem space. But of B it can only be inferred that it is low, of O that it is even, and of N that it is high if and only if B is low. Hence, box 5 is consistent with $3 \times 48 = 144$ assignments in the basic problem space, and the 5 admissible boxes jointly are consistent with $35 \times 48 = 1680$ assignments in that space.

Each of the five admissible assignments in the abstract space can be taken as the starting point for a search in the basic problem space to determine whether there is an actual solution to the problem consistent with the abstract solution in question. The exploration trees for these searches are shown in Figure 5.11. The searches work from right to left, making maximum use of the inferences that can be drawn from the constraints specified in the boxes. Within each column of DONALD+GERALD, they generate on the most constrained letter first—e.g., in column 3, they generate on E, rather than A.

The 1680 possible assignments remaining after search in the abstract space represent a factor of 216 reduction from the 9! possible assignments in the basic space. Of course this reduction does not really measure the utility of the search in the abstract space, since we would not need to look at all 9! possibilities in searching in the basic space. However, the searches displayed in Figure 5.11 also explore far fewer than 1680 possibilities—only 17, in fact. This number can be compared with the total of 87 for Figure 5.5 and of 23 for Figure 5.7. Hence, in terms of the number of final nodes that will be reached before a solution is discovered, the search in the abstract space appears to be relatively efficient. Of course, all three searches suffer in efficiency from failing to infer promptly that $E = 9$. It should be added that the search in the abstract space requires considerable processing to take advantage of the multiplicity of constraints that are implicit in the partial results attained along the way.

Both of the last two spaces we have described are examples of spaces that abstract from the full detail of the original space. Thus, they are not spaces in which a problem solver can solve the entire problem, for he cannot express in them all the information about the solution. Rather, they are spaces in which plans can be forged, which can then be used to guide further action in a fully detailed space.

SUMMARY

Our purpose in presenting so many variations on a theme is to provide a firm foundation on which to examine the behavior of some humans attempting to solve the DONALD+GERALD=ROBERT task. Even though we have not exhausted all possible representations of this task, we stand a good chance of recognizing which one a given human is using—especially if he has had little exposure to cryptarithmetic. (If he is a cryptarithmetic buff, the tables may be turned and we may learn a thing or two ourselves.)

It remains an open question, of course, whether humans will operate within a problem space as we have defined it, or, if so, whether they will use the heuristic devices we have set out. That is the topic for the next two chapters. We would not expect a human subject to operate in our simpler spaces; these form a base line from which the intelligence that he shows can be measured. In fact, since we know generally that humans do not have the ability to keep track of large amounts of information and operate in highly systematic ways, our measure of the size of spaces like the basic problem space assures us that a subject who knew only enough to operate in such a space would find the problem difficult or impossible to solve.

6

CRYPTARITHMETIC:
Behavior of a Single Subject,
S3, on
DONALD+GERALD=ROBERT

The last chapter has given us tools enough to start the analysis of human data. The job of this chapter is to examine in detail the behavior of a single individual subject, S3, during a single integrated problem solving attempt on DONALD+ GERALD=ROBERT. The data are a transcript of the subject's verbalizations during the course of problem solving—what is called a *protocol*. The protocol also includes additional data, about either the subject or the environment, that bears on the total performance. In the present case these augmentations include some indications that S3 had written down various assignments, and some remarks of the experimenter, E.

Many issues must be dealt with in handling this first instance of behavioral analysis. One set of issues derives from the theoretical analyses that have occupied our attention up until now:

1. Can the subject be viewed as working in some problem space?
2. If so, can one identify his problem space at the degree of detail that we have been using in our analyses?

3. Can the subject's behavior be viewed as making use of the sorts of problem solving organizations we have introduced—e.g., search strategies, heuristics, and so on?
4. Can one actually describe an IPS that behaves like the subject—and to what degree of detail?

A second set of questions concerns the treatment of the data:

5. How does one extract information from verbal behavior?
6. What ways are there of inducing the program from the information so extracted?
7. How much information about the behavior is really given by the protocol?

A third set concerns the testing of theory:

8. How does one compare the induced IPS with the behavior it is supposed to explain?
9. More generally, how does one compare two streams of history-dependent, meaningful behavior?
10. To the extent that the theory is inexact (as it must be), how can we evaluate the goodness of approximation?

And, finally, a fourth set of questions is concerned with generality:

11. Are the mechanisms that describe this one subject unique to him?
12. If not, how does one extract the parts that are not idiosyncratic?
13. To what extent are the IPS's that describe the subject dictated by the task environment, to what extent dictated by the processing mechanisms of the subject (i.e., by psychology)?

Direct answers to all these questions cannot be provided in this one chapter. However, evidence on a substantial number will emerge as the chapter goes along. Questions about generality will mostly be postponed to the next and later chapters. We have chosen to start by looking at a single problem solving attempt, and this obscures questions of communality. There is, of course, the generality of the task analysis of the previous chapter: if our subject settles neatly into this framework, we can have some expectation that other subjects will also (an expectation to be tested, of course).

One advantage of focusing on a single subject performing a single task is the bright light it shines on some of the other questions, especially those involving the representation of a human as an IPS. If this theory captures a substantial part of the reality of human information processing, then it should be expected to hold up when that processing is examined in detail. The level of detail of the present chapter (and others that examine individual behavior in different tasks) is beyond what one would want to consider most of the time; but it is quite appropriate when asking if the theory fits.

There is another reason for focusing on the individual problem solving attempt. Each such attempt is to be represented by a specific IPS operating in a specific task environment—by a symbolic system that generates behavior that corresponds to a segment of human behavior. Such a symbolic system, by the usual canons of science, is a theory of that behavior. Thus, the theory of human problem solving we set out in this book produces large numbers of highly specific little theories— *microtheories* would be an appropriate term.[1] Each of these microtheories can be viewed as a single data point, at which a more generalized theory is put to the test. Each data point requires this elaborate treatment because the data with which it makes contact are so sequentially interdependent that they cannot be unraveled meaningfully without the creation of a highly specific IPS. That is, the raw data (i.e., the verbalizations in the protocol) only make sense when seen through the lens of an appropriate IPS that unfolds their sequential dependencies.

Actually, as we shall see in Chapter 7, a great deal of analysis can be carried out at a more abstract level than the analysis presented in this chapter. However, the validity of the abstraction depends in part on the essential correctness of the kind of detailed analysis engaged in here. Also, even though they are more abstract, the efforts in Chapter 7 remain microtheories, explaining the behavior of individual problem solvers.

We will start with an overview of the protocol, then explore the subject's problem space, and finally attempt to write down an IPS that characterizes his behavior. We will not, however, carry the IPS quite to the level of detail or specificity of a program capable of simulation on a computer.

OVERVIEW OF THE PROTOCOL

The protocol was taken in the spring of 1960; the subject (S3) was a male college student at Carnegie Institute of Technology. The procedure was simple. The subject was seated at a table with a paper and pencil; the instructions of the puzzle were read to him and the sum, DONALD+GERALD=ROBERT, was written down in its conventional form. In addition, the subject was asked to speak aloud at all times while he worked, and his verbalizations were tape-recorded. The transcription of this tape—the protocol—is reproduced in full in Appendix 6.1 at the end of the chapter. No separate record is available of what the subject wrote down, although it is usually clear from the protocol when he wrote something (as in B9). Likewise, no separate timing information is available. However, since the protocol contains a total of 2186 words, and since other protocols under similar conditions average about two words a second, we can estimate the duration of this one at about 20 minutes. Timing information is not critical, since we have no way of making use of it in our analysis.

---

[1] We use this term even though it is used currently in a somewhat broader sense to denote a theory applying to a miniature domain of behavior, e.g., a theory of rat behavior in the T-maze.

The protocol has been broken up into short phrases, labeled B1, B2, . . . , B321. The numbered phrases include the remarks of both the subject and the experimenter. The phrasing is based on a naive assessment of what constitutes a single task assertion or reference. It is meant to facilitate reference and does not affect the analysis explicitly. However, the total number of phrases, 321, does give some indication of how many such assertions are present—one phrase every three to four seconds. Considering how much we sometimes suppose can go on in a few seconds of human thinking, this may seem a rather low density of data.

A fundamental question about such data is to what extent the phrases have an unambiguous meaning. Since the verbalizations are freely emitted, we can expect—and get—exchanges such as B169–B176 which includes "I still feel as though I'm baring my soul." In general, however, the task provides an extremely narrow context, which makes interpretation relatively easy.

It might seem that the verbalizations should be encoded into formal categories, in order to make clear what information was being used in the analysis. In fact there are objections in principle to such an encoding, if the content of the utterances is to be preserved.[2] Language is a device for encoding information. To recode it into another language that preserves *all* the meaning is hardly to encode it at all. To recode it into another language with substantial loss of meaning throws away the very data we hope to obtain by recording protocols.

Possibly, the verbalizations could be "cleaned up"—say, by removing some of the variability and redundancy of spontaneously spoken prose. But in practice, parts that are easy to code don't need it—e.g., B189: "I'm going to make R a 9" or B208: "that means that A + A has to equal 10." Parts that are not easy to code should be kept in their original form in order to extract any information they do contain—e.g., B16 and B17: "that are each—somewhere—" or B62–B65: "Now if the—oh, I'm sorry I said something incorrect here, I'm making—no, no, I didn't either." Breaking the utterance up into small phrases goes a long ways towards isolating a series of unambiguous "measurements" of what information the subject had at particular times. These measurements carry the main burden of the analysis; the ambiguous phrases that are left operate mostly as weaker checks of consistency.

We now turn to an analysis of S3's problem solving behavior. Various additional issues of interpretation will be dealt with as they come up in the context of the analysis.

THE SUBJECT'S PROBLEM SPACE

An examination of the protocol shows the following characteristics, which must be encompassed in a formal description of the subject's problem space.

---

[2] The difference between our situation, which argues against coding, and the more common situation in psychology where verbal data are coded as a matter of course, is that we wish to deal with the full content of the verbalizations—i.e., their meaning—and not just with the verbalizations as an indicator of a few underlying attributes (e.g., see Bales, 1970; Stone, Dumphy, Smith, and Ogilvie, 1966: Soskin and John, 1963; but also Pittinger, Hockett, and Danehy, 1960, for another example of a refusal to encode).

1. The subject writes some things down, but long periods go by with no writing. Thus, there is an internal problem space that is clearly different from the space of written, externalized actions.

2. Several kinds of internal actions occur: *assigning* digits to letters, *inferring* relations from the columns of the sum, and *generating* digits that satisfy certain relations. For example:

> B43: "if we assume that L is, say, 1." (assignment)
> B44: "we'll have 1 + 1 that's 3 or R. . . ." (inference)
> B26: "So R can be 1, 3, not 5, 7, or 9." (generation)

3. The relations that occur are *equality*, *inequality*, and *parity* (even-oddness). Equality must be kept separate from assignment, since the subject appears to distinguish throughout whether a digit has been *inferred to be equal* to a letter or has been *assigned* to that letter. Examples:

> B134: "A would have to equal 5." (equality)
> B58: "R has to be a number greater than 5." (inequality)
> B22: "which will mean that R has to be an odd number." (parity)
> B95: "Of course, this is all going on the assumption that R is 7—" (after B61: "so we'll start back here and make it a 7"). (assignment, distinct from equality)

4. The subject is able to consider *disjunctive sets*. Example:

> B74: "But now I know that G has to be either 1 or 2."

5. The subject uses the concept of a letter's being unconstrained (*free*) as well as the concept of a letter's being only constrained by membership in the remaining unassigned set of digits (in particular, being the *last* one). Examples:

> B242: "It looks then as though my solution for O is going to be independent of the rest of the column." (free)
> B248: "So it's probably going to be the last one I ever find." (last of the free set of digits)

6. Although the subject frequently states equations, these all correspond to reading a column; there is no evidence that he manipulates equations algebraically. (Such manipulations do show up clearly in protocols of other subjects.)

7. With respect to carries, the subject is able to *use* them in inferences, to *infer* them, to *seek* them, and (possibly) to *assign* them. For example:

> B70: "because 3 + 3 is 6 + 1 is 7." (use)
> B85: "which would mean that I was then carrying 1 into the left-hand column." (inference)

B261: "There's no place where I can get L + L to equal more than 10 so I could make . . . ." (search)

B221: "Suppose I would carry 2 from the column." (assignment)

The last example shows that the values of the carry cannot be restricted to 0 and 1 for this subject (recall the comments in Chapter 3 on whether the subject is limited to legal moves).

8. A few actions and kinds of information lie outside the range indicated above. These occur so rarely that they must be handled in an ad hoc fashion in any event. Examples:

B40: "Possibly the best way to get to this problem is to try different possible solutions." (reference to a method)

B50: "It's not possible that there could be another letter in front of this R is it? Is it or not?" (an operation to obtain information from experimenter)

FIGURE 6.1

problem space for S3

```
⟨digit⟩ :: = 0|1|2|3|4|5|6|7|8|9
⟨digit-variable⟩ :: = x|y
⟨general-digit⟩ :: = ⟨digit⟩|⟨digit-variable⟩
⟨digit-set⟩ :: = ⟨general-digit⟩ ∨ ⟨general-digit⟩|⟨general-digit⟩ ∨ ⟨digit-set⟩
⟨letter⟩ :: = A|B|D|E|G|L|N|O|R|T
⟨letter-set⟩ :: = ⟨letter⟩|⟨letter⟩ ⟨letter-set⟩
⟨carry⟩ :: = c⟨column-number⟩
⟨variable⟩ :: = ⟨letter⟩|⟨carry⟩
⟨column⟩ :: = column.⟨column-number⟩
⟨column-number⟩ :: = 1|2|3|4|5|6|7
⟨column-set⟩ :: = ⟨column⟩|⟨column⟩ ⟨column-set⟩
⟨assignment-expression⟩ :: = ⟨variable⟩ ← ⟨general-digit⟩|
    ⟨variable⟩ = ⟨general-digit⟩
⟨constraint-expression⟩ :: = ⟨variable⟩ ⟨parity⟩|⟨variable⟩ = ⟨digit-set⟩|
    ⟨variable⟩ ⟨inequality⟩ ⟨general-digit⟩|⟨variable⟩ ⟨qualifier⟩
⟨parity⟩ :: = even|odd
⟨inequality⟩ :: = >|<
⟨qualifier⟩ :: = free|last
⟨expression⟩ :: = ⟨variable⟩|⟨assignment-expression⟩|⟨constraint-expression⟩
⟨state-expression⟩ :: = ⟨expression⟩|⟨expression⟩ ⟨tag⟩
⟨tag⟩ :: = new|□|unclear|unknown|note
⟨knowledge-state⟩ :: = ⟨state-expression⟩|⟨state-expression⟩ ⟨knowledge-state⟩
⟨operator⟩ :: = PC [⟨column⟩]|GN|AV|TD
⟨goal⟩ :: = get ⟨expression⟩|get ⟨letter-set⟩
    check ⟨expression⟩|check ⟨column-set⟩
Particular sets:
    all-letters, free-letters
    all-digits, free-digits
    all-columns
```

We can now describe the problem space that appears to cover most of the protocol. It is a variant of the augmented problem space, as described in Chapter 5. Figure 6.1 gives its description, using BNF. We have included the elementary definitions, such as for ⟨digit⟩, to make the description self-contained.

The figure starts with the definition of the basic entities. The digits are expanded to the class ⟨general-digit⟩ by the inclusion of variables x and y for digits, since S3 on occasion goes through the form of processing a column without dealing with specific digits. The letters and carries are combined into the class ⟨variable⟩, since for several purposes these are equivalent for S3. Along with the basic entities we also define corresponding sets, ⟨digit-set⟩, ⟨letter-set⟩, ⟨column-set⟩ (sets of carries or variables never occur). Mostly sets are simply lists of the elements. We have used the disjunction sign ($\vee$) with digit-sets to permit us to write $(G = 1 \vee 2)$ rather than $(G = (1\ 2))$, $(G = 1\ 2)$ or $(G = 1, 2)$, all of which are either clumsier or somewhat ambiguous. At the bottom of the figure we list the names of several particular sets. The adjective *free* refers to those items (digits or letters as the case may be) that have not yet been assigned. Thus, free-letters is a list whose membership changes with time, as opposed to all-letters, which is a constant set (containing all the letters of ⟨letter⟩).

The figure then builds up to the definition of ⟨knowledge-state⟩ in two stages. First, it defines ⟨expression⟩ in terms of ⟨variable⟩, ⟨assignment-expression⟩, and ⟨constraint-expression⟩. Then it defines ⟨state-expression⟩ (the component of a knowledge-state) as an ⟨expression⟩ followed by a ⟨tag⟩. An ⟨expression⟩ represents a relation among variables and digits, e.g., $R > 5$ or $D \leftarrow 5$. A tag represents a mode of knowing; the open box, $\square$, is to be read *impossible* or *implies a contradiction*. Thus, with respect to a given expression, say $R > 5$, it is possible to have the following state-expressions:

$R > 5$	S knows that $R > 5$
$R > 5$ new	S has just come by the knowledge that $R > 5$
$R > 5\ \square$	S knows that $R > 5$ is impossible, given the rest of the state-expression
$R > 5$ unclear	S believes $R > 5$, but is uncertain of the grounds for believing it
$R > 5$ unknown	S is concerned for some reason with whether $R > 5$, but does not know whether it is true or not
$R > 5$ note	S knows that $R > 5$, and this fact has become important to other considerations

A single variable may also be an expression. Only two of the combinations with tags make semantic sense:

L	(no meaning)
L new	(no meaning)
L $\square$	S knows that no value of L is possible, given the rest of the state-expression
L unclear	(no meaning)

L unknown   S is concerned for some reason with the value of L, but does
not know what it is

L note   (no meaning)

The combinations labeled *no meaning* above do not occur in the protocol, so it makes little sense to assign them meanings. We could have excluded them formally from the BNF, but this would simply have complicated Figure 6.1.

Our renderings of these state-expressions are not to be taken as introducing concepts, such as belief, uncertainty, concerned, and so on, into the definition of the IPS. From an information processing view, what exists in the IPS is a representation of the knowledge-state as a set of state-expressions. Each state-expression is a symbol structure isomorphic to a sequence of symbols [e.g., the list $(R, >, 5,$ unclear)]. The reactions to these state-expressions are defined by the IPS program, and not by our natural language paraphrase above.

The ⟨*assignment-expression*⟩ contains both the assignment (←) and the equality (=), which, as we observed earlier, S3 distinguishes. The ⟨*constraint-expression*⟩ contains the various ways in which the possible values of a variable can be limited without necessarily being reduced to a single digit (hence representable by an assignment-expression). Each of these types corresponds to the forms discussed on page 167.

R odd   R is an odd digit (i.e., one of 1, 3, 5, 7, 9)
$G = 1 \lor 2$ G is either 1 or 2
$R > 5$ R is a digit greater than 5 (i.e., one of 6, 7, 8, 9)
O free   O is any digit at all from the digits that are left—i.e., from free-digits
O last   O is the last digit that will remain in free-digits

Again, the semantics of these relations is built into the IPS and not given by our explication, above.

The final part of Figure 6.1 gives the *operators* and the *goals*. We discuss the operators in detail below. The goals are of two types, *get* and *check*. Get refers to obtaining the associated expression:

get R   Obtain a value for R
get $c6 = 1$ Infer that $c6 = 1$

This last goal has a degree of wishful thinking about it, of course, since there may be no possibility that $c6$ could be 1, given the rest of the knowledge-state. S3, however, is capable of forming such a goal—that is, of attempting to obtain such a result, rather than, say, simply assuming it. Get ⟨letter-set⟩ represents the goal of obtaining all the letters of the indicated set. *Check* is a goal that operates with respect to some information that is already part of the knowledge-state. Again, check ⟨column-set⟩ means to check all of the columns in the set.

Four operators are given; these are used to generate new states of information from old. The operators provide the processing facilities that seemed to be required in an augmented problem space, as discussed in Chapter 5. Initially, we will describe them externally in terms of the information they use as input and the information they produce. This will be enough to identify them when they occur in the protocol. We will discuss later whether consistent algorithms can be fashioned to predict the occurrences of these operators.

PC[*column*] *Process column.* The input to PC is all the information in the current state about the three letters and two carries associated with a column. The output is one or more state-expressions that contain inferred information about some of the variables of the column. The specification of the variable about which information is to be obtained may or may not be determined prior to performing PC; if it is, we can write PC[column for variable]. Examples:

	INPUT					OUTPUT
column	*carry in*	*top* +	*middle* =	*bottom*	*carry out*	
1	0	D = 5	D = 5	T	?	$(T = 0)(c_2 = 1)$
2	1	L	L	R	?	(R *odd*)
6	?	D = 5	G	R ← 7	0	$(G = 1 \lor 2)(c_6 \text{ unknown})$

GN(*variable*) *Generate.* The input to GN is a variable with whatever information is known about it. The output is the set of admissible values (i.e., those consistent with the input information), *not* taking into account whether or not the values have previously been assigned to other letters. Examples:

INPUT	OUTPUT
L free	0, 1, 2, . . .
R odd	1, 3, 5, 7, 9
(R odd) (R > 5)	7, 9

AV(*variable*) *Assign value.* The input to AV is a variable with whatever information is known about it. The output is an assignment of a digit to that variable. If the digit to be assigned is determined prior to performing AV, we can then write AV(variable, digit). Examples:

INPUT	OUTPUT
L	L ← 1
R, 9	R ← 9

TD(*letter, digit*)   *Test admissible value.* The input to TD is a letter with
whatever is known about it, and a digit. The output is a
statement either that the digit is admissible or that it is
not. In the latter case the expression that caused the
failure is noted. TD determines (1) whether the digit
is already used for another letter, and (2) whether the digit
satisfies the known restrictions on the given letter. Examples:

INPUT	OUTPUT
L, 3	$+$
R, 5	(R = 5 □) (D ⟵ 5 note)

No operators have been defined either for writing information externally
or for reading values from the external display—i.e., the paper. As noted earlier,
the act of writing appears clearly enough in the protocol that its occurrence could
be indicated when it occurred. The same is not true of reading. There is never any
direct evidence when information stored in the external display is acquired. More
important, in this protocol the distinction between internally and externally stored
information (i.e., that L = 1 is written but R = 3, say, is not) does not seem to be
an essential part of the knowledge-state. Of course, only a successful total analysis
of the protocol without such discrimination proves this to be the case. The important effect of writing (if comparison is made with subjects not having pencil and
paper as external memory) is that S3 does not seem to have much difficulty in
remembering assignments.

The Problem Behavior Graph

The basic premise underlying the concept of a problem space is that the subject
can be viewed as searching through this space for a solution. Thus, if the structures
of Figure 6.1 do in fact represent the problem space for S3, we should be able to see
him wandering in this space throughout the task. We should be able to plot his
search tree, where each node in that tree can be characterized by an expression
given in the language of Figure 6.1, and each move to a new node in the tree can be
characterized by application of one of the four operators. For this latter to be the
case, not only must the operators apply to the node, but the new state of information must correspond to the additional information yielded by that operator.

In the previous chapters we have depicted a number of different search trees.
All of them have been overly simple in one respect: no part of any tree was searched
more than once. Repetition was prevented either by using systematic generators
(as in Figure 5.5, page 149, or by including specific tests for duplication (as in LT,
in Chapter 4). Also, in analyzing LT we had a program already in hand and wanted
to understand its behavior. Here our situation is reversed: we know nothing yet
about the subject's program; in particular, we have no assurance that he does not
search the same part of the problem space repeatedly. Thus we will introduce a
modification of the search tree, the *problem behavior graph* (PBG), which will

retain the full information about the dynamics of search, including repetitions. The rules for constructing a PBG are:

Rules for Problem Behavior Graph (PBG)

A state of knowledge is represented by a node.
The application of an operator to a state of knowledge is represented by a horizontal arrow to the right: the result is the node at the head of the arrow.
A return to the same state of knowledge, say node X, is represented by another node below X, connected to it by a vertical line.
A repeated application of the same operator to the same state of knowledge is indicated by doubling the horizontal line.
Time runs to the right, then down: thus, the graph is linearly ordered by time of generation.

FIGURE 6.2

problem behavior graph (PBG)

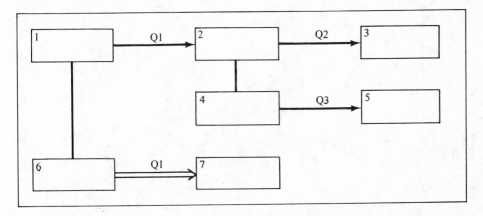

These rules are illustrated in Figure 6.2. The subject starts at node 1 in the upper left-hand corner. The first operator applied is Q1, producing the state of knowledge indicated by node 2. Then Q2 is applied, leading to node 3. At this point the subject returns to the same state of knowledge as in node 2; this is shown in node 4. Since the act of returning did not involve an operation—such as recalling the prior state, or abandoning the information produced by Q2—the move from node 3 to node 4 is not shown as an operation. At node 4, Q3 is applied to produce node 5, and then the subject returns (node 6) to the state of knowledge represented by node 1. Node 6 must be written on the line below nodes 4 and 5, since it occurred later in time. Q1 was applied again, as indicated by the double line emanating from node 6. The identity of the knowledge states at node 7, 2, and 4 is not indicated in the graph.

The problem solver is viewed as always being located at some node in the PBG —that is, as having the information about the problem that defines the node. But the act of search itself generates several additional kinds of information. One kind is *path* information: the subject knows something about how he got to the node.

FIGURE 6.3

problem behavior graph of S3

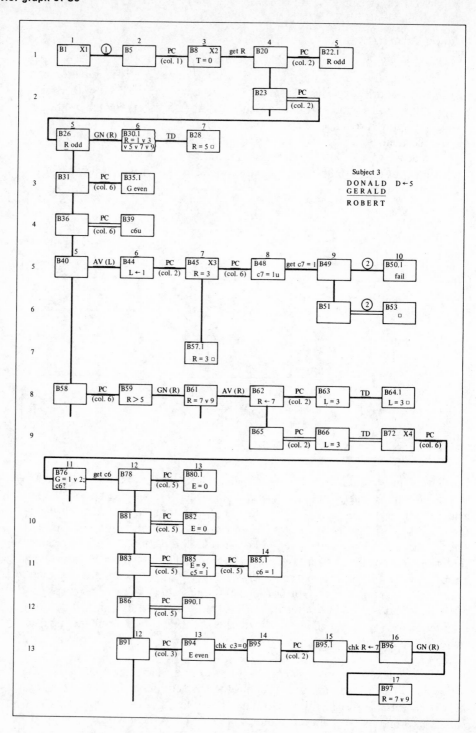

FIGURE 6.3 (cont'd)

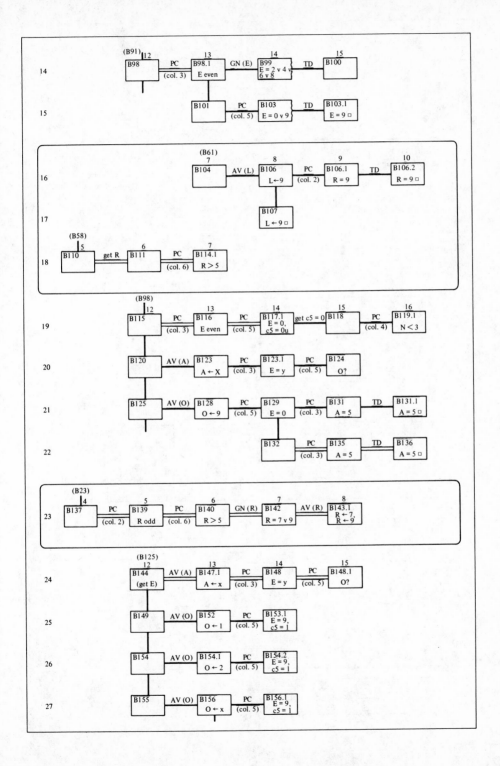

175

FIGURE 6.3 (cont'd)

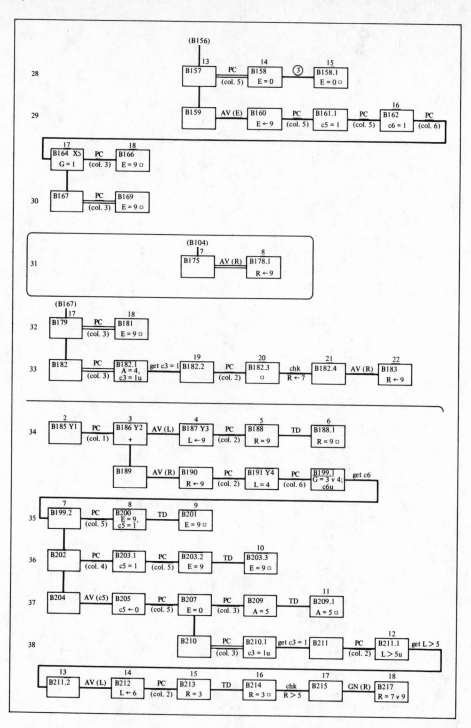

FIGURE 6.3 (cont'd)

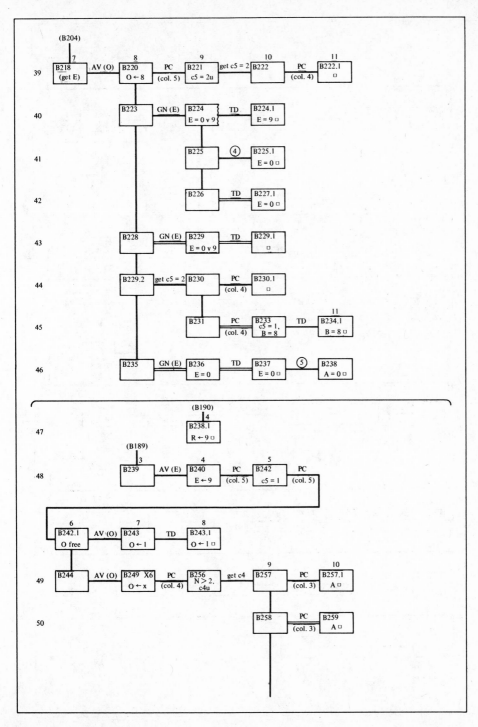

FIGURE 6.3 (cont'd)

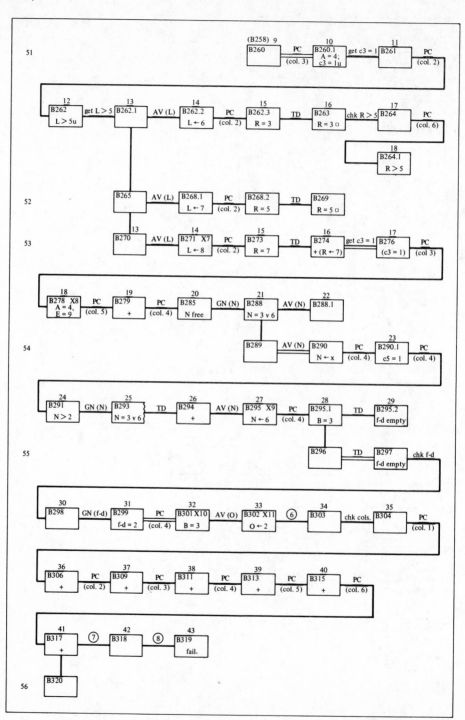

FIGURE 6.3 (cont'd)

B1	X1	DONALD
		GERALD
		ROBERT

B8	X2	5ONAL5
		GERAL5
		ROBER0

B45	X3	5ONA15
		GE3A15
		3OBE70

B72	X4	5ONA35
		GE7A35
		7OBE70

B164	X5	5ONA35
		1E7A35
		7OBE70

B185	Y1	DONALD
		GERALD
		ROBERT

B186	Y2	DONAL5
		GERAL5
		ROBER0

B187	Y3	DONA95
		GERA95
		ROBER0

B191	Y4	5ONA45
		GE9A45
		9OBE90

B249	X6	5xNA35
		197A35
		7xB970

B271	X7	5xNA85
		197A85
		7xB970

B278	X8	5xN485
		197485
		7xB970

B295	X9	5x6485
		197485
		7xB970

B301	X10	5x6485
		197485
		7x3970

B302	X11	526485
		197485
		723970

Notes for numbered operators

(1) Interaction with experimenter to define problem.

(2) Asking experimenter about c7 — i.e., on definition of the problem.

(3) Recall of information from B136; we have no operator for this.

(4) Experimenter interjects E = 0 □ (T = 0!).

(5) Digit based operation (given 0 □ find all letters affected)?

(6) Given a solution, to evoke checking behavior.

(7) Given a solution, to evoke finding all solutions.

(8) Shifting assignments, but how?

Since there may be many paths to the same node (as $3 + 5 = 8$, $2 \times 4 = 8$, $24/3 = 8$, and so on), the path information is not necessarily derivable from the state of knowledge as previously defined. It is possible to infer from the state which operators were applied, but it is not possible to determine either their order of application or whether they were applied more than once.

Another kind of additional information refers to *past attempts*. At node 4 (Figure 6.2) the problem solver must know that he has been in this state before and that Q2 was then applied. Otherwise (assuming no randomness in his behavior), being in the same state of knowledge as at node 2, he should apply Q2, rather than Q3. It is of course possible to return to the same situation without knowing the full history of past attempts; this may be the case at node 7, for instance. Both path information and information about past attempts are functions of a node, so that we should think of the state of knowledge in each node as being expanded to include them. (In fact, this is precisely the information that makes nodes 7, 2, and 4 separate nodes.)

An operator may be applied, or its application attempted, without any result—hence without any new state of knowledge occurring. In this case we still place a new node at the head of the arrow. This is a helpful convention, since the inference that no new information has been produced may occur late in the data analysis, or even remain in doubt.

Figure 6.3 shows the problem behavior graph (PBG) for the subject, using the conventions just set forth. Since no operations on the external display are shown, at those points where something was written down we have put an Xi in the upper right-hand corner of the box, for the name of the new external display. These displays are shown on the last page of the figure. Figure 6.3 has had to be folded rather badly to fit the tree onto page-sized sheets. Figure 6.4 shows the outline of the entire tree, and also provides a summary of the main problem solving episodes.

Each node in Figure 6.3 corresponds to an interval in the protocol. The B-number in the upper left of the node gives the approximate starting point of the interval; lines have been drawn across the protocol (in Appendix 6.1) at these points. Where the phrase divisions are not fine enough, decimals are used—e.g., B64.1—to indicate an occurrence somewhere after the phrase. A few items of information are sufficiently unique that it seemed inappropriate to add them to the formal definition of the problem space; these are indicated by circled footnote numbers—e.g., the number after B49. The only other convention is the one used at B30.1. Here each digit generated is tested by TD and one of them, $R = 5$, is rejected. Rather than depict the entire loop between GN and TD, we have simply shown node B30.1 with a jagged right-hand boundary to indicate that the B28 node is subordinated to the generator and executed repeatedly. This convention is used also at B99 and B103.

Let us see how the encoding goes. We adopt the point of view that anything that changes the knowledge-state, as defined in Figure 6.1, should be treated as an operator. (The four operators listed above are the end result of coding, of course, and were not chosen a priori.) Various other kinds of information, most notably what column is being considered, are not shown explicitly in this problem space.

Starting at the beginning, B1 is an exchange that is really outside the problem

FIGURE 6.4

problem behavior graph of S3—overview

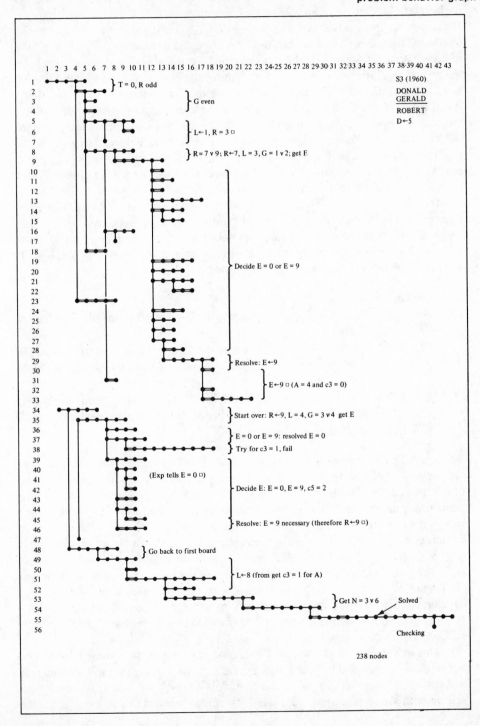

space, since it involves clarifying the rules for the subject. Not wanting to include it in the first real node, we simply indicate it by a special footnote (1). Likewise we indicate conventionally that the initial display, X1, is already set up by the experimenter. The second node, B5, provides a clear statement considering the two D's, asserting their value, and concluding that T is zero. The coding of this as the operator PC[*column 1*] is clear, but there are some open questions: (1) when did the inference actually occur; (2) why was column 1 considered; (3) did the subject have the goal of finding the value of T before he processed column 1; and (4) did he also conclude that $c2 = 1$? We do not need complete answers to all of these questions. As to the first question, we need only know the approximate sequence of processing, which is evident from the protocol. As to the second question, we have declared the selection of columns to be internal to the node and thus irrelevant to the problem graph. (We will return to this point later.) The third question is relevant, but we adopt the view that unless specific information is available we will not record conjectures about such matters. Finally, although it is plausible that $c2 = 1$ is inferred, since $5 + 5 = 10$, there is no immediate evidence for this. However, later behavior (B21) shows that in fact this information was retained.

We will find it useful to consider the next node, B8, in conjunction with node B20. In this the subject clearly is considering column 2, inferring that R is odd. If we write down what happens before this, we have:

B8–B9:   Writing prior result.

B10–B11:   Searching for a next step with no result in terms of our problem space.

B12–B13:   Another writing step, when the D in column 6 is noticed: conceivably new information is obtained, but certainly no evidence for it appears.

B14–B19:   Considering column 2, column 3, A, L, and R, searching a next step. No new information obtained in our problem space.

B20–B22:   Processing column 2.

The subject's concern with R, clearly indicated in B18 and B19, leads to the inference that the decision to process column 2 is based partly on the decision to obtain some information about R. Thus we attribute to B8 the goal of inferring the proper assignment for R (i.e., get R). The things occurring prior to B18 all belong within a node: the subject's writing operations and his (attempted) selection of columns on which to work. If the inference (to get R) were less clear, we would have only a single node for B8 to B22, whose operator would be PC[column 2]. In B18–B19 the immediate evidence is that the numbers of occurrences of the letters A, L, and R were noted. To count these the various columns must have been considered. There is no evidence that any processing of the columns occurred— i.e., any attempts to derive further information. We thus conclude that S is simply selecting the next column to work on.

This inference could be wrong. First, he could have derived some information but not have mentioned it. If this were the case, we can expect that this information will surface at some later point in the protocol—i.e., will be used in some context, arising without apparent antecedents. This appearance will allow us to draw the correct inference about the source of the information in B14–B19. Second, there may have been an unsuccessful attempt to derive new information. Then, we would know that our interpretation of the segment B14–B19 was wrong only if some regularity of S's behavior implied that he would have been processing the columns at this point.

In B23 and B25 the reasoning used in B20 and B22 is repeated. Why the subject repeats is not as apparent. It might be to check the processing—to insure that the inference is correct. That a correction can occur on a repetition is shown by the sequence B32–B35, yielding (G even), and the immediate repetition, B36–B38, leading to his realization that no such inference is possible. However, the repetition in B23–B25 may also be determined by the structuring of the experimental situation to get the subject to talk. In any event, we need to create a node, B22.1, for the result of his first PC[column 2] and then must back up for the repetition at B23.

In B26–B30 the subject generates the odd digits explicitly, following immediately upon his (confirmed) conclusion that R is odd. Thus the inference that GN(R) occurred is not problematic. It is also apparent that in the generation, the subject does not take into account what values are already assigned. That is, the already used digit, 5, is generated, then explicitly rejected, rather than skipped over. This supports the inference that the subject applied TD to the output of GN. It is not as clear, of course, that TD was applied to 1, 3, 7, and 9, since these were admissible and the subject gives no special indication of their acceptability. Thus, some assumptions of parsimony enter into the coding: if the subject applied TD sometimes and sometimes not, then he must have had a process to make this decision: but this process would have had to perform (uniformly) the same function as TD, namely, to determine if a digit were already assigned; consequently, it is simpler to assume that he applied TD uniformly. (A comment has already been made on the special notation in the graph for the repetition at node B30.1.)

B31 signals a pause, since the experimenter breaks in with a prod, urging the subject to talk. Since there is no evidence in what follows B32 that the subject used the refinement $(R = 1 \lor 3 \lor 7 \lor 9)$, rather than the more primitive information (R odd), we infer that he backed up in his search to the state of knowledge in B26. It is quite possible that some additional processing did go on from B30.1 during the pause, but since we have no evidence for it, we make no explicit note of it. If S3 obtained some new information, either it should show up at B31 (which it doesn't) or at some later time in terms of some facts whose origin would not be accounted for.

Our purpose is served in the last few pages if they give some appreciation of how one codes the data into the behavior graph. Most of the instances discussed so far are quite transparent. Similar discussion could elaborate the rest of the graph, but since we have examined above only 4 percent of the protocol, another 70 pages would be required. Much of it would be equally transparent (and equally dull); a few phrases would raise serious issues of interpretation. Following the protocol in Appendix 6.1, we have added notes that discuss most of these problematic cases. They are labeled by the corresponding B-numbers.

Although the detail itself is not very exciting, it is important to see what is going on in this phase of the analysis. We are trying to infer from the subject's verbalizations what he knows and what operations he performs at any point in time.

To do so, we must interpret his language—i.e., consider its meaning. Thus, if he says "R is odd," we infer that he knows R is odd. Of course, it is relevant, in principle, to ask whether the given utterance could have been made by chance. If the subject has been asked: "Is R odd or even?" then his answer that "R is odd" has a fifty-fifty chance of being true, whether the subject knows anything about R or not. As fortune-tellers know, one can often appear to give information by making general enough statements so that the a priori chances of falsification are remote.[3]

In our situation, the ensemble against which to view the subject's utterances is the language of the problem space. This makes it highly unlikely that "R is odd" will be uttered correctly by chance. More important than the probabilities is the web of inference that goes beyond a short utterance in isolation ("R is odd") and relates it to other utterances (e.g., "Two L's equal an R"). This web of inference varies in its coverage, and not all assertions can be made with considerable assurance.

There is much confusion in psychology about how to deal with verbal data. It is worth emphasizing that we are not treating these protocols as introspections. Actually, there are very few introspective utterances in them. An example does occur at B87:

B86: Exp: What are you thinking now?
B87: I was just trying to think over what I was just—

We treat this utterance only for the evidence it gives of the subject's knowledge or operation—in this case, essentially no evidence. The protocol is a record of the subject's ongoing behavior, and an utterance at time t is taken to indicate knowledge or operation at time t. Retrospective accounts leave much more opportunity for the subject to mix current knowledge with past knowledge, making reliable inference from the protocol difficult. Nor, in the thinking-aloud protocol, is the subject asked to theorize about his own behavior—only to report the information and intentions that are within his current sphere of conscious awareness. All theorizing about the causes and consequences of the subject's knowledge state is carried out and validated by the experimenters, not by the subject.

This technique of data analysis does depend on a human analyst's extracting the meaning of the linguistic utterances, proposing statements about the knowledge and operation to be attributed to the subject, and constructing the web of inference that supports these attributions. When psychology uses human analysts as instruments (e.g., in scoring tests or measuring interactions in small groups), the measurements are generally duplicated by several judges, and measures of reliability calculated. In working with protocols, we have not adopted these methods, believing it more appropriate to rely upon the persuasiveness of the web of inference.[4]

[3] There are some interesting computer programs that make effective use of this principle (Weizenbaum, 1966).

[4] In our judgment, the long-run solution to these questions of validity and reliability lies in mechanizing the procedure—in getting the human analyst out of the business of making the attributions and creating the web of inference. It is too early to report progress on current efforts toward mechanization.

The inputs to protocol analysis are the natural language strings produced by the human problem solver. The outputs are symbol structures interpreted as components of the problem solver's deep-structure representation of his knowledge-state and actions. The relations between the inputs and the outputs pose two kinds of linguistic problems: the problem of how the human problem solver generates the natural language strings from his internal representation in terms of deep structure; and the inverse problem of how we, the analysts, infer the deep structure from the strings that compose the protocols. These two problems are identical with the central problems of modern structural linguistics: the problems of synthesis and analysis, respectively.

We shall not address ourselves to the problem of synthesis, of how the problem solver generates his utterances. The problem is genuine, and important to linguistics, but its solution is not relevant to our theory of problem solving. That theory postulates only linguistic deep structure (the internal representations) and not surface structure.

The problem of analysis cannot be evaded in this way if we are to use protocols as data to test the theory. We can, however, stop somewhere short of constructing a full formal grammar to account for the translation from natural language strings to elements of deep structure. Instead, as we have just illustrated, we rely upon a systematic, but informal, set of procedures, combined with our own knowledge of the English language and our consequent ability to extract meanings from natural-language strings—to extract from the protocols the most directly obvious components of the underlying deep structures that are implicit in them.

Interpretation of the PBG

The problem graph is a projection of the total behavior of the subject into a space of our own devising. Thus, in interpreting the problem graph we must take into account the various possibilities for the true situation relative to what we see in the graph. Let us state first, in strong form, what the problem graph implies, following this with some possible qualifiers.

The successful encoding of S3's behavior into the problem graph of Figure 6.3 implies:

1. The subject's problem solving proceeds through the states of knowledge shown in the figure. That is, evidence exists that S3 had these various states of knowledge and proceeded on a path through them from the initial state to the solution.
2. The operators PC, GN, AV, and TD account for *all* his transitions to new states of knowledge. (Returns to prior states are governed by other processes.)
3. The operators, along with a set of processes for selecting operators, evaluating states of knowledge for termination, and selecting prior nodes

to which to return, constitute a sufficient set of processes for explaining the subject's behavior at the level of detail considered.

In short, S3's basic problem solving method is search, hence "trial and error," but in a space defined by intellectual operations of a moderate degree of sophistication (PC, GN, AV, TD). These operators provide a definition of basic competence, similar to the abilities that Gagné has tried to identify in somewhat simpler arithmetic situations (Gagné and Paradise, 1961; see also Resnick, 1969).

The true state of affairs can deviate from the stipulations above in several ways, either because of the sorts of information that the subject actually used or because of the complexity of the processes.

1. Up to this point none of the components—the operators or the selection and evaluation processes—have been spelled out in detail. It may be that the essential problem solving is done "inside" one or more of these. If this were so, the problem graph would have to be termed *superficial*, since, although a true enough description, it would not explicate the important processing steps. Note that the basic issue is not how much selection is performed within the components (e.g., by the operator-selection process), but whether the selection requires problem solving: either search in another space, or some other as-yet-unspecified intellectual process.

2. It may be that the analysis has gone too far—is too *disaggregated*. Thus, the graph may show the means used to carry out some larger plan or method without giving any clear indication about this higher organization. An analog would be the trace of the machine instructions carried out by a computer in executing a program. Excessive disaggregation would reveal itself in the capriciousness of various selections, viewed in terms of the local context, whenever the next action was in fact (but not explicitly) determined by the structure of the higher-level plan or method.

3. In the worst case, the present graph might be *epiphenomenal*. In this case, other processes using different (or at least additional) information from that represented in the PBG would actually be responsible for the problem solving. As a consequence of these other processes and information the subject would come to know (and reveal) the information contained in the graph.

To illustrate further the difficulties that arise from excessive aggregation (points 1 and 3), suppose that we had taken as our problem space one centered around the operation of writing assignments on paper. As true behaviorists we might well have done so, arguing that we had found an appropriate objective indication of an intermediate state in the course of problem solving.[5] Figure 6.5 gives a BNF definition of such a space, which we can call the *external problem space*, for S3. Figure 6.6 shows the problem graph we would have obtained. This

---

[5] See Moore and Anderson, 1954a, page 156, for just such a statement.

indeed is epiphenomenal. It contains very few clues as to the essential processes that are determining the sequence of actions. Indications of its incompleteness would arise as soon as one tried to specify the rules for operator selection in terms of the states of knowledge. For example, since there is no representation in the external space for the fact that $R = 7 \lor 9$, there is no indication of why R was assigned the value 7 at B61 and 9 at B189. Or again, not until B249 does any evidence occur for the subject's concern with E, O, and column 5, although these dominated his attention from B80 to B162 and from B219 to B243—almost half the total time.

FIGURE 6.5

external problem space for S3

$\langle\text{row}\rangle :: = \text{top}\,|\,\text{middle}\,|\,\text{bottom}$
$\langle\text{row-index}\rangle :: = t\,|\,m\,|\,b$
$\langle\text{column}\rangle :: = \text{col.1}\,|\,\text{col.2}\,|\,\text{col.3}\,|\,\text{col.4}\,|$
$\qquad\qquad \text{col.5}\,|\,\text{col.6}$
$\langle\text{column-index}\rangle :: = 1\,|\,2\,|\,3\,|\,4\,|\,5\,|\,6$
$\langle\text{entry}\rangle :: = \langle\text{digit}\rangle\,|\,\langle\text{blank}\rangle\,|\,\langle\text{digit-variable}\rangle$
$\langle\text{blank}\rangle :: =$
$\langle\text{place}\rangle :: = \langle\text{letter}\rangle\,|\,\langle\text{letter}\rangle\,\langle\text{column-index}\rangle\,|$
$\qquad\qquad \langle\text{letter}\rangle\,\langle\text{row-index}\rangle\,|\,\langle\text{letter}\rangle\,\langle\text{row-index}\rangle$
$\qquad\qquad \langle\text{column-index}\rangle$
$\langle\text{write-operator}\rangle :: = \langle\text{place}\rangle \longleftarrow \langle\text{entry}\rangle$
$\langle\text{knowledge-state}\rangle :: = \langle\text{display}\rangle$

		col.6	col.5	col.4	col.3	col.2	col.1
$\langle\text{display}\rangle :: =$	top	D $\langle\text{entry}\rangle$	O $\langle\text{entry}\rangle$	N $\langle\text{entry}\rangle$	A $\langle\text{entry}\rangle$	L $\langle\text{entry}\rangle$	D $\langle\text{entry}\rangle$
	middle	G $\langle\text{entry}\rangle$	E $\langle\text{entry}\rangle$	R $\langle\text{entry}\rangle$	A $\langle\text{entry}\rangle$	L $\langle\text{entry}\rangle$	D $\langle\text{entry}\rangle$
	bottom	R $\langle\text{entry}\rangle$	O $\langle\text{entry}\rangle$	B $\langle\text{entry}\rangle$	E $\langle\text{entry}\rangle$	R $\langle\text{entry}\rangle$	T $\langle\text{entry}\rangle$

From these observations it might appear that the use of a PBG to explain behavior would depend critically on the graph's representing precisely the right degree and level of aggregation of the behavior. If too aggregated, the graph would be superficial or epiphenomenal; if too disaggregated, it would fail to reveal the larger units of organization. In point of fact, the success of the method is not nearly so sensitive to the level of aggregation as these warnings would seem to imply. It is insensitive, basically, because the behavior under study is itself organized in a hierarchy of levels. The more detailed processes (the "subroutines") are carried out as components of more comprehensive acts. Thus, for example, a subject might process column 2 as one component of an act intended to infer an assignment for R.

Now the prices to be paid for disaggregating too far are, first, that we will be led to analyze in detail subprocesses that are not problematic for the subject,

FIGURE 6.6
problem behavior graph of S3 in external problem space

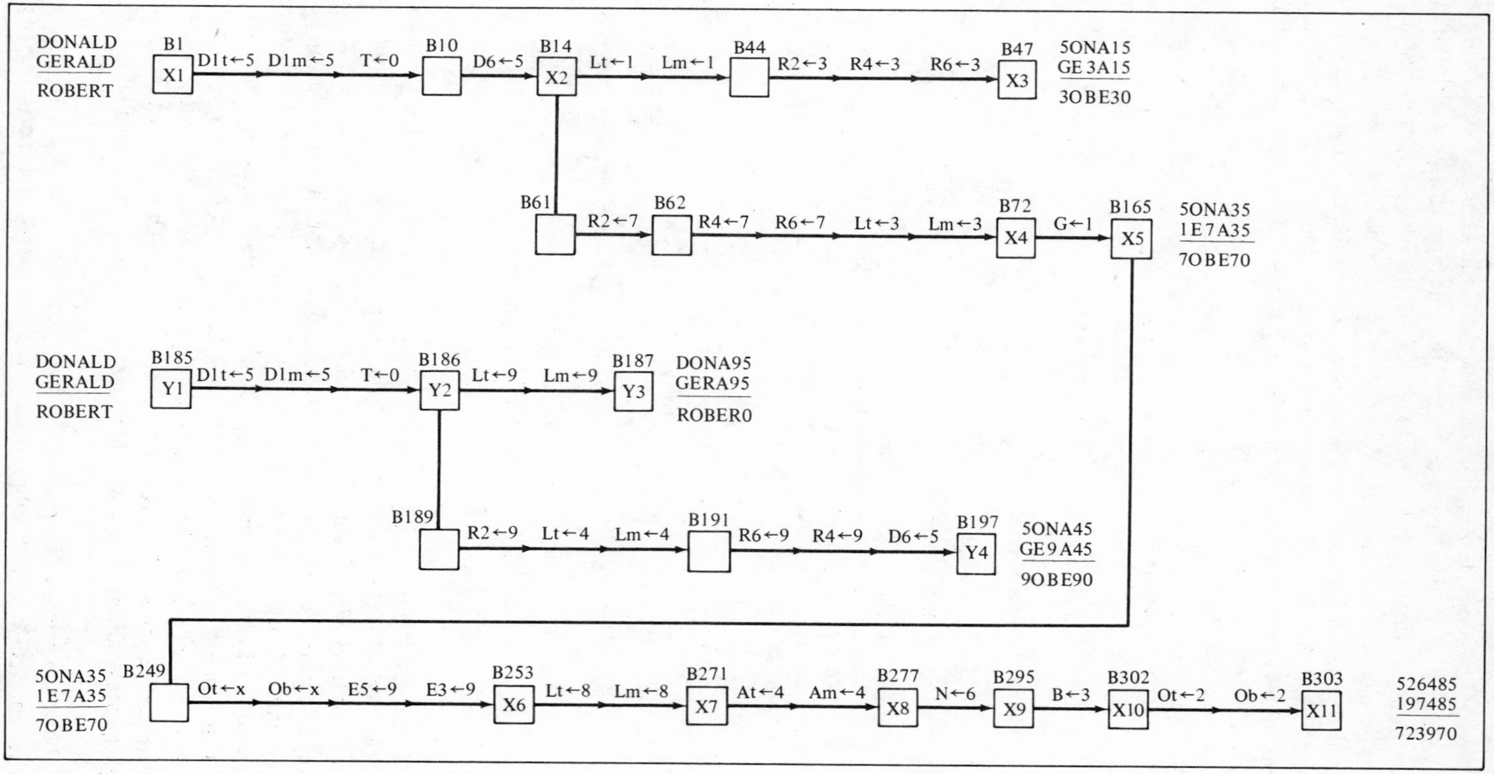

188

hence amount simply to doing what the task environment demands, and second, that we will have to look well beyond the local context of a particular behavior to explain why it occurred just where it did. The first price is not burdensome, and may be written off as an inefficiency of the technique. The second price may be somewhat heavier, but, as we shall see, it can be payed by constructing a comprehensive IPS to explain the behavior, and then testing the predictions of the IPS.

Excessive aggregation also exacts its price—and since aggregation means loss of information, the price may well be heavy, or even ruinous. The nature of the difficulty has already been illustrated in the comparison of the aggregated external problem space with the less aggregated space we have actually used to describe S3's behavior.

But notice that even in this case, where the aggregated graph clearly does not correspond with the space in which the subject is working, the graph may still provide a great deal of data for testing theories of his behavior. If we have reason to assume (from data on other subjects, from data on other problems attempted by the same subject, or on theoretical grounds) that the subject is working, say, in the augmented space, then we can construct an IPS, using the augmented space, to simulate the behavior; and we can predict the information in the aggregated graph by extracting the appropriate subset of information from the more complete simulated graph. Such prediction is likely to be successful (when the simulation theory embodied in the IPS is more or less correct) to the extent that the missing subprocesses represent doing what the environment demands. For example, in the specific case at hand, if the IPS were constructed on the assumption that the subject was actually working in the augmented problem space, then the fact that in the external (aggregated) space he tried the values 7 and 9 for R, and no others, would become understandable, and might even be predicted.

Thus, the problem behavior graph obtained from a protocol can be treated from either of two viewpoints. It can be treated as representing the subject's problem space, in which case it is essential that it describe information and behavior at the right level of detail—or at least at not too aggregated a level. Alternatively, the graph can be regarded simply as the experimenter's summary of the subject's protocol, described in terms of a space that may or may not correspond with the subject's problem space. In this case it can still be used to test how well a hypothesized IPS predicts the observed behavior.

It is extremely important for our purposes that this second interpretation of the problem behavior graph is available. First, there is no a priori reason why the subject's verbalizations, reported in his protocol, should give anything like a complete record of his state of knowledge at every moment. The frequency with which we should expect gaps and omissions, even in a fairly full protocol, has already been indicated in our detailed treatment of the behavior of S3.

Second, we may wish to use data for testing our theories where complete protocols have not been taken or reported. Later, we shall examine several sets of data in which only external behaviors were recorded (among them, some data of Bartlett's on DONALD+GERALD, and data of Moore and Anderson's on logic problems), and will find them highly informative even though they are far too aggregated to reveal the subjects' successive states of knowledge in their problem spaces.

Third, as should already be amply evident, protocol analysis detailed enough to construct the problem behavior graph is extremely costly. If we have carried out enough such analysis to hypothesize an IPS that we think will fit the subject's behavior in other problems, or the behavior of other subjects, then we can test the hypothesized theory with the help of more aggregated data that are easier to obtain from the protocol, and more convenient to manipulate and present. A large part of the evidence for our theory of problem solving in cryptarithmetic to be examined in Chapter 7 is of an aggregated kind. We will postpone a discussion of the techniques for analysis of aggregated data until we reach that chapter.

Prospectus

We return now to our analysis of S3's behavior at the level of his PBG. In constructing the graph, the first stage of our analysis has been completed. The verbal protocol of S3 has been encoded, with a relatively high degree of objectivity and reproducibility, and in very concrete terms, so that the content of the problem solving steps has been retained. This PBG goes a way toward answering some of the questions posed at the beginning of the chapter. The subject can be viewed as working in a problem space, and indeed we can specify that space in some detail. The task of extracting from the protocol the information required for the PBG has not proved difficult. The task's simplicity is due in part to the limited range of the subject's linguistic behavior, so that complicated interpretations are infrequent.

A number of the questions remain untouched. From one point of view the PBG is simply a basic description of the subject's behavior. Our task at this point is to build a bridge from that description to a full theory of human problem solving. In the next two sections of this chapter we will outline a program for producing (i.e., predicting) S3's PBG; then we will compare the program's predictions in some detail with the behaviors in the PBG to see how closely it matches them, and in what particular respects it fails. The program will not be described in completely closed terms, hence a certain degree of looseness will remain in fitting it to the data. We will try to comment on the significant points where further elaboration of the program would be required in order to test it with complete rigor.

As we shall see, the program for S3 will have several kinds of essential components. Most evident from the PBG, it will contain *processes for doing the arithmetic* —i.e., drawing inferences from the arithmetic relations specified in the problem. The process we have called PC will play a central role here, together with the other three processes, FC, GN, and TD, that are used with it to change the state of knowledge.

As a second component, the program will contain *processes for deciding what to do next*. Suppose that the subject, in processing a column, infers a new assignment of a digit to a letter (e.g., $D = 5$, hence, from column 1, $T = 0$). What task shall be program take up next? This component of the program may be thought of as the subject's (implicit or explicit) general strategy. The strategy is synonymous with the set of processes—it need not involve an overall plan, much less a conscious one.

As a third component, the program will contain implicit and explicit *assumptions about what the subject remembers* as he pursues his task, and about the circumstances under which he will evoke the information he has stored in memory.

If the program is to have any efficacy in solving the problem, its components have to bear some appropriate relation to the task environment. For example, the subject uses the inference, "If $y = 2x + 1$ (y and x integers), then y is odd." A subject who did not have this rule available, or did not think to use it, would face additional difficulty in solving the problem. One of the actual difficulties of S3 was that he made the invalid inference at an early point that $R = 7$ implies $L = 3$ and $c3 = 0$. By and large, however, the arithmetic operators we encounter in the program are determined by the task environment (the rules of arithmetic) rather than by the idiosyncracies of the subject.

The subject's strategy may also be strongly conditioned by the task environment. S3 approaches the task with the idea (which he considers abandoning only occasionally) that he can deduce the correct set of assignments of digits to letters without trying all possible combinations. It is, of course, an objective property of the task environment that this is possible, although another subject might very well not make use of it.

If we were to program a computer to perform the cryptarithmetic task, without any intent to simulate a human subject, we would probably construct the program so that any fact would be remembered, once it had been validly inferred. We will see as we proceed with our analysis of S3's behavior that a great deal of what is specifically psychological about it (as distinguished from what is a reflection of the structure of the task environment) revolves around the limitations and vagaries of the subject's memory.

With these introductory comments out of the way, we proceed with our construction of a program to account for the PBG.

ANALYSIS OF THE PROTOCOL: A PRODUCTION SYSTEM

The Problem Behavior Graph segments the total protocol into 238 parts, with each of which is associated one of a finite set of possible behaviors (the operator, together with its particular inputs and outputs). With each of these nodes is also associated a state of knowledge. If the subject employs definite processes for selecting, evaluating, and applying the operators, then within these 238 occurrences there may occur enough repetitions of essentially the same situation to allow us to induce what the processes are and to have some faith in their reality. Repetition of decision situations is the key issue, for if each situation called forth a unique process, then we could never verify that a proposed process was in fact the one used. Note, however, that the definition of the same decision situation is not given a priori. Each of the 238 states of knowledge is unique. Therefore the amount of repetition is defined after the fact by the nature of a proposed process and the proposed laws of its evocation.

If the essential problem solving is carried out in the space of Figure 6.1, then simple, definite algorithms should exist for the component processes for selecting, evaluating, and applying operators. These might use information not in the knowledge-state, but only information of a local kind or information already available in the subject's general fund (such as properties of integers). As we have seen, different organizations and heuristic rules are possible for effecting the selection, evocation, and evaluation of the operators of a problem space.

Since our data (the PBG) are a set of correspondences between states of knowledge and the actions that resulted, the production system turns out to be a natural form for an IPS. In particular, it seems well adapted to inducing the total program from the PBG, since each production, which is an actual component of the eventual program, is introduced to handle one or more situations where certain specific information evokes given operators. The total program, then, is the collection of these individual productions, plus the ordering of the productions that resolves conflict if several conditions are satisfied concurrently.

Production System for S3

The production system shown in Figure 6.7 purports to explain the behavior of S3 in the problem graph of Figure 6.3. These rules were induced by examining the problem graph in the light of the various notions of how problem solving might proceed in the cryptarithmetic task. The notation is that used in describing problem

FIGURE 6.7

production system for S3

P1: ⟨assignment-expression⟩ new ⟶
        FC(variable of expression) (⟹ column); PC[column]
P2: get ⟨variable⟩ | get ⟨variable⟩ = ⟨general-digit⟩ ⟶
        FC(variable) (⟹ column); PC[columns for variable]
P3: get ⟨letter.1⟩ ⟶ FA(letter.1) (⟹ column);
        AV(letter.2 of column); PC[column for letter.1]
P4: get ⟨variable⟩ and (⟨constraint-expression⟩ new) with variable ⟶
        GN(variable) (⟹ digit-set); size (digit-set) = small ⟶
        AV(variable)
P5: check ⟨column-set⟩ ⟶ GNC(column-set) (⟹ column); PC[column]
P6: ⟨expression⟩ unknown ⟶ (get expression)
P7: ⟨expression⟩ □ ⟶ (get variable of expression)
P8: check ⟨expression⟩ new ⟶ (get expression)
P9: get ⟨letter-set⟩ ⟶ FL(letter-set) (⟹ letter); (get letter)
P10: ⟨expression⟩ note ⟶ (check expression)
P11: ⟨letter⟩ = ⟨digit⟩ new | GN(⟨letter⟩) (⟹ ⟨digit⟩) ⟶
        TD(letter, digit)
P12: ⟨expression.1⟩ □ ⟶ FA(expression.1) (⟹ expression.2);
        (expression.2 □)
P13: ⟨operator⟩ ⟹ (⟨expression⟩ unclear) ⟶
        (get variable of expression); repeat operator(variable)
P14: check ⟨expression⟩ ⟶ FP(expression) (⟹ production);
        (get expression); repeat production on expression

spaces, except for a few additions, which will be noted in the discussion of individual rules.[6]

Several new processes have been introduced, in addition to PC, GN, AV, and TD. These all produce outputs that do not change the knowledge state as we defined it. They select columns, letters, or prior actions for consideration; i.e., they control attention. Because they do not change the state of knowledge, none of these was included in our original set of operators. They would be included if we were to operate in an expanded problem space that made control over the subject's attention explicit. We define these processes here at the same level as the operators.

FC(variable) — *Find column containing a variable.* The input to FC is the variable (letter or carry) for which it is desired to find the column. The column currently being attended to is also known.

FA(expression) — *Find the antecedent of expression.* The input is an expression. The output is the column or relation that was used in deriving the expression.

GNC(column-set) — *Generate columns.* The input is a set of columns. GNC generates the columns of the set from right to left.

FL(letter-set) — *Find letter.* The input is a set of letters (not letter occurrences). The output is a letter of the set. The display and current knowledge about letters are available to FL, so it can select, for instance, the particular letter, among those still undetermined, that occurs a maximum number of times in the display.

FP(expression) — *Find production that produced expression.* The input is an expression that was derived at some prior point in the analysis. The output is the production that yielded it. Thus, FP is essentially a recall process. (It differs from FA in outputting a production, rather than a column or a relation.)

We now provide a brief explanation of each of the productions.

P1. If a new expression determining an assignment (either = or ←) has been produced, then find a column that contains the variable involved in the expression, and process that column, PC[column]. If no column is produced by FC, then of course PC is not evoked; that is, the sequential action is conditional on appropriate outputs' being produced by prior actions. This production represents the subject's ability to take new information and apply it elsewhere to get yet more new information. Its evocation depends only upon some new information's

---

[6] As noted in the preface, this entire chapter is a rewritten version of Newell, 1967c. The changes in the problem space and the production system are primarily notational.

being available. Successful execution of the production removes the *new* tag from the recognized *assignment-expression;* thus the production will not be repeated.

P2. If the goal has been set to evaluate a variable, or establish a specific value for a variable ($\langle$variable$\rangle = \langle$general-digit$\rangle$), then find a column containing that variable (FC), and process that column for the variable (PC). Again, if no column is produced by FC, PC is not evoked. P2 can be applied repeatedly to the same variable, gradually to accumulate information about it. The goal can either be to get information about a variable, or to obtain some relation, as in (get $c5 = 1$). Both P1 and P2 have fundamentally the same action sequence, yet they derive from quite different concerns. The former is evoked by new information about a variable, the latter by the goal of getting such information.

P3. If the goal has been set to get the value of letter.1, find a column containing letter.1, then assign a value to the other letter, letter.2, that appears in the column, after which letter.1 may be determined using PC. P3 provides an alternative means for reaching a goal. It gives the appearance, whether justified or not, of being less arbitrary than simply assigning a value to letter.1.

Both P1 and P2 apply to variables—i.e., to letters or carries. P3, on the other hand, applies only to letters, although it could just as well have been generalized to include carries. However, S3 never performed P3 with carries. The principle of using the minimal necessary generality leads to P3 in its present form. On the other hand, both P1 and P2 did occur with carries as well as letters. This principle applies against the background of the problem space of Figure 6.1. Thus, for instance, there is genuine generalization in creating P1 with $\langle$assignment-expression$\rangle$ as the condition, since not all combinations of letters and digits occurred. However, to have fitted P1 to the exact combinations that did occur would have required an extensive enumeration. Thus, the organization of the problem space dictates the generalizations that take place: always use the smallest class in the problem space that covers the cases observed.

P4. If the goal has been set to evaluate a variable that is constrained in its set of possible values—i.e., occurs in a constraint-expression—generate its admissible values. If there are only a few values satisfying it, assign a value, AV(variable); otherwise do nothing. Again, as with P1, the tag, new, is stripped from the constraint-expression by P4.

P5. If the goal is to check a set of columns, generate the columns from right to left, executing PC on each. This production is evoked only once during the course of problem solving—namely, at the end—but it governs a rather long sequence of behavior.

P6. If an expression is relevant but unknown (i.e., has the tag, unknown) then set up the goal, get expression. That the expression is unknown is only evoked when some other process attempts to use it and finds that it is unknown. Thus, expressions do not exist in the knowledge-state for all things that are unknown. This illustrates that the knowledge-states are *not* to be interpreted as "all things that the observer can infer the subject could know are true."

P7. If it is known about a variable, v, that a certain fact is not possible—i.e., (expression ☐)—then set up the goal, get variable. This production does not represent the subject's attempt to deny the new information (which would lead to check-expression), but his acceptance of the information, which leads him to look for another value for the variable.

P8. If the goal is to check an expression that is new (that is, has not been derived before), set up the goal, get expression. Although P8 occurs only rarely, a fact may be assumed or become known without any explicit prior derivation of it. This production simply bridges the gap between the goals *check* and *get* in these situations.

P9. If the goal is to evaluate a set of letters, find one of them (by means of FL) and set up the goal of evaluating it. This production simply selects a member from a set. Its role is essentially to find something to work on when all else fails, since the initial problem is stated as: get all-letters.

P10. If an expression has been critical in determining some process, as expressed by the tag, note, then set up the goal, check expression. The production P10 has been stated unconditionally, but the degree of the subject's certainty about the expression, expressed in some manner, will also condition its evocation. For instance, the subject will not check D ← 5. Some, but not all, of this variation in certainty is taken care of by the fact that the tag, note, is removed from the expression by P10 (as is *new* by P1 and P4).

P11. Whenever a digit is newly derived as the value of a letter (letter = digit new), test if the digit is admissible (TD). The result is either +, indicating that the value is admissible, or a change of the tag from new to ☐ (i.e., letter = digit is a contradiction), along with the statement of the reason for the inadmissibility, (⟨expression⟩ note). P11 is also evoked when digits are generated in the context of obtaining values for a variable. Note that there is no similar check on the value of a carry.

P12. If it is determined that expression.1 is not possible, then find expression.2, which was used in deriving expression.1, and declare it not possible also (expression.2 ☐). This production provides backtracking on a succession of implications when a contradiction is discovered.

P13. If the result of an operator is unclear (i.e., has tag, unclear), then repeat Q, setting up as the goal, get variable, where the variable is the one involved in the unclear expression. The operator is normally, but not always, PC. The tag, unclear, requires further delineation. Addition of two digits, as in (5 + 5 = T), is always clear, but complex determinations, like the inference of (R odd) from (1 + L + L = R), are unclear—at least the first time encountered. Processes that lead to contradictions, and those from which no definite conclusion can be drawn, are also unclear.

P14. If the goal is to check an expression that has been derived previously, find the production used in that derivation and repeat it (after setting up the goal of getting the expression). P14 implies some memory of production occurrences.

The production system of Figure 6.7 is not complete. First, it does not specify the priority order of the productions. The order in the figure is essentially arbitrary. It can be seen that conflicts will in fact occur, since some productions have identical conditions (e.g., P2 and P3), and other productions have conditions that, although different, can both be satisfied at the same node (e.g., P1 and P2).

A more important gap than the priority ordering is the fact that not all the nodes of the problem graph are handled by the system. The productions were created from the regularities that were found in the PBG. Nodes that are either idiosyncratic in their behavior or unclear do not give rise to productions. Thus, the production system is incomplete from a task point of view. It is not capable of solving the task of DONALD+GERALD, nor many other cryptarithmetic tasks, without augmentation.

The productions of Figure 6.7 form an integrated system in at least one nonobvious way. The context in which the conditions are tested is provided by the products of the productions themselves, insofar as the system is complete. Thus the conditions can be adequate to make the right discriminations within the restricted context, even though they might be inadequate within a larger context.

We can summarize the relation of these rules to the evaluative and selective functions that are required for any system capable of generating a problem graph.

Operator Selection. The functions of P1, P2, P3, P4, P5, and P11 are to select one of the four operators, PC, GN, AV, and TD, to be performed. Two of these productions, P3 and P4, specify a pair of operators to be applied in sequence, if all goes well. In addition, P13 selects an operator indirectly, as does P14.

Evaluation. Terminal nodes occur either when an impossibility (□ tag) arises, or when the product of an operator is unclear. Termination on impossibility is implicit, in that none of the productions that can select new operators do so with a □ tag. Those that respond to □ select an old node from which to proceed, thus abandoning the current one. Positive evaluation to continue is implicit in the conditions of productions that do select operators. No special processes are required.

Node Selection. P12, P13, and P14 carry out the function of node selection. P13 and P14 determine the actual node to be used; P12 simply backs down the tree, eliminating nodes as candidates for restarting. Implicit in P12 is the retention of path information. Implicit also is the principle that if the subject is at a node and it isn't prohibited, then he selects it. This, in conjunction with path memory, is equivalent to a depth-first search strategy.

Goal Setting. The productions that create goals are P6, P7, P8, P9, and P10. Three of these, P6, P7, P10, along with P13, form one component of means-ends analysis, namely, immediate reaction to a difficulty by setting up a goal to deal with it. These control the hierarchic phrase-structuring of behavior, by setting up subgoals within subgoals.

Given the production system of Figure 6.7 we wish to evaluate how well it characterizes the problem graph. This involves first accounting for what the production system explains and what it does not. We can then analyze both the errors of omission (where the production system is silent on the behavior that occurs) and the errors of commission (where the system makes a specific, but wrong, assertion about behavior).

How Much Does the Production System Explain?

The first step in an accounting is to write down for each node what production, if any, seems to have been evoked. This is done on the protocol itself (Appendix 6.1), rather than on the problem graph, to permit comparison of the productions with the verbal behavior that is the main evidence for them.[7] We require a few conventions.

First, it is often the case that we cannot discern the information on which the production conditions are based, or can discern neither condition nor action. We use question marks (?) to indicate these cases. Sometimes we make a comment in English, especially when the behavior is clearly outside the problem space and is coded by a footnote on the problem graph. Examples:

B1	?:	(ask Exp. about rules)	(outside space)
B18	?:	get R	(evidence for action only)
B39	?:		(no production in evidence)

Second, several of the productions cover more than one node. We use a vertical arrow (↑) to indicate at a node that it is covered by the production named at the preceding node.

B22.1	P13:	PC unclear $\longrightarrow$ get R; repeat PC
B23	↑ :	PC[2](R) $\Longrightarrow$ (R odd)

Third, on occasion we need to indicate that TD is applied to several members of a generator. We do this by using a variable (d) for the input to TD. Sometimes

---

[7] As already noted, the analysis here is essentially the same as that in the earlier paper (Newell, 1967c). The productions alongside the protocol are nearly identical to those in the prior publication. The changes are due to some minor inconsistencies in coding that were discovered after publication of the earlier report. These changes have a slight effect on the actual numbers that occur in the various figures and tables in the remainder of the chapter, but in no case are the conclusions affected.

this appears to interrupt another production, since the TD is being applied to each output.

B59	P4:	get R $\longrightarrow$ GN(R) $\Longrightarrow$ 7, 9
B60	P11:	R = d $\longrightarrow$ TD(d, R) $\Longrightarrow$ +
B61	↑ P4:	AV(R) $\Longrightarrow$ R ← 7

A question of more substance arises from the fact that once a production occurs at some point in the protocol, a sequence of production occurrences is automatically generated by the outputs of one becoming the inputs of the next. Sometimes several members of this implied sequence happen within a node. An example occurs at B8, where FC $\Longrightarrow$ fail, so that two P1 productions occur within the node; another occurs at B7 (and several other places) where P11 produces an occurrence of TD for which no node occurs in the graph because TD $\Longrightarrow$ +. The question is whether to consider the set of production occurrences fixed in advance by the number of nodes in the problem graph or to expand it by the additional implied occurrences. We do the latter, consequently expanding the data set from 238 nodes to 275 production occurrences (an expansion of about 15 percent). Henceforth, when we refer to a node, we will mean a place where a production was (or should have been) evoked.

Now we are in a position to make an accounting of the productions. Considering each rule separately, the protocol provides all the positive occurrences. But there could also be a number of other nodes at which the conditions of the production were satisfied, but either some other production was evoked, or no recognizable production occurred (marked by ?). These are the negative instances. This information can be obtained by asking, for each node (i.e., each place where a production or ? occurs in the protocol) and for each production, whether its conditions are satisfied. These data appear at the end of the chapter in Appendix 6.2 in the *State-production Table*. This table was constructed by recording the expressions produced by the productions that actually occurred, and maintaining a goal stack. The horizontal lines in the table simply indicate when an exploration terminated and the arrows at the left show at what point the new exploration started. With this state information recorded, each production was matched at each context point and one of five marks made:

+	The conditions are satisfied and the production is evoked.
↑	The production was evoked at a prior node and is still in effect.
—	The conditions are satisfied but the production is not evoked.
?	The conditions may have been satisfied, but the production is not evoked.
blank	The conditions are not satisfied.

Notice that it is not possible for a production to be evoked when its conditions are not satisfied, for we do not recognize a production by its action part alone. For example, in B185 the action part is taken to be similar to that of P5, but a ? is coded for the production, since the condition for P5 (existence of the goal (check ⟨column-set⟩)) is not satisfied. However, we accept as evidence for the condition part either explicit data from the protocol or implicit data output by prior productions that have been evoked.

Figure 6.8 summarizes these data in a matrix. The columns refer to the productions that *did* occur at a node; the rows refer to the productions that *could have* occurred at a node. Thus the entry (i, j) of the (i)th row and (j)th column gives the number of times production i could have occurred, but instead production j did occur. The total number of times the (j)th production did occur is given by the diagonal entry (j, j). Each cell has two possible entries. The top one is the main one; it counts the nodes in which the conditions of a production were definitely satisfied, hence where the corresponding column of the State-production Table was marked with a plus (+) or minus (−). The lower number shows the additional nodes which were questionable, hence marked in the table with a question mark (?).

For any pair of productions, the symmetric pair of off-diagonal entries (i, j) and (j, i) tell how those productions fared against each other. If there were no nodes where conditions for both productions were satisfied, then both entries would be zero. We see that in the 10 cases in which P1 or P2 could have occurred, P1 did occur in 8, and P2 in 2. Similarly, in the cases in which either P3 or P4 could have occurred, P4 did occur 14 times and P3 did not occur at all (0).

These strong biases towards one production's dominating another are consistent with the imposition of a priority ordering on the set of production rules. We can attempt to impose a linear ordering on the productions, always placing production j above production i if the (i, j)th entry is greater than the (j, i)th entry. We do this in Figure 6.9.[8] In general this can lead to difficulties if there are intransitivities in the data, so that i precedes j and j precedes k, but k precedes i. However, we do not in fact meet this problem, since there are no intransitivities in the data. Note that the data are not everywhere equally numerous or unequivocal and that in several cases there are no data at all to specify the ordering. The three productions that are essentially isolates, P14, P5, and P8, are placed at the top, but they could equally well be anywhere in the ordering. The one additional rule we impose is that once a production is evoked, there is no opportunity for evoking new productions until its action part has run its course. Operationally, this means that ↑ has top priority of all.

The transitivity of the ordering does not imply that the priority system describes the data perfectly. Every nonzero entry above the diagonal in Figure 6.9 represents a case where the production lower on the priority order was in fact selected by the subject. The farther the entries are from the diagonal, the larger was the inversion.

---

[8] In constructing Figure 6.9 only the definite comparisons (the top entries in each cell) have been considered, and the questionable ones (? in the State-production Table) ignored. If the latter are added, however, the picture remains about the same. The tie between P12 and P10 is broken in the direction opposite from the way it is shown in Figure 6.9; in addition the ordering between P7 and P4 is reversed. Thus the four consecutive productions, P9, P4, P12, P7, would be reordered as P12, P9, P7, P4. This would introduce one intransitivity, in that the single comparison between P4 and P12 showed P4 to be preferred.

FIGURE 6.8

matrix of production occurrences (comparison of possible with actual occurrences)

PRODUCTION
DID OCCUR

	P1	P2	P3	P4	P5	P6	P7	P8	P9	P10	P11	P12	P13	P14	own ↑	↑	?
P1	35	2	0			3			0		24		3			18	6
P2	8	29	9	15		6	2			4	13		2			11	34
P3	4	16	9	14		3	1			4	9	1	7		16	19	19
P4		2	0	24			0		0	1	3	0	1		4		2
		2	2			1	3						2			4	3
P5					1										6		
P6	0	0	0			11			0		0						3
P7		0	0	1			8		0	5		9	11				9
P8								2									
					1												
P9	26					1		5	4		4	2	18	8	6		3	9
P10		0	0	0			0		0	7		4	3				3
							1					4	2				
P11	1	0	0	0		2			0		31		2			1	
	2					1							2			3	2
P12			0	1			5		0	4		10	11				9
P13	0	0	0	0			0		0	0	0	0	18		18		2
						1				1							1
P14															4		
own ↑															44		
↑																	
?																	38

PRODUCTION COULD OCCUR

FIGURE 6.9
matrix of Figure 6.8 reordered by priority

PRODUCTION
DID OCCUR

PRODUCTION
COULD
OCCUR

	P14	P5	P8	P6	P13	P11	P10	P4	P12	P7	P1	P2	P3	P9	own↑	↑	?	Ex
P14	4																	4
P5		1														6		7
P8			2															2
		1																
P6				11		0					0	0	0	0			3	11
					0		0											
P13						18	0	0	0	0	0	0	0	0	18		2	36
					1		1										1	
P11					2	2	31	0			1	0	0	0		1		31
					1	2					2					3	2	
P10						3	7	0	4	0	0	0	0				3	7
						2		4		1								
P4						1	3	1	24	0	0	2	0	0	4		2	28
						1	2			3		2	2			4	3	
P12						11			4	1	10	5	0	0			9	10
P7						11			5	1	9	8	0	0			9	8
P1				3	3	24					35	2	0	0	18		6	35
P2				6	2	13	4	15		2	8	29	9			11	34	29
P3				3	7	9	4	14	1	1	4	16	9		16	19	19	25
P9				5	6	18	2	1	8	4	26				4	3	9	4
own↑															44			
↑																		
?																	38	

Figure 6.10 provides a way of looking at the total performance of the production system. Some productions account for many items of behavior; some for only a few. Thus, one can add new productions, each increasing the total fraction of the protocol described, but with a diminishing marginal utility (especially if we view the extra production in the total description as a cost in terms of parsimony). In Figure 6.10 the productions are ordered by the total number of nodes they cover. P13 comes first with 38 occurrences; P8 comes last with 2.

FIGURE 6.10

summary of performance of production system for S3 on DONALD+GERALD=ROBERT

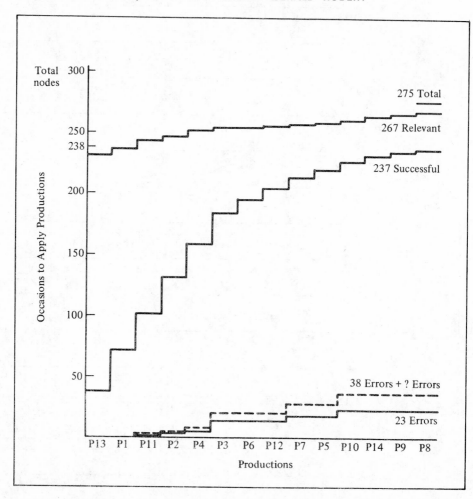

As we increase the number of productions in the system, two other changes occur simultaneously. The total number of nodes handled increases. Originally 238, the number of nodes in the PBG, it gradually increases to 275. As mentioned earlier, this increase is produced by carrying along subsequent evocations of productions to implied products as long as these are not contradicted by the data.

The top line in Figure 6.10 runs from 230 on the left to 267 on the right—8 nodes less than the total of 275 nodes. The smaller number is considered the relevant total, since eight contexts are clearly outside the problem space we are dealing with, involving conversations with the experimenter, discussions of the rules, and so on. The fraction of the protocol to which some production applies starts at 16 percent if P13 is the only production and climbs to 89 percent for all productions.

· Simultaneously with the increase in coverage, positive errors begin to occur—that is, nodes at which the wrong production is evoked. This is shown by the lower curve. The solid line, which corresponds to the definite errors, starts out at zero for P13 alone (since there is then no possibility of conflict of P13 with other productions) and climbs to 23 errors for the total system. The second (dotted) error curve adds the errors that have been labeled questionable; it rises to 38 for the total system. These error figures come from adding up the appropriate subsets of entries above the diagonal in the matrix in Figure 6.9.

If we penalize the system for its errors, then we might say that it had described $(237 - 23)/267 = 80$ percent of the protocol.[9] In fact, this number is not very informative, since it combines errors of omission (30) and errors of commission (23). Rather, we should be interested in understanding both of these types of errors to see why the system was unable to do better.

Errors of Omission

The failure to find a production (or sequence) that fits a segment of protocol has various causes, ranging from lack of data to inability to construct an appropriate mechanism. Below we discuss the types of failures under a series of ad hoc headings suggested by the omitted instances. Two instances illustrate more than one type of problem, so the total number of items listed is 40, rather than 38, the total number of ?-nodes.

Although we do not create a separate category, many of the failures are due implicitly to lack of information in the protocol. As a related point, it will be noted that most of the failures occur at terminations (26) or beginnings (8). However, failure to interpret the protocol leads to inferring termination, and not vice versa. Since lines of exploration are not very long, once the thread is lost, for whatever reason, it is unlikely to be picked up again until the subject has started a new line. In particular, the apparently obvious inference that, because most ?-nodes are terminals, the model makes most errors on evaluation is false. The frequency of such omissions is caused by the artifact just mentioned.

Evaluation. (B39, B119.1, B143.1, B183, B222.1, B238.1) There are several nodes where an evaluation is explicit, but we are unable to incorporate it. The decision to "forget it" at B39 is most explicit. B119.1 is an example where the subject clearly runs out of gas; but it is not clear how to stop the production system. In B143.1, S3 explicitly enunciates his options ($R \leftarrow 7$, $R \leftarrow 9$), then decides to keep the assignment ($R \leftarrow 7$). Part of the same dilemma is his decision to switch at B183 to ($R \leftarrow 9$), and also his decision to switch back at B238.1. In all of these episodes the subject

[9] If we add the questionable errors, we get $(237 - 38)/267 = 75$ percent.

shows some persistence, then finally backs down. We have no representation for this kind of evaluation process. A related pair of evaluations concern $(c_5 > 1)$. At B222.1 the subject chooses not to investigate $(c_5 > 1)$, whereas a little later, at B230, he does. The system only fails on one of these options, but in fact we face a general problem of formulating the effect of multiple branchings at the same decision point.

Selection of Prior Nodes.   (B97, B137, B175, B178.1, B217) Besides the immediate path and the initial situation, the subject appears to keep two additional nodes available in memory: the decision situation relating to the assignment of R and the one relating to E. A look at the total PBG in Figure 6.4 (page 181) reveals three substantial breaks in the continuity of the search (lines 16–18, 23, and 31). (The other apparent breaks, lines 7, 17, and 47, are all intermediate nodes where he backs up to a previous state.) The breaks are all oscillations between E and R, as is the one other that is hidden, when the subject decides to explore $(R \leftarrow 9)$ at line 34. We do not have any formulation that predicts these jumps. They might be handled partly by appropriate evaluation (a point already noted) in conjunction with a better treatment of the goal stack. That is, the return to E after a jump to R may occur because (get E) never leaves the goal stack, but is simply pushed down.

Memory Mechanisms.   (B158, B188.1, B275) A substantial number of memory mechanisms are assumed in the problem space as we have used it: knowledge of the current states, path memory, prior nodes, and a goal stack (see the State-production Table in Appendix 6.2). However, in a few places there is clear evidence of additional memory. At B158, the subject recalls that $E = 0$ leads to a contradiction (at B136). Although we assume memory of values assigned (required for the operation of TD), we do not provide for this more elaborate recognition that permits the subject by memory to go down the path he has traversed before. At B188.1 we have an immediate recovery from the error of setting $(L \leftarrow 9)$. Earlier, at B105, the error was the same, but the subject's process of recovering from it was much more involved. Although it is plausible that he would not stumble so badly the second time, we provide nothing in the production system to produce the quicker recovery. At B275 we have, first, a forgetting that is only partly explainable by the system, and then a recall for which we provide no mechanism.

The examples, though few, give the impression—strongly reinforced by much else known about human memory—that we need a more generalized memory, not completely tied to the service of the problem space. On occasion such a memory would deliver some information of value, although it could not be relied upon to do so.

Extensions of Production System.   (B90.1, B100, B110, B124, B148.1, B155.1, B201, B237, B238.1, B244, B303)   We include here examples of mechanisms that are similar to those incorporated in the production system, but which we were unable to formulate properly.

An important example is provided by operations that are digit-oriented. That is, instead of selecting a letter and finding a digit to assign to it, the subject sometimes selects a digit and finds a corresponding letter. The two examples in the protocol somewhat like this are close together. In B237 the subject, after asserting (E = 0 ☐), immediately asserts (A = 0 ☐). It appears the subject is finding all the letters that can't be paired with 0, now that he knows that 0 has already been assigned to T. In B238.1 the subject seems to be deciding whether to assign 9 to R or 9 to E; that is, the focus is the letter to be assigned to 9, not the digit to be assigned to a fixed letter.

A second important type of mechanism is induction, where the subject sees the general case from an examination of several specific instances. The one clear example is at B155.1, where the production system does not have too much difficulty incorporating the generation of values of O, but cannot make the inductive step to "Actually, that's almost the case no matter what the situation is—."

Most of the other mechanisms seem of lesser moment. The subject's third return to (get E) because he is unclear (B90.1), does not quite fit the production system. At B100 the subject makes the connection between "E is even" and "E cannot be 9," at least sufficiently to cause him to go back and check. There is no place yet in the system for such partial glimpses. At B110 the gap should be successfully bridged by setting up a goal to check, but this does not seem to work. B124 (and its repetition, B148.1) apparently involves the subject's seeing that, since he is already assigning a value to E (P3), he would be better off to assign the value to O rather than A. The key seems already to be in the behavior of the production system in producing (O unknown), since if the prior scheme didn't lead to determining O, then it would be preferable to assign O directly. However, there remains a gap from (O unknown) to his application of P3 at column 5. At B201 there is apparently a switch to exploiting (R ← 9), rather than (get E), once (R ← 9) becomes the focus of attention via (R ← 9 note). At B244 it is quite clear that the subject thinks initially in terms of the full digit set (*all-digits*) and then transforms his analysis to use only the remaining digits (*free-digits*). At B281–B282 the same reasoning process is repeated, but much more smoothly (and without an omission error, as it happens). The production system could probably be extended to handle this; the main requirement is to make the internal structure of GN and AV explicit. Finally, at B303 we have no means of evoking the final checking operation. We could have written a production that reacted to the final positive solution. Actually, this is only indicated in a negative way in the current system, by FL ⇒ fail. Thus, two productions would be required probably: one to say "Eureka"; the other to say, "if Eureka, then check."

Interaction with External Problem Space. (B185) The main justification for not making explicit the writing operations is that in this protocol they do not appear to affect very much what goes on in the internal problem space. B185 is one exception, not only in terms of the subject's ability to have two external displays, but also in his having a copy operation that takes information from one to build the other. A second example, not recorded as an omission, occurs at B12, where the response to finding D in c6 is to write 5 for D, rather than to process c6. We might have found more interactions, especially in attention control, if we had incorporated in the system a set of writing productions and thus tried to determine the conditions under which writing would be evoked.

Extensions of the Problem Space. (B1, B39, B50, B169, B224.1, B225, B317, B318, B319, B320) All but two of these, B39 and B169, constitute the situations that were so far outside the problem space that they were considered irrelevant to evaluating the performance of the production system. Several of these instances, B1, B50, B169, B224.1, B225, and B320, involve interactions with the experimenter. To handle these would require a quite new problem space (assuming that to be the appropriate construct), and one that should not be constructed on such skimpy data. However, if one had developed the general characteristics of such a model elsewhere, one might import it here with good effect. The extensions relate to areas immediately bordering the task itself: concern with the rules (B1, B50); concern with new methods (B39); concern with whether the top goal is to find a single solution or all solutions (B317, B318, B319); and the exit from the problem space to the larger world (B320). Some of these areas conceivably could be developed as problem spaces, but they would be more complex than the one we have worked with. For example, development of a space of methods for solving cryptarithmetic problems is decidedly nontrivial (as we shall note in the next chapter).

As to other types of behavior in this group, B169 is the one clear example of the injection of emotionally toned behavior. B224.1 and B225 are task-oriented behavior by the experimenter.

Blank Periods. (B30.1, B85.1, B103.1, B114.1) The last group of omissions are those that show extended periods of silence, usually broken by the experimenter's asking the subject to continue to talk. Clearly, the PBG of Figure 6.3 does not show the full extent of S3's exploration. However, if he obtained critical information about the solution during this period, we would expect it to show up at some later time. There is no clear evidence of this. It seems more likely that these silences are mainly periods when the subject does not know how to proceed.

Errors of Commission

The 38 errors (23 definite, 15 questionable) in which the wrong production was evoked according to the established priority scheme are best discussed by considering the various pairings. Table 6.1 analyzes the errors in this way. The top row, P3/P2, treats the cases where P3 was chosen over P2, although the priority ordering (Figure 6.9) indicates that P2 should be chosen over P3. The second column shows how far apart the two rules are in the priority ordering; in the case of P3 and P2 they are adjacent. The third column shows the number of occurrences of each preference. Thus in 25 co-occurrences, P2 was chosen 16 times and P3 9 times; thus the number of errors is 9, out of 25 co-occurrences. The next column gives similar numbers for questionable errors—in this case there were none. Finally, the nodes at which these errors occur are listed. Where questionable errors are recorded, we prefix the nodes with question marks (?) to distinguish them from nodes with definite errors. More than one error can occur at a node. This happened four times, in each case a questionable error occurring along with a definite error. We have noted these cases in parentheses; e.g., the bottom row shows that the single error of choosing P7 over P10 involved also choosing P7 over P12.

TABLE 6.1

errors of commission

ERROR PAIR	SEPARATION	DEFINITE ERRORS	QUESTIONABLE ERRORS	NODES
P3/P2	1	9/16		B40, B104, B120, B125, B144, B149, B186, B189, B218
P7/P12	1	5/9		B158.1, B203.3/2, B227.1, B229.2, B243.1/2
P12/P10	2	4/4	4/0	B106.2, B203.2, B234.1, B243.1; ?B136, ?B229.1, ?B238, ?B269
P2/P4	4	2/15	2/0	B116, B139; ?B111, ?B299
P2/P1	1	2/8		B85, B290.1
P1/P11	5	1/24	2/0	B207; ?B129, ?B278
P7/P4	2	0/1	3/0	?B158.1 (see P7/P12), ?B265, ?B269/2
P3/P4	5	0/14	2/0	?B104 (see P3/P2), ?B218 (see P3/P2)
P10/P13	2	0/3	1/2	?B94
P7/P10	3	0/5	1/0	?B227.1 (see P7/P12)
		23/	15/	

P3/P2, P3/P4. The difficulty here is that we do not have the appropriate discriminators to tell when P3 is evoked. The nine errors constitute *all* occasions on which P3 was evoked. P3 is clearly a secondary method; it is never evoked until after P2 has been tried at least twice.

The total number of errors (9) is deceptive, either as a measure of an amount of error or as a sample from which to diagnose what is wrong. There appear to be only three essentially independent evocations of P3: in getting R at B40, E at B120, and E at B218. The rest involves various degrees of repetition. B104 repeats B40, as does B186 when the subject starts over with $(R \leftarrow 9)$ instead of $(R \leftarrow 7)$; and B189 is an immediate repeat of B186 due to an error in executing the latter. B125 is the shift of B120 to try it on column 5 with O rather than on column 3 with A; this whole pattern is repeated in B144 and B149. Consequently, how many errors have really occurred here is quite uncertain. They are not independent, but the acts of repetition themselves are part of what is to be explained.

P7/P12, P7/P4. P7 is the production that converts a failure into a goal of establishing the value of the variable just affected. Of the eight occurrences, all but one are implicated in some error, so that P7 clearly is of marginal efficacy. Even more significant, when a moderately careful account is taken of goals (see State-production Table), five of the above eight occur when the goal is already at the top of the stack. Perhaps the same is true of (B243.1/2), for the system has been attending to obtaining O for some time before running into the difficulty that sets the goal of obtaining O. In the other two cases (B203.3/2 and B229.2) a genuine switch of attention is made by P7. Both of these involve the carry and are among the most obscure passages in the protocol. In short, with only slight modifications of the system one might dispense with P7 altogether.

207

P12/P10, P7/P10, P10/P13. The issue here is under what conditions a critical feature will trigger off the attempt to check it. As we observed earlier, we did not add additional discriminating conditions to P10, even though it is clear that discrimination is necessary. Thus, all four of the questionable errors on P12/P10 as well as the P7/P10 error are due to the subject's never checking (D ← 5 note) or (T ← 0 note), except the latter after the experimenter brings it to his attention. These are not open to much uncertainty. One can find plausible reasons in the four cases of definite error why there is little sense in checking. However, no clear pattern emerges, especially when these instances are viewed against the times when checking is evoked. More generally, there is a relatively thin line between getting a value and checking a value, and our explication of this distinction is only marginally satisfactory.

The one case where P10 is preferred over P13 is worth noting, since it is one of the few places in the protocol where a critical feature is generated by a process other than TD. The protocol at B94 is quite clear on the attention directed at (c3 = 0). However, it is possible that B95 reflects a much more general switch to a concern with R—this happens elsewhere in the protocol. In fact, B95 provides a nice instance of ambiguity about the antecedent of "this."

P2/P4. All four errors in this case involve repetition in some way, and show that our system is not explicit enough about exactly what things are remembered from the past and how processing is handled when guided by the past. The two definite errors (B116 and B139) both involve repeating the final path of a previous branched exploration. In both cases this implies not repeating the generation of values for the constrained variable. In one questionable error (?B111) it is unclear where the starting point is in repeating R; even if it were started from (R odd), the previous concern about whether to repeat the generation still applies. The issue in the last error (?B299) is a little different. In obtaining a value for B via PC [column 4] the subject is sidetracked because he errs in determining the set of available digits. Having cleared this matter up, the subject returns to get B. He now has a simple way to get to B via a repeat of PC (which is what he does), or he can generate values from the restricted set and assign one of them. This kind of choice only occurs at this one point in the protocol. In all other places where P4 occurs there is no such alternative.

P2/P1. One of these errors (B85) is simply an ambiguity. Both P1 and P2 lead to exactly the same result—namely, the determination of c6. The other error (B290.1) occurs in the midst of a context of processing larger than the new information that 1 is carried out of column 4. This test sequence requires first deriving (c5 = 1) and then returning to test N. Our production system is not constructed in this way. Even if one tried to model the method by a direct recall of (c5 = 1), the error would still occur. Here the system has not captured the higher level of organization adequately.

P1/P11. In all three of these errors the main question is whether the relation produced is new or not. It is clear generally that the subject does not evoke TD on old material. As we will see, the issue is critical for the subject—and not just for us—since the failure to evoke TD on $E = 0$ at B129 and again at B207 is part of *his* major difficulty in solving the problem. The definite error here occurs at B207; however, this may well be an analogous repetition for the $(R \leftarrow 9)$ case of the prior processing for the $(R \leftarrow 7)$ case. The correspondent of B207 is B129. This seems to be a questionable error (for us), since $(E = 0)$ has already occurred several times. The last questionable error (?B278) occurs very late in the protocol when $(E = 9)$ and $(A = 4)$ are rederived; it is not clear whether they should be treated as new or not.

Any discussion of errors is only partial and is fundamentally biased, since it takes place against a background of choices about how to fashion the production system. A number of these errors could have been transformed into nonerrors by modification of the production system. Of course an equivalent number of errors (actually somewhat more, in the cases investigated during the course of analysis) would have shown up elsewhere. Still, this discussion provides some feeling for the places where the system is weak, and what some remedial actions might be.

THE BASIC PROCESSES

So far in the analysis we have introduced a set of processes that have been defined only by rough input/output descriptions: the main operators, PC, GN, AV, TD, and the auxiliary processes, FC, FA, FL, FP, GNC. Our descriptions were sufficient for the purpose—namely, to identify the occurrences of a process of the specified type in the data. One can determine that a column is being processed, and even know exactly the information output, without being able to specify just how that output was produced.

The use we have made of these processes, both in the PBG and in the productions, implies that a single process is to be associated with each name, and not merely that these names stand for types of processes. That is, the processes are to be subroutines. We should be able to write down expressions for them in some process language, in such a way that the entire variation of output is determined by the variation of input. Stated otherwise: to predict the output of processes we should not have to appeal to information, other than the specified inputs, about the context in which they occur.

To the extent that this condition does not hold, the total errors in our description of the subject are underestimated, since some production occurrences will be judged correct when in fact an algorithmic specification of the basic processes that would be consistent with other occurrences of the process would lead to an error. Consequently, the errors in describing the basic processes need investigation. However, they should not necessarily be combined with the errors in the production system, since it is quite possible for the productions to be correct, even if the basic processes are faulty; e.g., the subject may make errors in arithmetic, while the processes postulate that he always adds correctly. The present context does not provide sufficient evidence to predict why such errors are made or when. Such errors are assigned properly to the processes underlying PC and do not invalidate the productions that use PC. At some point, of course, if such errors are too numerous, they compromise the entire system. But we have independent knowledge that human subjects do make errors of perception, memory, and elementary processing; hence a division of errors is appropriate.

To explicate the basic processes fully, we must postulate yet another set of processes (call them BB, for *basic-basic* processes) in terms of which the basic processes themselves can be described. Consideration of the basic processes shows that the BB-processes are at the level of elementary operations of perception, immediate memory, and accessing of long-term memory. FC, for example, involves a visual exploration of the board under the direction of already assimilated information about the structure of the task display; it might take less than a second. Even the most complex of our basic processes, PC, involves operations of the order of adding a pair of digits or recalling the known properties of a letter (e.g., $R > 5$). Thus, a model for the BB-processes is in fact a detailed model of immediate memory and immediate processing.

This volume is not the appropriate place for such an analysis. We will provide rather informal and incomplete treatment, examining the input/output correspondences for evidence of inconsistency or complexity of processing that seems incommensurate with regarding these processes as basic.

We group below, in six subsections, discussions of each of the nine basic processes. The numbers in parentheses in the section titles are the numbers of occurrences of each process. Each section also has a table that lists each occurrence with its input and output.

Process Column (88)

The most complex of the basic processes, PC, also occurs often enough to provide considerable information about its nature. If PC were simply a routine for adding pairs of numbers (as in $5 + 5 \Rightarrow T = 0$, $c2 = 1$), understanding its internal mechanism would be synonymous with understanding how a human does arithmetic. As noted above, this involves the detailed structure of immediate memory, and the detailed handling of attention. But even more is involved, since PC generates a rather wide variety of final responses. In fact, the power of S3's problem solving hinges strongly on the sophistication of PC. (This is evident if S3's behavior is compared with that of subjects whose PC admits only of simple arithmetic.)

Information about the 88 occurrences of PC is given in Table 6.2. The diversity of processing apparent in the table implies that even if PC is in some sense a single subroutine, it is a highly conditional one. Hence, the key question is whether some underlying uniform scheme of processing can yield this diversity. To provide some feeling for what is involved we can sketch a system that might perform somewhat in the manner of S3's PC operation (Figure 6.11). Basically, the system performs a series of arithmetic *operations*, taking an *operand* as input, to create a *value*, which can then be packaged with the *unknown* to form an output expression for PC. Operations can also affect the unknown, so that it is necessary to specify the *target* for each operation—i.e., either the value or the unknown.

FIGURE 6.11

arrangement of memory for PC

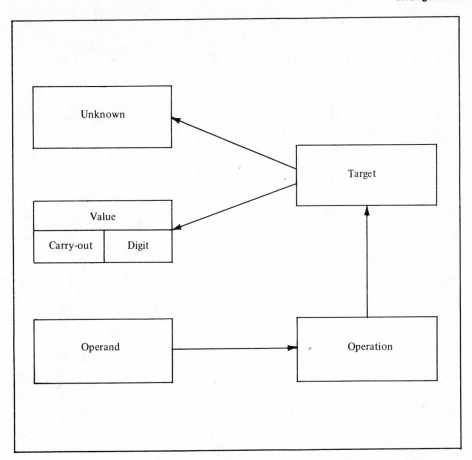

The system starts in the context of a particular goal and column, as depicted in Table 6.2, with all five elements of Figure 6.11 undefined. A set of productions, the initial productions of the system of Figure 6.12, define these elements from the context. The u-productions define the unknown, the v-productions define the value, the single o-production defines the operand, the t-productions define the target and the q-productions define the operator. After these first productions have done their work, everything is defined so that production p1 can be evoked to perform the operation. Following p1 are a number of a-productions that analyze the results of the operation, either causing new operations to be performed or simply packaging the output expression.

The complexities of PC arise in large part from the varieties of symbol structures that must be combined. Thus, the operations can be called upon to deal with digits, with parity-values (i.e., even and odd), with inequality-values (e.g., > 5),

TABLE 6.2
occurrences of PC

N	ITEM	GOAL	COLUMN	CARRY-IN	TOP	+ MIDDLE	= BOTTOM	CARRY-OUT	RESULT
1	B5		col.1	0	5	5	T		$T = 0$; $c2 = 1$
2	B20	R	col.2	1	L	L	R		R odd
3	B23	R	col.2	1	L	L	R		R odd
4	B32	R	col.6		5	G	R [odd]		G even
5	B36	G	col.6		5	G	odd		c6u
6	B44	R	col.2	1	1	1	R		$R = 3$
7	B47		col.6		5	G	3		$c7 = 1u$
8	B49	$c7 = 1$	col.7	[1]					□ (zln)
9	B58	R	col.6		5	G	R	0	$R > 5$
10	B62		col.2	1	L	L	7		$L = 3$
11	B65	L	col.2	1	L	L	7		$L = 3$
12	B74		col.6		5	G	7		$G = 1 \lor 2$; c6u
13	B78	c6	col.5		O	E	O		$E = 0$
14	B81	E	col.5		O	E	O		$E = 0$
15	B83	E	col.5		O	E	O		$E = 9$; $c5 = 1$
16	B85	c6	col.5	1	O	9	O		$c6 = 1$
17	B86	E	col.5		O	E	O		[unclear]
18	B92	E	col.3	0	A	A	E		E even; $c3 = 0n$
19	B95	$c3 = 0$	col.2	1	3	3	7	[0]	$+$; $R = 7n$
20	B98	E	col.3	0	A	A	E		E even
21	B101	E	col.5		O	E	O		$E = 0 \lor 9$
						[even]			
22	B106	R	col.2	1	9	9	R		$R = 9$
23	B108	R	col.2	1	9	9	R		$R = 9$
24	B111	R	col.6		5	G	R	0	$R > 5$
25	B115	E	col.3	0	A	A	E		E even
26	B116	E	col.5		O	E	O		$E = 0$; $c5 = 0u$
						[even]			
27	B118	$c5 = 0$	col.4		N	7	B	[0]	$N < 3$
28	B123	E	col.3	0	x	x	E		$E = y$
29	B123.1		col.5		O	y	O		Ou
30	B128	E	col.5		9	E	9		$E = 0$
31	B129		col.3	0	A	A	0		$A = 5$
32	B132	A	col.3	0	A	A	0		$A = 5$
33	B138	R	col.2	1	L	L	R		R odd
34	B139	R	col.6		5	G	R	0	$R > 5$
35	B147.1	E	col.3	0	x	x	E		$E = y$
36	B148		col.5		O	y	O		Ou
37	B152	E	col.5		1	E	1		$E = 9$; $c5 = 1$
38	B154.1	E	col.5		2	E	2		$E = 9$; $c5 = 1$
39	B156	E	col.5		x	E	x		$E = 9$; $c5 = 1$
40	B157	E	col.5		x	E	x		$E = 0$
41	B160		col.5		O	9	O		$c5 = 1$
42	B161.1		col.5		O	9	O		$c6 = 1$
43	B162		col.6	1	5	G	7	0	$G = 1$

FIGURE 6.13

differences for PC

	DIGIT	PARITY	INEQUALITY	QUANTITY
DIGIT	d-d use digit arithmetic undefine operand	d-p convert digit to parity	d-i use digit arithmetic undefine operand	d-q convert quantity to inequality
PARITY		p-p use parity arithmetic undefine operand	p-i convert parity to inequality	p-q even: ⟨letter⟩ ⟶ convert quantity to parity
INEQUALITY			i-i same sense ⟶ use digit arithmetic undefine operand	i-q convert quantity to inequality
QUANTITY				q-q same letter ⟶ use digit arithmetic undefine operand

production and the resulting output values. Initially, all elements are undefined. The first production evoked is u5, which defines T as the unknown. None of the conditions of the prior productions (u1 to u4) was satisfied. The next production, v1, defines 5 as the value. Next, production o1 defines the other 5 as the operand. Next, production t1 is evoked to determine that the operation will modify the value (rather than the unknown). The last of the defining productions, q1, specifies addition as the operation. At this point, p1 attempts to perform the addition. Since both the operand and the value are digits, this is possible, giving 10 for the value. Also, *operand* becomes undefined again (indicated by a ∅). The d-d in the column marked

FIGURE 6.14

operation of PC on 5 + 5 = T

Context:

N	ITEM	GOAL	COLUMN	CARRY-IN	TOP + MIDDLE = BOTTOM	CARRY-OUT	RESULT
1	B5		col.1	0	5 5 T		T = 0; c2 = 1

Trace of system:

PRODUC- TION	UNKNOWN	VALUE CARRY-OUT	OPERAND DIGIT	TARGET	OPERA- TION	CONVER- SION	RESULT
u5	T						
v1		5					
o1			5				
t1				value			
q1					add		
p1		1 0	∅			d-d	
a2							(T=0); (c2=1)

215

conversion indicates that this was a case of digit-versus-digit addition. The next pass through the production system evokes a2, which decomposes the 10 into a digit and a carry as shown and provides the output expressions.

Let us consider next a somewhat more complex case: the inference that R is odd (line 2 of Table 6.2). As shown in Figure 6.15, the processing proceeds similarly to the initial example through the first five productions, which define all the elements. Finally, p1 is evoked. It finds that the two inputs, value and operand, are both quantities with the same letter (L). Thus, they can be added to get 2:L. Next, production a5 converts the 2:L into even. After this, c1 sets operand to be 1. The operation is redefined as addition by production q1. Now p1 finds a parity-value for value versus a digit for operand (p-d). This condition evokes a conversion of the digit to a parity-value (see Figure 6.13), after which p1 can add them, to obtain odd as the final value. Production a10 produces the final result, (R odd).

FIGURE 6.15
operation of PC on 1 + L + L = R

Context:										
N	ITEM	GOAL	COLUMN	CARRY-IN	TOP +	MIDDLE =	BOTTOM	CARRY-OUT	RESULT	
2	B20	R	col.2	1	L	L	R		R odd	

Trace of System:							
PRODUC- TION	UNKNOWN	VALUE CARRY-OUT	OPERAND DIGIT	TARGET	OPERA- TION	CONVER- SION	RESULT
u3	R						
v1		L					
o1			L				
t1				value			
q1					add		
p1		2:L	ϕ			q-q	
a5		even					
c1			1	value	ϕ		
q1					add		
p1			odd			p-d	
p1		odd	ϕ			p-p	
a10							(R odd)

Figure 6.16 shows a case where the unknown is the target (line 10 of Table 6.2). The addition of the two L's produces 2:L; subtraction of the carry from the digit produces 6 as the new value of the digit; and, finally, a division is performed to produce (L = 3).

The system of Figures 6.11, 6.12, and 6.13 is not meant as a formal model of S3's PC operator. Although it explains many of the cases where S3 evokes PC, there are a number of minor variations with which it has trouble. For example, the handling of column 5 (O + E = O) is still awkward. Also, there remain a few concepts, such as trying for the maximum value (line 64 of Table 6.2), that are not represented in the production system. However, the main reason for our not wishing to consider the system a model of the subject's arithmetic is simply our desire to avoid a detailed consideration of his immediate memory and immediate processing.

What the system does show is (1) that it is possible to represent by a production system the kinds of inferences and operations carried out by S3's PC; (2) that there are no gross inconsistencies in S3's PC;[10] and (3) that a great deal of knowledge stored in S3's memory is required for such a diversified operator.

FIGURE 6.16

operation of PC on 1 + L + L = 7

Context:

N	ITEM	GOAL	COLUMN	CARRY-IN	TOP	+ MIDDLE	= BOTTOM	CARRY-OUT	RESULT
10	B62			1	L	L	7		L = 3

Trace of system:

PRODUC-TION	UNKNOWN	CARRY-OUT	DIGIT	OPERAND	TARGET	OPERA-TION	CONVER-SION	RESULT
u4	L							
v2			7					
o1				L				
t2					unknown			
q1						add		
p1	2:L			φ			q-q	
c1			1		value	φ		
q2						subtract		
p1			6	φ			d-d	
a8	L			2	value	divide		
p1			3	φ			d-d	
a10								(L = 3)

Writing the system as a production system reveals that no intricate numerical algorithm is required to do the task of PC. Each production constitutes a bit of partial knowledge that a human of the skills of S3 might have. This is also true of the entries in the conversion matrix of Figure 6.13.

One interesting regularity is apparent in Table 6.2. The carry from the previous column is attended to only after the other operands. There are eleven instances in the data in which some evidence is available on the order of addition (B20, B23, B36, B65, B182, B271, B276, B306, B309, B313, B315), and in all of these the carry is dealt with last. Furthermore, there is no evidence of any kind for the carry's being considered at any other position (such as picking up the first operand, adding in the carry, and then dealing with the second operand). This issue bears on another one—namely, whether the carry is not sometimes disregarded entirely. There are

[10] The original research report may be consulted for an earlier version of this production system, where an attempt was made to provide a trace for each entry of Table 6.2.

three occasions (B20, B32-36, B78-81-83), all at the beginning, where the carry is not attended to at first. However, it is always discovered eventually, and throughout the remainder of the protocol the assumption fits best that the carry will always be taken into account. Very often, of course, when the carry is 0 or when it is undefined, nothing in the protocol indicates explicitly that the carry has been noted.

Generate Variable (27), Assign Value (27)

These two processes (see Tables 6.3 and 6.4) are discussed together, since AV(variable) can be viewed as:

$$\text{AV(variable): GN(variable)} (\Longrightarrow \text{digit}); \text{associate(variable, digit)}$$

Associate (variable, digit) is essentially the operation that occurs in a standard paired-associate learning task, where variable is the stimulus and digit the response (or vice versa, since recall can be via either variable or digit, and this may modify

TABLE 6.3

occurrences of GN

N	ITEM	PROD.	VAR.	SET	RESULT	NOTES
1	B26	S4	R	odd	$1 \lor 3 \lor 5 \lor 7 \lor 9$	
2	B59	S4	R	odd, > 5	$7 \lor 9$	
3	B96	S4	R	odd, > 5	$7 \lor 9$	repeat B59
4	B98.1	S4	E	even	$2 \lor 4 \lor 6 \lor 8$	
5	B140	S4	R	odd, > 5	$7 \lor 9$	repeat B59
6	B150	↑S3	O	ds	1	
7	B154	↑S3	O		2	} one generation
8	B155	↑S3	O		interrupted	
9	B159	S4	E	$0, 9; -0$	9	
10	B178	S4	R	$7, 9; -7$	9	
11	B182.4	S4	R	odd, > 5	$7 \lor 9$	
12	B204	S4	c5	$0, 1; -1$	0	
13	B211.2	S4	L	> 5	6	
14	B215	S4	R	$7, 9$	$7, 9$	possible R odd, > 5 instead
15	B223	S4	E	$0, 9$	$0, 9$	
16	B228	S4	E	$0, 9$	$0, 9$	repeat B223
17	B235	S4	E	0	0	
18	B239	S4	E	$0, 9; -0$	9	
19	B242.1	S4	O	free(ds)	1	
20	B248	S4	O	free(fds)	ϕ	
21	B262.1	S4	L	> 5	6	
22	B268	S4	L		7	} one generation
23	B270	S4	L		8	
24	B285	S4	N	fds	$3, 6$	
25	B291	S4		fds	$3, 6$	repeat B285
26	B298	S4	N	fds	2	
27	B301/3	S4	O	fds	2	

the way the subject stores the information). Also, one of the components (variable) remains in view at all times, even though embedded in a display. Actually, 13 of the 27 occurrences of AV are essentially just associate, since a single value has been delivered externally, either by GN (in P4) or because P3 goes slowly enough for us to see the generation going on (B150–B154). Whether the association is actually made by creating symbol structures, as is implied by our formulation of the problem space with expressions (D ← 5), or by a designation such that (find digit of D ⇒ 5), is not determined. However, the performance of the system is not affected by the choice.

There are five cases where AV assigns a digit-variable as value—e.g., (O ← x) at B248. These symbols simply stand for a general value and are not more complex than digits. There is certainly no difficulty assuming that the associate process can associate such symbols. However, the assumption does imply additional structure to that shown above. In particular, some processes must evoke the bypassing of GN and the switch into the abstract mode. Not enough data exist in the present situation to pin down the mechanism; indeed it is clear that more than one mecha-

TABLE 6.4

occurrences of AV

N	ITEM	PROD.	VAR.	SET	RESULT	NOTES
1	B42	S3	L	ds	L ← 1	
2	B61	↑S4	R	7, 9	R ← 7	
3	B105	S3	L	7, 9; −7	L ← 9	
4	B120	S3	A	ds	A ← x	
5	B125	S3	O	ds	O ← 9	
6	B143	↑S4	R	7, 9	R ← 7, R ← 9	
7	B147	S3	A	ds	A ← x	repeat B120
8	B150	↑S3	O	1	O ← 1	
9	B154	↑S3	O	2	O ← 2	
10	B155/1	?	O	?	O ← x	
11	B159	S4	E	9	E ← 9	
12	B178	S4	R	9	R ← 9	
13	B182.4	S4	R	7, 9; −7	R ← 9	
14	B186	S3	L	9	L ← 9	repeat B105
15	B189	S3	R	9	R ← 9	
16	B204	S4	c5	0	c5 ← 0	only t
17	B211.2	S4	L	6	L ← 6	
18	B219	S3	O	−0, −9	O ← 8	
19	B239	S4	E	9	E ← 9	
20	B248	S4	O	ϕ	O ← x	
21	B262.1	S4	L	6	L ← 6	
22	B268	S4	L	7	L ← 7	
23	B270	S4	L	8	L ← 8	
24	B288	S4	N	3, 6	unclear	
25	B289	R1	N	3, 6	N ← x	
26	B294	S4	N	3, 6	N ← 6	
27	B301/3	S4	O	2	O ← 2	

nism is involved. B120 and its repetition, B147, involve a kind of planning; whereas B248 is a way to indicate that O is taken care of, even though its value is unknown until the end.

If we add the remaining nine cases of AV, which contain a buried GN, we have a total of 36 cases of GN. The main form of this process, accounting for 24 cases, starts at the low member of the set and generates values in ascending order. Included in this total are three cases in which the set has one or no elements. Also included is B98.1, which generates (E even) starting from 2 rather than from 0. This is undoubtedly what occurred (only programmers start counting from 0), even though for the problem at hand 0 is the correct starting place. (A consequence of this will be apparent later.)

A somewhat different mechanism seems to be operating in six other cases, which involve a two-element set, one member of which has been adjudged not to be possible ($\square$) just prior to the evocation of GN. The proximity to this new information implies that the basic set of values has not yet been modified; indeed, one can view GN as performing this updating. This could be accomplished, of course, by a generate-and-test, using GN and TD. However, with only a two-element set there is the strong possibility that there is a mechanism that amounts to the rule: pick the other one. The coexistence of the two mechanisms is possible, since unique clues for evoking it are clearly present. In general, an organism with a small immediate memory may be expected to handle small sets quite differently from large ones, which must necessarily involve serial generation.

This leaves six cases of GN unexplained. Three of these are unimportant, involving either incomplete GN's for which no information is available (B155, B288), or an already discussed unsatisfactory situation, which is probably digit-centered rather than letter-centered (B235). The final three cases give evidence both that a set of values exists and that generation begins with the top value in the set, rather than the bottom one (they involve generation of only a single value). In the two cases where (O ← 9)(B125) and (O ← 8)(B219) there are complexities involved that we can sense, but have not captured in our formal scheme. For instance, by assigning 9 to the letter O, the dilemma for (E = 0 ∨ 9) is resolved. Likewise, (O ← 8) is probably confused with (E = 8), since it evokes (c5 = 2) [or is determined by (c5 = 2), a shift of interpretation we explored, but discarded, at an earlier stage of the analysis]. The final case of generating from the top, at B294, leads to the selection of (N ← 6) instead of (N ← 3). This follows upon an extensive comparison of the consequences of each value, which apparently ended indecisively. The failure here is our inability to discover the additional considerations that went into the decision.

Test Digit (31)

TD(letter, digit) consists of two separate parts, as shown in Figure 6.17: one checks whether the digit is available; the other checks whether the digit satisfies all the constraints known to hold for the letter. For the present subject, who appears to work from letters to digits, if any letter is associated with the given digit, it presumably need not be tested to see if it is the given letter. That is, we find no instances in Table 6.5 (which gives TD occurrences) in which TD was evoked with a variable that already had a value. In the other direction, however, it is possible for the letter to be constrained, hence for the given digit to lie outside the admissible set for the letter. This happens in three cases, two for (R > 5) and one for (E even). Whether these two parts of TD are done in the order shown, the inverse order, or as a single access to a compound stimulus (letter, digit) is unclear. The order may vary with the circumstances, letter first and then digit, when a new assignment is being proposed, but digit first during a generation of digits. Such variation, of course, requires either that TD be two different processes or that there be enough conditional structure in TD to permit adaptation to circumstances. Additional structure is indicated, at least for B229, where two values of E are discarded, one because T = 0, the other because R ← 9.

TABLE 6.5

occurrences of TD

N	ITEM	PRODUCTION	LETTER	DIGIT	RESULT OF TEST	NOTES
1	B7	P11	T	0	+	
2	B28	P11	R	$1 \lor 3 \lor 5 \lor 7 \lor 9$	$R = 5 \square (D \leftarrow 5n)$	
3	B45	P11	R	3	+	
4	B60	P11	R	$7 \lor 9$	+	
5	B63	P11	R	3	$L = 3 \square (R = 3 \square n)$	
6	B66	P11	L	3	+	
7	B84	P11	E	9	+	
8	B99	P11	E	$2 \lor 4 \lor 6 \lor 8$	+	
9	B103	P11	E	9	$E = 9 \square (E \text{ even } n)$	
10	B106.1	P11	R	9	$R = 9 \square (L \leftarrow 9n)$	
11	B131	P11	A	5	$A = 5 \square (D \leftarrow 5n)$	
12	B135	P11	A	5	$A = 5 \square (D \leftarrow 5n)$	repeat
13	B163	P11	G	1	+	
14	B188	P11	R	9	$R = 9 \square (L \leftarrow 9n)$	repeat
15	B190/2	P11	L	4	+	
16	B200	P11	E	9	$E = 9 \square (R \leftarrow 9n)$	
17	B203.2	P11	E	9	$E = 9 \square (R \leftarrow 9n)$	
18	B209	P11	A	5	$A = 5 \square (D \leftarrow 5n)$	
19	B213	P11	R	3	$R = 3 \square (R > 5n)$	
20	B224	P11	E	9	$E = 9 \square (R \leftarrow 9n)$	
21	B229	P11	E	$0 \lor 9$	$E = 0 \lor 9 \square$ $(T = 0n, R \leftarrow 9n)$	
22	B233	P11	B	8	$B = 8 \square (O \leftarrow 8n)$	
23	B236	P11	E	0	$E = 0 \square (T = 0n)$	
24	B243	P11	O	1	$O = 1 \square (G = 1n)$	
25	B262.3	P11	R	3	$R = 3 \square (R > 5n)$	
26	B268.2	P11	R	5	$R = 5 \square (D \leftarrow 5n)$	
27	B273	P11	R	7	+	
28	B293	P11	N	$3 \lor 6$	+	
29	B295.1	P11	B	3	$B = 3 \square (\text{f-d} = \phi n)$	
30	B300	P11	B	3	+	
31	B301	P11	O	2	+	

The only other noteworthy occurrence of TD is at B295.1, where the subject becomes aware that if he permits the conclusion that $B = 3$, no other digits will be available, even though a letter (O) is still unassigned. Clearly this inference does not come from the program as given in Figure 6.12, but requires other processing. If our model had some way of handling noticing, this event could be handled differently (as could B202–203, which raises some of the same issues).

FIGURE 6.17
program for TD

TD(letter.1, digit.1);
1. find letter of digit.1,
        if letter $\neq$ letter.1 stop TD and report
            (letter.1 = digit.1 □), (letter = digit.1 note);
2. generate constraint-expression of letter.1:
3.   test if constraint-expression admits digit.1,
                if yes continue,
                if no stop TD and report
                    (letter.1 = digit.1 □), (constraint-expression note),
        if completed stop and report +.

Find Column (64)

The defined input to FC is the variable whose column is being sought. Thus, we require additional mechanism when more than one column involves the given variable. Table 6.6 shows the alternative outputs in the column labeled *Others*. For a carry, both the column that determines it and the adjacent column that uses it are listed. Among the 64 cases there are ten that are repetitions of other occurrences of FC (noted in column labeled *Notes*) and another eight that have uniquely determined columns; these raise no further issues. For the other 46, the key feature seems to be whether the sought-for variable has been processed on the current column or not. This is indicated in the table by a yes or no in the column labeled *Column Done?*, which is left blank if the subject is not attending to any particular column. Suppose we assume the rules:

Rule 1: If current column is unprocessed for the variable ($-$), always select current column.

Rule 2: If current column is already processed for variable ($+$), do not select current column.

The first rule accounts for six cases. The second rule accounts for 30 cases, in that it reduces the set from which selection must occur to either one or no elements. These cases are labeled *rule 1* and *rule 2*, respectively, in the column labeled *Notes*.

TABLE 6.6
occurrences of FC

N	ITEM	PRODUC-TION	LETTER	CUR. COL.	COL. DONE?	CANDIDATE LIST RESULT	OTHERS	NOTES
1	B5	P1	D			col.1	col.6	col.1 most constrained
2	B10	P1	T	col.1	yes	ϕ	col.1	col.1 out by rule 2
3	B12	P1	D	col.1	yes	col.6	col.1	col.1 out by rule 2
4	B20	P2	R			col.2	col.4, col.6	col.2 most constrained
5	B32	P2	R	col.2	yes	col.6	col.2, col.4	col.2 out by rule 2, col.6 most constrained.
6	B47	P1	R	col.2	yes	col.6	col.2, col.4	col.2 out by rule 2, col.6 most constrained
7	B49	P2	c7	col.6	yes	col.7	col.6	col.6 out by rule 2
8	B58	P2	R	col.6	no	col.6	col.2, col.4	col.6 by rule 1
9	B62	P1	R	col.6	yes	col.2	col.4, col.6	col.6 out by rule 2, col.2 most constrained
10	B72	P1	L	col.2	yes	ϕ	col.2	col.2 out by rule 2
11	B74	P1	R	col.2	yes	col.6	col.2, col.4	col.2 out by rule 2, col.6 most constrained
12	B78	P2	c6	col.6	yes	col.5	col.6	col.6 out by rule 2
13	B85	P2	c6	col.5	no	col.5	col.6	col.5 by rule 1
14	B86	P2	E	col.5	no	col.5	col.3	repeat
15	B92	P2	E	col.5	yes(?)	col.3	col.5	col.5 out by rule 2(?)
16	B95	P2	c3	col.3	yes	col.2	col.3	col.3 out by rule 2
17	B98	P2	E			col.3	col.5	repeat
18	B101	P2	E	col.3	yes	col.5	col.3	col.3 out by rule 2
19	B111	P2	R			col.6	col.2, col.4	repeat
20	B115	P2	E			col.3	col.5	repeat
21	B116	P2	E	col.3	yes	col.5	col.3	repeat
22	B118	P2	c5	col.5	yes	col.4	col.5	col.5 out by rule 2
23	B123.1	P1	E	col.3	yes	col.5	col.3	col.3 out by rule 2
24	B129	P1	E	col.5	yes	col.3	col.5	col.5 out by rule 2
25	B138	P2	R			col.2	col.4, col.6	repeat
26	B139	P2	R	col.2	yes	col.6	col.2, col.4	repeat
27	B148	P1	E	col.3	yes	col.5	col.3	repeat
28	B160	P1	E	col.5	no	col.5	col.3	col.5 by rule 1
29	B161.1	P1	c5	col.5	no	col.5	col.4	col.5 by rule 1
30	B162	P1	c6	col.5	yes	col.6	col.5	col.5 out by rule 2
31	B164/1	P1	G	col.6	yes	ϕ	col.6	col.6 out by rule 2
32	B165	P1	E	col.5	yes	col.3	col.5	col.5 out by rule 2
33	B179	P2	E			col.3	col.5	repeat
34	B182.2	P2	c3	col.3	yes	col.2	col.3	col.3 out by rule 2
35	B191	P1	L	col.2	yes	ϕ	col.2	col.2 out by rule 2
36	B197	P1	R	col.2	yes	col.6	col.2, col.4	col.2 out by rule 2, col.6 most constrained
37	B199.2	P2	c6	col.6	yes	col.5	col.6	col.6 out by rule 2
38	B203	P1	R			col.4	col.2, col.6	note col.2, not col.4, most constrained
39	B203.1	P1	c5	col.4	yes	col.5	col.4	col.4 out by rule 2
40	B206	P1	c5	col.5	no	col.5	col.4	col.5 by rule 1
41	B207	P1	E	col.5	yes	col.3	col.5	col.5 out by rule 2

TABLE 6.6 (cont'd)

N	ITEM	PRODUC-TION	LETTER	CUR. COL.	COL. DONE?	CANDIDATE LIST RESULT	CANDIDATE LIST OTHERS	NOTES
42	B211	P2	c3	col.3	yes	col.2	col.3	col.3 out by rule 2
43	B212	P1	L	col.2	no	col.2	ϕ	unique
44	B222	P2	c5	col.5	yes	col.4	col.5	col.5 out by rule 2
45	B230	P2	c5	col.5	yes	col.4	col.5	col.5 out by rule 2
46	B240	P1	E			col.5	col.3	neither most constrained
47	B242	P1	c5	col.5	no	col.5	col.4	col.5 by rule 1
48	B255	P1	c5	col.5	yes(?)	col.4	col.5	col.5 out by rule 2(?)
49	B257	P2	c4	col.4	yes	col.3	col.4	col.4 out by rule 2
50	B261	P2	c3	col.3	yes	col.2	col.3	col.3 out by rule 2
51	B262.2	P1	L	col.2	no	col.2	ϕ	unique
52	B264	P2	R	col.2	yes	col.6	col.2, col.4	col.2 out by rule 2 col.6 most constrained
53	B268.1	P1	L	col.2	no	col.2	ϕ	unique
54	B271	P1	L	col.2	no	col.2	ϕ	unique
55	B276	P1	c3	col.2	yes	col.3	col.2	col.2 out by rule 2
56	B278	P1	A	col.3	yes	ϕ	col.3	col.3 out by rule 2
57	B278/2	P1	E	col.3	yes	col.5	col.3	col.3 out by rule 2
58	B279	P2	N			col.4	ϕ	unique
59	B290	P1	N	col.4	no	col.4	ϕ	unique
60	B290.1	P2	N	col.4	no	col.4	ϕ	unique
61	B295	P1	N	col.4	no	col.4	ϕ	unique
62	B299	P2	B	col.4	no	col.4	ϕ	repeat
63	B301	P1	B	col.4	yes	ϕ	col.4	col.4 out by rule 2
64	B302	P1	O	col.5	yes	ϕ	col.5	col.5 out by rule 2

We are left with ten cases in which one column was selected from a set of two or three eligible columns. Almost all (eight) involve the selection of a column for R; one involves the initial selection of a column for D, and the remaining one the selection of a column for E after the final decision has been made to assign E the value 9. Any variation on a rule that selects the most constrained column will account for all these cases except B203 and B240. With such a rule, the subject would select either column 2 or column 6 for R in preference to column 4, and column 1 for D in preference to column 6. One must be careful in evoking such a mechanism, however, since it can imply considerable computation and comparison of all columns before a selection is made. This clearly does not occur. For example, B12 makes it highly probable that the subject did not select the initial column for D (at B5) by a deliberate comparison of column 1 and column 6. Of the two cases not explained by maximum constraint, one (B203) appears to involve a genuine anomaly (already discussed) in which the concern for R leads the subject to evoke P1 on (R ← 9), rather than to consider (E ← 9). In the other case (B240) we have no clues why column 5 should have been selected over column 4 after (E ← 9).

We can summarize these mechanisms in a program (Figure 6.18). However, we must remember that FC is highly perceptual, and that such a sequential program is likely to be a poor representation of the actual process.

FIGURE 6.18
program for FC

FC(letter):
1. generate columns:
2.   test if column contains letter,
          if false continue generation;
3.   test if column = current-column,
          if true go to 5;
4.   insert column on candidate-list,
          continue generation;
5.   test if current-column processed for letter,
          if true continue generation,
          if false stop FC and report current-column.;
6. test if candidate-list empty,
    if yes, stop and report fail;
7. test if candidate-list has one element,
    if yes, stop and report element;
8. select most-constrained-element from candidate-list
    stop and report most-constrained-element.

Find Antecedent (19), Find Production (4)

These two processes (presented in Tables 6.7 and 6.8) are grouped together because the essential component in both is the recall of past behavior. Both FP and the FA in production P12 clearly call for some past information. But even in the use of FA in P3, which on the surface simply calls for a relation that determines the input variable, the result is never a new relation, but always one that has been used already. Thus, in B42, which concerns the assignment of L to (get R), it seems implausible to think of FA as choosing between three columns for R (as in FC). Rather, it returns to column 2, which was used to derive (R odd).

With this view there is very little to say about the mechanisms of FA and FP without a more detailed model of memory. Table 6.7 for FA shows that for ten cases there are no alternatives to the output provided, and that five others are repetitions of prior sequences. This leaves four cases that are worth some discussion. Two of these have to do with whether an assignment for O could have been evoked by FA. In the PBG these assignments do precede the evocation of the production in question (always P12). In fact, no consequences follow from the assignment of values, but incorporation of this assignment would seem to require a memory that keeps track of connections in addition to the tree ordering. The other two cases (B120, B125) belong together as one, since B125 is a parallel version of B120, with column 5 and O substituted for column 3 and A, respectively. This in itself reveals that at B120 there was a choice between column 3 and column 5 as a way of determining E. However, we have no mechanism to propose for making this initial selection.

We do deal with two different forms of memory in these processes: with path

225

TABLE 6.7

occurrences of FA

N	ITEM	PRODUC-TION	VARIABLE	RESULT	NOTES
1	B42	P3	R	col.2, L	no alternatives
2	B56	P12	$c7 = 1$	$R = 3$	no alternatives
3	B105	P3	R	col.2, L	repeat B42
4	B106.2	P12	$R = 9$	$L \leftarrow 9$	no alternatives
5	B120	P3	E	col.3, A	col.5
6	B125	P3	E	col.5, O	parallel B120, col.3 (but already used)
7	B136	P12	$A = 5$	$E = 0$	$O \leftarrow 9$ but hypothetical as the line disappears
8	B147	P3	E	col.3, A	repeat B120
9	B149	P3	E	col.5, O	repeat B125
10	B186	P3	R	col.2, L	repeat B105
11	B189	P3	R	col.2, L	repeat B186
12	B203.3	P12	$E = 9$	$c5 = 1$	no alternative (not $R \leftarrow 9$ □)
13	B219	P3	E	col.5, O	no alternatives (once col.5 is constrained at B217)
14	B229.1	P12	$E = 0 \vee 1$	$c5 = 0 \vee 1$	no alternatives (not $O \leftarrow 8$)
15	B234.1	P12	$B = 8$	$c5 > 1$	no alternatives
16	B238	P12	E	$R \leftarrow 9$	$O \leftarrow 8$ possibly?
17	B243.1	P12	$O = 1$	O free	no alternatives
18	B264.1	P12	$R = 3$	$L \leftarrow 6$	no alternatives
19	B269	P12	$R = 5$	$L \leftarrow 7$	no alternatives

TABLE 6.8

occurrences of FP

N	ITEM	PRODUCTION	ACTION
1	B95.1/2	P14	repeat S4 on $R \leftarrow 7$
2	B182.4	P14	repeat S4 on $R \leftarrow 7$
3	B214	P14	repeat S4 on $R > 5$
4	B263	P14	repeat S2 on $R > 5$

memory in FA, and with production-occurrence memory in FP. These are probably not distinct but are all interwoven in the memory of past behavior. However, we can shed little additional light on how this works.

Generate Column (2), Find Letter (4)

Both of these processes are represented by so few instances that nothing can be said about their internal mechanisms (Tables 6.9 and 6.10). They both are postulated in response to needs for sufficiency—e.g., it is not possible to add up a sequence of columns serially (B304–B316) without sequencing through the columns.

The only instance of FL that offers food for thought is the extended attempt at B14–B18 to select a letter for processing. The subject clearly is considering letters and their multiple occurrences. Thus a mechanism that chooses the unprocessed letter occurring the maximum number of times in the problem will be as good an approximation as one can get, even though it may differ from the actual process the subject goes through.

TABLE 6.9
occurrences of GNC

N	ITEM	PRODUCTION	INPUT	RESULTS
1	B185	?		col.1
2	B303	P5	col.3	col.1 to col.6

TABLE 6.10
occurrences of FL

N	ITEM	PRODUCTION	INPUT	RESULTS
1	B14	P9	letters: all $-$T, D	R
2	B278	P9	letters: N, B, O	N
3	B301	P9	letters: O	O
4	B302	P9	letters: ϕ	ϕ

SUMMARY OF THE ANALYSIS

We have finished the detailed analysis of S3's behavior. A problem behavior graph was constructed from his protocol; a set of operators was defined to account for the transformations of his state of information as he moved through the graph; a set of productions was proposed to account for his choices of moves or directions of exploration; and the details of fit were scrutinized between the production system and the PBG. All of this analysis shows how a verbal thinking-aloud protocol can be used as the raw material for generating and testing a theory of problem solving behavior. A sizable fraction (75 to 80 percent) of the units of behavior was accounted for by the production system, and our detailed scrutiny of the discrepancies gives no reason for supposing that the remainder of the behavior is intrinsically incomprehensible or random. On the contrary, most of the inadequacies of the model appear to be due either to the lack of a detailed account of attention and memory mechanisms or to missing data. We can now characterize S3 with respect to his arithmetic processes, his strategies, and his memory structures and processes.

The subject's processes for drawing inferences from the columns of the crypt-arithmetic problem are very close to those that are ideal for this task environment, and to those we postulated in the infer-consequences process in Chapter 5. S3 is able to infer properties of numbers (R odd) as well as to limit the possible assignments numerically (G = 1 $\lor$ 2). He makes inferences about the carries into and out of a column as well as the letters in the column.

In two respects S3's arithmetic processes fall short of what is demanded by the task environment. First, he is not always sure that his inferences are correct; hence, he must sometimes check them by repeating them. Second, occasionally they are actually *not* correct, the inference to L = 3 from R = 7 being a notable example. The uncertainties and errors seem sometimes to be associated with a vagueness in S3's distinction between necessary and sufficient conditions. Thus, L = 3 is consistent with the hypothesis that R = 7; hence S3 infers that L = 3 from R = 7. On the other hand, S3 notices in column 5 that (E = 0 $\lor$ 9) is consistent with O + E = O; it requires some experimentation to convince him that this conclusion is necessary. Apart from these two (not inconsequential) deviations from the ideal, S3 knows, and uses, all the arithmetic that could be of help to him in this task environment. The environment is not, in this sense, a test of or a measure of his arithmetic knowledge and skills.

S3's Strategy

The subject's main strategy (depth-first search, means-ends analysis) for deciding what to do next when one process has been finished is also an effective one in this task environment, and is very similar to the strategies described in Chapter 5. He substitutes known values for the letters in the display, inferring what consequences he can; if he obtains new information, he substitutes this back into the display. Thus, he substitutes D $\leftarrow$ 5 in both columns 1 and 6. When this leads to no result, he follows the carry, c2 = 1, into column 2, finds that R is odd, and takes this information into column 6 where R appears again, and combining it with what he finds in column 6, concludes that (R = 7 $\lor$ 9). Similarly (B91) when his examination of column 5 yields (E = 9 $\lor$ 0), he turns immediately to the other occurrence of E, in column 3, and begins to process that column. The bulk of the protocol consists of passages concerned focally with the value of R, and involving columns 2 and 6; and passages concerned with E, and involving columns 5 and 3.

We know (as S3 did not) that the problem can be solved, at least down to a single assignment, by following this precise strategy; and S3 would have solved it in this way if he had not had such difficulties determining that E = 9. Even before he arrived at these difficulties, however, he did retreat from this strategy and introduce a certain amount of less selective search. When his initial processing of columns 2 and 6 did not lead to a precise value for G or R, he decided (B40) to try different possible solutions (forward search). As we have seen, he only did so to a very limited extent. His initial trial of L $\leftarrow$ 1 led into a blind alley. He then (B61)

divided his exploration into two cases: R = 7 and R = 9, pursuing these separately
(B61–B182, B183–B238, respectively, see also Figure 6.4)—even to the extent of
starting two different written solutions for the two cases.

229

Cryptarithmetic:
*Behavior of
a Single Subject*

S3's Memory

The way in which S3 holds information in memory, and the fallibilities of his
memory, have already been discussed at length. In general, he keeps cognitive
strain at relatively low levels by trying not to make highly conditional hypotheses—
one of the by-products of using a reasoning strategy rather than a forward search
strategy. He does, however, remember whether he is considering the case (R = 7)
or the case (R = 9), and that other results may be conditional on these assumptions.

S3 generally remembers properties of the letters that he has deduced—e.g.,
(R = 7 $\vee$ 9) and (E = 9 $\vee$ 0)—but not always just how he derived them. Hence,
he sometimes repeats derivations to check whether they rest on untested assumptions. His failure to recall T = 0 in order to refute E = 0 is not completely explained, although it is consistent with some features of his program—i.e., evoking
TD only on new results.

The analysis of the chapter has become increasingly particularistic. It has
considered only the behavior of a single individual working on a single problem,
and moreover it has focused more and more on the minute detail of that behavior.
If the reader felt somewhat stifled by the extended series of investigations of the
bits and pieces of S3's protocol, we can admit to a good deal of empathy. The
detail has, however, provided preliminary answers to some more of the questions
posed at the beginning of the chapter.

The subject seems to make use of several of the mechanisms of problem solving
we have investigated in earlier chapters. This shows up in his overall strategy, as
we have just summarized it, and also in a number of particular heuristics, such as
the column selection process, FC. Furthermore, one can pass from the general
observations on the use of heuristics to a precisely defined IPS (or almost so, for
we stopped short of a full program). The way in which this IPS was specified—the
production system—makes the relation of the program to the search in the problem
space (i.e., the PBG) transparent. The degree of detail assimilated to the IPS is
substantial. Although this degree cannot be given precise meaning, no appreciable
chunk of raw data (the verbalizations of the protocol) is left unresponded to,
down to the level of individual linguistic utterances.

With respect to the induction of programs from the data, the present chapter
has provided a number of techniques:

1. The formalization of the problem space, including both the knowledge
    states and operators, so that it becomes easier to determine what
    changes of knowledge are occurring.
2. The Problem Behavior Graph (PBG), which is a way of plotting the
    subject's search through the problem space.

3. The production system, which permits one to extract the regularities of behavior at a node of the PBG.
4. The determination of the priority ordering of the production system, by minimizing the number of errors it makes in predicting behavior.
5. The display of the performance of the production system in a graph that shows both its coverage and its errors, compared with the addition of new productions.

These steps all operate in the context of an information processing theory of problem solving. But within that framework they are tools of data analysis. The last item in the list also provides at least one way in which to quantify how much behavior is being explained by a given IPS. No statistical theory of significance underlies the numbers so obtained, but they are not less useful for that.

The present analysis has had least to say about generality, and about what parts of the IPS of S3 are determined by his psychology and what parts by the nature of the task environment. These questions are the subject of the next chapter.

APPENDIX 6.1

Protocol for Subject S3 on Donald + Gerald = Robert

$$\begin{array}{ll} \text{Problem:} & \text{DONALD} \qquad D = 5 \\ & \text{+GERALD} \\ & \overline{\text{ROBERT}} \end{array}$$

PHRASE NUMBER	PROTOCOL		INFERRED PRODUCTIONS
B1*	Each letter has one and only one numerical value. . . .	?:	[ask E about rules]
B2	(E: One numerical value.)		
B3	There are ten different letters		
B4	and each of them has one numerical value.		
B5*	Therefore, I can, looking at the two D's . . .	P1:	$D \leftarrow 5 \rightarrow$ FC(D) ($\Longrightarrow$ col.1); PC[col.1] ($\Longrightarrow$ T = 0 new)
B6	each D is 5;		
B7	therefore, T is zero.	P11:	$T = 0 \longrightarrow$ TD(T, 0) ($\Longrightarrow$ +)
B8*	So I think I'll start by writing that problem here.		
B9	I'll write 5, 5 is zero.		
B10	Now, do I have any other T's?	P1:	$T = 0 \longrightarrow$ FC(T) ($\Longrightarrow$ fail)
B11	No.		
B12	But I have another D.	P1:	$D \leftarrow 5 \longrightarrow$ FC(D) ($\Longrightarrow$ col.6) (no PC)[col.6]

*Asterisks refer to the notes that follow the protocol.

B13	That means I have a 5 over the other side.	
B14	Now I have 2 A's	P9: get all-letters $\longrightarrow$ FL(all-letters) ($\Longrightarrow$ R); get R
B15	and 2 L's	
B16*	that are each . . .	
B17	somewhere . . .	
B18	and this R . . .	
B19	3 R's . . .	

B20	2 L's equal an R. . . .	P2: get R $\longrightarrow$ FC(R) ($\Longrightarrow$ col.2); PC[col.2 for R] ($\Longrightarrow$ R odd new)
B21	Of course I'm carrying a 1.	
B22	Which will mean that R has to be an odd number.	

B22.1		P13: PC unclear $\longrightarrow$ get R; repeat PC

B23	Because the 2 L's . . .	$\uparrow$: PC[col.2 for R] ($\Longrightarrow$ R odd)
B24	any two numbers added together has to be an even number	
B25	and 1 will be an odd number.	

B26	So R can be 1,	P4: get R $\longrightarrow$ GN(R) ($\Longrightarrow$ 1 $\vee$ 3 $\vee$ 5 $\vee$ 7 $\vee$ 9)
B27	3,	
B28*	not 5,	P11: R = d $\longrightarrow$ TD(R, d) ($\Longrightarrow$ (R = 5 $\square$) (D $\longleftarrow$ 5 note))
B29	7,	
B30	or 9.	

B30.1*		?:

B31	(E: What are you thinking now?)	
B32	Now G. . . .	P2: get R $\longrightarrow$ FC(R) ($\Longrightarrow$ col.6); PC[col.6 for R] ($\Longrightarrow$ G even new)
B33	Since R is going to be an odd number	
B34	and D is 5,	
B35*	G has to be an even number.	

B35.1		P13: PC unclear $\longrightarrow$ get G; repeat PC

B36	I'm looking at the left side of this problem here where it says D + G.	$\uparrow$: PC[col.6 for G] ($\Longrightarrow$ c6 unknown)
B37	Oh, plus possibly another number,	
B38	if I have to carry 1 from the E + O.	

B39*	I think I'll forget about that for a minute.	?:

B40*	Possibly the best way to get to this problem is to try different possible solutions.	
B41	I'm not sure whether that would be the easiest way or not.	
B42	Well, if we assume . . .	P3: get R $\longrightarrow$ FA(R) ($\Longrightarrow$ col.2); AV(L) ($\Longrightarrow$ L $\longleftarrow$ 1);
B43	if we assume that L is, say, 1,	

B44*	we'll have 1 + 1 that's 3 or R....	↑: PC[col.2 for R] ($\Longrightarrow$ R = 3 new)
B45 B46	We'll put in a 3 here, and one here.	P11: R = 3 new $\longrightarrow$ TD(R, 3) ($\Longrightarrow$ +)
B47	Well, 5 plus something has to equal 3 in that case....	P1: R = 3 new $\longrightarrow$ FC(R) ($\Longrightarrow$ col.6); PC[col.6] ($\Longrightarrow$ c7 = 1 unknown)
B48*	I suppose it's....	P6: c7 = 1 unknown $\longrightarrow$ get c7 = 1
B49	Well, not, ...	P2: get c7 = 1 $\longrightarrow$ FC(c7) ($\Longrightarrow$ col.7); PC[col.7 for c7] ($\Longrightarrow$ □ (z1 note)) [z1: letter at bottom of col.7 does not exist]
		P10: z1 note $\longrightarrow$ check z1
B50	it's not possible that there could be an- other letter in front of this R is it?	?: check z1 $\longrightarrow$ ask(E) ($\Longrightarrow$ fail)
B50.1		P13: ask(E) unclear $\longrightarrow$ get z1; repeat ask(E)
B51 B52	Is it or not? (E: No.)	↑: ask(E) ($\Longrightarrow$ z1 (from E))
B53 B54 B55* B56 B57	It's not ... all right ... so if ... if that couldn't be a 13 on the left side, then R cannot be 3.	P12: c7 = 1 □ $\longrightarrow$ FA(c7 = 1) ($\Longrightarrow$ R = 3); (R = 3 □)
B57.1		P7: R = 3 □ $\longrightarrow$ get R
B58	R has to be a number greater than 5,	P2: get R $\longrightarrow$ FC(R) ($\Longrightarrow$ col.6); PC[col.6 for R] ($\Longrightarrow$ R > 5 new)
B59 B60	which means that it can be either 7 or 9.	P4: get R $\longrightarrow$ GN(R) ($\Longrightarrow$ 7 $\vee$ 9) P11: R = d $\longrightarrow$ TD(R, d) ($\Longrightarrow$ +)
B61*	So we'll start back here and make it a 7.	↑P4: AV(R) ($\Longrightarrow$ R ← 7 new)
B62*	Now if the....	P1: R ← 7 new $\longrightarrow$ FC(R) ($\Longrightarrow$ col.2); PC[col.2] ($\Longrightarrow$ L = 3 new)
B63* B64	Oh, I'm sorry, I said something incor- rect here. I'm making....	P11: L = 3 new $\longrightarrow$ TD(R, 3) ($\Longrightarrow$ (L = 3 □) (R = 3 note))
B64.1		P13: PC unclear $\longrightarrow$ get L; repeat PC
B65	No, no, I didn't either.	↑: PC[col.2 for L] ($\Longrightarrow$ L = 3 new)
B66 B67 B68 B69 B70 B71	R is going to be a 7, then this will be 7, and that will be 7, and it's the L's that will have to be 3's, because 3 + 3 is 6 + 1 is 7.	P11: L = 3 new $\longrightarrow$ TD(L, 3) ($\Longrightarrow$ +)
B72*	Now, it doesn't matter anywhere what the L's are equal to ...	P1: L = 3 new $\longrightarrow$ FC(L) ($\Longrightarrow$ fail)

B73	so I'm independent of L when I get past the second column here.		
B74*	But now I know that G has to be either 1	P1:	R ⟵ 7 new ⟶ FC(R) (⟹ col.6); PC[col.6] (⟹ (G = 1 ∨ 2) (c6 unknown))
B75	or 2,		
B76	depending on whether or not E + O is greater than 10	P6:	c6 unknown ⟶ get c6
B77*	or greater than 9.		
B78	Now I have this O repeating here in the second column from the left;	P2:	get c6 ⟶ FC(c6) (⟹ col.5); PC[col.5 for c6] (⟹ E = 0 new)
B79	that is, itself plus another number equal to itself.		
B80	This might indicate that E was zero. . . .		
B80.1		P13:	PC unclear ⟶ get E; repeat PC
B81	In fact, it might have to necessarily indicate that.	↑:	PC[col.5 for E] (⟹ E = 0 new)
B82	I'm not sure.	P13:	PC unclear ⟶ get E; repeat PC
B83	Or, E could be 9	↑:	PC[col.5 for E] (⟹ (E = 9 new) (c5 = 1 new))
B84*	and I would be carrying 1,	P11:	E = 9 new ⟶ TD(E, 9) (⟹ +)
B85	which would mean that I was then carrying 1 into the left-hand column.	P2:	get c6 ⟶ FC(c6) (⟹ col.5); PC[col.5 for c6] (⟹ c6 = 1 new)
B85.1*		?:	
B86	(E: What are you thinking now?)	P2:	get E ⟶ FC(E) (⟹ col.5); PC[col.5 for E] (⟹ [unclear])
B87*	I was just trying to think over what I was just . . .		
B88	about the possibility . . .		
B89	the implications of an O + another number equaling an O,		
B90*	and what that necessarily implies.		
B90.1		?:	
B91	Let's see. . . .		
B92	I have two A's equaling an E.	P2:	get E ⟶ FC(E) (⟹ col.3); PC[col.3 for E] (⟹ (E even new) (c3 = 0 note))
B93	Therefore, E has to be an even number,		
B94*	because I know I'm not carrying 1.	P10:	c3 = 0 note ⟶ check c3 = 0
		P8:	check c3 = 0 ⟶ get c3 = 0
B95*	Of course, this all going on the assumption that R is 7.	P2:	get c3 = 0 ⟶ FC(c3) (⟹ col.2); PC[col.2 for c3 = 0] (⟹ + (R ⟵ 7 note))
B95.1		P10:	R ⟵ 7 note ⟶ check R ⟵ 7
		P14:	check R ⟵ 7 ⟶ repeat P4

B96	R could be 9 also.	P4:	get R $\longrightarrow$ GN(R) ($\Longrightarrow$ 7 $\vee$ 9)
B97	Well, maybe I'll just continue to try to work this through again.	?:	
B98*	If E has got to be an. . . .	P2:	get E $\longrightarrow$ FC(E) ($\Longrightarrow$ col.3); PC[col.3 for E] ($\Longrightarrow$ E even)
B98.1		P4:	get E $\longrightarrow$ GN(E) ($\Longrightarrow$ 2 $\vee$ 4 $\vee$ 6 $\vee$ 8)
B99*	Now, wait a second.	P11:	E = d $\longrightarrow$ TD(E, d) ($\Longrightarrow$ +)
B100	I got something out of this.	?:	[9 not in generated set]
B101	E has to be an even number	P2:	get E $\longrightarrow$ FC(E) ($\Longrightarrow$ col.5); PC[col.5 for E] ($\Longrightarrow$ E = 0 $\vee$ 9)
B102	and E + O = O. . . .		
B103	E cannot be 9.	P11:	E = d $\longrightarrow$ TD(E, d) ($\Longrightarrow$ (E = 9 $\square$) (E even note))
B103.1		?:	[change R, use 9]
B104	(E: What are you thinking now?)		
B105*	I'm going back over these L's here and try to think what would happen if they are ni . . .	P3:	get R $\longrightarrow$ FA(R) ($\Longrightarrow$ col.2); AV(L) ($\Longrightarrow$ L $\longleftarrow$ 9 new)
B106*	rather . . .	$\uparrow$:	PC[col.2 for R] ($\Longrightarrow$ R = 9 new)
B106.1		P11:	R = 9 new $\longrightarrow$ TD(R, 9) ($\Longrightarrow$ (R = 9 $\square$) (L $\longleftarrow$ 9 note))
B106.2		P12:	R = 9 $\square$ $\longrightarrow$ FA(R = 9) ($\Longrightarrow$ L $\longleftarrow$ 9); (L $\longleftarrow$ 9 $\square$)
B107	Let's see, how did I arrive at the point of that?	P13:	PC unclear $\longrightarrow$ get R; repeat PC
B108	This is going to be a little confusing to start trying to trace back here.	$\uparrow$:	PC[col.2 for R] ($\Longrightarrow$ unclear (L $\longleftarrow$ 9 $\square$))
B109	What's the reasoning here?		
B110	I'm thinking in the back of my mind what this R was.	?:	[vacuous?]
B111	I decided that R had to be greater than 5,	P2:	get R $\longrightarrow$ FC(R) ($\Longrightarrow$ col.6); PC[col.6 for R] ($\Longrightarrow$ R > 5)
B112	because that was given		
B113*	and R + G,		
B114	or rather, D + G = R.		
B114.1*		?:	
B115	I know you're wondering what I'm thinking.	P2:	get E $\longrightarrow$ FC(E) ($\Longrightarrow$ col.3); PC[col.3 for E] ($\Longrightarrow$ E even)
B116*	I'm still trying to look at this second column here, where E + O = O,	P2:	get E $\longrightarrow$ FC(E) ($\Longrightarrow$ col.5); PC[col.5 for E] ($\Longrightarrow$ (E = 0) (c5 = 0 unknown))
B117	and A + A = E.		

B118	Then again, that's assuming that N is less than 3,	P2:	get $c_5 = 0 \longrightarrow$ FC(c_5) ($\Longrightarrow$ col.4); PC[col.4 for $c_5 = 0$] ($\Longrightarrow$ N < 3 new)
B119	because I don't want to be carrying 1 into that E + O column.		
B119.1		?:	
B120	I think I'll try once more here . . .	P3:	get E $\longrightarrow$ FA(E) ($\Longrightarrow$ col.3); AV(A) ($\Longrightarrow$ A $\longleftarrow$ x new);
B121	just trying to sort of bluff my way through this.		
B122*	That is, just assume some value for A,		
B123	so I can get that E.	↑:	PC[col.3 for E] ($\Longrightarrow$ E = y new)
B123.1		P1:	E = y new $\longrightarrow$ FC(E) ($\Longrightarrow$ col.5); PC[col.5] ($\Longrightarrow$ O uncertain)
B124*	I can do better than that.	?:	
B125*	I. . . .	P3:	get E $\longrightarrow$ FA(E) ($\Longrightarrow$ col.5); AV(O) ($\Longrightarrow$ O $\longleftarrow$ 9 new)
B126	I know that E + O has to equal O,		
B127*	and, at most, O is going to be 9;		
B128*	in which case E would be zero.	↑:	PC[col.5 for E] ($\Longrightarrow$ E = 0)
B129	If E is zero.	P1:	E = 0 $\longrightarrow$ FC(E) ($\Longrightarrow$ col.3); PC[col.3] ($\Longrightarrow$ A = 5 new)
B130	A + A. . . .		
B131	But A can't equal 5. . . .	P11:	A = 5 new $\longrightarrow$ TD(A, 5) ($\Longrightarrow$ (A = 5 ▢) (D $\longleftarrow$ 5 note))
B131.1		P13:	PC unclear $\longrightarrow$ get A; repeat PC
B132	That is, A + A would equal E	↑:	PC[col.3 for A] ($\Longrightarrow$ A = 5 new)
B133	and if E were zero,		
B134	A would have to equal 5;		
B135	but A can't equal 5.	P11:	A = 5 new $\longrightarrow$ TD(A, 5) ($\Longrightarrow$ (A = 5 ▢) (D $\longleftarrow$ 5 note))
B136*	And. . . .	P12:	A = 5 ▢ $\longrightarrow$ FA(A = 5) ($\Longrightarrow$ E = 0); (E = 0 ▢)
B137*	See. . . .	?:	$\longrightarrow$ get R
B138	I decided that R had to be an odd number,	P2:	get R $\longrightarrow$ FC(R) ($\Longrightarrow$ col.2); PC[col.2 for R] ($\Longrightarrow$ R odd)
B139	and has to be greater than 5,	P2:	get R $\longrightarrow$ FC(R) ($\Longrightarrow$ col.6); PC[col.6 for R] ($\Longrightarrow$ R > 5)
B140	which leaves only 7	P4:	get R $\longrightarrow$ GN(R) ($\Longrightarrow$ 7 $\vee$ 9)
B141	and 9.		

B142	I think that reasoning is correct.	
B143	Well, at worst I have only two solutions to work on in that case, starting from that point.	↑: $AV(R) (\Longrightarrow (R \leftarrow 7)$ $(R \leftarrow 9))$
B143.1		?:
B144	Let's see, what do I want that E to be?	
B145*	I think that you're absolutely right.	
B146*	It might take a full 30 minutes.	
B147*	$A + A = E. \ldots$	P3: get $E \longrightarrow FA(E) (\Longrightarrow$ col.3$)$; $AV(A) (\Longrightarrow A \leftarrow x)$
B147.1		↑: PC[col.3 for E] $(\Longrightarrow E = y)$
B148	$E + O = O.$	P1: $E = y$ new $\longrightarrow FC(E) (\Longrightarrow$ col.5$)$; PC[col.5] $(\Longrightarrow O$ uncertain$)$
B148.1		?:
B149	I'd better start back at this O here.	P3: get $E \longrightarrow FA(E) (\Longrightarrow$ col.5$)$;
B150	What values could O have?	↑: $GN(O) (\Longrightarrow 1)$; $AV(O, 1)$ $(\Longrightarrow O \leftarrow 1)$;
B151	Suppose O were 1	
B152	and E would have to be 9,	↑: PC[col.5 for E] $(\Longrightarrow (E = 9) (c5 = 1))$
B153	and I'd have to be carrying a 1.	
B153.1		↑: [return to GN]
B154*	Suppose . . .	↑: $GN(O) (\Longrightarrow 2)$; $AV(O, 2)$ $(\Longrightarrow O \leftarrow 2)$;
B154.1		↑: PC[col.5 for E] $(\Longrightarrow$ $(E = 9) (c5 = 1))$
B154.2		↑: [return to GN]
B155*	s'pose. . . .	↑: $GN(O)$?: $\longrightarrow AV(O) (\Longrightarrow O \leftarrow x)$
B156*	Actually, that's almost the case no matter what the situation is. . . .	↑P3: PC[col.5 for E] $(\Longrightarrow (E = 9) (c5 = 1))$
B156.1		P13: PC unclear $\longrightarrow$ get E; repeat PC
B157	Unless E is zero. . . .	↑: PC[col.5 for E] $(\Longrightarrow E = 0)$
B158*	But E can't be zero. . . .	?: $E = 0 \longrightarrow$ [recall col.3] $(\Longrightarrow E = 0 \ \square)$
B158.1		P7: $E = 0 \ \square \longrightarrow$ get E
B159*	Therefore, E might have to be 9	P4: get $E \longrightarrow GN(E) (\Longrightarrow 9)$; $AV(E)$ $(\Longrightarrow E \leftarrow 9)$
B160	and I have to carry	P1: $E \leftarrow 9 \longrightarrow FC(E) (\Longrightarrow$ col.5$)$; PC[col.5] $(\Longrightarrow c5 = 1$ new$)$
B161	in order to have the $O =$ the O.	
B161.1		P1: $c5 = 1$ new $\longrightarrow FC(c5) (\Longrightarrow$ col.5$)$; PC[col.5] $(\Longrightarrow c6 = 1$ new$)$

B162*	In that case, it looks like G is going to be 1,	P1:	c6 = 1 new ⟶ FC(c6) (⟹ col.6); PC[col.6] (⟹ G = 1 new)
B163	because I am going to be carrying 1.	P11:	G = 1 new ⟶ TD(G, 1) (⟹ +)

B164*	I think I'll tentatively put that in there.	P1:	G = 1 new ⟶ FC(G) (⟹ fail)
B165	And I'll call E....	P1:	E ⟵ 9 new ⟶ FC(E) (⟹ col.3); PC[col.3] (⟹ E ⟵ 9 ☐)

B166	Let's see, E can't be 9 though.	P13:	PC unclear ⟶ get E; repeat PC

B167	It doesn't look like E can be 9,	↑:	PC[col.3 for A] (⟹ E ⟵ 9 ☐)
B168	because A + A has to equal E.		

B169*	Am I irritating you being so far off the course?	?:	
B170	(E: No.)		
B171	I still feel as though I'm baring my soul to my mind here.		
B172	(E: What are you thinking now?)		
B173	Well, I see you here pacing around the room.		
B174	You have me all worried.		

B175	Now I'm going back to see if I've made some obvious fallacy.	?:	⟶ get R
B176	(E: You haven't made any obvious fallacies.)		
B177*	I sort of thought....		
B178	Of course, I did have the choice of making this R a 9.	P4:	get R ⟶ GN(R) (⟹ 9); AV(R) (⟹ R ⟵ 9 new)

B178.1		?:	

B179	I seem to be running into trouble the way I am here.	P2:	get E = 9 ⟶ FC(E = 9) (⟹ col.3); PC[col.3 for E = 9] (⟹ ☐)
B180	Having trouble getting this E....		

B181	I can't make E a 9.	P13:	PC unclear ⟶ get E; repeat PC

B182*	If that were 4 + 4 plus....	↑:	PC[col.3 for A] (⟹ (A = 4 new) (c3 = 1 unknown))

B182.1		P6:	c3 = 1 unknown ⟶ get c3 = 1

B182.2		P2:	get c3 = 1 ⟶ FC(c3) (⟹ col.2); PC[col.2 for c3 = 1] (⟹ ☐ (R ⟵ 7 note))

B182.3		P10:	R ⟵ 7 note ⟶ check R ⟵ 7

B182.4		P14:	check R ⟵ 7 ⟶ repeat P4
		↑P4:	get R ⟶ GN(R) (⟹ 7 ∨ 9); AV(R) (⟹ R ⟵ 9 new)

B183	I think I'll make myself another model on the other side,	?:	
B184	and compare these two.		

B185*	Now I had a column 5 + 5 = 10.	?:	⟶ GNC (⟹ col.1); PC[col.1] (⟹ +)

B186* Now the change I'm going to make is that I'm going to make L a 9.	P3: get R $\longrightarrow$ FA(R) ($\Longrightarrow$ col.2); AV(L) ($\Longrightarrow$ L $\longleftarrow$ 9 new)
B187* Which means . . .	$\uparrow$: $\qquad\qquad$ PC[col.2 for R] ($\Longrightarrow$ R = 9 new)
B188* I'm sorry. . . .	P11: R = 9 new $\longrightarrow$ TD(R, 9) ($\Longrightarrow$ (R = 9 $\square$) (L $\longleftarrow$ 9 note))
B188.1	?:
B189 I'm going to make R a 9,	P3: get R $\longrightarrow$ FA(R) ($\Longrightarrow$ col.2); AV(R) ($\Longrightarrow$ R $\longleftarrow$ 9)
B190 which means that L has to be 4.	$\uparrow$: $\qquad$ PC[col.2] ($\Longrightarrow$ L = 4 new) P11: L = 4 new $\longrightarrow$ TD(L, 4) ($\Longrightarrow$ +)
B191* I wish that L appeared somewhere else, B192 since I can get it within at least 1 B193 or 2 of right. B194* Now, since R equals 9, B195 and in the far left-hand total is going to be a 9, B196 and the R in GERALD is going to be 9. B197 Now instead of G plus 5 being 9,	P1: L = 4 new $\longrightarrow$ FC(L) ($\Longrightarrow$ fail) P1: R $\longleftarrow$ 9 new $\longrightarrow$ FC(R) ($\Longrightarrow$ col.6); PC[col.6] ($\Longrightarrow$ (G = 3 $\vee$ 4) (c6 unknown))
B198 G can be either 3 B199 or 4.	
B199.1	P6: c6 unknown $\longrightarrow$ get c6
B199.2	P2: get c6 $\longrightarrow$ FC(c6) ($\Longrightarrow$ col.5); PC[col.5 for c6] ($\Longrightarrow$ (E = 9 new) (c5 = 1 new))
B200 Of course now my E can't be a 9,	P11: E = 9 new $\longrightarrow$ TD(E, 9) ($\Longrightarrow$ (E = 9 $\square$) (R $\longleftarrow$ 9 note))
B201 since I've used the 9 for R.	?:
B202* And also am using R as 9 instead of a 7 B203 makes me think it more likely that I'm going to be carrying 1 into that E + O column.	P1: R $\longleftarrow$ 9 $\longrightarrow$ FC(R) ($\Longrightarrow$ col.4); PC[col.4] ($\Longrightarrow$ c5 = 1 new)
B203.1	P1: c5 = 1 new $\longrightarrow$ FC(c5) ($\Longrightarrow$ col.5); PC[col.5] ($\Longrightarrow$ E = 9 new)
B203.2	P11: E = 9 new $\longrightarrow$ TD(E, 9) ($\Longrightarrow$ (E = 9 $\square$) (R $\longleftarrow$ 9 note))
B203.3	P12: E = 9 $\square$ $\longrightarrow$ FA(E = 9) ($\Longrightarrow$ c5 = 1); (c5 = 1 $\square$) P7: c5 = 1 $\square$ $\longrightarrow$ get c5
B204* Oh, or zero. . . .	P4: get c5 $\longrightarrow$ GN(c5) ($\Longrightarrow$ 0); AV(c5) ($\Longrightarrow$ c5 $\longleftarrow$ 0 new)
B205* Suppose I were to. . . . B206 This implies that E is zero perhaps.	P1: c5 $\longleftarrow$ 0 new $\longrightarrow$ FC(c5) ($\Longrightarrow$ col.5); PC[col.5] ($\Longrightarrow$ E = 0 new)

B207	But as soon as E is zero	P1:	$E = 0$ new $\longrightarrow$ FC(E) ($\Longrightarrow$ col.3); PC[col.3] ($\Longrightarrow A = 5$ new)
B208*	that means that $A + A$ has to equal 10,		
B209	and I don't find any way to do that.	P11:	$A = 5$ new $\longrightarrow$ TD(A, 5) ($\Longrightarrow (A = 5 \square)$ (D $\longleftarrow$ 5 note))
B209.1		P13:	PC unclear $\longrightarrow$ get A; repeat PC
B210	Let's see. . . .	↑:	PC[col.3 for A] ($\Longrightarrow c3 = 1$ unknown)
B210.1		P6:	$c3 = 1$ unknown $\longrightarrow$ get $c3 = 1$
B211	If I could get L to be more than 5. . . .	P2:	get $c3 = 1 \longrightarrow$ FC(c3) ($\Longrightarrow$ col.2); PC[col.2 for $c3 = 1$] ($\Longrightarrow L > 5$ unknown)
B211.1		P6:	$L > 5$ unknown $\longrightarrow$ get $L > 5$
B211.2		P4:	get $L > 5 \longrightarrow$ GN(L) ($\Longrightarrow$ 6); AV(L) ($\Longrightarrow$ L $\longleftarrow$ 6 new)
B212*	On the other hand $L + L$ has to equal R	P1:	L $\longleftarrow$ 6 new $\longrightarrow$ FC(L) ($\Longrightarrow$ col.2); PC[col.2] ($\Longrightarrow R = 3$ new)
B213	and R has to be greater than 5.	P11:	$R = 3$ new $\longrightarrow$ TD(R, 3) ($\Longrightarrow (R = 3 \square)$ $(R > 5$ note))
B214	So I'm in sort of a dilemma in that case.	P10:	$R > 5$ note $\longrightarrow$ check $R > 5$
		P14:	check $R > 5 \longrightarrow$ repeat P4
B215	Now I really think that R is either 7	P4:	get R $\longrightarrow$ GN(R) ($\Longrightarrow 7 \lor 9$)
B216	or 9.		
B217	And let's get back to $E + O$.	?:	$\longrightarrow$ get E
B218	Something we're missing here.		
B219*	Suppose O were something like 8.	P3:	get E $\longrightarrow$ FA(E) ($\Longrightarrow$ col.5); AV(O) ($\Longrightarrow$ O $\longleftarrow$ 8 new);
B220	8 plus something has to equal 8.	↑:	PC[col.5 for E] ($\Longrightarrow c5 = 2$ unknown)
B221	Suppose I would carry 2 from the column.	P6:	$c5 = 2$ unknown $\longrightarrow$ get $c5 = 2$
B222*	That's sort of difficult in this particular problem.	P2:	get $c5 = 2 \longrightarrow$ FC(c5) ($\Longrightarrow$ col.4); PC[col.4 for $c5 = 2$] ($\Longrightarrow \square$)
B222.1		?:	[vacuous?]
B223	I sort of keep coming up with idea that E should equal zero, or 9.	P4:	get E $\longrightarrow$ GN(E) ($\Longrightarrow 0 \lor 9$)
B224	Of course I've used the 9. . . .	P11:	$E = d \longrightarrow$ TD(E, d) ($\Longrightarrow (E = 9 \square)$ (R $\longleftarrow$ 9 note))
B224.1		?:	[interrupted]
B225*	(E: You've used the zero, too.)	?:	$\longrightarrow (E = 0 \square)$ (0 used note) [from E]

B225.1	P13:	TD unclear $\longrightarrow$ get E = 0; repeat TD
B226* Yeah, that's certainly true.	$\uparrow$:	TD(E, 0) ($\Longrightarrow$ (E = 0 $\square$)) (T = 0 note))
B227 I used the zero.		
B227.1	P7:	E = 0 $\square$ $\longrightarrow$ get E
B228 Well, I'm getting into problems here if I can't make E either zero	P4:	get E $\longrightarrow$ GN(E) ($\Longrightarrow$ 0 $\vee$ 9)
B229 or 9,	P11:	E = d $\longrightarrow$ TD(E, d) ($\Longrightarrow$ (E = 0 $\vee$ 9 $\square$)) (T = 0 note) (R $\longleftarrow$ 9 note))
B229.1	P12:	E = 0 $\vee$ 9 $\square$ $\longrightarrow$ FA(E) ($\Longrightarrow$ c5 = 0 $\vee$ 1); (c5 = 0 $\vee$ 1 $\square$)
B229.2	P7:	c5 = 0 $\vee$ 1 $\square$ $\longrightarrow$ get c5 > 1
B230* and it doesn't seem as though I'm going to be able to carry more than 1 in any case.	P2:	get c5 > 1 $\longrightarrow$ FC(c5) ($\Longrightarrow$ col.4) PC[col.4 for c5 > 1] ($\Longrightarrow$ $\square$)
B230.1	P13:	PC unclear $\longrightarrow$ get c5 > 1; repeat PC
B231 That is true.	$\uparrow$:	PC[col.4 for c5 > 1] ($\Longrightarrow$ (c5 = 1) (B = 8 new))
B232* The most I could have any column total to would be 18.		
B233* And even that can't occur	P11:	B = 8 new $\longrightarrow$ TD(B, 8) ($\Longrightarrow$ (B = 8 $\square$) (O $\longleftarrow$ 8 note))
B234* unless the column immediately preceding equals 0.		
B234.1	P12:	B = 8 $\square$ $\longrightarrow$ FA(B = 8) ($\Longrightarrow$ c5 > 1); c5 > 1 $\square$
B235* I've used the zero,	P4:	get E $\longrightarrow$ GN(E) ($\Longrightarrow$ 0)
B236 so E can't be a zero.	P11:	E = 0 $\longrightarrow$ TD(E, 0) ($\Longrightarrow$ (E = 0 $\square$)) (T = 0 note))
B237 and A can't be zero.	?:	($\Longrightarrow$ (A = 0 $\square$)) (T = 0 note))
B238* I'm finding difficulty in making it a 9.	P12:	E $\square$ $\longrightarrow$ FA(E) ($\Longrightarrow$ R $\longleftarrow$ 9); (R $\longleftarrow$ 9 $\square$)
B238.1	?:	
B239 We'd better make E a 9.	P4:	get E $\longrightarrow$ GN(E) ($\Longrightarrow$ 9); AV(E) ($\Longrightarrow$ E $\longleftarrow$ 9 new)
B240* I'm going to have to carry 1	P1:	E $\longleftarrow$ 9 new $\longrightarrow$ FC(E) ($\Longrightarrow$ col.5); PC[col.5] ($\Longrightarrow$ c5 = 1 new)
B241 in order to satisfy the other conditions.		
B242* It looks then as though my solution for O is going to be independent of the rest of the column.	P1:	c5 = 1 new $\longrightarrow$ FC(c5) ($\Longrightarrow$ col.5); PC[col.5] ($\Longrightarrow$ O free new)

B242.1	P4:	O free $\longrightarrow$ GN(O) ($\Longrightarrow$ 1)
B243 But....	P11:	O = d $\longrightarrow$ TD(O,1) ($\Longrightarrow$ O = 1 $\square$) (G = 1 note))
B243.1	P12:	O = 1 $\square$ $\longrightarrow$ FA(O) ($\Longrightarrow$ O free); (O free $\square$)
	P7:	O free $\square$ $\longrightarrow$ get O
B244 No, it's not either,	?:	[shift to free-digits instead of all-digits]
B245 because I'm only going to have ...		
B246 I only have 10 letters to use ...		
B247 10 numbers to use for 10 letters.		
B248* So it's probably going to be the last one I ever find.	P4:	O free $\longrightarrow$ GN(O) ($\Longrightarrow$ fail); AV(O) ($\Longrightarrow$ O $\longleftarrow$ x)
B249 I'll put an x in here for the O.		
B250 Make E a 9,		
B251* which leaves my right hand ...		
B252 (noise) ...		
B253 which leaves this left-hand solution.		
B254* Now, R is 7.		
B255 I have to have it so it carries 1 into the E + O column.	P1:	c5 = 1 new $\longrightarrow$ FC(c5) ($\Longrightarrow$ col.4); PC[col.4] ($\Longrightarrow$ (N $\geqslant$ 3 new) (c4 unknown))
B256 Yeah, this is looking pretty good right now.	P6:	c4 unknown $\longrightarrow$ get c4
B257 I guess I still have a problem.	P2:	get c4 $\longrightarrow$ FC(c4) ($\Longrightarrow$ col.3); PC[col.3 for c4] ($\Longrightarrow$ A $\square$)
B257.1	P13:	PC unclear $\longrightarrow$ get A; repeat PC
B258 Yes, I have an awful problem here.	$\uparrow$:	PC[col.3 for A] ($\Longrightarrow$ A $\square$)
B259 I can't make A + A = 9 very well.	P13:	PC unclear $\longrightarrow$ get A; repeat PC
B260 A + A....	$\uparrow$:	PC[col.3 for A] ($\Longrightarrow$ (A = 4 new) (c3 = 1 unknown))
B260.1	P6:	c3 = 1 unknown $\longrightarrow$ get c3 = 1
B261 There's no place where I can get L + L to equal more than 10,	P2:	get c3 = 1 $\longrightarrow$ FC(c3) ($\Longrightarrow$ col.2); PC[col.2 for c3 = 1] ($\Longrightarrow$ L > 5 unknown)
B262 so I could make....	P6:	L > 5 unknown $\longrightarrow$ get L > 5
B262.1	P4:	get L > 5 $\longrightarrow$ GN(L) ($\Longleftarrow$ 6); AV(L) ($\Longrightarrow$ L $\longleftarrow$ 6 new)
B262.2	P1:	L $\longleftarrow$ 6 new $\longrightarrow$ FC(L) ($\Longrightarrow$ col.2); PC[col.2] ($\Longrightarrow$ R = 3 new)
B262.3	P11:	R = 3 new $\longrightarrow$ TD(R, 3) ($\Longrightarrow$ (R = 3 $\square$) (R > 5 note))
B263 Well, then the problem is over here on this R....	P10:	R > 5 note $\longrightarrow$ check R > 5
	P14:	check R > 5 $\longrightarrow$ repeat P2

B264	This R, it seems to me, has to be greater than 5.	P2:	get R $\longrightarrow$ FC(R) ($\Longrightarrow$ col.6); PC[col.6 for R] ($\Longrightarrow$ R > 5)
B264.1		P12:	R = 3 $\square$ $\longrightarrow$ FA(R = 3) ($\Longrightarrow$ L $\leftarrow$ 6); (L $\leftarrow$ 6 $\square$)
B265*	Now, suppose these were real big numbers,	P7:	L $\leftarrow$ 6 $\square$ $\longrightarrow$ get L > 5
B266	not just little . . .		
B267	not 10, but way more than 10.		
B268	Suppose that was something like 7. . . .	P4:	get L > 5 $\longrightarrow$ GN(L) ($\Longrightarrow$ 7); AV(L) ($\Longrightarrow$ L $\leftarrow$ 7 new)
B268.1		P1:	L $\leftarrow$ 7 new $\longrightarrow$ FC(L) ($\Longrightarrow$ col.2); PC[col.2] ($\Longrightarrow$ R = 5 new)
B268.2		P11:	R = 5 new $\longrightarrow$ TD(R, 5) ($\Longrightarrow$ (R = 5 $\square$) (D $\leftarrow$ 5 note))
B269*	No, make it even bigger. . . .	P12:	R = 5 $\square$ $\longrightarrow$ FA(R = 5) ($\Longrightarrow$ L $\leftarrow$ 7); (L $\leftarrow$ 7 $\square$)
		P7:	L $\leftarrow$ 7 $\square$ $\longrightarrow$ get L > 5
B270	Make it 8.	P4:	get L > 5 $\longrightarrow$ GN(L) ($\Longrightarrow$ 8); AV(L) ($\Longrightarrow$ L $\leftarrow$ 8 new)
B271	If we let L be 8 and 8	P1:	L $\leftarrow$ 8 new $\longrightarrow$ FC(L) ($\Longrightarrow$ col.2); PC[col.2] ($\Longrightarrow$ R = 7 new)
B272	and the 1 carried would be 17,		
B273*	so my R is still 7.	P11:	R = 7 new $\longrightarrow$ TD(R, 7) ($\Longrightarrow$ +)
B274*	Now, I sort of forgot why I was going through all this trouble.		
B275	Oh, yes, I wanted to carry 1 into the A + A column,	?:	[recall (get c3 = 1)]
B276	which will make A now equal to 4 + 4,	P1:	c3 = 1 new $\longrightarrow$ FC(c3) ($\Longrightarrow$ col.3); PC[col.3] ($\Longrightarrow$ (A = 4 new) (E = 9 new))
B277	and the 1 I am carrying gives me a 9 for the E,		
B278	which satisfies the requirements in the second column from the left.	P1:	A = 4 new $\longrightarrow$ FC(A) ($\Longrightarrow$ fail)
		P1:	E = 9 new $\longrightarrow$ FC(E) ($\Longrightarrow$ col.5); PC[col.5] ($\Longrightarrow$ +)
		P9:	get all-letters $\longrightarrow$ FL(all-letters) ($\Longrightarrow$ N); (get N)
B279	Now I have an R + N,	P2:	get N $\longrightarrow$ FC(N) ($\Longrightarrow$ col.4); PC[col.4 for N] ($\Longrightarrow$ N free new)
B280	7 + something = B.		
B281*	This looks like I'm getting into the in- dependent part of the solution right now.		
B282*	Of course, it all has to satisfy the fact that I have 10 letters for 10 numbers.		
B283*	I rather feel I'm pretty close to it right now.		
B284	Let's see what I am doing here.		

B285* I just need. . . .	P4:	get N $\longrightarrow$ GN(N) ($\Longrightarrow$ 3 $\vee$ 6)
B286* I'm only two numbers short, aren't I?		
B287 3 and a 6.		
B288* So I'll make the . . .	$\uparrow$:	AV(N) ($\Longrightarrow$ [unclear])
B288.1	P13:	AV unclear $\longrightarrow$ get N; repeat AV
B289* suppose I make the N a. . . .	$\uparrow$:	AV(N) ($\Longrightarrow$ N $\leftarrow$ x new)
B290* Well, I have to carry 1 in that column.	P1:	N $\leftarrow$ x new $\longrightarrow$ FC(N) ($\Longrightarrow$ col.4); PC[col.4] ($\Longrightarrow$ (B = y new) (c5 = 1 new))
B290.1	P2:	get N $\longrightarrow$ FC(N) ($\Longrightarrow$ col.4); PC[col.4 for N] ($\Longrightarrow$ N > 2 new)
B291 Well, 3	P4:	get N $\longrightarrow$ GN(N) ($\Longrightarrow$ 3 $\vee$ 6)
B292 or 6,		
B293 either one would do it.	P11:	N = d $\longrightarrow$ TD(N, d) ($\Longrightarrow$ +)
B294 Suppose I make this a 6.	$\uparrow$P4:	AV(N) ($\Longrightarrow$ N $\leftarrow$ 6 new)
B295* Now, this R plus N is 7 + 6. . . .	P1:	N $\leftarrow$ 6 new $\longrightarrow$ FC(N) ($\Longrightarrow$ col.4); PC[col.4] ($\Longrightarrow$ B = 3 new)
B295.1	P11:	B = 3 new $\longrightarrow$ TD(B, 3) ($\Longrightarrow$ (B = 3 $\square$) (free-digits empty note))
B295.2	P13:	TD unclear $\longrightarrow$ get B; repeat TD
B296 Have to make B a. . . .	$\uparrow$:	TD(B, 3) ($\Longrightarrow$ (B = 3 $\square$)) (free-digits empty note))
B297 I must be missing another number here.	P10:	free-digits empty note $\longrightarrow$ check free-digits empty
	P8:	check free-digits empty $\longrightarrow$ get free digits
B298 Yeah, I'm missing 2 also.	P4:	get free-digits $\longrightarrow$ GN(free-digits) ($\Longrightarrow$ 2)
B299 7 and 6 is 13,	P2:	get B $\longrightarrow$ FC(B) ($\Longrightarrow$ col.4); PC[col.4 for B] ($\Longrightarrow$ B = 3 new)
B300 so B becomes 3,	P11:	B = 3 new $\longrightarrow$ TD(B, 3) ($\Longrightarrow$ +)
B301 which leaves me a 2 for O.	P1:	B = 3 new $\longrightarrow$ FC(B) ($\Longrightarrow$ fail)
	P9:	get all-letters $\longrightarrow$ FL(all-letters) ($\Longrightarrow$ O); (get O)
	P4:	get O $\longrightarrow$ GN(O) ($\Longrightarrow$ 2); AV(O) ($\Longrightarrow$ O $\leftarrow$ 2 new)
	P11:	O = 2 $\longrightarrow$ TD(O, 2) ($\Longrightarrow$ +)
B302 Now I think I may be satisfied.	P1:	O $\leftarrow$ 2 new $\longrightarrow$ FC(O) ($\Longrightarrow$ fail)
	P9:	get all-letters $\longrightarrow$ FL(all-letters) ($\Longrightarrow$ fail)
B303 Probably better check the addition.	?:	$\longrightarrow$ check all-columns
	P5:	check all-columns $\longrightarrow$ GNC (all-columns)

B304*	5 and 5 is 10,	↑: (⟹ +)	(⟹ col.1); PC[col.1]
B305	carry 1;		
B306	8 and 8 is 16	↑:	(⟹ col.2); PC[col.2]
B307	and 1 is 17	(⟹ +)	
B308	carry 1;		
B309	4 and 4 is 8	↑:	(⟹ col.3); PC[col.3]
B310	and 1 is 9;	(⟹ +)	
B311	7 and 6 are 13,	↑: (⟹ +)	(⟹ col.4); PC[col.4]
B312	carry the 1;		
B313	9 and 2 are 11	↑:	(⟹ col.5); PC[col.5]
B314	and the 1 is 12;	(⟹ +)	
B315	5 and 1 is 6	↑:	(⟹ col.6); PC[col.6]
B316	and 1 is 7.	(⟹ +)	
B317	Just for the sake of really giving a complete answer,	?:	[get another solution]
B318*	I imagine you could shift these numbers around here a little bit to make this. . . .	?: (⟹ fail)]	[method: shift assignments
B319*	Well, I really don't know how to check.	?:	
B320	I think I've completed the problem.	?:	[end]
B321	(E: That's right.)		

Notes to Protocol

B1   The exchange deals with the definition of the problem, hence is outside the problem space.

B5   The subject has been told that $D \leftarrow 5$ prior to the start of the tape.

B8   We do not encode writing operations.

B16   After identifying A's and L's, searching for more occurrences. The pattern shows for R in B18–B19.

B28   "not 5" shows S3 is generating and testing at same time.

B30.1 Don't know what S3 does after GN.

B35   Shows S3 has ignored carry.

B39   Don't know what the decision is based upon; however, there is no place to go as long as assignments are not made (see B40).

B40   One of the few indications of development (or change) of methods.

B44   S3 is writing 3's at col.2, col.4, and col.6.
–B46

B48   "I suppose it's [not possible]." Determined by repeat in B50.

B55   Precursor to B56.

B61   "back here" indicates col.2.

B62   "Now if the [R is 7, L must be 3]."

B63   The difficulty is R = 3 □ coupled with a general confusion between L and R. The continuation through B71 adds support: "it's the L's that will have to be 3's." B105 and B186, where S3 assigns $L \leftarrow 9$ and not $R \leftarrow 9$, confirms this.

B72   Evidence for FC being evoked after new information derived (L = 3).

B74   Note that S3 says $G = 1 \lor 2$ not $G = 2 \lor 1$. This latter would be expected if he worked without c5 and then remembered it later.

B77   Probably "or less than 9"; but could be a restatement with slight correction of "greater than 10." The ambiguity is created by (1) "whether or not," which would normally be followed by only the single condition, and (2) "greater," which is ambiguously $>$ or $\geq$ in casual conversation.

B84   Taken as $c5 = 1$, since B85 states $c6 = 1$ as a consequence.

B85.1   Don't know how much further S3 goes—e.g., to col.6 and $G = 1$; thence to S1, which gives $FC(G)$ ($\Longrightarrow$ fail).

B87   Clearly reworking col.5, but unclear whether any information derived.

B90   Note the "necessarily" and the parallelism of phrasing to B81.

B94   Is the emphasis a precursor to his checking $c3$ rather than following up on E even?

B95   An alternative interpretation is that S3 simply reflects on the contingency of the current line of attack; however, the concern with $c3$ in B94 makes the chosen interpretation more plausible.

B98   "If E has got to be an [even number]." Note the "an"; also compare B93 and B101. The assumption is that S3 starts counting from 2 and not from zero; otherwise might have seen ($E = 0 \;\square$) ($T = 0$ note).

B99   It is unclear what clue evokes the possibility that $E = 9 \;\square$ but does not yet settle it.

–B100   That $E = 9$ has not occurred in the generation is a possibility. In B101–B103, S3 goes through the argument as if for the first time.

B105   "they are ni[ne]" makes clear the assignment is misplaced from $R \longleftarrow 9$ to $L \longleftarrow 9$. This (and B186) might be due to the use of production S3, which to get x assigns a value to a different variable, y.

B106   The confusion, starting here and running to B109, stems from the assignment error. But why so confused, rather than simply recognizing the misassignment? The peculiarities of PC with $L \longleftarrow 9$ make it plausible:

    (1) $9 + 9 + 1 = 19$; thus get $R = 9$, which is the true assignment.

    (2)   Thus, to assign $R \longleftarrow 9$ would seem to lead back to $L \longleftarrow 9$, as given above. (That this is not necessary, since $4 + 4 + 1 = 9$ as well, would not be apparent.)

    (3) $TD(R, 9)$ leads to rejecting $L \longleftarrow 9$; but once $L \longleftarrow 9$ is rejected then $TD(R, 9)$ ($\Longrightarrow +$)!

B113   Can make nothing substantive of the slip.

–B114

B114.1   Might have to go on to $R = 7 \lor 9$ as he did in B137–B143.

B116   The phrasing of B116, B117, is col.5, col.3. However, the subsequent behavior concerning col.4, which refers to carries into col.5, indicates that a repetition of the reasoning from E even (col.3) to $E = 0$ (col.5) to $c4 = 0$ (col.4) is going on. Hence the order is col.3, col.5.

B122   An explicit statement of production P3, implying the ability to go over a method in a particular context without carrying through the calculation in detail.

B124   Do better than to assign A to get E; namely, assign O to get E. Is this better because it is closer to the difficulty; namely E in col.5?

B125   Precursor to B126.

B127   Why $O \longleftarrow 9$ rather than $O \longleftarrow 1$? Perhaps because S3 excludes $E = 9$; perhaps because by maximizing O he maximizes chance of getting $c6 = 1$.

B128   If $O \longleftarrow 9$ and $E = 0 \lor 9$, then $E = 0$; however, probably PC.

B136   "and [that means E can't equal zero]."

B137   "[Let's] see." Precursor to B138.

B145   Outside the problem space.

B146   Outside the problem space.

B147   The designation of col.3, col.5 followed by the assignment of values to O makes it plausible that a repeat of B120 to B124 is occurring. An alternative—less structured and less attractive—is that he simply "considers" each in turn.

B154   "Suppose [O were 2]." The grounds for inferring a generation comes from B150, which announces it explicitly, and the parallelism between B154 and B151.

B155   "S'pose [O were . . .]." Unclear whether he actually sets up another value ($O \longleftarrow 3$) or senses the fact that the reasoning would give the same answer (as indicated by B156).

B156   Subject has induced the general form from a sequence of cases. We have coded this as the assignment of a general variable ($AV(O)$ ($\Longrightarrow O \longleftarrow$ x)) and the carrying through of a symbolic calculation in PC. PC certainly has these capabilities (B122–B123, B249–B250). An alternative is a mechanism for inducing directly from the invariance of the internal process in PC for the different specific values of O. There need not be any checking with O ← x—i.e., no performance of PC after O ← x.

B158   Recalls B128–B136. Not (E = 0 □)(T = 0 note).

B159   "might have to be" indicates the force of "E = 0 ∨ 9 and E = 0 □ therefore E = 9" rather than PC(col.5). Also supporting is the "have to carry" (B160), which indicated E = 9 imposed from outside col.5.

B162   The only reference to G = 1 until it shows in checking the answer (B135). Apparently
–B165   G = 1 was recorded (B164) but E = 9 was not (B165–166). Thus, when going back to the first display, the E must be written in (B250) but the G = 1 is already there.

B164   There is little evidence for FC(G); the production system demands it and there is no evidence against it.

B169   The only major interaction on nontask matters with the experimenter.
–B176

B177   Unclear what he thought (that R ← 7 was necessary?).

B182   Indicates either (1) awareness that c3 might be 1, or (2) a consideration of whether it might be so. The decision to try the alternative route (R ← 9) is probably influenced by the fact the 9 > 7, but clearly does not represent any detailed consideration of whether R ← 9 implies c3 = 1 (it is independent of it, of course).

B185   Simply copying over the first column, not rederiving it. However, still does a PC.

B186   Note the error: means R ← 9. Compare B63 and B105.

B187   "which means [that R has to be 9]."

B188   The fact that he catches himself more readily than at B105 may indicate some learning. This might simply be recall of recovery at B105.

B191   Good indication of P1 evoked when there is no column to be found. See also B10, B72.

B194   Writing in R ← 9.
–B196

B202   This appears to be a place where the noting of R ← 9 for TD leads to attending to
–B203   the R in col.4 rather than get E in col.5. Clearly, sees that R ← 9 in col.4 leads to c5 = 1, rather than working back from col.5 (where in fact E = 9 □ leads to c5 = 0).

B204   Now checks col.5 and sees that T = 0 is implied.

B205   "Suppose I were to [make c5 = 0]."

B208   Does not consider A + A = 0.

B212   Clearly does not see L ← 8 or L ← 9, since he thinks L > 5 implies R < 5. This might be done by general reasoning; trying L ← 6 seems more plausible.

B219   Why O ← 8? Clearly means O from B220. Two alternatives:
–B221   (1)   Since E = 0 ∨ 9, not select O = 0 ∨ 9. If generating from top (see B127), then O ← 8 is next. However, why generate from top?
       (2)   Confuse O with E so that E = 9 □ implies try E (= O) ← 8). Getting implies this, since O ← 8 does not imply anything about c5.
       We chose the latter interpretation.

B222   c > 1 is not possible with only two addends. However, S3 is not completely sure.

B225   Apparently, the experimenter can contain himself no longer. Too bad.

B226   This makes it clear that B158 did not mean (E = 0 □)(T = 0 note).

B230   Confirms B222.

B232   Either (1) max = 9 + 9 and ignore carry or (2) max = 9 + 8 + (c = 1). We don't have to choose.

B233   "that" = sum = 18.

B234   Shows still O ← 8.

B235   Probably digit-oriented action: (x = 0 □)(T = 0 note) with x = E and x = A. How-
–B237   ever, current production system doesn't accommodate this.

B238   "it" = R (not E), as evidenced by B239.

B240   "carry" = c5 and the "conditions" are col.5 (not col.3; see B257).
–B241

B242   "independent" means can be chosen arbitrarily—e.g., by GN. Whether GN (⟹ 1)

−B247 and (O = 1 □) (G = 1 note) in order to see that this is not possible, is only a conjecture (although the production system generates it).

B248 Clearly GN (O) (⟹ fail), but there is no mechanism to realize it will be the last one and
−B249 to put O ⟵ x.

B251 Starts to correct current version (R ⟵ 9), then switches to earlier one (R ⟵ 7).
−B253

B254 Reading off R ⟵ 7 in col.4.

B265 Making L > 6. Confirms L ⟵ 6 at B211−B214.
−B268

B269 Sees 7 + 7 = 15 □ (D ⟵ 5 note).

B273 This is a check of R ⟵ 7 but not one that requires "check," since all right at col.2.

B274 Trouble with goal stack. Not implausible because of duration since get c3 = 1. How-
−B275 ever, exact mechanism of forgetting and of recall obscure.

B281 Coded simply as analogous to col.5 and O (B242-B249), since B and N are mutually undetermined. However, could be more to it. "From now on all letters are undetermined"; or "the independent part is localized here in col.4 and col.5."

B282 Note that there is little hesitancy in asserting here what took substantial effort in B244−B249.

B283 Unclear whether evaluation is more than a way of summarizing that all terms left are "independent." Might be evoked because can't go further, but needs to indicate (to himself) that the failure doesn't mean it can't be done.

B285 "I just need [N and B]."

B286 Error: short 2, 3, 6. Unclear why error is made. Possibly, O ⟵ x leads to need 2,
−B287 leads to generating the first two digits. But then why 3 ∨ 6 and not 2 ∨ 3?

B288 "So I'll make the [N]. . . ." Cannot decide on whether N is 3 or 6.

B289 Repeat of B288.

B290 "that column" = col.5.

B295 "Now this R plus N is 7 + 6, [which is 13]." . . . "Have to make B a [3]." Detects
−B296 difficulty from checking with TD, since there are no more digits, and aware (peripherally) that O still to go. However, not a clear inference, so repeats. The break in sentence between B295 and B296 is the clue that something is going on. Alternatively could get B = 3 and start to process col.5 before realizing free-digits is empty; however, seems like too much processing.

B304 Note in all the additions that the carry comes after adding digits of column.
−B316

B318 Unclear exactly what is being tried in attempting to get another solution.

B319 "Well, I really don't know how to check [that there aren't other solutions]." Subject was trying to be "complete" in B317−318—i.e., get all solutions.

APPENDIX 6.2

State-production Table

The following abbreviations are used in the table:

        n = note [e.g., (R = 3 n) is (R = 3 note)]
        u = unknown [e.g., (c6 u) is (c6 unknown)]
        a-l = the set of all letters
        a-c = the set of all columns
        f-d = the set of free digits (those not assigned)

The bracketing arrows on the front side of the *result* column show where backup occurs. Entries are written in the goal stack only when some change occurs. When it is necessary to show what has been sitting in the goal stack (e.g., when a backup occurs), the contents of the goal stack are put in parentheses.

ITEM	RESULT	GOAL STACK	P1	P2	P3	P4	P5	P6	P7	P8	P9	P10	P11	P12	P13	P14	?	ERROR
B1	D ← 5	a-l																
B5	T = 0		−	+													+	
B8	+ / fail		−	+	−	+	+						+					
B20	R odd	R, a-l																
B22.1			+	−	−			−	−	−	−	−			+			
B23	R odd	R, a-l												←				
B26	R = 1 ∨ 3 ∨ 5 ∨ 7 ∨ 9		−	−	−	+												
B28	R = 1 ∨ 3 ∨ 7 ∨ 9		−	−	−	−												
B30.1			−	−	−	−							+		+		+	
B31	G even	(R, a-l)	+	−														
B35.1			−	−														
B36	c6 u	G, R, a-l	−	−				−					+		+			
B39			−	−										←			+	
B40	L ← 1	R, a-l	+	+	←								+		+			P2
B44	R = 3		−	−				+				+						
B45	+	a-l	−	+														
B48	c7 = 1 u	c7 = 1, a-l							−	−	−							
B49	□ (z1 n)	1s	+															
B50.1	fail	z1 n, c7 = 1, a-l										+			+			
B51		a-l, z1 n, c7 = 1, a-l													+		+	
B53	c7 = 1 □	a-l						−	−	−				←				

ITEM	RESULT	GOAL STACK	P1	P2	P3	P4	P5	P6	P7	P8	P9	P10	P11	P12	P13	P14	?	ERROR
B57.1	R = 3 □	(a-l)						+				−						
B58	R > 5	R, a-l	+	−	−	−	−											
B59	R = 7 ∨ 9	(R, a-l)	−	−	+	−	←						+					
B61	+	a-c																
B62	R ← 7		+	−						−	−	−	+	−		+		
B63	L = 3			−														
B64.1	□ (R = 3 n)							−					−			+		
B65	L = 3	L, a-l											+		←		
B66	+	a-l	−							−	−	−	+	+			
B72	fail				+	+									?		
B76	G = 1 ∨ 2; c6 u	c6, a-l					+					−	−		+		
B78			+	−			+								+		
B80.1	E = 0		−						−	−	−		−				
B81	E = 0	E, c6, a-l	−	−									−	←	+		
B82	E = 0	c6, a-l	−	−									−	+			
B83	E = 9, c5 = 1	E, c6, a-l	−	−									+	←			P1
B85	+	c6, a-l	−	+													
B85.1	c6 = 1	a-l	−	−						−						+	
B86	[unclear]	(E, a-l)	+	−									−	−		+	
B90.1			−	−				+	+							+	
B91	E even, c3 = 0 n	(E, a-l)	+	−										?		+	?P13
B94		c3 = 0 n, E, a-l	−	−			+										

249

ITEM	RESULT	GOAL STACK	P1	P2	P3	P4	P5	P6	P7	P8	P9	P10	P11	P12	P13	P14	?	ERROR
B95		$c3 = 0, c3 = 0\,n, E, a\text{-}l$	+									+						
B95.1	$+(R \leftarrow 7\,n)$	$c3 = 0\,n, E, a\text{-}l$														+		
B96		$R \leftarrow 7\,n, c3 = 0\,n, E, a\text{-}l$															+	
B97	$R = 7 \vee 9$	$c3 = 0\,n, E, a\text{-}l$				+										−		
B98		$(E, a\text{-}l)$	+	−														
B98.1	E even	$(E, a\text{-}l)$		−		+							+				+	
B99	$E = 2 \vee 4 \vee 6 \vee 8$			−	−													
B100	+			−	−													
B101	[9 not in set]	$(E, a\text{-}l)$	+	−									+				+	
B103	$E = 0 \vee 9$			−	−									−				
B103.1	$E = 9 \;\square$			−	−	?	?											
B104 (B61)	$L \leftarrow 9$	$(R, a\text{-}l)$	−	−	+	?	?	−										P2, ?P4
B106	$R = 9$	$a\text{-}l$	−	−	↑	?	?			−	−	−	+	+				
B106.1	$\square\,(L \leftarrow 9\,n)$		−															
B106.2																		P10
B107	$L = 9 \;\square$	$(R, a\text{-}l)$ / $R, a\text{-}l$		−	−	?	?	−	−				−	−	+	↑		
B110 (B58)	[unclear]	$(R, a\text{-}l)$		−	−	?	?						−		−		+	?P4
B111	$R > 5$			+	−	?	?				−						+	
B114.1						−												
B115 (B98)	E even	$(E, a\text{-}l)$	+	+				+										
B116	$E = 0, c5 = 0\,u$	$a\text{-}l$	−								−		?					
B117.1		$c5 = 0, a\text{-}l$									−							
B118	$N < 3$	$a\text{-}l$			+											+	P4
B119.1																		

ITEM	RESULT	GOAL STACK	P1	P2	P3	P4	P5	P6	P7	P8	P9	P10	P11	P12	P13	P14	?	ERROR
B120		(E, a-l)						−										P2
B123	A ← x		−	+		−												
B123.1	E = y		−	←		−									?		+	
B124	O u		+	−		−												
B125		(E, a-l)																P2
B128	O ← 9		−	+									?					
B129	E = 0	a-l	−	←					−	−	?	?	+		+			?P11
B131	A = 5		+						−				−					
B131.1	□ (D ← 5 n)			−							?							
B132	A = 5	A, a-l																
B135	□ (D ← 5 n)	a-l	−					−		−	?	+	−	←		+	
B136				−								+	+					?P10
B137 (B23)	E = 0 □	(R, a-l)	−	−					−		−	−					+	P4
B139	R odd		−	+	+													
B140	R > 5		−	−	←													
B142	R = 7 ∨ 9		−	−							?					+	
B143.1	R ← 7, R ← 9		−	−													
B144 (B125)	A ← x	(E, a-l)	+	−	+													P2
B147.1	E = y		−	←													
B148	O u		−	−			−									+	
B148.1			+	−													
B149		(E, a-l)	+	−													P2
B152	O ← 1		−	←						−		?					
B153.1	E = 9, c5 = 1	a-l	−	←													

251

ITEM	RESULT	GOAL STACK	P1	P2	P3	P4	P5	P6	P7	P8	P9	P10	P11	P12	P13	P14	?	ERROR
B154	O ←— 2	(E, a-l)	−	−	←													
B154.1	E = 9, c5 = 1	a-l	−	−	←													
B154.2			−	−	←	?							?				+	
B155		(E, a-l)								−									
B156	O ←— x	a-l	−	−	←								?	+				
B156.1	E = 9, c5 = 1		−	−	←					−								
B157	E = 0	(E, a-l)	−	−						−			?	←			+	
B158	E = 0 □	a-l						+		−			−						
B158.1			−			?												P12, ?P4
B159	E ←— 9	E, a-l			+		+			−									
B160	c5 = 1	a-l		+						−									
B161.1	c6 = 1			+						−			+						
B162	G = 1	(a-l)	−		−					−									
B164	+ / fail			+						−									
B166	E = 9 □			+				+		−				+					
B167		E, a-l	−	−				−					−	←			+	
B169	E = 9 □		−	−		?												
B175 (B104)		(R, a-l)	−	−	−												+	
B178.1	R ←— 9	R, a-l				+				−							+	
		a-l	−															
B179		(E, a-l)	+	−				−					−	+				
B181	E = 9 □		−	−		?												

252

ITEM	RESULT	GOAL STACK	P1	P2	P3	P4	P5	P6	P7	P8	P9	P10	P11	P12	P13	P14	?	ERROR
B182								+					−			←		
B182.1	$A = 4, c3 = 1\ u$	E, a-l	−	−	−													
B182.2	$\square\ (R \leftarrow 7\ n)$	$c3 = 1$, E, a-l	−	+	−									−				
B182.3		E, a-l	−	−	−							+						
B182.4		$R \leftarrow 7\ n$, $c3 = 1$, E, a-l					+									+		
B183	$R \leftarrow 9$	$c3 = 1$, E, a-l	−	−					−								+	
B185	+	R, a-l		+									+				+	P2
B186	+		−	−						−	−							
B187	$L \leftarrow 9$		−		←					−	−							
B188	$R = 9$	a-l	−															
B188.1	$\square\ (L \leftarrow 9\ n)$		−					+	−			−	+	−			+	
B189	$R \leftarrow 9$	(R, a-l)	−	+														P2
B190	$L = 4$	a-l	−		←													
B191	+ fail		+	+				+										
B199.1	$G = 3 \lor 4;\ c6\ u$	c6, a-l		+	−													
B199.2	$E = 9, c5 = 1$	(c6, a-l)	−	−				+	−				+	−				
B200	$\square\ (R \leftarrow 9\ n)$																	
B201									−			+	+	−			+	
B202 (B199.2)	$(R \leftarrow 9)$	(c6, a-l)	+	−									+	+				
B203.1	$c5 = 1$		+	+	−				+				+					P10
B203.2	$E = 9$		−	−	−			−	+			−		−				P12
B203.3	$\square\ (R \leftarrow 9\ n)$ $c5 = 1\ \square$		−															

ITEM	RESULT	GOAL STACK	P1	P2	P3	P4	P5	P6	P7	P8	P9	P10	P11	P12	P13	P14	?	ERROR
B204	$c5 \leftarrow 0$	c5, c6, a-l	−	−			+											
B205	$E = 0$	c6, a-l	+	+									−					P11
B207	$A = 5$		+	+								−	+					
B209	$\square$ (D $\leftarrow$ 5 n)		−	−									−	−				
B209.1												?		+	+			
B210		A, c6, a-l												←				
B210.1	$c3 = 1$ u	c3 = 1, A, c6, a-l		−				+										
B211	$L > 5$ u			+				+										
B211.1		L > 5, A, c6, a-l																
B211.2	$L \leftarrow 6$	A, c6, a-l					+											
B212	$R = 3$		+	−														
B213	$\square$ (R > 5 n)		−	−					−		+		−					
B214		R > 5 n, R = 3, A, c6, a-l										+			+			
B215		A, c6, a-l					+											
B217	$R = 7 \lor 9$			−								?	?				+	
B218	$O \leftarrow 8$	E, a-l	−	+	?	?												P2, ?P4
B220	$c5 = 2$ u			←	?													
B221				−	?													
B222	$c5 = 2$ $\square$	c5 = 2, E, a-l	+	−				+	−									
B222.1				−									−				+	
B223	$E = 0 \lor 9$	(E, a-l)		−			+											
B224	$\square$ (R $\leftarrow$ 9 n)	(E, a-l)		−								−	+					
B224.1				−													+	
B225 (B224)	$E = 0$ $\square$	(E, a-l)	−	−														
B225.1				−					−			−			+		+	

ITEM	RESULT	GOAL STACK	P1	P2	P3	P4	P5	P6	P7	P8	P9	P10	P11	P12	P13	P14	?	ERROR
B226		$E = 0$, a-l	−											−	↑			P12, ?P10
B227.1	$\square\,(T = 0\,n)$	a-l				+		+			−	?						
B228 (B223)		E, a-l	−	−	−						−		+	+				?P10
B229	$E = 0 \vee 9$		−	−				−			−	?		+				
B229.1	$\square\,(T = 0, R \leftarrow 9)$	a-l																
B229.2	$c5 = 0 \vee 1\ \square$	(E, a-l)	−					+						−				P12
B230	$c5 = 2\ \square$	$c5 = 2$, E, a-l	+												+			
B230.1		E, a-l	−					−						−				
B231	$c5 = 1, B = 8$	c5, E, a-l	−								−		+					P10
B233	$\square\,(O \leftarrow 8\,n)$	E, a-l	−	−										−				
B234.1			−	−	−	+		−					+	+	↑			
B235	$c5 > 1\ \square$	(E, a-l)	−	−	−			−			−			−				
B236	$E = 0$	a-l									−	?	+					
B237	$\square\,(T = 0\,n)$							−			−	?		−			+	?P10
B238	$A = 0\ \square\,(!)$							−		+	−			+				
B238.1 (B190)	$R \leftarrow 9\ \square$	(a-l)						−			−			−			+	
B239 (B189)	$E \leftarrow 9$	E, a-l	−	−		+					−							
B240	$c5 = 1$	a-l	+	+							−							
B242	O free		−			+					−		+	+				
B242.1	$O = 1$										−			−				P10
B243	$\square\,(G = 1\,n)$							−			−							P12
B243.1	O free $\square$							+										
B244	(O free)	O, a-l	−	−		+											+	

ITEM	RESULT	GOAL STACK	P1	P2	P3	P4	P5	P6	P7	P8	P9	P10	P11	P12	P13	P14	?	ERROR
B249	O ← x	a-l	+							−	−							
B256	N > 2, c4 u							+										
B257	A □	c4, a-l		+	−								−	+				
B257.1																		
B258	A □	A, c4, a-l	−	−							−			←				
B259	A □	a-l	−	−				−			−		−	←				
B260	A = 4, c3 = 1u	A, a-l	−															
B260.1				−						−			−			←		
B261	L > 5 n	c3 = 1, a-l		−				+										
B262			−	+				+										
B262.1	L ← 6	L > 5, a-l					+											
B262.2	R = 3																	
B262.3	□ (R > 5 n)	a-l	+							−								
B263			−					−										
B264	R > 5 n, R = 3, a-l																	
B264.1	R > 5	a-l	+					−		−	+		−	+				
B265	L ← 6 □	(L > 5, a-l)		?				+					−		+			?P4
B268.1	L ← 7	L > 5, a-l		+						−		+						
B268.2	R = 5	a-l	+	−				−		−	?						?P10
B269	□(D ← 5 n)																	
B270	L ← 7 □	(L > 5, a-l)		?				+		−			+					?P4
B271	L ← 8	L > 5, a-l	+	+						−								
B273	R = 7	a-l		−						−		+				+		
B274	+																	

ITEM	RESULT	GOAL STACK	P1	P2	P3	P4	P5	P6	P7	P8	P9	P10	P11	P12	P13	P14	?	ERROR
B276	c3 = 1		+										?					?P11
B278	A = 4, E = 9		+	+														
	fail				+						−							
	+						←					+						
B279	N free	N, a-l		−	+													
B285	N = 3 ∨ 6	(N, a-l)		−	−								−					
B288				−	−								?					
B288.1	[unclear]			−	−	+	←							+				
B289	N ← x	N, a-l	+	−	−													P1
B290	B = y, c3 = 1		−	−	+													
B290.1	N > 2			−	−	+							+		←			
B291	N = 3 ∨ 6			−	−	−	←											
B293	N = 3 ∨ 6																	
B294	+		+	−											+			
B295	N ← 6	a-l	−							−	−	−		−				
B295.1	B = 3												+					
B295.2	☐ f-d = φ n																	
B296	☐ f-d = φ n	B, a-l	−	−	−	?							+	−	←			
B297		f-d n, B, a-l	−	−					+									
		f-d, f-d n, B, a-l						−				+						
B298	f-d = 2	B, a-l		+	−	+	?				−							?P4
B299	B = 3	a-l											+					
	+		+								−							
	fail				−													
B301	O ← 2	O, a-l		−	−	+					−							
	+	a-l	−	+							−	+	+					
	fail																	
B302																		

257

ITEM	RESULT	GOAL STACK	P1 P2 P3 P4 P5	P6 P7 P8 P9 P10	P11 P12 P13 P14	?	ERROR
B303	fail	empty				+	
B304		a-c n		?			
B306	$T = 0, c_1 = 1$		— ←				
B309	$R = 7, c_2 = 1$		— ←				
B311	$E = 9, c_3 = 0$		— ←				
B313	$B = 3, c_4 = 1$		— ←				
B315	$O = 2, c_5 = 1$		— ←				
B317	$R = 7, c_6 = 0$	empty	— ←				
B318						+	
B319						+ +	
B320						+	

7

CRYPTARITHMETIC:
A Broader
View

How can we decide whether the theory developed for subject S3 explains the behavior of other subjects—and to what extent it succeeds in doing so? In its literal form, the theory comes close to being a specific computer program (we have already explained in what respects it falls just short of being that). Used as a general theory, it would predict that other subjects, confronted with DONALD+ GERALD=ROBERT, will behave exactly as S3 did and will produce identical protocols.

Clearly that prediction will fail—we shall see shortly exactly how it fails. But what is important is the manner and extent of its failure. We will not be surprised if the basic processes of other subjects differ to some extent from those of S3—if their arithmetic processes, for example, corresponding to PC, are different from his in a number of details. Nor will we be surprised if these basic processes are organized into somewhat different productions and operate in a somewhat different problem space.

Whether the theory developed for S3 is simply a specific description of idiosyncratic behavior or whether it has broader significance depends on the extent of these differences and upon the circumstances in which they appear. In this chapter we will examine the similarities and differences between S3 and the other subjects at three levels. We begin, in the first section, with a comparison of the subjects' problem spaces, and we find that a number of subjects work in an augmented space closely similar to the one used by S3.

In the second section we compare behavior at the level of *episodes*—which reveal the major features of the search paths followed by the subjects. The similarities and differences in these paths will give us clues for identifying the similarities and differences among different subjects' productions and among their underlying basic processes. We will not undertake formal comparisons of protocols at the level of detail of the previous chapter; rather we will depend on diagrams depicting the organization of the episodes in each subject's protocol to give us a sufficiently tight framework to diagnose and identify the causes of difference at more detailed levels. To the extent that the basic processes, productions, and problem spaces used by the various subjects differ significantly, these differences should cause the subjects to pursue somewhat different paths through the problem space. We can trace backwards from the differences in paths to the underlying causes for divergence—i.e., the program differences.

Generalizing along another dimension—the task—we turn in the third section to a different cryptarithmetic problem, CROSS+ROADS=DANGER. Here we ask to what extent the IPS's hypothesized to deal with the previous problem are adequate to explain behavior in the face of this variant task. We examine two protocols, one of which is supplemented with synchronized gross eye-movement data. The eye-movement data permit us to ask whether the details of our information processing model are consistent with a second kind of independent evidence, in addition to verbalization, about the subject's moment-to-moment behavior.

PROBLEM SPACES

In the last chapter we were able to characterize S3 as working in a problem space, and to specify that space in detail both in terms of the kind of knowledge that constitutes its elements and the operators for acquiring new knowledge. We then proceeded to describe the details of S3's behavior by means of a production system. But even without the production system, the problem space already contains important information about the subject's capabilities. Once the problem space is fixed, intelligence is constrained to selecting among the operations it admits, on the basis of the kinds of information it makes available.

It is of interest, then, to learn something of the variety of potential problem spaces—those that are possible for a task, and those among them that humans use. In Chapter 5 we did explore some possible problem spaces for cryptarithmetic, classifying them according to the entities explicitly referred to, and the relations and predicates that could be applied to these entities. Thus, for example, the basic problem space—that obtained directly from the problem statement—is denoted (letter digit ←) since it admits only expressions of the form ⟨letter⟩ ← ⟨digit⟩, which relate a letter to a digit by the act of assignment.

We did not characterize separately the operators associated with each space. The basic kinds of operators appropriate to a space follow rather directly from the description of the states in that space—e.g., the basic problem space requires an operator for adding assignments. However, a given type of knowledge might be compatible with variant sets of operators. For instance, one might employ a delete-assignment operator in a (letter digit ←) space—that is, an operator that didn't simply return to an early state in the problem space when a contradiction was reached, but deleted a particular assignment from the current set, leaving all the others intact. Problem solving in this space would be very different from problem solving in the basic space, which has only the assignment operator. The modified space could be better or worse than the basic one, depending on the extent to which subsets of letters and columns were independent of each other.

A second example casts some light on how selection of a problem space fixes the operators in general, but not in detail. For the augmented space in which S3 worked, (letter digit carry ← = inequality parity), we were able to give plausible reasons (in Chapter 5) why the four operators PC, AV, GN, TD should be the appropriate ones. We did not specify the detail of these operators. For PC, at least, a good deal of variation is possible. Similarly, it is conceivable that TD could be split into two operators, one testing whether a given digit was already assigned, and another whether the proposed assignment was compatible with the known constraints of the letter (e.g., if $L > 5$, and $L ← 3$ is proposed, then TD fails). Each of these operators might be evoked on independent cues (probably to the detriment of the power of the problem solving).

Our concern in this section is with the problem spaces that humans actually use, rather than with the range of possible spaces. Of course a human *can* use any problem space we can specify, although possibly not in reasonable time nor without error, unless he is supplied with external memory and computational aids. Thus our interest centers on the spaces that in fact are used. However, we are not yet ready for a serious ecological study (as proposed, say, by Egon Brunswick, 1956) of how often various problem spaces will be encountered in naturally occurring environments. Rather, we wish to ask two prior questions: Does the concept of a problem space apply to the problem solving behavior of other humans besides S3? Is there enough variation in the problem space from one subject to another so that it becomes a psychological datum of interest, rather than a simple reflection of the demands of the task environment?

Augmented Problem Space

The augmented problem space—the one used by S3—appears to be the space used by most technically educated people when they encounter the DONALD+ GERALD task. For instance, of the eight short written protocols reproduced by Bartlett (1958), at least five clearly use the augmented space.

The protocol of Bartlett's subject I (his subjects are identified by Roman numerals) is reproduced in Figure 7.1. The data are only a written summary prepared by the subject, but they provide ample evidence of his problem space. First, the relations of equality, inequality, and parity are mentioned explicitly. Assignment is little used (because S is rather good at inferring) but is evident in lines 7 to 9. Thus, all the various elements of the augmented knowledge space are present. Similarly, each of the four operators appropriate to that space is used. We show this to the right of the figure by restating the subject's actions in terms of PC, GN, AV, and TD. More important than their mere occurrence is the fact that all the various relations occur both as input and as output to these operators, for this shows that the subject really can use the information contained in the knowledge state to move to a new knowledge state.

Figure 7.1 shows that the subject was working at least part of the time in a space that included the augmented space. Only by indirection does it show that the subject did not use additional inference operations in the space, or that there were not times when all the sophistication so apparent at other points in the protocol was inaccessible to him. These issues are not critical for the case at hand, partly because we understand the task well enough so that the sufficiency of the reasoning is apparent, and partly because we believe from general experience that human competence does not fluctuate violently over short periods of time in nonstressful situations.

FIGURE 7.1

protocol of Bartlett's Subject I

1.	Given D = 5, then $5 + 5 = T$		$\therefore$ T $= 0$	PC[col.1]
2.	O + E = O $\therefore$ E must be either nought which is			PC[col.5]
		impossible or 9 and N + R > 10	E $= 9$	TD(E, 0)
3.	L + L + 1 (carried) = R $\therefore$ R is an odd number;			PC[col.2]
		but also D(5) + G = R, so		PC[col.6 for R]
		R is 7 or 9, but E is 9	$\therefore$ R $= 7$	GN(R)
				TD(R, 9)
4.	D(5) + G + 1 (carried) = R and R is 7		$\therefore$ G $= 1$	PC[col.6]
5.	A + A = E and R is 9 $\therefore$ A $= 4$, and L + L > 10		A $= 4$	PC[col.3]
6.	L + L + 1 (carried) = R and R is 7		$\therefore$ L $= 8$	PC[col.2]
7.	N + 7 > 10 and as only 2, 3, 6 are now available		$\therefore$ N $= 6$	GN(free-digits)
				AV(N)
8.		and	B $= 3$	PC[col.4]
9.		and	O $= 2$	AV(O)

SOURCE: Bartlett (1958, p. 51)

However, with other protocols such issues can be more troublesome. For instance, Figure 7.2 shows the most obscure of the protocols reproduced by Bartlett, that belonging to subject VII. It is clear that the subject does not have strong inference capabilities using PC, at least at the beginning where he is mostly making assignments. There is no evidence that he uses parity, inequality, or disjunctive sets. However, once he makes the correct inference at column 5 (line 6), that E = 9, he simply asserts that "things fit in easily." We are left substantially uninformed about what processes he used for the fitting.

Rather than belabor examples where the data are insufficient, let us look at

FIGURE 7.2

protocol for Bartlett's Subject VII

1. Substituted 5 for D.
2. Juggled with the figures 0-9, substituting until this stage was reached:

$$
\begin{array}{l}
\text{DONALD} \\
5 \quad\quad 3\,4\,5 \\
\text{GERALD} \\
\underline{6\,9 \quad 3\,4\,5} \\
9 \quad\quad 6\,9\,0
\end{array}
$$

3. Progress was now difficult, as there were O, N, G, B to equal 1, 2, 7 or 8. About ten minutes was spent trying to make these numbers fit in and as it proved impossible to do this the attempt was given up.
4. Decided to begin again with

$$
\begin{array}{l}
\text{DONALD} \\
5 \quad\quad 5 \\
\text{GERALD} \\
\underline{\quad\quad\quad 5} \\
0
\end{array}
$$

5. Wrote out a list of the letters with their corresponding numbers as known, thus:

$$
\begin{array}{l}
A \\
B \\
D = 5 \\
E \\
G \\
L \\
N \\
O \\
R \\
T = 0
\end{array}
$$

6. Now realized that O + E had to give the O of ROBERT and so E had to be 9.
7. The numbers now seemed to fit in easily. They were identified in the order L = 8, A = 4, R = 7, G = 1.

   In comment on the whole process this operator declared stage 3 to be the difficult one. It was hard to break away from an approach which nevertheless was leading to nothing definite. Once stage 6 was achieved the rest was "much easier," for all the numbers now seemed to "fit in."

SOURCE: Bartlett (1958, p. 56)

our own subjects, for whom we do have complete protocols in the same style as S3's. Of the four subjects, three—S4, S5, and S8—clearly work in the augmented problem space. The other, S6, does not, and we will discuss his protocol later. The protocols for the first three subjects are reproduced in Appendices 7.1, 7.2, and 7.3 at the end of the chapter. To show that S4, S5, and S8 worked in the augmented problem space, we present in Figures 7.3, 7.4, and 7.5 illustrations from their respective protocols of mention of the various elements of the knowledge state and of the use of the four operators. We select examples showing that the various bits of knowledge are used as inputs to the operators, and do not occur only as outputs. As with Bartlett's protocols, our figures do not prove that other problem spaces were not used. However, a perusal of the actual protocols settles the issue with reasonable certainty.

That all these subjects, both Bartlett's and ours, worked in the augmented problem space does not mean that all their problem solving activity was identical.

FIGURE 7.3

evidence for problem space of S4

Use of carries:
    B50:   Knowing that O plus 9 is equal to O,
    B51:   must make N plus R some number greater than 10,
    B52:   in order to make the fifth column come out correctly.
Use of inequalities:
    B37:   So L must be some other digit greater than 5,
    B38:   in order to have the two A's equal to 9.
Use of parity:
    B53:   So we know that R must be an odd number,
    B54:   because the two D's added to 10.
Use of disjunctions:
    B9:   And looking at the left-most column, you can see that R is either 1 or 2 greater
           than G,
Use of PC:
    B28:   And to have O plus E equal to O,
    B29:   this means that E is 1 less . . .
    B30:   It means that E must be 9.
Use of GN:
    B44:   And knowing that the two L's add to some number greater than 10,
    B45:   they must be either 6, 7 or 8.
Use of TD:
    B22:   And that must make G a 1,
    B23:   because G must be either a zero or a 1,
    B24:   for D plus G to be equal to R.
    B25:   And you know that T is zero.
Use of AV:
    B17:   So just to guess L a 3 could be some help.
    B18:   Could you make L a 3?

FIGURE 7.4

evidence for problem space of S5

Use of carries:

    B78: Um . . . if A is 4, 8, 9,

    B79: carry 1 there.

    B80: So that will have to be er . . .

    B81: L can be si . . . 6 I guess.

Use of inequalities:

    B331: R has to be greater than 5

    B332: and less than 10.

    B333: It has to be 6, 7, 8, or 9.

Use of parity:

    B335: And um . . . can't be an even digit

    B336: since we are carrying an odd . . . carrying 1 and adding two the same, multiplying by 2.

    B337: So it'll have to be odd.

Use of disjunctions:

    B288: so R has to be 7 or 9.

    B289: So L has to be 3 or 4.

Use of PC:

    B215: OK. In order for E to be 9,

    B216: A has to be 4.

    B318: E would have to be . . E would have to be 9.

    B319: Since 1 plus 9, if you carry 1, equal 11,

    B320: which would equal 1, right?

Use of GN:

    B157: Now we have . . what numbers left?

    B158: 2 and 3.

    B159: OK. No we have to have more than that, 2, 3, 4, 5.

    B160: We have 2, 3 and 6 left.

Use of TD:

    B356: E would have to be um . .

    B357: Make it zero.

    B358: No. T is already zero.

Use of AV:

    B450: Make L 3,

    B451: R would be 7.

    B452: If we make L 2,

    B453: R would be 5,

    B454: So that cannot . . .

    B455: Make L 1,

    B456: R would be 3.

    B457: But we have zero is already 1, or O is already 1.

There was substantial variation, as we shall see. However, it does mean that they all were using essentially the same intellectual tools, so that their strategies and heuristics can meaningfully be compared.

FIGURE 7.5

evidence for problem space of S8

Use of carries:
    B539: If I use 2 [for N]
    B540: that'll force me to make B 9.
    B541: Well, that will give me no carry over again [to col.5]

Use of inequalities:
    B411: Now if I make A anything higher than 6
    B412: this isn't going to do me any good
    B413: 'cause I'm going to have a carry over of 1

Use of parity:
    B69: So er . . . looks, looks like E has got to be an even number.
    B70: You get it by adding A and A.
    B71: But that doesn't tell me too much.

Use of disjunctions:
    B37: So R . . . R is 7 or 9.
    B38: And in other . . . in other words it's either a number you get by adding er . . . 3 and 3 plus 1,
    B39: and the number you get by adding 4 and 4 plus 1.
    B40: So L is either 3 or 4.

Use of PC:
    B585: That . . . that gives me two numbers here, which when added up give me a 9 (laughs) or 19.
    B586: Er . . . So, unless I'm completely bawled up, there must be a carry over from this column here.
    B596: Er . . . So I've got a 1 carry over.
    B597: And A and A add up to 9.
    B598: So this means that A could be 4

Use of GN:
    B15: The number GERALD is going to be er . . . less than five hundred thousand.
    B16: G will either be 1, 2, 3, or 4, I guess.
    B185: (Yawns) OK. So R is 7 and 9.
    B186: (laughs) That gives L is 3, 4, 8 or 9.

Use of TD:
    B358: And er . . . I didn't use 2, [for A]
    B359: 'cause that adds up to 4, and [for E but L = 4]
    B360: And I've eliminated 3,
    B361: 'cause that's G according to my assumption.
    B362: And 5 is the next number,
    B363: and I've used that [T = 0]

Use of AV:
    B53: So er . . . let's let er . . . L equal to 3, and see what that gets us.
    B54: See if I can remember that L has to be either 3 or 4.
    B55: Put down 3 for L.

More Basic Problem Spaces: An Example

    In the augmented problem space it is possible to make substantially maximal inferences from arithmetic relations, given information about the ranges of the participating letters, information restricting them to small sets of digits, statements of inequalities, or parity statements. We would expect not to find a subject working in a basic space and using only the options of (1) assignment, and (2) checking whether two given digits sum to a third (as in $3 + 3 = 9$?). For if a problem solver can add well enough to check columns, he can probably also add well enough to infer that if $R = 3 + 3$, then $R = 6$. Nevertheless, we might expect to find problem spaces that are more impoverished than the augmented space we have been considering so far. Indeed, we will present one example in some detail.[1] We do not mean by this simply a protocol from a subject who isn't as competent arithmetically as the subjects we have looked at so far. For as we descend in arithmetic skill, say toward young children whose arithmetic competence is low, we may get behavior that is not characterizable at all as working in the basic problem space.

Our example is the protocol of subject S6, an adult who had not gone to college and whose arithmetic and symbolic skills were below those of the other subjects we have worked with. He abandoned the problem unsolved after 25 minutes.

S6's protocol consists mostly of assignments, punctuated by his sometimes summing columns where the digits had been assigned. There is no evidence that he makes use of inequalities, digit-set, or parity information. From some of his assignments it can be inferred that additional column processing occurred, but always starting with the two upper digits as inputs (e.g., $3 + 3 = E$ or $3 + 3 = 9$?). A striking feature of the subject's behavior is that he permits inconsistencies in assignments to stand for substantial periods of time. The experimenter recorded on the display the digits assigned, and S6 simply allowed, for example, column 6 ($D + G = R$) to remain as $5 + 8 = 7$ for four minutes.

We are concerned with what such features indicate about the subject's problem space. S6 appears to divide his display into two parts: a right-hand set of columns, which are considered to be *firmly* assigned, and the remaining columns to the left, which are considered to be tentatively assigned. Apparently he assigns digits to letters that appear only in the left-hand columns without dealing with the consequences of the assignments for those columns. The important inference we draw from this about his problem space is that S6 retains the knowledge of which columns have been assigned definitely, and which tentatively.

The subject's protocol consists of 130 phrases, most of them separated by short statements of the experimenter, as he makes an assignment, or asserts that he cannot do so (thus the protocol runs from B1 to B240). Since we do not wish to analyze the entire protocol in detail, but only describe the problem space, we have reproduced a single segment of it in Figure 7.6 (the entire protocol can be found in Appendix 7.4). On the right-hand side we note the operations on the problem space that can be inferred to occur. The sample of behavior was selected to show as many different operations as possible; thus, it is atypical of the subject's behavior, underrepresenting the large number of assignment statements he makes in the full protocol.

---

[1] One of Bartlett's subjects (V) appears systematically to use inequality information but not parity information and to ignore prospective carries (i.e., ones he has not previously calculated). However, the record is too brief to use him as an example.

FIGURE 7.6

fragment of S6's protocol

			6 5 4 3 2 1 D O N A L D G E R A L D <u>R O B E R T</u>
			↓
			5 1 9 2 3 5 8 4 7 2 3 5 <u>7 1 6 4 7 0</u>
B69	390	Er . . . make the . . . make the O . . . make the O . . .	PC[col.5 for O] ($\Longrightarrow$ O $\longleftarrow$ 5)
B70	417	(E: Please talk.)	TD(O, 5) ($\Longrightarrow$ □ (D = 5))
B71	420	Er . . . make the O 4.	AV(O) ($\Longrightarrow$ O $\longleftarrow$ 4) TD(O, 4) ($\Longrightarrow$ □ (E = 4))
B72	422	Ch . . . change the . . .	AV(E) ($\Longrightarrow$ fail)
B73	425	Take 4 from the E and make the A . . . the O 4.	MD(O, E) ($\Longrightarrow$ O $\longleftarrow$ 4, E undefined)
			↓
			5 4 9 2 3 5 8 E 7 2 3 5 <u>7 4 6 E 7 0</u>
B74	432	(E: E is no longer 4. O is 4.)	
B75	435	Ooops . . . Change that back. Change that back.	BU(E) ($\Longrightarrow$ E $\longleftarrow$ 4, O undefined)
B76	437	Keep the E as 4, please.	
			↓
			5 O 9 2 3 5 8 4 7 2 3 5 <u>7 0 6 4 7 0</u>
B77	442	(E: E is 4. O is no longer 4.)	
B78	445	Right. Ok. Make um . . . make the O . . . make the O . . .	PC[col.5 for O] ($\Longrightarrow$?)
B79	465	3, 4, 5, 6.	GN(used-digits) ($\Longrightarrow$ 2, 3, 4, 5, 6,
B80	475	Make the O . . . oh . . . make the O the th . . . make the O 1.	7, 8) AV(O) ($\Longrightarrow$ O $\longleftarrow$ 1)
			↓
			5 1 9 2 3 5 8 4 7 2 3 5 <u>7 1 6 4 7 0</u>
B81	492	(E: O is 1.)	
B82	495	Right. Er . . .	
B83	502	(E: Please talk.)	
B84	510	Make the G . . . make the G . . . make the G se . . .	PC[col.6 for G] ($\Longrightarrow$?)
B85	527	(E: Please talk.)	
B86	530	G has to stay as 8,	
B87	532	O as 1.	
B88	540	5 and 5's 10.	PC[col.1] ($\Longrightarrow$ T = 0, c2 = 1)
B89	545	Er . . . (whistles) 3 and 6 and 1 is 7 . . . 1 is 7.	PC[col.2] ($\Longrightarrow$ R = 7, c3 = 0)
B90	562	2 and 2. E is 4.	PC[col.3] ($\Longrightarrow$ E = 4, c4 = 0)
B91	567	E has to stay as 4.	

B92	572	Er ... 9 and 7 are 16.	PC[col.4] ($\Longrightarrow$ B = 6, c5 = 1)
B93	580	4, 5 and 1 is 6 ... er ...	PC[col.5] ($\Longrightarrow$ O = 6 □ (O ← 1))
B94	585	Make the O 6.	AV(O) ($\Longrightarrow$ O ← 6)
B95	592	Make the R 8.	TD(O, 6) ($\Longrightarrow$ □ (B ← 6))
B96	594	(E: O is 6.)	MD(O, B) ($\Longrightarrow$ O ← 6, B undefined) AV(B) ($\Longrightarrow$ B ← 8)
B97	597	(E: I'll have to change B then.)	(E: TD(O, B) ($\Longrightarrow$ □ (B ← 8)))
B98	599	Pardon me.	
B99	600	(E: I must change B, because B is 6.)	
B100	605	Right. You're ... Change the B to er ... to er ... se ... er ... 8.	AV(B) ($\Longrightarrow$ B ← 8) [repeated]
B101	612	(E: G is 8.)	(E: TD(B, 8) ($\Longrightarrow$ □ (G ← 8)))
B102	615	OK. Change the G to 1.	AV(G) ($\Longrightarrow$ G ← 1)

$$\downarrow$$

$$5\ 6\ 9\ 2\ 3\ 5$$
$$1\ 4\ 7\ 2\ 3\ 5$$

| B103 | 617 | (E: G is 1) | |

$$\overline{7\ 6\ 8\ 4\ 7\ 0}$$

B104	622	(E: and B is 8.)	
B105	627	Um ... 9 and 7 is si ... 16.	PC[col.4] ($\Longrightarrow$ B = 6 □ (B ← 8))
B106	632	6 and 4 are 10.	PC col.5 ($\Longrightarrow$ O = 0 □ (O ← 6))
B107	640	Oh. Er ... change the ... change the B to 9	EX(N, B) ($\Longrightarrow$ N ← 8, B ← 9)
B108	657	and the N to 8.	

$$\downarrow$$

$$5\ 6\ 8\ 2\ 3\ 5$$
$$1\ 4\ 7\ 2\ 3\ 5$$

| B109 | 660 | (E: B is 9,) | |

$$\overline{7\ 6\ 9\ 4\ 7\ 0}$$

| B110 | 662 | (E: and N is 8.) | |

The problem space we have induced for S6 from this protocol is shown in Figure 7.7. The knowledge state consists of the assignments he has made to each letter, plus a column, *next-column*. All columns to the right of next-column are considered firm. All letters occurring to the right of next-column are considered to be firmly assigned; all others are only tentatively assigned. His current knowledge state also contains his current goals, as well as strictly temporary information. Knowledge of the assignments already made appears to be kept externally on the display (as written by E on request by S), so that all S6 remembers internally are next-column, the goal stack, the immediate products of operators, and the column at which he is currently working (which need not be the same as next-column).

There are seven operators: four that make assignments (AV, MD, EX, AEX), one that processes columns (PC), one that tests if proposed values of assignments are legitimate (TD), and one that retracts steps or backs up (BU). Each of these is described briefly in Figure 7.7. We can illustrate most of them from Figure 7.6.

Since the figure presents only one or a few instances of each operator, we tabulate in Table 7.1 the number of occurrences of each operator in the entire protocol. The occurrences are divided into various subclasses that will be explained as we take up the operators. We do not present a PBG for S6, since, as we shall see, his search through the problem space does not have any structure that lends itself to graphical display.

FIGURE 7.7

problem space of S6

⟨letter⟩ :: = A | B | D | E | G | L | N | O | R | T
⟨digit⟩ :: = 0 | 1 | 2 | 3 | 4 | 5 | 6 | 7 | 8 | 9
⟨next-column⟩ :: = col.1 | col.2 | col.3 | col.4 | col.5 | col.6
⟨expression⟩ :: = ⟨letter⟩ ⟵ ⟨digit⟩
⟨expression-set⟩ :: = ⟨expression⟩ | ⟨expression⟩, ⟨expression-set⟩
⟨knowledge-state⟩ :: = ⟨next-column⟩, ⟨expression-set⟩

AV(letter)	*Assign-value.* Assign an unused digit to letter.
MD(letter.1, letter.2)	*Move-digit.* Assign to letter.1 the digit currently assigned to letter.2; make letter.2 unassigned.
EX(letter.1, letter.2)	*Exchange.* Assign to letter.1 the digit currently assigned to letter.2; and assign to letter.2 the digit currently assigned to letter.1.
AEX(letter)	*Assign-exchanged-digit.* Assign to letter the digit that has just become unassigned by the previous assignment.
TD(letter, digit)	Test if digit is assigned to another letter.
PC(column for letter)	Process column, possibly for a value for a given letter. Add top + middle to get a value for bottom. PC is applicable only if top and middle have digits assigned. (Occasionally more complex processes occur.)
BU(letter)	*Back-up.* Return to letter the previous digit assigned to it. Any other letter assigned that digit becomes undefined.

TABLE 7.1

operator occurrences in S6's protocol

Assignments	61
AV	49
MD	2
EX	3
AEX	7
Process column (PC)	42
digit + digit = letter	30
digit + letter = digit	4
unclear	8
Test digit (TD)	32
by S6	11
by E	21
Back up (BU)	4

Assignment. The main assignment operator, AV, assigns a digit to a letter. The digit either (1) is not in use, or (2) has just been produced by PC (and may already be assigned to another letter). Figure 7.6 starts with a situation in which all ten digits have already been assigned; hence it does not often show AV assigning an unassigned digit [case (1), above]. Nevertheless this does happen at B80, since in assigning O ⟵ 4 and then reconsidering the assignment (B73, B75), S6 leaves both O and the digit 1 unassigned. He then assigns O (AV(O)) at B80. We even see him generating the digits in his search for an available value. This generation, by the way, is seen in only two other places in the protocol, always in exactly the same circumstances. Thus, S6 has no GN(letter) operator of the kind possessed by all subjects who use the augmented problem space. Examples of the operation, AV, using a digit already assigned to another letter [case (2) above], occur at B71 and at B94.

Figure 7.7 claims S6 uses three other assignment operators: move-digit (MD), exchange (EX), and assign-exchanged-digit (AEX). These are required because S6 rapidly arrives at a tentative full assignment of digits to letters (9 assigned by B30, all 10 by B69). From that point onward, any new assignment must use a digit already assigned. It is clear that the subject comes to view each new assignment as moving a digit from one letter to which it had previously been assigned, to another (MD). The first example in Figure 7.6 occurs at B73, where S6 says "Take 4 from E and make . . . ."

MD occurs only twice and is a transition to EX, where the subject constructs a single operator to make more than one assignment. By exchanging digits, he avoids making an assignment that violates the problem constraint, which says that each digit can be assigned to only one letter. An example of EX (the first) occurs at B107. The new operator is clearly marked by the fact that S announces two assignments at once. EX is in turn a transition to AEX, in which S makes an assignment and then lets E evoke TD (by asserting that the inconsistently assigned digit must be changed on the letter to which it was previously assigned). Then S assigns the just-released digit. Many apparently inappropriate assignments are made this way. The first AEX occurs at B133, and this is also the time of the last EX. Of the 21 TD's evoked by E, 70 percent occurred after this point (with only 40 percent of the time remaining).

Column Processing. The subject does a substantial amount of column processing (42 instances). In essentially all cases the two upper digits are given. In most cases the lower digit is given as well, so that the process is really a check on the consistency of the assignments. Figure 7.6 contains the longest explicit arithmetic sequence in the protocol (B88 to B93), where the subject adds from right to left in a fully assigned situation until he reaches a column (5) that does not check. The limitations on the subject's PC are evident here, since when he adds up column 5 ($O + E + c5 = O \Rightarrow 4 + 1 = 5, + 1 = 6,$) he then sets the letter O to 6 without observing that O also appears as one of the upper digits. Since, in the protocol segment, all the digits are always assigned, there is no opportunity in Figure 7.6 for a column to be processed when the lower letter is unassigned; however, this does happen elsewhere in the protocol.

In two or three places in the protocol one might argue that the subject is engaged in more complex reasoning, but each instance implies several types of action that are not supported anywhere else in the behavior. For instance, at B24 after assigning $O \leftarrow 4$ and getting

$$
\begin{array}{cccccc}
5 & 4 & N & 2 & 3 & 5 \\
6 & E & R & 2 & 3 & 5 \\
\hline
R & 4 & B & E & R & 0 \\
\end{array}
$$

S6 says "Er... Make the E 9." He could have reasoned that $E = 0 \lor 9$ with $c5 = 0 \lor 1$ correspondingly. But he never shows any awareness of this possibility later, nor does he ever take a carry from an uncompleted column into account. Thus, we conclude that the selection of 9 rather than some other value was not guided by PC. In particular, of course, it was not guided by the application of PC to column 4, which would have implied that $E = 4$ or 5. This example, by the way, shows how S6 could leave obvious consequences and inconsistencies untouched on the display.

As Table 7.1 shows, there were four reasonably clear instances where S6 inferred a value for a letter that occurred on the top of the display. For example, at B126 the display was:

$$
\begin{array}{r}
5\ 4\ 3\ 6\ 8\ 5 \\
9\ 2\ 7\ 6\ 8\ 5 \\
\hline
7\ 4\ 1\ 2\ 7\ 0
\end{array}
$$

S6 first produced $E = 9$ and followed it by $G = 2$. It is not necessary to assume that the answers were obtained by transposition and subtraction; they could also be obtained by trying values and verifying. Considering that each of the four instances took from 10 to 30 seconds, a generate-and-test process is plausible. Three of the four cases (the two above and one other) occurred in the last minutes of the attempt, just before S6 gave up. Thus, it is fair to characterize S6's PC as extremely rudimentary, very close to what would be available in the basic problem space.

Testing Assignments. The operator TD occurs explicitly at several places in the protocol, even though the devices embedded in the assignment operators usually serve to keep conflicts from occurring (as in the exchange at B107). None of the explicit uses of TD appears in Figure 7.6. The shift of the test from TD to the assignment operators is due partly to the experimenter's stepping out of his passive role and gradually taking on the responsibility for not allowing multiple assignments. However, occasionally cases slipped by the experimenter, and then were caught by S6. At B41, for example, having assigned 7 to both R and N, he says "Er... something's wrong here. We have N and R both as 7's."

Backup. The final operator listed in Figure 7.7 retracts a single step. In the augmented problem space, subjects engage in a substantial amount of trial and error, backing up each time to some previous knowledge state. This is what makes a PBG representation interesting, since it reveals the search pattern. S6, on the other hand, almost never backs up; instead, he keeps all the digits fully assigned and simply makes reassignments to deal with local difficulties as he encounters them. Therefore one needs to recognize explicitly the few places where he retracts an action rather than simply continuing to a new one. An instance occurs at B75 in Figure 7.6; its character is clear from the subject's language.

These backups are relevant to the last point we want to discuss in relation to S6's problem space. One of its novel aspects is next-column, which divides the display into a firm and a tentative part, and which (we claim) S6 keeps in memory during the course of problem solving. The evidences for this claim are indirect, but of several kinds. First, we define next-column operationally as the first column from the right that contains either an undefined letter or an inconsistency. We include only inconsistencies that do not depend on the carries from or into adjacent columns. In Figure 7.6 the arrow over the display shows next-column, determined according to this definition. All letters occurring in columns to the right of next-column are *firm*, all others are *tentative*. Then, the following is the case:

1. Whenever a choice is made of a letter to change, a tentative letter is always changed in preference to a firm letter. Such choices occur among the letters of an inconsistent column and between the two letters of a TD conflict. A total of 27 conflict situations occur that pit a firm letter against a tentative one, and the tentative one is changed in 22 cases— i.e., in all but 5 cases.
2. All four backups occur after a failure in the rule above, when a firm letter is changed in preference to a tentative one. Thus, four out of five of the failures to maintain firm letters are, in fact, lapses that are immediately caught and the status quo maintained.
3. On those few occasions (3) when a firm letter is changed, the new next-column is attended to immediately.
4. When attending to next-column, the assignment always makes the column consistent, insofar as that is possible from S6's PC. That is, S6 always makes the attempt at consistency with next-column, though sometimes, as in B94 in Figure 7.6, the result is not objectively correct. There are 13 cases where this attempt at consistency occurs.
5. Generally, the only inconsistencies that S6 discovers are in next-column (18 cases out of 21). Thus, it is next-column that is supposed to be consistent, not any of the others farther left. On at least one occasion (B88 to B94, shown in Figure 7.6) S6 makes explicit the strategy of working from right to left until he encounters an inconsistent column, which he then tries to make consistent.

This concludes our discussion of S6 and his problem space. We have been rather explicit, both about its character and the evidence for establishing it. We have done this partly to document the existence in human behavior of spaces other than the augmented problem space, since the latter will seem natural to most readers of this book. We have done it also to emphasize that much is known about a problem solver's power once his problem space is known. Of course, the problem can be solved in the space used by S6, but the solution process is not easy, for it requires extensive search.

Other Problem Spaces

We could proceed to take up separately a number of other problem spaces, as we have done with the augmented and basic problem spaces. But it happens that one of our subjects (S8), in attempting the cryptarithmetic problem LETS+

WAVE=LATER, carried out an initial search for different ways to approach the problem. This prelude, which lasted about 25 minutes, constitutes a fascinating source of data on problem spaces in cryptarithmetic. Consequently, we will examine this segment of his protocol. S8 finally settled on using the augmented problem space for LETS+WAVE=LATER, and continued to use it without further ado in the next task, which was DONALD+GERALD=ROBERT, discussed later in the chapter.

The protocol for S8's search for a problem space (as we will refer to this behavior of S8 to keep it distinct from his problem solving on DONALD+GERALD) is contained in Appendix 7.5 at the end of the chapter. We have annotated it on the right-hand side of the page but we will not discuss it in detail. In Figure 7.8 we extract from it the seven problem spaces that S8 unearthed in his attempt to approach the task. Before we turn to these main items of interest, we offer a few comments on the protocol.

The subject proceeds by attempting to characterize the task in various ways (e.g., B6: "All right. So I'm adding up two four-digit numbers er . . . to get a five-digit number.") and seeing if these evoke methods to deal with the task. If he evokes a method, he makes a preliminary evaluation of its feasibility. If the evaluation turns out negative (as it does repeatedly), he looks for a new characterization, or picks up again a method that he has looked at earlier and dropped. The subject has just finished the task AA+BB=CBC, which he solved by fairly exhaustive search in the space of equal-digit numbers, 11, 22, 33, . . . (see discussion below). Assessing the same techniques to be inapplicable to his new task, he then searches rather widely. The analysis on the right side of the protocol in Appendix 7.5 shows he generated fourteen methods, which employ seven different problem spaces. Toward the end the subject becomes somewhat discouraged:

B132: I . . . I have the feeling that I'm er . . . I'm being dull here,
B133: but I er . . . can't er . . . I'm really . . . I'm really stymied at this point.
B134: I mean, I . . . I haven't at . . . attempted to substitute any numbers or anything yet,
B135: but er, . . . I realize maybe that's what you want me to try and do.
B136: But er . . . I haven't done it because I'm convinced that it's futile.
B137: I mean, I might accidently stumble on the right answer,
B138: but I think that is a skillion to one shot.

Finally, however, he begins to make some trial assignments, the commitment to this course occurring when he changes his estimate of the probability of success by becoming aware that there might be many solutions:

B226: Ah! Well now wait a minute. Is it possible, I wonder? Is it er . . . possible that a prob . . . this problem has got more than one solution?
B227: Maybe a lot of solutions, one of which I could pick out er . . . just by starting at the beginning.

At this point the search for a problem space ends and he starts working in the augmented problem space.

The subject does not see himself as searching for a problem space, but rather for a method or approach to the problem. But that he is engaged in the latter search is explicit:

B40: I'm er . . . really at a loss as to how to attack this problem.

B167: I'm just about ready to throw in the towel I'm afraid
B168: 'cause I can't think of a method to attack this problem.
B169: If I could just think of a way to attack it, but I can't.

Each method, however, implies a definite problem space, which we can infer.

The subject does on a few occasions derive significant problem information during this search. For example, he settles for himself whether a carry can be greater than 1 (it can't). He does this, however, not in a direct attempt to solve the problem, but as a subtask in determining whether an approach, that of adding up vertical columns, is hopeless because the carry isn't known. He sums up his extensive considerations on the carry by commenting on column 2 (he has been discussing all columns):

B217: Either T and V, or T plus V plus 1, will give me either E or the number the second digit of which is E.
B218: So I . . . I guess you could start eliminating on this basis.

FIGURE 7.8

the seven problem spaces found by S8

Basic problem space	
Element:	A collection of letter-digit assignments
Operators:	Assign a digit to a letter
	Unassign a letter
	Test if a digit (and/or a letter) is unassigned
Initial element:	No assignments
Final element:	Element satisfying the addition and exclusion tests
Augmented problem space	
Element:	A collection of letter-digit and carry-digit relations: assignment, equality, inequality, parity, disjunction
Operators:	Assign a digit to a letter
	Test if a digit (and/or a letter) is unassigned
	Process a column to derive new relation
	Generate the digits still possible for a letter or carry
Initial element:	No relations
Final element:	Element with assignments satisfying the addition and exclusion tests
Number problem space	
Element:	A set of three numbers, one associated with each word of the problem

FIGURE 7.8 (cont'd)

Operators:	For a given word obtain another number that fits its pattern (e.g., as ABAB yields 1212, 1313, 2323, . . .), taking into account excluded and forced values from other words.
	Test if three numbers satisfy the addition test
Initial element:	No numbers, just the three words from the display
Final element:	Three numbers that satisfy the addition test

Algebra problem space

Element:	A collection of equations, whose variables are letters and carries A set of admissible values for each variable.
Operators:	Substitute add subtract transpose, etc. Test if two equations have the same value but different variables
Initial element:	The collection of equations corresponding to the columns of the display
Final element:	A solved set of equations for the letters

Word-meaning problem space

Element:	A collection of meaningful words and phrases, including numbers
Operators:	Associate semantically in LTM to obtain yet other words and phrases Associate semantically to a number that fits the pattern of an initial word
Initial element:	The words of the display
Final element:	A set of numbers, which will then satisfy the addition and exclusion tests

Cryptogram problem space

Element:	A rule that maps the letters into digits, using the positional relations of the letters in the alphabet as the basis of the rule
Operators:	Construct another rule, expressed in a language involving relations in the alphabet (e.g., next, distance between letters, distance from ends, etc.)
Initial element:	No rule
	The set of letters to be mapped into the ten digits
Final element:	A rule that will produce a digit assignment meeting the addition test (the exclusion test being satisfied by construction)

Typographical problem space

Element:	A recognition process that sees in the shape of each letter a digit, i.e., a mapping from typographical features of letters to digits (e.g., I 1, Z 2, E 3, etc.)
Operators:	Select various ways of viewing the letters, so as to produce the recognition of a digit (e.g., symmetry, as in E and 3, deletion, as in H and 4, etc.)
Initial element:	No letters recognized as digits
	The set of letters to be so recognized (e.g., R and N, as well as O and S)
Final element:	All the letters recognized as digits, which will then satisfy the addition test (the exclusion test being satisfied by the recognition process)

The various problem spaces considered by S8 are shown in Figure 7.8. The figure lists them in the order in which we shall discuss them, from the most familiar to the least. S8 came across them in a different order, which can be reconstructed from the references to the places in the protocol where the spaces are discussed. The first two spaces listed, the basic problem space and the augmented problem space, hardly need further discussion here. As we have seen above in discussing S8's discouragement, he refers to the basic space explicitly, and wants no part of it. One other passage shows this clearly:

B54: If you ... if you substituted letters for numbers at random that er ...
B55: the solution of this problem is virtually ... is virtually hopeless
B56: er ... without er ... either an enormous amount of time
B57: or else (laughs) some sort of machine to process data.

Number Problem Space. The essential feature of this space is that each of the words is viewed as a number (i.e., WAVE is a four-digit number, hence in the thousands), and some way is sought to limit the admissible values of this number so that instances can be generated. The subject gets essentially nowhere with this space in the present problem, but it is the one that he used almost exclusively in the AA+BB=CBC problem, as mentioned earlier. Without going into detailed analysis of the latter protocol, we can give a passage from it that shows how clear-cut the evidence is:

... so they're not going to be 11 and 22.
Or they're not going to be er ... 11 and 33.
And they are not going to be er ... 22 and 44.
And not going to be 33 and 44.
Let's see what's ....
They won't be er ....
Let's see. The next highest would be er ... let's see. 33 and 55 ...
22 and 66 just about ...
that just about gets me to 99.

In the present protocol, since there is no such way of viewing the numbers, the evidence that S6 considers this space comes from comments about trying to find patterns in the numbers—for example:

B172: On examination er ... these numbers er ... the letters in these numbers don't tell me anything about the numbers.
B173: L, E, T, S. There is no letter repeated with a number.
B174: These numbers don't have any pattern at all.
B175: I mean L, E, T, S could be anything, or virtually anything.

Algebra Problem Space. We have already defined this space in Chapter 5 and used it there to provide a parsimonious solution attempt to the DONALD+ GERALD problem. It involves representing the carries by variables, writing one algebraic equation for each column, and then manipulating the equations by substitution, addition, and subtraction. The space does not in fact show up to any great extent in the protocols we have examined. When it does, the subject usually only approaches its formulation and then backs off, finding it too difficult. In the present case S8 tries twice. His attempt runs like this:

B122: So (cough) I keep coming back to the idea of er ... I keep coming back to the idea of ... of trying some sort of algebraic equation

B123: but the more you think about this the more ridiculous it gets.
B124: I mean I'd start with S and E
B125: er ... which will give me a number added together will ... er ... going to give me a number that's either R or else a number the second ... two-digit number, the second digit of which is R ....
B126: Right away I ... I have no idea er ... what to work with.

His difficulty stems from his inability to invent (discover?) a way to represent the carries explicitly. Another difficulty derives from his experience with algebraic equations in continuous variables—namely, his belief that the number of unknowns should not exceed the number of equations:

B41: Er ... I don't think it can be attacked algebraically,
B42: er ... although I can't claim to be a whiz at math.
B43: It looks like er ... if ... if I could set up any kind of equation or equations I'd have too many unknowns.
B44: Um ... because even though the letters are repeated, they are not repeated enough. I'm pretty sure of that.
B45: That's sort of a guess.

Thus the algebraic space is simply beyond the mathematical sophistication of this subject (a college undergraduate), although if one were to set that space up for him, he could probably maneuver in it.

Word-Meaning Problem Space. It is an irrelevant feature of cryptarithmetic problems that they use patterns of letters that make up standard English words. Any other set of distinct variables would do as well. For example:

L E T S	$D_7D_2D_4D_1$	S E N D	B Q K X
W A V E	$D_8D_6D_5D_2$	M O R E	U T C Q
L A T E R	$D_7D_6D_4D_2D_3$	M O N E Y	U T K Q A

are essentially the same problem. However, when English words are used, these *could* be a source of information, and the prevalence of anagram problems even makes this a plausible possibility. For instance, in the problem

$$
\begin{array}{r}
B\ I\ L\ L \\
W\ A\ S \\
\hline
K\ I\ N\ G
\end{array}
$$

if one detected the clue that BILL → William → William the Conqueror → 1066, so that B = 1, I = 0, L = 6, the problem is almost solved.

The subject tried several times to create such a problem space, always (of course) without success:

B153: Er ... I don't imagine it's possible that the words would have any significance: LETS, WAVE, and LATER.

B154: Er . . . This doesn't seem likely that the er . . . numbers LETS . . . the words LETS, WAVE, and LATER would give me any clues to any four-digit or five-digit numbers.

B155: Er . . . They certainly don't.

B156: So, I think that idea can be . . . more or less be rejected.

There is a question of whether such clues can be viewed as forming a problem space in the sense in which we have been using the word. It seems to us that they can, but we do not wish to press the issue, nor have we the data to establish it. As indicated in Figure 7.8, the elements of this problem space would be words with meanings, the intitial elements are the words given in the cryptarithmetic task, and the desired elements are word meanings that satisfy two conditions: that they correspond to the initial elements and that a number is associated with them having the same number of digits as there are letters in the word. The operators are those used to search long-term memory. This sketch of the space doesn't settle the issue, since no good models of long-term memory are available to provide more precise definitions of these operators. Nevertheless, the sequence of actions that takes us from BILL to 1066 gives an indication of what they must be like.

Cryptogram Problem Space. It is possible to search for a single rule that assigns to every letter a unique digit. The simplest example is $A \leftrightarrow 1$, $B \leftrightarrow 2$, $C \leftrightarrow 3$, ... Once the rule is found, it is only necessary to write down the specific correspondences and verify that the sum is correct. The plausibility of such a rule's existing is enhanced by the fact that in cryptarithmetic each letter is assigned a different digit.

There is, of course, no such rule available for the LETS+WAVE task (nor is it easy to manufacture one after the fact from the solution). S8 does go in search of one:

B99: Of course, there are other possibilities, I guess.

B100: Er. . . . Maybe a number er . . . could count er . . . the num . . . the number er . . . it could count as er . . . the number of letters from the front of the alphabet that it was, if it was near the front,

B101: or the number it was back from the end if it was near the end.

B102: I don't know if I could fit L into this.

B103: I'll count, A, B, C, D, E, F, G, H, I, J.

B104: No, that would make L 12.

B105: So that idea's not good.

B106: There's no way for it to work that'll work for it to make L a one-digit number.

This bit of behavior is the second round of S8's trying to find a global rule, his first attempt foundering on the failure of the simplest assignment rule ($A \leftrightarrow 1$, and so on). Here, S8 not only thinks of a more sophisticated rule, but immediately tests it out, and when it doesn't work abandons it.

One of Bartlett's subjects (VI) apparently worked in this same cryptogram problem space. His written record, reproduced as Figure 7.9, speaks for itself. He records two distinct possible coding rules and undoubtedly considered several others.

The question can also be raised here whether this is a problem space in the sense we have defined it. The answer is a somewhat more clear-cut affirmative than in the case of the word-meaning space. The elements of the cryptogram space are rules (functions from the letters to the digits). These rules are expressed in some language, although we have not described such a language here. The operators of the space are the means of composing new rules in this language. A few such rules may be given directly in memory—e.g., the simple one that assigns the integer i to the (i)th letter. But all the rest must be constructed. For instance, S8 clearly

FIGURE 7.9

protocol of Bartlett's Subject VI

DONALD = 526485
GERALD = 197496

ROBERT   723970

1. Tried putting letters in alphabetical order, against numbers 0–9 in numerical order: no good.
2. Wrote down every other letter, beginning with D and wrote the numbers from 5–0, 1–4 against them: no good.
3. Wrote down letters as they occurred in the problem against numbers in numerical order: no good.
4. Tried the letters and numbers by shifting the possible pairs: no good.
5. Wrote down the problem again with 5 in place of D, and 0 in place of T. No new ideas occurred to me so left the problem for several days.
6. Realized that there was no formula and for half an hour wrote in different numbers but failed.
7. Finally hit on a combination but it was not the right one for I had to have one more letter than was needed; e.g.

5 2 8 4 6 5
7 9 3 4 6 5

1 3 2 1 9 3 0

8. A friend noticed what I was doing and told me that I had got 0, E, and A right.
9. Wrote the problem down again, substituting the numbers known to be correct for the letters, and guessing the others until all that could not be correct were eliminated. Finally achieved the result as stated.

(This operator expressed the belief that he would have found the required result more quickly had he not been so eager to put in the figure three, this being his favourite number so that he wished it to occur more than once.)

SOURCE: Bartlett (1958, p. 55)

attempts to meet the demands of the problem in trying to invent a rule that works from both ends. It is doubtful that he knew about it from some previous experience and simply remembered it rather than generating it.

The assurance that we can construct problem spaces whose elements are rules comes not from the analysis given here but from several programs that have been developed to find concepts of various kinds defined in terms of rules (Simon and Kotovsky, 1963; Evans, 1964; Johnson, 1964; D. Williams, 1969). Though these programs are not cast in the form of a definition of a problem space, they all provide the essential ingredients for such a definition.

Typographical Problem Space. The last problem space listed involves possible correspondences between the surface features of the letters themselves and the digits they signify—an onomatopoetic approach, if you will. S8 is quite clear what he is searching for:

B83: I guess it's also possible that certain numbers le . . . letters look like numbers.

B84: For example an E looks a lot like a 3.

B85: But er . . . I don't er . . . I'm afraid I'm not going to get very far with this idea,

B86: because er . . . I can't see any other letters there that look too much like numbers.

B87: Er . . . I. . . . Well . . . you might say . . . I guess you might say that a 2 looks like an S.

B88: Let's see. A 1 doesn't look like anything down there.

B89: And if you wanted a 1 then you . . . that method you would put an I in there obviously.

The subject proceeds to check out all the digits through 7. But the record quoted is sufficient to show, not only that he is pursuing the idea deliberately, but that he engages in some reasonable testing of it (B89).

Of all the approaches mentioned, this one is least easily put in the form of a problem space, although we have given the desiderata in Figure 7.8, along with the others. The search is for a mapping from the typographical features of letters to the digits, just as in the cryptogram problem space the search is for a function from the position of the letters in the alphabet (or other sequence) to the digits. But whereas in the cryptogram space we could conceive of spaces of rules there, and could even raise the possibility of search operations in long-term memory in the word-meaning problem space, it is not so easy here. Still, the EPAM program for simulating verbal learning (see Chapter 2, pages 34 to 36) makes use of features to discriminate among letters, and could be used to simulate judgments of similarity like those expressed by the subject in the passage quoted above. Something is known, from the work of Eleanor Gibson (1966), about the specific cues used by children to discriminate letters, and a great deal more is known about features used in auditory discrimination of phonemes. With this information we might at least sketch out possible procedures for search in a space of similarity criteria.

Summary

We have now examined a number of problem spaces. All have appeared in the context of attempts by humans to solve cryptarithmetic problems. Some have been presented with extended evidence of their character as problem spaces, others have been sketched less formally. A number of spaces, especially those that were more briefly noted, are not capable of supporting successful problem solving for this task (or so we experimenters believe). For these, especially, it is not easy to demonstrate the existence of a space within which a human's search will reside while problem solving.

Our purposes in dwelling on the variation of problem space are twofold. First, we want to emphasize the psychological reality and usefulness of the concept of problem space. For this we must not only present evidence that subjects other than S3 work in problem spaces, but we must show some variation among the spaces. Second, we want to bring out the fact that the problem space comes rather close, for this class of problem, to constituting a definition of the situation, or world view. Definition of the subject's problem space provides a precise identification of what it is that he knows, has available by way of intellectual tools, and will extract out of the situation.

Nothing we have said so far deals with the stability of the subject's problem space. We have not presented evidence that the subject must work in his given problem space, or that even a small hint, such as "Note that R is odd—why don't you try to use such information," would not change the problem space for the remainder of the task. Indeed, S8 spends his time deciding what problem space he wishes to enter. When he does finally move into the augmented space, all of the alternative spaces disappear from view. What we *have* shown is that in these cryptarithmetic tasks the problem space is a useful construct for describing the gross features of a human subject's behavior.

PROBLEM SOLVING STRATEGIES

Knowing in what problem space a problem solver is working tells only part of the story. Major variations of behavior and performance still occur, to be explained and understood. With S3 on DONALD+GERALD we were able to describe the additional structure of his information processing, so that we came to understand the additional elements that entered into his behavior. The full structure is embodied in the production system described in the last chapter, but we can extract its main aspects. In the following list we deliberately ignore everything that is determined directly by the problem space.

1. He attended to whatever columns were relevent to the subgoal at hand (partly embodied in FC).
2. When he obtained new information, he attempted to exploit it (partly embodied in P1).
3. When he lacked some information, he attempted to obtain it (partly embodied in P2).
4. When he discovered inappropriate assignments (i.e., reached a dead end), he was able to back off to the last prior state of knowledge that was not disconfirmed (partly embodied in P12).

5. Whenever he obtained any new information, he always checked to see if it was consistent with the previous assignments (partly embodied in P11).

These items do not exhaust the implications of the productions, but they do reveal the kind of information the productions contain—what might be called S3's problem solving *strategy*. Actually, we know from the analysis of Chapter 6 that there are limits in the extent to which S3 followed these generalizations, and that some of the departures from them (e.g., the failure to evoke TD on E = 0) account for much of the inadequacy in his problem solving.

We would like now to explore two questions. To what extent do other human subjects use these same strategies and, insofar as their strategies differ, how? Second, to what extent are these strategies demanded by the task, and to what extent are they psychological? In considering these questions we should limit ourselves to a set of subjects who use the same problem space. Thus, we will consider S3, S4, S5, and S8, all of whom work in the augmented problem space.

We will conduct the analysis at a more aggregated level than we did for S3—for three reasons. (1) The production system does not always reveal as clearly as possible the role of the task environment; the aggregated technique we shall use appears somewhat better in this regard. (2) Creating the production system requires substantial effort; our alternative technique is somewhat easier to apply, yet still captures much of what goes on. (3) We wish to introduce as many tools as possible for dealing with problem solving data. Since different tools serve different purposes and have different costs, one should not be tied to any single way of analyzing data.

We turn first to describing this alternative data analysis technique, before going ahead with the analysis of the three new subjects, S4, S5, and S8. In doing so, we will briefly reanalyze S3's behavior so as to have a comparable base.

The Episode Abstract

In Chapter 3 we considered how to define the task environment with respect to a given problem solver. We introduced the notion of invariances in the task environment—that is to say, aspects that can clearly be viewed as demands of the task environment. Any problem solver who does not take account of these essential aspects does not solve the problem. Therefore, if the problem solver wants to solve the problem and does, we can expect to see the reflection of these invariant demands in his behavior.

Next, we strengthened this view by introducing the concept of the intelligence of the problem solver. Given any particular upper limit to intelligence, certain aspects of the task environment become invariant and are revealed by the behavior of all successful problem solvers with intelligence below that limit. That is, although these aspects are not completely invariant, solution paths that do not exhibit them require higher intelligence than is available to the problem solvers in question (e.g., such paths might involve inventing a new mathematics for cryptarithmetic tasks, still undiscovered, that would reduce the solution to execution of a simple algorithm). But also on the other side, with any particular lower limit on intelligence, certain aspects of the task environment become *obvious*, which is to say, they can be assumed to be discovered readily by all problem solvers whose intelligence exceeds these limits.

Finally, we defined episodes of behavior as those intervals during which a problem solver of a particular level of intelligence was doing the obvious things, in the above sense. The boundaries of the episode are reached when he faces the problem of doing something that is not obvious to him, given his intelligence. Behavior can be aggregated into episodes, so as to focus attention on the features of behavior that are most relevant to assessing a subject's problem solving abilities. In Chapter 3 we illustrated these notions with some everyday examples but did not attempt to make them operational. We are now in a position to do so with respect to cryptarithmetic.

The key problem in creating an objective way of episoding protocols is introducing an operational concept of intelligence. We argued in Chapter 3 that intelligence is a useful construct in our context, and that we were not begging any serious questions by using it. Nevertheless, we did not attempt to operationalize it there, since the context was not sufficiently specific. Let us make clear what we want from such a concept. We put ourselves in the position of a scientific analyst who is given a definition of the task environment and a definition of the subject's intelligence:

1. There should be an operational meaning for the phrase "the subject will obviously do X in situation Y."
2. There should be an operational meaning for the phrase "the subject must show behavior X if he is to solve problem Y in situation Z."

The appropriate construct for intelligence starts with the problem space. If we know what problem space a subject is operating in, we already know a good deal about what behavior is obvious. If a subject in the augmented problem space wants to know what digits are available for assignment to a letter, he simply applies GN. For a subject in a less powerful problem space, this same task might require a painstaking accounting of all the values already assigned. It is not enough, however, merely that the operators in the space be obvious. Some notion is required of when an operator will be applied, or more precisely, when it will *obviously* be applied. For this, we consider that in all of the cryptarithmetic problems there is a global goal, which is to accumulate knowledge about the assignments. That is, a problem progresses from the initial state, which is completely void of information about the assignments, to the final state, in which knowledge is complete (and proven correct). Thus, there is a gradient in the space. This gradient has very little directive value in problematic situations (e.g., should R ← 7 or R ← 9 be assigned?). However, it has great directive value if there is some obvious knowledge available for the asking—it directs that the knowledge should be obtained.

FIGURE 7.10

choices at a node in the augmented problem space

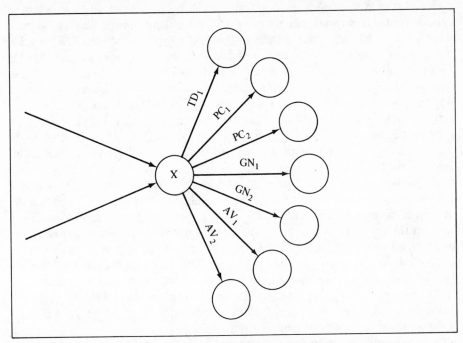

Consider the node marked X in the augmented problem space of Figure 7.10. From this node radiate a number of actions, each labeled with an operator. These operators are all variants of PC, AV, GN, or TD. The variations can be subtypes, as in the three assignment operators of S6 (though he was in the basic space), or they can have specialized operands—e.g., the letter for GN or the column for PC. Now, the application of some of these operators can lead to validated new information—that is, to information that is true provided that the knowledge held at node X is true. Nodes produced by PC, TD, and GN all create this possibility, although they need not produce new information in fact [e.g., GN(letter) *may* only reveal what was already known about *letter*]. Other nodes, those produced by AV, do not produce new validated information, but only the possibility of it later on. The assumption that the problem solver will obtain new information if it is seen to be available implies that he will move to nodes where new information becomes available. However, the problem solver must see that a given node will produce new information before he will move to it. We make the following assumption:

Any *immediate* node from a given node that adds validated knowledge is obvious.

Thus, we say that any problem solver in the augmented problem space will see and acquire any information that is only one step away in the problem space, but that he will not see his way across boundaries of conjecture. He will, of course,

285

cross these from time to time, but such actions represent outcomes of his decision strategy that we wish to observe.[2]

With the analysis just given, we can divide the problem space into potential episodes. That is, we can create subsets of the problem space by connecting each node to those that are obvious from it. One and only one of these nodes, the one containing the most information, constitutes the *head* of the episode and contains the information that any S will obtain if he enters into the episode at all. We can now view the movement within an episode from entry to head as an obvious response to a demand of the task environment—*demand*, because any rational man would acquire this information. Hence we can ignore within-episode detail, and concentrate analysis on the moves from episode to episode.

We are making an empirical assertion. We are assuming that no S who has achieved the status of working in the augmented problem space will be blind to such opportunities for immediate gain of knowledge. If this assertion is false, its failure will be evident from the protocols, and we will have to look for a modified definition of *obvious*. Our analysis of S3's protocol should give us some confidence, since in the main he clearly meets the conditions. S6, however, does not satisfy the assumption. As we saw on page 267, S6 left columns with obvious inferences untouched—e.g., column 2 with $3 + 3 = R$. This is so, independent of the fact that he divided all his columns into firm and tentative, where contradictions in the tentative part were simply not considered as representing firm assignments. However, S6 works in a version of the basic problem space, and it is plausible that a different criterion of obviousness is required for it.

The same assumption about obviousness can be made in terms of the production system. The assumption asserts that productions P1, P7, P11, and P12 are included in all subjects' programs. These represent all the ways in S3's production system for responding immediately to new information to derive still other new information. The one production missing is the derivation of new information from GN when the set turns out to be small; for example, if it is known that R is odd and there is only one odd number unassigned, then R has to be that. This case never really came up in S3's DONALD+GERALD task, so it is unknown whether he would make this obvious inference or not. We could include it as:

P15: $\langle$constraint-expression$\rangle$ new $\longrightarrow$ GN(variable of constraint-
expression) ($\Longrightarrow$ digit-set)
(size(digit-set) $= 1$) $\longrightarrow$ AV(variable)

Thus, we could do our episoding systematically by applying the mini-production system consisting of the five productions just given. Every node the system could reach from a starting node would be within a single episode.

This last way of looking at episoding reemphasizes the remark made earlier: that we are not asserting that the subject becomes immediately aware of all the

---

[2] We could define *obvious of degree n* if we assume that the problem solver sees across *n* conjectural steps. However, as *n* increases, we come more and more to have an artificial measure, analogous to the assumption that chess players look ahead a fixed number of moves. The assumption we use above does not suffer much from this arbitrariness. Empirically, a more extended definition does not seem needed.

obvious consequences. It may take appreciable time for him to find them, and we may find substantial segments of the protocol devoted to becoming aware of the obvious—for example, all the phrases in S3's protocol that correspond to the productions listed above. In fact, each such segment of behavior will appear to the observer to constitute a small self-contained phase of highly organized activity—which is why we call it an episode.

Reanalysis of S3. To make these ideas concrete, let us go back and reanalyze S3's protocol on DONALD+GERALD. Having the complete analysis of the prior chapter, we can see what is happening when we describe his behavior in terms of episodes.

As an aid in doing this, we review in Figure 7.11 the essential features of the DONALD+GERALD task. There is a series of information sources, the columns,

FIGURE 7.11

essential structure of DONALD+GERALD=ROBERT

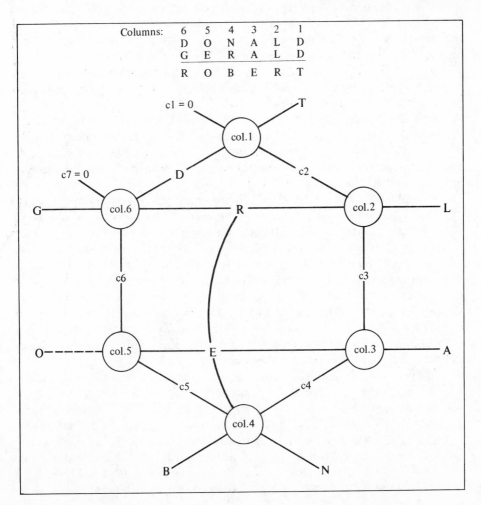

each of which imposes constraints on a subset of the variables. In the figure, the information sources are represented by nodes, and the variables are linked to these nodes by lines. Starting at any of the nodes, a subject can attempt to generate new information; if he is successful, he can move to any other node that is affected by the new information. The gist of our assumption of obviousness is that if a subject starts at a node and obtains new information, he keeps going until no more information can be inferred. Such a sequence of inferences constitutes an episode.

The one source of information that is not represented in the figure is the exclusiveness of assignments. In its most obvious form it requires that no two letters be assigned the same digit. But it has less obvious forms—for example, that digits greater than five cannot be assigned to more than four letters. We explored a problem space in Chapter 5 that made use of such inferences, using an abstracted set of values: greater or less than five and even or odd. In the augmented problem space there is no apparent way for these inferences to be made except through TD and GN. The former operator simply makes the elementary check as to whether a digit is available for assignment or is outside the admissible range for the variable being tested. The latter operator takes into account only the range of the variable and the specific digits that are excluded by virtue of already being assigned to other letters. Thus, we can ignore more subtle inferences in defining the boundaries of the episodes. (If it turned out that all such available subtle inferences were routinely made by users of the augmented problem space, we would have to revise our definition of obviousness.)

Episodes are generated by assuming a state of knowledge, starting at the corresponding node in Figure 7.11 and tracing out the sequence of inferences until all obvious information has been generated. If we did this for all possible states of knowledge, we would be able to construct an objective map of potential episodes against which to examine the behavior of a subject.

Actually, if we were to draw the map and examine it, we would see that many of the sequences were essentially the same—that is, involve the same line of reasoning in Figure 7.11. For instance, the starting states of two sequences might differ only in having different amounts of information irrelevant to the episode. Then the two sequences would be in one-to-one correspondence and at the end would still differ by the same additional (irrelevant) information. Again, two sequences might differ by one's having an additional piece of relevant information; then it would proceed somewhat further than the other. We need not consider every possible episode sequence in the total space, but only the characteristic types of sequences—*episode schemas* might be an appropriate term—that provide the essential inferential structure of the task environment shown in Figure 7.11.

In Figure 7.12 we show the most important episode schemas for DONALD+ GERALD. In order to exhibit the structure of the task, we have ignored the special information that $D \leftarrow 5$, which is clearly adventitious. We have labeled each episode schema mnemonically by the columns that are processed during the episode. Thus 1-2-6 is the episode schema in which we start with the assumption that $D \geq 5$, infer in column 1 that T is even, then in column 2 that R is odd, then in column 6 that $R > 5$, then that $R = 7 \lor 9$, and finally that $G < 5$. The episode is essentially the same if we begin it with the knowledge that $D \leftarrow 5$, although in

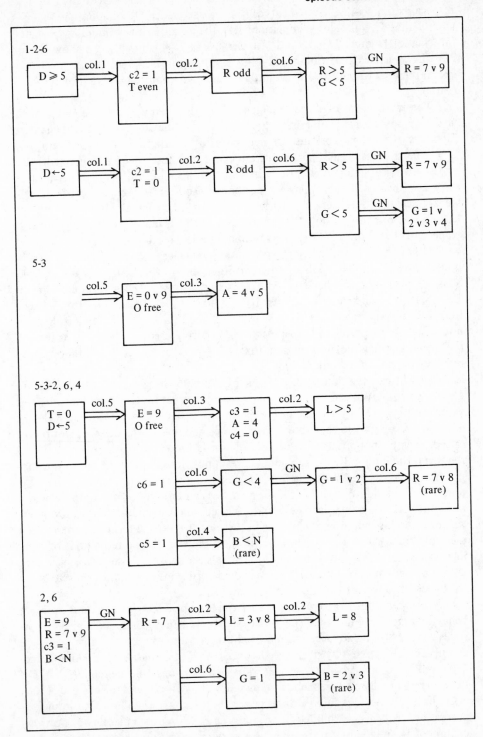

FIGURE 7.12

episode schemas for DONALD+GERALD=ROBERT

this case the information obtained about T increases to include the knowledge that T = 0. This additional information is not unimportant, of course, since it permits immediate refinement of the 5-3 sequence by eliminating the possibility that E = 0. This elimination may then lead to the obtaining of further information about L, G, B, and N (schema 5-3-2-4-6). Finally, we show schema 2-6, the sequence that obtains all the remaining information about the letters, except the final resolution of B, N and O, which still requires a small trial-and-error search.

The importance of these schemas is that they represent the demands of the task environment for problem solvers who work in the augmented problem space. Elements of all these episodes are necessary to the solution of the problem (e.g., E = 9 must be arrived at somehow, either through inference or assignment). But once the subject enters any episode he will run through it to the end, because the steps are obvious. Thus, when we see these episodes in the behavior of subjects, we are seeing the reflections of the demands of the task environment, and we learn about our subject only that he has attained a certain level of adaptivity with respect to the environment (always assuming adequate motivation).

Although we have written the processing sequences assuming that the column inferences will be taken up in a particular order, many other orderings are possible. This is especially true whenever a correct value is assigned to a variable. Thus, if L ← 8, then it will be concluded that R = 7, hence G = 1; also that c_3 = 1, hence that E is odd, therefore that E ≠ 0—even if some of these other relations happen not to have been established previously. The ordering used in Figure 7.12 is the one that occurs when the information that D ← 5 is processed first, followed by response to the critical fifth column.

We will call the description of a subject's behavior in terms of episodes an *episode abstract*. With this preparation we can construct for S3 the episode abstract shown in Figure 7.13 Each line of the figure represents a single episode. On the far left are the B-numbers that show where the episode begins in the protocol reproduced in Appendix 6.1. In the second column is the name of the episode (its E-number). In column 3 we give the new presuppositions or facts that lead the subject into the episode. On the right of the page we describe the episode in the same notation we used in Figure 7.12. If the episode is an instance of one of the schemas in Figure 7.12, we note this in column 4. We record on separate lines the few intervals of behavior that are not episodes in the sense we use the term here, describing them informally in brackets. They are primarily rehearsals and repetitions of prior inference sequences. However, not all rehearsals are shown; those occurring within an episode are subsumed under the episode description, which aims only to show the logical structure of the information generated.

A comparison of the episode abstract in Figure 7.13 with the total problem behavior graph in Figure 6.4 (page 181) shows that they correspond nicely. Episodes consist of long advances with only short backups; the start of a new episode can usually be detected by the subject's retreat to a prior base state of knowledge.

Looking at the abstract, we see that two portions (the beginning, E1–E4, up to the point where S3 erroneously concludes that c_3 = 0; and the end, E16–E19, after the experimenter's intervention) correspond, almost literally, to the principal processing sequences exhibited in Figure 7.12. Moreover, these two portions contain substantially all the analysis necessary to solve the problem. This part of

FIGURE 7.13

episode abstract for S3 (bold face indicates assignments entered on external display)

```
      DONALD
      GERALD
      ──────
      ROBERT
```

(1) B	(2) E	(3) INSTIGATOR	(4) E-SCHEMA	(5) EPISODE
B5	E1	**D ← 5**	1–2–6	$\overset{1}{\Rightarrow} T=0 \overset{2}{\Rightarrow} R\ odd \overset{GN}{\Rightarrow} R=1 \vee 3 \vee 7 \vee 9 \overset{6}{\Rightarrow}$ c6 unknown
B40	E2	**L ← 1**	2–6	$\overset{2}{\Rightarrow} R=3 \overset{6}{\Rightarrow} c7=1 \,\square\, (c7=0)$ (from E) reject R L
B58	E3		6	$\overset{6}{\Rightarrow} R>5 \overset{GN}{\Rightarrow} R=7 \vee 9$
B62	E4	**R ← 7**	2–6	$\overset{2}{\Rightarrow} L=3 \overset{6}{\Rightarrow} G=1 \vee 2$

```
5 ONA 3 5
GE 7 A 3 5
──────────
7 OBE 7 0
```

(1) B	(2) E	(3) INSTIGATOR	(4) E-SCHEMA	(5) EPISODE
B78	E5	get E	5–3–5	$\overset{5}{\Rightarrow} (E=0) \vee (E=9, c5=1, c6=1) \overset{3}{\Rightarrow} E\ even \overset{5}{\Rightarrow} (E=9\ \square)$
B104	E6	review	2–6	[confuse L ← 9 with R ← 9] $\overset{26}{\Rightarrow} R>5$
B115	E7	get E	3–5	$\overset{3}{\Rightarrow} E\ even \overset{5}{\Rightarrow} E=0 \overset{3}{\Rightarrow} A=5 \,\square\, (D\leftarrow 5)$
B137	E8	review	2–6	$\overset{2}{\Rightarrow} R\ odd \overset{6}{\Rightarrow} R>5 \overset{GN}{\Rightarrow} R=7 \vee 9 \overset{AV}{\Rightarrow} (R\leftarrow 7) \vee (R\leftarrow 9)$
B144	E9	get E	5	$\overset{5}{\Rightarrow} O \overset{5}{\Rightarrow} E=9, c5=1, c6=1 \overset{6}{\Rightarrow}$ **G = 1**

```
5 ONA 3 5
1 E 7 A 3 5
──────────
7 OBE 7 0
```

(1) B	(2) E	(3) INSTIGATOR	(4) E-SCHEMA	(5) EPISODE
B166	E10	E = 9	3–2	$\overset{3}{\Rightarrow} E=9 \,\square\, (c3=0) \overset{2}{\Rightarrow} R\leftarrow 7 \,\square\,$ construct second display

```
5 ONAL 5      5 ONA 3 5
GERAL 5       1 E 7 A 3 5
─────────     ──────────
ROBER 0       7 OBE 7 0
```

(1) B	(2) E	(3) INSTIGATOR	(4) E-SCHEMA	(5) EPISODE
B185	E11	**R ← 9**	2–6–5–3	$\overset{2}{\Rightarrow} L=4 \overset{6}{\Rightarrow} G=3 \vee 4 \overset{5}{\Rightarrow} E=0 \overset{3}{\Rightarrow} A=5 \,\square\, (D=5)$ reject E = 0
B210	E12	(E = 0 □)	3–2	$\overset{3}{\Rightarrow} c3=1 \overset{2}{\Rightarrow} L>5 \overset{AV}{\Rightarrow} L\leftarrow 6 \overset{2}{\Rightarrow} R=3 \,\square\, (R>5)$
B218	E13	get E	5	$\overset{5}{\Rightarrow} E=0 \vee 9 \overset{GN}{\Rightarrow} E=0 (R\leftarrow 9) [E: E=0 \,\square\, (T=0)]$
B225	E14	T = 0	4	$\overset{GN}{\Rightarrow} E=0 \vee 9 \,\square\, \overset{4}{\Rightarrow} c5=2 \,\square\, \Rightarrow R\leftarrow 9 \,\square\,$ return to first display

```
5 ONA 3 5
1 E 7 A 3 5
──────────
7 OBE 7 0
```

(1) B	(2) E	(3) INSTIGATOR	(4) E-SCHEMA	(5) EPISODE
B239	E15	**E = 9**	5–4–3	$\overset{5}{\Rightarrow} c5=1, 0\ free \overset{4}{\Rightarrow} N>2 \overset{3}{\Rightarrow} A \,\square\, \Rightarrow L>5$
B262	E16	get L > 5	2–3	$\overset{GN2}{\Rightarrow} L\leftarrow 8 \overset{2}{\Rightarrow} R=7, c3=1 \overset{3}{\Rightarrow} A=4, E=9$
B279	E17	next column	4–5	$\overset{4GN}{\Rightarrow}$ **N = 6, B = 3** $\overset{5}{\Rightarrow}$ **O = 2** solution
B303	E18	check solution		$\overset{1}{\Rightarrow} \overset{2}{\Rightarrow} \overset{3}{\Rightarrow} \overset{4}{\Rightarrow} \overset{5}{\Rightarrow} \overset{6}{\Rightarrow}$ solution

the protocol can be characterized as task-determined; but what about the remainder, when S3 was struggling with the contradictions generated by his error?

The nature of this middle portion of the protocol can also be described parsimoniously in terms of the principal sequences—but with the addition of the erroneous premise that $(c3 = 0)$, and with the omission of the forgotten fact that $T = 0$. In E5, E7, E9, and E12, S3 is following schema 1-2-6, once to calculate consequences of assuming that $R = 7$, twice to check previously derived facts about the value of R, and the last time to calculate the consequences of assuming that $R = 9$. (In this last case, sequence 5-3 follows sequence 1-2-6, terminating in a contradiction.)

In E6, E8, E11, and E13–E14, sequence 5-3 is followed, in the first case until the inference (E even) is derived, in the latter three cases until a contradiction is reached. The contradiction leads S3 to change either his currently held value of E or his assumed value of R. The contradictions all involve, directly or indirectly, the fact that in column 3 (E even) implies $A = 5$, which is incompatible with the known fact that $D = 5$. But (E even) cannot be abandoned because $c3 = 0$ is held to be true.

Having reanalyzed S3's behavior in terms of episodes, we can now examine the other three subjects by means of their episode abstracts.

Subject 4

The episode abstract of S4 is shown in Figure 7.14 (full protocol in Appendix 7.1). S4 was the most efficient of our five subjects in solving the problem, taking only about ten minutes. The directness of his route is revealed clearly by the brevity of his abstract. After processing column 1, he considers the possibility that $L = 3$, taking path 1-2-6, ignoring the carry, c2, and concluding that $G = 1$. From column 6 he notices the solution for column 5, and he follows path 5-3 back to column 3 and column 2. Next (E4), his attention apparently called to R by column 4, he finds $R = 7$ by schema 1-2-6, using $E = 9$ to eliminate the alternate value for R. He now (E5) checks from right to left the entries he has already made. Because he has not erased $L = 3$ from column 2, he obtains $E = 8$ in column 3, but discovers the contradiction when he reaches column 5. Retracing this path (schema 5-3, E5 and E6), he corrects L to $L = 8$, then arrives at the remaining values, working from right to left.

Subjects 3 and 4 made the same error—leaving the tentative value $L = 3$ on the display—but S4 recovered from the error much more rapidly than S3. We may speculate as to the reasons. S4 evidently recalled $T = 0$ when processing column 5, hence arrived at the definite conclusion that $E = 9$, instead of the alternative, $E = 9 \lor 0$. Since he knew that $E = 9$, he was able to infer definitely that $R = 7$. On his first exploration of schema 5-3 (E3), he followed the path to its conclusion, $L > 5$, in column 2, even though $L = 3$ was written in the display—evidently he remembered at that moment that this value had been assigned tentatively. The fact that S3 was faced with a number of alternatives ($E = 0 \lor 9$,

FIGURE 7.14

episode abstract for S4

(1) B	(2) E	(3) INSTIGATOR	(4) E-SCHEMA	(5) EPISODE
		DONALD		
		GERALD		
		ROBERT		
B3	E1	D ← 5	1–6	$\xRightarrow{1} T = 0 \xRightarrow{6} R > G$
B17	E2	L ← 3	2–6	$\xRightarrow{2} R = 6 \xRightarrow{6} G = 1, c6 = 0$
B28	E3	c6 = 0	5–3–2	$\xRightarrow{5} E = 9 \xRightarrow{3} c3 = 1 \xRightarrow{2} L > 5 \xRightarrow{3} A = 4 \xRightarrow{5} c5 = 1$
				reject L ← 3
		5 ON 4 3'5		
		1 9 6 4 3 5		
		6 OB 9 6 0		
B53	E4	get R	2–6	$\xRightarrow{2} R \text{ odd} \xRightarrow{6} R > 5 \xRightarrow{GN} R = 7$
		5 ON 4 3 5		
		1 9 7 4 3 5		
		7 OB 9 7 0		
B63	E5	next column	4–5	$\xRightarrow{4} (c3 \square \xRightarrow{3} c3 = 0 \xRightarrow{2} E = 8) \xRightarrow{4} \xRightarrow{5} E = 9 \square \text{ reject } E = 8$
B78	E6	E = 9	3–1–4–5	$\xRightarrow{3} c3 = 1 \xRightarrow{2} L = 8 \xRightarrow{4} N ← 6, B = 3 \xRightarrow{5} O = 2 \text{ solution}$

$R = 7 \vee 9$) made it harder for him to fix on a particular point as the source of the contradiction. Thus, small but crucial differences in memory about previous results had a large effect on ease of recovery from error.

Another difference between the two protocols is the greater noticeability in S4's of a systematic right-to-left search to check the partial results he had thus far achieved. S3 always generated columns via FC, hence never systematically (until he made a final check after finding the solution).

Subject 5

S5 (Figure 7.15, full protocol in Appendix 7.2) was even more ready than S4 to work from right to left, trying alternative assignments of letters—assigning R, inferring L, assigning A (E2–E4). In E3, following schema 2-6-5 he makes the same mistake ($R = 7 \Rightarrow L = 3$) made by the two subjects previously discussed, but this error turns out not to cause him later troubles. Working from right to left, he follows path 3-5-6 in reverse direction (E4 to E5), but infers that $E = 9$. However, at the same moment, he makes the incorrect inference that $O = 1$, a conclusion that leads him to a sequence of apparent contradictions from E6 through E21, at which point he discovers the source of his difficulty. Thus, the erroneous belief that O = 1 plays the same mischievous role for S5 as L = 3 plays for S3.

It is highly instructive to see exactly how this error occurs, for it represents another instance of confusion between necessary and sufficient conditions. When S5 processes column 5 carefully for the first time (E4), he works from the top of the column to the bottom, trying values for O, then for E. He rejects O = 0 because of his knowledge that T = 0, then tries O = 1, finding that the latter value is satisfactory, provided that E = 9. Hence, he never explores other possible values for O, and never discovers that O = 1 is not necessary for column 5.

FIGURE 7.15
episode abstract for S5

		DONALD		
		GERALD		
		ROBERT		
(1) B	(2) E	(3) INSTIGATOR	(4) E-SCHEMA	(5) EPISODE
B10	E1	D ← 5	1	$\overset{1}{\Rightarrow} T = 0$
B15	E2	E ← 9	2-6-5	$\overset{2}{\Rightarrow} L = 4 \overset{6}{\Rightarrow} G, c6 = 1 \overset{5}{\Rightarrow} E = 9$
B34	E3	L ← 3	2-6-5	$\overset{2}{\Rightarrow} R = 7 \overset{6}{\Rightarrow} G = 2 \overset{5}{\Rightarrow}$ get E
B40	E4	get E	3-5-6	$A \leftarrow 4, 1 \overset{3}{\Rightarrow} E \overset{5}{\Rightarrow} O = 1, E = 9, c6 = 1 \overset{6}{\Rightarrow}$ $G = 1 \square$ erase L R
		5 1 N A L 5		
		G 9 R A L 5		
		R 1 B 9 R 0		
B70	E5	E = 9	3-2	$\overset{3}{\Rightarrow} A = 4, c3 = 1 \overset{2}{\Rightarrow} L > 5$
B80	E6	L ← 6	2-6-4	$\overset{2}{\Rightarrow} R = 3 \overset{6}{\Rightarrow} G = 7 \overset{4}{\Rightarrow} N, B \square (c3 = 0)$ reject L
B141	E7	L ← 7	2-4-6-5	$\overset{2}{\Rightarrow} L \leftarrow 8, R = 7 \overset{4}{\Rightarrow} N = 6, B = 3 \overset{6}{\Rightarrow} G = 2 \overset{5}{\Rightarrow}$ $c6 = 0 \square (c6 = 1)$ reject L
B176	E8	review	2-3	$L \overset{GN}{\Rightarrow} 8, 7, 6, 5, 4 \overset{2,3}{\Rightarrow} L > 5 \Rightarrow L \leftarrow 6, 7$ erase everything
B210	E9	review	5-3	$\overset{5}{\Rightarrow} E = 9 \overset{3}{\Rightarrow} A = 4$
		5 1 N 4 L 5		
		G 9 R 4 L 5		
		R 1 B 9 R 0		
B222	E10	L ← 7	2	$\overset{2}{\Rightarrow} R = 5 \square (D = 5)$
B230	E11	L ← 6	2-6	$\overset{2}{\Rightarrow} R = 3 \overset{6}{\Rightarrow} G = 7 \square (c7 = 0) \overset{6}{\Rightarrow} R > 5$ erase G R L
B252	E12	R > 5	2	[confuse L with R] $\overset{2}{\Rightarrow} L = 9$, erase E $\overset{2}{\Rightarrow} R = 9 \square$ erase L, E = 9
B277	E13	R > 5	6-2	$\overset{6}{\Rightarrow} R = 7 \vee 9 \overset{2}{\Rightarrow} L = 3 \vee 4 \overset{TD}{\Rightarrow} L = 3$ erase A E

FIGURE 7.15 (cont'd)

```
        5 1 N A L 5
        G E R A L 5
        ─────────
        R 1 B E R 0
```

B303	E14	$L = 3$	2–3–5–6	$\overset{2}{\Rightarrow} R = 7 \overset{3}{\Rightarrow} E \overset{5}{\Rightarrow} E = 9 \overset{6}{\Rightarrow} G = 1 \;\square\; (O = 1)$ erase L R
B330	E15	review	6–2	$\overset{6}{\Rightarrow} R > 5 \overset{2}{\Rightarrow} R \text{ odd} \overset{GN}{\Rightarrow} R = 7 \lor 9 \overset{TD}{\Rightarrow} R = 9$ $(R = 7\; \square)$
B344	E16	$R = 9$ (erase E)	2–6–5–3	$\overset{2}{\Rightarrow} L = 4 \overset{6}{\Rightarrow} G = 3, c6 = 1 \overset{5}{\Rightarrow} E = 0 \;\square\; (T = 0)$ $\overset{3}{\Rightarrow} A \text{ reject R}$
B368	E17	get R	6–2–5–3	$\overset{65}{\Rightarrow} R, L = 3 \overset{2}{\Rightarrow} R = 7 \overset{5}{\Rightarrow} E = 9 \overset{3}{\Rightarrow} A = 4\frac{1}{2} \;\square$ reject R, $A = 4$
B387	E18	review		$R \overset{GN}{\Rightarrow} R = 9 \;\square\; (E = 9) \text{ erase E A}$

```
        5 1 N A 3 5
        G E 7 A 3 5
        ─────────
        7 1 B E 7 0
```

B408	E19	$R = 9$	2–3–5	$\overset{2}{\Rightarrow} L = 4 \overset{3}{\Rightarrow} E = 8 \overset{5}{\Rightarrow} E = 9, O = 1 \;\square\; \text{erase R L}$ $E = 9, A = 4$
B434	E20	get L	2–6	$L \overset{GN}{\Rightarrow} 9\text{-}0\text{-}9 \;(\overset{2}{\Rightarrow} L = 8, R = 7 \overset{6}{\Rightarrow} G = 1 \;\square$ $(0 = 1)) \Rightarrow L = 8$

```
        5 1 N 4 L 5
        G 9 R 4 L 5
        ─────────
        R 1 B 9 R 0
```

B499	E21	$L = 8$	2–6–5	$\overset{2}{\Rightarrow} R = 7 \overset{6}{\Rightarrow} G = 1 \;\square\; (O = 1) \overset{5}{\Rightarrow} \text{erase O}$
B510	E22	O free	5–6–4	$\overset{5}{\Rightarrow} O = 2 \overset{6}{\Rightarrow} G = 1 \overset{4}{\Rightarrow} N = 6, B = 3 \overset{5GN}{\Rightarrow} O = 2$ solution

Holding the conclusion that $E = 9$, S5 now follows schema 3-2 back to column 2, trying possible values of 6, 7, and 8 for L (since $L > 5$ had been inferred). For each assignment of L, he works back from right to left trying to complete column 4 and column 6 by assignment of the remaining digits. Because of his assumption that $O = 1$, each time, he arrives at one or another contradiction. After repeating this sequence twice (E6–E7 and E10–E11), he now tries assigning each of the alternative values, 7 and 9, to R, making use of the erroneous inference that $L = 3 \lor 4$. These attempts lead again to contradictions (E14–E18), then to a careful reexamination of column 5 (E19–E20), whence the error is discovered and the solution found.

On first impression it seems that S5 handles his conflicts in an unsystematic way, sometimes rejecting the assignment that evokes the conflict, sometimes keeping it and rejecting the one established earlier. Certainly a direct perusal of the protocol makes it appear this way. However, S5 has in fact a consistent scheme for deciding which of the two conflicting expressions to reject.[3] Like all subjects

---

[3] We are indebted to R. Van Horn for an initial analysis of the protocol, which first uncovered S5's consistent reaction to conflicts.

who work in the augmented problem space, S5 distinguishes an assignment from an inference (e.g., R ← 9 from R = 9). But he also distinguishes information that is truly known (e.g., D = 5), which we will call *facts*, from two forms of inference: information derived from a column and information derived by exhaustion of values (e.g., if R = 7 ∨ 9 and R ← 7 has been shown to lead to contradictions, then R = 9 by exhaustion). Thus each expression is tagged with one of five tags:

a   assignment
da derived from an assignment
df derived from a fact
de derived by exhaustion
f   fact

An expression belongs to the first category (a) only if it has the form (⟨letter⟩ ← ⟨digit⟩). It is a fact (f) only if given directly on the display or by the experimenter. Thus D = 5, c7 = 0, and O + E = O are facts. Things derived from facts, no matter how immediately, belong to category df, e.g., T = 0, E = 0 ∨ 9. The other three classes are hereditary: if something is derived from D = 5 (f), then it is derived from a fact, hence is tagged df (e.g., T = 0). If something is derived from a df, in turn, it is also tagged df (e.g., R odd). From the evidence, S5 does not distinguish gradations within category; e.g., something is not less well established if it is reached through several steps of inference.

S5's decision rule, when faced with two conflicting expressions, is simply to reject the one that is higher in this order. Thus, assignments (a) yield to anything, expressions derived from assignments (da) yield to expressions derived from facts (df), and (most important) knowledge derived from facts loses to knowledge derived by exhaustion (de). If two expressions belong to the same category, then S5 rejects the most recent.

There are 58 instances in S5's protocol where two expressions come into conflict. Figure 7.16 gives the basic data on how these conflicts were resolved. Each cell shows the number of conflicts between two categories in which the category named in the column was rejected in favor of the row category. Entries above the diagonal indicate a failure of the decision rule. For example, there were 13 conflicts between da and df where the da-expression was rejected. Looking at the symmetric cell, there were only 3 conflicts between these categories where the df-expression was rejected.

Finding all the instances of conflicts and determining how the elements are to be classified requires a study of the protocol in more detail than is shown in the episode abstract. In Appendix 7.2, along with the protocol, we have given a PBG for S5 that provides these data and a table of all the conflicts. (Table A7.2.1)

As we can see from Figure 7.16, the particular decision function describes S5 rather well. Out of a total of 54 decisions between expressions belonging to different categories (the off-diagonal entries), 87 percent were consistent with the decision rule (47/54). All four decisions on the diagonal are consistent with the rule of rejecting the most recent.

As important as the general agreement is the nature of the failures. Six out

FIGURE 7.16

REJECTED

		a	da	af	de	f	
	a	1	0	1	0	0	2
	da	1	0	3	0	1	5
ACCEPTED	df	9	13	2	2	0	26
	de	1	3	9	1	0	14
	f	2	8	0	1	0	11
		14	24	15	4	1	58

of the seven exceptions were almost immediately retracted. Sometimes S5 was simply exploring extreme possibilities. For example, two of the failures (B458 and B460) result from an attempt to see if $L \leftarrow 0$ would work, first abandoning $T = 0$ and then questioning the experimenter on $D = 5$ (i.e., attempting to abandon it). Another example occurs at B167, where S5 has attained a complete assignment, ending with $G = 2$ (da). He infers from column 6 that $c6 = 0$ and then discovers that $c6 = 1$ already from column 5 and the previously established $E = 9$ (df). He rejects $c6 = 1$ (i.e., $E = 9$) momentarily (hence violating the rule) and considers whether the situation can be saved by $E \leftarrow 8$. He concludes that it can't and abandons the entire line.

Decision rules such as the one we are examining here are not absolute. They are not part of the structure of the problem solver, but are part of his program. Thus, they are always open to revision; indeed, successful problem solving may require overruling a decision rule. Thus, "errors" in a matrix, such as Figure 7.16, are not necessarily to be viewed as "noise." Some of them may reflect higher decision rules coming into play. For example, the one entry above the diagonal that is not retracted almost immediately (B421) rejects $R = 9$, which has been established by exhaustion (de), in favor of $E = 9$, which has been established by processing column 5 (df). But a perusal of the protocol shows that in this case the study of column 5 was especially careful and done with S5's back against the wall, so to speak. For instance, he has just finished rejecting $E = 9$ in favor of $R = 9$ in the prior decision. Thus, this was *the* time to abandon the principle.

Like S3, S5 several times (E15, E18) when in difficulties rehearses the facts he has previously derived. Like S3's, S5's difficulty in pinpointing the source of his contradiction is related to the fact that at each moment he is faced with several alternatives and contingencies. The contradiction generally arises at the end of a long line of reasoning, involving several possibly fallible steps and assumptions. Thus, E7, which should have led to a solution, arrives at a contradiction because 1 has already been assigned to O, hence only 2 is left as a possible value for G in column 6.

Although superficially the course of search shown in S5's abstract is quite different from that in S3's, we see that the underlying processes are basically the same. The long middle segments of the two protocols follow different courses (though both share preoccupation with schemas 2-6-5 and 5-3) largely because they are predicated on different errors. The difficulty of both subjects is a difficulty in localizing and removing the source of error. As long as the subject is not certain that he has tried all possibilities, he continues to explore alternatives, more or less systematically. When he is convinced that there is a genuine contradiction for all alternatives, he identifies it fairly rapidly.

Subject 8

S8 (Figure 7.17, full protocol in Appendix 7.3) took even longer than the others—nearly an hour—to solve the problem. After determining, as the others did, that $R = 7 \lor 9$ (following schema 2-6), he shows an even stronger propensity than S5 to work from right to left, as he would in working an actual arithmetic problem, systematically trying out all admissible assignments of the letters. Assigning R, he infers L (or vice versa), then tries alternative values for A in column 3, beginning with 1, and working systematically upward. The only fact that he uses to make his search more selective is $R = 7 \lor 9$.

Notice that as soon as S8 deduces the crucial fact that $E = 9$ (E22), he abandons the right-to-left forward-search strategy for the reasoning strategy employing the select-column process used by the other subjects, and arrives almost immediately at the answer. Hence, the essential parts of his reasoning are E1–E2 (schema 1-6-2), and E22–E23 (schema 5-3-2), which are almost the same as the essential parts of the three protocols previously analyzed.

The difficulties that S8 encountered in solving the problem did not arise primarily from errors that led to apparent contradictions. (He did make the usual error, that $R = 7$ implies $L = 3$, in E2, but this was corrected in E8, and hence did no harm.) Instead, he stuck so systematically to his right-to-left search that he seldom came to column 5, and when he did, it was always with a value assigned previously to E from his processing of column 3. Because of the several "iffy" assumptions on which he was proceeding at any moment, he had no reason to localize the error in that assignment. As a matter of fact, his one important piece of unsystematic behavior occurred when, the third time that he reached column 5, he took seriously the special properties of that column—that $O + E = O$. There is no convincing evidence in the protocol as to why he processed it differently on this third occasion.

In one sense, S8 had "bad luck." His strategy required him to consider three major cases (see E7): $(R = 7)$ and $(L = 3)$; $(R = 7)$ and $(L = 8)$; $(R = 9)$ and $(L = 4)$. Because $R = 7$ allowed two alternatives for L, but $R = 9$ only one, he "reasonably" decided to explore the latter hypothesis first (E10–E17). Because 3 precedes 8 in the order of the digits, he decided to explore $L = 3$ before $L = 8$ (E18–E23). Even if he had not arrived at the conclusion that $E = 9$ in E22, he would sooner or later have arrived at the correct answer (barring a mistake along the way!). During the systematic search phase of his protocol, S8 experienced considerable difficulty keeping in memory just where he was and what alternatives he had tried.

FIGURE 7.17

episode abstract for S8

DONALD
GERALD
$\overline{\text{ROBERT}}$

(1) B	(2) E	(3) INSTIGATOR	(4) E-SCHEMA	(5) EPISODE
B7	E1	D ← 5	1–6	$\xrightarrow{1} T=0 \xrightarrow{6} G = 1 \vee 2 \vee 3 \vee 4$
B23	E2		6–2	$\xrightarrow{6} R>5 \xrightarrow{2} R\text{ odd} \xrightarrow{GN} R = 7 \vee 9 \xrightarrow{2} L = 3 \vee 4$
B46	E3	L ← 3	2–6–3	$\xrightarrow{2} R=7 \xrightarrow{6} G = 1 \vee 2 \xrightarrow{3} E\text{ even}$
B78	E4	R ← 9	6	$\xrightarrow{6} G = 3 \vee 4$

5 O N A 3 5
G E 7 A 3 5
$\overline{7\ O\ B\ E\ 7\ 0}$

(1) B	(2) E	(3) INSTIGATOR	(4) E-SCHEMA	(5) EPISODE
B94	E5	A ← 1	3–6	$\xrightarrow{3} E=2 \xrightarrow{6} G=2\ \square$
B110	E6	A ← 2	3–6	$\xrightarrow{3} E=4 \xrightarrow{6} G=1$ going nowhere erase G E R A L

5 O N A L 5
G E R A L 5
$\overline{R\ O\ B\ E\ R\ 0}$

(1) B	(2) E	(3) INSTIGATOR	(4) E-SCHEMA	(5) EPISODE
B136	E7	review	2	$\xrightarrow{2} L = 3 \vee 4,\ R = 7 \vee 9 \Rightarrow L = 8 \vee 9$
B158	E8	L = 8 ∨ 9 possible	6–2	$\xrightarrow{6} R = 6 \vee 7 \vee 8 \vee 9 \xrightarrow{2} R\text{ odd} \xrightarrow{GN} R = 7 \vee 9 \xrightarrow{2} L = 3 \vee 4 \vee 8 \vee 9$ nowhere
B197	E9	AV(R)	2	$R = 7 \vee 9 \xrightarrow{2} (R=9, L=4) \vee (R=7, L=3 \vee 8)$
B217	E10	R = 9, L = 4	6–3	$\xrightarrow{6} G = 3 \xrightarrow{3GN} A \leftarrow 1 = \text{first}$

5 O N A 4 5
3 E 9 A 4 5
$\overline{9\ O\ B\ E\ 9\ 0}$

(1) B	(2) E	(3) INSTIGATOR	(4) E-SCHEMA	(5) EPISODE
B244	E11	A ← 1	3–4–5	$\xrightarrow{3} E=2 \xrightarrow{4} N=7, B=6 \xrightarrow{GN5} O=8\ \square$ (E = 2) erase A N E G
B291	E12	col.5	5	$\xrightarrow{5} (E=0) \vee (E + c5 = 0) \Rightarrow c5$ unknown
B298	E13	review	3	$R = 9, L = 4$ (erase B) $\xrightarrow{3GN} A \leftarrow 3$ next
B313	E14	A ← 3	3–4–5–6	$\xrightarrow{3} E=6 \xrightarrow{4} N=2, B=1, c5=1 \xrightarrow{5} \xrightarrow{6} G=3\ \square$ erase A N R E B
B349	E15	review	6–3	$\xrightarrow{6} G=3 \xrightarrow{3GN} A \leftarrow 6$ next
B369	E16	A ← 6	3–4	$\xrightarrow{3} E=2 \xrightarrow{4GN} N, c4=1 \xrightarrow{4} N=B \xrightarrow{3} A \geqslant 6\ \square$ erase A E G
B425	E17	review		$A \xrightarrow{GN} A\ \square,\ R=9\ \square \xrightarrow{GN} R=7$ erase R L

FIGURE 7.17 (cont'd)

```
        5 O N A L 5
        G E R A L 5
        ―――――――――
        R O B E R 0
```

B434 E18   R = 7   2–3–6 $\overset{2}{\Rightarrow}$ L = 3 ∨ 8 $\overset{AV}{\Rightarrow}$ L ← 3 $\overset{AV}{\Rightarrow}$ A ← 1 $\overset{3}{\Rightarrow}$

             E $\overset{6}{=}$ 2 ⇒ G = 1 ∨ 2 □ erase A E

B467 E19   A ← 2   6–3–4–5 $\overset{6}{\Rightarrow}$ G = 1 $\overset{3}{\Rightarrow}$ E = 4 $\overset{4GN}{\Rightarrow}$ N = 9, B = 6, c5 = 1

             $\overset{5}{\Rightarrow}$ □ erase A N E B

B516 E20   review   A $\overset{GN}{\Rightarrow}$ A ← 4 next

```
        5 O N A 3 5
        1 E 7 A 3 5
        ―――――――――
        7 O B E 7 0
```

B529 E21   A ← 4   3–4–5 $\overset{3}{\Rightarrow}$ E = 8 $\overset{4GN}{\Rightarrow}$ N = 6, c5 = 1 $\overset{5}{\Rightarrow}$ □ ⇒

             c5 = 0 ∨ 1

B561 E22   c5 = 0 ∨ 1   5 $\overset{5}{\Rightarrow}$ E = 9, c5 = 1

B582 E23   E = 9   3–2–3 $\overset{GN}{\Rightarrow}$ R = 7 $\overset{3}{\Rightarrow}$ c3 = 1 $\overset{2}{\Rightarrow}$ L = 8 $\overset{3}{\Rightarrow}$ A = 4

B610 E24   next column   4–5–6 $\overset{4GN}{\Rightarrow}$ N = 6, B = 3 c5 = 1 $\overset{5}{\Rightarrow}$ O = 2 $\overset{5}{\Rightarrow}$ c6 = 1

             $\overset{6}{\Rightarrow}$ G = 1 solution

B648 E25   check solution $\overset{1}{\Rightarrow}$ $\overset{2}{\Rightarrow}$ $\overset{3}{\Rightarrow}$ $\overset{4}{\Rightarrow}$ $\overset{5}{\Rightarrow}$ $\overset{6}{\Rightarrow}$ solution

Summary

We can say of the four subjects (S4, S3, S5, S8) that their programs show close resemblances. All four had the necessary command of arithmetic knowledge, though they were not beyond making mistaken inferences. All four had both the column selection strategy and right-to-left search strategies in their repertoire, although they showed varying degrees of readiness to use the one or the other. In a certain sense, all four "preferred" the column selection strategy, which permitted them to solve for the unknowns one by one, as in solving simultaneous algebraic equations, rather than making arbitrary conditional assignments. They all eventually recognized the central importance of the inference, E = 9. All four subjects showed severe limits in the amount of information about the problem that they were able to retain, and some of their difficulties were traceable to these limits. In particular, they appeared to retain derived properties of the letters better than they retained a memory of the path they had used to achieve any particular inference.

Thus, although the actual courses taken by the protocols in the four cases were noticeably different, the divergence does not imply fundamental differences in the programs governing the subjects' behavior. The component processes and the range of component strategies appear to be largely alike in all four cases.

It is not difficult to construct a common program that, through minor variations in priority and in the breadth of inferences drawn can produce protocols resembling those of any of these subjects. For we have seen that the differences in the paths they took can be accounted for almost entirely by (1) differential priorities for the several strategies, and (2) differences in the particular errors of reasoning or memory committed. We have, it is true, only rudimentary indications of the causes for the occurrence of the latter.

In Figure 7.18 we show the episode abstracts that would be produced from a simple version of such a program. For definiteness we assume that the program will follow FC whenever any information is produced, either about a letter or a carry. This procedure expands an episode to its maximum limit. An episode terminates whenever no further inferences can be made, or when a value for a letter is obtained by exhaustion (e.g., R = 7 $\lor$ 9 and E = 9 implies R = 7), hence not from a column. If there is no specific instigator for a new episode, then the program scans from right to left to obtain next-column. Assignments, if any, are always to be made for letters in next-column.

In version α no assignments are made on a trial-and-error basis. If definite information cannot be extracted by processing a column, it is temporarily passed over for the next column. Abstract α can be seen to bear some resemblance to the abstract for S4.

In version β, if the admissible assignments for a letter have been narrowed down to not more than 2, these are explored in turn. Otherwise, as in α, the columns are scanned. The resulting abstract has some resemblance to S3's. This resemblance is greatly increased (abstract γ) if the reasoning is degraded slightly. In γ it is assumed that the possibility of a carry into column 3 is ignored, resulting in the erroneous inferences that L = 3 (E2) and L = 4 (E4). It is also assumed that when a branch terminates, the information developed during that branch is rejected completely—thus, that E = 9 is not seen as independently valid (E3).

Abstract δ simulates a subject who is not capable of drawing the inference that E = 9 from column 5, though he is capable, of course, of seeing that there is a contradiction if other specific values are assigned to E. With this degradation of reasoning ability, we must give up the restriction on assignments adopted in version β: any letter, if selected, can be assigned digits. Abstract δ can be seen to bear some relation to S8, except that (1) S8 chose to start with R $\leftarrow$ 9, L = 4, rather than R $\leftarrow$ 7, L $\leftarrow$ 3, and (2) S8 did finally discover that E = 9 and then immediately arrived at a solution.

Even these simple, and rather rigid, simulation programs exhibit, by means of relatively minor parametric changes, a range of individual differences that correspond rather well with the differences among our subjects. The lesson to be drawn from the simulations is that in large combinatorial spaces, small causes can bring about great divergences between search paths. Direct comparison of temporal sequences in behavior may therefore exaggerate the underlying differences among the programs generating the behavior. The commonalities can be detected by inducting a family of programs sufficiently rich in capacity for minor variation to generate a number of different paths.

FIGURE 7.18

episode abstracts for simulation programs

Abstract α: No trial and error

E	INSTIGATOR	E-SCHEMA	EPISODE
E1	D ← 5	1–6	$\overset{1}{\Rightarrow} T = 0,\ c2 = 1 \overset{6}{\Rightarrow} R > 5,\ G < 5 \overset{6}{\Rightarrow} R\ \text{odd} \overset{GN}{\Rightarrow} R = 7 \vee 9$
E2	next column	5–3	$\overset{5}{\Rightarrow} E = 9,\ c5 = 1,\ c6 = 1 \overset{3}{\Rightarrow} A = 4,\ c3 = 1,\ c4 = 0 \overset{GN}{\Rightarrow} R = 7$
E3	R = 7	2–6	$\overset{2}{\Rightarrow} L = 8 \overset{6}{\Rightarrow} G = 1$
E4	next column	4	$\overset{4}{\Rightarrow} N = 6,\ B = 3 \overset{GN}{\Rightarrow} O = 2$ solution

Abstract β: Assign if only two alternatives

E	INSTIGATOR	E-SCHEMA	EPISODE
E1	D ← 5	1–6–2	$\overset{1}{\Rightarrow} T = 0,\ c2 = 1 \overset{6}{\Rightarrow} R > 5,\ G < 5 \overset{2}{\Rightarrow} R\ \text{odd} \overset{GN}{\Rightarrow} R = 7 \vee 9$
E2	R ← 7	2–6	$\overset{2}{\Rightarrow} L = 3 \vee 8 \overset{6}{\Rightarrow} G = 1 \vee 2$
E3	L ← 3	2–3–5	$\overset{2}{\Rightarrow} c3 = 0 \overset{3}{\Rightarrow} E\ \text{even} \overset{5}{\Rightarrow} E = 9\ \square\ (E\ \text{even}) \Rightarrow E = 9,\ c5 = 1,\ c6 = 1$
E4	L ← 8, E = 9	2–3–6	$\overset{2}{\Rightarrow} c3 = 1 \overset{3}{\Rightarrow} A = 4 \overset{6}{\Rightarrow} G = 1$
E5	next column	4	$\overset{4}{\Rightarrow} N = 6,\ B = 3 \overset{GN}{\Rightarrow} O = 2$ solution

Abstract γ: β with c3 = 0 error

E	INSTIGATOR	E-SCHEMA	EPISODE
E1	D ← 5	1–6–2	$\overset{1}{\Rightarrow} R = 0,\ c2 = 1 \overset{6}{\Rightarrow} R > 5,\ G < 5 \overset{2}{\Rightarrow} R\ \text{odd} \overset{GN}{\Rightarrow} R = 7 \vee 9$
E2	R ← 7	2–6	$\overset{2}{\Rightarrow} L = 3,\ c3 = 0\ \text{[error]} \overset{6}{\Rightarrow} G = 1 \vee 2$
E3	next column	3–5	$\overset{3}{\Rightarrow} E\ \text{even} \overset{5}{\Rightarrow} E = 9,\ c5 = 1,\ c6 = 1\ \square\ (E\ \text{even})$ [reject E = 9]
E4	R ← 9	2–6	$\overset{2}{\Rightarrow} L = 4,\ c3 = 0\ \text{error} \overset{6}{\Rightarrow} G = 3 \vee 4$
E5	next column	3–5	$\overset{3}{\Rightarrow} E\ \text{even} \overset{5}{\Rightarrow} E = 9,\ c5 = 1,\ c6 = 1\ \square\ (R \leftarrow 9)$ [reject E = 9]
E6	R ← 7 review	2	$\overset{2}{\Rightarrow} L = 3 \vee 8 \overset{GN}{\Rightarrow} L = 8$
E7	L = 8	2–3–5–3–6	$\overset{2}{\Rightarrow} c3 = 1 \overset{3}{\Rightarrow} E\ \text{odd} \overset{5}{\Rightarrow} E = 9,\ c5 = 1,\ c6 = 1 \overset{3}{\Rightarrow} A = 4,\ c4 = 0 \overset{6}{\Rightarrow} G = 1$
E8	next column	4	$\overset{4}{\Rightarrow} N = 6,\ B = 3 \overset{GN}{\Rightarrow} O = 2$

Abstract δ: No E = 9 inference

E	INSTIGATOR	E-SCHEMA	EPISODE
E1	D ← 5	1–6–2	$\overset{1}{\Rightarrow} T = 0,\ c2 = 1 \overset{6}{\Rightarrow} R > 5,\ G < 5 \overset{2}{\Rightarrow} R\ \text{odd} \overset{GN}{\Rightarrow} R = 7 \vee 9$
E2	R ← 7	2–6	$\overset{2}{\Rightarrow} L = 3 \vee 8 \overset{6}{\Rightarrow} G = 1 \vee 2$
E3	L ← 3	3	$\overset{3}{\Rightarrow} c3 = 0,\ E\ \text{even}$

FIGURE 7.18 (cont'd)

$$
\begin{array}{l}
\text{E4} \quad 5\,O\,N\,A\,3\,5 \\
\phantom{\text{E4} \quad} G\,E\,7\,A\,3\,5 \\
\phantom{\text{E4} \quad} \overline{7\,O\,B\,E\,7\,0}
\end{array}
$$

E4	A ← 1	3–5	$\overset{3}{\Rightarrow} E = 2 \overset{5}{\Rightarrow} \square$
E5	A ← 2	3–5	$\overset{3}{\Rightarrow} E = 4 \overset{5}{\Rightarrow} \square$
E6	A ← 4	3–5	$\overset{3}{\Rightarrow} E = 8 \overset{5}{\Rightarrow} \square$
E7	A ← 6	3–5	$\overset{3}{\Rightarrow} E = 2 \overset{5}{\Rightarrow} \square$
E8	A ← 8	3–5	$\overset{3}{\Rightarrow} E = 6 \overset{5}{\Rightarrow} \square$
E9	A ← 9	3–5	$\overset{3}{\Rightarrow} E = 8 \overset{5}{\Rightarrow} \square$
E10	L ← 8	2	$\overset{2}{\Rightarrow} c3 = 1,\ E \text{ odd}$

$$
\begin{array}{l}
5\,O\,N\,A\,8\,5 \\
G\,E\,7\,A\,8\,5 \\
\overline{7\,O\,B\,E\,7\,0}
\end{array}
$$

E11	A ← 1	3–5	$\overset{3}{\Rightarrow} E = 3 \Rightarrow \square$
E12	A ← 2	3	$\overset{3}{\Rightarrow} E = 5 \ \square \ (D \leftarrow 5)$
E13	A ← 3	3	$\overset{3}{\Rightarrow} E = 7 \ \square \ (R \leftarrow 7)$
E14	A ← 4	3–5–6	$\overset{3}{\Rightarrow} E = 9 \overset{5}{\Rightarrow} c5 = 1,\ c6 = 1 \overset{6}{\Rightarrow} G = 1$
E15	next column	4	$\overset{4}{\Rightarrow} N = 6,\ B = 3 \overset{GN}{\Rightarrow} O = 2 \text{ solution}$

CROSS+ROADS=DANGER

So far we have used a single task, DONALD+GERALD=ROBERT. By the nature of our analysis this is not as severe a limitation as it might seem. For we have not treated the task as an unanalyzed "variable" against which to plot our subject's behavior (as occurs in intelligence testing, or even in many experimental investigations, such as those on functional fixity or the *Einstellung* effect). Rather we have attempted to discern the specific mechanisms whereby each bit of task-oriented behavior is produced. If the theory is any good at all, these same mechanisms should operate in the same way in any cryptarithmetic task.

Nevertheless, it would be comforting to verify that the same information processing behavior shows up in a new task. Let us look briefly, then, at one other, CROSS+ROADS=DANGER. This was solved successfully by S4 immediately after (with a ten-minute break) he had done DONALD+GERALD, and was also attempted by another subject, S2 (for whom the main interest lies in his eye-movement data).

The task itself is somewhat more difficult than DONALD+GERALD, insofar as no key step exists that unlocks the puzzle. Figure 7.19, parallel to Figure 7.11, shows how the variables enter into the constraints. The immediate processing sequences are given in Figure 7.20. We have included in the diagram an initiation from R ← 6, since S4 was given this information as a start (just as he was given D ← 5 in DONALD+GERALD). Progress is quite easy to begin with, taking full information from columns 1 and 2. However, there seems to be no way to extract any general information from the left-hand three columns, despite the fact that they are coupled by three letters (R, O, and A) that occur more than once. Even if one attempts to write the equations for the task, assuming the two rightmost columns to be correctly filled in (S = 3, E = 4, R ← 6), one gets

$$c5 + C + 6 = 10 + A$$
$$c4 + 6 + O = 10c5 + N$$
$$O + A = 10c4 + G$$

FIGURE 7.19

essential structure of CROSS+ROADS=DANGER

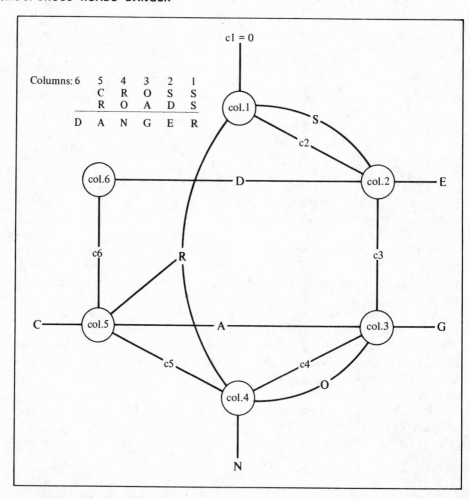

FIGURE 7.20

episode schemas for CROSS+ROADS=DANGER

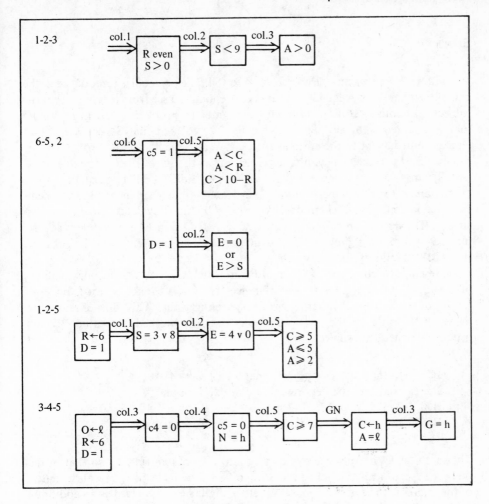

from which the best that can be obtained is:

$$G + 10 = C + N + 11(c5 - c4)$$

The factor involving the two carries can take on values of $+1$, 0, and -1, but it can be seen that -1 leads to a contradiction. Consequently, $c5 = 0$ and $c4 = 1$ is not possible. This same conclusion follows directly and more generally from the reasoning:

$$(R > A) \supset (O + R > O + A) \supset (c4 + O + R \geq O + A + c3)$$
$$\supset (c5 \geq c4) \supset (c4 = 1 \supset c5 = 1)$$

But this is not a very strong conclusion and leaves almost all the trial-and-error search still to be carried out. The line of reasoning just exhibited, by the way,

305

is a good example of reasoning that is *not* possible for someone working in the augmented space.

Subject 4

Figure 7.21 gives the episode abstract for S4. The protocol is reproduced at the end of the chapter in Appendix 7.5. It is easy enough to see from the figure that the subject is essentially still operating in the augmented problem space. In E1 we see that $R \leftarrow 6$ leads to the inference that $S = 3 \lor 8$, and that S4 derived $D = 1$ almost immediately. In the episode abstract we also see iterations through the assignments of variables, including a generation of the set of digits available for C (at E9); and we note numerous successful applications of TD (e.g., at E5). More to the point is to ask whether a more sophisticated problem space than the augmented space is being used. There doesn't seem to be much evidence for such a possibility. The derivation of $E = 4 \lor 0$ from $S = 3 \lor 8$ in E1 was actually accomplished by rapid assignment and calculation, as can be seen from the protocol (B17–B19). Similarly the derivation of $A = 2 \lor 3$ and $O = 2 \lor 3$ in E5 appears to represent a combination of GN and PC in which $G \leftarrow 5$, and the unavailability of the digits 0 and 1 leads to the inference that (4, 1) cannot be used, but only (2, 3), consequently that either letter can have either value. This form of reasoning, in which the order of the two variables is not distinguished, shows up clearly a little later, where the subject says:

> B58: In that case G must be equal to A plus 4.
> B59: And the numbers remaining are 2, 4, 5, and 7 . . .
> B60: 2, 3, 4, 5, and 7.
> B61: And 3 and 7 are the only numbers fitting this.

The fact that S4 has neglected the carry into the column (in E5), so that in fact there is no set of available values that sum to $4 (= 5 - 1)$, helps to reveal the nature of the inference. The use of unordered sets of digits may be viewed as an additional augmentation of the problem space, but except for this we can conclude that the problem space for S4 is the same one he used on DONALD+GERALD.

Scanning the episode abstract, we see that S4 promptly exhausted the immediate information in the problem, recognized the situation (B29: "You really can't tell anything about the rest of the letters, what digits correspond to them"), and went into a systematic attempt to assign values. Note, however, as confirmation of his use of the augmented problem space, that he did not see the more subtle inference that $c4 = 1$ implies $c5 = 1$. The task requires at least a double assignment before any real consequences flow, and the figure makes the effect of this on S4's behavior clear—the assignments with G and O (namely column 3) when $S \leftarrow 8$ and with C and O (namely columns 5 and 4) when $S \leftarrow 3$. With each assignment, the episode is immediately completed, and the contradiction found.

The subject makes a substantial number of errors, each of which has been noted in the figure. In each case there is rapid recovery once the contradiction has been found. However, the recovery never involves the subject's discovery that

FIGURE 7.21

episode abstract for S4 on CROSS+ROADS=DANGER

(1) B	(2) E	(3) INSTIGATOR	(4) E-SCHEMA	(5) EPISODE
		5 4 3 2 1		
		C R O S S		
		R O A D S		
		D A N G E R		
B6	E1	R ← 6	1–5–2	$\overset{1}{\Rightarrow} S = 3 \vee 8 \overset{5}{\Rightarrow} D = 1 \overset{2}{\Rightarrow} E = 4 \vee 0$
B20	E2	S ← 8	2	$\overset{2}{\Rightarrow} E = 0$
		C 6 O 8 8		
		6 O A 1 8		
		1 A N G 0 6		
B26	E3	next column	3–4	$\overset{3}{\Rightarrow} 0 \overset{4GN}{\Rightarrow} 0 = 3 \vee 7$ [not clear in protocol]
B30	E4	G ← 7	3–5	$\overset{GN}{\Rightarrow} 0 = 3 \overset{3}{\Rightarrow} A = 4 \overset{5}{\Rightarrow} C = 7 \vee 8 \ \square \ (G \leftarrow 7, S \leftarrow 8)$
B35	E5	G ← 5	3–4–6	$\overset{3}{\Rightarrow} 0 = 2 \vee 3, A = 2 \vee 3 \overset{GN}{\Rightarrow} O = 3 \overset{4}{\Rightarrow} N = 9 \overset{3}{\Rightarrow} A = 2, G = 5 \overset{6}{\Rightarrow} C = 6 \ \square \ (R = 6)$
B52	E6	O ← 3	3–4	$\overset{3}{\Rightarrow} N = 9, \ c5 = 0 \overset{5}{\Rightarrow} C \geqslant 4, A > 1 \overset{4NG}{\Rightarrow} O \leftarrow 3 \ \square$ [not clear in protocol]
B56	E7	O ← 4	3–4	$\overset{3}{\Rightarrow} G = 7, A = 3 \overset{4}{\Rightarrow} N = 0 \ \square \ (E = 0)$
B63	E8	O ← 3	3–4–5	$\overset{3}{\Rightarrow} G = 7, A = 4 \overset{4}{\Rightarrow} N = 9 \overset{5}{\Rightarrow} C = 6 \ \square \ (R = 6) \Rightarrow S \leftarrow 8 \ \square$
B69	E9	S ← 4	2–5	$\overset{2}{\Rightarrow} E = 4, \ c3 = 0 \overset{5}{\Rightarrow} C = 5 \vee 7 \vee 8 \vee 9$ [O = 3 left on display, but disregarded]
		C 6 O 3 3		
		6 O A 1 3		
		1 A N G 4 6		
B84	E10	C ← 5	5–4	$\overset{5}{\Rightarrow} A = 2, \ c5 = 1 \overset{4}{\Rightarrow} O > 4 \Rightarrow N < 6, N \neq 0 \ \square$ (0 ∨ 7 ∨ 8 ∨ 9 free)
B85	E11	C ← 7	5–4	$\overset{5}{\Rightarrow} c5 = 1 \overset{4}{\Rightarrow} O > 4 \Rightarrow N < 6 \ \square$ (as per E10) not certain [E10 and E11 not clear in protocol]
B88	E12	C ← 8	5–4	$\overset{5}{\Rightarrow} A = 4 \vee 5 \overset{4}{\Rightarrow} O = 5 \vee 7 \vee 9$
B96	E13	O ← 5		$\overset{GN}{\Rightarrow} A = 4 \ \square \ (E = 4) \overset{GN}{\Rightarrow} O = 7 \vee 9$
B99	E14	O ← 7	4–3	$\overset{4}{\Rightarrow} c4 \leftarrow 0, N = 3 \overset{GN}{\Rightarrow} A = 5 \overset{3}{\Rightarrow} G = 2 \ \square \ (c4 = 1)$
B105	E15	c4 ← 0 [still O ← 7]	3–4–5	$\overset{3}{\Rightarrow} A = 2, G = 9 \overset{4}{\Rightarrow} N = 3 \overset{5}{\Rightarrow} A = 5$
B112	E16	A = 5	5–4	$\overset{5}{\Rightarrow} c5 = 1 \overset{GN}{\Rightarrow} O \leftarrow 7, 9 \overset{4GN}{\Rightarrow} N = 3 \vee 4, 6 \ \square \Rightarrow A = 5 \ \square, C \leftarrow 8 \ \square$ [C = 8, O = 3 left on display, but disregarded]
		C 6 O 3 3		
		6 O 5 1 3		
		1 5 N G 4 6		
B123	E17	C ← 9	5–4–3	$\overset{5}{\Rightarrow} A = 5, \ c5 = 0 \overset{4}{\Rightarrow} O = 2, N = 8 \overset{3}{\Rightarrow} G = 7$ solution
B130	E18	record and check		C = 9, O = 2, G = 7, N = 8 solution

he has made an error, rather than simply a set of incompatible assignments. Since a considerable part of the protocol, some six and one-half episodes out of 21, was generated because of the errors, they were not costless. However, they never caused S4 the kind of difficulties that S3 and S5 had in DONALD+GERALD.

In the episode abstract there are three selection behaviors that are not explained by the hypothesis of systematic generation. One of these is the selection of S ← 8 before S ← 3. There is no cue in the protocol as to why this occurs. S4 generates assignments for G from large digits downwards, but for O upwards and, later, for C upwards. The second anomaly is the choice of column 3 to work on after columns 1 and 2 have been exhausted (starting at E3). Here we may conjecture that S4 is simply working from right to left, a rational strategy, since he knows the value of the carry into column 3 ($c3 = 1$), but does not know it for either of the other candidate columns (4 and 5).

The final act of selection in the abstract is the order of assignments to G, O, A, and C. As one can see from the figure, in the first half of the protocol (S ← 8), the subject assigns G, then O, then C (in E5). This order appears to be determined by the column considerations. But in the second half of the protocol (S ← 3) the subject switches to the order: C, then O, then A, but with O after A in E12. The issue boils down to the selection of C (column 5?) after $E = 4$ in E9 (as opposed to column 3 in the corresponding situation earlier), and the retention of $A = 5$ in passing from E16 to E17.

In sum, S4 operates on this new problem essentially as he did on DONALD+GERALD: he uses the same problem space and exhibits the same level of episoding. We have not tried to compare the two protocols of S4 in detail, since the episode abstract appears to be too crude an instrument for such comparison. Likewise, though we noted above a number of decisions and errors that remained unexplained, there is no indication whether or not they could be understood in terms of the fine structure of the programs.

Subject 2

Figure 7.22 shows the episode abstract for another subject (S2), also a college sophomore, on CROSS+ROADS=DANGER. We have shown only the first few minutes of the behavior (382 seconds), but this is sufficient to confirm much of what we found with S4. Actually, the experimental arrangements were a little different. First, the subject was wearing an eye-movement helmet. Second, assignments were not written on the display (which was a projected slide); rather, the subject could ask the experimenter to remember an assignment and could call for it at any later time. This does make a difference in the operations used by the subject, as we shall see later, but not one that shows up in the episode abstract.

There are clear indications that S2 works in the augmented problem space. First of all, the derivation of $D = 1$ in the first episode, and the derivation of $C \geq 6$ in the second, imply his use of a reasonable PC operator. The TD operator appears to be routinely applied and is more than minimal—note the conclusion that $A = 0$ is not possible since it makes $O = G$, even though neither of these has an assigned value. The assignment operator (AV) is used systematically. The evidence for a GN operator, except as associated with assignment, is not explicit, but later in the protocol S2 says:

B305: S equals 3,
B306: R is six, and C
B307:
B308: can be five,
B309: seven, or eight.

Thus S2 uses all of the operators that are associated with the augmented problem space. Moreover, he does not seem to use any others of greater power. For instance, at E4, knowing that 1 and 2 are unavailable for assignment (as indicated by his immediate recognition of that fact after generating $A = 1$ and $A = 2$, respectively) S2 might have made the inference that $C \geq 9$, hence $C = 9$. In fact, 3 is not available either ($E = 3$), but E6 shows that S2 does not recollect this fact—thus that, even if he had the reasoning mechanism described above, he would not have excluded $C = 9$.

FIGURE 7.22

episode abstract for S2 on CROSS+ROADS=DANGER

(1) E	(2) B	(3) INSTIGATOR	(4) E-SCHEMA	(5) EPISODE
		5 4 3 2 1 CROSS ROADS ——— DANGER		
T1.8	E1	S ← 1	1–5	$\xrightarrow{1} R = 2 \xrightarrow{5} D = 1 \;\square\;$ reject S
T91.2	E2	S ← 2	1–5	$\xrightarrow{1} R = 4 \xrightarrow{5} C \geqslant 6$
		C 4 0 2 2 4 0 A 1 2 ——— 1 A N G E 4	[display does not hold values. E holds them in memory, on call by S2]	
T130	E3	C ← 6	5–2–3	$\xrightarrow{5} A = 0 \xrightarrow{2} E = 3 \xrightarrow{3} O = G \;\square\; \xrightarrow{3} A > 0$
T223	E4	C ← 7	5	$\xrightarrow{5} A = 1 \;\square\; (D = 1)$
T240	E5	C ← 8	5	$\xrightarrow{5} A = 2 \;\square\; (S = 2)$
T264	E6	A ← 3	5–3	$\xrightarrow{5} C = 9 \xrightarrow{3} O + 3 = G$
T294	E7	O ← 5	3–4	$\xrightarrow{3} G = 8 \xrightarrow{4} N = 9 \;\square\; (C = 9)$
T352	E8	get N (still 0 ← 5)	4	$\xrightarrow{\text{GN}} N \leftarrow 7 \xrightarrow{4} R = 2 \;\square\; (S = 2)$

In all other ways, the fragment of S2's behavior looks unexceptional, and we need not tarry further with it at this level. At the level of analysis being used, we have little to learn from either S4 or S2 except that moving to a different task within the same environment (CROSS+ROADS instead of DONALD+GERALD) still leads to behavior analyzable in the same terms. The same problem space, the augmented one, is used. The demands of the task show up in the same way—that is, as episodes involving immediate generation or obvious implications. The subjects proceed from episode to episode with essentially systematic assignment of variables. But this was what needed confirmation.

Only if we wish to fix more closely the mechanisms that realize the behavior that is grossly exhibited in the episode abstract is analysis worth pursuing. Additional analysis could be carried out at the level of the production system, as developed for S3. Such analysis concentrates on the fine structure of the sequential linkage of behavior, to make clear how that sequence is controlled within the problem space. At a still lower level lie the mechanisms that implement the operators and remember informaton. In all of the protocols, errors of immediate memory have been significant. In S2's behavior, for instance, we already noted how his failure to recall that $E = 3$, so that $A \leftarrow 3$ was not possible (E6), vitiates the remainder of the episodes shown in Figure 7.22.

Since we have eye-movement data for S2, it is worthwhile to extend the analysis of his protocol. Mostly, the additional analysis will provide evidence at the level of the production system, although a few more facets of the structure of his immediate memory and immediate processing will emerge.

Subject 2: Detailed Analysis Using Eye-Movement Data

The data on Subject 2 came from a study by Arnold Winikoff (1967) to explore whether eye-movement data could aid the analysis of problem solving behavior. Although our use of the data about S2 requires additional analysis beyond that done in Winikoff's study, a brief review of the latter will provide a starting point.

Our investigations of human problem solving alternate between two strategies. One is to examine the behavior of an individual problem solving attempt in as much detail as possible. The aim is to determine whether the information processing theory really describes the fine structure of behavior. Chapter 6 was an example of such analysis, and others will be provided in Chapters 9 and 12. The other strategy is to ask more broadly whether the theory fits the facts from a substantial range of situations, trading off breadth for depth. We have followed this strategy in the episode abstracts in this chapter and will use it in other analyses in Chapters 10 and 13.

It is the first strategy—the detailed one—that concerns us now. We wish to acquire as much information as possible about the subject's behavior during a given period, using the data both to induce and to verify the IPS that models the behavior. The verbal protocol, although posing problems of interpretation, has the great virtue of providing a relatively high density of data per minute of subject behavior. (A moment's consideration reveals that running the subject for longer sessions in order to collect more data is not an equivalent strategy, since it provides more opportunity for new elements—facts, methods, external stimuli—to enter the situation, hence introduces more degrees of freedom.) Gross eye movements provide additional data, gathered in parallel with the verbal report, hence increase the number of "points" the theory must fit without increasing the number of degrees of freedom available for the fitting. Winikoff's study was addressed to this issue. It employed a small number of subjects (4) but secured a large amount of data (15 minutes per subject with eye-movement data every fifth of a second). Three of the tasks used were cryptarithmetic (including S2) and the other was chess.

A commercially available adaptation of the Mackworth Eye Marker Camera[4] was used to record where, on the display, the subject's eyes were pointing at each instant of time. The recording technique involves reflecting a spot of light from the cornea and bringing it via an optical path composed of mirrors and lenses to focus on a frame of film that is being exposed to the situation viewed by the subject. When the eye moves, the spot is reflected at a slightly different angle and hence comes to bear at a somewhat different place on the film. Under proper calibration, the spot on the film coincides essentially with the point to which the eyes are oriented. The accuracy can be as good as $\pm 1°$ horizontally and $\pm 2°$ vertically.

Since the subject's head moves frequently, the entire camera assembly is mounted on a helmet, moving with the head. Somewhat better accuracy is possible if the mechanical system composed of head and helmet is held in one place by having the subject bite a rod attached to the helmet. However, since we wanted our subjects to talk continuously while problem solving, we used the somewhat cruder system. Eye movements have been taken with instrumental arrangements over the last half century, and the arrangement used is in no way exceptional. More details can be found in Winikoff (1967). The camera is shown in Figure 7.23. The frames were taken at 0.2-second intervals so that almost no fixations were

FIGURE 7.23
eye-movement camera

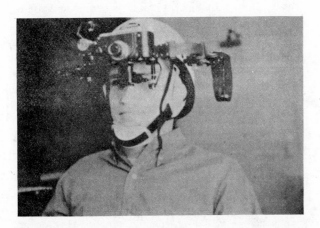

[4] Westgate Instrument Corporation, Dayton, Ohio. (See also Mackworth and Mackworth, 1958.)

missed. Time markers were placed on the audio tape from the camera, so that the speech and the eye movements could be coordinated. However, coordination is not perfect, since the time is marked on every tenth frame (thus, every 2 seconds) and a human had to make the coordination between the heard time and the word.

The results of the study fall into two parts. The first concerns the eye movements themselves, the second their relation to the problem solving behavior. With respect to eye movements, in a stationary display, such as a cryptarithmetic display or the page of a book, eye movements consist of a series of *fixations*, during each of which the eyes are focused on a fixed position of the display. Each fixation is followed by a *saccade*, in which the eyes jump to another position somewhere in the display.[5] Almost no time is taken by the saccade itself, and apparently nothing is seen while the eyeball is in transit, so that all the vision time may be divided up into fixations, each localizable on the display. Thus the fixation is the natural unit of analysis, and it has been so used in many prior studies—e.g., reading studies that analyze the record in terms of number of fixations per line, average length of fixation, and number of regressive fixations (those that jump back to a prior place in the text) (e.g., Tiffin, 1937).

The field of vision itself has two parts, a foveal part with high resolution and a peripheral part with relatively low resolution but high sensitivity to certain visual stimuli (e.g., moving stimuli). Acuity falls off rather rapidly with distance from the center of the fovea. Thus, in order to see an object a subject moves his eyes so that the object falls somewhere within the foveal region of clarity. The size of this region is affected by many things, such as the visual task to be performed (e.g., judging two vernier lines to coincide versus recognizing a well-printed character) and the surrounding visual field (e.g., whether there are other letters close by). In displays like the one used in the cryptarithmetic tasks, the region of clarity is about $2°$ in radius, that is to say, the region is about the width of a letter. Thus, if the eye spot is located on the D in column 2, then the subject is probably not looking at any of the adjacent letters (S, A, E, or S) and is certainly not looking at any letters further away than the adjacent ones. (Whether he actually is *seeing* the D is of course another matter; the evidence is only that he is *looking* at it.)

Two other points are worth noting. Generally, more fixations are directed to the upper half of the total visual field than to the lower half and more to the right half than to the left (Buswell, 1935). If we look at the distribution of number of fixations (or of fixation time, it would make no difference) for S2 on CROSS+ ROADS (Table 7.2), we see that there is indeed a very strong vertical effect, although the column structure of the task obscures any left-right effect that might exist. Thus, there are very few fixations on the lower row of the display. This effect is enhanced (and the dominance of the top row obscured) by the fact that the top and

---

[5] The eye is also capable of continuous movements when tracking a slowly moving object. Similarly, the eye is always engaged in small fast oscillations (about 50 per second, with a few seconds of arc amplitude), as well as in micro-saccades (about 5 per second with amplitudes from 15 seconds of arc up). Although much studied recently, none of these aspects of eye movements concerns us here (Yarbus, 1967).

bottom rows are relatively easy to read compared with the middle row (Mackworth, 1965). The same generalizations hold for all of Winikoff's subjects.

The final, and important, point to be noted is that the task involves looking at a display that does not change over the course of the problem solving attempt. The subject learns about the letters, the columns, and their relationships by looking at the display, but after the first orientation he does not obtain information that was unavailable earlier. This contrasts with the situation in many studies of eye movements (e.g., watching a radar scope) where, if the subject doesn't look at a given part of the display at a certain time, he cannot, hence will not, acquire new stimulus information present there at just that time.

TABLE 7.2

		3	C:	232	R:	133	Q:	140	S:	145	S:	100	Row 1:	753
		12	R:	206	O:	85	A:	92	D:	97	S:	112	Row 2:	604
	D:	9	A:	58	N:	12	G:	11	E:	13	R:	25	Row 3:	128
Column Total		24		496		230		243		255		237	Total:	1599

Fixations to the right of the board: 23
Fixations to the left of the board: 1
Fixations above the board: 20
Blinks: 70

One of the main results of Winikoff's investigations was that the cryptarithmetic eye-movement data could be aggregated into units of 1 to 20 seconds in duration (called *EMA*'s for *eye-movement aggregates*).

1. *Attention unit:* a series of fixations devoted predominantly to a single task-relevant locale in the display.
2. *Scan unit:* a series of short fixations that wander widely over the display.
3. *Transition unit:* a short series of brief fixations interposed between attention units.
4. *Excursion unit:* a short series of brief fixations within an attention unit that leave the locale of that unit (and then return to it).[6]

The interpretation to be given to these units is already indicated by their names. An attention unit is to be interpreted as caused by the subject's attending to problem solving concerned with the part of the display that the attention unit designates. The scan unit is to be interpreted as the subject's engaging in some kind of search.

[6] In Winikoff's study the term *transition unit* was used to cover both the transition units and the excursion units defined here, since the interpretation given to them is the same. We adopt separate names to avoid continual reference to *within-unit transitions* and *between-unit transitions*. In fact, the operational definitions of the two kinds of units differ slightly.

The transition and excursion units are not regarded as having problem solving significance. (They may function in some lower level of control process not analyzed here.)

Operationally, these units are defined by a set of rules, realized in a multiple-pass ALGOL program, which aggregates the time series of frames automatically. Each aggregate specifies the letter occurrences on the display at which the subject is looking.

> *Setup:* Define task-relevant areas for CROSS+ROADS=DANGER to be columns (a set of input parameters to the program).
>
> *Pass 1:* Aggregate the fixations.
>
> *Pass 2:* Aggregate consecutive fixations that lie within the same task-relevant area (same columns). Absorb nonfitting fixations as excursions if they are short (a preset parameter) and short compared to the surrounding unit (another preset parameter).
>
> *Pass 3:* Aggregate series of form ABAB into C (where C is the union of the places in A and B) if certain conditions are met on A and B (preset parameters).
>
> *Pass 4:* Aggregate series of the form ABA into A (i.e., absorb B into A) if certain conditions are met on A and B (preset parameters).
>
> *Pass 5:* Label the remaining intervals as either scan units or transitions depending on their durations (cutting point determined from the distribution of lengths given by the output of pass 3).

TABLE 7.3

	TRANSITION UNITS				SCAN UNITS							
Number of occurrences	27	20	24	23	7	6	2	3	3	3	3	7
Duration (secs)	.2	.4	.6	.8	1.0	1.2	1.4	1.6	1.8	2.0	2.1	>2.1

As can be seen, several parameters influence the decisions about whether to aggregate or not. Winikoff's study includes an analysis of sensitivity of the aggregation to these parameters, showing that the aggregation remains quite stable with small variations in their values.

The aggregation program attempts to find attention units, building them up in a manner analogous to bottom-up grammatical recognition. Thus, large attention units are likely to be made up of smaller attention units, although the hierarchy does not become very deep. In creating these units the program is prepared to discard (i.e., to label as transitions and excursions) various brief fixations that do not fit. The residual—the part that is not incorporated in attention units—is assigned to scan units (regarded as meaningful) or transition units (regarded as nonmeaningful) on the basis of total duration. Table 7.3 shows the distribution of durations of these residuals for S2. There is a sharp drop in their number at 1.2 seconds. This indicates that the long nonattention units are not simply the tail of a single homogeneous distribution to which the attention units also belong and justifies the use of a cutting point. (All the experiments in Winikoff's study show the same phenomena.)

Figure 7.24 shows a small sample of the raw data. As indicated at the top of the figure, the places on the two-dimensional display (letter occurrences) have been laid out horizontally. A fixation shows as a single vertical line in the appropriate column; its duration is indicated by the length of the line. We have indicated the attention units and scan units by boxing the set of eye movements included in each unit. The transitions and excursions are left unmarked. Excursions can be seen clearly—for example, in attention unit 9 (SSR); however, other attention units (e.g., 11) do not contain any excursions. Similarly, transitions sometimes occur (e.g., between 7 and 9) and sometimes do not (e.g., between 16 and 17). Because of the way in which scan units are defined, excursions within a scan unit or transitions between a scan unit and an attention unit are not possible (they would be assimilated into the scan). Similarly two scan units cannot be adjacent.

Figure 7.25 shows several attention and scan units in the correct geometrical perspective. The size of each dot is proportional to the length of the corresponding fixation. We have had to displace some of the fixations slightly so as to make the diagram intelligible; thus the fine structure of placement around a letter is an artifact of the diagram. An additional implication of the attention-unit interpretation can now be appreciated: that the within-unit distribution and sequence has no interpretation in information processing terms. A more microscopic understanding of the process would no doubt show this to be false, just as our interpretation of transitions and excursions as meaningless is undoubtedly false at a finer level of detail. Nevertheless, Winikoff's study disclosed no reliable way of interpreting these aspects of eye movements.

With the last remark we have already alluded to the second main result of the eye-movement study: namely, that the attention and scan units correspond closely with the problem solving behavior inferred from the verbal protocol. This can already be seen to some extent in Figure 7.24, where S2 is looking continuously at column 1 (SSR) while processing it, and later at column 2, toward the bottom of the figure. On the other hand, some attention units, such as RON at EMA10, provide no direct indication in the verbal behavior that the subject was processing column 4. Of course, it could be that a model of the information processing of S2 would indicate that column 4 was indeed considered, and then the RON attention unit could be taken as confirming evidence.

Winikoff undertook a general evaluation of the correspondence between the problem solving behavior and the eye-movement units. Evaluation is not straightforward for four distinct reasons. First, we now have two measures of eye movement: individual fixations and the eye-movement aggregates, just defined. These measures are correlated, since the aggregates are made up of fixations. Thus, if we find a relation between problem solving behavior and the eye-movement aggregates, it may not have anything to do with the aggregation per se, but only with particular fixations within the aggregate. That is, it might be better not to aggregate at all but to look directly for correspondence with fixations.

The second difficulty in evaluation arises from the measurement of problem solving behavior. This is to be induced from the verbal behavior. Even if verbal behavior and eye movements correspond, this might not have anything to do with the inferred problem solving, but rather with some other feature of the verbal behavior. More particularly, some of the inferred problem solving is based on surface features of the utterances; e.g., in Figure 7.24 at EMA9 S2 says "S plus S has to equal R." That the eyes look at S, S and R may as easily be predicted from the occurrence of S, S and R in the utterance as from the inference that S2 was processing column 1.

The third difficulty is that even under ideal conditions (of our hypothesis that eye movements and problem solving are related) we would expect the correspondence to be imperfect. We would expect the absence of *inconsistency*, but there should be numerous cases where the eye movements indicate behavior that is not verbalized or is only ambiguously verbalized. Similarly, various types of behavior may not produce associated eye movements (though of course the eyes will be looking somewhere at the time). Lack of complete correspondence is not entirely unwanted from the point of view of using eye movements to supplement the verbal protocols (and not just to verify them). Their usefulness clearly depends on giving information in addition to that obtainable from the verbal behavior.

Finally, several possible measures might be used in the evaluation. With respect to the eye movements, one can measure numbers of units or total duration, and both may be meaningful. For errors one can count eye movements that do not correspond to problem solving, or problem solving for which there are no eye movements. For problem solving one must specify the inferential technique. The better the technique, the greater will be the difference between the surface indications from the verbal behavior and the inferred problem solving, but also the greater will be the effort required. Last, any comparison will produce a certain rate of false positives (places where a correspondence is asserted but where none exists), and the number of correspondences can be increased at the expense of increasing the number of false positives. Thus a particular degree of correspondence must be evaluated relative to some null model of chance correspondence. This is important, because several different analyses need to be compared—i.e., analyses using fixations with those using aggregates, and analyses using surface behavior with those using inferred problem solving—and each of these comparisons has a different chance level as a base line.

It is not our purpose to review Winikoff's entire study here, but only to indicate in a general way its setting and results. Our detailed treatment of the data for S2 below obviates the need to do more. Winikoff compared three correspondences: between fixations and surface verbalizations, between fixations and inferred problem solving, and between eye-movement aggregates and inferred problem solving. The levels of all correspondences far exceed chance, so there is little doubt about their reality. Almost always there is improvement in fit as we go from (fixations, verbalizations) to (fixations, inferred problem solving) to (aggregates, inferred problem solving). This is exactly the direction of improvement that would justify using the correspondence between aggregates and problem solving.

There is better correspondence if one measures total duration rather than numbers of units (whether of fixations or aggregates). This is plausible, since the larger the unit, the more likely there is to be a correspondence, both statistically and also if the supposed relationship really holds. The latter follows from the somewhat arbitrary cutoff of short durations, so that a number of small units were classified as attention or scan units that probably should be transitions. The improvement with the shift from fixations to aggregates is more pronounced than that from surface verbalizations to inferred problem solving. This is also plausible, since the inferences about problem solving were made at the level of the problem behavior graph. In the one chess protocol analyzed, for instance, where the PBG yielded little beyond the surface verbalizations, there was no improvement.

In its net result, Winikoff's study provides confidence that we can use eye-movement aggregates as an additional measure to supplement verbal behavior. In a good many instances the two sets of data will simply corroborate each other, but in some cases the eye movements can be expected to add significant information. From a more general viewpoint, of course, the confirmation of the information processing models by an independent source of data provides additional assurance that this is an essentially correct way to view human problem solving.

Subject 2's Production System. With Winikoff's study as background, we can now look at the data for S2. As usual, we give the protocol at the end of the chapter (Appendix 7.6), but arranged somewhat differently from the other protocols. Beside the verbalizations, there is a time line (in seconds) along which are marked the attention and scan units. At the left of the protocol we have portrayed these units on small CROSS+ROADS=DANGER displays, showing only (1) the letters covered, for the attention units, or (2) the path followed (but not the sequence), for the scan units. Beside each unit we note the time it started, its duration, and, where needed, a negative number showing how much of the unit consisted of excursions. Thus, the large attention unit EMA9 is shown as starting at 14.2 seconds, lasting 8 seconds, and including 1.2 seconds of excursions. (For comparison, the detail of this unit can be seen in Figures 7.24 and 7.25). To the right side of the human data we give the productions and intermediate products of a hypothesized IPS that models S2's behavior. We now wish to describe this processing system.

Since our aim is to see whether an IPS can describe in detail S2's verbal behavior plus his eye movements, we have constructed a production system for him, just as we did for S3 in Chapter 6. By now we can do this without providing motivation for the general scheme, commenting only on the relatively unique features. The following system is based only on the first 206 seconds of the protocol (through episode E3). Figure 7.26 gives the problem space. Of the four operators (PC, AV, GN, and TD) that we have come to expect any subject to use who works in the augmented problem space, only three (PC, AV, TD) occur in the figure. Although we know from the total protocol that S2 does generate values (GN), this does not happen during the first 200 seconds.

One new operator, RV, is postulated, which recalls the value of a variable. This operator appears to enter because of the relatively indirect way in which S2 records values—by uttering them to the experimenter with later retrieval by request. However, the inclusion of RV as an explicit operator is based directly on eye-movement data, since S2's eyes return to the original place of assignment or derivation whenever he tries to recall the digit associated with a letter. There is rarely any indication of this in the verbal behavior. Thus, such an operator might have been part of our other subjects' programs without our being aware of it. It might be thought that S2 would have operators for the acts of verbal recording and

FIGURE 7.24

sample of raw eye-movement data

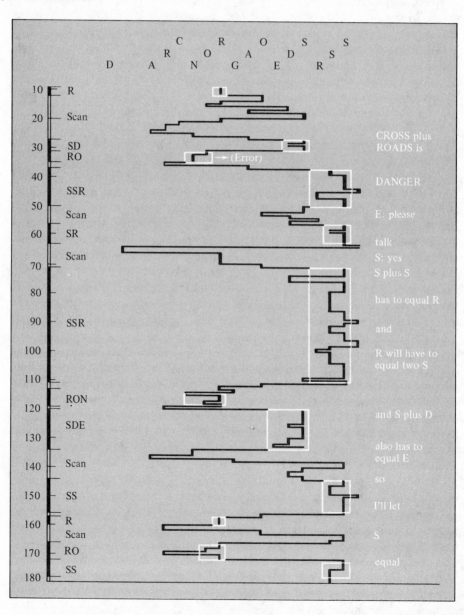

FIGURE 7.25
sample of detailed EM

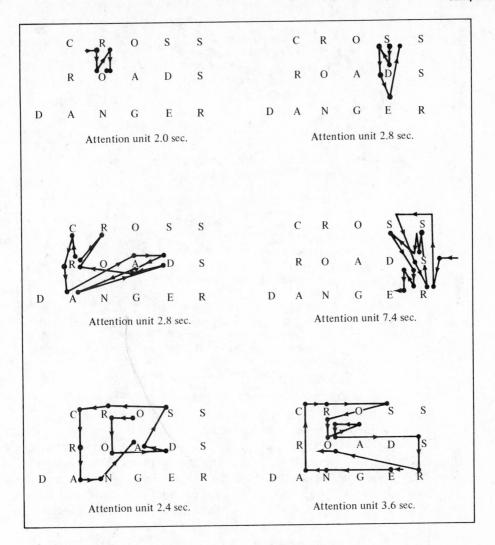

retrieving. However, no indications of such operators are apparent in the initial segment of behavior that we are analyzing. There is an operator, RA, for recalling the antecedent situation, which represents memory of the path that the subject has followed in the problem space. It is similar to operator FA for S3.

We have specified the knowledge state for S2 somewhat more completely than for S3, including in it not only the sequence of expressions known to him at each given point of time, but also his stack of goals. As with S3, the knowledge state still does not contain an explicit representation of the path information (recalled by RA). Since the subject does not seem to make errors in his recall of such information, we do not have any basis for determining its structure or content.

FIGURE 7.26

problem space for S2 on CROSS+ROADS=DANGER

$\langle$letter$\rangle$ ::= A$\,|\,$C$\,|\,$D$\,|\,$E$\,|\,$G$\,|\,$N$\,|\,$O$\,|\,$R$\,|\,$S
$\langle$digit$\rangle$ ::= 0$\,|\,$1$\,|\,$2$\,|\,$3$\,|\,$4$\,|\,$5$\,|\,$6$\,|\,$7$\,|\,$8$\,|\,$9
$\langle$carry$\rangle$ ::= c1$\,|\,$c2$\,|\,$c3$\,|\,$c4$\,|\,$c5
$\langle$column$\rangle$ ::= col.1$\,|\,$col.2$\,|\,$col.3$\,|\,$col.4$\,|\,$col.5$\,|\,$col.6
$\langle$variable$\rangle$ ::= $\langle$letter$\rangle|\langle$carry$\rangle$
$\langle$object$\rangle$ ::= $\langle$letter$\rangle|\langle$digit$\rangle$
$\langle$relation$\rangle$ ::= $\leftarrow|=|\langle$inequality$\rangle$
$\langle$inequality$\rangle$ ::= $\geq|\leq|>|<$
$\langle$tag$\rangle$ ::= $\square|$new
$\langle$expression$\rangle$ ::= $\langle$variable$\rangle\langle$relation$\rangle\langle$object$\rangle|$
    $\langle$variable$\rangle\langle$relation$\rangle\langle$object$\rangle\langle$tag$\rangle$
$\langle$expression sequence$\rangle$ ::= $\langle$expression$\rangle|$
    $\langle$expression$\rangle\langle$expression sequence$\rangle$
$\langle$operator$\rangle$ ::= $\langle$main operator$\rangle|\langle$find operator$\rangle|$
    $\langle$recall operator$\rangle$
$\langle$main operator$\rangle$ ::= PC$|$AV$|$TD
$\langle$find operator$\rangle$ ::= FNC$|$FC
$\langle$recall operator$\rangle$ ::= RA$|$RV
$\langle$goal type$\rangle$ ::= get $\langle$variable$\rangle|$do $\langle$main operator$\rangle|$
    check $\langle$variable$\rangle|$use $\langle$column$\rangle|$recall $\langle$letter$\rangle$
$\langle$signal$\rangle$ ::= null$|+|-|$i$|$i$-$
$\langle$goal expression$\rangle$ ::= $\langle$goal type$\rangle\langle$signal$\rangle|\langle$goal type$\rangle\langle$column$\rangle\langle$signal$\rangle$
    $\langle$goal type$\rangle\langle$column$\rangle\langle$variable$\rangle\langle$signal$\rangle$
$\langle$goal sequence$\rangle$ ::= $\langle$goal expression$\rangle|\langle$goal expression$\rangle\langle$goal sequence$\rangle$
$\langle$goal stack$\rangle$ ::= $\phi|\langle$goal sequence$\rangle$
$\langle$knowledge state$\rangle$ ::= $\langle$goal stack$\rangle\langle$expression sequence$\rangle$

Figure 7.27 defines the production system, along with the conventions used. We have endeavored to make these productions as much like those of S3 as possible (Figure 6.7, page 192). Thus, we have used the same names for analogous productions. Only one production has no counterpart in S3's set, the one having to do with recall; we give it a new name, P16. In the condition part of the productions, we have not distinguished what is in the goal stack from what is in the expression sequence, since this distinction is clear from the form of the expressions.

This production system for S2 differs from that of S3 in several ways. The original P1 production is now split into three parts. The two conditions ($\langle$letter$\rangle$ = $\langle$digit$\rangle$ and $\langle$letter$\rangle \leftarrow \langle$digit$\rangle$) are handled separately, since with assignment ($\leftarrow$) attention is already located at the correct column, so that FC is unnecessary. Also, P1 for S2 produces the goal of using a column, and P1″ evokes the processing of that column, whereas in the P1 production for S3 these two functions were tied together. The split is required to handle the option of executing AV as well as PC (as given in S3). P2, on the other hand, is identical for both production systems. P3 is more direct for S2 than for S3. Similarly, P4 is much simpler in the present system and does not appear to have any generation associated with it. P5 (for S3)

FIGURE 7.27

production system of S2

P1: $\langle$letter$\rangle = \langle$digit$\rangle$ new $\longrightarrow$ FC(letter) ($\Rightarrow$ column); (use column).

P1′: $\langle$letter$\rangle \longleftarrow \langle$digit$\rangle$ new $\longrightarrow$ (do PC)

P1″:   use $\langle$column$\rangle \longrightarrow$ PC.

P2:   get $\langle$variable$\rangle \longrightarrow$ FC(variable) ($\Rightarrow$ column); PC[column for variable].

P3:   use $\langle$column$\rangle$ and PC[column] ($\Rightarrow$ fail) $\longrightarrow$ AV($\langle$letter$\rangle$ above, column).

P4: $\langle$letter$\rangle$ $\langle$inequality$\rangle$ $\langle$digit$\rangle \longrightarrow$ (do AV(letter)).

P7: $\langle$letter$\rangle \longleftarrow \langle$digit$\rangle$ $\square \longrightarrow$ (do AV(letter)).

P9: $+|$ $-|$ empty $\longrightarrow$ FNC($\Rightarrow$ column); (use column).

P11:   ($\langle$letter$\rangle = \langle$object$\rangle$ new) and not (do TD) $\longrightarrow$ (do TD(letter, object)).

P12: $\langle$letter$\rangle = \langle$digit$\rangle$ $\square \longrightarrow$ RA($\Rightarrow$ expression); (expression $\square$).

P14:   check $\langle$variable$\rangle \longrightarrow$ RA(letter) ($\Rightarrow$ production); repeat production.

P16:   recall $\langle$letter$\rangle \longrightarrow$ RA(letter) ($\Rightarrow$ column); RV(letter, column).

Operation of goal stack:

SIGNAL	INTERPRETATION	ACTION ON GOAL STACK
none	new goal	[goal used to select next production
+	success	pop stack if another goal in stack
−	fail	pop stack if another goal in stack
i	interrupted	continue with top goal
i−	conditionally interrupted	if subgoal succeeds (+) then set signal to i; if not then set signal to (−)

Operation of production actions:

New goals push the stack, unless top goal has signal (+, −), in which case the top goal is replaced.

New goals are created by actions (producing expressions with goal-types) or by operators.

The top goal in the stack may acquire additional (or modified) specifications:

a goal-type is never added, but may be modified (from *use* to *do*) when an operator is added,

an operator is added when one is executed in a production (if not part of a new goal):

a column is added when one is produced by a find operator (FC, FNC);

a variable is never added;

the signal is added or modified by the stack operation or by the operator.

does not appear, since the protocol segment that we deal with does not include any final checking.

Two of the goal-setting productions of S3 have close analogs for S2. In responding to contradiction (P7), however, S2 sets up the goal of assigning a new value, rather than simply setting up the general goal of getting a value (as with S3). This difference may turn out only to reflect the small segment of protocol we are examining for S2. As the basic driving mechanism (P9), S2 uses FNC, which finds the next column in the standard right-to-left sequence, while S3 used FL, which finds an appropriate letter. In this respect S2 resembles S5 and S8 more closely than S3.

321

P11 and P12 exist in essentially the same form for both subjects. P11 evokes TD, which checks the constraint that one letter must correspond to one digit. P12 backs down a chain of implications: if the consequent is false, then the antecedent must also be false.

Of the two productions that cause repetition, S2 has only P14, which recalls a prior production in order to check the inference about a letter.

In summary, the two production systems are basically similar, the present one, if anything, being somewhat simpler than S3's (e.g., in assignment in P4 and no repetition as in P13). Some of the differences (e.g., missing productions P6, P8, and P10) reflect an altered scheme for handling the goal stack, to be described below, and thus may be more apparent than real. However, the small differences that do exist can generate substantial differences in behavior.

The right-hand side of the protocol (Appendix 7.6) of S2 shows a goal stack and a set of expressions. The top goal and the expressions constitute the information S2 uses to select the next production to be executed—thus this information constitutes the relevant short-term memory of his problem space. It does not constitute his full knowledge state, of course, since assignments and deductions made earlier along the path are not represented. Presumably, these are stored in long-term memory.

The mechanics of the goal stack are not handled by productions, but rather by the set of rules stated in Figure 7.28. The goal stack is either empty (ϕ) or holds a sequence of *goal expressions*. Each goal expression consists of a *goal type* and a *signal* giving the goal's operational status, plus possible additional defining information (e.g., the name of a column or a variable). Operations on the stack, shown in the figure, are performed in response to the *signal* and take precedence over all other actions. The stack should be thought of as automatic in operation, not taking appreciable time, and not having any implications for eye movements. Whether to set up a new goal or add to a current one is determined by the productions themselves. For instance, in P1′ *do PC* is an instance of a goal type; hence, execution of P1′ would push the existing goal down in the goal stack (changing its signal to i) and establish at the top of the stack the goal of doing PC. But in executing P1″ the existing goal of use-column would not be pushed down, but would be modified to *do PC[column]*. The only *signal* that requires explanation is the conditional fail (i-). This occurs when a goal (e.g., do PC) establishes a subgoal (e.g., get S), such that there is nothing more to do toward the goal unless the subgoal produces some new information. Thus there is no need to return to the original goal if the subgoal fails. One could equally well have a problem solving system that always returned to the prior goal, and only then determined whether there was more to do. However, this would have different implications from the present scheme for the eye movements.

A feature of the present system that differs from the system for S3 is that the operators produce goals directly. In the system describing S3 the operators produced expressions that were then converted into goals by other productions (P6, P10). These intermediate products have been eliminated in the existing scheme.

FIGURE 7.28

conditions on operators

PC: Add from top to bottom:
   if value exists and not in STM $\Rightarrow$ (recall ⟨letter⟩).
 With all operands obtained:
   if digits exist for all three $\Rightarrow$ test (presumably).
   if digits exist for top and middle $\Rightarrow$ sum and $+$.
   if only one digit and not subgoal $\Rightarrow$ (get bottom) (get above).
   if no digits exist $\Rightarrow$ $-$.
 (Not stated: when to produce checks.)

AV: If value is known $\Rightarrow$ (recall ⟨letter⟩).
 If not $\Rightarrow$ (get ⟨letter⟩).
 Assign from bottom of range.

TD: If digit is unassigned $\Rightarrow$ $+$.
 If digit is assigned $\Rightarrow$ (recall ⟨digit⟩).
 If two letters have same value:
  reject the dependent one.
  if independent, reject the assignment.
 Recognize that two different letters may not equal each other.

FNC: Find right-most column that is not completed.

FC: Find unique column containing letter (other than current column).
 If carry $\Rightarrow$ find prior column.
 If multiple columns, find the most constrained.

S2's Behavior. We now summarize the behavior of S2 in terms of the production system. We urge the reader to follow through the protocol at least part of the way in order to get a feeling for the degree of correspondence between predictions and behavior. To help in this we have added to Appendix 7.6 some pages of commentary that "talk through" the first seconds of the protocol.

We can proceed, as we did for S3, to look at the amount of behavior accounted for by each production as it is added to the system, and to count the errors of various types. Two complications arise. First, we have two measures of behavior, eye movements and verbalizations, which are essentially incommensurable. Second, there are no errors of omission for the verbal behavior, corresponding to the "?" used in S3—that is, there are no verbal phrases that do not fit the corresponding production. This is partly an artifact arising from having the operator produce subgoals. In several cases these outputs (though plausible) do not follow from any general rules that could be written to describe the operator's internal behavior. Thus, we must count certain operator outputs as ad hoc and these are equivalent to breaks in the continuity of productions. To make this evident, we give in Figure 7.28 a set of rules for each of the operators; and we mark all the productions in Appendix 7.6 that have outputs not accounted for by these rules.

We need to set up correspondences between the production system and the expected eye-movement aggregations. This is accomplished through two observation rules:

1. The subject will always have an attention unit at the column specified in the top goal of the stack; in addition the attention unit will cover (or emphasize) the letter specified by the top goal, if it exists.
2. The subject will scan the display whenever he selects a new column, undirected by the previous problem solving (i.e., by FNC), or when a directed search (FC) fails.

These two rules follow Winikoff's study in discarding transitions and in setting the boundary between attention units and transitions according to the internal criteria of the aggregation program. In fact, many occurrences of FC appear to be associated with transitions. Furthermore, many small attention units that occur in proximity to a scan appear to make sense as part of an enlarged scan.

We can adopt a set of observation rules that shift the boundary between scan and attention units somewhat, and that attribute significance (for FC and FNC) to transitions. We can also add a few plausible ad hoc interpretations. This set of correspondences may be termed the *maximum* rules. We can call the rules used in the Winikoff study the *minimum* rules. The true state of affairs undoubtedly lies somewhere between these two sets of rules for correspondence.

Several quantities can now be calculated for each production:

1. Number of nodes of the PBG covered.
2. Number of ad hoc outputs of operators.
3. Number of eye-movement units that correspond with productions.
4. Amount of time of the eye-movement units that correspond.
5. Number of productions that do not have corresponding eye movements.
6. The number of eye-movement units that do not have corresponding productions (these are not assignable to individual productions).

Items 3, 4, and 5 have different values for the regular (minimum) analysis and the reinterpreted (maximum) analysis. Items 1 and 2 do not change.

These quantities are the basis for the curves of Figure 7.29. The productions are listed in order of the number of nodes of the PBG, from P1″, covering the most (18), to P4, covering the least (1). The number of eye-movement units covered does not equal the number of PBG nodes covered, since several productions may be accounted for successfully by a single attention unit. For example, both PC and the following TD occur typically during one long attention unit. We have arbitrarily given equal fractional credit for the number of eye-movement units accounted for by each (item 3 above). Similarly, we have used an arbitrary, but somewhat plausible distribution of time (item 4 above), based on the cases where the productions occur in isolation. Thus, the durations assigned to each production type are approximate (though the totals over all productions are exact), but give some indication of which productions are accounting for the bulk of the protocol. Differences between the totals for the number of eye-movement units and for the time in the two accountings of the eye movements arise because transitions are not counted in the minimal accounting, but are counted in the maximal one.

In Figure 7.29 we plot all these quantities in the same manner as we did for S3, cumulating as we add new productions. Since we have many disparate measures, we normalize everything to percentages. Thus, the curve is strictly concave, and rises to 100 percent, since coverage is complete. The other curves are all necessarily monotone, but may have small departures from concavity. Correspondingly, the number of ad hoc operator outputs rises to about 10 percent of the total, occurring

FIGURE 7.29

summary of performance of production system for S2 on CROSS+ROADS=DANGER

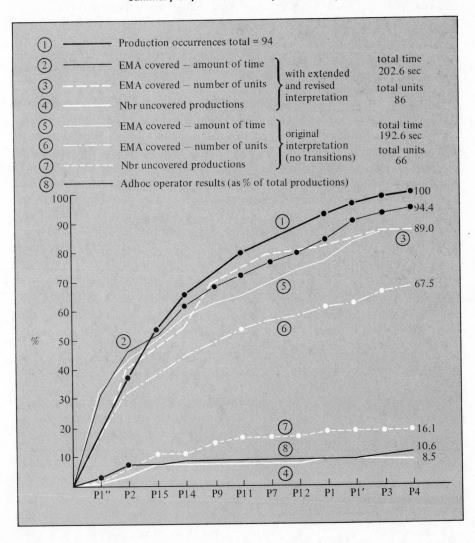

mostly in the two main productions, P1″ and P2. With respect to the eye movements, there is better coverage of time than of number of units, as one would expect from the original Winikoff study. One can have one's choice between a minimum figure of 67.5 percent coverage of units and 87.5 percent of time and a maximum figure of 87 percent of units and 94.4 percent of time. The bulk of the increase in coverage comes from the systematic parts of the reinterpretation (items 1 and 2 on page 324) rather than from the additional ad hoc reinterpretations.

Let us note a few interesting features of the protocol as interpreted by the production system. One is the use of recall. The subject seems always to return to the point of original assignment (or derivation) to obtain a value of a letter. It is as if he had available in immediate memory the fact that he knew the value. One cannot determine whether the shift of eyes is related to the actual recall, is an aid to it (i.e., part of a confirming act), or simply follows upon the recall. Precise time measurements between verbalization and eye movements might help to resolve the issue, but could not be definitive, given possible lags between seeing and talking. These recalls can be seen clearly at T59.6 (where a verbalization accompanies the recall); and at T128.8, where it can be inferred from the protocol that the subject goes through the sequence $(C + R \geq 10) \Rightarrow (C \geq 10 - R) \Rightarrow (C \geq 6)$, and in obtaining the value of R $(= 4)$ goes back to column 1 for 1.8 seconds. The protocol is consistent with such recall at all points where it might occur (eight possible cases). However, the positive evidence is not equally strong in all cases. It is good in six cases and requires reinterpretaion in two. One of the latter occurs at production 67 (T154.0), which shows only a scan back to column 1 to obtain the value of R. The other case occurs at production 76 (T167.2), where attention is fixed at column 2, and recall has moved the eyes to column 1 to recall S, then returns them to column 2 (all within EMA at T158.4), and now should move them to column 5 or 6 to recall D $= 1$. In fact there is a relatively short EMA at column 3 (OA) and a long transition unit (.8). However, if one examines the unit and transition in concert one gets the pattern shown in Figure 7.30. Thus, it is plausible that this supports the recall production. Verbally, the action is consistent, in that the subject explicitly states that D $= 1$ and then goes on to add up the column to get E $= 3$.

FIGURE 7.30

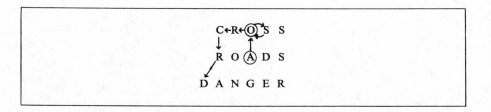

We have not in general "opened up" the attention units and examined whether more detailed correspondences exist or not. In a few cases, however, we have done so to check the interpretation. An example is given by the 8.8-second unit that occurs just before the incident discussed above (namely, at T158.8). The production system indicates a PC on column 2, then a recall to column 1 (for S), then a return to column 2 to continue the PC. The EMA indicates columns 1 and 2 jointly. If we disaggregate it, we get the sequence shown in Figure 7.31. This clearly corresponds to the production system.

FIGURE 7.31

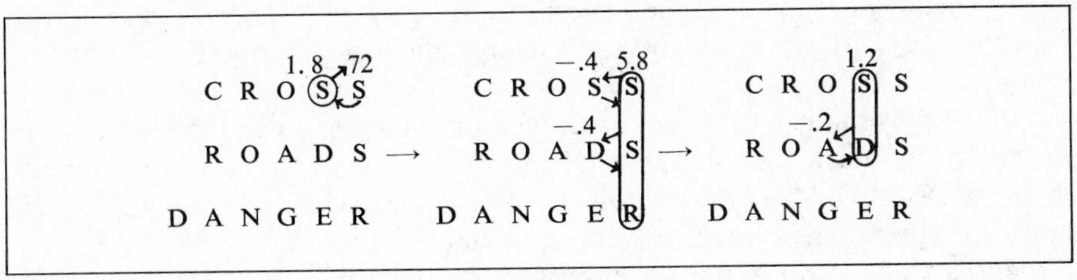

A major implication of the present analysis is the assignment of meaning to the transitions, made possible by the finer-grained analysis here (i.e., developing the production system) as compared with the original study carried out by Winikoff. However, this is not the place to pursue the matter in detail. In particular, the function of the excursions (i.e., the within-unit transitions) needs to be considered also. Occasionally, as in the example above, it turns out that the aggregation program has simply over aggregated, but in general this is not the case.

We can summarize the results of the analysis as follows. We have taken a small (200-second) segment of protocol and found an IPS that fits extremely closely all the data, both verbal protocol and eye movements. The fit is better than with S3 on DONALD+GERALD. Undoubtedly this is due in part to the shortness of the segment studied (200 versus about 1000 seconds). However, it seems also to be due to the additional fine-grained evidence provided by the eye-movement data. Note, for instance, that the productions are about half again as dense in this comparison as in the one for S3 (.47 productions per second versus .32). The production system for S2 is very much of a piece with the system describing S3 and, by extension, with the general structure of the behavior of other subjects who used the augmented problem space. Thus, the eye-movement data substantially support the reality of these information processing models.

CONCLUSION

We are now at the end of the trilogy of chapters devoted to explaining human problem solving in the task environment of cryptarithmetic. In the first of the three chapters, Chapter 5, we analyzed the task environment itself and described a series of problem spaces that could be used to represent and solve cryptarithmetic problems. In the second chapter, Chapter 6, we carried out a detailed analysis of the problem solving behavior of a single subject on a single task—the DONALD+ GERALD problem. We determined that his behavior could, in fact, be represented as taking place in one of the problem spaces we had proposed in the previous chapter—the augmented problem space—and that his search in that space could, in fact, be described and explained fairly accurately and in fair detail by postulating a program in the form of a production system capable of operating in the augmented problem space. The largest part of Chapter 6 was given over to deriving a problem behavior graph from the subject's thinking-aloud protocol, and to testing the veridicality of the production system against the data of the problem behavior graph.

In the present chapter we have extended this analysis to the behavior of four other subjects (and, more briefly, to data on still other subjects reported by Bartlett) on the DONALD+GERALD problem, and the behavior of two subjects on another cryptarithmetic problem. To carry out the extended analysis, we have introduced two additional tools: a procedure for episoding behavior that enables us to treat the data in more summary and less painful ways than are required to produce and analyze the full problem behavior graph, and procedures for obtaining and analyzing eye-movement data in conjunction with the verbal protocol.

The picture of problem solving in the cryptarithmetic task environment that emerges from the extended analysis provides additional confirmation for the general conclusions reached in the previous chapter. It proved possible to characterize the problem spaces in which the subjects were operating. Three of the four subjects who did the DONALD+GERALD task in our laboratory operated in essentially the same augmented problem space as that used by S3, and the fourth subject in a simpler and more basic problem space. As the episode abstracts showed, a very large part of the behavior of the subjects could be accounted for as behavior demanded by the task in the problem spaces within which they were working. Some of the behavior, however, was determined by particular errors they made, and these errors were themselves not predicted by the theory. The errors were of simple kinds—generally involving either elementary faults of reasoning (confusing sufficient with necessary conditions) or lapses of memory. Explaining them would call for detailed data on memory processes that were not obtainable from the protocols.

From these three chapters, then, there begins to emerge a detailed, if particularistic, theory of human problem solving and some reasons for confidence in the technical devices that have been used to obtain the data and extract the theory from it. In moving, in the present chapter, from examination of the behavior of a single subject to a comparative study of a number of subjects, we have taken the first cautious step toward generalizing the theory. We now take the next step— devoting another trilogy of chapters to problem solving in a second task environment, discovering proofs for theorems in a formal system.

Our job of tool building is complete in all essentials. In the tasks that will occupy us in the remaining chapters, we will use the same tools as we have used in studying cryptarithmetic: verbal thinking-aloud protocols, definitions of problem spaces and production systems, problem behavior graphs, and episode analyses. We shall see how well these tools work in tasks other than the one in which we have developed them.

APPENDIX 7.1

S4 on DONALD+GERALD

[Time (T) in seconds; triangles (△) mark 5-second intervals.]

B   T

DONALD
GERALD
‾‾‾‾‾‾‾‾
ROBERT

| B1 | 2 | (E: Here is another problem) △ |
| B2 | 10 | (E: I will give you that D is 5 △ in this problem. △ Please talk.) △ |

E1

5 ONAL 5
GERAL 5
‾‾‾‾‾‾‾‾
ROBERT

B3	22	Well, D.... Giving D 5
B4	25	automatically makes △ T a zero.
B5	27	Could you make T a zero?
B6	29	(E: T is a zero.) △
B7	32	Because 5 plus 5 is equal to 10,
B8	34	and that's simple from the problem. △
B9	40	And looking at the leftmost column, △ you can see that R is △ either 1 or 2 greater than G,
B10	47	but that doesn't seem to help very much at this point. △
B11	55	In the second column having the two △ L's equal,
B12	60	and also △ the two A's equal in the third △ column,
B13	70	doesn't seem to help too △ much at this point either. △
B14	80	Knowing that the two L's △ are equal, △
B15	87	if I just took a guess at one of the L's, △
B16	95	this ... △ this might give me some insight into how about ... △ how to go about the problem.

E2

B17	105	So just to guess △ L a 3 would be some help.
B18	110	Could you make L △ a 3?
B19	112	(E: L is 3.)
B20	114	That would make R a 6. △
B21	117	(E: R is 6.) △
B22	124	And that must make G △ a 1,
B23	130	because G must be either △ a zero or a 1,
B24	132	for D plus G to be equal to R.

B **T**

B25	135	And you know △ that T is zero.
B26	137	So that makes G a 1.
B27	139	(E: G is 1.) △

E3

B28	145	And to have △ O plus E △ equal to O.
B29	155	this △ means that E △ is 1 less. . . . △
B30	167	It means that E must be 9.
B31	169	Would you make E a 9? △
B32	172	(E: E is 9.) △
B33	177	Also in ROBERT. △△
B34	190	And that △ makes the guess of L a 3 △ a bad guess, △
B35	202	because the two A's cannot be equal to 9
B36	204	since they must be a whole digit. △
B37	210	So L must be △ some other digit greater than 5, △
B38	217	in order to have the two A's equal to 9.
B39	219	The two. . . . △
B40	222	A must be 4
B41	224	in order to have the two add to 9. △
B42	227	Would you make A a 4?
B43	229	(E: A is 4.) △
B44	235	And knowing △ that the two L's add to some number △ greater than 10,
B45	245	A [they] must be either △ 6, 7, or 8. △
B46	255	And △ given that the D is 5, △△
B47	267	and knowing that the two O's . . . . △
B48	272	O must be. . . . △
B49	277	You can't tell. . . . △
B50	282	Knowing that O plus 9 is equal to O, △
B51	290	must make N plus R △ some number greater than 10, △
B52	297	in order to make the fifth column come out correctly. △

E4

```
  5 O N 4 3 5
  1 9 6 4 3 5
 ─────────────
  6 O B 9 6 0
```

B53	305	So △ we know that R △ must be an odd number, △
B54	317	because the two D's added to 10. △
B55	325	So we could try △ making R . . . △
B56	335	R must be △ 1 greater than D. . . .
B57	340	No, △ R doesn't have to be 1 greater than D. △
B58	350	R must be some number between 6 △ and 9
B59	352	and the other. . . .
B60	355	The only odd number △ in that range is 7.
B61	360	So could you change R △ to 7?
B62	365	(E: Change R from 6 △ to 7. R is 7.) △

E5

```
  5 O N 4 3 5
  1 9 7 4 3 5
 ─────────────
  7 O B 9 7 0
```

B63	375	Can see now that the first △ three columns are correct,
B64	380	but that doesn't necessarily △ mean that they're the correct digits for the problem. △

B65	390	N △ now must be. . . . △
B66	400	The only numbers left are 2, △ 6, and 8. △
B67	407	And they must go to O, N, and B. △
B68	415	I can now see △ an error △ in the third column. △
B69	427	(. . . ? . . .) E, △
B70	432	could you change E to an 8,
B71	435	because 4 plus 4 is . . . △ is not equal to 9.
	440	(E: I will change △ E from 9 to 8. E is now 8.) △
B72	450	So the numbers now remaining are 2, △ 6, and 9. △
B73	460	And △ they must go to the let . . . △ the letters O, B, and N. △
B74	475	And △ seeing that O plus △ 8 is equal to O . . . △
B75	490	must make E △ a 9, △
B76	497	for reasoning which I gave previously. △
B77	505	So that must make some other △ digit wrong.

E6

B78	510	So we could △ change △ E △ back to a 9
B79	525	and make L △ an 8.
B80	530	Could you change E to 9 △ again,
B81	535	and make L △ an 8
B82	540	in order to have the first two △ columns come out correctly?
B83	542	(E: Change E from 8 to 9. E is now 9.) △
B84	547	L from 3 to 8.
B85	549	(E: L from 3 to 8. L is now 8.) △

$$
\begin{array}{r}
5\,O\,N\,4\,8\,5 \\
1\,9\,7\,4\,8\,5 \\
\hline
7\,O\,B\,9\,7\,0
\end{array}
$$

B86	555	So the remaining digits △ are now 2, △ 3, and 6. △
B87	567	If N were 6,
B88	570	then B △ would be 3,
B89	572	which would . . . △ is one of the remaining digits. △
B90	577	And if 6 plus 7 is equal to 13, △
B91	582	making B a 3
B92	584	and carrying 1 into the next column,
B93	585	would only leave 2 △ for the O.
B94	590	And 2 plus 9 is equal to △ 11, plus the carry is equal to 12,
B95	592	making the second O the required 2. △
B96	597	And adding 1 to the last column,
B97	600	and making the problem △ come out correctly.
B98	605	So if you make N a 6, B a 3, △ and O a 2,
B99	607	I believe that solves it.
B100	609	(E: N is 6.)
B101	610	(E: B is △ 3.)
B102	612	(E: O is 2.) △

$$
\begin{array}{r}
5\,2\,6\,4\,8\,5 \\
1\,9\,7\,4\,8\,5 \\
\hline
7\,2\,3\,9\,7\,0
\end{array}
$$

B103	617	(E: Is that your solution?)
B104	618	Yes.
B105	619	(E: Right. That is the correct solution.) △

[Time (T) in seconds; triangles (△) mark 5-second intervals].

B   **T**

DONALD
GERALD
_____
ROBERT

| B1 | 5 | (E: This is another problem. △ It's task number 4.) △ |
| B2 | 15 | (E: And I will give you that D is 5. △ Please talk.) |

5 O N A L 5
G E R A L 5
_____
R O B E R T

B3	17	OK. D is 5 is. . . . △
B4	25	Five . . . six letters △ in the first row,
B5	27	and six in the second.
B6	29	Six in the third. △
B7	32	Five different ones in the first. △
B8	37	Six different ones in the second.
B9	40	Five △ different ones in the third.
E1		
B10	42	OK. If D is 5,
B11	44	T is zero. △
B12	47	Put T zero.
B13	49	(E: T is zero.) △
B14	55	Right. △ And L is repeated. △
E2		
B15	65	So, △ if we make R . . . △ we'll make R 9 △
B16	77	since it is also on the end line. △
B17	82	It's also the first digit.
B18	83	That'll make it. Make R 9.
B19	84	(E: R is 9.) △
B20	90	Make L △ 4.
B21	92	(E: L is 4.)
B22	94	4 and 4 is. . . . △
B23	97	Nope that won't work, △
B24	102	'cause G would also have to be . . .
B25	104	No . . . not necessarily. △
B26	107	Yes it would too. △
B27	112	(E: Please talk.)
B28	115	If G . . . △ G would also have to be 4
B29	117	unless we carry 1 from the column before. △
B30	122	But in order to carry 1. . . . △
B31	127	we have E and zero. △
B32	135	E plus O would have to be △ some two-digit number
B33	137	which would probably make E 9 or something. △

E3

B34	145	So we'll make er . . . △ make L 3,
B35	147	and R 7. △
B36	152	(E: Change L from 4 to 3. L is 3.) △
B37	157	(E: R from 9 to 7. R is 7.) △
B38	162	Make G 2.
B39	164	No don't do that yet. △

E4

B40	170	We'll make A . . . △
B41	175	A plus A is △ E.
B42	180	So if we make A △ 4,
B43	182	E would be 8. △△
B44	192	(E: Please talk.)
B45	195	OK. We'll make A . . . △ make A 1. △
B46	205	E would be 2, △ 2.
B47	210	We'd have to have E plus zero to equal △ zero again. △
B48	220	So, △ if we make △ A plus A to equal . . . △ equal um . . . △
B49	240	Well, let's see. △ Make G 1
B50	245	and carry 1 from △ the previous column. △
B51	252	We already have T zero,
B52	255	so △ zero has to be 1. △
B53	262	Zero would have to be 1, since T is already zero. △
B54	267	Make zero 1. △
B55	272	(E: Make O . . .)
B56	273	O 1.
B57	274	(E: 1. O is 1.) △
B58	277	Right. E will have to be. . . . △△ ·
B59	290	Um . . . E will have to be △ 8. △
B60	297	E will have to be 9. (clears throat)
B61	299	Make E 9. △
B62	302	(E: E is 9)
B63	305	Right. △ Make △ si . . . 1 6,
B64	315	OK. △ E will be 9.
B65	317	Erase the L and R. △
B66	322	(E: Erase the L and R. L is no longer 3.)
B67	323	Because I won't . . .
B68	324	(E: R is no longer 7.) △
B69	327	'Cause I am going to use that different.

E5

$$
\begin{array}{r}
5\ 1\ N\,A\,L\,5 \\
G\ 9\ R\,A\,L\,5 \\
\hline
R\ 1\ B\,9\,R\,0
\end{array}
$$

B70	330	OK. △ So I'll carry 1 there.
B71	332	R is no longer 7. △△
B72	342	E is 9.
B73	345	So A △ would be 4.
B74	347	Make A 4. △
B75	352	(E: A is 4.)
B76	354	We'll carry 1 over, △
B77	357	which will make . . . △
B78	365	Um . . . △ if A is 4, 8, 9,
B79	367	carry 1 there. △

E6

B80	372	So that will have to be er . . .
B81	375	L can be si . . . △ 6 I guess.
B82	377	Make L 6.
B83	379	(E: R is 6.) △
B84	382	No, wait. Don't do . . . don't make it 6. △
B85	387	Make it . . . You are making R 6, I said make L.
B86	389	(E: R is 6.) △
B87	392	No, don't do that.
B88	394	(laughs) I don't want R 6
B89	395	I wanted um . . . △ I wanted L to be 6.
B90	400	(E: Right. Erase △ 6 from R.)
B91	402	Right.
B92	403	(E: L is 6.)
B93	404	Make L 6. △
B94	407	And that'll make R 2,
B95	409	or R 3.
B96	410	That's right, it'll make R 3. △ OK.
B97	415	(E: Right. △ R is 3.)
B98	420	Right. △ In that way G will be 7, △
B99	427	since we are carrying 1.
B100	428	Make G 7.
B101	429	(E: G is 7.) △
B102	435	OK. Now we've got △ 9.
B103	440	We've used up 1, △ 3, 4.
B104	442	We've 2. △
B105	447	We've used up 5, 6, 7 △
B106	452	and we have 2 and 8 left.
B107	455	Oh. △ Oh ho.
B108	457	N will have to be . . . △△
B109	467	N will have to be 8. △
B110	472	3 [B?] is 11, 12. △△
B111	482	That doesn't work either.
B112	484	N will have to be um . . . △
B113	490	There is only two numbers left . . . two digits left, △ 2 and 8.
B114	492	If it's 8, △
B115	497	that can't be.
B116	500	So we'll △ have to make er . . . △
B117	510	change L to raise R, △ I think.
B118	512	Make L 7. △
B119	517	Erase everything back . . .
B120	519	(E: Erase.)
B121	520	everything . . . △ everything from D down.
B122	522	(E: Everything from B ?)
B123	525	Erase everything △ but this first column.
B124	527	(E: Ah. G is no longer 7.) △
B125	532	(E: R is no longer . . .)
B126	533	No don't erase that 7.
B127	534	OK, that's it.
B128	535	(E: 3. △ Um . . .)
B129	537	Leave that second column like it is.
B130	539	(E: L is no longer 6.) △
B131	542	Right.

B132	543	(E: And anything else.)
B133	544	Erase the A and E. △
B134	547	(E: △ is no longer 4.)
B135	549	(E: E is no longer 9.)
B136	550	No, leave △ E 9.
B137	552	(E: E is 9.) △
B138	560	OK. △ OK. You can leave A 4 then too. △
B139	567	Make △ 4 again.
B140	569	(E: A is 4.)

E7
$$
\begin{array}{r}
5\ 1\ N\ 4\ 6\ 5 \\
G\ 9\ 3\ 4\ 6\ 5 \\
\hline
3\ 1\ B\ 9\ 3\ 0
\end{array}
$$

B141	570	OK. Make um . . . △ L er . . . △ 7.
B142	577	(E: L is 7.) △
B143	582	Let's see if this works.
B144	585	OK, that'll make R △ 5.
B145	590	Hm. Have to make L . . . △ se . . .
B146	592	L can't be 7.
B147	595	Have to make L △ 8, I guess.
B148	597	Try 8.
B149	599	Make L 8. △
B150	602	(E: Change L from 7 to 8. L is 8.) △
B151	607	16.
B152	609	That'll make R 7. △
B153	612	Make R 7.
B154	613	(E: R is 7.)
B155	614	Since we've carry 1. △
B156	617	9, 9 right. △
B157	622	Now we have . . . what numbers left?
B158	624	2 and 3. △
B159	630	OK. No, we have to have more than that, △ 2, 3, 4, 5.
B160	632	We have 2, 3, and 6 left. △
B161	640	Make △ N 6. △
B162	647	(E: N is 6.)
B163	648	B is 3.
B164	649	(E: B is 3.) △
B165	652	G is 2.
B166	654	(E: G is 2.) △
B167	657	That's not a solution. △△
B168	663	OK. So. . . . △△
B169	677	That's not a solution, so. . . .
B170	680	Let's see. △ If you have E is 8
B171	682	you have 8 and 1. △
B172	690	Have to be △ 1,
B173	695	'cause zero . . . △ or O is 1.
B174	697	And E would have to be 9. △△△
B175	712	(E: Please talk.)

E8

B176	714	And if we make er . . . L. . . . △
B177	717	since 8 don't work,
B178	718	and 7 don't work,
B179	719	and 6 don't work,

CRYPT-
ARITHMETIC

B180	720	and △ 5 is already used,
B181	722	and 4. . . . △
B182	727	Have to make E 9. △△
B183	740	er . . . 7, △ 9 right.
B184	742	13 carry 1, right. △
B185	747	OK. Make er. . . . △
B186	752	We'll have to change everything. △
B187	757	Change the first column.
B188	759	No. . . . Leave the second one, right
B189	760	and change △ the next three.
B190	762	(E: Sorry.)
B191	764	Erase the first column.
B192	765	(E: First . . . △ this column?)
B193	767	Yeah. Erase G and R.
B194	769	(E: G is no longer 2.)
B195	770	(E: And R is no longer △ 7.)
B196	772	Then erase the middle. △
B197	777	N, A, and L, erase those.
B198	778	(E: N is no longer 6.)
B199	779	(E: B is no longer 3.) △
B200	781	Erase L.
B201	782	(E: Erase L.)
B202	783	Uh . . . huh.
B203	784	(E: L is no longer 8.) △
B204	790	And if we make um . . . △ L . . . △ ts. . . . △
B205	802	Erase A. △
B206	807	(E: Sorry.)
B207	808	Erase A.
B208	809	(E: A is no longer 4.) △
B209	815	Right. △ And E is no longer 9, maybe. △

E9

B210	822	If er. . . . △△
B211	835	A plus A would have to be equal to . . . △ to 9, △
B212	842	since E has to be 9. △
B213	847	O plus E to equal O, △
B214	852	E has to be 9. △
B215	860	OK. △ In order for E to be 9,
B216	862	A has to be 4. △
B217	867	We can carry 1.
B218	870	OK. △ Make A △ 4.
B219	877	(E: A is 4.) △
B220	882	And if we carry 1. . . . △△
B221	892	(E: Please talk.)

E10

```
    5 1 N 4 L 5
    G 9 R 4 L 5
    _____
    R 1 B 9 R 0
```

B222	895	If we make L △ 7, it makes R 5. . . .
B223	897	Wait.
B224	898	(E: Sorry.)
B225	899	That makes R 5. △
B226	902	But D is already 5. △

B227   907   And T is already zero. △△
B228   917   (E: Please talk.)
B229   920   Altogether △ we have er. . . .

E11
B230   922   Let's see, we make um L 6. △
B231   927   R would be 2 . . . 3. △
B232   932   Make L 6
B233   934   and R3. △△
B234   942   OK. Make L 6.
B235   944   (E: L is 6.) △
B236   947   And R is 3.
B237   949   (E: R is 3.) △△
B238   960   And er . . . △ G will have to be ts . . . △ 7. △
B239   972   Make G 7,
B240   974   (E: G is 7.) △
B241   977   since 5 and 7 is 12 and 1 will be 13.
B242   979   No. △
B243   985   Oh, I see. R has to be △ greater than 5,
B244   987   but less than 10
B245   990   So △ R. . . . △
B246   997   Erase G
B247   998   and erase R.
B248   999   Erase L.
B249   1000   (E: G is △ no longer 7.)
B250   1002   (E: R is no longer 3.)
B251   1004   (E: And L is no longer 6.) △

E12
B252   1010   In order for R to be △ greater than 5
B253   1012   and less than 10,
B254   1015   L will △ have to be . . . which is . . . let's see 6, 7, △ 8, and 9.
B255   1027   Since we are carrying 1,
B256   1029   that leaves 6 and 8 out. △
B257   1032   Have to be 7 and 9. △
B258   1037   Can't be 7,
B259   1038   so it'll have to be 9. L'll have to be 9.
B260   1039   Erase E.
B261   1040   (E: Erase △ E.) △
B262   1047   Make L 9.
B263   1049   (E: L is 9.) △
B264   1052   18, 19.
B265   1054   R can't be 9 either. △△△
B266   1067   (E: Please talk.)
B267   1070   If R can't △ be 9,
B268   1072   L has to be 7. △
B269   1080   No. △
B270   1085   R could be △ 6, 7, △ 8.
B271   1095   Ah . . . R △ could be 6, 7, 8, or 9.
B272   1097   Not L.
B273   1100   OK, △ erase L again.
B274   1102   (E: L is no longer 9.)
B275   1103   That was a mistake.
B276   1104   I had the letters mixed up. △

CRYPT-
ARITHMETIC

E13

B277	1107	R could be 6, 7, 8, or 9. △
B278	1115	So △ if it's . . . △ um . . . 6, △
B279	1127	that would make G zero.
B280	1129	Make E 9. △
B281	1132	(E: E is 9.)
B282	1135	Yes. △ Make G zero.
B283	1137	That's already zero.
B284	1140	It's 7, △
B285	1142	that would make um. . . . △
B286	1147	Well, it can't be 6, △
B287	1152	and it can't be 8,
B288	1154	so R has to be 7 or 9. △
B289	1160	So L has to be △ 3 or 4.
B290	1162	So L has to be 3, △
B291	1167	since A is 4.
B292	1170	Erase △ A too.
B293	1172	(E: A is no longer 4.) △
B294	1177	L has to be. . . . △
B295	1182	R would be 9.
B296	1185	Can you make L △ 4,
B297	1187	R would be 9.
B298	1189	E is already 9. △
B299	1192	(E: Please talk.) △
B300	1197	OK. If you make L. . . . △
B301	1202	Erase E.
B302	1204	(E: E is no longer 9.) △

E14

```
5 1 N A L 5
G E R A L 5
R 1 B E R 0
```

B303	1210	Right. △ Make L △ 3.
B304	1217	(E: L is 3.) △
B305	1222	R will be 7. △
B306	1227	Make R 7.
B307	1229	(E: R is 7.) △△
B308	1237	Make um. . . . △
B309	1242	E still has to be 9, △△
B310	1255	since zero plus E △ is equal to zero or O. △△
B311	1267	4.
B312	1270	Oh my, so △ O would have to be equal to z . . . or E rather. △
B313	1277	(E: Please talk.) △
B314	1282	How can. . . . △
B315	1290	Oh, I see . . . △ that could be two digits, right?
B316	1292	(E: Please talk.) △
B317	1300	If er . . . △ A plus A equals E, △
B318	1310	E would have to be . . . △ E would have to be 9. △
B319	1320	Since 1 plus 9, △ if you carry 1, equal 11,
B320	1324	which would equal 1, right? △
B321	1327	G would have to be 1 that way. △△
B322	1337	(E: Please talk.)
B323	1339	OK. L can't be. . . . △
B324	1342	Erase L and R.

B325   1344   (E: L is no longer 3.) △
B326   1347   L and R erase.
B327   1349   (E: R is no longer 7.) △
B328   1352   Make E 9. △
B329   1357   (E: E is 9.) △

E15
B330   1362   Right. Now R has to be . . . △△
B331   1372   R has to be greater than 5 △
B332   1377   and less than 10. △
B333   1382   It has to be 6, 7, 8, or 9. △△
B334   1392   (E: Please talk.)
B335   1395   And um . . . can't be △ an even digit
B336   1400   since we are carrying an odd . . . △ carrying 1 and adding two the same, △
              multiplying by 2. △
B337   1412   So it'll have to be odd.
B338   1414   It'll have to be 7 or or 9. △
B339   1420   Um . . . Can't be △ 7, △
B340   1430   since G would be △ 2. △
B341   1437   (E: Please talk.)
B342   1439   If we made um . . . △
B343   1442   but T is zero.

E16
B344   1445   OK, if we made R △ 9. △
B345   1452   Erase E.
B346   1455   (E: E is no longer 9. △ R is 9.) △
B347   1462   Make L 4.
B348   1464   (E: L is 4.) △
B349   1467   That's 9. △
B350   1475   Now, if we make △ um . . . make E △ equal to . . . △
B351   1487   R is 9.
B352   1490   G would have to be △ 4 or less, △
B353   1497   4 or 3. △
B354   1502   E would have to be 9, △△
B355   1512   since D is 5. △△
B356   1522   E would have to be um . . . △
B357   1527   Make it zero.
B358   1530   No. △ T is already zero. △
B359   1540   A is . . . △ A is 1, △
B360   1547   or O is 1.
B361   1550   Make that △ 2,
B362   1552   that would be 4. E would be 4. △
B363   1557   O would be 5.
B364   1559   That can't be. △
B365   1562   D is 5. △△
B366   1572   L is 4. △
B367   1577   (E: Please talk.) △

E17
B368   1582   If G was 1, △
B369   1587   R would be 6. △
B370   1592   6. . . .
B371   1593   If G is 2 . . .
B372   1594   6, 7, 8, or 9.

B373	1595	R has to be 6, 7, 8, △ or 9.
B374	1600	OK. △ Can't work with 9.
B375	1602	Can't work with 7. △
B376	1610	Make L △ 3
B377	1612	and R 7.
B378	1615	(E: Change L from 4 to 3. L is △ 3.)
B379	1617	R is 7.
B380	1619	(E: R from 9 to 7. R is 7.) △△
B381	1627	OK. Make er. . . . △△
B382	1637	E 9. Make E 9.
B383	1639	(E: E is 9.) △
B384	1645	OK. △ That means A would have to be . . . oof . . . 4 and a half. △△
B385	1657	Make A 4.
B386	1659	(E: A is 4.) △

E18

B387	1662	Make. . . . △△△
B388	1677	(E: Please talk.)
B389	1680	Make um . . . △ R 7. . . .
B390	1682	Make R 9. △
B391	1687	Neither one work. △△
B392	1700	R has to be either 7 △ or 9. △
B393	1707	R has to be odd. △△
B394	1717	And . . . △
B395	1722	(E: Please talk.)
B396	1725	has to △ be greater than 5. △△
B397	1735	(. . . ? . . .) too big.
B398	1737	Can't be 6. △
B399	1742	Can't be 7. △
B400	1747	Could be 9. △
B401	1752	Can't be 8. △
B402	1757	Make R 9. △
B403	1762	(E: Um . . . E is 9.)
B404	1764	Change everything. △
B405	1767	(E: E is no longer 9.)
B406	1768	A is no longer 4.

E19

```
    5 1 N A 3 5
    G E 7 A 3 5
   ─────────────
    7 1 B E 7 0
```

B407	1769	(E: A is no longer 4.)
B408	1770	(E: R △ is changed from 7 to 9. R is 9.) △
B409	1777	That means L is 4.
B410	1779	(E: L is changed from 3 to 4.) △△
B411	1790	And um. . . . △ Now △ make E . . .
B412	1797	E plus O equal O.
B413	1800	(yawns) △ We have. . . . △
B414	1807	Make E 8,
B415	1810	zero . . . △ O 2. △
B416	1817	or O 1. △
B417	1822	8 and 1 is 9, and 1 is zero. △△
B418	1832	(E: Please talk.)
B419	1834	If we make O . . . △
B420	1837	O can only be 1. △

B421	1842	E can only be 9. △△
B422	1852	Uh . . . huh. △
B423	1857	(E: Please talk.)
B424	1859	Change R. △
B425	1861	(E: R is no longer 9.)
B426	1862	Make E 9.
B427	1863	(E: Sorry.)
B428	1864	E 9. △
B429	1867	(E: E is 9.) △
B430	1872	And make A 4.
B431	1874	(E: A is . . . L is 4.) △
B432	1877	Change L.
B433	1879	(E: L is no longer 4. A is 4.) △

E20

B434	1885	Right, △ Make L △ 8. △ L. . . .
B435	1897	No, don't do that yet.
B436	1899	If we make L 8, R would be 7. △△
B437	1907	(E: Please talk.)
B438	1909	Make L 9,
B439	1910	R would be △ 8. △
B440	1917	Make L 9,
B441	1919	R would be 8. △△
B442	1927	But E is 9.
B443	1930	If we make △ L 4, △
B444	1937	5. △△
B445	1947	(E: Please talk.)
B446	1948	If we make L 4
B447	1949	and R will be 9. △
B448	1952	And E would be what? 8,
B449	1954	No. △
B450	1957	Make L 3, △
B451	1962	R would be 7.
B452	1965	If we make L △ 2,
B453	1967	R would be 5,
B454	1969	so that cannot. . . . △
B455	1972	Make L 1, △
B456	1977	R would be 3.
B457	1979	But we have zero is already 1, or O is already 1. △
B458	1982	If we make um. . . . △△
B459	1992	D has to equal 5.
B460	1994	(E: D is 5.) △△
B461	2002	If we make L 1,
B462	2004	R is 3. △
B463	2007	That can't be.
B464	2009	If we make L 2, △
B465	2012	R is 5, △
B466	2017	and that can't be. △
B467	2022	If we can make L 3,
B468	2024	R is 7. △
B369	2027	Doesn't work.
B470	2029	If we make L4, △
B471	2032	R is 9. △
B472	2037	But E has to be 9. △△

B473	2047	So, make L 5,
B474	2048	which it can't be.
B475	2049	We'll make L 6, △
B476	2052	R would be 2. △
B477	2057	That can't be . . .
B478	2059	R would be 3. △
B479	2062	Make L 7,
B480	2064	R would be 5. △
B481	2067	Make L 8, △
B482	2072	R would be 7. △
B483	2077	Make L 8, △
B484	2082	and R 7.
B485	2085	Change L △ to 8
B486	2087	and R to 7.
B487	2089	(E: L is 8.)
B488	2090	(E: R △ is 7.) △
B489	2097	That won't work △
B490	2105	'cause G would have to be △ 1, △
B491	2112	and er . . . O is already 1. △△
B492	2122	(E: Please talk.)
B493	2125	So we make er . . . L 9, △
B494	2132	and R. . . . △
B495	2137	No. L can't be 9 either, △
B496	2142	'cause then R would be 9. △
B497	2147	It can't be 7. △△
B498	2157	(E: Please talk.)

E21

$$5\ 1\ N\ 4\ L\ 5$$
$$G\ 9\ R\ 4\ L\ 5$$
$$\overline{R\ 1\ B\ 9\ R\ 0}$$

B499	2158	If L is 8,
B500	2159	R is 7. △
B501	2162	G would got to be 1, △
B502	2167	which it cannot be. △
B503	2172	Couldn't make O 2.
B504	2174	All right, make O 2. △
B505	2177	O, change it to 2. △
B506	2181	or just . . . just erase it.
B507	2182	(E: Change O . . . .)
B508	2183	Don't change it to anything. Just erase it.
B509	2184	(E: O is no longer 1.) △

E22

B510	2190	OK. Make that . . . △ better . . . make it 2. △
B511	2197	(E: O is 2.) △
B512	2202	Right. Make G 1. △
B513	2207	(E: G is 1.) △
B514	2215	Right. OK. Now that makes 6 △ and 1 is 7,
B515	2220	11, and need 1 in there to be 12. △ Right.
B516	2222	4, 8 and 1 is 9, △
B517	2227	carry 1, that's 8.
B518	2230	What's left? △ 1, 2 that's 3, and 6. △△

B519 2242 (E: Please talk.)
B520 2245 Wait. 3 and 6 △ is left. △
B521 2252 So, take the 2 off of O.
B522 2254 (E: O is no longer 2.) △
B523 2260 Right. △ So there is 2, 3, and 6 △ left.
B524 2270 If we make R . . . △ If we make um . . . N △ equal to 2 . . .
B525 2277 make N equal to 3. △△
B526 2287 (E: Please talk.)
B527 2290 E [B] will be um . . . △ 1.
B528 2295 No, △ B will be. . . .
B529 2297 Make N equal. . . .
B530 2300 Oh. OK. Make R. . . . Make N △ 6,
B531 2302 and B 3.
B532 2303 (E: N is 6.)
B533 2304 (E: And B is 3.) △
B534 2306 O is 2.
B535 2307 (E: O is 2.)
B536 2308 I thought I was carrying 1.
B537 2309 That's the solution. △

$$
\begin{array}{r}
5\ 2\ 6\ 4\ 8\ 5 \\
1\ 9\ 7\ 4\ 8\ 5 \\
\hline
7\ 2\ 3\ 9\ 7\ 0
\end{array}
$$

B538 2315 Sure. . . . △ Right?
B539 2316 (E: Is that your solution?)
B540 2317 Hm.
B541 2318 (E: Fine. Yes, that's the correct solution.)
B542 2319 I thought I was carrying 1 there. △
B543 2325 (E: Good. △ That . . . that . . . that was fine.) △
B544 2332 (E: Especially when you were in difficulties you talked.)
B545 2335 No, △ I thought I was △ carrying 1.
B546 2342 All that time I wasn't.
B547 2344 (E: OK. Um. . . .) △
B548 2347 On the last part I mean. △

TABLE A7.2.1

S5 on DONALD+GERALD=ROBERT resolution of contradictions

NBR	B NO.	EVOKER	TYPE	CONFLICT	TYPE	REJECT	COMMENTS
1	B24	G = 4	da	L = 4	da	G	
2	B33	E = 9	df	R ← 9	a	R E	
3	B49	O ← 0	a	T = 0	df	O	
4	B64	G = 1	da	O = 1	df	G	
5	B108	B = 5	da	D = 5	f	B	
6	B111	c4 = 1	da	c4 = 0	df	c4 = 1	
7	B115	c4 = 1	da	c4 = 0	df	c4 = 1	
8	B146	R = 5	da	D = 5	f	R	

NBR	B. NO	EVOKER	TYPE	CONFLICT	TYPE	REJECT	COMMENTS
9	B167	c6 = 0	da	c6 = 1	df	c6 = 1	inconsistent (retracted)
10	B174	E = 9	df	E ← 8	a	E ← 8	
11	B180	L ← 5	a	D = 5	f	L	
12	B182	R = 9	da	E = 9	df	R	
13	B204	R = 4	da	A = 4	df	A	inconsistent, speculative (retracted)
14	B225	R = 5	da	D = 5	f	R	
15	B227	c2 ← 0	a	c2 = 1	df	c2 ← 0	
16	B242	c7 = 1	da	c7 = 0	f	c7 = 1	
17	B259	L = 9	de	E = 9	df	E	
18	B265	R = 9	de	L = 9	de	R L	both are locked together
19	B283	G = 0	da	T = 0	df	G	
20	B285	G = 1	da	O = 1	df	G	
21	B290	L ← 4	a	A = 4	df	L	
22	B292	L = 4	de	A = 4	df	A	
23	B295	R = 9	de	E = 9	df	R	inconsistent (retracted)
24	B300	c3 = 0	de	c3 = 1	df	c3 = 1	
25	B311	c3 = 1	df	c3 = 0	de	c3 = 1	
26	B317	A = 5	de	D = 5	f	A	(could be de or df)
27	B322	G = 1	df	O = 1	df	G	(G = 1 could be de or dfe)
28	B340	c6 = 0	da	c6 = 1	df	c6 = 0	
29	B343	E = 0	da	T = 0	df	E	obscure
30	B345	R = 9	de	E = 9	df	E	
31	B351	E = 9	df	R = 9	de	E	
32	B353	G ← 4	a	L = 4	de	G	
33	B355	E = 9	df	R = 9	de	E	
34	B257	E = 0	df	T = 0	df	E	
35	B360	A ← 1	a	O = 1	df	A	
36	B364	O = 5	da	D = 5	f	O	
37	B366	E = 4	da	L = 4	de	E	abandons L and R a moment later
38	B384	c3 = 1	df	c3 = 0	da	c3 = 0	take 4½ to be c3 = 1
39	B403	E = 9	df	R = 9	de	E	E = 9 by E
40	B421	E = 9	df	R = 9	de	R	inconsistent, but possibly E = 9 de
41	B442	L ← 9	a	E = 9	df	L	
42	B448	R = 9	da	E = 9	df	E	inconsistent (retracted)
43	B454	R = 5	da	D = 5	f	R	
44	B457	L ← 1	a	O = 1	df	L	
45	B458	L ← 0	a	T = 0	df	T	inconsistent (retracted)
46	B460	D ≠ 5	da	D = 5	f	D	inconsistent (retracted)
47	B464	L ← 1	a	O = 1	df	L	
48	B466	R = 5	da	D = 5	f	R	
49	B472	R = 9	da	E = 9	df	R	
50	B474	L ← 5	a	D = 5	f	L	
51	B480	R = 5	da	D = 5	f	R	
52	B489	G = 1	da	O = 1	df	G	
53	B495	R = 9	da	L ← 9	a	R L	both are locked together
54	B502	G = 1	de	O = 1	df	O	
55	B518	B = 1	da	G = 1	de	B	
56	B518	B = 4	da	A = 4	df	B	
57	B524	B = 0	da	T = 0	df	B	
58	B528	B = 1	da	G = 1	de	B	

problem behavior graph of S5 on DONALD+GERALD=ROBERT

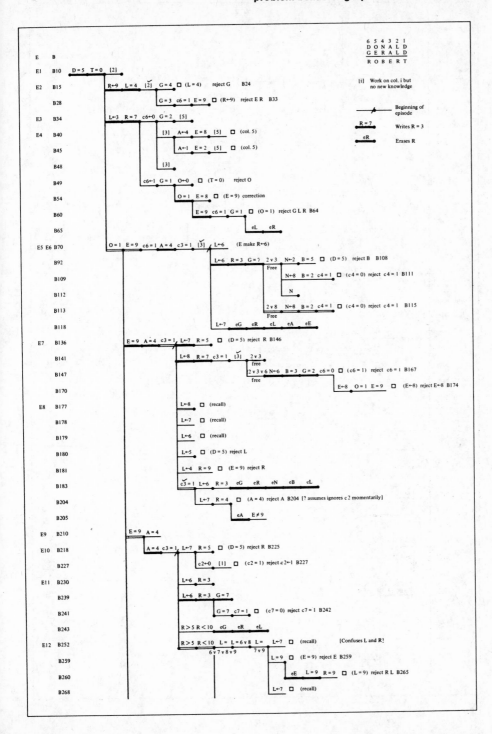

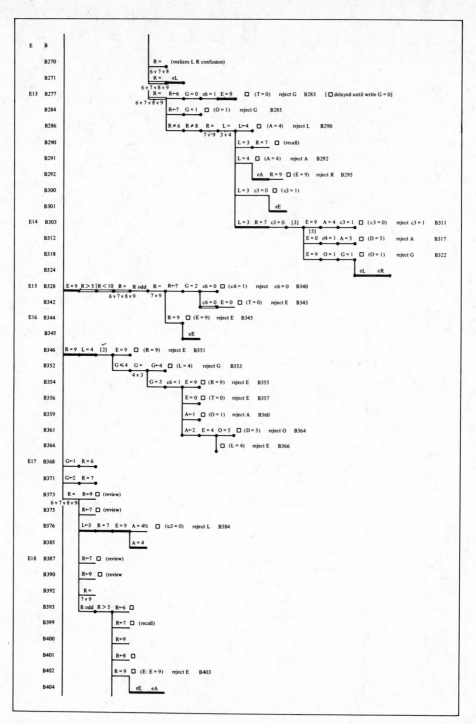

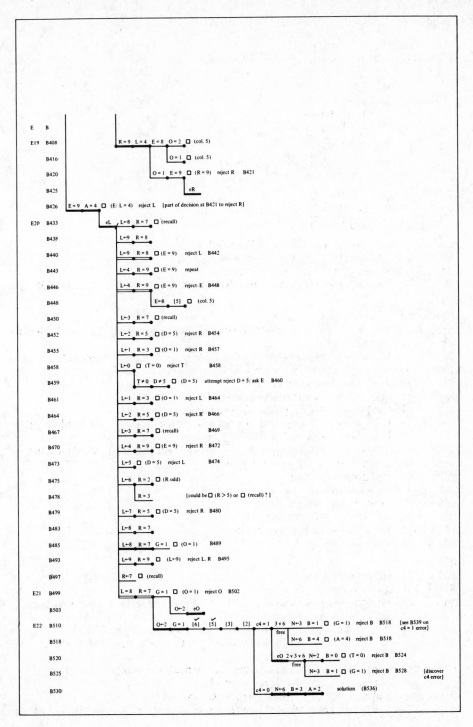

347

S8 on DONALD+GERALD

[Time (T) in seconds; triangles (△) mark 5-second intervals.]

B	T	

DONALD
GERALD
ROBERT

| B1 | 5 | (E: OK. This is task △ number 4.) |
| B2 | 10 | (E: I will give you △ that D is 5.) |

5 ONAL 5
GERAL 5
ROBERT

B3	15	(E: Here's the problem. △ Please talk.)
B4	17	All right. D . . . the D is . . . oh, I see. △
B5	22	It's er . . . er . . . (laugh) it's a. . . . △
B6	27	You've got some names for me this time: DONALD, GERALD, and ROBERT.

E1
B7	30	And the D is 5 △ is given.
B8	35	OK. So I have △ two sitch . . . six-digit numbers that add up to a △ six-digit number.
B9	45	So two numbers in the hundred thousands that add up to △ hundred thousand.
B10	50	(coughs) All right. △ (coughs) So △ you've given me that D is 5.
B11	60	Um. . . . △ That's interesting.
B12	65	Oh. . . . Well . . . well that gives me △ T,
B13	67	but T doesn't fit in anyplace else, you ratfink. △
B14	75	Erm. . . . So △ D is in the five hundred . . . the . . . the . . . the number △ DO-NALD is . . . is in the five hundred thousands.
B15	85	The number GERALD is △ going to be er . . . less than five hundred thousand. △
B16	92	G will either be 1, 2, 3, or 4, I guess. △
B17	97	Or I guess it could be. . . .
B18	98	No it couldn't. . . .
B19	99	Yeah, it could be zero. . . . △
B20	105	All right. △ Well, OK. Put in er. . . .
B21	110	No, of course that can't be △ zero,
B22	112	T is zero.

E2
B23	113	Put in zero for T.
B24	114	(E: T is zero.) △
B25	120	All right. (coughs) △ So er . . . in the next er . . . addition △ column gives me L and L, which add up to R. △
B26	135	Erm. . . . Let's see. R appears in the . . . is △ the first digit of ROBERT.
B27	140	Erm. . . . △ R has got be to a number . . . it's got to be a number from 6 △ to 9, ob . . . obviously.
B28	150	Well, not △ obviously I guess, but er . . . it must be a number from 6 to 9
B29	155	because . . . △ it's . . . it's greater than D. △
B30	165	And er . . . so △ (coughs) R might be 6, 7, 8, or 9. △
B31	175	And it's a number which △ you can get by doubling a small number and adding △ a 1 to it.
B32	182	And it is 6, 7, 8, or 9.

B   T

B33	185	So △ it must be an odd number.

B33   185   So △ it must be an odd number.

B34   187   It's not 8. △

B35   192   It's . . . so R is 7 or 9. (coughs) △

B36   197   I mean . . . it . . . it . . . it couldn't be 8 because. . . . △

B37   202   So R . . . R is 7 or 9.

B38   205   And in other . . . in other words it's △ either a number you get by adding er . . . 3 and 3 △ plus 1,

B39   212   and the number you get by adding 4 and 4 plus 1.

B40   215   So △ L is either 3 or 4.

B41   220   Er. . . . Is there someplace △ you could write down these er . . . △ er . . . little things for me?

B42   227   (E: No.)

B43   229   OK.

B44   230   (E. Not unless you make an assignment, then . . . △ then I'll write it down.)

B45   232   OK. I see. All we can put down on there is the numbers. △

E3

B46   237   All right. So L is either 3 or 4. △

B47   242   Now is there someplace else here that I can get evidence from L.

B48   245   It doesn't appear △ again.

B49   247   That leaves R either 7 or 9.

B50   250   So △ I can get some evidence about R.

B51   255   It. . . . It appears over there △ but that doesn't really tell me whether it's 7 or 9, I'm afraid,

B52   260   'cause I . . . I don't know how big a number GERALD △ is.

B53   265   So er . . . △ let's let er . . . L equal to 3, and see what that gets us. △

B54   272   See if I can remember that L has to be either 3 or 4.

B55   273   Put down 3 for L.

B56   274   (E: L is 3.) △

B57   277   (coughs) OK. With the 1 carry over that makes R equaled to 7. △

B58   282   So put down 7 for R. △

B59   287   (E: R is 7.)

B60   290   All right. △ So, if R △ is equal to 7. . . .

B61   300   Now er . . . that gives me △ er . . . a sort of a limited restriction er . . . that sort △ of restricts G for me now.

B62   310   Er. . . . △ It looks . . . it looks like G has got to be △ er . . . 1 or 2.

B63   317   And I haven't eliminated either of those numbers yet. △

B64   325   Er. . . . So . . . △ 7. . . .

B65   330   All right. So △ E is an even number. . . .

B66   332   Let's see. That doesn't. . . .

B67   334   So D [G] is 1 or 2. △

B68   337   That doesn't help me at all now. (coughs) △

B69   345   So er . . . looks, looks like △ E has got to be an even number.

B70   347   You get it by adding A and A. △

B71   352   But that doesn't tell me too much. △

B72   360   Boy! This is getting me △ bogged here already.

B73   362   This . . . this isn't panning out too terribly well. △

B74   367   Hm. . . . Let's see, is there a better way to do this? △

B75   372   There's gotta be a better way.

B76   375   D and D and D. △ I've got that D over there for 5. △

B77   382   I'm calling R 7.

E4

B78   385   Let's see—my alternate possibility for R was △ 9.

B79   387   If I made R 9,

B80	390	That would make G like △ equal to 3 or 4.
B81	395	That ... that .. I can't eliminate that, △ there is no reason why....
B82	397	G only appears once.
B83	400	Let's see. △ (coughs) All right. △ T only appears once too. △
B84	415	All right. So.... △ Let's see A ... △ A is ... er ... △ nice even number.
B85	430	So △ erm.... △ Let's see. △ Oh, boy! △ Ts. △ All righty. △
B86	457	Let's just for the sake of argument.... △
B87	462	No, that isn't going to get me anyplace,
B88	465	If I start △ substituting numbers in.
B89	467	Just isn't getting me anyplace.
B90	470	There's got to be a pattern △ to this .. (coughs) for this lousy thing, △ pattern-type solution. △
B91	485	So △ a method ... a method, △ there must be a better method.
B92	495	Hm.... △△ Oh well.... OK. △ I'll try ... I'll....
B93	507	Maybe if I just blunder on I'll get a better idea.

E5

$$5\,O\,N\,A\,3\,5$$
$$G\,E\,7\,A\,3\,5$$
$$\overline{7\,O\,B\,E\,7\,0}$$

B94	510	Let's call A △ 1.
B95	512	Put in a 1 for A.
B96	513	(E: A is 1.)
B97	514	A is 1.
B98	515	OK. △ So still working under the assumption that R is 7,
B99	517	that means G has to be 2, △
B100	521	'cause it was either 1 or 2.
B101	522	And I've used 1 for A.
B102	523	So put 2 by G.
B103	524	(E: G is 2.) △
B104	530	Um ... hm ... OK. So ... er ... (... ?...) Beautiful. △ G and E are both 2.
B105	535	Er.... △ Well, OK. So △ let's get rid of the 1's and the 2. △
B106	546	All right. Would you erase the 1's and the 2.
B107	547	(E: A is no longer 1.)
B108	548	No.
B109	549	(E: G is no longer 2.) △

E6

B110	552	Er.... A is 2 now.
B111	554	Put 2 down. △
B112	557	(E: A is 2.)
B113	558	Um ... hm. And G is 1.
B114	559	(E: And G is 1.) △
B115	562	(coughs) And E is 4.
B116	564	(E: And E is 4.) △
B117	570	All righty. So △ we'll just get △ me with the next er.... △ (coughs)
B118	582	N and R add up to B.
B119	584	And R is 7. △
B120	587	Oh, oh. △
B121	592	(E: Please talk.)
B122	595	This er ... this method isn't △ any good.
B123	597	It ... it ... it doesn't even....
B124	600	I was continuing △ with it hoping I ... it would suggest some ... some systematic attack, △ some practical attack.
B125	607	Er.... This is systematic I guess.

B126   610   But er . . . △ er . . . it's strictly for people who have a thousand years to do it. △

B127   617   And I . . . it's not suggesting a better method

B128   620   so I er . . . am going to abandon all . . . all △ this . . . this er . . . procedure all together. △

B129   630   And er . . . I'd like you to er . . . erase all . . . △ all the numbers except your er . . . 5's of course,

B130   632   and the zero.

B131   634   (E: G is no longer 1.) △

B132   637   (E: E is no longer 4.)

B133   638   (E: R is no longer 7.)

B134   639   (E: A is no longer 2.) △

B135   642   (E: And L is no longer 3.)

E7   5 O N A L 5
                    G E R A L 5
                    ─────────────
                    R O B E R 0

B136   645   OK. . . . △ So now. All right. △ So I did establish △ that L must be either 3 or 4. △

B137   662   I think I established this.

B138   665   And R was 7 △ or 9. △

B139   672   I forget how I did that but. . . . (laughs)

B140   675   Let's see. Well, △ L and L are two numbers that add up to R. △

B141   682   No, but wait a minute. Hold it.

B142   684   L and L could be two numbers. . . . △

B143   687   What did I do?

B144   690   L and L could be two numbers that add up to er . . . a two △ digit number the second digit which is R.

B145   695   Why did I say it had to be △ 3 or 4?

B146   700   Did I have er . . . △ did I have some . . . some other reason for doing that, △

B147   707   or did I just say that because I was too dumb to know any better? △

B148   715   Er. . . . △ Oh yeah er. . . . Oh yeah er. . . . I put some limitations on △ R.

B149   725   All right. There're some limitations on R. Well wait a minute. △ There are some limitations on R er. . . .

B150   730   It has △ to er . . . be 6, 7, 8, or 9. △

B151   740   But then these two lousy numbers . . . L and L △ could add up to 16.

B152   745   Or . . . △ or they could. . . . Yeah . . . ts. . . .

B153   750   Oh. L and L could add up to 16 △ or they could add up to 18.

B154   755   Right. L . . . L and △ L could be 8 or 9, as well as 3. . . .

B155   760   L could be . . . △ L could be 3, 4,

B156   762   or it can be 8 or 9. △

B157   770   Hm. . . . Let's see, 3, 4, △ I'm on the dumb side. △ (coughs)

E8
B158   777   All right. There has to be some. . . . △

B159   785   Well it doesn't have to be but if the problem is going to be solved △ er . . . by me here, ha, there has △ to be some better way than this.

B160   795   Eliminating, ha, △ eliminating er . . . L down to 4 numbers is really not much of △ an accomplishment.

B161   805   L has to be 3, 4, se . . . △ 8, or 9.

B162   810   But I'm afraid △ that doesn't do me any good. △

B163   817   (coughs) Oh, my. Oh. What do △ I do about . . . ? All right. Let's see what I do about R. △

B164   827   Well I do have R. . . . I do have. . . . Let's see. △ Well I do have R, I guess. △

B165   840   No, wait a minute. OK. R is si . . . △ 6, 7, 8, or 9. △

B166	847	That's what I said about R. △
B167	855	And . . . △ originally from the . . . from. . . .
B168	860	And △ it can't be 7 or 9,
B169	865	Because L and L add up to it. △ Or add up to a number the second digit which is △ R.
B170	875	So I've still. . . . I have established that R . . . △ that R . . . I guess that I have R eliminated to . . . to two numbers. △
B171	885	Er. . . . △ No wait there, hold it. Whoa. A 1 carry over . . . a 1 carry over.
B172	889	Er . . . I forgot about the carry over. △
B173	895	So er . . . △ Let's see. Do I haven't eliminated the 7 and 9? △
B174	902	Yeah. Right, it . . . it . . . it can't be 6 or 8. △
B175	907	So I know R that is 7 or 9. △△
B176	917	But . . . ts. . . . △
B177	925	Darn it. This. . . . △ That doesn't seem to be getting me anyplace though. △
B178	932	So R is 7, or else it's 9.
B179	935	Now R appears △ as first number of ROBERT.
B180	937	Now then. . . . △
B181	942	And it's the third number of GERALD. △
B182	950	Well the third number, that's . . . that's not significant. △ That . . . that has no significance at this point.
B183	952	It can't help me at all. △
B184	957	That's too far in.
B185	960	(yawns) OK. △ So R △ is 7 and 9.
B186	967	(laughs) That gives L is 3, 4, 8, or 9. △
B187	972	Yeah, and it could be 9. △
B188	980	My my. Ts. (yawns) △ Oh, boy! L . . . L only appears in these two places. △
B189	987	So there's no way for me to narrow L down any more. △
B190	995	Boy, there must be some . . . some △ sort of △ progressive type thing that I △ could use. △
B191	1012	I just don't believe it. △
B192	1017	(E: Please talk.)
B193	1020	All right. Um. . . . △ Again . . . again I . . . I seem to be licked almost before I've started. △
B194	1030	I haven't really accomplished anything except △ getting R down as one of two numbers.
B195	1035	Even if I knew what number △ R was, er, I . . . I don't think this △ in itself would help me.
B196	1045	I don't think I can get anything by proceeding on the assumption △ that R is one or the other. △

E9

B197	1055	(coughs) All right. Er. . . . △ Well maybe I can. △ Er. . . . Drat. △
B198	1070	Well R is △ 7 or 9.
B199	1075	So (yawns) if I picked 9 △ for R for example, that'll get. . . .
B200	1080	If I assume that R is 9, that'll give me two △ numbers for L, instead of four. △
B201	1090	Er . . . L will then have to be er . . . △ either 4 △ or 8. △△
B202	1107	Er . . . and 4 and 4 is . . . and carry 1 will give me 9. △
B203	1112	8 and 8 are 17.
B204	1115	No, wait a minute. Er it . . . it has △ to be either 4 or 9.
B205	1117	Say I haven't est. . . . △
B206	1122	All right. R has to be an uneven number. △
B207	1130	So . . . △ wait a min . . . wait a . . . wait a minute. Hold the phone. △ Hold the phone here.
B208	1140	Er . . . if R △ is 9,

B209	1142	then L would have to be either 4 or 9, △
B210	1150	er . . . 'cause 9 and 9 are 18 and 1 △ carry over would give me 9.
B211	1155	So if I proceed on the assumption △ that R is 9,
B212	1160	that establishes L △ as 4.
B213	1162	Now, let's see. Suppose R was 7. △
B214	1167	If R was 7, then this would leave me with the . . . 3 and 8. △
B215	1172	3 and 3,
B216	1174	and 8 and 8.

E10

B217	1175	Yeah. △ Well, it seems to be a more productive course to assume that R is 9. △
B218	1182	So write down 9 for R.
B219	1184	(E: R is 9.) △
B220	1190	Now, if R is 9, △ then L er . . . △ L . . . is going to have to be 4. △
B221	1202	So write down L for 4.
B222	1204	(E: L is 4.) △
B223	1207	Write down 4 for L rather.
B224	1210	All right. △ Let's see if that got me anyplace. △
B225	1220	Well, △ I guess that . . . that gives me the G again.
B226	1225	I mean G more or less has to be 3 △ or 4.
B227	1227	So put down a 3 for G.
B228	1228	(E: G is 3.) △
B229	1232	Yeah. That really isn't going to help me, I'm afraid, △
B230	1237	until . . . until the end, if I can get along further along than this. △
B231	1242	So now I'm back to er . . . the beautiful position of picking an A now. △
B232	1250	Er. . . . Well. △ I've staggered this far. △ Er. . . . I'll play (. . . ? . . .) and (. . . ? . . .), and see what I get. △
B233	1262	Er. . . . Let's see. If A is 1,
B234	1265	then I can let △ E be equal to 2.
B235	1267	I haven't eliminated that yet.
B236	1268	If A is 2,
B237	1269	that's no good, △
B238	1272	'cause E will have to be 4.
B239	1275	OK. A can . . . A can be 3, △ though.
B240	1277	It can be 4.
B241	1279	It can't be 5. △
B242	1282	Maybe 6.
B243	1284	Oh well. Let's start at the beginning. △

E11

$$5\ O\ N\ A\ 4\ 5$$
$$\underline{3\ E\ 9\ A\ 4\ 5}$$
$$9\ O\ B\ E\ 9\ 0$$

B244	1287	Put a 1 down for A.
B245	1289	(E: A is 1.)
B246	1290	Yeah. △ All right. And put a 2 down for E.
B247	1292	(E: E is 2.) △
B248	1300	OK. Now △ er. . . . △ Ts. So I have N and R adding up △ to B. Beautiful.
B249	1312	R is 9. △
B250	1320	Er. . . . All right. I've got 1, 2 △ and 3, 4, and 5 all used up, and 9. △
B251	1327	Hold it. Let's start at the next available. . . .
B252	1330	Let's see. The next available number △ will be 6.
B253	1332	That would give me 5 for B.
B254	1334	I've already used that. △

B255	1337	Then the next available number is 7.
B256	1340	That would give me △ 6 for B.
B257	1342	I haven't used that.
B258	1345	So er . . . △ make N 7.
B259	1347	(E: N is 7.)
B260	1350	Um . . . hm. 7 and 9 △ are 16.
B261	1352	Make B 6.
B262	1354	(E: B is 6.)
B263	1355	OK. △ I'm going to have a 1 carry over,
B264	1360	so that's going to be . . . give me △ the sum of 3 on the other side. Uh . . . huh. △ That's going to be . . . give me 3 on the other side.
B265	1370	I'm going to need another number that'll give me another △ carry over,
B266	1372	because I've 5 and 3 adding up to 9. △
B267	1380	So. . . . Ooops. So O △ is going to be a number which when added to E. . . . △
B268	1390	Oh ho, yek. Let's look △ at this again. (Coughs)
B269	1395	The △ E gives me a two-digit number, the first digit which is 1, of course, the second digit △ of which is O again. △
B270	1410	Hm. . . . Mother Machree. △ Oh, that's an interesting little angle.
B271	1415	I haven't gotten △ anyplace with this because I obviously
B272	1420	E . . . △ E just can't work as 2 in this position, I'm afraid.
B273	1425	I could use . . . △ Let's see.
B274	1427	Nope. 8 is about the only number I've got left here. △
B275	1435	I got 1, 2, 3, 4, 5, 6, 7 △ and 9 used.
B276	1437	So A would . . . O would sort of have to be 8. △
B277	1445	But er . . . that isn't going to work out too cool is this one, △ I'm afraid,
B278	1447	because 8 and 2 is not equal to 18 unfortunately. △
B279	1455	Er. . . . So er . . . △ I think we'd better er . . . er . . . △ fall back.
B280	1465	Let's see. To the point . . . the point where I assumed △ that R was equal to 9.
B281	1467	and L was equal to 4. △
B282	1472	If. . . . I think we can get rid of 1.
B283	1474	Erase the 1's, please. △
B284	1477	(E: A is no longer 1.)
B285	1479	Erase the 7's please. △
B286	1482	(E: N is no longer 7.)
B287	1485	Er. . . . Erase the er . . . △ R and L.
B288	1487	So [No (?)] erase the 2's and 3's.
B289	1489	(E: E is no longer 2.) △
B290	1492	(E: And G is no longer 3.)

E12

B291	1495	All right. So now we'll look at the other end of this △ problem.
B292	1500	This . . . this . . . this business here, where △ I have zero and E adding up to either zero △ or a f . . . two-digit number the first digit △ of which . . .
B293	1512	Wait, hold. This could be ze. . . .
B294	1515	Oh. It's zero or E △ plus a carry over which I don't know.
B295	1520	Yeah. Oh. △ Um . . . hm. No dice, no dice.
B296	1525	OK. △ Erm. . . . △ All right, I started on that er . . . unproductive track by letting A equal to 1. △
B297	1537	That didn't. . . .

E13

B298	1539	Well I'm still . . . I'm still using the assumption that R is 9. △
B299	1542	It has to be 9 or 7, I think.
B300	1545	But I'm . . . I'm still . . . I used the assumption that R is △ 9,

B301	1547	because this allows me to set L at 4.
B302	1549	And it gives me more . . . more to work with. △
B303	1552	So we'll go back to A again.
B304	1554	It didn't work out as 1.
B305	1555	So. . . . △ And it is not going to work out as 2.
B306	1560	Er . . . oops, excuse me. △ How er . . . erase the L [the L = the. . . . Well, (?)]. Would you please erase the 6.
B307	1562	(E: B is no longer 6.) △
B308	1567	Yeah. I overlooked that one.
B309	1568	Er . . . it's . . . it's not going to work as 2,
B310	1569	'cause I've already used 4. △
B311	1572	What need to . . . work is 3,
B312	1573	because I haven't used 6 yet.

E14

B313	1574	So let A equal to 3. △
B314	1577	(E: A is 3.)
B315	1580	Yeah. And er . . . △ let er . . . E equal △ 6.
B316	1587	(E: E is 6.)
B317	1590	Okey-doke. Um . . . △ hm. . . . All right. So I've got an N. △
B318	1597	I'm trying to remember what I let N equal last time. △
B319	1602	Er . . . I guess I let it equal to the next number I could use. △
B320	1607	Well I haven't used. . . .
B321	1609	If I use 1, er . . .
B322	1610	that'll give me zero △ for B,
B323	1612	and I've already got that one.
B324	1615	If I use 2, △ er . . .
B325	1617	that'll make B equal to 1. △
B326	1625	And er . . . I haven't used that yet △ on this board.
B327	1627	Let er . . . N equal to 2.
B328	1630	Put 2 down △ for N, please.
B329	1632	(E: N is 2.)
B330	1633	And er. . . . Put B down for 1.
B331	1634	(E: B is 1.) △
B332	1637	And that gives me a 1 carry over.
B333	1640	Er. . . . △ So er. . . . (Coughs) △ Hm. △ Hello there. △ Ts. Oops. △
B334	1665	I'm going to be . . . no matter . . . no matter how you slice it . . . △ oh . . . how you slice it, B . . . G is going to be . . . have to be 3 or 4.
B335	1670	I've already △ used both those numbers.
B336	1675	Erm. . . . △△ As a matter a fact I . . . I've forced G to be equal to 3. △
B337	1687	Yes, that's right. I forced G to be equal to 3 when I made the assumption that L was equal to 4. △
B338	1695	Er . . . All right. Er. . . . △ Erase the 3's.
B339	1697	(E: A is no longer 3.) △
B340	1702	And erase the 2.
B341	1704	(E: N is no longer 2.) △
B342	1707	And erase the 9's.
B343	1708	(E: R is no longer 9.)
B344	1709	And erase the 6.
B345	1710	(E: E is no △ longer 6.)
B346	1715	Oh, boy! △ Oh, erase the 1, too.
B347	1717	I didn't see it.
B348	1719	(E: B is no longer 1.)

B   T

E15
```
5 O N A 4 5
G E R A 4 5
─────────
R O B E R 0
```

B349	1720	OK. △ So I assumed that L is equal to 4.
B350	1725	So I made the mistake not realizing △ I used up 3 also.
B351	1727	Er. G must be 3. △
B352	1732	So er . . . put a 3 down to G.
B353	1734	(E: G is 3.)
B354	1735	OK. So . . . △ oops. Oh, boy! Now I've lost △ my train of thought.
B355	1742	I tried A with 1 I think,
B356	1744	and and it didn't work out.
B357	1745	Ha. △ I don't remember why, but I think it didn't work out.
B358	1750	And er. . . . △ I didn't use 2,
B359	1752	'cause that adds up to 4. △
B360	1757	And I've eliminated 3,
B361	1759	'cause that's G according to my assumption. △
B362	1762	And 5 is the next number,
B363	1763	and I've used that.
B364	1764	And after that that gives me 6, △
B365	1767	which would make it . . . E would equal to 2.
B366	1770	OK. △ Er. . . . Let's let er. . . . △△
B367	1782	Well, I probably . . . I probably go wrong again here.
B368	1784	But let's let A equal to 6. △

E16

B369	1787	Put a 6 down for A.
B370	1789	(E: A is 6.)
B371	1790	All right. So △ put a 2 down for E.
B372	1792	(E: E is 2.)
B373	1795	All right. △ Now let's . . . review the available numbers △ for N.
B374	1805	Er . . . △△ I haven't done anything with R yet, have I? △
B375	1817	(. . . ? . . .) I guess I didn't have a number down for R before. △
B376	1822	Oh. Hm. △△
B377	1832	(E: Please talk.)
B378	1835	Er. . . . Oh, you. . . . Oops. I had △ you . . . I had you erase a 9 that I didn't want you to erase.
B379	1837	Er. . . . Oh er . . . R has to be 9. △
B380	1842	Put down a 9 for the R, please.
B381	1844	(E: R is 9.)
B382	1845	According to this assumption I'm using R has △ to be 9. I'm assuming that R is 9.
B383	1847	I think I established that it had either to be 9 or 7.
B384	1850	All △ right. So let's take a look at the available numbers for N now. △
B385	1857	It can't be 1.
B386	1860	'cause that would give me am . . . zero △ for B,
B387	1862	and I've used zero.
B388	1863	And it can't be 2,
B389	1864	'cause I've used 2.
B390	1865	It can't be △ 3, 4, 5, or 6. △
B391	1872	And it can't be 7,
B392	1875	'cause that would give me △ 6 for. . . .
B393	1877	Now I've. . . . Whoa . . . whoa. I have a carry over.
B394	1880	I've got 10 △ there. I've got 10 there, not 9.

B395	1882	All right. I've got a carry over, now. △
B396	1884	So . . . 10. . . .
B397	1890	So, I . . . I can't use △ 1,
B398	1892	'cause that would make B 1 also.
B399	1895	I can't use △ 2
B400	1897	'cause that would make B. . . .
B401	1899	Oh, I've used 2. △
B402	1902	I've used 3, 4, 5, and 6.
B403	1904	Now to make it se. . . . △
B404	1910	Er. Oh. Oh, oh. △ I can't make it anything,
B405	1915	because er . . . △ any. . . .
B406	1917	Oh. I'm adding it to 10,
B407	1920	so anything I'm . . . anything △ I have for 10,
B408	1925	er . . . since I have a carry over here, △ er . . . anything. . . .
B409	1927	It's going to make N or B equal, △
B410	1932	with a carry over of 1.
B411	1935	Now if I make A △ anything higher than 6
B412	1937	this isn't going to do me any good
B413	1939	'cause I'm going to have a carry over of 1
B414	1940	and I'm still going △ to have this contradiction here.
B415	1945	So er. . . . △ Let's see now. Where did the fault lie.
B416	1950	It must go back △ to the assumption . . . to my very first assumption, △ that er . . . R was equal to 9.
B417	1957	Let's see. R is equal to 9. △
B418	1962	Now let R equal to 9. △
B419	1970	And er. . . . Well. Erase . . . △ erase the 6's, please.
B420	1972	(E: A is no longer 6.)
B421	1974	And erase the er 2's and 3's. △
B422	1977	(E: E is no longer 2.)
B423	1979	Er. . . . Erase the 3's also . . . the 3 also. △
B424	1982	(E: G is no longer 3.)

E17

B425	1984	All right. So, my assumption R was △ 9.
B426	1990	Er . . . I er . . . △ all right. I eliminated 1 for A. △
B427	1997	I can't use 2.
B428	1999	I eliminated 3. △
B429	2002	I can't use 4 or 5. △
B430	2005	I can't use anything higher either.
B431	2010	OK. So △ I'm . . . um . . . um . . . unless I've got lost. . . .
B432	2015	If I haven't △ got lost in the . . . in the confusion, er . . . △ then I've. . . . If I haven't got lost in the confusion, I've △ proved that R is 7. △
B433	2035	Er. . . . So er . . . △ erase the 9's

E18   5 O N A L 5
              G E R A L 5
              ———————————
              R O B E R 0

B434	2037	and make R equal to 7. △
B435	2042	(E: R is no longer 9. R is 7.)
B436	2044	OK. R is 7. △
B437	2047	OK. Now get rid of the 4's L.
B438	2049	(E: L is no longer 4.) △
B439	2052	OK. Now I believe I have a couple of options for L.
B440	2055	Er. . . . I've got △ a 1 carry over,

B441	2057	so I can make L equal to 3,
B442	2060	or I can △ also make L equal to 8, um . . .
B443	2064	which will give me 17.
B444	2065	So let's △ start with the simplest case.
B445	2067	We'll make L equal to 3.
B446	2069	So write . . . write down a △ 3 for L.
B447	2072	(E: L is 3.)
B448	2075	(coughs) △ Now. . . . All △ righty. This gets me △ back to A again, with a whole new set of. . . . △
B449	2092	Well I can't use anything I've gotten before.
B450	2095	Okey-doke. △ Let's say I'll let A equal to 1.
B451	2097	That'd give me 2 for. . . . △△
B452	2107	Well that's not a contradiction yet.
B453	2109	It will be in a minute, probably. △
B454	2112	So let A equal to 1.
B455	2115	We'll △ start from the bottom up.
B456	2117	Put a 1 down for A.
B457	2119	(E: A is 1.) △
B458	2122	And er . . . will you write down a 2 for E.
B459	2124	(E: E is 2.) △
B460	2130	OK. △ (yawns). △ Now er. . . .
B461	2137	(E: Please talk.) △
B462	2145	All right. Er. . . . Wait a minute. △ Er. . . . Erase the 1's and the 2 please . . . the 2's please.
B463	2150	(E: A is no longer △ 1.)
B464	2152	(E: E is no longer 2.)
B465	2154	Get them out of the way.
B466	2155	That's so they won't confuse my △ small mentality.

E19

B467	2157	I . . . I've already. . . .
B468	2160	I . . . I can do some . . . I must be able to do △ something with G over here.
B469	2165	Now, er . . . it must be either △ 1 or 2.
B470	2170	Er. . . . So I can't use △ both 2 and a 1 over here.
B471	2175	So er . . . △ a 1 . . . a 1 is no good.
B472	2177	So I've eliminated 1. △
B473	2185	So er . . . let's let A equal △ to 2.
B474	2187	Put down a 2 for A.
B475	2189	(E: A is 2.) △
B476	2192	Right you are. And put down a 1 for G.
B477	2194	(E: G is 1.) △
B478	2197	Um . . . hm. OK. Now let's use 4 for E.
B479	2200	Put down a 4 △ by the E's.
B480	2202	(E: E is 4.)
B481	2205	(coughs) All right. △ Now . . . this gets us back to using the △ available numbers for N.
B482	2215	I've used 1, 2, △ 3, 4, and 5.
B483	2220	If I use △ 6
B484	2225	that'll force me to use a 3 for △ B.
B485	2227	If I use. . . .
B486	2229	I can't use a 7, △
B487	2232	because I've used that.
B488	2234	If I use an 8,
B489	2235	that'll force me to use a 5 △ for B.

B490	2237	and I've used that. △
B491	2242	If I use a 9,
B492	2245	I use a 6 for △ B
B493	2247	and I haven't eliminated that yet.
B494	2250	Er . . . let N equal to 9. △
B495	2252	Put down a 9 for the N.
B496	2254	(E: N is 9.) △
B497	2257	See, I don't have any carry over yet do I? Right.
B498	2260	Er. . . . Put down a 6 by △ the B. . . .
B499	2262	(E: B is 6.)
B500	2265	All right. (coughs) Now, △ let's look at what I've got left over for . . . △ er. . . .
B501	2275	OK. I've got △ a 1 carry over. △
B502	2285	And er . . . OK. △ A 1 carry over fouls me up,
B503	2290	'cause I need something . . . △ for O.
B504	2292	I need a number which, when added to 5, gives me O. △
B505	2300	(laughs) All right. So, let's see. What have △ I eliminated?
B506	2305	Er . . . er . . . △ I go back now to the step where I used 2 for A.
B507	2310	Because I had already eliminated △ the 1.
B508	2315	All right. △ Er. . . . Erase the 2's.
B509	2317	(E: A is no longer 2.) △
B510	2322	Erase the 9.
B511	2325	(E: N is no longer △ 9.)
B512	2327	Erase the 4.
B513	2329	(E: E . . . E is no longer 4.) △
B514	2332	Erase the 6.
B515	2334	(E: B is no longer 6.)

E20

B516	2335	OK. I thought . . . △ I eliminated 1 for A. △
B517	2342	Now I've eliminated 2.
B518	2344	And 3 is out.
B519	2345	So △ let's let A equal to f. . . .
B520	2347	Let's see I . . . I'm just . . . just say it so I get it straight.
B521	2350	I'm still △ working on the assumption that L is 3
B522	2352	and not 8 which it can also be. △
B523	2357	So let's let er. . . . Let's see I've eliminated 1, 2, 3, △
B524	2362	and 3 are no good. △
B525	2367	Let's see. Have I eliminated 4 for A? △
B526	2375	Er . . . △ What was I using . . . ?
B527	2377	I was using a 2 last time.
B528	2379	I want a 3 in other words.

E21

$$\begin{array}{c} 5\ O\ N\ A\ 3\ 5 \\ \underline{1\ E\ 7\ A\ 3\ 5} \\ 7\ O\ B\ E\ 7\ 0 \end{array}$$

B529	2380	So put down a 4 △ by the A's.
B530	2382	(E: A is 4.)
B531	2385	Okey-doke. △ Er. . . . So let E equal to 8. △
B532	2392	Put down an E by the 8.
B533	2393	Excuse me. Put down an ei . . . E by the 8.
B534	2394	(E: E is 8.) △
B535	2397	Or put down an 8 by the E. △
B536	2405	All righty. Now let's see what I've got for er. . . . △ Let's see what I've got for er . . . for N. △

B   T

B537	2412	1, er. . . .
B538	2414	2 isn't eliminated. △
B539	2417	If I use 2
B540	2419	that'll force me to make B 9. △
B541	2422	Well, that will give me no carry over again.
B542	2425	So for O I'll need something that'll . . . △ I'll need something that will er. . . .
B543	2432	Yeah, △ well. I'll need a carry over there, in that column. △
B544	2440	Er. . . . So . . . △ 1,
B545	2442	so . . . so 2 is no good.
B546	2445	3, △ 4, and 5 have been used.
B547	2450	So let's have that N equal △ to 6.
B548	2452	That'll give me the carry over of 1. △
B549	2457	That means I'll need a number which when added to 9. . . .
B550	2460	Let's have . . . er. . . . △ Let's . . . a carry over of 1.
B551	2465	That means I'll need number whi . . . △ which when added to 9. . . .
B552	2467	No, that's no good. △
B553	2475	Er . . . △ er. . . . Wait a minute. What am I △ doing to myself? Er. . . . Oh △ boy! What am I doing to myself. △
B554	2492	Oh, my. The carry over always has to be either a zero or a 1. △
B555	2500	That . . . but this business here of zero of O plus △ E. . . .
B556	2505	Ah, △ ahm . . . OK. △ Er. . . . Let me . . . let me. . . . △
B557	2517	Get rid of the 4's. Erase the 4's please.
B558	2519	(E: A is no longer 4.) △
B559	2522	Right. And erase the 8's please.
B560	2524	(E: E is no longer 8.) △

E22

B561	2530	OK. Now, in this column over here zero, E, zero, △ I've got a zero or naught △ plus O plus E △ giving me some number the first of which digit is O, △ or else giving me O.
B562	2550	Now this △ is clearly impossible.
B563	2555	Er . . . let me . . . △ O plus E couldn't give me O obviously.
B564	2557	T is zero.
B565	2560	That's all △ used up.
B566	2565	And er . . . so er . . . △ an O plus E cou . . . plus it . . . △ couldn't give me a number er . . . the first digit of △ which is O either.
B567	2580	Er. . . . So △ there must be a carry over of 1. △
B568	2590	And △ this must mean that E is equal to 9. △△
B569	2602	So put down a 9 by the E. △
B570	2607	(E: E is 9.)
B571	2609	Now we've a couple of them out.
B572	2610	Oh. Oh, Oh. △ (screeches) Yeah. △ Oopsy-daisy. △
B573	2625	E is 9. △ E is gotta to be 9.
B574	2630	Let me see. Does E △ have to be 9.
B575	2632	What else could it be.
B576	2635	You've got △ zero in . . . odd . . . you've O, E, O. △
B577	2642	Must be 9 with a 1 carry over.
B578	2645	So it something like 5 plus 10, that'll be △ 15 down here.
B579	2647	6 plus 10 is 16. △
B580	2652	So er. . . . △
B581	2657	(E: Please talk.) △

E23

| B582 | 2662 | So if E is 9. |
| B583 | 2664 | and R has to be 7, |

B584	2665	so I think I've said 'cause R has to be 7 △ or 9.
B585	2670	That . . . △ that gives me two numbers △ here, which when added △ up give me a 9 (laughs) △ or 19.
B586	2690	Er. . . . So, unless I'm completely bawled up, △ there must be a carry over from this column here. △
B587	2697	So let's see if this gets me any place now.
B588	2699	So this must mean. . . . △
B589	2702	I've . . . I had L down to the . . . two numbers. I guess.
B590	2705	It had to be an 8 △ or 3.
B591	2707	So get rid of those 3's, there. △
B592	2712	(E: L is no longer 3.)
B593	2713	Yeah. And put down an 8.
B594	2714	(E: L is 8.)
B595	2715	I going to commit △ hari-kari if this doesn't get me any place.
B596	2720	Er. . . . △ So I've got a 1 carry over.
B597	2725	And A △ and A add up to 9.
B598	2730	So △ this means that A could be 4
B599	2732	or it could be. . . .
B600	2735	Well, △ 9 and 9 are 18.
B601	2737	Well, so A must be 4.
B602	2740	So put in △ a 4 for A.
B603	2742	(E: A is 4.)
B604	2745	(coughs) Oh △ boy! Well have I got any big contradictions yet? △
B605	2755	Er . . . △ let's see if this adds so far.
B606	2757	5 and 5 are 10. △
B607	2762	6 and 7,
B608	2764	carry the 1 to 9.
B609	2765	It adds up △ so far.

E24

B610	2770	OK. △ Now the next number is N.
B611	2772	What are the number available . . . numbers available for N. △
B612	2777	1 is used. △
B613	2782	2 is no good. △
B614	2787	Er. . . . △
B615	2792	(E: Please talk.)
B616	2795	2 is no good, because it would give 9 △ for B,
B617	2797	and we have already used 9.
B618	2799	3 is no good,
B619	2800	because that would give you zero △ for B,
B620	2801	and we have used zero.
B621	2802	4 is no good
B622	2803	'cause we've used it.
B623	2804	5 we've used. △
B624	2807	6
B625	2809	will give you 3 for B, △
B626	2811	and we haven't used 3 yet.
B627	2812	Put in a 6 for N.
B628	2813	(E: N is. . . .)
B629	2814	Er. . . . Put in a 6 by N. △
B630	2817	(E: N is 6.)
B631	2819	And make B equal to 3.
B632	2820	Er. . . △ put it . . . put a 3 by the B.
B633	2822	(E: B is 3.)

**CRYPT-
ARITHMETIC**

B634	2825	OK. △ Now we've got a carry over of 1. △
B635	2832	Like we need it.
B636	2834	And so O. . . . △
B637	2837	I'm going to need another carry over of 1.
B638	2840	Er . . . I guess I'm . . . △ have I used everything?
B639	2842	Let's see. 1. △
B640	2847	I've used 1. △
B641	2852	OK. Put in. . . .
B642	2854	Haven't used 2 yet I guess. △
B643	2857	Put in a 2 by the O.
B644	2859	(E: O is 2.)
B645	2860	All righty. △ Ah. △ Ye gads. Oh, yeah. Yeah, there's a carry over. △
B646	2872	All right, and that'll give you another carry over. △

E25

```
    5 2 6 4 8 5
    1 9 7 4 8 5
   ─────────────
    7 2 3 9 7 0
```

B647	2877	All right. Let's add this dumb number up.
B648	2880	5 and 5 are 10, △ carry the 1.
B649	2882	8 and 8 are 16, that gives you 7, carry the 1.
B650	2885	4 and 4 △ are 8 and 1 is 9.
B651	2887	6 and 7 are 13, carry the 1. △
B652	2892	2 and 10 are 12, carry the 1.
B653	2894	6 and 1 are 7. △
B654	2897	Q.E.D. That's my solution. △
B655	2902	(E: Fine. Good, that's the correct solution. Thank you very much.) △
B656	2910	Oh. Bongo, bongo, bong. △ (laughs) △
B657	2917	Oh . . . if I . . . it was so simple . . . It was. . . . △
B658	2922	Over there in the end there, if I could've just seen that I had to have a 1 carry over,
B659	2925	I could've got along so △ quickly.
B660	2927	I . . . I can't . . . I don't know. . . .
B661	2930	I couldn't get rid of that idea in my mind that er . . . △ that I could have a carry over besides zero and 1. △

APPENDIX 7.4

S6 on DONALD+GERALD

[Time (T) in seconds; triangles (△) mark 5-second intervals.]

B   T

B1	2	(E: Here is the next task,)
B2	5	(E: and I will △ give you a cl . . . a clue for this one, that D △ is 5. △ Righty.) △
B3	25	(E: Here is task number 4. D is 5. △ Please talk.)
B4	30	Er. . . . △ (whistles) Make the △ T 3. △
B5	42	(E: T is 3.) △
B6	47	Er . . . change the T . . . △ change the T to. . . . △
B7	57	The D has to stay 5? △

B8	62	(E: Yes.)
B9	64	D has to stay 5. [Said by E?]
B10	65	And you can't change △ the T to zero?
B11	67	(E: Sorry.)
B12	70	You . . . you cannot change the T △ to zero, can you?
B13	72	(E: You can. Yes.)
B14	74	Well, make the T zero. △
B15	77	(E: T is zero.)
B16	80	Right. △ OK. Make the L △ 3.
B17	87	(E: L is 3.) △
B18	95	Er . . . make the A △ 2.
B19	100	(E: A △ is 2.) △
B20	110	Er . . . make the △ er . . . G △ 6.
B21	117	(E: G is 6.) △
B22	125	Make the △ O 4. △
B23	132	(E: O is 4.) △
B24	137	Er . . . make the △ E 9.
B25	142	(E: E is 9.) △△
B26	155	Make the N △ 7.
B27	157	(E: N is 7.) △
B28	162	Make the R 8.
B29	164	(E: R is 8.) △△
B30	172	Er . . . change the R to 6.
B31	174	Oh . . . G is 6. △
B32	180	Er . . . △ 6, 7.
B33	182	(E: Please talk.)
B34	185	Change the R to △ 7.
B35	187	(E: R is 7.) △△
B36	200	Make the E △ 4. △
B37	210	Er . . . change △ the O . . . change the O to △ 1.
B38	217	Make the E 4.
B39	219	(E: O is 1.) △
B40	222	(E: E is 4.) △
B41	230	Right. Er. . . . △ Something's wrong △ here. We have N and R both as 7's.
B42	237	(E: Ah, yes.) △
B43	245	Er . . . change the N △ to . . . change △ the N to 6.
B44	252	(E: G is 6.) △
B45	257	G is 6.
B46	260	Er . . . change the N △ to 8.
B47	262	(E: N is 8.) △
B48	270	Change the er . . . make the △ R . . . △ make the R . . . △△ make the R er . . . △ 6.
B49	292	(E: G is 6.) △
B50	297	Pardon me.
B51	298	(E: G is 6 already.)
B52	299	G is 6.
B53	300	Change the si . . . △ G to 9.
B54	302	(E: G is 9.) △
B55	307	Make the R 6.
B56	310	(E: R △ is 6.) △
B57	317	Oops . . . 6, 7. △
B58	322	(E: Please talk.) △
B59	327	Er . . . change the R back to 7.

**CRYPT-
ARITHMETIC**

B60	329	(E: R is 7.) △△
B61	340	Er . . . change △ the N to . . . △ (whistles) △ change the . . . change the N to △ ni . . . 9. △
B62	362	(E: G is 9.)
B63	365	Change △ the 9 . . . change G 9 to er . . . G . . . △ G 8. Make the G an 8.
B64	375	Make the △ N a 9.
B65	377	(E: N is 9.)
B66	379	(E: G is 8.)
B67	380	Right. △ Er . . . make the B 6.
B68	382	(E: B is 6.) △
B69	390	Er . . . △△ make the . . . △ make the O . . . △△ make the O. . . . △
B70	417	(E: Please talk.)
B71	420	Er . . . make the △ O 4.
B72	422	Ch . . . change the. . . .
B73	425	Take 4 △ from the E and make the A . . . the O 4. △
B74	432	(E: E is no longer 4. O is 4.)
B75	435	Oops. . . . △ Change that back. Change that back.
B76	437	Keep the E as 4, please. △
B77	442	(E: E is 4. O is no longer 4.)
B78	445	Right. △ OK. Make um . . . △ make the O . . . △ make the O. . . . △
B79	465	3, 4, △ 5, 6. △
B80	475	Make the O . . . △ oh . . . △ make △ the O the . . . △ make the O 1.
B81	492	(E: O is 1.)
B82	495	Right. △ Er. . . . △
B83	502	(E: Please talk.) △
B84	510	Make the G . . . △△ make the G . . . △ make the G se. . . . △
B85	527	(E: Please talk.)
B86	530	G has △ to stay as 8.
B87	532	O as 1. △
B88	540	5 and 5's △ 10. 5 and 5 is 10.
B89	545	Er . . . △ (whistles) △ 3 and 6 △ and 1 is 7 . . . 1 is 7. △
B90	562	2 and 2. E is 4. △
B91	567	E has to stay as 4. △
B92	572	Er . . . 9 and 7 are 16. △
B93	580	4, 5 △ and 1 is 6 . . . er. . . .
B94	585	Make △ the O 6. △
B95	592	Make the R 8.
B96	594	(E: O is 6.) △
B97	597	(E: I'll have to change B then.)
B98	599	Pardon me.
B99	600	(E: I must change B, △ because B is 6.)
B100	605	Right. You're. . . . Change the B to er . . . △ to er . . . se . . . er . . . △ 8.
B101	612	(E: G is 8.)
B102	615	OK. Change the G △ to 1.
B103	617	(E: G is 1) △
B104	622	(E: and B is 8.) △
B105	627	Um . . . 9 and 7 is si . . . 16. △
B106	632	6 and 4 are 10. △
B107	640	Oh. er . . . △ change the . . . △△ change the △ B to 9
B108	657	and the N to 8.
B109	660	(E: B △ is 9,)
B110	662	(E: and N is 8.)
B111	665	7's △ 15,

B112	670	4. Er . . . △ er . . . △ 10, △
B113	682	14. [4 10 (?)] Er. . . .
B114	685	Change the O △ to . . . change the O to △ 1,
B115	695	and make the G △ 6.
B116	697	(E: O is 1.) △
B117	702	G 6.
B118	704	(E: And G is 6.) △△
B119	712	4 and 1 are 5,
B120	715	and that will be 4 . . . △ 5 and 4 are 9. . . .
B121	720	Er . . . △ change the △ er . . . △ change the △ R from 7 to 6.
B122	740	(E: R △ from 7 to 6.)
B123	742	(E: But G is 6.) △
B124	750	Yeah. Well, well change the . . . the G to . . . er . . . △ change the . . . G △ to er . . . △ 1.
B125	762	(E: R is 6.)
B126	763	(E: G is 1.)
B127	764	(E: But O is 1.) △
B128	770	Change the O to . . . △ er . . . 7. △
B129	777	(E: O is 7.) △△
B130	790	Er. . . . Change the . . . △ change the L to △ 2.
B131	797	(E: L is 2.) △
B132	802	(E: But A is 2.) △
B133	807	Change the A to 3.
B134	809	(E: A is 3.) △△
B135	820	Change the . . . △ er . . . change the er . . . R to 4 △
B136	827	and the E to 6.
B137	829	(E: R is 4,) △
B138	832	(E: and E is 6.) △
B139	840	(E: Please △ talk.)
B140	845	Er . . . △ change the . . . (whistles) △ change the L . . . △ L to 8. △
B141	862	(E: L is 8.) △
B142	867	(E: But N is 8.) △
B143	875	Er . . . change the er . . . 8 to . . . △ N to 2.
B144	877	(E: N is 2.) △
B145	882	Change the R to 6.
B146	884	(E: R is 6.) △
B147	887	(E: But E is 6.)
B148	890	Right. △ Change the er . . . E △ to er . . . △ 4.
B149	902	(E: E is 4.) △
B150	907	(. . . ? . . .) and 1 is 7. △
B151	915	Change the E to . . . △ change the E to 9. △
B152	922	(E: E is 9.)
B153	925	(E: But △ B is 9.)
B154	930	Change the B to . . . △ change the B to △ 7. △
B155	942	(E: B is 7.)
B156	944	(E: But O is 7.)
B157	945	(laughs) Change . . . △ change the O to △ 4.
B158	952	(E: O is 4.) △
B159	960	OK. △ Change the R to 7.
B160	964	(E: R is 7.) △
B161	970	(E: Sorry. △ But B is 7.) △
B162	977	Change the B to 6. △
B163	982	(E: B is 6.)

CRYPT-
ARITHMETIC

B164	984	17. △
B165	987	3 and 3 and 6 and 1 is 7. △
B166	995	Change the . . . change the er . . . △ A to . . . △ to 6. △
B167	1007	(E: A is 6.)
B168	1009	(E: But B is 6.) △
B169	1015	Er. . . . Change the B △ to 9.
B170	1017	(E: B is 9.)
B171	1019	(E: But E is 9.) △
B172	1025	Change the △ E 9 to E 2.
B173	1027	(E: E is 2.) △
B174	1032	(E: But N is 2.) △
B175	1037	Change the N to . . . to er . . . △△
B176	1050	to 1, 2, 3, △ 5.
B177	1052	Oh . . . change the N to 9. △
B178	1057	Oh, B . . . B is 9.
B179	1060	Change △ the N to . . . △△ change the N to f . . . 3. △
B180	1077	(E: N is 3.) △
B181	1082	Er. . . . △
B182	1087	(E: Please talk.) △
B183	1095	Change . . . △ change the th. . . . △
B184	1102	(E: Please talk.)
B185	1104	Change the B to 1. △
B186	1107	(E: B is 1.)
B187	1110	(E: But G △ is 1.)
B188	1115	Change the G △ to . . . to . . . △ er. . . . (whistles) △
B189	1127	Change the B to . . .
B190	1130	2, 3, 4, 5, 6, △ 7, 8. . . .
B191	1132	Change the B to 9.
B192	1134	(E: B is 9.) △△
B193	1142	No, I wanted the B as 1
B194	1144	and the G as 9.
B195	1145	(E: B △ is 1,)
B196	1147	(E: and G is 9.)
B197	1149	1's 11.
B198	1150	OK. △ Er . . . △ change the O to 7.
B199	1157	(E: O is 7.) △
B200	1162	(E: But R is 7.)
B201	1164	But R is 7. △
B202	1167	Change the R to 4. △
B203	1172	(E: R is 4.)
B204	1175	Oh, oh, oh, oh, wait . . . wait just a minute. △ Leave that the way it was.
B205	1177	(E: R is 7.) △
B206	1185	Ah . . . (whistles) change the . . . △ change the . . . △ er. . . . △
B207	1197	(E: Please talk.) △
B208	1202	Change the O to 2. △
B209	1207	(E: O is 2.)
B210	1209	(E: But E is 2.) △
B211	1215	Change the O to △ 4. △
B212	1221	No. O. . . .
B213	1222	(E: Sorry, O is. . . .)
B214	1223	O. O to 4. O to 4.
B215	1224	(E: O is 4.) △△
B216	1235	Er . . . △ ch . . . change the . . . △ er . . . △ E to ni. . . .

B217   1250   Er ... △ change the ... △ change the G to 2. △
B218   1262   (E: G is 2.)
B219   1264   (E: But E is 2.) △
B220   1270   OK. Change the G △ to. ... △
B221   1277   (E: Please talk.)
B222   1280   Change ... (splutters) △ change the G △ to 4.
B223   1287   (E: G is 4.)
B224   1289   (E: But O is 4.) △
B225   1292   Change the O to um ... 9. △
B226   1297   (E: O is 9.) △
B227   1302   Change the D to. ... △
B228   1305   No D has got to stay the same way as it is. ...
B229   1310   Change the △ D to. ...
B230   1312   Leave the D the same. △
B231   1317   Change the R to. ... (whistles) △
B232   1322   (E: Please talk.) △
B233   1326   I give up.
B234   1327   (E: You give up.)
B235   1328   Fuff.
B236   1329   (E: OK.) △
B237   1332   Huh?
B238   1333   (E: You give up?)
B239   1334   Yeah, I give up. I. ...
B240   1335   (E: Fine. OK. △ We'll go on to the next task then.)

APPENDIX 7.5

S8 prelude to LETS+WAVE (Problem Spaces)

[Time (T) in seconds; triangles (△) mark 5-second intervals.]

B   T

                              L E T S
                              W A V E
                              ――――――――
                              L A T E R

B1   2   (E: This is task ... task number 3.)
B2   4   All right. △
B3   6   (E: It's a harder one.)
B4   8   Hm.
B5   10   (E: Please talk.) △△

E1   *Numerical problem space (#1)*
B6   20   All right. So I'm adding up △ two four-digit numbers er ... △ to get a five-digit
                number.
B7   30   Adding up two numbers in the thousands er ... △ to get a number in the ten
                thousands.
B8   35   See what repeated number I have △ down there.

**CRYPT-
ARITHMETIC**

B9	38	I've got two L's. △
B10	42	I've got two E's. (coughs)
B11	45	I've got △ two T's.
B12	50	One S. △

E2   *Basic problem space (#1)*

B13	55	Well er . . . this not . . . this problem here, △ er . . . is er . . . I think not going to be solved by the method that . . . that . . . △ I used the hit-and-missed method to solve the simpler one.
B14	65	Er. . . . This one is △ obviously going to be too complicated for that. △
B15	72	Much too complicated to solve with er . . . a process of elimination, △ or hit and miss, or whatever you want to call it.
B16	80	So I'm going to have to er . . . △ er . . . I'm going to have to try and er . . . △ try and work out s. . . . △
B17	92	At least I think it's going to be complicated to solve with hit and miss. △
B18	100	Of course, if . . . it's made somewhat simpler, or it's made somewhat simpler by the fact that I have △ repeated numbers,
B19	105	but er . . . not simple enough . . . I don't think it's made △ simple enough that er . . . I can consider a process of elimination, △ or a er . . . a hunt-and-peck type er . . . method to solve the problem. △△

E3   *Numerical problem space (#2)*

B20	125	So er . . . I er . . . △ guess I could er . . . △ more or less figure out what range these numbers are in. △
B21	137	They are numbers in the thousands that add up to a number in the ten thousands. △
B22	145	(coughs) So again their . . . their . . . their sum will be er . . . △ just like the . . . the last . . . their . . . their sum . . . their sum will er . . . be er . . . △ of these two numbers in . . . in the thousands will △ be er . . . greater than △ ten thousand.
B23	162	So they're not . . . you know.
B24	165	And er . . . △ I guess it automatically has to be less than twenty thousand, doesn't it? △
B25	172	So er. . . . But it will be greater than ten thousand.
B26	174	There would be a lot that weren't. △
B27	180	I don't really think that . . . that this information is terribly useful △ to me.

E4   *Word-meaning problem space (#1)*

B28	182	I notice that you . . . you have words there. △
B29	187	That obv . . . obviously doens't mean anything, but it's an interesting observation. △
B30	192	Letters that make words. △

E5   *Numerical problem space (#3)*

B31	200	OK. So all I know so far is that er . . . that numbers △ in the thousands, some of which will be . . . er. . . .
B32	205	No. △ I can only use numbers the sum of which will be greater than er . . . △ er . . . ten thousand.
B33	215	There are obviously △ not any obvious simple numbers
B34	220	because er . . . in neither of the two numbers on top △ is there er . . . a number repeated. △
B35	230	I . . . I can't say anything much about these er . . . △ numbers, I think,
B36	235	except, well, that S and E obviously aren't zero. △ (coughs)
B37	240	Because they add up to R △ and not S or E. △
B38	250	They add up to a number the second . . . the first digit of which is . . . △ is R in anyway . . . the second digit of which is R. △ (coughs) △ Er . . . △
B39	267	(E: Please talk.)
B40	270	I'm er . . . really at a loss as to how to attack △ this problem.

E6		*Algebra problem space* (#1)
B41	272	Er . . . I don't think it can be attacked algebraically, △
B42	277	er . . . although I can't claim to be a wiz at math. △
B43	285	It looks like er . . . if . . . if I could set up any kind of equation or equations △ I'd have too many unknowns.
B44	290	Um . . . because even though the letters are repeated, △ they are not repeated enough, I'm pretty sure of that.
B45	293	That's sort of a guess. △
B46	300	I don't think I can set up an equation based on . . . on . . . △ on the way that arith . . . arithmetic addition is done. △
E7		*Basic problem space* (#2)
B47	310	Er . . . and er . . . △ I can't solve this problem by substitution either. △
B48	320	So er . . . △ I er . . . I'm really at a loss as to how to proceed. △
E8		*Cryptogram problem space* (#1)
B49	330	Is it er . . . is it possible △ that er . . . there's something in this er . . . △ that you . . . did you put something into this problem er . . . other than what you have explained?
B50	340	For example, △ is it possible that there's any significance er . . . △ any . . . any relationship between the letter's position in the alphabet and the number it represents? △
B51	352	[E: (. . . ? . . .)]
B52	355	All right. Well, △ er . . . if I'm overlooking something obvious △ then I'm overlooking something obvious.
E9		*Basic problem space* (#3)
B53	365	But on the surface it looks to me like er . . . △ this problem. . . .
B54	368	If you . . . if you substituted letters for numbers at random △
B55	375	that er . . . the solution of this problem is △ virtually . . . is virtually hopeless,
B56	380	er . . . without er . . . △ either an enormous amount of time
B57	385	or else (laughs) some sort of of machine △ to processes data.
B58	390	In other words without time enough to make an enormous △ number of substitutions
B59	395	and without a . . . a device that could make an enormous er . . . number of △ substitution quickly.
E10		*Cryptogram problem space* (#2)
B60	400	(coughs) So △ er . . . I might try and er . . . think of some er . . . △ connection between letters and numbers er . . . △
B61	413	that er . . . you, or who ever invented the problem, might have put in there. △
B62	420	Now, er . . . △ if it's a relationship between numbers and positions of letters in the △ alphabet,
B63	430	it'd have to . . . it . . . it's not . . . △ it's not a . . . it's not the most elementary one. obviously,
B64	435	because there are 26 letters △ in the alphabet, and I'm only concerned with 10 digits.
B65	440	And there're obviously △ er . . . letters in this problem that are . . . are beyond the . . . the first ten. △
B66	447	And er . . . there are letters scattered all over the alphabet. △
B67	452	Er. . . . Well not exactly, but. . . .
B68	455	Well, △ yeah you got L which is sort of in the middle.
B69	460	And er . . . △ A and E at the beginning
B70	463	and R and T comes at the end. △
B71	467	V is at the end.

B   T

E11   *Cryptogram problem space* (#3)

B72	470	So, er . . . △ (coughs) if er . . . there was any substitution △ I guess that it . . . it'd have to be some sort of based on groups. △
B73	482	like say the first two letters of the alphabet represented one number.
B74	485	And it . . . △ it have to be some groups of two and some groups of three, to △ er . . . get you to come out with 26. △
B75	500	And er . . . offhand △ er . . . this doesn't look like a very promising idea.
B76	505	Maybe I should just junk △ the entire idea, that there's a . . . that there's some other clue that you've put in here. △
B77	515	Er. . . . △ But er . . . be . . . for . . . because you have . . . well, we have R and . . . △ we have R, S, and T all in this problem. △
B78	530	And they △ come together. They adjoin each other in the alphabet. △
B79	538	And er . . . so, if this method that I outlined were used, er . . . △ R, S, and T couldn't be three different numbers.
B80	545	Er. . . . △ This wouldn't be possible.
B81	550	They could be . . . they . . . they can only re . . . these letters can only represent two △ different numbers at the most.
B82	555	So I have to er . . . junk △ that idea I'm afraid, they're . . . that . . . that you've . . . you've put something in here, at least △ in that form.

E12   *Typographical problem space* (#1)

B83	565	I guess it's also possible that certain number le . . . △ letters look like numbers.
B84	568	For example an E looks a lot like a 3. △
B85	575	But er . . . I don't △ er . . . I'm afraid I'm not going to get very far with this idea,
B86	580	because er . . . △ I can't see any other letters there that look too much like numbers.
B87	585	Er . . . △ I. . . . Well . . . you might say . . . I guess you might say that a 2 looks like an S. △
B88	592	Let's see. A 1 doesn't look like anything down there.
B89	595	And if △ you wanted a 1 then you . . . you were using that method you would put an I in there obviously. △
B90	605	So er . . . a 4. . . . Let's see. Does a 4 △ look particularly like a. . . . [A (?)]
B91	607	No.
B92	610	A 5? Well again △ a 5 looks sort of like an S.
B93	613	Er . . . 6? △
B94	620	Well this idea isn't er . . . △ isn't panning out I'm afraid.
B95	622	7?
B96	624	No. △
B97	630	So (coughs) er . . . working on the assumption that △ I couldn't solve this problem △ er . . . unless you have some △ relationship between numbers and letters that's △ er . . . that's er . . . independent of the problem itself, △
B98	655	er . . . I really can't er . . . △ I really can't think of any. △

E13   *Cryptogram problem space* (#4)

B99	662	Of course, there are other possibilities, I guess. △
B100	670	Er. Maybe a number er . . . △ could count er . . . the num . . . the number △ er . . . it could count as er . . . the number of letters from the △ front of the alphabet that it was, if it was near the front,
B101	685	or the number it was back △ from the end, if it was near the end.
B102	687	I don't know if I could fit L into this.
B103	690	I'll count. A △ B, C, D, E, F, H, G, I, J. △
B104	697	No, that would make L 12.
B105	699	So that idea is no good. △
B106	702	There's no way that'll work for it to make L a one-digit number.
B107	705	(coughs) △ I guess it would be 20. . . .
B108	710	It'll be 14 from the back I guess, △ or 13 . . . 14.
B109	715	But er. . . . △ So, I guess er . . . there is nothing like that in the problem. △

E14   *Review* (#1)
B110   725   So if er . . . it's er . . . really possible that I can △ solve this problem,
B111   730   then er . . . I must be overlooking some simple △ method.
B112   735   Er . . . I haven't been able to figure out any relationship △ between the letters of
               the alphabet and the . . . and the numbers △ that you have sort of concealed in the
               problem.
B113   745   Er . . . so △ I . . . I think I more or less eliminated substitution.
B114   750   This . . . this idea is totally △ in . . . tri . . . substitution and trial and error.
B115   755   This method, which I more or less used △ on the first problem, is totally impracti-
               cal in this one. △
B116   762   So, there must be some er . . . simple thing.
B117   765   Either . . . there are two possibilities . . . △ there's either a simple method that I am
               overlooking completely because I just haven't seen it,
B118   770   or else △ er . . . nobody is really expected to solve this problem by you, △
B119   780   but you're just interested in how △ it is attacked.
B120   781   But. . . . Well I know you're interested in how it is attacked
B121   783   but it's . . . it's possible that I'm not really expected to be able to solve it. △

E15   *Algebra problem space* (#2)
B122   790   (coughs) So (coughs) △ I keep coming back to the idea △ of er . . . I keep coming
               back to the idea of . . . △ of trying some sort of algebraic equation,
B123   805   but the more you think about this the more ridiculous △ it gets.
B124   808   I mean I'd start with S and E
B125   810   er . . . △ which will give me a number added together will . . . er . . . going to give
               me a number that's either R △ or else a number the second . . . two-digit number,
               the second digit of which is R . . . △
B126   825   Right away I . . . I have no idea er . . . △ what to work with.
B127   830   Er . . . in other words the the number will give me △ R minus 10 if the sum of S
               and E is greater than 10, △
B128   840   where it will give me just (yawns) R △ if if the sum of S and E is less than 10.
B129   845   And do I. . . . I obviously △ can't be attacking it . . . er . . . I can't be attacking it,
               △ trying to set up any equations.
B130   855   This . . . this would be . . . this . . . △ this idea is more or less fantastic. △

E16   *Review* (#2)
B131   865   (coughs) S . . . △ oh, my. This is . . . this is really tough.
B132   870   I . . . △ I have a feeling that I'm er . . . I'm being dull here, △
B133   880   but I er . . . can't er . . . △ I'm er . . . I'm really . . . △ I'm really stymied at this
               point.

E17   *Basic problem space* (#4)
B134   890   I mean, I . . . I haven't at . . . △ attempted to substitute any numbers or anything
               yet,
B135   895   but er . . . I realize maybe that's △ what you want me to try and do. △
B136   902   But er . . . I haven't done it because I'm convinced that it's futile. △
B137   907   I mean, I might accidently stumble on the right answer
B138   910   but I think that is a skillion △ to one shot.
E18   *Numerical problem space* (#4)
B139   915   So er. . . . △ Let's see. What are the repetitions in this?
B140   917   There isn't enough repetition.
B141   920   You haven't got . . . I don't believe you have one this . . . △ you don't have one
               that appears three times even.
B142   925   Er. . . . You've △ got a couple of T's in there,
B143   927   and er . . . a couple A's,
B144   928   and a couple of E's,
B145   929   only one L, △

B146	931	only W,
B147	932	no a couple of L's.
B148	933	only one W,
B149	934	one one V, △
B150	936	only one S.

E19   *Word-meaning problem space (#2)*

B151	940	Er . . . △ now then. △ Let's see. I don't imagine. . . .
B152	950	Getting back to the idea that you might have △ er . . . planted a clue in there, er . . . independent of the problem, △
B153	957	er . . . I don't imagine it's possible that the words would have any significance . . . LETS, WAVE, △ and LATER.
B154	965	Er. . . . △ This doesn't seem likely that the er . . . numbers LETS . . . the words LETS, WAVE, and LATER △ would give me any clues to any four-digit or five-digit numbers. △
B155	976	Er. . . . They certainly don't.

E20   *Augmented problem space (#2)*

B156	978	So, I think that idea can be . . . more or less be rejected. △
B157	985	Er . . . △ I mean. . . . Let's see now. △ This is er . . . △ this is rather tricky.
B158	1000	Let's see. S and △ E, starting on the end . . . on the right hand where you . . . △ where you'd begin addition, give you R or a two-digit number the second digit △ of which was R.
B159	1013	S doesn't appear anyplace else in the problem. △
B160	1017	E is up there on the top line.
B161	1020	It is . . . this is . . . this is really going △ to get me noplace.
B162	1022	As . . . as I went further on in this method I . . . I . . . it . . . △ I'd have the same old problem.
B163	1030	I mean, as I got in the middle I . . . I'd have △ er . . . I'd never know △ whe . . . whether I was adding up and getting a one-digit number or △ whether I was adding up and getting a er. . . . △ a two-digit number. △

E21   *Review (#3)*

B164	1053	So er. . . . △
B165	1056	(E: Please talk.)
B166	1058	I don't . . . I don't know whether you're. . . . △
B167	1062	I'm just about ready to throw in the towel I'm afraid. △
B168	1067	'cause I can't think of a method to attack this problem.
B169	1070	If I △ could just think of a way to attack it, but I can't.
B170	1075	It er . . . △ it just . . . just er . . . looks too er . . . △ too complicated to me,
B171	1085	to yield △ to any technique that I could . . . that I could think of . . . △ er . . . to △ yield to any technique that I could think of.

E22   *Numerical problem space (#5)*

B172	1100	On examination er . . . △ these numbers er . . . the letters in these numbers don't tell me anything about the numbers.
B173	1105	L, E, △ T, S. There is no letter repeated within a number.
B174	1110	These numbers don't △ have any pattern at all.
B175	1115	I mean L, E, T, S could be anything, △ or virtually anything.
B176	1120	Er . . . Ah, I said △ it . . . it's obvious that neither S nor E is zero. △
B177	1127	But er . . . I mean this information does me little good. △

E23   *Augmented problem space (#2)*

B178	1135	Er . . . I got to be over . . . △ I must be overlooking something simple.
B179	1138	What is it? △
B180	1142	Oh, my. Let's see, now. If. . . . △
B181	1150	Is there any . . . any . . . any pattern △ at all here?

B182	1155	Er.... △ I can't work at all the individual's vertical sums
B183	1160	because I △ er ... I really △ never have any clue to the carry over, △
B184	1172	(coughs) I mean, the carry over from one sum to the next △ one er ... could be 1, △
B185	1185	or working from carry △ overs from previous sums could ... could build it up more △
B186	1192	er ... so that er ... it ... it could be 2.

E24   *Augmented problem space (#3)*

B187	1195	Er.... △ Like for example suppose that er ... S and E were er ... △ were ... were 9 and 8, △
B188	1207	and er ... T ... T and V were ... were 6 and 7. △
B189	1212	So, 9 and 8.
B190	1215	Well that ... that obviously △ won't work.
B191	1217	Just er ... say they were 6 and 5.
B192	1220	So let's say 9 △ and 8 are 17.
B193	1225	And I carry △ 1.
B194	1230	And ... Well ... △ let ... let's make S and E, say er ... 5 and 6.
B195	1232	5 and 6 are 11
B196	1234	and I carry 1. △
B197	1237	Let's say T and V were 9 and 8.
B198	1240	So △ the most I ... carry over I'm going to have here....
B199	1245	From the first column the most △ carry over I can have is 1.
B200	1248	It might be zero. △
B201	1255	But could this build me up to a number for the second △ summation that'd be over 20?
B202	1258	No, it can't. △
B203	1265	Er ... I don't know. Something gave me △ the idea that I could get a bigger carry over.
B204	1270	I guess △ I should have been adding long enough that I know I can't, △
B205	1277	least until I get to the end.
B206	1280	Let's see. △ No, there's no way that this is possible.
B207	1285	First two numbers can't add up △ to anything over 20, obviously,
B208	1290	so the carry over must be 1. △
B209	1295	So 1 added to the second two really can't get me △ over 20 either
B210	1300	The high ... the ... the highest they could be is 9 △ and 8.
B211	1303	So I guess it'd be a 1 carry over in each summation. △
B212	1310	Er.... △ So △ S and E △ added together would give me, as I said pre ... repeatedly, △ either R or ... or a two-digit number the second digit of which is R. △
B213	1335	Then T and V added together △ will give me △ er ... T and V add together △ will give me either △ E, △
B214	1358	or T and V added to either plu....
B215	1360	T and V △ will give me either E or er ... △ a number the second ... a two-digit number the second digit of which is E.
B216	1370	Or ... △ that's not exactly....
B217	1375	Either T and V, or T plus V plus 1 △ will give me either E or the number the second digit of which is E. △

E25   *Augmented problem space (#4)*

B218	1382	So I ... I guess you could start eliminating △ on this basis.
B219	1390	Er ... △ if I.... Maybe if I started substituting for S △ and E. △
B220	1405	I could er ... work this △ problem out by some way. △
B221	1415	Er.... △ Let's see. If I let S and E be, say for example 1 and 2,
B222	1420	that'd △ give me 3 for R.
B223	1425	So a T and V △ (yawns) would have to add up to △ er ... either 12 or 13 ... either 11 or 12, △

B T

B224 1437 'cause depending on which . . . whether I plan on making S 1 or. . . . △

B225 1442 So, er. . . . △

E26 *Problem redefinition*

B226 1450 Ah! Well now wait a minute. Is it possible, I wonder? Is it possible, I wonder? △
Is it er . . . possible that a prob . . . this problem has got more than one solution?
△

B227 1460 Maybe a lot of solutions, one of which I could pick △ out er . . . just by starting at
the beginning. △

E27 *Augmented problem space* (#5)

B228 1467 Er. . . . Let's let S equal 1, △

B229 1472 and E equal 2.

B230 1473 Would you put 1 and 2 up there for S and E.

B231 1474 (E: S and 1.)

B232 1474 Yeah.

B233 1475 (E: E is 2.) △

$$\begin{array}{c} \text{L 2 T 1} \\ \text{W A V 2} \\ \hline \text{L A T 2 R} \end{array}$$

B234 [S continues to work in augmented problem space but does not solve problem within
time limits.]

APPENDIX 7.6

S4 on CROSS+ROADS
A. Protocol

B T

$$\begin{array}{c} \text{C R O S S} \\ \text{R O A D S} \\ \hline \text{D A N G E R} \end{array}$$

B1 2 (E: Here is the next problem. Please talk.) △

B2 10 The two S's △ can be seen . . . are identical △ in the first column.

B3 17 (E: I'm sorry. I must. . . . My apologies. I should give you that R is 6.) △

B4 22 Oh.

B5 24 (E: R is 6.)

E1 $$\begin{array}{c} \text{C 6 O S S} \\ \text{6 O A D S} \\ \hline \text{D A N G E 6} \end{array}$$

B6 25 Since R is 6 △ and the two S's are equal,

B7 30 S must be equal to 3, △ or 8.

B8 35 And D △ must be equal to 1,

B9 40 because △ C plus R can't be greater than 19,

B10 45 or greater than △ 16 in this case.

B11 47 So D must be a 1. △

B12 52 Would you make D a 1?

B13 54 (E: D is 1.) △

B14	57	And seeing that two S's are equal, △
B15	65	they must be either 3 or △ 8.
B16	67	If they are 8, △
B17	72	then E would be zero.
B18	75	If they △ are 3,
B19	77	then E would be 4. △

E2

B20	85	So let's try the S's as △ 8.
B21	87	Could you make the S an 8?
B22	89	(E: S is 8.) △
B23	95	That would make E △ a zero.
B24	97	Would you make E a zero?
B25	100	(E: E is △ zero.)

E3

```
        C 6 O 8 8
        6 O A 1 8
      ─────────────
      1 A N G 0 6
```

B26	105	Can see that O plus A △ is equal to G,
B27	110	and 6 plus O is △ equal to N.
B28	115	See that △ O. △
B29	125	You really can't tell anything about △ the rest of the letters, what digits correspond to them. △

E4

B30	135	You can see that if △ G were a 7,
B31	137	A would be a 4, △
B32	145	and △ then that would make C either a 7 or an 8. △
B33	152	But that is impossible
B34	154	because both 7 and 8 have been used. △

E5

B35	160	So if G △ were a 5, △
B36	170	that would make O a 2 △ or 3
B37	172	and A a 2 or 3. △
B38	180	If we make △ O a 3, △
B39	187	then that would make N a 9, △
B40	192	and A a 2
B41	195	and C △ a 5.
B42	200	Er. . . . That might be △ a solution.
B43	202	So let's try making O a 3. △
B44	207	(E: O is 3.)
B45	210	That makes △ N a 9, △
B46	217	and A a 2,
B47	219	and G a 5. △△
B48	230	That △ can't be right
B49	237	because, △ if we make A a 2 now △
B50	242	that would make C a 6,
B51	245	but 6 △ has already been used. △

E6

B52	255	We know that C △ is 4 or greater. △
B53	265	And C △ cannot be 1. △
B54	272	C cannot be 1 because of the D. △
B55	280	See that 3 is . . . is an impossibility with . . . △ for O.

E7

| B56 | 285 | So we could try △ O △ as a 4 |

B **T**

B57	295	and △ A. . . . △
B58	305	In that case △ G must be equal to A plus △ 4.
B59	315	And the numbers remaining are 2, 4, 5 △ and 7. . . . △
B60	322	2, 3, 4, 5, and 7.
B61	325	And △ 3 and 7 are the only numbers △ fitting this.
B62	335	So △ if O is a 4. . . .

E8

B63	337	O is a 3,
B64	339	A is a 4, △
B65	342	and G is a 7, △
B66	350	making N △ a 9.
B67	352	That won't work. △△
B68	362	Maybe the two S's are wrong. △

E9

B69	370	If we were to make △ one of the S's a 3, △△
B70	382	then that would force E to be 4. △△
B71	395	Could you make the S's a 3, △ instead of 8?
B72	400	(E: Change the S from 8 to 3. △ S is 4.)
B73	402	No, 3.
B74	405	(E: S is 3. △ S is 3.) △
B75	412	That makes E a 4. △
B76	417	Could you make E a 4?
B77	419	(E: Change E from zero to 4.) △
B78	425	Er. . . . The numbers that are left are zero, 2, 5, △ 7, 8, and 9. △
B79	435	Know that △ C must be △ 5,
B80	442	because that. . . . △
B81	450	The C can be 5, 7, △ 8, or 9.
B82	452	Zero and 2 are impossibilities for C △
B83	457	because D cannot be a 1 in that case. △

E10

```
        C 6 O 3 3
        6 O A 1 3
       ───────────
       1 A N G 4 6
```

B84	465	So, △ guessing again. △△

E11

B85	480	C △ could be. . . . △
B86	487	It's unlikely that C is a 5 or a 7, △
B87	495	unless O is greater △ than 4. △

E12

B88	505	So we could say that C △ was 8.
B89	510	That would make △ A a 4 or a 5. △
B90	520	Could try △ C as an 8. △
B91	527	(E: C is 8.) △
B92	535	And that makes △ A a 4 or 5.
B93	540	And O △ can't be 2 △
B94	547	and can't be zero. △
B95	555	So O must be 5, △ 7, or 9. △

E13

B96	562	And if C is 5 . . . or O is 5. △
B97	567	then A would be 5.
B98	570	So O must be 7 △ or 9.

E14

B99	575	If O △ was 7,

B100   580   then N △ is most like a 3. △
B101   587   So if A were 5, △
B102   592   and O were 7, △
B103   597   then G would be 2. △
B104   602   But that wouldn't work either. △

E15
B105   607   If O were 7
B106   609   and A were 3, △
B107   612   the G would be 9, △
B108   620   and N △ would be 3
B109   622   and A 5. △
B110   627   Could you make A a 5?
B111   629   (E: A is 5.) △△

E16
B112   640   And △ if △ O were made a 7 . . . △
B113   652   O must be either 7 or 9, △
B114   660   in order to have the C plus R △ equal to A.
B115   662   If O were 7, △
B116   670   then N would be either 3 △ or 4.
B117   675   So that's △ impossible.
B118   680   And △ if O were 9, △
B119   687   N must be a 6. △
B120   692   But R is 6. △
B121   700   So A △ must not be a 5. △
B122   710   If A . . . if A is not a 5, △ then C △ must not be an 8. △

E17   C 6 O 3 3
                       6 O 5 1 3
                      ——————————
                     1 5 N G 4 6

B123   725   C △ would also △ be a 9, △
B124   740   in which case △ things might work out.
B125   742   C is a 9, △
B126   750   then O △ could be a 2, △
B127   757   and N an 8,
B128   760   and A △ being left as △ a 5, △
B129   772   making G a 7. △

E18
B130   777   Could you make C a 9?
B131   779   (E: Change C from 8 to 9. C is 9.) △
B132   785   And make △ O 2.
B133   790   (E: Change O from 3 △ to 2. O is 2.)
B134   792   And G 7 △
B135   797   and N 8.
B136   798   (E: G is 7.)
B137   799   (E: N is 8.) △

                       9 6 2 3 3
                       6 2 5 1 3
                      ——————————
                     1 5 8 7 4 6

B138   805   And I think that's the er . . . solution. △ Yes.
B139   810   (E: Fine. △ Good. That's the correct solution. △ That was good.)

APPENDIX 7.6

B. Eye Movements

TIME	DURATION	EMA	VERBALIZATIONS	NUMBER	PRO-DUC-TION	OPERA-TOR	GOAL STACK*	EXPRESSIONS
1.8	.6	C R O S S / R O A D S / D A N G E R						
				1	P9	FNC	∅	
2.4	3.0 scan	C R O S S / R O A D S / D A N G E R						
5.4	.8	C R O S S / R O A D S / D A N G E R						
6.2	.8	C R O S S / R O A D S / D A N G E R	CROSS plus ROADS is					
8			DANGER.	2	P1″	PC	use Col.1	

7.4   2.6   CROS(S)
      −.2   ROAD(S)
             DANGE(R)

9

10   Exp: Please

11

12   talk. S: Yes

13

14   S plus S

15

16   has to equal R

17

3 INT attend Exp; PC Col.1 i

4 ANS

5 cont PC ANS Exp +; PC Col.1;
            PC Col.1

10.0 1.2 CROS S
     scan ROAD S
          DANGER

11.2 1.4 CROS(S)
          ROAD(S)
          DANGER

12.6 1.6 CROSS
     scan ROADS
          DANGER

14.2 8.0 CROS(S)
     −1.2 ROAD(S)
          DANGE(R)

*To conserve space "do" is deleted in the goal type

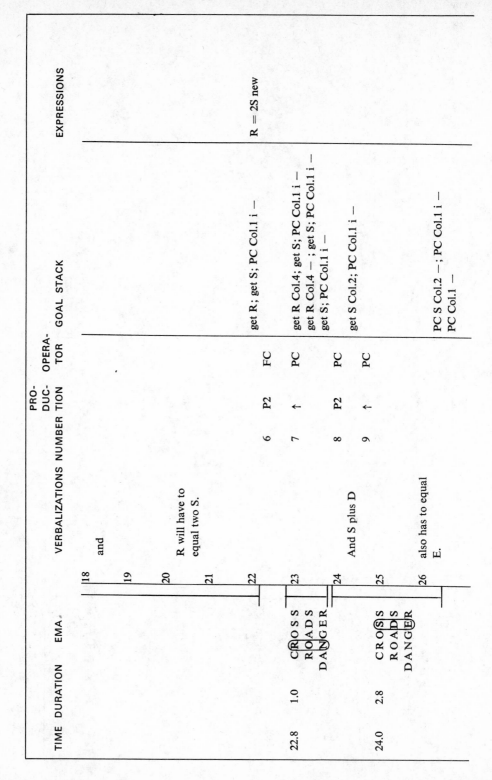

TIME	DURATION	EMA	VERBALIZATIONS	NUMBER	PRO-DUC-TION	OPERA-TOR	GOAL STACK	EXPRESSIONS
			and	18				
				19				
			R will have to equal two S.	20				
				21				
				22	6	P2	FC	get R ; get S; PC Col.1 i —	R = 2S new
22.8	1.0	CR(O)SS ROADS DAN(GE)R		23	7	↑	PC	get R Col.4; get S; PC Col.1 i — / get R Col.4 — ; get S; PC Col.1 i — / get S; PC Col.1 i —	
			And S plus D	24	8	P2	PC	get S Col.2; PC Col.1 i —	
24.0	2.8	CRO(S)S ROADS DAN(GE)R	also has to equal	25	9	↑	PC	PC S Col.2 —; PC Col.1 i — / PC Col.1 —	
			E.	26					

	P	FNC/AV	Notes
10	P9	FNC	use Col.1
11	P3	AV	
12	P2	FC	get R; AV S Col.1 i
13	↑	PC	get R Col.4; AV S Col.1 i
14	cont	AV	PC R Col.4 –; AV S Col.1 i; AV S Col.1 i
15	P1′	PC	AV S Col.1 +

S ← 1 new

Time		Display	Line	Text
26.8	2.0 scan	CROSS-S / ROAD/S / DA—NGER	27	
28.8	2.4 / –.2	CROSS(S) / ROAD(S) / DANGER	28	
			29	So
			30	I'll let
31.4	.6	C(R)OSS / ROADS / DANGER	31	
32.0	1.2 scan	CROSS / ROAD'S / DANGER	32	S
33.2	1.2 / –.2	C(R)OSS / R(O)ADS / DANGER	33	
			34	equal . . .
34.4	1.2	CROSS / ROAD(S) / DANGER	35	Let S equal
			36	
35.8	.6	CROSS / ROADS / DANGER(O)	37	

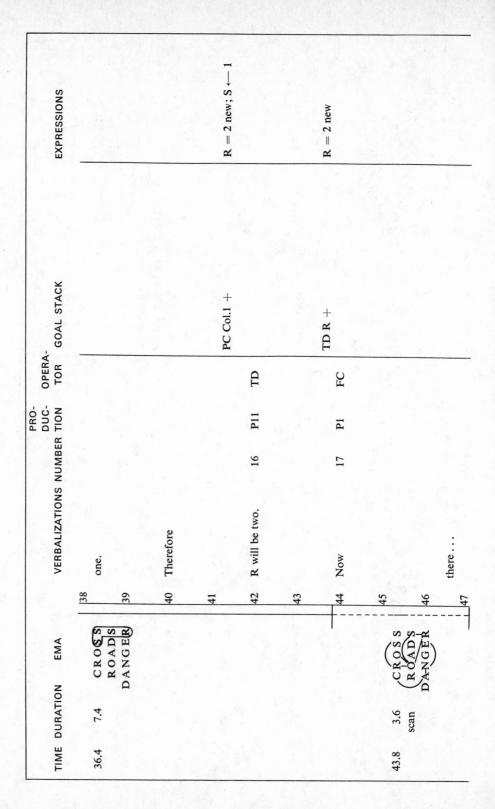

	CROSS ROADS DANGER					
47.4						
.8	48	there is R	18	P1″ PC	use Col.4; use Col.5	R = 2 new
48.2	49					
2.0	50	plus O	19	P1″ PC	PC Col.4 —; use Col.5 use Col.5	R = 2
50.2	51					
2.8	52	and C plus R.	20	P9 FNC	PC Col.5 —	
−1.2	53					
53.2	54	So I'll,	21	P1″ PC	use Col.2	
1.0	55					
−.2	56	letting S plus D			PC Col.2 —	
54.8	57					
2.8						
−.4						

TIME	DURATION	EMA	VERBALIZATIONS	NUMBER	PRO-DUC-TION	OPERA-TOR	GOAL STACK	EXPRESSIONS
		58		22	P9	FNC	use Col.2	
58.4	1.2	CRO(S)S						
	−.4	ROADS						
		DANGER						
		59		23	P3	AV	recall S ⟨replace A ∨ S Col.2⟩	
				24	P5	RA	recall S Col.1	
		60	So let the S	25	↑	RV		
59.6	2.2	CRO(S)S	already equals					
	−.4	ROAD(S)	one.					
		DANGER						
		61						
		62		26	P9	FNC	recall S Col.1 +	S ⟵ 1
61.8	.6	CROSS						
		ROADS						
		DANGER						
		63						
62.4	2.2	CR-O-SS						
	scan	ROAD-S	And					
		DANGER						
		64						
		65		27	P1″	PC	use Col.2	S ⟵ 1
		66	S plus					
64.6	4.2	CRO(S)S						
	−.2	ROADS						
		DANGE(R)						

Time		Diagram	Line	Utterance	No.			Annotation
			67					
68.8	1.2 −.2	CROSS ROADS DANGER	68 69	D equals E.	28	P2	FC	get E; get D; PC Col.2 i —
70.0	1.8 scan	CROSS ROAD-S DANGER	70 71	And there's no other E				
71.8	.8	CROSS ROADS DANGER	72	in the word.				
73.0	.8	CROSS ROADS DANGER	73		29	P2	FC	get E —; get D; PC Col.2 i — get D; PC Col.2 i —
74.4	1.0	CROSS ROADS DANGER	74	But	30	↑	PC	get D Col.6; PC Col.2 i —
		CROSS ROADS DANGER	75	D				
			76		31	cont	PC	get D Col.6 +; PC Col.2 i — PC Col.2 i

D = c6 new

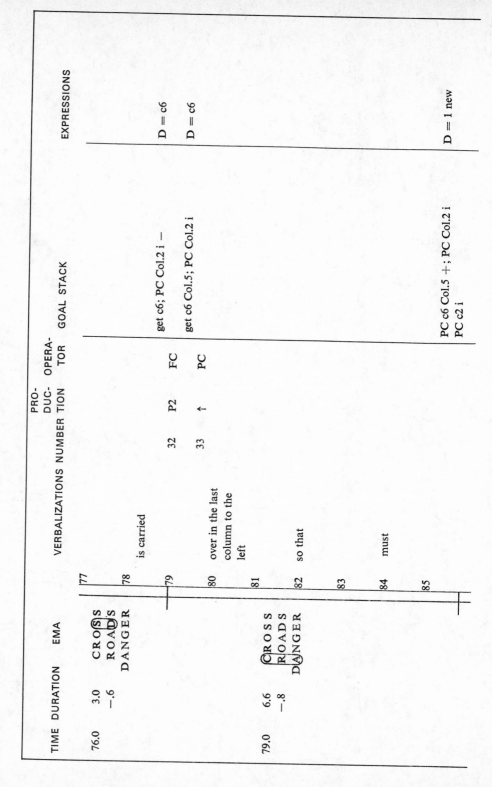

TIME	DURATION	EMA	VERBALIZATIONS	NUMBER	PRODUCTION	OPERATOR	GOAL STACK	EXPRESSIONS
76.0	3.0	CRO(S)S ROA(D)S DANGER		77				
	−.6		is carried	78				
				79	32	FC	get c6; PC Col.2 i −	D = c6
			over in the last column to the	80	33 ↑	PC	get c6 Col.5; PC Col.2 i	D = c6
			left	81				
79.0	6.6	(C)ROSS ROADS (DA)NGER	so that	82				
	−.8			83				
			must	84				
				85			PC c6 Col.5 +; PC Col.2 i PC c2 i	D = 1 new

Line	Prod	Op	Description	Result
34	P11	TD	recall S; TD D i; PC Col.2 i	D = 1 new
35	P15	RA	recall S Col.1; TD D i; PC Col.2 i	D = 1 new
36	↑	RV	recall S Col.1 +; TD D i; PC Col.2 i	S ⟵ 1; D = 1 new
37	cont	TD	TD D i; PC Col.2 i	
38	P7	AV	TD D −; PC Col.2 −	S ⟵ 1☐; D = 1 new
39	P2	FC	get S; AV S Col.1 i	D = 1 new
40	↑	PC	get S Col.2; AV S Col.1 i	D = 1 new
41	P14	RA	check D; AV S Col.1 i	D = 1?
42	↑	PC	check D Col.5; AV S Col.1 i	D = 1?

Value	Δ	Line	Display	Text
85.6	.8	86	CRO(S)S / ROADS / DANGER	be a one.
		87		
86.4	4.6 / −.4	88	CRO(S)S / ROADS / DANGER	Therefore S cannot be one.
		89		
		90		We'll change S.
		91		
91.2	1.8 / −.4	92	CRO(S)S / ROADS / DANGER	To begin
		93		
93.0	3.2 / −.2	94	(CRO)SS / (ROA)DS / DANGER	with we'll let D equal one.
		95		

TIME	DURATION	EMA	VERBALIZATIONS	NUMBER	PRO-DUCTION	OPERA-TOR	GOAL STACK	EXPRESSIONS
		96		43	cont	AV	check D Col.5 +; AV S Col.1 i AV C Col.1 i	D = 1
96.6	2.8	97 CROS(S) ROAD(S) DANGER						
		98	And let S equal					
		99		44	P2	FC	get S; AV S Col.1 i	D = 1
99.4	2.0 −.6	100 CRO(S)S ROADS DANGER		45	↑	PC	get S Col.2; AV S Col.1 i	D = 1
		101						
		102	uh	46	cont	AV	get S Col.2 −; AV S Col.1 i AV S Col.1 i	
		103						
101.4	8.4 −.6	104 CRO[S S] ROAD[S] DANGER	say two.	47	P1′	PC	AV S Col.1 +	S ⟵ 2 new
		105						

48	P11	TD	PC Col.1 +	R = 4 new; S ← 2
49	P1	FC	TD R +	R = 4 new
50	P1″	PC	use Col.5	R = 4 new
51	P14	RA	check Col.2; PC Col.5 i	R = 4 new
52	↑	PC	check c2 Col.1; PC Col.5 i	R = 4 new

106

107

108 Therefore, R

109

110 will equal four.

110.4   1.2
         −.2

111 CROSS
     ROADS
     DANGER

112

113

112.4   3.6

114 CROSS
     ROADS
     DANGER

115

TIME	DURATION	EMA	VERBALIZATIONS	PRODUC-TION NUMBER	OPERA-TOR	GOAL STACK	EXPRESSIONS
			116			check c2 Col.1 +; PC Col.5 i	t2 = 0 new
						PC Col.5 i	
			117				
			118 And C plus R	53 cont	PC		
			119				
			120				
			121				
116.0	12.8	CROSS	122 has to equal				
	−.6	ROADS	123				
		DANGER	124 ten or				$C + R \geq 10$

125				
126	greater.			
127				
128	Therefore C must equal	54	P15	RA	recall R; PC Col.5 i	$C \geq 10 - R$
129		55	↑	RV	recall R Col.1; PC Col.5 i	$C \geq 10 - R$
130	six				
131		56	cont	PC	recall R Col.1 +; PC Col.5 i PC Col.5 i	$R = 4; C \geq 10 - R$
132	or greater.				
133		57	P4	AV	PC Col.5 +	$C \geq 6$ new
134					
135					

128.8   1.8
         −.4

CROS Ⓢ Ⓢ
ROADS
DANGER

130.6   8.4
         −.8

Ⓒ R O S S
Ⓡ O A D S
D Ⓐ Ⓝ G E R

NUMBER	VERBALIZATIONS	PRODUCTION NUMBER	OPERATOR	GOAL STACK	EXPRESSIONS	TIME	DURATION	EMA
136	So we'll let C							
137								
138	equal							
139								
140	see C equal six.	58	P1′	PC	AV Col.5 +	C ← 6 new			
141								
142	And A is zero.	59	P11	TD	PC Col.5 +	A = 0 new; C ← 6	139.6	3.6 / −.2	CROSS ROADS DANGER
143		60	P1	FC	TD A +	A = 0 new			
144					use Col.3	A = 0 new	143.2	1.8 / scan	CROSS ROADS DANGER

A = 0 new

61	P1″	PC	check A	A = 0?
62	P14	RA	check A Col.5 i	A = 0?
63	↑	PC	recall C; PC A Col.5 i	A = 0?
64	P15	RA	recall C Col.5; PC A Col.5 i	A = 0?
65	↑	RV	recall C Col.5 +; PC A Col.5 i PC A Col.5 i	C ← 6; A = 0?
66	cont	PC		
67	P15	RA	recall R; PC A Col.5 i	C ← 6; A = 0?
68	↑	RV	recall R Col.1; PC A Col.5 i	C ← 6; A = 0?
			recall R Col.1 +; PC A Col.5 i PC A Col.5 i	R = 4; C ← 6; A = 0?

145.0 2.2 −.4	145	CROSS ROADS DANGER	
	146		
147.2 .6	147	CRO(S)S ROADS DANGER	
	148	CROSS ROADS DANGER	So we'll let
	149		
	150		C equal six.
148.0 6.0 −.2	151	CROSS ROADS DANGER	
	152		
	153		
154.0 1.0 scan	154	CRO-S ROADS DANGER	
	155	DANGER	

TIME	DURATION	EMA	VERBALIZATIONS	NUMBER	PRODUCTION NUMBER	PRODUCTION	OPERATOR	GOAL STACK	EXPRESSIONS
155.0	3.4	CROSS ROADS DANGER		156	69	cont	PC		A = 0; R = 4; C ← 6
				157	70	P9	FNC	PC A Col.5 +	
			So we'll go back	158	71	P1″	PC	use Col.2	
				159					
			to S plus D.	160	72	P15	RA	recall S; PC Col.2 i	
				161					
158.4	8.8	CROSS ROADS DANGER	S	162	73	↑	RV	recall S Col.1; PC Col.2 i	S ← 2
	−.8			163				recall S Col.1 +; PC Col.2 i	
			equals two	164	74	cont	PC	PC Col.2 i	

75	P15	RA	recall D; PC Col.2 i	S ← 2
76	↑	RV	recall D Col.5; PC Col.2 i	S ← 2
77	cont	PC	recall D Col. 5 +; PC Col.2 i PC Col.2 i	D = 1; S ← 2
78	P11	TD	PC Col.2 +	E = 3 new
79	P1	FC	TD E +	E = 3 new

165

166

167

168 and S plus

169

170 D equals one.

171

172 Therefore E

173

174 equals three.

175

167.2
1.2
-.2

CRO(S)S
RO(A)DS
DANGER

169.2
5.4
-.4

CRO(S)S
ROADS
DAN(G)E(R)

TIME	DURATION	EMA	VERBALIZATIONS	NUMBER	PRO-DUC-TION NUMBER	OPERA-TOR	GOAL STACK	EXPRESSIONS
174.6	1.8 −.6	CROSS ROADS DANGER		176				
				177				
				178				
				179				
					80	P9	FNC	∅	E = 3 new
					81	P1''	PC	use Col.3	
177.2	3.6 −.6	CROSS ROADS DANGER						
			Now we have O	180				
				181				
					82	P2	FC	get O; PC Col.3 i	
			plus A. Let's	182				
					83	↑	PC	get O Col.4; PC Col.3 i	
180.8	1.6	CROSS ROADS DANGER						
				183				
					84	cont	PC	PC O Col.4 −; PC Col.3 i / PC Col.3 i	
182.4	1.2	CROSS ROADS DANGER	see	184				
					85	P15	RA	recall A; PC Col.3 i	

183.6	3.6 scan	CROSS ROADS DANGER	185						
			186						
186.8	.8	CROSS ROADS DANGER	187		86	↑	RV	recall A Col.5; PC Col.3 i	A = 0
187.6	2.0 scan	CROSS ROADS DANGER	188	A	87	cont	PC	recall A Col.5 +; PC Col.3 i / PC Col.3 i	A = 0
			189		88	P14	RA	check A, PC Col.3 i	
189.6	5.6	CROSS ROADS DANGER	190	has to equal zero	89	↑	PC	check A Col.5; PC Col.3 i	A = 0
			191						
			192	uh, C					
			193						
			194	plus R.					

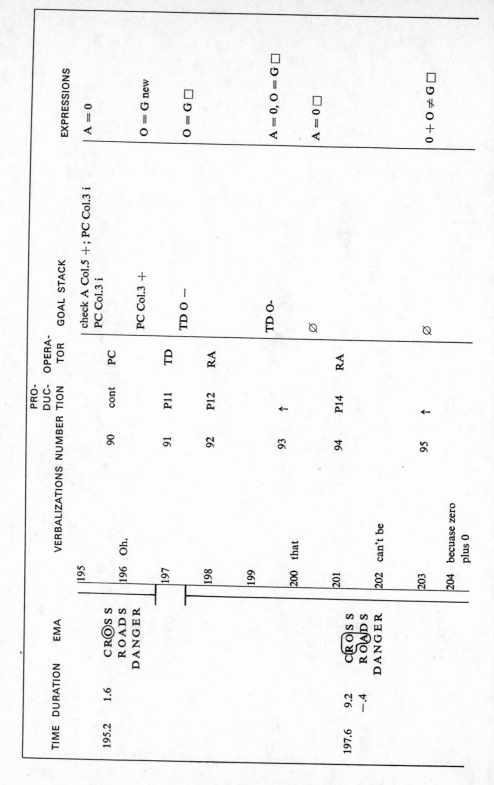

TIME	DURATION	EMA	VERBALIZATIONS	NUMBER	PRODUCTION NUMBER	PRODUCTION	OPERATOR	GOAL STACK	EXPRESSIONS
195.2	1.6	CR(O)S S ROADS DANGER		195				check A Col.5 +; PC Col.3 i PC Col.3 i	A = 0
			Oh.	196	90	cont	PC		O = G new
				197	91	P11	TD	PC Col.3 +	O = G □
				198	92	P12	RA	TD 0 −	O = G □
				199					
			that	200	93	↑		TD 0-	A = 0, O = G □
				201	94	P14	RA	∅	A = 0 □
197.6	9.2 −.4	CR(OS S RO(A)DS DANGER	can't be	202					
				203	95	↑		∅	
			becuase zero plus 0	204					0 + O ≠ G □

205				
206	won't equal G.			
207	96	P7	AV	∅	get C, AV C i
208				

End of first quarter

T1.8   Initially the goal stack is empty. This evokes FNC, which finds the next unprocessed column, i.e., column 1. It records this by setting up the goal (use col.1). During FNC there is a general orientation to the display.

T7.4   (use col.1) evokes P1″, which starts to process the column.

T10.0   The experimenter interrupts the processing of column 1 with a request that the subject talk. When E first interrupts, there is a short scan of the eyes, then a brief return to column 1, then another scan when subjects says "Yes." We have put in a new goal type (*attend*) and two new operators, INT (to handle the interrupt) and ANS (to generate the answer), in order to show the orderly retention of the goal (PC col.1). No additional behavior is exhibited that would serve to define these operators or the attend goal type.

T14.2   S having answered the E successfully, the goal stack pops to bring (PC col.1 i) to the top, which then evokes the continuation of PC. There is a long (8-second) EMA on column 1 while PC is processed. This obtains the expression ($R = 2S$ new), which we parenthesize, since it is not admitted by the problem-space definition of Figure 7.27 and represents only an intermediate product. Another example of an intermediate product that is articulated occurs at T116.0. The actual output from PC is two goals (get R) and (get S). The evidence for this is (1) the EMA at T22.8 and the EMA and remark at T24.0, and (2) the similar behavior at T64.6 where (get E) and (get D) are produced from PC operating on column 2. Without the eye-movement evidence, the utterance at T24.0 would probably be taken to indicate an occurrence of FNC (which, of course, remains an alternative explanation, with some other explanation for the EMA at T22.8 to column 4).

T22.8   The goal (get R) evokes P2, from which first FC finds column 4 and then PC operates on it, leading to no information. At each step the (get R) goal acquires some additional specifications, first a column from FC, then a failure signal from PC. This leads to popping the stack, to reveal the goal (get S).

T24.0   A similar sequence of goal specification and then failure takes place for (get S). This leads to popping the stack again to reveal the PC goal that produced the two subgoals. This goal has been marked by the signal i−, which is to be interpreted as a failure if all subgoals fail and as an interruption if a subgoal succeeds. That is, if (get S) or (get R) produced an expression, then (PC col.1) would have continued. (An instance where it does continue occurs at T76.0.) Goals are marked conditionally interrupted (i−) only when it is known at the time of interruption that there is nothing else to do if the subgoals fail. This occurs only when the operators themselves generate subgoals and thus have this information available. An alternative processing structure would be always to return to the supergoal, simply exiting immediately from it if there is nothing more to do. However, this would imply that the eyes should return to the column of the supergoal. In the present case we would expect a return to column 1, before the scan at T26.8. (Actually, the little display is deceptive, since it makes it look as if the scan first went to the top S in column 1 and then out to G and A; in fact it went the other way—from N to A to G to the S of column 1 and back to column 2.)

T26.8   The top goal is now − (fail). It is not popped (see Figure 7.28), since it is the last goal in the stack. FNC is evoked via production P9. Thus, P9 is the backup production that drives the system when there is nothing else to do. It determines that S2 will work basically from right to left, as in doing a standard addition problem. In this case, it returns S2 to column 1, since that is the rightmost column that is unspecified. Again, FNC is associated with a scan of the entire display.

T28.8   The eye movements reveal that S attends to column 1. However, since PC has been tried and failed, production P3 (rather than P1″) is evoked, leading to the assignment operator, AV. The condition of P3 requires memory of path behavior. Here the information is available in the immediate past. Possibly a representation should be used that makes the information available in an expression in STM (e.g., as information associated with column 1 per se). The AV operator (similarly to the PC operator) evokes subgoals about the other letters in the column. Thus, AV does not simply make the assignment; it first sets up the subgoal (get R).

T31.4   The goal (get R) again evokes P2, which evokes FC to get column 4 and then PC to operate on column 4. The evidence for this lies in the eye movements, and also in the break in the utterance at T34, indicating that attention is somewhere other than on the assignment itself. However, from the break alone we would be hard put to verify what sort of attention displacement had occurred. There is a scan at T32.0. Possibly this should be combined with the short attention unit at T31.4, all as part of the eye movements associated with FC. Our model is not quite precise enough to tell.

T34.4   Attention returns to column 1 with the return of (AV S col.1 i) to the top of the stack. In general, attention is always directed at the column of the top goal. Though no information was forthcoming, from the subgoal (get R) an assignment is still made (notice that the AV goal was marked i and not i— when it was pushed down). AV now produces the assignment (S ← 1 new); i.e., it starts at the first digit, which is 1, rather than 0.

T36.4   The situation now is that AV has succeeded (AV S col.1 +) and a new expression is available (S ← 1 new). Under these conditions P1′ is evoked, rather than P9, though the conditions of both are satisfied. A long EMA occurs on column 1 that corresponds to the PC operation of adding 1 and 1 to get 2. Addition of two digits need not take very long, when a human is set to do the task. In the midst of other problem solving activities, as here, it seems to take several seconds. The result, of course, is (R = 2 new). This evokes P11 and TD, which does not produce any significant output, i.e., (TD R +). (Thus P11 dominates P1, whose condition is also satisfied.) There is no direct evidence for TD. The eye movements stay at column 1 and there is no indicative verbalization. TD occurs here because of the structure of the production system. Later on, of course, direct evidence occurs for TD, when there is an illegal assignment (e.g., T86.4).

T43.8   Following the generation of some new information, P1 is evoked to make use of it. First FC is executed, as evidenced by the long scan. This leads to the generation of two goals, (use col.4) and (use col.5). Both the eye-movement evidence and the utterances confirm that both columns were considered. EMA at T47.4, which attends to column 5 before column 4, makes it appear that both columns were generated and column 5 remembered before any column processing occurred. This is what the production of the two goals accomplishes. We have other evidence for the generation of more than one goal by P2 (T14.2 and T64.6). Furthermore, P2 goes from column 4 to column 5 without any return to column 1, which would be expected if there were a second independent attempt to use (R = 2 new) by, say, evoking P1 again. Thus, the evidence for FC finding the two columns is reasonably good. If this is the case, however, why didn't FC find both columns at the earlier occasions (T22.8, T32.0)? There is certainly a difference in the occasions: namely, whether one is looking for information or whether one has information in hand. But it is not clear that this ought to create the difference—i.e., to make the earlier FC's more tentative.

T48.2   The two goals lead to successive applications of PC to the two columns, each of which fails to generate any new information. This empties the goal stack (down to the last failed PC) and paves the way for another application of FNC (at T53.2), which directs attention to column 2, column 1 having been fully specified.

3

LOGIC

8

LOGIC:
Task Analysis

In Part III, consisting of Chapters 8 through 10, we examine human performance in a second task—solving problems in a simple system of symbolic logic. In a sense this label for the task is misleading, since the subjects whose behavior will be examined were not told that they were concerned with symbolic logic, but instead that they were to "recode" certain strings of symbols into other, specified, strings, using a given set of rules to transform the strings. The task was developed by O. K. Moore and Scarvia Anderson (1954a).

THE TASK

The subject, facing a blackboard, has before him (Figure 8.1) a sheet of paper with twelve rules for manipulating parenthesized expressions containing letters connected by *dots* (·), *wedges* (∨), *horseshoes* (⊃), and *tildes* (~). The connectors stand respectively for *and*, *or*, *implies*, and *not*. However, the subject is not told this and in fact does not discover this interpretation; hence, he treats the connectors

405

FIGURE 8.1

rule sheet used by subjects with logic problems

RULES FOR HANDLING THE CODE

** Arrows Show Direction In Which Recoding May Take Place **

First Set

1. AvB ─────→ BvA
   A·B ─────→ B·A

   Use only with wedge or dot.
   Trade places. No sign changes.

2. A⊃B ─────→ ~B⊃~A

   Use only with horseshoe.
   Trade places. Two sign changes:
   A part and B part.

3. AvA ←──→ A
   A·A ←──→ A

   No sign change.

4. Av(BvC) ←──→ (AvB)vC
   A·(B·C) ←──→ (A·B)·C

   No place changes. No sign changes
   Only grouping changes.

Second Set

5. AvB ←──→ ~(~A·~B)

   Use only with wedge or dot.
   Three sign changes: A part,
   B part, and total wedge or
   dot expression.

6. A⊃B ←──→ ~AvB

   Use only with wedge or horseshoe.
   One sign change: A part.

7. Av(B·C) ←──→ (AvB)·(AvC)
   A·(BvC) ←──→ (A B)v(A·C)

   No sign changes.

Third Set

8. A·B ──→ A
   A·B ──→ B

   Use only with major dot and positive total expression. No
   sign changes.

9. A ───→ AvX

   X may be any coded expression.
   No sign changes

10. A
    B ───→ A·B

    A and B represent two lines of the
    message. No sign changes.

11. A⊃B
    A ───→ B

    A⊃B line must be positive;
    horseshoe must be major connective.
    No sign changes.

12. A⊃B
    B⊃C ───→ A⊃C

    Both horseshoe lines must be
    positive. Horseshoes must be
    major connectives. No sign
    changes.

entirely in terms of their syntactic properties and without reference to semantic meaning.[1]

The rules of Figure 8.1 show that expressions of certain forms (at the tails of the arrows) can be *transformed* into expressions of different forms (at the heads of the arrows). Transformations designated by double-headed arrows can occur in either direction. Unlike the form of logic considered in Chapter 4 for LT, double negation is handled implicitly. That is, the rules make changes in sign, so that multiple negation signs never arise. Thus R2 (A $\supset$ B $\rightarrow$ $\sim$B $\supset$ $\sim$A) can be applied to $\sim$P $\supset$ Q by setting A = $\sim$P and B = Q; it yields $\sim$Q $\supset$ P as a result, rather than $\sim$Q $\supset$ $\sim\sim$P.

A problem is formulated in this task environment by giving the subject a set of expressions and requesting that he transform these ("recode" was the phrase used) into another specified expression. Figure 8.2 gives a number of problems: three practice problems, $\alpha 1$–$\alpha 3$, and sixteen regular ones that systematically vary the number of given expressions between one and four. [It is also possible to construct problems with several desired expressions, the task being either to obtain any one of them, or to obtain all. Such problems have been investigated by Anderson (1957), but we will not consider them here.]

The organization of the blackboard is illustrated in Figure 8.3, which shows the solution to problem D1 (S4's solution,[2] in fact). The experimenter instructs the subject that his task is to obtain the desired expression (written in the upper right quadrant), using the twelve rules. We will always call the desired expression L0, and the given expressions L1, . . . , Ln. The subject can ask the experimenter at any time to apply one of the rules to an expression (or pair of expressions, respectively) that is already on the blackboard. If the transformation is legitimate, the experimenter writes down the new expression in the left-hand column (continuing the numbering), with the name of the rule in the right-hand column beside it. Thus, there is at each moment an external record of the rule applications officially made up to that moment, and these form the base for subsequent actions. The expressions in the lower left quadrant are called the derived expressions. As soon as one of them is the same as L0, the problem is solved.

We have data from two groups of subjects: (1) sixty-four subjects (run by Carpenter, Moore, and others at Yale University[3]) each of whom attempted all of

[1] The tilde ($\sim$), standing for *not*, is a partial exception, since many subjects notice that, in appearance and properties, it resembles *negative* or *minus*—for example, that pairs of tildes, like pairs of negatives and minus signs, cancel.

[2] None of the subjects in cryptarithmetic was a subject in logic (or in chess). Thus, S4 is simply a particular subject in the logic task environment.

[3] We are grateful to O. K. Moore and his associates for their kindness in allowing us to use their data and in providing us with a complete copy of the raw data sheets. Their experiment was run as part of a study of the effect of alcohol on problem solving, but since the design of their experiment was carefully counterbalanced, and all subjects and problems received the same range of alcohol treatments, and since the effects of the alcohol were small, we have used throughout the data for all subjects on each problem. For the Yale group's analysis of these data, see Carpenter, Moore, Snyder, and Lisansky (1961). They show that the largest amounts of alcohol (equivalent to about three martinis!) caused about a 30 percent decrement in performance, and smaller amounts no significant decrement. (The relative numbers of problems solved with 0, 1, 2, and 3 units of alcohol were 1, 1.1, 1.1, and 0.7, respectively. *Op cit.*, p. 201.)

FIGURE 8.2

PROBLEM		GIVEN L'S	LO
α1	L1	R·(~P ⊃ Q)	(Q ∨ P)·R
α2	L1	~S·(S ∨ ~Q)	~Q
α3	L1	(P·Q) ∨ (P·~P)	P ⊃ Q
A1	L1	(~P·Q) ∨ (P·~P)	Q
A2	L1	P·(Q·R)	T·T
	L2	~(R ⊃ T) ⊃ ~(P·Q)	
A3	L1	P ∨ (Q ∨ R)	~Q ⊃ ~S
	L2	~(Q ∨ R)	
	L3	S ⊃ ~P	
A4	L1	P ∨ Q	P ∨ T
	L2	~R ⊃ ~Q	
	L3	S	
	L4	R ⊃ ~S	
B1	L1	(P·~P)·(R ⊃ T)	Q ∨ S
B2	L1	(P ∨ Q) ⊃ ~(~R ∨ P)	~Q
	L2	~[~(S·Q) ∨ R]	
B3	L1	~P ⊃ Q	Q ∨ S
	L2	~R ⊃ Q	
	L3	~P ∨ ~R	
B4	L1	(P ∨ P) ⊃ ~Q	(S·R) ∨ T
	L2	Q ∨ R	
	L3	R ⊃ S	
	L4	P	
C1	L1	(P ∨ Q)·(Q ⊃ R)	P ∨ (Q·R)
C2	L1	(P·Q) ∨ (P·T)	Q ∨ R
	L2	T ⊃ (P·R)	
C3	L1	~S	~ Q
	L2	R ∨ S	
	L3	(P ⊃ Q) ⊃ ~R	
C4	L1	P ⊃ Q	~P ∨ (~T·R)
	L2	~R ⊃ (P·Q)	
	L3	Q ⊃ ~T	
	L4	(P·Q) ⊃ ~P	
D1	L1	(R ⊃ ~P)·(~R ⊃ Q)	~(~Q·P)
D2	L1	(P ∨ Q) ⊃ R	~P ∨ S
	L2	R ⊃ S	
D3	L1	(P ⊃ Q) ⊃ ~R	~Q
	L2	R ∨ S	
	L3	~S	
D4	L1	(P ∨ Q) ⊃ (R ∨ S)	S
	L2	P	
	L3	~T ⊃ ~(Q ∨ R)	
	L4	~T	

FIGURE 8.3

display for logic task (showing S4's solution to D1)

1.	$(R \supset \sim P) \cdot (\sim R \supset Q)$	$\sim (\sim Q \cdot P)$
2.	$(\sim R \lor \sim P) \cdot (R \lor Q)$	Rule 6 applied to left and right of 1.
3.	$(\sim R \lor \sim P) \cdot (\sim R \supset Q)$	Rule 6 applied to left of 1.
4.	$R \supset \sim P$	Rule 8 applied to 1 (left).
5.	$\sim R \lor \sim P$	Rule 6 applied to 4.
6.	$\sim R \supset Q$	Rule 8 applied to 1 (right).
7.	$R \lor Q$	Rule 6 applied to 6.
8.	$(\sim R \lor \sim P) \cdot (R \lor Q)$	Rule 10 applied to 5. and 7.
9.	$P \supset \sim R$	Rule 2 applied to 4.
10.	$\sim Q \supset R$	Rule 2 applied to 6.
11.	$P \supset Q$	Rule 12 applied to 6 and 9.
12.	$\sim P \lor Q$	Rule 6 applied to 11.
13.	$\sim (P \cdot \sim Q)$	Rule 5 applied to 12.
14.	$\sim (\sim Q \cdot P)$	Rule 1 applied to 13. QED.

the sixteen regular problems, with a time limit of fifteen minutes per problem; (2) ten subjects (run at Carnegie Institute of Technology) who attempted one to six problems each, with a time limit of thirty minutes per problem. The subjects in the Yale experiments were undergraduates, those in the Carnegie Tech studies undergraduate and graduate students. The problems used in the Carnegie Tech studies were chosen from among those used at Yale (and, in addition, the α-problems).

In both studies the subjects instructed the experimenter aloud to make specified transformations on the blackboard. The list of transformed expressions, together with the expressions transformed in each case, the rule applied, and the time elapsed constitute the data in the Yale experiment. In the Carnegie study, times were not recorded, but the subjects were instructed to think aloud, thus providing protocols.

In the Carnegie Tech study the subjects had studied the rules and solved (or were helped to solve) the three relatively easy practice problems ($\alpha 1$–$\alpha 3$). They then attempted problem D1, followed by C1. Protocols were not taken for all problems for all subjects. In all of our analyses, we will consider all the protocols that are available for a particular problem.

As in the chapters on cryptarithmetic, we will first analyze the task environment, then examine some human behavior in detail, then take a broader view. Throughout, we will respond directly to the nature of the task and to the data, relatively independently of the analysis of cryptarithmetic in the previous section. Therefore, we will be asking once again (1) whether humans can be described as working in problem spaces, (2) what sorts of problem solving organizations and heuristics they exhibit, and (3) to what extent their behavior is determined by the demands of the task environment or by their own characteristics, respectively.

Our exploration of the task environment will first take up the basic problem space in which all behavior in these problems occurs. Then, instead of considering a number of alternative problem solving schemes, we will focus on a single program called the General Problem Solver (GPS). We will consider GPS here only as an example of a problem solving IPS for logic, leaving to the next chapter its use as a model for human behavior.

Finally, we will examine somewhat more closely the sources of problem difficulty, drawing on some of the data of the 64 Yale subjects, because (as we have remarked often already) human data are often best viewed as revealing the structure of the task environment.

THE PROBLEM SPACE

The logic problems shown in Figure 8.2 can be formulated in the natural basic problem space in which the elements are logic expressions and the operators are the given rules. In this space, the initial state is the one (or several) logic expressions L1 (L2, . . .) and the final desired state is L0. The actual knowledge state consists of all expressions derived to a given point, each application of an operator (if successful) adding a new expression to the collection. Some of the operators (the rules) take as input a single expression, and some (R10, R11, and R12) take as inputs a pair of expressions.

Since these are clearly search problems, we can get a feeling for the size of the search by assuming various simple search schemes, as we did in Chapter 4, along the lines of the British Museum algorithm. As the simplest scheme we might assume that the twelve operators are applicable at each point, so that to find the seven-step proof of D1 (embedded in Figure 8.3) would require threading a 12^7 ($\sim 4 \times 10^7$) maze. A moment's examination of the operators, however, reveals some opposing effects on the size of the maze. On the side of decreased growth, not every operator is applicable to every expression. In fact some, like R7, rarely are. On the side of increased growth there are three factors. First, many operators can be applied to subexpressions as well as to the total expression (e.g., R6 transforms $P \vee (Q \supset R)$ to $P \vee (\sim Q \vee R)$). Second, operators that take two expressions as inputs add new expressions to the system in proportion to the square of the number of available expressions, rather than linearly with the number of available expressions as we have assumed in positing simple exponential growth. This can be seen most strikingly with R10, which combines any two derived expressions to form their conjunction, thus assuring growth at exactly the square of the number of previously derived expressions. The third factor leading to growth is R9, which permits creation of arbitrarily large numbers of new expressions at any time, simply by substituting an arbitrary expression for the X.

These complications require more subtlety in estimating the size of the search space. All three of the expanding effects we have just listed are related to the size of the expressions involved. The number of subexpressions to which operators may apply depends on expression size, and both R9 and R10 produce expressions that are larger than their input expressions. But the starting and terminal expressions (L1 and L0) provide approximate bounds on the sizes of plausible intermediate expressions (and on the constants, e.g., P, Q, . . . , that should be introduced in forming new expressions for R9).

The situation may usefully be viewed as in Figure 8.4, where the total problem space is depicted schematically as a series of concentric rings, each ring representing the expressions of a given size. We can measure the size of an expression by the

FIGURE 8.4

graphic representation of logic-problem space

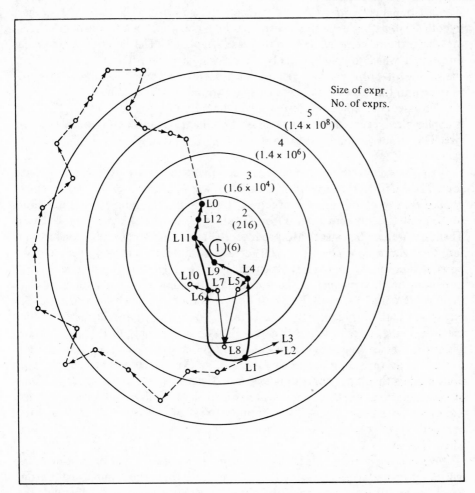

[4] The number of expressions is given by $e(n) = g(n) \cdot 2^s \cdot 3^c \cdot t^n$, where s is the number of signs, c is the number of connectives, t is the number of terms, and $g(n)$ is the number of distinct ways of parenthetically grouping an expression of n terms. The formula is really a function of just n and t, since $c = n - 1$, $s = n + c = 2n - 1$, and

$$g(n) = \frac{1}{n}\binom{2n - 2}{n - 1}.$$

number of terms (constants or variables) it contains, and the number of possible expressions containing n terms can then be determined. We have written these (approximate) numbers in the figure, assuming that only three distinct letters (e.g., P, Q, R) are used.[4] The number of expressions increases by a factor of approximately 100 with each increase of one in size of expression. Thus the number of expressions rises much faster than the increase in area on the figure indicates.

Solving a problem requires a trip from one point in the area to another. Two such trips are shown in the figure for problem D1, which starts with a four term expression (L1), searching for a two-term expression (L0). The rather direct search (solid line) corresponds to the solution shown in Figure 8.3; the other, hypothetical, path (dashed line) corresponds to going the long way around—making things more complex before they are simplified. The latter is an unlikely direction in which to search, initially, and we will have something to say later about the nature of problems that require such excursions. For the moment we are interested in the growth of the search space within each size domain.

To assess the latter, we must evaluate the frequency with which each operator is applicable to expressions of a given size, producing expressions of another given size. This is not very difficult to do if a little care is taken in enumerating possible cases.

To show how these numbers are computed, consider expressions of size four. These derive from applications of R1, R2, R4, R5, and R6. R1, for instance, applies to any of the three connective locations in an expression of size four, but only if the connective is ($\vee$) or ($\cdot$)—that is, only two out of three cases. Therefore R1 can be expected to produce $3 \cdot (\frac{2}{3}) = 2$ four-term expressions from a four-term expression. The assessment for R4 is a little more subtle. There are two possible subexpressions to which R4 might apply. Its applicability might be thought to depend on the structure of the four-term expression—e.g., on whether it is of the form ((A B)(C D) or (A(B(C D)))—but it doesn't. For each subexpression R4 requires that the two connectives be both ($\vee$) or both ($\cdot$), and furthermore that the sign of the subpart be positive—e.g., R4 does not apply to $P \vee \sim(Q \vee R)$. These requirements give frequencies of $(\frac{2}{3})(\frac{1}{3})(\frac{1}{2})$ for each of the two opportunities, so that the average contribution of R4 is $\frac{2}{9}$ of an expression. Not all the contributions are less than one. For instance, if we consider the generation of expressions of size four from an expression of size two, then R9 will apply to each possible expression of size two, thus contributing a total of 216 expressions. This high productivity, of course, is the very reason why R9 (and similarly R10) is to be used with discretion.

We can use these productivities to estimate the number of expressions that will be available at each stage of search, starting from some initial expression. From the numbers of expressions of different sizes at each stage, we compute the numbers at the next stage. The top curve of Figure 8.5 shows the total number of expressions of all sizes resulting from such a calculation (taking into account only expressions with ten or less terms). Since the growth of expressions is exponential, we plot the logarithm of the number of expressions as the ordinate (thus a growth of $10^{\alpha t}$ appears as a line of slope α). We have started with a single expression of size four, corresponding to L1 of Problem D1. The actual growth rate turns out to be about thirty-fold per step.

FIGURE 8.5

growth of numbers of expressions (for specified limits on maximum size of expression)

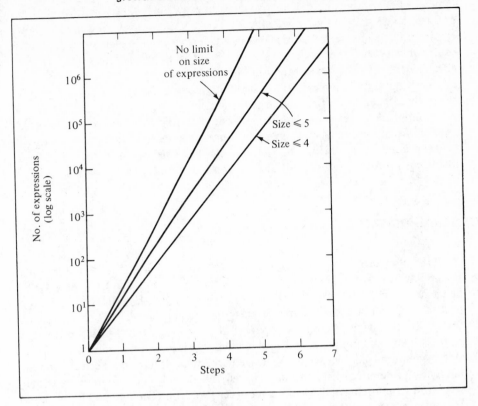

Many of the assumptions behind such an estimate reflect gross aspects of problem solving strategy. For instance, in computing the curve of the figure we ignored the contributions of R9 and R10, since these would swamp the calculations. But it is also plausible to exclude them, since even a brute-force problem solver could not afford to use them very often. Another assumption behind the upper curve is that all expressions of whatever size will be kept, and in fact many expressions of small size are generated by generating large ones and then breaking them up. We might expect a problem solver to discriminate against large expressions—this is exactly the strategy that the direct path of Figure 8.4 suggests. Since we have stratified the expressions of the space by size, it is easy to examine how strong the effect of such discrimination might be. The two lower curves of Figure 8.5 assume that no expressions greater than 5 (or greater than 4) will be generated. Thus, the middle curve assumes the problem solver is willing to consider expressions a little more complex than the original four-term expression. The lower curve rejects any additional complexity at all. As we see, with these limits on size of expressions, the growth rate becomes much smaller, declining to about 12 and 9 per step, respectively. It is still large enough to preclude brute-force forward search.

This sort of rough estimation of the size of search spaces might also be carried out for other assumptions. For instance, as Figure 8.4 shows, only a limited total

413

number of distinct expressions of small size exist—6 of size one, 216 of size two, etc. But our calculation scheme does not take this limit into account; it permits the number of expressions in each size category to grow indefinitely—as it would for a problem solver that did not check for duplicates. Alternatively, if duplicates were eliminated, the number of expressions in a category would reach an asymptote at some value, say half the maximum size. Allowing for duplicates, however, has small effect on the overall growth rate, one too slight to show on the graph of Figure 8.5. The limitation becomes effective first with the smallest expressions, which have relatively little effect on the total growth rate.

Simplified models like this one provide a feeling for the amount of search required to find solutions by simple procedures. These calculations provide us with a background against which to view the mechanisms and heuristics of a more intelligent processing system (GPS) that works within this same space.

GPS, THE GENERAL PROBLEM SOLVER

GPS is a problem solving program developed initially by the authors and J. C. Shaw in 1957.[5] It grew out of the work on LT, described in Chapter 4. GPS's first task environment was the Moore-Anderson logic task, just as we have described it. GPS obtained its name of "general problem solver" because it was the first problem solving program to separate in a clean way a task-independent part of the system containing general problem solving mechanisms from a part of the system containing knowledge of the task environment. It has since been applied to a number of different tasks (Ernst and Newell, 1969), and other programs essentially similar in structure have worked on yet other problems (Quinlan and Hunt, 1968). However, our concern in this chapter is with logic. We will describe GPS in a task-independent way (indeed that is the natural way to describe it), but we will not assess its suitability to other task environments.

GPS operates on problems that can be formulated in terms of *objects* and *operators*. An operator is something that can be applied to certain objects to produce different objects (as a saw applied to logs produces boards). The objects can be characterized by the *features* they possess, and by the *differences* that can be observed between pairs of objects. Operators for a given task may be restricted to apply only to certain kinds of objects; and there may exist operators that apply to several objects as inputs, producing one or more objects as outputs (as the operation of adding two numbers produces a third number, their sum).

Various kinds of problems can be formulated in a task environment containing objects and operators: to transform a given object into another; to find an object possessing a given feature; to modify an object so that a given operator may be applied to it; and so on.

To specify problems and subproblems, GPS has a discrete set of goal types. We shall introduce two of these initially:

[5] An extensive treatment of GPS can be found in Ernst and Newell (1969), which includes references to other papers on GPS.

Transform Goal Type: Find a way to *transform* object.1 into object.2 (The objects, 1 and 2, may be any objects defined in specifying the task environment. The phrase "way to transform" implies "by applying a sequence of operators from the task environment.")

Apply Goal Type: *Apply* operator to object.1 (or to an object obtained from object.1 by admissible transformations).

An example of a transform goal is: Find an expression (L0) from an initial expression (L1). An example of an apply goal is: Apply a rule (R7) to an expression (L1).

With each goal type is associated a set of methods related to achieving goals of that type. The principal heuristics of GPS are embedded in the methods, so that the executive organization is quite simple.[6] As shown in Figure 8.6, when an attempt is made to achieve a goal, the goal is first evaluated to see whether it is worth achieving and whether achievement seems likely. If so, one of the methods is selected and executed. This leads either to success or to a repetition of the loop.

FIGURE 8.6

GPS executive program

```
achieve (goal):
1.     evaluate (goal),
            if reject stop and report fail;
2.     select method for goal,
            if none stop and report fail;
3.     apply method to goal,
            if succeed stop and report succeed,
            go to 1.
```

The executive in Figure 8.6 does not fully reflect the control structure of GPS, for in general the methods attempt to achieve a goal by creating subgoals, whose achievement is to aid in achieving the main goal. The methods then evoke the executive [i.e., the program: achieve(goal)] in order to attempt the subgoal. Thus, the methods are recursive, so that the attempt to achieve one goal leads to other goals, and these, in turn, to still others. In this way the methods form an organized, cooperating system of heuristics (though each method independently remains a rational approach to achieving goals of its goal type). This recursive structure makes GPS basically a depth-first problem solver, since each method attempts everything appropriate to achieving a subgoal before returning control to the method of the subgoal that evoked it.

---

[6] The version of GPS described in Ernst and Newell (1969) is more elaborate, but the simpler structure described here will serve our purposes.

The main methods of GPS jointly embody the heuristic of means-ends analysis (which we touched on briefly in the cryptarithmetic task). Means-ends analysis is typified by the following kind of common-sense argument:

> I want to take my son to nursery school. What's the difference between what I have and what I want? One of distance. What changes distance? My automobile. My automobile won't work. What is needed to make it work? A new battery. What has new batteries? An auto repair shop. I want the repair shop to put in a new battery; but the shop doesn't know I need one. What is the difficulty? One of communication. What allows communication? A telephone . . . and so on.

This kind of analysis—classifying things in terms of the functions they serve, and oscillating among ends, functions required, and means that perform them—forms the basic system of heuristic of GPS. More precisely, this means-ends system of heuristic assumes the following:

1. If an object is given that is not the desired one, differences will be detectable between the available object and the desired object.
2. Operators affect some features of their operands and leave others unchanged. Hence operators can be characterized by the changes they produce and can be used to try to eliminate differences between the objects to which they are applied and desired objects.
3. If a desired operator is not applicable, it may be profitable to modify its inputs so that it becomes applicable.
4. Some differences will prove more difficult to affect than others. It is profitable, therefore, to try to eliminate "difficult" differences, even at the cost of introducing new differences of lesser difficulty. This process can be repeated as long as progress is being made toward eliminating the more difficult differences.

To incorporate this heuristic in GPS, we expand the vocabulary of goal types to include:

Reduce Goal Type: Reduce the *difference* between object.1 and object.2 by modifying object.1.

The core of the system of functional analysis is given by three methods, one associated with each of the three goal types, as shown in Figures 8.7 and 8.8. The first figure presents methods in the traditional way, in a flow diagram; the second uses the notation of this book. The *transform method*, associated with the transform goal type, consists in: (1) matching object.1 to object.2 to find a difference between them; (2) setting up the *reduce subgoal* of reducing the difference, which, if achieved,

FIGURE 8.7

GPS methods—flow diagram

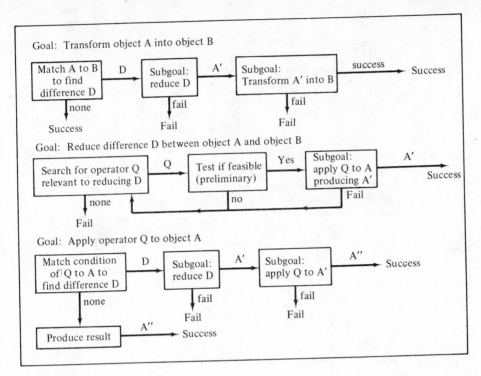

produces a new transformed object, object.3; (3) setting up the *transform type subgoal* of transforming object.3 into object.2. If this last goal is achieved, the original transform type goal is achieved. The match in step (1) tests for the more important differences first.

The apply-operator method, for achieving an apply type goal, consists in: (1) determining if the operator can be applied to the object immediately, and if so, applying it; (2) if not, setting up the *reduce* subgoal of reducing the difference that has been discovered between the object and condition(operator), the input form of the operator; (3) if the difference is reduced successfully, setting up the *apply* subgoal of applying the operator to the new object just produced. If the operator is applied in either (1) or (3), the new object is produced from product(operator), the output form of the operator. This method is appropriate where the operator is defined by two forms, one describing the input or conditions and the other the output, or product. The logic task has operators of this kind. Variants of this method exist for an operator defined by a program, described iteratively or recursively.

The *reduce method* for achieving a reduce type goal consists in: (1) searching for an operator that is relevant to reducing the difference; (2) if one is found, setting up the apply type goal of applying the operator, which, in case of success, produces the modified object.

417

FIGURE 8.8
GPS methods-program

Transform-method (transform object.1 into object.2) ($\Longrightarrow$ operator-list):
1. Match object.1 to object.2 ($\Longrightarrow$ difference),
    if no difference stop and report achieved;
2. Create-goal(reduce difference on object.1) ($\Longrightarrow$ goal);
3. Achieve(goal) ($\Longrightarrow$ new-object),
    if fail stop and report fail;
4. Create-goal(transform new-object into object.2) ($\Longrightarrow$ goal);
5. Achieve(goal),
    if fail stop and report fail,
    if achieved stop and report achieved.

Apply-operator-method (apply operator to object) ($\Longrightarrow$ new-object):
1. Match condition(operator) to object ($\Longrightarrow$ difference),
    if no difference go to 6;
2. Create-goal(reduce difference on object) ($\Longrightarrow$ goal);
3. Achieve(goal) ($\Longrightarrow$ modified-object),
    if fail stop and report fail;
4. Create-goal(apply operator to modified-object) ($\Longrightarrow$ goal);
5. Achieve(goal) ($\Longrightarrow$ new-object),
    if fail stop and report fail,
    if achieved stop and report achieved;
6. Copy product(operator) ($\Longrightarrow$ new-object),
    stop and report achieved.

Reduce-method (reduce difference on object) ($\Longrightarrow$ new-object):
1. Find-relevant-operator for difference ($\Longrightarrow$ operator),
    if fail stop and report fail;
2. Create-goal(apply operator to object) ($\Longrightarrow$ goal);
3. Achieve(goal) ($\Longrightarrow$ new-object),
    if fail go to 1,
    if achieved stop and report achieved.

GPS at Work: A Simple Example

This system of heuristics already gives GPS some problem solving ability that we can apply to the logic problems. To do so we must provide correlative definitions for objects, operators, and differences. These are summarized in Figure 8.9. From the definition of the problem space for logic given earlier, it is easy to see what corresponds to the objects and operators and to the initial and desired objects. However, the differences constitute new information, unique to means-ends problem solving in the problem space. (Other problem solving programs in this space would not use differences.)

We must also associate with each difference the operators that are relevant to modifying it. This is accomplished explicitly by the *table-of-connections* in Figure 8.9. Finally, we provide criteria of progress, in terms of a list of the differences in order of difficulty.

FIGURE 8.9

symbolic logic task environment

Differences. The differences apply to subexpressions as well as total expressions, and several differences may exist simultaneously for the same expressions.

Δt   A variable appears in one expression but not in the other.
E.g., $P \lor P$ differs by $+t$ from $P \lor Q$, since it needs a Q; $P \supset R$ differs by $-t$ from R, since it needs to lose the P.

Δn   A variable occurs different numbers of times in the two expressions.
E.g., $P \cdot Q$ differs from $(P \cdot Q) \supset Q$ by $+n$, since it needs another Q; $P \lor P$ differs from P by $-n$, since it needs to reduce the number of P's.

Δs   There is a difference in the "sign" of the two expressions;
E.g., Q versus $\sim Q$, or $\sim(P \lor R)$ versus $P \lor R$.

Δc   There is a difference in binary connective; e.g., $P \supset Q$ versus $P \lor Q$.

Δg   There is a difference in grouping;
E.g., $P \lor (Q \lor R)$ versus $(P \lor Q) \lor R$.

Δp   There is a position difference in the components of the two expressions;
E.g., $P \supset (Q \lor R)$ versus $(Q \lor R) \supset P$.

Connections between Differences and Operators. A $+$, $-$, or $\times$ in a cell means that the operator in the column of the cell affects the difference in the row of the cell. $+$ in the first row means $+t$, $-$ means $-t$, etc.

	R1	R2	R3	R4	R5	R6	R7	R8	R9	R10	R11	R12
Δt								−	+	+	−	×
Δn			×				×	−	+	+	−	×
Δs		×			×	×						
Δc					×	×	×					
Δg				×			×					
Δp	×	×										

Criteria of Progress. All differences in subexpressions are less important than differences in expressions. For a pair of expressions the differences are ranked: $+t$, $-t$, $+n$, $-n$, Δs, Δc, Δg, Δp, from most important to least. E.g., Δs is the more important in comparing $\sim(P \lor Q)$ with $R \supset Q$, while Δc is the more important in comparing $\sim P \lor Q$ with $P \supset Q$.

[To be augmented by a coordination statement: Li $\longleftrightarrow$ objects; Ri $\longleftrightarrow$ operators.]

A simple illustrative logic problem, $\alpha 1$, and its solution are shown in Figure 8.10. The object, L1, being given, GPS is required to derive the object, L0. The problem is stated to GPS in the form of a transform goal: (Goal 1) find a way to transform L1 into L0. By Figure 8.8, this goal type calls for the transform-method. Comparison of L1 with L0 shows that they have the difference Δp, for the R is on the left end of L1, but on the right end of L0. GPS now erects the reduce type goal: (Goal 2) reduce ΔP between L1 and L0. This type of goal calls for application of the reduce-method. Since the table-of-connections (Figure 8.9) shows that R1 is relevant to reducing Δp, GPS erects the goal: (Goal 3) apply operator R1 to L1. The reader can follow the remaining steps that lead to the solution from Figure 8.10. The resulting derivation may be summarized:

$L1 = R \cdot (\sim P \supset Q)$	L0: $(Q \lor P) \cdot R$
$L2 = (\sim P \supset Q) \cdot R$	apply R1 to L1
$L3 = (P \lor Q) \cdot R$	apply R6 to left(L2)
$L4 = (Q \lor P) \cdot R$	apply R1 to left(L3)
	$L4 = L0$, QED

FIGURE 8.10

trace of GPS on problem α1

Given L1: $R \cdot (\sim P \supset Q)$
Given L0: $(Q \lor P) \cdot R$

Goal 1: Transform L1 into L0
   Goal 2: Reduce Δp between L1 and L0
      Goal 3: Apply R1 to L1
         Goal 4: Transform L1 into condition(R1)
         Produce L2: $(\sim P \supset Q) \cdot R$

Goal 5: Transform L2 into L0
   Goal 6: Reduce Δc between left(L2) and left(L0)
      Goal 7: Apply R5 to left(L2)
         Goal 8: Transform left(L2) into condition(R5)
            Goal 9: Reduce Δc between left(L2) and condition(R5)
         Rejected: No easier than Goal 6

Goal 10: Apply R6 to left(L2)
      Goal 11: Transform left(L2) into condition(R6)
      Produce L3: $(P \lor Q) \cdot R$

Goal 12: Transform L3 into L0
   Goal 13: Reduce Δp between left(L3) and left(L0)
      Goal 14: Apply R1 to left(L3)
         Goal 15: Transform left(L3) into condition(R1)
         Produce L4: $(Q \lor P) \cdot R$

Goal 16: Transform L4 into L0
   Identical, QED

Note: The version of GPS to which this trace belongs is slightly different from the version of Figure 8.8. It creates a transform goal to carry out the match of step 1 of the apply-operator method. See goals 4, 8, 11 and 15, which would be absent from a trace produced by the GPS of Figure 8.8.

A More Complex Example

GPS can solve problems more difficult than the simple one illustrated. Figure 8.11 gives the trace of the solution of D1, leaving out some of the intermediate detail of Figure 8.10, but still showing all the goals. To solve D1 requires some way of handling operators with two inputs (R10, R11, and R12); for selecting a rule like R12 (A $\supset$ B, B $\supset$ C $\Longrightarrow$ A $\supset$ C) with one expression (the current one) in hand does not determine to which of the two inputs the expression should correspond, nor whence the other input should come. If we view these as "difficulties," then it

FIGURE 8.11

trace of GPS on problem D1

```
L0:   ~(~Q·P)                                              0
L1:   (R ⊃ ~P)·(~R ⊃ Q)                                    1
G1:   Transform L1 into L0                                 2
  G2:   Delete R from L1                                  26
    G3:   Apply R8 to L1 (⟹ left)                         30
          Produce L2:   R ⊃ ~P                            66

  G4:   Transform L2 into L0                              68
    G5:   Add Q to L2                                     77
          reject                                          78

  G2:   (Reinstated)                                      80
    G6:   Apply R8 to L1 (⟹ right)                        83
          Produce L3:   ~R ⊃ Q                           120

  G7:   Transform L3 into L0                             122
    G8:   Add P to L3                                    131
          reject                                         132

  G2:   (Reinstated)                                     135
    G9:   Apply R7 to L1                                 140
      G10:   Change connective to ∨ in left(L1)          163
        G11:   Apply R6 to left(L1)                      168
               Produce L4:   (~R ∨ ~P)·(~R ⊃ Q)          202

      G12:   Apply R7 to L4                              205
        G13:   Change connective to ∨ in right(L4)       258
          G14:   Apply R6 to right(L4)                   263
                 Produce L5:   (~R ∨ ~P)·(R ∨ Q)         300

        G15:   Apply R7 to L5                            303
          G16:   Change sign of left(right(L5))          356
            G17:   Apply R5 to right(L5)                 360
                   Produce L6:   (~R ∨ ~P)·~(~R·~Q)      400
                          too complex                    401
            G18:   Apply R6 to right(L5)                 408
                   same as L4 (reject)                   441

  G2:   (Reinstated)                                     475
    G20:   Apply R3 to L1                                477
      G21:   Add term to right(L1)                       513
             find nothing                                518

  G2:   (Reinstated)                                     526
    G22:   Apply R11 on L1                               531
      G23:   Select input from R11 for L1                535
             Select A ⊃ B ⟷ L1                           540
      G24:   Apply A ⊃ B to L1                           543
      G25:   Change connective to ⊃ in L1                557
        G26:   Apply R5 to L1                            562
               Produce L7:   ~((~R ⊃ ~P) ∨ (~(~R ⊃ Q))   605
                      too complex                        606
```

421

FIGURE 8.11 (cont'd)

G27: Apply R7 to L1	616
G28: Change connective to · in right(L1)	663
G29: Apply R6 to right(L1)	669
Produce L8: $(R \supset \sim P) \cdot (R \lor Q)$	707
G30: Apply R7 to L8	710
Produce L9: $((R \supset \sim P) \cdot R) \lor ((R \supset \sim P) \cdot Q)$	769
too complex	770
G31: Apply R7 to L1	794
already failed	796
G2: (Reinstated)	817
G32: Apply R12 to L1	822
G33: Select input from R12 for L1	826
Select $B \supset C \longleftrightarrow L1$	832
G34: Apply $B \supset C$ to L1	835
G35: Change connective to $\supset$ in L1	849
G36: Apply R5 to L1	855
already rejected	857
G37: Apply R7 to L1	866
already rejected	868
G38: Apply R7 to L1	881
already failed	883
G32: (Reinstated)	885
G33: (Reinstated)	887
Select $A \supset B \longleftrightarrow L1$	900
G39: Apply $A \supset B$ to L1	903
G40: Change connective on L1	917
G41: Apply R5 to L1	923
already failed	925
G42: Apply R7 to L1	934
already failed	936
G43: Apply R7 to L1	963
already failed	965
G44: Transform L1-set into L0	987
G45: Select expression from L1-set for L0	995
Select L3	1004
G46: Transform L3 into L0	1006
already rejected	1008
G1: (Reinstated)	1010
Select G2	1040
G1: (Reinstated)	1042
Select G8	1073
G8: (Reinstated)	1076
G47: Apply R11 to L3	1083
G48: Select input from R11 for L3	1086
Select $A \supset B \longleftrightarrow L3$	1091
G49: Apply $A \supset B$ to L3	1093
Produce Q11: $\sim R \supset Q, \sim R \Longrightarrow Q$	1121
G50: Apply Q11 to L1-set	1123
G51: Select expression from L1-set for Q11 input	1031
fail	1033

422

FIGURE 8.11 (cont'd)

G8: (Reinstated)	1152
G52: Apply R12 to L3	1156
G53: Select input from R12 for L3	1159
Select B ⊃ C ⟷ L3	1164
G54: Apply B ⊃ C to L3	1167
Produce Q12: A ⊃ ~R, ~R ⊃ Q ⟹ A ⊃ Q	1202
G55: Apply Q12 to L1-set	1205
G56: Select expression from L1-set for Q12 input	1212
Select L2	
G57: Apply Q12 to L2	1222
G58: Change position on L2	1232
G59: Apply R2 to L2	1238
Produce L10: P ⊃ ~R	1270
G60: Apply Q12 to L10	1273
Produce L11: P ⊃ Q	1306
G7: (Reinstated)	
G61: Transform L11 into L0	1321
G62: Change connective to · in L11	1331
G63: Apply R6 to L11	1336
Produce L12: ~P ∨ Q	1369
G64: Transform L12 into L0	1371
G65: Change connective to · in L12	1381
G66: Apply R5 to L12	1384
Produce L13: (P · Q)	1418
G67: Transform L13 into L0	1420
G68: Change position on L13	1430
G69: Apply R1 to L13	1434
Produce L14: (Q·P)	1470
G70: Transform L14 into L0	1473
Identical, QED	1497

is natural for GPS to handle them in the same way it handles all other difficulties—i.e., by setting up a reduce type goal to remove the difficulty.[7]

The scheme can be seen in its entirety in the trace from goal G52 to G60 in the figure. In G52 the attempt to apply R12 to L3 produces the difference of a single expression (L3) versus a set of expressions (the inputs to R12). The subgoal (G53) to reduce this difference results in selecting B ⊃ C to correspond to L3. A similarity test is performed here, but of course the two inputs of R12 (A ⊃ B and B ⊃ C) appear equivalent to GPS, which simply selects one of them. Then, in G54 this input is applied to L3. The result, however, is not a new expression, but a partially specified operator, Q12, which is a one-input operator of the form A ⊃ ~R ⟹ A ⊃ Q. Q12 arises from making the substitutions of B = Q and C = ~R in R12. This new operator is now applied to the set of expressions

---

[7] There are other ways to handle two-input operators. For example, the version of GPS discussed in Ernst and Newell (1969) has an additional method for multiple-input operators and an additional goal type to select an element from a set.

available—i.e., to the expressions on the display. This input is set up by the method for applying operators, though it could be handled as well simply by creating an apply goal with no input at all, generating thereby another difference (to find an input), so that the display satisfied this goal.

The attempt to apply Q12 in G55 produces the difference of a single expression (A ⊃ ~R) versus a set of expressions (the display), leading to the selection of L2 (P ⊃ ~R). A similarity test is again used here to perform a substantial selective function, since there are a total of nine expressions to choose from. Notice that the partially specified operator carries additional information in its input about the expression that was needed, namely A ⊃ ~R instead of just A ⊃ B.

L2 having been selected, Q12 is now applied to it. Since L2 is not in quite the right form, and since Q12 is handled like any other single-input operator, there results a difference of position, an operator (R2) for reducing it, and a reapplication (G60) of Q12 to the result, L10. This finally produces the desired expression (L11: P ⊃ Q) which has both P and Q, but no R's. From here it is three short steps to the final solution.

Looking at the overall performance of GPS, we see that it first attempts to eliminate terms, and in doing so considers in turn each of the rules that might eliminate something: R8, R7, R3, R11, and R12. Each rule is rejected, though sometimes not without extensive exploration. Sometimes paths are rejected because the expressions become too complex and sometimes because GPS remembers that the result has already been tried and either failed or was rejected. Having exhausted direct ways to eliminate the R's, GPS looks over the whole set of expressions (in G44) to see if perhaps it should make a direct attempt to go from some available expression to the final solution. Since expressions can be generated for other purposes, e.g., to make an operator applicable, an interesting expression may already have been generated. This process is handled in a way similar to the two-input operators. A goal of transforming from the entire display to L0 is created, which produces a difference of a set of expressions versus a single expression (L0), and the goal of selecting one expression from the set. The one chosen is immediately rejected, since it had been tried already in G7.

At this point GPS starts selecting goals as new starting points. The selection of G2 comes to nothing, but the selection of G8 (add P to L3) proves fruitful, leading after a small detour on R11 to the R12 sequence we just examined, and on to the solution. This selection of goals is a form of working forward; thus, though GPS has just rejected working on L3 in G46, it is prepared in G47 to ignore its previous negative evaluation ("adding terms is too difficult") and work on L3.

We can plot the search that GPS engaged in while solving problem D1. Figure 8.12 shows the PBG, taking as operators the rule applications, which is equivalent to viewing GPS as working in the basic problem space. It is clear that something is missing, for the PBG leaves to the imagination, for example, why the sequence of rules 5 and 6 is performed in the third line. The guiding role of R7 is nowhere apparent. This suggests that we should view the goals as operators as well, so that the attempt to apply R7 would show up on the PBG, even though no successful application of it ever occurs.

FIGURE 8.12

problem behavior graph of GPS on problem D1 (basic problem space: rule applications as operators)

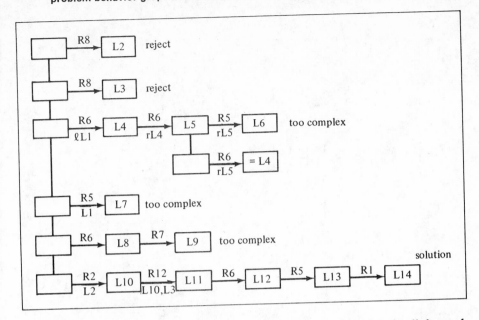

There are actually two ways to modify the PBG. One is to include all the goals as operators. We show a fragment of such a PBG in Figure 8.13. Each of the lines in the figure corresponds to a goal in Figure 8.11, as labeled on the box at the beginning of the line. Goals that produce a product have an arrowhead; goals that do not, have none. Thus, both the initial transform goal (abbreviated *get* L0) and the initial reduce goal of deleting a term (abbreviated —t) have no arrowheads, while the goal of applying R8 to produce the left-hand side does have an arrowhead, since it produces L2. State information, such as a new expression or an evaluation, appears in the box. A goal without an arrowhead is stored in the goal stack and provides context for what follows. When the subgoals are finished (whether successfully or not), the goal in the stack is reapplied. Thus, after G3 the initial goal is taken up again. We indicate this by the double line. For another example, in the third line of the PBG, the goal of applying R7 (G9) recurs after each attempt to deal with a difficulty in applying it.

The alternative to putting in all the goals as operators is to show only the transform and apply goals, taking the differences to be state information associated with the corresponding transform or apply goal. Figure 8.14 shows the total search in this form. The differences (—t, +t, Δc, and so on) now are given in the boxes. A table of abbreviations (—t for delete term, and so on) is given on the figure. This form of the PBG, which compresses the horizontal scale somewhat, is the form we will use for the PBG's of our subjects. Actually, it represents an alternate way to organize a GPS program, in which data structures are not created for reduce type goals, but differences are simply associated with the corresponding transform and apply goals.

425

FIGURE 8.13

fragment of PBG of GPS on problem D1 (all goals as operators)

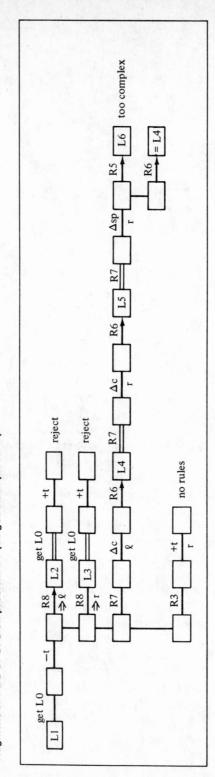

FIGURE 8.14
PBG of GPS on problem D1 (only apply and transform goals as operators)

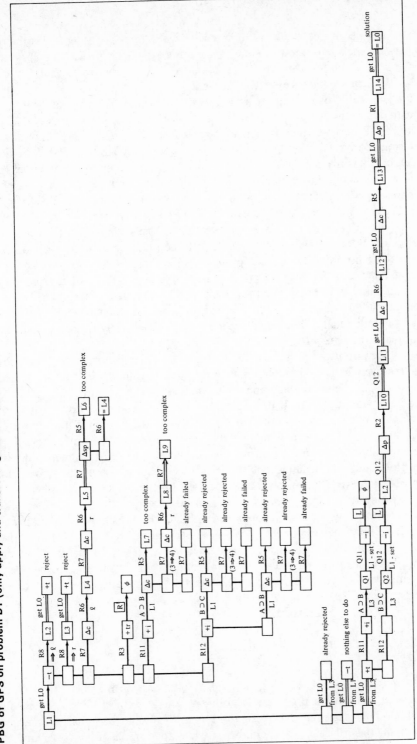

Before turning to other GPS heuristics, a comment is in order on the relation between the size of the very small space actually searched in solving a problem and the size of the problem space, as estimated in an earlier section of this chapter.

The problem space was viewed as the space that is generated by starting with a set of initial objects and working outwards from these to the other objects that can be reached from them, without imposing any particular direction on the search. When means-ends analysis is used, we are given both the initial and the terminal objects. Searching by the technique of generating and removing differences has the general effect of limiting the search to objects that lie between, or nearly between, the initial and terminal objects, respectively. It also generally finds paths between start and termination that are relatively short and direct.

How much search will actually be required to solve problems with means-ends analysis will depend upon the exact structure of space and operators. If the differences between any two objects can be factored into a set of elementary differences, which do not interact and each of which is associated with an elementary operator that removes it without introducing new differences, then solving problems will be an entirely purposeful activity, with no trial and error whatsoever. Interactions among differences, or, what is the same thing, unavailability of operators to handle all the individual differences independently, will generally make a certain amount of search necessary (Ernst, 1969).

The important point is that, so long as the search need never extend beyond a relatively narrow band joining initial with terminal objects, the size of the search space remains small and *independent* of the size of the problem space. The (possibly infinite) expanse of the problem space beyond this narrow band becomes simply irrelevant to the problem solver. By taking account of the characteristics of the goal object it is seeking to reach, the problem solver extracts from the situation an enormous amount of information about the direction in which it should explore, and almost immediately rules out of bounds all but a tiny portion of the problem space. (It can, of course, be wrong—the only path between two small expressions might pass through a very large expression.)

Means-ends analysis is to be distinguished from a simple working-backwards method, like that used by LT. Working-backwards methods start from the goal object, using information about it to anchor the search. In fact, GPS works forward. But means-ends analysis uses information about the relation between both terminals, thus imposing a far more powerful directionality on the search than the other procedure.

Planning as a Problem Solving Technique

A second system of heuristic used by GPS is a form of planning that allows GPS to construct a proposed solution in general terms before working out the details. This procedure acts as an antidote to the limitation of means-ends analysis in seeing only one step ahead. It also provides an example of the use of an auxiliary problem in a different problem space to aid in the solution of the initial problem.[8] Planning is incorporated in GPS by adding a new method, the planning method, to the repertoire of the transform type goal.

This *planning method* (see Figure 8.15) consists in (1) abstracting by omitting certain details of the original objects and operators, (2) forming the corresponding problem in the abstract problem space, (3) when the abstract problem has been solved, using its solution to provide a plan for solving the original problem, (4) translating the plan back into the original problem space and executing it. The power of the method rests on two facts. First, the entire machinery of GPS can be used to solve the abstract problem in its appropriate task environment; because of

FIGURE 8.15

planning method

Planning-method (transform object.1 into object.2):
1. abstract(object.1) ($\Longrightarrow$ abstract-object.1);
2. abstract(object.2) ($\Longrightarrow$ abstract-object.2);
3. create-goal(transform abstract-object.1 into abstract-object.2) ($\Longrightarrow$ abstract-goal);
4. achieve(abstract-goal) ($\Longrightarrow$ abstract-operator-list),
        if fail stop and report fail;
5. initialize current-object = object.1;
6. generate abstract-operator-list:
7.   find operator of abstract-operator;
8.   create-goal(apply operator to current-object) ($\Longrightarrow$ goal);
9.   achieve(goal) ($\Longrightarrow$ current-object),
            if fail stop generation.,
        if stopped go to 4:
10. create-goal(transform current-object into object.2) ($\Longrightarrow$ goal);
11. achieve(goal),
        if fail go to 4,
        if achieved stop and report achieved.

the suppression of detail, this is usually a simpler problem (having fewer steps) than the original one. Second, the subproblems that make up the plan are collectively simpler (each having fewer steps) than the original problem. Since, unless reliable en route evaluations can be made, the exploration required to solve a problem generally increases exponentially with the number of steps in the solution, replacement of a single large problem with several smaller problems, the sum of whose lengths is about equal to the length of the original problem, may reduce the problem difficulty by whole orders of magnitude.

Figure 8.16 shows the planning method applied to D1.[9] The particular ab-

[8] See the work of H. Gelernter (1960) on theorem-proving programs for plane geometry, where the geometric diagram provides another example of a very powerful auxiliary problem space, though not one in which planning occurs.

[9] A complete planning method was never fully implemented for GPS. GPS did plan with rules R1–R9. but not with the two-line input rules (R10–R12).

FIGURE 8.16

planning method applied to problem D1 (see footnote to Fig. 8.10)

Given L1: $(R \supset \sim P) \cdot (\sim R \supset Q)$
Given L0: $\sim (\sim Q \cdot P)$

Goal 1:   Transform L1 into L0   [Method No. 1 failed; now
   Abstract L1 and L0   Method No. 4 is tried.]
      Produce A1:   (PR)(QR)
             A0:   (PQ)
   Goal 2:   Transform A1 into A0 [using abstracted operators]
   Several plans are generated [details are omitted]

      P1:   R8, R11, R12
      P2:   R8, R8, R12
      P3:   ...

Goal 3:   Apply P1 to L1
   Fails [details are omitted]

Goal 4:   Apply P2 to L1
   Goal 5:   Apply R8 to L1
      Goal 6:   Transform L1 into condition(R8)
         Produce L2: $R \supset \sim P$

   Goal 7:   Apply R8 to L1
      Goal 8:   Transform L1 into condition(R8)
         Produce L3: $\sim R \supset Q$

   Goal 9:   Apply R12 to L2 and L3
      Goal 10:   Transform L2 and L3 into condition(R12)
         Goal 11:   Reduce Δp between L3 and condition(R12)
            Goal 12:   Apply R2 to L3
               Goal 13:   Transform L3 into condition(R2)
                  Produce L4: $\sim Q \supset R$

      Goal 14:   Transform L2 and L4 into condition(R12)
         Produce L5: $\sim Q \supset \sim P$

Goal 15:   Transform L5 into L0
   Goal 16:   Reduce Δs between L5 and L0
      Goal 17:   Apply R2 to L5
         Fails [details are omitted]
      Goal 18:   Apply R5 to L5
         Goal 19:   Transform L5 into condition(R5)
            Goal 20:   Reduce Δc between L5 and condition(R5)
               Goal 21:   Apply R5 to L5
               Reject
               Goal 22:   Apply R6 to L5
                  Goal 23:   Transform L5 into condition(R6)
                     Produce L6: $Q \vee \sim P$

         Goal 24:   Transform L6 into condition(R5)
            Produce L7: $\sim (\sim Q \cdot P)$

Goal: 25   Transform L7 into L0
   Identical, QED

straction scheme that is illustrated ignores differences among connectives, signs, and the order of symbols (Δc, Δs, and Δp). For example, $(R \supset {\sim}P)\cdot({\sim}R \supset Q)$ becomes $(PR)(QR)$. The operators are similarly abstracted, so that $A \lor B \rightarrow B \lor A$ becomes $(AB) \rightarrow (AB)$—i.e., the identity operator—and $A\cdot B \rightarrow A$ becomes $(AB) \rightarrow A$. All the abstracted operators are shown in Figure 8.17. The abstracted problem, transform A1 into A0, has several solutions in the abstracted problem space. One of these may be summarized:

A1: (PR)(QR)	A0: (PQ)
A2: (PR)	Apply R8 to left(A1)
A3: (QR)	Apply R8 to right(A1)
A4: (PQ)	Apply R12 to A2 and A3
	A4 = A0 QED

FIGURE 8.17

abstract operators and table of connections

RULE	BASIC SPACE	PLANNING SPACE
R1	$A \lor B \rightarrow B \lor A$ $A\cdot B \rightarrow B\cdot A$	Identity
R2	$A \supset B \rightarrow {\sim}B \supset {\sim}A$	Identity
R3	$A \lor A \leftrightarrow A$ $A\cdot A \leftrightarrow A$	$AA \leftrightarrow A$
R4	$A \lor (B \lor C) \leftrightarrow (A \lor B) \lor C$ $A\cdot(B\cdot C) \leftrightarrow (A\cdot B)\cdot C$	$A(BC) \leftrightarrow (AB)C$
R5	$A \lor B \leftrightarrow {\sim}({\sim}A\cdot{\sim}B)$	Identity
R6	$A \supset B \leftrightarrow {\sim}A \lor B$	Identity
R7	$A \lor (B\cdot C) \leftrightarrow (A \lor B)\cdot(A \lor C)$ $A\cdot(B \lor C) \leftrightarrow (A\cdot B) \lor (A\cdot C)$	$A(BC) \leftrightarrow (AB)(AC)$
R8	$A\cdot B \rightarrow A$ $A\cdot B \rightarrow B$	$AB \rightarrow A$
R9	$A \rightarrow A \lor X$	$A \rightarrow AX$
R10	$\left.\begin{array}{l}A\\B\end{array}\right\} \rightarrow A\cdot B$	$\left.\begin{array}{l}A\\B\end{array}\right\} \rightarrow AB$
R11	$\left.\begin{array}{l}A \supset B\\A\end{array}\right\} \rightarrow B$	$\left.\begin{array}{l}AB\\A\end{array}\right\} \rightarrow B$
R12	$\left.\begin{array}{l}A \supset B\\B \supset C\end{array}\right\} \rightarrow A \supset C$	$\left.\begin{array}{l}AB\\BC\end{array}\right\} \rightarrow AC$

**Table of Connections
in Planning Space**

	R3	R4	R7	R8	R9	R10	R11	R12
Δt				$-$	$+$	$+$	$-$	$\times$
Δn	$\times$		$\times$	$-$	$+$	$+$	$-$	$\times$
Δg		$\times$	$\times$					

Transforming A1 into A0 is the abstract equivalent of the problem of transforming L1 into L0. The former is solved by applying the abstracted operators corresponding to R8, R8, and R12 in sequence. Hence (Figure 8.16, goal 4) a plan for solving the original problem is to try to apply R8 to L1 [obtaining a new object whose abstract equivalent is (PR)], applying R8 to the other side of L1 [obtaining an object corresponding to (QR)], applying R12 to the objects thus obtained, and, finally, transforming this new object (which should be an abstract equivalent of L0), into L0. Each of the first three parts of this plan constitutes an apply type goal in the original task environment—that is, requires the application of a specified operator to a specified expression. These three apply goals are goals 5, 7, and 9, respectively, in Figure 8.16. The first two are achieved almost trivially, and the third requires only five subgoals. The result is the expression L5, which is to be transformed to L0, as indicated by goal 15. Note that implementing the plan involves only operators that become the identity operator upon abstraction.

Like the other heuristics, the planning heuristic offers no guarantees that it will always work. It may generate no plan, a single plan, or several. More serious, a plan may turn out to be illusory—it may prove impossible to carry out. The first plan generated in the illustrative problem, for example—R8, R11, R12—does not provide a basis for a valid derivation when it is translated back to the concrete original task environment. The time wasted in fruitless efforts to execute invalid plans must be counted in evaluating the planning heuristic. But even when allowance is made for this cost, the heuristic remains a very powerful one.

The specific abstraction scheme we have introduced to illustrate the *planning-method* was set forth without any motivation. It consists in ignoring differences among connectives, signs, and the order of symbols. Under this abstraction, four of the operators (R1, R2, R5, R6) coincide with the identity operator, hence become irrelevant. We will call the differences and operators that are eliminated by the abstraction *inessential* differences and operators, respectively, and those that remain the *essential* differences and operators. Let us refer to the abstraction just used as the *standard* abstraction. Is there anything in the structure of the task environment that makes the standard abstraction particularly appropriate or salient?

For any given set of differences there is a definite set of possible abstractions. Each subset of the differences becomes a possible basis for an abstraction. Thus, the six differences that we have introduced (Δt, Δn, Δc, Δs, Δg, Δp) provide $2^6 = 64$ possible bases. We have already expressed the standard abstraction by (Δs, Δc, Δp), a list of the three differences that are to be ignored. Another possible basis would be (Δs), for abstracting from signs alone. This abstraction, for example, sends L1: $(R \supset \sim P) \cdot (\sim R \supset Q)$ into $(R \supset P) \cdot (R \supset Q)$. Still another basis would be (Δt, Δg), for abstracting from the identity of terms and the structure of expressions. This basis sends L1, above, into $(X \supset \sim X \cdot \sim X \supset X)$. Another possibility is (Δn, Δc, Δs), which abstracts from any ability to count numbers of occurrences, as well as from connectives and signs. A possible representation for L1 under this abstraction is the graph structure:

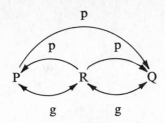

Information about order (p) and about grouping (g) is still preserved by the abstraction, as well as the identity of terms. No linear representation achieves this.

The criteria for a good abstraction are complex, involving three distinct aspects:

1. The size of the planning space and the difficulty of solving problems in it.
2. The number of spurious solutions that are obtained in the planning space.
3. The size of the implementation space (the original space) and the difficulty of solving problems in it.

Some features of the problem situation remain invariant under abstraction. The total depth of the problem (the sum of the depth in the planning space and the depths of all of the implementation problems in the original space) is fixed. Shortening the depth in planning space lengthens the total depth of the implementation problems, and vice versa.

It might be thought that all possible bases need to be considered, but the difference ordering used by GPS eliminates many of them. A difference is not considered for inclusion in the abstraction basis if differences higher in the ordering are retained in the planning space. Thus, if differences in terms (Δt) are retained, then connective differences (Δc), being lower in the ordering, are not abstracted. Details of the strategy for using the difference ordering are not important (one could conceive of a strategy that tried to remove all the low-order differences first, in order to "see" the major difference as clearly as possible). However, an abstraction scheme that abstracted from two differences in the ordering, but not from the ones between these two, would violate the ordering. Thus, the basis (Δp, Δt) is not consistent with the difference ordering that GPS uses (it is, of course, consistent with some other difference orders).

Thus, if the difference order is given, as well as the differences themselves, then the possible planning spaces are determined by the five possible divisions of the ordered list of differences into two parts, the top set being the essential differences and the bottom set the inessential differences. Figure 8.18 lists these possibilities for GPS. It also shows which operators become identity operators, hence become inessential. If we abstract only from Δp, only R1 becomes an identity; abstracting from all differences turns all operators into the identity operator—if all expressions are indistinguishable then operators change nothing.

FIGURE 8.18
possible abstractions for GPS

ABSTRACTION	BASIS	INESSENTIAL OPERATORS
1	Δp	R1
2	Δp Δs	R1 R2
3	Δp Δs Δc	R1 R2 R5 R6
4	Δp Δs Δc Δg	R1 R2 R5 R6 R4
5	Δp Δs Δc Δg Δn	R1 R2 R5 R6 R4 R3 R7
6	Δp Δs Δc Δg Δn Δt	R1 R2 R5 R6 R4 R3 R7 R8 R9 R10 R11 R12

Exactly where should the split be made? At least three different considerations suggest themselves: efficiency in heuristic search, the effect of abstraction on the applicability of operators, and analogy.

The effort required for heuristic search tends to increase geometrically with depth of search. Hence, an abstraction should be efficient to the extent it decreases the depth of search in both abstract and original spaces. The maximum depth is likely to be minimized by dividing the differences more or less equally between the two spaces—i.e., by splitting the list of differences near the middle, rather than toward either end.

However, it is important also that in the abstract space limits on the applicability of operators should not prevent paths from being followed through successive steps to a possible problem solution. In the case of logic expressions, for example, if differences among connectives were retained in the abstract space, it would be about as difficult to trace plans to their conclusion as to solve the problem in the original space. Hence, a workable abstraction must remove differences among connectives, and abstract at least to (Δp, Δs, Δc), which is the standard abstraction we have been considering. It might be feasible to go one step further and abstract also from Δg; but adding the next difference, Δn, to the list loses much of the structure of the task. We are left, therefore, with two plausible abstractions: (Δp, Δs, Δc) and (Δp, Δs, Δc, Δg).

An analogy with physical objects provides an entirely different basis for choosing an abstraction. If we think of expressions as physical objects, the differences fall into two subsets. Δn and Δt determine what materials (the letters) are contained in an expression, while Δs, Δc, Δp, and Δg determine how these materials are connected together and arranged. Then a problem may be viewed as a two-stage task: first obtaining the materials of which L0 is composed, then manipulating these materials to arrange them in the right form. On this analogy, (Δn, Δt) become the essential differences, to be retained in the planning space, while all the other differences become inessential.

Of course this is just an analogy; the structure of the task environment is determined completely by the operators and the syntax of the expressions. Nevertheless, the analogy leads to substantially the same essential-inessential distinction as the one we are using (and will continue to use in our discussion of logic problems).[10] Since the material-arrangement distinction is familiar from everyday situations, the abstraction our subjects used may have been suggested to them by this analogy rather than by the formal features of the task.

In summary, three different plausible criteria lead to an essential-inessential distinction much like the one we have introduced—although whether Δg should be regarded as essential or inessential is left ambiguous by these criteria. Since only R4 would be handled variously by the two alternatives that remain, and since this rule enters rarely into the problems we shall treat in detail (C1 and D1), we can leave the ambiguity unresolved.

This account of abstraction assumes that both the differences and the difference-ordering are given at the outset of the problem solving attempt. Changes in either of these could alter the set of essential differences. We do not yet know how to approach the question of abstraction in this broader setting.

Developing the Task Information

In the formulation of GPS for logic, we simply gave GPS all the information it needed about the differences: what they were, what operators were relevant to them, and what order was desired. This information constitutes most of what GPS knows about the structure of the task environment. Similarly, in planning, the basis of abstraction was simply given to GPS. In both of these instances this is appropriate, for our interest is in asking whether GPS can provide a model for some human problem solving, and these features seem essentially fixed for a human subject at the start of an experimental session. The subject has dealt previously with symbolic parenthesized structures and with operations on them, and he holds in long-term memory a great deal of structure which he is prepared to transfer immediately to the new task. (Indeed, were this not so, much training would be required before the subject could operate in the task environment.)

Nevertheless, it is worth examining briefly the extent to which these informational aspects reside in the task environment and whether GPS could itself have derived them (if it were given additional general principles).

The *table of connections* is the easiest to derive (Newell, 1962), for an operator is relevant to those particular differences that it reduces. But these can be found simply by matching the output expression of the operator to the input, and with exactly the same match process that is used elsewhere in GPS. Figure 8.19 shows the differences so derived. They can be seen to be exactly the ones in the table of connections. The essential fact is that the operators and objects determine the structure of the task environment, and we have merely found a way of extracting a relevant part of that information.

[10] A different analogy would split the differences into those having to do with the *content* of an expression (Δs, Δc, Δt) and those having to do with *structure* (Δp, Δg, Δn). But this analogy is not consistent with the ordering of the differences and does not seem to have influenced the abstractions the subjects actually used.

FIGURE 8.19
derivation of table of connections by matching operator conditions and products

	MATCH	DIFFERENCES
R1	A ∨ B to B ∨ A	Δp
	A·B to B·A	Δp
R2	A ⊃ B to ∼B ⊃ ∼A	Δp, Δs
R3	A ∨ A to A	Δn
	A·A to A	Δn
R4	A ∨ (B ∨ C) to (A ∨ B) ∨ C	Δg
	A·(B·C) to (A·B)·C	Δg
R5	A ∨ B to ∼(∼A·∼B)	Δs, Δc
R6	A ⊃ B to ∼A ∨ B	Δs, Δc
R7	A ∨ (B·C) to (A ∨ B)·(A ∨ C)	Δn, Δg, Δc
	A·(B ∨ C) to (A·B) ∨ (A·C)	Δn, Δg, Δc
R8	A·B to A	Δt, Δn
	A·B to B	Δt, Δn
R9	A to A ∨ X	Δt, Δn
R10	A to A·B	Δt, Δn
R11	A ⊃ B to B	Δt, Δn
R12	A ⊃ B to A ⊃ C	Δt, Δn

It is also possible to derive the differences themselves, and this has been done in at least two programs (Ernst and Newell, 1969; Quinlan and Hunt, 1968). However, since one cannot eliminate *all* perceptual processes, the derivation of the differences comes down to deriving differences relevant for a *given* task environment from a set of generalized primitive (perceptual) differences, such as are implied by the basic definition of logic expressions (e.g., connectives can be discriminated, one from the other, and, as a class, from signs and terms, and so on). The existing schemes that obtain their own differences do so at the price of working with quite elementary differences. Thus, they do not use differences like Δn (number of variable places). The one theoretical proposal to develop more sophisticated differences (Newell, Shaw, and Simon, 1960b) was never actually implemented. Figure 8.20 shows the difference structure for a particular logic operator (Newell, 1962). Again, the key information is contained in the operators, requiring only an appropriate process to extract it.

Recently a program has been written that produces a difference ordering from given differences and operators (Eavarone, 1969). It is based on a relation that must hold between an ordered difference and the operators it evokes, if the more difficult (i.e., higher) difference is to be taken care of first. If all of the operators relevant to removing a difference produce higher differences in the output expressions, then any attempt to take care of the higher differences first is doomed to failure—they are just reintroduced again. Hence, it must be possible to write the table of connections as a triangular array, if we list the differences vertically in order. Figure 8.21 shows the table of connections for logic written this way.

FIGURE 8.20

difference structure of an operator

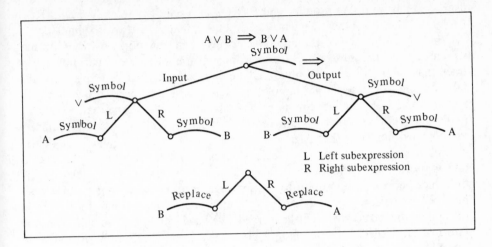

FIGURE 8.21

triangularized table of connections for logic task environment

	R8	R9	R10	R11	R12	R3	R7	R4	R5	R6	R2	R1
Δt	×	×	×	×	×							
Δn	×	×	×	×	×	×	×					
Δg							×	×				
Δc							×		×	×		
Δs									×	×	×	
Δp											×	×

(Boldface = essential rule and difference)

Given the information as to which operators are relevant to which differences, the program determines whether there exists an ordering that produces a triangular array. The program also has some additional heuristics for selecting a particular ordering, if several satisfy the main criterion. The program did in fact produce an ordering for logic that is consistent with the ordering we have used (there were slight differences in formulation).

No program has produced its own planning space. As we saw earlier, achieving this hinges on two issues. Conceptually, the main issue is which differences are going to be taken as essential, which inessential. This, in turn, depends mostly on the difference ordering. Thus, given a scheme, such as Eavarone's, that will produce an ordering, most of the selection of an essential-inessential distinction has been accomplished. The second issue is the development of a representation for the abstract space that permits problem solving to occur in it. No general

437

investigation of this issue has yet been carried out. For some kinds of features (e.g., Δs, Δc, Δt) the matter is trivial. One can either delete the feature from the expression, as we did in producing (RP)(RQ), or use a constant value, e.g., (R $\vee$ P) $\vee$ (R $\vee$ Q). For other differences, such as Δn, matters are not so simple.

In summary, each of the additional kinds of information used by GPS has its source in the structure of the task environment, and we can see in part how to extract that information by simple analytic processes. It can also be extracted by induction from a series of examples. Inductive learning processes have both advantages and disadvantages compared to analytical processes. They can be simpler (if the induction demanded is not too sophisticated), and they do not require a fully formed model of the space. On the other hand the knowledge is gained at much greater cost in terms of processing (it is extracted bit by bit, so to speak) and is more contingent. In fact, the difference between the two is exactly the difference between theory and observation in science. However, our purpose here has been to expose the nature of the task environment rather than to explore in detail how that structure might be learned. We have sought only to show that the information needed for developing a planning scheme is relatively accessible to the IPS itself.

SOURCES OF PROBLEM DIFFICULTY

After this intensive examination of a single problem solving program, we can gain a different sort of perspective on the nature of the task environment by trying to explain, using the data from the 64 Yale subjects, why certain of the problems were much more difficult than others. In Table 8.1 the sixteen problems are listed in order of difficulty, as measured by the numbers of subjects who solved them. They are arranged from the most difficult, B2 solved by 5 subjects and C1 by 6, to the least difficult, D1 and C3 solved by 24 subjects each.

The problem name is listed in the first column of the table, the number of subjects who solved it in the second column, subdivided to show the number who found each of the major variant solutions for those problems that have more than one. The third column shows the median solution time for the successful subjects. The fourth column gives the number of steps, omitting the initial given expressions (which range from 1 to 4). The fifth column is a measure of the size and number of expressions that are involved in the proof—the number of binary connectives in the proof is the actual measure used. The sixth column lists the constructions (to be explained presently), if any, involved in the proof. The last column shows the number of applications of essential rules in the solution, excluding (for reasons that will become apparent) applications of R8 and those applications of R9 that added an expression as the very last step.

Examining Table 8.1, we observe that all of the solutions involving more than ten steps appear in the upper half of the table (the first seven problems). Every problem, however, has at least one solution involving not more than eight steps; two (B1 and D1) have six-step solutions, and most have solutions of seven steps. The variation in median solution time is small, and, with one exception, median times over ten minutes correspond to solutions having more than ten steps. As a matter of fact, the median solution time is approximately one minute per step.

Only four of the twelve solutions for the seven harder problems contain *less* than ten connectives, and only one of the eleven solutions for the nine easier

TABLE 8.1

Moore-Anderson problems arranged according to difficulty

PROBLEM	NUMBER CORRECT	MEDIAN TIME	NUMBER STEPS	NUMBER CONNECTIVES	CONSTRUC-TIONS	ESSENTIAL STEPS
B2	5 { 2 / 2 / 1	11 / 8 / 13	11 / 7 / 12	19 / 8 / 11	(5, 7, 8) / (9) / (9), (9)	2 / 2 / 4
C1	6	6	7	10	(10, 7)*	3
B3	8 { 3 / 5	10 / 6	11 / 7	20 / 6	(10, 7) / —*	3 / 3
D4	9	7	7	5.	(9)	4
C4	10	9	7	10	(10, 7)	4
A3	12 { 5 / 6 / 1	12 / 7 / 12	11 / 8 / 7	16 / 8 / 10	(4, 5) / (9) / (9)	4 / 3 / 3
D2	14	7.5	7	13	(5, 7)	2
A2	17 { 17 / 0	4.5 / —	7 / 9	8 / 7	— / —	3 / 3
B4	17 { 14 / 3	7 / 7.5	7 / 7	5 / 5	— / (9)	5 / 5
C2	17	7	7	12	—	3
A1	19	8	7	8	—	2
B1	20	7	6	6	—*	2
D3	22	8.5	8	7	—	2
A4	23	6	7	4	—	3
D1	24	7	7	6	—	1
C3	24	6	8	7	—	2
"Difficult"	9.1	8.1				
"Easy"	20.3	6.8				

*See text for further discussion of special properties of these problems.

problems contain *more* than ten connectives. There is some correlation, of course, though not a perfect one, between number of steps and number of connectives.

All but one of the twelve solutions of difficult problems contain constructions, but only one solution (found by three subjects) of the easier problems. Except for Problem B4, the solutions of the easier problems contain one, two, or three essential steps. Except for Problems B2 (two of the three solutions) and D2, the solutions of the harder problems contain three or four essential steps.

Several of the characteristics shown in the table correlate, therefore, with problem difficulty, but the feature that correlates most closely is the presence or absence of constructions. We turn now to a discussion of this concept.

The term *construction* is borrowed, of course, from elementary geometry. Proofs of certain theorems in geometry require auxiliary lines, or other figures, to be constructed that are not contained in the problem statement. Constructions substantially increase problem difficulty, for the student must decide whether a construction is necessary, and if one is, which lines he should construct, out of the infinite number that are possible.

As long as the proof is restricted to figures in the original problem statement, the number of segments, angles, triangles that might be proved equal or homologous is very limited. The possibility of constructions throws the student into an immensely larger problem maze, in which he needs new selective heuristics if he is to generate the right possibilities and not lose his way.

Consider, for example, the problem discussed by Wertheimer (1945) of finding the formula for the area of a parallelogram. The key, as he points out, is to drop perpendiculars from one side to the other (see Figure 8.22). Once this is done—

FIGURE 8.22

finding the formula for the area of a parallelogram

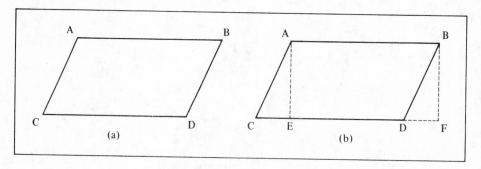

once the right construction has been discovered—the problem is seen to be equivalent to finding the area of a rectangle, obtained by adding and subtracting equal triangles, ACE and BDF, respectively, from the original parallelogram.

The Nine Dot Problem (Chapter 4, page 90) is another example of difficulties introduced by constructions. As long as the subject limits himself to lines bounded by the dots, he has only a small number of possibilities before him—not including any solutions. The problem difficulty lies in answering the ill-defined question: "What can I do that I haven't tried?" This question is likely to be answered successfully only if the problem solver has an appropriate set of generators and selective heuristics for obtaining a *few* possibilities in a larger space.

In the logic problems, the given expressions and goal expression in the problem statement define a limited set of expressions that can be derived without excessive search—i.e., those obtainable by (1) *simplifications* of one or more of the given expressions (e.g., applications of R8), (2) rule applications that promise directly to *reduce differences* between the given expressions and L0, (3) applications of rules that *conspicuously fit* the forms of given expressions, and (4) expressions obtained by *inessential* steps.[11] The inessential rules generate small closed subsets of expressions, while changes in the direction of simplification and difference-reduction will also not generate a large space of new possibilities. The complexity of the original expression sets an upper bound on the size and complexity of expressions that can be obtained by simplification or by application of rules that fit expressions particularly closely, while the characteristics of given expressions and goal place bounds on wanderings motivated by the aim of reducing the differences between them. These wanderings can only produce expressions that are in some sense between the givens and the goal.

From these considerations, we can define a *construction* as a rule (1) that produces a more complex object as output than the object that is its input (or more complex than any one of the inputs, if there are more than one) and (2) does so in such a way that there is no *direct* prior justification for producing this additional complexity. Simplifications and inessential transformations fail to satisfy the first of these two conditions, hence are not constructions. Applications of rules to reduce differences with the goal expression and applications of rules that fit conspicuously an expression already obtained do not satisfy the second condition, hence are not constructions. All other rule applications are constructions.

Construction, in this context, thus becomes roughly comparable to *nonobvious step* as we used that phrase in the cryptarithmetic chapters. However, the two terms are not quite synonymous, and we shall have to postpone a discussion of their relation until we have taken up the topic of episoding and looked at more of the human behavior in the logic tasks.

Our interest at present is in the difficulty of problems. We predict difficulty by postulating that subjects will generally be able to generate those expressions that can be obtained without constructions from others previously generated, and that those problems will therefore be difficult that cannot be solved without making constructions.

The principal types of steps that should be regarded as constructions are certain applications of R5, R7, R9, and the two-line rules (R10, R11, R12). R9 and R10 both produce outputs of increased complexity and can be used to produce a large number of different output expressions. R5, applied in the direction that adds a tilde to the whole expression being operated upon, and R7, applied in the direction that increases the size of the expression, both increase complexity but do not proliferate large numbers of new expressions. The geometric analogy to the distinction between the constructions of R5 and R7, on the one hand, and R9 and R10, on the other, is the distinction between drawing a line between two existing vertices (thus, a construction, but not one permitting wide choice) and drawing a line to new vertices not previously existing in the diagram.

The two-line rules (especially R11 and R12) may be regarded as constructions when their application must be preceded by an otherwise unmotivated generation of one or both of the inputs.

---

[11] Some empirical justification for inclusion of classes (1) and (3) in this list can be found in Anderson (1957), p. 302. The author observes. "The subject first rearranges one or more premises into a more workable form. The initial restructurings are probably suggested by the premises themselves and the forms of the rules and are not importantly dependent on the goal to be deduced."

In Appendix 8.1 to this chapter we show the solutions to the sixteen problems that are summarized in Table 8.2. Using these as examples, we can see under what conditions applications of R7 and R9 are to be regarded as constructions.

Constructions with Rule 7.   Consider Problem A1. The expression L1 is of the form, $(X \cdot Y) \vee (X' \cdot X)$, which is so close to one of the forms of R7 as immediately to suggest that rule. We will therefore not consider application of R7 in this problem to be a construction. Next, consider Problem C1. The final step in solving the problem is to apply R7 to $(P \vee Q) \cdot (P \vee R)$. But in order to do this, the input part of this expression must first be generated. This is done by obtaining $P \vee Q$, then $P \vee R$, and then using R10 to put them together with a dot. We will consider the sequence of R10 followed by R7 to be a construction, since in working forward, a large number of possible pairs of expressions might be generated as candidates for R10. The sequence, R10, R7, occurs also in one solution of B3, and in the solution of C4.

Now, consider L3 in the solution of D2. By means of three inessential steps, this expression is changed into a form where R7 can be, and is, applied. The path here, involving R5 followed by R7, is sufficiently indirect, perhaps, to be regarded as a construction. However, since problem D2 is only of borderline difficulty, we need not insist on classifying this path as a construction.

Constructions with Rule 9.   Consider Problem A4. The goal, L0, is $P \vee T$. The letter T occurs nowhere in the given expressions. Hence, an obvious route to the solution is to obtain P, then transform it into $P \vee T$ by R9. In this, and comparable, cases the application of R9 is not a construction, for it is motivated by examining the difference in variables between given and goal expressions.

Now consider D4. In this solution, R9 is used to produce $P \vee Q$ from P, and the output used for R11. The letter Q is absent from the goal expression, and actually present in two of the given expressions. Hence, adding it with R9 is a construction. Similar kinds of applications of R9 occur in two solutions of B2, two solutions of A3, and one solution of B4.

Other Constructions.   There is only one other sequence of transformations that should probably be regarded as a construction. The first solution of A3 requires R4 and then R5 to be applied to L5 in order to obtain $\sim R$, which is subsequently used as an input to R11.

If we accept these criteria for determining which transformations are to be regarded as constructions, then we see from Table 8.1 that constructions were involved in all but one of the solutions of the seven hard problems, while no construction was involved in any of the solutions of the nine easier problems, except one solution employed by three subjects. Among the problems not involving constructions, there is also some inverse correlation between number of solvers and number of essential steps.

Some Statistical Evidence.   We can subject the distinction between constructions and other steps to several kinds of tests, empirical and theoretical. First we will examine some statistical data, then approach the problem with simulation.

Figure 8.23 shows, for eight of the problems, the number of subjects who wrote down various specific expressions that lie along the paths to solutions. From these, we can determine which steps were the difficult ones. We can also obtain evidence that in certain situations steps are logically linked in either of two ways: (1) that the first of a pair of transformations was carried out by subjects in order to carry out the second, or (2) that the second was obvious, once the first had been executed. The evidence for this would be that almost all subjects who carried out the first in fact also carried out the second. We will encounter eleven instances of this phenomenon in the eight problems. However, let us take up the problems in order.

FIGURE 8.23

frequency of various paths for selected Moore-Anderson problems

Problem A1 (19)

Problem A2 (17)

Problem B3 (9)

(One subject applied both R12 and R10)

Problem C1 (6)

FIGURE 8.23 (cont'd)

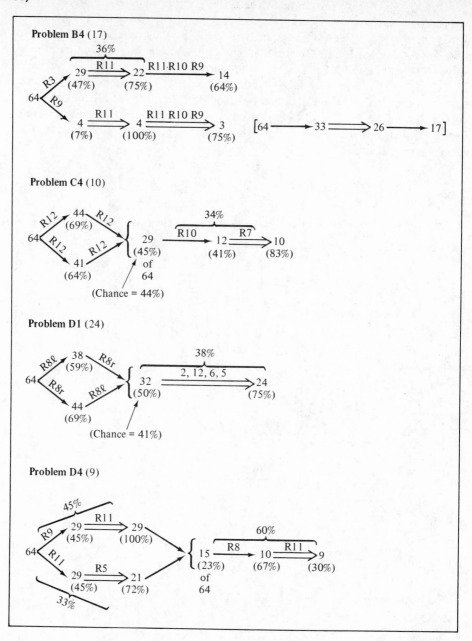

In Problem A1, three-fifths of the subjects applied R7 to L1 (after inessential transformation), and half of these discovered the remaining steps (simplification by R8, then R11) to solution. This is characteristic of the statistics for the easy problems.

Problem A2 provides an example of linked transformations. Only half of the subjects found the regrouping of L1 by R4, but four-fifths of these went on to apply R11. We may conjecture that many of them worked backwards, applying Rule 4 in order to obtain the expression P·Q as input for the R11 application. Two-thirds of these went on to solve the problem.

Two solution paths are shown for Problem B3. Let is look first at the lower path (the first solution in Table 8.2). Only six of the subjects applied R10, but all but one of these went on to use R7, and three solved the problem. The evidence is strong that R10 was used in order to apply R7. In the other path, twelve subjects derived an expression equivalent to $\sim Q \supset Q$ or $Q \vee Q$, and half of these applied R3 and R9 to obtain the solution. Since the two applications of R12 can be motivated by the aim of eliminating unwanted letters, it is not obvious why so few subjects found this path. It is possible that $\sim P \supset Q$ and $P \supset Q$ looked so much alike as to discourage subjects from supposing that anything could be gained by working with the two expressions together—but this explanation is entirely ad hoc.

In Problem B4, similarly to A2, the most difficult step was to consider applying R9 or R3 at the outset. More than half of the subjects who did this solved the problem (17 out of 33), although they had to take a whole sequence of essential steps. Each essential step, however, removed an unwanted letter.

The diagram for Problem C1 shows the detail of some of the inessential, as well as the essential, steps. Note again that subjects who got R10 almost all followed through with R7. The construction was not the only difficulty, however, for only one-quarter of the subjects applied R12. The difficulty of this problem also involved the phenomenon of functional fixity. It is the only problem in which the same term, $P \vee Q$, is put to two distinct uses in the solution. It is used as the left-hand input to R10 after it has previously been used to construct one of the inputs to R12. We will later present evidence that some subjects were deterred from "using up" $P \vee Q$ by R12 because they could see that they wanted that expression as one of the components of L0.

Problem C4 provides another example of the R10–R7 construction, where, again, 10 out of 12 subjects who made the former transformation made the latter. Half of the subjects lost the trail while eliminating Q and (P·Q), and only a third of the remainder carried through the construction.

We have already examined the statistics of D1 at length. Moving to Problem D4, we see that three principal subproblems are involved. The R9–R11 construction can be seen in the upper left part of the diagram. Only half of the subjects applied R9, but all of those went on to apply R11. A large fraction of these failed to obtain $\sim R$, needed for the elimination of the letter R.

We conclude that these data are generally consistent with our construction hypothesis. In particular, they point to certain steps that are strongly linked— where the subject was very likely operating with a plan to carry through both steps. The data do not indicate that subjects generally constructed a full plan for problem solution before making transformations. If they had done this, we would expect very low transition probabilities through the remainder of the chain. Instead, we see a picture of steady attrition, hastened at difficult steps and slowed down somewhat between linked steps.

Interpretation by Simulation. Our hypotheses about problem difficulty can be examined further by a technique similar to the one we used with Problem D1. We can postulate a certain processing system, and ask which expressions that system would generate for each problem, and whether it would, in fact, solve the problem.

The assumptions are these. We postulate (simplification) that R8 will be applied to all positive main expressions with dots as main connectives, that inessential rules will be applied when useful to make essential rules fit, and, in particular, that R2 and R5 will be applied when this will reduce the number of tildes. We postulate that R11 and R12 will be applied to eliminate unwanted letters, and that R7 will be applied when one of the given expressions is of the form (AB)(AC) (conspicuous fit). Finally, we postulate that R9 will be applied as the last step when L0 is of the form $A \lor B$, and B does not occur in the given expressions (reduce differences).

As the reader can verify by hand-simulating it, a processor obeying these postulates would solve all but one (B1) of the six easiest problems (i.e., A1, D3, A4, D1, and C3), and none of the harder ones. It would fail with B1 because that problem calls for using R9 and *then* R11. The processor in B1 would generate P and $\sim$P; to solve the problem, it would have to add $Q \lor S$ to one of these expressions by R9, then cancel out the P's with R11. It is possible that the semantic interpretation of this problem ("P and not P") helped some of the subjects to find the solution, hence it made it easier than we would have estimated from its formal structure.

In Problem C2 the processor would fail to find the final sequence, R7–R8. In B4 it would fail to use R with R11, since R appears in L0, hence should not be eliminated. In A2 the processor would fail to use R10 to form P·Q after obtaining P and Q separately. These are the three problems that come next in order of difficulty. The processor would fail on all of the seven difficult problems, because none of its heuristics would cause it to make any constructions. Thus, we may regard the hypothetical processor as a crude first approximation to the heuristics employed by those subjects who solved the easier problems but not the harder ones.

SUMMARY

Our task analysis of the Moore-Anderson logic problems has been somewhat narrower than the one we made for cryptarithmetic in Chapter 5. We described the basic problem space and provided some estimates of the size of that space when objects are generated in it exhaustively from an initial object. Rather than ring many changes on the problem space and the heuristics that could be used within each space, we presented an existing problem solving program, GPS, that works in the basic space of logic. GPS, however, does not just do simple forward search. In fact, we used it to introduce several important ideas about problem solving.

1. **Goal Structures.** Rather than simply attributing goal significance to an object in the task environment, as we did in LT, we used a special symbol structure for the goal. The goal is a symbol structure that holds information not only about the desired object but also about the various methods of attaining the goal and the history of past attempts.

2. **Means-Ends Analysis as a Problem Solving Heuristic.** The central idea is the selection of means (i.e., operators) with a view towards the ends (the goal to be achieved). Several requirements must be satisfied before means-ends analysis can be effective: differences must exist to form the bridge between the perceptual world (the objects) and the action world (the operators); and these differences must be ordered so that some additional sense of direction can be imposed on the search.

3. **Difficulties Lead to Goals to Overcome Them.** This device accounts for much of the recursive flavor of GPS, since its reaction to being unable to apply an operator is to set up a goal of applying it. However, this is a rather dangerous heuristic, since it throws away a source of selectivity (namely, to work only with operators that are applicable), and can thus lead to following blind paths forever, unless curbed.

4. **An IPS Constructing Its Own Structures.** We showed the possibility that an IPS can create differences and the connections between differences and the operators relevant to them, making use of information available in the definition of the task environment.

5. **Constructions.** An operation that serves to increase complexity in the absence of strong guidelines was called a construction. With the available conceptual apparatus, we were able to make the concept operational for the logic task environment. We were then able to understand the relative difficulty of the various problems as a combination of the requirements of a construction and the effect of large search spaces. As an independent measure of difficulty we used the behavior of the 64 Yale subjects.

6. **Planning Spaces.** We have emphasized repeatedly the possible existence of multiple problem spaces, especially in the analysis of cryptarithmetic. The planning space is indeed another problem space. However, unlike the various spaces in cryptarithmetic, it is not richer than the base space (as the augmented space was), but impoverished—that is, it consists of less detail. Thus, its role is to guide action, rather than to serve as the site of the main problem solving, and we have an example where a single problem solving attempt oscillates between two spaces.

In this chapter we have already made some use of human data (in looking at the sources of difficulty). Thus, we already have some evidence in hand that our information processing analysis makes sense in application to human behavior. We are now ready to examine that issue more deeply.

APPENDIX 8.1

Principal Solutions of Moore-Anderson Logic Problems

Problem A1

L1: $(\sim P \cdot Q) \lor (P \cdot \sim P)$	L0: Q
L2: $(\sim P \cdot Q) \lor (\sim P \cdot P)$	R1 to right(L1)
L3: $\sim P \cdot (Q \lor P)$	R7 to L2
L4: $\sim P$	R8 to L3 ($\Longrightarrow$ left)
L5: $Q \lor P$	R8 to L3 ($\Longrightarrow$ right)
L6: $P \lor Q$	R1 to L5
L7: $\sim P \supset Q$	R6 to L6
L8: Q	R11 to L4,L7 QED

(length = 7)

Problem A2

L1: $P \cdot (Q \cdot R)$	L0: $T \cdot T$
L2: $\sim (R \supset T) \supset \sim (P \cdot Q)$	
L3: $(P \cdot Q) \supset (R \supset T)$	R2 to L2
L4: $(P \cdot Q) \cdot R$	R4 to L1
L5: $(P \cdot Q)$	R8 to L4 ($\Longrightarrow$ left)
L6: $R \supset T$	R11 to L3,L5
L7: R	R8 to L4 ($\Longrightarrow$ right)
L8: T	R11 to L6,L7
L9: $T \cdot T$	R3 to L8 QED

(length = 7)

second solution

L4: P	R8 to L1 ($\Longrightarrow$ left)
L5: $Q \cdot R$	R8 to L1 ($\Longrightarrow$ right)
L6: Q	R8 to L5 ($\Longrightarrow$ left)
L7: $P \cdot Q$	R10 to L4,L6
L8: $R \supset T$	R11 to L7,L3
L9: R	R8 to L5 ($\Longrightarrow$ right)
L10: T	R11 to L9,L8
L11: $T \cdot T$	R3 to L10 QED

(length = 9)

Problem A3

L1: $P \lor (Q \lor R)$	L0: $\sim Q \supset \sim S$
L2: $\sim (Q \lor R)$	
L3: $S \supset \sim P$	
L4: $\sim P \supset (Q \lor R)$	R6 to L1
L5: $S \supset (Q \lor R)$	R12 to L3,L4
L6: $\sim (Q \lor R) \supset \sim S$	R2 to L5
L7: $\sim S$	R11 to L2,L6
L8: $\sim S \lor Q$	R9 to L7
L9: $Q \lor \sim S$	R1 to L8
L10: $\sim Q \supset \sim S$	R6 to L9 QED

(length = 7)

448

second solution

L4: (Q ∨ R) ∨ P	R1 to L1
L5: ~(Q ∨ R) ⊃ P	R6 to L4
L6: P	R11 to L2,L5
L7: P ⊃ ~S	R2 to L3
L8: ~S	R11 to L6,L7
L9: ~S ∨ Q	R9 to L8
L10: Q ∨ ~S	R1 to L9
L11: ~Q ⊃ ~S	R6 to L10 QED

(length = 8)

third solution

L4: ~Q·~R	R5 to L2
L5: ~R	R8 to L4 (⟹ right)
L6: ~P ⊃ (Q ∨ R)	R6 to L1
L7: S ⊃ (Q ∨ R)	R12 to L6,L3
L8: ~S ∨ (Q ∨ R)	R6 to L7
L9: (~S ∨ Q) ∨ R	R4 to L8
L10: R ∨ (~S ∨ Q)	R1 to L9
L11: ~R ⊃ (~S ∨ Q)	R6 to L10
L12: ~S ∨ Q	R11 to L5,L11
L13: Q ∨ ~S	R1 to L12
L14: ~Q ⊃ ~S	R6 to L13 QED

(length = 11)

Problem A4

L1: P ∨ Q	L0: P ∨ T
L2: ~R ⊃ ~Q	
L3: S	
L4: R ⊃ ~S	

L5: S ⊃ ~R	R2 to L4
L6: ~R	R11 to L3,L5
L7: ~Q	R11 to L2,L6
L8: Q ∨ P	R1 to L1
L9: ~Q ⊃ P	R6 to L8
L10: P	R11 to L7,L9
L11: P ∨ T	R9 to L10 QED

(length = 7)

Problem B1

L1: (P·~P)·(R ⊃ T)	L0: Q ∨ S

L2: P·~P	R8 to L1 (⟹ left)
L3: P	R8 to L2 (⟹ left)
L4: P ∨ (Q ∨ S)	R9 to L3
L5: ~P ⊃ (Q ∨ S)	R6 to L4
L6: ~P	R8 to L2 (⟹ right)
L7: Q ∨ S	R11 to L5,L6 QED

(length = 6)

Problem B2

L1: $(P \lor Q) \supset \sim(\sim R \lor P)$	L0: $\sim Q$
L2: $\sim[\sim(S \cdot Q) \lor R]$	

L3: $(\sim R \lor P) \supset \sim(P \lor Q)$	R2 to right(L1)
L4: $(S \cdot Q) \cdot \sim R$	R5 to L2
L5: $\sim R$	R8 to L4 ($\Longrightarrow$ left)
L6: $\sim R \lor P$	R9 to L5
L7: $\sim(P \lor Q)$	R11 to L3,L6
L8: $\sim P \cdot \sim Q$	R5 to L7
L9: $\sim Q$	R8 to L8 ($\Longrightarrow$ right) QED

(length = 7)

second solution

L3: $(S \cdot Q) \cdot \sim R$	R5 to L2
L4: $\sim R$	R8 to L3 ($\Longrightarrow$ right)
L5: $\sim(P \lor Q) \lor \sim(\sim R \lor P)$	R6 to L1
L6: $\sim(P \lor Q) \lor \sim(P \lor \sim R)$	R1 to right(L5)
L7: $\sim[(P \lor Q) \cdot (P \lor \sim R)]$	R5 to L6
L8: $\sim[P \lor (Q \cdot \sim R)]$	R7 to L7
L9: $\sim P \cdot \sim(Q \cdot \sim R)$	R5 to R8
L10: $\sim(Q \cdot \sim R)$	R8 to R9 ($\Longrightarrow$ right)
L11: $\sim Q \lor R$	R5 to L10
L12: $R \lor \sim Q$	R1 to L11
L13: $\sim R \supset \sim Q$	R6 to L12
L14: $\sim Q$	R11 to L4,L13 QED

(length = 12)

third solution

L3: $(S \cdot Q) \cdot \sim R$	R5 to L2
L4: $(S \cdot Q)$	R8 to L3 ($\Longrightarrow$ left)
L5: Q	R8 to L4 ($\Longrightarrow$ right)
L6: $Q \lor P$	R9 to L5
L7: $P \lor Q$	R1 to L6
L8: $(P \lor Q) \supset (R \cdot \sim P)$	R5 to right(L1)
L9: $R \cdot \sim P$	R11 to L7,L8
L10: R	R8 to L9 ($\Longrightarrow$ left)
L11: $R \lor \sim Q$	R9 to L10
L12: $\sim R \supset \sim Q$	R6 to L11
L13: $\sim R$	R8 to L3 ($\Longrightarrow$ right)
L14: $\sim Q$	R11 to L12,L13 QED

(length = 12)

Problem B3

L1: $\sim P \supset Q$	L0: $Q \lor S$
L2: $\sim R \supset Q$	
L3: $\sim P \lor \sim R$	

L4: P ⊃ ~R	R6 to L3
L5: P ⊃ Q	R12 to L2,L3
L6: ~Q ⊃ ~P	R2 to L5
L7: ~Q ⊃ Q	R12 to L1,L6
L8: Q ∨ Q	R6 to L7
L9: Q	R3 to L8
L10: Q ∨ S	R9 to L9 QED

(length = 7)

second solution

L4: P ∨ Q	R6 to L1
L5: R ∨ Q	R6 to L2
L6: Q ∨ P	R1 to L4
L7: Q ∨ R	R1 to L5
L8: (Q ∨ P)·(Q ∨ R)	R10 to L6,L7
L9: Q ∨ (P·R)	R7 to L8
L10: (P·R) ∨ Q	R1 to L9
L11: ~(P·R) ⊃ Q	R6 to L10
L12: ~(P·R)	R5 to L3
L13: Q	R11 to L12,L13
L14: Q ∨ S	R9 to L14 QED

(length = 12)

Problem B4

L1: (P ∨ P) ⊃ ~Q	L0: (S·R) ∨ T
L2: Q ∨ R	
L3: R ⊃ S	
L4: P	

L5: P ∨ P	R9 to L4
L6: ~Q	R11 to L5,L1
L7: ~Q ⊃ R	R6 to L2
L8: R	R11 to L6,L7
L9: S	R11 to L3,L8
L10: S·R	R10 to L8,L9
L11: (S·R) ∨ T	R9 to L10 QED

(length = 7)

second solution

L5: P ⊃ ~Q	R3 to L1
L6: ~Q	R11 to L4,L5
L7: ~Q ⊃ R	R6 to L2
L8: R	R11 to L6,L7
L9: S	R11 to L3,L8
L10: S·R	R10 to L8,L9
L11: (S·R) ∨ T	R9 to L10 QED

(length = 7)

Problem C1

L1: $(P \lor Q) \cdot (Q \supset R)$		L0: $P \lor (Q \cdot R)$
L2: $P \lor Q$		R8 to L1 ($\Longrightarrow$ left)
L3: $Q \supset R$		R8 to L1 ($\Longrightarrow$ right)
L4: $\sim P \supset Q$		R6 to L2
L5: $\sim P \supset R$		R12 to L3,L4
L6: $P \lor R$		R6 to L5
L7: $(P \lor Q) \cdot (P \lor R)$		R10 to L2,L6
L8: $P \lor (Q \cdot R)$		R7 to L7 QED

(length = 7)

Problem C2

L1: $(P \cdot Q) \lor (P \cdot T)$		L0: $Q \lor R$
L2: $T \supset (P \cdot R)$		
L3: $P \cdot (Q \lor T)$		R7 to L1
L4: $Q \lor T$		R8 to L3 ($\Longrightarrow$ right)
L5: $\sim Q \supset T$		R6 to L4
L6: $\sim Q \supset (P \cdot R)$		R12 to L2,L5
L7: $Q \lor (P \cdot R)$		R6 to L6
L8: $(Q \lor P) \cdot (Q \lor R)$		R7 to L7
L9: $Q \lor R$		R8 to L8 ($\Longrightarrow$ right) QED

(length = 7)

Problem C3

L1: $\sim S$		L0: $\sim Q$
L2: $R \lor S$		
L3: $(P \supset Q) \supset \sim R$		
L4: $S \lor R$		R1 to L2
L5: $\sim S \supset R$		R6
L6: R		R11 to L1,L4
L7: $R \supset \sim (P \supset Q)$		R2 to L3
L8: $\sim (P \supset Q)$		R11 to L5,L6
L9: $\sim (\sim P \lor Q)$		R6 to L7
L10: $P \cdot \sim Q$		R5 to L8
L11: $\sim Q$		R8 to L9 ($\Longrightarrow$ right) QED

(length = 8)

Problem C4

L1: $P \supset Q$		L0: $\sim P \lor (\sim T \cdot R)$
L2: $\sim R \supset (P \cdot Q)$		
L3: $Q \supset \sim T$		
L4: $(P \cdot Q) \supset \sim P$		

L5: P ⊃ ~T	R12 to L1,L3
L6: ~P ∨ ~T	R6 to L5
L7: ~R ⊃ ~P	R12 to L2,L4
L8: R ∨ ~P	R6 to L7
L9: ~P ∨ R	R2 to L8
L10: (~P ∨ ~T)·(~P ∨ R)	R10 to L6,L9
L11: ~P ∨ (~T·R)	R7 to L10 QED

(length = 7)

Problem D1

L1: (R ⊃ ~P)·(~R ⊃ Q)	L0: ~(~Q·P)
L2: R ⊃ ~P	R8 to L1 (⟹ left)
L3: ~R ⊃ Q	R8 to L1 (⟹ right)
L4: ~Q ⊃ R	R2 to L3
L5: ~Q ⊃ ~P	R12 to L2,L4
L6: Q ∨ ~P	R6 to L5
L7: ~(~Q·P)	R5 to L6 QED

(length = 7)

Problem D2

L1: (P ∨ Q) ⊃ R	L0: ~P ∨ S
L2: R ⊃ S	
L3: (P ∨ Q) ⊃ S	R12 to L1,L2
L4: ~(P ∨ Q) ∨ S	R6 to L3
L5: (~P·~Q) ∨ S	R5 to left(L4)
L6: S ∨ (~P·~Q)	R1 to L5
L7: (S ∨ ~P)·(S ∨ ~Q)	R7 to L6
L8: S ∨ ~P	R8 to L7 (⟹ left)
L9: ~P ∨ S	R1 to L8 QED

(length = 7)

Problem D3

L1: (P ⊃ Q) ⊃ ~R)	L0: ~Q
L2: R ∨ S	
L3: ~S	
L4: S ∨ R	R1 to L2
L5: ~S ⊃ R	R6 to L4
L6: R	R11 to L3,L5
L7: R ⊃ ~(P ⊃ Q)	R2 to L1
L8: ~(P ⊃ Q)	R11 to L6,L7
L9: ~(~P ∨ Q)	R6 to L8
L10: P·~Q	R5 to L9
L11: ~Q	R8 to L10 (⟹ right) QED

(length = 8)

Problem D4

L1: $(P \lor Q) \supset (R \lor S)$ L0: S
L2: P
L3: $\sim T \supset \sim(Q \lor R)$
L4: $\sim T$

L5: $\sim(Q \lor R)$ R11 to L3,L4
L6: $P \lor Q$ R9 to L2
L7: $R \lor S$ R11 to L1,L6
L8: $\sim Q \cdot \sim R$ R5 to L5
L9: $\sim R$ R8 to L8 ($\Rightarrow$ right)
L10: $\sim R \supset S$ R6 to L7
L11: S   R11 to L9,L10   QED

(length = 7)

9

LOGIC:
GPS and Human
Behavior

In this chapter we wish again, as in Chapter 6, to address questions of detail. We have cast our task analysis of the Moore-Anderson logic into the form of a single program, GPS, operating in a definite problem space—namely, the basic one consisting of logic expressions as nodes and the twelve legal rules as operators. Does a human subject when working these logic problems behave in a GPS-like way? Does he do so at a convincing level of detail? From our experience with cryptarithmetic our aspirations should be high—aiming to leave only modest amounts of task behavior unexplained.

The situation we face is not entirely simple. First, we are permuting historical sequence. GPS was the first program ever developed as a detailed simulation of human symbolic behavior. It followed the development of the Logic Theorist, which was compared only generally with human problem solving (Newell, Shaw, and Simon, 1958b). The cryptarithmetic task was tackled after logic. We have reversed the order of presentation, because some of the basic issues are more transparent in the cryptarithmetic situation than in logic.

Furthermore, GPS was constructed by detailed study of some of the same protocols that are to be discussed. This means only that the explanation that GPS offers is partially adapted to the data, just as is any model that contains parameters. It does not mean that the fit of program to data is tautological, for GPS can be an adequate description only to the extent that the subject's behavior is indeed GPS-like. All aspects of GPS—its methods, heuristics and organization—are defined independently of subjects' behaviors in terms of the task environment and the theory of problem solving enunciated in Chapter 4. Therefore, there is no a priori reason why humans should behave this way, or why any particular person should, even if some other person does.

Finally, and this is the one complexity of real importance, GPS is not a single program. Several specific variants have run on computers, but these variants, all called GPS, differ in many respects. The variations are not limited to settings of parameters—even such nonnumerical parameters as tables of connections. For instance, GPS at one time or another has had five basic underlying IPS structures, the differences among them affecting the representation of both methods and data structures. There has been one change of programming language. Similarly, various methods have been added and subtracted from time to time. Thus, the questions to be raised in this chapter deal with the *GPS-like* behavior of the subjects, although we will be at some pains to point out those aspects that fit closely to particular existing forms of GPS and those that don't.

BEHAVIOR ON PROBLEM α1

Consider first a single protocol: S9 on Problem α1.[1] This was a relatively simple training problem, the first problem the subject attempted after studying the twelve rules. In Figure 9.1 the protocol of S9 is shown on the left. On the right side of the same figure is a computer trace of a particular version of GPS solving the same problem. With the trace there is no need for a PBG, either of the protocol or of GPS's behavior.

The language of the subject is much less stylized than the language of the computer program. To fit the theory, we must, for example, interpret a sentence such as, "I'm looking at the idea of reversing these two things now," as equivalent to "Construct the difference-reduction goal of eliminating the difference in position of corresponding subparts in objects L0 and L2." We have already seen that making such a translation is, in practice, not too difficult. Having made it, we can determine in detail the similarities and differences between the programs of the subject and the computer, respectively.

---

[1] This analysis is essentially identical to that in Newell and Simon (1961c), except that the GPS trace in Figure 9.1 was produced by a working version of the program, whereas the tree in the referenced paper was hand-simulated.

FIGURE 9.1

comparison of GPS with subject S9 on problem α1

Given L0: (Q ∨ P)·R
Given L1: R·(~P ⊃ Q)

(E: What are you looking at?)

Goal 1: Transform L1 into L0
  Goal 2: Change position in L1
    Goal 3: Apply R1 to L1
      Produce L2: (~P ⊃ Q)·R

I'm looking at the idea of reversing these two things now.
(E: Thinking about reversing what?)
The R's . . .
Then I'd have a similar group at the beginning . . .
But that seems to be . . .

Goal 4: Transform L2 into L0
  Goal 5: change position in left(L2)
    Goal 6: Apply R2 to left(L2)
      Produce L3: (~Q ⊃ P)·R

I could easily leave something like that 'til the end,
except then I'll . . .

Goal 7: Transform L3 into L0
  Goal 8: Change term sign
      left(left(L3))
    Rejected

(E: Applying what rule?)
Applying . . . for instance, 2.
That would require a sign change.

Goal 5: (reinstated)
  Goal 10: Apply R1 to L2
    Rejected, not desirable

(E: Try to keep talking if you can.)

  Goal 11: Apply R3 to L2
    Rejected, not desirable

Well . . . then I look down at R3 and that doesn't look any too practical.

  Goal 12: Apply R4 to L2
    Rejected, not desirable

Now 4 looks interesting. It's got three parts similar to that and there are dots, so the connective . . . seems to work easily enough, but there's no switching of order.

  Goal 13: Apply R5 to L2
    Rejected, not desirable

I need that P and a Q changed, so . . . I've got a horseshoe there.

  Goal 14: Apply R8 to L2
    Rejected, not desirable

That doesn't seem practical any place through here.

  Goal 15: Apply R8 to L2
    Rejected, not desirable
  Goal 16: Apply R1 to Left(L2)
    Goal 17: Change connective
      of left(L2)

I'm looking for a way, now, to get rid of that horseshoe. Ah . . . here it is, R6.

      Goal 18: Apply R6 to
        left(L2)

So I'd apply R6 to the second part of what we have up there.
(E: OK. To L1 you apply R6.)

        Produce L4:
        (P ∨ Q)·R

(E: writes L2: R·(P ∨ Q))
And now I'd use R1.

      Goal 19: Apply R1 to
        left(L4)

(E: R1 on what part? You can use it with the entire expression or with the right part.)

        Produce L5: (Q ∨ P)·R

I'd use it in both places.
(E: Well, we'll do them one at a time . . . Which do you want to do first?)
Well, do it with P and Q.
(E writes L3: R·(Q ∨ P))
(E: Now the entire expression?)

Goal 20: Transform L5 into L0
  Identical, QED

Yeah.
(E: On L3, R1.)
(E writes L3: (Q ∨ P)·R)
And . . . that's it.

Let us consider some of the differences visible in the example that represent inadequacies of GPS in this form as an accurate theory of the subject's behavior. Observe that the subject solves the entire problem in his head and then asks the experimenter to write the actual transformations on the blackboard. The GPS program, in the version shown here, makes no provision for such a distinction between the internal and external worlds; hence, the trace corresponds only to the subject's covert (but verbalized) problem solving. For example, GPS and the subject both discover in the same sequence the correct rules for transforming the problem expression, but the subject officially applies these rules in the reverse order.

Another difference, characteristic of these data (and, as we have seen, of protocol data in general), is that a number of things appear in the trace that have no correspondents in the human protocol—most prominently, the reference here in the trace to R5 and R8. We cannot tell whether these omissions indicate an error in the theory or whether the subject noticed the rules in question but failed to mention them aloud—and hence that the program makes a genuine prediction of covert behavior.

Correspondences with GPS

In contrast to these differences, there is some striking correspondence in detail between the computer trace and the subject's protocol. First, in noticing differences between pairs of expressions, both GPS and the subject pay most attention to differences in the positions of symbols, next most attention to the presence or absence of signs ($\sim$), and least attention to differences in connectives. This shows up, for example, in the refusal of both to use R2 to reorder the expression (after either mentioning or trying it), because applying the rule also changes a sign. Second, of the several possible paths to solution of the problem, both program and subject chose an application of R6 and two applications of R1.

The version of GPS shown here is different in one important detail from the version described in the previous chapter (compare that one's behavior on $\alpha 1$ in Figure 8.10, page 420). In the version of Figure 9.1 the *reduce-method*, as it sequences through the rules looking for one to apply, generates the differences of each rule. This is necessary, since the rule is being applied at the main connective, but the relevant difference is on the left-hand side. We mentioned in the description of GPS the construction of the operator-difference connection by GPS itself; this is an application of that procedure. The reduce-method as a whole remains the same, of course, only the find-relevant-operator being different. Figure 9.2 describes the process.

In summary, although this is a miniscule sample of behavior, there is little doubt, not only that S9 was working in the same problem space as GPS, but that his program was GPS-like in many ways.

For this problem there are, in fact, six distinct solution paths of length three, all of them essentially permutations of the one used by the subject and GPS. For, expressed in functional terms, the problem calls for three changes to be carried out, and these can be carried out in any order ($3! = 6$). In the words of S11, whose protocol we will examine in a moment: "You've got to change the places of the R to the other side; and you have to change the signs, tilde, and horseshoe to wedge; and you've got to reverse the places from P and Q to Q and P."

Thus, like the clicking safe (Chapter 4), the problem is factorable into subproblems, the solution of each of which can be recognized from the form of the resulting expression, and each of which can be carried out with a single operation. For reference, we list the six paths in Figure 9.3. (PQ) identifies the subexpression containing P and Q. The only element of interdependence among subproblems is that the operation required to reverse P and Q is R2 if their connective is still ⊃, but R1 if the connective has previously been changed to ∨.

FIGURE 9.2

find-relevant-operator: S9 version of GPS

Find-relevant-operator(difference) (⟹ operator):
1.   generate rules:
2.   find left of condition of rule (⟹ input);
3.   find left of product of rule (⟹ output);
4.   match input to output (⟹ rule-difference),
                if ≠ difference continue,
                if = difference stop process and report rule.,
          stop and report fail.

FIGURE 9.3

the six paths for problem α1

Path. 1:   (R1 to α1, R2 to (PQ), R6 to (PQ))
Path. 2:   (R1 to α1, R6 to (PQ), R1 to (PQ))
Path. 3:   (R2 to (PQ), R1 to α1, R6 to (PQ))
Path. 4:   (R2 to (PQ), R6 to (PQ), R1 to α1)
Path. 5:   (R6 to (PQ), R1 to α1, R1 to (PQ))
Path. 6:   (R6 to (PQ), R1 to (PQ), R1 to α1)

In Appendix 9.1 are given the protocols of S9 and four other subjects. There are close similarities among all five protocols. Some of these similarities derive from the fact that all the subjects are working in the same task environment—as we have noted, all paths to the solution are trivial variants on a common theme.

Similarities among the Subjects

But the similarities in behavior of the subjects go beyond the dictates of the task requirements. All of the subjects map out the solution partially or fully, before they ask the experimenter to carry out the official transformations. These initial statements are expressed partly in terms of functions to be performed [S9 (B26): "I'm looking at the idea of reversing these two things now"], partly in terms of rules to be applied [S15 (B16–B17): "Well, use R1 and switch the two around"]. Only one subject, S10, mentions features of the expression that are *not* to be changed [(B11–B14): "R4 will not apply because there's not an inner grouping change. Oh! there's no major sign change . . . no major connective change either"]. He does this after he notices that a particular rule, R4, would alter a feature that is to remain constant. Presumably, he compares the output of R4 with the goal expression and notices the new difference that has been introduced.

All five subjects mention first the reversal of left and right sides of the whole expression. Three of them (S9, S14, S15) then mention the change in connective followed by the commutation of the P-Q terms; two of them (S10, S11) mention these transformations in the reverse order. Thus, all five subjects discuss path.1 or path.2. All except S15, however, actually carry out the solution along path.6, while S15 uses path.2. None of them, at either stage, interposes the transformation of the whole expression between the two operations on the parts. Only S9 and S15 mention considering R2, and both are troubled by the changes in tildes it produces. Thus, all five subjects use R1 rather than R2 to interchange P and Q in their final solutions.

The Repertory of Subprocesses

The number of distinguishable subprocesses discernible in the five protocols is small. First, there is the process of *matching* two expressions to discover one or more differences between them. All five subjects clearly match L1 with L0 at the outset. The difference in order of terms in the total expression is uniformly noticed before the differences in the P-Q terms. However, the similarity of $(Q \lor P)$ to $(\sim P \supset Q)$ is taken into account in all of the matchings, even though these subexpressions occur in different locations in their respective total expressions. [That is, no subject proposes to transform R into $(Q \lor P)$ or $(\sim P \supset Q)$ into R.]

The differences discovered by the match processes are usually expressed in active, functional terms—that is, in terms of actions to remove them—rather than purely descriptively. There occur such phrases as: "connective change," "change places," "inner grouping change." Occasional descriptive phrases, "they're in different order," are conspicuous by their rarity.

The match processes are used not only to compare L1 with L0, but also to discover the applicability of rules by matching expressions with their input forms and to discover the functions of rules by comparing their outputs (*product*) with their inputs (*conditions*). There is an explicit example in the protocol of S9 (B39–B41): "Now 4 looks interesting. It's got three parts [i.e., Match L1 to *condition*(R4)]

. . . but there's no switching of order [i.e., Match *product*(R4) to *condition*(R4)." This use of the match processes to compare rule inputs with outputs is important, for it leads to characterizing rules in terms of their functions, independently of the expressions to which they are applied.

A second kind of subprocess apparent in the protocols is one that searches for an operator relevant to reducing a difference or to performing a function. As in GPS, the process is evoked by the statement of a difference to be reduced or function to be performed. In GPS, these are synonymous; not so in the protocols, as we shall see in a moment. An example of the latter (S9, B45–B46) is: "I'm looking for a way, now, to get rid of that horseshoe. Ah . . . here it is, R6." A probable example of the former (S15, B27–B46) is: "Now I'm trying to make it into $Q \vee P$ . . . $Q \vee P$ . . . . Well, if I use 2, the, ah, no, if I use 2 and that gives me . . . let's see, I have $\sim P \supset Q$, and using R6, $\sim Q \supset P$ . . . will give me $Q \vee P$, wouldn't it?" The difference is that in the first example the input and output of a rule are evidently compared to find that the rule eliminates a horseshoe, while in the second example the rule is actually applied to a concrete expression, an output obtained, and this matched with the desired output to see if the specified difference has been removed.

A third kind of subprocess is a search for a rule that is applicable and produces an apparently desirable result. Thus, in S9's protocol (B37–B41): . . . then I look down at R3, and that doesn't look any too practical. [Inapplicable, two parts of expression not identical]. Now 4 looks interesting It's got three parts similar to that . . . and there are dots, so the connective . . . seems to work easily enough [applicable], but there's no switching of order [undesirable]."

One final distinction is needed between two classes of subprocesses that find a rule relevant to a difference or function: there may already be an association stored in memory between the function or difference and one or more rules (the GPS *table-of-connections*), or it may be necessary to search the rules more or less systematically to find one that performs that function. Since this is the first problem these subjects have solved, they have not yet stored in memory much of a table of connections, hence there are numerous examples in the protocols of rule searches motivated by functions to be performed. It is usually easy to distinguish these rule searches from those mentioned in the last paragraph: if the function has already been specified, the applicability of the rule is not examined until after its function has been determined. However, S9 (and the GPS trace modeled on him) behaves differently. Searching for a rule to interchange P and Q, he considers applying the rules 3 and 4 before he notices that they do not perform the desired function.

In S9's protocol, and probably in S15's, there occurs an instance where no applicable rule appears to perform a desired function (S9, B42–B44): ". . . need that P and a Q changed, so . . . I've got a horseshoe there. That doesn't seem practical anyplace through here"), and the subject then searches for a way to remove the difficulty so that a rule can be applied (S9, B45): "I'm looking for a way, now, to get rid of that horseshoe"). Thus, at least one event, and perhaps others, in the procotols corresponds to GPS's find-relevant-operator subprocess.

In summary, the protocols are all explicable in terms of a small number of subprocesses that are contained in GPS, or describable in GPS-like terms. As a reflection of the fact that the subjects have not yet learned which rules perform which functions, rule searches to find an applicable rule that would do something useful, and to find a rule to perform a specific function, are frequent. On the other hand, all the subjects already are applying a match process whose outputs are expressed in functional language. They know what needs to be done in the language of functions that they have brought to the task from their knowledge of algebra and from everyday life, but they don't know how to do it without trying out their available (unfamiliar) tools, one by one. We can expect to see more evidences of a table-of-connections in behavior in later problems, and in this we will not be disappointed.

BEHAVIOR ON PROBLEM D1

The problem labeled D1 was one of the sixteen given to the Yale subjects. It was usually given to the Carnegie subjects immediately after the three training problems. It was one of the two easiest of the problems for the Yale subjects, 24 out of 64 solving it in the fifteen minutes allowed. However, only one of the sixteen subjects who encountered it at the first of the four one-hour problem solving sessions solved it, four who received it at the second session, five at the third, and fourteen of the sixteen who received it at the fourth session (i.e., after they had practice, successful or unsuccessful, with at least twelve previous problems). Hence, it was not really easy in an absolute sense for subjects who had not had extensive practice with such problems. Five of the seven Carnegie subjects for whom we have protocols solved problem D1 in the half hour allowed them.

The Task Environment

The shortest-path solution of Problem D1 involves six steps from L1, as shown in Figure 9.4. A few permutations of steps are possible: for example, L2 and L3 may be interchanged, or both L3 and L4 may precede L2. However, other modifications will lengthen the solution. If Rule 2 is applied to L2 instead of L3, a later application of R1 or R2 will be needed to reverse the order of P and Q. Thus, a subject may take seven instead of six steps without wasting any (i.e., taking any steps that are not part of his final solution).

FIGURE 9.4

shortest solution path for problem D1

L1: $(R \supset \sim P) \cdot (\sim R \supset Q)$	L0: $\sim (Q \cdot P)$
L2: $(R \supset \sim P)$	R8 to left(L1)
L3: $(\sim R \supset Q)$	R8 to right(L1)
L4: $(\sim Q \supset R)$	R2 to L3
L5: $(\sim Q \supset \sim P)$	R12 to L2,L4
L6: $(Q \lor \sim P)$	R6 to L5
L7: $\sim (\sim Q \cdot P)$	R5 to L6

A functional description of the solution might run like this: L1 is split in two parts by two applications of R8. One of these parts [preferably $(\sim R \supset Q)$] is commuted (R2) so that the product can be combined with the other, by R12, to eliminate the R's. In the resulting expression in Q and P, the horseshoe connective is changed to dot by first changing it to wedge (R6), then from wedge to dot (R5). Even more succinctly, the task is to eliminate the R's from L1 and to combine the Q and P in a single expression. This is accomplished by the sequence R8, R8, R12, together with appropriate applications of R2, R6, and R5 to change connectives.

What clues does the task environment provide to suggest the correct path, short of an exhaustive search? A match between L1 and L0 detects the need to delete R. This is an *essential* difference, as we used that term in the discussion of planning in Chapter 8. It suggests that we consider the various paths that solve the problem in the abstract space. We show five such plans in Figure 9.5. These are not all that could be generated, but they will serve us for the analysis of the subjects' behavior on Problem D1. The schematic expressions belong to the abstract

FIGURE 9.5

possible paths for the solution of D1

path.R7	Use R7 to separate R from Q and P; then eliminate R by R8:
	R7 to (RP)(RQ) $\Rightarrow$ R(PQ)
	R8 to R(PQ) $\Rightarrow$ PQ
path.R9	Use R8 to obtain left(L1). Then add Q by R9, regroup by R4, and eliminate R by R8:
	R8 to (RP)(RQ) $\Rightarrow$ (RP)
	R9 to (RP) $\Rightarrow$ (RP)Q
	R4 to (RP)Q $\Rightarrow$ R(PQ)
	R8 to R(PQ) $\Rightarrow$ (PQ)
path.R10	Use R8 twice on both sides of L1 to extract P and Q, respectively. Combine Q and P with R10:
	R8 to (RP)(RQ) $\Rightarrow$ RP
	R8 to RP $\Rightarrow$ P
	R8 to (RP)(RQ) $\Rightarrow$ RQ
	R8 to RQ $\Rightarrow$ Q
	R10 to Q, P $\Rightarrow$ QP
path.R11	Remove the R from half of L1 by two successive applications of R8, leaving a P (Q, respectively). Use this R, together with other half of L1, by R11, to cancel the second R. By R10, combine P with Q, and change connectives to get the final expression:
	R8 to (RP)(RQ) $\Rightarrow$ RP
	R8 to RP $\Rightarrow$ R
	R8 to (RP)(RQ) $\Rightarrow$ RQ
	R11 to RI RQ $\Rightarrow$ Q
	R8 to RP $\Rightarrow$ P
	R10 to Q, P $\Rightarrow$ QP
path.R12	Use R8 to obtain the right and left sides of L1. Then eliminate R by R12. This is the path leading to the solution.
	R8 to (RP)(RQ) $\Rightarrow$ RP
	R8 to (RP)(RQ) $\Rightarrow$ RQ
	R12 to RP, RQ $\Rightarrow$ PQ

space; i.e., they are the original expressions with connectives, signs, and the order of symbols ignored. For convenience, we have labeled each path by the essential rule that seems most characteristic of it.

The main features of the paths for Problem D1 are depicted in another way in Figure 9.6. This figure shows how various new expressions can be derived from the original expressions in the abstracted space by the rule applications. Each concentric circle contains the expressions of a particular size—expressions with a single letter in the innermost circle, those with two letters in the second circle, and so on. Each of the transformations shown in Figure 9.6 may be employed as a component of several of the paths of Figure 9.5.

FIGURE 9.6

graphic view of paths in D1

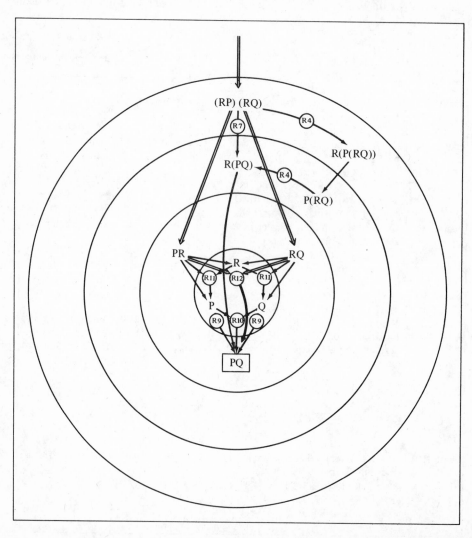

In two of these schemes (path.R11 and path.R10) the R's are eliminated by successive applications of R8 (path.R10) or R8 combined with R11 (path.R11), and the resulting fragments combined with R10. In two others (path.R7 and path.R12) the elimination is accomplished by R7 followed by R8 (path.R7) and by R12 (path.R12). In the latter scheme (path.R12) in particular, R8 is used, not to eliminate or delete letters, but to divide the total expression, L1, into two separate parts to which the two-line rule, R12, can be applied. In the final plan (path.R9) R8 is used to eliminate (RQ), and later again to remove the remaining R. These are not the only paths that might be considered, as we shall see from the protocols, but they are the most important.

Of these potential paths to a solution, only the fifth (path.R12) is actually operative; the others cannot be carried out. The attempt to extract a single letter (path.R4 or path.R10) by successive applications of R8 fails because R8 can be applied only to positive expressions with dot main connectives. But the connective of left(L1) or right(L1) cannot be changed to a dot without making the entire expression negative; hence R8 cannot be applied a second time.

The attempt by path.R7 fails, because L1 cannot be transformed into an expression to which R7 is applicable. The two R's cannot be given the same sign without having different connectives in the two expressions, or the R's in the wrong positions. The reason for this is most easily understood from Figure 9.7, which shows the effects of all possible applications of R1, R2, R5, and R6, the four inessential rules (see Chapter 8) that change tildes and connectives and permute the order of terms around the main connective. It can be seen that, starting with any one of the six expressions in the figure, each of the other five, and only these five, can be obtained by applications of these rules.

Now consider all binary expressions composed of two fixed subexpressions, A and B. Independently there can be three connectives, two orders (AB and BA), and three signs (one for A, one for B, and one for the expression) each positive or negative. Thus, there are $3 \times 2 \times 2^3 = 48$ expressions. Since from Figure 9.7

FIGURE 9.7

effects of applying inessential rules: the equivalence class of AVB

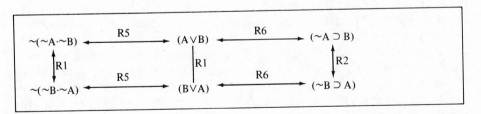

exactly six subexpressions form an *equivalence class* under the four inessential transformations, there must be exactly $48/6 = 8$ such classes. Any two expressions belonging to the same class can be obtained from each other by the application of rules R1, R2, R5, R6; no expressions belonging to different classes can be so obtained.

As we observed in Chapter 8, the inessential rules do not add terms to expressions, delete terms, or change the grouping of terms in subexpressions. The term *form-preserving* would perhaps be more descriptive, since subjects almost uniformly regard the expressions belonging to a single equivalence class as highly similar. The term *inessential* alludes to the observation, discussed in Chapter 8, that we can plan problem solutions in terms of the *essential* rules that must be applied, considering the *inessential* rules as means for making minor adjustments in expressions to fit together the segments of the plan of major transformations. Labeling a rule *inessential* does not imply that it can be ignored in determing the feasibility of a plan.

To apply R7 to an expression similar to L1, we would have to transform L1 into $(R \lor P) \cdot (R \lor Q)$, or $(R \cdot P) \lor (R \cdot Q)$, or something similar with tildes in front of *both* R's. But it can be seen from Figure 9.7 that the sign of R in any subexpression with a wedge or dot connective obtained from L1 is determined by the connective; hence *different* changes cannot be produced in the two signs of R without obtaining different connectives in the two subexpressions containing R.

This result is by no means obvious. A person who did not have Figure 9.7 before him might not be sure that he could not put L1 in a form for application of R7 by appropriate use of the four inessential rules. Hence, the infeasibility of path.R7 is also not obvious. If a subject were attempting to carry out this scheme, we would expect him to generate one or more expressions from L1 by commuting it or applying Rules 1, 2, 5, or 6 to the subexpressions of L1. We will call such expressions the *equivalence class of L1*. The entire set of expressions that can be obtained by operating on the main expression of L1 as well as on its parts will be called the *extended equivalence class of L1*. Since there are three binary expressions involved, there are $6^3 = 216$ expressions in each extended equivalence class.

On the other hand, a person attempting to follow path.R11 or path.R10 might be expected to generate expressions $(R \supset \sim P)$ or $(\sim R \supset Q)$, or both, together with other members of their equivalence classes.

So far, we have considered the match between L0 and L1 as the source of clues to guide search in solving the problem. The initial expression, L1, can also be compared with the expressions that result from applying various rules to it. If these new expressions are simpler than L1, in terms of some measure, this *simplification* might be used as a clue that the step is appropriate. Thus, the application of R6 might be justified not only for the reasons given previously, but also because it produces expressions simpler than L1. Simplification might also be applied working backward from L0. Since L0 is a negative expression, it can be simplified by applying R5 to produce $(Q \lor \sim P)$, a positive expression with only one tilde within. If a subject carried out all these simplifications, he could replace the original problem by the new problem of obtaining $(Q \lor \sim P)$ from $(R \supset \sim P)$ and $(\sim R \supset Q)$. Whether the new problem is any easier to solve is not our immediate concern: the point is the motivation of the transformations suggested.

A still weaker clue might be the *applicability* or apparent applicability of a particular rule. Applying a rule because it applies is a little like climbing a mountain because it is there. Thus, L1, which has the shape (RP)(RQ), looks quite similar to the right side of R7—(AB)(AC). This similarity may suggest the application of

R7. We have seen in our discussion of α1 that subjects sometimes scan the list of rules looking for those that might be applicable. However, as we noted in the task analysis in Chapter 8, rules vary widely in the likelihood that they will be applicable. It makes no sense to apply R9 *because* it is applicable—since R9 is always applicable.

All of these aspects of problem structure, and perhaps others, could be used by an information processing system for its selection of paths along which to search for a solution to D1.

Comparison of GPS with a Protocol of Subject S4

As a first step toward understanding the behavior of human subjects confronted with Problem D1, we compare, in a manner similar to our earlier comparison for α1, an initial segment of a subject's protocol (S4) for D1 with a trace of a version of GPS for the same initial period. (A trace for the entire problem with a somewhat different version of GPS was shown in Figure 8.11.) The trace and the protocol are shown side by side in Figure 9.8.[2] (The entire protocol for S4 is given in Appendix 9.2.)

The GPS Trace. First, consider the GPS trace. The initial problem is to transform L1 into L0. Matching L1 to L0 reveals that there are R's in L1 and no R's in L0. This difference leads to the formulation of a reduce goal, which for readability has been given its functional name, *Delete*. The attempt to reach this goal leads to a search for rules, which finds R8. Since there are two forms of R8, both of which are admissible, GPS chooses the first. (Variants of rules are not indicated but can be inferred easily from the trace.) Since R8 is applicable, a new object, L2, is produced. Following the method for transform goals, at the next step a new goal has been generated: to transform L2 into L0. This in turn leads to another reduce goal: to restore a Q to L2. But this goal is rejected by the evaluation, since adding a term is treated by the system as more difficult than deleting a term. GPS then returns to goal 2 and seeks another rule that will delete terms. This time it finds the other form of R8 and goes through a similar excursion, ending with the rejection of R8 altogether.

Returning again to goal 2 to find another rule for deleting terms, GPS obtains R7. It selects the variant $(A \lor B) \cdot (A \lor C) \rightarrow A \lor (B \cdot C)$, since only this one both decreases terms and has a dot as its main connective. R7 is not immediately applicable; GPS first discovers that there is a difference of connective in the left subexpression, and then that there is one in the right subexpression. In both cases it finds and applies R6 to change the connective from horseshoe to wedge, obtaining successively L4 and L5. But the new expression reveals a difference in sign, which leads again to R6—that is, to the same rule as before, but perceived as accomplishing a different function. R6 produces L6, which happens to be identical

[2] The analysis given here is essentially identical to that in Newell and Simon (1961a).

L0: $\sim(\sim Q \cdot P)$
L1: $(R \supset \sim P) \cdot (\sim R \supset Q)$
Goal 1: Transform L1 into L0
  Goal 2: Delete R from L1
    Goal 3: Apply R8 to L1
      Produce L2: $R \supset \sim P$

  Goal 4: Transform L2 into L0
    Goal 5: Add Q to L2
      reject

  Goal 2: (reinstated)
    Goal 6: Apply R8 to L1
      Produce L3: $\sim R \supset Q$

  Goal 7: Transform L3 into L0
    Goal 8: Add P to L3
      reject

  Goal 2: (reinstated)
    Goal 9: Apply R7 to L1
      Goal 10: Change connective to $\vee$
          in left(L1)
        Goal 11: Apply R6 to left(L1)
          Produce L4:
            $(\sim R \vee \sim P) \cdot (\sim R \supset Q)$

    Goal 12: Apply R7 to L4
      Goal 13: Change connective to $\vee$
          in right(L4)
        Goal 14: Apply R6 to
          right(L4)
          Produce L5:
            $(\sim R \vee \sim P) \cdot (R \vee Q)$

    Goal 15: Apply R7 to L5
      Goal 16: Change sign of
          left(right(L4))
        Goal 17: Apply R6 to
          right(L5)
          Produce L6:
            $(\sim R \vee \sim P) \cdot (\sim R \supset Q)$

    Goal 18: Apply R7 to L6
      Goal 19: Change connective
          to $\vee$ in right(L6)
        reject
      Goal 16: (reinstated)
        nothing more
    Goal 13: (reinstated)
      nothing more
  Goal 10: (reinstated)
    nothing more

Well, looking at the left hand side of the equation, first we want to eliminate one of the sides by using R8. It appears too complicated to work with first

Now ... no ... no ... I can't do that because I will be eliminating either the Q or the P in that total expression.
I won't do that at first

Now I'm looking for a way to get rid of the horseshoe inside the two brackets that appear on the left and right sides of the equation.
And I don't see it.
Yeh, if you apply R6 to both sides of the equation, From there I'm going to see if I can apply R7.
(E writes L2: $(\sim R \vee \sim P) \cdot (R \vee Q)$)

I can almost apply R7, but one R needs a tilde. So I'll have to look for another rule.
I'm going to see if I can change that R to a tilde R. As a matter of fact, I should have used R6 on only the left hand side of the equation. So use R6, but only on the left hand side.
(E writes L3: $(\sim R \vee \sim P) \cdot (\sim R \supset Q)$)

Now I'll apply R7 as it is expressed.
Both .. excuse me, excuse me, it can't be done because of the horseshoe. So ... now I'm looking ... scanning the rules here for a second, and seeing if I can change the R to a $\sim$ R in the second equation, but I don't see any way of doing it.
(Sigh) I'm just sort of lost for a second.

with L4, although GPS does not notice the identity here. This leads, in goal 19, to redetection of the difference in connective, whereupon the goal is finally rejected as representing no progress over goal 13. Further attempts to find alternative ways to change signs or connectives fail to yield anything. This ends the episode.

Notice that GPS employs one of several possible means to avoid cycling indefinitely over the inessential rules in order to transform L1 into an appropriate input for R7. The actual means used is to apply a progress test to the successive differences between the expressions obtained and the desired expression (the input for R7). GPS arranges differences in a priority order. Removing a difference in connectives is progress, but reintroducing the connective difference in order to remove a sign difference is not. Hence, the latter brings the series of transformations to a halt. An alternative means would be to compare new expressions with those obtained previously, and to halt upon evidence of cycling. (The alternatives are not equivalent, for the same expression might be generated in different contexts.)

GPS and the Protocol. We now have a highly detailed trace of what GPS did. What can we find in the subject's protocol (Appendix 9.2) that either confirms or denies that the program is a detailed model of the symbol manipulations that S4 is carrying out? As with our analysis for problem $\alpha1$ with subject S9, we will carry out an informal comparison.

Let us start with the first sentence of the subject's protocol (B3–B4):

"Well, looking at the left-hand side of the equation, first we want to eliminate one of the sides by using R8."

We see here a desire to decrease L1 or eliminate something from it, and the selection of R8 as the means to do this. In its effect, this stands in direct correspondence with goals 1, 2, and 3 of the trace. We shall discuss later whether program and subject have the same motive for this step.

Let us skip to the third and fourth sentences (B6–B9):

"Now . . . no, no, I can't do that because I will be eliminating either the Q or the P in that total expression. I won't do that at first."

We see here a direct expression of the covert application of R8, the subsequent comparison of the resulting expression with L0, and the rejection of this course of action because it deletes a letter that is required in the final expression. It would be hard to find a set of words that expressed these ideas more clearly. Conversely, if the mechanism of the program (or something essentially similar to it) were not operating, it would be hard to explain why the subject uttered the remarks that he did.

One discrepancy is apparent, however. The subject handled both forms of R8 together, at least as far as his comment is concerned. GPS, on the other hand, took a separate cycle of consideration for each form. Possibly the subject followed the program covertly and simply reported the two results together. However, the fit would be better if GPS had proceeded somewhat as follows:

> Goal 2.   Delete R From L1
>   Goal 3.   Apply R8 to L1
>   Produces L2. $(R \supset \sim P)$, $(\sim R \supset Q)$
> Goal 4.   Transform L2 into L0
>   Goal 5.   Add Q to $(R \supset \sim P)$ or add P to $(\sim R \supset Q)$
>   Reject

Later, we will consider further evidence on this point.

Let us return to the second sentence (B5), which we skipped over:

> "It appears too complicated to work with first."

Nothing in the program is in simple correspondence with this statement, though it is easy to imagine some possible explanations. For example, this could merely be an expression of the matching—of the fact that L1 is such a big expression that the subject cannot absorb all its detail. On the other hand, it might derive from a working-forward goal of simplifiying expressions: given a large expression, find a rule that will simplify it. There are not enough data in the protocol to determine what part of the trace should correspond to this statement, so the sentence stands as an unexplained element of the subject's behavior.

Now, let us consider the next few sentences of the protocol (B10–B13):

> "Now I'm looking for a way to get rid of the $\supset$ inside the two brackets that appear on the left and right side of the equation, and I don't see it. Yeah, if you apply R6 to both sides of the equation, from there I'm going to see if I can apply R7."

This corresponds directly with goals 9 through 14 of the trace. The comment at the end shows that applying R7 is the main concern, and that changing connectives (inessential changes) is required in order to accomplish this. Further, the protocol shows that R6 was selected as the means. All three rule selections provide some confirmation that the subject, like GPS, made a preliminary test for feasibility in the reduce goal method. If there was not selection on the main connective, why wasn't R5 selected instead of R6? Or why wasn't the $(A \cdot B) \vee (A \cdot C) \rightarrow A \cdot (B \vee C)$ form of R7 selected?

However, there is a discrepancy between trace and protocol, for the subject handles both applications of R6 simultaneously (and apparently was also handling the two differences simultaneously), while GPS handles them sequentially. This is similar to the discrepancy noted earlier in handling R8. Since we now have two examples of such grouping of similar tasks, it is likely that there is a real difference on this score. Again, it would be better if GPS proceeded somewhat as follows:

> Goal 9.   Apply R7 to L1
>   Goal 10.   Change connective to $\vee$ in left(L1) and right(L1)
>   Goal 11.   Apply R6 to left(L1) and right(L1)
>   Produces L5. $(\sim R \vee \sim P) \cdot (R \vee Q)$

A common feature of both these discrepancies is that forming the compound expressions does not complicate the methods in any essential way. Thus, in the case involving R8, the two results stem from the same input form and require only the single match. In the case involving R7, a single search was made for a rule, and the rule was applied to both parts simultaneously, just as if only a single unit were involved.

The protocol provides information on two aspects that the program is not equipped to explain. First, the subject handled the application of R8 covertly, but commanded the experimenter to make the applications of R6 on the board. The version of GPS used here does not make any distinction between internal and external actions. To this extent it is not an adequate model. (Recall that a similar comment held for the GPS version that was run on α1.) The overt-covert distinction has consequences that run throughout a problem, since expressions on the blackboard have very different memory characteristics from expressions generated only in the head. Second, this version of GPS does not simulate the search process sufficiently well to provide a correspondent to "And I don't see it. Yeah, ..." For this, the system would have to have a facsimile of the rule sheet, and would have to distinguish search on the sheet from searches in the memory.

The next few sentences read (B15–B18):

"I can almost apply R7, but one R needs a tilde. So I'll have to look for another rule. I'm trying to see if I can change that R to a ∼ R."

Again the trace and the protocol agree on the difference that is seen. They also agree that this difference was not attended to earlier, even though it was present. Some fine structure of the data also agrees with the trace. The right-hand R, rather than the left-hand R, is viewed as having the difference (R to ∼ R), although either view is possible. This preference arises in the program, and presumably in the subject, from the language habit of working from left to right. It is not without consequences, since it determines whether the subject goes to work on the left side or the right side of the expression; hence, it can affect a whole subsequent stream of events. Similarly, in the R8 episode the subject apparently worked from left to right and from top to bottom in order to arrive at (Q ∨ P) rather than (P ∨ Q).

The next portion of the protocol is (B19–B20):

"As a matter of fact, I should have used R6 on only the left-hand side of the equation. So use number 6, but only on the left-hand side."

Here we have a strong departure from the GPS trace, although, curiously enough, the trace and the protocol end up with the same expression, (∼ R ∨ ∼ P)·(∼ R ⊃ Q). Both the subject and GPS found R6 the appropriate rule to change signs. GPS simply applied the rule to the current expression, whereas the subject went back and corrected the previous application. Nothing in the program corresponds to this. The most direct explanation is that the application of R6 in the inverse direction is perceived by the subject as undoing the previous application of R6. After following out this line of reasoning, he then takes the simpler (and less foolish-appearing) alternative, which is to correct the original action.

The final segment of the protocol episode reads (B22–B28):

"Now I'll apply R7 as it is expressed. Both . . . excuse me, excuse . . . . It can't be done because of the horseshoe. So . . . now I'm looking . . . scanning rules here for a second, and seeing if I can change that R to ∼ R in the second equation, but I don't see any way of doing it (sigh). I'm just sort of lost for a second."

The trace and the protocol are brought back into good agreement. Paths that begin to diverge do not often merge in this way. The protocol records the futile search for additional operators to remove the differences of sign and connective, always with negative results. The final comment of mild despair can be interpreted as reflecting the impact of several successive failures.

Summary. Let us take stock of the agreements and disagreements between the trace and the protocol. The program provides a complete explanation of the subject's task behavior through this episode with five exceptions of varying degrees of seriousness.

In two aspects, GPS is unprepared to simulate the subject's behavior: in distinguishing between the internal and external worlds, and in representing adequately the spaces in which the search for rules takes place. Both of these are generalized deficiencies that could be remedied.

The subject handles certain sets of items simultaneously by using compound expressions, while GPS handles all items one at a time. In the example examined here, this causes no striking differences in problem solving, but larger discrepancies could arise under other conditions. It is fairly clear how GPS could be extended to incorporate this feature.

In two cases, nothing in the program corresponds to some clear task-oriented behavior in the protocol. One of these, the early comment about "complication," seems to be mostly a case of insufficient information. The program is making numerous comparisons and evaluations that could give rise to comments of the type in question. Thus this error does not seem serious. The other case, involving the "should have . . ." passage, does seem serious. It clearly implies a mechanism (perhaps a whole set of them) that is not in GPS. Adding the mechanism required to handle this one passage could significantly increase the total capabilities of the program. For example, there might be no reasonable way to accomplish this except to provide GPS with a little continuous hindsight about its past actions.

The version of GPS we have employed to simulate these initial episodes of S4 in Problem D1 is different with respect to details of the differences it notices and the priorities it employs from the version used to simulate S9 in α1. In a basic sense, however, they must surely be regarded as the same program, and our ability to achieve an approximate fit to the behavior of two different subjects in two different problems gives us some confidence in the essential correctness of the main processes incorporated in the program structure.

Aggregate Data on Problem D1

Before we analyze intensively the protocol data from our other subjects, we can get a comprehensive view of behavior in Problem D1 from the performance of the 64 Yale subjects. These data will check our characterization of the task environment. They also will throw light on the question of whether thinking-aloud instructions modify the problem solving process in significant ways. Finally, they will provide a background against which the protocol data can be examined.

Table 9.1 shows the number of steps taken by the twenty-four Yale subjects (out of sixty-four) who solved the problem, and also by the five Carnegie subjects (out of seven) who solved it under thinking-aloud conditions. Thirteen of the twenty-four solvers in the Yale group obtained solutions in six or seven steps, as did two of the Carnegie group. Thus, the distribution of steps appears quite similar for the two groups.

Returning to the entire group of 64 subjects, those who solved the problem and those who did not, we find that they wrote on the board a total of 118 different expressions, with a total of 519 occurrences, an average of 4.4 occurrences per expression. The main question we should like to answer about the expressions the subjects generated is to what extent they are the ones we would expect if the subjects were searching along one or more of the four paths described in the earlier discussion of the task environment. Is the behavior of the subjects highly idiosyncratic, or can it largely be accounted for in terms of salient characteristics of the task that are easily noticed by the subjects (and by us)?

We have previously (p. 465) defined an *equivalence class* of expressions as all the expressions that can be obtained from a given one by application of commutation (R1 and R2), change in connectives (R5 and R6), and change in signs (R2, R5, and R6). We have defined the equivalence class of L1 as the expressions that can be formed by replacing the left and right sides of L1 by all possible combinations of members of the equivalence classes of the respective subexpressions, and by commuting around the main connective, but not changing the connective. We have also defined an extended equivalence class that includes expressions obtained by changing the main connective also.

TABLE 9.1

number of steps taken to solve problem D1 by the Yale and Carnegie subjects who solved the problem

NUMBER OF STEPS	6	7	8	9	10	11	12	13	14	Total
NUMBER OF SUBJECTS:										
YALE	4	9	3	2	2	1	1	1	1	24
CARNEGIE		2			2		1			5

We would expect a pursuit of a solution along any of the four paths to generate primarily expressions belonging to: (1) the equivalence class of L1, (2) the equivalence classes of the left of L1 and the right of L1, and (3) the equivalence class of L0. For R8 applied to L1 gives a member of left(L1) or right(L1), and the corresponding equivalence classes will be generated in trying to secure positive expressions with dot connectives so that R8 can be applied to them again (path.R11 and path.R10). One or more members of left(L1) and right(L1) will also be generated along path.R12, as will members of the equivalence class of L0. The attempt to apply R7, along path.R7, will cause the subject to generate members of the equivalence class of L1.

These are the only expressions we can account for in a straightforward way by assuming that subjects will search along these four paths. What do the data show? They show that the vast bulk of the different expressions, and an even larger percentage of the occurrences of the expressions generated by the 64 subjects, is contained in these classes. Specifically,

1. Of the 72 members belonging to the equivalence class of L1, 42 actually occurred in one or more subjects' records.
2. Of the six members belonging to the equivalence class of left(L1), all occurred.
3. Of the six members belonging to the equivalence class of right(L1), all occurred.
4. Of the six members belonging to the equivalence class of L0, all occurred.

Table 9.2 gives the statistics of occurrences for these four classes and for the class of all others.

Thus, the four classes mentioned account for just over 50 percent of the totality of different expressions that occurred in the 64 records. But these expressions occurred, on average, very much more frequently than the others (7.3 times per expression, as compared with an average of 1.4 for expressions outside the four classes). Hence, the expressions of the four classes account for 84 percent—five-sixths—of all occurrences. Of the other "unusual" expressions 26 percent (29 percent of the occurrences) belong to the extended equivalence class of L1 ($\frac{15}{58}$ and $\frac{24}{82}$ respectively).

Every subject who generated an expression in the equivalence class of L0 solved the problem. We know that a solver must use at least three expressions in the class of L0 to change from a horseshoe connective to a dot connective. The 84 occurrences in the records of the 24 solvers exceeded this minimum by only 12 occurrences (0.5 occurrences per solver). The subjects milled about very little once they obtained a member of the equivalence class of L0. Of 32 subjects who generated expressions in *both* the equivalence class of left(L1) and right(L1), 24 (75 percent) solved the problem.

These data show that subjects working under thinking-aloud conditions generated much the same expressions as did the others. Our seven subjects generated 34 different expressions, with a total of 78 occurrences. Only three of these expressions (one occurrence each) were ones not used by the Yale subjects; one of these three belonged to the equivalence class of L1. Of the remaining 31 expressions, 30 belonged to the four classes above. Of the 68 occurrences in these four classes, 29 were expressions of the class of L1, 11 of the class of left(L1), 9 of the class of right(L1), and 10 of the class of L0. The two subjects who failed to solve the problem did not generate any members of left(L1), right(L1), or L0. The five solvers generated a total of 20 occurrences of expressions belonging to left(L1) and right(L1), and 19 belonging to L0, as compared with the 15 of each category that would be the minimum for five solutions. Hence, relatively few superflous expres-

TABLE 9.2

CLASS	DIFFERENT EXPRESSIONS	TOTAL OCCURRENCES	OCCURRENCES PER EXPRESSION
L1	42	151	3.6
left(L1)	6	84	14.0
right(L1)	6	115	19.1
L0	6	87	14.5
Total:			
Four classes	60	437	7.3
Other	58	82	1.4
Grand Total	118	519	4.4

sions were generated. All of these data suggest strongly that the thinking-aloud instructions did not modify the directions of search for the problem solvers.[3]

The thinking-aloud protocols also contain evidence for expressions that subjects generated in their search but did not ask the experimenter to write on the board. These occur in various contexts. Sometimes subjects apply a rule mentally, calculate the output, and consider whether it is desirable. If it is not, they do not ask the experimenter to make the transformation. For example, S4 on D1 sees at the outset that he could obtain his L4 and his L6 by applying R8 to L1, but he does not make these transformations because each eliminates a letter that he needs for L0. All expressions of these kinds in S4's protocol belong to the equivalence classes of L1, left(L1), and right(L1) and the extended equivalence class of L1.

Sometimes, subjects work backward from L0—deriving $Q \lor \sim P$, for example. Sometimes they consider what expression they would have to have in order to make a rule applicable. S4, for example, considers that if he had $(R \lor Q)$, he could then apply R7 to derive $R \cdot (P \lor Q)$, then R8 to derive $(P \lor Q)$. These latter two classes of expressions provide important evidence for the path that the subject is searching, hence, again confirm our interpretation. In the protocols we have examined, the expressions clearly considered by the subjects but not written down fall in the

---

[3] This is not meant as a general statement about the effects of thinking-aloud instructions on behavior. Dansereau and Gregg (1966) found no difference in the times taken by subjects to do mental multiplication problems in silent and thinking-aloud conditions. We are not familiar with other studies that bear directly on the question. Most of the research on "effects of verbalization" is concerned either with verbal *instruction* or with the effects of requiring subjects to state reasons for what they are doing or to verbalize the principles inherent in problem solutions. See, for example, Gagné and Smith (1962), and the literature they cite. Effects of verbalization demonstrated under these conditions have no relevance to the question of whether thinking aloud changes the course of problem solving behavior. Because of the crucial importance of thinking-aloud behavior for our understanding of problem solving, the latter question deserves further study.

categories we have just described, hence support use of the expressions written down to obtain a general characterization of the problem-solving activities.

The Equivalence Class of L1.   The expressions of the equivalence class of L1 are particularly interesting in the light of our earlier examination of S4's protocol in the episode where he was attempting to apply R7. We would expect this kind of search to explain many or most of the expressions generated in this equivalence class.

Let us review the situation faced by S4, and by any subject trying to put L1 in a form where R7 can be applied. Consider the match of L1 to the input of R7:

$$(R \supset \sim P) \cdot (\sim R \supset Q)$$
$$(A \lor B) \cdot (A \lor C)$$

Three differences may be noted: $\sim R$ for R in right(L1), and horseshoe for wedge in the connective of left(L1) and of right(L1). To remove the first, the problem solver can apply R6 to right(L1); to remove the second, he can apply R6 to left(L1); to remove the third, R6 to right(L1). The first and third transformations lead to $(R \supset \sim P) \cdot (R \lor Q)$; the second leads to $(\sim R \lor \sim P) \cdot (\sim R \supset Q)$. If, after having changed one connective, he now changes the other, with R6 to the appropriate side, he obtains $(\sim R \lor \sim P) \cdot (R \lor Q)$. It may be observed in Figure 9.7 that S4's L2 is the last of these three expressions (the experimenter allowed him to apply R6 to both sides of L1 in one step), while his L3 is the second of the three expressions above. These are two of three occurrences of expressions of the class of L1 in S4's protocol.

These expressions are not peculiar to S4. In our other Carnegie subjects, all three occcur in S5's protocol, accounting for five of the 15 occurrences of expressions in the class of L1. In S8's protocol, the second and third expressions occur among four occurrences of class L1 expressions. S9 and S10, who did not make preparations to apply R7, generated none of these three expressions. S11 generated the second (twice) and the third, his only L1 class expressions. S15 commuted L1, then generated the analog of the first expression, then one other expression of this equivalence class.

The records of the 64 Yale subjects reveal the same picture. There were, in all, 122 applications of rules to transform L1. Of these, 24 were applications of R6 to left(L1), 11 were applications of R6 to right(L1), 34 were applications of R8 to obtain a member of right(L1), and 28 were applications of R8 to obtain a member of left(L1), eight were applications of R1 to L1, presumably to match the order of (QP) in L0, 11 were applications of R2 to left(L1), in five cases preparatory to applying R8. The remaining six applications, together with the six applications of R2 not accounted for above, amount to just 5 percent of the transformations of L1. The 95 percent accounted for above fit one or more of the five paths, some 30 percent (35) apparently preparatory to applying R7.

Given the expression $(\sim R \lor \sim P) \cdot (\sim R \supset Q)$, we might expect the further step of applying R6 to the right side. In 13 rule applications, this occurred four times. (We do not know how many subjects considered it but abandoned it because it changed the sign of R.) R8 was also applied four times. Similarly, in 13 rule applications to $(R \supset \sim P) \cdot (R \vee Q)$, R6 was applied four times to the left side. R8 was also applied four times.

In total, the expression $(\sim R \vee \sim P) \cdot (\sim R \supset Q)$ was generated by the 64 subjects 26 times, $(R \supset \sim P) \cdot (R \vee Q)$ ten times, and $(\sim R \vee \sim P) \cdot (R \vee Q)$ 19 times. The only other expressions in this equivalence class generated more than six times are the two mentioned above [apply R2 to left(L1) (nine times); apply R1 to L1 (eight times)]. In seven of the 19 cases where $(\sim R \vee \sim P) \cdot (R \vee Q)$ was generated, it was not further transformed. (In the 36 cases where the two expressions leading to it were generated, further transformations were made in 31 cases.)

The evidence is therefore convincing that expressions in the class of L1 were generated by the subjects in both conditions largely in anticipation of applying R7. We might ask why some of these subjects generated expressions like $(P \supset \sim R) \cdot (R \vee Q)$, as they did. When we examine S5's behavior, we will see that such expressions are readily explained as attempts to achieve by various indirect paths what the subject could not do directly by altering the sign of one R and changing both connectives to wedges. Subjects cycled on the structure of Figure 9.7 until they became convinced that indirect paths were as infeasible as direct ones for making R7 applicable to derivatives of L1.

The Equivalence Classes of Left(L1) and Right(L1).   Expressions of these classes arise from the application of R8 to L1 or its derivatives. Figures 9.9 and 9.10 show

FIGURE 9.9

frequency of occurrence of expressions in equivalence class of left(L1)

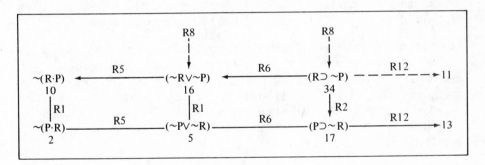

FIGURE 9.10

frequency of occurrence of expressions in equivalence class of right(L1)

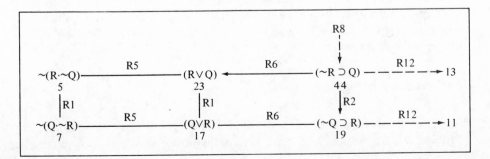

the principal transformations of expressions of these classes in the records of the 64 subjects. These figures have the same structure as Figure 9.7. transformations to forms with dot connectives are probably largely explainable as attempts to delete the R's by a second application of R8, thwarted by the fact that the expressions cannot be made positive. In 24 cases, expressions of each class, with horseshoe connectives, serve as inputs to R12, the crucial step in solving D1. We have already remarked that the five subjects in the thinking-aloud condition who obtained expressions in this class used them pretty directly as inputs to R12.

The Equivalence Class of L0.   Figure 9.11 provides the same data for expressions of the equivalence class of L0. Initially derived by R12 with horseshoe connectives,

FIGURE 9.11

frequency of occurrence of expressions in equivalence class of L0

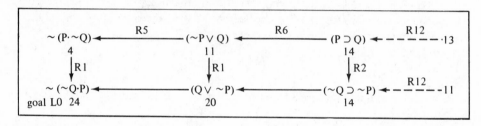

the connectives were changed to dot, and the expressions, if necessary, commuted. All but two of the 63 transformations that occurred were in the directions pointing toward the goal expression, $\sim(\sim Q \cdot P)$. We have already commented that the behavior of the subjects in the thinking-aloud condition was similar.

Miscellaneous Expressions.   Plausible accounts can be given of the paths of the problem solvers even in many of the cases where miscellaneous expressions were generated. Subject 62, for example, used R9 to generate $(R \supset \sim P) \vee Q$, then manipulated this, using R4 among other rules, in a series of eight steps, into $\sim R \vee \sim(\sim Q \cdot P)$, but then was unable to eliminate the left-hand side. Plans calling for R9 followed by R4 probably account for 20 of the 43 miscellaneous expressions, and 27 of their 58 occurrences.

Summary.   The generation of expressions by subjects can be explained parsimoniously by postulating that they are seeking to follow paths suggested by noticeable differences between L1 and L0, and noticeable features of these expressions. There is little that seems random about this generation, once we understand the problem structure. Whether the subject is only vocalizing his rule applications, or whether he is also thinking aloud while trying to solve the problem, has no detectable effect on the paths he follows.

The Protocols for Problem D1

Now let us take a closer look at the seven thinking-aloud protocols for Problem D1 (Appendices 9.2 to 9.8). So far we have only looked at the beginning of the protocol of S4. The previous sections already provide us with enough under-standing of the particular task, D1, and of the way humans cope with it, to structure the data analysis considerably. We have seen that the solution attempts of the subjects, whether correct or incorrect, revolve around making various essential transformations (those that delete or diminish an R), and that in the pursuit of this the members of the various equivalence classes are generated. Furthermore, from the behavior on $\alpha 1$ and also from the bit of D1 examined, the means-ends opera-tions of GPS not only generated a directed exploration of the equivalence classes, but did so in the same way as human subjects. In $\alpha 1$, of course, the entire problem remained within one equivalence class (since only changes of sign, order, and con-nective were required to solve the problem); but in S4's attempt to apply R7 we have an almost perfect example of an exploration of an equivalence class (of L1) in or-der to achieve an essential step (two R's diminished to one and factored out).

This suggests that we can episode the protocols at the level of goals that attempt essential changes. Once an essential step has been decided upon, some *obvious* inessential steps will need to be executed to permit the essential rule to be applied. Within each episode, behavior will be predominantly GPS-like. Whether the initiation and termination of episodes, so defined, is again GPS-like or involves other methods is not clear and is not of concern for the moment.

The expectation that episodes exist in logic, and the prediction about their internal nature, are basically still hypotheses, to be tested. We defined the concept of episode abstractly in Chapter 3 as a segment of obvious behavior performed in pursuit of a goal, given the general intellectual level of the problem solver. In Chapter 7 we were able to give this concept concrete operational character for cryptarithmetic by relying on the solver's tendency to acquire new knowledge, so that any problem solver would follow a path to obvious new information—and information would be obvious if it could be obtained without positing a new assignment. But the logic task has a different structure and requires a correspond-ingly different notion of episode.

The characteristic feature of the logic task is that, in one way or another, the subject arrives at an essential rule that he wishes to apply but that is inapplicable to the current expression. This may come about in one of several ways:

1. in responding to an essential difference, without further concern for the consequences;
2. in responding to a general principle, such as simplification;
3. in deciding to apply an operator because its input is similar to that of the current expression;
4. in developing a plan involving several rules, and then beginning to imple-ment the first rule of the plan.

In the initial segment of S4's protocol we have seen examples only of item 1 and possibly item 2. We will not examine the other possibilities until Chapter 10. But it is not important, for present purposes, to understand the exact mechanisms that give rise to a commitment to apply an initially inapplicable essential rule. All subjects make such commitments repeatedly in the course of problem solving.

The decision to apply an essential rule initiates an episode. The obvious steps taken to make the rule applicable constitute the body of the episode. The analysis assumes that the problem solver can (hence will) go through the GPS-like means-ends cycle in which a difference is detected, a relevant operator selected and applied, and the result evaluated by attempting to reapply the original essential operator that initiated the episode. The relevant operator may be obtained by direct association from the difference (i.e., functional description) to the operator. But it may also be obtained by a search of the rule sheet with a corresponding test for the desired function. The operator may be a rule to modify the current expression, but it may also be a search of the display for an existing expression that already satisfies the desired conditions. In both cases of search—of the rule sheet and of the display—there is immediate feedback about the success or failure of the search, so that the continuity of the episode is not broken.

An episode usually terminates with failure to apply the essential rule. Since there is seldom any sharp indication that a rule is not applicable to some (inessential) variant of the available expressions, the subject may continue within an episode for a very long period of time (e.g., several minutes) before acknowledging failure. Although an available result within an episode is obvious (by definition), hence should be obtained with alacrity, it is *not* obvious that a result is *not* available. For the latter involves exhausting the space of inessential transformations, rather than just finding a single path through this space to a desired expression.

If perchance the essential operator is applicable, then the episode may continue to the application of one (or more) additional essential rules. This can happen because the episode was initiated by a plan (item 4 above), or by following a general principle, such as simplification (item 2). Thus a separate episode does not correspond to each concern with an essential rule, but rather to each decision to follow a path, as we described these earlier.

Episodes can arise in two other ways. One is the direct attempt to reach the goal expression. Such an episode is exactly the same as the ones above, with the goal expression in place of the operator condition. As we noted, each of the attempts to solve $\alpha 1$ constituted a single episode of this type, since no essential operators were involved.

The second way episodes can arise is by the adoption of a specific method. For instance, a subject may decide to work forward, applying each operator in turn and evaluating its probable usefulness. Once such a method has been adopted, a sequence of future actions becomes highly predictable—one might even say, obvious. For it is obvious that a subject who is working forward in this particular way will consider R4 after R3 and R5 after R4, independently of the content of the rule. His actions are obvious because they derive from the steps of a method to which he has become committed. Hence the behavior following upon the adoption of a method constitutes an episode. The case is exactly analogous to a plan, where the next essential rule does not initiate a new episode, because it is obvious, given the plan.

Episodes, since they are tied to goals, can be hierarchical, with one episode embedded in another. This is especially possible in the logic task, where—as we shall see—subjects can become committed to following particular paths for long

FIGURE 9.12

episode abstract for S4 on problem D1

E	B	INSTIGATOR	E-SCHEMA	EPISODE
		L0: $\sim(\sim Q \cdot P)$		
		L1: $(R \supset \sim P) \cdot (\sim R \supset Q)$		
E1	B3	eliminate		$\overset{R8}{\Rightarrow}$
E2	B10	?	path.R7	$\overset{R7}{=\!=}\overset{R6}{\Rightarrow} L2, (L1) \overset{R6}{\Rightarrow} L3$
		L2: $(\sim R \vee \sim P) \cdot (R \vee Q)$		
		L3: $(\sim R \vee \sim P) \cdot (\sim R \supset Q)$		
E3.1	B29	eliminate	WF	$(L1) \overset{R8}{\Rightarrow} L4$
		L4: $R \supset \sim P$		
E3.2	B35			$\overset{R12}{=\!=}\overset{\boxed{L}}{\Rightarrow} (L2, L3) \overset{R12}{=\!=}$
E3.3	B38			$\overset{R11}{=\!=}$
E4	B40		path.R7	$\overset{R10}{=\!=}\overset{R7}{=\!=} (L5) \overset{R6}{\Rightarrow} L6, (L1) \overset{R6}{\Rightarrow} L7 (\overset{R12}{\Rightarrow}) \overset{R7}{=\!=} L8$
		L5: $\sim R \vee \sim P$		
		L6: $\sim R \supset Q$		
		L7: $R \vee Q$		
		L8: $(\sim R \vee \sim P) \cdot (R \vee Q)$		
E5	B59	E	review	(eliminate) $\overset{R8,R11,R12}{=\!=\!=\!=\!=}$ (path.R7) $\overset{R10}{\Rightarrow}$
E6	B72		path.R7	$\overset{R7}{=\!=}$
E7	B97		WF	$\overset{R1-R12}{\Longrightarrow}$ path.R7
E8	B124		path.R7	$\overset{R7}{=\!=}\overset{R2}{=\!=}\overset{\boxed{L}}{=\!=} (L2, L4)$ notice R12
E9	B132	R12	path.R12	$(L2,L4) \overset{R12}{=\!=}\overset{R2}{\Rightarrow} L9,L10 (L6,L9) \overset{R12}{\Rightarrow} L11$
		L9: $P \supset \sim R$		
		L10: $\sim Q \supset R$		
		L11: $P \supset Q$		
E10	B149	E	review	
E11	B157	get L0		$(L11) \overset{R6}{\Rightarrow} L12 \overset{R5}{\Rightarrow} L13 \overset{R1}{\Rightarrow} L14$ solution
		L12: $\sim P \vee Q$		
		L13: $\sim(P \cdot \sim Q)$		
		L14: $\sim(\sim Q \cdot P)$		

periods of time, during which they may adopt various methods, thus initiating subepisodes.

We can use S4, the subject discussed earlier in comparison with GPS, to illustrate the episoding of a logic task. We show in Figure 9.12 the episode abstract for S4 and in Figure 9.13 the PBG, to permit evaluation of the reality of the episodes from two different viewpoints. The legend for the PBG is given at the end of the figure. The operators are the goals of applying a rule and of transforming one expression into another (abbreviated in the figure as *get*). The inputs to an operator are sometimes given with the operator; when they are missing, they are the current

FIGURE 9.13
problem behavior graph of S4 on problem D1

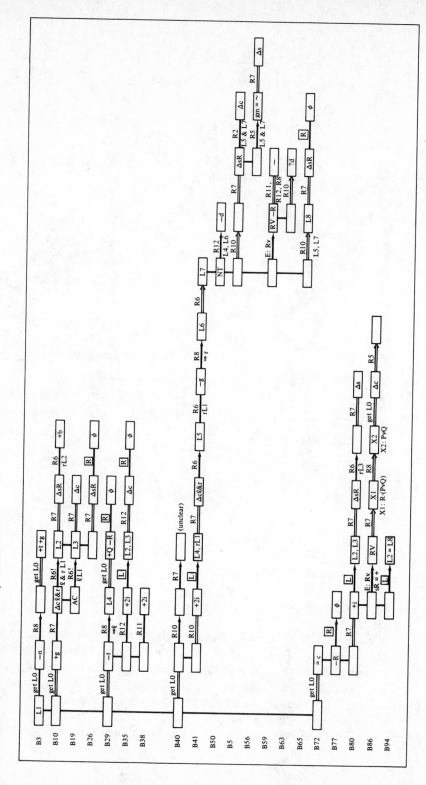

FIGURE 9.13 (cont'd)

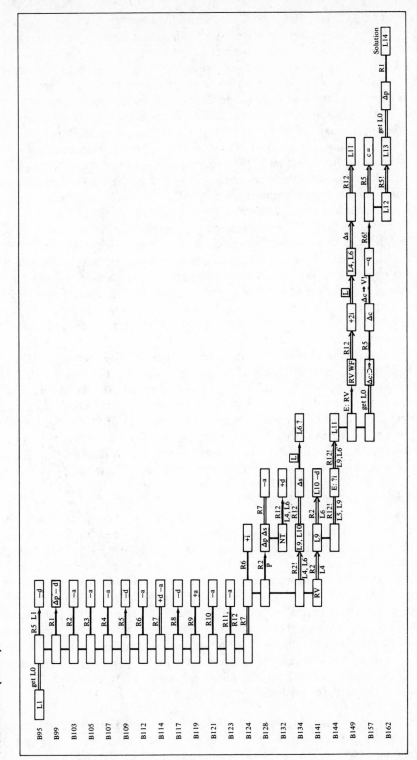

expressions, as taken from the PBG. The information written in the boxes is the state information—either the expression under consideration or differences and features that have been derived from it.

It is necessary to take goals as operators, rather than just the rules themselves, since attempts at application of rules are a salient feature of the logic task. We could either take the goal of reducing a difference as an operator, along with the apply and transform goals, or treat the differences as state information associated with the appropriate apply or transform goal. We chose the latter alternative. Thus differences may appear as operators in the PBG when they are used explicitly as operators (e.g., "remove a term") to produce an output and then proceed with the analysis. No good example occurs in the PBG of S4, though at B158 he attempts to command E to change a wedge, then realizes he has named the operator in terms of the associated function rather than by its proper name (R6).

We indicate that an operator is applied successfully (whether covertly or overtly, abstractly or in full detail, accurately or with error) by putting an arrowhead on the line between boxes. Then the contents of the following box describe the result of that application. We indicate that an operator is not applied by omitting the arrowhead. Then the contents of the following box describe the difficulty in applying the operator. The operator (actually, the goal of applying the operator) will then be in the goal stack. A later reapplication of it will be indicated by a double-lined connection.

The beginning of S4's PBG, from B3 through the line starting at B26, constitutes the part simulated by GPS, as described earlier in the chapter. The reader can clarify the various conventions just described by comparing the two descriptions. (In the PBG we do not show two distinct applications of R8, since this appears to be a feature of the GPS simulation and not of S4's actual behavior.)

S4's behavior breaks into eleven episodes, one of which (E3) consists of three subepisodes. Each of the episodes is clearly delineated in the PBG as a separate cluster of search. Most of the episodes derive from the attempt to follow one of the paths, either path.R7 or path.R12. But one episode provides a clear example of working forward (indicated in the PBG by the WF at B99). There are a few other such notes on the PBG (e.g., AC at B19, for the avoid-consequences method). These will be discussed further in describing within-episode behavior.

Examination of the protocol in Appendix 9.2 will show that both the initiation of episodes and their termination are often marked by distinctive language. For example, the working-forward episode is intiated by (B99): "I'm looking through them one at a time to see just in what way they might help rearrange the expression," and terminated by (B123–B124): ". . . nor 11 or 12 [the last rules to be looked at]. So 7 seems to be the only one that can help me . . . ." Thus, episoding simply on the empirical basis of boundaries where the subject "changes direction" or "does something different" would coincide with the present episoding in many cases. The present scheme for episoding, of course, provides a basis for understanding why episodes exist and for explaining their extent.

Overview of Episodes.   Figures 9.14 to 9.19 give the episode abstracts for the other six protocols of D1, formed acccording to the scheme of the preceding section. The protocols themselves are reproduced at the end of the chapter (Appendices 9.2 to 9.8), with the episode boundaries marked. The few uncertainties in processing the data are footnoted at the appropriate places in the protocols themselves.

Most of the protocols begin with some characterization of the problem expressions and the differences between L1 and L0. The transformation required is most often expressed as "I must eliminate the R's," sometimes followed by, "I must group the Q and P."

There are some strong hints that the specific way in which the subject represents the problem, hence phrases the task, influences the paths he evokes and tries. For example, R8 may be viewed as a means for eliminating half of L1:

FIGURE 9.14

episode abstract for S5 on problem D1

E	B	INSTIGATOR	E-SCHEMA	EPISODE
		L0: $\sim(\sim Q\cdot P)$		
		L1: $(R \supset \sim P)\cdot(\sim R \supset Q)$		
E1	B3	input from R7	path.R7	$\overset{R7}{=}\overset{R2}{\Rightarrow}$ L2
		L2: $(R \supset \sim P)\cdot(\sim Q \supset R)$		
E2	B39	get Q	path.R10 with R12 for R8	L1,L2 $\overset{R12}{=}\overset{R5}{\Rightarrow}$ L3 $\overset{R6}{\Rightarrow}$ L4 $\overset{R12}{=}\overset{get\ P,Q}{\Longrightarrow}\overset{R10}{=}$
		L3: $\sim(\sim(R \supset \sim P) \vee \sim(\sim Q \supset R))$		
		L4: $\sim((R \supset \sim P) \supset \sim(\sim Q \supset R))$		
E3.1	B95	WF	path.R7	L1 $\overset{R7}{=}\overset{R6}{\Rightarrow}$ L5 $\overset{R6}{\Rightarrow}$ L6 $\overset{R2}{\Rightarrow}$ L7
		L5: $(\sim R \vee \sim P)\cdot(R \vee Q)$		
		L6: $(R \supset \sim P)\cdot(R \vee Q)$		
		L7: $(P \supset \sim R)\cdot(R \vee Q)$		
E3.2	B140	get sign R = +	path.R7	L5 $\overset{R1}{\Rightarrow}$ L8 $\overset{R6}{\Rightarrow}$ L9 $\overset{R2}{\Rightarrow}$ L10 = L6,L8 $\overset{R1}{\Rightarrow}$ L11
		L8: $(\sim P \vee \sim R)\cdot(R \vee Q)$		
		L9: $(P \supset \sim R)\cdot(R \vee Q)$		
		L10: $(R \supset \sim P)\cdot(R \vee Q)$		
		L11: $(\sim R \vee \sim P)\cdot(R \vee Q)$		
E3.3	B182		path.R7	L11 $\overset{R5}{\Rightarrow}$ L12 $\overset{R1}{\Rightarrow}$ L13 $\overset{R5}{\Rightarrow}$ L14 $\overset{R1}{\Rightarrow}$ L15 = L5 = L11
		L12: $\sim(R\cdot P)\cdot(R \vee Q)$		
		L13: $\sim(P\cdot R)\cdot(R \vee Q)$		
		L14: $(\sim P \vee \sim R)\cdot(R \vee Q)$		
		L15: $(\sim R \vee \sim P)\cdot(R \vee Q)$		
E4	B220	get Q	$(QR)(QR) \Rightarrow QQ \Rightarrow Q$	L1 $\overset{R12}{\Rightarrow}\overset{R8}{\Rightarrow}\overset{R12}{=}\overset{R10}{\Rightarrow}$ cycle
E5	B247	get sign R on right = $\sim$	path.R7	L15 $\overset{R6}{\Rightarrow}$ L16 $\overset{R2}{\Rightarrow}$ L17 $\overset{R6}{\Rightarrow}$ L18 E terminates attempt
		L16: $(\sim R \vee \sim P)\cdot(\sim R \supset Q)$		
		L17: $(\sim R \vee \sim P)\cdot(\sim Q \supset R)$		
		L18: $(\sim R \vee \sim P)\cdot(Q \vee R)$		

S4 (B3–B5): First we want to eliminate one of the sides by using R8. It appears too complicated to work with first.

Alternatively, R8 may be viewed as a means for obtaining the two subexpressions as separate lines:

S9 (B17–B18): Well, I can split those up, using Rule 8.

FIGURE 9.15
episode abstract for S8 on problem D1

E	B	INSTIGATOR	E-SCHEMA	EPISODE
		L0: ~(~Q·P)		
		L1: (R ⊃ ~P)·(~R ⊃ Q)		
E1	B4	get L0	WF	L1 $\xrightarrow{R1,R3,R4,R7}$
E2	B23	group P Q	path.R7	L1 $\xrightarrow{R7}$⇒ L2 $\xrightarrow{R6}$ L3 $\xrightarrow{R7}$
		L2: (~R ∨ ~P)·(~R ⊃ Q)		
		L3: (~R ∨ ~P)·(R ∨ Q)		
E3	B56	get L0	WF	L1 $\xrightarrow{R1,R8}$ $\xrightarrow{R7,R4}$⇒ $\xrightarrow{R8}$
E4	B85	notice R4	path.R4	L3 $\xrightarrow{R4}$⇒ L4 $\xrightarrow{R5}$ L5 $\xrightarrow{R4}$
		L4: ~(R·P)·(R ∨ Q)		
		L5: ~(R·P)·~(~R·~Q)		
E5	B135	group P Q	WF	$\xrightarrow{R1,R7}$
E6	B152	get L0	R8 to part	$\xrightarrow{R8}$⇒ⓁL5 $\xrightarrow{R8}$⇒ⓁL3 $\xrightarrow{R8}$ R5,R8
E7.1	B177	notice R9	path.R9	$\xrightarrow{R2}$⇒$\xrightarrow{R8}$⇒$\xrightarrow{R9}$ plan.R9
E7.2	B204	plan.R9	path.R9	L3 $\xrightarrow{R8}$ R5,R6,R2
E8	B247	get L0	WF	L1 $\xrightarrow{R8,R3}$ $\xrightarrow{R11}$ $\xrightarrow{R8,R8}$
E9	B286	get L0	review	L1 $\xrightarrow{R1,R8}$
E10	B299	get L0	do something different	L1 $\xrightarrow{R5}$⇒ L6 $\xrightarrow{R6}$⇒ $\xrightarrow{R8,R8,R6,R5}$
		L6: ~(~(R ⊃ ~P) ∨ ~(~R ⊃ Q))		
E11	B367	eliminate term	path.R9	L1 $\xrightarrow{R8}$⇒ L7 $\xrightarrow{R8}$$\xrightarrow{R6,R5}$ L1 $\xrightarrow{R8}$⇒ ~R ⊃ Q ; $\xrightarrow{R8}$$\xrightarrow{R6,R5}$
		L7: R ⊃ ~P		
E12.1	B437	eliminate term	WF	L1 $\xrightarrow{R2}$⇒ ~R ⊃ Q $\xrightarrow{R10}$⇒ⓁL7 $\xrightarrow{R10}$
E12.2	B453		path.R12	~R ⊃ Q,L7 $\xrightarrow{R12}$$\xrightarrow{R2}$⇒ plan.R12
E13.1	B457	plan.R12	path.R12	L1 $\xrightarrow{R8}$⇒ L8 $\xrightarrow{R2}$⇒ L9,L7 $\xrightarrow{R12}$⇒ L10[error] $\xrightarrow{R6}$⇒ L11 $\xrightarrow{R5}$⇒ ~(~Q.~P)
		L8: ~R ⊃ Q		
		L9: ~Q ⊃ R		
		L10: ~Q ⊃ P error		
		L11: Q ∨ P		
E13.2	B505	change sign(P)		L10,L11 $\xrightarrow{R8,R2}$

FIGURE 9.16

episode abstract for S9 on problem D1

E	B	INSTIGATOR	E-SCHEMA	EPISODE
		L0: $\sim(\sim Q \cdot P)$		
		L1: $(R \supset \sim P) \cdot (\sim R \supset Q)$		
E1	B3	get L0		$\overset{R5}{\Rightarrow}$ L0 [use sometime]
E2	B6	group P and Q	path.R12	$L1 \overset{R12}{=\!=} \text{split} \overset{R10,R9,R8}{=\!=\!=\!=\!=} \overset{R12}{\Rightarrow} \sim P \supset Q \overset{R2,R5}{=\!=}$ plan.R12
E3	B34	plan.R12	review	$L1 \overset{R8}{\Rightarrow} \text{group} \overset{R12}{\Rightarrow} \overset{R2}{\Rightarrow} \text{plan.R12}$
E4	B47	plan.R12	path.R12	$L1 \overset{R8}{\Rightarrow} L2 \overset{R2}{\Rightarrow} L3$ [error], $L1 \overset{R8}{\Rightarrow} L4$ $\overset{R12}{=\!=} \overset{R2}{\Rightarrow} L5$ [L3 error discovered]
		L2: $R \supset \sim P$		
		L3: $\sim R \supset P$ [error]		
		L4: $\sim R \supset Q$		
		L5: $\sim Q \supset R$		
E5	B81	plan.R12	path.R12	$L3,L4 \overset{R12}{\Rightarrow} L6 \overset{R6}{\Rightarrow} L7 \overset{R5}{\Rightarrow} L8 \overset{R1}{\Rightarrow} L9$ solution
		L3: $P \supset \sim R$ [correct]		
		L6: $P \supset Q$		
		L7: $\sim P \vee Q$		
		L8: $\sim(P \cdot \sim Q)$		
		L9: $\sim(\sim Q \cdot P)$		

FIGURE 9.17

episode abstract for S10 on problem D1

E	B	INSTIGATOR	E-SCHEMA	EPISODE
		L0: $\sim(\sim Q \cdot P)$		
		L1: $(R \supset \sim P) \cdot (\sim R \supset Q)$		
E1	B3		WF	$L1 \overset{R6,R2,R3}{=\!=\!=\!=\!=}$
E2	B13	group	WF	$L1 \overset{R6,R5,R8}{=\!=\!=\!=\!=}$
E3	B19		WF	$L1 \overset{R11,R12}{=\!=\!=} \overset{R8}{\Rightarrow} \overset{R12}{\Rightarrow} \text{plan.R12}$
E4	B25	plan.R12	path.R12	$L1 \overset{R12}{=\!=} \overset{R2}{\Rightarrow} L2, L1 \overset{R8}{\Rightarrow} L3, L2 \overset{R8}{\Rightarrow} L4, L2$ $\overset{R8}{\Rightarrow} L5 \overset{R12}{\Rightarrow} L6$ $\overset{R6}{\Rightarrow} L7 \overset{R5}{\Rightarrow} L8 \overset{R1}{\Rightarrow} L9$ solution
		L2: $(P \supset \sim R) \cdot (\sim R \supset Q)$		
		L3: $R \supset \sim P$		
		L4: $P \supset \sim R$		
		L5: $\sim R \supset Q$		
		L6: $P \supset Q$		
		L7: $\sim P \vee Q$		
		L8: $\sim(P \cdot \sim Q)$		
		L9: $\sim(\sim Q \cdot P)$		

FIGURE 9.18

episode abstract for S11 on problem D1

E	B	INSTIGATOR	E-SCHEMA	EPISODE
		L0: $\sim(\sim Q \cdot P)$		
		L1: $(R \supset \sim P) \cdot (\sim R \supset Q)$		
E1	B3	get L0	WF	$L1 \overset{R2,R8,R12,R6}{=\!=\!=\!=\!=\!=}\rfloor$
E2	B39	get L0		$L1 \overset{R2}{=\!=}\rfloor \text{ group P Q} \overset{R12,R7}{=\!=\!=\!=}$
E3.1	B94	notice R4	path.R4	$L1 \overset{R4}{\Rightarrow} R \cdot (\sim P \cdot (\sim R \supset Q)) \overset{R8}{\Rightarrow} \sim P \cdot$ $(\sim R \supset Q) \overset{R4,R8}{=\!=\!=\!\Rightarrow} \sim (R \cdot \sim Q) \overset{R8,R3}{=\!=\!=}\rfloor \text{ plan.R4}$
E3.2	B161	plan.R4	path.R4	$L1 \overset{R4}{=\!=} \overset{R6}{\Rightarrow} L2 \overset{R5}{\Rightarrow} \sim (R \cdot P) \overset{R4}{\Rightarrow} \overset{R8}{=\!=}\rfloor$
		L2: $(\sim R \vee \sim P) \cdot (\sim R \supset Q)$		
E4	B196	eliminate $\sim R$'s	path.R7	$L2 \overset{R7}{=\!=} \overset{R2}{\Rightarrow} L3 \overset{R6}{\Rightarrow} L4 \overset{R7}{=\!=}$
		L3: $(\sim R \vee \sim P) \cdot (\sim Q \supset R)$		
		L4: $(\sim R \vee \sim P) \cdot (Q \vee R)$		
E5	B255	eliminate R's	path.R4	$L4 \overset{R4}{=\!=} \overset{R6,R3}{=\!=\!=}\rfloor$
E6	B276	eliminate $\sim R$'s	WF	$L4 \overset{R8}{=\!=}$

FIGURE 9.19

episode abstract for S15 on problem D1

E	B	INSTIGATOR	E-SCHEMA	EPISODE
		L0: $\sim(\sim Q \cdot P)$		
		L1: $(R \supset \sim P) \cdot (\sim R \supset Q)$		
E1	B3		WF	$L1 \overset{R1,R3,R8}{=\!=\!=\!=\!=\!=}\rfloor$
E2	B9	group, eliminate	WF	$L1 \overset{R7}{=\!=} \overset{R1}{\Rightarrow} L2 \overset{R6}{\Rightarrow} L3 \overset{R5}{\Rightarrow} L4 \overset{R8,R7}{=\!=\!=}$
		L2: $(\sim R \supset Q) \cdot (R \supset \sim P)$		
		L3: $(R \vee Q) \cdot (R \supset \sim P)$		
		L4: $\sim(\sim R \cdot \sim Q) \cdot (R \supset \sim P)$		
E3	B50		WF	$L1 \overset{R2,R5,R4}{=\!=\!=\!=\!=}$
E4	B67	eliminate	path.R12	$L1 \overset{R8}{\Rightarrow} L5,L6 \overset{R12}{=\!=} \overset{R6}{\Rightarrow} L7,L5 \overset{R2}{\Rightarrow} L8 \overset{R12}{\Rightarrow} L9$ $\overset{R6}{\Rightarrow} L10 \overset{R1}{\Rightarrow} L11 \overset{R5}{\Rightarrow} L12 \text{ solution}$
		L5: $R \supset \sim P$		
		L6: $\sim R \supset Q$		
		L7: $\sim R \vee \sim P$		
		L8: $P \supset \sim R$		
		L9: $P \supset Q$		
		L10: $\sim P \vee Q$		
		L11: $Q \vee \sim P$		
		L12: $\sim(\sim Q \cdot P)$		

S4's fomulation deters him from applying R8: "No, no, no, I can't do that because I will be eliminating either the Q or the P in that total expression." The protocol of S15 illustrates the effect of moving from the one viewpoint to the other (end of his first episode):

S15 (B45–B47):   Number 8 would get rid of them completely, and I can't.
. . .

(B67–B70):   Going to 8, again, I would get one side of that, and you could get either side. How about doing 8 twice on L1, and getting A and B separately?

Most of the episodes in the protocols are compatible with the five plans. All the solvers, of course, employ path.R12. S4, S5, and S8 are occupied extensively, and S10 and S11 briefly, with path.R7 and variants of it. Variants of path.R11 are prominent in S5's protocol, and of path.R10 in S8's. S11 is a special case, which we will take up later. Here, we wish merely to observe that in only one of his seven episodes (E6) does he follow any of the paths we have described.

The path.R12 episodes are all highly similar, as we remarked earlier, and relatively simple. After the subjects have used R12 to generate $(P \supset Q)$, they all note the difference in connective with L0 and proceed to remove it, then to commute the resulting expression, with few or no comments other than their instructions to the experimenter to apply specific rules. As in the cryptarithmetic problems, the protocols are fuller of comments about differences and possible operators when difficulties are being encountered than when the sailing is smooth.

Given the goal of applying R12, a GPS to simulate these episodes would have to evoke the subgoal of obtain-two-inputs, then the operator R8, applied twice (recall the discussion in Chapter 8). However, S4 and S8 started along path.R12 only after they had applied R8 to L1 for other reasons. Hence, a GPS to simulate them would be simpler than the one required for the other three solvers. However, it would have to be able to initiate problem solving from any of the displayed expressions. Once R12 has been applied, almost any version of GPS would discover and apply the final transformations (change connective, change position) in much the same way that the five subjects did.

With this overview of the episodes, we can turn to the separate tasks of assessing the within-episode behavior and then the initiation and termination of episodes.

Within-Episode Behavior.   These are 49 episodes in all. Of these, some 35 last long enough to contain some within-episode behavior—that is, consist of more than an opening gambit that leads nowhere and terminates. Each of these could be considered in detail and analyzed both for its similarity to other episodes and for the ability of GPS-like mechanisms to provide an adequate simulation of it. However, this would extend an already long treatment of these data. Instead we will examine just one sequence of episodes, S5's attempt to apply R7, and then provide a summary accounting of the mechanisms used within all the episodes.

S5 failed to solve the problem, and three out of his five episodes are related to path.R7 (the attempt to apply R7). These three episodes can conveniently be considered together, since the two intervening ones (E2 and E4) were short and appeared to have little impact on the bulk of his behavior. This preoccupation with R7 throughout the subject's protocol is shown in several ways. For one, he generated far more members (15) of the equivalence class of L1 than did any other subject. In fact, when questioned afterward by the experimenter, he said (B296–B302):

> Well, maybe I was stuck on one track. Indirectly, I kept doing the same thing over and over again, switching around terms, and I kept ending up with the wrong sign in the wrong place. I was unable to apply R7 to it in the first place. There must be some way it'll fall out real easily. It looks very easy. It looks like you can do it in only a few steps if you knew the right ones. I was just horsing around trying to get it into that form that would work.

The nature of S5's "horsing around" is revealed clearly by Figure 9.20, which shows the steps he used to generate lines 6 through 18. As can be seen from his episode abstract (Figure 9.14), L5 is the first line he generates in E3, on becoming aware of the connective difference in applying R7 to L1. He applies R6 to both sides of L1 to get L5. The protocol segment divides into three subepisodes, designated in the figure E3.1, E3.2, and E3.3, respectively. In the protocol, the division between E3.1 and E3.2 is marked by a pause that causes the experimenter to ask (B165): "What are you doing now?" (There is no such pause within any of the subepisodes.) The division between E3.2 and E3.3 is even more strongly marked by a passage in which S5 briefly interrupts the path.R7 scheme to consider one or two others.

All three subepisodes are concerned with trying to change the sign of one of the R's in an expression like $(\sim R \lor \sim P) \cdot (R \lor Q)$. In E3.1, S5 tries to remove the tilde from the R in the left-hand subexpression by going around the right-hand cycle of Figure 9.7—i.e., by changing the connective, then changing the sign, then changing the connective back again. He tries to do this in both directions [see Figure 9.20 (E3.1)].

In E3.2, S5 tries to do the same, but this time by going around the left-hand cycle of Figure 9.7—i.e., by changing to a dot, instead of a horseshoe, and back. In E3.3 he gives up trying to remove the tilde from the R in the left-hand subexpression and instead tries to add one to the R on the right. Again, he goes around the right-hand cycle of Figure 9.7, this time noticing his lack of progress a little sooner than he did in E3.1. (The goals in all three subepisodes are clearly verbalized in the protocol.)

Analyzed in this way, S5's attempts to apply R7, though futile, are understandable and systematic. Since he has not analyzed the effects of successive rule applications, as we have in Figure 9.7, he hopes that he can change a sign by following one of the cycles of connective changes in that figure. Being unable to look more than a step or two ahead without putting the transformations on the blackboard, he must carry out an extensive search to convince himself he will always come back to the same expression without the desired change in sign. All the

FIGURE 9.20

attempts by S5 to apply R7 in problem D1

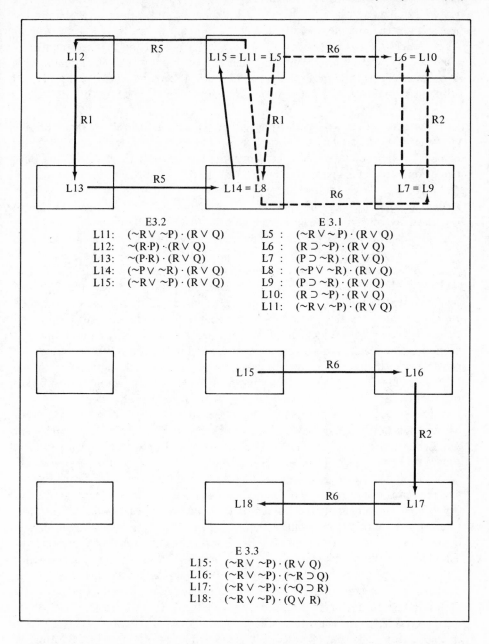

E3.2
L11: $(\sim R \lor \sim P) \cdot (R \lor Q)$
L12: $\sim(R \cdot P) \cdot (R \lor Q)$
L13: $\sim(P \cdot R) \cdot (R \lor Q)$
L14: $(\sim P \lor \sim R) \cdot (R \lor Q)$
L15: $(\sim R \lor \sim P) \cdot (R \lor Q)$

E 3.1
L5 : $(\sim R \lor \sim P) \cdot (R \lor Q)$
L6 : $(R \supset \sim P) \cdot (R \lor Q)$
L7 : $(P \supset \sim R) \cdot (R \lor Q)$
L8 : $(\sim P \lor \sim R) \cdot (R \lor Q)$
L9 : $(P \supset \sim R) \cdot (R \lor Q)$
L10: $(R \supset \sim P) \cdot (R \lor Q)$
L11: $(\sim R \lor \sim P) \cdot (R \lor Q)$

E 3.3
L15: $(\sim R \lor \sim P) \cdot (R \lor Q)$
L16: $(\sim R \lor \sim P) \cdot (\sim R \supset Q)$
L17: $(\sim R \lor \sim P) \cdot (\sim Q \supset R)$
L18: $(\sim R \lor \sim P) \cdot (Q \lor R)$

verbalizations in this part of the protocol are consistent with this interpretation of his actions.

We have already discussed at length the path.R7 episodes of S4 and the GPS trace simulating them. The priority ordering of differences in that version of GPS would prevent it from following S5's more extensive explorations, since it would

491

not change connectives (R6 and R5) in order to achieve a change in sign of a term, as S5 repeatedly did. However, to achieve this kind of behavior is not simply a matter of changing the priorities, as a little hand-simulation of a revised version would show. S5 has the goal of eliminating the tilde before R—i.e., transforming $(\sim R \vee \sim P)$ into either $(R \vee \sim P)$ or $(R \vee P)$—by applying the inessential rules along indirect as well as direct paths. Hence, a program would simulate this kind of behavior, generating the expressions of Figure 9.20(a) and 9.20(b), if it generated all paths from an initial expression, using the inessential rules, until it detected a cycle.

The accounting we have just given of S5 addresses itself to the GPS-like character of his behavior only by indirection. We have shown quite clearly that his behavior is almost all devoted to attainment of a single essential goal. And we have made some assertions about the changes in GPS to simulate it, but we have not really detailed these. Is there some way, short of simulation, that can give us a feeling whether the behavior within an episode is GPS-like, rather than being generated by other mechanisms, such as exhaustive search?

GPS can be described by a collection of steps: the act of matching and then trying to reduce a difference, the act of selecting a rule that is relevant to a high-priority existing difference, the response to the inapplicability of a rule by trying to make it applicable, and so on. These are sufficiently integrated acts that they can be recognized in the protocols without much difficulty. The comparisons of GPS with the protocol materials earlier in the chapters provide numerous examples. Other steps, such as the deliberate search through the rules, trying each one and examining the result, can also be clearly discerned in the protocols. Such steps are possible rules in a heuristic search scheme, through not specifically included in the GPS described in Chapter 8. Other parts of the protocols (within the episodes) may not be identifiable at all with any step that makes sense.

Thus, one possible analysis is to list the different types of steps that occur within an episode and see how much of the behavior is GPS-like. The convenient representation for this is the PBG. Consider the PBG of S4, which was shown in Figure 9.13 (page 482). There are 79 instances of a rule application in this graph, ignoring the transform goals (e.g., get L0), but counting the scans of the display and the scans of the rule sheets for rules where none was found (e.g., the 🄻 and 🅁 in the line starting at B35). Each of these operator occurrences can be classified according to the mechanism that evoked it. These mechanisms can mostly be determined directly from the PBG itself, without further resort to the protocol. Thus, to take the familiar line at B10, the first R7 is in response to a difference (g+: group terms) derived from the goal of getting L0, hence constitutes an example of means-ends analysis towards the goal object. The next operator, R6, is in response to a difference (Δc: change connective) that occurs because R7 is not applicable, hence constitutes an example of means-ends analysis to make a rule applicable. The next operator, R7, is the reapplication of the first R7 after an attempt has been made to remedy the difficulty; and the last operator, R6, is again in response to a difference (ΔsR) from R7, thus constitutes a second example of means-ends analysis for operator applicability.

We have developed PBG's for all seven subjects on Problem D1. These appear in the appendices along with the corresponding protocols. The same conventions are used as for the PBG of S4 in Figure 9.13. In Table 9.3 we show the mechanisms found in the entire set of protocols, along with the number of occurrences of each and their relative frequency. There occur variants of three basic methods: means-ends analysis, working forward, and working backward. Within each of these classes are subvarieties, most of which are already familiar. We have already seen numerous examples of means-ends analysis (a) working toward the goal expression and (b) attempting to make an operator applicable. Within the latter category it is possible to distinguish overcoming a difficulty (the common case) from adding additional specifications and correcting an error.

TABLE 9.3

total frequencies of occurrences of GPS-like mechanisms in seven protocols for problem D1

Means-ends analysis	258		
towards goal object		89	
operator applicability		151	
overcome difficulty			143
further specify			5
resolve uncertainty			3
avoid consequences		18	
avoid difficulty			17
prepare desired result			1
Working forward	41		
systematic scan and evaluate		37	
input form similarity		3	
do something different		1	
Working backward	2		
output form similarity		2	
Repeated application	230		
after subgoal		93	
to overcome difficulty			58
to further specify			11
to resolve uncertainty			2
to avoid consequences			12
to correct error			8
to process interruption			2
implementation		97	
for plan			84
to command experimenter			13
review		40	
Other	27		
noticing		6	
repeated application		11	
new application		10	
Total	558		

An important form of means-ends analysis that we haven't yet met is the *avoidance of consequences.* Consider a situation involving an operator that is applicable (hence nothing need be done to make it applicable) but that has both desirable and undesirable consequences. A simple GPS-like system would merely take the resulting expression and attempt to remove the undesirable consequences. The method of avoiding consequences involves searching for a rule to apply *beforehand,* so that when the given rule is subsequently applied it retains the desired consequence, but *does not have* the undesired one. A clear example of this mechanism can be seen in S8's protocol, when he goes down the same path as S4 does initially, trying R8 and discovering that it throws away a P or Q (B61–B70):

> Oh! Wait a minute, I see something. I don't know if it's any good. On R8 ... ah ... across a, a dot major connector. I can take either, ah ... the whole thing will equal either one, A or B. But the ... ha ... trouble is, the final answer is in Q and P, and there's, either one of the terms are either Q ... have both Q and P in it. But ... the only way I can think to get rid of it ... R8 would work if I could apply R7. Why can't I apply R7?

There is no question that R8 can be applied. R8 accomplishes something desirable (eliminating an R) and something undesirable (eliminating either a P or Q). R7, by grouping the P and Q, would fix things up so that R8 would only do the desirable thing.

Most of the examples of avoiding consequences couple a good effect and a bad one that are seemingly independent. There is one other case that really represents a form of preparation to obtain a positive consequence. S5 has continually been trying to change the sign of R to make it positive, in order to apply R7. He has just produced L14 (B196–B203):

> [E writes L14: $(\sim P \lor \sim R) \cdot (R \lor Q)$.]
> Let's see, if we used R6 on that we'd get a $P \supset R$ and we want to change the sign of the A term. . . .
> We want to apply R1 to L14 . . . that's what we want to do.
> (E: Where?)
> Within the first term.
> [E writes L15: $(\sim R \lor \sim P) \cdot (R \lor Q)$.]

Thus, applying R6 produces a consequence: the change of sign of the A term, which is the $\sim P$ of $(\sim P \lor \sim R)$. But this is not the desired consequence—the change of sign of R. What to do? Apply R1 beforehand to prepare the expression for changing the sign of R by bringing the sign into the position where R6 can affect it. There is no way a standard GPS could conclude here that R1 was appropriate. Nor does R6 have both a bad and a good consequence, one of which is to be removed, unless one says that the change of sign is good, but the place where it changes is bad. Rather, R6 could provide a good consequence, but does not.

We have already seen examples of the main type of working forward: iterating through the rules systematically and evaluating each one. S4 provided us with a perfect example (see the PBG, Figure 9.13). There are two other types of working forward, which occur but rarely. Two cases of working forward by similarity of input form occur together in S11's protocol at the point where he has applied R7 mentally, obtaining an expression of the form A(BC) (though it is not clear exactly how much detail he perceives). He considers what to do with the new expression (B84–B93):

B84:	Now let's see . . . 7	apply R7 to L1
B85:	Let's see . . . that would combine the B and the C	($\Rightarrow$ A(BC))
B86:	At my sheets	find rule
B87:	Uh, let's see now . . . I could spread it	apply R7 to result
B88:	No, that wouldn't do any good	($\Rightarrow$ (AB)(AC))
B89:	B . . . I've knocked out B; and C	
B90:	which is what I had in the first place . . . what I started off.	evaluate
B91:	4 . . . what would that give me?	apply R4 to result
B92:	No, that wouldn't do any good,	($\Rightarrow$ (AB)C)
B93:	not unless I reversed it.	evaluate

This basic sequence is evident. The argument is that, once the result was obtained, the rules to consider were selected purely on the basis of the three-term form of the expression. There is no evidence that any comparison against L0 was made, so that no means-ends analysis entered. Nor did S11 consider the rules systematically, since many other rules are also applicable, e.g., R1, R5, possibly even R8, if S11 thinks the connective is a dot.

The one example of doing something just because it is different is provided by S8 (B298–B310):

I was reading about that last night. Don't stay in a rut. All right, let's look at something altogether different then. What can we do with the quantity as a whole? I've been trying to look at the parts, what can we do as a whole? I can convert that dot into a, ah wedge, and that'll change the sign. And then, ah well, we . . . . Let's try it. I, ah, I can't see that in my mind too well, I . . . . Let's apply R5 to L1 and see if we get anything from it.

Although it takes S8 a while to crank up to it, there is ample evidence that (1) he generates R5 in order to do something different, (2) although he tries to evaluate the contemplated action he is unsuccessful, so that (3) he finally applies the rule simply to obtain the new results. This is confirmed, of course, by the fact that there is nothing functional about the result:

$$\text{L6:} \quad \sim(\sim(R \supset \sim P) \lor \sim(\sim R \supset Q))$$

Since working backward rarely occurs in Problem D1, we need not illustrate it here, but we will discuss it extensively in Chapter 10.

A very large fraction of the operators that occur in the PBG are repetitions of prior applications. In the PBG of S4 these are shown by double-lined connections between boxes. Most of these occur after an attempt to attain a subgoal—i.e., the prior goal of applying an operator is kept in a goal stack and reevoked after the remedial attempt of the subgoal. We have classified the reapplications by the types of remedial action attempted. Besides actions relating to difficulty, specification, and uncertainty about the output of the operator, there also occur reapplications after errors (e.g., stating the wrong input) and after an interruption irrelevant to the problem solving (e.g., a request by E for a review of why S did what he did). We have also included here reapplication of the desired operator after an attempt to avoid consequences. The main reason for listing all these subcases is to show the predominance of the one we understand best—i.e., the reattempt after trying to overcome a difficulty. But all the varieties arise from the same basic mechanism, the goal stack.

The second type of repetition is aimed at implementing an operator that has already been applied and its results examined. These repetitions can be detected in the PBG by the occurrence of an operator with an arrow, where no expression was generated on the display. If, after carrying the problem solving forward, the subject returns and applies the operator all over again, then the latter application is an implementation. Often this is intended to produce an actual result on the display, but sometimes it is intended simply to carry the calculation forward again covertly. This activity constitutes a variety of planning. Since it is very important, we will devote a section of Chapter 10 to it; we will not discuss it further here.

A special type of implementation is labeled *command*. This term indicates a repetition that commands E to apply a rule, and where no other function is served except to get the result on the display. This happens when the subject has carried the calculation through in detail in his head and already knows all there is to be known about the result. Usually, of course, when the subject commands E to apply a rule, he has not thought through the result in detail, and thus he is using E to perform a calculation of consequences for him.

The final kind of repetition is a *review*—a recapitulation of a past sequence of actions. This may happen when the S himself is trying to understand what has gone on, or it may be evoked by E, in an attempt to elicit information for the record.

Most of the behavior in the reviews is strictly reproductive (when it is not, it is classified otherwise). But one review that occurs for diagnostic purposes deserves description, since it is the only one of its kind in all the protocols. At the very beginning of E5, S5 is returning to another bout of trying to make R7 applicable, after attempting an abortive plan in E4 to obtain an isolated Q. He reviews the situation as follows [starting at the beginning of the episode (B247–B255)]:

> Gosh I wish that other method would work. . . . If we could only get an R in that first term instead of a $\sim$R. . . . There ought to be a rule for changing that. For all the stuff I've gone through I should have had it someplace along here. Someplace I must have reversed something where I shouldn't have. Looking at L13 . . . I reversed it there because of . . . on R1. . . . Well if I left it the same as it was on R12 [L12] and applied R5 again.

S5 hypothesizes what he has done wrong and then searches for a previous step that confirms this hypothesis. He actually works his way backward from L13 to the prior expression (L12) and then tries something new. Thus, this is an example of avoiding consequences, as well. However, the interesting behavior is the generation of a diagnostic hypothesis.

The category labeled *other* contains those operator occurrences that are not determinably GPS-like in their basic character. It contains at least one distinguishable subtype, *noticing*, where the subject in working on one thing sees something else that is useful. These instances are usually quite clear in the protocol. For example, S4 is concerned with how to make R7 apply [right after the working-forward sequence whose termination (B124) was quoted on page 484] when the following occurs (B126–B136):

> In order to make number 7 apply, R6 has got to be used in some way. Now, if I applied R2, it would switch the right and left hand side. You get a sign change, but that wouldn't do any good. I just saw something. I don't know if it would help me or not, but if I applied R2 to 4 and 6 . . . . [E: Shall I do it?] Yeah, but the reason I'm doing that is so I can apply R12.

This is the critical juncture where S4 sees path.R12. He clearly was not looking for it, though he was prepared in the sense of being concerned with R2, which is needed to make R12 applicable. Not all of the noticings are as critical as this, though many of them are as clearly marked.

The rest of the *other* category consists of applications where it is not possible to determine from the protocol what mechanism evoked the rule. Since it is possible to determine whether the application is a repetition or not, we have shown the two separately, just to indicate that the obscurities are not all of one kind.

Table 9.3 is remarkable not for the diversity of mechanisms, but for their small number, and because most of them belong to the main types that we already understand: GPS-like means-ends analysis, working forward, repetition from the goal stack, and implementation of plans. Between them, these types account for 82 percent of the occurrences, to which should be added the 9 percent that are essentially reproductions of past behavior (review and commands to E). This leaves, essentially, the avoid-consequences method, the noticings, and the items for which too few data are available. The general character of avoiding consequences is clear enough as an elaboration on means-ends analysis, but we have not really considered it in detail. The same is partly true of planning and of working backward (though we did consider the basic mechanism of planning in detail in Chapter 8), but we will examine these two mechanisms more thoroughly in the next chapter.

We must be careful as to what we infer from accounts such as Table 9.3. These data are analogous to the results obtained by a centrifuge: we have dissolved the total behavior into a collection of little bits, each to be classified only in terms of a single property. Specifically, we have destroyed much of the integrated character of the behavior. We have also ignored the selective rules used to get operators and the rules used to terminate attempts. Although each instance in isolation possesses a plausible selection or evaluation rule, we have not considered the consistency of such rules over all the behavior. We *have* shown that no other collection of problem solving mechanisms seems to be required to account for the data, and that more complete descriptions of the problem solving behavior of the subjects will probably fit within a GPS-like framework.

A number of questions of methodology can be raised about Table 9.3. The use of the PBG overstates the GPS-like character of the behavior, since it tends to fill in the gaps in a "plausible" fashion—i.e., a GPS-like fashion.

One partly methodological issue that does have substantive interest is the distribution of mechanisms by subject. Table 9.4 shows a somewhat aggregated version of Table 9.3 broken out by subject. It is ordered from left to right according to the total number of operator occurrences (equivalently, phrases or time). It shows, first of all, a strong stability of the major categories, suggesting that these are indeed dictated by the general structure of the task along with a basic GPS-like mechanism for a problem solver. That the nonsolvers (S11 and S5) do not differ much from the solvers reinforces this interpretation. The only interesting subject differences are the almost complete absence of the *other* category for the efficient solvers (S10, S9, and S15) and the gradual increase of avoid consequences and review as the protocols get longer. These variations are to be expected, since the good solvers in this task simply never have occasion to depart from the basic mechanisms.

It is also relevant to inquire how much behavior is not reflected in the tables at all. Of course, there is considerable behavior related to aspects of the PBG that do not enter into the considerations of Table 9.3—e.g., all the transform goals, evaluations, and so on. But the PBG itself comes close to exhausting the total behavior in the protocol. This may be verified directly by an examination of the protocols. However, to give one summary indication: of the 176 phrases that occur in S4's protocol, only 19 do not have their primary content reflected in the PBG shown in Figure 9.13 and thus might be candidates for additional problem solving mechanisms. In fact, most of these are phrases not relevant to the task.

In making the tabulation in the previous tables we have not distinguished the within-episode behavior from the initiators of the episodes. The within-episode behavior, as measured by numbers of rule applications, completely swamps the initiation, so that the character of the results would not be changed by deleting the initiators. However, of the 40 rule applications associated with episode initiation, 50 percent of them belong to the *other* category and these applications account for 75 percent of all items in that category. Thus, the behavior within episodes is, if anything, even more consistently GPS-like than the tables show.

Initiation of Episodes. We have seen by numerous examples that the behavior of our subjects within each episode can generally be explained in considerable detail by positing GPS-like organizations of processes that differ relatively little from subject to subject (except, perhaps, for S11). This is not enough, however, to explain the whole course of each subject's problem solving behavior, or the reasons why different subjects followed such different courses. To understand the organization of the episodes, our explanation must incorporate processes for initiating episodes and for terminating them.

The table of connections in GPS, and the ordering of differences in that table, provides a definite mechanism for initiating episodes from a given pair of initial expressions. These given expressions may be L1 and L0 of the problem statement; subsequently, they may be one or two derived expressions, written on the blackboard or held in the subject's memory, and the input form of one of the rules; or

TABLE 9.4
frequencies of occurrence of GPS-like mechanisms in protocols, by subject

	S10	S9	S15	S4	S11	S5	S8	TOTALS
Means-end analysis	9 37%	15 47%	29 48%	30 38%	46 52%	54 50%	75 45%	258 46%
towards goal object	6	8	16	9	19	5	26	89
operator applicability	3	7	13	20	26	44	38	151
consequence avoidance				1	1	5	11	18
Working forward	4 17%		8 13%	11 14%	2 2%	1 1%	15 9%	41 7%
Working backward		2 6%						2 1%
Repeated application	11 46%	14 44%	22 37%	31 39%	35 39%	48 44%	69 42%	230 41%
after subgoal	4	7	7	13	19	21	22	93
implementation	7	7	12	7	12	19	33	97
review			3	11	5	8	14	40
Subtotal	24 100%	31 97%	59 98%	72 91%	83 93%	103 95%	159 96%	531 95%
Other	0 0%	1 3%	1 2%	7 9%	6 7%	5 5%	7 4%	27 5%
Total	24 100%	32 100%	60 100%	79 100%	89 100%	108 100%	166 100%	558 100%

they may be a derived expression and L0; or a derived expression and one held in memory by working backward from L0. We have seen examples of all of these in the protocols. Whatever the source of the pair of expressions, the transform goal of GPS can match to find a difference between them, set up the subgoal of reduce-difference, find and apply operators, set up new subgoals in order to make their application possible or to exploit the results of their application, and so on.

In a trace of GPS we would count as initiating a new episode a match, and subsequent processing, that was not evoked as a subgoal of a currently active goal. Essentially, this is the same criterion that we have used in dividing the subjects' protocols into episodes. (This statement needs one qualification: when the goal of reducing the differences between L1 and L0 evokes only the process of searching the rules, the actions resulting from the independent consideration of each new rule are regarded as a separate episode.)

At the beginning of his consideration of the problem, the subject (or GPS) has available only L0, L1, and the rules as sources of differences that might initiate episodes. In the protocols, three variant types of initiation can be distinguished more or less clearly: (1) matching L0 and L1 to form differences (e.g., "eliminate the R's" "group Q and P"); (2) finding rules that will simplify L1 (by some criterion); (3) searching for rules that apply to L1. Intuitively, the third process seems more primitive than the second, and the second more primitive than the first, where primitive means less specifically adapted to the particular task at hand. The GPS we have described employs only category (1); an extended GPS could add (2) and (3) in that order. It would still not capture all the variants visible in the protocols. Most (not all) of the subjects begin with a more or less complete match of L0 with L1, although perhaps some (S4, S8) begin with the goal of simplification, and some rule searches occur in the interest of goals whose statement in the protocols is vague (S8, S11, S15).

After one or more episodes have been initiated, and new expressions written down, new properties of the situation may be held in memory (compare such facts as "R is odd" in the cryptarithmetic task, or "after N-N5, checkmate is threatened" in chess), and the new expressions may serve as inputs for matching with L0 or with the rules. Two of the five solvers (S4 and S8) evoked path.R12, which uses R8 twice to obtain inputs for R12, *after* having generated one or both of the subexpressions with R8 in the interest of some other goal.

Except at the outset, in all the protocols, searches through the rules or through previously generated expressions occur primarily after episodes have been terminated, and when the subjects do not have specific goals in mind. To this extent, the less primitive initiators take precedence over the more primitive. S4, for example, has two principal episodes along path.R7, each followed by a rule search; S10 searches the two-line rules after a path.R7 episode. Particularly clear is S4's comment (B33–B34): "I'm just scanning the rules, not in search of anything in particular. I can't find anything that's going to help me." The same kinds of comments are prominent in S4's protocol on Problem C1, to be examined in the next chapter (see Appendix 10.7). For example, in B59–B67, he says: "So now I'm lost . . . hmm . . . I'm looking over the rules to see if 10, 11, or 12 will fit any of the four expressions [that he has generated]. I'm lost, so I'm just sort of looking to see if any of the rules will change . . . the expressions around. Well, I'm just lost for the moment—so

I'm going to go through the rules again to see which one will apply to the original expressions." He repeats almost the identical statement in B77–B82 of his protocol on Problem C1.

Termination of Episodes.   Differences of the same general magnitude exist in the ways in which episodes are terminated. As in GPS, an episode terminates when the goal has been attained, or when the subject can think of nothing more to do to advance toward it. But "think of nothing more" is a highly ambiguous phrase that cloaks essential differences among subjects. S4 abandons path.R7 after generating only two expressions with (B27): "but I don't see any way of doing it" and after his second attempt, in which he wrote no new expressions (B71), "but as yet I can't find a way." S5, on the other hand, went through the elaborate search for indirect routes that we have already described. S8, like S4, gives up after generating two expressions, with (B56): "Here I am, well, now where am I?"

We can apply a label like *stereotypy* to S5's persistent behavior on path.R7, but unless we find consistency in such a trait from one problem to another, its presence is neither testable nor useful for prediction. Even worse, we cannot generalize to say that such persistence necessarily reduces a subject's problem solving effectiveness. If S4 had been *more* persistent the first time he considered R12 as a means for eliminating R's (B36, B37): "Right now, I'm looking at equations 2 and 3 and thinking of applying . . . . Oh, R12 doesn't apply," he would have found the solution much sooner.

SUMMARY

In this chapter we have undertaken to test how well GPS serves as a theory of human problem solving in the Moore-Anderson logic task environment. In this context "GPS" refers to several variants of the program, described in Chapter 8, which employ means-ends analysis as a principal problem solving heuristic, and which are organized to divide their general problem solving capabilities from their knowledge about specific task environments.

To test GPS we used a number of thinking-aloud protocols taken in our own laboratory together with more aggregative data gathered at Yale from 64 subjects. We found that subjects who talked aloud while solving the problems explored very much the same parts of the problem space as subjects who did not. In the case of both groups of subjects, the subjects' behavior was of the kind we would predict from the GPS simulations.

The data in this chapter were restricted to two problems—one a very simple problem, where we were able to compare protocols with a GPS simulation in considerable detail, the other a more difficult (but not extremely difficult) problem from Moore and Anderson's set. For the latter problem we showed how a task analysis, based on the distinction between essential and inessential steps, and upon the notions of construction and planning introduced in the previous chapter, was adequate to explain to a considerable extent why the subjects' explorations remained mostly in limited, specified portions of the problem space.

Most of the analysis of Problem D1 was concerned with the microstructure of search in that problem—that is, with the behavior within each of the separate episodes of each protocol. In the next chapter we will round out our discussion of the adequacy of GPS as a theory of problem solving in this environment by taking up a number of additional topics, including: some alternative interpretations of the program organization for initiating new episodes and of the planning processes used by subjects; the subjects' behavior on a more difficult problem, C1; and some observations on individual differences and on learning.

APPENDIX 9.1

Protocols on Problem α1

S9 ON PROBLEM α1

B1	[E writes L1:..R·($\sim$P $\supset$ Q)]
B2	[E writes L0: (Q $\vee$ P)·R]
B3	(E: Well, there's the problem.)
B4	(E: See if you can recode it as that.)
B5	Very interesting.
B6	(E: Now, what do you see . . . what do you think of, what are you looking at?)
B7	Well, I figured it must be a problem like this . . . something of this nature where you're given the beginning and the end . . .
B8	when we got to R8,
B9	rather than a strict decoding job or a strict addition to making a code out of this.
B10	(E: Well, you want to see whether you can get something . . . beginning to end.)
B11	Right. I'd gathered that,
B12	so I'd already started to work on this halfway through.
B13	I made a system out of this so I'd know exactly what I wanted.
B14	So here . . . like on R10 I made a note here . . .
B15	that addition in 9 I had a choice
B16	and 4 is a group change.
B17	So in all these now I have a . . . notes as to exactly what I can do with them.
B18	And the next thing I'd do . . . I'd finish these before I'd even start on that ordinarily.
B19	So I'd have a complete system worked out
B20	because if I just started looking at these rules, it's just about a hit-and-miss operation.
B21	(E: Well, we'd like you to work on this if you can.)
B22	OK.
B23	(E: Start off with the hit and miss. . . .)
B24	(E: You'll get familiar with them so that you know them.)
B25	(E: What are you looking at?)
B26	I'm looking at the idea of reversing these two things now.
B27	(E: Thinking about reversing what?)
B28	The R's. . . .
B29	Then I'd have a similar group at the beginning,
B30	but that seems to be. . . .
B31	I could easily leave something like that till the end,
B32	except then I'll. . . .
B33	(E: Applying what rule?)

B34   Applying . . . for instance, 2.
B35   That would require a sign change.
B36   (E: Try to keep talking if you can.)
B37   Well . . . then I look down at R3
B38   and that doesn't look any too practical.
B39   Now 4 looks interesting.
B40   It's got three parts similar to that and there are dots, so the connective . . . seems to work
        easily enough,
B41   but there's no switching of order.
B42   I need that P and a Q changed,
B43   so . . . I've got a horseshoe there.
B44   That doesn't seem practical anyplace through here.
B45   I'm looking for a way, now, to get rid of that horseshoe.
B46   Ah . . . here it is, R6.
B47   So I'd apply R6 to the second part of what we have up there.
B48   (E: Want to do that?)
B49   Yeah.
B50   (E: OK. To L1 you apply R6.)
B51   [E writes L2: $R \cdot (P \vee Q)$]
B52   And now I'd use R1.
B53   (E: R1 on what part? You can use it with the entire expression or with the right part.)
B54   I'd use it in both places.
B55   (E: Well, we'll do them one at a time. . . . Which do you want to do first?)
B56   Well, do it with P and Q.
B57   [E writes L3: $R \cdot (Q \vee P)$]
B58   (E: Now the entire expression?)
B59   Yeah.
B60   (E: On L3, R1.)
B61   [E writes L4: $(Q \vee P) \cdot R$]
B62   And . . . that's it.
B63   (E: That's it all right. OK . . . that wasn't too hard.)

S10   ON PROBLEM α1

B1   [E writes L1: $R \cdot (\sim P \supset Q)$]
B2   [E writes L0: $(Q \vee P) \cdot R$]
B3   Oh, there's an interchange of signs.
B4   See. . . .
B5   (E: What are you doing now?)
B6   Oh . . . I'm looking at the second set of rules,
B7   but I don't think . . .
B8   R4 is collecting terms . . .
B9   but they're in different order.
B10   Should I talk louder?
B11   R4 will not apply
B12   because they're not an inner grouping change.
B13   Oh, there's no major sign change . . .
B14   no major connective change either.
B15   Um . . . try R1. . . .
B16   No.
B17   Try inside the expression. . . .

B18	Oh, R6. A ⊃ B implies, or is, ~A ∨ B.
B19	Hum, that would be ~P ⊃ Q.
B20	R6 would apply for inside the parenthesis.
B21	Involves R6 and R1.
B22	I don't ...
B23	I'm supposed to recode that to that?
B24	(E: Yeah.)
B25	All right. Apply R6 inside the parenthesis.
B26	(E: R6 to L1.)
B27	[E writes L2: R·(P ∨ Q)]
B28	(E: Is that right?)
B29	No.
B30	Well, that's right ... what I told you to do.
B31	Now I have to apply R1 inside the parenthesis.
B32	(E: R1 to L2)
B33	[E writes L3: R·(Q ∨ P)]
B34	Now R1 to the whole expression.
B35	(E: To L3....)
B36	[E writes L4: (Q ∨ P)·R]
B37	(E: And that's what we want.)
B38	(E: Well, that was easy.)

S11 ON PROBLEM α1

B1	[E writes L1: R·(~P ⊃ Q)]
B2	[E writes L0: (Q ∨ P)·R]
B3	(E: Now what are you doing?)
B4	You've got to change the places of the R to the other side,
B5	and you have to change the signs tilde and horseshoe to wedge,
B6	and you've got to reverse the places from P and Q to Q and P.
B7	So let's see ... see, R1 is similar to it
B8	because you want to change places with the second part....
B9	Oh, let's see, R4.
B10	Oh that's no good because you've got to change the signs....
B11	A tilde B, R5.
B12	No....
B13	Let's see.... A dot ... 7,
B14	No....
B15	(E: Try to keep talking.)
B16	Q tilde P,
B17	no ... Q wedge ... Q wedge P....
B18	You can only use it with a dot....
B19	(E: You can only use what with a dot?)
B20	Actually, it doesn't seem like any of these apply ...
B21	because you've got to change the signs....
B22	Like on R5 you've got to change it to a tilde ...
B23	the whole thing is changed....
B24	R7 is out ...
B25	R9 is out
B26	because you have a set form in there.
B27	Let's see, 10, 11, 12,

B28	they're out. . . .
B29	R1,
B30	that's out.
B31	R2 . . .
B32	that's out,
B33	R3 . . .
B34	that's out.
B35	R4. . . . A dot B . . .
B36	parenthesis change on that,
B37	so R4 is out. . . .
B38	R5. . . . A wedge . . .
B39	that's out. . . .
B40	R7 . . .
B41	that's out.
B42	Let's try them backwards now.
B43	Let's see, two sign changes.
B44	(E: What are you doing now?)
B45	I'm trying to change the R, the first part . . . to another expression,
B46	and that expression to another one.
B47	If I can do it. . . .
B48	Let's see . . . oh, let's see . . . use 1
B49	to change the $R \cdot (\sim P \supset Q)$ to parenthesis tilde P tilde Q not R. . . .
B50	Let's see.
B51	(E: Now where are you?)
B52	Actually nowhere.
B53	5, tilde P, B. . . .
B54	That's no good.
B55	(E: You're doing a lot of thinking without talking about it.)
B56	Ah . . . let's see . . . R7, A dot . . .
B57	That wouldn't apply. . . .
B58	$\sim P \supset Q$
B59	Got them reversed. . . .
B60	$(\sim P \supset Q) \cdot R$. . . .
B61	Let's see 4 . . . that's dots
B62	so that's out.
B63	I've got to change that horseshoe to a wedge.
B64	10, 11, or 12 . . .
B65	I can take out entirely. . . .
B66	You've got to use two lines for that. . . .
B67	9 would be out,
B68	because in set 1 you have to apply Q P to that . . . and X is any expression. . . .
B69	(E: What was your reason there?)
B70	About 9?
B71	(E: Yeh. It's out. Why?)
B72	X is any expression whatsoever in that you can define it,
B73	and you have to have just an expression, A,
B74	and here you have two.
B75	So that would be out.
B76	(E: Well, actually R9 is applicable any time,)
B77	(E: because you can consider this A.)
B78	The whole thing's A.
B79	(E: Add anything at any time.)
B80	(E: I just want to correct your misconceptions.)
B81	Oh, that still doesn't apply

B82	'cause if I use that as A,
B83	I have an A wedge . . .
B84	and this I don't need.
B85	(E: You may not want to use it, I just say you can use it.)
B86	The only thing I can figure out, as far as I can see, is change the expression ($\sim P \supset Q$) to parenthesis Q, what you have up there.
B87	Dot . . . parenthesis B·C. . . .
B88	That's out.
B89	(E: You looked at 4 and then at L1 and decided that they don't look alike?)
B90	Yeh, that's out.
B91	Q wedge P. . . .
B92	I don't know why we can't throw out that horseshoe.
B93	(E: You're looking at the rules to see what can change that horseshoe?)
B94	If there is anything. . . .
B95	2, A $\supset$ B . . . tilde B.
B96	No.
B97	I've still got that horseshoe in there.
B98	Let's see what . . . 6, A $\supset$ B, $\sim$A $\supset$ B. . . .
B99	If I have A as R,
B100	then you have to reverse the positions on it . . .
B101	and the sign of A has to stay the same,
B102	so . . . my R has to stay the same . . .
B103	and it changes here.
B104	(E: Well, how do you mean?)
B105	6 is A $\supset$ B changes to $\sim$A $\supset$ B.
B106	(E: $\sim$A $\vee$ B)
B107	Wedge B, I'm sorry.
B108	But for one thing A and B reverse
B109	and the sign of A changes
B110	and the dots between the two have to stay the same . . . has to be the major connector.
B111	But in 6 the major connector is a wedge.
B112	(E: You know that some of the rules can be applied simply within the parenthesis.)
B113	(E: Some of the rules can be applied to either the whole expression or to just the part in parentheses.)
B114	(E: Then there are other rules, such as 8, which can be applied to only the whole expression . . . only to the major . . . part of it.)
B115	In other words in those parentheses like 6, I could use P and Q as A and B.
B116	(E: That's right.)
B117	Huh . . . A $\supset$ B . . .
B118	that would change it to $\sim$P $\supset$ Q . . .
B119	the tilde would make the P positive,
B120	so that would be P $\vee$ B or wedge Q.
B121	So if I just applied 6 to that part I would come out with P $\vee$ Q. . . .
B122	So if that's the case. . . .
B123	So I would apply 6 to that part, that part there.
B124	(E: You tell me what you want me to do.)
B125	Apply 6 to 1.
B126	(E: R6 to L1.)
B127	So I would come out with R·(P $\vee$ Q). . . .
B128	[E writes L2: R·(P $\vee$ Q)]
B129	To reverse that
B130	I could apply 1 to the first part of that, to it again,
B131	and I would have oh that would be R parenthesis. . . .
B132	[E writes L3: R·(Q $\vee$ P)]

B133   All you do is reverse that

B134   so I can use the second part of A,

B135   and ah with B equal to $(Q \lor P)$.

B136   So you come out with . . .

B137   that's the second part of 1 on that . . .

B138   so I'll come out with $(Q \lor P) \cdot R$,

B139   and that's what you want.

B140   [E writes L4: $(Q \lor P) \cdot R$]

B141   (E: That's it. You've done it. OK.)

B142   (E: So you've learned that you can apply some of these rules just within the parenthesis.)

B143   Yeh.

S14 ON PROBLEM α1

B1   [E writes L1: $R \cdot (\sim P \supset Q)$]

B2   [E writes L0: $(Q \lor P) \cdot R$]

B3   And you want me to solve it just as it stands.

B4   Well, my first feeling is that we want to get the R on the left

B5   and somehow invert the Q and the P.

B6   See what we have here about dots and inverting.

B7   R7 is $A \cdot (B \lor C)$ and you can convert it to $(A \cdot B) \lor (A \cdot C)$.

B8   That doesn't seem to be applicable here, though.

B9   Let's see, R6 seems to relate wedges and horseshoes.

B10   This might be good.

B11   It also involves a change in sign,

B12   so the portion $\sim P \supset Q$ could be changed to $P \lor Q$.

B13   So then we have $R \cdot (P \lor Q)$.

B14   So applying the second part of R7. . . .

B15   No, we don't want to do that.

B16   I've got $R \cdot (P \lor Q)$ on the left

B17   and we want to change that to $(Q \lor P) \cdot R$.

B18   That R4 . . . you can change $A \cdot (B \cdot C)$. . . .

B19   (E: What are you considering now?)

B20   I'm gazing randomly at rules.

B21   Well, I think we can. . . .

B22   Instead of applying the rule to the whole,

B23   I think we might try applying it in segments.

B24   I think we can say it [it's] $R \cdot (P \lor Q)$.

B25   What do we have?

B26   I've forgotten.

B27   That's the answer if we apply R1 to segments of this.

B28   Now you change a horseshoe into a wedge by applying. . . .

B29   What can we apply?

B30   Oh, yes, we had changed $\sim P \supset Q$ into $P \lor Q$,

B31   applying R1 to the portion in parentheses.

B32   We can then say that $P \lor Q$ can be recoded as $Q \lor P$,

B33   and applying the same rule again to the total expression, saying the parenthetical expression is portion B,

B34   we can say that $(Q \lor P) \cdot R$ been recoded from the step before that.

B35	(E: You tell me to apply certain steps here. I'll do it and see how it comes out.)
B36	OK. Apply R6 to the portion within the parentheses on the left.
B37	And we come out with $R \cdot (P \lor Q)$.
B38	[E writes L2: $R \cdot (P \lor Q)$]
B39	Correct. Now to the portion within the parentheses, apply part one of R1.
B40	(E: To L2 we apply R1.)
B41	[E writes L3: $R \cdot (Q \lor P)$]
B42	Correct. Now to total expression 3 we apply R1
B43	and we get $Q \lor P$.
B44	[E writes L4: $(Q \lor P) \cdot R$]
B45	And that's what you want to go for.
B46	Am I introspecting all right?
B47	(E: Well, you could do a little more. What you're specifically doing all the time might be helpful.)
B48	(E: And you can ask me to write anything . . . apply any rule or step at any time you want.)
B49	(E: You don't have to see the entire answer before you tell me to do something.)
B50	Oh, I can tell you to do things and you're my handwriting. I see.
B51	(E: That's right.)
B52	I was under the impression you were going to observe me doing this in my mind.
B53	(E: No.)
B54	OK.
B55	(E: No, that's why we use the board.)

S15 ON PROBLEM α1

B1	[E writes L1: $R \cdot (\sim P \supset Q)$]
B2	[E writes L0: $(Q \lor P) \cdot R$]
B3	(E: What comes into your head?)
B4	Number 1.
B5	These complex. . . .
B6	Do you work them like I did that one where you use two rules at one time?
B7	(E: I don't think you use more than one at a time anywhere.)
B8	No, I mean actually there is more than one rule used there?
B9	(E: Oh, yeh, yeh. Well, what are you doing?)
B10	Oh, you want me to work it?
B11	(E: Yeh.)
B12	Oh, I thought you were waiting for the tape.
B13	Now do I have to get what is over in 2?
B14	(E: Yeh.)
B15	I'll have to remember that.
B16	Well, use R1
B17	and switch the two around
B18	and then, ah, then use R6. . . .
B19	(E: What did you say?)
B20	You use R6 on the second part
B21	and you get ah, $(P \supset \sim Q)$ and $(P \supset \sim Q) \cdot R$. . . .
B22	(E: What are you thinking about?)
B23	Trying to find something that will apply to that
B24	so I can get Q.

B25	(E: Apply to what?)
B26	Q. . . . Well to the part that is first.
B27	Now I'm trying to make it into Q ∨ P.
B28	Well. . . .
B29	(E: Just keep telling me what you're doing.)
B30	Q ∨ P. Huh. . . .
B31	(E: Now you're looking at the rule sheet.)
B32	I'm looking at the rule sheet trying to find a rule.
B33	(E: What rule?)
B34	I looked at R2
B35	but it doesn't work,
B36	because it will change both the signs.
B37	(E: OK.)
B38	So, I . . . scanning now.
B39	(E: What are you looking for?)
B40	Well, if I use 2,
B41	then, ah. . . .
B42	No, if I use 2
B43	and that gives me. . . .
B44	Let's see, I have ∼P ⊃ Q, that would give me Q horseshoe, no it will give me ∼Q ⊃ P
B45	and using R6
B46	∼Q ⊃ P . . . ∼Q ⊃ P will give me Q . . . that will give me Q ∨ P. Wouldn't it?
B47	I use 2
B48	and that would give me Q ⊃ ∼P.
B49	Yeh. Change it around fine.
B50	No, that won't work.
B51	We have to have a horseshoe expression in it.
B52	Could you write that up there . . . what I told you first?
B53	(E: What do you want me to do?)
B54	Ah, interchange the first two.
B55	In other words. . . .
B56	(E: In L1 apply rule. . . .)
B57	R1.
B58	[E writes L2: (∼P ⊃ Q)·R]
B59	Yeh, now . . . (mumbles) . . .
B60	(E: What did you say?)
B61	Not anything . . . just mumbled.
B62	(E: Say something.)
B63	All right, all right.
B64	I'm looking for a horseshoe that I can use to change that.
B65	If I use 6 that will give me P ⊃ ∼Q, P ⊃ ∼Q.
B66	And then use 2
B67	that would give me Q ⊃ ∼P, no, yeh, Q ⊃ ∼P.
B68	Can't get rid of that tilde.
B69	(mumbles). . . .
B70	If I say something wrong can you scratch it out after?
B71	(E: Oh, yeh.)
B72	(E: Just keep talking.)
B73	OK, OK . . . one way. . . .
B74	(E: What's that?)
B75	I was looking at the third set and they're all one way.
B76	Can't change it the other way.
B77	Using 6. . . .
B78	It can't go in reverse.

B79	Try using 6
B80	and that will give me P $\lor$ $\sim$Q.
B81	(E: No, 6 will give you P $\lor$ Q in parenthesis.)
B82	Oh, that's right.
B83	(E: dot R.)
B84	Dot R.
B85	[E writes L3: (P $\lor$ Q)·R]
B86	And I want Q $\lor$ P, huh.
B87	Now I've got a wedge.
B88	Oh, using R1,
B89	P $\lor$ Q becomes Q $\lor$ P.
B90	And then that will give me what you have over there.
B91	(E: That's right.)
B92	[E writes L4: (Q $\lor$ P)·R]
B93	(E: That's what we have.)

APPENDIX 9.2

S4 on D1

B	T*	
B1		[E writes L0: $\sim$($\sim$Q·P)]
B2		[E writes L1: (R $\supset$ $\sim$P)·($\sim$R $\supset$ Q)]
E1		
B3		Well, looking at the left-hand side of the equation, first we want to eliminate one of the sides
B4		by using R8.
B5		It appears too complicated to work with first.
B6		Now. . . .
B7		No, no, I can't do that
B8	30	because I will be eliminating either the Q or the P in that total expression.
B9		I won't do that at first.
E2		
B10		Now I'm looking for a way to get rid of the horseshoe inside the two brackets, that appear on the left- and right-hand side of the equation.
B11	60	And I don't see it.
B12		Yeah, if you apply R6 to both sides of the equation,
B13	90	from there I'm going to see if I can apply R7.
B14		[E writes L2: ($\sim$R $\lor$ $\sim$P)·(R $\lor$ Q)]
B15		I can almost apply R7,
B16		but one R needs a tilde.
B17	120	So I'll have to look for another rule.
B18	150	I'm trying to see if I can change that R to a $\sim$R.
B19		As a matter of fact, I should have used R6 in only the left-hand side of the equation.
B20	180	So use number 6, but only on the left-hand side.
B21		[E writes L3: ($\sim$R $\lor$ P)·($\sim$R $\supset$ Q)]
B22		Now, I'll apply R7 as it is expressed.

*Times are indicated at 30-second intervals.

B23		Both. . . .
B24		Excuse me, excuse. It can't be done
B25		because of the horseshoe.
B26	210	So. . . . Now I'm looking . . . scanning the rules here for a second, and seeing if I can change that R to ~R in the second equation,
B27		but I don't see any way of doing it.
B28	240	(sighs) I'm just sort of lost for a second.

E3.1

B29	270	Well, I'm going to start on the first equation again.
B30		Hmm . . . apply R8 and eliminate . . . and just come out with an A.
B31	300	Now, I'm just wandering here . . . I just want to see. . . .
B32		[E writes L4: R ⊃ ~P]
B33	330	I'm just scanning the rules, not in search of anything in particular.
B34		I can't find anything that's going to help me.

E3.2

B35	360	Now, I'll start back on equation 1 again.
B36	390	Right now, I'm looking at equations 2 and 3 and thinking of applying. . . . (pause)
B37		Oh, R12 doesn't apply.

E3.3

B38		So I'm still looking at steps 2 and 3 and seeing if there's a way to. . . .
B39	420	No, I don't see a thing that would help me there.

E4

B40		I'm just looking. . . . (long pause)
B41	450	Use R6 on 4.
B42		[E writes L5: ~R ∨ ~P]
B43		Well, I want to get it with the wedge there.
B44		I also want to get the right-hand side of the equation with the wedge and a. . . . (pause)
B45		Yeah. Now use your number 8 on equation 1.
B46	480	Only get B this time instead of A.
B47		[E writes L6: ~R ⊃ Q]
B48	510	Now, apply R6 to that one too.
B49		[E writes L7: R ∨ Q]
B50		Oh, I see something between 4 and 6 that maybe I can apply rule. . . .
B51		No, applying R12 won't help me,
B52		because I can get an R anyhow.
B53	540	Now I'm looking at 5 and 7.
B54		Now I'm looking at R2,
B55		but R2 doesn't apply.
B56	570	(sigh) So . . . use rule number. . . . Let's see. . . .
B57		I was going to say use R5 on 5 and 7 there,
B58		but I get a minus expression. That's right.

E5

B59		(E: Will you explain what you're trying to do overall.)
B60		Well, I was trying to eliminate the R's by some . . .
B61	600	either by rule number 11 or 12 or 8.
B62		Can't see a way to do it.
B63		Now, I'm looking at R10.
B64	630	I don't know whether that would help me or not.
B65		If I applied R10 to number 5 and number 7.
B66	660	During the last two or three steps just wandering more than anything.
B67		[E writes L8: (~R ∨ ~P)·(R ∨ Q)]

B68	690	Now, I'm looking . . . I was looking for a rule where I could get both R and P positive on the left-hand side of the equation,
B69		and then apply R7.
B70		And that's what I'm looking for now,
B71	720	but as yet I can't find a way.

E6

B72	780	Yeah . . . well, I started back at the beginning,
B73		since I'm getting noplace down there.
B74		I'm trying to. . . .
B75	810	I'm just a little lost . . . I don't know where to go.
B76	840	So now I'm looking at the equation in the expression and the answer, and I see that the dot is a major connective in both expressions and. . . .
B77	870	So, now . . . I'm looking at the rules to see if there's any way I can get rid of those R's again.
B78		I don't. . . .
B79	900	I'm sort of stuck. . . .
B80	930	Now I'm looking at 2 and 3 again.
B81		The problem seems to be to get that R into a tilde,
B82	960	and I can't find any way to do that.
B83		If I tried R6 on 3.
B84		No, that wouldn't do it,
B85	990	R would be positive.
B86		(E: Why do you want to make R positive?)
B87		Well, then I can apply R7,
B88	1020	in which I get $R \cdot (P \vee Q)$.
B89		I can eliminate the R
B90		and then change the wedge to a dot expression.
B91		I'll need number 5 before I can follow through,
B92		but I can't find a way to change the sign of the R.
B93	1050	I'm lost. . . . (long pause)
B94	1080	Well, I'm looking at equation number 2 and number 8 and I find I have the same thing.
B95	1110	Well, I'm clear back at the beginning again.
B96		No. . . .

E7

B97		I was going to say apply R5 to 1,
B98		but that won't give me anything.
B99	1140	I'm looking through them one at a time to see just in what way they might help rearrange the expression.
B100		Now . . . 1.
B101		Would be just the idea of switching the idea around,
B102	1170	which actually is no help there.
B103		2.
B104		Doesn't apply.
B105		3.
B106		Doesn't apply.
B107		4.
B108		Doesn't apply.
B109		5.
B110		Would apply,
B111		but I can't see in what direction it would help me.
B112		6.
B113		Doesn't apply.

B114		Now I was trying to make 7 apply.
B115		I think that would help me.
B116		But I can't find a way to make it apply.
B117		8 applies,
B118		but it doesn't do me any good.
B119		9.
B120		Applies.
B121		10.
B122		Doesn't apply,
B123	1200	nor 11 or 12.

E8

B124		So 7 seems to be the only one that can help me . . .
B125	1230	if I can only get it into the proper form.
B126		In order to make number 7 apply,
B127		R6 has got to be used in some way.
B128		Now, if I applied R2,
B129	1260	it would switch the right- and left-hand side.
B130		You get a sign change,
B131	1290	but that wouldn't do any good.

E9

B132		I just saw something.
B133		I don't know if it would help me or not,
B134	1320	but if I applied R2 to 4 and 6. . . .
B135		(E: Shall I do it?)
B136		Yeah, but the reason I'm doing that is so I can apply R12.
B137		[E writes L9: $P \supset \sim R$]
B138		[E writes L10: $\sim Q \supset R$]
B139		I don't think that will help,
B140	1350	because I think there are too many signs wrong.
B141		Now, actually, actually, well, then. . . .
B142	1380	In other words, I didn't want to apply it to number 6.
B143		I just wanted to apply it to number 5.
B144	1410	That way I can use number 12 on 5 and 9.
B145		(E: 5 and 9 you say, this one and this one? [pointing])
B146		No, 5 and 9.
B147		9 and 6. Yeah. Excuse me.
B148		[E writes L11: $P \supset Q$]

E10

B149		(E: Can you explain how you decided to use this step?)
B150	1440	Well, I was going through them rule by rule,
B151		and if the only one I haven't considered at all was 12.
B152		I mean, so I looked to find my two expressions . . .
B153		I remembered that I had it broken up . . . broken it into different expressions . . . into the right- and left-hand sides.
B154		I had . . . I remembered they had horseshoes in them already, like in number 12.
B155		So I just rearranged them to get . . . so as to get signs correct.
B156	1470	That's what it gives me . . . right.

E11

B157		So . . . now, I have to find a way to change the horseshoe in a dot.
B158		Oh, first of all, I'll change it to a wedge.
B159	1500	Oh, excuse me, you apply R6.
B160		First, I'll change it to a wedge expression,

513

B161		and then see if I can change it from a wedge expression to a dot expression.
B162		[E writes L12: $\sim P \vee Q$]
B163		Now, by applying R5 to that, I believe....
B164	1530	Yeah, apply R5 to that.
B165		[E writes L13: $\sim(\sim Q \cdot P)$]
B166	1560	Now, just apply R1 to the inside of the parenthesis.
B167		[E writes L14: $\sim(P \cdot \sim Q)$]
B168		On this one, I discovered that some kind of ...
B169		I just ... I, I used a couple of rules there
B170		and just wandering someplace.
B171		I found actually by reconsidering everything that I had done.
B172		I came up with the answer by just using something that I really hadn't thought would work.
B173	1590	I just was wandering.
B174	1620	By looking back over what I did, I came up with the answer.
B175		I can see by this one that it helped by knowing just what the answer was.
B176	1650	I knew exactly that I had to eliminate the R, and....

APPENDIX 9.3

S5 on D1

B1	[E writes L1: $(R \supset \sim P) \cdot (\sim R \supset Q)$]
B2	[E writes L0: $\sim Q \cdot P)$]
E1	
B3	Well, this problem is a little different
B4	because in the answer we want one part out of each of the two parts of L1.
B5	Offhand it looks as if we might be able to ...
B6	if we fudge around a little bit to apply this rule....
B7	Let's see which one is it....
B8	Yeah, L1 is almost in the form to which we can apply R7
B9	except that in one bracket it's a $\sim R$ instead of an R....
B10	So I want to change that $\sim R$ into an R term.
B11	Let's see ... so we have a horseshoe and we want to change the horseshoe into another horseshoe
B12	except ... well except with a regular R instead of a $\sim R$.
B13	Let's see ... if we use R6
B14	we get a wedge in there....
B15	We don't particularly want that.
B16	I think we could apply R2....
B17	I think it doesn't make too much difference which term we apply it to....
B18	Apply it to the second term of L1....
B19	Apply R2....
B20	Oh, wait a minute ... wait a minute, that only goes one way,
B21	we can't do it.
B22	(E: Yes, you can.)
B23	Yeah, but that wasn't what I was thinking of ...
B24	I was thinking of going in the other direction.

B25   (E: If you want to apply this to the right-hand side of L1 you can.)

B26   Going to the left?

B27   (E: Yes, all they mean here is you change both signs.)

B28   OK. Yeah, I don't know what I was thinking of.

B29   [E writes L2: $(R \supset \sim P) \cdot (\sim Q \supset R)$]

B30   The first term stays the same,

B31   we reverse the order of the second term,

B32   and the sign on the second term. . . .

B33   Now wait a second . . . yeah, OK.

B34   Oh . . . that isn't too good either

B35   because we want to . . .

B36   I'd like to reverse the order of the second term of L2,

B37   but there isn't a rule here that will do this without changing the punctuation mark.
      (sigh)

E2

B38   (E: What are you doing?)

B39   I was just wondering. . . .

B40   Umm . . . I see a method where we could possibly get an individual Q . . .

B41   with those two lines like we did before. . . .

B42   Get a Q all by itself.

B43   I believe . . . let's see . . . we could fudge lines 1 and 2 around

B44   so we could apply R12 . . .

B45   and from this we could get an individual Q.

B46   I was thinking of . . .

B47   then it would be necessary to get a P

B48   and then horse around with it some more.

B49   Those are both dots

B50   and in order to use R12

B51   both lines need a horseshoe.

B52   R12 can't be used if its negative.

B53   In other words we couldn't use R5 to change it into. . . .

B54   That changes into wedges anyway. . . .

B55   We don't want a wedge,

B56   we need a horseshoe. . . .

B57   Let's see we want to go from a dot to a horseshoe.

B58   The only way we could do that is possible. . . .

B59   We may have to use R5 to go to a wedge

B60   and R6 to go to a horseshoe. . . .

B61   Let's apply 5 to L2 to get. . . .

B62   [E writes L3: $\sim(\sim(\sim R \supset \sim P) \vee \sim(\sim Q \supset R))$]

B63   Yeah, I just noticed though that this won't work too well

B64   because the whole bracket is negative. . . .

B65   I don't think we can apply R6 to it as it stands . . .

B66   to get it into a horseshoe form?

B67   (E: Yes.)

B68   Can R6 be applied to what's inside of the brackets?

B69   (E: Yes.)

B70   OK, then we might try that then.

B71   [E writes L4: $\sim((R \supset \sim P) \supset \sim(\sim Q \supset R))$]

B72   We may be getting a little complicated.

B73   Now let's see what we have there. . . .

B74   Uh, huh. That's in a horseshoe form.

B75	It would be possible to get L1 into the same form . . .
B76	by the same two steps. . . .
B77	However, they're both going to have a minus and a bracket in front of it
B78	and if I'm right we're not allowed to apply R12 to that. . . .
B79	Is that correct?
B80	(E: Correct.)
B81	We can't apply R12 to it. . . .
B82	Some way we've got to get rid of that tilde. . . .
B83	We want to use the method. . . .
B84	Let's see the only. . . .
B85	That would be R5 again
B86	and that would be going backwards . . . from where we're going . . .
B87	ehhhh (disgust).
B88	That's not going to do us a heck of a lot of good. . . .
B89	Now I'm trying to think. . . .
B90	Let's see there is the possibility of using R10 for something
B91	but I think that's going to complicate it much too much.
B92	If I could get a separate P and Q,
B93	then I could use R10
B94	to get it into the form of the answer.

E3.1

B95	Maybe I could go back to. . . .
B96	Let's see we haven't used R7 yet. . . .
B97	R7 looks like it has some possibilities,
B98	because we probably get the P and Q both with the same signs in the one term.
B99	L1 has both horseshoe expressions. . . .
B100	We can't use R7 as is. . . .
B101	We could change the horseshoe into wedges by R6. . . .
B102	But if we had it into wedges,
B103	let's see . . . oh, yeah, they've got tilde on that other R there. . . .
B104	That would change when you use R6. . . .
B105	Let's see . . . Let's apply R6 to L1 and see what happens.
B106	(E: Can't be applied.)
B107	It can be applied in each bracket can't it?
B108	(E: I beg your pardon, you're right.)
B109	We'd better try it in both brackets
B110	because we have to have both wedge expressions.
B111	[E writes L5: $(\sim R \vee \sim P) \cdot (R \vee Q)$]
B112	That changes the sign on the first term . . .
B113	still going to be off by a sign.
B114	Yeah, OK, now . . . we're a little bit closer to being able to apply R7
B115	but we still have to change the sign on one of those two terms.
B116	So that we could work backwards on R7
B117	and get a term that had a B·C in it . . . or something like that.
B118	R6 changes the sign
B119	but that's going to put us right back where we started from. . . .
B120	R1 doesn't change any sign. . . .
B121	R2 would change both signs. . . .
B122	Yeah, let's apply R2 to the first term of L5.
B123	(E: Can't.)
B124	Oh . . . you're right. . . .
B125	OK, let's apply R6 to the first term of 5 first. . . .

516

B126	That'll go back to a horseshoe
B127	and then use the horseshoe to change the signs with R2. . . .
B128	What I should have done was just change the last term on that other.
B129	I keep going backwards here.
B130	[E writes L6: $(R \supset \sim P) \cdot (R \vee Q)$]
B131	All right now we want to use R2 on the first term of L6.
B132	[E writes L7: $(P \supset \sim R) \cdot (R \vee Q)$]
B133	OK, now we want to apply R6 to. . . .
B134	Wait a minute . . . maybe not . . .
B135	maybe we do. . . .
B136	Just see if we're going to have . . .
B137	that 6 part changes the sign on A part but keeps the same order. . . .
B138	That wouldn't do us too much good
B139	unless we could use this horseshoe again. . . .

E3.2

B140	Uh (disgust).
B141	Let's see now, I just got through applying R2, L7, didn't I?
B142	We want to get a plus R,
B143	we want to change the sign of the B part there.
B144	Let's see, there's some way we could reverse the term. . . .
B145	Let's see . . . well, I can see how we could do it. . . .
B146	Back in L5 if we. . . .
B147	Yeah, we're going to have to backtrack again. . . .
B148	L5, we're going to have to apply R1 to the first term in L5 . . .
B149	in other words with a $\sim P$ . . . . OK.
B150	[E writes L8: $(\sim P \vee \sim R) \cdot (R \vee Q)$]
B151	OK, now let's go to R6 on L8 and see where this takes us . . . left-hand side.
B152	[E writes L9: $(P \supset \sim R) \cdot (R \vee Q)$]
B153	Now we're at a horseshoe. . . .
B154	We want to . . . let's see now . . . if we. . . .
B155	Oh, I see . . . now we'll apply R2 to L9 and see what happens here . . . the first part of it. . . .
B156	I may have changed that sign twice.
B157	[E writes L10: $(R \supset \sim P) \cdot (R \vee Q)$]
B158	Now we're back in the same form we were in 10.
B159	I managed somehow to change that sign twice.
B160	I wanted to get a. . . .
B161	If I applied R6 to it again
B162	I still would get a minus R back . . . $\sim R$ . . . I didn't particularly want. . . .
B163	Let's see, we just got through applying R2 to it, didn't we.
B164	Oh, here . . . this is . . . let's see. . . .
B165	(E: What are you doing now?)
B166	Looking for some way of switching back to where we were before and a. . . .
B167	Let's go back to L8 and apply R1 to the first term . . . see what happens. . . .
B168	If there were only some way of switching horseshoes around.
B169	[E writes L11: $(\sim R \vee \sim P) \cdot (R \vee Q)$]
B170	OK, now we've got a wedge and we want to get it to a horseshoe. . . .
B171	Hmm. Try R6. . . .
B172	What happened to our horseshoe. . . .
B173	Oh, I see we left that behind. . . .
B174	OK, I lost track of where we were going . . . of what I was trying to do. . . .
B175	I want to get it into a form to use R7.

517

B176   Two terms with wedges connected, by a dot, the first term is the same. . . .

B177   OK. In other words I still want to change that minus R to an R.

B178   Let's see, we have a horseshoe expression here . . .

B179   changes the order and size.

B180   Yeah, in here the trouble is that A gets its sign changed twice

B181   if you use rules 2 and 6.

E3.3

B182   Still not much better off than we were before. . . .

B183   See that same expression back here at 5.

B184   One way possibly to do it would be use R5 in there. . . .

B185   to reverse the order [?], . . .

B186   change the signs twice. . . .

B187   No [Now? Know?] that's going to introduce that other deal. . . .

B188   Let's try a R5 on the first term of 11.

B189   [E writes L12: $\sim(R \cdot P) \cdot (R \vee Q)$]

B190   OK, we'll apply a R1 to the first term of L12.

B191   [E writes L13: $\sim(P \cdot R) \cdot (R \vee Q)$]

B192   OK, now we want to apply a R2 to L13.

B193   That kind of brings us right back to where we started?

B194   (E: R2?)

B195   Uh, no not R2 . . . what am I talking about . . . R5.

B196   [E writes L14: $(\sim P \vee \sim R) \cdot (R \vee Q)$]

B197   Let's see, if we used R6 on that

B198   we'd get a $P \supset R$

B199   and we want to change the sign of the A term. . . .

B200   We want to apply R1 to L14 . . . that's what we want to do.

B201   (E: Where?)

B202   Within the first term.

B203   [E writes L15: $(\sim R \vee \sim P) \cdot (R \vee Q)$]

B204   OK, now rule. . . .

B205   What happened here . . . hah. . . .

B206   We wanted a horseshoe here someplace. . . .

B207   Doggone it, what am I thinking of. . . .

B208   Let's see . . . I was thinking I was going to have to use a R6 again,

B209   but it's already in the form we want it . . .

B210   except for that . . .

B211   I'm back where I started from again.

B212   How many times have I had that on there . . . hah?

B213   Let's see now back at L13 I had a $P \cdot R$ and what did I do to . . .

B214   use R5 to get it back into a wedge . . .

B215   (sigh) . . . We didn't really. . . .

B216   What I really want is a $P \cdot \sim R$.

B217   Can't change signs with just one term with a dot . . .

B218   (sigh) . . . Oh . . . well, let's try something else. . . .

B219   We've had that 15 so many times now. . . .

E4

B220   We change that dot. . . .

B221   On R12 there's no reason why A and B can't be the same, is there?

B222   (E: No.)

B223   We've had that same form so many times. . . .

B224   We could just eliminate it

B225   if we could just get it into the form of number 12

B226   and we're just going to get it . . . an $(R \vee Q) \supset (R \vee Q)$

B227	and then we can change those horseshoes into a wedge
B228	and the wedge into a dot
B229	and a dot into just an R $\vee$ Q
B230	and then into just a plain Q. . . .
B231	So we've got to change those dots eventually into horseshoes
B232	so eventually we can use R12. . . .
B233	We're going to get rid of that term altogether and quit horsing around with it.
B234	If you want to go from a dot to a horseshoe
B235	I guess we're going to have to go from a. . . .
B236	Then you'll introduce those brackets again
B237	if we use R5 . . .
B238	which won't do us too much good. . . .
B239	Maybe we can . . . R1 will just reverse the order.
B240	Hmm . . . that way it won't work
B241	because we'll have that minus times the bracket no matter what we do there.
B242	I'm looking at R10 . . . A and B could be the same
B243	and then you'd have an A·A
B244	and then an A·A equals A,
B245	but we'd just be back where we started from.
B246	It wouldn't do us any good. . . .

E5

B247	Gosh I wish that other method would work. . . .
B248	If we could only get an R in that first term instead of a $\sim$R. . . .
B249	There ought to be a rule for changing that.
B250	For all the stuff I've gone through I should have had it someplace along here.
B251	Someplace I must have reversed something where I shouldn't have.
B252	Looking at L13 . . . I reversed it there
B253	because of . . . on R1. . . .
B254	Well if I left it the same as it was on R12 [L12]
B255	and applied R5 again
B256	I'd be right back to L11
B257	which would be the same as what I had.
B258	That doesn't do any good. . . .
B259	Let's see, R6 is the only one that changes one sign. . . .
B260	Only . . . the A part gets the sign change when you use R6 . . .
B261	that changes from a horseshoe to a wedge. . . .
B262	I've used that so many times. . . .
B263	Let's see . . . maybe instead of trying to get the first term R positive
B264	we could try to get the $\tilde{\text{s}}$econd term R negative.
B265	That might do it easier.
B266	We want a horseshoe and then a dot . . .
B267	and back to a horseshoe. . . .
B268	Try R6 to the second part of L15.
B269	Which is the same as several other lines. . . .
B270	[E writes L16: $(\sim$R $\vee$ $\sim$P)·($\sim$R $\supset$ Q)]
B271	Now we have a horseshoe. . . .
B272	We can reverse the sign of the horseshoe by. . . .
B273	No, we don't have a horseshoe. . . .
B274	Oh, yeah, we have a horseshoe over there. . . .
B275	I was looking at the first term.
B276	We have a horseshoe. . . .
B277	If we change the order and the sign. . . .
B278	Apply R2 . . . let's apply R2 to 16 . . . to the second part of 16,
B279	[E writes L17: $(\sim$R $\vee$ $\sim$P)·($\sim$Q $\supset$ R)]

problem behavior graph of S5 on D1

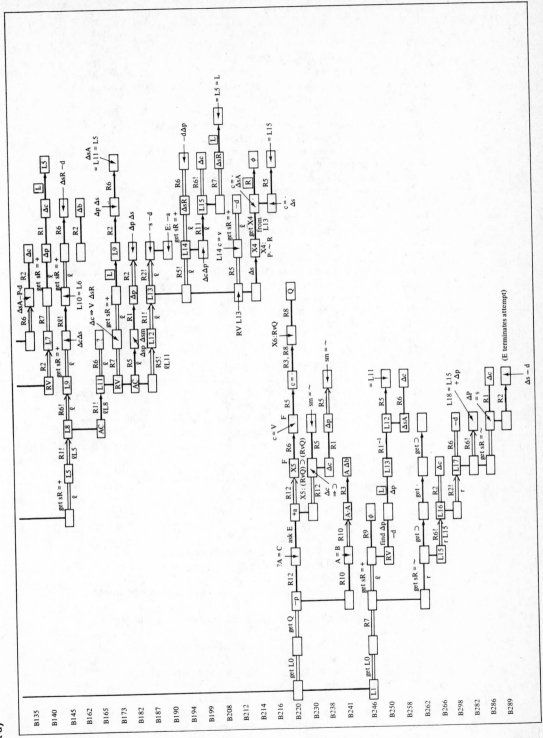

B280   Q R . . . fine.

B281   Now . . . if apply R6 to that

B282   all we're going to get is. . . . (sigh)

B283   I don't think it's going to get us anything that'll do us much good. . . .

B284   We'll see what happens.

B285   [E writes L18: $(\sim R \vee \sim P)\cdot(Q \vee R)$]

B286   That's kind of the same place we were before . . .

B287   except we have the order reversed. . . .

B288   Hah . . . oh gee . . . if we could only change the order of that second term of 17 . . .

B289   but leaving the signs the same. . . .

B290   We can't do it directly because the horseshoe. . . .

B291   There's always a sign change when you change the order by R2. . . .

B292   Let's see. . . .

B293   [E terminates attempt.]

B294   We didn't get too far on this one.

B295   (E: What did you think about this problem?)

B296   Well, may be I was stuck on one track . . .

B297   indirectly I kept doing the same thing over and over again, switching around terms

B298   and I kept ending up with the wrong sign in the wrong place.

B299   I was unable to apply R7 to it in the first place. . . .

B300   There must be some way it'll fall out real easily.

B301   It looks very easy . . . it looks like you can do it only a few steps if you knew the right ones.

B302   I was just horsing around trying to get it into that form that would work.

B303   (E: Why were you trying to use R12?)

B304   No, that was part way through that I was using R12.

B305   I was trying to use R7 at the beginning and then near the end again

B306   and in the middle for some reason I tried R12.

B307   Well actually I had two different strategies for the whole thing.

B308   At first I was trying to get a separate Q and a separate P

B309   and I got discouraged on that idea somewhere along the way that didn't seem to work out too easily . . .

B310   because with a separate Q and a separate P by using R10

B311   you could get it into a dot form

B312   and it would be easy to change the signs around

B313   and get it into the form of the answer.

B314   So that was one possibility

B315   and then I was also looking at R7. . . .

B316   I don't know why I was so interested in using R7. . . .

B317   I felt if I could get something in the form of the right-hand side of R7 I could go over toward the left-hand side of R7.

B318   (E: Is that possibly because R7 worked on the previous problem?)

B319   I don't think so. . . .

B320   In fact I didn't even remember that I'd used R7 on the last one.

B321   Maybe it was, but I don't think so.

B322   Then if I got it in the form of the left-hand side of R7,

B323   I could change that into a dot by R5

B324   and then I could take that thing and after playing around with it awhile

B325   maybe getting it into . . . so I could use R8

B326   and just get the B part of the left-hand side of R7

B327   which would give me something pretty close to the answer. . . .

B328   The P and Q would be there with a dot between them . . .

B329   maybe the signs would be wrong.

B330   It probably takes only half a dozen steps.

B	T*	
B1	0	[E writes L1: $(R \supset \sim P) \cdot (\sim R \supset Q)$]
B2	1	[E writes L0: $\sim(\sim Q \cdot P)$]
B3	2	(E: OK. There's the problem.)

E1

B4	3	Got a lot of tildes, huh? △
B5	5	[E: $(R \supset \sim P) \cdot (\sim R \supset Q))$ △△
B6	13	(E: and you're supposed to get $\sim(\sim Q \cdot P))$ △
B7	20	Wow, △ well I guess . . . △ I suppose I'm going to have to handle each one of the parentheses separate. △
B8	29	First, I'll look for a, ah . . . I think I'll look for a . . . △ something with a connector, with a dot connector as the major connector. △
B9	37	Now I can see here . . . set . . . R1. △
B10	41	I could reverse them,
B11	44	but, ah, I can't see any point △ in that right now.
B12	48	Ah. △ If they were the same. . . .
B13	50	I can't use R3. △
B14	56	Ah, △ rule, R4 △ and R7. . . .
B15	62	I can . . .
B16	64	well △ no I can't use them
B17	68	because they require . . . △ they require the same or else . . . ah . . . the same minor and major △ connector.
B18	76	Or else R7 has, ah . . . has no △ horseshoe.
B19	80	Ah . . . △ I don't see any, see anything I can do on the . . . △ do on the scale of the whole. △
B20	92	I guess I'll △ have to take it down separately.
B21	96	So, they're both △ horseshoes.
B22	100	Maybe . . . maybe the same △ rule will apply to each one.

E2

B23	104	Ah . . . △ see △ I want to get it . . . one quantity, get a tilde in front of it,
B24	112	and I want to get △ a tilde in front of it △
B25	117	and a dot minor connector. △
B26	124	Ah . . . △ R6,
B27	128	I can rearrange . . . △ rearrange the ah, △ inner workings of 1
B28	134	and change the horseshoe to a wedge. △
B29	140	Let's . . . let's do that, △ apply R6 to part of 1,
B30	144	because, mm, if I get those △ in wedges,
B31	146	I may be able to use rule . . . ah, 7. △
B32	149	(E: OK, 6 to the first part of L1.)
B33	150	[E writes L2: $(\sim R \vee \sim P) \cdot (\sim R \supset Q)$]
B34	152	Yeh . . . △△△△△△ well, △ ah . . .
B35	180	(E: The first part changes to △ $\sim R \vee \sim P$.) △
B36	188	Yeah, △ doggone. See that, that △ that, if I change the second part,
B37	196	that would work out real nice for △ R7,
B38	200	except that a, a tilde △ would make it a different term.
B39	202	Is that, is that all right?

*Times were recorded at 4-second intervals. The times shown are interpolated.

B40	204	See I'll have a $\sim$R, $\triangle$ ah, wedge $\sim$P then in second, ah . . . across $\triangle$ the . . . connected by a point . . . I'll have $\sim$R or $\triangle$ I'll have it straight . . . a positive R, just R.
B41	216	So apply it to that $\triangle$ too,
B42	218	we'll have . . . and that'll give us. . . .
B43	219	Apply R6 to the second part of 1. $\triangle$
B44	221	(E: Uh hum, all right.)
B45	222	Or you can apply it to 2, that's all right. $\triangle$
B46	228	Yeah that, $\triangle$ that should do it,
B47	232	but ah . . . I don't seem $\triangle$ to quite get this.
B48	236	I can't get these . . . ah . . . $\triangle$ math signs. I keep getting 'em mixed up with the tildes, the negative $\triangle$ math signs, ya know.
B49	244	(E: So, $\triangle$ the second part is now R $\vee$ Q.)
B50	246	[E writes L3: $(\sim$R $\vee$ $\sim$P)$\cdot$(R $\vee$ Q)]
B51	248	Yeh, well that, that, that's $\triangle$ exactly R7. That, that, that $\triangle$ applies.
B52	254	I can get, ah . . . and from that I'll get. . . .
B53	256	But you see, $\sim$R $\triangle$ and R, are they different terms?
B54	258	(E: They're different.)
B55	260	Well $\triangle$ then, that doesn't fit in R7. . . .

E3

B56	264	So, here I am. . . . $\triangle$ well . . . $\triangle$ ah. . . $\triangle$ esh . . . $\triangle$ now where am I?
B57	280	Ah. $\triangle\triangle$ I could reverse them around,
B58	288	but I don't think $\triangle$ that's going to do anything,
B59	290	working as a whole again. $\triangle$
B60	293	I, I, I can't see. . . .
B61	296	Oh! $\triangle$ Wait a minute, I see something. $\triangle$
B62	301	I don't know if it's any good.
B63	304	On R8 . . . ah . . . $\triangle$ across a, a dot major connector.
B64	308	I can take either, ah . . . the whole thing $\triangle$ will equal either one, A or B.
B65	312	But the . . . ha . . . $\triangle$ trouble is, the final answer is in Q and P, $\triangle$
B66	320	and there's, neither one of the terms are either Q . . . have $\triangle$ both Q and P in it. $\triangle$
B67	325	But . . . the only way I can think to get rid of it. . . .
B68	326	R8 would work
B69	327	if I could apply $\triangle$ R7.
B70	332	Why can't $\triangle$ I apply R7?
B71	336	Maybe $\triangle$ R4.
B72	338	They're, they're the perfect ones
B73	340	'cause then I can get rid $\triangle$ of that one term.
B74	344	I have to get it so that a P $\triangle$ and a Q are in the same quantity . . . same parenthesis.
B75	346	So maybe . . . um. . . . $\triangle\triangle$
B76	356	Yeh but I, I, I can't see anything . . . that, $\triangle$ ah, does it.
B77	358	R7 seems to be everything.
B78	360	I'll have to rearrange $\triangle$ that so I can get that in there.
B79	364	Ah. . . . $\triangle$ wait, if I can apply one $\triangle$ rule,
B80	390	and reverse it . . . ah . . . just . . . ah . . .
B81	372	that's taking $\triangle$ an individual quantity, and change the sign $\triangle$ on the R and not on the other one,
B82	380	then I'm $\triangle$ all right.
B83	384	Ah $\triangle$ such as, ah . . . $\triangle$ well (laugh) $\triangle$
B84	396	Let's see . . . now . . . $\triangle$ I don't see anything $\triangle$ that I can do that with unless . . . ah.

E4

B85	404	Oh, here's an idea, △ on . . . on R5 I see that I can convert the inners to △ dots
B86	410	and if I have all dot connectors,
B87	412	then I can apply △ R4.
B88	414	See what I mean? △
B89	420	Let's see now, ah, what would that give △ me?
B90	422	I'd be changing all them signs,
B91	424	course that wouldn't really △ matter.
B92	428	Let's see, if I had a dot △ for a major connector and inner connector, and ah . . .
B93	432	then I could apply △ R4,
B94	434	and then from R4 I can apply 8.
B95	436	And △ 8's gonna get me real, and that'll get me real close. △
B96	444	Ah . . . △ I dunno.
B97	448	Well, let's apply . . . R5 △ to ah, L3.
B98	452	(E: OK. △ which part?)
B99	456	Well, △ ah . . . apply it to both parts.
B100	460	otherwise △ R4'll never △ work.
B101	466	(E: Let's do it one at a time.)
B102	468	All right, then I don't . . . I don't know where that's going to get △ me. Ah.
B103	470	(E: R5 eh.)
B104	471	(E: Now when we do the first thing mmm.) △
B105	476	Oh, I didn't see that △ R3. . . .
B106	480	Oh, △ oh, no, no, OK, I was thinking of △ R3,
B107	486	but . . . they're not like terms so I can't do that. △△△
B108	497	[E writes L4: ~(R·P)·(R ∨ Q)]
B109	500	(E: OK, △ in this step I did it to the A part and got △ ~(R·P)·(R ∨ Q). △△
B110	513	Yeh, now you want. . . .
B111	516	(E: Now I apply it to the next one, the B △ part.)
B112	518	[E writes L5: ~(R·P)·~(~R·~Q)]
B113	520	Gee, I, I keep △ wanting to multiply them tildes out,
B114	522	and get positive.
B115	524	He could △ do that.
B116	528	No, he couldn't do that . . . △ tilde.
B117	532	(E: The B part is how changed △ to be ~(~R·~Q).)
B118	544	Now, △ that'll give me. . . . △
B119	549	I could apply R4 . . . couldn't I?
B120	550	Or could I? △
B121	553	No, I don't think I could. . . . △
B122	557	It seems to me I'm up a tree. . . . △
B123	564	Ah . . . △ I, I, I can't seem to apply R4, △
B124	569	unless I call the second complex quantity C
B125	572	but th, that's △ that's stretching it. △
B126	577	Or is it?
B127	580	You could call the whole second complex quantity C, △ couldn't you?
B128	582	(E: Uh-huh.)
B129	584	And ah, △ well if we apply R4 to that,
B130	588	I would △ get a real messed up number. △
B131	593	I, I don't think I will
B132	596	because, ah, △ I may get into three terms there, △
B133	601	and that'll give me too complex a number.
B134	604	I, I've got to do something △ else,

E5

B135	606	I, I don't know if that's right or not. △
B136	609	I've got to look for something with dots. . . . △

525

B137	613	Can't see any dots. △
B138	617	I'll have to . . . ah. . . . △
B139	624	Well, I can still invert them, if that △ would mean anything. . . .
B140	626	No, wouldn't mean thing. △
B141	632	Gotta get Q and P in the same quantity . . . △ and. . . . △△
B142	641	The only thing I know. . . . △△
B143	649	See. . . . △△
B144	657	I can't see a thing,
B145	658	must be way off base. △
B146	661	I don't see a thing.
B147	664	I guess I'm going △ to have to . . .
B148	666	gonna run out of ideas here. △
B149	672	Sure hate to start over △ once I got that . . . been on the track,
B150	674	but I, I, I guess I'll have to.
B151	676	I, I, I don't think I'm . . . working up a blind △ alley here. △

E6

B152	684	Well, let's look back △ at the original one and see if I can see anything.
B153	688	Ah, △ I like that conversion into ah wedges, △
B154	696	but ah, △ I don't know if it'll get me anywhere.
B155	700	If I can, wonder △ if I can eliminate ah right inside that, through, through a wedge, △
B156	705	or I could through a dot. △
B157	712	Oh, I have an idea, how about if I, ah, take, ah, apply △ R8,
B158	716	oh, yeh I get it, △ ah, just to part of ah, △ step 5,
B159	724	and ah, that is the same △ as A point B
B160	726	and I'll get just B from it, I'll get just P. △
B161	729	See, what I mean?
B162	730	I'll apply R8 △
B163	731	and I'll end up getting. . . .
B164	736	Ah, oh wait a minute, positive . . . △ it has to have a positive total expression. △
B165	741	(E: Uh-huh.)
B166	744	Well in that case, let's go back then △ to L3.
B167	746	No, L3 is no good.
B168	748	Oh, every time I change △ it I get a, a, a title, a teetle, a what do you call it?
B169	750	(E: Tilde.) △
B170	753	. . . tilde (laugh), a tilde in front of it. △
B171	757	I get a, see, if I have the tilde in front of it
B172	758	in order to have the dot, △
B173	761	and I have to have the dot △
B174	765	in order to apply R8. △,
B175	769	Well, I have to get rid of that tilde, △
B176	776	and keep the dot . . . in front of the total △ expression. △

E7.1

B177	784	Well, oh, △ oh, I could, I could △ do one other thing.
B178	792	Ah is L5, △ ah, in the whole total expression, is that considered negative?
B179	796	No, △ it isn't, is it?
B180	800	When both components are △ tildes, is that necessarily the whole thing negative? △
B181	805	(E: Do you mean can you apply R4 to L5?) △
B182	809	No, I want to apply R8.
B183	812	It has △ to have a positive total expression.
B184	816	If I apply △ the whole . . . I can. . . .
B185	818	(E: It can be applied by dropping out either this A part or this B part.)

B186	820	Yeh, △ I would like to drop out the A part, △
B187	825	because by using R9
B188	826	I may be able just to add something sometime. △
B189	829	(E: Do you want me to apply?)
B190	830	Well, wait a minute there, I'll need one other thing. △
B191	833	Eventually if I can use R9,
B192	834	I, I, think I could get rid of the R. . . . △
B193	840	And . . . I have to look for something △ with a, just a △ dot connector.
B194	845	Let me think ahead a little bit. . . .
B195	846	Ah, just with a dot connector,
B196	847	can I get rid of that. . . . △
B197	849	Oh, sure, I can apply it again,
B198	850	and just drop it out. △
B199	856	Oh, no, the whole thing is, the whole expression △ is negative, the, ah, the negative expression. △
B200	861	It would be nice just to eliminate everything
B201	862	and add what you wanted, △
B202	865	and with 8 and 9 you can do that.
B203	866	(chuckle) But these happen to be △ tildes.

E7.2

B204	872	Ah. . . . △ let's see, somehow I've got to get rid of that R. △
B205	880	If I decide to ah . . . decide △ to do it that way. △
B206	885	I don't see a thing. △
B207	889	Unless I revert it back into something else. △
B208	893	I could get it into R ∨ Q △
B209	897	by R5 backwards, R ∨ Q, △
B210	901	R ∨ Q, and like I have there,
B211	904	and ah . . . △ what would that △ do? △
B212	913	And I'd have to get rid of, still have to get rid of the R. . . . △
B213	920	And, ah . . . △ I don't see a thing that I could do.
B214	924	I guess I'm up the wrong tree △ again mmm. △△
B215	933	Hmmm, nuts. . . . △
B216	937	Ah, let me think, ah where can I go? △
B217	944	I, I, I guess, darn △ R8 looks so attractive and so close.
B218	948	I △ just can't get rid of that tilde, always △ negative.
B219	956	There's no other way of converting ah, dots to ah wedges is △ there,
B220	958	let's see, or wedges to dots? △
B221	961	Even in the beginning, can I convert a horseshoe to a dot. . . .
B222	964	Somehow △ I . . . I don't see a thing. △
B223	972	No, △ it's the only, only way . . . △ the only steps in converting major connectors are ah 5 and △ 6. △
B224	988	And, ah, you, you have to go through it that △ way . . . dot to wedge and wedge to horseshoe.
B225	992	And ah . . . △ it makes the △ whole expression. . . .
B226	1000	Oh, △ hey, I see something on R2, ah, △ working with a horseshoe. △
B227	1009	If I would, instead of jumping the gun there and converting . . . △
B228	1016	if I originally converted the signs △ by just, just reversing △ them and changing the signs.
B229	1024	That △ would make everything the opposite all the way down the line. . . . △
B230	1029	I'd still . . .
B231	1030	that doesn't get rid of the tildes in front.
B232	1032	Darn, that's the only thing △ that's bothering me.
B233	1036	Are the tildes in △ front.
B234	1038	See, I . . .

B235   1040   All the way down the line they would be △ just opposite

B236   1042   if I'd do that first.

B237   1044   I, I, △ I'd converted them into wedges, that've been, it would be positive. △

B238   1052   Well, the, △ the jump would have been when I converted into △ dots . . .

B239   1058   the total expression keeps negative. △△

B240   1065   Gee whiz, that's the problem. △

B241   1072   Well, may be I better do something △ altogether different.

B242   1074   Try it over. △

B243   1080   Ah, △△ well, △ I don't see a thing. . . .

B244   1092   Ah. △ (sigh) It sure was harder than it was △ yesterday,

B245   1098   at least it seems to be right now. △

B246   1101   (E: What are you looking at?)

E8

B247   1102   I'm just looking at right, right at the beginning.

B248   1104   I, I'm △ going to have to start all over I think.

B249   1108   Now I gotta get △ a dot, gotta to get into dots,

B250   1112   but I've have to get rid of a whole △ term.

B251   1116   I've gotta convert the △ sign. . . .

B252   1118   I gotta do everything to it.

B253   1119   I gotta convert the sign, △

B254   1124   I gotta, get into one △ quantity,

B255   1128   I gotta get a, a dot as the major △ connector.

B256   1129   Oh, wait a minute, I see something.

B257   1132   Um, △ I see that, ah, △ that it,

B258   1138   I don't have to change the dot necessarily, △

B259   1141   since the dot's still the major connector in the final answer.

B260   1144   If △ I can just get rid of the R in each term,

B261   1146   I've got it knocked. △

B262   1152   Now, how can you get rid of a term with △ a horseshoe?

B263   1154   I don't think you can. △

B264   1157   That's all right I can get rid of something else.

B265   1160   The only △ place. . . .

B266   1162   Well, R8, you can get rid of something. △

B267   1165   And ah △. . . .

B268   1176   Well, that's the only thing I see that you can get rid

B269   1178   or R3,

B270   1180   but ah, they have to be △ identical.

B271   1182   I'd never change a letter.

B272   1184   Ah, △ rule . . . the only other thing △ that looks interesting is △ R11.

B273   1196   But I don't know how I can get them in the △ same line.

B274   1200   See I . . . cause I'd have to eliminate a △ term.

B275   1202   If I can eliminate it,

B276   1204   I'd be OK in △ anything.

B277   1208   'Cause if I take △ part of the quantity, △ that is, the t' . . . that, that's considered the total expression then,

B278   1216   and it's negative, it's negative, it's got a tilde in front of △ it.

B279   1218   Because as soon as you convert it to a dot,

B280   1220   you put a tilde △ in front of it.

B281   1224   And there's nothing I can do △ to change that tilde. △

B282   1232   Gee whiz, a tilde times a tiddle, tiddle, tilde doesn't make △ a positive does it?

B283   1236   Makes a △ negative. △

B284   1241   Doggone. △

B285   1245   There's a. . . . △△

B286   1253   Must be something to that.

E9

B287 1256 Well, △ what else can we do in the beginning? △
B288 1261 If I reverse them what am I doing? △
B289 1265 Ah, nothing.
B290 1260 Got to think up something to △ get it.
B291 1272 I can't think △ as well when I'm talking,
B292 1274 but I gotta to keep talking. △
B293 1280 Ah, △ gotta get an idea. Where's an idea.
B294 1284 Let's see. △ Gotta get a . . . got to get rid △ of a term.
B295 1292 The only way I can get rid of △ a term is with points. . . .
B296 1294 I'm in that rut. I'm in that one thing all the time.
B297 1296 I gotta change my △ attitude.
B298 1298 I was reading about that last night. △

E10

B299 1301 Don't stay in a rut. △
B300 1308 All right, let's look at something altogether different △ then.
B301 1312 What can we do with the △ quantity as a whole?
B302 1314 I've been trying to look at the parts,
B303 1316 what can we do as a △ whole?
B304 1320 I can convert that dot △ into a, ah wedge,
B305 1322 and that'll change the sign. △
B306 1328 And then, △ ah well, we. . . . △
B307 1336 Let's △ try it.
B308 1338 I, ah, I can't see that in my mind too well, I. . . .
B305 1340 Let's apply R5 △ to L1
B310 1344 and see if we get anything △ from it.
B311 1346 (E: Oke.)
B312 1347 'Cause that'll change, that'll change the sign. △
B313 1349 Even the outside sign . . . the total expression. △△
B314 1360 But what will △ that gimme me. △
B315 1365 Oh, I think I see something that's good,
B316 1368 because if that's △ outside is changed,
B317 1372 then I can convert it into a △ horseshoe,
B318 1374 everything will be opposite,
B319 1376 and just work it in a horseshoe for △ a while,
B320 1378 keep it in a horseshoe all the way down to the end, △
B321 1381 and if I convert it back,
B322 1384 it's OK if the whole expression is negative △ then
B323 1388 because, because ah, △ the answer to the expression is negative.
B324 1392 Yet △ I won't be able to get rid of anything I'm afraid,
B325 1396 'cause you have to have it in a dot △ to get rid of any. . . .
B326 1398 Ah, no, except the same thing you have to get. △
B327 1401 [E writes L6: $\sim(\sim(R \supset \sim P) \vee \sim(\sim R \supset Q))$]
B328 1402 Now what does that give me?
B329 1403 Is that what. . . .
B330 1404 (E: You've got △ $\sim(\sim(R \sim (P \supset \vee \sim(\sim R \supset Q).)$ △△
B331 1416 Gee △ whiz. Oh, △ brother!
B332 1421 If I can reverse that,
B333 1424 and change those inside t' △ tildes,
B334 1426 to get them out of there
B335 1428 then I can eliminate them as separate terms. △ I think. △
B336 1433 But can you reverse them.
B337 1436 Let's see, is △ there any way you can reverse them around a wedge?
B338 1438 And. . . . △

529

B339   1441   Yes, you can in there, R1,
B340   1444   but that doesn't change any △ signs.
B341   1448   And . . . △ ah . . . △ can't seem to do a thing △ there.
B342   1460   I guess △ nothing I can do there is, ah. . . .
B343   1464   Oh, △ wait, if in R6,
B344   1468   if I, if I change it, the major term to △ horseshoe,
B345   1470   you change just A, △
B346   1473   which would be an advancement
B347   1476   because ah △ if I get A's sign changed,
B348   1480   then I've got, △ I've got a term there that's positive, right?
B449   1484   Or is that major t . . . is that tilde △ outside the brackets considered that negative too?
B350   1488   See, △ if I take that out
B351   1490   and apply R8 to just that part,
B352   1492   is that considered the total △ expression positive?
B353   1494   (E: No.)
B354   1496   Then △ I can eliminate some . . .
B355   1500   Oh, no, because its a △ horseshoe
B356   1502   and you have to change it to a dot,
B357   1504   and when you do dat, △ you're gonna get it. You're gonna get it right in △ the ear.
B358   1512   You're gonna get △ a negative sign △ again.
B359   1520   I got it around a wedge, △ and ah. . . . △
B360   1525   Gee is that right?
B361   1528   That's not △ right, the way you got that written up there is it? △
B362   1533   Oh yes, I guess it is. Yeh, it's right. △
B363   1540   I don't know what I did here, but ah, △ it seems to me. . . . △
B364   1545   Naw, I guess that's nothing.
B365   1548   I was △ thinking that if I could convert it backwards,
B366   1550   I was gonna get a different answer,

E11

B367   1552   but I wouldn't, of △ course. △
B368   1557   What can I do.
B369   1558   They were positive to begin with around a dot. △
B370   1561   I can eliminate one whole term.
B371   1564   I can apply △ R8 anytime I want
B372   1566   and eliminate a whole term.
B373   1568   What's △ that gonna give me?
B374   1570   I tried that once before, didn't I? △
B375   1573   No, not exactly. △
B376   1577   I might be better off trying something like that. △
B377   1581   It's too complicated now.
B378   1584   If I, if I just eliminated a whole △ term. . . .
B379   1586   I've got things right in front of me
B380   1588   and I'm trying △ to eliminate something all the time. △
B381   1596   (sigh) Well, △ ah, now, which term to eliminate △ is the question.
B382   1602   Ah, I, I want to eliminate one
B383   1604   because, ah, I'll △ eliminate . . . I want to use . . . to be able to ah, eliminate another word, another thing again. △
B384   1609   Ah, now, I don't know if you're gonna follow me on this,
B385   1610   but here's the way I feel. △
B386   1613   I'll eliminate one of these terms,
B387   1616   the one I don't eliminate, I'll take that, △ change it to a dot,
B388   1620   and eliminate that △ letter, see.

B389 1622 That leaves me with just a **P** or **Q**.
B390 1624 Then △ I can add on,
B391 1626 through R9.
B392 1628 I △ think I'm getting it now.
B393 1630 Now the question is . . . △
B394 1633 I don't want it to be negative. △
B395 1637 See, I could choose the wrong one and get. . . .
B396 1640 Well, I, △ I'd better write it, get △ it written down
B397 1646 'cause I think I've got it now.
B398 1648 Let's apply R8 to △ the total expression, in the beginning, rule, L1. △ Apply R8
            to that. △
B399 1660 And let's take, ah, △ let's have it apply the ah, oh, △ I don't know. . . .
B400 1666 Let's, well let's see, convertin', when you ah, from a horseshoe to a dot, you'll ah,
            in . . . will ya invert △ them . . . reverse them anytime?
B401 1670 No. △
B402 1673 So let's take ah. . . .
B403 1676 Oh, △ that's going to gimme trouble. . . .
B404 1678 Well, let's take the first one. 's OK.
B405 1679 (E: Take the first one and drop the second one, is that it?)
B406 1680 OK, △ yeah, that sounds pretty good.
B407 1682 I, I, I, I won't be able to see,
B408 1684 but at least I know I'm on the right △ track
B409 1686 so if it doesn't work out,
B410 1687 I'll try the other one. △
B411 1689 [E writes L7: R ⊃ ~P]
B412 1690 (E: You have (R ⊃ ~ P).) △
B413 1696 Now, if I want to change that to a △ dot. . . .
B414 1700 Ah nuts, I'm gonna run △ into trouble, I know.
B415 1704 I'm gonna get a negative total expression . . . △△ any way you look at it.
B416 1712 Son of a gun! △ Aw, man. △
B417 1720 Well, I . . . the only △ way I can get a negative total expression △ is when I have a
            dot
B418 1726 and that's the only time I don't want it. △
B419 1732 I don't see anything where I can get a negative total △ expression
B420 1736 even △ down, through the other steps the. . . .
B421 1740 Pardon me . . . I'd be △ nowhere.
B422 1742 I'd . . . I don't see a thing that. . . .
B423 1744 The only place I have a neg, negative △ total expression is when I have a dot. △
B424 1749 And that's exactly when I don't want it, △
B425 1753 'cause I can't apply R8. △△
B426 1764 See, if I converted that, what I have △ there,
B427 1768 I'd end up with △ ~R ∨ ~P, △
B428 1776 and that would give me △ ~(R·P), △ ~(R·P) △ in with the total expression. △
B429 1789 Boy, oh boy. △△
B430 1800 Well, △ I can only apply that to part.
B431 1804 Even if I had △ that, ~(R·P). △
B432 1812 Even △ if I took the other one, if I was only sittin' there with △ ~R ⊃ Q. △
B433 1824 I would get from that △ R ∨ Q,
B434 1828 and from that I would get △ tilde △ ah, △ ~(~R ∨ ~Q). △
B435 1841 That gives me nothing. △
B436 1845 Sure up the wrong tree here. △

E12.1
B437 1852 Well, doggone, △ ah . . . △ can't do it, △ can't do a thing. △
B438 1868 Maybe I'd better start over again, over △ and over and over.

B439 1872 I'm looking, △ looking at this part. . . .
B440 1876 Everyone △ I see is a horseshoe. △
B441 1884 Boy, △ let's see, △ ∼R ⊃ Q. △
B442 1893 Looking across the sheet here and. . . . △
B443 1900 I never thought of two lines, maybe I can do something △ with two lines,
B444 1902 but ah. . . . △
B445 1905 Hey, here's an idea, R10. △
B446 1912 Ah. If I apply △ R8 to the, to the next line △
B447 1917 that would just give me what I have I guess. △
B448 1921 I'd have ah, and ya know
B449 1924 and I'd drop the ah . . . I'd drop the B △ part ah . . . the A part and
B450 1926 I'd have A and B, △
B451 1929 and that would give me A·B.
B452 1930 Doesn't change any signs either, does it?

E12.2
B453 1932 "No change in △ signs. A and B represent two l . . . △ lines of the message." △
B454 1941 Maybe I can get a R12 out of it. △
B455 1948 Ah can you . . . what do you do when you . . . can you invert a △ horseshoe?
B456 1950 Yeah, when you change the signs.

E13.1
B457 1952 Wait a minute, here's an idea, △ ah, ahm, yeah, △ on just the B part. . . . △
B458 1964 If I apply R8 to the first △ one and, and get the B out of it,
B459 1966 invert it
B460 1967 and change the signs,
B461 1968 that △ gives me two positive R's.
B462 1970 Aha! I'm gettin' it, I'm gettin' it.
B463 1972 Apply R8 to the first step, and △ take . . . △ and that's the second part and get just B.
B464 1973 [E writes L8: ∼R ⊃ Q]
B465 1980 (E: OK, on L8 △ you have ∼R ⊃ Q.) △
B466 1985 Right. Now then apply R2 to L8. △△
B467 1993 (E: OK.)
B468 1996 Apply R2, △ R2 to L8.
B469 2000 Agh! Yuk, yuk, yuk. And we're gonna cancel some R's out, △ that's what we're gonna do.
B470 2001 [E writes L9: ∼Q ⊃ R]
B471 2008 (E: You get △ ∼Q ⊃ R.)
B472 2012 Uh huh. That's △ fine. Now then, you take 7 △ and 9 as two lines △
B473 2024 and cancel the R's △ according to R12.
B474 2026 (E: Uh-huh.)
B475 2028 And △ you'll get . . .
B476 2032 you apply R12 to sev' . . . rul' lines 7 and △ 9
B477 2034 and you'll get ∼Q ⊃ P. △
B478 2037 And that's gettin' close all the time. △
B479 2041 That's for L10 now.
B480 2042 [E writes L10: ∼Q ⊃ P]
B481 2043 (E: Tilde Q horseshoe P.) [Error: should be ∼Q ⊃ ∼P.]
B482 2044 Horseshoe P. △ [Said concurrently with "horseshoe P" above, confirming error.]
B483 2046 That's applying R12 to 7 and 9. △
B484 2052 Now I've got to change it to a dot, from a horseshoe to a △ dot,
B485 2054 and I go through a couple of steps.
B486 2055 I think it will work out perfect.

B487	2056	I'll just take a △ chance.
B489	2060	Apply R6 to that, △ to L10, that's it. △
B489	2068	And I should get ah, △ ah Q ∨ P. △
B490	2073	[E writes L11: Q ∨ P]
B491	2074	(E: Q ∨ P.)
B492	2076	Now apply △ R5 to that. . . .
B493	2080	Oh, oh! △ Don't tell me I'm gonna get all the way down there and one lousy tilde △ is gonna be wrong.
B494	2088	Well, △ mmm. I am.
B495	2092	If I apply △ R5,
B496	2096	I'll get △ ∼(∼Q·∼P),
B497	2100	and △ the answer is positive P. △
B498	2105	Talking about close as you can git and not git it. △
B499	2112	Ahm. We gotta do something △ here.
B500	2116	Ah, △△ well, what △ the heck. △ I had it in the horseshoe form.
B501	2132	What good would that △ do?
B502	2136	Ah. If I had △ it in the dot form △ anyhow,
B503	2142	what can I do? △
B504	2146	Don't think I can do anything. △

E13.2

B505	2152	Let's see, we're △ really close here.
B506	2156	L10 seems to be the key △ line, ah, ∼Q ⊃ P.
B507	2160	What else can I do △ to that? ∼Q ⊃ P. △
B508	2165	Yeah, I can, I have to be able to do something else to that . . . △
B509	2169	change the signs around somethin'.
B510	2172	I gotta get △ P negative.
B511	2176	Well, △ how about this? I △ could, I, I, I, I could in L10,
B512	2182	instead of, instead of, doing △ L11,
B513	2185	then applying R6 to it,
B514	2188	let's △ apply . . .
B515	2190	Oh, its a dot.
B516	2192	Oh △ never mind,
B517	2193	I was going to apply R8. △
B518	2200	Ahm. △ Well now that's interesting, △ can't do anything. △
B519	2209	If I invert them,
B520	2212	What am I doing △ around that? △
B521	2217	Getting a positive Q and a minus P △
B522	2224	and ah, △ that's not doing a thing. △
B523	2229	(Sigh) Right this close and I can't get it.
B524	2232	(E: And your time is about △ up.)
B525	2236	(E: Ah, do you want to quit △ or do you want . . . do you think you have any hot leads on it?) △
B526	2241	None with the exception I'm that close.
B527	2244	See, I, I can get △ ∼(∼Q·∼P)
B528	2248	and its supposed to be △ positive P.△
B529	2256	Well, △ I guess I've had it. △ I don't see a thing. △
B530	2265	[E turned off recorder and showed S the correct solution. E's error in L10 was discovered, and the recorder turned back on.]
B531		(E: OK, I guess we'll credit you with the correct solution then,)
B532		(E: because I got △ that line wrong.)
B533		(E: It should be ∼Q ⊃ ∼P.)
B534		Yeh.
B535		(E: And from there you could go to the correct △ solution.)

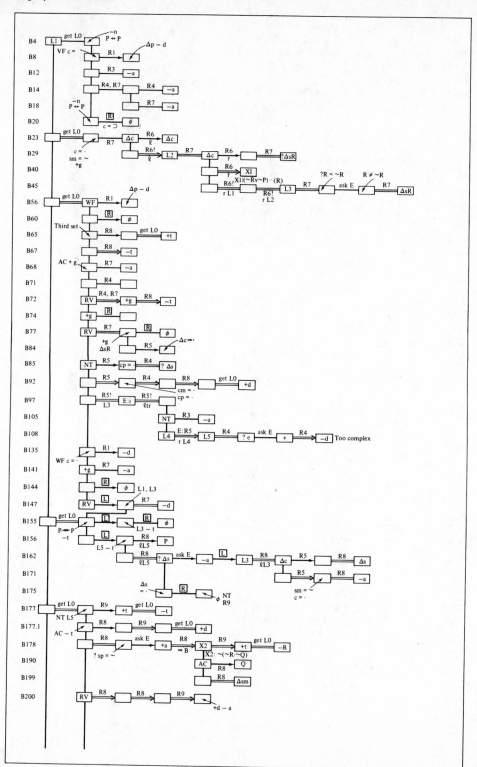

534

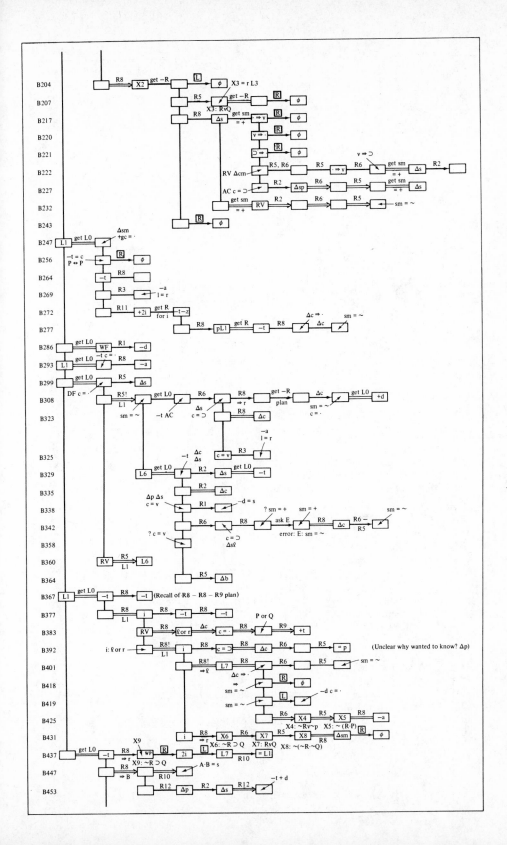

535

(cont'd)

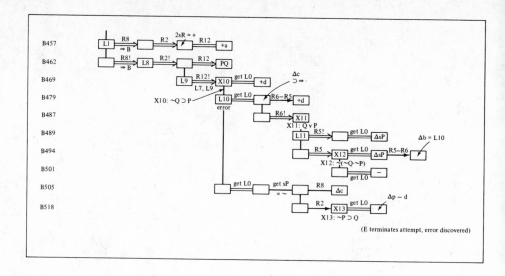

B457	
B462	
B469	
B479	X10: ~Q ⊃ P
B487	
B489	
B494	
B501	
B505	
B518	

(E terminates attempt, error discovered)

APPENDIX 9.5

S9 on D1

B1	[E writes L1: (R ⊃ ~P)·(~R ⊃ Q)]
B2	[E writes L0: ~(~Q·P)]
E1	
B3	Well, the tilde on the outside reminds me of R5.
B4	But inside R5 there's a dot,
B5	so it figures I might get something out of that later on.
E2	
B6	I require a Q and a P . . . Q and a P,
B7	and there's a Q in the second part, a P in the other,
B8	and there's two R's in there.
B9	So I could drop both those R's,
B10	and see . . . split those terms up.
B11	Now what could I do with that?
B12	Nothing seems handy. . . .
B13	10 doesn't seem . . . at all for that
B14	and 9, neither . . .
B15	nor . . . yes, 8
B16	Now . . . how to get a tilde expression.
B17	Well, I can split these up,
B18	using R8. . . .
B19	And let's see now R4, R2 rather, works within these things.
B20	So two sign changes. . . .
B21	Oh, can I work backwards from the final thing?
B22	(E: Uh huh.)
B23	Well, then I'd like to apply R5 to what we have on the end there.

536

B24   (E: I mean you can work backwards in your mind,)

B25   (E: but you have to work on L1.)

B26   OK. Well, let's see, I'll work R5 backwards from the finish . . . work with R5 backwards.

B27   Three sign changes . . .

B28   that would get rid of the tilde on the outside,

B29   would have to make the P with a tilde . . . $\sim$P.

B30   So then I have a $\sim$P

B31   and the Q would have to be positive.

B32   So I think I have to change then, the $\sim$R $\supset$ Q.

B33   And I can do that using R2.

E3

B34   So let's split it up, first of all.

B35   Wait a second, still missing one step aren't I. . . .

B36   Had to combine all this business,

B37   and that . . . oh, what step is that?

B38   Hum . . . R6,

B39   that's not handy at all.

B40   Hum . . . now I forgot how I can combine these.

B41   I'd have to drop these R's . . .

B42   I thought I had a way to drop these R's a moment ago,

B43   Hum . . . see, R12 gives me A times C and the B's would drop out.

B44   But then I'd have to reverse one of those.

B45   That I could do in R2,

B46   so let's try that.

E4

B47   Let's split those two up,

B48   using rule . . . where is it . . . using R8, that's right.

B49   (E: Which part do you want?)

B50   Either one,

B51   I'll take 'em both.

B52   (E: Well, we'll keep the A part here . . . R $\supset$ $\sim$P . . . drop the B part.)

B53   [E writes L2: R $\supset$ $\sim$P]

B54   OK, and with that I. . . .

B55   Let's see, what'll have. . . . The R's will have to go out.

B56   So, let's see, we'll reverse that right now, using R2.

B57   (E: R2 to L2 . . . that gives you $\sim$R $\supset$ P.) [Error: should be P $\supset$ $\sim$R.]

B58   [E writes L3: $\sim$R $\supset$ P]

B59   This might give me an extra step.

B60   Now, we'll split the other part off.

B61   (E: Apply R8 to L1 . . . giving you L4. [E writes L4: $\sim$R $\supset$ Q.]

B62   Well, now, see I need the Q before the P,

B63   so that would have to be the top line if I use R12.

B64   So I'd have to reverse that, too.

B65   I think this is going to get me into trouble before I'm done.

B66   Wait a second, I was thinking of another step before.

B67   Well, let's do this anyway and see what happens. . . .

B68   See if I can remember what I forgot.

B69   (E: What do you want me to do?)

B70   Uh . . . let's reverse that 4,

B71   using the same thing as we did in 2.

B72   (E: Apply R2 to L4.)

B73   (E: You get R $\supset$ $\sim$Q.)

problem behavior graph of S9 on D1

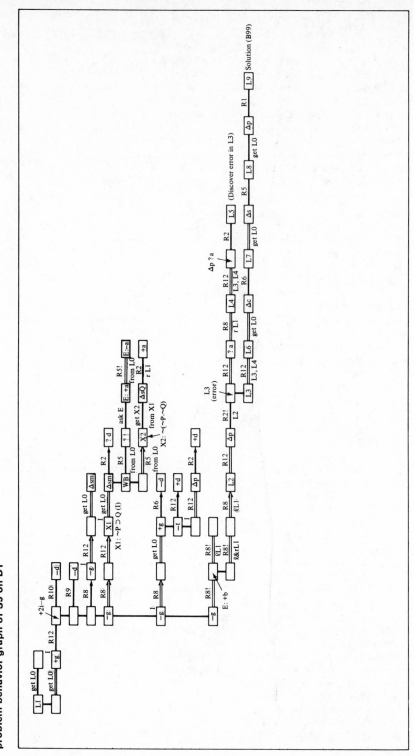

B74   (E: No, you don't either . . . not at all. You get ~Q ⊃ R.)

B75   [E writes L5: ~Q ⊃ R]

B76   Is that right in L3 now? Is from 2 to. . . .

B77   (E: Yeah. . . .)

B78   (E: No, wait a minute . . . L3 is wrong, too.)

B79   I thought something was wrong

B80   and I don't think we need L5 at all.

E5

B81   (E: That's right. P ⊃ ~R.)

B82   [E rewrites L3: P ⊃ ~R]

B83   OK . . . now if P is second that'll have to be the bottom line.

B84   Then I wouldn't have needed L5 anyway.

B85   Then using lines 3 and 4, applying R12 with . . . with L4 on top and L3 on bottom.

B86   [E writes L6: P ⊃ Q]

B87   I got P ⊃ Q . . . P ⊃ Q.

B88   And now if I apply R6. . . .

B89   (E: 6 to L6?)

B90   Right.

B91   [E writes L7: ~P ∨ Q]

B92   ~P ∨ Q.

B93   What the heck happened now? What'd I do, mix these up again?

B94   Oh, well that's OK.

B95   Now apply R5 to that.

B96   (E writes L8: ~(P·~Q)]

B97   Now I simply reverse what's inside,

B98   using R1.

B99   [E writes L9: ~(~Q·P)]

B100   (E: That's the answer.)

B101   Am I doing enough talking now?

B102   (E: Yes, pretty good. The more the merrier, though.)

APPENDIX 9.6

S10 on D1

B1   [E writes L1: (R ⊃ ~P)·(~R ⊃ Q)]

B2   [E writes L0: ~(~Q·P)]

E1

B3   OK. I'm going to look the first card over before I start writing down any rules.

B4   I'll examine it very carefully.

B5   Um . . . a horseshoe expression. . . .

B6   Both of them are horseshoe expressions.

B7   And for those you may use R6 . . .

B8   R2.

B9   Now, if I got them both alike,

B10   I could . . . I could probably eliminate. . . .

B11   No, I can't get them both alike.

B12   So . . . I will. . . .

E2

B13 Oh, I don't have a Q and P in either expression,

B14 so I have to get them together somehow.

B15 A ⊃ B . . . is A ∨ B.

B16 What expressions involve two parts?

B17 There is A·B or. . . . (long pause)

B18 I'm getting confused . . . again.

E3

B19 I'll try the third set

B20 because that's where we may interchange things.

B21 If I could change. . . .

B22 If I could get them on two separate lines.

B33 Hum . . . the thing to do is to try to eliminate the R's.

B24 Therefore I'll have to use something like R12.

E4

B25 But before I can do that . . . I have to . . . um . . . interchange,

B26 or make that one R a ∼R . . . in the parenthesis.

B27 So I will . . .

B28 and still have it a horseshoe . . .

B29 which will be. . . .

B30 Oh . . . no,

B31 R2.

B32 Now, apply R2 to the first parenthesis, L1.

B33 [E writes L2: (P ⊃ ∼R)·(∼R ⊃ Q)]

B34 All right. Apply R8 to L1, eliminating the B expression,

B35 [E writes L3: R ⊃ ∼P]

B36 All right. Oh! No, excuse me.

B37 You'll have to apply it to L2 instead. I'm sorry.

B38 'Cause I wanted to get rid of the R.

B39 (E: Leaving this?)

B40 Yes . . . leave the first one.

B41 [E writes L4: P ⊃ ∼R]

B42 All right. Now apply it to L2 again, eliminating the A expression.

B43 [E writes L5: ∼R ⊃ Q]

B44 All right, now apply R12 to L4 and L5.

B45 [E writes L6: P ⊃ Q]

B46 OK. Um . . . now, apply R6 to L6.

B47 [E writes L7: ∼P ∨ Q]

B48 All right now, apply R5 to L7.

B49 [E writes L8: ∼(P·∼Q)]

B50 All right, apply R1 inside the parenthesis.

B51 [E writes L9: ∼(∼Q·P)]

B52 (E: All done.)

B53 Well!

B54 (E: How did you see to do that, I mean what did you see. . . .)

B55 Well, I knew I had to eliminate the R's,

B56 and there were two parentheses there,

B57 and the only way I could eliminate the R's was by R12,

B58 because that's the only rule with two expressions . . . with two lines of two expressions each.

B59 (E: When did you know you had it?)

B60 I was sure . . . L8,

B61 because I wanted to just keep going ahead instead of stopping to ah . . . figure it out.

B62 Seem to be a little sharper than I was yesterday.

problem behavior graph of S10 on D1

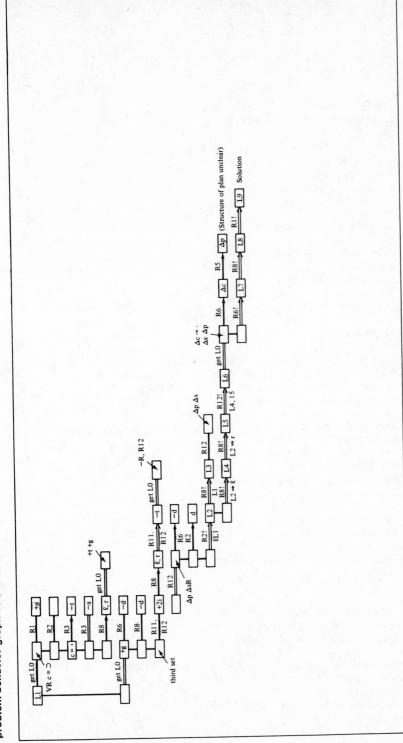

B1	[E writes L1: $(R \supset \sim P) \cdot (\sim R \supset Q)$]
B2	[E writes L0: $\sim(\sim Q \cdot P)$]

E1

B3	Uh-huh, let's see now . . . remove all R's,
B4	horseshoe, change the sign on the Q from the horseshoe to the tilde . . .
B5	change the sign on P from tilde to a dot before it. . . .
B6	Let's see . . . the major connective remains the same . . . its a dot.
B7	And the final expression is negative . . .
B8	with a tilde in it.
B9	I'm looking over the sheet . . . see what I can do on it. . . .
B10	Let's see whether I can . . . take the first expression, $R \supset \sim P$,
B11	and remove the R
B12	and change the sign on the P. . . .
B13	See . . . sheets. . . .
B14	Let's see, $R \supset P$ yields 2,
B15	using R as A
B16	and P as B or $\sim P$ as B.
B17	That would give me $\sim R \supset P$. . . .
B18	What good would that do me, now?
B19	See . . . R . . . $\sim R \supset P$.
B20	Seems like I have to remove R's first . . .
B21	(mumbles) sheets.
B22	Let's see, I can't remove one of the expressions
B23	because I have the letters I need . . . one is in each one. . . .
B24	So I have to work on 'em separately to get what I want.
B25	I'm on the sheets just looking it over. . . .
B26	Let's see, if I can split 'em up into two lines. . . .
B27	Let's say you have R as . . . gotta' use R as B for number 12.
B28	Now I have what?
B29	$B \supset A$. . . .
B30	No, I could use P as C.
B31	Nope, let's see . . . would that work?
B32	Hum . . . no . . . because I have a B in front both times
B33	and I need $A \supset B$, $B \supset C$.
B34	No, I can't reverse them. . . .
B35	Let's see . . . all right, equation 6 . . . what can I do on that?
B36	Well, let me . . . $(\sim R \supset Q)$
B37	That would make it R wedge . . . $R \lor Q$. . . .
B38	And let's see . . . $R \lor Q$ . . . hum.

E2

B39	Let's see now, P has a tilde in front of it in L1.
B40	And the Q has no sign in front of it except for the horseshoe. . . .
B41	Oh, let's see now. Oh . . . equation 2 . . .
B42	If I can get the. . . .
B43	Let's see now . . . I think that's going to work . . . very good . . .
B44	if I can put the $\sim P$ in place of the $\sim R$.
B45	And that would make the expression, $\sim P \supset Q$.
B46	Let's see . . . what good would that do me?

B47	If I had $\sim P \supset A$ in the second parenthesis. . . .
B48	That's similar to 2,
B49	'cause you're using P as A
B50	and B is Q.
B51	You could change that to $\sim B$
B52	which would make the Q . . . $\sim Q$.
B53	Yeah, that would make it $\sim Q \supset P$.
B54	Let's see now, could there be anything to . . . change the horseshoe to a dot?
B55	Let's see now . . . sheet. . . .
B56	I'll work first on changing it around
B57	and then getting rid of the $(R \supset \sim R)$ . . . parenthesis R horseshoe $\sim R$. . . .
B58	I'll get rid of the R's that way. . . .
B59	Now, what would change them first. . . .
B60	Let's see, I'd have that. . . .
B61	Actually I have four numbers of figures in there.
B62	How could I do that?
B63	Hum . . . I could . . . change the $\sim Q$. . . .
B64	cancel it out in the second expression. . . .
B65	I could use that as A for. . . .
B66	Let's see now, I want the horseshoe in there.
B67	Can use 7 right off the bat. . . .
B68	Let's see now . . . what could I work with that has a horseshoe in it?
B69	2. . . .
B70	That would make it . . . working on the second expression . . . $\sim R \supset Q$. . . .
B71	Let's see . . . using R as A
B72	and Q as B,
B73	change it to $R \supset \sim Q$. . . .
B74	No . . . no . . . change it to $\sim Q \supset R$.
B75	Let's see, that's $\sim Q \supset R$.
B76	Ummm . . . that would make it change places again. . . .
B77	Let's see . . . $A \supset B$ in 6. . . .
B78	That would change the expression to $R \supset \sim Q$.
B79	Yeah . . . that would give me the R . . . R's are equal.
B80	So I could convert the expression.
B81	So I could use that as A.
B82	So I have what. . . .
B83	$(A \supset B) \cdot (A \supset C)$. . . .
B84	Now let's see . . . 7. . . .
B85	Let's see . . . that would combine the B and the C. . . .
B86	At my sheets. . . .
B87	Uh, let's see now . . . I could spread it. . . .
B88	No that wouldn't do any good. . . .
B89	B . . . I've knocked out B and C
B90	which is what I had in the first place . . . what I started off.
B91	4 . . . what would that give me?
B92	No, that wouldn't do any good,
B93	not unless I reversed it,

E3.1

B94	and what could I use for C . . . let's see . . . C.
B95	Could use it as $(\sim R \supset A)$. . . .
B96	Nope, gotta' change the horseshoe around to a dot or a wedge. . . .

543

B97 Hum . . . now that changes horseshoe from a dot to a wedge . . . er . . . a . . . to a wedge or a dot.

B98 That's 6. . . .

B99 I'd have to what . . . put a dot in between the two.

B100 So, what can I do . . . with equation 4. . . .

B101 I'll have to change the dot or the first line for any reason. . . .

B102 See, if I use $R \supset \sim P$ as A,

B103 No, that wouldn't do any good.

B104 Or maybe it would.

B105 If I used the $R \supset \sim P$ as A and B.

B106 and I changed the horseshoe to a dot. . . .

B107 Let's see now . . . in equation 4, I would have $(A \cdot B) \cdot C$. . . .

B108 So, let's see, the dot, the major connective in L1 wouldn't have to change,

B109 and it would come out A, which is R . . . $A \cdot (B \cdot C)$, which would be what, $\sim P \cdot (\sim R \supset A)$. . . .

B110 Now let's see . . . A. . . .

B111 No.

B112 Let's see . . . if I used the expression $B \cdot B$ as B,

B113 I could get rid of the A with R8, so just give me B,

B114 which is the expression $(B \cdot C)$.

B115 Let's see now what would I have left. . . .

B116 I'd have $\sim P \cdot (\sim R \supset Q)$.

B117 Now if I worked on the second half of that I'd get rid of $\sim R$. . . .

B118 Let's see . . . that would have . . . I could have the expression $\sim R \supset Q$. . . .

B119 Let's see what would work on that.

B120 Using $\sim R$ as A

B121 and Q as B . . .

B122 what expression would just give me B. . . .

B123 Rule line 8 . . . R8, I mean, would give me just B . . .

B124 but then I have to have a dot as a major connective. . . .

B125 Now what would give me from a horseshoe to a dot. . . .

B126 See here on the sheets . . .

B127 I can't use 5 on that

B128 because the whole expression would be negative. . . .

B129 And can't apply that on 8.

B130 See . . . if I use 6,

B131 that would give me from a horseshoe to a wedge. . . .

B132 And from the wedge,

B133 using R1, I can get to what?

B134 Nothing.

B135 Sooo . . . looking it over again. . . .

B136 See now, what did I do?

B137 Remove the A . . . before. . . .

B138 Let's see now . . . what about 11.

B139 See . . . I have $\sim R \supset Q$,

B140 using that as A and B. . . .

B141 Now, if I could only. . . .

B142 Let's see now . . .

B143 no, 'cause to come out on that I have to remove the R. . . .

B144 I'd only have B left anyway. . . .

B145 So no sense in going through that.

544 B146 Let's see . . . (sighs) . . . R6 gives me a wedge . . .

B147   and R5 from that . . .
B148   that would give me tilde . . . uh positive A dot $\sim$Q. . . .
B149   Now if I just work from that . . .
B150   I still can't use 8
B151   because the whole expression is negative.
B152   So what would I have if I removed the tilde.
B153   What would remove the tilde for me?
B154   R3 wouldn't work
B155   because the sign doesn't change.
B156   R6 . . . going back to that . . .
B157   I just applied it to that expression. . . .
B158   Let's see . . . If I used R9 . . .
B159   could give me an expression I don't want with a wedge in between as a major connective.
B160   I better go back and see what I was doing. . . .

E3.2
B161   Let's see . . . using A as R
B162   and $\sim$P as B
B163   and the expression $\sim$R $\supset$ Q as C. . . .
B164   Uh . . . I better work on the first expression first.
B165   So that would be A $\supset$ B
B166   and I want to get it to what?
B167   Let's see . . . horseshoe. . . .
B168   What rule did I use?
B169   Let's see, 5,
B170   why did I apply that?
B171   That turned out to be tilde parenthesis tilde . . . no . . . $\sim$R dot tilde . . . er . . . a [A?] . . . dot P. [$\sim(\sim$R$\cdot$P)]
B172   Let's see . . . yeah, apply R5 to the first expression L1.
B173   (E: Tilde parenthesis, tilde. . . .)
B174   (E: No, wait a minute, you can't do that.)
B175   Why not?
B176   (E: Well, you've got the wrong connective.)
B177   Oh, wrong connective, fine. . . .
B178   R6, then, to the expression.
B179   [E writes L2: ($\sim$R $\vee$ $\sim$P)$\cdot$($\sim$R $\supset$ Q)]
B180   All right, let's see now . . . uh . . . I want to get rid of the tildes in there. . . .
B181   Could use R5 in there. . . .
B182   That will give me $\sim$(R$\cdot$P).
B183   Now, how do I apply that to 4. . . .
B184   R would be A,
B185   which I can remove with R8 . . . I think. . . .
B186   Yeah, and I'd just have B$\cdot$C. . . .
B187   Yeah . . . I think . . . I still have that tilde in there I think. . . .
B188   See now, $\sim$R wedge. . . .
B189   Wait a minute . . . $\sim$(R $\vee$ P) would gimme. . . .
B190   Oh . . . let's see, R5 would give me $\sim$(R$\cdot$P). . . .
B191   Uh . . . see, can I remove that tilde in front of the expression?
B192   Hum . . . Let's see what would work on that.
B193   See . . . maybe two horseshoes . . .
B194   or wedges. . . .

B195   And now I have to get rid of the $\sim R$'s.

E4

B196   Using $\sim R$ as A,

B197 $\sim P$ as B

B198   and Q as C. . . .

B199   What could work on that?

B200   R7 . . . what would that give me?

B201   If I change the Q . . .

B202   or let the Q the same . . .

B203   I'd just have to change the horseshoes to a wedge.

B204   How will I do that without changing the signs.

B205   If we were using it as $A \supset B$.

B206   Yeah . . . could be R6. . . . That would give me what?

B207   That would give me $R \lor Q$.

B208   Then let's see what would I have to do. . . .

B209   The R. . . .

B210   I could go back to 4

B211   and use $\sim R$ as A.

B212   Let's see . . . $\sim P$ as B

B213   and in the second expression as C . . .

B214   I would have what?

B215   Let's see I would have $A \lor B$ . . .

B216   dot in the middle would have to change to a wedge. . . .

B217   Hum . . . the simplest way?

B218   Hum . . . hum. . . .

B219   Dot. . . .

B220 $A \lor B, A \lor C$ on 7. . . .

B221   Now what would do that?

B222   I do want to change the Q to $\sim Q$.

B223   See, if I use 2 on it,

B224   it's A equal to $\sim R$

B225   and Q as B,

B226   that would change to $\sim Q \supset R$

B227   and then using 6 to that . . . that would change it again to . . . what . . .

B228   Q. . . .

B229   No, that would change it back to $\sim R \lor Q$. . . .

B230   That would be right.

B231   Then I would have $(A \lor B) \cdot (A \lor C)$ . . .

B232   which would change it to $A \lor (B \cdot C)$.

B233   No [Now?], it would be A equal to the R. . . .

B234   Let's see, was that $\sim R$? Yes, A equal $\sim R$.

B235   I have $A \lor B$ . . . would be equal to the expression $B \cdot C$. . . .

B236   Now how could I remove the A?

B237   Well, with 8

B238   I have to change the wedge to a dot. . . .

B239   Oh . . . let's see. let's see . . . before I forget again . . . apply R2 to L2 on that second expression.

B240   [E writes L3: $(\sim R \lor \sim P) \cdot (\sim Q \supset R)$]

B241   Uh huh. . . . Now I want to use 6 . . .

B242   using $\sim Q$ as A . . .

B243   B as R.

B244   Reverse them again

B245 and then you come out with what I want as far as R7 is concerned.
B246 All right . . . so you apply R6, L3 to the second expression.
B247 [E writes L4: $(\sim R \lor \sim P) \cdot (Q \lor R)]$
B248 Uh huh. Now, wouldn't that be R6. . . .
B249 Let's see now . . . that didn't get me anywhere did it?
B250 Use 6 . . . hummm.
B251 So may be I can discard 6 and then start. . . .
B252 Let's see . . . 3 and 4?
B253 Hummm . . . how did I goof up on that?
B254 Still, I could use the expression $Q \lor R$ as C

E5

B255 and $\sim R$ as A
B256 and $\sim P$ as B . . .
B257 So what would that give me?
B258 $(A \lor B) \cdot C$ . . .
B259 Hum . . . what would change the dot to a wedge as a major connective?
B260 Or, in the parenthesis, the wedge to a dot . . .
B261 Hum . . . oh let's see. Now if I apply 6 to 4 . . . first expression, I have what?
B262 No, I can't . . .
B263 I think maybe I could . . .
B264 because in reversing it I would have R . . . no, that would give me a horseshoe . . .
B265 I don't want that.
B266 Why don't we change that dot . . . major connective . . . to a what?
B267 To a wedge . . . hm.
B268 Let's see, $A \lor A$, R3 . . .
B269 Can't use that.
B270 What's safe to use on that?
B271 How would the first parenthesis on L4 . . .
B272 Would give me what?
B273 $A \lor B$ . . .
B274 if only that was a dot . . .
B275 Let's see, of course. . . .

E6

B276 No, that wouldn't do any good . . . on R8.
B277 'cause that would remove the Q
B278 (E: Well, your time is about up. . . .)
B279 (E: We usually give about one half hour per problem.)
B280 (E: What do you think held you up?)
B281 I don't know. . . .
B282 I think it was just mostly working on the signs . . . I was working on 'em.
B283 (E: Want to see one way to do it?)
B284 Any way would be OK.
B285 [E explains solution in detail, finally getting L9: $(Q \lor \sim P).$]
B286 Uh huh . . . and that's what you want.
B287 (E: Yes, that's what you want to apply R5,)
B288 (E: so applying 5 to 9 you get the answer . . . $\sim(\sim Q \cdot P).$)
B289 Looks mighty simple that way.
B290 (E: Think you would have figured it out with more time?)
B291 Frankly, I doubt it . . .
B292 'cause I was completely off . . . I was working in a completely different direction. . . .
B293 So I doubt if I would have come around to that.

problem behavior graph of S11 on D1

B157
B159
B161
B175
B190
B191
B196
B211
B221
B230
B240
B247
B251
B252
B255
B262
B269
B272
B276

R6 Δb
R9
X3 v X

B · C ?s
φ
R8
R4
R5 X5   X5: ~ (R · P)   R4
R4 ?1   X5
R5 X4   Δs
R5   X4: ~ R · P   ☐R
R4 Δc   R51: ~ ~ R · P   Δcm → v
AB = φL1   φL1   E: Δc   R...
R7 Δc   get L0   R8   Δc
get L0   R6   R7   X6: (~ Rv ~ P) · (R V Q)   ~t   +a
L2   X6: (~ Rv ~P) · (R V Q)   R7   Δs   φ   R7
Recall   R4 = r X6   ☐R   Q v R
R7 Δc   R2   R6   ~ R v Q   X7: ~ R v (B · C)
Δc AC   ~ Q ⊃ R   R6   R7   X7   Δp   Δp
Δs   rL2   L3   Δs   L4, Δb
R2!   R6! r   L4
r   R6   ~a
RV   L4   Δc   ☐L
L3   rL3   R7
C = Q V R   φ   ~d c = ⊃
Δc℘   R6   ℘
v ⇒   R3   ~a
☐R   Δcm   R6   ~d c = ⊃
Δcm → v   Δc℘
get L0
L4   R8   +Q
L4 ~t   ⇒ ℘   (E terminates attempt)

549

B1	[E writes L1: $(R \supset \sim P) \cdot (\sim R \supset Q)$]
B2	[E writes L0: $\sim (\sim Q \cdot P)$]
E1	
B3	I could use number 1,
B4	Ah . . . did you say in number 3, those two A's would be different? I mean it could be two different expressions?
B5	(E: No they have to be similar.)
B6	They have to be the same. [Said by E?]
B7	That could be 1 or 8 to start off with. . . .
B8	And get $\sim (\sim Q \cdot P)$.
E2	
B9	Hum, ah, if I could get rid of . . .
B10	if I could only get one thing out of each part of that.
B11	Well, first I'd have to change that horseshoe to a dot.
B12	or that dot in the middle to something else.
B13	If I used 1
B14	and switch them around, what would that give me?
B15	Ah, I would change the positions . . .
B16	then I will have a Q on that side.
B17	Use 1 and change the positions to start.
B18	[E writes L2: $(\sim R \supset Q) \cdot (R \supset \sim P)$]
B19	Now, there aren't any . . . no . . . there aren't any horseshoes that I could get a single expression out of.
B20	The Q changes the sign.
B21	But if I use 6
B22	that will change the horseshoe to a wedge.
B23	Using the wedge in 1. . . .
B24	Apply 6 to the first part of number 2.
B25	[E writes L3: $(R \vee Q) \cdot (R \supset \sim P)$]
B26	Oh, you can't work on them individually?
B27	(E: Yes you can.)
B28	I didn't mean that . . . I mean $(\sim R \supset Q)$ changed to R . . . I mean $(R \supset \sim Q)$.
B29	Can I do that?
B30	(E: Well, this is applying to the first parenthesis, is that what you meant to do?)
B31	Yeh.
B32	(E: That is the only way you can apply 6 to the first parenthesis on L2.)
B33	You can do that?
B34	(E: Yeh. You can get this . . . this what I got . . . $R \vee Q$.)
B35	Oh, there's only one sign change . . .
B36	that's no good.
B37	I wanted a $\sim Q$.
B38	I have a wedge. . . .
B39	The $\sim P$ has to be a P, that's right.
B40	Use 5 reversed in L3.
B41	[E writes L4: $\sim (\sim R \cdot \sim Q) \cdot (R \supset \sim P)$]
B42	That gets me nowhere too.
B43	Or does it? I have my $\sim Q$ and my outside tilde.
B44	Now, let's get this worked out.
B45	Number 8,
B46	would get rid of one of them completely,
B47	and I can't.

B48	Two expressions . . . you'd get A B, and A C if I use 7,
B49	and I can't use 7.

E3

B50	Going back to the original, I could. . . .
B51	No . . . couldn't use 2 . . .
B52	the dot.
B53	How about going back to the original and applying. . . .
B54	No . . . never mind . . . 5 wouldn't do any good.
B55	Humph. I need two lines for the third set.
B56	They either have to be in the second set or the first.
B57	The only ones involving the dot in the middle are 5, 1, 7, and 4.
B58	I can take (R ⊃ ~P) to be a single thing?
B59	(E: Yes.)
B60	Oh, in L4 I still have that horseshoe in there.
B61	And if I apply 5 to 1
B62	I will get A, B and the whole thing is positive. . . .
B63	I will get negative . . . parenthesis . . . I guess you have to use square brackets . . . negative square brackets parenthesis . . . no . . . negative square brackets, negative parenthesis R horseshoe tilde P, (R ⊃ ~P), wedge . . . [~(~(R ⊃ ~P) ∨ . . .]
B64	I can't get a wedge in there. . . .
B65	The only one that will get rid of an expression is 3
B66	and that won't work.

E4

B67	Going to 8 again,
B68	I would get one side of that,
B69	and you could get either side.
B70	How about doing 8 twice on 1? And getting A and B separately?
B71	(E: OK. 8 to L1.)
B72	[E writes L5: R ⊃ ~P]
B73	(E: 8 to L1 again.)
B74	[E writes L6: ~R ⊃ Q]
B75	Now, I have two horseshoe expressions.
B76	but I can't apply 12,
B77	because even if I reverse them,
B78	I'm not going to get the same B.
B79	Hummm, wait, I need ~Q.
B80	One sign change in 6.
B81	Which would be the R. . . .
B82	Apply 6 to 5.
B83	[E writes L7: ~R ∨ ~P]
B84	Now, I've got two A's the same.
B85	And I have a horseshoe and wedge.
B86	Oh man!
B87	I applied 6 to 5.
B88	Changed that to a dot. . . .
B89	If I use 6 to 6,
B90	change that also to a wedge.
B91	I can't go to 1. . . .
B92	That would be switching a wedge to a dot
B93	using 5 and changing signs.
B94	There must be some way of doing these separately though.
B95	I've got two horseshoes,
B96	but I don't have the same B.

B97	How can I switch the two around?
B98	Using 2 would switch them,
B99	but it would switch signs. . . .
B100	Ah . . . applying 2 to 5
B101	would give me P $\supset$ ~R . . . P $\supset$ ~R.
B102	Apply 2 to 5.
B103	[E writes L8: P $\supset$ ~R]
B104	Uh hum. P $\supset$ ~R.
B105	Still don't give me the right B.
B106	Let's see, 6. . . .
B107	Oh, if I used L8 as A B and L6 . . . A B, B C,
B108	I would get P . . . P $\supset$ Q . . . P $\supset$ Q.
B109	Well, we'll try again.
B110	Apply 6 and 8, R12.
B111	[E writes L9: P $\supset$ Q]
B112	Now, apply 6 to 9.
B113	[E writes L10: ~P $\vee$ Q]
B114	Oh, I thought by using 5
B115	I could change their places,
B116	but I can't.
B117	I have ~P $\vee$ Q, and going to 1,
B118	~P $\vee$ Q would give you Q $\vee$ ~P.
B119	Now, Q $\vee$ ~P. . . .
B120	Oh, apply R1 to 10.
B121	[E writes L11: Q $\vee$ ~P]
B122	Right. Now, I've got a Q and P
B123	and if I apply 5 to 11,
B124	I think it will give it to me.
B125	[E writes L12: ~(~Q·P)]
B126	Right. Let's see, how many steps did I make?
B127	I had to start with 5.
B128	(E: Right.)
B129	And then 6 was no good. Right?
B130	(E: 6 was right. You had to have 5 and 6.)
B131	Oh, it was 7 that didn't get me anywhere.
B132	(E: Yeh, it was 7.)
B133	Well, then I reversed the order of them by changing it to 8,
B134	and from there you could sort of get it.
B135	I sort of figure that 2 or 4 should give me something. . . .
B136	They didn't.
B137	4 didn't give me anything. . . .
B138	Of course, that tilde in the front . . . if I could have kept it.
B139	Well that's finished.
B140	Try another one.
B141	(E: Well you got it.)

problem behavior graph of S15 on D1

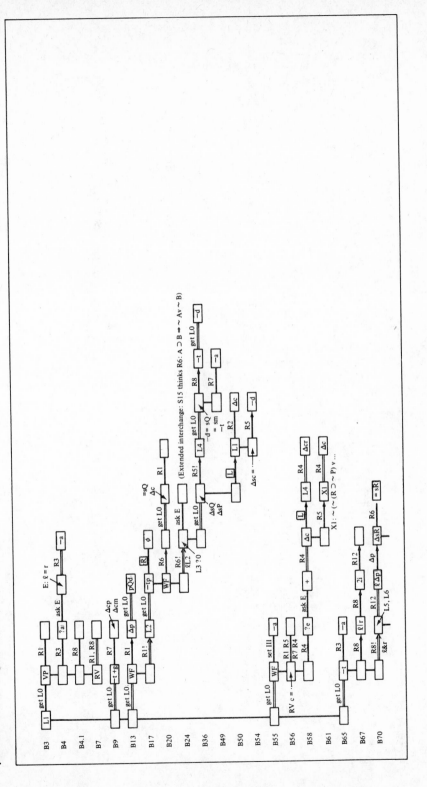

554

(cont'd)

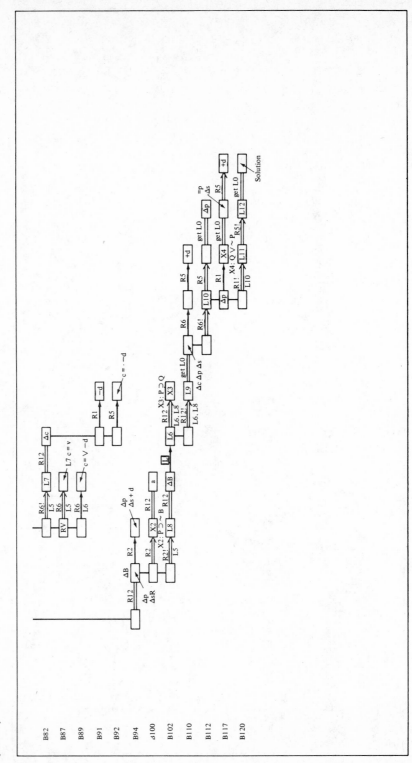

B82
B87
B89
B91
B92
B94
∆100
B102
B110
B112
B117
B120

LOGIC:
a Broader View

In the last two chapters we have been occupied with the basic questions of whether a human subject who is solving problems in logic can be described as an IPS—and with enough fidelity to support an information processing theory of human problem solving. Instead of confining our attention to the behavior of a single subject, as in the corresponding chapter on cryptarithmetic, we examined data from several subjects, most of it relating to performance on a single problem. We particularized our hypothesis by considering an IPS having the characteristics of GPS and asking to what extent the mechanisms and organization of that program corresponded with the subjects' behavior.

In the present chapter we continue our exploration of human behavior in the logic tasks but address ourselves to some additional important questions. The previous analysis has established the GPS-like character of the human problem solving within individual episodes—the subjects' frequent use of functional analysis, the emergence of goal structures, the formulation of subgoals to reduce differences between expressions and the input forms of operators. In the first part of this chapter we will take a closer look at the macrostructure of the protocols—the arrangement and evocation of episodes. This will involve us in the topic of planning, for we shall ask to what extent the processes that bring about the broad organization of the protocols resemble, or differ from, the planning processes described for GPS in Chapter 8.

The topic of planning and organization will be followed by the analysis of the data on the behavior of a number of subjects on another problem, C1, which is substantially more difficult than D1. We shall see to what extent the data can be explained in terms of the theory that has emerged from our previous analysis, and will introduce one new heuristic—working backwards—that appears more prominently in the C1 protocols than in the protocols examined previously.

Following the discussion of problem C1, we will take up two important topics that lie outside the main goals of our undertaking, but which we cannot ignore completely. As the first of these, we will consider what our data teach us about individual differences among subjects. As a second, and related, problem we will examine the behavior of a single subject over a series of problems in order to gain some insight into his learning processes.

PLANS AND THE ORGANIZATION OF EPISODES

In Chapter 9 we confined our analysis largely to within-episode behavior on problem D1, hence did not face the question of how the subjects selected the goals that initiated episodes. GPS, as described in Chapter 8, provides two different possible answers to the question, and, as we shall see, a whole range of additional possibilities lie somewhere between these two.

In the basic version of GPS the question never really arises, for the program makes no distinction between essential and inessential differences. If the program incorporates two particular heuristics, however, combined with a specific ordering of the differences, its behavior may give the appearance of responding to a distinction between these two classes of differences. The two heuristics are:

1. Attempt to reduce the most serious differences first.
2. Do not create reduce-difference subgoals for apply-operator goals if the differences in question are serious, but abandon the apply-operator goal instead.

If, now, the differences are so ordered that all of the essential differences precede all of the inessential differences, GPS will set up the goal of reducing the most serious essential differences, will go through an episode of using inessential operators preparatory to applying an essential operator to achieve that goal, and then, successful or not, will continue on to the next essential goal.

In the version of GPS that incorporates the planning method, a similar organization is brought about in a different way. The planning routine constructs a plan by finding a solution for the abstracted problem in the planning space. Each step in that solution, which is an essential operator, is transformed into a subproblem–a goal–in the original problem space. Subsequently, an episode is devoted to handling each of the subproblems so defined.

It would be easy to detect which of these two procedures was responsible for the organization of a particular protocol. For, if the planning routine were used, the initial portion of the protocol would reveal only abstracted actions in the planning space, while the later portion of the protocol would consist of episodes in the original problem space arranged in the order of the preceding plan.

Things would be a little more complicated if the subject evolved several plans before trying to implement any one of them, or if he evolved new plans after he had failed to execute a previous one. Ignoring the specifics of the GPS planning scheme, we can say that a subject is planning if his protocol contains the following kinds of behavior:

1. He considers abstracted transformations of expressions—that is, transformations in which he does not specify all the details of the output and/or input expressions.
2. He considers sequences of at least two such consecutive transformations, so that the second operation is contemplated without detailed knowledge of the input to it, or of the feasibility of accomplishing the previous operation.
3. After developing such a sequence of consecutive transformations, he engages in a series of episodes to carry out the steps of the sequence in the original problem space.

Planning, by this looser criterion, may be partial and incomplete. A subject may use planning for a portion of a problem but omit it for other portions. He may show no explicit signs of alternating consciously or systematically between the problem space and the planning space but may move quite flexibly from the one to the other. The nature of the abstraction he uses—what differences are essential, what differences inessential—could change from one time to another (although we do not, in fact, find convincing evidence of any such changes in our protocols).

The GPS planning routine was developed, inductively, after examining some of these human protocols. Planning activity is very prominent in many of the protocols—particularly those of the more successful subjects, and of the subjects who had accumulated some experience from previous problems. The GPS routine, however, must be regarded as a formalized and stylized description of the less formal and less comprehensive processes we find in the protocols. There is a stiffness and deliberateness in GPS's movement back and forth between problem space and planning space that contrasts with the subjects' flexibility.

Planning: S8 on A4

Four of the six protocols for subject S8 give an excellent picture of the kind of flexible planning just described, and we will use them to illustrate it in depth. For S8, we have protocols for problems D1, C1, A2′, B2, A4, and C3, which he worked on in that sequence. (The protocols are reproduced in Appendices 9.4,

10.9, 10,1, 10.2, 10.3, and 10.4, respectively.) Later we will have something to say about what he learned in the course of working these six problems, but for the moment we are not concerned with changes through time, and we will first take up A4, then D1, C3, and B2.

Problem A4 is:

$$L1: P \lor Q \qquad\qquad L0: P \lor T$$
$$L2: \sim R \supset \sim Q$$
$$L3: S$$
$$L4: R \supset \sim S$$

After the experimenter wrote these initial expressions on the blackboard, S8 said (B14–B33):

> Well, one possibility right off the bat is when you have just a $P \lor T$ like that the last thing you might use is that R9. I can get everything down to a P and just add a $\lor$ T. So that's the one thing to keep in mind.
> Well, maybe right off the bat, I'm kinda jumping into it, I maybe can work everything down to just a P; I dunno if that's possible.
> But I think it is, because I see that steps 2 and 4 are somewhat similar; if I can cancel out the R's, that would leave me with just an S and Q;
> and if I have just an S and Q, I can eventually get step 3, get the S's to cancel out and end up with just a Q;
> and if I end up with just a Q, maybe the Q's will cancel out; so you see, all the way down the line. I dunno, it looks too good to be true, but I think I see it already.

This talk took approximately a minute and a half. By the end of it, S8 had a plan. It is easy to see how we infer it from his remarks, all of which are prior to applying any rule. In the first two segments he sets up the subgoal of obtaining P by itself, since with this, R9 would give the final answer. For him to discover this, he must ask what rule and what input would give $P \lor T$, where T appears nowhere in the input expressions, and then, having found R9, what input to R9 would give $P \lor T$ as output. This process of discovery is clear in the first segment, and the acceptance of the result in the second.

In the third segment, S8 groups L2 with L4 as inputs to an operation that will "cancel out" the R's. Thus, the subject must be considering R12, as is confirmed later in his protocol. Notice, however, that R12 cannot be applied to L2 and L4 as they stand. One or the other must be reversed, and until this is done, it is not known whether the two R's will have, as required, the same sign. Thus we can infer that S8 decided to apply R12 without knowing for certain whether it could be made applicable.

In the operation of the basic GPS, without planning, the decision to apply a rule occurs before its feasibility is tested; but this decision then creates an apply-operator goal and initiates immediate activity to test feasibility and (if feasible) to apply the rule, or (if not feasible) to set up subgoals to make it feasible. In the present situation, however, S8 merely describes some essential features of the result:

"just an S and Q." There is no indication he knows that such a result could be obtained.

Our subject then goes on, in the fourth segment, to take this abstract result together with L3 as inputs to an operation that will "cancel out" the S's—clearly R11 is intended, as is also confirmed later in the protocol. In the fifth segment S8 moves on again, characterizing the (hypothetical) result as "just a Q" and combining it with L1 to get the Q's to "cancel out." The final result, which the subject doesn't enunciate, but clearly perceives, is a P by itself—the goal S8 set for himself at the beginning of the passage.

Now S8 has a plan to solve the problem, which we schematize in Figure 10.1.

FIGURE 10.1

S8's plan for A4

Transform (L1,L2,L3,L4) into $P \lor T$
   Transform (L1,L2,L3,L4) into P
      Cancel R's
         Apply R12 to (L2,L4) ($\Longrightarrow$ (SQ))
      Cancel S's
         Apply R11 to (result,L3) ($\Longrightarrow$ Q)
      Cancel Q's
         Apply R11 to (result,L1) ($\Longrightarrow$ P)
   Apply R9 to P($\Longrightarrow P \lor T$)

The symbols (SQ), (Q), (P) represent the abstracted expressions that S8 postulates as the outputs of the rule applications. The structure of Figure 10.1 and the protocol from which it was constructed provide evidence of planning as we defined it earlier. The plan is not a complete solution, and it may not even be feasible. The subject does not know whether R12 can be applied, nor what expression would result from the application—except that it would contain S and Q. Hence, he does not know whether either the second or third steps of the plan are feasible, nor the exact form of the final result (which might be $\sim P$ instead of P).

Of course, S8 may have worked out the solution in full detail and simply not mentioned that detail as he worked. We can test that by seeing how he implements the plan. If our analysis is correct, he should go back to the goal of applying R12, work it out in detail, then move on to the two successive applications of R11. We would not expect much hesitation or exploration in moving from one of these episodes to the next, but a certain amount of search and problem solving *within* each episode. Here is the remainder of the protocol (B34–B68):

Steps 2 and 4, we'll have to do something about them. If I invert step 4—L4, that is—apply R2 to it; I will have an $S \supset \sim R$. Good. OK. Apply R12 to L4.

(L5: $S \supset \sim R$)

Now apply R12 to L2 and L4—2 and 5, I mean.

(L6: S ⊃ ~Q)

Right. Get rid of the R's.

Now apply R11 to L6 and L3. Oh, that's it—too easy! Something's going to backfire. (Experimenter asks "That'll give you what?") I think just ~Q.

(L7: ~Q)

Now you have P ∨ Q and ~Q. I would like to apply R11 to 1 and 7, but I'm first going to change L1 to a horseshoe. So change L1 to a horseshoe— apply R6 to it. I think this is it—I think we got it.

(L8: ~P ⊃ Q)

Yeah. Oh it would, wouldn't it! OK. Apply R2 to L8. Hey, I think this is going to work real fine.

(L9: ~Q ⊃ P)

Now apply R11 to L9 and L7.

(L10: P)

Heh, heh, heh, heh, heh, I feel good now. Well, apply R9 to L10 and that's it.

(L11: P ∨ T)

The evidence that S8 has not previously worked out all the details, but is genuinely solving problems in applying the plan, is substantial—among others: "we'll have to do something," "too easy, something's going to backfire," "I'm first going to change . . . so change . . . apply," "I think this is it," "I think this is going to work real fine."

Planning: S8 on D1

The second case, part of S8's protocol on our familiar problem D1, illustrates unsuccessful planning. Failure is particularly informative because it shows that the whole of a plan has not been thought through. The subject has already worked for some time on the problem, and has generated the expressions shown in Figure 10.2.

Lines L2 through L5 are reminiscent of path.R7 discussed in the last chapter. However that may be, the protocol continues (B368–B416):

What can I do? They were positive to begin with around a dot. I can eliminate one whole term. I can apply R8 anytime I want and eliminate a whole term. I tried that once before, didn't I? No, not exactly. I might be better off trying something like that. It's too complicated now.

FIGURE 10.2

S8 on D1
initial transformations L1 through L6

L1: $(R \supset \sim P) \cdot (\sim R \supset Q)$	L0: $\sim(\sim Q \cdot P)$
L2: $(\sim R \vee \sim P) \cdot (\sim R \supset Q)$	R6 to left(L1)
L3: $(\sim R \vee \sim P) \cdot (R \vee Q)$	R6 to right(L2)
L4: $\sim(R \cdot P) \cdot (R \vee Q)$	R5 to left(L3)
L5: $\sim(R \cdot P) \cdot \sim(\sim R \cdot \sim Q)$	R5 to right(L4)
L6: $\sim(\sim(R \supset \sim P) \vee \sim(\sim R \supset Q))$	R5 to L1

If I, if I just eliminated a whole term ... I've got things in front of me and I'm trying to eliminate them all the time. Well, now, which term to eliminate is the question.

I want to eliminate one because I'll want to eliminate another thing again. I don't know if you'll follow me on this, but ... I'll eliminate one of these terms; the one I don't eliminate, I'll take that, change it to a dot and eliminate that letter; see, that leaves me with just a P or a Q. Then, I can add on, through R9. I think I'm getting it now.

Now the question is ... I don't want to be negative. I could choose the wrong one ... I'd better get it written down because I think I've got it now. Let's apply R8 to the total expression, in the beginning, step 1. Apply R8 to that.

When you convert from a horseshoe to a dot, will you invert—reverse them? No. So let's take, oh, there's going to be trouble ... well, let's take the first one.

(Experimenter asks, "Take the first one and drop the second one?")
Yeah, that sounds pretty good, except that I won't be able to see ... but at least I'm on the right track and if it doesn't work out, I can try the other one. (L7: $R \supset \sim P$)

Now, if I want to change that to a dot, ah nuts, I'm going to run into trouble, I know. I'm going to get a negative total expression, any way you look at it. Son of a gun! Aw man. . . .

The third segment of this protocol fragment expresses a clear plan: Apply R8 to L1 ($\Rightarrow$ (RP) or (RQ)); change connective ($\Rightarrow$ (R·P) or (R·Q)); apply R8 to eliminate R ($\Rightarrow$ P or Q); apply R9 ($\Rightarrow$ (PQ) or (QP)). The proposed sequence of operations is described in terms of functions to be performed: eliminate, add on. Only once is a connective mentioned—the need to change the connective to a dot after the first application of R8 to enable the second application of R8. Except for the (undefined) operation to make this change in connective, S8 mentions only essential operations.

There is conclusive evidence that the subject has not worked out, and is unaware of, the inessential operations he has not mentioned, and the details— tildes and connectives—of the expressions that will be produced by the operations. First of all, the segment following the one in which the plan is stated indicates that he had not yet decided whether to eliminate the left or the right of L1. Even more telling evidence is that the plan, when he tries to implement it, does not work —S8 discovers that he cannot transform the connective in L7 into a dot without making the expressions negative, hence that he cannot apply R8 a second time to eliminate the R. S8 discovers this difficulty by proceeding methodically to execute the plan. When he is unable to overcome the difficulty, he abandons the plan.

Planning: S8 on C3 and B2

S8's planning behavior on Problem C3 is quite similar to his planning on A4, already discussed. The planning portion of his protocol (Appendix 10.4) is brief (B11–B23):

$$L1: \sim S \qquad\qquad L0: \sim Q$$
$$L2: R \lor S$$
$$L3: (P \supset Q) \supset \sim R$$

$\sim$ Q again. Well, we're up to all the tricks on how to get $\sim$ Q. There is only one Q in the whole thing, and right off the bat I see one thing, if it's possible. I would say rearrange L2 so you can cancel the S's out, with 1, 2, and you end up with just an R; and work it out so line 2 and 3 will cancel out, because that's a horseshoe connector. See what I mean? We're going to apply R11 to cut them out right off the bat.

Thus, the plan is to eliminate the S's by applying R11 to L1 and L2 (modified), getting R; then to eliminate R between R and L3 by another application of R11. As in the previous examples, S8 proceeds right through the plan, working out the details as he goes, and hardly hesitating between getting one result and moving to the next stage in the plan. The whole problem proceeds so smoothly and quickly that only a few interpretive remarks (e.g., "I guess if we're going to apply rule 11 we are going to have to . . . ") and small hesitations (e.g., "I think I see . . . I don't see everything . . .") show that S8 did not have the full solution already when he stated the plan. Notice that the plan does not go all the way to a solution. After executing the plan, S8 still needed to eliminate the P from $\sim$(P $\supset$ Q), and there is no evidence that he had anticipated exactly how he could do this.

For a final case, S8 on Problem B2 (Appendix 10.2), we give only the plan; the implementation was quite devious and took a long time (B5–B24):

$$L1: (P \lor Q) \supset \sim(\sim R \lor P) \qquad L0: \sim Q$$
$$L2: \sim(\sim(S \cdot Q) \lor R)$$

$\sim Q$. Not too much doubt about that. First you've got to eliminate everything down.
When I see a $\sim Q$ it reminds me of one I had the other day: $T \cdot T$. Since there's a Q in both steps 1 and 2, if we get it down to just $\sim Q \cdot \sim Q$ that will be equal to just $\sim Q$. So I think that's what we're going to get it down to. I dunno, it just strikes me that way.
If we can get it down to just a Q in each line. In fact, if I want to work it backwards to get it to $\sim Q \cdot \sim Q$, why, if I can get it down to $\sim Q$ in each line, I can apply R10, and just put it that way.
So that seems to be the things—try and—work each line separately and try to get it down to a $\sim Q$. I don't know yet. Well, let's look at it first.
If I am going to go by that theory and try to get it down, maybe I should change the major connector in L1 to a dot . . .

The plan indicated by this passage may be schematized thus:

> Transform L1 into $\sim Q$.
> Transform L2 into $\sim Q$.
> Apply R10 to these $\Rightarrow \sim Q \cdot \sim Q$.
> Apply R3 to this $\Rightarrow \sim Q$.

This plan has several noteworthy features beyond those shown in previous plans. First, it was generated from a strategy taken from a specific prior problem (which S8 had not solved). More intriguing, the plan is incredibly redundant. Success in achieving *either* of the first two goals would solve the problem. There would be no need to use R10 to put the two expressions together in order to use R3 to take them apart again! Nevertheless, this is indeed S8's plan. It is amply confirmed by the five minutes of behavior that followed this protocol segment, as S8 struggled (of course unsuccessfully, since it is infeasible) to execute the plan.

Similar analysis could be made of the planning behavior of the other subjects, but we will refer the interested reader to the full protocols in the Appendix. We have perhaps sufficiently illustrated the fact that the subjects did, indeed, employ planning procedures, and we have shown in general how these planning procedures differed from the more formal planning routine that we described for GPS.

S8's abstractions correspond well with the distinction between essential and inessential rules. His plans are concerned with R11, R12, R8, R9, R10, and R3—and not at all with R1, R2, R5, or R6. The evidence is strong that at least five of the other subjects, in Problem D1, used a distinction close to the essential-inessential distinction.

We might ask where the subjects derived this particular distinction, but we can only conjecture as to the answer. One plausible conjecture is that it represents a transfer of distinctions familiar to them from other mathematical tasks. In algebra, for example, persons who are proficient automatically simplify expressions, whenever they can, by combining similar terms, arranging the terms in patterned ways, and so on. A scheme described in Newell, Shaw, and Simon (1959b) for doing trigonometric identities with GPS (hand-simulated but never actually implemented on the computer) also illustrates the distinction between *essential* trigonometric manipulations [e.g., replacing $(\sin^2 + \cos^2)$ by 1] and *routine* algebraic manipulations [e.g., combining $(a \sin x + b \sin x)$ into $(a + b) \sin x$].

An alternative conjecture is that the essential-inessential distinction might arise from experience in manipulating material objects. Using R8 to disassemble an expression into parts that can be manipulated separately appears less drastic to several subjects than using R8 to delete part of the expression.

A third conjecture is more perceptual in character: that subjects distinguish perceptually between (1) objects maintaining an identity through time, and (2) the possibly changeable properties of objects (basically, the ancient philosophical distinction between essences and accidents). Thus, R7 "really" changes an object to an object having a new form (alternatively: changes the entire form of the object), while R1 "merely" rearranges the parts of an object.

The distinction between operating *upon* an object and changing it into a *new* object appears in protocols of subjects who are solving algebra story problems (Paige and Simon, 1966). The following is a striking illustration. The problem was for the subject to set up the equation corresponding to: "If a certain number is multiplied by 6 and the product increased by 44 the result is 68. Find the number." Two different protocols read as follows:

1. We'll call the number n. It says that if we multiply it by 6 and add 44 to it, the result is 68. This presents a simple equation of 6n plus 44 equals 68.
2. The unknown is a certain number, which would be x. Multiply x by 6. Write down "6x" please. "Increased by" means "add," so you put a plus 44. "The result is"—indicates "equals"—write please—"68".

The repeated use of "it" in the first protocol to refer to the result of the partially completed calculation indicates that, in the subject's representation, there is an entity that we could call "the result so far," which is progressively modified but retains its identity. For the second subject, the process is represented much more as one of assembling a symbolic object (the final equation) out of a set of parts.

In this section we have emphasized and illustrated the use of planning to organize individual episodes into a total problem-solving effort. We return to the observation at the beginning of the section that the effort may also be organized without planning, as, indeed, it is in the basic GPS and in the protocol of S4 on D1 that we compared with GPS in the last chapter. We call the reader's attention to the many protocols in the Appendices that give little or no evidence that the effort was being guided by planning. Our earlier discussion provides a general indication of the nature of the organization of the protocols in these cases.

By analyzing the relative difficulty of the sixteen problems attempted by the subjects, we developed the notion that problem difficulty was closely connected with the need to make constructions in order to solve a problem. We also saw that, in some cases, constructions could be avoided and the difficulty of the problem reduced by working backward from the goal expression, L0. The difficult problem C1 gives us additional data for testing our ideas about the sources of problem difficulty.

Aggregate Data on Problem C1

An analysis of the expressions that were generated both by the Yale subjects and by the Carnegie subjects while attempting problem C1 gives a picture very similar to the one we found in our analysis of the corresponding data for problem D1. Almost all of the expressions generated by the subjects belong to a small number of equivalence classes that are related in simple ways to the classes of L1 and L0 and the path between them. Table 10.1 shows the distribution of different expressions generated, and of total occurrences by equivalence classes for the Yale subjects.

TABLE 10.1

expressions obtained by Yale subjects on problem C1

EQUIVALENCE CLASS	DIFFERENT EXPRESSIONS	TOTAL OCCURRENCES	OCCURRENCES PER EXPRESSION
L1	23	134	5.8
Extended L1	12	20	1.7
Left(L1)	5	92	18.4
Right(L1)	6	73	12.2
R $\lor$ P	4	33	8.2
(P $\lor$ Q)·(P $\lor$ R)	1	7	7.0
L0	1	6	6.0
Rule 9	46	88	1.9
All other	23	34	1.5
On path and R9—total	86	433	5.0
Other	35	54	1.5
Grand total	121	487	4.0

Looking first at numbers of distinct expressions, about a quarter (34) belong to the equivalence classes of L1 and its left and right sides. Another 10 percent

(12) belong to the extended equivalence class of L1; a third (46) to classes obtained from those previously mentioned by applying Rule 9; and 5 percent (6) to the classes leading to the solution; leaving only 20 percent (23) in the "all other" category.

As with problem D1, total occurrences are even more strongly concentrated in a few classes than are numbers of distinct expressions. The equivalence class of L1 accounts for more than a quarter of all occurrences, and the equivalence classes of its left and right sides for more than a third. Now the R9 and "all other" categories together add up to only one quarter of the total occurrences. We can say that the subjects did not stray very far from the set of expressions obtainable from L1 by relatively simple transformations.

The similarity demonstrated for problem D1 between the Yale subjects and the Carnegie subjects shows up equally clearly in problem C1. Thinking-aloud instructions did not substantially influence what part of the problem space the subjects explored. In Table 10.2 the distribution of total occurrences of expressions among classes is compared for the Yale and Carnegie subjects. Although the Carnegie subjects generated a few more lines, per subject, than did the Yale subjects (9.8 as compared with 7.6), the occurrences distributed themselves among the classes in strikingly similar ways, as comparison of the third and fourth columns of the table shows.

TABLE 10.2

comparison of expressions obtained by Yale and Carnegie subjects on problem C1

EQUIVALENCE CLASS	Total Occurrences		Percent of All Occurrences	
	YALE	CARNEGIE	YALE	CARNEGIE
L1	134	32	28	33
Extended L1	20	2	4	2
Left(L1)	92	14	19	14
Right (L1)	73	14	15	14
$(R \lor P)$	33	13	7	13
$(P \lor Q) \cdot (P \lor R)$	7	3	1	3
L0	6	3	1	3
Rule 9	88	15	18	16
All other	34	1	7	1
Total	487	97	100	100
No. subjects	64	9		
Av./subject	7.6	9.8		

Sources of Problem Difficulty on C1

The protocols of nine subjects on Problem C1, reproduced in Appendices 10.5 to 10.13, give us additional data for testing our ideas about the sources of problem difficulty. Episode abstracts for each subject on this problem are presented in Figures 10.3 to 10.11. Of the nine subjects, three succeeded in solving C1, while six failed.[1] For six of the subjects we have protocols for both Problems D1 and C1. Of these six, two (S8 and S9) solved both D1 and C1, two (S4 and S10) solved D1 but not C1, and two (S5 and S11) failed to solve either problem. These results are consistent with our classification of C1 as more difficult than D1 (Table 8.1).

FIGURE 10.3

episode abstract: S2 on problem C1

E	B	INSTIGATOR	E-SCHEMA	EPISODE
		L0: $\quad$ P $\lor$ (Q·R)		
		L1: $\quad$ (P $\lor$ Q)·(Q $\supset$ R)		
E1	B3	get L0 delete Q		L1 $\overset{R8}{\Rightarrow}$ L2 $\overset{R6}{\Rightarrow}$ L3,L1 $\overset{R8}{\Rightarrow}$ L4 $\overset{R6}{\Rightarrow}$ L5 $\overset{R8}{=\!=\!\dashv}$
		L2: $\quad$ Q $\supset$ R		
		L3: $\quad$ ~Q $\lor$ R		
		L4: $\quad$ P $\lor$ Q		
		L5: $\quad$ ~P $\supset$ Q		
E2	B34	WF	path.R12	L2,L5 $\overset{R12}{\Rightarrow}$ L6[error], L4 $\overset{R7}{=\!=\!\dashv}$ $\overset{R6}{\Rightarrow}$ L7,L6 $\overset{R2}{\Rightarrow}$ L8 $\overset{R6}{\Rightarrow}$ L9 $\overset{R7}{=\!=\!\dashv}$ $\overset{R5}{=\!=\!\dashv}$
		L6: $\quad$ R $\supset$ ~P [error]		
		L7: $\quad$ ~R $\lor$ ~P		
		L8: $\quad$ P $\supset$ ~R		
		L9: $\quad$ ~P $\lor$ ~R		
E3	B57	review	path.R12	$\overset{R7}{=\!=\!\dashv}$ L4,L9 $\overset{R10}{\Rightarrow}$ $\overset{R7}{=\!=\!\dashv}$ get sign(P) = +
E4	B72	get sign(P) = +		L2,L4 $\overset{R5}{=\!=\!\dashv}$
E5	B91	review	path.R12	$\overset{R10}{\Rightarrow}$ $\overset{R7}{\Rightarrow}$
E6	B100	get sign(P) = +	WF	L5 $\overset{R3,R2,R6}{=\!=\!=\!=}$ = L4 $\overset{R1,R4,R9}{=\!=\!=\!\dashv}$
E7	B113	WF R12		L6,L8 $\overset{R12}{=\!=\!\dashv}$
E8	B129		WF	L9 $\overset{R8}{=\!=\!\dashv}$ $\overset{R5}{=\!=\!\dashv}$ L10 $\overset{R8,R7}{=\!=\!=\!\dashv}$
		L10: $\quad$ ~(P·Q)		
E9.1	B139	get L0	path.R7	L1 $\overset{R6}{\Rightarrow}$ L11 $\overset{R7}{=\!=\!\dashv}$ $\overset{R8}{\Rightarrow}$ L12 $\overset{R1}{\Rightarrow}$ L13,L12 $\overset{R4}{\Rightarrow}$ L14
		L11: $\quad$ (P $\lor$ Q)·(~Q $\lor$ R)		
		L12: $\quad$ ~Q $\lor$ R		
		L13: $\quad$ R $\lor$ ~Q		
		L14: $\quad$ Q $\supset$ R		
E9.2	B175			L4,L12 $\overset{R10}{\Rightarrow}$ L15 $\overset{R7}{=\!=\!\dashv}$ $\overset{R2}{\Rightarrow}$ L16,L5 $\overset{R12}{\Rightarrow}$ L17,L2 $\overset{R12}{\Rightarrow}$ L18 E terminates attempt
		L15: $\quad$ (P $\lor$ Q)·(~Q $\lor$ R)		
		L16: $\quad$ R $\supset$ ~P		
		L17: $\quad$ R $\supset$ Q		
		L18: $\quad$ Q $\supset$ Q		

[1] One of the failures (S2) was probably caused by an error of the experimenter in putting an expression on the blackboard. Hence, the box score should probably read: four solutions, five failures.

FIGURE 10.4
episode abstract: S3 on problem C1

E	B	INSTIGATOR	E-SCHEMA	EPISODE
		L0: $P \lor (Q\cdot R)$		
		L1: $(P \lor Q)\cdot(Q \supset R)$		
E1	B3	get L0 rearrange	path.R7	L1 $\overset{R7}{=}\overset{R6}{\Rightarrow}$ L2 $\overset{R1}{\Rightarrow}$ L3 $\overset{R7,R4}{\Longrightarrow}$, L3 $\overset{R5}{\Rightarrow}$ L4 $\overset{R7}{=}$
		L2: $(P \lor Q)\cdot(\sim Q \lor R)$		
		L3: $(Q \lor P)\cdot(\sim Q \lor R)$		
		L4: $\sim(\sim(Q \lor P) \lor \sim(\sim Q \lor R))$		
E2	B49	eliminate Q	WF	$\overset{R11}{=}$
E3.1	B52	return	path.R7	L3 $\overset{R6}{\Rightarrow}$ L5 $\overset{R2}{\Rightarrow}$ L6,L7 $\overset{R7}{=}$
		L5: $(\sim P \supset Q)\cdot(Q \supset R)$		
		L6: $(\sim Q \supset P)\cdot(Q \supset R)$		
		L7: $(\sim Q \supset P)\cdot(\sim R \supset \sim Q)$		
E3.2	B80		path.R7	L7 $\overset{R6}{\Rightarrow}$ L8, L1 $\overset{R1}{\Rightarrow}$ L9 $\overset{R6}{\Rightarrow}$ L10 $\overset{R2}{\Rightarrow}$ L11 $\overset{R7,R6}{=}$ L7 = L11
		L8: $(\sim Q \supset P)\cdot(Q \supset R)$		
		L9: $(Q \lor P)\cdot(Q \supset R)$		
		L10: $(\sim Q \supset P)\cdot(Q \supset R)$		
		L11: $(\sim Q \supset P)\cdot(\sim R \supset \sim Q)$		
E3.3	B139		path.R7	L11 $\overset{R6}{\Rightarrow}$ L12 $\overset{R6}{\Rightarrow}$ L13 $\overset{R5}{\Rightarrow}$ L14 $\overset{R1}{\Rightarrow}$ L15 $\overset{R5}{\Rightarrow}$ L16 $\overset{R7}{=}$
		L12: $(Q \lor P)\cdot(\sim R \supset \sim Q)$		
		L13: $(Q \lor P)\cdot(R \lor \sim Q)$		
		L14: $(Q \lor P)\cdot\sim(\sim R\cdot Q)$		
		L15: $(P \lor Q)\cdot\sim(\sim R\cdot Q)$		
		L16: $\sim(\sim P\cdot\sim Q)\cdot\sim(\sim R\cdot Q)$		
E4	B182	E: review	path.R7	$\overset{R7}{\Rightarrow} Q \lor (R\cdot P) \overset{R4}{\Rightarrow} (Q \lor R)\cdot P$ E terminates attempt

FIGURE 10.5
episode abstract: S4 on problem C1

E	B	INSTIGATOR	E-SCHEMA	EPISODE
		L0: $P \lor (Q\cdot R)$		
		L1: $(P \lor Q)\cdot(Q \supset R)$		
E1	B3	get L0	WF	L1 $\overset{R1,R2,R3,R4,R5,R6,R7}{=\!=\!=\!=\!=\!=} \overset{R8}{\Rightarrow}$ L2
		L2: $Q \supset R$		
E2	B18	get L0	WF	L1 $\overset{R8}{\Rightarrow}$ L3,L2 $\overset{R12}{=}\overset{R6}{\Rightarrow}$ L4 $\overset{R12}{\Rightarrow}$ not desirable
		L3: $P \lor Q$		
		L4: $\sim P \supset Q$		
E3	B29	get L0	WF 2i	L2,L3,L4 $\overset{R10,R11,R12}{=\!=\!=}$
E4	B32	WF	path.R10	L3 $\overset{R10}{=}\overset{R8}{=}\overset{R5}{=}$
E5	B40	WF	path.R7	L1 $\overset{R7}{=}\overset{R6}{\Rightarrow}$ L5 $\overset{R7}{=}\overset{R6,R5}{=\!=}$

FIGURE 10.5 (cont'd)

E	B	INSTIGATOR	E-SCHEMA	EPISODE
		L5: (P ∨ Q)·(~Q ∨ R)		
E6	B60	get L0	WF	L2,L3,L4,L5 $\overset{2R}{=\!=}$ L3,L5 $\overset{R11}{=\!=}$
E7	B74	get L0	WF	L1 $\overset{R7}{=\!=}$ $\overset{R6}{\Rightarrow}$ = L5
E8.1	B79	get L0	WF	$\overset{\boxed{R}}{\Rightarrow}$ φ
E8.2	B86		WF	$\overset{R1,R2,R3,R4,R5,R6,R7,R8,R9,2i}{=\!=\!=\!=\!=\!=\!=\!=\!=\!=\!=}$
E9	B103	get L0	WF	L2,L4 $\overset{R12}{=\!=}$ $\overset{R2}{\Rightarrow}$
E10	B109	get L0	WF	L1 $\overset{\boxed{R}}{\Rightarrow}$ φ
E11	B113	get L0	WF	L3 $\overset{R5}{\Rightarrow}$ L6
		L6: ~(~(P ∨ Q) ∨ ~(~Q ∨ R))		
E12	B124	get L0	WF	L2,L3,L4,L5 $\overset{2iR}{=\!=}$ $\overset{R12}{=\!=}$
E13	B130	get L0	path.R7	L5 $\overset{R7}{=\!=}$ $\overset{R1}{\Rightarrow}$ L7 $\overset{R7}{=\!=}$
		L7: (Q ∨ P)·(~Q ∨ R)		
E14	B141	get P at left		L5$\overset{R11,R12}{=\!=\!=\!=}$
E15	B146	get P		$\Rightarrow$ $\overset{R9}{}$ P $\overset{R11}{\Rightarrow}$ $=\!=$

FIGURE 10.6

episode abstract: S5 on problem C1

E	B	INSTIGATOR	E-SCHEMA	EPISODE
		L0: P ∨ (Q·R)		
		L1: (P ∨ Q)·(Q ⊃ R)		
E1	B3	get right(L0)		L1 ⇒ QR $\overset{R6}{\Rightarrow}$ $\overset{R5}{\Rightarrow}$
E2.1	B13	get L0	WB	L0 $\overset{R7^{-1}}{\Rightarrow}$ (P ∨ Q)·(P ∨ R)
E2.2	B21	get (P ∨ Q)·(P ∨ R)	path.R7	L1 ⇒ (P ∨ Q), L1 $\overset{R6}{\Rightarrow}$ L2,L1 $\overset{R2}{\Rightarrow}$ L3 $\overset{R7}{\Rightarrow}$ Q(PR)
		L2: (P ∨ Q)·(~Q ∨ R)		
		L3: (P ∨ Q)·(~R ⊃ ~Q)		
E3	B45	get L0	path.R10	L1 $\overset{R8}{\Rightarrow}$ L4 $\overset{R6}{\Rightarrow}$ L5,L2 $\overset{R8}{\Rightarrow}$ L6 $\overset{R8}{=\!=}$ $\overset{R5}{=\!=}$
		L4: Q ⊃ R		
		L5: ~Q ∨ R		
		L6: P ∨ Q		
E4	B81	get L0	path.R9	⇒ P $\overset{R9}{\Rightarrow}$ P ∨ (QR),L6,L1 $\overset{R11}{=\!=}$ $\overset{R3,R1,R6,R4}{=\!=\!=\!=}$
E5	B108	notice R4	path.R9.R4	L6 $\overset{R9}{\Rightarrow}$ (P ∨ Q) ∨ R $\overset{R4}{\Rightarrow}$ P ∨ (Q ∨ R) $\overset{R5}{\Rightarrow}$
E6.1	B120	get P	WF	L6 $\overset{R8}{=\!=}$ $\overset{R5}{\Rightarrow}$ L7 $\overset{R8}{=\!=}$
		L7: ~(~P·~Q)		
E6.2	B138		path.R11	L6 $\overset{R3}{\Rightarrow}$ $\overset{R9}{\Rightarrow}$ L8 $\overset{R1}{\Rightarrow}$ P ∨ (P ∨ Q) $\overset{R4}{\Rightarrow}$ (P ∨ P) ∨ Q $\overset{R3}{\Rightarrow}$ = L6
		L8: (P ∨ Q) ∨ P		
E6.3	B148			L6,L8 $\overset{R11}{=\!=}$ L8 $\overset{R1}{\Rightarrow}$ L9 $\overset{R6}{\Rightarrow}$ L10 $\overset{R2}{\Rightarrow}$ L11 $\overset{R11}{=\!=}$

FIGURE 10.6 (cont'd)

E	B	INSTIGATOR	E-SCHEMA	EPISODE
		L9: P ∨ (P ∨ Q)		
		L10: ~P ⊃ (P ∨ Q)		
		L11: ~(P ∨ Q) ⊃ P		
E6.4	B172			$L8 \overset{R12}{=\!=}\overset{R6}{\Rightarrow} L12 \overset{R2}{\Rightarrow} L13 \overset{R12}{=\!=} L6 \overset{R9}{\Rightarrow} L14 \overset{R6}{\Rightarrow}$ $L15,L13 \overset{R12}{=\!=}\overset{R2}{\Rightarrow} L16$
		L12: ~(P ∨ Q) ⊃ P		
		L13: ~P ⊃ (P ∨ Q)		
		L14: (P ∨ Q) ∨ (Q·R)		
		L15: ~(P ∨ Q) ⊃ (Q·R)		
		L16: ~(P ∨ Q) ⊃ P		
E7	B204	review		$\Rightarrow P ⊃ (P ∨ Q) \overset{R12}{\Rightarrow} P ⊃ (Q·R) \overset{R6}{\Rightarrow}$ $\sim P ∨ (Q·R), \sim P ⊃ \sim(Q ∨ P) \overset{R12}{\Rightarrow}\overset{R6}{\Rightarrow}$
E8.1	B216	get sign right(L13) = ~		$L13 \overset{R2}{=\!=}\overset{R6}{\Rightarrow} L17 \overset{R1}{\Rightarrow} L18 \overset{R6}{\Rightarrow} L19$
		L17: P ∨ (P ∨ Q)		
		L18: (P ∨ Q) ∨ P		
		L19: ~(P ∨ Q) ⊃ P		
E8.2	B249			$L18,L6 \overset{R11}{=\!=}$
E8.3	B255			$L15,L17 \overset{R12}{=\!=}\overset{R6}{\Rightarrow} L20 \overset{R12}{\Rightarrow} \sim P ⊃ (Q·R) \overset{R6}{\Rightarrow}$ $P ∨ (Q·R)$

FIGURE 10.7

episode abstract: S8 on problem C1

E	B	INSTIGATOR	E-SCHEMA	EPISODE
		L0: P ∨ (Q·R)		
		L1: (P ∨ Q)·(Q ⊃ R)		
E1	B3	get L0	path.R7	$L1 \overset{R4,R7}{=\!=}\overset{R1,R2,R6}{=\!\!\longrightarrow}\overset{R7}{=\!=}$
E2	B24	get L0	path.R9	$L1 \overset{R8}{\Rightarrow} L2 \overset{R8}{=\!=}\overset{R5}{=\!=} L2 \overset{R11}{=\!=}\overset{R8}{\Rightarrow} Q ⊃ R \overset{R8}{=\!=}\overset{R6,R5}{=\!=}$
		L2: P ∨ Q		
E3	B61	get L0	path.R7	$\overset{R10}{=\!=} P ∨ Q, right(L1) \overset{R2,R6}{\Rightarrow}\overset{R10}{\Rightarrow}\overset{R7}{=\!=}$
E4	B86	get P	WF	$L2 \overset{R1,R3,R4,R5}{=\!\!=\!\!=\!\!=\!\!\longmapsto}\overset{R2}{\Rightarrow} \sim P ⊃ Q \overset{R2}{\Rightarrow} \sim Q ⊃ P$ notice sign(Q)
E5	B107	sign(Q)	path.R7	$\sim Q ⊃ P \overset{R7}{=\!=} right(L1) \overset{R6}{\Rightarrow}\overset{R2}{\Rightarrow} \sim R ⊃ \sim Q$ $\overset{R7}{=\!=}\overset{R12}{=\!=} notice\ R12$
E6	B116	R12	path.R12	$L2 \overset{R6}{\Rightarrow} L3 \overset{R2}{\Rightarrow} L4,L1 \overset{R8}{\Rightarrow} L5 \overset{R2}{\Rightarrow} L6,L4 \overset{R12}{\Rightarrow} L7$
		L3: ~P ⊃ Q		
		L4: ~Q ⊃ P		
		L5: Q ⊃ R		
		L6: ~R ⊃ ~Q		
		L7: ~R ⊃ P		

FIGURE 10.7 (cont'd)

E	B	INSTIGATOR	E-SCHEMA	EPISODE
E7	B143	get L0 from L7	WF	$L7 \xrightarrow{R2,R6}\!\mid L7,L2 \xrightarrow{R12\ R10} L7.L2 \xrightarrow{R7}$
E8.1	B171	R7	path.R12	$L7 \xrightarrow{R2} \xrightarrow{R10} \xrightarrow{R7} \xrightarrow{R6} \xrightarrow{R7}$ plan.R7
E8.2	B181	plan.R7 from L7	path.R12	$L7 \xrightarrow{R2} L8,L3 \xrightarrow{R6} L9 = L2,L8 \xrightarrow{R6} L10,L9$ $\xrightarrow{R10} L11 \xrightarrow{R7} L12$

L8: $\sim P \supset R$
L9: $P \vee Q$
L10: $P \vee R$
L11: $(P \vee Q)\cdot(P \vee R)$
L12: $P \vee (Q\cdot R)$

FIGURE 10.8

episode abstract: S9 on problem C1

E	B	INSTIGATOR	E-SCHEMA	EPISODE
		L0: $P \vee (Q\cdot R)$		
		L1: $(P \vee Q)\cdot(Q \supset R)$		
E1	B3	get L0	path.R7	$L1 \xrightarrow{R7,R4\ R6}\!\mid \Rightarrow L2 \xrightarrow{R1\ R7}$
		L2: $(P \vee Q)\cdot(\sim Q \vee R)$		
E2	B25	eliminate		$\xrightarrow{R} \phi$
E3	B27		path.R7	$L1 \xrightarrow{R2} L3 \xrightarrow{R6} \sim R \vee \sim Q \xrightarrow{R7}$
		L3: $(P \vee Q)\cdot(\sim R \supset \sim Q)$		
E4	B68	eliminate	WF	$\xrightarrow{R3} \xrightarrow{R8\ R12} \xrightarrow{R9\ R1}$ plan.R9.QR
E5	B77	plan.R9.QR	path.R9′	$L1 \xrightarrow{R8} \xrightarrow{R6} L2 \xrightarrow{R8\ R5}$
E6	B86	get L0	WB	$L0 \xrightarrow{R7^{-1}} (PQ)(PR) \Rightarrow P \vee Q,$ get $P \vee R \xrightarrow{R12}$ $\xrightarrow{R9} P \xrightarrow{R9} P \vee R$
E7.1	B108	R9	path.R9′	$L1 \Rightarrow P\mid Q\cdot R \xrightarrow{R9} Q\cdot R \xrightarrow{R9\ R1}$
E7.2	B112	get Q·R	path.R9′	$Q \supset R \xrightarrow{R6\ R5}$
E7.3	B114	get P	path.R9	$P \vee Q \xrightarrow{R8\ R5\ R11}$ get Q
E8.1	B117	approach.R4-R7	WF	$Q \supset R \xrightarrow{R4,R7\ R6,R5}$
E8.2	B133		WB for QR	$Q \vee R \xrightarrow{R6^{-1}} \sim Q \supset R \xrightarrow{R12} Q \supset R, L3 \xrightarrow{R12\ R6}$ $L4, Q \supset R \xrightarrow{R12} \sim P \supset R$
		L4: $(\sim P \supset Q)\cdot(\sim R \supset \sim Q)$		
E8.3	B155	plan.R12	path.R12	$L4 \xrightarrow{R8} L5,L1 \xrightarrow{R8} L6,L5 \xrightarrow{R12} L7$
		L5: $\sim P \supset Q$		
		L6: $Q \supset R$		
		L7: $\sim P \supset R$		
E9	B172	get L0 from L7	path.R12	$L7 \xrightarrow{R6} L8 \xrightarrow{R10} L1 \xrightarrow{R8} L9,L8 \xrightarrow{R10} L10 \xrightarrow{R7} L11$ solution
		L8: $P \vee R$		
		L9: $P \vee Q$		
		L10: $(P \vee Q)\cdot(P \vee R)$		
		L11: $P \vee (Q\cdot R)$		

FIGURE 10.9

episode abstract: S10 in problem C1

E	B	INSTIGATOR	E-SCHEMA	EPISODE
		L0: $P \lor (Q \cdot R)$		
		L1: $(P \lor Q) \cdot (Q \supset R)$		
E1.1	B3	get L0	WB	$L0 \overset{R4^{-1}}{=\!=} L1 \overset{R4}{=\!=} \overset{R5}{=\!=}$
E1.2	B8		WB	$L0 \overset{R7^{-1}}{\Rightarrow} (P \lor Q) \cdot (P \lor R)$
E2	B16	get L0, keep PQR	WF	$L1 \overset{R12,R5,R1}{=\!=\!=\!=|}$
E3	B28	R8		$L1 \overset{R8}{\Rightarrow} Q \supset R, P \lor Q \overset{R8}{=\!=} \overset{R5}{=\!=} Q \supset R \overset{R6}{\Rightarrow} \overset{R5}{=\!=}$
E4	B43	eliminate Q	path.R11	$\overset{R11}{=\!=} Q \cdot R, P \lor Q \overset{R6}{\Rightarrow} \overset{R2}{=\!=} \overset{R11}{=\!=} L1 \overset{R6}{\Rightarrow} L2$
		L2: $(\sim P \supset Q) \cdot (Q \supset R)$		
E5	B67	R9	WB	$L0 \overset{R11}{\Rightarrow} P \overset{R9}{=\!=}$
E6	B75	L2	path.R11	$L2 \overset{R6,R5}{=\!=|} \overset{R2}{\Rightarrow} L3 \overset{R5}{=\!=} \overset{R11}{=\!=}$
		L3: $(\sim Q \supset P) \cdot (Q \supset R)$		
E7	B91	eliminate Q	WF	$L1 \overset{R7,R6}{=\!=\!=} (\sim P \supset Q)| \overset{R1,R6}{=\!=\!=} (\sim Q \supset P)| \overset{R6}{\Rightarrow} L4$
				$\overset{R7,R1}{=\!=\!=} (P \lor Q), (R \lor \sim Q)| \overset{R5}{=\!=}$
		L4: $(P \lor Q) \cdot (\sim Q \lor R)$		
E8	B111	R11	path.R11	$L1 \overset{R11,R8}{=\!=\!=|} \overset{R6,R5}{=\!=} (Q \cdot R)| \text{get } Q| \overset{R10}{=\!=}$
E9	B121	L0	WB	$L0 \overset{R10^{-1}}{=\!=} \overset{R9^{-1}}{=\!=} L1 \overset{R5,R8,R10}{=\!=\!=\!=} L4 \overset{R5}{\Rightarrow} L5 \overset{R5}{\Rightarrow} L6 \overset{R8}{=\!=}$
		L5: $\sim(\sim P \cdot \sim Q) \cdot (\sim Q \lor R)$		
		L6: $\sim(\sim P \cdot \sim Q) \cdot \sim(Q \cdot \sim R)$		
E10	B156	R7	WF	$L1 \overset{R7,R5}{=\!=\!=} (\sim P \cdot \sim Q) \overset{R6}{\Rightarrow} (\sim Q \lor R) \overset{R5}{\Rightarrow} \sim(Q \cdot$
				$\sim R) \overset{R2}{=\!=} (Q \supset R) \overset{R2,R6}{=\!=\!=} (Q \lor R) \overset{R5}{\Rightarrow}$
		L7: $(P \lor Q) \cdot (\sim R \supset \sim Q)$		$(\sim Q \lor \sim R), (P \lor Q) \overset{R1}{\Rightarrow} (\sim Q \lor \sim P),$
		L8: $(P \lor Q) \cdot (R \lor \sim Q)$		$(\sim Q \lor \sim R) \overset{R7}{\Rightarrow} Q \lor (\sim P \cdot \sim R)$
		L9: $\sim(\sim P \cdot \sim Q) \cdot \sim(\sim R \cdot Q)$		$L1 \overset{R2}{\Rightarrow} L7 \overset{R6}{\Rightarrow} L8 \overset{R5}{\Rightarrow} L9| \text{reviews}$
E11	B207	L0	WB	$\overset{R11,R10}{=\!=\!=} L0 \overset{R5}{\Rightarrow} \sim(\sim P \cdot \sim(Q \cdot R))| \overset{R5}{=\!=} \overset{R3}{=\!=} \overset{R12}{=\!=}$
				$\overset{R4}{=\!=} \overset{R10}{=\!=}$

FIGURE 10.10

episode abstract: S11 on problem C1

E	B	INSTIGATOR	E-SCHEMA	EPISODE
		L0: $P \lor (Q \cdot R)$		
		L1: $(P \lor Q) \cdot (Q \supset R)$		
E1	B3	get L0	WF	$L1 \overset{R7,R2,R8,R6,R4}{=\!=\!=\!=\!=} \overset{R7}{\Rightarrow} Q \supset (R \cdot P)$
E2	B43	eliminate Q	WF	$L1 \overset{R8,R1,R12}{=\!=\!=\!=} \overset{R5}{=|} \Rightarrow \sim(\sim P \cdot \sim Q)$

FIGURE 10.10 (cont'd)

E	B	INSTIGATOR	E-SCHEMA	EPISODE
E3.1	B58	R7	WB	$L0 \xrightarrow{R7^{-1}} (P \vee Q)\cdot(P \vee R) \Longrightarrow$ get $P \vee R \xrightarrow{R12}$
E3.2	B80	R12 uncertainty		[extended discussion with E on applying R12 to parts]
E4	B116		path.R7	$L1 \xrightarrow{R7} \xLongequal{R1,R6,R5} \xrightarrow{R7}$
E5.1	B154		path.R9′	$L1 \xLongequal{R9} \xrightarrow{R8} L2 \xLongequal{R9} L3 \xrightarrow{R1} L4 \xLongequal{R2,R5,R6}$
		L2: $Q \supset R$		
		L3: $(Q \supset R) \vee P$		
		L4: $P \vee (Q \supset R)$		
E5.2	B206	path.R9	AC	$L1 \xrightarrow{R8} Q \supset R \xrightarrow{R8} \xLongequal{R5} \xLongequal{R2} \xrightarrow{R6}$ E terminates attempt

FIGURE 10.11

episode abstract: S13 on problem C1

E	B	INSTIGATOR	E-SCHEMA	EPISODE
		L0: $P \vee (Q\cdot R)$		
		L1: $(P \vee Q)\cdot(Q \supset R)$		
E1	B3	split		$L1 \xrightarrow{R8} \xLongequal{R8} \xLongequal{R6,R5}$
E2	B17			$L1 \xLongequal{R12} \xrightarrow{R6}$
E3	B27		path.R7	$L1 \xLongequal{R7} \xrightarrow{R6} L2, L1 \xrightarrow{R6} L3 \xLongequal{R7}$
		L2: $(\sim P \supset Q)\cdot(Q \supset R)$		
		L3: $(P \vee Q)\cdot(\sim Q \vee R)$		
E4.1	B64		WB	$L0 \xrightarrow{R7^{-1}} (P \vee Q)\cdot(P \vee R) \xrightarrow{R1} \xLongequal{R12}$
E4.2	B84	get $(P \vee Q)\cdot(P \vee R)$	WF	$L3 \xLongequal{R8} \xLongequal{R1,R2,R3,R4,R5}$
E4.3	B108			$L3 \xLongequal{R11} \xrightarrow{R8} P \vee Q \xLongequal{R9} (P \vee Q) \vee R$
E5	B120	get $(P \vee Q)\cdot(P \vee R)$		$L1,L2 \xLongequal{R12} \xrightarrow{R8} \xrightarrow{R10}$ notice R10
E6.1	B140	get $(P \vee Q)\cdot(P \vee R)$	path.R12	$\xLongequal{R10} \xrightarrow{R8} P \vee Q$, get $P \vee R \xLongequal{R12} \xrightarrow{R8} Q \supset R \xrightarrow{R12} \sim P \supset R \xrightarrow{R6} P \vee R$ plan.R12
E6.2	B174	plan.R12	path.R12	$L2 \xrightarrow{R8} L4, L2 \xrightarrow{R8} L5 \xrightarrow{R12} L6 \xrightarrow{R6} L7$
		L4: $\sim P \supset Q$		
		L5: $Q \supset R$		
		L6: $\sim P \supset R$		
		L7: $P \vee R$		
E7.1	B194	get $(P \vee Q)\cdot(P \vee Q)$		$L7 \xLongequal{R9}$ recall plan
E7.2	B206			$L7 \xLongequal{R10} L3 \xrightarrow{R8} L8, L7 \xrightarrow{R10} L9 \xrightarrow{R7} L10$ solution
		L8: $P \vee Q$		
		L9: $(P \vee Q)\cdot(P \vee R)$		
		L10: $P \vee (Q\cdot R)$		

Sources of Difficulty: Construction

In C1 the last step in getting from L1: $(P \lor Q) \cdot (Q \supset R)$ to L0: $P \lor (Q \cdot R)$ calls for applying R7 to $(P \lor Q) \cdot (P \lor R)$, the latter expression having previously been assembled from its two components by R10. Note that the left-hand component can be obtained immediately from left(L1) by R8, but that obtaining the right-hand component involves indirection: after L1 is divided by two applications of R8, and the connective changed to a horseshoe in the left component, the two are combined again by R12, eliminating the Q's and leaving $(\sim P \supset R)$.

Now the R10, R7 sequence is a construction, by our previous definition, but it can be avoided by working backwards. Taken by itself, the task of obtaining $(P \lor R)$ from $(P \lor Q) \cdot (Q \supset R)$ would not be regarded as a hard problem—in

FIGURE 10.12

possible paths for the solution of C1

path.R4	Eliminate extra Q from L1,
	R4 to (PQ)(QR) $\Rightarrow$ Q(P(QR))
	R8 to Q(P(QR)) $\Rightarrow$ P(QR)
path.R7	Eliminate extra Q from L1 by R7, then regroup by R4
	R7 to (PQ)(QR) $\Rightarrow$ Q(PR)
	R4 to Q(PR) $\Rightarrow$ (PQ)R
	R4 to (PQ)R $\Rightarrow$ P(QR)
path.R9	Extract P from left (L1) by R8; add QR by R9
	R8 to (PQ)(QR) $\Rightarrow$ PQ
	R8 to PQ $\Rightarrow$ P
	R9 to P $\Rightarrow$ P(QR)
path.R9'	Extract QR from right(L1) by R8; add P by R9
	R8 to (PQ)(QR) $\Rightarrow$ QR
	R9 to QR $\Rightarrow$ P(QR)
path.R10	Same as path.R9, but use R10 to recombine
	R8 to (PQ)(QR) $\Rightarrow$ PQ
	R8 to PQ $\Rightarrow$ P
	R8 to (PQ)(QR) $\Rightarrow$ QR
	R10 to P, QR $\Rightarrow$ P(QR)
path.R11	Extract PQ and Q by R8; use R11 to get P; add QR by R9 or R10:
	R8 to (PQ)(QR) $\Rightarrow$ PQ
	R8 to (PQ)(QR) $\Rightarrow$ QR
	R8 to QR $\Rightarrow$ Q
	R11 to PQ, Q $\Rightarrow$ P
	R9 to P $\Rightarrow$ P(QR)
	(or R10 to P $\Rightarrow$ P(QR))
path.R12	Get PQ and QR by R8; combine by R12 to get P R. Combine PQ and PR by R10, and use R7 to get P(QR)
	R8 to (PQ)(QR) $\Rightarrow$ PQ
	R8 to (PQ)(QR) $\Rightarrow$ QR
	R12 to PQ, QR $\Rightarrow$ PR
	R10 to PQ, PR $\Rightarrow$ (PQ)(PR)
	R7 to (PQ)(PR) $\Rightarrow$ P(QR)

fact it has the same structure as D1. What makes the whole problem hard—according to our earlier explanation—is to discover that $(P \lor Q)$ and $(P \lor R)$ are wanted; and this can be discovered by working backward.

Some seven paths can be described that have some a priori plausibility as routes for solving C1. We would expect most of the expressions that subjects derived to relate to one or another of these seven paths, which are depicted in Figure 10.12.

Only the seventh plan, path.R12, is feasible; none of the others yield solutions of the problem. Path.R9 should produce expressions belonging to the equivalence class of left(L1), and expressions obtained by applying R9 to these. Path R9′ should produce expressions equivalent to right(L1). Path.R10 and path.R11 should produce expressions from L1, left(L1), and right(L1). Path.R7 should produce expressions from the equivalence class of L1 (since, as in D1, R7 is not actually applicable). Path.R12 should produce expressions from the equivalence

FIGURE 10.13

graphic representation of paths in C1

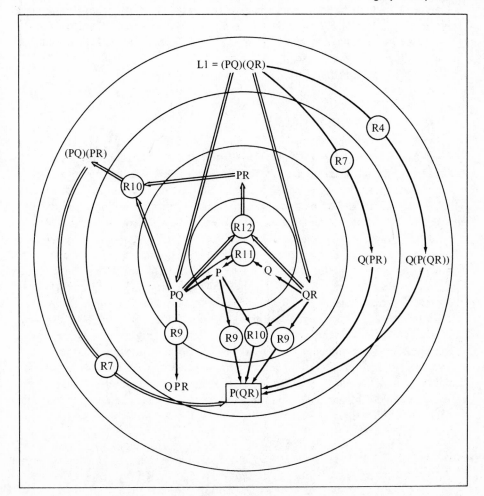

classes of right(L1) and left(L1), but also the class of $(\sim P \supset R)$ and of the two final expressions, $(P \lor Q) \cdot (P \lor R)$ and L0. The expressions generated by the nine subjects are limited to these classes, with two exceptions: (1) as a result of the experimenter's error, S2 generated six expressions derived from the incorrect expression $(P \supset \sim R)$; (2) on a path resembling path.R10, S5 generated eleven expressions like $(P \lor Q) \lor P$ and two like $(P \lor Q) \lor (Q \cdot R)$, which he tried to combine to eliminate the $(P \lor Q)$ by R12.

If we include S2 as a solver, then only the four subjects who solved the problem applied R12 to obtain $(\sim P \supset R)$; and conversely, all who applied that rule solved the problem. Before we investigate the significance of this fact, another fact should be mentioned. Three of the four solvers discovered, by working backwards, that L0 could be obtained from $(P \lor Q)$ and $(P \lor R)$ by R10 and R7. The fourth, S8, derived $(\sim P \supset R)$ without previously noticing that fact. However, three of the five nonsolvers (S5, S10, and S11) also discovered the R10–R7 possibility by working backward but did not use it successfully. Unless we can explain these anomalies, our previous hypotheses about the source of problem difficulty will fail, for the R10–R7 sequence is the only construction required. We therefore will concern ourselves first with the working-backward episodes in the protocols, with particular reference to S5, S10, and S11. (We might observe that S5 and S11 failed to solve Problem D1 also, hence dismiss them as weak problem solvers; but this would not explain the causes of their weakness, nor why S10, who solved D1 readily, failed on this problem.)

Working-Backward Episodes

S2, in his first episode (Figure 10.3), simplifies L1 by obtaining its two sub-expressions with R8. He then searches for applicable rules, finding and applying R12. At this point he notices the possibility of applying R7 and appears to notice that the term, (PQ), that he has just derived is an appropriate input for this step. Unfortunately, at this point the experimenter made an error in writing down an expression, and S2, working with the incorrect instead of the correct expressions, failed after persistent attempts to apply R10 and R7, and abandoned the plan for another. Even allowing for the error, there is considerable mystery in this protocol as to why S2, after actually deriving the two expressions, $(P \lor Q)$ and $(P \lor R)$, required for input to R10 and R7, did not see how to carry through the plan.

Near the beginning of his protocol, S5 notices that $(P \lor Q) \cdot (P \lor R)$ would give the answer by R7, and that he already has $(P \lor Q)$ (Figure 10.6, E2). However, looking at L1, and influenced by the two Q's in that expression, he immediately transforms the subproblem into one of applying R7 to L1 (path.R4), which he is unable to do. He then goes off to another plan, which he pursues with great persistence as he did his infeasible plan in D1. The critical passage near the beginning of the protocol is this (B19–B25):

> If we had a $P \lor R$ and a $P \lor Q$, we could get the answer directly by R7. We have a $P \lor Q$: we also have a $Q \supset R$. A $Q \supset R$ can be changed into a wedge by R6, except that we are going to have a sign problem again—and— let's try it anyway. Let's try R6, second part of L1.

> What I'm doing, and I think it's wrong—maybe I'll go back—I'm trying to get the expression into something to which R7 will apply, but once I get there it's only going to give one a P and a Q . . . a Q and an R plus a P, plus R or P, R term—that won't do me any good.

S5's difficulty, therefore, arises from failing to evolve a plan for obtaining the appropriate inputs to R7—he never considers using (P ∨ Q) and (Q ⊃ R) in combination to obtain (P ∨ R).

S8 begins somewhat as S2 did (Figure 10.7). Initially, he considers path.R7— R7 to L1, then R4—but recalls from his experience with D1 the impossibility of changing signs in L1 to fit R7. He then looks at L0, whose main connective, wedge, suggests path.R9 to him. This leads him to rules like R8 and R12 that cancel terms, so that he soon has derived (P ∨ Q), (Q ⊃ R), and (∼R ⊃ P). He does not have any definite plan in mind, for he then says (B143–B145): "There I am. I don't know what I'm going to do with it though. Well, maybe if I look at these for a minute, I can see something more that applies."

Shortly thereafter, he announces the plan, path.R12, but the events leading up to it are unclear. Whatever the exact steps, S8 basically solved the problem by working forward, applying a simplification heuristic, and examining the simplified expressions for the possibilities of new operations.

S9 also begins by noticing path.R7 (Figure 10.8). Since he did not struggle with the signs in L1 of Problem D1, he did not learn from that problem about the properties of the equivalence class of L1. Hence, he tries for some time to put L1 in shape for R7. After abandoning this tack, he soon tries going backward from L0, stating clearly (B94–B95): "We've got the PQ, but the PR we still have to get."

He considers using R12 to cancel Q from (PQ)(QR), but then distracts himself by considering path.R9. He soon returns to R12, applies it, and carries through to the conclusion.

S10, who worked backwards from L0 but failed to solve the problem, has a very instructive protocol (Figure 10.9). We quote the relevant passage, near the beginning, in full (B8–B19):

> I keep looking at the second expression, trying to work backwards, which isn't too good. I'll just see. P ∨ (Q·R) would be P . . . oh, it'd be R7 . . . (P ∨ Q)·(P ∨ R). Now in the first expression there is (P ∨ Q)·(Q ⊃ R), which isn't consistent, because there's only one P. All right . . . um . . . let's see . . . we have to keep a P, a Q, and an R. Therefore we couldn't use R12, because it eliminates Q's . . . after you get done with all the other rigamarole.

He then abandons path.R12, and never returns to it. Now S10 had previously solved D1; and in doing so, he had used R12 "to eliminate R's." In fact, early in his D1 protocol he says (B23–B24): "Hmm . . . the thing to do is to try and eliminate the R's. Therefore I'll have to use something like R12." Thus, on C1, he views an application of R12 as "eliminating" the Q's, hence as removing (P ∨ Q), which he needs for the subsequent application of R7. We have here a clear example of *functional fixity* (Duncker, 1945). Since (P ∨ Q) is to function as one of the inputs for R10 and thence R7, it cannot be "consumed" as an input for R12.

A very similar piece of reasoning appears in the protocol of S11 (Figure 10.10). He discovers that R7 applied to (P ∨ Q)·(P ∨ R) would yield L0. Comparing the needed expression with L1, he observes (B72–B82):

> So the step I use to get the final expression is P ∨ Q, which is the first expression I started out with . . . the only thing actually I'd have to work on is to change the Q ⊃ R to . . . P ∨ R. That doesn't help much because I'd have to change the first expression to get it and I'd have to change the results back to P ∨ Q. Let's see now . . . what could I do? Well, let's try to change the horseshoe to a wedge again . . . A ⊃ C on 12 . . . that would give me what I wanted . . . but in doing so, I'd have to take out the Q.

Here again, the subject assumes implicitly that P ∨ Q is "consumed" by its use with R12, hence is not later available for R10.

Finally (Figure 10.11), S13 also works backwards from L0, also is troubled by the dual role of P ∨ Q, but finally overcomes the difficulty. From the expression (P ∨ Q)·(∼Q ∨ R), he observes (B67–B71):

> We're going to have to get . . . (P ∨ Q) which we have, ·(P ∨ R) . . . I just want to get the ∼Q to P. No, how can I get that? Ah, probably by using two lines. . . . (B92–B94): I could break it apart, but I don't want to break it apart though. It looks like I'm going to have to though.

Somewhat later (B160) he comments: "I must remember that . . . I want to get a P ∨ R from somewhere out of two expressions." Shortly thereafter, he derives P ∨ R, and comments immediately (B194): "Now, if we can get that back into the expression" [i.e., into (P ∨ Q)·(∼Q ∨ R), mentioned above, replacing (∼Q ∨ R)]. Later, at (B215): "If I can get from somewhere just a P ∨ Q . . . ," he finds his way to the solution.

There is no very solid ground for speculating why S13 was able to overcome the difficulty about the double function of P ∨ Q, while S10, S11, and S5 were not. Nor do we know why these three subjects were troubled by the problem, while S2 and S9 applied the working-backwards idea without difficulty. What we do know is that representing the functions of certain operators as *canceling* or *eliminating* a symbol can deter a subject from applying the operator if he also knows the symbol will be needed for another function.

We can now see also the reason why, among the Yale subjects, a sizable fraction (37.5 percent) of those who applied R12 went on to solve the problem (Figure 8.23). In our protocols, R12 was occasionally applied in the interest of simplification, or some similar working-forward motivation. Both S2 and S8 appear to have applied it without previously working backward from L0 to discover that P ∨ R was needed. However, the latter path was the more common one for arriving at the need for R12. But a subject who noted in this way that P ∨ R must be obtained would simultaneously note that P ∨ Q must be retained, hence, as we have seen, would be reluctant to alter the latter. The argument against double functions would show up as a failure to apply R12.

Double-function phenomena do not require the introduction of any basic mechanisms beyond those already contained in GPS. Suppose that, before an operator is applied officially—i.e., to write a new expression on the board—it is checked to see whether the differences it will produce are larger or more serious than those it removes. If the answer is yes, it will not be applied. Now the use of this test in this problem situation is fallacious, since any expression in the logic problems can exist in as many copies as desired, hence is not destroyed by transformation. If the problem expressions were made of wood, and the transformations accomplished by saws and drills, then the test as described would be entirely appropriate. A piece of wood that has been fashioned into the leg of a chair cannot also be used in manufacturing the chair back.

The double-function test is in fact often quite relevant in chess, as we shall see. If a Knight is guarding a Bishop, then it cannot simultaneously protect a pawn. That is to say, it can guard *either*, but not *both*, in the face of a simultaneous assault. Failure to note that a piece is overburdened by multiple functions, and that in actually performing one it may become disabled from performing the others, is a frequent source of chess blunders (or, conversely, for the player who exploits his opponent's overburdened piece, a source of combinations).

Conclusion

We conclude that for subjects who worked forward, the R10–R7 construction made problem C1 difficult. Such subjects would have to apply R12 for some reason unconnected with the actual solution path (as S2 and S8 did) in order to hit upon the path. For subjects working backward, the problem difficulty stems primarily from functional fixity arising from the double function of the subexpression (P $\vee$ Q).

EXTERNAL MEMORY

The logic task has two displays: the rule sheet, which is static, and the board, which slowly accumulates information available for further use. These external memories have important effects on performance of the task. It would be a very different matter for a subject to do a problem such as C1 (or even D1) in his head, even if the rules were perfectly memorized.

The role of external memories is doubly important for us in the light of the concept of a problem space. The element of the problem space is identified with the momentary status of the problem solver, from which he moves forward by selecting and applying an operator, or backward by recalling a prior element of the space. The element of the space is what the problem solver knows. It is precisely the knowledge that is immediately available to him, either for inputs to the operators or for selecting an operator and evaluating the position.

In describing the logic task initially in Chapter 8 we took the element of the problem space to be the logic expression and the operators to be the twelve rules—essentially the basic space as defined by the experimenter. Subjects tend to have a single logic expression currently in view and to operate on it with a rule that produces a simple new logic expression, which then becomes the current expression. Upon failure with the current expression, subjects tend to fall back to some other single expression, the board display acting as the repository for expressions that may be recalled.

In using the PBG in Chapters 8 and 9 we modified this specification by taking as the operators the goals, rather than the rules. The current goal provides a substantial amount of the information used in selecting the next operator, so that the adoption of a new goal (such as to apply an operator) changes the state of knowledge substantially. Therefore, it must be included as part of the problem-space element.

The issue raised by external memories is exactly the opposite of that raised by the goals. All the information in the knowledge state is considered to be available, but is all the information in the external memories available? If not, then it is not part of the knowledge state. But if it is available, then how does the external memory fit into our conception of the problem space?

First of all, there is little doubt about the differential accessibility of the contents of the external memories in logic. The subjects have to search them repeatedly. More important, they soon get to know some parts of the information on the displays but not other parts. They know R5 and R6 well enough to apply them without reference to the rule sheet, but not R4 or R11. They know the current expression being worked on, but they may be unaware for some time that this current expression is already on the display at a different line.

There are four ways in which an external memory can be incorporated into a problem space:

1. It can act as a repository for elements of the space that are not current but can be reached by recall mechanisms, rather than by operators that generate new knowledge.
2. It can be wholly external to the knowledge state, so that operators that access the memory and search it have the same status as any other operators in the problem space: when successful they generate new knowledge that becomes part of the knowledge state.
3. It can be incorporated into the processing at a node, in such a way that all the relevant information in the external memory is in fact available.
4. It can be an extension or adjunct to the current knowledge state, with some of its information available, but not all. We will call a knowledge state, along with any such adjuncts, the *extended knowledge state*.

The first three alternatives simply assimilate the external memory to the conception of a problem space as developed so far. The last one, the extended knowledge state, is a genuine elaboration. Which role a given external memory plays for a given problem solver is primarily an empirical matter, though to some extent it may be a question of convenience of description. If there are several external memories, they may play distinct roles. And the same external memory may change its role over time—for instance, as the problem solver becomes acquainted with its contents.

The experimental arrangements used for the three tasks considered in this book were not designed to obtain good information about the use of external memory. The eye-movement studies, one in cryptarithmetic and one to be considered later in connection with chess, are perhaps exceptions, although in these, the external memories were entirely static. However, enough information can be gleaned from the protocols at least to illustrate and clarify the four possibilities listed above. In Chapter 9 we classified all of the operator occurrences in the seven protocols on problem D1. Among these 500-odd occurrences were 18 instances of searches of the board, and many instances of returns to some earlier expression, such as the initial one. In addition, there is abundant evidence of searches of the rule sheet for the operators. Let us consider, then, each of the four roles that an external memory might play.

Stock of Prior Nodes

Subjects in the logic task engage primarily in a depth-first search in which each newly generated expression succeeds the last as the current expression. Indeed, it is this feature that permits us to characterize, to a first approximation, the knowledge state as consisting of a single logic expression. When the current expression is evaluated as undesirable, the subjects fall back to some other one in the display. Most commonly, this is either the prior one or the initial expression. Actually, the subjects avoid entering a new expression on the display until they think it represents progress. Thus, most of the backing off to the immediate prior expression occurs at the covert level, returning to the most recent expression that has been entered on the board. The evidences for these behaviors are widespread and clear in the protocols. Examination of the PBG's in the appendices of Chapter 9 for problem D1 will provide an easy index to them, especially the return to L1. Let us give just one example of each kind of return. In problem D1, S4 terminates a fruitless attempt (ending at L8) to follow path.R7 in these terms (B69–B73):

> ... and then apply R7. And that's what I'm looking for now, but as yet I can't find a way. Yeah ... well, I started back at the beginning, since I'm getting noplace down there.

The return to the original expression for the function of starting over could hardly be clearer.

In problem C1, S3 is trying to apply R7 and has obtained expression L3 (B28–B29):

> [E writes L3: $(Q \lor P) \cdot (\sim Q \lor R)$]
> No rule to the problem that the Q's aren't the same sign.

A moment later he tries applying R5 to L3. The attempt is clearly experimental (B37–B44):

> [E: Apply 5 to the left-hand side of 3?]
> No, to the entire expression of 3.
> [E: Entire expression.]
> Yeah. Now right now I'm not thinking of anything, I'm just waiting to see what that's going to look like.
> [E writes L4: $\sim(\sim Q \vee P) \vee \sim(\sim Q \vee R)$]
> I don't think that helped any at all.
> [E: Why not?]

After answering E's question, S3 proceeds (B52–B53): "Let's see now, disregarding L4, getting back into what we wanted, changing the Q to $\sim$Q. ..." Here we have an instance of backing up one node on the display, where the functional significance of the step is evident.

Almost all the movement on the display is consistent with depth-first search and backup. Only occasionally is the display actually searched for a new starting place, independent of the genesis of the prior expressions—corresponding to a search-and-scan strategy as performed by some of the artificial problem solvers that keep a subproblem list. One example occurs in an attempt by S8 in D1 to eliminate an R from a subexpression directly (i.e., to ignore the constraint that R8 applies only to main expressions). The display consists of five expressions:

$$L1: (R \supset \sim P) \cdot (\sim R \supset Q)$$
$$L2: (\sim R \vee \sim P) \cdot (\sim R \supset Q)$$
$$L3: (\sim R \vee \sim P) \cdot (R \vee Q)$$
$$L4: \sim(R \cdot P) \cdot (R \vee Q)$$
$$L5: \sim(R \cdot P) \cdot \sim(\sim R \cdot \sim Q)$$

S8 has just given up on an extended attempt to follow path.R7 (B152–B158):

> Well, let's look back at the original one and see if I can see anything. Ah, I like that conversion into ah wedges, but ah, I don't know if it'll get me any-where. If I can, wonder if I can eliminate ah right inside that, through, through a wedge, or I could through a dot. Oh, I have an idea, how about if I, ah, take, ah, apply R8, oh, yeh, I get it, ah, just to part of ah, L5,. ...

R8 cannot be applied to a subexpression as S8 soon discovers. But our interest in the above segment of behavior is that S8 clearly has left L5 and returned to L1 (another example of backing up all the way). He then searches the display. He looks at L3, reevoking path.R7, which he immediately discards. Still looking at L3, he generates the strategy of eliminating an R in a subexpression. Since this is not possible with wedges, he moves to dots and L5. We cannot tell whether he moved from wedge to dot and then searched, or whether he simply continued his scan of the display while considering the new strategy. In any event, his final statement makes the strategy clear, as well as the selection of L5 as the current expression.

L5 happens to be the most recent expression, but there is little doubt about the manner in which it was generated.

583

Logic:
A Broader View

External Source of New Knowledge

If none of the information in an external memory is known to the problem solver, then searching it and extracting data from it must be an operation like any other information generating operation. This is obviously the role played by references, books, maps, letters, and so on. The set of operators in the problem space is then inhomogeneous, some being search operators for these external memories, others being inference operators, and so on. But there is no reason for all the operators to be of one kind, like the twelve rules in logic. In fact, the operators of cryptarithmetic were also inhomogeneous. There must be rules to select search operators of external memories, just as there are for the twelve logic operators, and these rules must depend only on knowledge in the current state.

The rule sheet in logic hardly operates in this fashion, since the subjects become familiar with it, even before they tackle their first problem. Although we could introduce an operator for searching the rule sheet and could detect its operation, especially at the beginning of the first few problems, it would soon meld in with direct recollection of the operators, or (more often) with checking a partial recollection.

The display of expressions on the board, since it is generated by the subject himself, also seems unlikely to be an entirely external source of information. But there are a few instances in which the subject responds to a difficulty by a search of the display for an alternative expression, rather than for a rule to modify the current expression. One example is provided by S8 right after the sequence just quoted (which gives the relevant expressions) (B162–B167):

I'll apply R8 [to left(L4)] and I'll end up getting. . . .
Ah, oh wait a minute, positive . . . it has to have a positive total expression.
[E: Uh huh.]
Well, in that case, let's go back then to L3. No, L3 is not good.

The sequence is a standard means-ends cycle to remedy a difficulty in applying an operator:

apply R8 to left(L5)   [left(L5): $\sim(R\cdot P)$]
     change sign of main expression   [left(L5) is considered main]
          search display for expression with sign(main) positive
               $\Rightarrow$ left(L3): $\sim R \lor \sim P$
     apply R8 to left(L3)
          change connective from wedge to dot
               reject

With this parallelism of function, it is hard to deny the search of the display the same status as a rule application.

Part of Knowledge State

All of the information in the knowledge state must be in some memory: in the subject's STM, his LTM, or in some external memory. The definition of the knowledge state is functional: it contains the knowledge available for application when the subject is in a particular state. Hence, the criterion for including an external memory as part of the knowledge state is simply whether all its contents that are relevant to selection and specification of operators, or as inputs to operators, are in fact available. They may be available even though not all contents of the external memory are equally accessible.

In our analyses of the subjects' problem solving in logic we have tended to treat the rule sheet in exactly this fashion, not distinguishing whether a subject knows the rule (i.e., has it in some internal memory) or finds it in the sheet. To a first approximation this procedure has proved quite adequate, especially after the subjects have acquired some familiarity with the rules. Structurally, the assumption also makes sense, since the external memory for rules is on a single sheet of paper, open to continual visual search by the subject. However, we have not examined closely exactly which rules are evoked in a subject's attempt to find a relevant operator. Thus, we have not put this assumption to any stringent test. It has been enough to note that when the subject is reducing a difference, the rules satisfy functional requirements, and when he is working forward they satisfy some requirements of applicability, but do not satisfy functional requirements.

As we have noted, usually only the current expression in the display on the board is part of the current knowledge state, the rest being only a memory for prior nodes to which to return. Structurally, as long as the display contains only a few expressions, it could undoubtedly be part of the knowledge state, if the subject's problem solving program so required. When the display becomes rather large, and the expressions are complex (e.g., the four-term expressions in D1 and C1), then the memory becomes truly external to the current state. The best evidence for this is the failure of our subjects to detect duplications immediately. For instance S4 on D1 generates L8: $(\sim R \lor \sim P) \cdot (R \lor Q)$ by R10 at B67 and does not notice that this is the same expression as L2 until B93–B95:

> I'm lost. . . . (long pause)
> Well, I'm looking at equation number 2 and number 8 and I find I have the same thing. Well, I'm clear back at the beginning again.

The important additional information in the last statement is that discovering the duplication has the effect of sending S4 back to start over. That is, the discovery of the duplication is not a matter of indifference to S4, but indicates failure to progress. This is true in general. Thus, S5 (on D1), in discovering a duplication (actually a triplication) between L15, L11, and L5, says (B211–B213):

> I'm back where I started from again. How many times have I had that on there . . . hah? Let's see now back at L13 I had a P·R and what did I do to. . . .

Thus, S5 abandons L15 after discovering the duplication.

Extended Knowledge State

If an external memory is being used in a routine way, but is not totally available, even when relevant, how should one view it? We can introduce the notion of an *extended knowledge state*, which contains additional information that is available to the problem solver at a node in the problem space, but not all the information that is in the external memory. For such a concept to be operational, rather than just a relabeling of the phenomena, we must be able to define the accessing functions used by the problem solver, so that we can describe what information is actually available to him. Thus, instead of describing the current knowledge state of the subject as the contents of memories X and Y, we describe it as the contents of memory X plus what can be obtained from memory Y by retrieval program P.

Under such a definition, an external memory, such as the display of logic expressions, may be available for some functions, but not for others. We have noted the limited ability of our subjects to detect duplication. Another use of the display is to find inputs to two-line rules (recall the way GPS scanned the display to obtain a second input for R12 in Figure 8.16, page 430). There are several instances of such searches in the protocols, where a two-line rule is obtained. There is no behavioral indication that any of the expressions in the display is unavailable. Indeed, when the subject engages in a deliberate scan of the display, all of its expressions become as available as the information in the immediate knowledge state. The subjects duplicate expressions because they do not search the display each time they generate a new expression, but rely instead on noticing the occurrence of a duplicate. If a deliberate search were incorporated in their programs, duplications would be caught immediately in most cases.

As we noted at the beginning of the section, the experimental arrangements do not provide sufficient information to formulate a set of accessibility functions for the external memories. Thus, we cannot exhibit in detail an extended knowledge state for the logic task. An informal feeling can be obtained about a subject's access to the rule sheet by scanning the protocols. When working forward the subjects select almost entirely on the basis of the connective. Here is S10 at the beginning of D1 (B3–B8):

OK. I'm going to look the first card over before I start writing down any rules. I'll examine it very carefully. Um . . . a horseshoe expression. . . . Both of them are horseshoe expressions. And for those you may use R6 . . . R2.

S10 announces that he is working forward; he then states the criterion of search explicitly and finally retrieves the two expressions that involve horseshoes, R6 and R2.

As we noted in Chapter 9, the subjects usually describe the situation functionally. Then the search for rules involves two conditions—function and feasibility (based on the connective). Sometimes, when first attempts at finding a rule fail, search is made by function alone, without reference to feasibility. A sequence from S8 on D1 illustrates both these cases. He has returned to reconsider L1 again (B260–B272):

If I can just get rid of the R in each term, I've got it knocked. Now, how can you get rid of a term with a horseshoe? I don't think you can. That's all right, I can get rid of something else. The only place. . . . Well, R8, you can get rid of something. And ah. . . . Well, that's the only thing I see that you can get rid of a term or R3, but ah, they have to be identical. I'd never change a letter. Ah, rule . . . the only other thing that looks interesting is R11.

The first statement defines the function. The next defines a search with connective and function, leading (correctly) to nothing. The protocol then is explicit about the modification of criteria, which is carried out by obtaining three rules, R8, R3, and R11, that delete terms but are not filtered for applicability. Of course, once S8 obtains the rule he then does concern himself with whether it can be applied, but the search of the rule sheet is carried out without such concern.

Only rarely do subjects engage in searches that involve more than one functional condition and one applicability condition. This is one of the prominent features of the searches of the rule sheets, not so much in excluding relevant operators as in letting through irrelevant ones, which must then be considered further. S5 on D1 provides an explicit example of a search with multiple criteria. He is (as usual) trying to apply R7, this time to L17:

L17: $(\sim R \lor \sim P) \cdot (\sim Q \sim R)$
(B288–B290): Hah . . . oh gee . . . if we could only change the order of that second term of 17 . . . but leaving the signs the same. . . . We can't do it directly because the horseshoe. . . .

Needless to say, no rule is found that satisfies the three conditions: the function of changing position, the function of not changing signs, and applicability to a horseshoe connective.

The rule sheet is actually a complexly structured memory (see Figure 8.1 on page 406), with three sets of rules, marked off by lines, and with descriptions written below each rule. This is the form originally used in the Yale studies and simply adopted by us for the same tasks. The details of this memory structure have effects, though they are hard to pin down systematically from our data. For example, the functional descriptions used by the subjects are no doubt affected by the wording used on the rule sheet. Also the grouping of the rules into subsets has an effect. For instance, it explains an important feature of S8's behavior at the beginning of D1. He starts out with a forward search (B8–B11):

> First, I'll look for a, ah . . . I think I'll look for a . . . something with a connector, with a dot connector as the major connector. Now I can see here . . . set . . . R1. I could reverse them, but, ah, I can't see any point in that right now.

He then proceeds to examine equally explicitly R3, R4, and R7, finally concluding with (B19): "Ah . . . I don't see any, see anything I can do on the . . . do on the scale of the whole."

What happened to R5 and R8? A plausible explanation for R5 is that the dot connective appears on the right-hand side of the rule in the upper right corner of the sheet. Rules 1, 3, 4, and 7 all appear on the left. S8 simply did not see that R5 satisfied the search condition. A plausible explanation for R8 is that it belongs to the third set, which was not examined at all by S8. Of course, it is possible that the two rules were examined, without verbalization. While there is no explicit evidence on R5, there is good evidence on R8 that confirms our interpretation. After a prolonged bout with trying to apply R7, S8 returns to the beginning (B55–B63):

> Well then, that doesn't fit in R7. . . . So, here I am. . . . Well . . . ah . . . esh . . . now where am I? Ah. I could reverse them around, but I don't think that's going to do anything, working as a whole again. I, I, I can't see. . . . Oh! wait a minute, I see something. I don't know if it's any good. On R8 . . . ah . . . across a, a dot major connector.

It seems evident that S8 is again working forward, just as he was in the segment from B8 to B19 (compare the wording). It is also clear that he finds R8 in this search, and that this is the first time he has seen this rule as a possibility. Thus, R8 was indeed overlooked in the first search, and probably because of the structure of the rule sheet.

Summary

Although we have been only illustrative in dealing with the role of external memory in the logic task, enough evidence has been presented to show that it can be incorporated in the process in several different ways, and that all of these show up to some extent in logic. Since the logic task is dominated by the basic means-ends cycle, the structure of the two external memories can be ignored to a first approximation. In other tasks this clearly would not be so.

The concept of an *extended knowledge state* would appear to be a necessary modification of our notion of the knowledge state. Much information in external memories can be acquired within the processing at a single node of the problem space by a glance or quick scan of a display. But the information in the external memory may not be totally available, owing to characteristics of the problem solver's program for accessing it. Still, we need some way of talking about what information can actually be brought to bear at the next step in solving the problem. The extended knowledge state provides this modified concept.

INDIVIDUAL DIFFERENCES AND LEARNING PHENOMENA

At various points in this analysis we have alluded to changes that took place in the problem solving procedures of the subjects over a series of problems.[2] We have mentioned, for example, that most of the solutions (14 of 24) of D1 by the Yale subjects were obtained by the one-fourth of the subjects who had already had experience with at least twelve other problems. We have also alluded to differences in the problem solving styles of different subjects.

In looking for individual differences among the subjects we can examine:

1. The problem spaces in which they work.
2. The operators they apply.
3. The differences they notice.
4. Their ordering of differences.
5. Their abstracting procedures, and their distinctions between essential and inessential.
6. Their methods.

When we carry out this examination, what strikes us first is the similarity among the subjects, and the subtle nature of the differences that distinguish them. With some qualifications for S11, whose idiosyncrasies will be discussed below, all subjects work in essentially the same problem space, apply the same operators, use the same differences, generally order the differences in about the same way, make similar kinds of abstractions (and the same distinctions between essential and inessential rules), and apply almost the same methods.

Nevertheless, differences are detectable among the protocols, and these differences are significant enough to make some of the subjects substantially better problem solvers than the others. In the next section we examine in some detail the differences we discovered.

[2] Carpenter, Moore, Snyder, and Lisansky (1961) show that the number of solutions obtained by their subjects increased more or less linearly from the first problem session to the fourth.

We might expect learning phenomena and individual differences to be inter-connected. Some individual differences might take the form of a greater range and sophistication of techniques available to one subject than to another. In such a case, we might expect practice to alter the style of the less sophisticated subject in the direction of the more sophisticated. Any kind of learning—whether this or some other—that occurred would also reduce the consistency of style of a given subject over a sequence of problems.

We can identify several aspects of style from the protocols:

1. Number of rule applications carried out. Subjects may be more or less consistent in being relatively quick or relatively slow to write new expressions on the board.
2. Forward search of rules to find rules applicable to given or derived expressions.
3. Search of rules to find a rule to perform a desired function or reduce a specified difference (as contrasted with direct association from function to rule).
4. Working backwards from L0 to find expressions that will yield L0.

If we inspect this list of stylistic differences, we see that they relate mostly to the methods employed. Number of rule applications would depend on the availability of generators (and the strength of stop rules). The second category relates to a method like "Find operator to transform X." The third relates to a method like "Find operator to perform function F." The fourth relates to the working-backwards method.

Use of the two rule-search methods implies that the subject has not stored in memory the forms of the rules or their functions (table of connections). Thus, these are "primitive" methods that we would expect to disappear as the subject replaces them by direct recognition processes.

In Figure 10.14 we show the initial segments of the protocols of two subjects, S9 and S11, each for two problems, D1 and C1. (It should be kept in mind that the subjects attempted D1 *before* C1.) By comparing vertically, we can look for similarities derived from working in a common task environment—the same problem. By comparing horizontally, we can detect characteristics of individual style that persist across problems.

First, at a superficial level, we notice some striking consistencies in manner of expression that identify the two subjects. In S9's protocols these include "Well, . . . reminds me of . . . , but" or "Well . . . suggests to me, but." "I require" or "I need," "so," "drop." In S11's protocol we have "Uh-huh, let's see now," "remove," "change," and "What can I do on it?"

At a deeper level, the processes of comparing L1 with L0 are quite different

FIGURE 10.14

comparison of verbal styles S9 and S11 on problems D1 and C1

	D1 L0: ~(~Q·P) L1: (R ⊃ ~P)·(~R ⊃ Q)	C1 L0: P ∨ (Q·R) L1: (P ∨ Q)·(Q ⊃ R)
S9	Well, the tilde on the outside reminds me of R5. But inside R5 there's also a dot, so it figures I might get something out of that later on. I require a Q and a P . . . Q and a P, and there's a Q in the second part, a P in the other, and there's two Rs in there. So I could drop both those Rs and see . . . split those terms up. Now, what could I do that with?	Well, that suggests to me R7 and R4, but I have a horseshoe in that, and, let's see, I'll need a Q and an R and a P. So I have to drop the Q and switch that horseshoe. And that I can do handily enough using R6.
S11	Uh-huh, let's see now. Remove all Rs, horseshoe, change the sign of the Q from the horseshoe to the tilde, change the sign on P from tilde to a dot before it. Let's see, the major connective remains the same . . . it's a dot and the final expression is negative, with a tilde in it. I'm looking over the sheet . . . see what I can do on it.	Hum. Let's see now. The only thing to remove is the horseshoe. The Q is taken out of the first expression, the dot is the major connective to change to a wedge, and the horseshoe in Q ⊃ R is changed to a dot. Let's see, what can I do on the first expression . . .

for the two subjects. In both cases, the form of L0 (or possibly, in C1, of L0 and L1) reminds S9 of a rule. The central problem, as he characterizes it, is in both cases getting the letters and number of occurrences in L1 to agree with those in L0. S11, on the other hand, particularly in D1, makes a symbol-by-symbol match between L1 and L0, with little or no abstraction of the detail of connectives. Particular locatable segments of L1 are to be transformed to particular parts of L0 (". . . change the sign on P from tilde to a dot before it," "The Q is taken out of the first expression.")

In Table 10.3 we compare for problems D1 and C1 the styles of all six subjects for whom we have protocols for both problems.

First, we notice great individual consistency in the number of expressions written down. On both problems, S11 works almost entirely in his head, writing down only three expressions each time; while S5 produces 17 expressions in the one case, 19 in the other. Only S4, who solved D1 (after writing 13 expressions) but failed to solve C1 (writing only 6), exhibits inconsistency in this respect. Notice that the two extreme cases, S11 and S5, were both subjects who solved neither problem.

Four of the six protocols contain extensive searches of the list of rules at one or more points. Each subject was entirely consistent in this respect, either making such searches or not on both problems. The two who did not search were a non-solver, S5, and a solver, S9.

One subject, S8, frequently searched through and scrutinized, in both problems, the expressions he had already written down. He and S4 were the only two

TABLE 10.3

styles of subjects on problems D1 and C1

		S9	S8	S4	S10	S5	S11
Solved problem:	D1	x	x	x	x		
	C1	x	x				
Expressions written:	D1	8	11	13	8	17	3
	C1	10	11	6	8	19	3
Searches rules:	D1		x	x	x		x
	C1		x	x	x		x
Searches expressions:	D1		x				
	C1		x				
Persistent:	D1					x	
	C1				x	x	
Works backwards:	D1	x					
	C1	x			x	x	x
Gives general characterization:	D1	x	x*		x	x	x
	C1	x			x	x	x

*Characterizes problem, but not at beginning of protocol.

subjects who obtained both left(L1) and right(L1) in D1 before considering the plan of applying R12.

S5, on both problems, and S10 on C1, showed great persistence in pursuing a particular infeasible plan, this being the source of most of the expressions generated. Statements do not recur in their protocols restating the overall problem goals.

As we have already remarked, four subjects worked backward from L0 in C1, and one of these, S9, also did so in D1. The two subjects who did not do this in either problem, S4 and S8, were the same ones who, as noted above, were successful in working forward in D1.

The four subjects who worked backward also gave a characterization of the problems at the beginnings of their protocols. S11's characterization, as we saw in Figure 10.14, was highly particularistic. The others were similar to S9's. S8 characterized D1 in general terms at several points in his protocol, but not at the beginning.

There are considerable consistencies, therefore, in the behavior of each subject, and substantial differences among subjects. Arranging the subjects in the apparent order of their problem solving power, we might describe them as follows:

S9   generates clear general plans, working both backwards and forward, which he executes with moderate difficulty.

S8   is initially much less planful, works forward, searching the rules when necessary, scans the new expressions as he generates them, and reformulates the problem with the new information obtained. In solving the problems he writes 22 expressions while S9 writes 18.

S4   resembles S8 in his behavior, but appears less resourceful in generating new expressions that give him new insights as he proceeds.

S10   generates plans and works backwards, but sometimes persists with a single subgoal, and sometimes searches through the rules for an applicable one.

S5   resembles S10 and S9 in characterizing the problem broadly and in planning, but in each case he becomes preoccupied with a subgoal and does not get back to the main goal.

S11   concerns himself with the detail rather than the broad structure of the problems, and spends much time in searching for rules he can apply, but without applying them unless the outcome has an obvious use.

In terms of our earlier classifications of strategies for applying means-end analysis, S5 provides a clear example of the depth-first strategy, and his inability to solve the problems can be attributed to the stereotypy this produces. S8, on the other hand, fits the pattern of a scan-and-search strategy, frequently reviewing the expressions he has generated and continuing his search from those that seem currently the most promising. Most of the subjects operate alternately in terms of abstractions and of the detail of the concrete problem space, but S9's protocols perhaps exhibit this alternation most clearly. He accomplishes most of his problem solving in terms of the abstracted expressions.

Idiosyncrasies of S11

As significant as the differences among the subjects is the fact that all of them operate in the problem space defined by the expressions and rules, and all of them use the same basic processes of finding differences, finding relevant operators, and applying operators. The range of individual differences appears narrower than the range of difference among subjects in the cryptarithmetic problems.

Even S11, the most idiosyncratic of the subjects, does not appear to work in a different problem space. His idiosyncrasy shows up in several ways, so that it is not easy to distinguish causes from symptoms. First of all, he instructed the experimenter to write down very few expressions—only two, in fact. His preference for working in his head had several consequences (or causes!). His plans appear vaguer than those of the other subjects, and there appears to be a less close connection between plans and rules. He is going to group the terms in L1 "somehow," and the feasibility of the "somehow" is never tested very carefully. Since he does not generate new expressions, these are not available to him for scanning to generate possible new goals (he cannot follow a search-and-scan strategy, because of the limits upon what he can hold in his head).

At one point in his protocols S11 appears to be confused about the syntax of the logic expressions, forming inappropriate subexpressions. Toward the beginning of his protocol on D1 (B4–B5) he says he must "change the sign on the Q from the horseshoe to the tilde . . . change the sign on P from tilde to a dot before it." These phrases imply that he is matching symbols in a linear string without first detecting the hierarchical phrase structure, and hence that he is unaware of the difference in function between binary connectives like the horseshoe or dot and the unary connective, tilde.

S11 carries out, in his head, numerous manipulations, particularly with the inessential rules. But these seem only distantly connected with the functions he names. His manipulations are generally with specific detailed expressions, and he does not often temporarily ignore details of signs and connectives as the other subjects do.

In fact, S11 appears at several points to be preoccupied with avoiding introducing tildes into the expressions; while other subjects generally treat tildes as details, to be adjusted with inessential transformations, except when a tilde, by making a whole expression negative, makes certain rules inapplicable to it.

The main symptoms, then, of S11's idiosyncrasy are not that he works in a different problem space from the other subjects but that (1) he does less planning and abstraction, and shows little ability to move from functional statements to their implementation with specific rules, (2) he places heavy demands on his short-term memory by working mostly in his head, (3) differences in tildes are more important to him than to the other subjects, and (4) he sometimes employs an inappropriate syntax in parsing the logic expressions.

We stress that these are symptoms, rather than a fundamental characterization of S11 as an IPS. If and when we are able to provide the latter, we will have gained a great deal of insight into the causes of major differences in human problem solving abilities from one person to another. From the fact that S11 can be regarded as working in the same problem space as the other subjects, we see that in this case these differences seem to stem from subtle differences in strategy and in the management of short-term memory.

Learning

In speaking of the *style* of a subject, we have been concerned only with behavior over a pair of immediately successive problems. We cannot tell from this evidence whether a subject would retain the same style over a much longer range of experience. In particular, we cannot tell whether, or how rapidly, the weaker problem solvers would gradually acquire the style of the stronger, or whether rule searches would gradually disappear from a subject's protocols as he learned the functions and conditions for applicability of each of the rules.

S8's Learning. To throw some light on these questions, we shall take up next the behavior of S8, for whom we have a series of six protocols, beginning with D1 and C1 and continuing through problems A2′, B2, A4, and C3.

Problem A2′ is a variant of A2, produced by a typographical error. In A2′, L0 is T·T, L1 is P·(Q·R) and L2 is ∼(P ⊃ T) ⊃ ∼(P·Q). One solution plan is:

Plan.R11 Extract PQ and P from L1
R4 (⟹ (PQ)R)
R8 (⟹ PQ)
R8 (⟹ P)
Obtain T from L2
R11 (PQ, (PQ)(PT)) (⟹ PT)
R11 (P, PT) (⟹ T)
Double T
R3 (⟹ T·T)

A2′ is a problem of moderate difficulty. We recall that B2 is a difficult problem, while C3 and A4 are easy. S8 failed to solve A2′, but solved the other three, as well as D1 and C1.

Table 10.4 summarizes the style of S8 in each of the problems he attempted, where the items are the same as in Table 10.3. For comparison, the style of S9 in the two problems of Table 10.3 is shown in the final column of Table 10.4. A

TABLE 10.4

changes in style—S8 (and comparison with S9)

| | S8 | | | | | | S9 | |
PROBLEM:	D1	C1	A2′	B2	A4	C3	D1	C1
Expressions written	11	11	18	15	11	11	8	10
Solved problem	×	×		×	×	×	×	×
Searches rules	×	×						
Searches expressions	×	×	×	×				
Persistent								
Works backward			×	×	×		×	×
Gives general								
characterization				×	×	×	×	×

gradual shift of the style of S8 in the direction of S9's style is clearly apparent from the table.

After problem C1, S8 no longer searches through the rules. The protocols for the last four problems have many comments that show he now knows the functions of the rules:

A2′: (B5) Well, the first thing I think of when I see the two lines is ... sometime or another we are going to have to apply either R11 or R12.
(B12–B13) ... I've got too many terms there; some of them will have to be canceled out.

B2: (B62–B63) I want to change that wedge to a dot. And we'll do that by R5.

A4: (after solving) I don't have to refer to that paper much any more; I'm starting to remember the rules as I look at them.

C3: (B80–B86) (after solving) As soon as I see a term any more it reminds me of a certain rule, and that's the one. Actually these rules are separate; they seemed to be close together in the beginning . . . all mixed up. But now they're really getting far apart. I see a term, and it's there.

S8 continues to generate expressions working forward for the first three or four problems, and to scan these expressions to determine how to proceed, but no longer does this in the last two problems. (This change may not represent learning, but may simply reflect the fact that the problems were sufficiently easy that he did not have to conduct searches.) He works backward from L0 for the first time in A2′, and does so in all succeeding problems. On the last three problems S8 characterizes the problem at the outset, and on each of the last two he outlines a correct plan for its solution.

Quite early—toward the end of problem D1—S8 learned that a horseshoe could be changed to a dot by applying R6 followed by R5, and that this sequence would have the side consequence of putting a tilde before the expression, or removing one if it were already there. He evoked this same compound operation subsequently in problems A2 (B20–B22) and C3 (B65–B73).

Summarizing these changes, we can say that S8 (1) gradually acquired a table of connections, or associations, between features and differences on the one hand, and rules on the other; (2) shifted from a working-forward style to a style based on abstract characterization of the main problem features and planning; (3) learned that certain goals can be achieved by fixed sequences of certain operators.

S9's Learning. We can also test whether this particular movie will run in reverse. For we have protocols for S9 with the three practice problems, α1, α2, and α3, which he attempted just before D1 (Table 10.5). Will these earlier protocols of S9 show any of the characteristics of S8's earlier behavior?

TABLE 10.5

changes in style—S9 (and comparison with S8)

PROBLEM:	S8		S9—Problems					S8
	D1	C1	α1	α2	α3	D1	C1	C3
Expressions written	11	11	3	9	4	8	10	11
Solved problem	×	×	×		×	×	×	×
Searches rules	×	×	×	×	×			
Searches expressions	×	×						
Persistent								
Works backward						×	×	
Gives general characterization					×	×	×	×

In problem α1 (Appendix 9.1), S9 makes notes on his rule sheet, indicating the functions of the various rules (B13–B20): "I made a system out of this so I'd know exactly what I wanted. So here . . . like on R10 I made a note here . . . that addition; in R9 I had a choice; and R4 is a group change. So in all these I now have notes as to exactly what I can do with them . . . because if I just started looking at these rules, it's just about a hit-and-miss operation." S9 then proceeds by noticing differences, then searching the rules to find one appropriate for the difference.

In problem α2 (Appendix 10.14) S9 runs into difficulty, because he does not know that expressions can be split up, and the parts used as inputs to two-line rules. Hence, he fails to solve the problem. There are several extensive rule searches (e.g., B80–B94). In problem α3 (Appendix 10.15) he characterizes the problem fairly completely at the beginning (B4–B7) and conducts one extensive search through the rules (B19–B49).

In summary, S9's behavior on the practice problems resembles S8's early behavior more closely than S9's subsequent behavior, but it is beginning to shift toward the latter on the third training problem. He is clearly aware that one of his learning tasks is to learn the rules and their functions. He gives no evidence that he is aware of learning to plan and to characterize the main features of the problems.

CONCLUSION

In Part III we have ranged widely through the territory of logic problems. The landscape has resembled strongly what we have previously encountered in cryptarithmetic. The exploratory behavior of the human problem solvers in this environment reflected the structure and appearance of the landscape as viewed and explored by IPS's having limited capacities to detect patterns, to infer consequences, to remember paths of exploration, and to learn heuristic generalizations about the character of the landscape. The subjects behaved, in short, very much like a number of variant versions of GPS.

As a first approximation, the range of paths that a group of subjects will explore in a problem of this kind can be predicted by assuming that they will make exploration and solution plans based on (1) comparing starting point with desired goal, applying appropriate operators to reduce differences; (2) simplifying the initial expressions; (3) applying operators whose inputs strikingly resemble given expressions. To varying degrees, subgoals are set up to find operators that will modify expressions to make them fit operators that have been selected for application. The behavior of all of the subjects and all versions of GPS fit this first approximation. The variations provide second approximations. The variations lie in a number of dimensions:

1. Subjects differ (as does the same subject at different stages of learning) in the way in which they characterize the initial problem. They appear to learn gradually which differences should be given first priority in planning solutions, and which can be removed in the process of fitting operators to expressions.

2. Subjects differ in their persistence in pursuing a subgoal once it is formulated and, conversely, in their readiness to return to a consideration of the overall problem.

3. Subjects differ in the relative priority they give to working forward and to restructuring the problem in terms of information acquired while exploring, as compared with working backward and in the framework of a definite plan.

4. Subjects differ in the cues they use to detect cycling and lack of progress toward a goal.

5. Subjects differ in the extent to which they try to explore paths mentally, as against writing expressions on the board where they can examine them.

6. Subjects differ in the extent to which operators are associated in memory directly with differences or features, so that searches are not required to find appropriate operators.

7. Subjects acquire generalized knowledge that certain differences are not remediable (e.g., changing a single sign without changing a connective), hence should be signals for terminating exploration. They acquire generalized knowledge that certain goals can be achieved by fixed sequences of specific operators.

To a large extent these differences can be detected in protocols and used to account for the variety in style of the explorations of various subjects. We have shown also how relative problem difficulty is related to the presence or absence of particular capabilities in programs, and how the solvability of a problem can be estimated from the structure of the program.

APPENDIX 10.1

S8 on A2′

B1	[E writes L1: P·(Q·R)]
B2	[E writes L2: $\sim(P \supset T) \supset \sim(P \cdot Q)$]
B3	[E writes L0: T·T]
B4	Oh boy. Well, the first thing 1 think of when I see the two lines is . . .
B5	ah . . . sometime or another we are going to have to apply either rule 11 or 12.
B6	So, ah . . . and I would imagine since there's. . . .
B7	No, it could be either 11 or 12.
B8	I was going to say it matches 11, but not necessarily.
B9	I think the trick is. . . .
B10	Well, the major connectors are going to have to be horseshoes,
B11	because I am eventually going to work towards using rule 11 or 12.
B12	I've got too many terms there,
B13	some of them will have to be canceled out.
B14	So, ah . . . the major connector in L1 is a dot.
B15	Now, if I made that a horseshoe, where would I be?
B16	Well . . . ah . . . let's make it a horseshoe.

B17	It's going to give me negative terms, that's for sure.
B18	And negative terms are what I want,
B19	because in L2 they're negative terms.
B20	So I'll apply R5, first of all, to L1.
B21	And then we'll apply R6 to L3.
B22	Right off the bat. Get rid of the horseshoe.
B23	(E: R5 to L1.)
B24	Yeh.
B25	(E: Oh, the other way around.)
B26	(E: To the whole expressions or to just the parenthesis?)
B27	No, to the whole expression.
B28	Oh, yes, I see something . . . I might be jumping the gun
B29	because . . . ah . . . I see in the second . . .
B30	I want to get like quantities
B31	and I see that the second one has a P and a Q in it.
B32	[E writes L3: $\sim(\sim P \lor \sim(Q \cdot R))$]
B33	Ah, no, I don't like that at all.
B34	I should apply rule 4 or 7, I bet.
B35	In fact, I should apply R4 to. . . .
B36	Yeh. I should have applied R4 to L1 first.
B37	That would change the connectors and everything.
B38	That's going to be much better.
B39	[E writes L4: $(P \cdot Q) \cdot R$]
B40	Yeh, that's what I want . . . dot R.
B41	Well, now I see something else.
B42	Ah . . . if I apply R8 to that and get rid of the R,
B43	that leaves me with just $P \cdot Q$
B44	and that gives me the possibility of applying R11.
B45	So let's apply R8 to L4.
B46	(E: R8 to L4.)
B47	And that leaves what? That should leave me with just the A term, $P \cdot Q$.
B48	[E writes L5: $P \cdot Q$]
B49	Fine, now let's reverse around that horseshoe.
B50	Let's apply R2 to L2.
B51	Yeh, it even changes the sign.
B52	This is really working out perfect, so far.
B53	[E writes L6: $(P \cdot Q) \supset (P \supset T)$]
B54	Now apply R11 to lines 5 and 6,
B55	and the $P \cdot Q$'s cancel out.
B56	[E writes L7: $P \supset T$]
B57	$P \supset T$, right.
B58	Starting to get on to this a little bit.
B59	Now, that must be right.
B60	And now I want to get $T \cdot T$ from that.
B61	Well, back to that old rule.
B62	I wish I could remember what I did in the other ones. . . .
B63	I ended up with a horseshoe and I want to get into a dot,
B64	because I want to drop the T,
B65	but I can't get into a dot
B66	because it will give me a negative quantity.
B67	Well, ah . . . gee whiz . . . what'll I do?
B68	What can I apply?
B69	I'm thinking about 9 . . . for some reason 9 catches my eye.
B70	I could call that the A term, the whole expression, put that in parenthesis and add a wedge something.
B71	I wonder if that would prove anything?

B72   I don't think so. . . .

B73   Might get me into trouble.

B74   Of course, I could add anything I wanted.

B75   Ah . . . if I added the right stuff, could I come up with just a T?

B76   I don't know if you see what I mean.

B77   I'm looking for rule 4 and 7.

B78   I don't know if I see anything. . . .

B79   I don't eliminate any terms in rules 4 and 7,

B80   but if I added the right thing. . . .

B81   Too bad you can't work R10 backwards.

B82   That has a. . . .

B83   Can't seem to do it.

B84   Well, I guess R9 is out.

B85   I'm sitting here with a horseshoe . . . what can you do with a horseshoe?

B86   I can switch . . . reverse them.

B87   What would that do?

B88   Or . . . I could take double lines.

B89   What would that be?

B90   Ah . . . hey, I see a P Q up there, a P·Q.

B91   You can take any two lines out and apply R2 [R12?], can't you?

B92   I'd end up with Q T, I bet I could end up with a Q T,

B93   but a . . . no I wouldn't . . .

B94   well maybe. . . .

B95   You have to have what . . . a horseshoe between them?

B96   If I tried to convert L5 to a horseshoe, what would I get?

B97   I would get an . . . oh . . . a negative quantity . . . the whole thing would be negative.

B98   I was thinking about canceling out with R12,

B99   but I've got it down to P ⊃ T.

B100   Should be able to do something with that.

B101   You want to get to T·T.

B102   Let's work backwards once. . . .

B103   How on earth would you ever get T·T?

B104   Since you have only one T to begin with,

B105   that means you have to either work them into double quantities

B106   and then apply R4. . . .

B107   Hey, that's an idea . . . apply R4 . . . and you can apply it backwards.

B108   Wait a minute . . . just thinking here . . . rule 4 and 7 again seem to be the tricks.

B109   I can add anything I want.

B110   Well, right after that I'd have to get into a dot or a wedge,

B111   whatever is convenient.

B112   And, I can add anything I want with a wedge connector.

B113   Now, if I added a P ∨ T,

B114   and I converted that into a wedge there,

B115   that means they'd all be in wedges. . . .

B116   And if I converted that into a wedge, what would I have?

B117   Doggone, I'd have a negative P.

B118   Well, I could add a negative P,

B119   what's the difference,

B120   and then you'd apply . . .

B121   I'd have to apply R7,

B122   since I'd have two quantities.

B123   So if I applied R7 I would get . . .

B124   I'd have to have dots in there instead of a wedge connector,

B125   and I would have to have a wedge connector.

B126   Getting things all jumbled up here in my mind.

B127   Well, if I changed that to a dot, what would I have?

B128	Oh, a horseshoe, a dot . . .
B129	its all balled up.
B130	I'd eventually get a $\sim(A \cdot \sim B)$.
B131	And then I can add a tilde. . . .
B132	What's the difference? . . . no signs change.
B133	I could add a tilde quantity A . . . anything . . . T for instance.
B134	So then I have a T,
B135	and I can take it backwards.
B136	You know I think that's it.
B137	Because if I take it backwards,
B138	I'm going to end up with the two T's in the same quantity and the tilde T outside connected with a dot.
B139	And if they're connected with a dot, you can always drop one of them.
B140	I think I've got it.
B141	First of all, to L7, we have to convert that to a dot,
B142	and we do that with R6,
B143	and then right away R5.
B144	(E: Convert it to a wedge?)
B145	Yeh, and from a wedge you apply R5
B146	and get it into a dot.
B147	[E writes L8: $\sim P \vee T$]
B148	OK. Now let's get it into a dot.
B149	[E writes L9: $\sim(P \cdot \sim T)$]
B150	OK. That's all right.
B151	Now we can call that expression A, and we can add anything we want with a wedge according to R9.
B152	Now we are going to have to watch what we add.
B153	We are going to have to apply R9 to L9. That's for sure.
B154	So put that up,
B155	and just what we're going to add yet, I don't know.
B156	Well, start off at the beginning. . . .
B157	You can't change it, can you?
B158	[E writes L10 (first part): $\sim(P \cdot \sim T)$]
B159	Now we will add wedge,
B160	and I think we had better add exactly the same thing . . .
B161	Besides, you can have two $\sim$ T's and call one B and one C,
B162	because that's how I missed so many questions on that test.
B163	(E: Now you're adding the same thing.)
B164	[E writes L10: $\sim(P \cdot \sim T) \vee \sim(P \cdot \sim T)$]
B165	Yeh, now if ah . . . now that should apply to the second part of R7 in reverse very nicely, that is . . . from right to left, the second part.
B166	So apply R7 to L10,
B167	and you get. . . .
B168	I don't know what you'll get. . . .
B169	What do you do about that tilde quantity?
B170	(E: I don't think it applies now.)
B171	Well, it doesn't say anything about it not being negative . . .
B172	These sheets only tell you what you can't do.
B173	(E: That's right.)
B174	And it doesn't say it can't be negative.
B175	(E: Well, what would you get?)
B176	I don't know . . . if the whole quantity is negative,
B177	I can only think in terms of mathematics.
B178	(E: I don't think it's applicable.)
B179	Heck, well I would get, forgetting about the signs, $P \cdot (P \vee T)$,
B180	and by R8 I can drop it see.

B181	Oh, it would probably be $\sim P \vee \sim P$,
B182	and by R8 I can drop the P
B183	because they are connected by dots,
B184	and then I have $\sim P \vee \sim T$.
B185	Then if I convert....
B186	Yeh, ha, ha, and there would probably be a tilde outside.
B187	If I converted that to a dot,
B188	I would get $T \cdot T$.
B189	Here's what I think L10 goes into....
B190	But I guess your solution isn't this way, huh?
B191	I say, L10, if you apply R7 to it,
B192	it will be $P \cdot \sim (\sim T \cdot \sim T)$.
B193	(E: Well, maybe that's what you hope it will be,)
B194	(E: but I don't see how R7 will bring it into that.)
B195	(E: I don't think R7 is applicable here when you have a tilde outside the parenthesis.)
B196	Well, darn it.
B197	(E: It would be nice if it was changed into that.)
B198	Yeh, it would work out.
B199	Well, at least I know it won't work that way,
B200	so I guess I had better try something else.
B201	OK. Here we go, all the way back.
B202	Well, what are we going to look at.
B203	Let's not go back too far.
B204	Well, we know that all the way up to L7 is pretty good, I think.
B205	Kind of proud of that.
B206	But, I was sitting there with $P \supset T$.
B207	Now what do we have back there that we can do something with?
B208	What can I get that into?
B209	I see by R11....
B210	No, that won't exactly work....
B211	I was thinking of canceling them out . . . line 6 or 7,
B212	but I have an A B with a B underneath,
B213	and if I invert it
B214	I will get a negative sign.
B215	That'll never work.
B216	What else can I do?
B217	I like this R10 suddenly,
B218	because you can take any two lines and connect them with a dot,
B219	which means that I can take any two lines up there, connect them with a dot,
B220	and drop one of them out.
B221	So what can I get from that?
B222	I have to keep T in my terms all the time.
B223	That's for sure because....
B224	And what's the closest I've gotten to $T \cdot T$?
B225	I've got $\sim (P \cdot \sim T)$. What can I do with that?
B226	Right in front of me I've got $\sim P \vee T$.
B227	If I changed that to a dot,
B228	I'd have the total quantity, sonofagun, tilde the quantity.
B229	I would have applied R8,
B230	and ended up with just T.
B231	That would have been nice.
B232	Well, what can you do?
B233	Maybe I should go back to the original.
B234	What else can I do to it?
B235	I extracted the $P \supset P$ [$P \supset T$] from the first . . . from the original.
B236	Now let's extract something else, maybe.

B237   I dunno, though.
B238   T horseshoe T [T, horseshoe T ?].
B239   I don't see anything else that would be worthwhile.
B240   T is the only thing I really want
B241   and maybe I can work that. . . .
B242   I like R11, too.
B243   If I could get just a plain P
B244   it would cancel out
B245   and I would end up with my T.
B246   I don't know why I want to end up with T.
B247   Maybe I can apply R12.
B248 $P \supset T$.
B249   Now if I ended up with anything horseshoe P,
B250   for instance, I have $P \cdot Q$.
B251   If I convert that into a horseshoe,
B252   that's the big step again,
B253   and that would give me a $P \cdot Q$ into a horseshoe,
B254   would reverse all the signs,
B255   and get negative quantity
B256   and I don't see how we can cancel out negative quantities.
B257   What can I do to it?
B258   See, I want maybe to apply R12.
B259   I'll need something horseshoe P,
B260   preferably $T \supset P$.
B261   What can I get to get that.
B262   Oh, I have a $P \cdot Q$. . . .
B263   I don't see much at all, now . . . it keeps getting dimmer and dimmer.
B264   Gee, what do I have down below?
B265   Nothing.
B266   Gee, I wish I could apply R7.
B267   What can I do with that $P \supset T \ldots P \supset T$.
B268   No sense going around it there.
B269   That's something.
B270   Let me look through here.
B271   Oh . . . what can I do with a horseshoe alone. . . .
B272   You can invert it,
B273   and you can change it,
B274   or you can use 11 and 12 . . .
B275   Those are the only things you can do with a horseshoe.
B276   Well, if I change it, I can then. . . .
B277   Oh, oh, I see something.
B278   R3, working backwards,
B279   R3 says that $T \cdot T$ is equal to T.
B280   So that all I have to do is end up with a T
B281   and I've got it,
B282   because I can apply R3
B283   and get $T \cdot T$.
B284   Let's work backwards.
B285   If I had just a T,
B286   how would I go about getting $P \supset T$?
B287   That might be taking too big a jump,
B288   so I'd apply the wedge rule
B289   and I'd have a $T \lor P$.
B290   And if I change it to a horseshoe,
B291   I'd have to change the sign of the A part,
B292   and it would be $\sim T \supset P$.

B293   Boy, you know that's darn close
B294   because you know. . . .
B295   Oh, I can add minus P. . . .
B296   I think I've got it.
B297   Take down L7 and apply R2 to it
B298   I think I've got it for sure.
B299   If I can remember what I said.
B300   [E writes L11: $\sim T \supset \sim P$]
B301   Yeh, $\sim T \supset \sim P$.
B302   Now convert that to a wedge.
B303   It doesn't work out.
B304   If I convert it to a wedge, I'll get $T \supset \sim P \ldots T < \sim P$.
B305   Now we have to drop the wedge $\sim P$.
B306   Working backwards you are allowed to do it that way.
B307   I worked it backwards and it worked out.
B308   What did I do?
B309   I said that I wanted $T \cdot T$
B310   and that is equal to T.
B311   Well, if I have a T. . . .
B312   Oh, I was working forward, not backwards.
B313   I applied R9 to T,
B314   but what the heck, that's working forwards again,
B315   'cause you can't apply the opposite to R9.
B316 $\sim T$.
B317   Now I should get that into $T \lor \sim P$.
B318   What can you do?
B319   You can get that into a dot,
B320   but that will give you a negative quantity.
B321   Doggone, well, if that isn't something.
B322   Thought I had it the other way.
B323   Of course, that's kind of cheating anyway.
B324   Now what are we going to do?
B325   Still can't do a thing with that.
B326   Still can't. . . .
B327   Wait, wait a minute, what am I thinking of.
B328   They're both in horseshoes.
B329   Can I cancel anything. . . .
B330   No, not a $\sim P$, a P.
B331   That will never do.
B332   What a mess.
B333   I can get them into dots,
B334   and get a dot connector.
B335   Oh wait, that's an idea, going back to that dot connector.
B336   That's working on what I did before, but on a little different basis though.
B337   If I can get them into. . . .
B338   Oh, I've got an idea . . . my trouble before in applying R7 was the fact
B339   that I had the minor connectors as dots,
B340   which gave me negative quantities which didn't apply the rule.
B341   If they are not dots,
B342   I don't have negative quantities,
B343   and that means I will be able to apply the rule.
B344   Why do I want to go all the way to 7?
B345   Oh, I see why, I got an idea, because the major connector was a wedge
B346   before, so the minor connectors had to be dots.
B347   But if I apply R10 to L7 and anything,
B348   7 and 11,

B349	then I'd have a dot for a major connector, and I could have wedges.
B350	And that will mean, since they are already similar,
B351	that I will be able to work into something that won't be a negative quantity.
B352	If I apply R2 to L7. . . .
B353	Oh, I already did that and got L11.
B354	Well, if I do it again,
B355	and get L12
B356	and connect them with dots,
B357	and change the sign
B358	and the minor connector into a wedge,
B359	I'll have the $(T \vee \sim P) \cdot (T \vee \sim P)$.
B360	And with that I can take out the T.
B361	After I've got it, and have $T \cdot (\sim P \vee \sim P)$.
B362	By R8 I can drop the second part
B363	and have just T,
B364	and from T I get $T \cdot T$.
B365	To L7 apply R2 again.
B366	(E: That will take you back to L11.)
B367	That's all right.
B368	(E: You've got L11.)
B369	No, from L7 apply R2
B370	and you get L12.
B371	Now to L12 do the same thing.
B372	(E: Oh, I see, oh, OK.)
B373	Now let me think.
B374	(E: 11 and 12 are the same.)
B375	[E writes L12: $\sim T \supset \sim P$]
B376	Now, to L11 apply R6.
B377	We've got it.
B378	[E writes L13: $T \vee \sim P$]
B379	And do the same thing to L12 to get L14, apply R6.
B380	[E writes L14: $T \vee \sim P$]
B381	Right. Now apply R10 to lines 13 and 14,
B382	and they'll be connected by dots, ha, ha.
B383	[E writes L15: $(T \vee \sim P) \cdot (T \vee \sim P)$]
B384	Yeh. Now apply R7 to L15.
B385	[E writes L16: $T \vee (\sim P \cdot \sim P)$]
B386	Sonofagun, that's right, doggone.
B387	I've got a wedge. . . .
B388	Got my connectors mixed up.
B389	Yeh, that's it, wouldn't you know it.
B390	Now wait a minute, wait a minute, I can still do it.
B391	Sure, if I change the wedge into a . . . dot,
B392	it's going to give me a negative.
B393	After all that.
B394	Well, maybe I can work in separate steps.
B395	I can easily drop one of the $\sim P$'s
B396	by applying R8 just to that.
B397	And that will give me $T \vee \sim P$,
B398	which I could have gotten from L7,
B399	without going through all of this.
B400	Sonofagun.
B401	What can I do with that major connector besides convert it?
B402	I can reverse around it.
B403	What can you reverse. . . .
B404	Or can you invert?

B405	Oh, you can invert without changing signs or anything, just plain invert.
B406	Well, I should have known that wouldn't give me anything
B407	because when you create two lines identical,
B408	that's going to get you into a paper bag.
B409	Well, ah . . . I can get just a ~P,
B410	and then I'll have T ∨ ~P.
B411	Oh, I see something.
B412	L8 says just the opposite.
B413	If I can change wedges into horseshoes,
B414	I can apply R12.
B415	By changing them into horseshoes
B416	all you do is change the sign into the first one.
B417	But then I'd have T ⊃ T.
B418	Well, I don't want to think this out, I want you to write.
B419	Apply . . . this is round-about . . . apply R3 to just part of L16.
B420	(E: R3 to L16. How do you do that?)
B421	Well, just part of it, on the B part.
B422	[E writes L17: T ∨ ~P]
B423	(E: You have that all sorts of places.)
B424	Oh, I do, don't I. OK.
B425	Then let's take T ∨ ~P, and L8 is ~P ∨ T, I can cancel out the ~P's I guess,
B426	and get T ∨ T.
B427	No you can't.
B428	You have to change it to horseshoes.
B429	Change line 13 or 14 into horseshoes by R6.
B430	[E writes L18: ~T ⊃ ~P]
B431	Yeh. And then you can do that to L8.
B432	[E writes L19: P ⊃ T]
B433	Darn, can't even apply that rule.
B434	(E: I think we better quit.)
B435	I think I lost that one.

APPENDIX 10.2

S8 on B2

B1	[E writes L1: (P ∨ Q) ⊃ ~(~R ∨ P)]
B2	[E writes L2: ~(~(S·Q) ∨ R)]
B3	[E writes L0: ~Q]
B4	(E: You're going for ~Q.)
B5	~Q. Not too much doubt about that.
B6	First you've got to eliminate everything down.
B7	When I see a ~Q it reminds me of one I had the other day, T·T.
B8	Since there's a Q in both steps 1 and 2,
B9	if we get it down to just ~Q·~Q,
B10	that will be equal to just ~Q.
B11	So, I think that's what we're going to get it down to.
B12	I dunno, it just strikes me that way.
B13	If we can get it down to just a Q in each line,
B14	in fact, if I want to work it backwards to get it to ~Q·~Q,
B15	why, if I can get it down to ~Q in each line,
B16	I can apply R10,

B17	and just put it that way.
B18	So that seems to be the thing . . . try and . . .
B19	work each line separately
B20	and try to get it down to a $\sim$Q.
B21	I don't know though yet.
B22	Well let's look at it first.
B23	If I am going to go by that theory and try to get it down,
B24	maybe I should change the major connector in L1 to a dot.
B25	But in a way I think I can't,
B26	because it will make the whole term into negative.
B27	That won't do any good.
B28	Oh, I know something else.
B29	On the second line, if I change that major connector to a dot,
B30	that will enable me to change the signs.
B31	The whole thing will be negative,
B32	and I will be able to drop a term.
B33	So apply R5 to L2.
B34	[E writes L3: $(S \cdot Q) \cdot \sim R$]
B35	Fine. Then according to R8
B36	I would get. . . .
B37	Oh, let's let that ride,
B38	because right off the bat I would say drop the $\sim$R.
B39	But I see a $\sim$R in the above term,
B40	and maybe will [we'll] be able to cancel out eventually.
B41	Anyhow, let's leave that there for the time being. . . .
B42	I'll try to remember that I can drop either one of them anytime I want.
B43	Well, wait a minute now.
B44	No, no.
B45	Let's apply R8 to L3 and drop just the $\sim$R.
B46	[E writes L4: $S \cdot Q$]
B47	Then you can apply R8 again to L4 and get Q.
B48	I can't see too far into the future yet,
B49	but at least I have one line down to a . . .
B50	[E writes L5: Q]
B51	a Q.
B52	Let's try to get L1 down to a Q.
B53	That's going to be a little bit rough,
B54	because I can't change it to a dot
B55	and I can't drop one of the terms.
B56	What else can I do?
B57	Well, I can apply. . . .
B58	I know what I can do . . .
B59	I can apply R8 eventually to just one part of the term.
B60	Now what I mean is let's apply rule. . . .
B61	I want to change it to a dot, the minor connector of the second part, part B, see in L1 . . .
B62	I want to change that wedge to a dot.
B63	And we'll do that by R5.
B64	(E: R5 to L1.)
B65	See, that'll get us to a dot
B66	and then we can drop part of that.
B67	We'll call that term A and B.
B68	This is what will [we'll] change.
B69	[E writes L6: $(P \vee Q) \supset (R \cdot \sim P)$]
B70	Yeh. Now I can drop either the R or $\sim$P if I want.
B71	Maybe I jumped the gun there because. . . .

B72	Oh, wait a minute. . . . As I look at that I see a P in the other term, too.
B73	You know, one way of killing two birds with one stone would be that rule 7 or 4 again.
B74	If I can get them separated and get a dot between.
B75	That means I will be working with the second part of 7 or 4.
B76	And it will probably be, yeh, R7.
B77	You see I can get those two things together
B78	but I need a wedge for a major connector though.
B79	Well, that doesn't seem too difficult.
B80	To L6 apply R6.
B81	[E writes L7: $\sim$(P $\vee$ Q) $\vee$ (R $\cdot \sim$P)]
B82	All right, now I want to get that other minor connector to a dot,
B83	in order to apply 7B.
B84	So apply R5 to just the A part of L7.
B85	[E writes L8: ($\sim$P$\cdot\sim$Q) $\vee$ (R$\cdot\sim$P)]
B86	Well, ah, according to R1,
B87	I can invert them around a dot without any trouble.
B88	So apply R1 to L8, just the B part.
B89	[E writes L9: ($\sim$P$\cdot\sim$Q) $\vee$ ($\sim$P$\cdot$R)]
B90	Good. Now apply R7 to part B, to L9.
B91	(E: 7 to 9.)
B92	[E writes L10: $\sim$P$\cdot$($\sim$Q $\vee$ R)]
B93	The only thing that worries me is the $\sim$Q.
B94	That's the final answer,
B95	and I have a Q in L5. . . .
B96	Well, maybe it will work out.
B97	Ah, I can drop either one of them
B98	by applying R8.
B99	I will probably drop the $\sim$P,
B100	because I can't see any sense in keeping that.
B101	Sitting here with a $\sim$Q $\vee$ R.
B102	Then what happens after that?
B103	Well, while I'm looking at it,
B104	apply R8 to L10 and end up with a $\sim$Q $\vee$ R.
B105	[E writes L11: $\sim$Q $\vee$ R]
B106	Now what.
B107	L5, L11, two key lines.
B108	I wish L5 was a $\sim$Q.
B109	Well, what can you do to a wedge. . . .
B110	Let's see, you can convert them,
B111	but that won't do any good.
B112	Reverse them.
B113	They're not the same,
B114	so I can't use L3.
B115	4 and 7 never work.
B116	I could change it to a dot. . . .
B117	That wouldn't do anything . . .
B118	just make it a negative term,
B119	kind of mix it up.
B120	I could change it to a horseshoe.
B121	But if I change it to a horseshoe, I could be in a mess,
B122	'cause I'd end up up with a $\sim$R.
B123	If I applied R6 to it,
B124	it would make it a Q $\supset \sim$R.
B125	And lines 5 and 11 would cancel the Q's.
B126	I'd end up with just a $\sim$R
B127	and I need a $\sim$Q.

B128	That's a sonofagun.
B129	Oh, I got an idea, got an idea.
B130	Remember, I jumped the gun, remember back on L3, I can drop either one.
B131	Let's apply R8 to L3 and drop the other one,
B132	and end up with just a $\sim$R.
B133	[E writes L12: $\sim$R]
B134	Yeh, now we're getting somewhere.
B135	Now apply R6 to L11.
B136	Reverse it.
B137	No, make it a horseshoe and change the sign.
B138	Oh, wait, that won't quite do it.
B139	[E writes L13: Q $\supset$ R]
B140	Oh, that's not so good.
B141	(E: Q $\supset$ R.)
B142	Oh, yes it is,
B143	because I can apply R2 to it
B144	and reverse them around.
B145	Apply R2 to 13.
B146	[E writes L14: $\sim$R $\supset$ $\sim$Q]
B147	OK, apply R11 to lines 12 and 14,
B148	and that gives you the answer.
B149	Hallelujah!
B150	(E: That gives you the answer, $\sim$Q.)
B151	[E writes L15: $\sim$Q]

APPENDIX 10.3

S8 on A4

B1	(E: This has got a lot of things to start with.)
B2	I keep thinking about the past ones.
B3	Every one, the way I got it, I would be on the wrong track.
B4	And then it would be right there plain as the nose on my face.
B5	And like the one I didn't get at all . . . like the one I didn't get. . . .
B6	Steps 5 and 7 were so similar.
B7	I kept saying "5 and 7," "5 and 7," and I couldn't even see it.
B8	It's always the obvious.
B9	[E writes L1: P $\vee$ Q]
B10	[E writes L2: $\sim$R $\supset$ $\sim$Q]
B11	[E writes L3: S]
B12	[E writes L4: R $\supset$ $\sim$S]
B13	[E writes L0: P $\vee$ T]
B14	Well, one possibility right off the bat is when you have just a P $\vee$ T like that,
B15	the last thing you might use is that R9.
B16	I can get everything down to a P
B17	and just add a wedge T.
B18	So, that's one thing to keep in mind.
B19	Well, maybe right off the bat,
B20	I'm kinda jumping into it,
B21	I maybe can work everything down to just a P.
B22	I dunno if that's possible.
B23	But I think it is,

B24	because I see that steps 2 and 4 are somewhat similar.
B25	If I can cancel out the R's,
B26	that would leave me with just an S and Q,
B27	and if I have just an S and Q,
B28	I can eventually get L3, get the S's to cancel out,
B29	and end up with just a Q.
B30	And if I end up with just a Q, maybe the Q's will cancel out.
B31	So you see, all the way down the line.
B32	I dunno, it looks too good to be true,
B33	but I think I see it already.
B34	Steps 2 and 4,
B35	we'll have to do something about them.
B36	If I invert step 4, L4 that is . . .
B37	apply R2 to it . . .
B38	I will have an $S \supset \sim R$.
B39	Good.
B40	OK. Apply R2 to L4.
B41	[E writes L5: $S \supset \sim R$]
B42	Now apply R12 to L2 and L4 . . .
B43	2 and 5, I mean.
B44	[E writes L6: $S \supset \sim Q$]
B45	Right. Got rid of the R's.
B46	Now apply R11 to L6 and L3.
B47	Oh, that's it . . . too easy!
B48	Something's going to backfire.
B49	(E: That'll give you what?)
B50	$\sim Q$.
B51	[E writes L7: $\sim Q$]
B52	Now you have $P \lor Q$ and $\sim Q$.
B53	I would like to apply R11 to 1 and 7,
B54	but I've first going to have to change L1 to a horseshoe.
B55	So change L1 to a horseshoe.
B56	Apply R6 to it.
B57	I think this is it . . . I think we got it.
B58	[E writes L8: $\sim P \supset Q$]
B59	Yeh. Oh, it would, wouldn't it!
B60	OK, Apply R2 to L8.
B61	Hey, I think this is going to work real fine.
B62	[E writes L9: $\sim Q \supset P$]
B63	Now apply R11 to L9 and L7.
B64	[E writes L10: P]
B65	Heh, heh, heh, heh, heh, I feel good now.
B66	Well, apply R9 to L10,
B67	and that's it.
B68	[E writes L11: $P \lor T$]

APPENDIX 10.4

S8 on C3

B1	These things must get real difficult when they get into the coding part. . . .
B2	They must have more than three letters.

B3	(E: Yeh. I'll tell you about that.)
B4	[E writes L1: ~S]
B5	[E writes L2: R ∨ S]
B6	[E writes L3: (P ⊃ Q) ⊃ ~R]
B7	Oh boy.
B8	(E: That's what you've got to start with.)
B9	(E: And you're going for ~Q again.)
B10	[E writes L0: ~Q]
B11	~Q again.
B12	Well, we're up to all the tricks on how to get ~Q.
B13	There is only one Q in the whole thing.
B14	And right off the bat I see one thing, if it's possible.
B15	I would say rearrange L2
B16	So you can cancel the S's out,
B17	with L1, L2.
B18	And you end up with just an R.
B19	And work it out so L2 and L3 will cancel out,
B20	because that's a horseshoe connector.
B21	See what I mean?
B22	We're going to apply R11
B23	to cut them out right off the bat.
B24	Ah, I guess we're going to have to do something.
B25	I guess if we're going to apply R11,
B26	we are going to have to get the major connector in L2 into a horseshoe.
B27	So we'll see what we get if we change L2
B28	when we apply R6.
B29	Ah, that's going to work right out.
B30	[E writes L4: ~R ⊃ S]
B31	Well, apply 2 to it.
B32	Change the signs
B33	and change it around.
B34	[E writes L5: ~S ⊃ R]
B35	That's good.
B36	Now apply R11 to L1 and L5
B37	and end up with just R.
B38	[E writes L6: R]
B39	Just R.
B40	Now ah . . . if we apply R2 to L3,
B41	you are going to change the signs around . . .
B42	reverse it and change the signs.
B43	So apply R2 to L3.
B44	[E writes L7: R ⊃ ~(P ⊃ Q)]
B45	Oh, I think you've got a mistake up there.
B46	(E: Could be.)
B47	It's not much . . . it doesn't mean anything.
B48	On line . . . in your second step in the fourth quadrant.
B49	Is that applying R2 to L3?
B50	That's applying it to L4.
B51	(E: Oh.)
B52	I don't think it will mean anything.
B53	(E: Which did you want to do?)
B54	You worked it out the right way,
B55	but you wrote it down wrong.
B56	(E: I see, you wanted to apply R2 to L4.)
B57	Now you can apply R11 to L6 and L7
B58	(E: 11 to 6 and 7, OK.)

B59	I see something.
B60	[E writes L8: ~(P ⊃ Q)]
B61	That tilde right away strikes a bell.
B62	Since it is a negative quantity.
B63	I bet, if we changed it. . . .
B64	Oh, this is going to work right out.
B65	Let's change it to a dot,
B66	because the negative quantity will then be positive.
B67	Apply R6 to L8.
B68	Everything's gonna work out real nice.
B69	(E: That will give you. . . .)
B70	That will be (~P ∨ Q).
B71	I think you can do that with a negative expression. . . .
B72	[E writes L9: ~(~P ∨ Q)]
B73	Yeh, sure. Because you're going to apply R5 to L9 now.
B74	(E: You want 5 to 9.)
B75	[E writes L10: P·~Q]
B76	P on Q. Yeh.
B77	Now you can apply R8 to L10 and drop the P.
B78	And there you are.
B79	[E writes L11: ~Q]
B80	As soon as I see a term anymore, it reminds me of a certain rule,
B81	and that's the one.
B82	Actually, these rules are separate.
B83	They seemed to be close together in the beginning . . . all mixed up.
B84	But now they're really getting far apart.
B85	(E: Uh huh.)
B86	I see a term and it's there.
B87	(E: Uh huh. I can see how.)
B88	See how I get on.
B89	(E: Kinda short today.)
B90	Yeh. I should've played dumb and made more money.

APPENDIX 10.5

S2 on C1

B1	[E writes L1: (P ∨ Q)·(Q ⊃ R)]
B2	[E writes L0: P ∨ (Q·R)]
E1	
B3	Well, now on this one, we want to change. . . .
B4	Get rid of the Q in that first part, I can see that.
B5	Get rid of the Q and also change it to a dot . . . from a dot to a wedge function.
B6	R8 seems to be a nice one to get rid of some of the terms,
B7	but I don't know if I want to or not, yet.
B8	Um . . . let's see, if I change . . . well, let's see, if I change the . . .
B9	or if I could invert it that would. . . .
B10	Well, I can take either one.
B11	Apply R8 to that and let's see. . . .
B12	(E: Want 8?)
B13	8 to that,

B14	but I want to see which one I want to keep.
B15	Ah . . . yeah . . . may as well . . . I want to keep Q ∨ R.
B16	[E writes L2: Q ⊃ R]
B17	Q ∨ R . . . I mean not Q . . . Q ⊃ R.
B18	Now, Q ⊃ R can be written as a wedge function.
B19	So that would be applying R6 to that.
B20	[E writes L3: ∼Q ∨ R]
B21	Now . . . um . . . let's see. If I keep. . . .
B22	Apply R8, also to L1, and keeping the other one, keeping the P ∨ Q. . . .
B23	[E writes L4: P ∨ Q]
B24	P ∨ Q . . . . Now, looking over my . . . see what I have to do with wedges.
B25	Can write 'em as dot functions,
B26	but that's not going to help.
B27	Horseshoe . . . P ∨ Q can also be. . . .
B28	Apply R6 in a reverse way to 4
B29	is tilde . . . ∼P ⊃ B.
B30	[E writes L5: ∼P ⊃ Q]
B31	Now if I could change these to one of the dot functions . . .
B32	not too much I can change it to a dot function. . . .
B33	Use R8.

E2

B34	Horseshoes, R12 . . . uses horseshoes and there I could write . . . ah. . . .
B35	Yeah, I could apply R12 to L2 and L5.
B36	Let's see, and that would make Q would be on top.
B37	[E writes L6: R ⊃ ∼P] [Error: should be ∼P ⊃ R.]
B38	R horseshoe tilde. . . .
B39	Okay, now looking . . . now I see a correlation in R7 with the answer,
B40	so if I can get these all wedges. . . .
B41	If I apply R6 to L6
B42	and that will give me ∼R . . . ah . . . ∼P.
B43	[E writes L7: ∼R ∨ ∼P]
B44	Let's see, how can I change my horseshoes around?
B45	Either that. . . .
B46	Go back and apply R2 also to R6 [L6]. . . .
B47	(E: That'd be ∼R . . . no, beg your pardon . . . P ⊃ ∼R.)
B48	[E writes L8: P ⊃ ∼R]
B49	Let's see, yeah, now if I apply R6 to that . . . to, what step number is that . . . 8, 6 to 8.
B50	[E writes L9: ∼P ∨ ∼R]
B51	Uh huh, let me see, that'd still give me the same thing.
B52	The only difference is that it's switched around.
B53	Uh . . . that'll give me negative function
B54	if I change that to dots.
B55	So I'm not going to change it.
B56	Somehow if I could get rid of my signs . . . don't like the negative signs.

E3

B57	Trying to get a correlation in . . . somehow in 7, that's (A ∨ B)·(A ∨ C).
B58	So that would be P ∨ Q . . . be P ∨ Q. . . .
B59	(E: I'm sorry, what did you want?)
B60	I was just thinking on trying to . . . using R7 in there,
B61	but before I could do it, before I'd want to get that far, I'd want to change my tildes to positive numbers.
B62	I practically have it, I think.
B63	If I could change those positive letters somehow.
B64	Um . . . sign changes aren't too frequent

B65   and then they don't give me the right ones.

B66   I could . . . well, I could get close to the answer

B67   if I applied R7 to. . . .

B68   Hum, wait a minute. This would mean I'd have to get these in dot functions first of all.

B69   That would mean applying R10 to step . . . ah . . . let's see, that would be steps 4 and 9, I think.

B70   (E: R10 to 4. . . .)

B71   No, but that won't work because . . . huh uh, that won't work.

E4

B72   That won't work because I've got to get a positive P instead of a negative P

B73   in order for my A's to fit into what I want in 7.

B74   So somewhere I've got to go back and look in my steps and see somewhere I can change . . . um. . . .

B75   I can change Q to wedge R.

B76   I'm back on L2.

B77   I'm going back on my steps

B78   because I think I'm on the right track,

B79   but I somehow I've got to change my . . .

B80 $\sim Q \vee R. \sim Q \vee R$ . . .

B81 $P \vee Q$. . . .

B82   And I changed my wedges.

B83   I can change my wedges . . . I can change 'em to dots,

B84   but I don't want that.

B85   Either that . . . A, B yields $A \cdot B$,

B86   that would give me dots.

B87   Ah . . . if I apply R10 . . . R10 to um . . .

B88   Let me see, taking 2 and. . . .

B89   Wait a minute, wait a minute . . . that's a different sign.

B90   That won't work.

E5

B91   Apply R10 somewhere

B92   and that would give me a dot function,

B93   but the only trouble is I don't know where to apply it.

B94   I can feel it, but I don't know where to put it.

B95   1 and. . . .

B96   No, that seems like too complicated a function

B97   if I'm going to apply R10 back on step 1 and another step.

B98   Um . . . somehow apply R7 and R10 to get what I want.

B99   But that doesn't seem to be working out.

E6

B100   Where am I now . . . I'm at $\sim P \vee Q$

B101   and R3 doesn't help me too much.

B102   And R2 will change the signs to wedges . . .

B103   if I went back and changed all the signs to wedge

B104   then that won't give me . . .

B105   but that's just reverses it . . .

B106   and R6 to get me what I want . . .

B107   wedges, wedges, wedges.

B108   I can invert. . . .

B109   I can get a more complicated function if I use something like that.

B110   I can't use 9. . . .

B111   Double function on 10 . . . would give me a dot,

B112   but that's not going to help too much I don't think.

E7

B113   Or 12 will give me something. . . .

B114   I've got to have B there . . . positive Q's anywhere . . . that are wedges . . . horseshoe . . . [few words garbled].

B115   Try R12 on 6 and 8.

B116   (E: R12 on 6 and 8.)

B117   So that gives me P horseshoe . . . 6 and 8 would give me. . . .

B118   (E: Sorry . . . sorry)

B119   That would give me R just. . . .

B120   (E: All right . . . 6 and 8, apply 12.)

B121   That won't work. Can't do it.

B122   (E: No, that won't work.)

B123   On . . . that came out with a horseshoe . . . I can't work it on 6 and 8,

B124   'cause I forgot the sign there.

B125   P $\lor$ Q . . . $\sim$P. . . .

B126   I'm trying to apply a two-line rule,

B127   but I don't know where it would get me anywhere.

B128   And I don't have the right signs in there to change.

E8

B129   Ah . . . let's see, on 9, if we rewrote that . . .

B130   applying R5 to 9.

B131   So that would give me tilde P wedge dot R, I think.

B132   [E writes L10: $\sim$(P$\cdot$R)]

B133 $\sim$(P$\cdot$R). . . .

B134   I can't apply R8

B135   'cause it's got no negative sign in front . . .

B136   um . . . P$\cdot$R, P wedge Q, R . . . [(PR)(PQ), R . . . ? PR, PQ, R . . . ? PR, P(QR) . . .?]

B137   7,

B138   if I could get somehow wedges into dots.

E9.1

B139   See, P . . . looking at the beginning step, I have part of what I want in that, P $\lor$ Q.

B140   And that will give me P wedge, I mean Q$\cdot$C, and what I . . .

B141   that's a horseshoe R, isn't it?

B142   So I would have to apply a rule on the horseshoe,

B143   that would give me a negative . . .

B144   applying R6 to part of that would give me . . .

B145   wouldn't give me what I wanted, I don't think.

B146   Ah . . . we'll apply it anyway.

B147   Apply R6 to the second part of L1,

B148   so that I would get dot. . . .

B149   [E writes L11: (P $\lor$ Q)$\cdot$($\sim$Q $\lor$ R)]

B150   This is A . . .

B151   still not what I want I don't think.

B152   'Cause I want two A's in there

B153   and I've got P and a negative Q

B154   and I've got to change that to get a P $\lor$ C.

B155   Hum . . . that would give me a negative Q.

B156   Applying rule . . . what rule is that. . . .

B157   Applying R8 to the second part of that step . . .

B158   to give me a negative. . . .

B159   (E: 11?)

B160   Repeating myself again.

B161 $\sim$Q $\lor$ R . . . hum. . . .

B162   (E: Second part?)

B163   Yeah, well that would just give me. . . .

B164	(E: R8?)
B165	Yeah . . . A·B will just give me B . . . leads to B.
B166	(E: Oh, I see, you want to drop the . . . [garbled]. . . .)
B167	No, I want to drop the first part and keep the second part.
B168	[E writes L12: ~Q ∨ R]
B169	Now, apply R1 to that.
B170	[E writes L13: R ∨ ~Q]
B171	Wedges . . . apply R6 to step 13.
B172	No, apply it to step 12.
B173	That will give me a positive Q . . . horseshoe R ` . . . yeah, Q ⊃ R.
B174	[E writes L14: Q ⊃ R]

E9.2

B175	I'm back to where I started from again.
B176	I don't exactly see where I'm going now.
B177	Somehow what steps I can apply give me. . . .
B178	Ah, let me see. R10 applied to 4 and 8.
B179	No, can't apply it to 4.
B180	4 and 12.
B181	(E: R10 to 4 and 12.)
B182	[E writes L15: (P ∨ Q)·(~Q ∨ R)]
B183	Let me see. If I could change my signs around some way . . .
B184	and the wedges.
B185	The only way I can change the signs is to change the connectives,
B186	and I don't want to change the connectives,
B187	'cause that isn't going to help me any at all.
B188	I don't have anywhere I can use R3.
B189	I can change my signs on my wedges to double negatives. . . .
B190	See, would that help if I applied that to step 7.
B191	Apply R2 to step 7.
B192	That will give me negative P . . . negative P. . . .
B193	(E: R2 to 7. OK.)
B194	Negative P, positive R. Now. . . .
B195	(E: 2 to 7?)
B196	2 to 8, rather.
B197	So . . . gives me R . . . negative P.
B198	[E writes L16: R ⊃ ~P]
B199	Ah . . . which I can apply 5 and 16. . . .
B200	Apply R12 to that. . . .
B201	(E: You want to apply 12 to 16 and what?)
B202	No, 5 to 16. Apply R12 . . . 5 and 16, apply R12.
B203	(E: Both 5 and 16. . . .)
B204	No, to line . . . step 5 and step 16, we apply R12. OK.
B205	(E: OK, 12 to 5 and 12 to 16.)
B206	[E writes L17: R ⊃ Q]
B207	R ⊃ Q. R ⊃ Q. . . .
B208	Now, apply . . . let's see. . . .
B209	(E: Well, I think you have to go now.)
B210	Yeah, I have to go now.
B211	(E: Or would you like one more try?)
B212	Well, I was going to apply step 12 . . . R12, rather . . . to 2 and 17,
B213	which would give me Q ⊃ Q.
B214	(E: 2 and 17. . . .)
B215	Gives me Q ⊃ Q.
B216	[E writes L18: Q ⊃ Q]
B217	(E: OK, Jack, thanks a lot.)

APPENDIX 10.6

S3 on C1

B1	[E writes L1: $(P \lor Q) \cdot (Q \supset R)$]
B2	[E writes L0: $P \lor (Q \cdot R)$]
E1	
B3	Well, this looks like more of a problem of rearranging.
B4	First of all . . . start right away rearranging the P and Q on the left-hand side.
B5	And, I guess R7 . . . applying R7.
B6	I see that in the answer we want a single P and a single Q.
B7	So I guess we're going to have to eliminate one of the Q's.
B8	Let's see . . . rule . . . R7.
B9	R7 can't be applied as it is . . .
B10	'cause of the horseshoe.
B11	Let's see, the horseshoe is eliminated from the answer,
B12	so . . . if we applied R6 to the right-hand side of number 1 . . . first expression. . . .
B13	[E writes L2: $(P \lor Q) \cdot (\sim Q \lor R)$]
B14	R7 . . . getting into the left hand as an expression of the set on the left-hand side. . . .
B15	Why don't we apply R7 to the first line.
B16	(E: Left-hand side?)
B17	Uh huh.
B18	No, R7 to the entire expression.
B19	(E: The left-hand side of the problem. . . .)
B20	No, we can't do that because. . . .
B21	Let's see, if . . . we'd have to switch the first expression around
B22	and then the Q's would have to be the same.
B23	Let's see, we can switch the left-hand side.
B24	Change the Q and P.
B25	That's R1. . . .
B26	(E: What number do you want to apply that to?)
B27	I'll apply it to the left hand of 2.
B28	[E writes L3: $(Q \lor P) \cdot (\sim Q \lor R)$]
B29	No rule to the problem that the Q's aren't the same sign.
B30	Ah . . . right now I'm going to take another glance at R4
B31	because if we could get into the . . . expression like the left-hand side of R7,
B32	then the brackets could be changed around so that we could get P and. . . .
B33	No, wait . . . Q and an R into a parenthesis.
B34	Let's see, to change Q to positive
B35	wait, maybe we can use R5.
B36	What I'm thinking about now is . . . what would R5 look like, taking equation 3 as the right-hand side of R5.
B37	(E: Apply 5 to the left-hand side of 3?)
B38	No, to the entire expression of 3.
B39	(E: Entire expression.)
B40	Yeah. Now right now I'm not thinking of anything,
B41	I'm just waiting to see what that's going to look like.
B42	[E writes L4: $\sim(\sim(Q \lor P) \lor \sim(\sim Q \lor R))$]
B43	I don't think that helped any at all.
B44	(E: Why not?)
B45	Well, because of the tildes . . . because we're going to run into trouble with all the tildes there.
B46	Looking at example 5, I was sort of mislead right into it . . . into thinking I could get it into left-hand form without the tildes,
B47	but we didn't have any tildes to start with

B48	and using R5 we just put them in.

E2

B49	Right now I'm just sort of glancing through the third set, and seeing if any of them might apply there.
B50	Right now I'm thinking in terms of R11 there.
B51	That . . . 11 . . . that just can't be used.

E3.1

B52	Let's see now, disregarding L4,
B53	getting back into what we wanted, changing the $\sim Q$ to Q. . . .
B54	We have the wedge there. . . .
B55	What I'm looking for now is whether there are any rules whereby I could change either the wedge or the horseshoe so that Q comes out positive,
B56	but I don't think there's anything.
B57	I haven't been able to see it.
B58	Let's see, I'm looking at the right-hand side of. . . .
B59	I'll have to look at the left-hand side to see if we might be able to change the left-hand side so that. . . .
B60	Let's see, changing the. . . .
B61	Oh, yeah . . . if R6 is applied to the . . . now, if it's applied to the left-hand side. . . .
B62	Oh, wait a minute.
B63	(E: Left-hand side of what?)
B64	On the first equation, apply R6 to the left-hand side. (mumbles)
B65	[E writes L5: $(\sim P \supset Q) \cdot (Q \supset R)$]
B66	I'm sort of wondering whether I had changed P and Q too soon.
B67	Now, let's see, we have. . . .
B68	With horseshoes we can only switch that around.
B69	Wait . . . if we apply R2, we change the sign of both. . . .
B70	(E: Both what?)
B71	If we apply R2 to both sides of number 5 . . . first to the right hand and then to the left. . . .
B72	(E: Want me to do this?)
B73	I think so, working between the parenthesis.
B74	(E: 2 and 5 . . . first to the left-hand side. . . .)
B75	[E writes L6: $(\sim Q \supset P) \cdot (Q \supset R)$]
B76	[E writes L7: $(\sim Q \supset P) \cdot (\sim R \supset \sim Q)$]
B77	Doggone! Tilde horseshoe $\sim Q$.
B78	Now . . . what I'm thinking of right now is sign manipulation, getting the Q's the same sign and. . . .
B79	So that we can use R4 on that . . . number 7, rather.

E3.2

B80	The only thing I can think of now is applying R6 to a. . . .
B81	Wait, before you write anything down.
B82	Ah . . . we'll be changing from a horseshoe to a wedge.
B83	Wait, we have to end up with either the wedge or a dot.
B84	Change . . . apply R6 to equation 7.
B85	We only change one sign and we. . . .
B86	(E: Which . . . what one do you want?)
B87	R6. . . .
B88	(E: Which side?)
B89	Apply it to the first side. . . .
B90	Wait, R6 is a. . . . Wait. . . .
B91	(E: I beg your pardon.)
B92	Shouldn't that be a wedge? $Q \lor P$.
B93	[E writes L8: $(Q \lor P) \cdot (\sim R \supset \sim Q)$]
B94	Now, if we apply the. . . .

B95	No, that. . . .
B96	Let's see, if we change the order first of all. . . .
B97	Go back to number 5.
B98	If we change before we. . . .
B99	Number. . . .
B100	Let's see, where did we do that?
B101	In . . . take the 5th equation there.
B102	If before we change that to a horseshoe.
B103	Let's see, we did that in number 1, right?
B104	We'll take number 1 first and change, interchange the Q and P.
B105	Let's see, that. . . .
B106	(E: Going to do that?)
B107	(E: . . . follow through . . . better than doing it in your head.)
B108	OK, why don't you.
B109	Q would become the negative in 5. . . .
B110	Yeah, go ahead and do that.
B111	(E: 1 to 1 to change the order around, that right?)
B112	[E writes L9: $(Q \lor P) \cdot (Q \supset R)$]
B113	Yeah. $Q \lor P$, $Q \supset R$.
B114	Now we, let's see, we applied R6 then.
B115	(E: To the inside. . . .)
B116	To the . . . yeah, to the left-hand expression.
B117	That would be $(\sim Q \supset P) \cdot (Q \supset R)$.
B118	[E writes L10: $(\sim Q \supset P) \cdot (Q \supset R)$]
B119	All right, now then, if we applied R2,
B120	changing the horseshoe to the wedge. . . .
B121	Or now, what did we do there?
B122	Let's see, we were changing (mumbles). . . .
B123	We did that to get the Q's the same.
B124	Let's see, we have . . . let's see, if you apply R2 to the right-hand side. . . .
B125	[E writes L11: $(\sim Q \supset P) \cdot (\sim R \supset \sim Q)$]
B126	Now let's see, number 1 would change it to the wedge
B127	and that was what . . . R6. . . .
B128	This would change the sign of the first one. . . .
B129	(E: 6 to 11?)
B130	Now wait, just a minute . . . before you do that.
B131	Somehow we seem to have . . . we're winding up with the same. . . .
B132	How did we end up with the same equation when we changed it?
B133	See what I mean . . . number 11 is the same as number 7.
B134	And what I wanted to do is change the order of those . . . the P and Q.
B135	Let's see, where did I. . . .
B136	(E: Not the same place as the first one.)
B137	[garbled]
B138	(E: Which one do you want me to work with?)
E3.3	
B139	Apply it to both.
B140	No, wait . . . apply it to the first line.
B141	This will give us. . . .
B142	[E writes L12: $(Q \lor P) \cdot (\sim R \supset \sim Q)$]
B143	Now if you apply it to the second side . . .
B144	change the Q.
B145	It'll be R. . . .
B146	(E: Well, I may as well do it.)
B147	OK.
B148	[E writes L13: $(Q \lor P) \cdot (R \supset \sim Q)$] [Error: should be $(Q \lor P) \cdot (R \lor \sim Q)$]
B149	You changed something

B150   because number 8 and 13 aren't the same.
B151   You got a positive R this time.
B152   Let's see, we have Q and R in the parenthesis.
B153   The only step is different is . . . rule 1 and 2.
B154   Now let's see, if you change from a horseshoe, or from a wedge . . . to a dot, that's three changes.
B155   I'm thinking of the right-hand side now . . . and would that be legal if the outside were negative?
B156   (E: I'm sorry, no it wouldn't.)
B157   Apply R5 to L13 . . . the right-hand expression.
B158   (E: OK.)
B159   (E: Ooops . . . sorry. R5 to the right hand of 13. Horseshoe connective.)
B160   Oh, that's a horseshoe, isn't it?
B161   Wait . . . no, that should be. . . .
B162   Wait, you applied 6 to 12. . . .
B163   (E: That's my fault, I'm sorry.)
B164   [E corrects L13: $(Q \lor P) \cdot (R \lor \sim Q)$]
B165   [E writes L14: $(Q \lor P) \cdot \sim (\sim R \cdot Q)$]
B166   And now we have . . . we apply R1 to the . . . R1 to the left-hand side.
B167   Change around P and Q.
B168   [E writes L15: $(P \lor Q) \cdot \sim (\sim R \cdot Q)$]
B169   Now we have the wrong connective in the. . . .
B170   (E: What are you trying to. . . .)
B171   Can we change the. . . .
B172   What I've been trying to do is change the right-hand side to fit the right-hand side of R7.
B173   And if we change. . . .
B174   Oh no, if we change from the dot back to the wedge. . . .
B175   No, wait.
B176   If you apply the . . . change the wedge in the left-hand expression to dot,
B177   that'll give us . . .
B178   (E: You want on 15 or. . . .)
B179   Yeah, on 15. Now wait . . .
B180   go head . . . R5, left hand, left-hand side.
B181   [E writes L16: $\sim (\sim P \cdot \sim Q) \cdot \sim (\sim R \cdot Q)$]

E4

B182   (E: Now, what are you trying to do?)
B183   Well, this didn't turn out the way I thought it would.
B184   What I was thinking of is going back to the expression in the right hand of number 13.
B185   You can have two minor connectives that are different and still with one the Q would be the right sign,
B186   but the minor connectives would be wrong to apply R7.
B187   (E: Now, what are you doing?)
B188   I'm just looking at it sort of frustratingly.
B189   I think the general idea that I had that . . . assuming that's right . . . that to get it into the right-hand form of R7 . . .
B190   then you could move it . . . you could change it to the left-hand side.
B191   Then you could apply R4.
B192   I see a problem that would arise there, too, anyway.
B193   (E: What would be the problem there?)
B194   Oh, well . . . 'cause what I was thinking of eventually getting it to was so I have a Q and R within the parenthesis and the P outside,
B195   but there would be a . . . there would be the wedge . . . would be the major connective and. . . .
B196   That's right, though. That's what we want.
B197   That wouldn't be the problem at all.

B198   You see, essentially what I want to do is to get into the form where I could take out the Q

B199   and make it Q $\lor$ (R$\cdot$P)

B200   and then ... using R4

B201   I could change the parenthesis and make it Q ... then it would be Q $\lor$ R

B202   and the wedge and the dot would be in the wrong places.

B203   (E: Well, I'm sorry ... that's all.)

B204   Yeah.

B205   (E: You have any general feelings about these problems, or. ...)

B206   Gee, I hope the defense of our country isn't resting on people like me to defend.

B207   (E: Well, these are pretty hard ones.)

B208   (E: What do you tend to do when you do get frustrated? I mean ... in the sense that. ...)

B209   The one thing I did was sort of to check whether the main idea I had in the first place would work out.

B210   And that's why I thought I wouldn't run into that problem where the signs were different.

B211   And that was just about at the end of the half hour.

B212   I s'pose if I had gone on,

B213   why I'd have probably looked for another. ...

B214   Well, I would have checked out to see whether the dots and the wedge could be changed around.

B215   Or tried to figure out another general method of solving the problem.

B216   (E: There anything different about the way you handled this problem and the last one?)

B217   Well, in this one I tried to keep in mind more the rules.

B218   One rule that I know that I tend to forget is the working with the various ... with two different lines ... a two-line rule.

B219   I kinda just completely forget about it

B220   and every once in a while I sort of check one against the other.

B221   But in this one, I didn't see too much use in using it

B222   because I know there were several lines there where R11 couldn't be used

B223   'cause that's a horseshoe.

B224   But I more or less checked to see whether canceling out would help any ... removing the A term.

B225   But since we wanted all three of the letters in the final answer,

B226   I didn't ... more or less tended to forget about that ... the idea of eliminating.

B227   The first time I was thinking more in terms of eliminating

B228   and this one ... more in terms of rearranging.

B229   Otherwise, the main method used to go about the problem, I think would be the same.

B230   I mean I kind of look for a general idea

B231   and then start working backwards or forwards

B232   to check out whether the actual operations correspond with the general idea.

APPENDIX 10.7

S4 on C1

B1   [E writes L1: (P $\lor$ Q)$\cdot$(Q $\supset$ R)]

B2   [E writes L0: P $\lor$ (Q$\cdot$R)]

E1

B3   Well, first, I'm going to check down the rules to see which rules apply to it.

B4	Hmm . . . R1 will apply.
B5	R2 will not.
B6	R3 will not.
B7	R4 will not.
B8	5 will.
B9	6 won't.
B10	7 won't.
B11	8 will. . . .
B12	Let's try R8 . . . apply it and come out with a B.
B13	[E writes L2: Q ⊃ R]
B14	Now to change. . . .
B15	I'd like to get that part of it to look like the expression in the parentheses in the answer,
B16	so try to find a rule to change that horseshoe to a dot.
B17	And I haven't got one. . . .

E2

B18	So start again. . . .
B19	Well apply R8 to the left-hand side.
B20	[E writes L3: P ∨ Q]
B21	This problem may be similar to the last one.
B22	Now I see right away that R12 would apply to 2 and 3,
B23	if I could get a horseshoe in L3.
B24	So I'll look for a way to change the. . . .
B25	Let's see . . . R6 to 3.
B26	[E writes L4: ~P ⊃ Q]
B27	Mmm . . . that doesn't seem to do anything . . . mmmm.
B28	(E: What are you doing?)

E3

B29	I'm just sort of lost.
B30	I'm trying to see what rules might apply . . . either 10, 11 or 12 to 2, 3 or 4.
B31	Hmm, I'm just looking through the rules to see if any of the rules will help me.

E4

B32	I'm just lost. Hmmm.
B33	Now I'm trying to see if there's some way I can isolate P on one side. . . .
B34	The wedge. . . .
B35	I was going to say apply R5,
B36	but I see the rule will make the whole expression minus. . . .
B37	So R10 won't apply to it.
B38	I'm just looking through the rules now.
B39	Hmm. I'm just lost. . . .

E5

B40	If I can change in the original expression . . . if I can change the horseshoe to a wedge.
B41	I can apply R7. . . . Yeah, I can apply R7.
B42	So . . . (sighs) apply, apply R6 to the right-hand side of 1.
B43	[E writes L5: (P ∨ Q)·(~Q ∨ R)]
B44	Now apply R7 to 5 . . . going to the left.
B45	(E: From left to right?)
B46	From right to left.
B47	(E: It doesn't fit.)
B48	Hmm . . . oh yeah, I see that it doesn't.
B49	Now I'm looking for a way to make it fit . . .
B50	a rule which will reverse either . . . which will reverse the Q's.
B51	Apply. . . .
B52	No. . . .
B53	If I apply R5 to the left-hand side. . . .
B54	No that won't work

B55   because it will give me a dot.

B56   So now I'm looking for a way to change the left-hand side.

B57   I can change the left-hand side so that the Q will be on the left of the wedge,

B58   but it will be the wrong sign.

B59   So now I'm lost.

E6

B60   Hmm. . . . I'm looking over the rules to see if 10, 11, or 12 will fit any of the four expressions in section 3.

B61   (E: Why are you looking at those rules?)

B62   To . . . umm . . . well because tilde. . . .

B63   Well, I don't really know. . . .

B64   I'm lost

B65   so I'm just sort of looking to see if any of the rules will change around . . . will change the expressions around.

B66   Well, I'm just lost for the moment. . . .

B67   So I'm just going to go through the rules again to see which one will apply to the original expression.

B68   (E: What are you doing now?)

B69   I'm looking at 3 and 5 and I see that they'll fit. . . .

B70   Oh, excuse me, wrong connective.

B71   I was going to say they'll fit R11,

B72   but they won't.

B73   I'm just lost right now.

E7

B74   If I could find a way to change the right-hand side of the expression to a wedge . . .

B75   I did that in 5. . . .

B76   Didn't work.

B77   I'm just lost right now.

B78   (E: Explain what you're looking at please.)

E8.1

B79   I'm not really looking at anything.

B80   I'm just looking at all of them trying to find something between them that I can use one of the rules on . . . if they'll fit one of the rules.

B81   I just don't see anything.

B82   (sighs) Hmmm. . . . I'm looking through to see which will fit the first expression and also if I think they'll help me.

B83   I see several that will fit,

B84   but I've already tried them

B85   and they don't help.

E8.2

B86   Number 1 will fit the left-hand side,

B87   but I can't see that it will do me any good.

B88   Number 2 will fit the left-hand side

B89   but still won't do any good.

B90   Number 3 will not fit. . . .

B91   Number 4 will not fit. . . .

B92   Number 5 will fit the left-hand side

B93   but . . . but I don't have any use for just changing the dots. . . .

B94   But let's see . . . remembered something, about ten minutes ago

B95   I wanted to get a dot in my expression. . . .

B96   I can't remember what it was.

B97   Number 6 I've already applied twice

B98   and number 7 doesn't apply.

B99   Number 8 I tried.

B100	Number 9 no good.
B101	Number 10, 11, or 12 don't apply to the original expression.
B102	So I'm just sort of lost.

E9

B103	Right now looking at 2 and 4 to see if there's some way I can apply R12 to them to make....
B104	I can't see a way of applying it.
B105	If I can get number 4 with the Q to the left of the horseshoe,
B106	then it becomes a minus....
B107	Hmm, that's no good.
B108	Just lost.

E10

B109	(E: What are you doing now?)
B110	Nothing . . . I don't even know what to look at.
B111	Now I'm looking at the original expression, but I've tried everything . . . I've tried just about every rule which I think will help me.
B112	I'm just lost . . . just lost.

E11

B113	Will R5 apply on expression 5?
B114	(E: Yes.)
B115	I don't know what reason for applying it,
B116	but apply it and see what happens.
B117	[E writes L6: $\sim(\sim(P \lor Q) \lor \sim(\sim Q \lor R))$]
B118	No, I can see that . . . I can see that didn't help much. That didn't help at all.
B119	So I'll disregard that one.
B120	I just don't know what to do.
B121	Well, I'll look at expression 6 to see if there's anything there . . .
B122	any rule that might change that around.
B123	No, I can't see anything there. . . . (sighs)

E12

B124	So I'll try looking at 2, 3, 4, and 5 again.
B125	I'm just sort of lost.
B126	I've tried switching the Q to the left of the horseshoe in number 2. Yeah.
B127	Just looking, that all....
B128	Nothing there to do . . . hmmm....
B129	Just lost . . . hmm . . . just lost. (sighs)

E13

B130	By looking at the answer I can see that R7 is probably used someplace.
B131	Now if I can only get one of my expressions to fit the right-hand side of R7.
B132	And 5 almost fits,
B133	if I can just switch a couple around,
B134	by applying R1 to the left-hand side of 5,
B135	I get Q in the right place,
B136	but with the wrong sign.
B137	[E writes L7: $(Q \lor P) \cdot (\sim Q \lor R)$]
B138	Now all I have to do....
B139	But still that won't give it to me
B140	because Q isn't the one I want on the left-hand side of the wedge.

E14

B141	What I'm looking at is 5....
B142	If I could find a way to replace the right-hand side of the equation with an expression with P in . . .

B143	which would mean using . . . I don't know what rule . . .
B144	11 or 12 . . .
B145	(sighs) I'm just lost.

E15

B146	If I can get P isolated . . . just by itself,
B147	I could . . . could I apply R9 and substitute?
B148	(E: Yes.)
B149	Well . . . that would mean using R11 in some way.
B150	I don't see any way to do it.
B151	I'm still looking for a way to isolate P.
B152	[E terminates attempt.]

APPENDIX 10.8

S5 on C1

B1	[E writes L1: $(P \lor Q) \cdot (Q \supset R)$]
B2	[E writes L0: $P \lor (Q \cdot R)$]

E1

B3	That looked complicated when you put it up,
B4	but now it looks easier.
B5	I don't know if it is or not.
B6	Let's see, the first thing is we give a . . .
B7	the right-hand part of L1 is the same letters as we want in the right-hand part of the answer,
B8	except we want to change the horseshoe to a dot.
B9	Ah, let's see if we could get a . . . if we could possibly get a $Q \supset R$ by itself. . . .
B10	Let's see, we could change the horseshoe to a wedge, and the wedge to a dot eventually.
B11	We'll have to. . . .
B12	That looks like a possibility.

E2.1

B13	Also, that answer is in the form of the left-hand side of R7,
B14	so that if we could get a $P \supset Q$ . . .
B15	which we already have . . . that would be the right-hand side . . . the first term of the right-hand side of R7,
B16	and then we want a dot,
B17	which we already have,
B18	and then we could want a $P \lor R$. . . .
B19	So let's see now. If we had a $P \lor R$ and a $P \lor Q$,
B20	we could get the answer directly by R7.

E2.2

B21	We have a $P \lor Q$. . . .
B22	We also have a $Q \supset R$.
B23	A $Q \supset R$ can be changed into a wedge by R6 . . .
B24	except that we're going to have a sign problem again . . . and. . . .
B25	Let's try it anyway . . . let's try R6 . . . second part of L1.
B26	[E writes L2: $(P \lor Q) \cdot (\sim Q \lor R)$]
B27	OK, now we can reverse the order of the wedge. . . .
B28	And their signs are going to be wrong.
B29	So if we applied R2 to L1.

B30   [E writes L3: $(P \lor Q) \cdot (\sim R \supset \sim Q)$]

B31   Yeah . . . now . . . the only way of going from that horseshoe to a wedge is with R6.
   . . .

B32   Let's see, we want to have a positive Q . . . eventually.

B33   Let's see, we had a. . . .

B34   Let's see, what did we do here?

B35   We applied R2 to L1 . . . that gives us that.

B36   We'd like to change the order . . . we'd like to have a. . . .

B37   Here, let's work on the first term of that.

B38   (E: First term of what?)

B39   What I'm doing . . .

B40   and I think it's wrong . . .

B41   maybe I'll go back . . .

B42   I'm trying to get that expression into something to which R7 will apply.

B43   But once I get there, it's only going to give one a P and a Q . . . a Q and an R plus, a
   P plus R or P R term. . . .

B44   That won't do me any good, anyway

E3

B45   I think I'll go back to the beginning and start over.

B46   OK, here's something we can do . . . we can take. . . .

B47   Oh, yeah, this ought to be simple . . .

B48   now we'll take . . . let's apply R8 to L1.

B49   Let's see, we'll keep the B part.

B50   [E writes L4: $Q \supset R$]

B51   OK, now we have $Q \supset R$.

B52   What we want is a $Q \cdot R$.

B53   We want to go from a horseshoe to a dot.

B54   Yeah, OK, so the only way to do that is to go via R6, I guess.

B55   R6 to L4.

B56   I think we're going to get it now . . . maybe.

B57   [E writes L5: $\sim Q \lor R$]

B58   OK, that's that . . . we got a horseshoe . . . we want to go from a horseshoe . . . oh,
   gosh, to a dot . . . we want to get a dot. . . .

B59   But now if we . . . let's see. . . .

B60   (E: What are you trying to do?)

B61   Hah . . . I'm trying to get a $Q \cdot R$

B62   because . . . see, I could also apply R8 to L2

B63   and eventually I think I can get a separate P out of that.

B64   In fact, let's do that now,

B65   and I'll come back to this other thing later.

B66   Let's apply R8 to L2 . . . keep the A part

B67   so we'll have a $P \supset Q$.

B68   (E: wedge?)

B69   Yeah, $P \lor Q$.

B70   [E writes L6: $P \lor Q$]

B71   The only trouble with that is you use R5

B72   to get that into a dot . . .

B73   and we could use R8

B74   just to get just the P part of it . . .

B75   except R8 only works with positive. . . .

B76   And we're going to get a negative

B77   when we use R5.

B78   That's the same thing that was holding me up on L5 there.

B79   Now let's see how can we get around that?

B80   There must be some way to get rid of the doggone. . . .

E4

B81 Another way to get the answer is to . . .

B82 if I can get a P, an individual P,

B83 I can use R9 and make X equal to $Q \cdot R$.

B84 That's an easy way to do it . . .

B85 hah . . . that's kind of cheating as a matter of fact. . . .

B86 So if we can get an individual P out of this someplace

B87 we're all set.

B88 How are we going to get an individual P?

B89 We have a $P \supset Q$.

B90 If we . . . I was looking at R11 . . . applying that between 1 and 6 or . . .

B91 which could be done eventually,

B92 but all that would give me is what I have there anyway . . . the $P \lor Q$.

B93 Let's see . . . $A \lor A$ equals A . . .

B94 that's no good.

B95 We can reverse the position with R1,

B96 then when you get it to a dot,

B97 you'll have that minus in front of it. . . .

B98 We could go from a wedge to a horseshoe

B99 and then what can we do with a horseshoe?

B100 What is there interesting that we can do with a horseshoe?

B101 If we change to a horseshoe . . .

B102 you use a horseshoe in R11,

B103 but then we'd have to have an individual A which would be the Q part,

B104 which wouldn't do us too much good.

B105 Any place where we could get an individual letter would be tremendous.

B106 R4 just regroups series of three

B107 which won't do us any good.

E5

B108 Let's see now . . . it would be possible to use R9 . . .

B109 add anything I wanted to onto 6

B110 I could regroup then by 4.

B111 That wouldn't do me much good anyway.

B112 Let's see, I could get a $P \lor (Q \lor R)$

B113 by using R9

B114 and then R4.

B115 It would be the same as the answer except I'd have a wedge instead of a dot.

B116 In order to change that wedge to a dot,

B117 I'm going to have to introduce that tilde bracket

B118 and change all the signs around . . .

B119 which doesn't do us too much good.

E6.1

B120 I think I'll go back and try to get an individual P out of expression 6 . . . an individual P.

B121 What I want to do is change the wedge into a dot

B122 so that I can use R8.

B123 Maybe we can do it anyway. . . .

B124 Yeah, we could apply R8 to just the inside of an expression?

B125 (E: What expression are you thinking of?)

B126 Well . . . ummm. . . apply 5 to 6 . . . L6.

B127 This is what I thought of a while ago,

B128 and I didn't think it could be done . . .

B129 I don't know if it could or not.

B130 [E writes L7: $\sim (\sim P \cdot \sim Q)$]

B131 (E: You cannot apply R8 because this must be a positive total exp ession.)

B132 Right . . . that's what I figured,

B133	so that wouldn't work.
B134	If I could do that, it would be very easy.
B135	Let's see . . . is there any way to get rid of a negative term.
B136	I don't believe there is . . . with that dot.
B137	Let's see, that method won't do us too much good. . . .

E6.2

B138	Oh, here's a. . . .
B139	Let's use R9 on L6.
B140	(E: What do you want me to add?)
B141	Add Q. . . .
B142	No . . . hah . . . I want to add P. . . .
B143	Q won't work because. . . .
B144	[E writes L8: $(P \lor Q) \lor P$]
B145	OK, now if we use. . . .
B146	No . . . well, let's see. I can change the order of that, can't I?
B147	Wait a second now . . . $P \lor P$ equals P,

E6.3

B148	so, I'll end up with the same thing I. . . .
B149	Let's see . . . OK, now, yeah, now, R11 . . . possibly. . . .
B150	Let's see yeah, between 6 and 8 there.
B151	If I can use R11
B152	I've got to change L8 into a horseshoe
B153	and I've got to keep the signs and everything like it is now
B154	and then I can get an individual P.
B155	Except I need a horseshoe connective there
B156	so I've got to change that wedge to a horseshoe
B157	but if I do it. . . .
B158	Let's change the order of that with R1.
B159	[E writes L9: $P \lor (P \lor Q)$]
B160	OK, now we'll apply R6 to that.
B161	[E writes L10: $\sim P \supset (P \lor Q)$]
B162	Now if we try to reverse the order back by R2,
B163	we're going to end up with. . . .
B164	Both signs are changed. . .
B165	that won't work.
B166	Better forget it. . . .
B167	That's going to give me the wrong sign.
B168	[E writes L11: $\sim (P \lor Q) \supset P$]
B169	That would be real nice if the signs were reversed on that.
B170	Now let's see . . . where did I reverse the order.
B171	I reversed the order back on L8 and . . .

E6.4

B172	I get a minus there. . . .
B173	Let's see . . . OK, yeah, let's try R8.
B174	(E: R8 on what?)
B175	I don't mean R8, I mean R6 on L8. . . .
B176	See what we come up with.
B177	[E writes: L12: $\sim (P \lor Q) \supset P$]
B178	That's R6, huh . . . good. . . .
B179	Now we go over to R2.
B180	(E: On what?)
B181	L12.
B182	I'm aiming toward using R12 eventually.
B183	[E writes L13: $\sim P \supset (P \lor Q)$]

B184	Now wait . . . yeah, now . . . I wish that was a positive P on that. . . .
B185	If so, I could have the answer in about two steps.
B186	(E: How could you get the answer in two steps if that were a positive P?)
B187	Well, here's the next step I want to do. I want to take 6 and add to it by R9, Q·R. . . .
B188	I don't think that'll work.
B189	[E writes L14: (P ∨ Q) ∨ (Q·R)]
B190	OK, now, let's see what's going to happen here. . . .
B191	Now we've got to change that. . . .
B192	In order to use R12,
B193	we've got to change that wedge to a horseshoe. . . .
B194	Let's use R6 and see what happens . . . hah. . . .
B195	[E writes L15: ~(P ∨ Q) ⊃ (Q·P)]
B196	Oh, great . . . well, now, if I had L13 again with the signs reversed,
B197	which I can by R2.
B198	Let's apply R2 to L13.
B199	I think we have it now . . . hah.
B200	[E writes L16: ~(P ∨ Q) ⊃ P]
B201	Oh, no, does that reverse them?
B202	Oh, I forgot that reversing . . . well, hmm.
B203	(E: Now what are you doing?)

E7

B204	I'm sitting . . .
B205	I was close there for a second.
B206	Now let's see what we can do here to fix this thing up.
B207	Let's see, I was trying to get a. . . . If I could get a positive P horseshoe (P ∨ Q),
B208	then by R12
B209	I can get P ⊃ (Q·R).
B210	Now, let's see, in order to change that horseshoe into a wedge
B211	we've got to use R6
B212	and that changes the sign again.
B213	So, what we'll want is a minus P horseshoe Q·R. . . .
B214	So what we want actually is 13 with a minus sign in the second term.
B215	And that will give it to us . . . the answer in several steps.

E8.1

B216	How are we going to get 13 except with a sign.
B217	Let's see, 13 is a horseshoe.
B218	We can . . . let's see . . . R2 reverses both signs. . . .
B219	We don't want to do that.
B220	We want to reverse one sign.
B221	So we can do that by applying R6 to L13.
B222	We'll get. . . .
B223	(E: Do you want me to do that?)
B224	We might as well to see what it'll look like.
B225	It's going to be the same as L9.
B226	[E writes L17: P ∨ (P ∨ Q)]
B227	What we want is that thing with two minus signs.
B228	Now we can reverse the order by R1 if we wanted to,
B229	but let's see, that won't do us much good. . . .
B230	Or will it,
B231	because when we switch it back to a horseshoe
B232	we're going to have a. . . .
B233	Let's see, it should come out opposite of what we had before. . . .
B234	Let's see . . . let's try R1 on that now . . . the whole expression.
B235	(E: 1 on step 17?)
B236	Yes, OK.

B237	[E writes L18: (P ∨ Q) ∨ P]
B238	Now let's go back to 6 again . . . see what we get.
B239	(E: 6 to what?)
B240	18. . . .
B241	Isn't that going to put us right back where we started?
B242	[E writes L19: ∼(P ∨ Q) ⊃ P]
B243	Yeah, we've seen that before.
B244	Let's see, that's interesting now . . . why. . . .
B245	now if I didn't reverse it,
B246	and I applied 6 to the same expression on a row
B247	I wouldn't end up with what I started with.
B248	We get a minus P.

E8.2

B249	Oh, here we go . . . here we go . . . here's the answer . . . here's the answer . . . here's the answer.
B250	Take 18 and divide 6 by rule. . . .
B251	(E: Step 18 using 6?)
B252	Oh, wait a second, OK, forget it.
B253	No, this is not the answer . . .
B254	I was going to use R11,

E8.3

B255	but that wasn't right,
B256	because we've got wedges instead of horseshoes.
B257	Apply R6 to L17.
B258	[E writes L20: ∼P ⊃ (P ∨ Q)]
B259	Now, what the heck do we have here. . . .
B260	OK, now that's what we want.
B261	Let's see where's our. . . .
B262	Oh, we have to have a minus sign on the second term
B263	in order to use 15 with it with R12,
B264	which would give us the answer in two steps.
B265	(E: would you explain how R12, if you could apply it, would give you the answer in two steps?)
B266	Well, you see step 15 here. . . .
B267	Well, if I had a tilde out in front of that 20 . . . the second part of it,
B268	then I could use R12
B269	and I'd get a ∼P ⊃ (Q·R).
B270	And changing that to a wedge
B271	I'd get a P ∨ (Q·R) . . . see?
B272	But I still haven't succeeded in getting a tilde in front of that second expression there.
B273	[E terminates attempt.]

APPENDIX 10.9

S8 on C1

| B1 | [E writes L1:   (P ∨ Q)·(Q ⊃ R)] |
| B2 | [E writes L0:   P ∨ (Q·R)] |

E1

| B3 | Well right away I look at the major connector—a dot, |
| B4 | and I look at the answer, and see that the major connector is a wedge. |

B5	I can see some possibilities of eventually applying R4 or R7,
B6	because they both have the common term Q in them.
B7	Now, if I can maybe reverse the one quantity.
B8	Oh . . . let's say . . . if I want to apply rule 4 or 7
B9	I'm going to have to reverse the second quantity,
B10	because you can't use a horseshoe. . . .
B11	You have to have a wedge in there. . . .
B12	That might mess me up.
B13	Well, let's look at it anyhow.
B14	If I do reverse just that, that's going to give me what?
B15	That's going to give me R. . . .
B16	Ah, I don't want to reverse it.
B17	Say I wanted to just change the horseshoe to a wedge . . .
B18	I would get $\sim Q \supset R$.
B19	And if I'd reverse the other ones around. . . .
B20	Can you reverse just a wedge?
B21	Yes you can. . . .
B22	I'd get a Q and a $\sim Q$.
B23	That'll never work.

E2

B24	Let's see what else we can do.
B25	Let's look at the answer.
B26	P . . . I want just P. . . .
B27	Oh . . . I see a P and a wedge.
B28	That could eventually lead to R9,
B29	because in the end, you can add anything you want . . . with R9.
B30	In fact, that kind of looks like it.
B31	My problem now is to eliminate everything right down to P.
B32	Well, with the dot,
B33	we can apply R8 right off the bat to L1.
B34	And you'll get. . . .
B35	[E writes L2: P $\vee$ Q]
B36	Now all you have to do is get that down to P.
B37	I know it's going to be rough,
B38	because in order to apply R8,
B39	I have to change it to a dot.
B40	And that will again give me a tilde quantity.
B41	And we can't do that.
B42	So let's look at the double-line rules,
B43	because sometimes you can cancel out the right terms,
B44	and it would be real easy.
B45	Oh, I see that I have R11,
B46	and if I can get just the B term out of that. . . .
B47	Would it be possible to get everything down to a Q?
B48	Well, if you applied R8 to the first part,
B49	and canceled that out,
B50	and you had the Q $\supset$ R left,
B51	and if I converted that to a wedge,
B52	that would give me a $\sim Q \vee R$,
B53	and that would give me. . . .
B54	I can't see a thing that would give me just Q.
B55	I'd be there with a tilde wedge R.
B56	How could I get a $\sim Q$. . . .
B57	How do you get rid of the R there?
B58	I would have to change it to a dot

B59	and that would go through the same thing again.
B60	Darn it. . . .

E3

B61	Let's see, what else can I do?
B62	Wait, R10 looks interesting.
B63	If I get an A term and a B term, I can get a dot between them.
B64	Well, the only B term I can get is a. . . .
B65	Hey . . . if I'm sitting there with tilde wedge R
B66	and I do have three terms,
B67	so maybe I can eventually apply R7,
B68	and I'd put a dot in between those two terms.
B69	Then I could apply R7 backwards,
B70	and end up with P. . . .
B71	Gosh no . . . I won't be able to have a common term,
B72	because one Q is always tilde and the other Q is always just plain Q.
B73	If I look up here . . .
B74	somehow if I can get rid of that $\sim$Q and get just plain Q
B75	when I have it in a wedge form. . . .
B76	Well, if I just invert the second quantity, $Q \supset R$,
B77	I would get $\sim R \supset \sim Q$.
B78	And if I changed that to a wedge,
B79	that would be real nice. . . .
B80	That would give me a positive R horseshoe $\sim$Q.
B81	I'd still have the $\sim$Q.
B82	I don't seem to be able to get rid of that.
B83	Well, I guess I won't be able to apply R4 or R7.
B84	Well, 4 isn't necessary,
B85	but 7 works out real nice.

E4

B86	Well, let's look at something else.
B87	I like the idea of getting rid of everything but the P.
B88	That looks awful easy.
B89	I've got to get rid of everything but the P.
B90	That's the trick.
B91	Is there any possibility of getting rid of a wedge?
B92	or inverting it . . . or anything?
B93	I can invert it.
B94	That doesn't prove a thing.
B95	I can. . . .
B96	No, they're not the same,
B97	so I can't use R3.
B98	I can't do anything with R4
B99	I can make a dot out of it . . . R5 . . .
B100	but that will make it a negative quantity.
B101	Well, R6,
B102	I can change it to a horseshoe,
B103	if that'll do anything.
B104	If I change it to a horseshoe, that would give me a $\sim P \supset Q$.
B105	And then if I inverted it,
B106	I would have $\sim Q \supset P$.

E5

B107	That means I have two tildes, then, two negative tildes.
B108	Now, if I remember right, the other tilde was in wedge form by the time it was negative.

B109	Let me look again.
B110	Well, now if I just inverted the second term,
B111	I'd have $\sim R \supset \sim Q$.
B112	But then they're not in the right position.
B113	Oh, they're in the opposite position!
B114	And they're both horseshoes.
B115	I can cancel.

E6

B116	So I'd better apply R12.
B117	Let's try that. Apply R6 to L2.
B118	I don't know if that's going to give me anything or not.
B119	[E writes L3: $\sim P \supset Q$]
B120	Yeh, I'm starting to lose track of my sequence.
B121	This will do something,
B122	but I think I've lost track of what I was originally trying to do.
B123	Well, let's go through with it now . . . let's see what I have.
B124	Now apply R2 to L3.
B125	[E writes L4: $\sim Q \supset P$]
B126	Yeh, I'm going to eliminate all the P's,
B127	when what I was originally trying to do was to eliminate everything but the P.
B128	Well, let's see what I get anyhow.
B129	Now to L1, just the second part of L1, apply. . . .
B130	Oh, right off the bat, I'm going to have to apply R8 to get rid of part A.
B131	(E: To L1?)
B132	To L1.
B133	And that will give me just $Q \supset R$. . . .
B134	[E writes L5: $Q \supset R$]
B135	And then I can apply R2 to that.
B136	(E: R2 to L5.)
B137	Yeh. I think this is going to get me nowhere.
B138	[E writes L6: $\sim R \supset \sim Q$]
B139	Yeh. I don't know why,
B140	but I can apply R12 to lines L4 and L6.
B141	And I get $\sim R \supset P$.
B142	[E writes L7: $\sim R \supset P$]

E7

B143	There I am.
B144	I don't know what I'm going to do with it though.
B145	Well, maybe if I look at these for a minute, I can see something more that applies.
B146	At least I got rid of the Q,
B147	but I got an R back into the thing.
B148	Well, what happens if you . . . what can you do with a horseshoe?
B149	I can reverse it back,
B150	and get a $\sim P$ or horseshoe R.
B151	I dunno if I'm any better off than I was with the original thing, P wedge . . .
B152	and from that I can convert that to a . . . a wedge,
B153	and I get either tilde . . .
B154	I can end up with a $\sim P$. No, I'd end up with a positive P and a $\sim R$, horseshoe $\sim R$.
B155	Or I'd end up with a $R \supset P$.
B156	If I apply R6,
B157	I will get an $R \lor P$, I mean.
B158	$R \lor P$ . . . that doesn't seem to get me anywhere because. . . .
B159	Wait . . . oh wait . . . if I have an $R \lor P$. . . .
B160	I'm trying to think in terms of two-line terms.
B161	If I can get that into a wedge,

B162   or if I can get the original P $\vee$ Q into a horseshoe, I have what?

B163 $\sim$P $\supset$ Q.

B164   And I have $\sim$R $\supset$ P.

B165   Ah . . . I can't seem to do anything.

B166   Well, one thing I could do is put a dot in between them.

B167   Then where would I be.

B168   Back where I was.

B169   Not exactly . . .

B170   but it wouldn't help much.

E8.1

B171   If I invert L7, just reverse it.

B172   I will get $\sim$P $\supset$ R.

B173   I can take that and put a dot in between that and L3 anytime I want,

B174   and that leaves me with $\sim$P $\supset$ Q and $\sim$P $\supset$ R with a dot between them.

B175   The only trouble is . . . a wedge . . . there has to be a wedge in between to apply R7.

B176   Oh, you can easily convert it to a wedge

B177   and whatever happens to one has to happen to the other.

B178   And what will happen to it if I convert that back into a wedge?

B179   Where is R and P in a wedge?

B180   Or did I say I could do that?

E8.2

B181   Ah, just for the heck of it, put down . . . apply R2 to L7.

B182   All right, now I have that.

B183   [E writes L8: $\sim$P $\supset$ R]

B184   OK, if I apply R10 to L3 and L8. . . .

B185   See what I'm going to do?

B186   (E: Connect it with a dot.)

B187   Connect it with a dot.

B188   (E: R10 to 3 and 8, did you say?)

B189   Yeh. Because I want to apply R7.

B190   The only thing is that the minor connectors have to be wedges,

B191   so that means that I'll have to take each one individually.

B192   So maybe I should have done this beforehand.

B193   (E: Do you want this one first?)

B194   Well, a . . . before I do that, to save complications later . . .

B195   to L3 just apply R6 . . . to L3.

B196   (E: OK. We didn't apply 10).

B197   Uh huh.

B198   [E writes L9:   P $\vee$ Q]

B199   Uh huh. Ah, oh wait a minute, I'm working in circles.

B200   It gives you P $\vee$ Q?

B201   Well, maybe not.

B202   If you applied R6 to . . . a . . .

B203   That was kinda dumb.

B204   I just work that in circles.

B205   R9 and R2 are the same . . . L2 are the same.

B206   Now I really am mixed up.

B207   Well, what if you applied R6 to L8.

B208   Funny I didn't see that before.

B209   [E writes L10:   P $\vee$ R]

B210   Now that's something.

B211   Now apply R10 to L9 and L10.

B212   (E: OK.)

B213   I think I'm real close. I think I'm going to get it right now.

B214   Look, it's really dumb . . .

B215	I've worked in circles . . .
B216	2 and 9 are the same thing.
B217	[E writes L11: $(P \lor Q) \cdot (P \lor R)$]
B218	Now apply R7.
B219	Apply R7 and I guess that's it.
B220	It's pretty close to it.
B221	R7 to L11.
B222	[E writes L12: $P \lor (Q \cdot R)$]
B223	Eureka!
B224	(E: That's right.)

APPENDIX 10.10

S9 on C1

B1	[E writes L1: $(P \lor Q) \cdot (Q \supset R)$]
B2	[E writes L0: $P \lor (Q \cdot R)$]
E1	
B3	Well, that suggests to me rule 7 and 4,
B4	but I have a horseshoe in that.
B5	And let's see, I'll need a Q and an R and a P.
B6	So I have to drop the Q
B7	and switch that horseshoe.
B8	And that I can do handy enough using R6 . . .
B9	to the second part of what is up there in the beginning.
B10	So apply that.
B11	(E: OK, R6 to L1.)
B12	[E writes L2: $(P \lor Q) \cdot (\sim Q \lor R)$]
B13	Now, if I was to apply R7 going backwards . . .
B14	and then I'd need to get rid of the tilde in front of the Q before the end sometime or other.
B15	The P is all right
B16	and the R is all right,
B17	but that Q would have to be in the beginning for awhile.
B18	So I'd have to switch. . . .
B19	Let's see now, how can I get that first Q with a tilde or the second Q without a tilde.
B20	Well, I could switch it around
B21	using R1 in the first part of it,
B22	or. . . .
B23	Nothing suggests itself,
B24	but . . . or hum. . . .
E2	
B25	Well, maybe I could drop something out of that.
B26	That doesn't seem any too convenient yet either.
E3	
B27	Well, I still need something to change signs,
B28	and nothing seems to suggest itself.
B29	Well, if I had first applied R2 to that part,
B30	I would have had two sign changes,
B31	and that would have reversed the two,

B32   and reversed the two signs on the second part,

B33   so that would be then R, rather, $\sim R \vee Q$.

B34   I then could reverse both parts. . . .

B35   Would be OK.

B36   So, we'll do that first.

B37   So we'll apply to what we had in the very beginning, on the second part . . . R2.

B38   [E writes L3: $(P \vee Q) \cdot (\sim R \vee \sim Q)$] [Error: should be $(P \vee Q) \cdot (\sim R \supset \sim Q)$.]

B39   (E: That right?)

B40   Right. And now, to the second part, let's apply R6.

B41   (E: 6 to L3. . . .)

B42   Well, one second . . .

B43   That's going to give me trouble again,

B44   unless I switch it around now I guess.

B45   (E: You don't want to do that?)

B46   No, just wait a second, let me think. . . .

B47   It might work out.

B48   I've got . . . wait a second, I think we've got a mistake someplace.

B49   On 3, the second part, there's a horseshoe there yet, isn't there?

B50   Or did we get rid of the horseshoe?

B51   No, there is a horseshoe there.

B52   (E: You're right, there is a horseshoe.)

B53   (E: Applying R2, you don't lose that horseshoe, do you?)

B54   [E corrects L3: $(P \vee Q) \cdot (\sim R \supset \sim Q)$]

B55   No. And now, if we apply R6, then we get. . . .

B56   That leaves me in as much trouble as I was in before.

B57   I still have the wrong sign there. . . .

B58   The first sign changes only.

B59   Unless I can swing those horseshoes around again,

B60   but that doesn't seem practical either.

B61   So I guess we are on the wrong track.

B62   (E: You don't want to apply R6 to L3?)

B63   No, it won't get me anyplace.

B64   (E: OK, we won't do that then. All right we're not through on L4 yet . . . we haven't done it yet, I mean.)

B65   Now I'm still troubled with a wrong sign on the Q.

B66   I don't see any simple way of getting rid of that . . . getting rid of the tilde

B67   or adding a tilde in the first part.

E4

B68   But if I could drop something. . . .

B69   But nothing's doubled,

B70   so this doesn't seem practical either.

B71   If we split this whole thing up again,

B72   or could we work using R12 again.

B73   Well, that's one way of going about it . . . maybe. . . .

B74   Finally reversing everything,

B75   and then reversing everything

B76   after just incidentally adding the P.

E5

B77   Well, $Q \supset R$ . . .

B78   you want the Q and the R . . .

B79   I want a dot in there rather than a wedge.

B80   I can do that by . . .

B81   not by anything handy.

B82   Well, in L2 we got a wedge.

B83   Now if we should remove this whole section. . . .

B84	We're still stuck getting to a dot,
B85	and R5 is very inconvenient for that.

E6

B86	So the next most convenient thing would be using R7,
B87	which looks most practical.
B88	So I think I'll start looking for something going backwards from R7.
B89	Is that R7 what I want at all?
B90	No, I don't think it is . . . think it will be too handy.
B91	So if I look at that again . . .
B92	Q and an R . . . Q, R, P. . . .
B93	That would seem to double itself into . . . this is working backwards . . . from, rather, into P Q, P R . . . P Q, P R.
B94	We've got the P Q,
B95	but the P R, we still have to get.
B96	Well, let's check that.
B97	And that would be the system, then.
B98	I need the P Q.
B99	The P Q is already right there.
B100	Let's see A $\lor$ (B·C)
B101	and that would change to P $\lor$ Q . . . and P $\lor$ R,
B102	so we need a P $\lor$ R . . . P $\lor$ R.
B103	Well, that might give some trouble getting,
B104	though I might be able to get it out of using R12 in the second part of what we had in the beginning.
B105	But, if 1 could use R9
B106	and just get a P,
B107	that might be something, too.

E7.1

B108	Just get a P or a Q R.
B109	No, not quite . . . just get a P or get a . . . or, wait a second.
B110	If I have to reverse that now . . . if I have to reverse that afterward,
B111	then I'd start with (Q·R) $\lor$ P.

E7.2

B112	Let's see now . . . Q·R. How can I get that?
B113	Seems to suggest only complicated ways of arriving at that.

E7.3

B114	So how can I get down to single letters?
B115	Doesn't seem very convenient at all. . . .
B116	Getting down to single letters seems almost impossible in this.

E8.1

B117	Trouble is, I need a single letter to make a single letter.
B118	So there doesn't seem to be any practicality in that.
B119	Well, I guess we'll have to concentrate on 4 and 7 again, deriving something through that.
B120	Well, that presents a problem again in the second part of that . . . Q $\supset$ R . . . Q $\supset$ R.
B121	Well now . . . if I do what I was thinking of before. . . .
B122	Let's see now, thinking about R6 again.
B123	Going back in circles it seems.
B124	R6 . . .
B125	and that would give me R, or would it?
B126	Yeah, that would give me. . . .
B127	Let's see, we applied 6 in the beginning . . . didn't we?
B128	And then we applied 2. . . . (mike noise)
B129	My whole trouble seems to be signs this time.

B130	Well, if I use R5,
B131	I'd be stuck with a tilde in the front,
B132	so that's out altogether.

E8.2

B133	Well, I think I'm going to have to work backwards from this.
B134	So, in order to get a Q R which is possible . . . which is positive,
B135	Q $\vee$ R . . .
B136	would before that be $\sim$R Q, no, it'd be tilde . . . $\sim$Q . . . $\sim$Q $\supset$ R.
B137	Wait a second, $\sim$Q $\supset$ R, that sets itself up very nice.
B138	But that doesn't find me another horseshoe.
B139	Well, now let's see, if we apply to 3 in the first part, what we have up there, R6 going backwards
B140	so we have another horseshoe. . . .
B141	What will we have?
B142	Let me see we'd have $\sim$P . . . $\sim$P $\supset$ Q. Right?
B143	$\sim$P $\supset$ Q . . . $\sim$P $\supset$ Q. . . . $\sim$P $\supset$ Q.
B144	OK, let's try that.
B145	(E: 6 to L3.)
B146	[E writes L4: $(\sim$P $\supset$ Q)$\cdot(\sim$R $\supset$ $\sim$Q)]
B147	Well now let's see. If we take down from L1, the Q $\supset$ R
B148	and on L4 the $\sim$P $\supset$ Q
B149	and work diagonally.
B150	But what would be first?
B151	L1 would have to be on the bottom, 4 would have to be on the top.
B152	That would give me $\sim$P $\supset$ R.
B153	That sounds like something I wanted before . . . $\sim$P $\supset$ R. . . .
B154	I can't think of what.

E8.3

B155	Well let's see, let's do that. . . .
B156	This might be all on the wrong track, but. . . .
B157	(E: Do what?)
B158	Well, this is a whole bunch of steps.
B159	and you have to split L4,
B160	'cause I want the first part using R8
B161	and split L1 . . . I want the second part.
B162	(E: Well, tell me what to do.)
B163	OK. This is R8 again. Using R8, give me the first part of L4.
B164	(E: R8 on L4.)
B165	[E writes L5: $\sim$P $\supset$ Q]
B166	And applying R8 to L1, I want the second part.
B167	[E writes L6: Q $\supset$ R]
B168	Right. And now, applying R12 to this,
B169	I'd get $\sim$P. . . .
B170	(E: R12 to 5 and 6.)
B171	[E writes L7: $\sim$P $\supset$ R]

E9

B172	Right. Now, to make any use of that, I'd have to eliminate some. . . .
B173	That horseshoe in there.
B174	That looks rather convenient so far.
B175	Looking at what I have at the end, Q$\cdot$R and a P wedge.
B176	I'm looking at. . . .
B177	Let's see, what would happen . . .
B178	I need to change this thing first before I go any further.
B179	So I'd have to apply R6 to what I have on 7.
B180	I think that's next in order.

B181	(E: Want me to do that?)
B182	Yeah.
B183	[E writes L8: P ∨ R]
B184	P ∨ R . . .
B185	and I also have P ∨ Q.
B186	Now, would suggest I use 7 between those two,
B187	in order to be a simple way of hitching these two together . . . of putting one above the other.
B188	Well, using 10. . . .
B189	Well let's see now . . . get these in the right order.
B190	P would be A . . . would be equal to A in 7.
B191	(E: The order doesn't matter. I mean the order of the line doesn't matter.)
B192	Oh, I see. OK, now . . . did we. . . .
B193	OK, from L1 we take out the P ∨ Q
B194	and from L8 we take the P ∨ R
B195	and we apply R10
B196	and get. . . .
B197	(E: Want me to do all this?)
B198	Yeah.
B199	(E: Well, we're applying 8 to 1)
B200	[E writes L9: P ∨ Q]
B201	Oh, we have to do that first, that's right.
B202	OK, and then we'll combine what we have in L8 and L9.
B203	(E: What rule are we applying?)
B204	You'd have to apply 7
B205	and then I'd have B times C. . . .
B206	(E: 7 isn't a two-line rule. . . .)
B207	(E: What's the next step?)
B208	Oh, I'm still still skipping things.
B209	You have to apply 10
B210	and then 7.
B211	(E: All right, 10 to L8 and L9. . . .)
B212	(E: L10 becomes . . . want this first or. . . .)
B213	Well, let's see which I'll need.
B214	Now I have to look at 7 again for this.
B215	C will have to be R
B216	and B will have to be Q . . . B will have to be Q.
B217	So P ∨ Q comes first . . . P ∨ Q.
B218	(E: All right.)
B219	[E writes L10: (P ∨ Q)·(P ∨ R)]
B220	Now , . . using R7,
B221	putting those together. . . .
B222	[E writes L11: P ∨ (Q·R)]
B223	(E: Looks like the answer.)
B224	Yep. I think there must have been a shorter way of doing that.
B225	(E: Well, that's not bad. There weren't too many extra steps there.)

APPENDIX 10.11

S10 on C1

B1	[E writes L1: (P ∨ Q)·(Q ⊃ R)]
B2	[E writes L0: P ∨ (Q·R)]

E1.1

B3	All right. Hum . . . in a way that looks like R4 backwards.
B4	But . . . um . . . I'm afraid it isn't.
B5	It doesn't. . . .
B6	Would give us a negative sign which . . . couldn't get rid of.
B7	So we try . . . let's see.

E1.2

B8	I keep looking at the second expression, trying to work backwards
B9	which isn't too good.
B10	I'll just see.
B11	$P \vee (Q \cdot R)$ would be P. . . .
B12	Oh, it'd be R7 . . . $(P \vee Q) \cdot (P \vee R)$.
B13	Now in the first expression there is $(P \vee Q) \cdot (Q \supset R)$
B14	which isn't consistent
B15	because there's only one P.

E2

B16	All right . . . um . . . let's see . . . we have to keep a P, a Q, and an R.
B17	Therefore we couldn't use R12
B18	because it eliminates Q's . . .
B19	after you got done with all the other rigamarole.
B20	I keep trying to apply algebra.
B21	A dot expression. . . .
B22	"Use only with wedge or dot". . . .
B23	R5 . . .
B24	R1. . . .
B25	Neither of which seems to fit.
B26	This is . . . "a major dot and positive total expression" which we can maybe work in R8 . . .
B27	if I can figure something out.

E3

B28	If we got $P \vee Q$ on one line,
B29	and $Q \supset R$ on another. . . .
B30	The thing would be to change the $Q \supset R$ in some way.
B31	We can change it to $\sim Q \vee R$.
B32	Then . . . oh, I can't use the elimination.
B33	How to get rid of one of those R . . . Q's is the thing.
B34	Um . . . $P \vee Q$ . . . $P \vee Q$, $Q \supset R$.
B35	Perhaps change the $P \vee Q$ to a dot expression.
B36	That would make the entire expression negative.
B37	Um . . . let's see . . . minus . . . tilde . . . oh, $\sim(\sim P \cdot \sim Q)$
B38	and change the Q to a wedge expression . . .
B39	the second expression to a wedge expression would get $\sim Q \vee R$ . . .
B40	which we could change to a dot expression,
B41	making $\sim Q \cdot R$. Um . . . $\sim Q$ dot tilde . . . no, $Q \cdot \sim R$.
B42	Now . . . change the wedge to a dot . . . dot expression.

E4

B43	Um . . . eliminate . . . oh, the thing to do is eliminate one of the Q's
B44	by R11.
B45	All right. $Q \cdot R$.
B46	Now, $P \vee Q$ would equal, if we changed it to a horseshoe,
B47	would equal $\sim P \supset Q$.
B48	Now . . . $A \supset B$ is $\sim P$ . . .
B49	R2.
B50	Now, how do you eliminate one expression . . .

B51	by R8.
B52	All right, if we changed that to a dot we would get . . . change the first
B53	expression to a dot would equal . . . hum.
B54	The only way you can do it is R5
B55	and you get a negative expression.
B56	Um . . . have to work it around to R11 somehow.
B57	Try eliminating. . . .
B58	We'll try changing the other first. . . .
B59	Has to be a horseshoe expression.
B60	First expression changed to a horseshoe
B61	would equal $\sim$Q horseshoe . . . no, $\sim$P $\supset$ Q.
B62	Then . . . I'll work on the first expression.
B63	Apply R6 to the first parenthesis.
B64	[E writes L2: $(\sim P \supset Q) \cdot (Q \supset R)$]
B65	All right. Now . . . I want to get . . .
B66	oh . . . no, I want to get the Q alone.

E5

B67	Are we permitted to use R9?
B68	(E: Sure.)
B69	Just out of curiosity.
B70	(E: You can use any rule, any time.)
B71	OK.
B72	(E: 'Cept when it's unapplicable.)
B73	Yeah. I was thinking I might be able to work R11 by adding something on.
B74	But I'm not sure yet.

E6

B75	Um . . . I'll work with the first parenthesis for a while on L2.
B76	I'd like to change that to a wedge expression.
B77	So I'll use rule. . . .
B78	Oh, I already had a wedge expression. . . .
B79	What's the matter with me?
B80	Oh, apply rule . . . no, not R5.
B81	Um . . . try R2 on the first . . . first parenthesis in L2.
B82	[E writes L3: $(\sim Q \supset P) \cdot (Q \supset R)$]
B83	Now, that doesn't seem to have done much good.
B84	Uh . . . I'm afraid I've gotten off on the wrong track.
B85	Now . . . um . . . well, we'll see how it works changing. . . .
B86	No, not R5.
B87	Perhaps if I can get around to. . . .
B88	Oh . . . wait. R11, A $\supset$ B over A yields B, or is decoded to B.
B89	So here I'm putting chemical expressions now.
B90	The thing to do is to get an expression which would . . . ah . . . eliminate half.

E7

B91	Oh, R7 . . . try R7 with the top expression.
B92	Ah . . . you can do it backwards.
B93	Now, the thing to do is to get the first Q both positive and in a horseshoe expression, if that's possible.
B94	Yes, it is.
B95	That would give me . . . using it in the first parenthesis . . . it would give me $\sim$P $\supset$ Q,
B96	No . . . that's not what I want.
B97	Oh . . . no, I'd get $\sim$Q $\supset$ P. . . .
B98	Was thinking of applying R1 in the parenthesis.
B99	Oh . . . apply rule. . . .
B100	No, can't do that with a horseshoe.
B101	How 'bout. . . .

B102 Oh, apply R6 to the second set of parenthesis in L1.
B103 [E writes L4: (P ∨ Q)·(~Q ∨ R)]
B104 All right, now . . . hum . . . seems impossible to get those Q's in the same position.
B105 I could apply R7.
B106 Oh, now we have two wedges.
B107 Perhaps I could switch one of them around and make it a dot expression.
B108 Hum . . . P ∨ Q, ~Q ∨ R
B109 (sighs) I'm very leary of R5
B110 because of the negative expression.

E8
B111 R11 is a horseshoe expression . . . no sign changes.
B112 Therefore I'd have to eliminate. . . .
B113 Oh . . . Oh, I know what to do! I think.
B114 Um . . . even in 8 . . . 1 . . . 5 . . .
B115 which one will I eliminate?
B116 Um . . . it'd have to be a Q·R.
B117 Now, if I change that to a dot expression,
B118 would make the whole expression negative.
B119 If I get the Q by itself,
B120 I can now apply R8.

E9
B121 However . . . would probably be an expression similar to R10 . . .
B122 with the P alone and the Q times R by itself.
B123 Now . . . doggone!
B124 Um . . . A is . . . A ∨ X.
B125 Um . . . ~B ⊃ ~A . . . R2.
B126 But that has nothing to do with it.
B127 Q . . .
B128 see . . . R5, if I applied R5,
B129 I couldn't do it just inside the parenthesis, could I?
B130 That still wouldn't be a negative expression . . . er . . . a positive expression.
B131 (E: You can use 5 within the parenthesis . . . the entire expression would be positive but the parenthesis would be negative.)
B132 Hum . . . I want to get rid of . . . a . . . say, a P.
B133 Oh, that has to be a dot, though in R10.
B134 You have a P for one line and Q·R for another line.
B135 Oh! oh, perhaps I could do that because R5 is reversible.
B136 All right . . . um . . . what did I want to get rid of?
B137 Oh . . . apply R5 to the first set of parenthesis in L4.
B138 [E writes L5: ~(~P·~Q)·(~Q ∨ R)]
B139 OK. Um . . . now, apply R5. . . .
B140 Oh! I should have said apply R5 to the whole thing . . . to the other set of parenthesis . . . can you do that?
B141 (E: R5 to line 5.)
B142 [E writes L6: ~(~P·~Q)·~(Q·~R)]
B143 All right. Um . . . now, what I want . . . what I asked you before, was um . . . whether I could. . . .
B144 Oh, wait a minute . . . I think I messed myself up.
B145 Now, what I meant was, can I apply R8 inside the parenthesis even though there was a tilde in front of it?
B146 (E: No.)
B147 That's what I thought.
B148 (E: Apply to the whole expression . . . not to just one part of it.)
B149 Uh huh . . . the whole expression is positive.
B150 (E: That's right.)

B151	Um . . . let's see. (sighs) If I eliminated one side of the expression,
B152	I still couldn't apply R8
B153	and eliminate something in the parenthesis.
B154	So, that's out.
B155	I'm still worried about getting rid of the Q.

E10

B156	Back to the beginning. . . .
B157	How 'bout R7 . . . try that again.
B158	If I, no . . . that doesn't . . . if I could work around to R7 in some way.
B159	All right, if I apply R5 to the first parenthesis
B160	I would get minus or tilde $(\sim P \cdot \sim Q)$ dot . . .
B161	and in the second parenthesis I would get first, $\sim Q \vee R$
B162	and then $\sim(Q \cdot \sim R)$.
B163	OK, the, $Q \cdot \sim R$. . . .
B164	Now, why can't I get my . . . I cannot get the Q's around so that they're alike.
B165	If I switched them around
B166	I'd still have a positive Q and a negative Q.
B167	Oh, I know . . . I apply R2 to the second expression
B168	getting $\sim Q \supset \sim R$.
B169	Then I would apply rule . . . R6
B170	and get $Q \vee R$
B171	and then apply R5
B172	and get minus $(\sim Q \vee \sim R)$.
B173	Then, I would apply R1 to one of the . . . to the first expression
B174	getting $(\sim Q \vee \sim P) \cdot (\sim Q \vee R)$.
B175	Then work R7 . . .
B176	getting $\sim Q \vee (\sim P \cdot \sim R)$.
B177	Now, what good would that do?
B178	Well, hum . . . I think I better see that in writing,
B179	I can't remember all that.
B180	Um . . . what did I start with?
B181	All right, apply R2 to the second parenthesis in L1.
B182	[E writes L7: $(P \vee Q) \cdot (\sim R \supset \sim Q)$]
B183	Oh. OK, now apply R6 to the second set of parenthesis in L7.
B184	(E: All right . . . R6 . . .)
B185	Oh! I . . . I made a very bad mistake.
B186	I didn't notice that they reversed.
B187	That'll ruin my setup.
B188	(E: You don't want me to do that?)
B189	No, wait. Let's see . . . $\sim B \supset A$ would change to $B \supset \sim Q$.
B190	Oh, that's all right . . . that's OK. Go ahead.
B191	Oh, what did I have you do? oh . . . yes, to the second parenthesis.
B192	[E writes L8: $(P \vee Q) \cdot (R \vee \sim Q)$]
B193	All right, now apply R5 to both sets of parenthesis . . . individually, of course.
B194	[E writes L9: $\sim(\sim P \cdot \sim Q) \cdot \sim(\sim R \cdot Q)$]
B195	Dot Q?
B196	(E: Uh huh.)
B197	Oh . . . yeah, I did mess myself up. Doggone!
B198	(sighs) All right, we'll try something else.
B199	Oh . . . I see how I could've . . . oh, I know how I could eliminate that.
B200	In which part . . . where did I apply R2 to L1.
B201	Oh . . . then I got a horseshoe . . .
B202	then I applied R6 to L7
B203	which gave me . . . $R \vee \sim Q$.
B204	No, I still wouldn't. . . .
B205	Even by switching it around

B206   I couldn't make it any better.

E11
B207   Something tells me that there's a very easy solution to this problem.
B208   A ⊃ B over A is B.
B209   A over B is A times B.
B210   Hum . . . how to get Q·R over P.
B211   Now, Q·R over P changed, going backwards . . . I'll have to go backwards.
B212   Changed to a dot by R5
B213   would be . . . minus . . . would be ~P· tilde . . . oh, tilde the quantity ~P dot the
        quantity . . . tilde the quantity two [Q] times R . . . Q R in brackets.
B214   Now, if we had a horseshoe . . . hum . . . horseshoe. . . .
B215   I changed it to a wedge.
B216   One tilde would be gone,
B217   and we had tilde . . . tilde R dot Q [~(~R·Q) or tilde . . . ~R·Q].
B218   Now . . . P wedge . . .
B219   have to get a ~P somewhere.
B220   Well that's easy enough to do.
B221   No, it isn't.
B222   Not with R5.
B223   Now, look over all the rules again.
B224   Can't use 3. . . .
B225   Can't use . . . hum . . .
B226   I'm getting stuck.
B227   A horseshoe triangle . . . 12. . . .
B228   Figure out a way for that.
B229   A ⊃ B . . . hum . . . Q ⊃ R . . . P ⊃ Q.
B230   The horseshoes are the things that foul everything up.
B231   A . . .
B232   let's see now . . . don't get clutched.
B233   Now . . . I have to say something.
B234   P ∨ Q . . . P ∨ Q times R.
B235   (sighs) A wedge B wedge C is A wedge B wedge C.
B236   Now . . . it's sort of . . . maybe it's an uncodable expression.
B237   (E: You have any hot leads?)
B238   No, well . . . I have an idea of how it should be done.
B239   Something . . . well, I don't know if the idea is right,
B240   but something like . . . the same lines as R10 is the only way I can figure out.
B241   But . . . the wedge . . . the transition from the wedge to the dot makes such a complex
        expression that I just don't see . . . how it'll work.
B242   (E: Well, time's up.)
B243   Oh . . . I'm sorry . . . I didn't get it.
B244   (E: Don't be sorry.)
B245   (E: Want to see how it can be done?)
B246   Yes.
B247   [E outlines solution.]

APPENDIX 10.12

S11 on C1

B1   [E writes L1:   (P ∨ Q)·(Q ⊃ R)]
B2   [E writes L0:   P ∨ (Q·R)]

E1

B3	Hum. Let's see now . . . (sighs) . . . the only thing to remove is the horseshoe.
B4	The Q is taken out on the first expression,
B5	the dot is the major connective to change to a wedge,
B6	and the horseshoe and [in ?] Q horseshoe R is changed to a dot.
B7	Let's see, what can I do on the first expression . . . P $\lor$ Q. . . .
B8	Hum . . . see . . . just looking on the sheet. . . .
B9	Hum . . . let's see, what would that be. What expression would that be?
B10	That could be A $\lor$ B and B $\lor$ C . . .
B11	or B $\supset$ C . . . humm.
B12	I don't want to change any of the signs, yet.
B13	Hum . . . let's see . . . expression. . . .
B14	No.
B15	Adding that is what. . . .
B16	A·B . . . what could I do with that?
B17	Hum . . . see . . . using rule R8
B18	I could get A or B on that by itself.
B19	Let's see . . . what would I have then?
B20	Let's see . . . what would change the horseshoe to a dot . . . on the second expression.
B21	Uh huh . . . A $\supset$ B. . . .
B22	No, I don't think that would work on 6 . . .
B23	then using 5. . . .
B24	(E: What are you talking about?)
B25	Oh . . . I'm trying to change the horseshoe in the second expression to a dot.
B26	But, let's see, using 6. . . .
B27	That would give me ~Q $\lor$ R.
B28	Let's see what good would that do me though . . . if any . . . hum.
B29	I keep tildes out, so to speak . . .
B30	Let's see . . . just looking on the sheets.
B31	Let's see . . . 4 . . . what is that?
B32	That's what . . . P $\lor$ Q . . . huh uh.
B33	See, 7 . . . ah . . .
B34	fits slightly . . . very slightly.
B35	Let's see now, if I used 1 on that I'd have what?
B36	That'd change it from A·B to B·A,
B37	which would give me (Q $\supset$ R)·(P $\lor$ Q),
B38	and we're using R7.
B39	Let's see, that would give me what . . . (Q $\supset$ R)·(P $\lor$ Q).
B40	That would change it to what. . . .
B41	Hum . . . P wedge . . . no, Q horseshoe R dot P [Q $\supset$ (R·P)? (Q $\supset$ R)·P ?]. . . .
B42	What good would that do me?

E2

B43	Hum . . . let's try to remove the Q in the first expression. . . .
B44	See if I can do that first.
B45	P $\lor$ Q . . . if I could only change that P $\lor$ Q . . . to a dot.
B46	Hum . . . see R1 . . . B $\lor$ A?
B47	What good would that do me now?
B48	See . . . B $\lor$ A. . . .
B49	Let's see . . . I'm on 12 . . . can I work anything on that?
B50	Doesn't look it.
B51	Let's see . . . 5. . . .
B52	What good would that do me now?
B53	That would change it to ~(~P·~Q).
B54	Hum . . . I can't use 8
B55	'cause the whole expression is negative. . . . (sighs)
B56	Let's see . . . using Q $\supset$ R as B, and tilde. . . .

B57	Wait . . . no. . . .

E3.1

B58	Start at the beginning again. $(P \lor Q) \cdot (Q \supset R)$ . . . going to $P \lor (Q \cdot R)$.
B59	Hum . . . I wonder whether we could work it backwards. . . .
B60	I have P . . . be A,
B61	and B would be Q,
B62	and C would be R . . . so let's see.
B63	Using 7 . . .
B64	that would give me P . . . P $\lor$ Q . . . P $\lor$ Q dot . . . hum P $\lor$ R.
B65	Let's see, P $\lor$ Q is my first expression in that. . . .
B66	The dot is the major connective. . . .
B67	And let's see . . . what expression would I have? Uh . . . P $\lor$ R. . . .
B68	So let's see . . . going forward now, what would it be?
B69	Parenthesis Q . . . or how would the $(Q \supset R)$ give me parenthesis P. . . .
B70	No, wait a minute . . . (sighs) . . . (mumbles).
B71	P $\lor$ (Q·R) as a result of 7 . . . goes backwards to that,
B72	so the step I use to get the final expression would be P $\lor$ Q
B73	which is the first expression I started out with . . . dot P wedge . . . P $\lor$ R.
B74	Ah . . . the only thing actually I'd have to work on is to change the Q $\supset$ R to P wedge . . . P wedge . . . P $\lor$ R.
B75	That doesn't help much
B76	because I'd have to change the first expression to get it
B77	and I'd have to change the results back to P $\lor$ Q.
B78	Let's see now . . . what could I do?
B79	Well, let's try to change the horseshoe to a wedge again.

E3.2

B80	Hum . . . (sighs) . . . A $\supset$ C on 12. . . .
B81	That would give me what I wanted . . .
B82	but in doing so, I'd have to take out the Q.
B83	On . . . uh . . . 12 if you have two lines, and there's an expression in each one, can you apply 12 to just those two expressions in both lines?
B84	Like you have . . . A and B in one line and this is . . . you know, a complex expression,
B85	and B and C is the other.
B86	You can just apply the two you want?
B87	Or would that . . . uh . . .
B88	That didn't make much sense.
B89	Ah . . . I mean . . . let's say, if two complex expressions . . . and . . . a . . . the one expression you want on one line is two letters . . .
B90	and you use that as A and B,
B91	and the second line . . . you have two expressions, too, but you only want to use one
B92	and you have the letters B and C in there.
B93	Can you apply 12 to just those two expressions . . . actually you have four?
B94	If you can understand what I mean.
B95	(E: Does it help to see there that the horseshoes must be major connectives . . .
B96	(E: does that answer your question?)
B97	Well, I see that . . . yeah,
B98	but . . . well, I know how that's set up on that.
B99	But I mean if somehow I had . . . if somehow I got it around like that.
B100	(E: Well, I'm not sure that you mean . . .)
B101	(E: but if you had a horseshoe here . . . and a horseshoe on a similar line below, you could call this A and this B and this C.)
B102	(E: Answer your question?)
B103	Well, almost but not quite.
B104	If I . . . see . . . let's say L1 was . . . uh was part of it . . .
B105	and it's sort of hard to explain why . . . that's . . . I have to show you what I mean.

B106	(E: Well, you couldn't have used just this. . . .)
B107	Yeah . . . well, that's what I mean.
B108	(E: Because the horseshoe here is not the major connective.)
B109	If I had another line and I was . . . let's see . . . using L1 as an example and I had the second line as $(P \lor Q) \cdot (R \supset Q)$.
B110	Could I use the $Q \supset R$ as $R \supset Q$ only in line 12 . . . and come out with uh . . .
B111	(E: Not without doing something else.)
B112	(E: No, because this is not the major connective of this expression.)
B113	I see.
B114	(E: And this is not the major connective in the second expression.)
B115	Well, let's see . . . I can discard that idea. . . .

E4

B116	Let's see . . . the end result . . .
B117	I had to use 7 . . .
B118	because that would give me actually exactly what I want. . . . (sighs)
B119	Let's see now . . . if I change the Q's around in there in the first expression,
B120	I'd have what . . . $Q \lor P$
B121	I'd use on that . . . R1.
B122	So that'd give me $(Q \lor P) \cdot (Q \supset R)$.
B123	If I change the horseshoe to a wedge. . . .
B124	See . . . what could I use on that?
B125	6. . . .
B126	No . . . that changes Q to $\sim$Q.
B127	That'd make that a different . . . different altogether.
B128	(sighs) What could I work on that now?
B129	See . . . R4 . . .
B130	$A \lor B$ . . . ah. . . .
B131	Let's see. That would give me $\sim(\sim P \cdot \sim Q)$.
B132	Hummm . . . changing them around with R1 . . .
B133	give me $\sim Q \cdot \sim P$.
B134	But . . . I don't think that's what I want.
B135	See now, then I'd have to change the dot to a wedge
B136	to use 7
B137	if I worked 6 on the second expression on L1. . . . (sighs)
B138	Now, if I do that. . . .
B139	Nope . . . no, I couldn't do that.
B140	Gotta use all three letters in there . . .
B141	and the only thing that would bring that . . . let's see.
B142	Almost sure equation 7 would have to be my last equation to be used.
B143	Now to set it up so I can use it.
B144	Let's see . . . $(A \lor B) \cdot (A \lor C)$ . . . hum . . .
B145	A dot B . . .
B146	10 . . . what could I do on that?
B147	I've got to use all the . . . the whole line, though.
B148	Let's see now . . . using P as A,
B149	Q is B
B150	and R is C . . .
B151	then I'll have what . . . A B, B C.
B152	Hum . . . now let's use $P \lor Q$ as A
B153	and no, on second thought . . . still wouldn't make any difference . . .

E5.1

B154	if I use 4 like that.
B155	(sighs) . . . See . . . I can't change the dot to a wedge as the major connective . . . at least not yet.
B156	Let's see . . . 9?

B157	Would good would that do me?
B158	Nothing.
B159	Unless of course, I used P $\lor$ Q and R . . .
B160	the whole first line as A. . . .
B161	And let's see, that is what?
B162	What could I use in place of that?
B163	Hum . . . could I use dot P?
B164	Hum . . . (sighs) . . . no, that'd have to be wedge P . . . wedge P . . . wedge P . . . hum.
B165	Using 9
B166	first I'd completely remove P $\lor$ Q
B167	and use Q $\supset$ R as A.
B168	Let's see, I could get Q $\supset$ R. . . .
B169	Now wait a minute . . . yeah, (Q $\supset$ R) $\lor$ P.
B170	Now, using 1
B171	from that I'd have P $\lor$ (Q $\supset$ R).
B172	Now what would change the horseshoe in the second expression to a dot?
B173	Hum . . . let's see . . . looking over the paper . . . horseshoe to a dot . . . let's see now . . . horseshoe to a dot.
B174	See anything . . . I could use 6
B175	and that would give me a wedge.
B176	And let's see . . . what would change the wedge to a dot? hum . . . a wedge to a dot.
B177	Let's see now . . . 10. . . .
B178	No, I'd have to use the whole expression.
B179	That wouldn't do any good.
B180	Have to take it a step at a time.
B181	Apply R8 to L1.
B182	Which part do I want . . . the second half.
B183	(E: Keep the second half?)
B184	Yeah, keep the second half.
B185	[E writes L2: Q $\supset$ R]
B186	Then apply R9 to that using Q $\supset$ R as A, and add a wedge P there . . . in place of that.
B187	[E writes L3: (Q $\supset$ R) $\lor$ P]
B188	And then, using R1 on that . . . ah . . . first half. . . .
B189	[E writes L4: P $\lor$ (Q $\supset$ R)]
B190	Uh huh. Now . . . how can I change that horseshoe to a dot?
B191	Hum . . . let's see.
B192	They're not reversed . . . Q and R aren't reversed.
B193	So . . . let's see now . . . what can I do on it?
B194	Let's see now . . . 6
B195	would give me $\sim$A $\supset$ R . . . er . . . $\sim$Q $\lor$ R.
B196	What good would that do me now?
B197	(sighs). . . . Hum . . . what could I do on that?
B198	See . . . does 7 work on anywhere on that?
B199	Let's see . . . I'd have a wedge. . . .
B200	No, Q horseshoe there. . . .
B201	That wouldn't do me much good.
B202	I have what . . . see, if I used 5 on Q $\supset$ R. . . .
B203	That would give me $\sim$($\sim$Q $\cdot$ $\sim$R).
B204	Uh . . . that wouldn't be much help.
B205	Ah . . . let's see now . . . 6 . . . using. . . .

E5.2

B206	See I'd come out with $\sim$Q $\lor$ R.
B207	Huh uh . . . maybe . . . let's see . . . maybe I shouldn't have used 9 yet.
B208	Yeah . . . let's just work on Q $\supset$ R without the P in there.
B209	All right . . . Q $\supset$ R . . . hum . . . let's see.
B210	That's what I have to remove . . . the. . . .

B211	No, no . . . I have to remove the R's first
B212	and then remove the Q.
B213	Now what would do that?
B214	The only thing that would do it is to change the horseshoe to a dot.
B215	But that leads to too many complications
B216	Can't use 5
B217	'cause the expression has to be positive . . . hum.
B218	Go back to 1 again.
B219	See . . . R4 . . . see. . . .
B220	No, the dot louses that up . . . nope.
B221	Let's see . . . what can I do to that Q ⊃ R . . .
B222	change it to a delta Q . . . delta Q wedge R. . . .
B223	Still doesn't get me anywhere.
B224	Delta Q . . . uh . . .
B225	if only I could reverse 'em.
B226	Hum . . . let's see now . . . Q is A.
B227	R is B
B228	I have A ⊃ B . . .
B229	hum . . . and applying 2
B230	I'd have ∼R ⊃ ∼B . . . er . . . ∼Q.
B231	And then applying 6 to it and I'd have what . . .
B232	R wedge . . . R ∨ ∼Q.
B233	That isn't much good.
B234	Don't tell me the half hour's up already.
B235	(E: Yeah.)
B236	(E: What do you think was giving you the trouble here?)
B237	That horseshoe in there.
B238	(E: That horseshoe in step 4?)
B239	Yeah . . . or if I could just get that horseshoe out of 2.
B240	(E: Yeah.)
B241	I could then apply R9 to it.
B242	But I just can't seem to do it.
B243	(E: Well this is a pretty hard one,)
B244	(E: because you are applying two two-line rules.)
B245	That's what I was trying to do.
B246	[E outlines solution.]

APPENDIX 10.13

S13 on C1

B1	[E writes L1: (P ∨ Q)·(Q ⊃ R)]
B2	[E writes L0: P ∨ (Q·R)]
E1	
B3	Huh. Let's see.
B4	(E: What are you doing?)
B5	Just looking first.
B6	I notice that the second parts are the same except for the connective
B7	and the major connectives are different.
B8	Maybe it would be smart to work backwards
B9	although that one is not so obvious as the other one was.
B10	Ah, let's see. Maybe your best bet again would be to pull them apart,

B11	taking a lesson from the last one.
B12	Ah, if you changed, let's see . . . the horseshoe to a dot, the second part of it. . . .
B13	You can't do that. . . .
B14	You have to change it to a wedge
B15	and then to a dot.
B16	Oh, well, let's see . . . A $\supset$ B would equal $\sim$Q, oh no, yeh, $\sim$Q $\vee$ R $\sim$Q $\vee$ R . . . and ah . . . $\sim$Q $\vee$ R.

E2

B17	Let me think. We change the sign from the wedges.
B18	If you apply . . . them apart,
B19	R6 again in the first part,
B20	you would get $\sim$P, $\sim$P $\supset$ Q . . . $\sim$P $\supset$ Q. . . .
B21	Then you have like A $\supset$ B . . . B $\supset$ Q. . . .
B22	Ah . . . A B, B C . . . A B, B C. . . .
B23	They would have horseshoes inside. . . .
B24	Oh, oh, can't do that. . . .
B25	Horseshoes inside. . . .
B26	Major dot connector.

E3

B27	Maybe if you change them to. . . .
B28	Leave them in wedges might be better.
B29	[One sentence unclear.]
B30	'Cause R7, since it goes backward, looks basically the same as that last part.
B31	See if we can try that.
B32	Changing the wedge to a horseshoe
B33	using R6. . . .
B34	You would come up with ah. . . .
B35	Oh, everything seems blank.
B36	Using R6 to the first. . . .
B37	No . . . I want to get a dot between B and C.
B38	So there'll have to be wedges inside and we have a major dot connective.
B39	So we'll change a horseshoe to a wedge
B40	using R6.
B41	We have $\sim$P $\supset$ Q . . . $\sim$P $\supset$ Q . . . ah $\sim$P $\supset$ Q.
B42	Could you do that, Andy?
B43	Using R6. . . .
B44	(E: R6 on L1.)
B45	You get $\sim$P . . . ($\sim$P $\supset$ Q).
B46	[E writes L2: ($\sim$P $\supset$ Q)$\cdot$(Q $\supset$ R)]
B47	All right. We'll have to rely on 7
B48	because it does give us the right form.
B49	You have to have A B, A C,
B50	and you had it that way.
B51	Ah . . . you want to keep the horseshoes in, or do you?
B52	What am I babbling about?
B53	I want to get the wedges.
B54	I'm sorry Andy, will you erase that please?
B55	(E: We'll just leave it that way.)
B56	Using R6 on that again,
B57	I want to get wedges,
B58	I don't want those horseshoes.
B59	The first part's the same
B60	[E writes L3: (P $\vee$ Q)$\cdot$($\sim$Q $\vee$ R)]
B61	Right. OK, then you could say that is. . . .
B62	Still we don't have a R7.

B63   It's probably a kickback to it.

E4.1
B64   Ah. . . . You want to get it A B, A C.
B65   You have . . . A in the final is going to be P,
B66   and then you have Q R.
B67   We're going to have to get that expression to P wedge parenthesis . . . no, P ∨ Q, which we have, dot (P ∨ R).
B68   Hold on to that last part, P ∨ R . . .
B69   I just want to get the ∼Q to P.
B70   Now, how can I get that?
B71   Ah, probably by using two lines.
B72   You have to get a ∼Q to a P.
B73   Ah, everything's all right except that one letter.
B74   Well, maybe we can use two lines.
B75   You have, you've got to have a horseshoe connective. . . .
B76   We have dots.
B77   And I want to keep them.
B78   See if we can use R8.
B79   We'd have . . . according to R1, it would be A B over B C.
B80   And you've got dot connectives.
B81   Now if you changed them to horseshoes, you would get A C,
B82   which would be . . . ah . . . A C,
B83   but you're eliminating your P.

E4.2
B84   I know R7 is the ending,
B85   and everything's perfect except that one letter.
B86   Wait a minute . . . maybe I was wrong on my last assumption.
B87   Let's see, in order to get from the last part of 7 to the first part, looking at the end,
B88   we would have to have P ∨ Q in parenthesis, dot, yeh, P ∨ R.
B89   Yeh, I was right in that assumption.
B90   Ah, hummm. If you can use two lines . . . probably . . .
B91   that seems to be the only thing I can see . . . two lines.
B92   I could break it apart,
B93   but I don't want to break it apart though.
B94   It looks like I'm going to have to though.
B95   That one letter. . . .
B96   Well, what can we do . . . using the wedge in the first part we could reverse it away from the first part.
B97   R ∼Q . . . it would be R ∨ ∼Q.
B98   A B equals C using R1. . . .
B99   That doesn't do any good.
B100   R2, no.
B101   R3, no.
B102   R4 would be a dot,
B103   No . . . we don't have the right connectives to apply it.
B104   A B dot something.
B105   R5,
B106   we would get tilde outside . . . ∼Q dot,
B107   I don't want to change the connectives though.

E4.3
B108   R7 seems to be the key.
B109   Ah, let's see how you eliminate.
B110   You could rule [use?] R11.
B111   You could use R8,

B112	ah, and keep the first part of it which is good, P ∨ Q,
B113	and then . . . P ∨ Q . . .
B114	and saying that is A using R9,
B115	you could say that that is P ∨ Q parenthesis, and I want wedge R.
B116	Wait a minute. Wedge R . . . that would be three wedges.
B117	We can change the ∼Q to a P,
B118	that's all we need.
B119	Can't change one letter to another.

E5

B120	Maybe we should start back in the beginning.
B121	I like that start,
B122	probably started too soon, though.
B123	Maybe if you didn't use R6 the second time, if you didn't use it the second time
B124	you'd have A dot B over A dot C.
B125	[One sentence unclear.]
B126	But you could change it . . . one part to A and one part to B.
B127	So you have P ∨ Q over Q ⊃ R.
B128	Maybe it would be better the other way.
B129	I can't seem to see ahead.
B130	Wait, using R10 at the very end . . .
B131	you could get A over B.
B132	Let's see if we can get A over B.
B133	We can say the A part is good, generally speaking;
B134	the B part I don't like.
B135	I can change ∼Q ⊃ R to P ∨ R,
B136	and ah if we could use that part with a part with a P in it,
B137	I mean an R in it. . . .
B138	Let's see . . . I can't see anything. . . .
B139	I'm sorry I seem to be giving up all the time. . . .

E6.1

B140	I know R7 is it . . . at least I think it is,
B141	and in order to use R7 effectively you can't have a ∼Q.
B142	You have to have P.
B143	Now, how can I eliminate ∼Q? . . . and get a P in there?
B144	You can use R10,
B145	that might help a bit . . .
B146	you'd get P ⊃ Q over P ⊃ R. . . .
B147	No, that's not right . . . P over . . . to get a dot expression.
B148	Yeh, yeh, you'd get P ∨ Q over P ∨ R.
B149	All right, we can get the P ∨ Q.
B150	Do we have a P ∨ R anywhere?
B151	No. . . .
B152	That means we're going to have to condense somewhere.
B153	We can condense somewhere but we eliminate, ah, let's see, we have to eliminate a Q or a ∼Q . . . something with Q in the expression
B154	and we have to keep the P and R.
B155	Well, we have two expressions with Q's in and a P and R . . . the very first one.
B156	All right, going back to that . . .
B157	or we can go back to the second one. . . .
B158	Let's see, if we use that thing with. . . .
B159	[One sentence unclear.]
B160	I must remember that . . . I want to get a P ∨ R from somewhere out of two expressions.
B161	Now, we're probably going to have to go into dots or horseshoes to get it out.
B162	Wait, let's see what we can do.
B163	Condensing you can use horseshoes, horseshoes only for two lines.

B164	So maybe if . . . L2 is in horseshoes, so if we keep . . .
B165	in order to condense we get A ⊃ B, over B ⊃ C. A ⊃ B over B ⊃ C.
B166	Using L2 and R8, we get ∼P ⊃ Q over Q ⊃ R.
B167	That would give us A B, over B C.
B168	That would be ∼Q ⊃ R.
B169	Ha, ha, ha, . . . ∼P ⊃ R. . . .
B170	We want to get to ∼P ∨ R . . . no, no, no, P ∨ R.
B171	We want to get ∼P ⊃ R to P ∨ R
B172	using R6.
B173	We get ∼P wedge . . . we start with a horseshoe. . . .

E6.2

B174	Write this down before I forget this,
B175	I think I'm getting somewhere.
B176	What did I do now?
B177	I want to split them
B178	so I used L2 and I applied R8
B179	[E writes L4: ∼P ⊃ Q]
B180	and I got ∼P ⊃ Q over. . . .
B181	No.
B182	Now I apply it again to L2 and get Q ⊃ R.
B183	[E writes L5: Q ⊃ R]
B184	Then I want to apply R12 to that, L4 and L5,
B185	and I get ∼P ⊃ R.
B186	[E writes L6: ∼P ⊃ R]
B187	Now I want to change it to P ∨ R . . .
B188	Now you can get around that by using R6 I think.
B189	Using R6, now let me get this straight.
B190	You would change it to P ∨ R.
B191	Ha, ha. Yeh, use R6
B192	and you will come up with P ∨ R.
B193	[E writes L7: P ∨ R]

E7.1

B194	Now, if we can get that back into the expression.
B195	How to get it back though?
B196	It's probably all there and I just don't see it.
B197	I want to get it to A·B. . . .
B198	No, I want (A ∨ B)·(A ∨ C).
B199	And I have the A ∨ C part.
B200	I want a dot in the center
B201	and I want to get the A ∨ B part.
B202	How if I could. . . .
B203	Can't substitute, though.
B204	Oh, and I thought I was going great guns.
B205	Well, let's see. Ah, you can add by using R9. . . .

E7.2

B206	Oh, oh. I know what I wanted to use, I wanted to use R10 saying A over B equals A B.
B207	Well, I want . . . I have the B part which will be downstairs. . . .
B208	I want an A part above it which is going to be equal to P ∨ Q,
B209	Ah, but I don't have it.
B210	I have it in the expression, though . . .
B211	A B over . . . let's see . . . R7's the key.
B212	Maybe I shouldn't have dropped that one expression.
B213	Let's see, I've used R6 to L1 twice
B214	and I used R8 to get two separate expressions.
B215	If I can get from somewhere just a P ∨ Q . . .

B216	but I would have had to get it before that.
B217	Well, let's see . . . you can always say that A·A, A·B rather, is A.
B218	Wait, wait, wait . . . then you're going to. . . .
B219	Say we had used that beforehand, we'd have a P ∨ Q over a P ∨ R.
B220	That's it.
B221	Andy, use rule, can you squeeze it in somewhere before?
B222	(E: The order of lines doesn't matter.)
B223	Ah, oh, all right. Use R8 again on L3
B224	and you get P ∨ Q.
B225	Then using R10,
B226	that's it.
B227	[E writes L8: P ∨ Q]
B228	Hot dog, I think. . . .
B229	Wait, keep my fingers crossed. . . .
B230	Using R10 on L8 and L7
B231	we get (P ∨ Q)·(P ∨ R).
B232	[E writes L9: (P ∨ Q)·(P ∨ R)]
B233	And that, using R7 on that line,
B234	you can reverse the order at the top to get P wedge parenthesis, the B part which is Q·R.
B235	That's it.
B236	[E writes L10: P ∨ (Q·R)]
B237	Ah, I feel great. Finally.
B238	(E: Fine.)
B239	I knew that was the key and I just had to do it that way.
B240	(E: You almost gave up there once.)
B241	Yeh, I was giving up.
B242	(E: When did you know you had it?)
B243	I knew you had to use R7
B244	and that I figured was almost obvious.
B245	And then I figured to get two dot expressions
B246	you would have to use A over B, R10.
B247	And from that I just tried to get both of them apart and get them somewhere separate. . . .
B248	Ho, ho, do I get a ribbon?

APPENDIX 10.14

S9 on α2

B1	[E writes L1: ∼S·(S ∨ ∼Q)]
B2	[E writes L0: ∼Q]
B3	Try and get ∼Q?
B4	(E: Uh huh, see if that can be recoded as ∼Q.)
B5	Now . . . looking at R8.
B6	where I can drop some of this stuff.
B7	So, I'd use R1
B8	and reverse the whole expression.
B9	(E: That's what you want me to do to start with?)
B10	Yeah.
B11	(E: R1, L1.)
B12	[E writes L2: (S ∨ ∼Q)·∼S)]

B13	Right. Now, I'd use R8.
B14	(E: On L2 you'd use R8 . . . and which do you want to drop? You can drop either the A part or the B part.)
B15	I can drop either?
B16	Oh, then I wouldn't have bothered to use R1.
B17	I just want to get rid of the ~S.
B18	[E writes L3: S ∨ ~Q]
B19	And . . . now I'd use it again . . .
B20	or can I?
B21	(E: No.)
B22	Ah . . . that's right.
B23	I may as well start over again.
B24	(E: Now I don't make any mistakes on purpose here, but I may make some, so you watch what I do.)
B25	(E: I'll do exactly what you want me to do.)
B26	(E: Will you try to keep talking?)
B27	OK . . . I looked at R5
B28	and that looks like it might be what I'm looking for.
B29	So, let's apply R5 to this.
B30	[E writes L4: ~(~S·Q)]
B31	Does this work the same way as math . . . that that first tilde can be multiplied . . .
B32	(E: No. Just work within the rules here.)
B33	Hum . . . that's funny.
B34	But then there's only sign changes involved, wouldn't that be?
B35	(E: Yeah, here there are only . . . well, you've changed the connective here.)
B36	(E: You've changed the sign of both the A and B part,)
B37	(E: and you've changed the sign of the total expression, is what you've done.)
B38	Well, that's no help then at all.
B39	See, I figured the two tildes would make a positive.
B40	No such luck.
B41	Well, something else is necessary.
B42	Since I assume that there ought to be an easier way of getting at this.
B43	(E: What are you considering?)
B44	Well . . . I'm just looking at the first thing that we started off with again.
B45	None of these rules seems very practical now,
B46	since that sign change requires a tilde in front there.
B47	I'm looking for something that gives me less . . . or more practical than the one I already used.
B48	That would be number 3.
B49	but that doesn't seem very. . . .
B50	Now, all these in the third set, they have to be positive, right?
B51	This is correct?
B52	(E: Well, let's see . . . no, I don't think so. Only where it says does it have to be positive.)
B53	OK. . . .
B54	(E: Definitely, they don't all have to be positive.)
B55	I thought I remembered him saying something like that in there.
B56	Oh, it was possible that they might have to be positive, that was it.
B57	Now, let me see . . . if I should add something. . . .
B58	(E: Can't tell what you're thinking about unless you speak up.)
B59	Well, now I'm looking at these three different parts again . . .
B60	and I'm suggesting regrouping then . . . starting. . . .
B61	And forgetting about 2, 3, and 4 . . . that was on the wrong track.
B62	So . . . well, I've got it now . . . I've got this.
B63	OK . . . using R4 from the beginning . . .
B64	regroup it so that the. . . .

B65	No, that's not . . . won't work out, or will it?
B66	In R4, they have to be both dots or both wedges?
B67	(E: That's right.)
B68	I see. All right, let me see now. R7 has a dot and a wedge.
B69	OK, let me see now.
B70	I'll use R7, but which way?
B71	Since I want . . . I'll need this dot so I can drop the other half. . . .
B72	From R8 that would be.
B73	So, using the second part of R7, on . . . from L1, that is.
B74	(E: R7 to L1.)
B75	[E writes L5: $(\sim S \cdot S) \vee (\sim S \cdot \sim Q)$]
B76	There is a wedge in between.
B77	(E: Think that's right.)
B78	See now . . . as long as that wedge is in there, it doesn't seem too practical either.
B79	(E: You're doing a great many things now, that you're not talking about.)
B80	I'm just looking over these rules now.
B81	(E: We want to know what you're looking at . . . how you're figuring. . . .)
B82	(E: Even if it's wrong we want to have a record of it.)
B83	I see, well . . . I have . . . I keep thinking of a whole bunch of rules at one time.
B84	(E: Well, you can't look at 'em all at one time.)
B85	Well, I looked at R1 . . .
B86	and it doesn't seem to be any good at all at present.
B87	And number 2 refers to horseshoes,
B88	so that's out.
B89	3, just doubles.
B90	So 4 , . . let me see . . . would work with step. . . .
B91	No, it wouldn't.
B92	I'll keep 4 in mind.
B93	5 is that handy little thing . . .
B94	but it's a nuisance . . . trying to change the signs all over the place.
B95	But . . . if I should use it I wouldn't be able to use rule . . .
B96	whatever it is . . . R9.
B97	R8 or R9.
B98	I see an interesting idea.
B99	That's using R9 and then . . .
B100	that won't work . . . then using rule . . .
B101	I was thinking of using R9,
B102	then using R1,
B103	and then using R8,
B104	but that wouldn't work
B105	because I have to use 5 in between again
B106	and that would change all my signs
B107	and then I couldn't go on to R8 any more.
B108	So . . . looking back where we started in the beginning again.
B109	Now I'm looking at R4 which isn't. . . .
B110	I need a double wedge or a double dot.
B111	Trouble is, I can double and add with wedges
B112	but I can't very well do that with dots.
B113	Well . . . let's see . . . I think I've got an idea.
B114	That would require R7,
B115	R1 a couple of times,
B116	and R3 . . .
B117	and R8.
B118	So if I need R7, I need four terms the first . . . the first the same both times.
B119	So, then I'll use R3
B120	and double what I have in step 2.

B121	That . . . that doesn't seem to be very handy either.
B122	Well, let's try it.
B123	So then I have $(S \lor \sim Q) \cdot (S \lor \sim Q)$.
B124	(E: What do you want to do?)
B125	Double it . . . as in R3.
B126	(E: Apply what to what?)
B127	To step 2.
B128	(E: Apply 3 to step 2?)
B129	Uh huh.
B130	(E: Which part of it? I mean, do you want to have a wedge connective or a dot connective?)
B131	I think a dot connective now.
B132	[E writes L6: $((S \lor \sim Q) \cdot \sim S) \cdot ((S \lor \sim Q) \cdot \sim S)$]
B133	Wait a second . . . no, that's not what I meant.
B134	Using it on step . . . what do you call steps?
B135	Oh, I see . . . oh, I was referring to step 3.
B136	Numbers on the left are the steps, is that it?
B137	(E: Yeah, that's a line.)
B138	Oh, I see. So that's . . . then it's L3.
B139	(E: R3 to L3.)
B140	That's what I meant rather than what you have there.
B141	[E writes L7: $(S \lor \sim Q) \cdot (S \lor \sim Q)$]
B142	Now . . . you now have to go to R7.
B143	That would give me. . . .
B144	Well, that might even seem more practical to be used . . . if I apply that to L5 rather than 7.
B145	Apply 7 to L5.
B146	(E: R7 . . . L5 . . . and you're back to L1, so you'd get. . . .)
B147	I'm back to L5.
B148	(E: Yeah, I know)
B149	(E: but I mean you get this . . . $\sim S \cdot (S \lor Q)$.)
B150	Oh . . . wasn't very handy.
B151	[loud background noise obliterates speech] . . . slightly different.
B152	Well, then apply it to . . .
B153	that's the same as the beginning, eh?
B154	I've got a dot and a wedge . . . and if I applied that to L7,
B155	I'd get . . . S wedge. . . .
B156	Apply R7 to L7 on that.
B157	[E writes L8: $S \lor (\sim Q \cdot \sim Q)$]
B158	Now . . . oh, brother. . . .
B159	Still looking for a way to get rid of that wedge
B160	and if I do use that, such as in L5 . . . that would give me a negative
B161	and I couldn't use R8 . . .
B162	that seems to be the problem and I haven't solved it yet . . .
B163	to the whole thing.
B164	Well, I need another rule altogether.
B165	Well, let's see . . . maybe if I go from wedges to horseshoes. . . .
B166	Might get me out of this.
B167	So I look at R6 . . .
B168	that would give me a horseshoe
B169	and what could I do with horseshoes?
B170	2's . . . got something to do with horseshoes.
B171	and there are two sign changes,
B172	but I can't reverse with horseshoes. . . .
B173	So let me see. Now . . . now if I . . . oh, I think I dropped someplace else before the. . . .
B174	OK, now going back to L3 I apply R6

B175	and I arrive at. . . .
B176	Well, let's apply R6 and see what we get.
B177	[E writes L9: $\sim S \supset \sim Q$]
B178	Now. . . . (long pause)
B179	Well, there's another problem here. . . .
B180	If I work with horseshoes I can change it around and ditch those two tildes.
B181	But, I'm stuck with changing back again.
B182	Doesn't seem to be handy rule for that with horseshoes and all.
B183	Hum . . . I have there . . . ($\sim S \supset \sim Q$).
B184	That would give $Q \supset S$.
B185	Then if I'd apply R6.
B186	Nix, that wouldn't get me anyplace.
B187	The key still seems to lie with R5.
B188	No, that doesn't work with horseshoes either.
B189	Well, horseshoes won't work at all.
B190	So the idea is to work with R5
B191	and get rid of that tilde in the front somehow.
B192	So now I'm looking for something that will eliminate that tilde once I get it up there.
B193	I'll get it up there first
B194	and then eliminate it with R5. (long pause)
B195	OK . . . maybe this will be the answer.
B196	Well, now where was I? What looks handy?
B197	If I apply R2 . . . apply to what we have in 10.
B198	I apply R6 again.
B199	Probably end up right where I started from, but. . . .
B200	Let me see, that would get me. . . .
B201	That doesn't seem to be too profitable.
B202	Well, I have that . . . right in the beginning I have that dot in the middle. . . .
B203	That's OK.
B204	How'd I ever lose it?
B205	Well . . . working off what we have in 1, change the $S \vee \sim Q$ using R5.
B206	[E writes L10: $\sim S \cdot \sim (\sim S \cdot Q)$]
B207	Now, we've got all the dots.
B208	Now . . . if we apply R4 to that. . . .
B209	(E: Well, that's one thing that's not made clear in the instructions,)
B210	(E: but you really can't, when you have this thing as a negative expression . . . whne you have a thing within that parenthesis negative . . .)
B211	(E: 'cause I really don't know how that would be recoded, according to R4.)
B212	(E: If that parenthesis were positive, it would be applicable.)
B213	If that first parenthesis was positive. . . .
B214	(E: If the second syllable was positive, then you could apply R4, but that's what's keeping you from applying R4.)
B215	(long pause)
B216	That seems to mess everything up. . . .
B217	Seems to halt that idea right where I started.
B218	(E: Well, let's call a halt to this problem)
B219	(E: and I'll show you one way that it can be done.)
B220	(E: Let's consider now . . . L3 and L10 here are pretty good.)
B221	Would you do this by getting into a double line?
B222	(E: Yeah.)
B223	That's the next thing I was going to try.
B224	I didn't quite understand this 11 and 12 . . . how they fit.
B225	They could double,
B226	but they had arrows going only one way.
B227	(E: That's right. Well now, look at L10 here . . . this is an important thing.)
B228	(E: Now if you can get a $\sim S$ all by itself on a line you can apply R11)

B229	(E: and get rid of this, see . . .)
B230	(E: leaving the ~Q . . . by R11.)
B231	(E: OK, now how do you get ~S all by itself?)
B232	(E: Why you apply R8 on L1, dropping the B part)
B233	(E: leaving a ~S all by itself.)
B234	(E: So you've got a ~S somewhere here on a line . . . then you can apply R11 to this line and to L10)
B235	(E: leaving just ~Q,)
B236	(E: which is what you want.)
B237	Oh, I see.
B238	If you have two steps in a row, that's considered two lines . . . or what?
B239	(E: Yeah . . . well, they don't have to be in a row.)
B240	(E: You can combine any two lines anywhere on what you've done, from)
B241	(E: what you've done . . . L11, or L12, or L10.)
B242	They had arrows always from two lines to one line,
B243	but I couldn't quite figure out how you get up to two lines.
B244	(E: Well that would be the way you do it.)
B245	(E: Say you were going to solve it now.)
B246	(E: You would . . . L12 would be a ~S, so applying R8 to L1 like this,)
B247	(E: then L13 would be ~Q . . .)
B248	(E: by applying R11 to lines 10 and 12. See how that would look?)
B249	From L10 and L12?
B250	(E: Yeah.)
B251	10 and 12 . . .
B252	then use R11.
B253	Yeah, I see that.
B254	So now I can combine any two lines here
B255	and as those two are considered two lines, then I can use 11 and 12.
B256	(E: That is correct. You can use 10 and 12 . . . applying rules (mumbles).)
B257	(E: OK, well that's one thing where the instructions aren't too clear.)
B258	I figured you could only use those steps in special problems when you start out with two lines.
B259	(E: No, any two lines you've created yourself . . . you can use them.)

APPENDIX 10.15

S9 on α3

B1	[E writes L1: (P·Q) ∨ (P·~P)]
B2	[E writes L0: P ⊃ Q]
B3	Want P ⊃ Q.
B4	The first thing that I see is the P and Q together in the beginning so. . . .
B5	But there's a wedge in between the two big parts
B6	so it's difficult to get rid of the second part
B7	without going through a lot of extra work.
B8	So, then I look for a practical way of getting the dot into a horseshoe.
B9	And offhand, there isn't any as far as I can see,
B10	unless I use R6 and that will end me up with the wrong sign again.
B11	So . . . so then I look at R11.
B12	Oh, but R11 isn't reversible.
B13	But using R12, A and C,
B14	then I need an intermediate term of B.

B15 A and C, that would be P and Q.
B16 P [B?] would have to . . .
B17 a P and a Q.
B18 So, the handiest thing . . . change all this business into horseshoes, but . . .
B19 1, 2, 3, and 4. . . .
B20 (E: You're thinking without talking.)
B21 I'm still trying to think of a way to drop this thing easily and without too much trouble. . .
B22 half of this expression, at least . . .
B23 or to split it up conveniently.
B24 (E: Well, we want to see how you do that.)
B25 OK, Now, let's see, we have two dots connecting and a wedge in the middle.
B26 That R5 is very handy, but very confusing.
B27 Now, if I'd use R5, into what difficulties would that extra tilde in the front give me again?
B28 That would stop me from using R4 again, is that right?
B29 (E: Yeah, Well, let's see, how do you want to apply R5? To the total expression?)
B30 Ah . . . yeah.
B31 (E: Total expression . . . now that would make. . . .)
B32 (E: No, you couldn't use R4.)
B33 (E: See how that would come out.)
B34 (E: R5 would make this parenthesis negative and this parenthesis negative and you'd have the brackets with a negative outside that.)
B35 I see, that wouldn't work then.
B36 Then I couldn't use R8 anyway
B37 and I couldn't drop half the expression.
B38 (E: That's right.)
B39 But now, we have R7.
B40 With R7 I can go from four through three.
B41 That'd require the second part of R7 going backwards,
B42 and that would give me P, Q . . . wait a second.
B43 That'll give me P, Q, P.
B44 Let's do that, using R7.
B45 [E writes L2: $P \cdot (Q \lor \sim P)$]
B46 Now . . . P dot . . . P dot. . . .
B47 I'm looking at 11.
B48 I'd need a horseshoe there.
B49 Using 12 I'd need a horseshoe there and. . . .
B50 Well, just so I remember . . . I can have a P all by itself or. . . .
B51 Well, that means now, that I could have a P all by itself or $Q \lor \sim P$.
B52 Well, that's rather convenient.
B53 OK now, P . . . OK now, using . . .
B54 well, we'll have to use R6 then on the second part of 2.
B55 So let's . . . let's drop that P in the beginning.
B56 (E: R8 on L2?)
B57 Yeah.
B58 No, you'd have to use R1 first, right?
B59 (E: No.)
B60 Oh, you can . . . it doesn't make any difference.
B61 [E writes L3: $Q \lor \sim P$]
B62 Right. Now using R6. . . .
B63 (E: R6 on L3.)
B64 [E writes L4: $\sim Q \supset \sim P$]
B65 Horseshoe $\sim P$ . . . and we want P horseshoe. . . .
B66 Uh oh . . . where the heck?
B67 That would've been convenient if it was reversed, wouldn't it? Very convenient if it was reversed around.

B68   Hum . . . now I look at R12,
B69   but I'd have to change the sign and all that
B70   and that would be more trouble.
B71   So . . . now look around for a way to change those . . . all those signs.
B72   "No sign change". . . .
B73   "No sign change."
B74   Now, let's see . . . R2 . . . "Use only with horseshoe, trade places, two sign changes."
B75   Well, that's the answer then.
B76   (E: Yep, that's what you want.)
B77   (E: L4, use R2.)
B78   [E writes L5:   P ⊃ Q]

4

CHESS

CHESS:
Task Analysis

11

We now move to the third and last task area that we shall examine in detail. The same questions must be answered as before. Can a human in this new task environment (choosing a move in chess) be viewed as an IPS? If so, can we identify problem spaces, search strategies, heuristics, goal structures, and so on—all in the relatively precise fashion in which we have been able to identify them in logic and cryptarithmetic? What aspects of the problem solving system derive from the task environment and what from characteristics of the subject? Thus, one of the functions of this part is to confirm or qualify the analyses of the previous parts.

In addition, of course, each new task environment brings its quota of new phenomena—of new reasoning mechanisms, new representations, new heuristics, new problem solving organizations. Thus, the logic task revealed, more strongly than did cryptarithmetic, means-ends analysis and goal structuring. We can expect similar novelties to emerge from chess. The question is not whether they fit the somewhat specialized IPS frameworks of the previous task environments. Rather, we wish to understand the nature of the new phenomena—whether they can be described and understood in terms of the basic apparatus of information processing systems proposed in Part I.

First, as in the other parts, we shall analyze the task, then examine some behavior in detail, and finally we shall take a broader view of human chess playing.

Chess is a game. There are numerous reasons why games are attractive for research in problem solving: the environment is relatively closed and well defined by the rules of a game; there is a well-defined goal (or goals, since sometimes several top goals can be incompatible—e.g., winning and drawing); the competitive aspects of a game can be relied upon (in our culture) to produce properly motivated subjects (even when no opponent is present!).

We could have chosen any of a number of games, ranging from tic-tac-toe, through the world of Hoyle, to chess and Go, or even to a game of our own devising. Chess, however, is particularly attractive:

1. Selecting a move in chess is generally acknowledged to be a difficult problem solving task. Professional players can devote substantially full time to improving and maintaining their skills in it, and such players seldom reach the peak of their powers with less than ten years' experience. Moreover, after 200 years of intensive study and play, the game has not become barren or exhausted. Innovations, both in specific tactics and in strategy and concepts, continue to be introduced into master play.

2. The vast amount of recorded experience—virtually all serious games between grandmasters in the last century have been preserved—makes it relatively easy to evaluate the quality of a chess-playing program and to compare it in detail with the programs of human players of different strengths, different styles, and even different periods in the history of the game. The protocols produced by a chess program can be compared with human protocols in the same game positions, and the strength of the program can be determined accurately by pitting it against human players.

3. The task has already been used in previous researches, particularly in the work of A. de Groot with human chess players (de Groot, 1965) and the several chess programs that will be described in this chapter.

4. The irregularity of the structure of chess gives the task some of the flavor of everyday, garden-variety problem solving that is absent from tasks like proving theorems or solving puzzles. By irregularity we mean the peculiarity of the moves of the several pieces, the exceptional moves like castling, the strong boundary effects of the edges of the board, and so on. This point will be obvious to chess players, and may appear plausible to other readers.

Our analysis of chess, like our analyses of the other tasks, will have to include some rudiments of the technology. Admittedly, this is a more serious problem with chess than with the other tasks, precisely for the reasons just enumerated: it is a really difficult task with unlimited technical depth. However, we shall not assume that our readers are, or wish to become, chess players.[1] We shall assume that they do have familiarity with some board game such as checkers, tic-tac-toe, or Go, but we trust they will not be seriously handicapped in understanding the implications of our analysis for problem solving if some of the specific technical aspects are unfamiliar to them. The situation is helped, of course, by the objective of understanding chess in information processing terms, and thus avoiding a chess-dominated context.

The analysis proceeds along familiar lines. We first take up the basic structure of the environment: its problem space and the nature of its goals. It is necessary to understand how games differ from the puzzles and mathematical tasks we have been considering. Then, we describe various chess programs. Many have been reported in the literature, providing instructive contrasts in search strategy and heuristics. The discussion of these programs will provide an adequate starting point for considering human behavior in chess.

BASIC TASK ENVIRONMENT

Games like chess, checkers, and tic-tac-toe have an immediately defined basic problem space. The elements are the various board configurations—positions—and the operators are the legal moves defined by the rules of the game. The rules define a starting position (usually a given fixed position for all plays of the game), and some means is provided for recognizing a set of terminal positions (those that win, lose, or draw). The game itself moves in this problem space and any problem solver who wishes to play vicariously, but exactly, also moves in this space. If we consider at each position all of the legal moves available to the player whose move it is, they generate the so-called *game tree* (which is of enormous size for interesting games).[2]

The basic problem space for a game is analogous in important respects to the problem spaces we have defined for theorem proving (the various logic tasks) and for puzzles (cryptarithmetic). To choose a move in a game, one explores the game tree to learn the consequences of different moves; to discover a proof in logic one explores the proof tree to learn what path leads to the theorem; and similarly in exploring for the solution to puzzles.

Although the analogy is useful, it is not exact. Let us compare the situation in chess with that in LT, which is a typical formulation of a theorem-proving task.

---

[1] We remark that the authors (collectively) can be regarded as strong, but not expert, chess players, conversant with the literature of the game and able to understand the discourse of masters, although not able to emulate their practice. We have had valuable assistance from a number of stronger players, including Edward Lasker, Adriaan de Groot, and George Baylor. They have been very helpful in assessing the plausibility of our interpretations but should not, of course, be held accountable for our conclusions.

[2] The concept of game tree was apparently first formalized by Zermelo in 1912. The concept was used informally in books on chess and checkers several hundred years earlier. On the history of the concept, see Chapter 8 of König (1956).

First, in chess the legal moves are always a function of the current position. In logic (though not in cryptarithmetic) the operators, which are rules of inference, can depend on more than one logic expression as input (e.g., *detachment*). Thus, the basic problem space in logic is more like a web or lattice.

Second, in the proof tree (or lattice) all moves are made by one player, while in the game tree alternate moves are made by opposing players. A proof is demonstrated by exhibiting a single path that leads to the desired theorem. A winning move in chess is demonstrated by exhibiting a *subtree* of the game tree having a so-called minimax property: that *for each* move of the opponent at a given branch *there exists* a move for the player that leads through a succession of such branches to a winning position. (See the next section for the detail of this concept.) A proof is a definite plan, while a *win* is a strategy setting forth a tree of paths for all possible moves of the opponent (case analysis in proofs provides a situation that is somewhat closer to the game situation). This distinction has important consequences for the nature of game-playing heuristics, as we shall see.[3]

Third, we must not confuse the problem solving search tree, when there is one, with *either* the proof tree of theorems or the game tree of chess. The subproblem tree generated by the Logic Theorist, while it is working backwards, is not a tree of theorems, but a tree of propositions from which the theorem to be proved can be derived (with the help of axioms and previously proved theorems). In most extant computer game-playing programs the problem solving activity consists specifically of a search out along some or all of the branches of the game tree; but this is not an essential characteristic of a game-playing program. Indeed, we will describe some game-playing schemes that operate in spaces larger than the tree of legal moves.

A fourth important difference between theorem proving and games derives from a difference in irreversibility of actions. In theorem proving, the aim of the problem solving activity *is* to find the path that constitutes the proof. If the search actually takes place in a space of proofs (or potential proofs, as in the Logic Theorist), the task is to find a whole path, but there is no penalty for going down blind alleys during the search or for taking unnecessary steps, other than the cost of the search time.

In game playing, the aim of the problem solving activity in any given instance is to find a *move*—i.e., a first step on a path through the game tree. Once that move has been selected and made, it cannot be undone if it later proves to have been wrong. On the other hand, although the player may have explored a whole tree in evaluating the move he finally chose, he is not committed to following any particular path on that tree (or even sticking to the limits of the tree if it is smaller than the legal move tree) beyond his first move. After the opponent has replied, he can reconsider his whole future path.

Hence, in game playing, the first move in the game tree from the current position occupies a different role from subsequent moves. The latter are explored not with the aim of selecting a path or strategy, but solely for the information they may

---

[3] In this respect a closer analogy to the search trees that occur in games is provided by the *and-or* trees used in some theorem provers (Chapter 4, page 138) than by the *or* trees used in LT.

contribute to the evaluation of the initial move (i.e., the move to be made in the current position). From this standpoint, proof paths are of the essence of theorem-proving tasks, while paths in the game tree are only incidental, although they may have great informational value, to the task of choosing moves. It is impossible to conceive of a theorem prover that does not discover proofs; a game player that does not search in the game tree is wholly conceivable (Newman and Uhr, 1965).

A fifth difference between proving theorems and playing games is that the task in the former is to find *a* proof—any one will do—while the task in the latter is to find the *best* move, or, if there is no way of guaranteeing this, at least a very good move. The suitability of a move can be evaluated only in relation to an assessment of what other moves may be available. The one exception is the case where a move can be shown to lead definitely to a forced win (i.e., a win no matter what the opponent does). Here, as in the theorem-proving case, the problem solver need search no further unless esthetic criteria lead him to prefer one winning strategy (or one proof, respectively) to another.

CHESS-PLAYING PROGRAMS

A sizable number of chess programs have been constructed. They all operate within the basic problem space (occasionally augmented by abstract moves, such as *no-move*). Furthermore, they all reflect the same fundamental approach, already described clearly by Shannon in 1949 (Shannon, 1950):[4] playing chess consists of considering the alternative moves, obtaining some evaluation of them by means of analysis, and choosing the preferred alternative on the basis of the evaluation. The analysis—which is the hard part—can be factored into three parts. First, explore the continuations to a certain depth.[5] Second (since it is clear that the explorations cannot be deep enough to reach terminal positions), evaluate the positions reached at the end of each exploration in terms of the pattern of men on the chess board. Next, combine these *static-evaluations* according to a procedure called *minimaxing* to determine the *effective value* of the alternative. Finally, choose the move with the highest effective value.

The approach is fundamentally one of forward search. There are two new features, in comparison with logic and cryptarithmetic. First is the evaluation, which acts as a complete surrogate for the ultimate (but unforeseeable) desired

---

[4] The idea of a chess-playing automaton (including some fraudulent realizations of the idea) is much older than the digital computer. Proposals for chess-playing programs came forward almost simultaneously with the invention of the modern computer. Edward Lasker in *The Adventure of Chess* (1959) devotes Chapters 10 and 11 to the precomputer automata and the electronic chess player, respectively. Shannon's 1949 paper may be taken as the first substantial analysis of chess-playing programs, even though he did not there present a particular program.

[5] In games, there is an ambiguity in the unit for measuring depth. The term *move* is often used to refer to a player's move together with the opponent's reply—i.e., two moves in the literal sense. In giving depth measures we will, following Samuel (1959), use *ply* for a single move, so that move and reply are *two plies*.

position. This substitution is forced by the commitment to a sequence of irreversible moves long before the final position comes into view. The second new feature is the complex procedure for inferring effective values of alternative moves. This is forced by the two-person character of the game. The particular procedure used, *minimaxing*, is basic to all the programs for playing chess. Let us examine it carefully.

The rules of chess assure that the game can be described completely as a branching tree, the nodes corresponding to positions, the branches to legal moves from positions. It is intuitively clear, and easily proved, that for a player who can view the entire tree and see all the ultimate consequences of each alternative, chess becomes a simple game. Starting with the terminal positions, which have determinate payoffs, he can work backwards, determining at each node which branch is best for him or his opponent as the case may be, until he arrives at the alternative for his next move. We can then define the *minimax-value* for a position recursively as follows:

$$\text{minimax-value(terminal-position)} = \text{win} \mid \text{tie} \mid \text{loss}$$
$$\text{minimax-value(nonterminal-position)} = \text{best(minimax-value(next-position))}$$
$$\text{all legal next-positions}$$

The values *win, tie, loss* are relative to the player; likewise, the function *best* is relative to the player. Viewed consistently from one player, best means maximum when he is to move, minimum when his opponent is to move. Thus the name minimax arises because of the alternation of minimum and maximum for the definition of best.[6] A next-position is one reached by making a single move from the given position.

Figure 11.1 shows a situation (position X at the top of the figure) where White is to move and has three choices, W1, W2, and W3. White's move will be followed by Black's: B11 or B12 in case move W1 is made; B21 or B22 if move W2 is made; and B31 or B32 if move W3 is made. To keep the example simple, we have assumed that all of Black's moves lead to terminal positions with known payoffs. How should White decide what to do—what inference procedure allows him to determine which of the three moves is to be preferred? Clearly, no matter what Black does, move W1 leads to a draw. Similarly, no matter what Black does, move W2 leads to a loss for White. White should clearly prefer move W1 to move W2. But what about move W3? It offers the possibility of a win, but it also contains the possibility of a loss; furthermore, the outcome is in Black's control (see Figure 11.1). If White imputes sufficient analytic ability to his opponent, he must conclude that move W3 will end as a loss for White, and hence that move W1 is preferable. The possible win from move W3 is a chimera that can never be realized. Thus White can impute a value to position X (in this case, tie) by reasoning backwards from known values, . and he can then select the best move, W1, from the position.

To repeat: If the entire tree can be scanned, the best move can be determined simply by the minimaxing procedure. Unfortunately for this "simplicity," the tree

---

[6] It probably should have been called *maximin*, since it is invariably applied in a situation which first maximizes and then minimizes. But euphony is against it.

FIGURE 11.1

minimaxing in a game tree

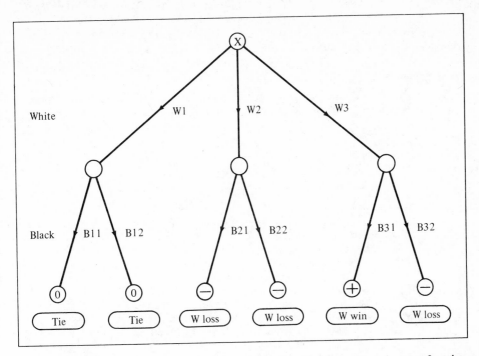

is so large that even current computers could discover only the minutest fraction of it in years of computing. There are something like 10^{120} continuations to be explored, with much less than 10^{20} nanoseconds available in a century to explore them.

We have presented minimaxing as if it would be applied to the exhaustive analysis of a game, taking into account only the evaluations and move possibilities given by the rules (win, tie, loss, and all legal moves). When it is used as a technique within a chess program, modifications must be made to incorporate static-evaluations and rules for generating moves other than the full legal set. Likewise, termination of the program must be possible before all possibilities have been exhausted. In Figure 11.2 we give a prototypic chess program that incorporates minimaxing with these other aspects.

The main process, called find-move, is concerned with the position initially given. The moves to be considered are generated by a process called base-moves. Each alternative base-move is made, yielding the corresponding next-position. This is evaluated by *analysis*, and the resulting value is used to decide whether a better move has been found than any previously analyzed. The program actually exhibits the process of obtaining the best-move by comparison and replacement, whereas in the recursive definition of the minimax function on page 668 this process was buried in the function *best*( ). We need to exhibit this processing structure to permit incorporation of a test, width-termination, to determine whether or not to continue.

The analysis process first determines whether the position is a terminal one (depth-termination) and, if it is, computes the static-value and quits. These two processes are sometimes combined, so that static-value is always executed, and failure to find a value is taken as a sign that further dynamic exploration should be made. Since the considerations that go into the decision to terminate may be quite distinct from those in the static-value, we have kept the two processes separate.

If the analysis is to be dynamic, then moves are generated by analysis-moves. Again, this might be the same generator as base-moves, used at the first level, but in several programs a distinct generator is used. This section of the analysis process parallels closely that of the find-move process: comparison of value, updating of

FIGURE 11.2

prototypic chess program

find-move(position) ($\Longrightarrow$ move):
1. initialize best-value = loss for player of position;
2. initialize best-move = resign;
3. generate base-moves(position):
4.   make base-move on position ($\Longrightarrow$ next-position),
        if fail continue generation;
5.   analyse(next-position) ($\Longrightarrow$ next-value);
6.   compare next-value to best-value for player of position,
        if better(next-value, best-value), base-move $\Longrightarrow$ best-move);
7.   test width-termination(best-value, width, position),
        if true stop generation,
        if false continue generation.
      stop and report 'best-move.'

analyse(position) ($\Longrightarrow$ value):
1. test depth-termination(position),
    if false go to 3;
2. compute static-value(position) ($\Longrightarrow$ value),
    stop;
3. initialize best-value = loss for player of position;
4. generate analysis-moves(position):
5.   make analysis-move on position ($\Longrightarrow$ next-position),
        if fail continue generation;
6.   analyse(next-position) ($\Longrightarrow$ next-value);
7.   compare next-value to best-value for player of position,
        if better(next-value, best-value);
8.   test width-termination(best-value, width, position),
        if true stop generation,
        if false continue generation;
9. compute adjusted-value(best-value, position) ($\Longrightarrow$ value).

Notes: make move on position computes depth of position.
        generate computes width of move.

Undefined: base-moves(position)
         analysis-moves(position)
         width-termination(best-value, width, position)
         depth-termination(position)
         static-value(position)
         adjusted-value(best-value, position)

the best-value found so far, and use of width-termination to indicate whether or not to continue. When the final best-value is available, a process, called adjusted-value, determines the actual output of analysis. Pure minimaxing implies that the best-value itself should be used, but several existing programs make some adjustment to this, hence require this last process.

Both depth of position in the search tree and order of generation of the moves from a position (called the *width*) are used frequently in making decisions about how to terminate search. We assume width and depth to be available automatically, without including in the figure processes for computing them.

At the bottom of Figure 11.2 we list the six processes that are undefined in the program. Existing chess programs can be specified almost completely by defining these processes in appropriate ways. We will look, in varying detail, at six programs,[7] all but one (Turing's) having run on a computer. They will provide a range of variation that will permit us to explore the task environment.

We will take up the programs in historical order. This coincides by and large with increasing sophistication, so that we deal at first (in the Turing program and the Los Alamos program) with the basic ways of realizing programs that fit the scheme above, and then move on to introduce additional organization and heuristics.

Turing's Program

In 1953 Turing (Chapter 25, Bowden, 1953) described a program along the lines of Figure 11.2 that was simple enough to be hand-simulated.[8] The additional six processes to be defined are given in Figure 11.3. The program considered all alternatives—that is, all legal moves. In order to limit computation, however, it was very circumspect about the continuations it considered. Turing introduced the notion of a dead position: one that in some sense was stable, hence could be evaluated without further search of the game tree.[9] For example, there is no sense in counting material on the board while an exchange of Queens is in process: the continuations should be explored until the exchange has been carried through—to the point where the material will not change with the next move. So Turing's program analyzed all the opponent's immediate replies (i.e., for depth $= 1$, the analysis-moves are all legal moves), but then considered further moves only from positions that were not dead. These are listed as the analysis-moves for depth > 1.

---

[7] There now exist a substantial number of chess programs in addition to the six we describe. Many of these have not yet been described in the technical literature (and may never be), although games have been published (Berliner, 1969; Rubenfeld, 1968; Smith, 1969; Scott, 1969). By all indications there will soon be a great many such programs.

[8] There is no a priori objection to hand simulation of a program, although experience has shown that it is almost always inexact for programs of any complexity. For example, there is an error in Turing's play of his program, because he—the human simulator—was unwilling to consider all the alternatives. He failed to explore the ones he "knew" would be eliminated anyway, and in one instance failed to select the move called for by the program.

[9] *Quiet* or *quiescent* would have been better terms but are seldom used.

Analysis terminated if no such moves were generated. The static-value of a position was limited to the value of material (mostly for computational reasons), but the program also considered a positional value at a depth of 1 (i.e., for the immediately succeeding position). We have indicated the evaluation in Figure 11.3 as a list, since the comparison of two values is to be lexicographic—material-value dominates, and only if material is the same does position-value count. We have spelled out the position-value in detail to give some feeling for the features involved. Finally, Turing did not work solely with simple minimax. Since only a subset of moves from a position were usually considered in the analysis, he allowed the static-value of the position itself to act as one more candidate in selecting the best. We have shown this as an adjusted-value that makes a final comparison between the best of the dynamic values and the static-value.

Only one published game, as far as we know, was played with the program (see Table 11.1). The program proved to be weak, for it lost against a weak human player (who did not know the program, by the way), although it was not entirely a pushover. Its play was rather aimless, and it was capable of gross blunders, one of

FIGURE 11.3

Turing chess program

base-moves:	all legal moves
analysis-moves:	depth = 1: all legal moves
	depth > 1: recaptures, captures of undefended man, captures of
	higher valued man, checkmates
width-termination:	never
depth-termination:	no analysis-moves
static-value:	depth = 1: (material-value position-value)
	depth > 1: material-value
where	material-value = material of player / material of opponent with
	$P = 1$, $N = 3$, $B = 3.5$, $R = 5$, $Q = 10$, Checkmate = 1000
	position-value = K-value + opponent-K-value + Q-value +
	sum(piece-value) + sum(P-value)
	K-value = mobility(K) − vulnerability(K) + castle-value
	where vulnerability(K) = mobility(Q at square(K))
	castle-value = 3 if castle is made
	2 if castle is legal
	1 if castle privilege is available
	mobility(X) = $\sqrt{\text{number of legal moves for X}}$
	where captures count as 2 moves
	opponent-K-value = .5 if opponent K in check
	1 if opponent K threatened with checkmate
	Q-value = mobility(Q)
	piece-value(X) = mobility(X) + defense-value(X)
	where defense-value(X) = 1 if X defended once
	1.5 if X defended twice
	P-value(P) = advancement-value(P) + P-defense-value(P)
	where advancement-value(P) = .2x(rank(P)−2)
	P-defense-value(P) = .3 if P defended by a piece
adjusted-value:	if all legal moves considered: best-value
	otherwise: best(static-value, best-value)

which cost it the game. The subtleties of the evaluation function were lost upon it, most of the numerous factors included in the position-value rarely influencing the move chosen. In summary, Turing's program was not a very good chess player, but it reached the bottom rung of the ladder of human play.

The Los Alamos Program

In 1956 a research group at Los Alamos programmed MANIAC I to play chess on a 6 × 6 board (Kister, *et al.*, 1957), and in 1958 a revised program was written for MANIAC II for the regular 8 × 8 board (though details were never published). The Los Alamos program is an almost perfect example of the simplest type of system realizing the framework. As shown in Figure 11.4, all base-moves are considered: all continuations are explored to a depth of four plies (two moves for Black and two for White); the static-evaluation function consists of a sum of ma-

TABLE 11.1

play of Turing's program (from Bowden, 1953)

	WHITE (MACHINE)	BLACK (HUMAN)
1	P-K4	P-K4
2	N-QB3	N-KB3
3	P-Q4	B-N5
4	N-B3	P-Q3
5	B-Q2	N-B3
6	P-Q5	N-Q5
7	P-KR4	B-N5
8	P-R4	N×Nch
9	P×N	B-KR4
10	B-N5ch	P-B3
11	P×P	O-O
12	P×P	R-N1
13	B-QR6	Q-R4
14	Q-K2	N-Q2
15	KR-N1	N-B4
16	R-N5	B-N3
17	B-N5	N×NP
18	O-O-O	N-B4
19	B-B6	KR-B1
20	B-Q5	B×N
21	B×B	Q×P
22	K-Q2	N-K3
23	R-N4	N-Q5
24	Q-Q3	N-N4
25	B-N3	Q-R3
26	B-B4	B-R4
27	R-N3	Q-R5
28	B×N	Q×B
29	Q×P	R-Q1 and wins

FIGURE 11.4
Los Alamos chess program (6 × 6)

base-moves:	all legal moves
analysis-moves:	same as base-moves
width-termination:	never
depth-termination:	depth > 4
static-value:	material-value + mobility-value
where	material-value = material of player / material of opponent
	mobility-value = number of legal moves
adjusted-value:	best-value + mobility-value

terial and mobility measures; the values are integrated by a minimax procedure, though there is an adjustment to the best dynamic value by adding in the intermediate mobility score. The best alternative in terms of the effective value is chosen for the move.

The MANIAC programs were again weak players. The programs were susceptible to serious blunders—a common characteristic, also, of inexperienced

TABLE 11.2

play of Los Alamos chess program (circa November 1958)

	WHITE	BLACK		WHITE	BLACK
1	P-K4	P-K3	26	B-K4	K-B2
2	Q-B3	P-Q4	27	B-R7	R-R1
3	P-Q4	P×P	28	B-B5	P-B4
4	Q-B3	P-QB3	29	K-B2	P-B5
5	P-KR4	B-Q3	30	N-B4	R-R3
6	B-K2	N-B3	31	P-B3	R-Q1
7	B-N5	P-KR3	32	N-K6ch	R×N
8	B×N	Q×B	33	R×R	K×R
9	N-Q2	P-K4	34	B×R	N-Q2
10	N×P	Q-Q1	35	R-Q1	K-K2
11	P×P	B×P	36	B×N	K-B2
12	Q×Bch	K-B1	37	P-N3	P×P
13	Q-B5ch	K-K1	38	P×P	P-R3
14	N-Q6ch	K-B1	39	B-B8	K-N2
15	N×Bch	K-K1	40	R-N1ch	K-B2
16	Q-K5ch	K-Q2	41	K-K2	K-K2
17	R-Q1ch	K×N	42	P-K4	K-B2
18	Q-B5ch	N-Q2	43	P-K5	K-B1
19	Q×P	R-B1	44	R-B1ch	K-N1
20	Q×P	R-KN1	45	R-N1ch	K-B1
21	Q×P	Q-K2	46	R-B1ch	K-N1
22	Q-K3	Q×Q	47	R-N1ch	K-B1
23	P×Q	R×P			
24	B-B3	R-KN1	Drawn by repetition of moves		
25	N-K2	N-K4			

human players. An example of a game played by the 8×8 program, taking both White and Black sides against itself, is shown in Table 11.2. The 8×8 program did apparently have some additional analysis-moves based on captures. The play is perhaps even less sophisticated than the hand-simulated play of Turing's program. Black (using the same program as White!) makes some remarkably foolish moves, which are matched only by White's allowing a draw by repetition of its checking moves.

There are, on the average, about 30 legal alternatives at each move. Thus, looking four plies ahead brings 30^4 continuations, almost one million, into consideration. (Even in the reduced, 6×6, game there were about 160,000.) To make a move in ten minutes, a processor executing the Los Alamos program would have to be capable of generating and evaluating a continuation in something less than one millisecond. To achieve this, the process must be very simple and straightforward (the MANIAC code was only about 600 instructions long). In a sense, the processor barely glances at each position it evaluates. The two measures in the evaluation function come directly from looking at continuations: changes in material are noticed if the moves are captures; the mobility score for a position is the number of new positions to which it leads—hence is computed almost without effort when exploring all continuations.

The Los Alamos programs test the limits of simplification in the direction of minimizing the amount of information required for each position evaluated, just as Turing's program tests the limits in the direction of minimizing the amount of exploration of continuations. These programs provide anchor points for a continuum along which chess-playing systems are distributed. They show that chess-playing programs can be constructed that, possessing very little in the way of complexity, play at the level of a human beginner. They throw doubt on the prospects of constructing a system at either extreme of the continuum that would rise very far above that level. All systems constructed subsequent to these two have attempted to combine computing power, absent from Turing's hand simulation, with appropriate selectivity, absent from the Los Alamos programs.

Bernstein's Program

In 1957–58 Alex Bernstein, a chess player and programmer at IBM, constructed a chess-playing program for the IBM 704 (for the full 8×8 board) (Bernstein *et al.*, 1958). His program takes an extremely important step in the direction of greater sophistication: only a fraction of the legal alternatives and continuations are considered. There is a series of subroutines, which we can call *plausible move generators*, that propose the moves to be considered. Each of these generators is related to some feature of the game: King-safety, development, defending own men, attacking opponent's men, and so on. The program considers at most seven alternatives, which are obtained by operating the generators in priority order, the most important first, until seven moves are accumulated. Figure 11.5 fills in the details.

The program explores continuations four plies ahead, just as the Los Alamos program did. However, it uses the plausible move generators at each stage, so that

FIGURE 11.5
Bernstein chess program

```
base-moves:              list of plausible move generators:
                            King-safety (if K in check)
                            Material gain, loss, exchange
                            Castling
                            Minor piece development
                            Occupancy of key squares
                            Occupancy of open files
                            Pawn moves
                            Piece moves
analysis-moves:          same as base moves
width-termination:       width > 7
depth-termination:       depth > 4
static-value:            material-value + mobility-value + area-control + King-safety-value
adjusted-value:          best-value
```

TABLE 11.3

play of Bernstein chess program (from Bernstein, 1958, p. 208)

	WHITE (MACHINE)	BLACK (HUMAN)
1	P-K4	P-K4
2	B-B4	P-QN3
3	P-Q3	N-KB3
4	B-KN5	B-N2
5	B×N	Q×B
6	N-KB3	P-B3
7	O-O	P-Q4
8	P×P	P×P
9	B-N5ch	N-B3
10	P-B4?	P×P
11	B×Nch	Q×B
12	P×P?	P-K5
13	N-N5	Q-N3
14	N-KR3	P-K6
15	P-B3	B-B4
16	R-K1	O-O
17	N-B3	P-K7 dis. ch
18	N-B2	B×P
19	P-KN3	P×Q=Q
20	N×Q	Q-B7
21	P-N3	QR-Q1
22	P-KR4	R×N
23	resigns	

at most seven direct continuations are considered from any given position previously generated. For its evaluation function it uses the ratio of two sums, one for White and one for Black. Each sum consists of four weighted factors: material, King defense, area control, and mobility. The program minimaxes and chooses the alternative with the greatest effective value. (There is no adjustment to the dynamic value.)

The program's play is uneven (see Table 11.3). Blind spots occur that are very striking; on the other hand it sometimes plays very well for a series of moves. It has never beaten anyone, as far as we know; in the game reported here it was beaten by a good player (Bernstein, 1958), and it was never pitted against weak players to establish how good it is.

Bernstein's program gives us our first information about radical selectivity in move generation and analysis. At seven moves per position, it examines only 2500 final positions four-ply deep, out of about 800,000 legal continuations. That it still plays at all tolerably with a reduction in search by a factor of 300 implies that the selection mechanism is fairly effective. Of course, the selections reflect the common and tested lore of the chess world, so that the significance of the reduction lies in showing that this lore is captured successfully in the mechanism.

Such radical selection should give the program a strong proclivity to overlook moves and consequences, for selective mechanisms in Bernstein's program have none of the checks and balances that exist in human selection on the chess board. And this is what we find. For example, in one situation (in an incomplete game not shown here) a Bishop was successively attacked by three pawns, each time retreating one square to a post where the next pawn could attack it. The program remained oblivious to this possibility, since the successive pawn pushes that attacked the Bishop were never proposed as plausible moves by the generators.

Every increase in sophistication of performance is paid for by an increase in the complexity of the program. The move generators and the components of the static-evaluation require varied and diverse information about each position. This implies both more program and more computing time per position than with the Los Alamos program. Bernstein's program contains 7000 instructions, the Los Alamos Program only 600 instructions, an increase by a factor of over 10. Although we do not have exact data, we estimate that both systems would require about the same average time per move on a processor of the same power—say half a minute per move on an IBM 360/65. Hence the increase in amount of processing per move in Bernstein's program approximately cancels the gain of 300 to 1 in selectivity that this more complex processing achieves—even though Bernstein's program is coded to attain maximum speed.

We have introduced the comparison in order to focus on the choice between computing speed and selectivity as sources of improvement in complex programs. It is not possible, unfortunately, to compare the two programs in performance level except very crudely. We need more games with each to provide reliable estimates of performance. Let us assume for purposes of argument that the Los Alamos and Bernstein programs are roughly comparable in performance. (On the skimpy evidence available, most chess players would probably assess Bernstein's program as the stronger.) To an approximation, then, we have two programs that achieve the same quality of performance with the same total effort by two different routes:

the Los Alamos program by using no selectivity and great speed, and the Bernstein program by using a large amount of selectivity and taking much more effort for each position examined in order to make the selection.

However, the similarity in the performance level of the two programs is an accident: selectivity is a very powerful device and speed a very weak device for improving the performance of complex programs. For instance, suppose both the Los Alamos and the Bernstein programs were to explore three moves deep instead of two, as they now do. Then the Los Alamos program would take about 1000 times as long (30^2) as it now does to make a move, whereas Bernstein's program would take about 50 times as long (7^2), the latter gaining a factor of 20 in the total computing effort required per move. The significant feature of chess is the exponential growth of positions to be considered with depth of analysis. As analysis deepens, greater computing effort per position soon pays for itself, since it slows the exponential growth in the number of positions to be considered. The comparison of the two programs at a greater depth is relevant, for the natural mode of improvement of the Los Alamos program is to increase the speed enough to allow explorations three moves deep. Furthermore, attempts to introduce selectivity in the Los Alamos program will be extremely costly relative to the cost of additional selectivity in the Bernstein program.

One more calculation might be useful to emphasize the value of heuristics that eliminate branches to be explored. Suppose we had a branching tree in which our program was exploring n moves deep, and let this tree have four branches at each node. If we could double the speed of the program—that is, consider twice as many positions for the same total effort—then this improvement would let us look half a move deeper $(n + \frac{1}{2})$. If, on the other hand, we could double the selectivity—that is, only consider two of the four branches at each node—then we could look twice as deep $(2n)$. It is clear that we could afford to pay an apparently high computing cost per position to achieve this selectivity.

To summarize, Bernstein's program introduces both sophistication and complication to the chess program. Although in some respects—e.g., depth of analysis—it still uses simple uniform rules, in selecting moves to be considered it introduces a set of powerful heuristics taken from successful chess practice, which drastically reduce the number of moves considered at each position.

Newell, Shaw, and Simon Program

Our own program for chess (hereafter called the NSS program), developed in 1958 with J. C. Shaw (Newell, Shaw, and Simon, 1958c), can be described in the same terms we have used for the others. Features of the earlier programs are clearly discernible: Turing's concept of a dead position, and the plausible move generators associated with features of the chess situation, used by Bernstein.

The program did introduce a second level of organization. There is a set of *goals*, each of which corresponds to some basic aspect of the chess situation—material balance, center control, and so on. Each goal has associated with it a generator of base-moves, a generator of analysis-moves, and a static-evaluation process (see Figure 11.6). These are three of the six processes needed to define a chess program in the style of Figure 11.2. Two processes, width-termination and depth-termination, are not specific to particular goals. The program contains no adjusted-value process.

Goals. The goals form a basic set of modules out of which the program is constructed. The goals are independent: they can be added to the program or removed without affecting the feasibility of remaining goals. At the beginning of each move a preliminary analysis establishes that a given chess situation (a "state") obtains, and this chess situation evokes a set of goals appropriate to it. A goal specification routine for each goal (see Figure 11.6) provides information that is used in this initial selection of goals. The goals are put on a list with the most crucial ones first. This current-goal-list then controls the remainder of the processing: the selection of alternatives, the continuations to be explored, and the static-evaluation. Inclusion of this level of organization requires a slight modification of the prototypic program of Figure 11.2. We show this in Figure 11.6 as the insertion

FIGURE 11.6
NSS chess program

base-moves: list of base-move generators a/c current-goal-list
analysis-moves: list of analysis-move generators a/c current-goal-list
width-termination: depth $= 1$:   first acceptable move
                       depth > 1:   alpha-beta procedure
depth-termination: no analysis-moves (unless limited by space)
static-value: list of static-values a/c current-goal-list
adjusted-value: best-value
goal-list: (material, center-control, development)

Modifications to prototypic program (Figure 11.2):
Insert in find-move after line 2:
2.1   initialize-goals ($\Longrightarrow$ current-goal-list);
Add new process:
initialize-goals(goal-list) ($\Longrightarrow$ list):
1.   generate goal-list:
2.   apply goal-specification of element to position ($\Longrightarrow$ status),
                   if fail continue generation;
3.   insert status on list..
material-goal: (goal-specification base-move-generator, analysis-move-generator, static-value)
center-control: (goal-specification base-move-generator, analysis-move-generator, static-value)
development: (goal-specification base-move-generator, analysis-move-generator, static-value)

of an additional initialization step in line 2.1 of find-move, followed by the definition of initialize-goals.

What kind of game the program will play clearly depends on what goals are available to it and chosen by it for any particular move. The purpose of this modular construction is to provide flexibility over the course of the game in the kinds of considerations on which the program spends its effort. For example, the goal of denying stalemate to the opponent is relevant only in certain endgame situations where the opponent is on the defensive and the King is in a constrained position.

Move Generation. The base-move generator associated with each goal provides alternative moves relevant to that goal. These move generators carry the burden of finding positive reasons for doing things. Thus, only the center control generator will propose P-Q4 as a good move in the opening; only the material balance generator will propose moving out of danger a piece that is *en prise*. These move generators correspond to the move generators in Bernstein's program, except that here they are used exclusively to generate base moves and are not used to generate the continuations that are explored in the course of analyzing a move. In Bernstein's program—and a fortiori in the Los Alamos program—identical generators are used both to find a set of base moves from which the final choice of next move is made, and also to find the continuations that must be explored to assess the consequences of reaching a given position. In our program the latter function is performed by a separate set of analysis generators.

Evaluation. Each move proposed by a base-move generator is assigned a value by an analysis procedure. As we said above, the base-move generators have the responsibility for finding positive reasons for making moves. Correspondingly, the analysis procedure is concerned only with the acceptability of a move once it has been generated. A generator proposes; the analysis procedure disposes.

The value assigned to a move is obtained from a series of evaluations, one for each goal. Thus, the value is a list, each component expressing acceptability or unacceptability of a position from the viewpoint of the corresponding goal. The material balance goal would assess only the loss or gain of material; the development goal, the relative gain or loss of *tempi*; the pawn structure goal, the doubling and isolation of pawns; and so on. The value for a component is in some cases a number—e.g., the material balance goal uses conventional piece values: 9 for a Queen, 5 for a Rook, and so on. In other cases, the component value is dichotomous, simply designating the presence or absence of some property, like the blocking of a move or the doubling of a pawn.

As in the other chess programs, the analysis procedure consists of three parts: exploring continuations to some depth, forming static evaluations, and integrating these to establish an effective value for the move. The analysis-move generators associated with the goals determine what branches will be explored from each position reached. At the final position of each continuation, a value is assigned using the static-evaluation routines of each goal to provide the component values. The effective value for a proposed move is obtained by minimaxing on these final static-values.

To be able to minimax, it must be possible to compare any two values, to decide which is preferable, or whether they are equal in value. Even though values are made up of many independent components (i.e., one for each goal selected), there must exist a complete ordering, independent of variation in the size and composition of the goal list. We use a lexicographic ordering: each component value is completely ordered within itself; and values of higher-priority components dominate lower-priority values, as determined by the order of goals on the goal list. To compare two values, then, the values on the first component are compared. If one move is preferable to the other with respect to this component, that move is preferred. If the two components are equal, then the values on the second component are compared. If these are unequal in value, they determine the preference for the entire value, otherwise the next components are compared, and so on.

It is still necessary to select the base-move to be played from the alternatives, given the values assigned to them by the analysis procedure. In the other programs, the final choice procedure was simply an extension of the minimax: choose the one with highest value. Its obviousness rests on the assumption that the set of alternatives to be considered is a fixed set. If this assumption is relaxed, by generating base-moves sequentially, then other procedures are possible. The simplest, and the one used in the NSS program, is *satisficing*: setting an acceptance level or aspiration level as final criterion and simply taking the first acceptable move. The executive routine proceeds down the goal list activating the move generators of the goals in order of priority, so that important moves are considered first. Thus the width-termination at depth 1 can be simply whether a move reaches a specified level of acceptability. If none reaches that level, the best move that was found is chosen.

Analysis. The *analysis-move generators* are the main agents of selectivity in the program. They determine for each position arrived at in the analysis just which further branches must be explored, hence the average number of branches in the exploration tree and its average depth. The base-move generators for the alternatives and the final choice procedure also affect the amount of exploration by determining what moves are considered. But their selection operates only once per move, whereas the selectivity of the analysis generators operates at each ply of the exploration. Hence the average depth of analysis varies geometrically with the selectivity of the analysis generators.

The exploration of continuations is based on a generalization of Turing's concept of a dead position. Turing applied this notion to exchanges, arguing that it made no sense to count material on the board until all exchanges that were to take place had been carried out. We apply the same notion to each feature of the board: the static-evaluation of a goal is meaningful only if the position being evaluated is dead with respect to the feature associated with that goal—that is, only if no moves are likely to be made that could radically alter that component static-value. The analysis-move generators for each goal determine for any position whether the position is dead with respect to their goal; if not, they generate the moves that are both plausible and might seriously affect the static-value of the goal. Thus the selection of continuations to be explored is dictated by the search for a position that is dead with respect to *all* the goals, so that, finally, a static-evaluation can be made. Both the number of branches from each position and the depth of the exploration are controlled in this way. Thus, for analysis (depth > 1) there are no separate width-termination and depth-termination processes (the *alpha-beta* procedure listed in Figure 11.6 with depth-termination will be discussed shortly). Placid situations will produce search trees containing only a handful of positions; complicated middle-game situations will produce much larger ones.

To make the mechanics of the analysis clearer, Figure 11.7 gives a schematic example of a situation. P_0 is the initial position from which White, the machine, must make a move. The arrow, M_1, leading to P_1 represents an alternative proposed by some move generator. The move is made internally (i.e., *considered*), yielding position P_1, and the analysis procedure must then obtain the value of P_1, which will become the value imputed to the proposed alternative M_1. Taking each goal from the goal list in turn, an attempt is made to produce a static-evaluation, For P_1 this attempt is successful for the first and second components, yielding values of 5 and 3 respectively. (Numerical values are used here to keep the picture simple; in reality, various sets of ordered symbols are used, their exact structure depending on the nature of the computation.) However, the third component does not find the position dead, and generates two moves, M_2 and M_3. The first, M_2, is considered, leading to P_2, and an attempt is made to produce a static-evaluation of it. This proceeds just as with P_1, except that this time all goal components find the position dead and the static-value (4, 3, 1) is obtained. Then the second move, M_3, from P_1 is considered, leading to P_3. The attempt to produce a static-value for P_3 runs into difficulties with the first goal component, which generates one move, M_4,

FIGURE 11.7

example of evaluation by NSS chess program

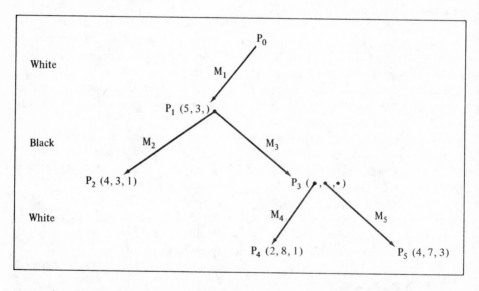

to resolve the instability of P_3 with respect to its feature. This move leads to P_4, which is evaluable, having the value (2, 8, 1). However, the second component also finds P_3 not dead and generates a single move, M_5, leading to P_5. This is also evaluable, having the value (4, 7, 3). The third component finds P_3 dead and therefore contributes no additional moves. Thus the exploration comes to an end with all terminal positions yielding complete static-values. Since it is White's move at P_3, White will choose the move with the highest value. This is M_5, the move to P_5, with a value of (4, 7, 3) (the first goal component dominates). The value of this move is the effective value assigned to P_3. Black now has a choice between the move, M_2, to P_2, yielding (4, 3, 1) and the move, M_3, to P_3, yielding (4, 7, 3). Since Black is minimizing, he will choose M_2. This yields (4, 3, 1) as the effective value of the alternative, M_1, that leads to P_1, and the end of the analysis.

Minimaxing is conducted concurrently with the generation of branches, permitting the operation of the so-called *alpha-beta procedure*.[10] This procedure, which lops off large numbers of irrelevant branches, is a consequence of the fact that each additional argument in a minimization (or maximization) can establish a new lower (or upper) bound. In general it works as follows. Suppose (Figure 11.8) at each node we keep track of the best-value found so far—the lowest at a minimizing node, the highest at a maximizing node. In the figure, suppose node.1 is a maximizing node and has alpha as the highest value so far; node.2, obtained from it along branch.i, is a minimizing node and beta is the lowest value so far. Then the move actually chosen at node.2 must have a value of beta or less—since beta is already in hand. Similarly, the move chosen at node.1 must have a value of alpha

FIGURE 11.8

the alpha-beta procedure

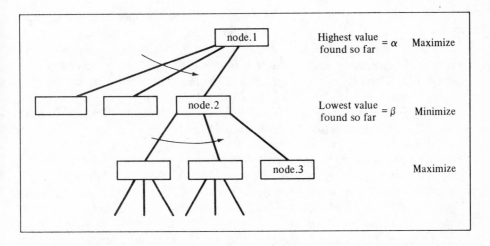

Highest value found so far $= \alpha$	Maximize
Lowest value found so far $= \beta$	Minimize
	Maximize

or greater—since alpha is in hand. Thus, if a move is ever found at node.2 that makes beta less than alpha, node.2 should be abandoned without further ado: for its eventual value is guaranteed to be less than alpha, and hence will be ignored at node.1 because alpha can be obtained there. Similarly, of course, at node.2 no move of value greater than beta is worthwhile, so that at node.3 (again a maximizing node) there is no sense in finding values greater than beta, since they will simply be ignored at node.2 in the course of minimaxing.

For a concrete example look at Figure 11.7. If P_5, which has a value of (4, 7,

---

[10] The name, coined by John McCarthy, came from the two limits used in the procedure, which were called alpha and beta. The procedure is similar to *branch and bound* procedures used in various management science combinatorial problems (e.g., Lawler and Wood, 1966).

3), had been generated prior to P_4, no further moves would have been generated from P_3, since it is already apparent that Black will prefer P_2 to P_3. The value of P_3 is at least as great as the value of P_5, since it is White's move and he will maximize.

The alpha-beta procedure is not a heuristic. The branches that it eliminates are guaranteed not to have any effect on the eventual value produced by mini-maxing—hence they can be ignored with impunity. A small processing cost is incurred, of course, since the various values of alpha and beta must be calculated and comparisons made at each node. However, the savings far exceed the costs. In the limit, the number of nodes examined may be reduced to the square root of the number that would have been examined without the alpha-beta procedure (Slagle and Dixon, 1969).

The alpha-beta procedure has been used in all game-playing programs after the first few. Providing that the relevant information about the best-value obtained so far by the opponent is available, it is a simple matter to add the alpha-beta test to the width-termination process. Actually, additional gains are possible by carrying forward the best-value obtained so far by the player of the position. Here, however, the problem is to know when a better value cannot be obtained by additional exploration, and this is indeed a heuristic matter. No regular algorithms for this case have come into use.

The analysis procedure we have described for the NSS program is not simple, either conceptually or technically. There are many ways to terminate search and reach an effective evaluation. There is no built-in rule that guarantees that the search will converge (except the external limits of space and time). Success depends heavily on the ability to evaluate statically. The more numerous the situations that can be recognized as having a certain value without having to generate continuations, the more rapidly the search will terminate. The number of plausible moves that affect the value is also of consequence.

Examples of goals.   Only three goals were fully developed and used in the NSS program: center-control, material-balance, and development. Schemata of the information for these three are shown in Figures 11.9, 11.10, and 11.11, respectively. These are the three goals appropriate to the opening phase of the game, and all three would be evoked at the start. Material-balance, of course, is relevant throughout the game. But in a more completely developed program, the other two goals would drop out as the game progressed and be replaced by goals more appropriate to later phases.

Goals are proposed in terms of the general situation—e.g., for the opening game. The list of actual goals is constructed for a particular position by applying, in turn, the specification of each of the potential goals. Whether any particular goal is declared relevant or irrelevant to the position depends on whether or not the position meets its specification. Consider first *center-control* (Figure 11.9), the simplest of the three goals. No special information needs to be gathered. The goal becomes irrelevant if all the center pawns have been moved to the fourth rank or beyond (or have been captured). The most important part of center-control is its base-move generator. It is concerned with the two primary moves: P-Q4 and P-K4. It will propose these moves if they are legal, and it is the responsibility of the analysis procedures (for all the goals) to reject the moves if there is anything wrong

FIGURE 11.9

schematic outline of center-control goal

Specification
Goal is always operative unless there are no more center pawns to be moved to the
fourth rank
No special information is needed

Base-move generator
(1) Move P-Q4, P-K4 (primary moves)
(2) Prevent the opponent from making his primary moves
move pawn to occupy Q4 or K4 squares
add an attacker to square
(3) Prepare own primary moves
add a defender to Q4 or K4 squares
eliminate a block to moving QP or KP

Static-evaluation
The number of blocks to making own primary moves

Analysis-move generators
None, static-evaluation is always possible

FIGURE 11.10

schematic outline of material-balance goal

Specification
A list of exchanges on occupied squares
separate lists for own and opponent targets
For each exchange
target man
list of attackers and list of defenders
including doubled attackers (defenders) on ranks, files, diagonals
ordered by low value of attacker (defender) first
taking into account necessary order of doubled men
static-exchange-value
from play-off of attacker and defender lists in order
terminating at maximum profit to attacker
assuming no indirect consequences elsewhere
(e.g., pins, discovered attacks, etc.)
Exchange list ordered on static-exchange-value
largest negative value (to target side) first
all exchanges of positive value to target side (i.e., safe) eliminated
A list of pinned men
with specification of source of pin and target of pin
Goal is operative if there are any exchanges for either side on the lists

Base-move generator
Generate exchanges from specification lists
in order on static-exchange-value
For each exchange generate moves
if target of exchange is opponent

FIGURE 11.10 (cont'd)

(1) capture target
    with first man from attacker list
    if attacker is pinned, try next attacker
    if otherwise rejected, stop on this exchange
if target of exchange is own
  (1) *no-move*
    (to see if attack is in fact damaging)
  (2) capture the attacker
  (3) add a defender
    not employed in another defense
  (4) move the target man
  (5) interpose a man between the attacker and the target
    not employed in another defense
    not if interposer can be captured
      evaluated statically
  (6) pin the attacker
    with man not employed in another defense
    not if pinner can be captured
      evaluated statically

Static-evaluation
  Basic value
    the sum of own material — opponent's material
      where $Q = 9, R = 5, B = 3, N = 3, P = 1$
  Adjusted-value
    play-off of exchanges (as unitary events)
      using static-exchange-values
      eliminating exchanges all of whose men have been taken in other exchanges
      permitting a side to disengage rather than prosecute an exchange
        if it has the move option

Analysis-move generator
  A position is dead
  (1) if there are no exchanges on the specification lists
    or (2) it is in the midst of an exchange, material is already lost, and the static-exchange-value is still negative (unlikely that loss can be recovered)
Generate move according to the basic move generator

FIGURE 11.11
schematic outline of development goal

Specification
  A list of undeveloped pieces
    separate lists for own and opponent pieces
    in order by KN, QN, KB, QB, Q, KR, QR
      (pawns are not included)
    criteria for being undeveloped

FIGURE 11.11 (cont'd)

N: in original position
B: in original position
R: not in good file position
    file not open through fourth rank
    R not in front of own pawns
    opponent R not behind own pawns
    opponent Q not on file
Q: on first rank
Goal operative if there are any undeveloped pieces

Base-move generator

(1) Generate developing moves
    in order from the specification lists
    criteria for a developing move
        N: N-B3
        B: (1) along centerward diagonal
               from far (rank 5) to near (rank 2)
               B-N5 only if it pins opponent N
           (2) along sideward diagonal
               rank 2, rank 3
        R: (1) move to good file
               centerward, sideward
           (2) castle
        Q: move to rank 2, rank 3
               centerward, forward, sideward
(2) Generate moves that prepare developing moves
    remove blocker of developing move
        in order on specification lists
        if own man blocking, move away
        if opponent blocking, add attacker
        first for moves with 1 block, then with 2

Static-evaluation

Value = (own tempi — opponent tempi), own blocked pieces
    tempi = sum of factors
        add 1 for developed B, R or Q
        add 1, 2, 3 for N on ranks (1 or 2), (3 or 4), (5 or more) respectively
        add 1 for castled K
        subtract 1 if castling privilege lost (and not castled)
        add 1 if *no-move*
    blocked piece
        undeveloped and and no legal developing move

Analysis-move generator

Position is dead
    if there are no undeveloped pieces
    or if the absolute change in static-value (for development) from the base position is
        greater than 1
Generate move
    (1) developing moves for the side on move
    (2) attacks on advanced opponent pieces
        by own men of lesser value
        an advanced man is beyond his fourth rank

with them—e.g., if the pawns will be taken when moved, So, after 1.P-Q4, P-Q4, the center-control move generator will propose 2.P-K4, but the evaluation routine of the material-balance goal will reject this move because of the loss of material that would result from 2. . . . , P×P. The center-control generator has nothing to do with tracing out these consequences.

If the primary moves cannot be made, the center-control move generator has two choices: to prepare them, or to prevent the opponent from making his primary moves. The program's style of play will depend very much on whether prevention has priority over preparation (as it does in our description of the generator above) or vice versa. The ordering in the figure, which puts prevention first, probably produces more aggressive and slightly better opening play than the reverse ordering. Similarly, the style of play depends on whether the Queen's pawn or the King's pawn is considered first.

The base-move generator tries to prevent the opponent's primary moves (whenever this subgoal is evoked) by first determining whether the opponent can make one of these moves (by trying the move and then obtaining an evaluation of it from the opponent's viewpoint). If one or both of the opponent's primary moves are not rejected, preventive moves will serve some purpose. Under these conditions, the center-control move generator will find moves that bring another attacker to bear on the opponent's K4 and Q4 squares or that pin a defender of one of these squares. Among the moves this generator will normally propose are N-B3 and BP-B4.

The base-move generator tries to prepare its own primary moves by first determining why the moves cannot be made without preparation—e.g., whether the pawn is blocked from moving by a friendly piece, or whether the fourth rank square is unsafe for the pawn. In the former case, the generator proposes moves for the blocking piece; in the latter case, it finds moves that will add defenders to the fourth rank square, drive away or pin attackers, and so on.

The evaluation routine for center-control is essentially negative—to assure that moves, proposed by some other goal, will not be made if they jeopardize control of the center. The possibility is ignored that a move generated for another goal will inadvertently contribute to center-control. Hence, the static-evaluation for center-control is only concerned that moves not be made that interfere with P-K4 and P-Q4. A typical example of a move that the center-control evaluation routine is prepared to reject is B-Q3 or B-K3 before the respective center pawns have been moved.

The second example of a goal is *material-balance* (Figure 11.10), which is much more extensive and complicated than center-control, and handles all questions about gain and loss of material in the immediate situation. However, it does not consider threats like pins and forks, where the actual exchange is still a move away; other goals must take care of these. Both the negative and positive aspects of material must be included in a single goal, since they compensate directly for each other, and material must often be spent to gain material.

A special data structure, consisting of all the exchanges, is obtained for material-balance, which operates primarily from this information. Each exchange is handled separately to obtain a static-exchange-value. This approximation to the "true" material-balance represented on the board is considerably better than just the static-value (the count of material) but considerably less accurate than a full dynamic analysis. Within each exchange, matters are handled quite appropriately, taking into account the order in which doubled pieces (such as a Queen preceding a Rook on a file) must capture. But no account is taken of interactions between exchanges (e.g., that an attacker cannot be used in two exchanges, or that execution of one exchange may remove a defender from the scene of another).

The static-exchange-value is used primarily to order the exchanges on the specification list, which governs, in turn the order in which moves are generated for resolving issues of material-balance. The base-move generator is the same as the analysis-move generator. They produce attacking moves for exchanges in which the opponent is the target and defensive moves for exchanges in which the side on move is the target. While the program does only one thing when attacking—i.e., capture—it has many ways of defending. In generating moves by function for a number of different goals, the same move may occur more than once. This duplication is detected at a more central spot in the executive.

A small first step is taken in the move generator to avoid overloading a man with multiple functions. Various defensive moves are only generated for men who do not already have a defensive function, as detected by the occurrence of the man on one of the lists of defenders. Although this is a limited concept of multiple function, it is an important notion.

The static-value is simply the balance of material, measured by the conventional values for the chess men. However, since search was usually terminated primarily for reasons of space (JOHNNIAC had a primary memory of only 4096 words, infinitesimal by today's standards), taking a forced static-value was much too crude an evaluation. Consequently, we adopted an adjusted static-value, which made use of the substantial information in the specification lists of exchanges. We played off the exchanges as if they were moves. When one player selected an exchange, his static-exchange-value was increased accordingly. Then the next player could select an exchange, and so on. The option to select the next exchange was allotted to the opponent of the player who made the last move on the previous exchange—it could be either player. The player holding the option could elect not to take any of the exchanges, but to terminate the playoff. This corresponded to making a defensive move or another attacking move and was considered always possible. Thus the playoff was not forced. This entire scheme still suffers from the basic simplification in the exchange analysis itself, namely, that it fails to take interactions into account. We did eliminate exchanges where no attackers were left by the time the playoff was evaluated, but this (though it handles many simple situations) is only a small corrective. Despite the simplifications, these adjusted values are very much better than the raw static-values.

The last goal is *development* (Figure 11.11). Like center-control it is concerned exclusively with the initial deployment in the game. Thus, it makes use of highly specific information (e.g., "develop a Knight to its B3 square"). Although the Knight will be credited as developed if it stands on any of a number of other squares, these other moves of the Knight will come about because other goals (such as material-balance) propose them. Another aspect of the highly particular nature of the development goal is the criteria it uses to decide whether a piece is undeveloped, hence should be put on the specification list.

The specification list controls the order in which moves are generated. Legal developing moves are proposed first. After all such moves have been generated, the base-move generator produces preparatory moves. To obtain these, the base-move generator employs a more fundamental generator that produces developing moves without regard to their legality. Each such move is described as having zero, one, or two blocking men—that is, men who stand in the way of making the move. The moves with zero blockers are the developing moves proposed at the first stage by the base-move generator. The other moves are used to generate a collection of blocking pieces against whom the preparatory moves are directed. If the blocker is the player's own man, then he can prepare development by moving it away. From development's viewpoint, one move is as good as another, as long as it clears the way. Thus, this goal simply generates legal moves, depending on the other goals to weed out the bad proposals. If the blocker is an opponent's man, then it is attacked in order to drive it away. Developing moves with one and two blockers are considered, but those with more than two are ignored.

The static value for development consists of two numbers. One is the *tempi* count (a rough approximation to that concept as it is used in the chess world). A *no-move* is assigned one tempo—which is exactly what a "standard" move should provide. (The program misplayed seriously when no-move was assigned no tempi.) The second component of the static value is the number of pieces that are wholly blocked from development. This is the number only for the side on move; there seems little reason to include the corresponding measure for the opponent. The tempi count and count of blocks must be combined to make position evaluations according to the scheme outlined earlier, which demands a single judgment about the developmental value of a position. The two counts are lexicographically ordered—tempi taking precedence over blocks.

The analysis-move generator for development is different from the base-move generator. No purpose is served in analysis by considering preparatory moves. However, there is good reason to consider attacking moves that drive away developed pieces, since these can affect considerably the stability of the development. Thus the analysis-move generator produces moves that attack advanced pieces (not pawns), with men of lower value.

Performance of the Program. Two kinds of experiments were performed with the NSS program to obtain some impression of its manner of coping with the task environment: it was matched against several human players, and its play was compared with several book games. Its speed of play was comparable to that of the Los Alamos and Bernstein programs: on a processor of the speed of an IBM 360/65, moves would take a second to half a minute.[11]

Perhaps the strongest game of the NSS program was played against one of the authors (HAS), who at the time was rated as a class A player. The program had

[11] That is, one hundred times longer on the JOHNNIAC, on which the programs actually ran (see footnote on page 110).

the three goals: material-balance, center-control, and development. It had no goals corresponding to King-safety, serious threats, or pawn-promotion, to say nothing of more subtle considerations. Nevertheless, the program, playing White, had rather the better of it for the first ten moves, until it ran out of things to do relating directly to development and center-control. Since an annotated version of the game has been published (Feigenbaum and Feldman, 1963, pages 66–70), we omit it here.

Another game, with the NSS program again playing White, and operating with the same three goals, is shown in Table 11.4. The opponent in this case was a weak player, and the program made several very strong moves (see especially moves 11 and 12), though not always for the right reasons. After the absence of a goal relating to attacks on the King caused it to miss the obvious and devastating double check on move 14, its position deteriorated rapidly. The last part of the game is a comedy of errors. White avoids mating threats only when they involve also the

TABLE 11.4

play of Newell, Shaw, and Simon chess program (May 1960)

	WHITE (JOHNNIAC)	BLACK (HUMAN)	
1	P-Q4	N-QB3	
2	P-K4	P-K4	
3	N-KB3	P-B3	
4	N-B3	B-N5	
5	B-QB4	R-N1	
6	B-K3	N-R4	
7	B-Q3	P-B3	
8	P×P	P×P	
9	N×P	P-Q3	
10	B×P?	R-R1	
11	Q-R5ch!	P-KN3	
12	N×NP	B×Nch	
13	P×B	Q-B3	
14	Q×N??	P×N	(14. N×Rch wins easily)
15	O-O	R-R4	
16	Q-R3	Q-K4	
17	P-R3	P-Q4?	(White notes mating threat)
18	P×P	B×P??	A comedy of errors
19	P×B?	R×P?	(19. R-K1 wins for White)
20	B-Q4?	Q-N4 mate	(White apparently doesn't see mate)

potential loss of a pawn! His opponent ignores the threat of a pin of his Queen on his King that (if NSS had possessed a goal that would have permitted noticing it!) would have rescued the program's game up to the very last move. Thus, the erratic play of the NSS program can be related directly to the presence and absence of specific goals. When the important considerations on the board relate to NSS's goals, the program's play is strong; when the goals relevant to the situations are missing, the program is blind. Its oversights are hard to distinguish qualitatively from those of the human opponent (the oversight by both of them of the Queen pin, for example).

Our understanding of the response of a system like NSS to its task environment can be enhanced by more systematic analysis of the process for choosing a move in particular situations. To this end, the behavior of the program was studied in the context of several games recorded in standard chess books. NSS was assigned the role of one of the players. Each time it made a move, this move was compared with the actual move in the recorded game. If they were not identical, the position was reset to agree with the book move, and NSS recalculated the value of that move, whereupon the game continued. A trace was printed out of all the continuations that NSS examined in its analysis, and from this trace it was possible to reconstruct the operation of the various move generators and evaluation processes.

FIGURE 11.12

position in opening play

Black

White

As an introduction to the kinds of inferences that can be made from data of this kind, let us examine a simple example. In Figure 11.12 the program is White and the play has been 1.P-K4, P-K4. Assuming that NSS has the three goals mentioned above, the material-balance base-move generator will not propose any moves, since there are no exchanges on the board. The center-control generator will propose P-Q4, which is the circled move in the figure. This move is rejected—as it should be—and it is instructive to see why. The move is proposed for analysis. Material-balance does not find the position dead since there is an exchange, and generates Black's move, 2. . . . , P×P. The resulting position is still not dead, and 3. Q×P, is generated. The position is now dead for material-balance, with no gain or loss on material. The first component of the static-evaluation is even. There are obviously no blocks to pawn moves, so that the center-control static-value is acceptable. However, the third component, development, finds the position not dead because there is now an exposed piece, the Queen. It generates replies that both attack the piece and develop—i.e., add a tempo. The move 3. . . . ., N-QB3 is generated. This forces a Queen move, losing a tempo for White. Hence development rejects the move, 2. P-Q4. (The move 3. . . . , B-B4 would not have caused rejection by development, since the Bishop could be taken.)

Let us consider next a whole game—the famous contest between Paul Morphy, the American champion of a century ago, and Duke Karl of Brunswick and Count Isouard, playing in consultation. Perhaps "contest" is not the right word, since the

TABLE 11.5

play of Newell, Shaw, and Simon chess program
in Morphy vs. Duke of Brunswick and Count Isouard

MOVE	WHITE (MORPHY)	BLACK (D & C)	BLACK (NSS)	POSITIONS CONSIDERED	MOVES CONSIDERED
1	P-K4	P-K4	P-K4	2	1
2	N-KB3	P-Q3	P-Q3	2	1
3	P-Q4	B-KN5	N-KB3	43	10(Y)*
4	P×P	B×N	P×P	6	1(N)*
5	Q×B	P×P	P×P	2	1
6	B-QB4	N-KB3	Q-KB3	14	3(N)
7	Q-QN3	Q-K2	N-QB3	58	20(Y)
8	N-QB3	P-QB3	P-QB4	2	1(N)
9	B-KN5	P-QN4	P-QB4	6	1(N)
10	N×P	P×N	P×N	2	1
11	B×Pch	N(N1)-Q2	N(N1)-Q2	5	2
12	O-O-O	R-Qsq	R-Qsq	7	1
13	R×N	R×R	R×R	36	2
14	R-Qsq	Q-K3	Q-B4	15	3(N)
15	B×Rch	N×B	N×B	4	1
16	Q-N8ch	N×Q	N×Q	2	1
17	R-Q8 mate				
	Average			13	3.0

* Y: Considered move chosen by D & C;
  N: Did not consider move chosen by D & C.

Duke and Count were not first-class players. But Sergeant (1957) says of this game: "No doubt the opposition was weak; but Morphy's method of overcoming it was most beautifully logical—a Damascus blade cutting a silk cushion." In our analysis, NSS modestly assumed the role of Black—of the Duke and Count.

Table 11.5 shows the play of the game. The first column gives the moves of Morphy (White), the second column, the actual moves of the Duke and Count (Black), the third column, the moves proposed by NSS (Black). The number of positions considered in the analysis of NSS is shown in the fourth column, and the number of moves considered in the fifth column.

The NSS program considers, on the average, only three alternative moves in each position. We have not counted the exact number of legal moves available, but the average in this game is very close to thirty, and probably slightly in excess of that number. Hence, the program considers only 10 percent of the legal moves. In fact, only on the third and seventh moves are more than three alternatives considered; and the program accepts the first move it considers in ten of the sixteen positions. In nine of the sixteen positions NSS proposes the same move as that adopted by the Duke and Count. In seven of these nine cases this is the first and only move considered.

The fact that there is agreement between the human players and NSS more than half the time gives strong evidence of the limits that the requirements of the situation placed on choice. Of course, we must be careful how we interpret the term *requirements*. The players only met the requirements as they perceived them; if they had perceived the *real* requirements, presumably they would not have lost the game in seventeen moves! Consider move 2, for example, where both Black players chose P-K3. This move was not demanded objectively by the situation. Although it is a well-known move in this position (Philidor's Defense), it is "old-fashioned" and no longer regarded as adequate for Black. What the situation requires here is N-QB3, the usual move, or N-KB3. NSS did not even consider these alternatives.

Black's sixteenth move, however, is objective enough, for it is the only legal move available. His fifteenth move can also be regarded as objective: although neither it nor any other move will avert disaster, this move is the only one that does not result in immediate loss of the Queen.

Not only does the NSS program limit its analysis to a few moves, it explores only a few continuations. The average number of positions considered in the sixteen moves is 13, and in only three cases is the number larger than 15. Thus, an average of a little more than four positions is generated for each move considered. These numbers may be compared with the seven moves and 2500 positions generally investigated by Bernstein's program, and the 30-odd moves and 800,000 positions investigated by the Los Alamos program. In terms of positions, there is an increase in selectivity over Bernstein's program by a factor of 200, and over the Los Alamos program by a factor of 60,000! And this great increase in selectivity is accomplished with no apparent loss in playing power, and with a gain in the opening part of the game. Partial repayment is made, however, in terms of the greater effort expended for each position examined. (The gain also comes from the alpha-beta procedure, which the earlier programs did not use.)

Let us consider one of the more problematic situations in the Morphy game—the position after 1. P-K4, P-K4; 2. N-KB3, P-K3; 3. P-Q4 (Figure 11.13) The

FIGURE 11.13

Morphy game: position after 3.P-Q4

Black

White

move actually made by the Duke and Count, B-N5, is followed in *Morphy's Games of Chess* by Sergeant's comment (1957, p. 149): "Following the bad example of Harrwitz." The earlier game in which Harrwitz played this move and lost to Morphy lasted, however, 59 moves; Emmanuel Lasker tried the same move (and lost) as late as 1889. When Sergeant remarks, then, (p. 101) that the move is "universally condemned by the analysts," he means that historical experience, in games among strong players, has shown it leads to bad consequences—not that its weakness can be determined by analysis in over-the-board play. Here the requirements of the situation do not reveal themselves easily or clearly.

The NSS program examined ten moves and 43 positions in this situation, which it evidently also found problematic (Figure 11.14). One of these moves was B-KN5, which it rejected because its analysis (erroneously) saw it leading to the loss of a pawn (3. . . . ., B-KN5; 4. P×P. P×P; 5. Q×Qch., K×Q; 6. N×P).

695

FIGURE 11.14

NSS program: analysis of reply to 3.P–Q4 in Morphy vs. Duke and Count
(the evaluation is shown in parentheses (abc). a is the material advantage, b the advantage in center control, and c the advantage in development)

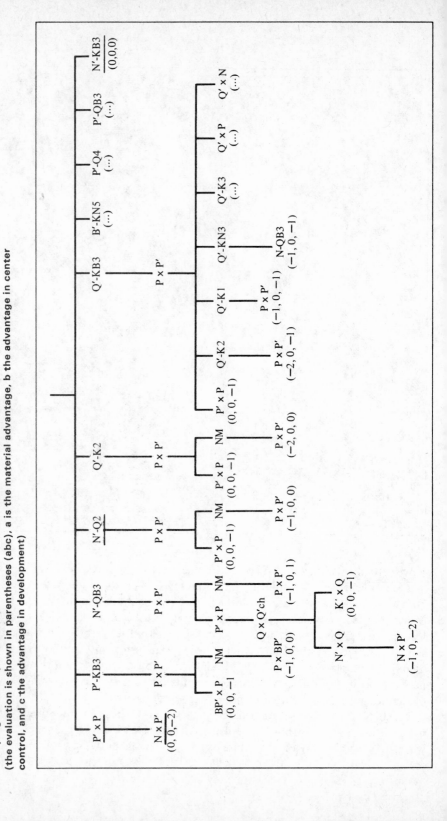

The other nine moves it considered included three of the four moves mentioned in a modern work on the opening game [the fourth move, P-KB4, not considered by NSS, is rated as inferior in *Practical Chess Openings* (Fine, 1948)]. One of these was the move actually chosen, N-KB3 (preferred by Nimzowitsch); the others were N-Q2, the move now usually played in this position, and P×P, both of which NSS considered slightly inferior to N-KB3. Twenty-three additional legal moves in the position were not even evoked by the move generators associated with the goals.

The moves considered by the NSS program in this position were proposed by material-balance to deal with the exchange that threatens Black with the loss of a pawn. One move countered the threat with an immediate exchange, five defended the pawn, one pinned the attacking Knight (B-N5), and three counterattacked. In its analysis of B-N5, the program failed to consider 4. P×P, B×N, since the exchange of Knight and Bishop did not seem to recover the lost pawn—in evaluating the exchange, the program did not see its interaction with the Knight's role on its K5.

Table 11.6 provides a final example of the play of NSS—the first ten moves of a game between Botvinnik, a former world champion, and Kmoch, a grandmaster. Only the beginning of the game is considered, since NSS does not have appropriate middle-game goals, but only the three goals of material-balance, center-control, and development. As before, NSS played Black.

Using again the criterion of the first satisfactory move (i.e., the first move considered whose value equals the precomputed static-value of the position), the NSS program considered an average of only two moves and 10.1 positions. In three of the ten moves in the table (moves 3, 5, and 10), the program chose the same move as Kmoch, while in two other cases (moves 1 and 6) it chose standard book moves. On the remaining five moves (2, 4, 7, 8, and 9) it did not consider the move chosen by Kmoch or shown in standard opening analyses. To a considerable extent this is due to its "trigger-happy" choice criterion, for in all cases except moves 1, 6, and

TABLE 11.6

play of NSS chess program in Botvinnik vs. Kmoch

MOVE	WHITE (BOTVINNIK)	BLACK (KMOCH)	BLACK (NSS)	POSITIONS CONSIDERED	MOVES CONSIDERED
1	P-K4	P-QB3	P-K3	5	3
2	P-Q4	P-Q4	P-K3	4	2
3	P×P	P×P	P×P	2	1
4	P-QB4	N-KB3	N-QB3	19	1
5	N-QB3	N-QB3	N-QB3	12	1
6	B-KN5	P-K3	P×P	35	7
7	P-QB5	B-K2	Q-QB2	8	2
8	B-QN5	O-O	N-Q2	6	1
9	N-KB3	N-K5	N-KN5	4	1
10	B×B	N×B	N×B	6	1
Average				10.1	2.0

9 it subsequently assigned a value to the move imposed on it (but not considered by it) at least as high as the value of the move it had previously chosen. In the first two of the exceptional cases (moves 1 and 6) the move it actually chose was a book move. Hence at moves 2, 4, 7 and 8, where it chose a different move from Kmoch's, the choice was sensitive to the order of move generation. Either a higher acceptance standard or a more complete set of positional goals would have forced the system into a more elaborate search before it selected a move.

One example will illustrate an important point made earlier—that the function of search in a game-playing program is quite different from the function of search in a theorem prover. The task of a game player is to choose a move; the game tree is explored only for the purpose of acquiring the information needed to evaluate moves—the exploration is not necessarily predictive of the future course of the game. At move 5, the NSS analysis of N-QB3 consists simply of examining the sequence of exchanges to evaluate material-balance when a dead position is reached. (5. ... , N-QB3, 6. P×P, N×P(Q4); 7. N×N, Q×N; 8. N-KB3, 8. N-K2, and 8. B-K3; 7. *no-move*, N×N; 8. P×N) This does not imply that these exchanges are a likely continuation of the game; in fact they are not, for the players will go on developing and struggling for control of the center.

The move called no-move requires comment. In situations where there are many alternatives, it frequently is possible to place a minimum value on the position by asking: "what would happen if I (or he, as the case may be) did nothing?" The NSS program incorporates this idea in order to curtail search, making the assumption that a no-move increases by exactly one tempo the value of a move for the player who makes it. In using the no-move procedure, the program takes a first timid step to extend the problem space beyond the basic space of legal moves.

The Kotok Program

Around 1960 a group of students at MIT, under the aegis of John McCarthy, produced a chess program, which became known as the "MIT chess program" or the Kotok program (Kotok, 1962). A variant of the program recently engaged in a four-game correspondence match with USSR chess programs, in which it did not fare very well (no author, 1967).[12]

Figure 11.15 gives the details of the program. It differs in two respects from prior programs. First, there is a single move generator, both for base-moves and analysis-moves, which operates by making each legal move and computing its static-value. Then the moves are generated in order on this value. Thus, no independent source of information goes into move generation; on the other hand all moves do get considered for inclusion. Second, the program adopts a fixed set of limits for width-termination, just as did Bernstein's program, but these limits are tapered to provide a deeper penetration. The limits given in the figure are typical; they clearly can be set to any values for a particular play. The static-value is, as

[12] The Russian programs appear to be descendants of the one described in Adelson-Velsky (no date).

FIGURE 11.15

Kotok chess program

base-moves:	plausible-move-generator
analysis-moves:	same as base-moves
where	plausible-move-generator(position)
	1. generate legal-moves(position):
	2. make legal-move on position ($\Longrightarrow$ next-position);
	3. compute static-value(next-position) ($\Longrightarrow$ value);
	4. insert legal move on move-list in order on value
	5. generate move-list.
width-termination:	alpha-beta procedure and
	$>$ width(depth): depth: 1 2 3 4 5 6 7 8
	width: 4 3 2 2 1 1 1 1
depth-termination:	no analysis-moves
static-value:	material-balance $+ (\frac{1}{60})$ center-control-value $+ (\frac{1}{15})$ development-value $+ (\frac{1}{20})$ pawn-structure-value
	where center-control-value and development-value are phased out as the game progresses
	material-balance:
	static exchange analysis
	with P $= 1$, N $= 3$, B $= 3$, R $= 5$, Q $= 9$, K $= 1000$
	center-control-value $=$ weighted sum of control of 16 center squares
	(1 to 8 points per square)
	development-value $=$ weighted sum for developed pieces
	with 1 to 4 points per man
	pawn-structure-value $=$ weighted sum for pawn features:
	open-file $= 8$, isolated P $= -1$, doubled P $= -3$
	backward P $= -5$, passed P $= 10$
adjusted-value:	best-value

in Turing's program, a sum of a large number of factors. However, material-balance is calculated by an exchange analysis similar to the one described for the NSS program.

In Table 11.7 we give the moves of a game played by the Kotok program (White) against an expert (Black) who gave the program odds of a queen—and lost. Taking immediate advantage of a mistake in Black's twelfth move, the program presses on to a win. Previous to its attack, the program had developed soundly, exchanging pieces whenever possible (which it should do, since it is ahead in material). The other games played by the Kotok program, though interesting, are not nearly as spectacular as this one.

The Greenblatt Program

A program constructed by Richard Greenblatt and his associates at MIT (Greenblatt, Eastlake, and Crocker, 1967), gives us our first really accurate information about playing strength in relation to human players. Since the program is under continual revision, its playing strength does not remain constant; our com-

TABLE 11.7

the Kotok chess program vs. an expert at odds of a Queen (1962)

	WHITE (KOTOK)	BLACK (EXPERT)		WHITE (KOTOK)	BLACK (EXPERT)
1	P-K4	P-K4	14	P×P	N-B3
2	N-KB3	N-QB3	15	P-N7ch!	N×Q
3	B-N5*	P-Q3	16	P×R=Qch	B-B1
4	O-O	P-KB4	17	N×P dis ch	K-Q2
5	B×Nch	P×B	18	N×R	B-K2
6	R-K1	N-KB3	19	Q×P	K×N
7	N-QB3	B-K2	20	R×B	N-B3
8	P-Q4	B-K3	21	Q-B7	K-B1
9	QP×P	QP×P	22	R×Pch	K-N1
10	P×P	B-Q4	23	R-N7ch	K-R1
11	N×B	N×N	24	R×Pch	K-N1
12	N×P	R-Q1?	25	Q-N7 mate	
13	Q-R5ch!	P-N3			

*Remove Black's Queen. The Ruy Lopez opening was agreed upon.

ments refer to its performance in the winter of 1966–67. The program has competed in at least two tournaments with rated players. In the first tournament it drew with a player rated at 1365 (class D), and lost four other games. It was provisionally given a rating of 1239 (class D). In the second tournament it defeated a player with a 1505 rating (class C), and lost four other games. Aside from a serious blindness about its own King safety, its play may even be of class B caliber.

The score of the program's tournament game with the class C player it defeated is shown in Table 11.8. In the first nine moves the program concerns itself systematically and vigorously with center-control and development. (White's third move loses a tempo but can hardly be viewed as amateurish, since the first three moves of both players are identical with a game between Mieses and Tarrasch at Berlin in 1920.) Black meanwhile loses time with premature pawn moves, and by the ninth move White has a distinct advantage in development. Black's eleventh move is a blunder, instantly exploited by White's surprising reply. On his fourteenth move Black falls into a trap that loses his Queen. The game is now won, but it is finished by White with a most elegant checkmate, beginning with the Queen sacrifice on move 20, and employing precisely the same motive as Morphy's checkmate of the Duke of Brunswick and Count Isouard. It should be observed that White's early success in this particular game is not unrelated to its ignoring considerations of its own King safety after Black's move 11.

The program's selection of several book moves is not an isolated incident. In a game in which, playing Black, it defeated H. Dreyfus (SICART Newsletter, October 1967, pp. 8–9), its first four moves were book, its human opponent being the first to depart from accepted lines. Similarly, the Kotok program, in two published games in which it played White, found book continuations for three and five

TABLE 11.8

Greenblatt chess program vs. class C player

	WHITE (GREENBLATT)	BLACK (CLASS C PLAYER)
1	P-K4	P-QB4
2	P-Q4	P×P
3	Q×P	N-QB3
4	Q-Q3	N-B3
5	N-QB3	P-KN3
6	N-B3	P-Q3
7	B-B4	P-K4
8	B-N3	P-QR3
9	O-O-O	P-QN4
10	P-QR4	B-R3ch
11	K-N1	P-N5??
12	Q×QP	B-Q2
13	B-R4	B-N2
14	N-Q5	N×P?
15	N-B7ch	Q×N
16	Q×Q	N-B4
17	Q-Q6	B-KB1
18	Q-Q5	R-B1
19	N×P	B-K3
20	Q×Nch!!	R×Q
21	R-Q8 mate	

moves, respectively, and in the latter case the opponent then departed from book.

The specifications of the Greenblatt program are given in Figure 11.16. Like the Kotok program, it generates its moves by engaging in a subsidiary generation of all legal moves, computing a plausibility score for each, and then ordering the moves for actual consideration on this basis. Unlike the Kotok program, its move plausibility value is entirely separate from its static-value. The plausibility value primarily reflects material and development, both being combined in a system of assigning weights to squares, and then scoring each move as a function of how it changes the coverage of weighted squares.

Again, like the Kotok program, the Greenblatt program shapes the search by controlling width-termination as a function of depth. The widths given in the figure correspond to tournament settings; smaller values are used in casual play. But, unlike the Kotok program, it uses this width value only as a basic value, and several things can increase it. For instance, one factor guarantees that a suitable diversity of pieces will be involved in the sample of moves considered. This is important in situations in which a threatened piece (e.g., the Queen) has a large number of squares to which it can retreat, and would (otherwise) preempt all the moves allowable by the base-width. Depth-termination is handled by the same strategy: a basic depth with extension for additional reasons. This, of course, is the same way the

FIGURE 11.16

Greenblatt chess program

```
base-moves:            plausible-move-generator
analysis-moves:        same as base-moves
width-termination:     alpha-beta procedure and
                       > base-width(depth)
                         ignoring safe-checks, moves leading to mates, and
                       diversity > diversity(position)
                         where diversity = number of distinct men making moves
                         where base-width:   depth:   1   2   3   4   5   6   7   8
                                             width:  15  15   9   9   6   6   3   2
depth-termination:     base-depth + plausible-capture + forced-defenses
static-value:          material-value + piece-ratio + pawn-structure-value + King-safety-
                       value + center-control-value
       where           material-value = material for player — material for opponent
                       piece-ratio = points to force exchanges when ahead
                                           in material
                       pawn-structure-value = points for opponent's
                                               backward pawns, isolated pawns,
                                               doubled pawns
adjusted-value:        best-value
plausible-move-generator(position):
1.     generate legal-moves(position):
2.             compute plausibility(move, position) (⟹ score);
3.             insert move on move-list in order on score.
4.     generate move-list.
plausibility(move, position) = sum of weighted factors
secondary-search requires modification of find-move in prototypic chess program:
6.     compare next-value to best-value for player of position,
               if not better go to 7:
6.1    make principal-variation on position (⟹ end-position);
6.2    analyze(end-position) with secondary-depth-termination (⟹ new-value);
6.3    compare new-value to best-value for player of position,
               if better(new-value, best-value), base-move ⟹ best-move);
```

other programs have handled depth. Search is carried to additional depth to examine plausible captures (a consideration universally included) and also forced defenses, a set of special conditions in which one might be able to get out of difficulties by making additional moves. Thus, the Greenblatt program moves some distance toward the structure of the NSS program, in which many separate kinds of reasons contribute to keeping the search going.

A new addition with the Greenblatt program, called secondary search, is shown at the bottom of Figure 11.16. Whenever a new alternative (i.e., a move at depth 1) has been found that is better than the reigning one, an additional search is conducted by traveling back out to the boundary of the previous search along the principal-variation. The principal-variation is the path that generated the minimax value for the newly discovered good move. Then the search is pushed a couple of plies further, and the resulting value is assigned to the alternative. With all the other chess programs the search has been conducted in a single sweep, applying whatever heuristics were available to shape and limit the search. The use of a one-level presearch to generate plausible moves was the first (small) modification in this uniform characteristic. The secondary search in the Greenblatt program introduces a more substantial modification.

To give some feeling for the search, in a 27-move game that the program played (and lost) against an expert, the median number of moves considered was 1057. The alpha-beta procedure was used a median number of 174 times to prune branches. The smallest number of moves considered was 162 (at the first move) and the largest number 16,613. The fact that the median was a little over 1000 shows that the pruning by the alpha-beta procedure rather more than compensated, on average, for the extra moves generated to reach dead positions. Thus, only the NSS program is more selective in its search than the Greenblatt program. The playing strength of the latter provides further evidence of the substitutability of small amounts of chess sophistication for large amounts of search.

SUMMARY

We have now examined six programs. They are not all the chess programs that have been written, but are all whose structure has been reported in the literature. (Exceptions are specialized programs: endgame players and the mating combinations program to be discussed in Chapter 13.) They are all very much of a type: forward search through a subtree of the tree of legal moves, selection heuristics, static-evaluations, minimaxing.

One additional feature common to them all has not been brought out—namely, that they all choose moves in a chess position rather than play a game of chess. The chess game is put together as a series of essentially independent move choices. Thus, for example, there is no difficulty having the program follow a book game, as we did with the NSS program, by forcing the program to make the book move, even if it differs from its own. If each move were based on a plan of play throughout the game, then this would not be possible in general, since the program would not know what to do with the arbitrary move forced upon it.[13]

The communality of the six chess programs with respect to some features should not obscure important differences with respect to others. One important difference is in the amount of search they perform. The Los Alamos program explores by far the largest game tree, the Bernstein program the next largest, and the Greenblatt program a smaller tree, while the NSS and Turing programs explore very small trees indeed. In the NSS program the severe limits on exploration stem from (1) the sharp distinction between move generation and continuation generation (as in Turing's program) and (2) the *satisficing* heuristic that accepts the first move meeting prior expectations. We have already seen examples where the former principle leads the NSS program to misevaluate a move, and cases where the latter

[13] Actually the NSS program did have to recompute some initial values of its evaluation function for a forced move, but this is a very modest connection between successive moves.

commits the program to a premature choice before it has even had an opportunity to consider the most promising moves. But the coin has another side. We have also seen many cases where the very first move the program generated (out of some thirty legal moves available) was a strong move—even one of the book moves in the position.

Another important variation among the several programs occurs in the generation of moves. The Bernstein program and, more extensively, the NSS program have many separate move generators corresponding to the individual functions to be served. The Kotok program and the Greenblatt program have a single move generator that generates all legal moves and orders them by an evaluation function. (In the Kotok program the evaluation is simply the static-value; in the Greenblatt program it is a special evaluation function.) These two approaches express, respectively, a concern that response be specificially adaptive, and a concern that possible candidate moves not be overlooked.

Two other significant variations should be noted, although they show up in only a single program and are more harbingers than well-explored features of program structure. One is the goal organization in the NSS program, which is part of the general emphasis in that program on functional analysis. The second is the secondary search in the Greenblatt program, which begins to relieve the program of the limitation of considering any given position only once.

Information required for intelligent behavior in a task environment as complex as chess can come from several sources. It can come from actual exploration of the specific environment, the specific game position. Apart from the characterization of the chess environment implicit in the static-evaluation function, this is the sole source of information to the Los Alamos program, and a major source to Bernstein's program.

On the other hand, information can be provided by chess theory as applied to the actual game position.[14] The move generators in the NSS program detect certain features of the position (e.g., a man under attack, or a pawn that can be moved to occupy, attack, or defend a center square) and find legal moves relevant to these features. The features detected are related to goals—gain of material, center-control, and so on—that have themselves been shown to be important to the final goal in chess, checkmating the opponent's King. These goals, their associated features, and the moves relevant to those features represent the main organization of known generalizations about chess.

The relation of moves to features is a relation of means to ends. The feature defines a possibility for gain (e.g., an enemy piece under attack) or for loss (e.g., one's own piece under attack). Moves are possible means, to be evaluated, for achieving the gain (e.g., capturing the piece) or averting the loss (e.g., interposing between attacker and attacked). Thus, NSS has a built-in knowledge of important possible means-ends relations. This knowledge enables the program to build a bridge directly from a present situation to possible actions for transforming it in desired directions, instead of being required to consider large numbers of actions,

---

[14] The term *theory* is used here with its usual meaning of general rules or principles. In the chess literature the same term is used, regrettably, to mean knowledge of the book moves in the chess openings—that is, knowledge of chess history.

systematically or at random, with the hope that some may turn out to be relevant to the desired goals in the given situation.

The NSS program also stores chess knowledge in the organization of its means-ends processes: specifically, in the sequential order in which goals are considered, the order in which features are detected, and the order in which relevant moves are generated. Material-balance is considered before center-control, and center-control before development. Moves of center pawns are considered, as means toward center-control, before preventive moves or preparatory moves.

In chess, as in real life, the amount of action that can be accomplished in a given time (in one move, in chess) is limited. In order to act effectively, it is not important, or even relevant, to consider all the things that might be nice to do. If the Queen is attacked, developing the Rooks becomes a secondary consideration, which is not even worth attending to unless it can be combined with the more important task of saving the Queen. This is the principal reason why the NSS program's first-acceptable-move rule produces sensible moves as often as it does: (1) the move is always proposed for a reason—it is relevant to a goal in the light of specific features of the position; (2) the most pressing problems and important considerations are taken up first; (3) since a single move exhausts the program's capacity for action there is no point in dealing with the less important features.

The NSS program illustrates a particular approach to the design of systems for coping with complex task environments. The program is aimed not only at making good moves, but at doing so for the right reasons—that is, in the light of consequences deduced from noticing certain circumstances in the situation. In a task environment as complex as chess, part of the success of play—of fitting behavior to the objective requirements of the situation—depends on the emergence of appropriate concepts. Without them, it will be impossible for a system, even a very fast one, to explore sufficiently to discover strong moves and to make reliable evaluations. Chess history can be written largely in terms of the gradual emergence of a few central concepts: piece values, mobility, development, center-control, and so on. One should not expect the equivalent of such a concept simply to emerge from computation in specific positions, where the computation is based on quite other features of the position.

12

CHESS:
Behavior
of a Single Subject

Our examination of chess has again provided us with a well-delimited set of notions about how a problem solver might work in a task environment. The problem space is the basic one, there is a search for consequences, and some fancy logic is used to integrate the results of the search. Within these bounds there is considerable freedom about how a problem solver might be organized. Some of this freedom we know is not for the human—he does not have the speed, memory, or precision of organization to examine 800,000 moves, taking only a speck of information from each one. As with the other tasks, extreme organizations simply provide background against which to appreciate and detect intelligence. However, some of the heuristic organization we have examined may well fit the human: plausible move generators, evaluation functions, rough-cut search, followed by fine-cut search, and so on.

We should also have tempered expectations about the current state of problem solving programs in chess. Unlike either cryptarithmetic or the elementary Moore-Anderson logic, chess is a deep task. Our investigation certainly was far less complete than with either of the other tasks, and existing chess programs are far from satisfactory. Whereas the reader probably felt he learned something about solving a cryptarithmetic task or the simple logic problems, we dare say he is no better a chess player for reading the previous chapter.

Still, the next step is to examine some human chess behavior and see what it looks like. The fundamental questions are the same as those asked for other tasks: can the human be viewed as an IPS, and if so can this IPS be described in sufficient detail to make the view scientifically plausible? What part of the human's program is dictated by basic aspects of the task, what part by features more properly psychological? What new mechanisms for reasoning or otherwise processing information are used in chess? As with the other tasks, we again start by treating a single situation in detail, in this case a single subject choosing a move in a given position. Even more than in logic and cryptarithmetic, a single position brings out only a part of the phenomena of chess. But we postpone to the next chapter a broader look.

INTRODUCTION

Figure 12.1 shows a middle-game position, called position A. It is taken from the study by de Groot (1965) that we have already mentioned (and which will be discussed in the next chapter). The subject is confronted with the position and asked to choose White's next move. He is allowed to take as long as he wants, which in practice means "a thorough analysis within the limits of normal over-the-board play." The subject is asked to talk aloud as he makes his analysis, and his talk is recorded on tape.

The subject, S2,[1] is a chess player of modest ability, who was active in a college chess club at the time the protocol was taken. He was by no means an expert or class A player, as these terms are used in chess ratings. His play is undoubtedly better than the chess programs discussed in the last chapter with the exception of the Greenblatt program. The latter program is very likely the better player.

The Position

As an introduction to the position of Figure 12.1 we can do no better than quote de Groot's opening comments upon it:

> Taken from a game between A. D. de Groot—C. Scholtens, April 10, 1936. White is on move. . . . This position mainly presents problems of a tactical nature. Through his last move (. . . Q-N3) Black has created a "hanging position" for his Bishop on K2; it is defended only by the exchangeable Knight on Q4 so that the Black Knight on B3 is somewhat tied down. There are all sorts of exchange possibilities in the center and the question is whether or

---

[1] Recall that names are reassigned to the subjects in each task. Thus S2 above is not the same person as S2 in cryptarithmetic or S2 in logic.

FIGURE 12.1

position A (from de Groot)

Black

White

not it is possible for White to make some profitable use of the tactical weaknesses in Black's position. If no such possibility should exist, White could best strengthen his position with some calm move.

From a thorough analysis, however, it appears that White is in a position to get the better of it; there is even a forced win. The winning move is 1. B×N/5. . . . (de Groot, 1965, section 26).

The move 1. B×N/5 was chosen by four out of five of the grandmasters who analysed it for de Groot. This is also the move selected by the subject. However, it cannot be concluded from this that his analysis is correct in its details; in fact, the subject appears to remain ignorant of several of the essential features of the position.

The Protocol

The subject's protocol is given in Appendix 12.1 at the end of the chapter. His words lie along the left-hand side of the page, segmented into short phrases and labeled like the other protocols. This segmentation reveals quite clearly, though informally, the information available in the protocol. To facilitate scanning, we have written opposite each phrase (where appropriate) the move or chess relation that is given by the phrase.[2] The notation is largely standard chess notation, the one departure being the use of a prime to indicate Black. Thus, $B \times N'/5$ means that the White Bishop takes the Black Knight on the fifth rank—the latter notation being necessary to distinguish the move from $B \times N'/6$. The prime is needed because we often refer to men or moves without sufficient context to determine sides. The rules of notation are given in Appendix 12.1 with the protocol.

We have noted the chess content only where it is clear, leaving the other phrases alone. For instance, at B16, "and the Bishop at Rook 2 is bearing down on the Knight," we write "B(R2) bears on N'." The N' is completely identified by the board context. It is necessary that "bear on" be defined rigorously, but in fact there is excellent consensus in the chess world on the term, and a check of all occurrences in the protocol reveals no idiosyncratic use. Utterances such as B138–B142: "Ah, let's see, we will play Knight takes Knight—play Bishop takes Knight. Bishop takes Knight—Knight takes Bishop. Then where do we stand—then we play Knight takes Knight and Black will play pawn takes Knight" require disentangling. The question is, which moves are corrections of previous moves and which are subsequent moves? The interpretation given is the only one consistent with the entire context. B134, "Now, Black's Kingside is in sad shape" is an example where we did not add a notation. It happens that the statement is not objectively true for most reasonable definitions of "sad shape." The subject does expand in B135 (which is precise) but the question remains whether B134 is just a prestatement of B135 or whether a more general concept is intended. Since no other occurrences of the phrase (or highly similar ones) exist in the protocol, we are left at sea. In any event, nothing is gained by paraphrasing the sentence.

Turning to the grossest features of the subject's behavior, we notice that he worked on the problem for almost 17 minutes, and that there appeared to be no difficulty in inducing him to talk. His average production of words is 115 per minute, ranging from a low of 90 to a high of 145. Chess has a well-developed argot for describing positions and their analyses. Thus the subject, who is fluent in this chess language, produces a stream of talk that is completely task-oriented, and singularly free from stumbles, breaks, and frustrated attempts at expression. All of the designatory phrases used in chess ("Bishop at Rook 2," "Knight under single attack," "Double up Rooks on the Queen file") are immediately at his service.[3]

[2] In the original study (Newell and Simon, 1965b) we developed an encoding for all the phrases of the protocol. However, since the analysis tends to work directly from the protocol phrases, there seems little need for such an intermediate coding. See the remarks in Chapter 6 on cryptarithmetic (p. 166).

[3] However, the total rate of flow of about two words per second is also typical of subjects in tasks where they have much more difficulty expressing themselves, providing one counts all the words, independently of whether they are used in complete phrases or not.

The subject's behavior falls naturally into a series of episodes, where relatively abrupt discontinuities of attention indicate boundaries of the episodes. We will carry out our analysis in terms of these episodes as given. At the end of the chapter we will return to the question of how the episodes in chess relate to the general notion of episode that we introduced in Chapter 3 and have used in both crypt-arithmetic and logic.

The description given in Figure 12.2 is appropriately enough viewed as a drama in which the subject struggles to discover which are the good and which the dangerous things in the situation. Since twenty-five episodes are too many for the reader to keep in mind (the subject did not have to keep them in mind, he only had to live them), we have grouped these into seven larger units, which we have called scenes. Each scene is simply a set of explorations that seem to be under the control of a common aim. Occasionally, however, interruptions can occur during a scene that are not devoted to the main concern of the scene.

FIGURE 12.2

episode abstract of S2 on position A

Scene 1:	Orientation (0 secs.)
	"OK, White to move . . . in material the positions are even."
E1:	Examines first the material situation, then (systematically) enumerates Black threats, then White ones. Is aware of Q'xNP threat.
Scene 2:	Explores 1.BxN'/5 (80 secs.)
	"The Bishop at Rook 2 can take the Knight, which would no doubt be answered by . . ."
E2:	Traces exchange until Q' is driven back to defend against double attack of (1) Q attack P' and (2) Q and B attack N'.
E3:	(Interrupt) Explores to see if Q-B3 (discovered in E2) is a good initial move; answer is negative.
E4:	Retraces exchange, re-examining arguments for Black's choices; concludes White wins a P.
E5:	Retraces exchange, examining counterattacks (3 . . . Q'xNP and 3 . . . Q'xQP) after 3.Q-B3; concludes White wins a piece for a P in this case.
Scene 3:	Searches widely (300 secs.)
	"Let's see if there's anything else here."
E6:	Explores 1.NxB': nothing.
E7:	Explores 1.NxBP': nothing.
E8:	Explores 1.NxNP': nothing.
E9:	Explores doubling Rooks on QB-file: nothing.
E10:	Explores K'side attack with Pawns: nothing.
Scene 4:	Re-examines 1.BxN'/5 (385 secs.)
	"the immediate exchange seems indicated if we can win a piece for a Pawn."
E11:	Retraces exchange, examining immediate counterattack (1 . . . Q'xNP); White wins a piece for a Pawn or two.
E12:	Retraces E11, examining a possible pin against White; concludes there is no threat.
E13:	Retraces exchange, considering retake by N'(B3), which apparently leaves B'(K2) undefended; discovers N' still defends B'(K2) (from Q4), but sees how to continue exchange and keep own B(N5) unthreatened.

FIGURE 12.2 (cont'd)

E14: Retraces original variation, but considers recapture by N'(B3) (discovered possible in E13) later in exchange; concludes the whole 1.BxN'/5 exchange is worth nothing for White.

Scene 5: Try something else (540 secs.)

"Now, Black's Kingside is in sad shape—"

E15: Discovers mating configuration (B-R6, Q-N7); B is well placed, but not easy to get Q in place; concludes that B'(K2) is difficulty.

E16: Explores 2.N-K4 in an attempt to get rid of B' (K2); concludes move is fruitless.

E17: (Interrupt in middle of E16) Examines whether 1.N-K4, which reveals R bearing on B'(B3), imposes a pin on Q' so it cannot capture NP; concludes there is no pin (return to E16).

E18: Worries about 1 ... Q'xNP after 1.N-K4, which threatens B(R2); sees that B must move and BxN' is only reasonable alternative; concludes that 1.BxN'/5 should be initial move.

Scene 6: Returns to BxN'/5 (735 secs.)

"... so let's take the Knight right away."

E19: Reviews responses to 1.BxN'/5; concludes that all lead to complications (which summarizes past explorations).

E20: Examines 1.BxN'/5, B'xB; tries new alternative for White (2.N-R4).

E21: Retraces E20; concludes advantage is with White; so Black will not respond 1.... B'xB.

E22: Examines 1.BxN'/5, P'xB; concludes the advantage (isolated P') is with White, so Black will not respond 1 ... P'xB.

E23: Examines 1.BxN'/5, N'xB; concludes that 2.NxN' makes this impossible for Black; hence Black will not respond 1 ... NxN'

E24: Concludes from E20-E23 that Black must play 1 ... P'xB; explores gain in terms of K' side attack.

Scene 7: Decides on BxN' (980 secs.)

"... so the best move is then Bishop takes Knight."

E25: Makes decision and gives next move, conditional on Black's response.

SEARCH BEHAVIOR

All of the analysis of the prior chapter leads to the hypothesis that the subject should spend a major part of his time in searching forward from the initial position for consequences. The space of this search should be essentially the basic space of legal moves. To verify this from the protocol and to refine the exact nature of that search is clearly a first order of business.

Perceived Relations and Dynamic Analysis

The protocol of the subject mentions both moves and relations on the board, the latter, of course, ultimately deriving from moves. Thus, B22 says "The Bishop at Rook 2 can take the Knight"; and from B23, "which would no doubt be answered by ... ," it is clear that the making of a move is being considered. On the other hand, B5 says "his Queen is threatening my Knight's pawn." This is true because $Q' \times NP$ is possible, but it does not mean that the move has been considered.

This distinction between moves and perceived relations is based, not on features of the board, but on characteristics of the information system that is processing the board. Like a system of axioms, all the future implications from any exploration in the game tree are *contained* in the present position (indeed, considering move sequences is just a way of extracting these remote relations). Any of these implications could in principle be *staticized* and made an object of present perception. Thus, *potential-forking-square* is just a description in terms of the present position of a situation that could be realized by several moves (i.e., by moving an appropriate piece to the square in question). Likewise, one could think of relations such as *the-ultimate-checkmater-of-the-King* as being as much presently perceived as *the-attacker-of-the-Rook*. That we normally know of no way to discover the former relation except by searching the tree of moves is only a limitation on ourselves (equivalent to the limitation on the beginner in discovering forks). Indeed, there are places in the endgame where one can speak of an *ultimately-promotable-pawn* without examining the forward move tree in the sense of a search.

We have labored this point at length, since the analysis of the subject's search behavior depends strongly on distinguishing where he perceives a static relation and where he considers a move. Our treatment of the protocol makes a choice in each case between these interpretations ("$P \times N$" and "Q-QB3" being examples of considered moves, "attack" and "pin" being examples of relations). In practice, making the distinction is not difficult for this protocol.

Search Behavior of S2

If we put together all the moves that the subject considered, we obtain the tree of exploration shown in Figure 12.3. This tree might have been badly discontinuous, with connecting branches missing owing to the subject's silence while traversing them. In actual fact, all the nodes in Figure 12.3 are mentioned explicitly by the subject, with the exception of the four enclosed by $\langle \ \rangle$, which are inferred. The dotted lines indicate cases where it is inferred that the subject did not propose a move; likewise, where nonspecific moves are given—e.g., Q-move—it is inferred that the subject was no more specific than is stated. The tree contains 64 positions, including the current one. There are also eight moves that are distinctly generated, but where it is inferred that the positions from those moves are never considered; these are indicated by branches with no small circle at their tips (e.g., R-exchange at the top of the figure). Thus, the subject examines about one new position every fifteen seconds.

The tree of Figure 12.3 does not reveal how the tree is generated. In Figure 12.4 we give the Problem Behavior Graph (PBG), which shows the search of S2 in the time order in which it is performed. We see immediately a distinctive pattern. The subject searches deeply without any appreciable branching (mostly without any branching at all). At the termination of each search he returns to the current posi-

FIGURE 12.3

exploration tree for S2 in position A

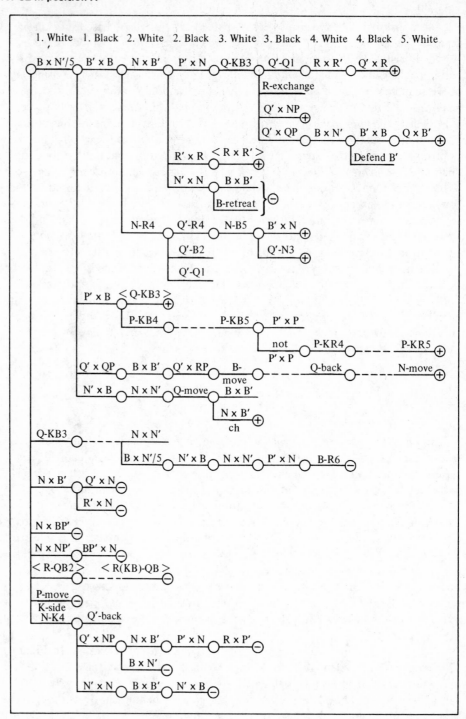

FIGURE 12.4

problem behavior graph of S2 in position A

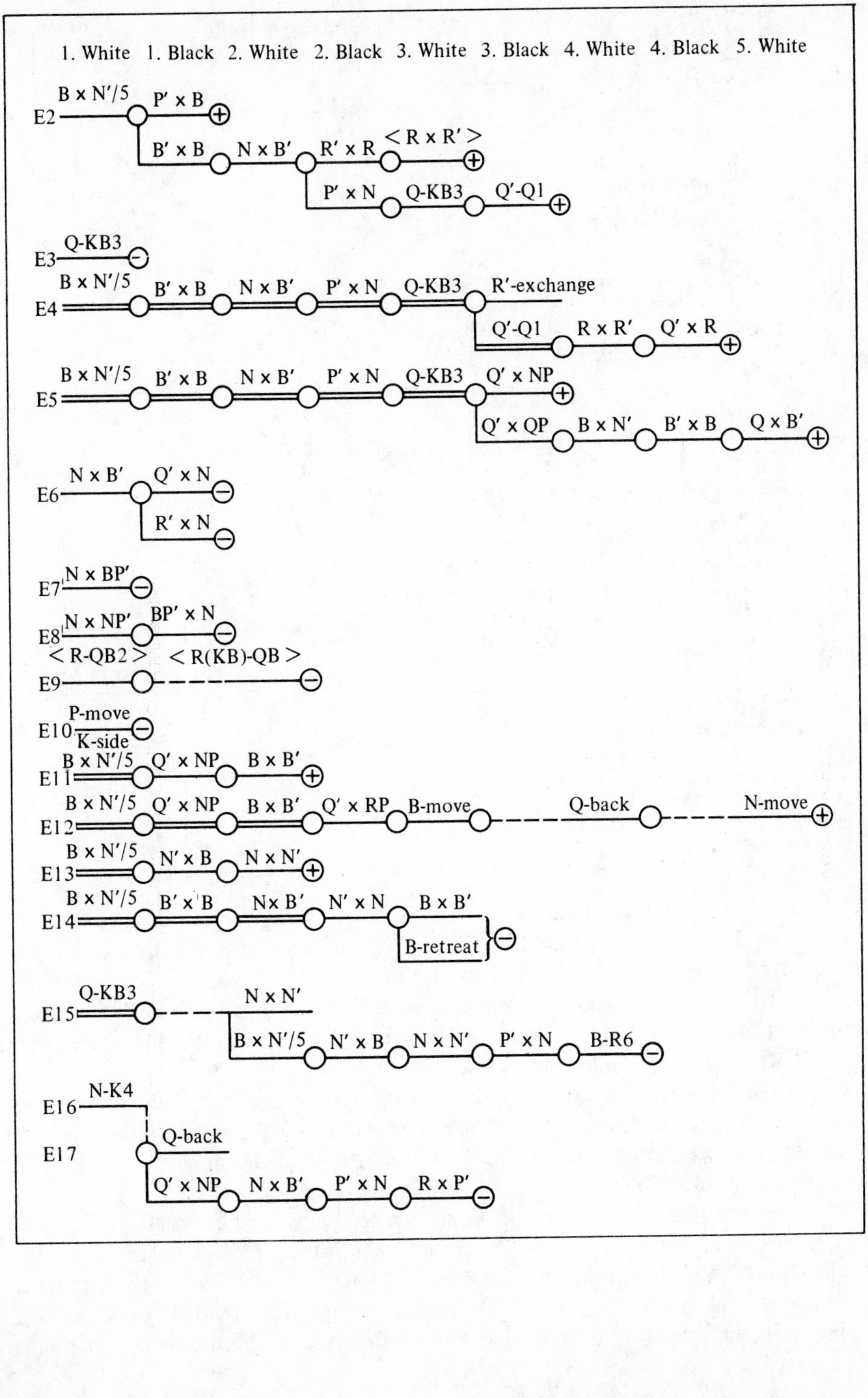

1. White   1. Black   2. White   2. Black   3. White   3. Black   4. White   4. Black   5. White

FIGURE 12.4 (cont'd)

1. White 1. Black 2. White 2. Black 3. White 3. Black 4. White 4. Black 5. White

E16 N-K4   N' x N   B x B'   N' x B

E18   Q' x NP   B x N'

E19 B x N'/5   P' x B

    B' x B
    N' x B

E20 B' x B   N-R4 < Q'-move > N-B5   B' x N

E21 B x N'/5   B' x B   N-R4   Q'-B2

    Q'-Q1

    Q'-R4   N-B5   Q'-N3

E22 B x N'/5   P' x B < Q-KB3 >

E23 B x N'/5   N' x B   N x N'   Q'-move   B x B'

    N x B'ch

E24 P' x B   P-KB4   ----   P-KB5   P' x P

    not   P-KR4   ----   P-KR5
    P' x P

E25 B x N'/5   N' x B   N x N'

    P' x B   P-KB4

    B' x B   N-R4   ----   N-B5

tion and starts over. Often he reconsiders an initial move already analyzed (among the 23 starts there are only eight distinct initial moves). Only when we get to E18 and beyond does the subject not go back to the start, but instead picks up at the point of the opponent's first response. Three of these cases (E20, E24, E25) have the same initial move ($B \times N'/5$), which has already occurred eight times; the other (E18) begins with N-K4, which has occurred just twice. As with the tree in Figure 12.3, all of the moves are explicitly mentioned, except those in $\langle \ \rangle$, so the evidence for returning to the start is direct. Thus, in search E24 there is no evidence for any specific consideration of the opponent's replies—only of the subject's own positive moves (B224 to B229).

The almost uniform return of the subject to the base position after each burst of exploration offers the means of segmenting the total problem into twenty-five episodes. E1, the orientation phase, does not show in Figure 12.4, since it contains no moves. The boundaries of these episodes are marked, not only by the discontinuity in the position considered but by evaluative and summarizing statements terminating an episode, and by proposals about what is to be done next, initiating another episode. Thus there is little doubt about the reality of the episodes in the organization of the subject's behavior.

Search Strategies

We can now ask what sort of information processing organization could have produced the search behavior shown in Figures 12.3 and 12.4. Whereas in describing the computer chess programs in the last chapter we could analyze the internal structure of existing programs and list the main mechanisms we discovered, here we must hypothesize mechanisms and then ask what behavior they lead to. At best, we can show that our hypothesized organization is sufficient to reproduce the subject's observed behavior. We cannot show it is necessary, although we may be able to show that some alternative organizations are incompatible with the behavior.

In designing search programs it is useful to distinguish the strategy of search from the information that is gathered during the search. The search strategy tells where to go next, and what information must be kept so that the search can be carried out. It does not tell what other information to obtain while at the various positions, nor what to do with the information after it is obtained. There may be strong interaction between the search itself and the information found, as in the decision to stop searching (depth-termination or width-termination), but we can often view this as occurring within the confines of a fixed search strategy.

The typical strategy in computer chess programs is the depth-first strategy, which follows directly from the prototypic chess program given in Figure 11.2 (page 670). Once a particular position has been generated, all deeper search beyond this position is carried out before that part of the tree is abandoned. This procedure is highly efficient memorywise, in that only a single line of positions from the base position (i.e., the one actually on the board) up to the position being considered needs to be kept in memory at a given time. (Usually, of course, only the moves are kept in memory, not the full positions, since the prior positions are regenerated from the current position and the move that led to it.)

The depth-first strategy is particularly suited to the requirements of the minimax inference procedure. Minimaxing derives the value of a dynamic position from the values of all one-level-deeper positions that are considered. The depth-first strategy makes all these values available sequentially with a minimum of memory and retrieval effort.

Figure 12.3, which shows the total set of positions covered by S2 in his search, would in fact also be the PBG generated by a depth-first search strategy, if we assume that the moves are considered in an appropriate order. Each node is considered once and only once. That it differs radically from the actual PBG (Figure 12.4) is obvious.

For comparison, Figure 12.5 gives a program for the alternative breadth-first strategy, which was used by LT. In Figure 12.6 we show how the search of Figure 12.3 would look as a PBG if generated by the breadth-first strategy of Figure 12.5.

FIGURE 12.5

breadth-first search strategy

breadth-first-search(position):
1.   generate moves(position):
2.   make move on position ($\Longrightarrow$ new-position),
          if fail continue generation;
3.   insert new-position on position-list at end.;
4.   select-and-remove first position from position-list
     if fail stop,
     otherwise go to 1 ($\Longrightarrow$ position).

Instead of going deeper and deeper, it completes all positions at one level before going on to the next. To do this, of course, all positions must be stored until they are considered. Thus, the PBG looks highly discontinuous, and we have labeled all the nodes that are saved in the figure, so that it is possible to keep track of what is going on. The difference in the number of the node being worked on and the node being generated tells how many positions are being kept in the position-list; it reaches a maximum of ten during the middle of the search.

In compensation for this storage, the breadth-first strategy avoids looking too deep in one part of the tree when something obvious is awaiting discovery at level 1 or 2 in an unexamined part of the tree. Although the breadth-first strategy has been used in some theorem-proving programs, it has not been used in any game-playing playing programs. Minimaxing with this search strategy, even though it can be done, requires more memory, effort, and organization than with depth-first search.

This excursion into the search strategies of programs is intended to lay the groundwork for considering what search strategy might generate the PBG of Figure 12.4. Clearly neither depth-first nor breadth-first will do. As a start, consider the strategy shown in Figure 12.7, called simple-progressive-deepening-search. It is divided into two parts, similar to the chess programs of the last chapter: one that generates base-moves and one that does the analysis. However, the analysis is not recursive (which would lead to depth-first search) but is a simple loop with only one move selected at each current-position.

By creating a list of base-moves and selecting moves from this list, repeated analyses of the same base-move will occur. It is implied that summary information is kept with each base-move in order to effect the selection of moves during analysis. We have indicated this by making analysis-move depend on the base-move (with its associated summary) as well as on the current-position. We have not indicated what the summary contains, or where it is generated, since the program of Figure 12.7 is meant simply to convey the search scheme itself.

Given this strategy, we would expect sequences of linear searches without any branching at all, going as deeply as necessary to get information. The summaries of the current state of analysis of base-moves permit different moves to be generated upon successive visits to the same position. The simple progressive-deepening strategy by no means describes Figure 12.4 exactly, but it is surely a closer approximation than either depth-first or breadth-first. One virtue of this strategy lies in

FIGURE 12.6

problem behavior graph for breadth-first search of position A

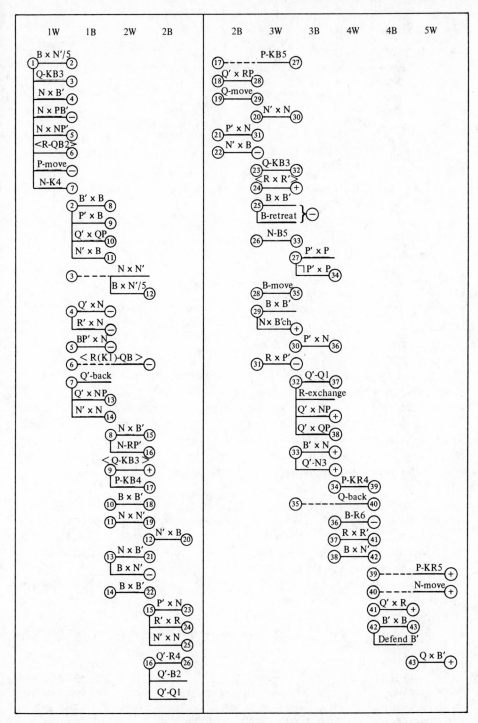

FIGURE 12.7

simple-progressive-deepening search strategy

```
simple-progressive-deepening-search(base-position):
1.   generate-base-moves(base-position):
5.         insert base-move on base-move-list;
3.         analyse(base-move, base-position);
4.         select move from base-move-list (⟹ base-move),
                 if succeed go to 3,
                 if fail continue generation.
analyse(base-move, base-position):
1.   make base-move on base-position (⟹ current-position);
2.   test termination(current-position),
          if true stop;
3.   select analysis-move(current-position, base-move) (⟹ current-move),
          if fail stop;
4.   make current-move on current-position (⟹ current-position),
          go to 2.
undefined:   base-moves(position)
             select move from base-move-list
             termination(position)
             select analysis-move(current-position, base-move)
```

lowering what Bruner called *cognitive strain* (Bruner, Goodnow, and Austin, 1956). No complicated internal housekeeping is needed to keep track of where the search is. Only a single position need be stored internally, and it can be stored in terms of the way it differs from the base position, which is under continual surveillance (thus providing a continuing memory of all the things that have not changed). The search strategy is even fail-safe in that if something goes wrong with an exploration—e.g., the subject loses track of what the current position is—then the search is simply terminated and the total analysis continues. The only loss is the effort spent in the abortive exploration.

The term *progressive deepening* is taken from de Groot (1965), who introduced it to indicate the tendency of his subjects to extend the analysis of a position successively. The version just given above is clearly a very simple case of such a strategy. To approach one step closer to what S2 was doing, consider the slight modification of the simple scheme shown in Figure 12.8.[4]

The process for base-moves remains the same. The analysis process is modified by replacing the selection of a single analysis-move with the generation of a set of analysis-moves and the consideration of each, before the selection of a single one for continuation. This is similar to the way the Kotok and Greenblatt plausible move generators work.

[4] In the original paper we referred to the two search strategies, here called simple-progressive-deepening and progressive-deepening, as progressive-deepening and modified-progressive-deepening, respectively. The present terminology seems more apt, since the first strategy is used primarily as a stepping-stone to the second.

FIGURE 12.8

progressive-deepening search strategy

```
progressive-deepening-search(base-position)
1.  generate base-moves(base-position):
2.       insert base-move on base-move-list;
3.       analyse(base-move, base-position);
4.       select move from base-move-list (⟹ base-move),
             if succeed go to 3,
             if fail continue generation.

analyse(base-move, base-position):
1.  make base-move on base-position (⟹ current-position);
2.  test termination(current-position),
         if true stop;
3.  generate analysis-moves(current-position, base-move):
4.       compute plausibility(analysis-move, current-position) (⟹ value);
5.       insert analysis-move on move-list in order on value.;
6.  select move from move-list (⟹ current-move),
         if fail stop;
7.  make current-move on current-position (⟹ current-position),
         go to 2.
```

This strategy will produce a sequence of explorations, each starting from the base position, but with the tree of each exploration resembling a skinny Christmas tree: the tree would have a main trunk, and at each node there would be a tuft containing a number of branches, each one move deep.

If we examine Figure 12.4 we see that of the fifteen instances of multiple branching eleven are exactly of this form. The contrary examples are in E2, E18, E24, and E25. Of these E2 is ambiguous. The subject referred to an exchange of Rooks (B28), and we are left to infer either that he considered first 2. . . . $R' \times R$ and then 3. $R \times R'$, or that the action of exchanging was a single conceptual act in some sense. We have already commented on E18 and E24, which appear to be truly cases of dropping back to the position defined by a familiar move. A similar comment applies to E25, which is a summary of the subject's behavior under different contingencies, and again drops back each time to the position after 1. $B \times N'/5$. Thus, in terms of the two features of the search—return to base position and single level tufts at each node—the progressive-deepening strategy seems a plausible description of the subject's PBG.

Given the search strategy, a number of additional processes must be specified in order to make a complete chess-playing system. Some of these fill out the undefined processes that are already explicit in the program in Figure 12.8. Others determine what additional information is to be gathered and to what use it is to be put. These parts form a single system, so that the shape of each one depends on the others. Thus our order of analysis in the paper begs somewhat the question of which features determine the others—of which are chickens and which eggs.

EPISODE GENERATION

According to the progressive-deepening strategy, episode generation and move generation within an episode are interwoven since the moves generated are determined by both the current-position and the present state of the base-move that is being explored. We first examine the episodes as wholes, viewing them as providing the context within which specific move generation operates.

Functions of Episodes

Since the subject makes a number of explicit statements about the function of each episode, the nature of an episode does not have to be inferred completely from the pattern of moves shown in Figure 12.4. These comments, which have already been reflected to some extent in the recitation of the drama, not only make good chess sense and good problem solving sense but are consistent with the subject's behavior throughout the episode. Consequently, we can accept the naive hypothesis that the episodes function in the total problem solving attempt pretty much as the subject indicates. The whole set of protocol statements is sufficiently interdependent that radically different interpretations for the episodes are not easy to manufacture. Table 12.1 provides for each episode a statement of its function, and its outcome (as positive or negative for White). We have also noted additional information that was discovered where this is relevant to later episodes—e.g., that Q-KB3 was discovered during E2. In the table, the term *explore* means to go down a new path, and the term *rework* means to go down the specified path again, for whatever reason. For the rework episodes we have added a brief characterization of what happened during the episode.

Rules for Episode Sequence

Each of the episodes is unique when put in the context of the previously occurring episodes. Nevertheless, it is possible to write down some rules that would generate a sequence of episodes not unlike that shown in Table 12.1. These rules are concerned with which base-move is selected for the next episode and what context governs the exploration of subsequent episodes of the same base-move. The rules do not describe behavior within an episode. Six rules are given below, and the protocol will be examined to see whether these rules are reflected in the subject's behavior. There is substantial evidence that the subject is observing the first three rules, and more limited evidence for the remaining three.

R1: The analysis of each base-move is independent of the analysis of other base-moves, except that it can be interrupted by other activity. That is,

TABLE 12.1

functions of episodes

EPISODE	FUNCTION	RESULT	R1	R2	R3	R4	R5	R6
E2	Explore 1. B×N'/5	+ new move Q-B3		+				
E3	Explore 1. Q-KB3	−			p		+	
E4	Rework E2 (extend)	+	+	+	+			
E5	Rework E2 (counterattack)	+	+	+	+			
E6	Explore 1. N×B'	−		+	p			+
E7	Explore 1. N×BP'	−			+			
E8	Explore 1. N×NP'	−		+	+			
E9	Explore Rooks on QB-file	−			+	+		
E10	Explore K-side P-move	−			+			
E11	Rework E2 (counterattack with loss)	+	+	+	+			
E12	Rework E11 (extend)	+	+	+	+			
E13	Rework E2 (recapture with loss)	+ new move N' recapture	+	+	+			
E14	Rework (N' recapture)	−	p		p		+	
E15	Explore Get B-R6, Q-N7	− need remove B'(R2)		+	+	+		
E16	Explore Remove B'(R2)	discover attack on B'(B3)						
E17	Explore Attack B'(B3)	−		+			+	
E16	Explore 1. N-K4 (continued)	−		+	+	+		
E18	Rework E16 (counterattack)	− B×N'/5 necessary	+	+	−	+		
E19	Summarize 1. B×N'/5				+		+	
E20	Rework E19 (B'×B) (explore 2. N-R4)	+	+	+	−			
E21	Rework E20 (extend)	+ not 1.... B'×B	+	+	+			
E22	Rework E19 (P'×B) (extend)	+ not 1.... P'×B	+	−	+			
E23	Rework E19 (N'×B) (extend E13)	+ not 1.... N'×B	+	+	+			
E24	Rework E22 (extend)	+		+		+		
E25	Choose 1. B×N'/5							−

Legend for rules: + confirm
$\quad\quad\quad\quad\quad\quad$ − disconfirm
$\quad\quad\quad\quad\quad\quad$ p another rule has priority

each episode in the analysis of a base-move is determined only by the results of the prior episodes of that base-move.

R2: The first episode of a base-move employs *normal* moves, and subsequent episodes utilize increasingly *unusual* moves. (*Normal* and *unusual* will be discussed below.)

R3: If the evaluation of an episode gives a favorable result, the analysis of its base-move is continued; if the evaluation is unfavorable, a different base-move is analyzed.

R4: When exploring, moves for the opponent may be considered that are favorable to self (in order to place an upper bound on the possibilities).

R5: The analysis of a base-move will be interrupted to pursue other moves, discovered during the episode, that seem to have merit either for self or for the opponent.

R6: Before a base-move is finally chosen, a check is made for other alternative base-moves.

Verification of Rules. Table 12.1 shows, for each episode, which rules are exemplified by that episode and whether the episode is confirming or disconfirming of the rule. There is not space (nor reader's patience) to deal individually with each of the 6×25 judgements, but let us note in general how each of the rules relates to the behavior.

R1 asserts that the total analysis can be factored into a set of little analyses, one for each base-move. The interaction between them is only one of allocation of effort, including the decision to abandon the analysis of a base-move because others have proved better.

It is difficult to refute this rule; one would have to find features within an episode derived from sources other than the prior episodes of the same base-move. Presumably one could recognize them if they occurred, but it is not easy to imagine examples. One apparent exception to R1 comes from the transposition of the move, N′ recaptures, from E13, where it was discovered, to E14. However, we view this instance as showing the priority of rule R5 (interrupting). It could hardly be considered a counterexample to R1, since E13 is part of the analysis of E2. Setting levels of aspiration (used in evaluating each episode) on the outcome of the episodes of all base-moves might be considered counterevidence to R1, but discussion of this point will have to wait until the section on evaluation.

R2 specifies the dependence of an episode on prior episodes of the same base move. It asserts that exploration goes from the normal to the unusual. The underlying model will be elaborated in the section on move generation; only the gross outlines are needed here. Consider the following responses to an attack: defend; counterattack threatening equivalent material; counterattack threating less material; move and ignore the attack. The normal response to an attack is to defend the man attacked. Each of the other responses is more unusual, and increasingly so, although they may be the correct response in the situation. R2 asserts that the subject has such a model of normal and unusual responses, and that each successive episode of the same base-move involves considering more unusual responses. The rule also considers a move to be unusual if it is considered again after prior analysis has shown the continuation to be bad to the side making the move. This phenomenon shows up in E4 and E23, where continuations shown to be bad for Black are extended without choosing alternative Black moves. The rule claims that the main information that is carried over from past episodes is what kinds of responses have already been considered (together with the current estimate of the worth of the base-move).

No assertion is made as to why certain responses are normal and others unusual—only that the subject has a consistent categorization of moves in such terms. In some sense, the normal response is the one that has the highest expectation of being the correct move; and the more unusual, the lower expectation. But the subject has no way of computing such an expectation prior to analysis.

Furthermore, no assignment of a quantitative expectation is required, only the ordering given by the classification. Thus the categorization is a priori, coming from a blend of personal experience and the publicly available knowledge of good chess play. Nor is the subject's classification necessarily correct. Many good players would consider a counterattack to be the normal response in many situations.

Table 12.1 shows that conformity to R2 is very consistent. Actually, verification depends on the details of move generation within an episode, which will be discussed further below. Roughly, conformity can be checked by noting the brief characterization of the rework episodes given in parentheses and assuming that the normal-to-unusual sequence is: explore, extend, counterattack, counterattack with loss, recapture with loss. Then each rework episode should be further down this sequence than its predecessor. (Also, the explore episodes should consist only of normal moves.)

R3 deals with the question of when to change base-moves. It says simply, "Stay with a winner, switch off a loser." A single disconfirmation of the soundness of the move is enough to cause the switch. Although changes in base-move usually involve generating a new move, R3 does not specify whether one is to obtain a new base-move or return to a different old one. Likewise, R3 does not specify at all how the new move shall be selected. In fact, there appears to be little that can be said from this one protocol in isolation about how base-moves are selected (but see the comparative data discussed in Chapter 13).

Of the 21 cases in Table 12.1 that are relevant to R3, 16 are confirmatory. Three cases (E3, E6, E14) show that other rules take priority (R5 and R6), and thus shed no light on R3. There are two negative instances, E18 and E20. In E18 the subject goes ahead and explores a second variation even though E16 turned out badly. Some light will be shed on this instance in discussing R4. In E19 the subject has just reviewed the 1. $B \times N'/5$ exchange with discouraging results, but decides to go ahead anyway in E20. Whether one calls this a negative instance or an irrelevant instance depends on whether E19 is viewed as an exploration or only as a summary.

R4 concerns the modification of the search rules in order to get special information. By biasing the choices of moves in favor of White, the subject is able to see if there is any possibility for a successful continuation. If the biased exploration were successful, one would expect additional episodes devoted to correcting the bias; unfortunately, the protocol does not provide good opportunities to test this. A problem posed by R4, and not answered in the rule, is how to bias the opponent's choices without opening the floodgates of foolishness, which would provide no useful information at all. Two hints are provided in the subject's behavior. One is to ignore the opponent's move altogether (the no-move); this at least leaves open what the opponent might do (E9, E24). The other is to permit the choice from the responses that are normal or almost normal, but which immediate evaluation might not indicate offer the best chance for the opponent (E15, E16, E18).

There are only a few cases relevant to R4, but the bias is sufficiently clear to make the rule important. No rule is given to determine when R4 is to be applied to an exploration; consequently, negative instances are not possible. E24 does provide a case where a biased exploration leads to positive results, but no critical follow-up occurs; on the other hand, the subject had concluded that the basic continuation (1. B×N/6, P'×B) was favorable to White.

The use of R4 is related to an important feature of the subject's behavior that has not been characterized in the rules. In general the episodes work forward, exploring the consequences of various base-moves. In this they agree with the basic philosophy of the computer chess programs. However, in E15, E16, and E18 a basically different approach is used. In E15 a future situation is envisioned (the mating configuration, B135), then an attempt is made to find a sequence of moves that leads to it. As a result of this activity, a difficulty is spotted [B'(K2)] and in E16 the goal is set up of removing this difficulty. Both E16 and E18 are devoted to achieving this goal. The search still works forward, but with a definite end in view. This kind of means-ends analysis, familiar to us from GPS, is not used in most existing chess programs, although we shall discuss a modest attempt in this direction later.

The condition that appears necessary for applying means-ends analysis is that a future situation can be specified in sufficient detail so that relevant differences can be found between the present state and the desired state. To assert in the present position that one wants to obtain a checkmate position does not permit any specific inferences, whereas to say that one wants to get the B at R6 and the Q at N7 defines a specific desired state of affairs. The amount of means-ends analysis in chess would depend strongly upon whether the positions being considered permitted highly specific future configurations to be envisioned. Three instances of the operation of R4 occur in these means-ends analysis episodes. Perhaps, having a specific goal in mind is what triggers the need to construct possible continuations that achieve that goal, even if they are not completely realistic.

R5 is a special form of the notion that moves can be considered independently of positions. An exploration may discover new moves to try as well as new facts about the base-move. This mechanism, in spite of its plausibility, has not been much used in chess programs.[5] Besides the idea of discovering moves in one context and using them in another, R5 also contains the idea of interrupting—i.e., of exploring the new move next. The protocol varies as to whether interruptions can terminate explorations (E18?), sidetrack them (E17), or only obtain priority to be the next episode (E3, E14).

Of the four relevant cases of R5, all are positive. E3 is completely explicit. E14 is a case of discovering that the N' can recapture the B in E13, and then trying it out at a different place in the 1. B×N'/5 exchange. One might argue that E14 is simply the next variation in the elaboration of the 1. B×N'/5 exchange. The interruptive character of E17 is fully shown by the return to E16 after E17 is complete. E19, of course, involves the return to an old move, rather than the discovery of a new move. Still, the move B×N'/5 shows up as the last move of the E18 exploration. There are no negative instances refuting R5; to have one would require discovering a move (and announcing it in the protocol) and then delaying its exploration for at least one episode.

[5] One exception is a program for finding checkmates in two moves (McCarthy, 1959); another is the MATER II program described in Chapter 13.

R6 is the heuristic for looking around when things go well. There is only one positive instance of it, but it is both so clear in the protocol and so important that we record it. E25 may be viewed as a negative instance (and we have so labeled it), since an insistent use of R6 would have required the subject to take one final survey of the whole position before committing himself to the move. The protocol gives no clue as to why R6 was evoked after E5, rather than earlier or later.

In summary, if we were to construct a program that operated according to rules R1 through R6, using suitable priorities, we would get some of the features of the episodic behavior shown by S2. These rules are not complete, however. For example, they do not determine how to choose a new base-move when switching is called for, when to shift to means-ends analysis, or when to declare a newly discovered move worth an interrupt. Also, they do not determine the internal structure of an episode. This last will be taken up in the next section, but the other questions will remain unanswered.

MOVE GENERATION

In this section we wish to construct a move generation scheme to be used at positions within episodes, and to compare the behavior of this scheme with the subject's behavior. We view this scheme as working within the progressive-deepening strategy and therefore fitting into the rules of episode generation we have just laid out. We must restrict our attention to those positions in Figure 12.4 in which move generation takes place. Thus, we exclude the base position and all terminal positions. We also exclude all of E19, the summary, and E25, the recapitulation of the final choice. And we ignore the three apparent branchings in E16–E18, E19–E20, and E23–E24, which are due to the subject's not returning all the way to the base position to start the next episode.

If we now consider Figure 12.4 with these restrictions, there are 74 positions in which move generation occurs. We should distinguish immediately the positions in which new moves are generated (53) from the positions in which moves that had already been made are repeated (21). The latter positions appear to pose primarily an issue of whether the position is one from which to start a variation. The decision need not involve any move generation at all, but only a diagnosis of the position on the basis of the prior analysis and the instructions for variation given to the episode. If no variation is to occur, then the subject simply repeats the move made previously.

Support for this interpretation of these *repeat* positions comes from the fact that in 20 of them only the repeated move is generated. The lone dissenter, in E4, involves a recollection of the Rook exchange in E2 (B50), and it is clear that the move was not considered seriously. In all events, there are no positions that pose choices between new moves and old moves.

Considering the positions where new moves are generated, the dominant fact is still that almost always only a single move is generated (43), although occasionally two (9) or three (1). Several features of these positions might provide a starting basis for understanding how the move generation may be accomplished. Thus, of the 10 positions with tufts (i.e., with multiple alternatives) 7 are Black and only 3 are White, the corresponding figure for single-move positions being 18 Black and 25 White. Thus the subject might be treating himself (White) differently from his opponent (Black). It is also noteworthy that 7 tufts are defensive and only 3 offensive (and the offensive tufts are not all White). The corresponding figure for single-move positions is 19 defensive and 24 offensive. It is plausible that multiple moves are generated for the player on the defensive (and hence constrained), whereas on the offensive a single aggressive move suffices. However, instead of pursuing either of these possibilities, we will take a different tack that will give us somewhat more specific information.

Move Generators for Specific Functions

Existing chess programs generate much larger sets of moves than we require. However, it is not easy to design single integrated processes that will turn out a large collection of plausible moves (e.g., the set of eight moves that the subject considers from the base position). As we indicated in Chapter 11, two solutions have been adopted in chess programs. One, in the Kotok and Greenblatt programs, is to generate all legal moves and pick the best one according to the evaluation function. The second is to develop specific generators devoted to specific functions, and to use higher routines to select these specific generators in order to obtain the total set of moves considered from a position. A cursory examination of the subject's protocol reveals considerable activity of this latter sort. For example, B46 says "Black must recapture," thus posing a function to be performed; and B47 follows with "and he can only do it by playing pawn takes Knight," thus generating the move (presumably the only one) that satisfies the function. If there had been several ways of recapturing, presumably they all would have been generated, and a tuft would have occurred at this position. B23 gives an example where a tuft did occur, the branches all representing recaptures. Although there is good evidence for move generation by function, there is little indication of combining the products of several separate generators. As we have already remarked, almost everywhere only a single move is generated.

Functions operate as intermediaries in the following way. Suppose a piece, Y, is moved so that $Y \times Z$ becomes possible. We then say Y *attacks* Z, which classifies the particular situation. From *attacks* we infer that a problem exists and obtain *defend* Z as a class description of a solution. Under *defend* is available a series of more specific functions that can accomplish this function: capture-attacker, add-defender, interpose-safe-man, pin-attacker, move-defender, and so on. At some point of elaboration, ways exist for generating actual moves that accomplish the functions—e.g., generate all moves that capture-attacker. Thus, we get from problem to solution via a string of functional characterizations, making connections between means and ends at a functional level.

This suggests that we specify for S2 the various situations that give rise to recognizable problems and thence to definite generators that provide moves to solve these problems. In any position, if S2 recognizes the situation, he simply generates the set of moves appropriate to a situation of that kind. A single move may be generated, or more than one; S2 takes whatever the generator produces. However, by implication, all the moves will serve the same function.

We view these specific functional generators as the means whereby rule R2 is carried out. Several move generators may apply to a single situation. These are then ordered by the subject from normal, to unusual. On any particular occasion, only one generator will be evoked. R2 asserts they are to be evoked in a specific order.

As discussed in the section on episode generation, we view these generators and their labels essentially as public knowledge (in the chess world), although obviously capable of being tinged with the subject's personal experience. For many of the situations, English-language function terms exist (e.g., "attack"), but there is no reason why there should always be such terms. However, we do expect other chess players of equal (or perhaps somewhat better) caliber to be able to recognize the same problem situations and to know what moves should be proposed to solve them. We will rely on this requirement, that the situations and generators exist in the domain of common chess knowledge, as a check against creating ad hoc generators to describe S2. In point of fact, there are no difficulties in interpretation for most of the cases in the present protocol.

Situation-Response Productions. We give in Table 12.2 a list of situations and the responses they invoke. The list includes defensive situations, situations in which the mover has the initiative, and situations where the mover's aim is to acquire information. Responses of this latter type are appropriate for analysis, but not for actual play. Opposite each description is a mnemonic code. This code indicates both the situation (to the left of the arrow) and the response (to the right of the arrow). Thus the first item is $x \longrightarrow r$, the x standing for the fact that a capture occurred (as in $B' \times B$) and the r standing for the response of recapturing. The rules are in the form of productions, comparable to those of Chapter 6. The list of Table 12.2 is by no means complete; it contains only those response situations that actually occurred in the protocol. The subject undoubtedly has available many more response schemes than come to light in this particular protocol.

All the productions in the table are extremely simple and well known in the chess literature. There can be little argument about their general familiarity to someone who plays any amount of chess and who has studied this literature. The information-gathering productions are seldom stated explicitly, of course, since they are part of the common sense of everyday living. However, some caution is indicated in the case of $g \longrightarrow g$, which implies that a plan is operating, from which decisions about continuing the plan are derived. Before $g \longrightarrow g$ can be inferred, we must infer the plan.

Assessment of the Productions

Figure 12.9 gives for each of the 64 new moves the mnemonic code of the production from Table 12.2 that appears to govern its generation. The figure permits

FIGURE 12.9

verification of move generators

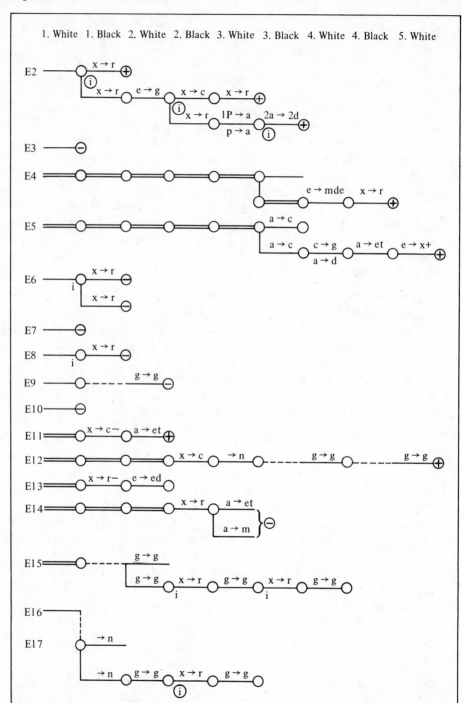

FIGURE 12.9 (cont'd)

1. White 1. Black 2. White 2. Black 3. White 3. Black 4. White 4. Black 5. White

an assessment of the extent to which our set of simple situation-response productions can account for the behavior of the subject. Overall, one might say that in the majority of positions (39) the account is reasonably good, and for an appreciable number (14) there is some reason to be dissatisfied. But this obscures the great variety of ways in which the rules can fail to account for move generation. Some of the "failures" can be explained, and some of the "successes" are not as solid as they appear on gross tabulation. Consequently, a certain amount of detailed treatment of the data is necessary.

Incomplete Generation. If the situation at a position evokes a production, we expect all moves generated by that production to be considered. Where this is not the case we have marked the position with an i (for incomplete). However, for some of these there is clear evidence in the protocols that the subject believed that he had generated them all. In these cases it is more reasonable to argue that the ap-

731

TABLE 12.2

situation-response productions for move generator

CODE	SITUATION	RESPONSE	N
	Defensive Situations		
x → r	Man captured last move →	Recapture with no apparent loss	11
x → c	Man captured last move →	Countercapture of equal value	1
x → c−	Man captured last move →	Countercapture with apparent loss	2
x → r−	Man captured last move →	Recapture with apparent loss	1
a → d	Man attacked, by man → of not lower value	Add defender	1
a → et	Man attacked, by man → of not lower value	Exchange target	8
a → ea	Man attacked, by man → of lower value	Exchange attacker	1
a → m	Man attacked, by man → of lower value	Move target away	5
a → c	Man attacked →	Counterattack of equal value	1
2a → 2d	Double attack →	Add double defender	1
	Initiative Situations		
iP → a	Opponent P isolated →	Attack P	2
p → a	Opponent man pinned →	Attack pinned man	1
e → ed	Opponent exchange, → just defended	Exchange defender	1
e → mde	Opponent exchange, → just defended	Move defender away by forcing its use in another exchange	2
e → x+	Opponent exchange, → underdefended	Capture target with gain	2
	Information Gathering Situations		
e → g	In midst of exchange →	Go on exchanging	1
c → g	Counterattacked →	Go on with primary attack,	1
g → g	In midst of plan, no → threat exists	Go on with plan	11
→ n	Assertion made about → situation	Take action, assuming negation, to test assertion	3

Legend: a—attack   g—go on   p—pin   (−)—with loss
         c—counterattack   i—isolated   r—recapture   (+)—with gain
         d—defend   m—move   x—capture
         e—exchange   n—negation

plication of the particular production was faulty, rather than that the overall scheme does not account for the subject's behavior. There still remain seven cases of incompleteness. These appear to be genuine failures. They suggest either additional considerations, not present in the simple rules of Table 12.2, or the requirement only to attain sufficiency, so that a single successful candidate will do.

There are four instances where the subject appears to believe his generation is complete, although objectively it is not. In E2, he ignores 1. ... N′×B, declaring the N′ to be pinned, which it is not. This error is repeated at the next move where he ignores 2. ... N′×N. Also in E2 the subject asserts that 3. ... Q′-Q1 is the only move that simultaneously defends both attacked men, but two other Q′ moves are also possible. In E17 the subject seems temporarily unaware of 2. ... R′×N, since he ignores 3. ... R′×R a move later.

Three cases (E6, E8, E21) of incomplete generation occur on the final move (i.e., at the position before the last one). In all these there is no need to do more than obtain a "typical" move to provide the evaluation. There are two cases (E17, E21) where not all the Q′ moves are generated—e.g., Q′-R3. These could have been eliminated by additional reasoning, or they could be a failure of the generator. Finally, there are two cases in E15 which are intimately tied up with rule R4 and biasing search in favorable directions.

More Than One Generator. To account for the small number of alternatives generated at each position, our scheme posits that only a single production is evoked. Positions in which only a single move is generated clearly conform to this. However, the tufts can provide counterexamples, and two cases out of ten show some evidence of multiple generators being evoked. Note that our one-position-one-generator hypothesis is somewhat ambiguous, since functions form a hierarchy. For example, the function of defense can be realized by adding a defender or moving away, and these might be functional equivalents as far as the subject is concerned.

One case of mixed generators occurs in E2 where 2. ... P′×N is clearly a recapture (x → r), whereas 2. ... R′×R is clearly a counterattack (x → c). This may be a case of interruption (R5). The subject shows a tendency to attend to the possibilities uncovered by a move (e.g., E17), and 2. ... R′×R is possible only because of 2. N×B′. A second case occurs at the end of E14. Here, two (perhaps equivalent) defenses for the B are considered. Note that one of them (B-retreat) is a generalized move. A parallel situation, but one that does not quite generate an actual move, occurs in E5 at 4. ... B′×B, where the subject remarks that Black must either recapture or defend his Bishop (B72). In one other tuft (E24) there is a pair of moves that are not functionally equivalent [2. ... P′×P and 4. ... not (P′×P)]. But as we show below, these are clearly generated by a single production (→ n).

Multiple Interpretation. It is possible for more than one production to account for a single generated move. However, it happens in only two cases here. The principle of making moves that serve more than one function is important and well known in chess. From an information processing viewpoint we would expect such a move to be generated from one production and then recognized as meeting the requirements of another. However the production 2a → 2d incorporates directly finding a double-function move. In any event, we should not treat cases of ambiguous interpretation as showing serious deficiencies in how our scheme accounts for the subject's behavior.

One case of multiple interpretation occurs in E2 at 3. Q-B3. This move can be generated by iP $\longrightarrow$ a, and the repetition of this function in E22 (B202 and B205) reinforces this interpretation. However, the move can also be generated by the production of a pinned man (p $\longrightarrow$ a), and it is clear that the subject considers the double threat (B34, B35). The second case of multiple interpretation occurs in E5 after the double threat, 3. Q-B3, and Black's counterattack, 3. ... Q'$\times$QP. The move, 4. B$\times$N', can be seen both as a way of adding a defender to the N'(K5) (a $\longrightarrow$ d), which the subject recognizes is in danger (B69), and as continuing the original attack to see what follows (c $\longrightarrow$ g).

No Generator. For two moves it does not seem possible to assign any of the situation-response productions, and for two others the assignment is quite uncertain. We have noted these four moves with a question mark.

The entire E20 episode is somewhat obscure. The subject needs an alternative White move, but his grounds for choosing 2. N-R4 are not evident. Likewise the follow-up, 3. N-B5, is perhaps an attempt to dislodge the defending B'(K2), since he apparently believes he is attacking the Q' (B193). The other unassigned move is 2. P-B4, which is clearly a move connected with initiating a K-side attack, but not one where it was possible to identify a familiar configuration that could determine the move.

Generation of Plans. In several situations the subject has developed a plan of action that implies a sequence of moves. The moves generated at eleven positions can be accounted for on this basis (g $\longrightarrow$ g). When implementing a plan, the subject seems to operate in a very exploratory way. Thus, all the positions where the opponent's move is skipped (the no-move) occur during these times, and the subject almost never generates alternative moves for implementing a plan. Some of the plans are so familiar that they could have been made into productions—e.g., doubling the Rooks in E9. Others, such as the means-ends analysis of E15, are clearly constructed for this particular situation. The technique of attempting to demonstrate a fact by assuming its negation and following out the consequences is used sufficiently often that we have made it a production ($\longrightarrow$ n). This technique generates a plan, since the next several moves are dictated by the attempt to elicit the pertinent consequences.

There are six instances of planning. Given a plan, the derivation of moves is easy. (1) The plan of E9, to double the Rooks on the QB-file, is not too clear in the protocol. (2) In E12 the attempt to show that the B is not pinned by showing that the N is not pinned is clearly stated. (3) The means-ends sequence of E15 has already been discussed. (4) In E17 the subject is concerned with determining whether the Q' has been tied down by the double attack on the B'(B3), and he does this by exploring the consequences of letting the Q' capture the NP. The final two plans occur in E24. (5) The exploration of the pawn push on the King side (2. P-B4) is clear enough, although its origin is obscure as we have mentioned. (6) The other plan is the attempt to determine the consequences of Black's not doing 3. ... P'$\times$P, and is clearly stated (B228).

Ordering of Generators. In many positions more than one production is applicable. The choice of generator is one means by which rule R2, which describes the sequencing of episodes, is carried out. In Table 12.2 the productions are given in priority order. Thus the normal response to a capture is to recapture ($x \rightarrow r$), after which (for the subject) comes a countercapture ($x \rightarrow c$), and then actions that entail loss. In many of the situations the protocol provides no opportunity for a series of responses—e.g., the initiative situations. From the protocol it appears that at each episode that reworks a previous episode the prior path is followed until a new production is applied to generate a variation. From this point on the subject carries out the search as an initial exploration, since all the subsequent positions are new.

Summary of Move Generation Analysis

The scheme of Table 12.2 is appealing in its simplicity. It says that the subject, through prior experience with chess and chess literature, has available a collection of fixed responses to specific classes of situations. Behavior directly follows recognition. The evocation of only a single generator and the specificity of the chess position itself yields the fact that the number of alternatives generated at a position is one or at most a few moves. The fact that most tufts are both Black and defensive is to be explained as a derivative characteristic of the generators that are appropriate to this particular base position. The attempt to verify this scheme in Figure 12.9 and the subsequent discussion shows both that the scheme can account for an appreciable number of move generations and that detailed consideration of each instance is required to make sense of the evidence.

Each item in Table 12.2 is based on a small exercise in logic—e.g., the idea behind defending an attacked man is that if he is defended, the opponent can no longer make a gain. In each instance in Figure 12.9 one could argue either that the subject has a preexisting production, as outlined, or that he brings to bear a more general problem solving mechanism to discover by reasoning the same moves that the scheme gives. Preexisting productions seem probable when the generated moves appear in the protocol immediately upon occurrence of the situation without evidence of substantial problem solving, but each instance must be argued on its own merits.

EVALUATION

The final question to be raised about S2's behavior is what evaluation is assigned when an episode terminates. The fundamental logic of the game—that one maximizes for self and minimizes for the opponent—is clearly used throughout. The subject operates as if permanent gain is unlikely from any position, so that discovery of any permanent gain can be used to terminate an episode. Thus any gain that a player has when it is still his opportunity to move can be considered permanent. Likewise, any loss that exists for a player at his move, for which there does not exist immediate compensation, can be considered permanent. This latter situation occurs especially just after a capture for which there is no immediate recapturing possibility. The departures from these terminating rules are most often deliberate counterattacks with loss and recaptures with loss. As we have seen, these are unusual responses and occur only in latter reworkings of an episode.

The dominant characteristic of the subject's evaluations is that they involve only a single feature of the position—e.g., a pawn isolated. At the end of each move (i.e., a move for White followed by one for Black) either the status quo is preserved, in which case search continues, or an advantage one way or the other exists, in which case the search terminates. Since almost always there is a single cause for the change in evaluation, this stands as the single evaluative feature. There is no balancing of a *pro* from one feature with a *con* from another. Thus the form of interaction implicitly provided for in the polynomial payoff functions of chess and checker programs, and capitalized upon when learning is attempted on the polynomial weights (Samuel, 1959), does not appear.

Table 12.3 shows the various evaluations used by the subject. Opposite each are the statements in the protocol where these can be found. They are not listed in any order. There are no occasions when more than one term appears in an evaluation. However, balancing of material does occur—e.g., a piece for a pawn. In a few instances there is a listing of specific conditions involved in preserving the status quo in addition to stating the advantage or disadvantage of the move.

TABLE 12.3

types of evaluations

Win material	B54, B76, B87, B97, B103, B218
Obtain no threat	B39, B85, B115, B123, B133, B158, B165
Remove threat	B36
Obtain open file	B28
Isolate pawn	B25, B202
Double men on file	B81, B83
Lose tempo	B89, B93, B170, B197
Put Queen out of play	B66, B75
Make retreating move	B190
No way to get Q on N7	B146
Make man hard to defend	B206
Remove control from square	B222
Lead to complications	B175
Put on pressure	B181
Mess up K-side	B230

Most of the terms in Table 12.3 are common chess terms with standard operational meanings—"isolate pawn," "lose tempo," "obtain open file," and so on. The subject uses only a few terms that are vague—"complications," "mess up," "pleasure." In this respect he differs from some of de Groot's subjects, whose protocols abounded in such general evaluations as "N-K4—take it away!" With such phrases one can still posit an underlying global, impressionistic, Gestaltlike evaluation. With our subject this is somewhat more difficult to do.

Closely allied to evaluation is the use of levels of aspiration—controlling search by setting a threshold such that only changes in the evaluation of the position that exceed threshold are used to terminate the search. Search starts with the threshold set at some reasonable level; if positions are obtained continually that exceed threshold, the aspiration level is raised; if few positions are found that exceed threshold, the level of aspiration is lowered. With the evaluative procedure that our subject is using, it is difficult to see such a mechanism in operation. One striking example of it does occur in the scene where the subject looks for new possibilities (E6–E10). The moves generated during this period are much poorer than the moves appearing elsewhere (e.g., 1. N × NP'). It appears as if the bars had been let down in order to gather in all the possibilities.

CONCLUSION

This concludes our study of S2 on position A, a detailed look at a person making an analysis of a chess position to decide upon a move. Although we have examined some parts extensively, a number of other aspects have been ignored or only hinted at. A list of the full specifications for a chess program using the progressive-deepening-search strategy reveals the missing parts: a move-generator for basic moves; a criterion for interruption; a criterion for applying a new production when reworking an episode; criteria for terminating analysis. There are also some levels of organization that we did not examine—most notably, the groups of episodes we called scenes. For example, a single organizing idea undoubtedly underlies all of the *search widely* scene (E6–E10).

Even the parts we did examine—episode generation, move generation, and evaluation—are incomplete. They represent what this particular task evoked from the subject's total repertoire. Many more situation-response productions would be needed to reflect the total chess information that S2 has, and the same is true of the evaluation. The rules of episode generation are in a somewhat different category, since they do not represent individual bits of chess lore. Nevertheless, they are incomplete, and reflect only the regularities evoked in this one position.

The limitations of the analysis of S2 should not obscure the evidence it has provided on several basic questions. We have seen that a human's behavior in one more task can be represented as search in a problem space, where this space can be specified with precision. In this case it is the basic problem space defined by the rules of the game augmented by a few abstract moves (such as no-move, Q-move, B-defense). Furthermore, within this space the search has a well-developed structure: the progressive-deepening-search strategy and the various rules for governing its details. Although we said very little about the underlying IPS, this entire program for behavior is clearly a symbolic system and hardly anything but an IPS could realize it concretely. It requires a basically serial processor with the ability to symbolize situations (how else to carry out the search and repeatedly go down the same path?), and to form and evoke associations (i.e., the productions).

We return for a moment to the definition of the episodes. We defined them directly from the protocol at hand, using the evidence it gave of breaks in activity. There is no question of the reality of these episodes, as the PBG shows. Each represents a return to the base situation in order to set out on a fresh exploration or to summarize the state of affairs to date. But the theoretical frame for episodes that we introduced in earlier chapters has not been in evidence so far. The original analysis on which this chapter is based (Newell and Simon, 1965) was carried out before the present notion of episode emerged, and it seemed wise to leave the analysis itself unchanged.

To review the concept of an episode: it is a stretch of behavior that is carried out by the problem solver because it is obvious. Any equally intelligent problem solver placed in the same starting position with the same goals will run through essentially the same episode. Sometimes, especially if the desired result is not in fact obtainable, the episode will encompass considerable search. Then the exact course of two problem solvers can be quite different, but the domain they explore, trying to reach the unobtainable, will be the same.

What is obvious behavior has to be determined separately in each task environment, or more precisely, each problem space. Particularized definitions were put forth for both previous task environments. What is the situation with respect to chess?

The situation-response productions provide an appropriate notion of obvious behavior. Given the set provided by the base-move, behavior runs off in terms of immediate action and reaction. Prior analysis through the same part of the tree conditions the behavior, in that more and more unusual moves are considered in successive analyses. But the decisions at each node along the path of the episode are reached without major reflection.

The situation at the base position is different. Each of the base-moves corresponds to a new exploration. It is significant that we did not try to define a base-move generator for S2, whereas we did propose move generators from the other positions. The lack of data about the base position, which occurs only once whereas the others occur many times, provides part of the reason for not proposing a base-move generator. But over and above the lack of data the base-move remains a significantly unobvious step, as compared with the exploration that follows. We would expect the exploration to be even more predictable if we had developed a more precise characterization of the instructions available at the beginning of the episode.

We will not try to give a more precise definition of an episode in chess, nor reexamine the detail of the protocol to see how well it fits. We do wish to suggest that the episodes we have seen in S2's chess protocol are consistent with the concept of episode introduced and used in the earlier parts of the book.

We did not dwell at length on the extent to which the task environment determined the subject's behavior. The relation of his program to the chess programs discussed at length in Chapter 11 is revealing in this regard. We remarked at the beginning of this chapter that our expectations for these programs should be modest, since chess is a much deeper task than either of the others we had chosen to study. Thus, it comes as no surprise that S2's problem solving organization falls outside those of the six programs—none of which use a scheme like progressive deepening. (The one partial exception is the secondary-search that has been added to the Greenblatt program.)

The similarity between S2 and the chess programs lies one level lower. Both work forward, searching for consequences. Both use the underlying logic of the game to reason backwards to an evaluation of a base-move. The separation between base-moves and the consequence-generating moves is very clear in S2's protocols, just as it is in the NSS program (e.g., compare the number of base-moves considered with the number of moves considered from advanced positions). Both S2 and the programs use move generators specialized to functions (although the Kotok and Greenblatt programs have taken a different path, avoiding special move generators). Both detect features of the board for evaluations (although none of the programs approach the one-feature-one-evaluation scheme used by S2.) Many of these common aspects of the computer and subject programs are to be ascribed to the demands of the task environment—there simply is no other way to construct systems that play chess, given certain gross features of the IPS, especially its seriality, its associative long-term memory, and the limited capacity of its short-term memory.

APPENDIX 12.1

A Chess Protocol on Position A of de Groot

E1
B1	OK, White to move. . . .
B2*	In material the positions are even.
B3	One, two, three, four, five, six . . . six pawns each.
B4	Black has what threats?
B5	His Queen is threatening my Knight's pawn
B6	and also he has one piece on my Queen's pawn . . .
B7	has a Rook in front of the Bishop,
B8	which will give him an open file.
B9	Let's see, all right, what threats do we have?
B10	We have his Knight under single attack
B11	protected by the Bishop.
B12*	We have his other Knight under attack
B13	protected by three pieces.
B14	The Queen is bearing down on the Knight's pawn

*Asterisks refer to notes listed at the end of the protocol.

B15	and the Rook is over here protecting the Knight	
B16	and the Bishop at Rook 2 is bearing down on the Knight.	
B17	All right, looks like we have something going on the King's side.	
B18	All Black's pieces are over on the Queen's side . . .	
B19	most of them out of play. . .	
B20	good chances for an attack perhaps.	
E2		
B21	See, what moves are there?	
B22	The Bishop at Rook 2 can take the Knight,	1. B × N′/5
B23	which would be no doubt answered by either Bishop takes Bishop or pawn takes Bishop.	1. . . . P′ × B
B24	Probably Bishop takes Bishop	1. . . . B′ × B
B25	to avoid isolating the pawn.	
B26	If we then play Knight takes Bishop,	2. N × B′
B27	he will then play pawn takes Knight or Rook takes Rook,	2. . . . P′ × N 2. . . . R′ × R
B28	but this would give White an open file if he exchanged	(3. R × R′)
B29	and this is doubtful.	
B30	This would isolate Black's Queen's pawn . . .	2. . . . P′ × N
B31	it would be protected only by the Knight	
B32	which is pinned,	
B33	therefore we could move the Queen to Bishop 3,	3. Q-KB3
B34	not only putting another threat on the Knight,	
B35	but also threatening an isolated pawn.	
B36	Both of them could not be protected simultaneously unless Queen to Queen 1.	3. . . . Q′-Q1
E3		
B37	All right, well, what about Queen to Bishop 3 immediately.	1. Q-KB3
B38	Queen to Bishop 3 immediately is not good . . .	
B39	it gives no threat on the Knight at Bishop 3	
B40	because it is protected by the Knight at Queen 4.	
E4		
B41	So let's follow this through again.	1. B × N′/5
B42	Bishop takes Knight	1. . . . B′ × B
B43	which will be answered by Bishop takes Bishop.	
B44	We will play Knight takes Bishop	2. N × B′
B45	threatening the Queen. . . .	

B46	Black must recapture	
B47	and he can only do it by playing pawn takes Knight.	2. ... P′×N
B48	Then if we play Queen to Bishop 3,	3. Q-KB3
B49	Black is forced. ...	
B50*	Oh, I was forgetting about the exchange of Rooks. ...	3. ... R′-exchange
B51	Black is forced to play Queen to Queen 1.	3. ... Q′-Q1
B52	If then we exchange Rooks,	4. R×R′
B53	Black must take the Rook with the Queen	4. ... Q′×R
B54*	and we would be able to win a pawn safely.	

E5

B55	However, I'll just go through again.	
B56	Bishop takes Knight,	1. B×N′/5
B57	Bishop takes Bishop,	1. ... B′×B
B58	Knight takes Bishop,	2. N×B′
B59	pawn takes Knight ...	2. ... P′×N
B60	Queen to Bishop 3,	3. Q-KB3
B61	White has the answer ... Black has the answer there.	
B62	Queen takes Knight's pawn if he wishes or Queen takes Queen's pawn.	
B63	Queen takes Knight's pawn is no trouble	3. ... Q′×NP
B64	because our Rook's pawn is protected by the Queen	
B65	and he has nothing else down there,	
B66	he's just putting his Queen farther out of play.	
B67	Queen takes Queen ... takes Queen's pawn ...	3. ... Q′×QP
B68	is a little worse.	
B69	Because then he's threatening our Knight.	
B70	So we ... so if we answer that by Bishop takes Knight,	4. B×N′
B71	he follows with what ... he follows with,	
B72	well, he must either take the Bishop or protect his Bishop at King 2.	4. ... B′×B
B73	If he takes it we answer it with Queen takes Bishop.	5. Q×B′
B74	therefore ... thereby protecting our Knight at King 5	
B75	and leaving Black's Queen out in the cold	
B76	and we have won a piece for a pawn.	

E6

B77	Let's see if there's anything else here.	
B78	Our Knight at King 5 can take the Bishop immediately,	1. N×B′

B79	but this . . . this hardly seems good . . .	
B80	Queen takes Knight,	1. . . . Q'×N
B81	then gives him two pieces on the file	
B82	or Rook takes Knight	1. . . . R'×N
B83	allows him to double up Rooks on the Queen Bishop file.	

E7

B84	The Knight at King 5 can take the pawn at Bishop 2,	1. N×BP'
B85	but this does not lead to any threat . . .	

E8

B86	can take the pawn at Knight 3 . . .	1. N×NP'
B87*	this is easily answered by Bishop's pawn takes pawn.	1. . . . BP'×N

E9

B88*	Both of our Rooks,	
B89	both of the Rooks cannot get into play more than two moves	(1. R-QB2)
		(2. R(KB)-QB)
B90	so they're out of the picture temporarily.	

E10

B91	A King side push of pawns	1. P-move-K-side
B92	to break up Black's King side	
B93	would take too long,	
B94	because we are after all under the necessity of protecting the Queen's Knight pawn	
B95	and also watching out for an attack on the Queen's pawn.	
B96	So, therefore	
B97	the immediate exchange seems indicated if we can win a piece for a pawn.	

E11

B98	All right . . . starts out with the Bishop at Knight 2 taking the Knight.	1. B×N'/5
B99	Black must recapture	
B100	or else he's lost a piece.	
B101	If he plays Queen takes Knight's pawn,	1. . . . Q'×NP
B102	then we can play Bishop takes Bishop if we wish	2. B×B'
B103	and we will come out a clear piece ahead for a pawn or two.	

E12

B104*	Let's see, now, Bishop takes Knight, Bishop at Knight 2 takes a Knight	1. B×N'/5
B105	followed by Queen takes Knight's pawn.	1. . . . Q'×NP
B106	Then we play Bishop takes Bishop we'd say,	2. B×B'
B107	then Black can play Queen takes Rook's pawn,	2. . . . Q'×RP

B108	and thus we cannot move our Bishop at Bishop 6	
B109	because if we did that	3. B(B6)-move
B110	we would put two pieces on our Knight at Bishop 3	
B111	which would be pinned in an attack by the Queen and the Knight, Queen and the Knight . . . Queen and the Knight . . . Queen and the Rook at Bishop 1 simultaneously.	
B112	So, it's pinned, however, it's protected twice	
B113	and we can break the pin	
B114	by moving the Queen back and then moving the Knight	4. Q-back 5. N-move
B115	so that is not a serious threat.	

E13

B116	So we play Bishop takes Knight . . .	1. B × N′/5
B117	Black must recapture,	
B118	if he doesn't he'll lose a piece or two for a couple of pawns.	
B119	He will not recapture . . . he will not recapture with the Knight . . .	
B120	yes, he can recapture with the other Knight.	
B121	If he recaptures with the other Knight,	1. . . . N′ × B
B122	we would of . . . we would play Knight takes Knight	2. N × N′
B123	therefore our Bishop at Knight 5 is immune	
B124	because his Queen is attacked.	

E14

B125	OK, Bishop takes Knight	1. B × N′/5
B126	followed by Bishop takes Bishop.	1. . . . B′ × B
B127	We then play Knight takes Bishop.	2. N × B′
B128	Again, Black can recapture with the Knight . . .	
B129	this was overlooked.	
B130	All right, Black recaptures with the Knight . . .	2. . . . N′ × N
B131	what do we have? The Bishop must either capture or retreat . . . there,	3. B × B′ 3. B-retreat
B132	we do not have very much.	
B133	So this exchange variation doesn't win us anything.	

E15

B134	Now, Black's King side is in sad shape . . .	
B135	There is a mate if we can get the Bishop down to Rook 6 and sneak the Queen in at Knight 7.	
B136	So, how do we do this?	
B137	An immediate Queen to Bishop 3.	1. Q-KB3

B138*	Ah, lets see, we will play Knight takes Knight	2. N×N'/5
B139*	play Bishop takes Knight. Bishop takes Knight . . .	2. B×N'/5
B140	Knight takes Bishop.	2. . . . N'×B
B141	Then where do we stand . . . then we play Knight takes Knight	3. N×N'
B142	and Black will play pawn takes Knight.	3. . . . P'×N
B143	Then . . . then what do we play?	
B144	We play Bishop to Rook 6.	4. B-R6
B145	If we play Bishop to Rook 6 we have the King trapped down there,	
B146	but there isn't any way to get the Queen . . . the Queen down into Knight 7	
B147*	because . . . because of the Bishop at Queen 2.	
B148*	Therefore it's necessary to get rid of the Bishop at Queen 2 before we can do anything for a mate.	

E16

B149	All right, the Bishop at Queen 2 . . .	
B150	Let's consider the move Knight to King 4.	1. N-K4

E17

B151	Knight to King 4 puts a couple of pieces on the Bishop at Bishop 3	
B152	and well, it doesn't really pin the Queen	
B153	Because the Queen has got . . . the Queen can go back and the Queen has Knight takes pawn,	1. . . . Q'-back 1. . . . Q'×NP
B154	which would get back the pawn we'd win	
B155	if we played Knight takes Bishop,	2. N×B'
B156	pawn takes Knight,	2. . . . P'×N
B157	Rook takes pawn. . . .	3. R×P'
B158	No, we don't have anything there.	

E16

B159	All right, but Knight . . . Knight to King 4	1. N-K4
B160	puts two pieces on the Knight . . . two pieces on the Knight at Bishop 3.	
B161	If he plays Knight takes Knight,	1. . . . N'×N
B162	we play Bishop takes Bishop.	2. B×B'
B163	This is easily answered by . . . Bishop takes Bishop . . . this is easily answered by Knight takes Bishop	2. . . . N'×B
B164	and then we cannot take the Knight which has . . . which is at Black's King 5.	
B165	So that move seems to be fruitless.	

E18

B166	We have to get the Bishop out of Rook 2	

B167	because if we do not get it out of Rook 2 . . . yeah, if we don't get the Bishop from Rook 2,	
B168*	Queen takes Knight . . .	1. . . . Q′×NP
B169	forces us to move it	
B170	thereby losing a move.	
B171	The only place the Bishop can go with any sense is to take the Knight,	2. B×N′/5
B172	so let's take the Knight right away.	

E19

B173	Takes the Knight . . .	1. B×N′/5
B174	then he can play pawn takes the Knight, Bishop takes Knight or Knight takes . . . play pawn takes Bishop, Bishop takes Bishop, or Knight takes Bishop.	1. . . . P′×B 1. . . . B′×B 1. . . . N′×B
B175*	All these lead into complications.	

E20

B176	Now let's see, let's try once again.	
B177	If he plays Bishop takes Knight, Bishop takes Bishop,	1. . . . B′×B
B178	then we can play Knight to Rook 4	2. N-R4
B179	attacking the Queen and defending our pawn at Knight 2 simultaneously,	2. . . . Q′-move
B180	with the possibility of moving next move into Bishop 5	3. N-B5
B181	putting a little more pressure on the . . . on Black	
B182*	and perhaps persuading his Bishop to take the Knight at Bishop 5.	

E21

B183	If we play Knight to Rook 4,	
B184	where can the Queen go?	
B185	If we play Bishop takes Knight . . .	1. B×N′/5
B186	to answer that Bishop takes Bishop,	1. . . . B′×B
B187	White follows with Knight to Rook 4.	2. N-R4
B188	The Queen can go nowhere on the Knight's file.	
B189	It can, of course, move to Rook 4 . . .	2. . . . Q′-R4
B190	can move to Rook 4 or it can retreat to Bishop 2 or Queen 1.	2. . . . Q′-B2 2. . . . Q′-Q1
B191	If it moves to Rook 4,	2. . . . Q′-R4
B192	then we can play Knight to Bishop 5,	3. N-B5
B193*	again threatening the Queen	
B194	forcing it to move back,	
B195	probably again . . . probably moving back to Knight 3	3. . . . Q′-N3
B196	and this Black would not do.	
B197	He's lost two moves.	
B198	Our Bishop at Bishop 5 is in a good position,	
B199	so therefore he will not take the Bishop with the Bishop.	

E22

B200	Again we play Bishop takes Knight	1. B×N′/5

B201	answered by pawn takes Bishop.	1. ... P′ × B
B202	This isolates a pawn ... it's a tactical disadvantage.	
B203	It's doubtful that he'd do this.	
B204	Besides	
B205	we can put two pieces on that pawn right away	(2. Q-KB3)
B206	and it would become hard to defend later on.	

E23

B207	So he will answer Bishop takes Knight with Knight takes Knight ... with Knight takes Bishop.	1. B × N′/5
B208	We'd answer it with Knight takes Bishop.	1. ... N′ × B
B209	Then if we play Knight takes Knight	2. N × N′
B210	the Queen is threatened	
B211	and must move.	2. ... Q′-move
B212	Well, therefore,	
B213	no he cannot answer it with Knight takes Knight	
B214	because if he does play Knight takes Knight, the Queen is threatened and must move no matter where it moves.	
B215	We can either play Bishop takes Bishop or Knight takes Bishop check.	3. B × B′
B216	Knight takes Bishop check is better	3. N × B′ch
B217	being at fork with the Rook,	
B218	therefore he'd lose at least a piece.	
B219	All right, so he cannot play Knight takes Bishop if we play Bishop takes Knight	

E24

B220	Therefore ... therefore he must play pawn takes ... pawn takes Bishop	1. ... P′ × B
B221	If he plays pawn takes Bishop ... what have we gained?	
B222	We have gained ... we have taken away one of the pieces ... one of the pawns on Bishop 5 square	
B223	thus making a pawn push more reasonable.	
B224	We can play pawn to Bishop 4,	2. P-KB4
B225	followed by pawn to Bishop 5.	3. P-KB5
B226	This will,	
B227	well, it won't force pawn takes pawn.	3. ... P′ × P
B228	However, we can if he does not take the pawn, we can push on the other side ... pawn to King Rook	3. ... not P′ × P 4. P-KR4
B229	followed by pawn to King Rook 5.	5. P-KR5
B230	This would mess up his King side	
B231	and leave him open to an attack	
B232	which should lead to an easy win.	

E25

B233	All right, so the best move is then Bishop takes Knight.	1. B × N'/5
B234	If it's answered with Knight takes Bishop	1. ... N' × B
B235	we play Knight takes Knight.	2. N × N'
B236	If it's answered with pawn takes Bishop,	1. ... P' × B
B237	we will play pawn to Bishop 4.	2. P-KB4
B238	If it's answered by Bishop takes Bishop,	1. ... B' × B
B239	we play Knight to Rook 4	2. N-R4
B240	and follow that up with Knight to Rook 5.	3. N-B5
B241	OK.	

Notes

B2	Refers to pieces and not men in light of B3.
B12	N(B3) rather than B(N2) in light of B16.
B50	Although "forgotten" implies a reference to B27 and B28, it is possible that the subject already sees 3. R × R'.
B54	The subject underestimates; in this position he can win a piece.
B87	"Bishop's pawn takes pawn" means BP' × N, since there is no pawn capture on the board.
B88	The subject is not explicit, but the only obvious way to bring the Rooks into play is by doubling them on the QB-file; the reference to "two moves" in B89 supports this interpretation.
B104	"Knight 2" is "Rook 2."
B138	1. N × N' is possible rather than 2. N × N', which would imply a shift in B139, B140, and so on. However, the comments in B145 and B146 support the choice of 2. N × N'.
B139	Possibly 2. N × N' is never considered and B138 is just a falter prior to B139.
B147	"Queen 2" means "King 2."
B148	See B147 note.
B168	1. N-K4 must be assumed, since otherwise the N defends B(R2). Also "Knight ..." must mean NP, since there is no Q' × N move.
B175	Apparently subject is summarizing the entire prior analysis and not making a new judgment at this point.
B182	"Persuade" implies that it is desirable for White to have N' × B, presumably to remove the B as a defender of the N(B3).
B193	N(B5) does not threaten Q'. If B192 were N(K5)-B4, then N(B4) would threaten Q'; but this seems most improbable in the light of subsequent behavior (e.g., B195).

CHESS:
a Broader View

Having examined in the first two chapters of this part a homogeneous set of chess programs and a single subject's behavior, we now take up a number of different topics related to chess playing. They not only provide some assurance that the prior material is not completely idiosyncratic, but also extend the analysis in various ways.

Few studies have been made of the psychology of playing chess. The most important work is that of de Groot (1965), originally done in 1938–42, which has recently been extended (de Groot, 1966; Jongman, 1968). Baylor has examined several protocols in his master's thesis (1965). Most other studies are so general in their comments as not to be relevant to analysis on an IPS level (e.g., Fine, 1967). Our first topic, then, will be to summarize the general view of chess playing that emerged from de Groot's study. We will follow this with a more detailed look at the way his grandmaster subjects handled position A, which will provide some direct check on the behavior of S2 studied in the last chapter. As the third topic, we will explore in more depth the phenomena of *defining the situation*, which show up strongly in de Groot's analysis, but are largely absent in the behavior of S2.

Next will come an investigation into a special class of chess situations: finding mating combinations. In the main this will be additional exploration of the task environment, with the help of a computer program that performs the task. This topic will add to our understanding of the relation of game playing to other tasks, since the mating-combinations program has some of the flavor of a theorem prover.

The final topic is the role of perception and noticing in chess. This aspect of behavior comes through more strongly in chess than in the two other tasks. All our tasks have perceptually simple displays, since we imposed this condition in selecting tasks for symbolic problem solving. But chess has a long and studied history, unlike either of the other tasks. Further, we used naive subjects for both cryptarithmetic and logic but experienced subjects for chess. There had been ample opportunity for our chess subjects to develop capabilities for recognizing subtle features of the task display, compared with those a novice would recognize (a novice in chess recognizes very little). Aspects of several studies can be brought to bear on this topic.

DE GROOT'S ANALYSIS

De Groot examined in great detail the protocols of a number of chess players who were analyzing positions in order to choose a move—essentially the same experimental situation as with our S2. De Groot also took protocols of his subjects, who were asked to talk aloud. Perhaps the chief difference in observational procedure is that we had tape recorders, whereas de Groot had to take notes. Thus, our protocols are more extensive. However, de Groot did go over the notes with the subject immediately after each session, something we did not do.

De Groot's subjects ranged from good club players to grandmasters (the best players in the chess world). Our subject would thus sit at the lower edge of de Groot's group, and his best subjects—the grandmasters—are incomparably better.[1] However, a summary of de Groot's main findings shows that his subjects and our S2 were alike in many ways. Similarly, the basic kinship of the human players to chess-playing programs is quite apparent.

Selective Search

Humans playing chess spend much of their time searching in the game tree for the consequences of the moves they are considering (de Groot, 1965, *passim*, but see especially pp. 100–130, 268–269). The search is highly selective, attending to only a few of the multitude of possible continuations. There is no evidence that the total number of different positions considered by a player, during an analysis

---

[1] Not quite. One can fill in the gap between S2 and a grandmaster with a sequence of other players, each of whom can nearly always beat the man below him and is nearly always beaten by the man above. There are four to five such players between S2 and a grandmaster, and perhaps three or four between a novice and S2.

lasting up to fifteen minutes or so, exceeds about one hundred. In position A, for example, the number of positions explicitly considered in protocols of five grandmasters ranged from 20 to 76 (de Groot, 1965, Table 12, p. 319). Evidence as to how many positions are considered is obtained by protocol analysis. The estimates err on the low side, since players may fail to mention positions they consider, but by no stretch of the uncertainties could the estimates be more than doubled.

Both facts mentioned above—that players do search, but that they search only a small space—reconfirm our view about existing computer chess programs. Programs that search thousands or tens of thousands of positions per analysis are almost certainly proceeding quite differently from humans; those programs that search very selectively are more relevant.

Chess Concepts

The description and analysis of chess positions involve the use of numerous classificatory terms, or concepts. These terms permit the features, or subpatterns, in the chess position that are relevant to its analysis to be described and referred to succinctly. A pattern, for example, that consists of Black pawns on Black's KB2, KN3, KR2, a Bishop on his KN2, a Rook on KB1, and his King on KN1 is a "fianchettoed short-castled position"—a phrase sufficient to allow a knowledgeable chess player to evoke the entire pattern of six pieces.

Superficially, the same kinds of elementary chess concepts are involved in human play as appear in chess programs: attacks, defenses, pins, open files, isolated pawns, and so on. This is to be expected, of course, since the chess programs are written by chess-playing programmers, who rely heavily on the standard chess literature. In programs, such concepts may appear in the condition parts of productions ("if piece is *attacked*, then . . ."), in the labels of actions (*checking move*), or in the evaluations of consequences of actions ("after the exchange, White has an *isolated pawn*"). However, the occurrence of the same concepts in both programs and protocols does not imply that they have precisely the same extensions, nor (more important) that the concepts are used in the same way in both cases. Concepts encapsulate information that may be used in a variety of ways.

Some concepts mentioned in human chess protocols are much more global than those listed above—for example, "a developed position," "control of the center," "a won position," "a weak King's side," "a closed position" (e.g., de Groot, pp. 150–157). Their counterparts in current chess programs occur mostly in the static-evaluation processes, and the correspondence does not seem very close. The chess programs of Chapter 11 do not shed much new light on these higher-level concepts. Subject 2 used such general concepts only occasionally—e.g., describing Black's position as in "sad shape."

With due regard for the differences in concepts and their use from one chess program (human or computer) to another, we conclude, nonetheless, that there are strong generic similarities deriving from the common reliance upon the standard vocabulary of chess and the kinds of underlying patterns that this vocabulary names.

Human chess analysis is broken up into separate episodes. As one would expect when a subject is plunged into a complex situation, initially he orients himself to the board position. He also sums up at the end, when finally picking the single move he will play. The number of episodes between these boundaries is variable, depending on the level of analysis. De Groot (pp. 102–116, 267) distinguishes three major phases (he included the initial orientation as a fourth): exploration, elaboration, and proof. But, as S2's protocol shows, within these phases many discontinuities occur in the problem solving process, marking the boundaries of still smaller episodes. Subject 2 showed clearly both an orientation phase (E1) and a summing-up phase (E25). But his episodic behavior in between is not so easily categorized in functional terms. However, identifying the features of different types of episodes considered individually is more important than attempting to find a characteristic phase sequence.

Progressive Deepening.   There often occurs what de Groot (pp. 266–274) calls progressive broadening and deepening: the analysis of a move is reworked repeatedly, going over old ground more carefully, exploring new side branches, and extending the search deeper. Indeed, some players start by constructing a sample variation to orient themselves to the position. This idea of "rough cut, fine cut," to use a term proposed by J. C. Shaw, is not prominent in computer chess programs, although the Kotok and Greenblatt programs do examine all legal moves statically in order to select the plausible moves for consideration at greater depth, and the Greenblatt program uses a single secondary search. S2's episodes showed this characteristic so strongly that we borrowed the term *progressive deepening* as a label for the search strategy he was using.

Exploration and Verification.   Some episodes are devoted to exploring for new information; others are devoted to proving or disproving a hypothesis (i.e., to verification). Players frequently select quite early a favorite move and then attempt to verify that it is better than the alternatives (de Groot, pp. 176–177, 194 ff). Search may be conducted in quite different ways in exploration and verification, since different information is sought. The general tendency in human behavior to deal with a complex world by a sequence of singular hypotheses rather than by narrowing possibilities deductively, using in full the incoming information, is well attested in concept attainment studies (Bruner, Goodnow, and Austin, 1956). In general, the human player has no way to squeeze all the information out of each new observation on the board; dealing with hypotheses seriatim throws away much information but makes the cognitive task manageable.

Although there are programs that create and test hypotheses (Feldman, 1963; Kochen, 1961), among chess programs only MATER II (to be discussed) makes even limited use of these mechanisms. They can all be found in one form or another in our subject. His use of negation in E17 and E24 is clearly a form of verification. Likewise, all of scene 3 (E6–E10) is clearly exploration. However, despite the fact that B × N′/5 is investigated time and again, there is little reason to view it as a deliberate favorite that he is trying to prove. S2 seems to return to it (scene 6) more because it is the only thing he has found of interest, than because he has a goal of proving it the right move.

Problem Definition

Human chess players attempt periodically to *redefine* the problem (de Groot, pp. 189, 227–239, 280–287). The redefinition, usually a conclusion based on the immediately prior analysis, is accepted as the new working assumption. These summaries are put forward in rather general terms, e.g., "In any case White will have to extract some profit from that weakness after all." One might be tempted to think of this as hypothesis formation, but it is not. Hypotheses can arise (and be accepted and hence worked on) without deliberate summarization; and likewise, after an attempt to redefine the problem, there is normally no testing activity devoted to proving or disproving the efficacy of the new problem definition. Nothing of the process of redefinition occurs in current computer chess programs, nor in our protocol of S2. We devote a section to it later on.

Position Evaluation

A major difference between human play and most chess programs lies in the evaluations of positions. The evaluations by de Groot's subjects were often rather elementary (de Groot, pp. 232–239), mentioning a single advantage (e.g., "and Black gains an open file"). This agrees with the behavior of S2 and is in contrast— although not in contradiction—to the rather elaborate polynomial evaluations that have been used in most chess and checkers programs. It does resemble more closely the NSS evaluation process. In human play there seldom occurs a balancing of many factors, some pro, some con, to arrive at an overall estimate. Sometimes de Groot's subjects used very global phrases such as ". . . and it's a won position for White," where it is not possible to see what structure or feature of the position leads to the evaluation. However, human players generally make evaluations at the terminal positions of each line of search (the static positions of chess programs) and make no explicit evaluations at intermediate positions (the dynamic positions of chess programs). In this respect, players and programs agree (de Groot, pp. 271–272).

Perceptual Processes

For all the aspects we have mentioned, there is evidence in S2's protocol to test whether or not he behaved in the manner indicated by de Groot's analysis— as he did with respect to progressive deepening and did not with respect to redefinition. One other aspect of human play is discussed in detail by de Groot (1965, pp. 321–334; 1966, pp. 35–48), for which protocols provide little evidence.

In trying to find measures to distinguish strong from weak players (other than making the correct move), de Groot was singularly unsuccessful with the statistics of search and analysis—e.g., the number of positions examined (pp. 317–320). (However, the worst of de Groot's players were good enough to play occasionally in local tournaments in Amsterdam.) He finally succeeded in separating strong from weak players by using perceptual tests involving the reproduction of chess positions after brief exposure to them (3–7 seconds). The grandmaster was able to reproduce the positions perfectly, and performance degraded appreciably with decrease in chess ability (pp. 328–329). De Groot was led to propose that perceptual abilities and organization were an important factor in very good play.

Since the protocol of S2 provides no direct evidence on perceptual processes, we will postpone to later in the chapter discussion of this aspect of human play. Instead, with this general view of de Groot's work as background, which shows good agreement with our analysis of S2, we will make a more detailed comparison of the behavior of de Groot's grandmasters on position A.

COMPARISON WITH DE GROOT'S PROTOCOLS ON POSITION A

The entirely qualitative comparison of the preceeding section needs to be supplemented by detailed examination. Especially is this true if we would understand to what extent communalities reflect the objective demands of the task environment, and to what extent they reveal common characteristics of human information processing systems. For this purpose, we can use the data that de Groot (1965)[2] has summarized from 19 protocols of subjects placed before position A: 5 grandmasters, 4 masters, and 11 players ranging from expert to club level. Sixteen of these protocols are reproduced in de Groot (pp. 409–421). One of the fullest of the protocols, that of the former World Champion M. Euwe, yielded the PBG shown in Figure 13.1, where it may be compared with the PBG of our subject.

The General Consensus

There are 56 legal base-moves available to a player in position A. Most of these were not mentioned by *any* of the 19 subjects. In fact, a total of only 22 different initial moves were mentioned by one or more subjects, and only 15 of these were mentioned by at least one of the nine subjects of master or grandmaster strength. The average number of different base-moves considered, per subject, was less than 5. One master considered 11; no other master or grandmaster considered more than 6.

There was a relatively high consensus among all the subjects (including ours) as to which base-moves deserved attention. A total of 94 moves (not all different) were mentioned by the 19 subjects; the seven moves mentioned by the largest num-

[2] Throughout this section all page references are to de Groot (1965).

FIGURE 13.1

problem behavior graph of M. Euwe in position A [from protocol in de Groot (1965)]

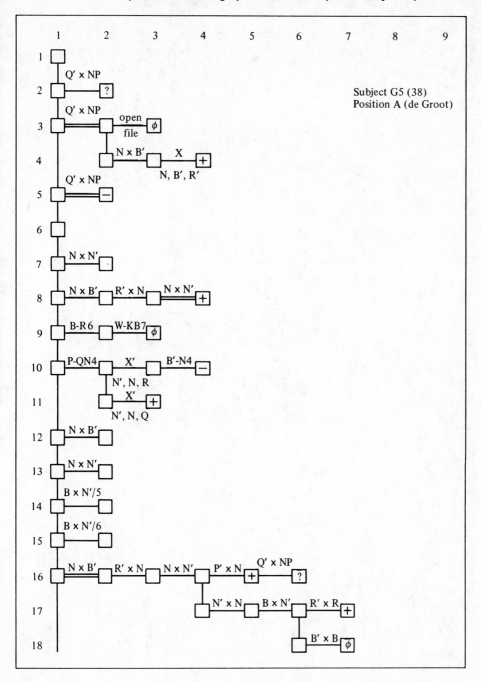

FIGURE 13.1 (cont'd)

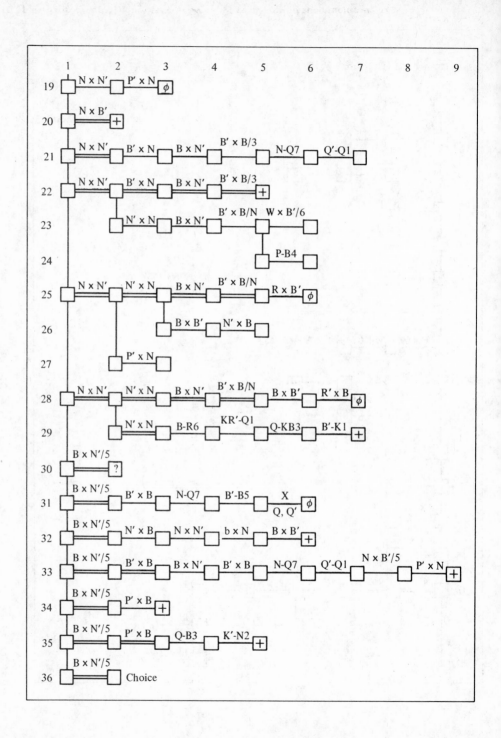

ber of subjects (16 to 6) accounted for about two-thirds ($\frac{62}{94}$) of all mentions. In almost all cases, the moves mentioned most often were the same for subjects of all levels of playing strength—from grandmasters to club players. In fact, six of these seven most popular moves were mentioned by at least one-third (3) of the masters and grandmasters, and six of the seven by at least one-third (4) of the other players. One item of disagreement between the two groups was 1. B × N'/5 (objectively the strongest move in the position), which was mentioned by all five grandmasters and chosen by four of them, but was mentioned only in three of the other de Groot protocols. (It was mentioned and chosen by our subject.) Conversely, P-KR4 was mentioned by two masters but by four weaker players (and chosen by one of the latter). Of the eight moves examined by our subject, four were among the popular seven. These four (B × N'/5, N × B', B-R6, N-K4), plus one other (Q-B3), account for almost all of his exploratory activity, the others being mentioned very briefly (see E3, E7, E8, E9, E10, E15). One of the four moves was chosen by four of the nonmasters, and another by three of the nonmasters (plus one grandmaster)— thus these two moves account for two-thirds of the moves chosen by the non-masters.

When we look closely at the entire search trees of moves mentioned by the five grandmasters and four masters, we see that the consensus extends even further (Figure 13.2). For the move 1. B × N'/5 (chosen by four grandmasters), three replies by Black were mentioned explicitly, two by eight of these players, and the other by seven. One branch explored by eight of them was the objectively correct reply, 1. . . . P' × B (the only one not resulting in material loss for Black), and there was considerable consensus again on White's possible next move—one move being examined by seven players and two others by three players each. A similar degree of consensus exists for the initial move N × B and its continuations. Moreover, the branches most explored by the grandmasters and masters account for a large proportion of the exploratory activity of S2, who was far from master strength. In fact, the production system we have outlined for his move generation would fit reasonably well the PBG's of these strong players.

How are we to account for this high degree of consensus? First, we may look at it from a sociological standpoint. All the players, even the weakest of those studied, belong to a common chess culture. This culture is transmitted in across-the-board play, in conversation among chess players, and in writing on chess (move-by-move reports and analyses of games among grandmasters, books on chess strategy and tactics). Most of the games of grandmasters have been published with annotations; three of the grandmasters in the sample (Euwe, Fine, and Keres) are authors of widely read books on chess, and a fourth (Alekhine) was noted for his analyses as well as his play.

Thus, all of these players know that the win of the exchange (Rook for Bishop or Knight) is usually decisive; that Bishops are usually slightly stronger than Knights; that dynamic analysis is necessary to evaluate exchanges; that Black's advanced KNP creates a possibility for a checkmate with Bishop and Queen; and many other things. They know, in fact, substantially all the heuristic principles that have been incorporated in existing chess programs and a great many more. They approach the position, therefore, with a common body of beliefs acquired through participation in a common culture. The beliefs are not identical, of course—else all the players would be grandmasters—but their commonality in terms of the task requirements is substantial.

In the cryptarithmetic and logic tasks analyzed earlier, there was also some common culture—a common understanding of elementary arithmetic processes, or of algebraic manipulation. But the subjects were not experienced specifically in the cryptarithmetic puzzles or logic tasks. The common elements in their approach to these puzzles stemmed in considerable measure from the structure and requirements of the tasks themselves.

Because of the vast size of the objective search space in chess, one cannot say with certainty what analysis of position A would be required to assess accurately the relative merits of alternative moves. Hence, what the task requires is itself sociologically defined. The best existing chess knowledge (the knowledge, presumably, shared by grandmasters) calls for certain analytic procedures, and certain criteria for evaluating their outcomes. Hence, the high degree of consensus among the grandmasters in their exploration of 1. B × N′/5 can be viewed either as participation in a common culture, or as a common response dictated by the requirements of the situation.

Let us carry this last example a little further. First, what is the objective character of the situation that leads the grandmasters and masters to pay particular attention to B × N′/5, while most of the weak players ignored that move? Two of the grandmasters comment near the beginnings of their protocols: "White's chances are in the attack; Black's in the endgame" (Flohr), and "White has to play for the attack; otherwise he has nothing" (Fine). Now Bishops are somewhat stronger than Knights—*but primarily in the endgame*. The general statement that Bishops are stronger than Knights is part of the lore of many chess players; the qualifying phrase is understood only in more sophisticated circles. We may speculate that the weaker players dismissed 1. B × N′/5 without analysis because of the general heuristic, while the stronger players considered the move because they intended to seek a decision before the endgame.

The actual dynamic analysis of 1. B × N′/5 by the stronger players was governed almost wholly by the objective requirements of the situation, although indirect evidence is needed to show that certain moves were seen that were not explicitly mentioned. Figure 13.2 shows the exploration tree that would be required to evaluate 1. B × N′/5 reasonably objectively (de Groot, pp. 89–90). This exploration would show that Black's reply 1. . . . B′ × B would lose a piece, while 1. . . . N′ × B would lose the exchange, leaving 1. . . . P′ × B as the only possible move. After 1. . . . P′ × B, White has new attacking possibilities.

Three of the five grandmasters dismissed the first two moves without mentioning their continuations; the protocols make it clear, however, that they saw the consequences. One grandmaster and one master mentioned continuations only for 1. . . . B′ × B and 1. . . . P′ × B. The others carried out analyses (not always detailed in their protocols) of all three moves to varying depth (essentially never beyond the point shown in our figure, except for 1. . . . P′ × B). All of the masters and grandmasters mentioned one or more possible moves for White after Black's reply, 1. . . . P′ × B. These moves were mostly related to occupying the now-open King's file (2. KR-K1), or making the position of Black's remaining Knight untenable (2. Q-B3, 2. N-N4).

FIGURE 13.2

composite exploration tree for position A

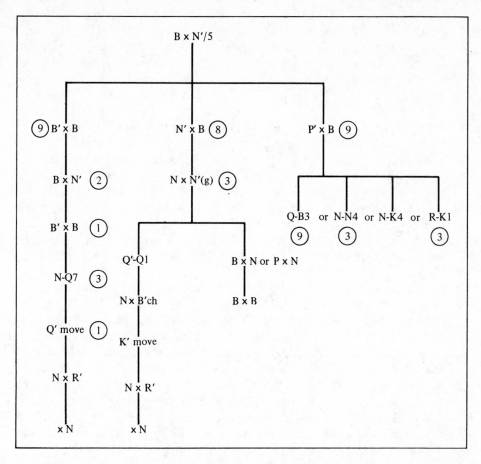

The move generation analysis made for our subject would apply quite well to the grandmasters' protocols. (This must be so, since essentially the same moves are examined.) Piece exchanges are examined dynamically, as is the undefended capture (1. ... Q′ × BP). The moves that are not exchanges, both initial moves and those at the ends of exchanges, are generally evaluated statically. Morever, the small set of these quiet moves that is considered—either initially or after exchanges—all relate directly to central features of the position: defense of the pawn on QN3, the pinned Knight on KB6, the potentially open King's file, and Black's weakened King's position.

Progressive Deepening

The most striking feature in the PBG's of the grandmasters that cannot be attributed to the task requirements, but rather to the players' information processing limits, is the progressive deepening. The grandmasters, like our subject, return to the base position with some frequency, and reexplore previously examined variations. There is very little branching without return to the base position. There is one exception in Keres' protocol, one in Fine's, and four in Euwe's (see Figure 13.1) —mostly after he has repeated a variation several times.

We have suggested earlier that the progressive-deepening strategy, which is so evident in chess protocols, is very likely attributable to the burden the exploration places upon short-term memory. To be sure, even with progressive deepening, the main sequence and outcome of each episode must be remembered so that it will not be repeated, but the branchings do not have to be held in memory while the sequence is being followed to its end. This interpretation is made more plausible by the fact, already noted, that in the last part of the protocol our subject (and also Euwe) does not always restart from the very first move of sequences after he has repeated them several times and has had adequate opportunity to fixate them in memory.

In the chess task, carried out under the standard chess rules that pieces may not be touched or moved, there is nothing comparable to the written display that is available in cryptarithmetic or logic for recording definite or tentative assignments. Thus, we expect to find that the difference in demands upon short-term memory is an important cause for differences in the organization of the problem behavior graphs for the two tasks.

We earlier proposed six rules governing the sequencing of episodes in our subject's PBG. How well do these fit the PBG's of the grandmasters? R1, asserting that the analysis of each base-move is independent of the analysis of the others, appears to be satisfied by all the PBG's. R2, that the first episode of a base-move employs normal moves, is not easily tested because of the paucity of variations in most of the protocols, but there are no obvious violations. R3, "stay with a good base-move, switch from a loser," is consistent with four of the protocols (one violation in Fine's) but not with Euwe's. In the latter protocol there are some six violations. Euwe proceeds in a more systematic manner than the other grandmasters, examining a substantial number of variations in a sequence that seems independent of immediate outcomes.

R4, considering less-than-optimum moves for the opponent, is represented in one to four cases in each of the grandmaster protocols, taking the form of no-moves for the opponent. R5, predicting interruption of analysis to pursue moves discovered during an episode, is not supported by any of the grandmaster protocols—probably because the grandmasters encountered no "surprises" in their analyses. R6, calling for a check on alternative moves before final choice of base-move, receives support only from Alekhine's protocol. But Alekhine is the only grandmaster who comes to the favorable move early in the analysis—it is the second base-move he considers. The others have already examined from two to five other (and unsatisfactory) moves before they hit upon the one chosen. Our subject also came on 1. $B \times N'/5$ at the very beginning of his analysis, and this perhaps explains his deliberate attempt to generate alternative base-moves.

Means-Ends Analysis in Chess

In position A, the protocols appear to be interpretable to a considerable extent in terms of forward search, where certain features of the position suggest directly certain kinds of responses that need exploration (e.g., G3, lines 2–9; M3, lines 2–4; cf. the productions for move generation of S2 in Chapter 12). However, explicit means-ends analysis is hardly evident in the protocols for position A, except (1) in the general strategic consideration, mentioned earlier, that an aggressive move must be sought since the endgame would be favorable to Black (e.g., G4, lines 5–6; M2, lines 1–3); and (2) in the interest expressed by several players in finding moves that attack Black's slightly weakened King's position (e.g., M1, lines 1–3; M2, lines 3–4; M3, lines 2–4). For the rest, the players, strong as well as weak, tend to work forward from the current position, evaluating the consequences of considerable moves.

This working-forward characteristic of the analysis is not entirely inherent in the nature of position A. In addition to the two general goals mentioned in the previous paragraph, there are several more specific targets that could be identified statically, and around which means-end analysis could be built. There is the defensive goal of protecting the pawn at QN2 (e.g., G2, lines 8–9; G4, lines 8–9; G5, lines 3–9), there is a hanging Black Bishop at K7 (guarded only by the Knight at Q5), and there is a potential square for forking Queen and Rook at Q7. Both of the latter two features are involved in the analysis of 1. B×N'/5 and 1. N×N', but in most of the protocols (however, see de Groot, p. 298) it seems evident that the features were discovered in the course of the dynamic analysis (e.g., G5, lines 9–18; M3, lines 42–43), or at least did not provide the motivation for that analysis (e.g., M1, lines 5–8).

De Groot also remarks (pp. 89–90) on the tactical character of position A as a partial explanation for the nature of the analysis. He cites numerous examples of means-ends analysis in protocols from positions of a more strategic character (see especially pp. 157–169). On the other hand, he produces considerable evidence that, especially for the stronger players, particular board features suggest specific move possibilities in a highly "automatic" (overlearned) way, and without the intervention of explicit, verbalized problem solving (see especially pp. 296–315, and the productionlike schema presented in footnote 20, p. 308). In the next section we shall explore a little more some of these strategic situations.

REDEFINITION OF THE SITUATION

In position A neither de Groot's subjects nor S2 redefined the chess situation in the course of the analysis. However, elsewhere in his book de Groot shows (pp. 218–227) that such redefinitions often occur in chess play. One can surmise that their relative paucity in position A is due to the nature of the particular task environment—to the tactical character of the position, just mentioned. Defining the situation is an important type of information processing to understand, since it contrasts sharply with search activity, which so far has been the mainstay of the cognitive activity in analyzing a chess position.

Let us examine a few instances of redefinition from de Groot's protocols. We leave out the initial orientation phase, since there is clear evidence that this first act of definition differs substantially from all the others.

In protocol (M4; C) the subject overlooks a key piece until line 57. The presence of this piece invalidates his favorable analysis of 1. . . . N'-K5, and he continues: "Oh! What nonsense. 2. . . . N'-B6 is no threat after 1. . . . N'-K5! Then, of course, other moves come into consideration."

Another kind of example is the protocol (M5; B-R7ch), where de Groot observes (p. 222) that "only at the very last does the subject decide on a calm move, even then reluctantly," the shift resulting from M5's ultimate conviction that his expectations about the value of the previously considered move had been excessive.

In a third case cited by de Groot, (G5; B), the subject does not change his intended move (1. . . . R'-N1), but makes the move in the context of a different plan than the one that suggested it initially. "For all that, the subject finds himself in the happy circumstance of not yet having to choose a plan: 1. . . . R'-N1 is playable in both plans . . . and does not spoil anything. There is a way out of the dilemma." (de Groot, p. 225)

These examples illustrate that redefinition may come about (1) because a feature of the situation is noticed that has been overlooked earlier, (2) because initial expectations about the value of a move have been disappointed, or (3) because exploration of a move relates it to outcomes and goals different from those that suggested it. In these situations the dynamic analysis of moves appears more as an information-gathering process than simply a forward search through a branching space. In the next two sections we will give further attention to the respective roles of information gathering and forward search in problem solving in chess.

CHECKMATING COMBINATIONS

An ironic piece of advice that chess players give to novices is: "Always check; it may be Mate!" The advice is ironic because most checking moves are easily refuted and result only in loss of time for the attacking player.

Nevertheless, series of checking moves that end in mate—mating combinations—provide much of the spectacular in chess, the brilliancies comparable to the final smashing cavalry charge of an (eighteenth-century) army that has first moved into position. Some of the recorded mating combinations are as many as eight or more moves deep (that is, sixteen plies), and these give rise to much of the mythology about the mnemonic and visualizing powers of grandmasters. Mating combinations are of especial interest in testing the limits of the concept of search, which is central to the theory of chess play being developed here. For mating combinations seem to require more search than is possible by the human with his limited processing abilities (Simon and Simon, 1962).

MATER

We shall describe here a mating combinations program (MATER) competent to discover many such combinations, including some of the more spectacular in chess history. MATER is a forward-search program built around two basic ideas:

(1) to generate only checking moves, and (2) to abandon a line of analysis as disadvantageous if it allows the opponent more than a very few (more than four, say)
legal replies. In addition to these two principles, MATER incorporates a few
important rules that determine the order in which the analysis tree will be explored.
The program is remarkably powerful in finding mating combinations, some involving sacrifices of Queens and other major pieces, and it accomplishes this with very
modest amounts of exploration (Baylor and Simon, 1965).

Mobility—more specifically, restricting the opponent's mobility—lies at the
heart of MATER. First, checkmate is itself a matter of mobility. The opponent is
checkmated when (1) his King is under attack; (2) he has no legal move, of the King
or other piece, that removes the King from attack. This means in particular that
all the squares adjacent to the King—to which he might consider moving—are
either blocked by his own pieces or under enemy attack. Thus, the checkmated
King is under attack *and* immobile.

Second, mobility is at the basis of the move generator in MATER. A checking
move, attacking the King, must be dealt with at once by a reply that relieves the
attack. Hence, checking limits severely the moves available to the opponent.
MATER generates checking moves, and all legal replies to each checking move.
(The reason for generating all legal replies will be explained presently.) Those checking moves that tend to restrict the opponent's mobility most severely—double
checks and discovered checks—are considered first.

Third, mobility is the main criterion for determining along which branches
of the search tree MATER will pursue its search. Of all the moves that have not
yet been evaluated, the one allowing the opponent the fewest replies is selected
next for exploration. A move that permits more than four replies is rejected out of
hand as unlikely to lead to checkmate.

Although MATER was written as a specialized program, taking advantage
of the various simplifications that were available, it can easily be viewed as a

FIGURE 13.3
program for MATER

base-moves:	checking moves
	with $\leq$ 4 replies
	ordered by number of replies (fewest first)
	subordered by double checks, no recaptures, others
analysis-moves:	own: same as base-moves
	opponent: all legal moves
	ordered by captures, K-moves, interpositions, others
	captures ordered by value of attacker, value of defender
width-termination:	none
depth-termination:	none
static-value:	own position:
	if no legal replies: *mate*
	if no checking moves: *no-mate*
adjusted-value:	best-value

version of the prototypic chess program used in Chapter 11 (Figure 11.2, page 670) to describe all of the regular chess programs that played full games. Figure 13.3 shows the specification of the missing routines in the same way as was used for the programs in Chapter 11 (e.g., compare Figure 11.5, page 676, which specifies the Bernstein program). The base-moves considered are all checking moves. These are produced in the order of the number of replies, the moves with fewest replies being produced first. Within this ordering double checks come first, then checks with no replies that recapture, then the rest in the order in which they happen to be generated. The list is cut off at moves with more than four replies.

For analysis, the moves of the attacking side are the same as the base-moves. All legal moves are considered for the defender. Those are considered first which are likely to foil a mating threat, so as to terminate fruitless exploration as quickly as possible.

The static-values are simply *mate* or *no-mate*. These are assigned in the attacker's position only. A position is assigned mate when there is a move to which there are no legal replies by the opponent. It is assigned no-mate when there are no base-moves—i.e., when the opponent cannot be checked with a move that restricts him to four or fewer replies.

With the forcing character of the attacker's moves, there is no need for separate limitations on the width or depth of search. Consequently, width-termination and depth-termination are simply absent from the program.

Since MATER is searching for a strategy that will decide the game irrespective of what the opponent does, it needs no static-evaluation other than mate and no-mate. Since the game is not going to continue if the search is successful, piece values and specific criteria like center-control have no significance. MATER will attempt sacrifices unhesitatingly if they permit continuing checks of the opponent's King. If MATER does not find a checkmating strategy, it simply halts—presumably shifting responsibility to some other (unspecified) program to suggest a move.

The program we have described would behave like MATER, with one exception. In MATER the tree of moves is retained via a web of associations that always gives access to the predecessors and successors that have been generated to any given move. MATER maintains a subproblem list identical in function to that described for LT in Chapter 4, which orders all moves on the entire tree by the number of replies (from fewest replies to most). MATER takes as its next move for analysis the one with the fewest replies, no matter where it is found on the tree.

When it selects a move from its subproblem list for analysis, MATER has to create the position corresponding to that move. It can do this via the tree of moves by finding out how the position of the new move differs from the current position. Jumping around the tree of moves in this manner extracts a price in additional processing, for the board position must be changed continually. However, the gain derived from growing the search tree from the most propitious node (the node at which the defender's choice is most restricted) is worth the extra housekeeping.

The program of Figure 13.3, like all those based on the prototype program, has basically a depth-first search strategy. It generates the same moves as MATER, but in a different order. However, owing to the alpha-beta cutoffs, the final trees might be very different, since MATER might establish good cutoffs earlier. If there were alternative mating sequences, the two versions could actually end up proposing different mates—though of course, they would be functionally equivalent.

As we have seen, humans do not employ the subproblem-list organization used by MATER, for the processing and memory requirements imposed by that organization are too severe. However, we have seen also that humans do not adopt a depth-first organization. Progressive deepening, the strategy they do use, involving a frequent return to old positions via reconstruction from the base position, can be seen as an attempt to move toward an organization having the freedom of the subproblem list, but consistent with the processing limitations of the human.

The Task Environment for Checkmating

What can we say about the task environment in which MATER operates? In the chapter on mating attacks in a standard work, Fine's *Middle Game in Chess* (1952, pp. 19–103), 129 positions are considered. In 51 of these 129 positions, checkmate can be forced by sequences of checking moves. In five other positions, which we will discuss later, the checking moves must be preceded by a move of a class known as one-move mating threats. In the remaining 73 positions, checkmate can be averted through a sacrifice of material by the defender, or the mate is not forced, as that term is defined by the MATER program.

It is only of slight interest to know that chess positions exist in which checkmate can be enforced by a series of checking moves. The matter becomes more interesting when some further questions are answered. First, are these positions unusual or pathological, or do they actually arise in play? The answer is that they arise quite frequently in tournament games, although relatively rarely nowadays in games between grandmasters of approximately equal strength. Second, do features of the position exist that signal the likelihood of a checkmating combination, or must the combination be discovered by "luck"? The answer is that reasonably reliable cues are almost always present. It is worthwhile to look for a checkmating combination when the opponent's King is exposed, or could be exposed by a capture, and when one's own pieces are quite mobile, while the opponent's are constricted. Even a rough measure of relative mobility would usually suffice as a signal.

Thus, in the chess task environment, situations arise with reasonable frequency in which checkmate can be enforced and in which this possibility is signaled by vulnerability of the opponent's King, combined with superior mobility. This raises the final question: is the structure of the task environment such that the checkmate can be discovered with a reasonable amount of search? The answer is that it often can. To make the answer more precise, we must define some measures of amount of search.

Consider the search tree of positions generated by a program attempting to discover a checkmate. Figure 13.4 is an example of such a tree from the position shown in Figure 13.5. We can call the number of positions on the tree that are actually examined the *size of the exploration tree*. The example shows an exploration tree of size 16. In general, however, more moves are seen than positions are

FIGURE 13.4
exploration tree for MATER I in Fine's position 36

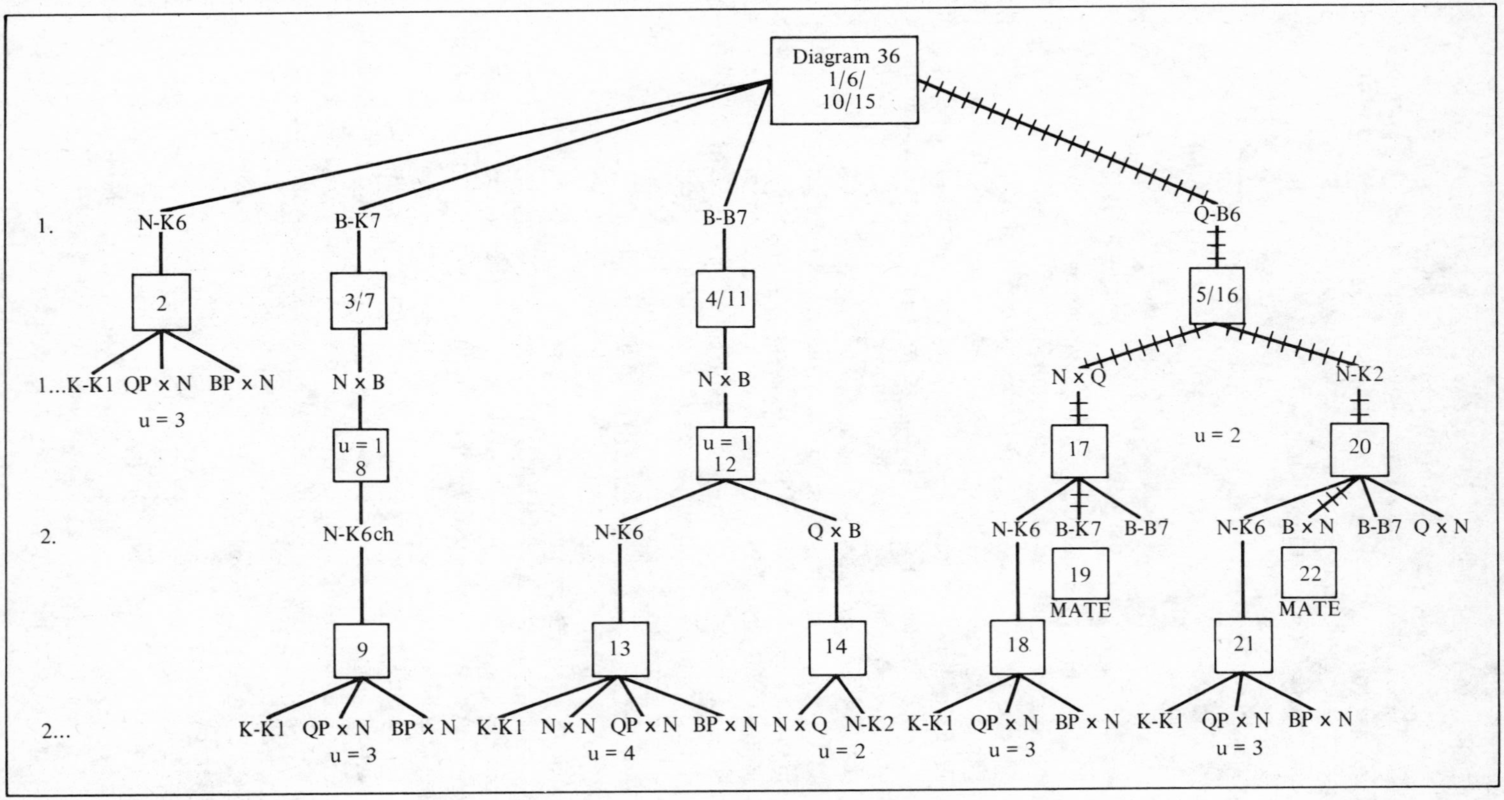

FIGURE 13.5

mating position (Fine's position 36)

Black

White

investigated—some moves put on the try-list remain unexplored, such as the replies to 1. N-K6ch in the example. The moves seen—uninvestigated and investigated—may be called the *discovery tree*. In Figure 13.4 the discovery tree is of size 36 (14 checks and 22 replies).

A subpart of the exploration tree is the *verification tree:* the branches that must be exhibited to prove that the combination is effective. It consists of the positions resulting from the single best move at each node for the attacker, and every legal move at each node for the defender. The verification tree is exactly analogous to the path leading to a theorem (i.e., a proof path) in the Logic Theorist. It is a tree in chess, instead of a single path, because all alternatives permitted to the defender must be tested. (In game-theory terms, the verification

767

TABLE 13.1

MATER's performance on 43 positions from Fine

N (POSITIONS)	DEPTH	Average number of Moves				
		V-SIZE	D-SIZE	$\dfrac{\text{V-SIZE}}{\text{DEPTH}}$	$\dfrac{\text{D-SIZE}}{\text{DEPTH}}$	$\dfrac{\text{D-SIZE}}{\text{V-SIZE}}$
15	2	3.5	15.5	1.8	7.8	4.4
11	3	5.4	24.6	1.8	8.2	4.6
14	4	9.9	61.5	2.5	15.4	6.2
2	5	11.0	56.0	2.2	11.2	5.1
1	8	17.0	108.0	2.1	13.5	6.4
43						

V-size = size of the verification tree, in moves
D-size = size of the discovery tree, in moves

tree is a strategy.) In the example of Figure 13.4, the branches of the verification tree are crosshatched. It includes five moves and six positions.

Achievement of MATER

MATER, set to work with no limit on computing effort, solves combinations that consist of uninterrupted series of checking moves provided that the defender has no more than four legal replies at any node in the verification tree. In the 51 mating positions in Fine that meet these conditions, MATER found solutions to 43. The program missed one combination entirely by failing to move a pawn that gave a discovered check—a program bug. It exhausted its available space in memory before finding the other seven combinations. Too much search was required, in these seven positions, to find the verification tree.

Table 13.1 shows certain measures of search behavior for the 43 positions in which MATER was successful: the depth of search to checkmate, the mean size of the verification tree necessary to prove the combination (V-size), measured in moves, and the mean size of the discovery tree generated in searching for mate (D-size), measured in moves.

This table characterizes the task environment of chess in mating-combination situations. It shows a fairly close correlation between depth and V-size—there are about two moves in the tree for each move (two plies) in depth. Thus, the tree varies more or less linearly, and not exponentially, with depth. This property of mating situations makes deep analysis possible. The D-size also grows only slightly more than proportionately to depth, and D-size maintains a nearly constant ratio to V-size of around five moves to one.

As a result of these characteristics of the task environment, MATER found quite deep combinations with a very modest amount of search—a fifteen-ply combination requiring a discovery tree of only 108 moves. An exponentially growing tree of depth fifteen, with only two branches per node, would have some 32,000 moves. Thus, in these forcing situations, the simple selective heuristics of MATER achieve a radical pruning of the tree.

A key heuristic in MATER is always to examine first those moves that permit the opponent the fewest replies. Variants of MATER that gave lower priority to this heuristic in determining what to explore next (in particular, depth-first exploration) were much less successful in finding mating combinations than the version we have described. The fewest-replies heuristic has a dual significance: on the one hand, it allows the opponent the fewest alternatives to find a way out of the mating net. On the other hand, it holds down the branchiness of the search tree, facilitating the discovery of the checkmate with relatively little search. In this task environment it is not possible to disentangle the contributions of these two factors to the heuristic's power.

The fewest-replies and checking-move heuristics illustrate the concept of holding the initiative in a competitive situation. Holding the initiative consists in taking actions that are so forceful that the opponent must devote all his effort to replying to them—to solving the problems they create. The side holding the initiative is able to determine the areas, so to speak, in which the struggle is waged, and the issues on which it will be decided.

An Extended Mating-Combinations Program

Additional insight into the structure of the task environment, and the nature of the relevant features in it, is provided by MATER II, an improved checkmating program developed by G. Baylor (1966). The aim of MATER II was to broaden the class of moves that could be considered in a mating combination beyond those that immediately place the King in check. The problem is to find ways of defining moves that are sufficiently threatening to lead rapidly into the kind of constrained checking situation handled by a MATER I type of organization. Two schemes were tried to obtain threatening moves. In one, candidate base-moves were obtained from moves generated at later plies from other bases, were tested to see if they threatened mate in one move, and if so, were tried as base-moves. In the second scheme, the control of the squares surrounding the King was assessed, and moves were sought that acquired sufficient control of these squares to present a threat of mate.

Figure 13.6 shows an organization corresponding to MATER II for the threatened-mate-in-one scheme. Again, we have departed from the actual program organization to stay within the schema of the prototypic chess program. The executive, shown at the top of the figure, has three parts. First, it uses a program called *search*, which is a slight modification of MATER I, to carry out an information-gathering exploration. (It may, of course, find the mate during this first search.) The entire tree of this search is retained, so that the executive, in its second phase, can scan it for candidate moves that might threaten mate in one. The test for the candidate is given at the bottom of the figure. It consists in making the move, then making a no-move for the opponent, and then seeing if there exists a move that mates. By this means, the executive builds up a list of moves that threaten mate in one. In the third phase, the executive again employs search, but this time with the mate-in-one threats as its base-moves.

MATER II, tested on all five positions from Fine that require an initial mating threat followed by checking moves, found the five checkmates. As examples, in two of these positions the search tree, eight plies deep in each case, contained 37 and 38 moves, respectively. Four out of 54 legal initial moves were considered

FIGURE 13.6
program for MATER II

Executive(position)
1. Search(base-moves = analysis-moves) (⟹ search-tree),
       if value = mate stop and report 'mate';
2. generate own-moves of search-tree (⟹ candidate-move):
3.   test-mate-in-one(candidate-move, position),
             if fail continue generating;
4.   put candidate-move on one-move-mate-threat-list, continue generating;
5. Search(base-moves = generate one-move-mate-threat-list), stop and report value

Search: prototypic-chess-program with:
    base-moves: parameter
    analysis-moves: own: all checking moves
                               with ≤ 4 replies
                               all replies are captures or interpositions
                               or a single reply of a K-move
                               ordered by number of replies (fewest first)
                         opponent: all legal moves
                               if in check ordered by captures, K-moves, interpositions,
                                 others
                               if one-move-mate-threat ordered by:
                                 captures, defense of mating square, K-moves, inter-
                                 positions, others
                               if in check ordered by:
                                 captures, K-moves, interpositions, others
    width-termination: none
    depth-termination: none
    static-value: own position:
                               if no legal replies: *mate*
                               if no checking moves: *no-mate*
    adjusted-value: best-value

test-mate-in-one(move, position):
1. make move on position (⟹ next-position),
       if fail stop and report 'fail';
2. make no-move on next-position (⟹ test-position);
3. generate legal-moves(test-position):
4.   test-mate(legal-move, test-position),
             if false continue generating,
             if true stop test-mate-in-one and report 'true'.,
         stop and report 'false'.

in the one case, 3 out of 37 legal initial moves in the second. Thus, the search trees of MATER II were of the same general size as those of MATER I.

The combination of the first and second heuristics of MATER II, described above, are of particular interest as another departure (along with the no-move) from limiting search to the tree of legal continuations. The high-priority search of step 1 above, if it does not lead to checkmate, is pursued for the purpose of gathering information about possible strong moves that are not checking moves. Chess players would call such searches *sample variations*. The moves thus discovered may or may not be legal moves in the initial position. As we have seen, before they are added to the list of moves to be tried, they are subjected to two tests: whether they are legal, and whether they constitute one-move mating threats.

Against the background of the chess programs in Chapter 11, MATER I and II permit one to delineate more clearly the role of search. Most important is that forward search remains the central mechanism in finding mating combinations. Owing to the structure of the task environment—plus some search heuristics that exploit this structure—the search space is more linear than exponential in the vicinity of a successful combination. Thus, to make a pun, search goes a long ways toward being a sufficient discovery mechanism.

But insofar as search must be highly selective, strong mechanisms must exist for noticing features of the board and building specialized strategies of search dependent on these features. In MATER II especially, where the program was extended beyond the limits of the basic general search heuristics (by accepting some nonchecking moves), such noticing programs provide the extra selectivity to make search successful. This is one of the few chess programs that extract information from one part of the search tree and apply it to another.

Some Evidence from Human Protocols

The analysis so far has been entirely task-oriented. Since in the main it reaffirms the general structure of chess programs, both machine and human, examined throughout the section, one can have some confidence that MATER I and II provide a first approximation to human behavior in finding mating combinations. We do have two protocols, gathered by G. Baylor (1965), for a mating position (Figure 13.4), in which a checkmating combination exists, which cast some light on the nature of this approximation.

The position in Figure 13.7 arose in a casual game among masters (Fine, 1952, p. 67). Checkmates are threatened on KN7 and KR7, although the former is protected by Black's Queen, Rook, and King, and the latter by the King. The winning move is N-N5. How does White discover it? One possible route is the following tree:

1. N-N5, $Q' \times Q$; 2. $N \times P'$mate.
     ... R'-N2; 2. R-Q8, R'-N1;   3. $Q \times RP'$mate.
                   ... other;   3. $Q \times R'$mate.
     ... Q'-N2; 2. $P \times Q'$ch, $R' \times P$; 3. R-Q8ch, R'-N1; 4. $Q \times RP'$mate.
     ... other;   2. $Q \times RP'$mate.

FIGURE 13.7

mating position (Fine's position 97)

Black

White

In fact, White can choose 1. N-N5 without seeing the combination to the end, since this move prevents 1. . . . Q'×Q, hence adds an attacking piece without loss of material.

The original mating program, MATER I, would not discover this checkmate, since N-N5 is not a checking move. MATER II first explores the checks, Q-N7 and Q×RP'. (See Figure 13.8 for MATER II's PBG.) The second of these leads to 1. . . . K'×Q, 2. N-N5ch. Although neither line leads to a checkmate, the move N-N5 has been discovered and placed on a special list. Now this move is tested to see if it threatens mate in one. It does (1. N-N5, no-move, 2. Q×RP'mate). Therefore, 1. N-N5 is analyzed, and is shown to force a checkmate by a series of checking moves.

FIGURE 13.8

problem behavior graph for MATER II in Fine's position 97

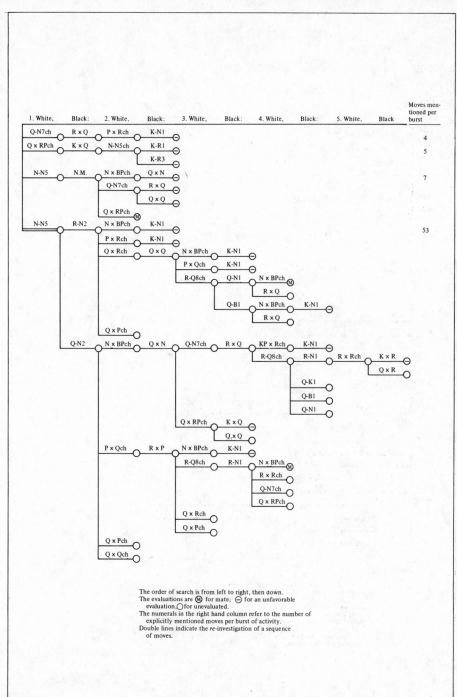

The order of search is from left to right, then down.
The evaluations are Ⓜ for mate, ⊖ for an unfavorable
   evaluation,〇for unevaluated.
The numerals in the right hand column refer to the number of
   explicitly mentioned moves per burst of activity.
Double lines indicate the *re*-investigation of a sequence
   of moves.

FIGURE 13.9

problem behavior graph for subject WT in Fine's position 97

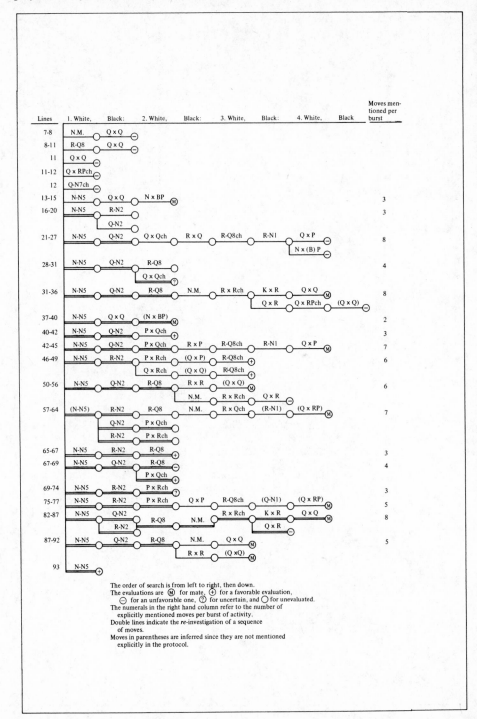

The order of search is from left to right, then down.
The evaluations are Ⓜ for mate, ⊕ for a favorable evaluation,
  ⊖ for an unfavorable one, ⑦ for uncertain, and ◯ for unevaluated.
The numerals in the right hand column refer to the number of
  explicitly mentioned moves per burst of activity.
Double lines indicate the *re*-investigation of a sequence
  of moves.
Moves in parentheses are inferred since they are not mentioned
  explicitly in the protocol.

The PBG of one of the two experts is shown in Figure 13.9. (The protocol of the other expert was less explicit.) Both experts found the combination, and did so by noticing N-N5. Neither the PBG shown in the figure nor the protocols of the two experts make explicit exactly how the move was noticed, but such evidence as there is suggests that N-N5 was evoked in both cases by means-ends analysis. In the PBG, for example, the player notes near the outset the possibility of a mate by Q×RP'. But since the pawn is defended by the Black King, the Queen's attack must be supported, and N-N5 provides that support. A somewhat similar line of reasoning appears in the other protocol, though less explicitly.

Although this process, like the one used by MATER II, makes the discovery of N-N5 depend on noticing Q×RP', there is an important difference. MATER II discovered N-N5, not as a preparation for Q×RP'—a means to make that move feasible—but as a move to continue the attack after Q×RP'. The function of the move at the time of its discovery is therefore different in the two cases. What is common between the human players and MATER II is that N-N5, once discovered, is explored in a new context—i.e., as a move that might initiate a mating combination. In this exploration, it is no longer monolithically connected, either as predecessor or successor, with Q×RP'.

Comparison of the two PBG's of Figure 13.8 and 13.9 reveals the characteristic difference in search strategy between chess programs and humans that is familiar from our earlier discussion. While MATER II employs a modified depth-first strategy, the human PBG reveals the usual progressive-deepening strategy.

We have now arrived at an emphasis on the problems of noticing selected features of the board, and linking them to actions via means-ends chains of reasoning. It is worthwhile to focus on the noticing process directly, which we do in the next (and last) section of the chapter.

PERCEPTUAL ASPECTS OF CHESS ANALYSIS

A large part of our discussion of the chess-playing protocols has been concerned with the tree of move continuations that the players construct in the course of their examination of consequences. Because of the role that this tree plays in the protocols, chess thinking has a working-forward flavor. At several points, however, we have seen another important element intruding into the picture. We have several times alluded to the role played by *noticing* in chess thinking. The players notice a small number of considerable moves, and do not notice (or at least do not mention noticing) the large number of remaining legal moves. As we saw in the last section, they also sometimes notice new moves or features in the course of their investigations, which then become the basis for additional explorations.

Moreover, during the first moments—for example, 15 seconds more or less—during which he is exposed to a new position, a skilled human player does not appear to engage in a search of move sequences. Instead, he appears to be occupied with perceiving the essential properties of the position—embodying some of the concepts mentioned earlier—which will suggest possible moves to him and help him to anticipate their consequences. He appears to be gathering information about the problem, rather than seeking an actual solution. The episode E1 of S2 (p. 739) is a good illustration of initial orienting behavior. De Groot (1965, p. 396) observes:

> From the analysis of protocols and from the additional experiments on chess perception we have learned that this is a first Phase of problem formation.
>
> The process in the first Phase is characterized by a perceptive and receptive, rather than actively organizing, attitude on the part of the subject. . . .

Subsequent research by de Groot (1966) and his students (e.g., Jongman, 1968), provides additional support for this conclusion. To understand thinking in chess, we must take account of perceptual processes as well as those that would usually be regarded as conceptual or cognitive. As we go along, we will mention additional phenomena that point in this same direction.

Perceptual and noticing mechanisms are essential constituents of chess programs, also, although we have not stressed them so much, concentrating instead on the nature of the search mechanisms. Consider MATER, for example. Among its subroutines that are employed in the service of higher-level routines for generating and testing moves is one that finds the direction between two given squares (notices, e.g., whether they lie on the same file); a second routine notices whether there is a piece on the rank, file, or diagonal between two given squares; another, whether a specified piece is under attack; another, whether a given square is under attack; another, whether a given square is defended; and so on.

All of these subprocesses operate directly in terms of the relations on the board—e.g., they have the knowledge embedded in them to look at the directions impinging on a square to determine whether the piece there is under attack.[3]

Turning next to the evidence on the initial perceptual processes of chess players, our best data come from records of eye movements gathered by de Groot and his associates (1966), Tichomirov and Poznyanskaya (1966), and Winikoff (1967). Both the problems of calibrating the instruments and the nature of the human visual apparatus make it impossible to establish with assurance the precise square to which a subject is attending at any given moment. A single fixation enables him to discover what pieces are standing on several neighboring squares. Peripheral vision also permits some information to be gathered about the status of even more distant squares. Indeed, such peripheral information is necessary to direct the eyes to new fixation points if the eye movements are to be other than random. Records of eye movements can only show the succession of fixations; they cannot show precisely what information is being processed at each moment. (Recall Chapter 7, page 312.)

---

[3] In general, plausible move generators contain such direct knowledge. Sometimes it can be pushed off—e.g., in the Kotok and Greenblatt move generators—by taking a generator over a larger class (i.e., all legal moves) and testing each move so obtained by a plausibility-evaluator. Here the direct knowledge lies in part in the legal move generator (though it too could conceivably be pushed off another level by generating all syntactically correct move data-structures and testing them for legality) and in part in the evaluator. The latter, of course, must be able to notice features of the situation directly.

The eye-movement data show rather consistently that the fixations of subjects move from one square of the board to another at a maximum rate of about four fixations per second. It appears that at each point of fixation the subject is acquiring information about the location of pieces at or near the point of fixation, together with information about pieces in peripheral vision (within, e.g., 2° of arc) that bear a significant chess relation (*attack*, *defend*, *block*, *shield*) to the piece at the fixation point.

To elucidate this hypothesis about the eye movements, and its implications, Simon and Barenfeld (1969) organized the noticing processes already contained in MATER into a new chess-perception program, PERCEIVER, that has some ability to simulate the initial sequences of the eye movements of human subjects. Carrying out the simulation requires stronger assumptions than simply that the human subjects are perceiving the relations among pieces on the board. It is necessary, in addition, to posit processes that will generate these perceptions in some particular sequence. The two basic assumptions incorporated in PERCEIVER are:

1. *Concepts.* The information being gathered during the perceptual phase is information about relations between pieces, or between pieces and squares. When the eyes are fixated on a particular piece, it is possible to detect neighboring pieces (a) that defend the piece in question, (b) that attack it, (c) that are defended by it, and (d) that are attacked by it. (Obviously, other relations could be added to the list.)

2. *Attention.* When attention is fixed on piece A, and one of the four relations mentioned above is noticed, connecting A with another piece, B, attention may return to A without change in fixation. If it does not, B will be fixated next.

Additional assumptions are needed to determine the detail of the program— including a process to specify an initial point of fixation (Jongman, 1968, pp. 131–137)—but the qualitative behavior of the program is not especially sensitive to variations in the detail of its structure.

Illustrative Comparison With Eye-Movement Data

Figure 13.10 shows the chess position used by Tichomirov and Poznyanskaya (1966, p. 5) in one of their experiments. Figure 13.11 shows the sequence of 20 fixations observed in an expert player during his first five seconds of looking at this position. Figure 13.12 shows the sequence of 15 simulated fixations produced by PERCEIVER in this position. On Figures 13.11 and 13.12, the ten squares are shaded that would probably be regarded by any good chess player as critical to understanding this position.

It is obvious that both the human expert (Figure 13.11) and PERCEIVER (Figure 13.12) were mainly occupied with the relations among pieces on these squares. By construction, all of PERCEIVER's fixations fell on squares occupied by pieces. Six of the human players' fixations fell on unoccupied squares. Nevertheless, the figures exhibit considerable concordance between the objects of

FIGURE 13.10

chess position used by Tichomirov and Poznyanskaya (1966)
(Black to play)

attention in the two cases. (For greater detail, see Simon and Barenfeld, 1969.) PERCEIVER's focus of attention on these particular relations does not rest on subtle or complex evaluations of what is important on the board. If attention follows a train of associations in such a web of relations, it will simply be brought back repeatedly to the points in the web where the density of relations is highest.

Reproductions of Positions from Memory

The example shows that a very simple program, using perceptual processes of the kinds already employed in computer chess programs, moves its attention about the board in a way that resembles the eye movements of a human subject.

FIGURE 13.11

**expert's eye movements for the first 5 seconds in position of FIGURE 13.10
[from Tichomirov and Poznyanskaya (1966)]**

Black

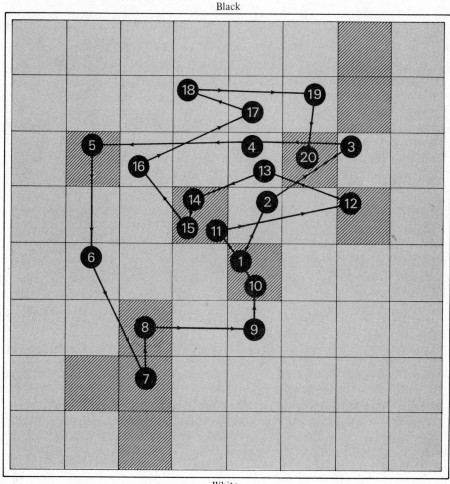

White

The next question is whether the information that can be extracted from a position by such perceptual processes is adequate to account for the ability of chess masters, already noted, to reproduce chess positions after brief exposure (five or ten seconds) to sight of the board. Notice that there are two parts to the human performance: (1) extracting from the chessboard the totality of information about the chess position, and (2) retaining all of this information long enough to reproduce the position from memory. After summarizing the experimental results, we must take up the question of retention, which is not elucidated by the PERCEIVER program.

Experimental Results. In a series of striking experiments, it has been shown that the ability of a subject to reproduce a chess position after a few seconds' exposure depends sensitively on (1) the subject's chess proficiency and (2) the meaningfulness of the position (de Groot, 1965, pp. 321–334; de Groot, 1966, pp. 35–48; Jongman, 1968, pp. 35–43). Meaningfulness can be manipulated by contrasting

FIGURE 13.12

eye movements simulated by PERCEIVER in position of FIGURE 13.10

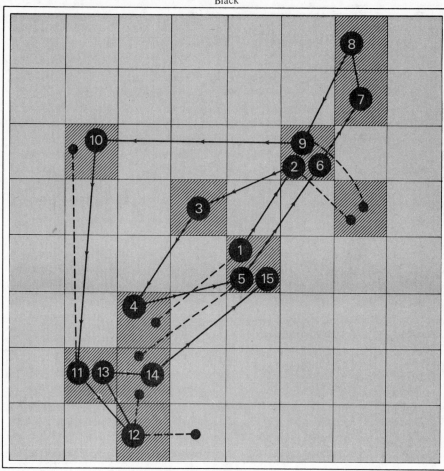

Black

White

the reproduction of positions from actual games (not known to the subjects) with the reproduction of boards having the same pieces as the game positions, but placed at random.

In summary, de Groot and Jongman report that (1) after five seconds' sight of the board, a grandmaster or a master can reproduce a chess position almost without error; (2) the weaker the player below this level, the more errors he makes—very weak players can place only half a dozen pieces correctly; and (3) with random boards, the performances of grandmasters and masters sink to the level of weak players, while the performance of weak players does not deteriorate further.

Any explanation of chess perception must be consistent both with these data and with what is known about STM and LTM. It is rather well established that (a) "seven plus-or-minus two" *chunks* can be held in STM; (b) probably not more than one chunk can be transferred from STM to LTM for each five seconds. A chunk here means any configuration that is familiar to the subject and can be recognized by him. (For a discussion of these facts, together with references, see Gregg and Simon, 1967, and also the discussion of Chapter 14.) If these two facts are accepted, then the information that allows a subject to reproduce a chess position after only five seconds' exposure must be mainly in STM. Further, if the position is reproduced perfectly, or nearly so, it must somehow be encoded as not more than, at best, nine chunks of information.

Proposed Explanation. An explanation of these phenomena is provided by combining the mechanisms of PERCEIVER with the discriminating and chunking mechanisms proposed by Feigenbaum in his EPAM (for Elementary Perceiver and Memorizer) theory for verbal learning (Feigenbaum, 1961; Simon and Feigenbaum, 1964; Gregg and Simon, 1967). We discussed the main outlines of EPAM in Chapter 2 (pages 34–36). In EPAM's discrimination processes, stimuli, or portions of stimuli that are found to match in their characteristics with symbols stored previously in memory, are recognized and replaced in STM by the symbol that designates them. Thus, if a configuration of relations in a stimulus is recognized as familiar, the whole configuration, consisting of as many parts as there are perceived relations, can be represented in memory by a single symbol. Hence, the STM, limited to holding a specified maximum number of symbols, can retain many more relations if they occur in familiar configurations than if they must be held independently in memory.

The familiar constellations referred to here are based upon the chess concepts discussed earlier in the chapter. If a player is familiar with the concept of Knight-pinned-on-Queen-by-Bishop, then, on scanning the board under consideration here, he can recognize the configuration embodying that concept, and needs only a single symbol to store it in short-term memory. The position of Figure 13.10 also embodies the concept of short-castled Black King (King on N1, Rook on B1), the concept of normally developed King's Knight (Knight on KB3), and the concept of fianchettoed King's Bishop (Bishop on KN2, with pawns on B2, N3, and R2). The player familiar with these concepts can designate each by a single symbol, hence each constitutes a single chunk in STM, and the four concepts together— four chunks—describe the positions of nine men.

But a more experienced player will likely also be familiar with the whole constellation, consisting of the conjunction of these four concepts. For him, the entire constellation of nine men can be designated by a single symbol, hence constitutes only one chunk in STM.

According to this explanation, clusters of related pieces in a position are recognized by chess masters as familiar constellations; hence each cluster is stored as a single symbol. Less skilled players have to describe the board as a larger number of simpler chunks—hence cannot hold all of the information required to reproduce the board in short-term memory. When the same number of pieces is arranged on the board at random, few of the resulting configurations are familiar even to grandmasters. They then need more symbols to describe the position than can be held simultaneously in short-term memory, hence they perform as poorly as weaker players.

The quantities demanded by this explanation are of the right order of magnitude. In the years required to attain mastership in chess, a player might be expected to acquire a "vocabulary" of familiar subpatterns comparable to the visual word-recognition vocabularies of persons able to read English, or the Kanji (or Kanji-pair) recognition vocabularies of persons reading Chinese or Japanese. These vocabularies are of the order of 10^4–10^5 symbols. Hence, sequences of seven such symbols could be used to encode 10^{28}–10^{35} [i.e., $(10^4)^7$–$(10^5)^7$] different total board positions.[4]

The number of chess positions that could arise from sequences of "reasonable" moves has been estimated to lie in the range from 10^{10} to 10^{15} (see Jongman, 1968, p. 33). This is well within the estimated vocabulary limits. That is, a vocabulary of the postulated size is sufficient to supply distinct seven-symbol descriptions to distinct chess positions.

Simon and Barenfeld (1969) suggest one possible encoding of the position of Figure 13.10 into eight symbols, representing eight constellations that would be familiar to many expert chess players:

1. The two center pawns, the two Knights and Queen attacking and defending them, and the blocking White pawn on K3 (six men).
2. Black's Knight, the Bishop attacking it, and Queen and Bishop defending it, and the two center pawns on which it bears (six men).
3. White's Queen's Knight's pawn, the Queen attacking it, the King and Queen defending it, and the Knight it defends (five men).
4. White's castled position on the Queen's side: two pawns, King, and Rook (four men).
5. White's Bishop on K2 (one man).
6. White's King's side: Rook and three pawns (four men).
7. Black's castled position: King, Rook, Bishop, Knight, and three pawns (seven men).
8. Black's Queen's side: Rook, Bishop, and three pawns, including the typically advanced Bishop's pawn (five men).

Obviously, there are different ways in which the relations on any given chessboard could be organized into familiar chunks, and different players of comparable skill may characterize and symbolize the board in somewhat different ways. What the analysis here shows is that the information known to be extracted by masters and grandmasters in their first perception of chess positions is consistent, in quantity and quality, with a hypothesized mechanism that (1) notices relations, in the manner of PERCEIVER, then (2) recognizes and chunks configurations of such relations, in the manner of earlier theories of human memory, such as EPAM. No significant new mechanisms seem to be necessary to account for the data on chess perception.

[4] A more conservative estimate would take account of the fact, to be mentioned presently, that the configurations in the corners of the board are highly stereotyped, hence perhaps only about 10^2 in number. The number of different positions made up of four such subpatterns and three other, less stereotyped, subpatterns describing the center of the board would be about $(10^2)^4 \cdot (10^5)^3 = 10^{23}$, which still provides sufficient variety.

In the data we have examined in this chapter, the grandmasters give clear evidence in their evaluations of seeing continuations that they do not mention explicitly. In general (but note the exception of subject G5), the protocols of the grandmasters are less full and explicit than those of the weaker players. This could be due to one of three causes: (1) the grandmasters might search more rapidly than other people, (2) they could simply report less, or (3) they could see the consequences of continuations without as much search as less talented players.

We have no evidence to show which of these explanations is correct. The most likely possibility is that the chessmaster uses his richer vocabulary of concepts to evoke condensed analysis programs that can be restricted to a small number of branches (evaluating exchanges to a dead position) and can abstract the dynamic analysis to avoid updating the position fully after each move (e.g., "counting out" exchanges without examining side effects or permutations of the order of exchange).

Thus, the chessmaster's ability to designate large configurations of relations enables him to evaluate certain situations without much detailed sequential calculation. With each familiar feature there can be stored in memory appropriate move generators and dynamic analysis programs. Thus, in position A, detection of Black's just-defended Knight on his KB3 can evoke in a chessmaster the moves that will attack this Knight—Q-B3, N-N4—which are among the moves most prominently mentioned after 1. $B \times N'/5$, $P' \times B$. Similarily, 1. . . . $P' \times B$, a capture by a pawn, leads the master to see that the King's file is now open, and evokes KR-K1, the other prominent "positional" move the masters considered. (Any capture involving a pawn may change the list of open files.)

This pattern of symptom-remedy has by now become familiar to us in a variety of contexts. It is means-ends analysis, for the moves generated are relevant to "remedying" the feature that serves as symptom. But the means-ends analysis is based on past experience, not present reasoning, hence it does not produce the explicit goal structures that are so visible in the operation of GPS. It is as "automatic" as "A headache? Take aspirin." It can be accomplished by a simple associational mechanism connected to a mechanism for recognizing features—i.e., by a production system.

CONCLUSION

In this chapter we have looked at a variety of data on human behavior in chess-playing situations. We first summarized the general picture of chess thinking the comes from de Groot's study, finding that it corroborates the more detailed, but narrow, analysis of our subject, S2. Then we compared in some detail the behavior of de Groot's grandmasters on position A. This permitted us to distinguish to some extent the demands of the particular task environment (position A) and to see what aspects of our subject's behavior could be explained by the particularities of the task environment. Such explanations had to be tempered by the role played by the sociology of chess, whereby the task is really defined only in comparison with other players' abilities to analyze the chess situation.

The rest of the chapter was devoted to pushing into corners of the chess situation not adequately explored by our detailed study. The first of these was the phenomenon of redefinition of the situation, which arises in positions that are more strategic in character than position A. The second was the mating-combination task, which permitted us to test whether search of the kind we had been considering in the first two chapters was sufficient for a task that appeared to require enormous searches. We found that it did, and we uncovered a few additional search heuristics along the way. Finally, we discussed perceptual and noticing mechanisms and related them to means-ends analysis.

THE THEORY

5

14

THE THEORY
OF
HUMAN PROBLEM SOLVING

In Chapters 5 through 13 we reviewed a considerable body of data that describes the task environments for three problem solving tasks and that provides detailed pictures of the behavior of human subjects when confronted with these tasks. In all this analysis we have remained within an information processing framework. But in other respects we have proceeded quite inductively, developing each theory of behavior largely from close observation of the behavior itself and adapting the theory to differences in task environment and response. It is now time to bring together what we have learned into a general theoretical statement about the processes of human problem solving, the characteristics of the information system that carries out the processes, and the nature of the task environments in which the processes operate.

Let us start with five very general propositions, which are supported by the entire body of analysis in the book and which pose the basic questions that this chapter must answer:

1. Humans, when engaged in problem solving in the kinds of tasks we have considered, are representable as information processing systems.
2. This representation can be carried to great detail with fidelity in any specific instance of person and task.
3. Substantial subject differences exist among programs, which are not simply parametric variations but involve differences of program structure, method, and content.
3. Substantial task differences exist among programs, which also are not simply parametric variations but involve differences of structure and content.
5. The task environment (plus the intelligence of the problem solver) determines to a large extent the behavior of the problem solver, independently of the detailed internal structure of his information processing system.

What theory of human problem solving fits these generalizations? Given the substantial differences among individuals and among tasks, does a single theory of problem solving exist, or only a congeries of separate theories? What is invariant over task and over problem solver that could constitute the basic theory? Further, what determines the aspects that are not invariant? For if we wish to understand the problem solving of many subjects over many tasks, the changed aspects are as important as the invariants. And overshadowing all: what can the theory of human problem solving be, when the shaping influence of the task environment seems to make the specifics of the problem solver's internal structure almost irrelevant?

These questions are not unique to our particular enterprise. In one guise or another they confront all attempts to develop human psychology. Both the specific variation in behavior by individual and by task, and the general predictability of intelligent behavior from the requirements of the task, are pervasive features of human behavior. Many answers to the questions have been proposed: postulating a representative subject, asserting that scientific psychology is only statistical (nomothetic), asserting that only what is common to all humans is scientific, abandoning all contents as too contingent to be of interest, or retreating to learning as the only fundamental topic of a scientific psychology. We propose below a different answer that seems to us both indicated by the studies of this book and supported by much additional evidence as well.

The shape of the theory we propose can be captured by four propositions:

1. A few, and only a few, gross characteristics of the human IPS are invariant over task and problem solver.

2. These characteristics are sufficient to determine that a task environment is represented (in the IPS) as a problem space, and that problem solving takes place in a problem space.
3. The structure of the task environment determines the possible structures of the problem space.
4. The structure of the problem space determines the possible programs that can be used for problem solving.

The main sections of this chapter develop these four propositions: the fundamental characteristics of the IPS; the problem space; the structure of the task environment; and the nature of the programs. Points 3 and 4 above speak only of *possibilities*, so that a fifth section must deal with the determination both of the actual problem space and of the actual program from their respective possibilities.

The evidence and analysis of this book provide various degrees of explication and support for the different parts of the theory. But each part requires description so that the total shape of the proposed theory can be seen. Before we enter on these sections, we sketch the general nature of the argument implied in the four propositions above, and comment on the scope of the theory.

The General Argument

The argument starts from the observation that adaptive devices shape themselves to the environment in which they are embedded. As we discussed thoroughly in Chapter 2, and have illustrated throughout the book, a system that is not flexible enough to meet the demands of its environment is not adaptive. Thus, only some rather general features of the structure of an adaptive IPS can show through to task behavior. In extreme environments, of course, this is not true, for (tautologically) these are environments where adaptation breaks down—and the structure of the IPS does consequently show through. But the environments studied in this book have no such extreme characteristics, at least for humans as intelligent and well educated as our subjects.

What features of an adaptive IPS will show through is not yet derivable a priori. These features have to do chiefly with the kinds of memories available to the IPS as characterized by memory sizes, rates of reading and writing, and accessing modes. It is noteworthy that with general-purpose computers, also, a few gross features of the devices largely determine performance, and these features are again memory sizes, and rates and ways of accessing. This characteristic of computers also arises because the flexibility of the program mediates between the detailed structure of the computer (its detailed order code and timing) and the structure of problems of practical concern (the situations to which it is to be adapted).

The particular memories and processing rates that characterize human beings determine that the problem space is a major invariant of problem solving—that all problem solving occurs in some problem space. The argument, as detailed later in the chapter, though not logically conclusive, has considerable force. IPS's with different characteristics from the human ones might not solve problems in the same way, and might not employ problem spaces to organize their efforts.

Although the IPS dictates that problem solving shall take place in some problem space, the task environment determines the structure of that space. For problem solving can be effective only if significant information about the objective environment is encoded in the problem space, where it can be used by the problem solver. There can be no guarantee, of course, that all the relevant information in the task environment is reflected in the problem space. Thus, the question remains of how the particular problem space used by a problem solver is determined. The studies in this book do not shed much light on the determining mechanisms. They do make it clear, however, that information about the general intelligence of the problem solver plus his knowledge in relevant domains is often sufficient to predict what problem space he will use. Thus, the task environment remains the overwhelming determinant of the problem space.

The question now turns to determining the actual program used by a problem solver. Since the function of the program is to search in the problem space, it must make the decisions necessary to operate in such a space: basically, select operators and evaluate knowledge states. Only that information is available for making these decisions which has been embedded in the problem space after its extraction from the task environment. Thus, the possible programs can be sharply categorized by the kinds of information available.

Again the problem solver selects a particular program out of the possible ones. And, again, the studies of this book do not much illuminate the mechanisms of selection or construction that determine which program will be used. But, as with the problem space, the selection is rather narrow and well structured.

The theory just outlined fits our five initial propositions. It provides much more, of course, in its concrete detail. But it also leaves a number of unfinished issues and poses a number of questions, some new and some simply refurbished. The question of scope is important enough to be taken up now; others will emerge in the ensuing discussion.

The Scope of the Theory

The very first figure we presented in Chapter 1 attempted to summarize the dimensions along which the human system could vary. The present study focused on a small slice from this total space. To quote that chapter (pp. 3-4):

> The present study is concerned with the performance of intelligent adults in our own culture. The tasks discussed are short (half hour), moderately difficult problems of a symbolic nature. The three main tasks we use—chess, symbolic logic, and algebra-like puzzles (called cryptarithmetic puzzles)—typify this class of problems. The study is concerned with the integrated activities that constitute problem solving. It is not centrally concerned with perception, motor skill, or what are called personality variables. The study is concerned primarily with performance, only a little with learning, not at all with development, or differences related to age. Finally, it is concerned with integrated activities, hence deemphasizes the details of processing on the time scale of elementary reactions (that is, half a second or less). Similarly,

long-term integrated activities extending over periods of days or years receive no attention.

Because our empirical study has kept close to the focus so delineated (though, as we noted, it is a focus, not a set of boundaries), the data upon which our theory is based are quite narrow. The arguments from the data are more general, however —especially those based on the relation of task environment to adaptive organism. Hence we believe that the theory we are putting forth is much broader than the specific data on which we are erecting it. Indeed, we have elsewhere used the same general approach to explore broader domains than those of this book,[1] but we have chosen here to hold to the rather specific focus enunciated above, rather than to assemble evidence from widely scattered realms of psychology.

In spite of the restricted scope of the explicit evidential base of the theory, we will put it forth as a general theory of problem solving, without attempting to assess the boundaries of its applicability. It is clearly broader than the three tasks. On the other hand, the evidence at hand is ill-suited to define the limits of its scope. From the nature of the arguments, of course, one can see some of the conditions that must be present for the theory to be valid (e.g., conditions that characterize the basic memory structures of the adult human IPS).

FUNDAMENTAL CHARACTERISTICS OF THE IPS

We devoted Chapter 2 to providing an explicit set of assumptions for an information processing system, defining such components as symbol, symbol structure, designation, memory, processor, information process, program, and primitive process. All the models of human behavior developed in the book have been instances of such a system, and these features of the IPS are present in all subjects performing all tasks.

But these assumptions leave much unspecified. They admit arbitrary programs, which in turn can generate arbitrarily varied behavior. In discussing specific situations, we even emphasized the remaining freedom of specification by using various programming organizations as the situation and data seemed to demand. Now we wish to see what else we can say about the basic characteristics of the IPS. We will review part of the material of Chapter 2, but only to the extent required to discuss the new assumptions.

Only a few additional characteristics of the IPS seem to be invariant over problem solver and task. (1) One such set of invariants are the size, access characteristics, and read and write times for the various memories in the human IPS.

---

[1] To be specific: concept formation (Gregg and Simon, 1967a; Newell and Simon, 1967; Simon and Kotovsky, 1963), algebra word problems (Paige and Simon, 1967), music (Simon and Sumner, 1968), verbal learning (Gregg and Simon, 1967b; Simon and Feigenbaum, 1964), creativity (Newell, Shaw, and Simon, 1962), administrative and organizational behavior (March and Simon, 1958; Simon, 1947), scientific discovery (Simon, 1966b), emotion (Simon, 1967a), and perception (Simon, 1967b; Simon and Barenfeld, 1969).

(2) Related to these invariants are the serial character of the information processing and the rate at which the elementary information processes can be performed. (3) Somewhat different in kind are two invariant aspects of the global program organization: its production-like and its goal-like character.

We will take up each of these characteristics below. We will be concerned not only with those that seem to affect problem solving performance, but also with other characteristics that are invariant in the human, but do not seem important for our theory.

The invariants to be discussed gain their relevance because of the way they determine and affect the information processing in problem solving situations. But the existence of many of them is independently validated by a variety of experimental psychological studies. We will not attempt an extensive review and evaluation of this external literature, partly because the demands of a serious review would exceed the limits in an already long and detailed book, and partly because, as we have stressed several times, only gross characterizations are relevant to problem solving. Much of the detail in the literature is too fine for application here.

Long-Term Memory (LTM)

The smallest units of information held in the memories of the IPS are symbols. There is no evidence that the human LTM is fillable in a lifetime, or that there is a limit on the number of distinguishable symbols it can store. Hence, we assume that the IPS has a potentially infinite vocabulary of symbols, and an essentially infinite capacity for symbol structures.

The human memory is usually described as associative. Associativity is achieved in the hypothesized IPS by storing information in long-term memory in symbol structures, each consisting of a set of symbols connected by relations. As new symbol structures are stored in LTM, they are designated by symbols drawn from the potential vocabulary. These new names can, in turn, be embedded as symbols in other symbol structures.

Unfortunately, we do not have operational specifications for the precise behavioral properties of the human associative memory. Thus, we do not know whether forms of associativity other than the one sketched above are needed. An example of such additional capability would be content addressing, whereby newly constructed symbol structures could designate stored symbol structures without previous assignment of addresses to the latter. The kind of associativity described above seems to be appropriate for the tasks we have examined in this book—even for the chess perception data in Chapter 13. But our tasks do not involve extensive processing in long-term memory, which might call for other forms of association.

Through learning, certain stimuli, or patterns of stimuli, from the input channels come to be designated by particular symbols—become recognizable. We call these recognizable stimulus patterns *chunks*. The stored symbols, then, serve as the internal representations for the corresponding stimulus patterns or chunks; and the chunks, on recognition, evoke their stored designators. The chunks are not innate, but develop through learning. For our subjects the letter D, the number 4, and a chess Bishop were all recognizable patterns. But for an experienced chess player, the configuration known as a fianchettoed short-castled position is also a single recognizable chunk, representable internally by a single symbol, although it is an arrangement of six chessmen.

Numerous experiments, especially reaction-time and recognition experiments, show that the time required to read a symbol structure from long-term memory is of the order of a few hundred milliseconds. So-called associative reaction times are obtained by requiring a subject to recognize a stimulus and then produce some sort of response associated with it (e.g., name a color or give the superordinate of a stimulus word). Such tasks, which involve both stimulus recognition processes and retrieval processes in LTM, typically give reactions times of one-half second to a second or a little more (Woodworth and Schlosberg, 1954, pp. 56–58). Although the times increase somewhat with all sorts of difficulties and uncertainties in the tasks, and with the size of the retrieval ensemble, in no case do they become much longer than this—the reactions never take many seconds. Moreover, reading LTM does not seem to call for scanning, which would produce read times proportional to size of memory.[2]

To write in LTM is another story altogether. Data from rote learning experiments indicate that to store (fixate) a symbolized internal representation of a stimulus containing K familiar subpatterns (including the capacity to recognize the newly formed chunk) requires about $5K$ to $10K$ seconds of processing time.

Much less systematic attention has been given in psychology to establishing this LTM fixation parameter than to determining reaction times. A number of experiments, however, yield data that support a time parameter of about five to ten seconds per chunk. Calculating time per chunk from learning time per syllable requires an estimate of the number of chunks that have to be fixated in learning each syllable, and an allowance for the fraction of the subject's total learning time that is spent in processes other than fixation (e.g., reading the stimulus, responding). On the basis of the EPAM model (Feigenbaum, 1961), it can be postulated that fixation of a low-meaningful CVC nonsense syllable pair in the paired-associate paradigm involves storing about seven new chunks (two for the stimulus, which need only be recognized, three for the three letters of the response syllable, and two for the pair). Similarly, fixation of each member of a list in the serial anticipation paradigm involves storing about four new chunks (one for each letter in the syllable, and one to add it to the series).

With these assumptions about numbers of chunks to be fixated, and without allowance for processes other than fixation, experiments reported by Underwood and Schultz (1960, in experiments 1, 4, and 7) give times of 13.0, 11.8, and 8 seconds per chunk with lists of eight paired-associate syllables, and (their experiment 3) 11.2 seconds per chunk for syllables in a serial list. The classical experiments of Hovland (1938a, b, and c) give 10 seconds per chunk for serial lists and (Hovland, 1949) 8 seconds per chunk for paired-associate learning. All of these experiments used college sophomores as subjects, and standard CVC syllables of relatively low association value. The slightly lower times reported by Hovland may reflect the

---

[2] There is, of course, behavior involving repeated accesses to LTM in attempts to remember something not retrieved "immediately," but such behavior does not fit the notion of a longer access time in the usual sense.

fact that he used the pronunciation method in his experiments, while Underwood and Schultz used the spelling method. If we estimate the number of chunks under the pronunciation method as only 6 and 3, instead of 7 and 4, for the two paradigms, respectively (assuming that a CVC syllable contains only two aural chunks), then Hovland's data would give 13.3 seconds per chunk with the serial anticipation method and 9.3 seconds per chunk with the paired-associate method. Bugelski's (1962) experiments showing the constancy of paired-associate learning time with different memory drum speeds also yield fixation times per chunk of about nine seconds for a wide range of drum speeds.

Not all experiments, however, are fully consonant with these, and much work still needs to be done to establish the fixation parameter firmly, and to determine the conditions that alter it. Ebbinghaus (1964) reported learning times of ten or twelve seconds per *syllable*—that is, two or three seconds per chunk—using himself as subject in serial anticipation experiments. The times reported by Lyon (1914) in his pioneering experiments with himself as subject were also in the neighborhood of three seconds per chunk. The fast fixation rates in these two series of experiments might be attributed to the experience of the subjects or their intelligence, but we simply do not know whether these factors can explain the difference. Experiments with mnemonic schemes appear to show also that responses that are familiar meaningful words can be learned in two or three seconds if associated "meaningfully" with previously overlearned stimuli. There is at least a hint—but little more—in these data that actually storing the new chunks requires much less time than indexing them for retrieval on presentation of the appropriate stimulus.

Until the fine structure of the fixation process is more thoroughly studied and better understood, however, and the factors accounting for differences in the speed of fixation determined, it is probably reasonable to take five to ten seconds per chunk as a typical fixation time, with some confidence that the parameter is correct within a half order of magnitude.

Little is known about the exact nature of the accessing potentialities that are created by fixation in LTM, except that the learner can exercise relatively little direct control over the process. The important fact, for our purposes, is that it takes at least a half order or full order of magnitude longer (i.e., five or ten times longer) to write in LTM than to read LTM. Thus, although an IPS can fixate some new symbols in LTM during the course of a ten-minute problem solving experience, the total number fixated will be modest (almost certainly less than fifty, since most of the IPS's activity will be devoted to processes other than fixation). This large difference between reading and writing times in LTM has much to do with the problem solving strategies that are available to a human IPS.

We have postulated that symbols in the memory of the IPS can designate not only familiar sensory patterns, but also processes of the IPS and output motor patterns (output messages). Learning very probably produces unitary designation of structures of primitive processes—of subroutines—as well. The available data certainly are not clear on these points, mostly because the matter has not hitherto been looked at in this way by experimentalists. Nor is the transition from discrete symbolic structures to continuous motor behavior well understood (but see Bernstein, 1967). But in the absence of contrary data we assume that these other designations, of processes and output motor patterns, are similar to designations of sensory patterns, and that symbolized processes and symbolized motor patterns require reading and writing times of the same order of magnitude as those for sensory patterns.

Short-Term Memory (STM)

The IPS has a short-term memory of very small capacity. It appears that the contents of STM at any given moment consist of a small set of symbols, each of which can designate an entire structure of arbitrary size and complexity in LTM. It is customary to measure the capacity of STM in symbols (or equivalently in chunks). Simple digit-span experiments show this capacity to be about five to seven symbols ["seven, plus or minus two," as George Miller (1956) put it in his well-known paper], and the capacity seems not to vary much over a wide range of tasks.

The STM seems to be immediately and completely available to the IPS processes. There are no studies that show convincingly how the accessing takes place. The memory is small enough so that it would be difficult to distinguish rapid serial scanning from direct addressing (i.e., a fixed set of cells holding the symbols) or from various content-addressing schemes. At the problem solving level such details make no difference at all. The STM can be defined functionally as comprising the set of symbols that are available to an IPS process at a given instant of time.

The details of how the IPS assembles and holds the inputs and outputs of its information processes are not known. It is most plausible to assume that these inputs and outputs must reside in STM at execution time. The evidence for this assumption is all circumstantial: again, the problem has not been posed experimentally in exactly these terms. But only a very few symbols can be retained in STM—perhaps not more than two—when even a simple processing task (e.g., counting backwards by threes) is interposed between presentation and recall. And almost all tasks that require attention, in some intuitive sense, subtract from the effective capacity of STM as measured by standard tests. It is plausible to suppose that the remaining "missing" capacity is being occupied by the inputs and outputs of the processes (and possibly by information for a stack of subprocesses).

There is good evidence that information in STM decays. (There is controversy—irrelevant here—over whether that decay is caused by interference among symbols in the memory or is a strictly time-dependent process.) For example, there is substantial evidence for rehearsal processes when a person has to maintain information in STM. The decay is another detail of memory that is unimportant for the explanation of problem solving. The reason is not far to seek. Since the problem solving activity is self-paced, the problem solver can adjust his rate and style of processing information so that he does not appear either to have a rapidly decaying STM or to rehearse. Decay and rehearsal might indeed have effects on problem solving—for example, a more reliable STM might permit problem solvers to work at somewhat faster rates. But the effect could be absorbed by the parameters measuring processing speed, hence an additional parameter would not be required to represent the time constant of STM decay.

The analysis above is only a first approximation, of course. STM errors may be caused primarily by decay in conjunction with rehearsal strategies. Such errors, according to the paragraph above, will occur infrequently, but when they do, they may have large effects: for example, S3 spent a long time on his cryptarithmetic problem because he did not recall that T = 0 so that E could not be 0. In fact, the argument from adaptivity breaks down here, precisely because the general processing program limits errors to low frequencies. To predict these errors, rather than taking them as exogenous events as we did in Chapter 6, could well require an explicit model of the decay of STM.

Elementary Processes

As postulated in Chapter 2 and repeated above, all processes take their inputs from STM and leave their outputs in STM (excepting only processes for reading or storing in other memories). How much processing an IPS can accomplish per unit of time depends on three parameters: (1) the number of processes it can do simultaneously, (2) the time it takes to do each process, and (3) the amount of work done by each individual process.

Serial Processing. As far as simultaneity is concerned, the answer is unequivocal: the human IPS is basically a serial system: it can execute one elementary information process at a time. This assertion is often misunderstood and equally often rejected, especially since the underlying physiological system is highly parallel. Let us be clear about it. Assuming that the IPS is serial does not imply that it accesses the various memories by means of a serial scan (i.e., a scanning process with read time proportional to memory size). The human LTM clearly does not operate this way and the STM *acts* as if it didn't, whether it does or not. Again, assuming an IPS to be serial does not imply that it cannot be aware of many things at once in the environment (or some other dynamic memory), in the sense of detecting and recognizing when a single one of them occurs. On the other hand, the statement that an IPS is a serial system asserts more than the bare logical necessity that behavior be serial if the information produced by a first process is required as input to a second. A serial IPS is one that can execute a single elementary information process at one time.

A paradigmatic experiment for seriality is the following: let there be some operation, Q, which the problem solver has learned well and which yields a final output of *yes* or *no*. Let this operation be performed on symbols of a given class. Then, present the IPS simultaneously with K symbols, $S_1, S_2, \ldots, S_K$, and ask it to give the K answers as quickly as possible. The IPS is a *serial machine* (with respect to operation Q) if the time required to give the K answers is proportional to K, and a *parallel machine* (with respect to Q) if the time is independent of K.

For example, suppose the task, Q, is to divide various numbers by a given integer, say 7. The output is *yes* if a number is exactly divisible by 7 and *no* if it isn't. A test with K = 1 is the number:

$$35642$$
$$69416$$

If the human IPS were a parallel processor, then it should do the second problem as fast as the first (due account being taken of the time required to state two results—*no, no*—versus one result, *no*). It is possible for an IPS to be parallel for two activities, but not parallel for three or four, since the processor may be capable of carrying along only two independent control sequences.[3]

In terms of this test, the human is a completely serial IPS for almost all information processing operations. There is some uncertainty whether this is true with respect to highly automated activities, since some parallelism then does appear, but with concomitant changes in the actual task being performed. With respect to motor activities, if the performing motor systems are physically independent then parallelism can exist. But whenever central control is involved, seriality reestablishes itself. The old trick of patting one's head with one hand while rubbing one's stomach in a clockwise direction with the other hand illustrates the extent—and limits—of parallelism in motor activity.

Processing Rate. The second factor determining how much processing the IPS can do is the unit time it takes to execute each information process. For elementary processes, memory access time provides an ultimate lower bound on processing time, for either a process takes as its inputs symbols already in STM or it gets the inputs from another memory (either LTM or the external environment). It can only avoid taking time to input from the latter memories, with their 100-millisecond access times, if it can get along with what is already in STM. But since this memory is very small, a process using no other inputs would soon have only itself to feed upon.

It would, of course, be possible for elementary processes to be much *slower* than the memory access time. Actually they appear not to be slower, for rather careful experiments show that the elementary processes in STM take times of the order of 40 milliseconds (e.g., Sternberg, 1966). This duration might as well be identified with the unit access time from LTM. Such an agreement, with processing times slightly shorter than access time, yields a satisfactory picture of a balanced system.[4]

Nature of Elementary Processes. The final factor that determines the speed of processing is how much work each process accomplishes. The elementary processes (those that take only 40 milliseconds) seem to be the simplest imaginable sorts of

[3] Indeed, some computers have existed (e.g., the SAGE air defense computer) that carried two numbers in each word (the x and y coordinates of a point) and operated simultaneously and independently on both.

[4] Evolutionary arguments might be used against the possibility of a processing time of, say, a microsecond. This would leave the system idle most of the time while waiting for the next symbol structure from LTM or the visual display. How would such a processing mechanism ever evolve?

compare and replace operations. In Chapter 2 we listed the basic types of elementary processes, observing that we were not in any position to select a specific unique set for our IPS, and that many alternative bases were sufficient to build up arbitrary programs. We are in no better position now to specify the set of basic processes, although later we will say a little more about it in discussing the production-like character of programs. The small size of STM does imply that most elementary processes involve only one or two input and output symbols. Otherwise they could not operate incrementally in a seven-symbol memory whose function is not only to hold the symbols for the immediate processes, but also to keep sufficient dynamic context (e.g., temporary symbols, place-keepers in processes and lists, local goals, and so on) to maintain coherence among the larger processes.

All more complex processes seem to involve either access to LTM or subdivision of the processes into sequences of subprocesses (i.e., into programs). For instance, if a man knows all two-digit by two-digit products, he can multiply 37×43 "instantly"—that is, almost as fast as 7×3—by reading the product out of LTM. If (more commonly) he knows only the 12×12 multiplication table, he may multiply 37×43 by carrying out a sequence of operations, involving, say, digit-by-digit multiplication and addition. One finds no experimental evidence for yet another process—quite different from either of the above—that computes 37×43 entirely within the STM.[5]

The analysis above implies that the time for a composite algorithm can be viewed as a sum of times for the elementary component processes (given the actual sequence executed). From an empirical standpoint, the matter is cloudy. While experiments have obtained simple linear times for linear searches (e.g., running down the alphabet) (Landauer, 1962), composite models of more complex processes run into difficulties (Olshavsky, 1965). One recent study on mental multiplication has had some success in predicting total times by adding up the component times (mostly memory transfer times) (Dansereau, 1969), but the evidence is still incomplete, and we will not attempt any detailed time accounting here.

Perception and Sensory Modality

One of the best-documented characteristics of human processing is that it has separate sensory systems for acquiring different kinds of information about the external environment. We even know a good deal about the physiology of the sensory systems and can trace their structure and function a good way toward the central nervous system. There is also by now good psychological evidence for the existence of very short-term sensory stores (with retention times of the order of a second at most) involving rather intricate mechanisms of masking, decay, and trans-

---

[5] It is doubtful whether any such process could be realized in the human. The computer algorithms that avoid dependence on long-term memory employ representations, such as binary, that simplify addition and multiplication. Such algorithms require processes for converting numbers from one base to another (e.g., $37 \times 43 \Rightarrow 100101 \times 101011$) and they also require substantial short-term memory to hold the intermediate results.

fer between these and the central STM. A general picture of the sensory system can be found in Geldard (1953) and in Gibson (1966), of the sensory stores in Neisser (1967) and in Haber (1969).

None of the data on problem solving appear to depend critically on the detail of any of these phenomena. Such detail might well be important for tasks different from those we have studied, but not for the particular phenomena we seek to explain. Moreover, such detail may be important in explaining the processes of reading information from the external environment, or writing it externally. For the purpose of understanding problem solving, however, the effects of the sensory processes can be summarized in simple ways—we need only postulate that externally written letters are recognized directly and produce corresponding internal symbols in short-term memory.

For example, the characteristics of the so-called visual buffer store have been determined (originally by Sperling, 1960) from tasks in which a subject is asked to recall a subset of information from a visual display a short time after he has seen it, but without forewarning (while he was actually looking at it) as to which part of the information he would be expected to retain. In our problem solving tasks, the external displays remain visible to the subject, hence the theory need not distinguish between information he retrieves from external displays and information he retrieves from the visual buffer store. The buffer store may be present and active in the system—it simply does not affect problem solving behavior significantly at the level of detail that we are considering, or cause inexplicable discontinuities of behavior.

Other details of the visual sensory system, including the system for visual pattern recognition, become irrelevant by reason of the nature of the problem materials. In all three classes of problems we have examined, the visual displays are rather simple arrangements of discrete elements that the subject can recognize immediately. In the cryptarithmetic task the elements are familiar roman letters and arabic numerals. In the logic task they are letters, punctuation marks, and a small set of symbols that the subjects are encouraged to recognize as *horseshoe*, *wedge*, *dot*, and *tilde*. In chess the elements are squares and chessmen, the latter belonging to six familiar types. Recognition of any of these elements, under the conditions of illumination and distance in which the experiments were run, is a nonproblematic process, requiring perhaps forty or fifty milliseconds, which we can take as an unanalyzed primitive process.

The geometric configurations of the elementary symbols are also rather simple in these tasks. In cryptarithmetic the symbols are arranged in a rectangle, in rows and columns. The subjects' previous experiences with the conventions of arithmetic encourage them to encode them that way, and there is no evidence that any subject treated the geometric pattern in any other way. In logic the expressions appear visually as horizontal strings of the elementary symbols. By interpretation of the parenthesis notation, they can also readily be encoded as phrase-structure trees, as we have already seen. These expressions are arranged, in turn, in a vertical column. In chess the board is an 8×8 square. The rules of the game encourage encoding the more complex geometric patterns according to the sixteen possible directions for legal chess moves.

These geometric characteristics of the visual displays, combined with the cultural expectations of the subjects, give some assurance that unknown properties of the visual pattern-recognition system were unlikely to exercise a major influence on behavior.

As another example, consider the effect of obtaining information in one or another sensory modality. For our theory the basic structural characteristics of LTM and STM are independent of the original sensory modalities of the information stored. What we mean by this postulate should be clear from the discussion of chess perception in Chapter 13. It does not mean that the IPS cannot distinguish between stored information that represents visual images, say, and information that represents aural images. As the analysis of chess perception shows, stored information acquires its modality, not by "hardware" differentiation between modes in the central structures, but by the specific ways in which these central capabilities are used to organize the information.

An internal encoding of information preserves the sensory modality to the extent that (1) stimuli that are similar (externally) in that modality have similar encodings, and (2) portions of stimuli that are directly related (externally) correspond to internal symbols with directly-coded relations—that is, to the extent that external and internal structures are isomorphic. As an example of the first aspect—similarity—we would regard an encoding of words as aural if both "taut" and "taught" had identical encodings. On the other hand, we might regard the encoding as visual if the representations of "tout" and "taut" were more nearly alike than those of "taut" and "taught."

The second aspect—relational isomorphism—is more subtle. It is illustrated by our earlier discussion of tic-tac-toe, Number Scrabble, and the magic square (Chapter 3). If Number Scrabble were being played without an external display, a subject's attempt to build a winning triplet from 3 and 9 would demonstrate that his internal representation was not visual, since these two numbers do not lie in a line in the magic square.

There is only modest evidence in the problem solving protocols for the role, if any, played by the sensory modalities in the internal encodings of information. In all three tasks, of course, the external visual stimulus, which was continually available to the subjects, played a major role. Hence, complete programs to represent performances on these tasks would have to include processes for scanning and recognizing components of these external displays.

External Memory (EM)

An IPS with only a STM and LTM possessing the characteristics we have described will behave very differently in a problem solving situation from an IPS, otherwise identical, that is also provided with external memories—paper, say, or a chessboard. The simplest evidence for this, if evidence is needed, is to compare the times required for a person to multiply two four-digit numbers with and without paper and pencil. The ratio of times is about 1 to 100.

Much of the difficulty in doing arithmetic mentally comes from the slow write times of internal LTM and the small size of STM. But the matter is deeper than that. Compare analyzing a chess situation with the board in view and not in view (i.e., blindfold analysis), or doing DONALD+GERALD given the display or entirely "in the head." Even when writing into the EM is not permitted, and only scanning it is allowed, dispensing with the external display makes the task much harder.

For our theory, specification of the EM's available to the problem solver is absolutely essential. These memories must be specified in the same terms as those we have used for the internal memories: symbol capacities, accessing characteristics, and read and write times (with decay times, if relevant). The problem solving program adopted by the IPS will depend on the nature of the available EM every bit as intimately as it depends on the nature of its "built-in" internal STM and LTM.

From a functional viewpoint, the STM should be defined, not as an internal memory, but as the combination of (1) the internal STM (as measured by the usual psychological tests) and (2) the part of the visual display that is in the subject's foveal view. The latter augmentation of the short-term store is, of course, a read-only memory. But it increases the short-term capacity and enhances the stability of the memory considerably.[6]

How, empirically, the two memories are merged is not clear, for again the appropriate experimental questions have not been asked. The merging issue is whether, in order to use any information in the EM to affect behavior, it must be read into the internal STM and symbolized there, or whether the foveal symbols in the EM, once recognized and remaining in foveal view, are part of the STM without further acts of reading and re-recognition. Reaction-time experiments do not address the question, since they almost always involve a change in external stimulus, after which, obviously, an act of recognition is required.

Similarly, it is not clear whether only the instantaneous foveal region can be merged with STM or whether a somewhat larger region, connected by adequately indexed saccades, might be available. To initiate saccadic processes takes times of the order of a hundred milliseconds, but so do rehearsals. Thus, the larger memory region could strongly affect the reliability and availability of dynamic information by permitting modified rehearsal strategies. The external augmentation is read-only memory, to be sure, but it can relieve the internal STM of maintaining fixed information that it must have. For all fixed information cannot be kept in LTM; accessing information is also required, to permit long-term information to be retrieved. The external augmentation could hold such information.

In short, although we have few independent data suited to defining precisely how EM can augment STM, the two components do appear to form a single functional unit as far as the detailed specification of a problem solving IPS is concerned.

Except for the phenomena just discussed, EM, like LTM, must be deliberately

---

[6] An auditory analog of this *attentional memory* would seem possible, except that most auditory information is highly time-varying, so cannot be used as an extension of memory. If continuous tones of varying pitch and intensity carry the information, then the analog probably does exist. It is not clear whether tactile and olfactory analogs exist, or whether they have to be sampled and input into internal STM as discrete symbols.

accessed both for reading and for writing. EM, like LTM, is essentially infinite in capacity. However, it is not associative, but rather must be accessed by means ranging from linear scanning to random accessing from addresses held in STM.[7] It takes a few hundred milliseconds either to read from a fixated domain to STM or to perform a saccade to another arbitrary point in the visual field. Thus, reading either from located domains of EM or from LTM requires times of the same order of magnitude.

There are, of course, more remote EM's, such as the work sheet on the side of the table, the sheet under the sheet now being worked on, nearby books, books in the library, and so on. Accessing times become increasingly large as more extensive motor behavior and physical distance are involved in retrieval.

The time to record a new structure in an appropriate EM tends to be much shorter than the time (five or ten seconds per symbol) required to record new structures in LTM. External writing time is, however, somewhat longer than the time required to write in STM. Furthermore, it depends critically on there being easily recorded external symbols to represent each of the internal symbols. If certain internal symbols do not have simple recordable external names, then storing in the EM may become very slow—even problematic. A beginning learner trying to write down the Chinese ideograms for words already fixated in his oral vocabulary would illustrate this well. Something like a second per symbol may be taken as the writing rate for overlearned symbols. The alphabet can be written in less than half a second per symbol (letter), and typists can type perhaps one symbol (word) per second, but the symbols in these instances are very simple and highly overlearned.

If we look at the EM's in our tasks, we see that all three had displays larger than could be held in immediate attention. Consequently, all three tasks involved scanning behavior as integral parts of the problem solving programs. The chess task had the peculiarity that no writing at all was permitted—the touch-move rule being enforced in the experiments. In the cryptarithmetic task the EM was a blackboard display. Most experiments with this task allowed digits to be written in physical association with the letter occurrences to which they were assigned. Information other than letter assignments was not permitted to be recorded [e.g., (R odd) or values of the carries]. In one experiment (S3) the subject was permitted to avoid part of his loss of information by maintaining two displays for two alternative hypothetical assignments of the digits. In another, where we had eye movements, no writing whatsoever was permitted on the display, but the subject was given a verbal-auditory EM for letter-digit assignments. In the logic task the EM was altered simply by annexing new logic expressions to the display without modifying or erasing those already there.

Each of these different arrangements of EM affected profoundly the problem solving programs that subjects used for the task. For instance, the progressive-deepening-search strategy, with its striking characteristic of returning to the initial position and retracing the search, stands out in chess where no external writing was allowed. In every example, the IPS's inferred to describe our subjects incorporated

---

[7] Actually, it is not known empirically whether or not eye movements to a previously known location in EM to pick up information require the use of STM.

the searches of the EM in their program structures. A problem solving program cannot be specified independently of its EM any more than it can be specified independently of its internal STM and LTM. Hence, one can predict the problem solving program of an IPS only after characterizing the EMs available to it.

Production-like Character of the Program

What can be said of the overall program organization of the problem solver? The most important aspect—the problem space—will be discussed in the next section. But even after the problem space has been specified, the program must still be organized in some way out of elementary processes. If we were talking of computers, we would ask what programming language is to be used. Here, since it is not clear to what extent behavior is governed by interpreted symbol structures and to what extent it is produced in some more direct way, we simply ask what the program organization is.

Throughout the book we have made use of a wide range of organizational techniques known to the programming world: explicit flow control, subroutines, recursion, iteration statements, local naming, production systems, interpreters, and so on. Does the empirical evidence permit any narrowing of this range? There are few experimental data beyond those provided in this book that are helpful for answering these questions. Not much is to be expected, of course, since such questions have not yet been posed experimentally.

From one viewpoint the question of program organization is as irrelevant to problem solving as the question of perceptual organization. For all programming languages have about the same power of expression—anything that can be stated in one programming language can be stated in the others.[8] If any reasonable organization were chosen, programs could be constructed to produce any of the behaviors that we have studied.

The reason for nevertheless concerning ourselves with program organization is twofold. First, to discuss problem solving systems in detail one must adopt *some* programming language. Failing to adopt any language precludes speaking on such topics as the structure of problem solving methods. One cannot, as with perception, simply ignore the detail. Second, the program representation may have second-order effects. For instance, adopting a particular representation may make it easier to determine in detail what program is being used, or easier to understand how learning and assembly of programs take place.

We confess to a strong premonition that the actual organization of human programs closely resembles the production system organization, which we used

---

[8] This may seem an exaggerated claim for computer programming languages. But many of the important differences among such languages as machine language, assembly language, FORTRAN, ALGOL, IPL, LISP, COMIT, SNOBOL, and so on, lie in naming ability, in data structures available, or in basic system features such as memory allocation. Given the associative character of long-term memory and the complete-accessing character of short-term memory, none of the above differences is relevant to the question of program organization as posed here.

extensively in cryptarithmetic and partially in chess. We cannot yet prove the correctness of this judgment, and we suspect that the ultimate verification may depend on this organization's proving relatively satisfactory in many different small ways, no one of them decisive. Let us list, without explicit support, some features of productions and production systems that point to their being an appropriate theoretical construct:

1. A production system is capable of expressing arbitrary calculations. Thus, it allows the human IPS the information processing capabilities we know he has.

2. A production system encodes homogeneously the information that instructs the IPS how to behave. In contrast, the standard control-flow system divides program information into the content of the boxes, on the one hand, and the structure of the flow diagram, on the other. In a production system this division does not exist, except to the extent that the ordering of productions carries additional information. Production systems are the most homogeneous form of programming organization known.

3. In a production system, each production is independent of the others— a fragment of potential behavior. Thus the law of composition of productions systems is very simple: manufacture a new production and add it to the set. This arrangement provides simple ways for a production system to grow naturally from incremental experience.

4. The production itself has a strong stimulus-response flavor. It is overly simple to identify the two constructs, since productions also have additional properties of matching, operand identification, and subroutine calling that are not apparent in any of the usual formulations of S-R theory [or even S-R theory extended to meet the demands of internal processing (Berlyne, 1965: Millenson, 1967)]. Nevertheless, productions might well express the kernel of truth that exists in the S-R position.

5. The productions themselves seem to represent meaningful components of the total problem solving process and not just odd program fragments. This is true in part because we, the scientists, sought to define them that way. Nonetheless it remains true that such an organization of meaningful pieces describes the data. (Later in the chapter we will provide some additional support for this assertion.)

6. The dynamic working memory for a production system is the STM (i.e., the memory on which its productions are contingent, and which they modify). This conception fits well the functional definition of the STM as the collection of information of which the subject is aware at any moment of time.[9] This is not the case with most other program organi-

---

[9] *Awareness* here means that the subject's immediately subsequent behavior can be a function of the given information. It does not mean that the subject can report that he has the information. For example, he may be too absorbed in the task to be "aware" in this monitoring sense; and interrupting to evoke a reporting program may result in the loss of the information from STM.

zation schemes (e.g., the GPS flow diagram in Figure 8.7 or the programs in sequential algebraic languages, such as that for LT in Figure 4.8) in which the relation to directly defined psychological constructs, such as STM, is not clear. All these other organizations contain implicitly an unknown amount of machinery that still requires psychological explanation.

For a production system it remains to specify the matching, the operand definition, the subroutining, and the sequential flow of control on the action side. All these seem amenable to explanation. For instance, each production may possess only a single action operator. In such a scheme the hypothesized action sequences—such as FC followed by PC in the productions for cryptarithmetic—would simply be our shorthand for an iteration through STM in which the output of the first production includes a unique symbol (a linking symbol) to identify the next stage of the action sequence. In this view, the subroutine pointer stack consists of the linking symbols in STM. In such a system almost all the program control apparatus is assimilated to the structure of STM.

In all events, the gap between program organization and the experimental psychology of immediate memory and processing seems smaller for production systems than for other program organizations.

7. There is an intriguing possibility that a production system offers a viable model of LTM. Possibly there is no LTM for facts distinct from the production system—that is, no basic distinction between data and program; rather the LTM *is* just a very large production system. If this were the case, the act of taking a new item into LTM would be equivalent to creating a new production (or productions). We will explore this suggestion a bit further in the section on the determination of programs.

8. A production system, unlike some other programming organizations, offers a nice balance between stimulus-bound activity and stimulus-independent activity. The production system itself is totally stimulus bound, if by *stimulus* one means the contents of the dynamic working memory (i.e., STM). All connection between two adjacent actions is mediated by the stimulus so defined. (As we commented above, this is not absolutely true for productions that have sequential action parts, but these may be eliminated in the way we have suggested.) But this stimulus is per se neither internal nor external, if we take the view that STM is a combination of the internal short-term store and the foveal parts of the visual field (plus of course the symbols that have just been stored in STM upon recognition of other external stimuli). If the vast majority of the productions executed are reactions to internally produced symbols, then the system will appear not to be stimulus bound. On the other hand, if almost all productions take as part of their condition an external symbol, then the system will appear to be very stimulus bound. Thus, the overly focused nondistractable character of programming models—which has seemed to some to be characteristic of them (Reitman, 1965; Neisser, 1963)—is not a structural feature of a production

organization, but depends on the particular productions that the system contains.

The explicit assumption that the IPS is organized as a production system makes its elementary processes more definite. Discriminating becomes simply the act of selecting the next production—that is, matching the conditions of productions to the contents of STM. This discriminative act may permit an indefinitely broad selectivity—the breadth depending on the number of productions available. At the most basic level, symbol structures are created by the action of a production's placing a new expression in STM. These new expressions may be assembled from parts of existing expressions, detected and designated by matching the production's condition to particular contents of STM. The elementary read operation is simply the operation of extracting these parts of the contents of STM.

It would be difficult—perhaps impossible—to determine for a production system whether new expressions were freshly created in STM or generated by modification of the previous contents. Suppose, in solving a cryptarithmetic problem, STM at one moment contains (A = 4 new), and a moment later simply (A = 4). The tag, *new*, might have been deleted, or another expression without the tag created. Our models of the immediate processor have not been detailed enough to distinguish between these two schemes.

The only other elementary processes a production system requires are processes to write in LTM and processes to interface with the external world. Explicit processes for shuffling information within STM are not needed, for the match process treats STM as a content-addressed memory. Retrieval from LTM, as we have noted, *is* just the process of selecting one production from memory (or, at least, this would be the most obvious way to arrange the memory). Exact specification of the remaining processes—writing in LTM and reading and writing in EM—lies outside the information that can be gleaned from the data we present in this book.

In summary, we do not think a conclusive case can be made yet for production systems as *the* appropriate form of program organization. Many of the arguments listed above raise difficulties. Nevertheless, our judgment stands that we should choose production systems as the preferred language for expressing programs and program organization. We will do so in the remainder of this chapter.

Goal-like Character of the Program

The final aspect of consistency in the human IPS, invariant over people and over tasks, is the existence of goals. Human behavior, viewed externally, clearly is goal-directed, and we have assumed as much throughout the whole book. This is not the question. The question is whether this goal-directedness has structural significance in the IPS. For teleological behavior can be obtained in many ways, as has often been remarked in the cybernetic literature. Thus, one can interpret water as "seeking its own level" or a stone as having the goal of falling.

We postulate for the IPS of the theory that it does have goals, where a goal is a symbol structure with certain characteristics:

1. A goal carries a test to determine when some state of affairs has been attained, in which case the goal is satisfied. This test, of course, may simply be a symbol structure to be fed to a testing process elsewhere defined.
2. A goal is capable of controlling behavior under appropriate conditions. We then say that the IPS is attempting to attain the goal. The control takes the form of evoking patterns of behavior that have a rational relation to the goal—i.e., methods for attaining the goal.

We have had to state these specifications very generally, since we have no good empirical information about the actual variety of goals. Goals seem to be highly diverse, but this diversity may have to do mostly with the many ways for specifying desired situations. The important question is whether goals are incorporated in symbolic structures like those defined above, or whether, alternatively, the equivalent behavior occurs because it is encoded into the program in other ways. In the former case, but not in the latter, we would say that the system has goals.

This book has offered examples of both kinds of behavior.

In cryptarithmetic, production P1 states: given a new piece of information about a letter, find an occurrence of that letter and attempt to use the new information. From observation of the subject's behavior, it can appear that he has the goal of using new information. Internally, in the program, there exists no data structure that *is* the goal; instead, a single production produces the behavior.

By way of contrast, production P2 states: to get the value of a letter, go to a location of an occurrence of that letter and process the column containing it. The "to get" condition of P2 is satisfied only if there exists an explicit symbolic structure that can be interpreted as the goal of obtaining the value of a letter. A system containing P2 uses goals.

Using goals has real consequences for the structure of the IPS. If there are goals, then the program must contain processes for creating goals, testing them, updating them, selecting methods for attempting them, evoking them, discarding them, and so on. Thus, a number of detailed specifications must be met by any IPS that represents human activity directed toward goals.[10]

Since directed activity does take place in a problem solving system, the important issue is to distinguish goal behavior from other forms of directed behavior. We can list a number of criteria for making the distinction, which all depend on the fact that the symbolized goal structure gives the system a way of remembering both that it has a goal and where it is along the way toward attaining that goal. Other systems for directed behavior are more stimulus bound, since they do not retain explicit data about progress toward goals in order to organize behavior. Thus, a key behavioral feature of goals is that they produce correlations of behavior over long time intervals.

---

[10] This argument is an instance of a more general principle: that the data types of an information processing system imply that the operations proper to those data types must be included in the repertoire of the system. Thus, knowing of a computer that its data types are addresses, boolean vectors, integers, and single-precision floating-point numbers goes a long way toward predicting its order code.

Some specific criteria for recognizing a goal-directed IPS are:

1. *Interruptibility*. If the IPS is removed or distracted from a situation, it later returns to directed activity at the same point.
2. *Subgoaling*. The IPS itself interrupts its activity toward a goal to engage in an activity that is a means to that goal, and then returns (often after considerable time lapse) to the activity directed toward the original goal, making use of the means produced by the subgoal.
3. *Depth-first subgoaling*. When the subgoaling behavior indicated above occurs to a depth of several goals, the evidence is particularly conclusive.
4. *Equifinality*. If one method for attaining a goal is attempted and fails, another method toward the same goal, often involving quite different overt behavior, is then attempted.
5. *Avoidance of repetition*. More generally, the system operates with memory of its history of attempts on goals, so as to avoid repetition of behavior.
6. *Consummation*. If the goal situation is attained, effort is terminated with respect to that goal.

The evidence for goal activity is abundant in the protocols we have studied. Thus, we conclude that the human IPS invariably has goal structures. However, it must not be assumed that all or most directed activity is achieved by means of goal structures.

Summary

In sum, the important characteristics of the human IPS that influence its programs for handling problem solving tasks are:

1. It is a serial system consisting of an active processor, input (sensory) and output (motor) systems, an internal LTM and STM and an EM.
2. Its LTM has unlimited capacity and is organized associatively, its contents being symbols and structures of symbols. Any stimulus configuration that becomes a recognizable configuration (chunk) is designated in LTM by a symbol. Writing a new symbol structure that contains K familiar symbols takes about 5K to 10K seconds of processing time. Accessing and reading a symbol out of LTM takes a few hundred milliseconds.
3. Its STM holds about five to seven symbols, but only about two can be retained for one task while another unrelated task is performed. All the symbols in STM are available to the processes (i.e., there is no accessing or search of STM).
4. Its STM and LTM are homogeneous, in that sensory patterns in all sensory modalities, processes, and motor patterns are symbolized and handled identically in STM and LTM.
5. Its elementary processes take times of the order of fifty milliseconds,

but the overall rate of processing is fundamentally limited by read rates from LTM and EM.

6. EM (the immediately available visual field) has access times of the order of a hundred milliseconds (the saccade) and read times to STM of the order of fifty milliseconds. Write times are of the order of a second per symbol for overlearned external symbols.

7. Its program is structured as a production system, the conditions for evocation of a production being the presence of appropriate symbols in the STM augmented by the foveal EM.

8. It possesses a class of symbol structures, the goal structures, that are used to organize problem solving.

THE PROBLEM SPACE

We postulate that problem solving takes place by search in a problem space. This principle is a major invariant of problem solving behavior that holds across tasks and across subjects.

In making this claim we should perhaps recall the scope of the theory being put forth. We do not know what part of all human problem solving activity employs a problem space, but over the range of tasks and individuals we have studied—a broad enough spectrum to make the commonalities nontrivial—a problem space is always used.

This statement does not mean that all behavior *relevant* to problem solving is search in a problem space. Initially, when a problem is first presented, it must be recognized and understood. Then, a problem space must be constructed or, if one already exists in LTM, it must be evoked. Problem spaces can be changed and modified during the course of solving. These activities, crucial to problem solving, need not themselves be searches in a problem space.

The statement that problem solving takes place by search in a problem space does mean that the human has a preferred problem formulation. In Chapter 3 we adopted a carefully neutral stance as to how problems were formulated. We defined two alternatives—the set-predicate formulation and the search formulation—and left open the possibility that there might be others. Any collection of symbol structures giving information about a task environment, together with interpreters to control the behavior of the IPS toward the achievement of some state of affairs, could constitute another problem formulation. However, the evidence we have gathered from the three tasks available to us indicates that a human will preferentially employ the search formulation.

The purpose of this section is twofold. First we need to review and summarize the concept of a problem space—introduced in Chapter 3 simply as the space (1) where problem solving takes place and (2) that contains not only the actual solution but possible solutions that the problem solver might consider. In subsequent chapters the problem space was given several concrete forms, each adapted to the task situation at hand.

Second, we wish to show that a number of the features of the problem spaces we have observed are consistent with the basic invariant characteristics of the IPS discussed in the previous section. The arguments are not so strong that we can claim to derive the existence and nature of the problem space from the IPS characteristics, but we hope to make the interdependence of the two structures plausible.

The Definition of Problem Space

A problem space consists of:

1. A *set of elements*, U, which are symbol structures, each representing a state of knowledge about the task.
2. A *set of operators*, Q, which are information processes, each producing new states of knowledge from existing states of knowledge.
3. An *initial state of knowledge*, u_0, which is the knowledge about the task that the problem solver has at the start of problem solving.
4. A *problem*, which is posed by specifying a set of final, desired states G, to be reached by applying operators from Q.
5. The *total knowledge available* to a problem solver when he is in a given knowledge state, which includes (ordered from most transient to most stable):
   (a) *Temporary dynamic information* created and used exclusively within a single knowledge state.
   (b) The *knowledge state* itself—the dynamic information about the task.
   (c) *Access information* to the additional symbol structures held in LTM or EM (the *extended knowledge state*).
   (d) *Path information* about how a given knowledge state was arrived at and what other actions were taken in this state if it has already been visited on prior occasions.
   (e) *Access information to other knowledge states* that have been reached previously and are now held in LTM or EM.
   (f) *Reference information* that is constant over the course of problem solving, available in LTM or EM.

To recall an example, in chess the elements of the problem space are chess positions; the operators are moves; the initial state is the given position; the final state depends on evaluations, but is related to checkmate; the extended knowledge state is the set of static relations among pieces that the problem solver has not yet extracted, but which are available through the display of the position in EM; the only other accessible knowledge state is the original position available in the display; path information includes (say) that the player has already looked at Bishop moves in the current position; temporary information is (say) the system's current position in a generator of all moves that defend a given man; and constant information includes the conventional values of the pieces, which are available in LTM for use in evaluating exchanges.

The concept of *available* in point 5 means that the information may be used in decision processes or in applying operators and will be forthcoming if it is called for. We distinguish in point 5 between the knowledge state itself, which is *directly* available, and the extended knowledge state, for which only access information is available. Similarly, the problem solver does not have available the information in the other knowledge states to which he might go if he were to abandon the current one, but he does have access information enabling him to recall them (if he did not, he could never get to them).

Invariant Features of Problem Spaces

A series of generalizations about the problem space hold for the tasks and subjects we have studied. We postulate these generalizations as invariant features of problem spaces used by humans:

1. The set of knowledge states is generated from a finite set of objects, relations, properties, and so on, and can be represented as a closed space of knowledge.
2. The set of operators is small and finite (or at least finitely generated).
3. The available set of alternative nodes in the space to which the problem solver might return is very small; in fact, it usually contains only one or two nodes.
4. The residence time in each particular knowledge state before generation of the next state is of the order of seconds.
5. The problem solver remains within a given problem space for times of the order of at least tens of minutes.
6. Problem solving takes place by search in the problem space—i.e., by considering one knowledge state after another until (if the search is successful) a desired knowledge state is reached. The moves from one state to the next are mostly incremental.
7. The search involves backup—that is, return from time to time to old knowledge states and hence the abandonment of knowledge-state information (although not necessarily of path information).
8. The knowledge state is typically only moderate in size—containing at most a few hundred symbols, more typically a few dozen.

We wish to relate the problem space, and these regularities describing it, to the basic characteristics of the IPS.

Residence Time

Earlier, we characterized the human IPS in terms of its seriality, the sizes and access times of its memories, and the speeds of its processes. In the last section we characterized the problem space and the knowledge state in terms of their sizes and their typical durations, or residence times, during problem solving. We believe that there are deep structural relations between the organization and parameters of the IPS and the problem space, respectively—that many characteristics of the latter are adaptations to constraints imposed by the former. In this section we will undertake to exhibit some of these structural relations.

Residence Times and the Size of the Knowledge State

We have defined the problem solver's knowledge state as that portion of his total knowledge which represents his dynamic information about the task. From the protocol data in all three tasks, the residence times in a knowledge state (i.e., the times between the moves that change current knowledge of the task) appear typically to be of the order of seconds. Table 14.1 gives the average durations for a subject in each of the tasks.[11] The durations range from two to eight seconds. The lowest average, from the PBG of S2 on CROSS+ROADS, was based on both protocol and eye-movement data, hence permitted a more fine-grained analysis (e.g., one that included recall operators) than the others. A move from one knowledge state to another generally means storage of some new information. Hence, we can infer something about the probable size of a knowledge state and the memories in which it might be stored from our knowledge of the speeds of the IPS's storage processes.

TABLE 14.1

average residence time in a knowledge state

SUBJECT AND TASKS	SECONDS
S2 on CROSS+ROADS	1.9
S5 on DONALD+GERALD	5.6
S2 on chess position A	6.2
S8 on logic problem D1	7.7

During very short time intervals—less than 100 milliseconds, say—symbols can be stored only in STM, where we would expect most of the within-state temporary symbols also to be held. Over residence times of several seconds, however, symbols can also be stored in LTM or EM. Hence the knowledge state can contain more information than is held in STM.

The increments of information from one knowledge state to the next are

[11] The average duration is total time divided by total number of nodes in the PBG. These averages have been calculated for only a few subjects, but we are concerned here with an order-of-magnitude estimate of average duration, and these illustrative data suffice for that.

limited by the amounts that can be stored during the residence interval. If a subject moves through the problem space at an average rate of five seconds per node, he cannot record very much information about the task in his LTM, which requires times of the order of 5K seconds to fixate a new symbol structure containing K symbols. But he can record *something*, especially if the knowledge is incremental.

The possibilities for storage of new information in EM are slightly more generous. Our tasks show that the subjects add to EM only sporadically, but then with a marked effect on their styles of problem solving. Slight differences in task structure (beyond the range we have studied) might make a real difference in strategies for external storage. For example, a man trying to solve complex equations, or a man writing a computer program, generally writes almost continually on scratch paper, thus putting a significant amount of his current knowledge into EM.

In summary, from a comparison of the memory write times of the IPS with the typical residence time in a single knowledge state, we can localize the current knowledge state as the content of STM together with a small quantity of information in LTM, plus a variable amount (a modest amount in our tasks) in EM.

Residence Times and Availability. By our definition of the current knowledge state, we require that the information in it actually be available to the problem solver in making his move to the next knowledge state. The information that is held in STM is immediately available. The same may be true for the part of the knowledge state that is in LTM, since it is retrievable within a few hundred milliseconds and without the execution of deliberate retrieval programs (e.g., it can be retrieved upon simple recognition of a familiar symbol in STM). There is a question as to whether this information will be retrieved when appropriate, but the situation is maximally favorable to its being called, for the information is both recent and in context. However, there is no absolute assurance that it will always be retrieved; in fact, some of the errors that plague problem solvers can be localized at this interface (e.g., in cryptarithmetic, S3's failure to recall that $T = 0$).

The situation with respect to EM is different. As long as information is within foveal view, it is effectively part of STM. But if it is outside the fovea, difficulties arise in guaranteeing its availability during the residence time of a knowledge state. Within an interval of several seconds, much external information can be accessed and read, but doing so requires explicit programs, especially for scanning it to bring the relevant parts within foveal view.

Hence, if all the information in EM is invariably to be available, the programs must be rather systematic and compulsive in their accessing behavior. Our observations of human behavior, especially in logic and chess, suggest that access to the EM depends on specific searches triggered by specific conditions (except for the initial orientation to a new external stimulus). Under these circumstances, it is necessary to define an *extended knowledge state* that is larger than the immediate knowledge state, but that can be accessed selectively within the course of processing during residence at a single node.

It follows also from these considerations that the immediate knowledge state is always kept small by the requirement of availability, but that the extended knowledge state may grow continually, provided the problem solver has appropriate selective accessing programs.[12]

Other factors are important in determining the sizes of the immediate and extended knowledge states held in EM. One of these is the actual physical limit on available EM—when the blackboard is filled, nothing more can be written unless something is first erased.

A second factor is more interesting, for it involves the cooperative action of internal LTM with EM. The most severe limit on LTM is the five-second-per-symbol write time; the most severe limit on EM is the search time to locate a relevant item for reading. It is sometimes efficient to store information in EM because it can be recorded rapidly, but to store *index entries* (i.e., accessing information) in LTM so that the EM can be read quickly. In fact, an EM of more than very modest size is almost useless for problem solving without such a complementary internalized index.

Processing Speeds and Residence Times. The information we possess about the processing rates of the human IPS provides another heuristic argument for expecting the typical residence time in a knowledge state to be a matter of seconds rather than minutes. What is the IPS doing during this time? It is exploring the extended knowledge state and then, on the basis of that exploration, selecting and executing an operator to obtain new knowledge—and thus move to a new knowledge state.

Our empirical knowledge of the operators actually employed shows that they are characteristically algorithmic subroutines (e.g., applying a rule in logic, processing a column in cryptarithmetic) that require a few seconds for execution by the human IPS.

But why could not the search for and the selection of the appropriate operator take several minutes? An extended search of this kind through a large knowledge state implies a commitment to spending much time deciding what to do, rather than making many small, incremental decisions, each on a new base of information. The problematic character of the task situations argues against the efficacy of the former procedure. The problem solver's information is not shaped precisely enough to permit him to engage profitably in such extended preparatory activity. A better balance between decision times and operator execution times provides a better use of the serial processing capacity—and implies residence times of the order of seconds, rather than minutes.

Cumulation of Knowledge

It is natural to think of problem solving as achieved by the accumulation of knowledge. It could hardly work in any other way. But from just this we would

---

[12] If we observe that the recognition process is a powerful selective accessing mechanism to the internal memory, then we see why the limits on content of the knowledge state in internal memory are so much broader than the limits for EM, which has no correspondingly powerful mechanism.

expect a different organization of knowledge from the one we have observed and described—instead of information organized in discrete current knowledge states, with some limited backup capability, we would have expected to find simply a single cumulative knowledge state. The IPS would never need to return to a previous state, but would simply add more and more information to the extended state. Indeed, LTM appears to work this way. With each week or year of life, we are informationally richer than we were before, and we never return to earlier states of ignorance or innocence until senility or pathologies overtake us.

Yet from our descriptions of behavior in problem spaces, it appears rather evident that search often does return to earlier knowledge states. The underlying reason for this phenomenon lies in the same properties of the IPS we have referred to previously. STM is too small to hold a continually growing knowledge state. If the cumulation were assigned to EM, the accessing cost would grow to unacceptable levels with the increase in information. Cumulation in LTM would avoid this disadvantage, but only by incurring large time costs for storing the information.

Memory Requirements for Backup. From time to time subjects abandon the current information state they have reached and return to a prior state. They do not, however, retain the information that would permit them to return to *any* node they have visited previously. On the contrary, at any given point in the search only one or two nodes are commonly available as backup to the current one. The reason for this is again to be found in the limits upon memory and, in particular, limits on the rate at which information can be stored.

Alternative knowledge states must be held in some memory. In view of the preemption of the STM by the current state and transient information, other states must be held primarily in LTM or EM. With either alternative, or both, the limiting factor is the number of such states that can be recorded in the times available. Of course the IPS could devote much, or most, of its time to storing such information, but only at the expense of slowing down its exploration and discovery of new information. In general, the programs we have studied avoid this expense, and they have, as a consequence, only rather rudimentary backup capabilities.

Reasons for Backup. The memory limitation argument implies only that the current knowledge state will not become arbitrarily large. It does not prove that information will be retained for returning to previous states. Indeed, some organizations of knowledge states do not make any provision for backup. For example, in cryptarithmetic (working in the basic problem space), when a contradiction arises from the assignments made up to a particular point, the contradiction could be resolved by changing one or more of the assignments independently of the order in which they were originally made—the order information would not need to be retained. In this case (as with S6 to some extent) the system would rarely return to a previous state of knowledge and then only by chance.

There are several reasons why a system will usually be more efficient that retains some capability for returning to previous knowledge states. A knowledge state may contain false information—as a result of errors in processing or recall. A knowledge state may also contain conditional information, where assumptions are made deliberately in order to work out their consequences (the conditional assignments of cryptarithmetic and the alternative moves of chess are both examples of conditional information).

In the cases either of error or of a rejected hypothesis it is desirable to abandon information if it proves inappropriate. If an error is discovered, then all the information in which the error is implicated through subsequent processing may need to be eliminated from the knowledge state. If a hypothesized alternative proves infeasible (e.g., a conditional assignment in cryptarithmetic leads to a contradiction) or undesirable (e.g., a sequence of chess moves is evaluated as unsatisfactory), all the inferred knowledge that depends on the hypothesis needs to be removed.

Insofar as increased search costs are incurred with increase in the size of the knowledge state, it may even be worthwhile to purge the current knowledge state of information that has been determined to be irrelevant. (Odd pages from the previous draft of a manuscript are best placed in the wastebasket, not left on the writing desk.)

Backup Mechanisms. Backup to a previous state may be more or less difficult. If the total knowledge state is a collection of symbol structures, each expressing a portion of the whole, abandonment of some symbol structures simply drops them out. Then the IPS automatically returns to a prior state—that state does not have to be stored as a separate, identifiable entity.

How the "dropping out" is accomplished is another matter. If the symbols were in EM, then dropping out may mean erasing them or discarding the workspace on which they were registered. It is much less clear from the evidence what capabilities the human IPS possesses for dropping out information from its internal memories. Symbols in STM can apparently simply be "written over," but it is possible that the only forgetting in LTM is that which results from modification or obliteration of the recognition capabilities that index it. In any event, elimination from LTM appears subject to very little, if any, systematic program control.

A quite different kind of backup capability is provided by the external displays, such as the chessboard. Here the initial problem state is recorded in an EM, from which it can be recovered with confidence. The presence or absence of a permanent external display of the initial problem state may largely determine the backup procedure actually adopted by the problem solver.

Noncumulative Memories. In problem solving, the knowledge state is by no means always stored in a way that facilitates returning to earlier states. When cryptarithmetic problems are solved in the basic problem space, moves from one knowledge state to another replace one piece of information with another, so that the earlier state is not recoverable from the external display and is not recoverable at all unless appropriate path information is kept elsewhere in memory.

A pure example of a noncumulative memory is the familiar 15-puzzle, shown in Figure 14.1. The state is changed in this puzzle by moving any one of the blocks adjacent to the empty space into that space. The aim of the game is to get from some initial arrangement of the blocks to one in which all the blocks are arranged in the order of their numbers.

It is extremely difficult to do this task in one's head because the number of

FIGURE 14.1

the 15-puzzle (the problem is to slide the small tiles about, making use of the single empty space, until they are arranged in ascending numerical order; in the position shown, this can be accomplished by moving the following pieces in sequence: 2-3-12-8-11-15-8-12-7-8-15-12-11-15.)

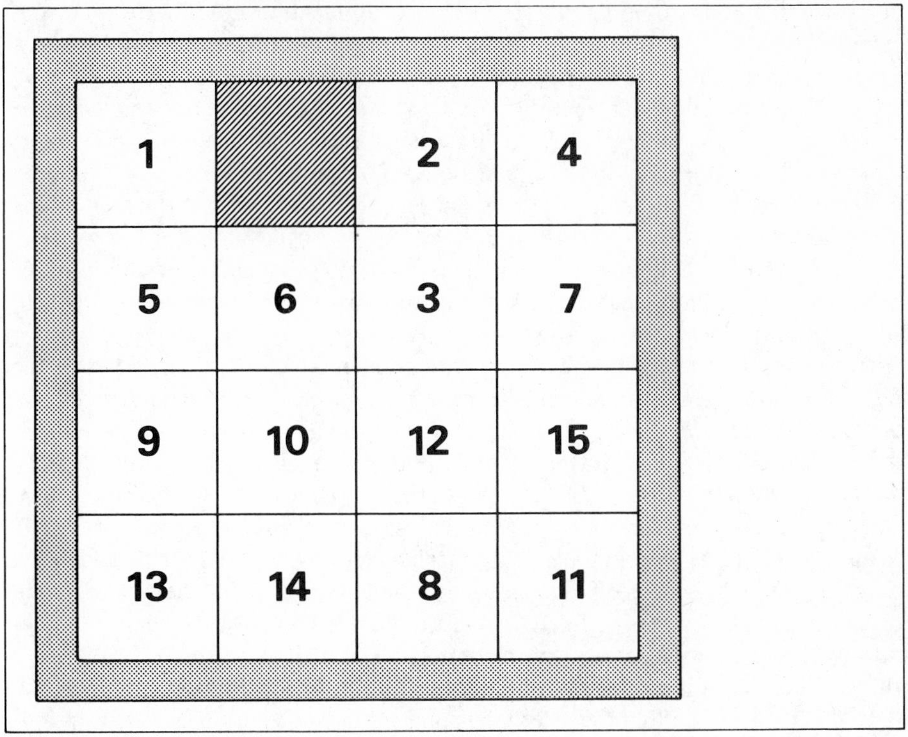

blocks is too large for STM. Most people try to solve the puzzle by manipulating the display—moving the blocks. But then their knowledge state consists almost entirely of the current state of the display. Their only ability to return to prior states depends on storing a few of the most recent moves in STM and restoring the display to a just prior one by performing the inverse operations.

Models and Descriptions. We can distinguish, roughly, two poles in the representation of the knowledge space. One of these, the *model*, is typified by the 15-puzzle, the chessboard, and by the cryptarithmetic display in the case where the problem solver enters on it the current set of assignments. In the case of a model, the current knowledge state can be viewed as a vector of fixed dimensionality. A move from one node to another consists in changing the values of one or more components of this vector. Previous knowledge states can be recovered only if previous values of vector components are retained, together with path information, or if the change operators that have been applied (or their inverses) are retained. In the chess mating combinations program described in Chapter 13, the latter mechanism was employed to permit arbitrary backup to previously visited nodes.

The use of the model format generally discourages return to prior states, since

817

the representation of the current situation itself is independent of the route by which it was reached. As we have just indicated, auxiliary information must therefore be retained in order to permit backup.

At the other pole from the model is the *description*, typified by the display of initial and derived expressions in the logic problems. In general, a description is a set of statements in some language (1) whose conjunction describes the current (extended) knowledge state and (2) whose validity is unconditional and does not depend on the node at which they are known.

In a description, statements that are known at one node may be *unknown* at another node (hence not part of that knowledge state), but they are not *false* at that node. The elements of a model can also be interpreted as statements, but only if they are made conditional—say, by subscripting them with the name of the node—so that they are only asserted to hold at a particular node.

Descriptions, unlike models, cumulate, hence do not require erasing in order to move to a new knowledge state. If the memory in which the description is held has ordering properties (e.g., a list on a sheet of paper), then the elements of a description will generally be entered in the order in which they are added to the state of knowledge. To this extent, some earlier states of knowledge can be recovered automatically by ignoring the subsequent items in the description.

An actual knowledge state can combine both model and descriptive aspects, of course. The part of the knowledge state held in LTM is apt to be descriptive, partly because some order information is almost always recorded with it, partly because there are no systematic erasing mechanisms, as required for a model. On the other hand, the part of the knowledge state held in EM—particularly if a formatted display is used—is likely to constitute a model. However, these generalizations have exceptions. When a problem is small enough to be solved in the head with STM alone, it is most apt to be represented by a model. On the other hand, we have already noted that the external display in the logic problems is description-like in character.

Long-term Cumulation. Because the external memory can accumulate information continuously and indefinitely (as with the logic display), we had to distinguish the immediate knowledge state from the extended knowledge state. If we take periods of time much longer than those needed to solve single problems—days, weeks, or years—then an indefinite amount of information can also accumulate in LTM. After such accumulation, the human IPS does not return to earlier states. Many terms are used to designate this longer-run cumulation: learning, education, training, experience, and so on. It is not necessary to distinguish among these here.

Thus, no sharp line can be drawn between the short-run cumulative changes in information during a problem solving session, which we have called moves in the problem space, and the long-run changes called learning. We must think of search as having a short-run component involving exploring and returning, riding atop a slower, gradual cumulation. Because of the time scales of the experiments, the tasks we explored have not provided much evidence of this two-level movement. We did, however, see some effects of learning in logic, and we can assert with reasonable assurance that it occurs generally.

We can now treat explicitly a property of the problem space that has been implicit throughout our discussion: that the space is in some sense closed under the operations that transform one current knowledge state into another. The closure we refer to is empirical and approximate, not formal. As with the other properties of the problem space, we wish to show that its (empirically) closed character is intimately related to the properties of the IPS.

Given other things we know about the problem solving human IPS, the closure property is not trivial. The human problem solver has an internal LTM in which is stored an enormous—essentially infinite—baggage. If we allow him to locomote, to reach a shelf of books, or even to glance freely around the laboratory, the totality of external information stored about him, to which he has access, is also essentially infinite. (*Infinite*, in this context, need mean only: far more than he could possibly scan during a problem solving session.) It is a striking fact that the problem solver usually evokes an extremely limited part of his internal store, and attends to an extremely limited part of his external environment. What is grossly irrelevant to the task in either of these memories could just as well not be there. We never detect either its presence or absence. [Exercise for the reader: from any one of the problem solving protocols reconstruct: (1) the extent of the subject's knowledge of Latin, ceramics, or modern history, or (2) a description of the room in which the experiment was performed.]

At any given point in its history, the IPS has available in its LTM a set of discriminations it can make, a set of relations and features it can notice, and a set of processing operations it can perform (nonproblematically). On exposure to a task a certain collection of such symbol structures and processes is evoked—in a later section we will discuss how this might come about. These structures and processes define the problem space: certain predicates can and will be noticed, certain operations can and will be performed. If the IPS is a production system, these two aspects of its performance will be determined by the condition and action parts, respectively, of its productions. Since the set of structures and processes—the productions, if you will—is finite, so also will be the problem space, at least initially.

The question is why it remains finite—why the IPS does not continually wander into new regions of LTM and EM. Our hypothesis is that the kinds of information produced by the problem solving processes—namely, the knowledge states —are all of a piece with the information initially evoked, and do not have associations, via the productions, with other materials in memory to evoke new information that would continually enlarge the problem space. If only algebraic operations are performed on algebraic expressions, then only new algebraic expressions are produced, and these evoke, in turn, only algebraic operations. Substitute for "algebraic" the name of any other task domain and the propositions remain true.

The closed character of a problem space is closely akin to functional fixity. The subject immerses himself in an informational environment that evokes only elements belonging to that environment. No *absolute* bar—independent of his production system—prevents him from generating ideas that go outside the standard problem space. Recall that S8, in cryptarithmetic, spent 40 minutes exploring alternative methods before settling in to the standard augmented problem space. In the tasks we examined, closure was the rule, but we can conceive of other tasks where a program might be evoked that would cause extensive search through LTM (e.g., free association) or actual physical search of the external environment (e.g., a manned landing on the Moon) or of a library (e.g., browsing).

Only in the case of at least approximate closure is it useful, or even operationally meaningful, to speak of problem solving as taking place in a problem space. The concept of problem space permits us to mark off a small portion of the internal and external memory and information sources, and to postulate the irrelevance of anything that lies outside the lines of demarcation. To assert that the problem solving takes place in this problem space is to say that the problem solving processes will never (or seldom) carry thought beyond these boundaries.

The closure of the problem space permits a relatively small production system to guide the behavior of the problem solver (or to describe it, from the viewpoint of the psychologist). The exact size of the production system does not seem to be an important descriptive parameter. It is certainly important that it be small enough to allow it to be discovered and analyzed. But additional productions come into use and into view with every new aspect of significant variety in the task environment. The point at which analysis stops is dictated by the frequency with which particular productions are evoked (recall Figures 6.10 and 7.29, which show the diminishing marginal explanatory utility of the successive productions for cryptarithmetic). The subject undoubtedly has other productions in LTM, especially to deal with error conditions, that we simply did not detect. In chess this was especially evident, for our catalog of productions for move generation (Table 12.2) was quite insufficient to cover the entire play of a chess game.

Possibly, in working on a task a *context* is somehow selected, so that a subset of the productions in LTM becomes the operative system; and there is then a boundary in LTM around it. While there is ample evidence for the presence of such context effects, nothing in our study identifies the context-establishing or context-maintaining mechanisms. It is quite possible that each production is selected, when it is to be used, from a very large set, which we simply never observe because the selection is limited, by the limited contents of STM, to a very small subset.

When Does the Problem Space Exist?

The concept of problem space is useful for describing behavior, therefore, only if the information accumulated during the course of the behavior remains pretty well confined within closed boundaries. Is the converse true: that whenever the sequence of knowledge states in observed behavior stays within a closed space, it is useful to regard that space as a *problem space*? Without trying to provide a definitive answer to what is essentially a question of word usage, we can illuminate the issues with some examples.

Provide a subject with paper and pencil and ask him to multiply 1492 × 1762. When he is done, his paper will look something like this:

$$1492$$
$$1762$$
$$\overline{2984}$$
$$8952$$
$$10444$$
$$1492$$
$$\overline{2628904}$$

There is no difficulty in describing his problem space, if he has one at all, just as we have done for the other tasks. Essentially, it is the space of all complete and incomplete arrays of the sort illustrated above (supplemented by information about the carries, which our subject presumably held temporarily in STM). It is clear enough from the display that the subject solved the problem by factoring it, more or less as follows:

$$(1492 \times 1762) = (1492 \times 2) + (1492 \times 6 \times 10)$$
$$+ (1492 \times 7 \times 100) + (1492 \times 1 \times 1000).$$

One could speak of the subgoals of carrying out the one-digit multiplications, shifting left, and performing the final addition.

If the subject were reasonably skilled in arithmetic, the description above, referring to goals, would not provide a veridical analysis of his behavior. If he provided a protocol, we would not expect to find goal statements in it, or evidences of explicit goal structures. In common-sense terms, we might not refer to him as solving a problem at all, but simply as following "mechanically" a well-learned algorithm for multiplication.

On the other hand, if the subject were interrupted in midstream—after the second multiplication, say—he would probably not start off from the beginning again, but would take up where he left off. If he were interrupted in the *middle* of a multiplication, however, he probably would redo that whole multiplication, not trusting his STM to retain the proper value of the carry. (That is, the acceptable interruption points would be points where no essential information was being held in STM.)

The "mechanization" of the algorithm appears to be a matter of degree along another dimension also. If our subject were an elementary school child, his protocol might reveal more or less definite traces of a verbal recipe he was following: "First, I must multiply by the digit on the right of the multiplier. . . ." At a very early stage, we might discover him actually listening to a teacher, and following her instructions step by step.

Finally, if we asked someone, fully able to execute the standard multiplication algorithm, to *explain* why it gave him the right answer, we might receive from him a more or less coherent reply, or none at all.

If the reader finds it difficult to reconstruct these various performances in his imagination, because he is too familiar with the multiplication algorithm, let him introspect about algorithms he knows less well—the algorithm for extracting square roots, say, or for checking multiplications by "casting out nines." He will be aware of a typical developmental sequence:

1. At the outset the algorithm is followed by reference, step by step, to a recipe stored in EM.
2. The recipe is memorized (stored internally) but still has to be executed by step-by-step interpretation.
3. The memorized recipe is "mechanized"—that is to say, compiled in the internal language of programs, so that it can now be executed directly and without interpretation.
4. More or less independently of the previous sequence, an understanding may be acquired of the logical justification for the algorithm—of why it works. Observe that a high level of mechanization can be achieved in executing the algorithm, without any evidences of understanding; and a high level of understanding can be achieved at a stage where the algorithm still has to be followed from an externally stored recipe. (The latter is likely to be true only of relatively elaborate algorithms—e.g., the simplex algorithm for linear programming.)

Essentially the same problem space can be used to describe the behavior, regardless of where it stands along these developmental sequences. The level of understanding is likely to affect performance primarily in recovery from error or interruption. Over longer periods of time it also affects the ease with which the subject acquires or retains the algorithm in memory, but that is an issue that goes beyond the scope of the present study. Finally, it may be exhibited in the subject's flexibility in adopting shortcuts and adapting the algorithm to special cases. A high degree of mechanization, on the other hand, may actually inhibit the use of special procedures for special cases.

Algorithms. When a subject is using a highly specific algorithm (e.g., the simplex algorithm for linear programming) to solve a problem in a highly mechanical way and with a low error rate (hence with little occasion to use procedures that stand outside the formal algorithm), it adds little to our knowledge about him to say that "he is engaged in problem solving activity." We might as well say that "he is carrying out the XYZ algorithm." None of the phenomena that make problem solving interesting are likely to appear in his behavior, precisely because the algorithm has been tailored (1) to guarantee solution of problems of the class in question, (2) to operate smoothly within the limits of the IPS with whatever specific EM aids are provided, and (3) to avoid searches as much as possible.

If we wish to have a term to refer to these arbitrarily varied sequences of behavior that are carried out under control of specific algorithms, we can call them *programmed activity*. They take place in problem spaces, but are to be distinguished (at least as a matter of degree) from the *unprogrammed activity*—i.e., less stereotyped and mechanized activity, involving search and backup—that we have treated in this book as problem solving behavior (March and Simon, 1958).

Planning. Problem solving within the context of a plan has somewhat the same flavor as executing a specialized algorithm, for plans are structurally identical to programs. They are symbolic structures, available in LTM (or in EM), that are used to guide action in exploring the problem space.

Plans involve exactly the same kind of commitment that we find in following algorithms like the simplex algorithm. Some prior activity—the development of the plan—results in a conviction that the plan is worth pursuing. Thereupon, there occurs implementation activity to carry out the plan. Plans, like those in the logic task, range from two-step affairs to rather lengthy sequences. There is no rigid boundary between behavior in which the subject is searching in the problem space (unprogrammed activity) and his behavior when he is following a predetermined plan (programmed activity). The programmed and unprogrammed aspects of his behavior are so interwoven that we have found it convenient to treat them both as interrelated components of his total problem solving activity.

Conclusion : Problem Space and IPS

In summary, we have discussed most of the regularities that problem spaces seem to possess, as listed in the beginning of this section. (The only listed item not mentioned is the nature of path information, where we have been silent because we have little to say.) We have tried to show the consistency between these regularities and the basic characteristics of the human IPS and to show, thereby, the plausibility of the idea that problem solving behavior takes the form of a search through a problem space.

We have not derived the problem space concept from the IPS characteristics, in the sense of showing that, given this kind of IPS, it is *necessary* that it search a problem space in order to solve problems. A proof, even if it exists, is well beyond the current state of understanding. To carry out such a demonstration, for instance, some way is needed to represent the set of all possible programs that accomplishes a given set of functions under specified structural limits. We know of no such representation.

TASK ENVIRONMENT AND PROBLEM SPACE

Having examined the nature of the problem space, we consider now the thesis that the structure of that space is largely determined by the structure of the task environment—more precisely, that the task environment delimits the set of *possible* structures of the problem space. For nothing forces a problem space to incorporate all aspects of the structure of the task environment, and indeed, all problem spaces are abstractions from that environment. But for the moment we will not be concerned with the differences between the possibilities and their realizations, which will be the topic of a later section.

In Chapter 3 we emphasized the impossibility of giving an objective description of the task environment—a description that is completely independent of the vantage point of the describer. In the light of this objection, we restate our basic thesis in the following symmetric pair of propositions:

1. The only aspects of the task environment that are relevant to solving a problem in a particular problem space are those that are reflected in the structure of that space.
2. The effectiveness of a problem solving scheme depends wholly on its reflecting aspects of the structure of the task environment.

The second proposition is obvious, since, by definition, problems lie in the objective task environment, hence only information about that environment can be relevant to their solution. The first proposition is demonstrated whenever we show, as we have for the tasks analyzed in previous chapters, that the behavior of the subject can be described as taking place in the problem space. Our task now is to show *how* structural information about the task environment is embedded in the problem space, and how this information is used in the problem solving process.

However difficult or impossible it may be to describe the task environment neutrally—that is, independently of its representation in terms of a particular problem space—the fact that it possesses certain structure—hence certain information that may be relevant to solving problems—is an objective fact, not dependent on the representation. Moreover, this structural information can be defined without reference to any properties of a problem solver who might use it.

In this section we will enumerate the decision points in the problem space at which information could be applied to aid problem solving. Then we will examine the possible sources of information in the task environment, giving special attention to two important special cases: factorability of the task environment, and the representation of task structure by variables. In order to make clearer, however, the *objective* character of the structure of the task environment, we will first take another look at the tic-tac-toe example that we have used in previous discussions of representation.

Invariance of Task Environment Structure

We have already defined one task that is isomorphic to tic-tac-toe: Number Scrabble. Let us now define still another isomorph.[13]

We draw a highly symmetric game tree. The tree is uniformly nine nodes deep, and each node (except the terminals) has exactly nine branches. The total number of branches is therefore 9^9, or a little less than four hundred million (387,420,489). The terminal branches are marked as *win*, *lose*, or *draw* for the first player. We give arbitrary names to the nodes and the branches.

This game tree is not quite isomorphic to the game tree for tic-tac-toe, but can be made so as follows: First, we identify each branch at any node of the new tree with the operation of placing an $\times$ or $\bigcirc$, as appropriate, in one of the nine squares of the tic-tac-toe display. After the first move, certain of these moves will be illegal, because the square will already be occupied. We place a marker on the branches corresponding to illegal moves. We now set the values on the remaining

[13] There are still others; see Michon (1967) and footnote 19, below.

legal terminal branches (362,880 in number) to correspond with the values for tic-tac-toe. With this modification, the new game tree represents tic-tac-toe, and could be used as a problem space for that game. (The tree could be pruned further, for along a number of subtrees the value of the game will be decided before the ninth move. We will simply disregard this inessential redundancy.)

There is nothing we can say about the new game tree that does not translate into a corresponding (and semantically synonymous) statement for tic-tac-toe or for number scrabble. The converse is equally true. In particular, we could play the new game by using the tic-tac-toe problem space, or vice versa. Hence, any structure that is present in the task environment can be expressed by translating into one of the problem spaces for which its expression is simple. The translation may itself be a complex process, but it certainly can be carried out by finite means.

For example, because of the symmetries possessed by the tic-tac-toe display, we can assign the common label, corner, to certain of the squares, and corner-moves to moves that occupy these squares. The geometric symmetries of the tic-tac-toe display will correspond to symmetries in the new game tree (marked for illegal moves)—that is, to its invariance under permutation of certain subtrees. Hence, the information about the symmetries—which can be used to reduce search—is present in the new game tree as surely as it is present in the tic-tac-toe display. A subset of the moves in the tree can be labeled corner-moves, and the term will have lost none of its structural significance, even if it no longer retains the specific geometric meaning it had in the tic-tac-toe representation.

Thus, although we have no way of talking about the structure of a task environment without somehow representing that environment, we *can* talk about alternative, isomorphic, representations of the *same* environment. We mean by the structure of the environment precisely the set of invariants that are preserved under translation from any one of these isomorphs to any other.

A problem space may contain more or less structure than the environment it represents. If it contains more (e.g., the fact that the tic-tac-toe array, as usually drawn, is square) some of this structure will be spurious. It will be at best useless, and possibly harmful to the problem solving process. If the problem space contains less structure than the environment, it may not permit maximum use of the structural information that is potentially available.

But presence or absence of structural information does not tell the whole story about problem spaces; if it did, the tic-tac-toe, number scrabble, and our tree space would all be equivalent from a problem solving standpoint—which they clearly are not. As we have seen throughout the book, there is also an issue of how *available* the information is in a particular representation—to what extent it can be incorporated explicitly in the current information state, or is readily derivable from that state. Let us summarize what determines this availability.

Decision Points in Problem Space

Structural information affects the efficiency of problem solving to the extent that it influences the choices the IPS makes at the decision points in its search through the problem space. A problem solving IPS is called upon to make four principal kinds of decisions:

1. At a knowledge state (a node in the problem space), to select an operator to be applied.
2. At a new knowledge state, to determine whether problem solving shall continue from this state or not.
3. At a knowledge state, to determine whether the knowledge state shall be remembered, so that return can be made to it at some later time.
4. At the decision to abandon a knowledge state, instead of continuing to search from it, to select another knowledge state as the backup state.

Backup Decisions. The main burden of the problem solving effort is sustained by the first pair of decisions—guiding search by selecting operators and by evaluating new states of knowledge. The second pair of decisions usually offers fewer opportunities for the application of structural information. For reasons of memory, already stated, only one or two prior information states are retained during problem solving as backup, and one of these is usually the initial state. The initial state served as a backup state in all our three tasks, but the backup state could instead be a recently visited state, as in the 15-puzzle.

When the knowledge state is descriptive—i.e., an accumulation of small symbol structures—what states are kept as backup generally depends on which component predicates are retained long enough (by use) to become part of the LTM. Thus no explicit decisions are made to keep particular backup states. In cryptarithmetic, decisions were made periodically to record predicates in EM (e.g., assignments on the display) instead of LTM, but these decisions recorded aspects of the current knowledge state, even though the information might later be used for backup. Other tasks might be found where the decision about what backup information to keep is a major aspect of the problem solving process, but it was not for the three tasks we studied.

Similarly, the decision about which prior state to return to seems to be handled in relatively automatic ways—and in any event, only one or two such states are usually available for choice. Much of the backup we observed simply resulted automatically from abandoning a knowledge state. Again, we must be careful not to extrapolate this observation beyond the types of tasks studied.

Search and Scan. A number of the most effective heuristic problem solving programs for computers make use of a *search-scan* strategy that is heavily dependent upon backup capabilities. The essential ideas of the strategy are these (recall Figures 4.4 and 13.3): (1) enough information is kept about prior nodes so that any knowledge state previously visited can be recovered; (2) an evaluation of its *promise* is made of each knowledge state from which search has not yet been undertaken; (3) each successive burst of search is made from the knowledge state that is most promising among those available at the moment, and the new nodes created are then evaluated.

Although strong arguments can be made for the effectiveness of this scheme in many kinds of problem spaces, it was not used by our subjects. Since the scheme would place heavy demands upon memory for backup information, its absence from the repertory of human problem solving programs that we encountered is a consequence of the structure of the human IPS.

Compound Problem Spaces.   The four decision points listed earlier in this section occur in all problem spaces, but there are some other aids to problem solving that may or may not be represented in any particular problem space: for example, the possibility of working backward, the possibility of working abstractly—as in planning—or the possibility of using various EM's.

These all provide means for extracting information about the structure of the problem space. We may think of them, as we did in Chapter 5, as permitting multiple problem spaces to be used simultaneously. There can exist a separate working-backwards problem space, a separate planning space, or a separate external problem space, in just the same way as there can exist an augmented problem space distinct from the basic one. The structure of the task environment, of course, determines whether such possibilities exist. Our present concern is only with the question of how, if they do exist, they permit structural information to be incorporated in problem spaces and used in solving problems.

As we saw in logic, human problem solvers do not always keep these different problem spaces entirely separate. Rather, they mix their behavior: planning and working-backwards processes are embedded in the main problem space. The decision to use either seems to be a local decision, made within the knowledge state and without switching problem spaces. The same is true of the scanning of EM's. We can think of these processes as offering additional operators that can be applied in the problem space—not as causing a change in space. Decisions about their application are then subsumed under the decision about which operator to apply at a knowledge state.

In summary, we can focus our attention on the two main decision points where operators are selected and new knowledge states evaluated. These two decision points are the crucial ones for applying knowledge of the task environment in order to enhance the selectivity of the problem solving search.

Information Sources

Structure in a problem space is equivalent to redundancy. By virtue of redundancy, information present in one part of the space becomes predictive—at least heuristically—of properties in another part of the space. Nodes in the problem space (knowledge states) are described or named in a state language. Nodes in the space are connected by sequences of operations, named or described in a process language. There are at least two ways—corresponding approximately to the two main decisions for the problem solver—in which structure can be exploited for problem solving purposes.

First, structure can contribute to problem solving if it correlates information in the state language, about one or more nodes, with information in the process language about the operators at those nodes. Such correlations may permit selectivity in the choice of operators.

Second, structure can be exploited if it correlates information in the state language about one node with information about another—information as to whether the two are connected, and how close they are. Such correlations may permit selectivity in deciding whether to proceed from a node, and in choosing a backup.

In addition to these two basic kinds of correlations, structure can also be exploited if it provides information about symmetries or other regularities in the problem tree, so that searches that are essentially repetitive may be avoided. Thus, recognition of the symmetry in tic-tac-toe reduces the number of distinct first moves from nine to three: center, side, and corner.

Formal Description of Structure. Speaking in general terms, problem solving is concerned with finding paths from initial states to desired states. The current state of knowledge contains at least information about the current state and the desired state (there must always be enough information to determine whether the goal has been reached). This information may be used to select the next operator (the first decision) or to decide whether to proceed from the current state (the second decision). In first approximation, we can describe the structural information in terms of the product space, of the set of current states U, the set of desired states G, and the set of operators Q: $U \times G \times Q$. Information relevant to the first decision takes the form of functions from $U \times G$ to Q. Information relevant to the second decision takes the form of predicates on $U \times G$, which can be evaluated *true* (continue from the node u_i) or *false* (discontinue search from u_i). Matters can be slightly more complicated, since the predicate may involve not only the current and desired states, but also other states that have previously been visited.

Consider structural information in the form of a function from $U \times G$ to Q. For each combination of desired state and current state, this function selects an operator to be executed. At one extreme—the worst case—the function might be definable only by a list, *in extenso*, of all the function values: one value for each pair of current and goal states. In general, such a function would be known only if the entire problem space had already been explored (by the problem solver or someone else). Hence, a problem space described only by such an arbitrary function would be no more tractable than a space with random connections between states and relevant operators—in fact, this is what one might mean by "random."

As an example of extensional definition of structure, consider a tic-tac-toe isomorph in which each of the nodes in the tree previously defined has an arbitrary, noninterpretable, name, and each branch also has such a name, unrelated to the names of the nodes it connects. With this representation, useful information for a player could only consist of a table of pairs, associating the name of each node with the name of the preferred branch at that node. But information can be given in this form even in the absence of any regularity of structure in the tree.

The actual problem spaces we have studied are far more manageable than this in at least two ways. First, they are at least approximately *factorable*. Second, the function relating states to operators can be defined more compactly and parsimoniously by the introduction of *variables*. In the next two sections—after one concluding comment in this one—we shall discuss these two concepts and their implications for search through a problem space.

Some Particular Information Structures.   The form of our definition of the operator selection function—as a function from $U \times G$ to Q—suggests that the operator to be applied depends both upon the current state and the desired state. In special cases it may, of course, depend on only one of these arguments, or on neither. Means-ends analysis provides an important class of examples where the function depends on both u and g—specifically, on their difference. In a pure *working-forward* strategy it may depend only on u, and in a pure *working-backward* strategy, only on g. If the operators are always tried in a fixed order of priority (as in some versions of the Logic Theorist), this priority ordering may be regarded as a constant function, determining q independently of both u and g.

In the same way, the predicate for evaluating the current state as a node from which to proceed may depend on both u and g or only upon u. A *progress test*, which falls in the former category, measures the distance of u from g. A *simplicity criterion*, which belongs to the latter category, rejects states that are too complex.

Factorability

Suppose that each state, u_i, in the problem space can be described in terms of the presence or absence of a number, n, of features. We can then write

$$u_i = (x_{i1}, x_{i2}, \ldots, x_{in})$$

where x_{ij} is *feature-present* or *feature-absent*. Initially, we will simplify matters further by assuming that g, the goal state, is invariant over all tasks, so that it can be omitted from explicit mention. Suppose, now that there exists a function from features to operators such that if feature j is present in state u_i, then operator g_i is relevant in state u_i. The notion is readily generalized to the case of a function from sets of features to operators, or from functions of features, and is equally readily generalized to the case where more than one operator may be associated with a given feature or function of features; but we will hold to the simplest case of a single-valued mapping from individual features to operators.

Since there are n features, there are 2^n discriminable states in the problem space. Owing to the factorability, however, we now need deal only with a function consisting of n pairs, instead of a function consisting of 2^n pairs. Moreover, if we know the space to have this structure, the mapping can be discovered after a search of only a small part of the total space.

As the next case, suppose that the relevance of an operator for reaching a desired state, g, from a current state, u_i, depends not upon the absolute features of u_i but only on the components, d_j, of a difference vector $d(g, u_i)$, where d_j has the value *difference-present* or *difference-absent*. That is, we define a relevance function from the set of difference vectors, D, to Q. This kind of relevance function, from D to Q, is the formal kernel of means-ends analysis. The assertion that means-ends analysis is a frequently powerful problem solving method is an assertion that relevance functions from D to Q can be defined in many task environments.

These kinds of functions from states to operators can be regarded appropriately as *factoring* the state space, because they make the relevance of a particular operator depend on only a single feature of the state, independently of which other features may be present or absent. A weak kind of interdependence may be reintroduced, however, by ordering the features. Then we might define an operator as relevant if its feature is present and no other feature is present that stands higher in the ordering.

In the limiting case, a problem space may be completely factorable. By this we mean that application of an operator that is relevant to a particular feature removes that feature, and affects no other. Suppose that the features are differences, as defined above. Then complete factorability implies that paths from an initial node to the goal node are permutable—the set of differences can be removed in any sequence by applying the corresponding relevant operators in the same sequence. Problem spaces with complete factorability will generally be rather uninteresting— the problems they define can be solved trivially once the function defining the structure of the space is given. The actual problem spaces we have examined are in certain respects nearly factorable, but not by any means completely factorable.

Where states in the problem space can be represented by vectors of factors, it may be possible to define abstracted spaces that retain most of the structural information in the original space but eliminate much detail. Such abstracted spaces are the planning spaces: the features and operators that are eliminated by abstraction are called *inessential*, while those that are retained are called *essential*. Where a subset of features and operators defines a completely factorable subspace, labeling this subset as inessential creates an abstracted space retaining most of the information that is important for finding paths in the original space.

The representation of states as vectors of features also facilitates the representation of task environments where the problem solution is not a single, specific goal state, but a set of features defining a whole class of states. Thus *checkmate* is not a specific arrangement of pieces on a chessboard, but a whole class of such arrangements.

The illustrations of these concepts in the problem spaces for cryptarithmetic, logic, and chess will probably already be more or less familiar from the analyses of those tasks in Chapters 5, 8, and 11, respectively, but we give some explicit examples later in this chapter.

Variables

Thus far we have considered problem spaces where the states are fixed vectors and the operators are associated with, and alter, specific features, or components, of these vectors. Many problem spaces contain another dimension of structure that provides much information for problem solving. In these spaces it is possible to describe whole classes of operators and states by *variables*. To apply an operator containing a variable, $q(x)$ say, to a specific state, $u(v)$, say, the value of the variable, x, in the operator is fixed to correspond with the value, v, that the variable takes in the description of the state. In the example, $q(x)$ becomes $q(v)$. The state that is reached by application of the operator q(v) depends on the value (here v) that has been assigned to the variable.

Thus, the *commute* operator of ordinary arithmetic takes any expression of the form A + B, where A and B are variables, and changes it to an expression of the form B + A, with the same values of A and B as in the input expression.

Operators containing variables serve as a form of abstraction, for they allow abstract paths to be defined from a whole class of states to the corresponding members of another class of states. Thus the commute operator of arithmetic takes all states of the class a + B (where a is now a particular number) into states of the class B + a. Hence, the structure of the space can be defined in terms of functions on such classes, and whole classes of paths can be searched simultaneously. In tracing paths through the space, there is complete freedom in determining at what stage the particular members of interest in a class will be selected. When, as is often the case, the selection can be postponed until a single member of the class has been identified, search is avoided entirely.

Variables may be viewed, alternatively, as devices for specifying that particular operators leave certain things invariant when they operate on a state. Thus, if an operator transforms A(B + C) into AB + AC, we may say that the position occupied by the A in the input expression *corresponds* to the positions occupied by A's in the output expression. The notation for variables allows us to specify that the symbol occupying these corresponding positions is left invariant by the operation. Thus, if an operator changes specific features of any state of a certain class, but is guaranteed to leave certain other features invariant, the latter features can be represented by variables, whose values specify the various states belonging to this class.

Static and Dynamic Information

The structural information we have discussed up to this point relates to the first decision: selecting an operator. Hence it involves functions from states to operators, connecting the language in which states of the world are described with the language in which processes that act on the world are described—the afferent language with the efferent. Information used to evaluate states (to measure the distance, for example, from the desired state) would not seem to involve the process language at all, for such information says nothing directly about operators.

This seems a little paradoxical if evaluations are to have any relevance for the problem solving process, which certainly involves the selective application of operators. The appearance of paradox vanishes when we note that operator selection is an application of foresight, while state evaluation is an application of hindsight. The first decision answers the question: which of several alternative operators shall I apply next in building this path toward the goal? The second decision answers the question: am I on a promising path to the goal, or would it be better to abandon it for another?

The first decision is made on the basis of information (the function of states onto operators) that allows a prediction of the relative promise of different actions.

The second decision is based on information (the evaluation function) that judges the efficacy of past actions. Since the results (i.e., the value of the current state) are now available, the evaluation may be regarded as the computation of the value of the sequence of actions that reached this state—i.e., the computation of a function of the current state to that action sequence. This computation takes the place of prior knowledge of the structure of the problem space.

Hindsight information is useful only if there is some capability for backup. For the information can be used only to leave the current path for some other path. Foresight takes information that is available statically, as part of the current knowledge state, while hindsight makes partial dynamic searches of alternatives in order to decide which offers greater promise for further search.

In some task environments it is possible to substitute static calculations on the current state for dynamic searches ahead from that state. Among the tasks we have studied, chess provides the best examples of staticizing dynamic information. Consider a chess position (Figure 14.2) in which Black's Queen (on her home square) is not under attack, but in which Black has a legal move for his King's Knight (now standing on his KB3). Consider a move of that Knight, and suppose that, after the move, White's Queen's Bishop (standing on his KB4) is attacking Black's Queen. This attack would be an important element in evaluating the position after the Knight move—hence in judging the move by hindsight.

But if we reexamine the original position, we see that essentially the same information can be obtained by foresight. Chess language has a substantial number of terms for describing positions—for example:

forking square: a square from which a piece (of a certain type) could attack two or more pieces simultaneously. (In Figure 14.2, K6 is a forking square from which a White Knight could attack the Rook and Queen.)

pinned piece: a piece so located that, if it were moved, another piece would come under attack. (In Figure 14.2 the Black Knight is pinned against its Queen by White's Bishop.)

Now, in the original position as described, Black's King's Knight is a pinned piece. This can be discovered from geometric properties of the position without actually making the Knight's move dynamically. The fact that the Knight is pinned might be used, in the way of foresight, to eliminate all Knight moves from consideration without actually trying any of them.

Describing the chess position statically has many advantages. One of these, already noted, is that the same static feature may be relevant to a number of dynamic paths. Another closely related advantage is that static features may persist over sequences of moves, hence reduce recomputational requirements. [Certain typical chess blunders are the reverse side of this coin. When static descriptions are used, care must be taken to revise them as the current state changes. Thus, a player may fail to notice that when a particular piece is moved to take advantage of a static feature—a forking square, say—another static feature dependent on that piece (e.g., a defended pawn) may disappear.] To the extent that the significant properties of a chess position can be described statically, it may become possible

FIGURE 14.2

static relations in a chess position: White's K6 is a *forking square* (Black's Q and R) for the N on Q4. The N on KB6 is a *pinned piece,* pinned by White's B on Black's Q

Black

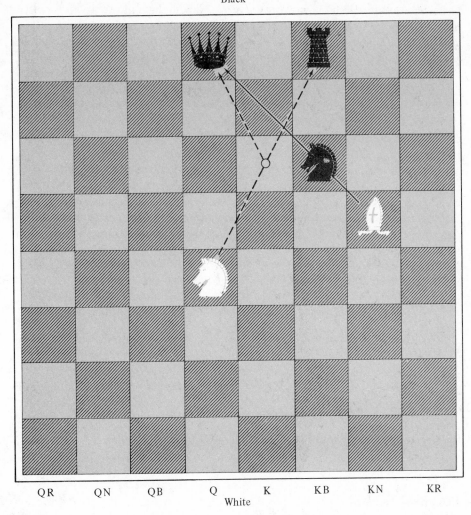

| QR | QN | QB | Q | K | KB | KN | KR |

White

to replace a large dynamic search of a tree of alternative move sequences by an analysis of the logical implications of the static properties. The distinction between dynamic and static analysis here is closely related to the distinction made earlier between models and descriptions, respectively.

Examples

Virtually all the forms of information about the structure of problem spaces that we have discussed in the preceding pages are illustrated by the three task environments examined in earlier chapters.

The basic notion of *feature* is, as we have just noted, well illustrated by the vocabulary for describing chess positions, which makes use of such terms as fork, pin, open file, attacked piece, weakened King's position, and so on. Each feature is correlated, in turn, with relevant moves that deal with the opportunity or threat, as the case may be, presented by the feature. Thus, the move of a Rook to a file is correlated with the feature that the file is open, a move of a defender with an attack on a piece, and a King's-side capture with a weakened King's position.

The logic task provides the best example of a problem space where the features take the form of differences between an initial state and a goal state. The notation for expressions in the logic task environment also makes explicit provision for variables. In addition, the logic task environment has provided us with our clearest examples of planning spaces and the distinction between essential and inessential features.

Information that can be acquired through dynamic analysis and hindsight is illustrated by the evaluation functions for chess positions, and also by the derivation of contradictions after making conditional assignments in the cryptarithmetic task environment. Information about the branchiness of the environment is illustrated most clearly in the problem space for the chess mating combinations program, MATER.

Summary

As this discussion shows, and as Chapters 5, 8, and 11, upon which it is based, showed in more detail, a great many of the characteristics of the problem solving systems we have studied can be inferred, at least in broad outline, from the structure of the environments in which they operate. To be effective in enormous problem spaces, problem solvers must be capable of extracting from the environments the information about their structure that is stored there. The forms this information takes condition the possible modes of its exploitation.

METHODS AND PROGRAMS

In this book we have described a number of specific methods that subjects use in working on tasks. Many of these have been given names: working forwards, working backwards, means-ends analysis, planning, and so on. For some of the problem solving mechanisms we have postulated, however, such as the production systems for cryptarithmetic, we developed a total system without analyzing it into labeled methods. Such a system might be viewed in toto as a single idiosyncratic method.

The task of this section is to describe the role that the methods play in the theory of problem solving. The essential point of this section is that methods are determined by the structure of the problem space. But this is not quite the whole story (nor the whole problem), so we need first to consider some preliminaries.

Methods were introduced in Chapter 4, as organizations for behavior that bear a rational relation to solving a problem. By rational is meant that if the premises of the method are granted, then it is possible for the method to produce a solution.[14] This is entirely a functional characterization. Structurally, methods are programs. Once a method is given, then behavior is determined, save for errors and interruptions.

The first issue we must settle resides right here. For, conceivably, methods could be taken as one level of organization and their realizations as programs could be another level. Certainly, methods can be stated so as to leave important aspects only partially or functionally specified. For example, the familiar method for solving quadratic equations includes the calculation of the square root of a certain quantity: *to find x such that* $ax^2 + bx + c = 0$, *compute*

$$x = -\frac{b}{2a} \pm \frac{1}{2a}\sqrt{b^2 - 4ac}$$

This statement does not specify what particular behaviors should occur in calculating this root (though it does specify certain other behaviors). The total method can take different lengths of time, have different chances of error, and so on, depending on the particulars of the subtasks. Similarly, if a method in chess, say, specifies reacting to a certain type of attack by adding a defender, the man in question is only partially specified (there may be several possible defenders), and therefore the detailed behavior (what man is actually moved) is not completely specified.

There exist indefinite gradations of these sorts of partial specifications, with correspondingly little indication of any separation between them. Thus, we identify method and program, permitting programs to contain functionally specified subprocesses and partially specified entities. This amounts to an inclusion of goals (or goal-creating processes) in programs, which has already occurred in particular examples given earlier in the book (e.g., the GPS methods in Figure 8.8, page 418).

A consequence of this definition is that no sharp distinction can be maintained between plans, as defined in Chapter 10, and methods. To paraphrase Polya (1945), a method is simply a plan that you use twice.

The Space of Methods

We have agreed to represent programs by production systems. Hence methods are to be represented as production systems, and the set of all methods is equivalent to the set of all production systems that will realize rational courses of action for

---

[14] As shown in Chapter 4, this is a minimal formulation of rationality. We do not need a more refined concept, which would permit distinguishing degrees of rationality— e.g., the "chances" of producing a solution. Our purpose here is only to establish the basic bond between method, goal, and environment.

some given goals and some environment. A specific problem solver has available some repertory of such methods, which come to control his behavior under various conditions.

This raises the second issue needing discussion. Although we are not concerned here[15] about how this control comes about—whether through selection, specialization, assembly, and so on—we *are* concerned with what methods make up the repertory. Only when we know what methods a subject uses are we prepared to say anything in detail about his behavior. We can, of course, make the conditional statement of what information he has if successful—i.e., he has the solution to the problem the method solves. But we can say little else—for instance, nothing about his chances of error.

In the process of task analysis and the investigation of the behavior of particular subjects we discover various methods. Thus gradually a library of methods builds up. These offer possibilities for behavior organization and permit us to derive consequences under the assumption that a subject comes under the control of one or another method. It thus becomes important whether the space of methods is very large, so that each subject has his own unique methods, so to speak, or whether only a much smaller number of common methods exists.

It appears that the variety of methods is quite modest, depending primarily on the structure of the problem space. However, this statement must be qualified in several ways. First, we are concerned only with the unprogrammed activity, as we used that term in a previous section—that is, with activity in which the situation is genuinely problematic to the subject. For it is clear that the set of all methods including ones like the quadratic formula and the simplex algorithm, is indeed very large and indefinitely varied. Restriction to the genuinely problematic puts limits on the ingenuity with which information can be extracted and fashioned to obtain an end. It is precisely such methods as the quadratic formula and the simplex algorithm that have to be discovered by someone highly skilled in the art and passed on to others for later use. Only rarely—exceedingly rarely—are such methods discovered and used by a problem solver who did not have them available initially. And when they are available, we consider the situation nonproblematic[16] (as we observed earlier, pages 822–823).

The second qualification is that the method (i.e., the production system) does depend on aspects of the total situation other than the structure of the problem space (as that was defined in the previous section). However, these other aspects can be specified in detail, and a more complete statement can be made. We will do this in the next subsection by analyzing the functions to be performed by a method.

The third and final qualification enters when we try to match the analysis just alluded to above with the actual variety of methods that seems possible. This will lead to a notion of mixtures of methods, which we will take up as soon as the functional analysis of methods is complete.

---

[15] But see the next section.

[16] It is theoretically conceivable that a problem solver could consist entirely of methods of this latter type, so that either it has a definite algorithm that it can apply, or it has no available adaptive behavior. In the light of evolution such a state of affairs could hardly exist for biological organisms.

The function of a method is to produce behavior rationally related to an end. We need to translate this general statement into more specific demands on the corresponding production systems.

Final Actions.　As we made clear in the last section, given the problem space, intelligence impinges on problem solving through a small set of decisions that determine goals, states, and operators. In different task environments these decision points differ both in their frequency of occurrence and the room they allow for the play of intelligence. Determination of goals and operators, and evaluations of new states, seem the important controlling decisions. Saving states, selecting old states for a retry, and rejecting goals usually offer less scope for intelligence. In any event a method is ultimately a device for generating a coordinated pattern of such decisions—one that produces rational behavior.

Sources of Information.　Again, as we emphasized in the last section, the only information that is available to make the decisions is information embedded in the structure of the task environment, as captured in the structure of the problem space. Thus, the main task of the method is to translate that information into the pattern of decisions. Any two production systems that provide identical translations— i.e., identical patterns as a function of problem-space information—are in some important sense the same method. In fact, as we shall see, all such methods often end up with a common name,

The information that is actually available to a production system comprises the symbol structures of the goals, states, and operators (and its own structure, of course). The correlations and redundancies that constitute problem-space structure are not symbolized directly, but are assumed, so to speak, by the method in the way it uses the information directly available to it in these symbol structures.

To illustrate the possibilities, let us consider some paradigmatic production systems for various methods. We take the problem space to be descriptive; that is, the state consists of an ordered conjunction of small *expressions* representing increments of knowledge (as in cryptarithmetic or chess). The conditions of productions can be conjunctions of features that match the expressions in the immediate memory. The actions of the productions can produce and place new expressions in the immediate memory or can tag existing expressions (e.g., expression: reject.)

Figure 14.3 shows a paradigmatic production system for working-forward. It consists of four types of productions. First are productions to recognize the solution state. These operate from features of the present state to produce the symbol *solution*. This symbol would trigger an action in the larger context in case a solution is found. Second are productions to evaluate the present state. These operate from the features of the present state and the new information [feature (expression: new)] to affix a tag of *reject*. This reject tag prohibits the rejected expression from entering into further problem solving (simply because productions for the latter have conditions that do not match expressions tagged with reject). Thus, in effect, these move the problem solver back to the prior knowledge state. Third are productions to determine how far to back up to a knowledge state from which to go

FIGURE 14.3
working-forward production system

CONDITION	ACTION	TYPE OF PRODUCTION
feature, ... feature	→ solution	recognize solution
.....	.....	
feature, ... feature	→ solution	
feature, ... feature (expression: new)	→ expression: reject	evaluate new state
.....	.....	
feature, ... feature (expression: new)	→ expression: reject	
feature (expression.1) ... expression.2: reject	→ expression.1: reject	backup
.....	.....	
feature (expression.1) ... expression.2: reject	→ expression.1: reject	
feature, ... feature	→ operator	select operator
.....	.....	
feature, ... feature	→ operator	

FIGURE 14.4
means-ends analysis production system

	CONDITION	ACTION	TYPE OF PRODUCTION
	feature, ... feature(expression: new)	→ solution	recognize solution
	.....	.....	
	feature, ... feature(expression: new)	→ solution	
A	feature, ... goal-feature	→ operator	select operator
	.....	.....	
	feature, ... goal-feature	→ operator	
B	feature, ... feature(expression: new)	→ goal	create difference goal
	.....	.....	
	feature, ... feature(expression: new)	→ goal	
	goal	→ operator	select operator
	.....	.....	
	goal	→ operator	

forward again. Detection of reject tags on some expressions causes such tags to be affixed to other information also. Fourth are productions to select the operator for the next forward move. This selection is based on the current state of knowledge, and may or may not depend on the newly added expression.

Working-forward gets its name from the use of information encoded in the current state to select operators to be executed next. That part alone is not sufficient to constitute a method. The rest of the productions complete it. Evaluative information needs to be added, since the operator selection cannot be very adaptive by itself (unless the system is only used in pursuit of a single fixed goal, in which case, the knowledge of the goal state can be built into the production system itself).

Figure 14.3 will also do to characterize what we called in Chapter 4 (page 94) the recognition method. This method consists simply of the productions for recognizing a solution and the productions for selecting an operator—i.e., for recognizing what needs to be done to produce a solution. As we noted in Chapter 4, this method is applicable in principle to any problem, the only condition being that the actual solution (more specificially, the operator that produces it) already be available in the problem solver's LTM.

Figure 14.4 shows a paradigmatic production system for means-ends analysis. The first type of production provides for recognition of final success. Productions of the second type, labeled A, select an operator as a function of the current state and the goal state. No state evaluation is provided; it is superfluous if the information about operator selection is sufficiently good. Concomitantly, backing up need not occur, since further action in the problem space can always be taken from the present (new) position. Not all means-ends analysis schemes are so powerful; generally some evaluation and backup occurs to provide additional adaptivity. We discuss this qualification further below.

There is a second way to select operators in means-ends analysis. It involves the two types of productions (B) in the figure. Operators may be selected solely as a function of goals. This might seem to be an unadaptive tactic, since it appears unresponsive to the current state, and thus the same operators would continue to be chosen forever. However, the goals themselves are created as functions of the current state, and hence encode by their occurrence information about the current state. We might think of these goals as *difference goals*; they describe either difficulties to be surmounted or gaps in information and specification to be filled. The forms A and B, though they are functionally equivalent in making operator selection depend on goal and state information, are nonequivalent in other ways. Existence of a goal implies continuing effort to reach that goal. Selecting an operator as a joint function of state and goal is a one-time action, leaving no trace other than the actual effects of the action upon the knowledge state.

These two paradigms cover the main ways in which the structure of the problem space can manifest itself. Some apparently distinct methods, such as *working-backward* and *planning* (finding the plan), are special cases of these schemes, in that they augment the collection of operators in various ways. However, there are other dimensions along which methods can vary.

Location of Information.   Any system with a diversity of memories must adapt its programs to deal with information in whatever memory it occurs. Information about states, goals, and operators can reside in STM, LTM, or EM. The accessing characteristics of the different memories lead to different-appearing production systems. Figure 14.5 shows these variants for operator selection. In group A the operators are part of the selection system itself, so that the act of selection leads immediately to the result of the operator appearing in STM. In group B the operators occur as separate production systems, and the selection operators simply

FIGURE 14.5

variations of operator selection with memory location

	CONDITION	ACTION	TYPE OF PRODUCTION
A	feature	$\longrightarrow$ expression	} LTM (contained in current
	. . . . .	. . . . .	production system)
	feature	$\longrightarrow$ expression	
B	feature	$\longrightarrow$ operator	} LTM (contained in separate
	. . . . .	. . . . .	production system)
	feature	$\longrightarrow$ operator	
C	feature	$\longrightarrow$ operator: do	} STM (contains name only)
	. . . . .	. . . . .	
	feature	$\longrightarrow$ operator: reject	
D	feature	$\longrightarrow$ select	
	select	$\longrightarrow$ find-next-operator	
	feature(operator)	$\longrightarrow$ operator: reject	
	. . . . .	. . . . .	} EM
	feature(operator)	$\longrightarrow$ operator: reject	
	feature(operator)	$\longrightarrow$ operator: do	
	. . . . .	. . . . .	
	feature(operator)	$\longrightarrow$ operator: do	

transfer control to them. Both of these types store the operators in LTM. Note that LTM is the most immediate memory for the operators, since knowing the operators (so that their selection can be embedded in a production system) implies having them in LTM.

STM is not large enough to hold operators. However, it must be possible to select (or reject) a single operator in STM and then to execute it. Productions in group C do this. Group D are productions that select and execute operators stored in EM. In this case the problem solver does not have in LTM a production system containing all operators and their selection criteria. Instead, he must search EM and evaluate each operator found there (for rejection or execution). This search is controlled by the tag symbol, *select*.

Similar variations exist for different ways of storing information about the current state and about the goal. We argued earlier that in the normal arrangement, information about the current state is mostly in STM with a small amount in LTM. Similarly, the current goal is in STM (with perhaps one or two other goals in the stack). The more pervasive higher goals are in LTM, though the top goal itself may well be recorded in the environment—say, on a blackboard. The major variation on this scheme is to record parts of the current state in EM; this is what gives rise to the extended knowledge state. Scanning programs are then required, similar to the one for the operators, to transfer information to the knowledge state in STM.

Assimilation/Interpretation. Methods differ as to whether their information is directly available to them or must be interpreted. The most striking example of

FIGURE 14.6

assimilated operators

Apply R1 to X:
1.　　connective(main) = (v | ·) ⟶ change positions of left and right.

Apply R2 to X:
1.　　connective(main) = ⊃ ⟶ change positions of left and right;
　　　　　　　　　　　　change sign(left); change sign(right).

Apply R3 to X (⟹ contract):
1.　　connective(main) = (v | ·) ⟶ compare left and right.
2.　　left and right same ⟶ write left.

Apply R3 to X (⟹ expand):
1.　　⟶ specify connective (⟹ v | ·); write connective for connective(main);
　　　　write X for left; write X for right.

Apply R4 to X (⟹ associate to right):
1.　　connective(main) = (v | ·) ⟶ compare connective(main) and connective(right).
2.　　connectives same ⟶ group left and left of right as left;
　　　　　　　　　　　write right of right as right.

this distinction in our problems was the contrast between subjects in logic who applied the rules from the rule sheet, as in a recipe (e.g., S11), and subjects who had assimilated the rules so that they could simply perform them (as did many subjects for the inessential rules, e.g., R1: A·B ⟹ B·A). Assimilation here means that the operation is available as a production system. Interpretation means that the controlling production system is an interpreter and the operator a symbolic structure. This symbolic structure might be available in either LTM or EM (or possibly even in STM, if the operator is represented by a very small symbol structure).

Figures 14.6 and 14.7 illustrate the distinction between assimilation and interpretation. Figure 14.6 shows the first four rules for the logic tasks as *assimilated productions*. The conditions for applicability of the rules have become conditions for evoking the productions. The output is expressed in terms of difference operators, such as change position, change connective, and so on. It is understood that the new expression to be produced is the input expression modified by these operators. Since the input is implicit throughout, we can, for example, abbreviate left-(input-expression) simply by *left*. Sometimes an additional production is required for a rule—for example, the first production in R3 (contract)—because the comparison of two complex expressions (left and right) cannot be handled as a simple recognition. The use of two productions for R4 is avoidable, but only at the price of having separate productions for the two forms of the rule (with wedge and dot connectives, respectively). A rather large number of productions is required for the total set of twelve rules, but their action is immediate.

Figure 14.7 shows a production system to *interpret* the rules of the logic task. The basic requirement is shown at the top of the figure: the input expression must

841

FIGURE 14.7
production system for interpreting an operator

Apply rule R to X:
1.   start ⟶ Match X to input-form(R).
2.   Match succeed ⟶ Produce output-form(R).

Match X to input-form:
1.   start ⟶ place X and input-form in stacks.
2.   variable defined ⟶ replace variable by definition.
3.   variable undefined ⟶ define variable = expression; pop stacks.
4.   term and term ⟶ compare terms; compare signs.
5.   terms same and signs same ⟶ pop stacks.
6.   expression and expression ⟶ compare connectives; compare signs.
7.   connectives same and signs same ⟶ find lefts; push into stacks.
8.   stacks popped and non-empty ⟶ find rights; replace top of stacks.
9.   stacks popped and empty ⟶ stop and report 'succeed'.
10.   otherwise ⟶ stop and report 'fail'.

Produce output-form:
1.   start ⟶ place output-form in stack.
2.   variable defined ⟶ replace variable by definition.
3.   variable undefined ⟶ specify expression for variable.
4.   term unwritten ⟶ write term.
5.   expression unwritten ⟶ write connective; find left; push into stack.
6.   sign = ∼ and unchanged ⟶ change sign.
7.   written ⟶ pop stack.
8.   stack popped and non-empty ⟶ find right; replace top of stack.
9.   stack popped and empty ⟶ stop and report 'succeed'.

---

be matched to the input-form of the rule, and, if the match is successful, the output-form used to produce the output expression. This latter process is not independent of the details of the match, but the communication between them is carried by the variables, which are defined during the match and then used during output.

The form of any interpreter is always dictated to some extent by the precise representations of the expressions to be processed. Since such details are beside the point here, we have tried to avoid cluttering up Figure 14.7 with them. Thus, we assume a tree-structure logic expression in which one can simply obtain the left and right subexpressions and write them down. Similarly, to keep the figure simple, we have used abbreviations in the same way as in Figure 14.6—e.g., *left* for left(expression) and even *lefts* for the left-hand expressions of both the input-form and the input-expression.

The details of operation of these production systems are not important, though the reader may find them instructive. Two stacks are required by the match to keep track of the corresponding positions in the two expressions being matched. One stack is required to process the output-form.

The important characteristic of the interpreter is that it must operate indirectly with two expressions, working through them symbol by symbol. The stacks are needed because the interpreter does not know how big either an expression or a rule will be. In the assimilated form, on the other hand, no uncertainty exists about these matters, since each rule is encoded inside its own production system. Thus, no stacks are required. On the other hand, the interpreter will work for any operators whatsoever, whereas the assimilated version is particularized to the rules shown. To add a new operator to the assimilated system requires the construction of a new set of productions.

Operators are not the only kind of information that may be held in unassimilated form. Everything in EM requires interpretation. Often this process is sufficiently immediate that we need not represent the interpretation in our model— e.g., the 5 written alongside the D in DONALD+GERALD is immediately interpreted as D = 5 when it is read into STM. But matters need not be so simple —e.g., a complex logic expression may be put on the blackboard and not be reread for some time.

Information in LTM can also be unassimilated. The verbal sequence corresponding to a sequential reading of A-horseshoe-B-yields-tilde-A-wedge-B can be remembered, and can be fed through the interpreter. In fact, though this book is not the place to elaborate on this point, the distinction between assimilation and interpretation provides a structural basis for distinguishing some varieties of meaningful versus rote ("mechanical") learning.[17]

This view of assimilation and interpretation implies that the production systems are not themselves interpreted systems. That is, we are representing by the symbolic structures such as Figure 14.6 an information processing system (a particular production system) that is realized directly (recall the extensive discussion of this point in Chapter 2, pp. 33–37). Actually, with present empirical knowledge we cannot know whether there is another mechanism that does interpret the productions. We do know that, if there is, it does not operate on the time scale of eip's. Even at 10 milliseconds per operation, there would be no way to interpret a production system so as to make *its* operation run at 100 milliseconds per operation (i.e., something like 1 ms per operation or faster would be required, even assuming parallel operation, to deal with the large number of productions that must be considered).

Feature Extraction. In all the examples of productions given here, as well as in most of the instances that occur in the book, the features to be responded to are given directly as the condition parts of productions. This need not be the way things work. An example of an alternative is the match process in logic (in GPS), where a complex comparison is made, leading to the production of a *difference* (a symbol structure that summarizes the match). This difference is then used to select an operator or a reduce goal. Thus, the paradigms originally given need possibly to be augmented by clusters of productions that compute features and differences.

---

[17] The distinction is all-or-none as it stands—either an interpretive program is being used or it isn't. However, in any complex material, parts will be interpreted and parts performed by assimilated production systems. For instance, most of our logic subjects, even when working from the rule sheet, matched and substituted for variables as assimilated operations. Only S11 seemed to spell out the fitting of a rule to an expression as if he were following a recipe (see Chapter 10, page 593).

However, the arguments given earlier about the short residence times within a knowledge state imply that these feature computations remain quite simple. For they occur prior to taking any action that the problem solver interprets as producing new knowledge. Only a small amount of effort would normally be tolerated. The examples of complex feature extraction that we have considered (e.g., the match) involve large expressions (not assimilable at a glance) that have to be scanned. Even here, the match does not in fact take very long (a second or two), so that it does not represent a terribly complex process, but it does require a separate production system.

Thus, our argument for simple feature computations rests on the postulated inability of the problem solver to withhold problem solving (so to speak) simply in the interests of information gathering (of a particular non-problem-oriented sort). When these assumptions fail, we may see quite different behavior. Orientation periods, which characterize the beginning of any new problem solving endeavor, provide an instance. Our best examples of these are in chess (recall the discussion of perception in Chapter 13, pages 775–783). These orientation operations build up the extended knowledge state. At some point, the subject then begins to explore the problem space by selecting and applying operators.

Parametrization and Variables. A final dimension of variation in production systems arises from the parametrization of information. Operators are given, not as fully specified sets of productions, but as forms with variables. The functional significance of parametrization was discussed in the last section. Parametrization permits the selection of one of a large number of possibilities (here operators) in a multistage fashion, in which, first, the form is selected and then the remaining degrees of freedom (variables) are removed one by one (sometimes with appreciable delay until a determining condition arises). Parametrization reflects another way of factoring—of dividing the selection of the appropriate operator into parts, so that each part can be attended to separately.

In terms of productions the usual effect of parametrization is to divide the totality of operators into *productive* operators (which produce new information) and *attentional* operators, which select an aspect of the current state (sometimes the extended knowledge state) for input to the productive operators. This division can work in two ways. In the first case, the two operators are coupled sufficiently closely that the attentional operator simply precedes the productive operator. An actual example is the use of FC before PC in the cryptarithmetic productions. There would be no reason for performing the attention operation, if the other did not follow. In the second case, when the productive operator is evoked, any gaps in its specification are symbolized as difficulties to be removed by other productions having that goal. The latter organization is much more flexible, of course, than the former. It is an instance of means-ends analysis.

Operators are the main type of knowledge that is parametrized. However, states can also contain variables, with a consequent major augmentation of the problem space. Goals are often parametrized as forms [e.g., check(letter)]. However, only rarely does there appear in our empirical data a real act of selection of the variable in a goal (though the absence of such acts may be an artifact of our particular tasks).

Summary. The nature and variety of production systems is not well enough understood to permit a definitive analysis of the structure of methods. However, the various functions we have described, with their structural counterparts, seem to cover the main sources of variation. The last three functions we discussed—dealing with the location of information, the need to interpret, and the effect of parametrization—account for some of the structural variability of methods. They do not alter the main function of a method—which is to effect a pattern of decisions about goals, states, and operators as a function of information embedded in the problem structure. They simply solve the subsidiary problems of effecting such a pattern, given the many ways information can be encoded.

Mixtures of Methods

The naming of methods, such as working-forward, implies that each method is a complete organization of action, that the problem solver has a discrete set of these methods, and that some method-selection mechanism evokes appropriate ones. The adaptation of the parts of a method to each other—they make sense only in the context of the total method—argues for this organization. Almost all multi-method artificial intelligence programs are organized this way (Moses, 1967; Ernst and Newell, 1969; King, 1969).

Although methods can contain functionally specified subparts, this still would seem to imply a large number of distinct methods to take account of the actual systems that characterize the behavior of human problem solvers. For instance, we mentioned at the beginning of this section that S3's cryptarithmetic production system might be thought of as an idiosyncratic method.

Alternatively, it is tempting to think of the named methods as really being ideal types and real problem solvers (especially human ones) as being mixtures of these types. To make such a view operational requires specifying what units of behavioral organization are to be used to construct the final methods.[18] The single production itself is too small a unit, since it leaves us simply with the class of all programs. However, it is possible that we can mix together production systems of various methods, so that the behavior is a composite of the several methods.

To illustrate this, Figure 14.8 shows the production system of S3 divided into clusters according to the method being used (simplified mnemonic renditions of the individual productions are used). The system is a mixture of two methods. Working-forward is realized by P1 and part of P4. Means-ends analysis is realized by productions P6, P7, and P10, which go from current state to goals that reflect differences, and productions P2, P3, and half of P4, which select operators for these difference goals. Production P13 contains the entire sequence of difference deter-

---

[18] Sociology has attempted to legitimize the analysis of ideal types as an appropriate paradigm for scientific analysis, without description of how real agents (institutions and individuals) are composed—only that they are, in some unspecified way, "mixtures." But this is simply a dodge in the face of phenomenal complexity. A viable theory of ideal types requires explicit laws of composition so that descriptions of actual agents are possible.

FIGURE 14.8

production system for S3 decomposed into basic methods

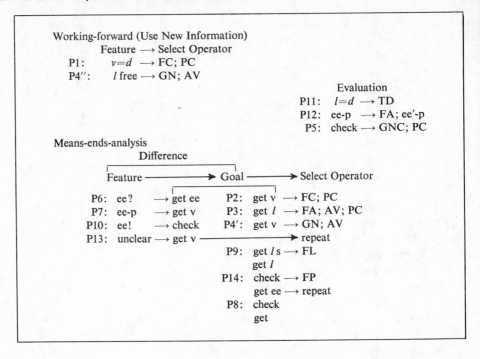

mination and operator selection. Productions P9 and P14 start with difference goals and generate other goals and (for P14) also select an operator. P8 transforms goal types from *check* to *get*. It is a substitute for adding the check goal to each of the productions, which has a get goal as condition. Both methods require evaluation, which is achieved in a common set of productions, P11, P12, and P5. This latter production constitutes the final evaluation of the problem. Working-forward controls behavior every time new information comes into the system, and means-ends analysis controls behavior whenever difficulties arise. Thus behavior oscillates back and forth between the two methods.

Whether all subjects' programs can be described as mixtures of basic clusters, or whether all ways of combining such clusters make sense, is not determinable here. Our empirical analyses are not cast into a sufficiently common form to answer such questions. Similarly, we have no way of getting at the psychological reality of mixing (which, at bottom, is the crucial issue). Nevertheless, the notion of describing the set of available methods as a set of basic functional clusters to be used separately or in mixtures appears both parsimonious and provocative.

Conclusion

We have now provided a partial analysis of methods as organizations of behavior for rational ends realized in production systems. The whole set of methods is clearly very large. But we have sought to reduce that large number to a small kernel. Mixtures of methods reduce the total to the ideal types. The functional analysis reduces the total still further by abstracting from the inessential variation of information location, parametrization, and the requirements for interpretation. Allowing methods to include functionally specified subparts reduces the total still more. We are left with a manageable space of methods that reflect the basic ways that information about the structure of the problem space can be mapped into patterns of operation selection, state evaluation, and goal creation.

This section argues that the method is not a completely independent variable to be added somehow to the specifications of the task environment, the goals of the problem solver, and the selection of the problem space. Clearly it is partly independent; a range of methods and mixtures is available, and a problem solver need not use all these methods, or the best ones. Which methods he does use is partly a measure of his intelligence and education. But his choices are highly circumscribed.

We end this section with a reminder that the analysis above is restricted to the methods available in problematic situations, and does not include the highly specific methods of science, mathematics, and the practical arts.

DETERMINATION OF INDIVIDUAL PROBLEM SPACES AND PROGRAMS

The two previous sections of this chapter have been devoted, respectively, to showing how the structure of the task environment determines the class of admissible problem spaces, and to showing how the problem space limits the range of possible problem solving programs. Now, we wish to describe how, when a subject is confronted with a problem solving task, these possibilities are narrowed down to a particular problem space and a particular problem solving program.

Associated with the question of what mechanisms are used to determine actual problem spaces and programs is the question of individual differences. So far we have been describing invariants over tasks and over persons. Yet we know that large individual differences exist, which must be reflected in some way in the actual problem space and program adopted by an individual problem solver on a given occasion.

This part of the theory is both tentative and incomplete. Most of the behavior that would be relevant to verifying, amending, and completing it takes place long before the subject arrives in the laboratory for his problem solving sessions. Much of the remainder occurs, especially if the task is unfamiliar to him, during the first minutes, or even seconds, when we are reading the task instructions to him. We have almost no record of pre-session behavior or history, and tantalizingly brief data on the initial response to the task.

If the determination of problem space and program are history-dependent, then the program will change gradually on the basis of experience in problem solving. Our information about such learning processes is also scanty. Their time scale is quite different from the time scale on which problem solvers search the maze representing a particular problem. The fact that we can represent the processes of a problem solver by a static program in a problem space that remains relatively fixed over many minutes shows that, except when a new task is presented, the performance program does not change much in the time it takes to solve a single problem, or a short series of problems. When we are interested in the development of the performance program, in learning, we must be prepared to follow behavior over hours of exposure to the task environment, rather than over minutes.

Only for a few subjects with the logic problems do we have a developmental sequence over a number of problems that reveals a growing sophistication in the program (Chapter 10). Moreover, none of our subjects could be described as naive, even initially, in any of the tasks. They were all familiar with the sets of symbols used in the logic and cryptarithmetic tasks, and with arithmetic and algebraic operations upon symbols of these general kinds. In chess, our subjects were even less naive. All were at least respectable amateur chess players who had devoted many hours of time to the game before they appeared in the laboratory, and de Groot's subjects were among the most experienced in the world. Under these conditions an initial performance program will be assembled with great rapidity as soon as the subjects are introduced to the specific experimental task, and this program will then remain relatively stable.

The Sources of Information

It is easy to identify the sources of information that can contribute significantly to the determination of a problem space and program at the moment when a subject is given task instructions in the laboratory:

1. The task instructions themselves, which provide more or less complete descriptions of objects and operators and of the initial state and goal state and which may offer or enforce a particular form of EM (the cryptarithmetic display, the chessboard).
2. Previous experience with the same task, or one nearly identical with it. In the limiting case, the instructions may simply evoke a program that is already available in LTM ("Would you care to play a game of chess?").
3. Previous experience with tasks that are recognized as somehow analogous to the given task—recognition evoked by the task instructions or by the initial attempts at task performance.
4. Stored programs in LTM of substantial generality that can be applied to any of a wide range of tasks.
5. Stored programs in LTM for constructing problem spaces and problem solving programs by combining information obtained from the external environment with information already stored in memory.
6. The course of problem solving itself, which may augment or modify the problem space or program or, on occasion, radically change one or both.

We will discuss the role of each of these information sources briefly, using the problem space and programs of our subjects as illustrations. The sources are not mutually exclusive, of course. Not only do they combine together as data and program (e.g., the construction programs of item 5, above, use the instructions as data), but different aspects of a given problem situation can be determined by different sources of information. Besides surveying the various mechanisms involved in determining problem spaces and programs, our discussion will prepare us to review briefly the nature of both task differences and individual differences.

Throughout this section we consider simultaneously determination of the problem space and of the programs that operate in it. There are significant differences between them; e.g., the instructions provide much more explicit information about the problem space than about the program. But many of the sources listed above—e.g., analogous tasks—are important for both. Since what we have to say about this aspect of the theory is illustrative, rather than systematic, there is little point to taking up problem spaces and programs, each in a separate section.

Task Instructions

In this chapter and in Chapter 3 we have insisted that we can know the objective task—"out there"—only through its particular representations. There is no neutral way of describing the task environment. As a consequence, task instructions do much more than define the task; they provide, in addition, a specific representation of it that can serve to define an initial problem space, and even parts of an initial problem solving program for the subject.

The game of tic-tac-toe, in its many forms, provides the basis for a critical experiment on this point. To the best of our knowledge, the experiment has not been performed, except informally with some of our friends as subjects. Its outcome is so obvious that perhaps it is not worth performing. Here is the experiment.

We define a task, which we shall call T. One of the representations of T is tic-tac-toe, another is number scrabble, and there are still others.[19] We define an experimental condition corresponding to each of these two representations: in condition C_i, T is described to the subject in its (i)th representation. Now our not very startling—but critically important—prediction is this: the problem space used by subjects in condition C_i will be the one defined by the ith representation. Subjects instructed to play number scrabble will use a problem space based on the objects and operators defined for number scrabble; those instructed to play tic-tac-toe will use a problem space based on the objects and operators defined for tic-tac-toe; and so on.

We put the matter in this tediously obvious way because the sources of the information that define the problem space are sometimes thought to be mysterious.

---

[19] Another isomorph is JAM, described by J. A. Michon (1967). JAM is the dual of tic-tac-toe, in the sense of projective geometry. The row, columns, and diagonals of tic-tac-toe become points in JAM, and the squares of the former become lines joining the corresponding points. The game is won by "jamming" all the lines through a single point, a move consisting of jamming a single line.

It is sometimes even argued that the "real" problem solving is not what we have called problem solving in this volume, but the preliminary sequence of processes that determine the problem space and program.[20] We see, on the contrary, that typical task instructions contain a large amount of information that can be used to define a specific problem space and program for working on the task—and that, indeed, this information is likely to determine which of various alternative representations a subject will use.

There is substantial corroboration for this assertion in our three tasks. In cryptarithmetic, which represented a new task to our subjects, the problem spaces used by them bore a close relation to the way the task was described in the instructions. To be sure, the subjects (all except S6) operated in the augmented problem space, rather than the basic problem space. But the very use of these descriptive labels for the two problem spaces reveals how close their relation is. The augmentation does not disturb the essential structure of the basic space, but only adds some additional relations to the knowledge state, with appropriate corresponding operators. None of our subjects used the algebraic problem space, nor any of the abstract spaces that are possible.

Similarly, in logic, all of our subjects constructed problem spaces that corresponded to the instructions. Their problem solving would have been quite different if they had been introduced to the task environment as a system of formal logic (i.e., with dot meaning *and*, wedge meaning *or*, and so on). For example, in problem A1 where L1 is $(\sim P \cdot Q) \vee (P \cdot \sim P)$ it is predictable that subjects would then worry over the contradiction $(P \cdot \sim P)$ in the right side of the expression, and what it might imply.

Previous Experience with the Same Task

Chess provides an almost perfect example of a task that is highly familiar to the subjects. Simply telling a subject that he is going to be shown a position in a chess game and that he is to behave exactly as if he were a player in that game—to choose a move—is quite sufficient to evoke from LTM the program he already has stored there for playing chess. We cannot expect the chess protocols to tell us anything at all about how a subject learned to play the game—although the first segment of his protocol may tell us a good deal about how he transfers to internal memory specific information about a new position when he sees it for the first time.

The same consideration applies to all the component tasks that subjects have to perform—e.g., addition and subtraction in cryptarithmetic, substitution in logic. In fact, a principal criterion for making a process an operator in a problem space is the fact that it represents a task in which the subject already has much experience and for which he has a performance program.

---

[20] The argument can be refuted simply by observing that if it were correct, and tasks from the same environment were presented sequentially to a subject, only the first of them would present him with a problem, since he would not need to determine a new problem space and program for the subsequent tasks.

If the given task bears a similarity to another task with which the problem solver is already familiar, then he may attempt to use the problem space and programs from the familiar one. To do so requires that the knowledge and structures be adapted to the new task. The result will be useful only if the initial recognition of similarity reflects fundamental isomorphisms between the structures of the tasks, and if the adaption is successful.

Our subjects provide examples of both functional and dysfunctional attempts to assimilate the given tasks to analogous ones. The most obvious dysfunctional example occurred in logic, where subjects tried to work with the tilde as if it were the negative sign of algebra. Two brief excerpts from S8, first on D1 and then on a later problem, A2, illustrate graphically both the difficulty and the pains that must be taken to avoid such assimilation even after it is recognized as inappropriate:

D1   B281:   Gee whiz, a tilde times a tiddle, tiddle, tilde doesn't make a positive does it?

B282:   Makes a negative.

B283:   Doggone.

A2   [Attempting to apply R7 to L10: $\sim (P \cdot \sim T) \lor \sim (P \cdot T)$]

B175:   (E: Well, what would you get?)

B176:   I don't know . . . if the whole quantity is negative,

B177:   I can only think in terms of mathematics.

The subjects undoubtedly paid a price for their interpretation of tildes as negative signs. But the cost was more than compensated by the general utility of the analogous problem space, from which the interpretation sprang. For the subjects obviously adapted the problem space and program they normally used for algebraic manipulation, and the common occurrence of the associative, distributive, and commutative laws made this identification largely worthwhile.

A more subtle example of adaptation of an analogous task comes from the use of arithmetic for cryptarithmetic. The similarity is obvious and is even stated in the cryptarithmetic instructions. A subject can attack the task in the same way in which he attacks an arithmetic addition: from right to left. In one sense this is dysfunctional, since information can be extracted from the constrained columns independently of their positions. At a less sophisticated level the adaptation is definitely functional, since it provides the problem solver with a systematic procedure. Without some such scheme he would have no way to decompose the problem into components that yield some definite information (recall the numerical problem space explored by S8).

An interesting positive example of analogy is available from logic. As we noted earlier, there is more than one possible source for the essential-inessential distinction. One is the familiar world of physical objects, in which one distinguishes manipulation and rearrangement of a given piece of material from removal or addition of material. This corresponds closely to the inessential-essential distinction, though of course it need not suggest it to a subject who has been introduced to the logic task as a formal problem. For him any such distinction must be based entirely on the twelve rules and the syntax of the expressions. Yet many of our subjects could have come to the distinction from this highly familiar analogy.

General Programs

Although the subjects are working on a specific task (e.g., logic or chess), they may in fact be using programs of substantially greater generality—using, in fact, exactly the same program in several tasks, but with different inputs and outputs.

For some component tasks, such as adding two numbers, this must be the case: each subject has a single program that accepts inputs representing digits and produces a representation of the sum (or difference) in STM. He does not have a special addition process for seeing that if he takes two pawns off the board six pawns are left, another for seeing that if he takes $N = 2$ from $B = 8$ six is left—whence $R = 6 + 1$ in column 4 of DONALD+GERALD. The arithmetic operation is indeed employed within a specific context in each case—an exchange evaluation in chess, say, and the column-processing operation in cryptarithmetic. But the same general program is being applied in both cases. The relevant input is the particular pair of digits being added or subtracted, not their interpretation as numbers of pawns or values of letters.

This case for generalized subroutines hardly needs belaboring when applied to low-level operations like arithmetic. The matter is otherwise for the problem solving programs. For it is not evident just how much communality can be extracted from a collection of problem spaces and packaged as a single process. For our human subjects there is also the empirical issue of whether they actually have such general programs, even if these are conceivable.

The programs we have described for the several tasks supply a variety of clues as to the existence of general programs. In cryptarithmetic, on the one hand, the production systems were specific to the task. Recall, for example, production P1:

P1: $\langle$variable$\rangle = \langle$digit$\rangle$new $\longrightarrow$ FC(variable) ($\Longrightarrow$ column); PC[column].

This is quite specific to cryptarithmetic. Although it expresses a very general proposition about what to do if one finds new information about an object, X, the production would only be evoked in cryptarithmetic, not in any other task—e.g., not in solving algebraic equations, where such a production would be equally meaningful. Possibly we should have written:

P1*: new-information(X) $\longrightarrow$ find(X) ($\Longrightarrow$ place); derive-consequences(place).

Although in Chapter 8 we used a not dissimilar production in a general production system for the algebraic problem space, there seemed to be no empirical grounds for asserting that the subjects were operating with such a general production, somehow identifying its terms with the specifics of the cryptarithmetic situation.

The situation is similar in chess. Although we described a single, general prototypic chess program such that all existing chess programs could be written simply by specifying various open subprocesses (e.g., base-moves), this chess executive is specific to chess. It certainly could not be used to do cryptarithmetic or logic.

On the other hand, GPS, the program we used to study the logic task, has substantial elements of generality. In describing GPS we did not discuss how it might operate in different task environments. But GPS is a program of exactly the sort required. The basic program operates in terms of very general symbolic structures representing objects, operators, features of objects, and differences between pairs of objects. The goals of GPS are formulated in just these general terms—e.g., transform object.1 into object.2. Likewise the methods are formulated without reference to anything more specific. Recall the method for the transform type goal (Figure 8.8, page 418) which refers to matching two objects, obtaining a difference, and setting up other goals in terms of differences and objects. Nowhere in the method is anything more task-specific required. The additional structures needed, such as the table-of-connections and the ordering of differences, are symbol structures that can be described exclusively in terms of the four basic concepts listed above.

To operate in a specific task environment, GPS requires a set of coordinating definitions that identify the terms object, operator, feature, and difference with specific classes of entities in the task environment, and that permit designation of individual elements of these classes. (Recall the discussion in Chapter 4, pages 91-92, of the structure of methods.) However, more than just a table of correspondences is required. There must also be programs that are specific to the task environment for detecting the features and differences and for applying the operators.

In any task environment for which these definitions can be framed, and the implied programs and correspondences supplied, GPS can attempt to solve problems. In the paper describing the original version of GPS, this flexibility was illustrated by the Moore-Anderson formulation of logic problems and by the task of solving simple trigonometric identities (Newell, Shaw, and Simon, 1959a). A later version, GPS-2-6, was able to work on eleven different tasks (Ernst and Newell, 1969), ranging from formal integration to various puzzles, to parsing a sentence, to series extrapolation.

To accomplish these feats of generality, GPS has to be given each of its tasks. In the early version of GPS this was done by supplying the necessary programs and tables in a simple scheme of program augmentation, due account being taken of the internal structure of the program. But in GPS-2-6, the later version, a special language was used to instruct GPS in new tasks. Figure 14.9 shows the instructions for a simple puzzle called Fathers and Sons (described in English at the top of the figure).

The instructions to GPS-2-6 (hereafter, just GPS) start with a list of coordinating definitions that link the words in the task with the basic terms in GPS's vocabulary. Thus, sail is an operator, a son (standing for son's location) is an attribute of an object (i.e., a type of feature), and so on. Then follows a description

FIGURE 14.9
instructions to GPS

A heavy father and two young sons have to cross a swift river in a deep wood. They find an abandoned boat, which can be rowed across, but which sinks if overloaded. Each young son is 100 pounds. A double-weight son is just as heavy as the father and more than that is too much for the boat. How do the father and the sons cross the river?

```
DECLARE      (
  BOAT = ATTRIBUTE
  D-L = FEATURE
  D-R = FEATURE
  FATHERS = ATTRIBUTE
  FINAL-OBJ = OBJECT-SCHEMA
  FROM-SIDE = LOC-PROG
  F-L = FEATURE
  F-R = FEATURE
  INITIAL-OBJ = OBJECT-SCHEMA
  SAIL = MOVE-OPERATOR
  SONS = ATTRIBUTE
  SIDES = SET
  S-L = FEATURE
  S-R = FEATURE
  TO-SIDE = LOC-PROG
  WEIGHT = EXPRES
  0–1 = SET
  0–1–2 = SET
  1–2 = SET
               )
TASK-STRUCTURES
  TOP-GOAL = ( TRANSFORM THE INITIAL-OBJ INTO THE FINAL-OBJ . )
  INITIAL-OBJ = ( LEFT ( SONS 2 FATHERS 1 BOAT BOAT )
                  RIGHT ( SONS 0 FATHERS 0 ) )
  FINAL-OBJ = ( LEFT ( SONS 0 FATHERS 0 )
                RIGHT ( FATHERS 1 SONS 2 BOAT BOAT ) )
  WEIGHT = ( X + X + Y )
  SAIL = $ SAIL THE BOAT FROM THE FROM-SIDE TO THE TO-SIDE WITH X
         FATHERS AND Y SONS IN IT . $
         ( CREATION-OPERATOR
         VAR-DOMAIN
         1.  THE FROM-SIDE IS AN EXCLUSIVE-MEMBER OF THE SIDES .
         2.  THE TO-SIDE IS AN EXCLUSIVE-MEMBER OF THE SIDES .
         3.  X IS A CONSTRAINED-MEMBER OF 0–1 . THE CONSTRAINT IS
             THAT THE WEIGHT IS IN-THE-SET 1–2 .
         4.  Y IS A CONSTRAINED-MEMBER OF 0–1–2 . THE CONSTRAINT IS
             THAT THE WEIGHT IS IN-THE-SET 1–2 .
         MOVES
         1.  MOVE THE BOAT AT THE FROM-SIDE TO THE BOAT AT THE
             TO-SIDE .
         2.  DECREASE BY THE AMOUNT X THE FATHERS AT THE FROM-
             SIDE AND ADD IT TO THE FATHERS AT THE TO-SIDE .
         3.  DECREASE BY THE AMOUNT Y THE SONS AT THE FROM-
             SIDE AND ADD IT TO THE SONS AT THE TO-SIDE . )
```

FIGURE 14.9 (cont'd)

```
SIDES = ( LEFT RIGHT )
0-1 = ( 0 1 )
0-1-2 = ( 0 1 2 )
1-2 = ( 1 2 )
S-L = ( THE SONS AT THE LEFT )
S-R = ( THE SONS AT THE RIGHT )
F-L = ( THE FATHERS AT THE LEFT )
F-R = ( THE FATHERS AT THE RIGHT )
D-L = ( THE BOAT AT THE LEFT )
D-R = ( THE BOAT AT THE RIGHT )
BASIC-MATCH = ( COMP-FEAT-LIST ( F-R S-R D-R ) )
COMP-OBJECTS = ( BASIC-MATCH )
DIFF-ORDERING = ( 1. ( F-L F-R )
                  2. ( S-L S-R)
                  3. ( D-L D-R ) )
TABLE-OF-CONNECTIONS = ( ( COMMON-DIFFERENCE SAIL ) )
LIST-OF-VAR = ( FROM-SIDE TO-SIDE X Y )
OBJ-ATTRIB = ( FATHERS SONS BOAT )
END
```

of the operators and of the initial situation and the final situation. This is followed by a statement of the goal. Finally, at the end, there is a statement of the difference ordering.

Missing from these instructions to GPS are any programs for executing operators or for detecting features and differences. Besides its central core of problem solving methods, GPS has two general types of operators and a single general scheme for detecting features and differences. GPS understands operators defined as forms—e.g., $A \cdot B \Longrightarrow B \cdot A$. It also understands operators defined as tests of applicability, followed by instructions for moving, copying, and rearranging parts of the input object. GPS can detect features that describe individual nodes in the object (a tree-structure expression) and differences formed by comparing corresponding features in two objects. Thus in logic it understands (connective of left = wedge) and (connective difference at left). For GPS to understand an operator, feature or difference designated in the instruction means that GPS has the programs to carry out any processes required by the general methods that involve that operator, feature, or difference.

The instructions to GPS bear a close resemblance to the instructions that must be given to a human—say, the English description of the task at the top of the figure (possibly prefaced by "Here is a little puzzle"). Due account must be taken of the limitations of GPS's access to the external world. The initial part of the explicit instructions to GPS have been acquired long ago by the human in building up his general vocabulary. Similarly, the word *boat* carries for the human information about capabilities for going back and forth across rivers with variable cargoes, which may be loaded and deposited at will. This has to be spelled out to GPS (in the definition of *sail*). Where a characteristic of the boat is not universal,

855

hence not part of the human's prior knowledge, it must be given to the human explicitly, just as to GPS—e.g., the load limitation of 200 pounds.

On the other hand, both GPS and the human come equipped with a general knowledge about what operators do. Both have built-in capacities for detecting features and differences. Thus, these do not have to be spelled out in either set of instructions, but only used. (Names have to be given to differences and features for GPS, of course, but naming is not to be confused with defining the concepts.) Similarly, in neither set of instructions is the connection between differences and operators spelled out. GPS, as well as the human, is able to determine relevance in terms of what it knows about operators and differences. On the other hand, GPS, in contrast with the human, is not able to order the differences. With the recent development of a scheme for deriving the order of differences (Chapter 8, pages 436–437), this part of the GPS instructions could now be dispensed with.

Thus, both the differences and the similarities between the instructions given to GPS and the instructions given to a human can be accounted for in terms of the knowledge they have already accumulated prior to the experiment—knowledge which can simply be evoked by designating phrases rather than having to be set forth explicitly. The differences that do exist between the sets of instructions stem from the rather careful choice in the case of the human of a story situation with familiar properties. These differences can be erased almost entirely by rephrasing the task:

> A slithy tove and two mimsy borogroves have to out-whiffle a frumious bandersnatch in a tulgey wood. They find a mome rath, which can be gyred awhiffle, but which outgrabes if frabjous. Each mimsy borogrove is 100 jub-jubs. A vorpal borogrove is just as slithy as the tove and more than that is uffish for the rath. How do the tove and the borogroves out-whiffle the bandersnatch?

Now the additional instructions given to GPS seem quite essential for the human as well (see Figure 14.10).

FIGURE 14.10

instructions for toves and borogroves task

```
DECLARE
  RATH = ATTRIBUTE
  D-L = FEATURE
  D-R = FEATURE
  TOVES = ATTRIBUTE
  FINAL-OBJ = OBJECT-SCHEMA
  FROM-SIDE = LOC-PROGRAM
  T-L = FEATURE
  T-R = FEATURE
  INITIAL-OBJ = OBJECT-SCHEMA
  OUT-WHIFFLE = MOVE-OPERATOR
  BOROGROVES = ATTRIBUTE
  SIDES = SET
  B-L = FEATURE
  B-R = FEATURE
```

FIGURE 14.10 (cont'd)

```
     TO-SIDE = LOC-PROG
     SLITHINESS = EXPRES
     0-1 = SET
     0-1-2 = SET
     1-2 = SET
                      )
TASK-STRUCTURES   (
     TOP-GOAL = ( TRANSFORM THE INITIAL-OBJ INTO THE FINAL-OBJ . )
     INITIAL-OBJ = ( LEFT ( BOROGROVES 2 TOVES 1 RATH RATH )
                         RIGHT ( BOROGROVES 0 TOVES 0 ) )
     FINAL-OBJ = ( LEFT ( BOROGROVES 0 TOVES 0 )
                       RIGHT ( TOVES 1 BOROGROVES 2 RATH RATH ) )
     SLITHINESS = ( X + X + Y )
     OUT-WHIFFLE = ( CREATION-OPERATOR
                       VAR-DOMAIN
                       1.  THE FROM-SIDE IS AN EXCLUSIVE-MEMBER OF THE
                           SIDES .
                       2.  THE TO-SIDE IS AN EXCLUSIVE-MEMBER OF THE
                           SIDES .
                       3.  Y IS A CONSTRAINED-MEMBER OF 0-1,  THE
                           CONSTRAINT IS THAT THE SLITHINESS IS
                           IN-THE-SET 1-2 .
                       4.  X IS A CONSTRAINED-MEMBER OF 0-1-2 , THE
                           CONSTRAINT IS THAT THE SLITHINESS IS
                           IN-THE-SET 1-2 .
                       MOVES
                       1.  MOVE THE RATH AT THE FROM-SIDE TO THE RATH
                           AT THE TO-SIDE .
                       2.  DECREASE BY THE AMOUNT X THE TOVES AT THE
                           FROM-SIDE AND ADD IT TO THE TOVES AT THE
                           TO-SIDE .
                       3.  DECREASE BY THE AMOUNT Y THE BOROGROVES
                           AT THE FROM-SIDE AND ADD IT TO THE
                           BOROGROVES AT THE TO-SIDE . )
     SIDES = ( LEFT RIGHT )
     0-1 = ( 0 1 )
     0-1-2 = ( 0 1 2 )
     1-2 = ( 1 2 )
     B-L = ( THE BOROGROVES AT THE LEFT )
     B-R = ( THE BOROGROVES AT THE RIGHT )
     T-L = ( THE TOVES AT THE LEFT )
     T-R = ( THE TOVES AT THE RIGHT )
     D-L = ( THE RATH AT THE LEFT )
     D-R = ( THE RATH AT THE RIGHT )
     BASIC-MATCH = ( COMP-FEAT-LIST ( T-R B-R D-R ) )
     COMP-OBJECTS = ( BASIC-MATCH )
     DIFF-ORDERING = ( 1.  ( T-L T-R )
                         2.  ( B-L B-R )
                         3.  ( D-L D-R ) )
     TABLE-OF-CONNECTIONS = ( ( COMMON-DIFFERENCE OUT-WHIFFLE ) )
     LIST-OF-VAR = ( FROM-SIDE TO-SIDE X Y )
     OBJ-ATTRIB = ( TOVES BOROGROVES RATH )
END
```

857

There is yet another way to obtain a specific problem space and problem solving program: construct it out of general components (subroutines and symbol structures) in response to the task instructions.

Perhaps the best example of this we have encountered is in S8's efforts to decide how to approach LETS+WAVE=LATER (Chapter 7, pp. 273 *ff.*). The organization he had used for the first problem (AA+BB=CBC) seemed inadequate to him. The task itself was sufficiently unfamiliar to S8 that he did not possess a set of preformed organizations that could simply be tried. Thus, his exploration involved constructing problem spaces. However, he hardly progressed far enough with any of them, except the augmented problem space, actually to construct any special problem solving programs.

Constructing a problem space involves constructing (1) a representation for the knowledge state, (2) operators to generate new knowledge, and (3) processes to test whether operators are applicable and whether positions are desirable. In all of the tasks we have been studying, the basic components for these constructs are highly overlearned and available in the subject's repertoire: addition, subtraction, comparison of symbols, representations for simple predicates (R odd), and so on. These components do not of themselves constitute column processors (PC), tests for digits (TD), or the more exotic components of S8's various problem spaces. However, their assembly into a space appears to take place exceedingly rapidly, in the first minute or two of problem solving, or even during the time the instructions are being assimilated.

Let us pose the issue a little more concretely. At B83, S8 considers for the first time the typographical problem space, trying to interpret letters as numbers with similar shapes (e.g., I = 1, Z = 2, E = 3, and so on). He has been considering rather extensively the cryptogram problem space, mapping the letters onto the numbers on the basis of their positions in the alphabet. The point of transition goes like this:

B79: And er . . . so, if this method that I outlined were used, er . . . △ R, S, and T couldn't be three different numbers.

B80: Er . . . △ this wouldn't be possible.

B81: They could be . . . they . . . they can only re . . . these letters can only represent two △ different numbers at the most.

B82: So I have to er . . . junk △ that idea I'm afraid, they're . . . that . . . that you've . . . you've put something in here, at least △ in that form.

[E11: Typographic problem space number 1]

B83: I guess it's also possible that certain number le . . . △ letters look like numbers.

B84: For example an E looks a lot like a 3. △

B85: But er . . . I don't △ er . . . I'm afraid I'm not going to get very far with this idea,

B86: because er . . . △ I can't see any other letters there that look too much like numbers.

B87:   Er . . . △ I . . . well . . . you might say . . . I guess you might say that
a 2 looks like an S. △

We have included a couple of phrases on each side of the transition, as well as the timing marks, to give some feeling for how long the transition takes.

The one point to be drawn from B79 to B81 is that S8 is deep in the consideration of a technical problem about the cryptogram space, namely, whether the occurrence of three consecutive letters, R, S, and T, invalidates a mapping scheme he has constructed which assigns A = 1, B = 1, C = 2, D = 2, and so on. From what we know of human processing in these tasks, S8 is definitely not considering other spaces at this point. In B82, S8 gives up on the cryptogram problem space. In the next phrase, without so much as a pause, he initiates a new approach. He follows this with a concrete example (B85) and with a general evaluation (B85, B86). He then continues with a more extended exploration, lasting until B96.

What is involved in constructing the typographic problem space? The space is *not* the particular mapping (E = 3, A = 4, I = 1, . . .), for this latter is an element in the space. The space consists of (1) a representation for such associations, (2) operators to generate such elements, and (3) test programs to see if an element is suitable. The representation of the element is simple—namely, just a set of correspondences. S8 obviously already is using this representation in the cryptogram space, where he has also been considering the assignments of digits to letters. There is also no difficulty about the tests. Basic ones, like rejecting (A = 4, H = 4, . . .) as not disjoint or (E = 3, L = 1) as not complete, are already formed and operational. The more complex test of whether a complete and disjoint set of assignments satisfies the addition test is postponable until after such an assignment set is generated, and no attention need be given to it in the interval between B82 and B83.

This leaves the second component, listed above, of the problem space: the operators that obtain assignments. We can safely assume that S8 does not have these operators available already. (The same might not be true of the cryptogram problem space, for S8 may well have played with cryptograms at some previous time.) The operators in this space are manipulations of how the symbols are perceived, so as to recognize them as digits rather than letters (Figure 7.8, page 276). Constructing a problem space means constructing some such operators in the immediate vicinity of B82.[21] That this is not impossible can be seen easily enough by the reader's rather rapid response to the written suggestion in the book that such operators exist.

This excursion back to S8's protocol is not meant to be a definite theory about the construction of problem spaces, but is intended to frame the problem appropriately, with the help of a concrete illustration. It does show that such constructions may be accomplished in rather short time intervals, so that the kind of data

---

[21] Perhaps no operators need be constructed precisely at B83. Instead, S8 may simply have noticed a single isolated letter-digit resemblance (E = 3). B85–86 is an attempt to find associations to the other letters, without yet developing any way of moving in the nascent space. Not until B87 are operators for the space in question.

we have dealt with in this book do not provide much evidence about them. The construction of problem spaces may appear exotic, and the fact that it may be done in a short time interval may seem to imply that substantially more processing per unit time is being accomplished than is allowed by our description of the IPS. This need not be the case, since the operators are built out of familiar components. Thus, the construction may imply a very large selection—i.e., a single organization is chosen from many possible ones—but it need not imply much processing.

There exist few synthetic program-constructing programs that provide insight into the possible structure of the human programs.[22] One exception is a program by Donald Williams (1969) that performs a number of concept-formation tasks from standard intelligence tests. The intelligence tests present first a set of instructions, consisting of a written description of a task and a few worked examples, followed by a series of problems in that task. Donald Williams' program, the *Example-Driven Problem Solver* (EDPS), assembles from the instructions a specific performance program, which it then uses to attempt all the tasks in the series. The program works entirely from the examples, having enough general context to dispense with the written instructions entirely. By examining these worked examples, EDPS determines the form in which the answer is to be given (whether a blank is to be filled in, an item that fits an induced rule selected, an item that fails to fit a rule selected, or the rule itself stated). It also determines what kinds of relations have to be detected in the problem material in order to find the answer. EDPS uses this information to construct a trial performance program and then tests it against the worked out examples. When it finally has a satisfactory program, it tackles the test items.

Although the range of tests it can handle is fairly limited (a limitation primarily of the task environment of intelligence tests), EDPS still provides an initial model of how a program might be assembled in response to task instructions. The processes it uses for program construction are not themselves problem solving processes but involve recognition of salient features of the task situation, coupled with direct actions to select the appropriate program components—i.e., direct means-ends analysis.

Modification during Problem Solving

The problem space and the specific set of methods used with it need not remain constant through a whole problem solving attempt. As footnote 21, above, indicated, the problem space may be constructed gradually as the need for the component pieces arises. Thus, the assumption that the subject is in a fully developed problem space with all its associated apparatus may be only an approximation to reality.

---

[22] There is an abundance of synthetic programs that construct programs (i.e., compilers), but since they all work from process descriptions of the programs to be constructed (their inputs are programs expressed in a higher-level language), they do not appear relevant here.

The protocol of S3 on DONALD+GERALD provides an illustration of sequential development of the problem space. He has just finished his first episode (E1) in which he established (T = 0, R odd), and failed to establish anything about G (first thinking it even, and then seeing that c6 is not known):

B39: I think I'll forget about that for a minute.
B40: Possibly the best way to get to this problem is to try different possible solutions.
B41: I'm not sure whether that would be the easiest way or not.

At this point he evokes production P3:

$$P3: \text{get } \langle \text{letter.1} \rangle \longrightarrow \text{FA(letter.1) } (\Longrightarrow \text{column});$$
$$\text{AV(letter.2 of column); PC[column for letter.1]}$$

This is the first time the assignment operator, AV, is executed, outputting (L ← 1). In our earlier analysis we characterized S3's problem space as containing AV from the beginning, and his program as containing P3 from the beginning—the above being the first occasion for its evocation. But it is also possible that the production was added to the problem solving program at this point. We do not, of course, have a very clear notion of what "adding a production to a production system" involves in terms of the structure of the IPS.

A less clear, but still instructive, example occurs with S8, also on DONALD+ GERALD, when he discovers towards the end of the session that the carry can take on values only of 0 or 1. He immediately finishes the solution at that point, getting E = 9 from the fact that E = 0 ∨ 9 and T = 0, and then traveling over (by then) familiar territory to make the rest of the inferences. S8 is emphatic about the importance of this discovery to him, both when it happens and immediately after the solution has been obtained. Here is the latter passage of the protocol:

B658: Oh . . . if I . . . it was so simple. . . . It was. . . .
B659: Over there in the end there, if I could've just seen that I had to have a 1 carry over,
B660: I could've got along so quickly.
B661: I . . . I can't . . . I don't know. . . .
B662: I couldn't get rid of that idea in my mind that er . . . that I could have a carry over besides zero and 1.

What changed with the sudden arrival of this knowledge (at B553 and B554)? A priori, it could have been the problem space, the specific program (the production system), or simply the knowledge state. It seems likely that what changed was a small aspect of the problem space—i.e., S8's general knowledge of the range of carries. We might conclude that the program had changed if the form of inference (i.e., that a letter must have a specific value because the other possibilities are exhausted) had been evoked here for the first time. But S8 drew inferences of this form several times earlier. Since S8 had no occasion to use the newly acquired general fact (carry = 0 ∨ 1) in the remainder of his protocol, we cannot be sure whether he changed his problem space or whether he only made a particular inference ($c5 = 0 \lor 1$), which would merely add to his knowledge state. S8's language, of course, takes the generalized form, so that we might expect his behavior on subsequent problems to be changed; but we do not have explicit evidence for this. Furthermore, the generality of a statement is not a reliable guide to interpretation. We refer the reader to E24 of S8's exploration of problem spaces (Appendix 7.5, page 373) some minutes before he began working on DONALD+ GERALD. There S8 explores the matter of carries thoroughly and arrives at the conclusion that the carry cannot be 2 or more.

The chess discussion in Chapter 13 on redefinition of the situation (page 761) is also relevant to the sorts of changes that occur in the problem space and in the program during problem solving. We can expect no changes to occur over the board in the basic problem space used for chess; all the chess subjects had too much experience with chess for this to happen. However, redefinitions could easily have been shifts of program to account for just such matters as whether the King-side was in fact in danger, or could be ignored; or who had the initiative. There is no way of classifying such redefinitions on the basis of their content and their gross function, since these evidences may not identify the specific changes in the problem solver's program and data structures.

Again, synthetic programs provide much less help than one would like, to explain progressive modification. There have been many programs that modify themselves in various ways (usually called learning programs), but few of them are instructive for our purposes. An exception is an interesting program that learns to play draw poker (Waterman, 1970). The problem solving program itself is cast as a production system, operating on a knowledge state made up of a fixed vector of features of the poker situation: the size of the pot, the opening bet, and so on. The program starts from a null production, which simply makes a random bet, and under the impact of play, gradually creates and adds new productions to the system. With reasonable amounts of experience the program comes to play quite passable draw poker.

Waterman used productions because of some of the same features that make them attractive to us: heuristics can be characterized as individual productions (or clusters of them) and the total system is simply the collection of such heuristics. Actually, Waterman's program is quite careful where it locates new productions, since their order in the system can have strong effects on behavior. The principle of location is conceptually simple: since productions near the head of the list screen later ones, it follows that productions representing specializations should precede productions representing more general rules of behavior.

The processes that add a production to the poker program are basically diagnostic programs that detect situations in which some specific feature of the program's behavior is unsatisfactory, and then fashion a specific production (or cluster) to remedy the situation. In this respect they respond in a fashion not unlike S3 above, who added production P3 because the existing production system (the one that produced E1, presumably a pure reasoning system) failed to offer a way of continuing. There is, of course, little reason for thinking that S3's program is similar structurally to the poker program, particularly since the construction and addition processes in the latter program are of substantial size and complexity.

However, they are no more complex than the problem solvers themselves, nor do they require processes other than the sorts of symbolic ones we have been considering in this book.[23]

Task Differences

We have described six different ways in which the actual problem space and problem solving programs can be determined. (In any actual instance, several ways may be involved simultaneously.) Only two of them, the first and last, focus primarily on the task presently facing the problem solver. The others—already having available the space for the task, adapting an analogous task, using general problem solving methods, and constructing the program and space out of available parts—all derive the capabilities on the present task from those on other tasks. (The first and the last do also, but in a less obvious way.) In all these four cases, how well the problem solver performs a task depends on how well he has done other tasks, for several tasks make use of some of the same processes and symbol structures.[24]

The problem space itself gives us some inkling of the communality among tasks, for we can say a good deal about behavior once we know what problem space is being used. Each problem space covers a range of tasks—for individual tasks can be defined by different starting and terminal points within the same space. S4 in cryptarithmetic operated in the same space for DONALD+GERALD and for CROSS+ROADS. S8 in logic operated in the same space through all his problems; and indeed, all of our six subjects who did both D1 and C1 used the same space for both. Here we know as much about task communality as we know about behavior on an individual task.

But communality is only one of the four mechanisms we outlined for transfer of information from different tasks. About the others we know very little. We will not understand generality of performance over task until the mechanisms identified in these previous sections are described in detail—or at least until some of their structural features are established. Moreover, we must describe versions of these mechanisms that are actually used by humans, instead of referring—as we have done in these sections—to synthetic programs that incorporate a few such mechanisms. We do not yet have mechanisms that are directly tested by behavioral data. Even the organization of GPS with respect to generality, although psychologically relevant, gains neither empirical support nor refutation from the kinds of data that are presented in Chapter 9. The various types of mechanisms for information transfer can all produce functionally identical problem solving programs (hence behaviors), so that separating the different mechanisms and obtaining adequate

[23] Independent of its specific interest for this section, Waterman's program provides strong reinforcement for the notion that production systems provide an appropriate representation for the IPS of a problem solver.

[24] In fact, we are discussing intertask transfer, a venerable topic in experimental and educational psychology. However, we wish to determine the underlying structural means for such transfer, rather than simply trying to express the facts of transfer, say, by correlating performance in different tasks.

descriptions of them may prove quite difficult. The relations among tasks inevitably depend on the actual structure of knowledge about the world—and thus bring us back to the quixotic task of describing all knowledge as a prerequisite to describing man's cognitive abilities. Yet a formal task is not simply an *example* of a task, as substitution is an *example* of an operation. Formal tasks occupy a very privileged position in the domain of all tasks. Nor is the notion of a resource and its control (recall the discussion in Chapter 11, page 705) just one among many concepts. The concepts of causality, time, space, seriation, and conservation, whose psychological study has been pursued by Piaget, have similarly general import. For all of these very general concepts, their actual content affects strongly the possibility of relations between tasks, and the possibility of learning programs whose function is to adapt programs and problem spaces in one task to the service of another.

In this respect GPS is a misleading model, and for that reason we discussed it as only one of several ways in which a specific program and problem space could be determined. For GPS suggests that there is a distinct level of task-free generality, neatly separated from the content of each problem space. If we were to take GPS as our model, task generality would then be bound up in the general mechanisms at this level (to be used in all tasks) and in the identifying processes that allow a task to be formulated so that the general mechanisms can be brought to bear on it. While such an organization is certainly possible, so are a number of others. Each form of organization implies a quite different relation between tasks.

Individual Differences

The world is populated by a great many problem solvers—some even say there are too many. Each is a distinct IPS, describable in terms of his processes and symbol structures and of their organization to solve problems in particular task environments. In what ways can these problem solvers differ, and what makes them different? In what ways are they the same, and what makes them the same?

The theory, as we have developed it so far, describes two levels of organizational commonality: (1) all humans are IPS's, hence have certain basic organizational features in common; (2) all humans have in common a few universal structural characteristics, such as nearly identical memory parameters. These commonalities produce common characteristics of behavior among all human problem solvers.

Both the structural constants and their consequences have been summarized earlier in the chapter, and do not need review. They still leave many degrees of freedom in human behavior. In fact, given all the invariant structure, a human IPS is still capable of almost arbitrary behavior in response to a task environment—everything from attempting the task to going to sleep, arguing with the presenter of the task, redefining the task, deliberately failing, ignoring the task, engaging in a sitdown strike for better working conditions, protesting over something not connected with the task—and so on and on. The structural limits provide only that he do these things in a certain style—not too fast, not remembering too much, using a goal structure to keep track of whatever goals he constructs and submits himself to, using a problem space when the current goal confronts him with a problem he wishes to solve.

The invariances we have described are not absolute. For instance, the size of STM, as measured by standard tests, varies considerably over the human population, and the variation is important for function. Differences in the capacity of STM, for example, probably play a large role in the functional difference between the very young and the mature, and between those we consider intellectually subnormal and those we consider normal. Even here, the range is small compared with the variation observable over the spectrum of man-made IPS's (which encompass STM's with capacities up to thousands of symbols, LTM's that store new symbols in a single operation time, and so on).

The behavioral significance of human differences in these parameters only emphasizes the strong role their constancy plays in the behavior of normally intelligent human beings, for whom they assume their characteristic values within only a small range of variation. In any event, our concern in this section is with those individual differences that are independent of variation in these parameters.

The theory postulates a second great source of commonality among human problem solvers—namely, the characteristics of task environments. If we put several humans in the same problem situation, if they have the same goals, and if they have sufficient ability to solve the problem, then many features of their behavior are given the same shape by the task environment. As we have seen, the shape imposed by the task is effective even if the humans are not quite able to solve the problem, for the same task features appear obvious to all of them and are responded to similarly.

Insofar as there are strikingly different ways of attacking a task, of course, there need be no behavioral similarity among several problem solvers, for they can follow different paths. The commonalities also depend on commonality of goals and situations.

The commonality enforced by rational response to the task is mediated through the IPS of the problem solver. It is not structural: any commonality among problem solvers must be represented in the IPS. Since the IPS can be factored into (1) basic structure, and (2) the contents of LTM (i.e., programs and data), it follows that any proposal for commonality among problem solvers not attributable directly to basic structure must be represented as an identity or similarity in the contents of the LTM's—in the production systems or in other stored memory structures.

The variables that are evoked in discussing why some people are different (and why others are the same) show this clearly. People differ, for purposes of behavioral science description, by virtue of culture, education, or socioeconomic class. That is to say, they differ because of particular experiences they have had, jobs they have worked at, people they have talked to, books they have read, and so on. The theory in its present form says little about what behavioral differences can be caused by all these differences in the contents of LTM. Correspondingly, it says little about the behavioral commonalities that are made by common culture, common education, common experiences. It proposes a system that, given enough time, can absorb any specification whatsoever—can become responsive to the full detail, say, of an encyclopedia (or a library of them). Hence the theory places the determination of differences and similarities of behavior directly upon the causes defining the content that will be stored in the human LTM. But these determinants of content are largely contingent upon the detail of the individual's life history. This does not mean that the determining processes are arbitrary or capricious or unlawful. It means that the contents can be as varied as the range of physical, biological, and social phenomena that surround the individual and from which he extracts them.

It is this fundamental characteristic of the human IPS that accounts for the elusiveness of psychological laws. Man is the mirror of the universe in which he lives, and all that he knows shapes his psychology, not just in superficial ways but almost indefinitely and subject only to a few basic constraints. This view should not be equated with the extreme form of cultural relativism sometimes espoused in anthropology, or the "man can be anything he wants" slogans preached by inspirational psychology. The universe that man mirrors is more than his culture. It includes also a lawful physical universe, and a biological one—of which man's own body is not the least important part. The view simply places the constraints upon the possible forms of human behavior in the environment rather than attributing these constraints directly to psychological mechanisms. It proposes limits on knowledge and how to obtain it, rather than limits on the ability to perform according to knowledge that has been assimilated.

Are there no other internal constraints on the forms of human cognition? First, as soon as the biological system—for our purposes, especially the sensory system—is pressed to a limit, various structural constraints come into play. There are not only general limits in sensory capacities, but all sorts of odd phenomena as well—after-images, illusions, ringing in the ears, and what not. Similarly, emotionality and altered states of awareness, such as drowsiness, are both internal and affect the operation of the IPS. These biological constraints are sources both of commonality (all human visual systems experience after-images) and of individual differences (hearing acuity can affect behavior substantially). But a *normal situation* is precisely one in which these biological limits are not exceeded, and it is to such normal situations that the theory of this book applies. In this sense, the theory is a first approximation, which is to be refined by introduction of the sensory and other biological limits as additional constraints upon behavior.

The other source to which we must look for constraints upon human cognition, hence for commonalities across all human problem solvers, is the set of processes by which the contents of the LTM of the human adult are acquired: the processes of development and learning. Since our studies have provided little information about them, we do not discuss them at length, but their existence must be acknowledged.

The human IPS must grow itself to its adult normal state, starting from a primitive neonatal state that is not yet well understood. At each moment of growth the ongoing changes in the cognitive system must be capable of being assimilated by the system that is already there, at the same time that the latter remains in reasonable working order. This requirement for a capacity to develop while performing may well imply certain structural similarities among all human cognitive systems, in addition to those discussed earlier in the chapter.

A similar possibility of commonality arises from the requirement that the human cognitive system be able to learn continually from the world around it. In this book we are working with systems that are creating new knowledge at all times, both in STM and LTM, and we have made the rather strong proposal that all increments of knowledge are cast in the form of productions. But we have not examined the acquisition process, and the acquisition mechanisms for productions that have been proposed (for example, Waterman's learning production system for poker) are not specific enough to answer the important psychological questions about the process. It is likely, however, that the capacity for learning within the time scales and amounts characteristic of normal humans implies additional invariant features common to all human cognitive systems.

Conclusion

In discussing how actual programs and problem spaces are determined within the limits set by the task environment and the basic structure of the IPS, we have not tried to specify, even speculatively, the actual process of determination. We have enumerated in some detail the sources of information that could be used in the determination. Appropriate bits of behavior of our subjects illustrated some of these. For others, we have not direct human behavioral evidence and have had to fall back on synthetic programs to illustrate the mechanisms concretely.

Next we discussed task differences and individual differences. Drawing on the detailed analyses of the previous three parts of the book, we summarized the relations among separate tasks, as the theory views these relations, and the sources of commonality and difference in cognitive behavior among human problem solvers.

Repeatedly, we have found ourselves concerned with the *content* of the problem solver's knowledge. Behavior is not simply a function of a few aggregative features of this content—of how much content there is, or how it is expressed. Behavior is a function of the specific detail of content, of the actual facts of the particular task in hand. And this content governs not just a partial aspect of the behavior of the IPS, but almost all aspects. The behavior of an IPS cannot be understood from syntax alone, abstracted from the vocabulary and semantics of what is being said and done. Methods and programs are themselves content.

Finally, we pointed to two additional sources of invariant structure in human behaviors: namely, the requirements that the human IPS be capable of developing and learning. The data of this book however, give us only glimpses of these aspects of human cognition.

SUMMARY

In this chapter we have drawn upon the empirical data that were presented and analyzed in the preceding nine chapters to construct a theory of human problem solving. Human problem solving, we have argued, is to be understood by describing the task environment in which it takes place; the space the problem solver uses to represent the environment, the task, and the knowledge about it that he gradually accumulates; and the program the problem solver assembles for approaching the task. We have tried to characterize environments, problem spaces, and programs, showing how the problem solver's program extracts some of the structural information that is embedded in the task environment in order to find solutions by means of a highly selective search through the problem space.

Our emphasis has been on the problem solver's performance program. In the last section of the chapter we brought to bear what evidence we could on the question of how the problem solver, in the face of a new task, generates an appropriate problem space and program and on the commonalities and differences among problem solvers. Our answers to these questions were sketchy, for these areas undoubtedly represent the largest and most important *terra incognita* on the map of the theory of human problem solving today.

To the extent that our data, and our understanding of those data, permit, we have now completed the task we set ourselves in Chapter 1. In the brief epilogue that follows, we wish to take leave of the readers who have been patient enough to follow us to this point.

EPILOGUE

We are now at the end of the trip through our data on human problem solving behaviors, and our explanations of those data in information processing terms. Problem solving behaviors, even in the relatively well-structured task environments that we have used in our research, have generally been regarded as highly complex forms of human behavior—so complex that for a whole generation they were usually avoided in the psychological laboratory in favor of behaviors that seemed to be simple: e.g., one-step mediations, like those involved in reversal experiments (Kendler, 1961).

The appearance of the modern computer at the end of World War II gave us and other researchers the courage to return to complex cognitive performances as our source of data. The computer was clearly a mechanistic device, behaving as it did because the laws of physics constrained it to. It was just as clearly a device capable of symbol-manipulating behavior at levels of complexity and generality unprecedented for man-made mechanisms—although this fact was obscured for a time, and still is for some, by the emphasis on numerical operations in the more common applications of computers. It is not surprising that many persons found in the computer new metaphors applicable to human cognitive processes and new hypotheses about the organization of mind and brain. This was part of the general insight of cybernetics, delayed by ten years and applied to discrete symbolic behavior rather than to continuous feedback systems.

In our work, the computer has been more than a metaphor. It has been an important tool, for it has permitted us to carry out, through simulation, detailed comparisons between theory and data, and to derive numerous empirical predictions from theory. But more important than the computer as hardware have been the new concepts of information processing systems and the new formalisms and languages for describing such systems with precision. The basic point of view inhabiting our work has been that programmed computer and human problem solver are both species belonging to the genus IPS. They do differ, of course, at the species level, and in ways our concepts describe: in memory organization, elementary processes, and program organization. In this book the computer has receded into the background and we have specified our IPS directly in terms appropriate to the study of human behavior.

When we seek to explain the behavior of human problem solvers (or computers for that matter), we discover that their flexibility—their programmability—is the key to understanding them. Their viability depends upon their being able to behave adaptively in a wide range of environments. A proper understanding of the intimate interdependence between an adaptive organism and its environment is essential to a clear view of what a science of an adaptive species can be like.

If we carefully factor out the influences of the task environments from the influences of the underlying hardware components and organization, we reveal the true simplicity of the adaptive system. For, as we have seen, we need postulate only a very simple information processing system in order to account for human problem solving in such tasks as chess, logic, and cryptarithmetic. The apparently complex behavior of the information processing system in a given environment is produced by the interaction of the demands of that environment with a few basic parameters of system, particularly characteristics of its memories.

This conception of problem solving behavior does not leave empty the gap between the task environment with its demands, and the basic IPS with its invariant characteristics. For there are mechanisms that fill this gap and produce the behavior. There are three layers of filling, so to speak. Proceeding inward from the task environment, there is the problem space, in which problem solving takes place as search; then the methods, which are the means whereby that search takes place; and finally the production system, which is the program organization whereby the methods are realized in terms of elementary processes and basic characteristics of the IPS.

We have attempted to show that a substantial fraction of all of these constructs flow directly from the basic two boundary conditions plus the assumption of adaptivity. Thus all this intermediate structure, which would constitute the heart of a classical mechanistic theory of human problem solving, although invariant, is for many purposes of explanation and prediction totally transparent. Only knowledge of the demands of the environment, the general level of intelligence of the human, and the basic cognitive limits of the IPS are required to explain behavior.

Thus we have an "inner" theory and an "outer" theory of human problem solving. We hesitate to evoke the standard image of thermodynamics and kinetic theory. For the relation there between macroscopic theory (thermodynamics) and microscopic theory (kinetic theory of gases) is statistical. But here the connecting link is just the opposite: adaptational. Matters are simple, not because the law of large numbers cancels things out, but because things line up in a means-ends chain in which only the end points count (i.e., equifinality). But in other respects the analogy with thermodynamics and kinetics is apt. In both cases the outer theory provides the main, gross results. The inner theory provides the fine structure. In our case the fine structure relates not only to the dynamic details over time, but also to the lapses from adaptation—errors, confusions, wrong explorations. Not all such details occur at the IPS level where we have worked, of course. They occur also in the underlying structure of the memories and processes, as investigated in the psychological laboratory, and even further down in terms of the physiology of the central nervous system.

The theory we set forth in Chapter 14, both in its central themes and in its details, extends beyond the base provided by our empirical studies of three tasks. The present empirical base gives strong clues to a general theory of human problem solving without defining the limits of the induction. Those limits that we could discern have been taken into account—indeed used to sense how the theory should be generalized. However, the gaps are not just those of extent—of not having examined 57 tasks ranging widely over various memory structures and demands on long-term memory. Many aspects of the basic IPS have not been explored in sufficient detail or with the appropriate experimental questions.

Does a production system represent adequately the immediately effective program? What are the exact characteristics of the *effective* STM—the internal STM plus the display-in-view? Are there auditory and other sensory extensions of similar type? Do place keepers for all processes (the subroutine stack) reside in STM? What are the specifications for associative accessing in LTM? What accessing information must be kept in what memories in order to access large displays (i.e., the extended knowledge state)? When a person is using scratch paper for a problem, how big is his effective STM (assuming residence time must be somewhat longer than a few hundred milliseconds)?

The list could be extended almost indefinitely. All of these questions can be extracted from the ongoing problem solving situation within which they arose, can be purified, and can then be explored experimentally. We are not voicing a complaint. Indeed, the work of the last ten years on immediate memory and the perceptual system has increasingly moved toward providing exactly the quantitative models of the memory systems that we seek. We wish only to observe that the theory as developed here poses many experimental questions.

Although we have framed the final version of the theory in general terms, we have not gone outside our self-imposed set of three tasks, either for additional verification or to show how the theory explains additional phenomena, both old and new. Some areas, such as concept attainment and rote memorization, were candidates for inclusion along with the three problem solving tasks. Not only do they have a large experimental literature, but a substantial amount of work has already been done by ourselves and others toward understanding them from an information processing viewpoint.

A number of isolated phenomena that usually make up the potpourri of topics grouped under thinking, such as functional fixity, the Einstellung effect, insight, incubation, and so on, must surely be included within the scope of a comprehensive theory. No extensive reanalysis of these phenomena from an information processing viewpoint has been carried out, but they speak to the same basic phenomena, so should yield to such an explanation. Indeed, functional fixity has been discussed at various places in the book.

Beyond this, one needs to move toward task environments of greater complexity and openness—to everyday reasoning, to scientific discovery, and so on. The tasks we tackled, though highly complex by prior psychological standards, still are simple in many respects. Success with these encourages pushing out the boundaries of rigorous analysis. The entire developmental continuum poses a substantial challenge, even though Piaget's monumental efforts have moved current perspectives a long way towards willingness to analyze the information processing capabilities and requirements at the different stages of development.

However, we have considerable respect for the demands of an information processing analysis. Sufficient unto the day (actually a decade) was the task thereof: to put forth in an empirically meaningful way a theory of human problem solving.

We view this volume, then, as a progress report on work that needs to be advanced in a great many directions. We do believe it describes some of the main information processing mechanisms that account for behavior in problem solving tasks, and embodies an essentially correct view of how to create a science of adaptive organisms. Our hope is that these investigations will stimulate others to extensions, emendations, or even refutations.

HISTORICAL ADDENDUM

In the text we have limited ourselves to references required by scholarly obligation. This is not the place to undertake a full-scale history of the developments leading up to the work reported in the book—nor are we the ones to undertake it. However, it seems appropriate to describe some of the antecedents of this work—particularly its less obvious connections with other streams of research—in somewhat greater detail than we allowed ourselves in the text. The following notes, then, are to be taken as a somewhat personal view of history.

World War II provides a convenient boundary between pre-history and history. The pre-history involves two main strands: one in psychology, and one in formal logic. The post–World War II history requires particular attention to the whole collection of ideas and activities sometimes assembled under the label of *cybernetics*, as well as to the exploitation of these ideas in artificial intelligence and in cognitive psychology.

Cognitive Psychology Before 1945

On the American side of the Atlantic Ocean there was a great gap in research on human complex cognitive processes from the time of William James almost down to World War II. Although the gap was not complete, it is fair to say that American cognitive psychology during this period was dominated by behaviorism, the nonsense syllable, and the rat. Hull's doctoral thesis (1920) on concept formation was a notable exception, but his desertion of this problem for others more compatible with the Zeitgeist is typical of the period. Not only that, it was widely interpreted as showing the futility of a direct approach to higher mental processes. In *A Study of Thinking* (1956), the only American psychologists mentioned more than casually for their pre-war work are Egon Brunswik (to whom the book is dedicated), Hull, and Tolman. The references to Hull are to his thesis, leaving Brunswik and Tolman as the real fore runners of the work, so far as American psychology is concerned.[1]

Of the leading American psychologists of this period, Tolman was the farthest from the dominant S-R position (except for those Gestalt psychologists who migrated from Europe). His relevance to the subsequent development of information processing psychology is clearly suggested by the titles of his principal book, *Purposive Behavior in Animals and Men* (1932), and of the best-known of his papers with Brunswik, "The Organism and the Causal Texture of the Environment" (1935). He treated man (and rat) as a goal-seeking, hence decision-making, organism, whose behavior was molded by the structure of the environment in which he sought to achieve his aims. Brunswik developed this same point of view by characterizing the structure of the environment in probabilistic terms—terms that would make natural the subsequent application of the concepts of information theory and game theory.

European psychology, less preoccupied than American with methodological rigor and more willing to use data from verbal protocols, had a more active record, during this period, of concern with the cognitive processes exhibited in complex behavior. From a longer list of names, we cannot omit mention, at least, of Bartlett in England, and Selz, Duncker, Wertheimer, Piaget, and de Groot on the Continent.

The specific trademark of Bartlett's *Remembering* (1932), allying his work with the Gestalt viewpoint, was its concern for the way in which information was represented "inside the head," and how it was modified by the processes that stored it there and retrieved it. A similar concern for central representations, and an even greater emphasis on central processes, characterizes the Würzburg school in general, and the work of Selz and his followers in particular.

The applications of this point of view to problem solving, especially by Wertheimer and Duncker, were hardly known in the United States until after World

---

[1] H. A. Simon, whose publication began before World War II, acknowledged James and Tolman as the principal sources of his psychological conceptions (*Administrative Behavior*, 1947, Chapter 5).

War II.[2] When post-war work on thinking and problem solving is examined, however, and the connections traced through concepts and citations, the lineages are clear. Our own work and de Groot's (which began before the war) owe large debts to Selz, while the works of Maier, Katona, Guetzkow, and Luchins, among others, develop the lines opened by the Gestaltists.

Apart from Tolman and Brunswik, we must mention one other viewpoint in pre-war American psychology that departs from the position of radical behaviorism. It is the "standard" viewpoint of physiological psychologists, which for our purposes is well expressed in the words of Boring: (*The Physical Dimension of Consciousness* (1933), preface to Dover edition, pp. vi-vii).

> A fact is a relation, and the simple basic fact in psychology is a correlation of a dependent variable upon an independent one. Ernst Mach made this point and B. F. Skinner took it up about the time this book was being written. He created the concept of "empty organism" (my phrase, not his), a system of correlation between stimulus and response with nothing (no C. N. S., the "Conceptual Nervous System"—his phrase, not mine) in between. This book does not go along with Skinner whose "empty organism" is made of "empty correlations," but rather argues that these correlations are early steps in scientific discovery and need to be filled—for the inquiring mind dislikes action at a distance, discontinuities that remain "unexplained." Thus my text undertook to assess the amount of neurological filling available in 1932—how much fact there was ready to relieve the psychophysiological vacuum—and it sought to formulate the requirements that more filling would have to meet.

We invite the reader's attention to Boring's last sentence, which contains the important implicit assumption separating the psychophysiological viewpoint (typified also by Lashley, for example) *both* from behaviorism and from the research we have mentioned as forerunner to our own. The assumption has two parts:

1. the "empty organism" is to be filled with explanatory mechanisms, an assumption that is accepted by all except the radical behaviorists; but also:
2. the explanatory mechanisms are to be neurological, an assumption that is not accepted by the psychologists whose views we have associated with ours.

Let us be entirely clear as to what the latter denial means. It is not a denial of in-principle reductionism—instead, it is an assertion that, by virtue of the complexity of the phenomena, the reduction of stimulus-response regularities to

---

[2] Similarly, before the war, Piaget's work was familiar to some American educational psychologists; hardly at all to American experimental psychologists. "Familiar" is perhaps not quite the right term, since there existed no way at that time for bringing that work, even when known, into any kind of relevant conceptual relation to the main stream of American behaviorism.

neural processes will have to be carried out in several successive steps, not just a single step. It is a denial modeled on the successful practice of physics and chemistry—and recently, of biochemistry and molecular biology—that accepts, in principle, the reduction of the most complex events to the laws of quantum physics, but carries out the reduction by erecting a number of layers of theory between gross biological phenomena and the sub-microscopic events of the atomic nucleus.

The implicit acceptance of the second part of Boring's assumption by virtually all American psychologists who were not behaviorists (except, again, those with views allied to Tolman's) erroneously identified explanation of stimulus-response correlations with neurophysiology. An important post-war example of this confusion was Hebb's insistence, in *The Organization of Behavior*, that his theory was to be regarded as physiological (Hebb, 1949, pp. xvi-xix).

Since the information processing theories discussed in this book represent a specific layer of explanation lying between behavior, on the one side, and neurology on the other, it is to be expected that we would resonate most strongly with those of our predecessors who admitted explanatory constructs of this kind. Whether these forerunners would be pleased to be regarded as "information processing theorists," or whether they would accept our operationalization of their vague (in our eyes) concepts are questions we do not feel called upon to answer. In this note we are acknowledging our intellectual debts, not representing our creditors.

The Influence of Formal Logic

The rise of modern formal logic, a product of the twentieth century—and, more generally, the spectacular development of abstract mathematics—has greatly enhanced the ability of a science to state its theories with rigor and precision. To build a successful scientific theory we must know what to say, and we must have a language in which we can express what we know. The greatest weakness of the antecedents of information processing psychology was the lack of a language to make its concepts clear and operational. Advances in knowledge that began with the formalization of logic by Peano, Frege, and Whitehead and Russell at about the turn of the century have provided that language.

Since the relation of formal logic to information processing theories is often misunderstood, we must expand our discussion a bit. Both logicians and psychologists agree nowadays that formal logic is not to be confused with human thinking. From the logician's viewpoint, they should not be confused because logical inference has objective, formal standards of validity which, if they must be given concrete existence at all, surely exist in Plato's heaven of ideas and not in human heads. We need not argue whether formalization of logic allows us to squeeze the last drop of intuition out of the act of inference; enough is squeezed out to make inference something quite different from a thought process.

From the psychologist's point of view, thinking must not be confused with logic because human thinking frequently is not rigorous or correct, does not follow the path of step-by-step deduction—in short, is not usually "logical."

If the logicians' and the psychologists' objections to confusing logic with thought are valid—and we agree that they are—what can be the possible contribution of formal logic to information processing psychology? The fundamental contribution was to demonstrate by example that the manipulation of symbols (at least *some* manipulation of *some* symbols) could be described in terms of specific, concrete processes quite as readily as could the manipulation of pine boards in a carpenter shop. The formalization of logic showed that symbols can be copied, compared, rearranged, and concatenated with just as much definiteness of process as boards can be sawed, planed, measured, and glued.

The persistence of concern with the mind-body problem can be attributed in part to the apparent radical incongruity and incommensurability of "ideas"— the material of thought—with the tangible biological substances of the nervous system. Formal logic, if it showed nothing else, showed that ideas—at least some ideas—could be represented by symbols, and that these symbols could be altered in meaningful ways by precisely defined processes. Even a metaphorical use of the similarities between logical manipulation of symbols, on the one hand, and thinking, on the other, had a profound liberating influence upon modes of conceptualizing thought processes, problem solving processes, decision-making processes. Simon (1944) used this metaphor explicitly as the framework for his research on administrative decision making and can testify to its crucial importance in the development of his own theorizing:

> Any rational decision may be viewed as a conclusion reached from certain premises. . . . The behavior of a rational person can be controlled, therefore, if the value and factual premises upon which he bases his decisions are specified for him (1944, p. 19).

Making this new operationality of symbols and their processing fully viable for psychology required seeing that "symbol manipulation" could refer to a much wider range of phenomena than simple deductive logic. The beginnings of this last, and crucial, generalization began to be visible at about the time of World War II, though it was not really completed until the modern computer had been fully developed.

Parallel to, and related to, the growth of formal logic was the progress that took place within economics in formal theories of rational decision making—the decision making of "economic man." Because economic man was patently too rational by human standards, his relevance for psychology was disputed or ignored. Nevertheless, economics was more and more explicitly concerning itself with *reasoning* about courses of action. The fact that it dealt only with reasoning that was logical, deductive, and correct postponed the recognition by economics and psychology of their common concerns. As matters turned out, it did not, ultimately, prevent that recognition.

The rational man of economic theory who began to emerge before the war was a close relative of the rational man of statistical decision theory—they grew up, in fact, in the same household. Statistics had, in turn, close historical links with philosophy, through concern with the foundations of probability and with the classical problem of induction. These links provided another tie between the emerging decision theory in economics and statistics, on the one hand, and the development of formal logic, on the other.[3]

One specific development in logic prior to World War II requires special mention. In their striving to handle symbols rigorously and objectively—as objects—logicians became more and more explicit in describing the processing system that was supposed to manipulate the symbols. In 1936, Alan Turing, an English logician, described the processor, now known as a *Turing machine*, that is regarded as the culmination of this drive toward formalization. At about the same time, Carnap, Church, Curry, and Post were introducing formalizations of the syntax of logic that subsequently provided models for the notions of "formal grammar" employed by modern linguistics.

Finally, we should mention a gradually growing belief that mathematics had a role to play in constructing theories of biological, psychological, and social phenomena parallel to the role it had earlier played in the physical sciences. Lotka's *Elements of Physical Biology* (1924) represented this point of view and foreshadowed some of the central concepts of cybernetics. Nicholas Rashevsky carried this kind of work forward in his theories of mathematical biophysics. Although there had been little contact of this work with psychology prior to the war, a number of psychologists (including Hull) were beginning to show strong interest in its potential.

What we have described is a powerful, growing Zeitgeist, having its origins around the turn of the century, involving a deep faith in mathematics as the language of science, but, more crucially, focused upon symbols and their manipulation in logical inference (if not in "reasoning") and decision. Symbols became, for the first time, tangible—as tangible as wood or metal. The Turing machine was an all-purpose planer and lathe for symbols. The stage was set, when World War II began, for the penetration of this new Zeitgeist into psychology.

THE POST-WAR SETTING

In Chapter 1 we suggested that 1956 could be taken as a critical year for the development of information processing psychology. That date occurs about a decade after the end of the war. Let us sketch how matters stood at the mid-fifties by reference to a few events and publications that occurred in that period.

The Cybernetic Revolution

The developments we have been tracing came to public notice at the end of World War II under the general label of *cybernetics*, a term that Norbert Wiener

---

[3] Readers familiar with contemporary statistics will recognize that we have used "decision theory" in a more generic sense than is usual—including, say, the contributions of R. A. Fisher and Neyman under this rubric as well as the later ones of Wald and the neo-Bayesians.

devised to embrace and characterize such elements as (1) information theory, (2) the theory of feedback systems (servomechanism theory, control theory), and (3) the electronic computer (Wiener, 1948). In other countries, particularly behind the Iron Curtain, where it has gained considerable currency, the term "cybernetics" is used even more broadly to encompass, in addition to the topics just listed, (4) game theory, (5) mathematical economics and statistical decision theory, and (6) management science and operations research.

Wiener has presented, in the first chapter of *Cybernetics*, his version of the history of these developments, to which the interested reader may refer; others have also given their accounts. Without repeating details, we offer several comments:

1. The broad use of the term cybernetics in Europe provides further confirming evidence for the unity of the Zeitgeist we have described, and for the roles we have attributed not only to logic but also to mathematical economics and decision theory in that *Zeitgeist*.

2. From the beginning, cybernetics had a strong concern with physiology, and with biological feedback mechanisms, thus linking back strongly to the *homeostasis* concepts of Claude Bernard, Lotka, Cannon, and Henderson. The considerable numbers of physiologists already attracted toward those concepts rapidly became acquainted with the cybernetic developments in other fields.

3. World War II did not produce the cybernetic developments; it more likely delayed them slightly. In particular, the ties with formal logic were especially evident in the earliest cybernetic publications, preceding and during the early years of the war: Shannon's master's thesis (1938), employing Boolean algebra for the analysis of switching circuits; the closely parallel Pitts-McCulloch paper (1943), providing a Boolean analysis of nerve networks; and the Rosenblueth-Wiener-Bigelow paper (1943) on "Behavior, Purpose, and Teleology."

4. Most of the figures prominent in these developments had early in their careers been deeply immersed in modern symbolic logic. Wiener had been a student of Russell's in Cambridge; much of von Neumann's work in the twenties and thirties was in logic; Shannon's and Pitts' and McCulloch's use of logic has already been mentioned.

5. Despite these intimate connections with logic, the computer as symbolic machine played a muted role in the early days of cybernetics. The main underpinnings were feedback (especially in continuous systems) and the information theory of Wiener and Shannon. Indeed, as late as the early fifties booklength expositions of cybernetics hardly mentioned the digital computer, and when they did it was only as "the biggest mechanism" (Ashby, 1956; Guilbaud, 1959). Analog and digital computers were treated on a conceptual parity, each taken to illustrate a form of encoding. And a perusal of Warren McCulloch's *Summary of Points of Agreement* at the end of the Macy Conference in Cybernetics (1955) makes a place for logic and for Turing machines, but none for symbolic mechanisms. These had to await the further development of programming.

It is well known, or at least widely believed, that work that too far anticipates its appropriate Zeitgeist is ignored, while work that is appropriate to the contemporary Zeitgeist is recognized promptly. Von Neumann's contributions to game theory in the twenties were known to few persons before 1940, Lotka was read by a few biologists, a few logicians were aware of the rapid strides of logic and the esoteric discoveries of Godel, Turing, Church, and Post. All this changed in the early post-war years.[4]

Biology and the various sciences of man did not long stay aloof from cybernetics. The feedback notions soon were being used, particularly by the physiologically inclined, and most enthusiastically in Great Britain (Ashby, 1952; Walter, 1953). The brain-computer metaphor suggested itself almost immediately—followed almost as immediately by warnings against taking the analogy seriously. The analogy, of course, that suggested itself initially, and against which these warnings were directed, was the one between the neurological organization of the brain and the wiring of the computer (von Neumann, 1956). Turing was one of the first to see that there was another level, the more abstract level of information processing, at which the analogy could be pursued more profitably. It is not at all surprising, in view of his conception in 1936 of the Turing machine, that he should have had this insight from the beginning.

Feedback concepts had considerable, but relatively unspecific, impact on psychology. But the influence of information theory was clear and precisely defined (Miller and Frick, 1949). Hick undertook to explicate and test a relation between response time and amount of information contained in the response, while others attempted to measure the information capacity of the human sensory and motor "channels."

Limits on the applicability of information theory to psychology gradually became clear. The high water mark had perhaps already been reached by 1955 (Quastler, 1955). Certainly by the time of Garner's monograph on *Uncertainty and Structure* (1962) information theory had receded to the status of a useful but specialized working tool for the analysis of variability.

---

[4] H. A. Simon can document from his own experience the dramatic change that took place during this period in the climate of ideas. When he first became interested (1935) in what he then called decision making and now calls information processing, he sensed vague affinities between his concerns and the lectures of Carnap on logic, Rashevsky on mathematical biophysics, and Schultz on mathematical economics and statistics. Through these teachers, he learned of Lotka, of recent developments in statistical decision theory, of Gödel—but not immediately of Church or Turing. He found a few other teachers and fellow-students who shared his vague sense of the Zeitgeist. His dissertation (published in 1947, with some revisions to take account of the publication of von Neumann and Morgenstern's book on game theory) reflected the intellectual climate of about 1940–42. The invisible college operated with some efficiency, then as now; for news of the new contributions, published in widely scattered journals and books, spread with great rapidity. His attention was called to the work of Shannon, Pitts and McCulloch, the servomechanism theorists, von Neumann and Morgenstern, and Wiener either before publication or within a few months thereafter. Similarly, the decision-making approach of his dissertation rapidly became known to cyberneticians working in economics and operations research.

The Würzburg and Gestalt Schools. The European work on thought processes was just beginning to be made available to Americans through translation and migration. The translations of Duncker's *On Problem Solving* and Wertheimer's *Productive Thinking* appeared in 1945; Humphrey, in *Thinking* (1951), provided the first extensive English-language discussion of Selz's research and theories; Katona's *Organizing and Memorizing* and a number of Maier's papers on problem solving had already appeared in 1940 but had almost been lost in the distractions of the war.

Concept Formation. The formalisms of information theory, statistical decision theory, and game theory had stimulated new interest in the classical research area of concept formation, and had suggested new research methods and theoretical concepts. Hovland's " 'Communication Analysis' of Concept Learning" was published in 1952; while George Miller's "Magic Number Seven" paper and the Bruner, Austin, and Goodnow *Study of Thinking* both appeared in the critical year 1956.

Human Factors. The war had produced a vast increase of research in human skills and performance—an area often referred to as "human factors" research. Moreover, much of this work was concerned with the human members of complex man-machine systems: pilots, gunners, radar personnel. As a consequence, the researchers not only were led to an emphasis on psychological processes, but were in a position to observe the analogies between human information processing and the behaviors of servomechanisms and computers. Broadbent's "A Mechanical Model for Human Attention and Immediate Memory" (1954) is illustrative both of the main research emphases (e.g., attention and short-term memory), and of the kinds of theoretical concepts that began to emerge.

There was considerable overlap in conceptions, personnel, and communication between the research in human factors and in concept formation. These areas provided a bridge, also, between the main stream of psychology and the newly emerging field of computer science, and a major route through which concepts drawn from the latter field began to be legitimized in psychology.

Linguistics

A long-standing concern with formalization and methodological clarity in linguistics received its own new impetus with Zelig Harris, *Methods in Structual Linguistics* (1951). The work of Chomsky, which was to redirect much of linguistics from a concern with structure to a concern with processing (that is, with generative systems) was just beginning (Chomsky, 1955), although it did not have much impact until a few years later (Chomsky, 1957). It is not possible for us, as outsiders, to assess the extent to which these developments in linguistics reflected the larger picture we have sketched. Some connections with logic are clear (e.g., Chomsky,

1954). But the efforts in the mechanical translation of languages (MT), which might be thought to demonstrate the close interconnection between linguistics and the computer, were made outside the main stream of linguistics (see Locke, 1955, for the early history).

Digital Computers

As we noted, the development of digital computers was a prominent event of the early post-war era. Their general theoretical character as universal machines was clearly understood; but they were viewed as primarily mathematical machines, that is, as devices that worked with numbers rather than symbols. Programming was still in a very rudimentary state. Although the first book on programming was published as early as 1951 (Wilkes, Wheeler, and Gill), the development of programming languages other than assembly languages only began towards the end of the period in question; for example, FORTRAN was begun in 1954 (Backus, et al., 1957). Thus, the powerful experience of working with a system that seemed to interpret symbols much as the user did was not available in the early fifties.

There was already some work using digital computers to simulate cognitive processes. Indeed, the use of mechanisms (robots) to illustrate psychological theories and enforce operationality has a long history, predating the computer. In an article on "Mind and Mechanism," Boring (1946) presents the view with his customary pungency and provides access to the earlier work. And with the cybernetic developments there was an additional pulse of mechanical robot building (Walter, 1953; Ashby, 1952). But all of these efforts were rather separate from simulation on the computer, which tended not toward activating mechanical beasts, but toward programming game playing and other symbolic activities. The first checker program was coded in 1952 (Strachy), and other game playing schemes are described in Bowden (1953). And Turing (1950), in a justly famous discussion, had put the problem of simulation in a highly sophisticated form.

THE CRITICAL YEARS: 1954–1958

We now turn from consideration of the general Zeitgeist in the early fifties to the events directly responsible for the theory in this book. The narrative necessarily becomes narrower in scope and somewhat more personal.

In late 1954 A. Newell initiated in earnest an effort to program a digital computer to learn to play good chess. The general context was the Systems Research Laboratory at RAND (later to metamorphize into the *System Development Corporation*), engaged in simulating an environment for an Air Defense radar center in order to understand its effectiveness (Chapman, et al., 1959). Thus the environment was a conceptual conglomerate of all the pieces we have been listing. But the proximate cause was the work of Selfridge and Dineen (reported in 1955), which seemed to make clear how computers were to become truly non-numerical processors.

In the first published description of this research effort, Newell (1955) said: "This is the means to understanding more about the kinds of computers, mechanisms, and programs that are necessary to handle ultracomplicated problems." The research undertaking was thus identified as "artificial intelligence" (though that name was not used); but the task to be examined was one of great psychological interest which had already been studied extensively by de Groot. The initial approach also established the precedents, followed in all of the subsequent work of our project, that artificial intelligence was to borrow ideas from psychology and psychology from artificial intelligence. Thus, Newell's programmatic description of his chess-learning problem proposed to use aspiration values and notions "of satisfactory solution" in evaluating chess moves, and discussed the necessity for "rules of thumb" (later called "heuristics") to chop down the enormous problem space to manageable size. Always following this course, the research pursued prior to 1957, although it had a heavy artificial intelligence emphasis, was carried on with one eye to its potential for psychology.

By the beginning of 1955, J. C. Shaw and H. A. Simon had associated themselves with Newell. Cliff Shaw had been concerned with the programming systems on JOHNNIAC, the computer built at RAND in the early fifties. Simon's early concerns have already been noted. His focus on limited rationality, satisficing and selective search at the juncture under discussion is summarized in Simon (1955, 1956). Considerable attention was being given to the programming language requirements for the project, and the relative advantages were being weighed of continuing with chess as the initial problem solving task as against first designing a theorem-proving scheme in geometry or logic. For several reasons, the latter tasks appeared to be somewhat simpler for an initial effort, and attention gradually shifted to them.

The work on programming language design moved in parallel with the substantive investigations through the autumn. By late October proving theorems in the propositional calculus (within the system of Whitehead and Russell) had been selected as the first target, and on December 15, 1955, the first successful hand simulation was carried out of the proof of a theorem in *Principia Mathematica* (Theorem 2.15), using essentially the methods and flow diagram that were incorporated in the Logic Theorist.

The formalization of this scheme, described in IPL-I (Information Processing Language I), was published in September, 1956, as has already been remarked in the text. It was announced, in less detail, in the unpublished RAND Report P-850, "Current Developments in Complex Information Processing" (May 1, 1956), a paper read by Newell in a series of lectures on computers and automation in Washington, D. C., May 2, 1956.

Programming Languages

The history of the programming languages employed in this research has been reported elsewhere (Newell, Tonge, Feigenbaum, Green, and Mealy, pp. xx–xxiv; see also Knuth, 1968, vol. 1, pp. 456–463). The first versions of LT actually run on a computer were programmed in IPL-II, and run on the JOHNNIAC computer at the RAND Corporation. The first complete machine proof of a theorem of *Principia Mathematica* (Theorem 2.01) was produced on August 9, 1956.

The suitability of the information processing languages for writing programs expressing psychological theories was not entirely accidental. They were designed, first and foremost, to handle complexity—unpredictable complexity. In arriving at the designs, every effort was made to take advantage of features of human memory thought to contribute to its flexibility—and, specifically, to exploit its "associative" organization. This cue from psychology was no doubt one important hint that pointed toward the list processing ideas.

The Dartmouth Summer Seminar

A research project in artificial intelligence had been organized at Dartmouth for June, 1956, by John McCarthy, Marvin Minsky, Nat Rochester, and Claude Shannon. Attendants at the seminar included a large percentage of all persons who were working actively in artificial intelligence at that time: McCarthy, Minsky, Rochester, Oliver Selfridge, Shannon, Ray Solomonoff, Trenchard More, Herbert Gelernter, Newell, and Simon. Many ideas for programs that would perform problem solving, pattern recognizing, or game-playing tasks were in the air, but the two concrete new schemes brought to the conference were the Logic Theorist and a program for proving theorems in the propositional calculus making use of the method of natural deduction, devised by Trenchard More (1957). More had constructed a flow diagram and hand simulated his scheme. The description of the Logic Theorist, later presented in September in Cambridge, was distributed to the group, and early debugging outputs were exhibited.

Marvin Minsky's well-known essay, *Steps Toward Artificial Intelligence*, although not published until several years later, was first drafted and circulated as a technical report late in 1956. It reflects very well the general body of knowledge in artificial intelligence that was pooled at the Dartmouth conference, and subsequently was itself an important document in organizing and codifying that knowledge.

Prior to the seminar, several persons and groups (including Minsky and Newell and Simon) had given some attention to proving theorems in geometry. This was an important topic of conversation at Dartmouth, giving impetus to the successful work of Gelernter and Rochester on this problem, which followed shortly thereafter. At the conference, Minsky prepared two sets of mimeographed notes on the geometry problem.

Human Problem Solving

The research up through the successful completion of LT in 1956 involved much more borrowing of ideas from psychology and human behavior to advance artificial intelligence than reverse borrowing from artificial intelligence to advance psychology. Psychology was very much on the research group's mind, however. The first file memorandum sketching a possible approach to EPAM (Elementary

Perceiving and Memorizing Program) is dated February 18, 1956. The notion of applying information processing ideas to human behavior in classical verbal learning tasks apparently was suggested while searching the standard psychological literature for clues to improved organizations of associative memories. E. J. Gibson's classical paper on stimulus and response generalization (Gibson, 1940) was perhaps the most important single source of the ideas that E. Feigenbaum subsequently developed into the EPAM program.

With respect to problem solving, however, serious attempts to interpret LT as a psychological theory got under way in the autumn of 1956. We had learned, meanwhile, that O. K. Moore and S. B. Anderson had used problems in logic theorem proving (disguised as "decoding" exercises) in their research on problem solving at Yale University (Moore and Anderson, 1954a and b). Their formal system was close enough to that of Whitehead and Russell to suggest using their task as a basis for comparing human behavior with the behavior of LT. With that end, Peter Houts, a graduate student at Carnegie Institute of Technology, began to make tape recordings of thinking-aloud sessions with subjects performing the Moore-Anderson logic task.

The first thinking-aloud tapes were transcribed in the spring of 1957, and their analysis was begun with a view to defining a computer program that would parallel, hence explain, the human behavior exhibited in them. It soon became clear that the LT organization did not fit the detail of human behavior at all well, and that the latter showed evidences of what we would now call the means-ends method.

Progress toward a new program was accelerated in discussion of the problem and of the transcriptions of the tape recordings with the members of a research seminar on organizational behavior that met on the Carnegie campus in the summer of 1957. During the summer and autumn, the analysis of the protocols gradually converged toward the first versions of the program that was christened the General Problem Solver. The general flow diagram of GPS was produced before the end of October, 1957, and the planning method was sketched a few days later (Newell, Shaw, and Simon, 1962).

The first published attempt to draw implications from the theorem-proving programs for the psychology of problem solving was the paper "Elements of a Theory of Human Problem Solving" in the *Psychological Review* for July, 1958. Written more than a year earlier, this paper was based on the experience with LT, hence emphasized the broad resemblances between the heuristic problem solving program and characteristics of human problem solving without attempting detailed comparisons of behavior. The "Elements" paper was organized around the thesis that "an explanation of an observed behavior of the organism is provided by a program of primitive information processes that generates this behavior." The methodological assumptions of the information processing approach to psychological theory were explored, and the relation of information processing theories of thinking to neurological, associationist, and Gestalt explanations discussed at some length. The "Elements" paper was thus the first explicit and deliberate exposition of the position now known as "information processing psychology"—although, in fact, that precise phrase was not used in the paper.

GPS (including the planning method) was first publicly described (though its name was not used) in "The Processes of Creative Thinking," a paper read on

May 14, 1958, at a University of Colorado symposium and again during June at the RAND Summer Seminar discussed below, but published only in 1962. This paper contained the first fragment of informal comparison of computer trace (hand simulated) with human thinking-aloud protocol.

Chess

Work on a chess program, which had been nearly dormant since 1955, was resumed toward the end of 1957. Meanwhile, discovery of de Groot's work, *Het Dencken van den Schaker* (1946), led to contact and collaboration with the author and his colleagues in Amsterdam that has continued down to the present. A history of computer chess programs, and a description of the NSS program, which became operational in 1958, can be found in "Chess-playing Programs and the Problem of Complexity" (1958, particularly pp. 322–331), and in Chapter 11 above, which also reviews the histories of psychological research on chess as a problem solving task and of chess-playing computer programs.

The RAND Summer Seminar

By the spring of 1958 extensive experiments had been carried out with LT; GPS had been conceived and hand simulated; the NSS chess program had joined its several predecessors as an operative program; the EPAM program was in process of construction; and the gathering and analysis of human protocol data were well underway. Research was also progressing at a lively pace at M.I.T. (Minsky and McCarthy), but with emphasis upon artificial intelligence rather than psychology. Apart from the RAND-Carnegie group and the M.I.T. group, however, there were no other large-scale programs of research on problem solving employing computer simulation as a main technique. Moreover, the communication was still weak between these efforts and the other main lines of development in information processing psychology, already mentioned. Among the most important of these were: (1) the burgeoning field of psycholinguistics, whose leading representative within psychology was George A. Miller of Harvard; (2) work in areas like concept formation, deriving from information-theoretic points of view (Carl Hovland of Yale was one of those pursuing this line of inquiry); and (3) research focusing on "vigilance," attention, and the processes of short-term memory—D. E. Broadbent's laboratory being an important example.

Under the auspices of a committee of the Social Science Research Council (Hovland, Miller, and Simon), a summer seminar was organized in 1958 at the RAND Corporation in Santa Monica, under the directorship of Newell and Simon, with the aim of acquainting a wider circle of social scientists, and particularly psychologists, with the computer simulation techniques and their application to the study of human behavior. Lectures and seminars were conducted principally by Newell and Simon, Hovland, Miller, Minsky, and J. C. Shaw. Programming instruction was provided in IPL-IV, then running on the RAND computer, and the curriculum was built mainly around the principal programs that had been constructed or were under construction—especially LT, GPS, the NSS chess program, and EPAM.

In addition to the group that planned and conducted the seminar, the participants included a number of persons who subsequently have played a significant role in developing computer simulation methods, relating those methods to "classical" psychological approaches, and "naturalizing" them on university campuses: Robert B. Abelson, Lawrence T. Alexander, Richard C. Atkinson, William F. Battig, Daniel E. Berlyne, Joseph D. Birch, Jack Block, James S. Coleman, Ward Edwards, Bert F. Green, Jr., Robert L. Hamblin, Lyle V. Jones, Edmund T. Klemmer, Gilbert K. Krulee, Nissim Levy, William N. McPhee, Irvin Pollack, Roger N. Shepard, Gerald H. Shure, and Donald W. Taylor.[5]

The importance of the RAND Seminar in bringing the work of the Carnegie-RAND group into effective relation with the other main streams of information processing psychology can be indicated from some of the subsequent work and writing of various of the participants.[6] Berlyne, in *Structure and Direction in Thinking* (1965), sought to show the relations of information processing psychology, Piagetian psychology, and Hullian learning theory. Abelson's "hot cognition" research (1963) represented one of the earliest attempts to bring concepts of motivation and emotion within the sphere of the information processing approach. Abelson, Coleman, and McPhee were also among the principals who organized the Simulmatics Corporation, an organization which, by its work and example, exercised a major influence in diffusing simulation methods into social psychology.

Green became the senior member of the team that produced the BASEBALL program (Green, Wolf, Chomsky, and Laughery, 1961), an important early investigation applying artificial intelligence ideas to information retrieval. He also directed the RAND Summer Seminars of 1962 and 1963. Hovland, with his student, E. B. Hunt, undertook to construct information processing models of concept formation behavior (see Hunt, 1962; also Shepard, Hovland, and Jenkins, 1961). Taylor extended the information processing approach to problems of motivation, and wrote several expository reviews on problem solving (1960). Shepard endeavored to make the case for information processing to the (then still very skeptical) verbal learning psychologists (1963).

These examples are by no means an exhaustive list of activities whose origin can be traced to the 1958 seminar or which received an impetus from it. Perhaps the most important of all, in terms of its subsequent influence in psychology, was the book *Plans and the Structure of Behavior* which Miller wrote in collaboration with Galanter and Pribram during the year 1958–59. The references and footnotes in that volume give a good picture of the role that the RAND Seminar and the previous work of the RAND-Carnegie group played in its conception, as well as the influence of the other channels of information processing psychology—and particularly the linguistic and "human factor" channels. The Miller, Galanter, and

---

[5] It is interesting that the first two articles in *Human Factors* using the phrase "information processing" prominently were written by Edwards and Klemmer.

[6] These effects of the seminar were further reinforced by additional summer seminars of the same kind held at RAND in the summers of 1962 and 1963.

Pribram book also gives an excellent picture of the "pre-historical" Zeitgeist that complements the account we have given here.

PAST INTO FUTURE

Thus, the basic ideas underlying the theory of this book emerged in the years from late 1954 through 1958. These years seem so critical to us that we have allowed ourselves an almost blow-by-blow account of the significant events of the period as they contributed to the development of this theory.

But the attempt at history—even parochial history—must stop with 1958. The years since this critical period have seen not only a continuation of work in information processing psychology, but a substantial broadening of the relevant efforts, bringing them into much wider domains of developmental psychology, psycholinguistics, and cognitive psychology.[7] The task of assessing these interwoven strands goes beyond the goals of this historical addendum. The review of Hunt (1968) (see also Reitman, 1965) gives access to the work done since 1958 in cognitive simulation, narrowly construed. There is simply no single source for the larger Zeitgeist, but see Newell (1970).

By terminating the history here, we do not wish to imply that all of the important ingredients of our theory had been mixed in by 1958 (though the first drafts of the book go back that far!). A number of the features of the theory, as it finally shapes up in Chapter 14, postdate the critical years. In particular, we would single out (1) the production systems as a preferred form for specifying the IPS and (2) the postulated relation between environment and organism. The genesis of other concepts is often clear. For instance, the problem space obviously derives via a continuous evolutionary path from the concept of heuristic search (first stated explicitly, as far as we can determine, in Newell and Ernst, 1965), which itself was simply an attempt to formulate what seemed common to many of the early artificial intelligence programs.

[7] The phrase "information processing psychology" itself provides an indication of this broadening. The term "information processing" originated in the late fifties in the computer field as a general descriptive term that seemed somewhat less contingent and parochial than "computer science," which also came into use during the same period. Thus, it was the name of choice for two of the encompassing professional organizations formed at that time: the *International Federation of Information Processing Societies* and the *American Federation of Information Processing Societies*. Although the transfer of the phrase from activities of computers to parallel activities of human beings undoubtedly occurred independently in a number of heads, the term was originally identified pretty closely with computer simulation of cognitive processes (see, e.g., Hilgard and Bower, 1966); that is, with the kind of effort from which arose the theory in this book.

But the term has come to apply to parts of human-factors research, to the study of concept formation, attention, short-term memory, verbal learning, and various forms of social psychology. In this, of course, there is not only a spread of the term from its locus as an alternative reading of "computer simulation," but an adaptation of the term directly from its root source in computer science as many psychologists recognized that they had been speaking "information processing psychology" for some time and sought to give a label to the emerging new Zeitgeist.

The production system was one of those happy events, though in minor key, that historians of science often talk about: a rather well-prepared formalism, sitting in wait for a scientific mission. Production systems have a long and diverse history. Their use in symbolic logic starts with Post (see, e.g., Post, 1941), from whom the name is taken. They also show up as Markov algorithms (Markov, 1954). Their use in linguistics, where they are also called rewrite rules, dates from Chomsky (1957). As with so many other notions in computer science, they really entered into wide currency when they became operationalized in programming languages, first in string manipulation systems (COMIT, see Yngve, 1958; and SNOBOL, see Farber, Griswold, and Polansky, 1964) and in compiler translation languages (Floyd, 1961). Thus, they were at hand when the data on human problem solving finally took a form (the PBG) which pointed to their usefulness. Our first use of them was in the chess analysis (Newell and Simon, 1965), which forms the basis of Chapter 12; but it was not until the work on cryptarithmetic (Newell, 1966), presented in Chapter 6, that the connection became fully explicit.

Our view on the shaping of the organism's behavior by the task environment, which is the central concern of Chapter 3 but permeates the book, also has a long history, for the issue has always been very much alive in economics and the related social sciences. Thus, much earlier, one of us could say, "If there were no limits to human rationality, administrative theory would be barren. It would consist of the single precept: 'Always select that alternative, among those available, which will lead to the most complete achievement of your goals.'" (Simon, 1947, p. 240). If one substitutes "psychology" for "administrative theory," one has an adequate statement of the problem addressed in Chapter 3. Yet this theme does not figure prominently in the papers on computer simulation, either ours or others. Nor, to the best of our recollection, was it raised by the critics of simulation. In our own formulations the theme returns again in full force in *The Sciences of the Artificial* (Simon, 1969).

A final element of the theory on which we may comment is the notion of symbolic system, as it is set forth in Chapter 2. From formal logic, information processing inherited an emphasis upon syntax—upon games with arbitrarily defined rules, played with symbol tokens. The meanings of symbols—what they denote—play a muted role in this scheme. When we reintroduce the relation of the information processing system with its environment, with the real world, the reference of symbols again becomes a central concern. Even without external reference, complex processes operating on complex memory structures require addressing schemes so that one symbol can denote another.

Semantics, the denotative aspect of symbol systems, has reemerged as a central concern in information processing, and one reflection of this reemergence is the emphasis on the relation of denoting in our discussion of such systems.

Milton somewhere spoke of "the never-ending flight of future days." We have here reached the point where past joins future—a proper point for a historical addendum to end.

BIBLIOGRAPHY

Author unknown. (1967) Stanford-Russian Chess Match. *SICART Newsletter*, No. 4, 11–12, June 1967. (Published by ACM.)

Abelson, R. P. (1963) Computer simulation of "hot" cognition, *in* S. S. Tompkins & S. Messick (eds.) *Computer Simulation of Personality*. New York: Wiley.

ACM. (1967) *SICART Newsletter*, No. 6, 8–9, October 1967.

Adelson-Velsky, G. M., Arlasarov, B. L. & Uskov, A. C. Programme for playing chess, *in Report on Symposium on the Theory and Computing in the Upper Mantle Problem*. (Translation from Russian; source and date unknown.)

Anderson, S. B. (1957) Problem solving in multiple-goal situations. *Journal of Experimental Psychology*, 54: 297–303.

Ashby, W. E. (1952) *Design for a Brain*. New York: Wiley.

Atkinson, R. C., Bower, G. H. & Crothers, E. J. (1965) *An Introduction to Mathematical Learning Theory*. New York: Wiley.

Backus, J. W. (1960) The syntax and semantics of the proposed international algebraic language of the Zurich ACM-GAMM Conference *in Information Processing*. Paris: UNESCO.

Bales, R. F. (1970) *Personality and Social Roles*. New York: Holt, Rinehart & Winston.

Bartlett, F. C. (1932) *Remembering*. Cambridge: Cambridge University Press.

Bartlett, F. C. (1958) *Thinking*. New York: Basic Books.

Baylor, G. W., Jr. (1965) Report on a mating combinations program. SP-2150. Santa Monica, California: System Development Corporation.

Baylor, G. W., Jr. & Simon, H. A. (1966) A chess mating combinations program. *AFIPS Conference Proceedings, 1966 Spring Joint Computer Conference*, 28:431–447. Washington, D. C.: Spartan Books.

Berliner, Hans J. (1969) Chess playing program. *SICART Newsletter*, No. 19, 19–20, August 1969.

Berlyne, D. E. (1965) *Structure and Direction in Thinking*. New York: Wiley.

Bernstein, A. (1958) A chess-playing program for the IBM-704. *Chess Review*, 208–209, July 1958.

Bernstein, A., Roberts, M. deV., Arbuckle, T. & Belsky, M. A. (1958) A chess-playing program for the IBM-704. *Proceedings of the 1958 Western Joint Computer Conference*, 157–159.

Bernstein, N. (1967) *The Coordination and Regulation of Movement*. New York: Pergamon Press.

Boring, E. G. (1933) *The Physical Dimensions of Consciousness*. Watkins Glen, N. Y.: Century.

Boring, E. G. (1946) Mind and mechanism. *American Journal of Psychology*, 59: 173–192.

Bowden, B. V. (ed.) (1953) *Faster Than Thought*. New York: Pitman.

Broadbent, D. E. (1954) A mechanical model for human attention and immediate memory. *Psychological Review*, 64: 205.

Broadbent, D. E. (1958) *Perception and Communication*. New York: Pergamon Press.

Brookes, M. (1963) *150 Puzzles in Cryptarithmetic*. New York: Dover.

Bruner, J. S., Goodnow, J. J. & Austin, G. A. (1956) *A Study of Thinking*. New York: Wiley.

Brunswik, Egon (1956) *Perception and the Representative Design of Psychological Experiments*. Berkeley: University of California Press.

Bugelski, B. R. (1962) Presentation time, total time, and mediation in paired-associate learning. *Journal of Experimental Psychology*, 63: 409–412.

Buswell, G. T. (1935) *How People Look At Pictures*. Chicago: University of Chicago Press.

Carpenter, J. A., Moore, O. K., Snyder, C. R. & Lisansky, Edith S. (1961) Alcohol and higher-order problem solving. *Quarterly Journal of Studies on Alcohol*, 22: 183–222.

Chapman, R., *et al.* (1959) The System Research Laboratory's air defense experiments. *Management Science*, 5: 250–269.

Chomsky, A. N. (1953) Logical syntax and semantics: their linguistic relevance. *Language*, 31: 36–45.

Chomsky, A. N. (1956) Three models for the description of language. *IRE Transactions on Information Theory*, IT-2(3): 113–124.

Chomsky, A. N. (1957) *Syntactic Structures*. The Hague: Mouton.

Chomsky, A. N. (1965) *Aspects of the Theory of Syntax*. Cambridge, Mass.: M.I.T. Press.

Collins, N. L. & Michie, E. (eds.) (1967) *Machine Intelligence 1*. New York: American Elsevier.

Dale, E. & Michie, D. (eds.) (1968) *Machine Intelligence 2*. New York: American Elsevier.

Dansereau, D. (1969) An information processing model of mental multiplication. Unpublished doctoral dissertation, Carnegie-Mellon University.

Dansereau, D. & Gregg, L. W. (1966) An information processing analysis of mental multiplication. *Psychonomic Science*, 6: 71–72.

Dewey, John (1910) *How We Think*. Boston: D. C. Heath.

Dineen, G. P. (1956) Programming pattern recognition. *Proceedings of the 1955 Western Joint Computer Conference*, 7: 94–100.

Duncker, K. (1945) On problem solving. *Psychological Monographs*, 58: 5 (Whole No. 270).

Ebbinghaus, H. (1964) *Memory*. New York: Dover.

Edwards, W., Lindman, H. & Phillips, L. D. (1965) Emerging technologies for making decisions, *in* T. M. Newcomb (ed.) *New Directions in Psychology*, 2: 259–325. New York: Holt, Rinehart & Winston.

Elsasser, W. M. (1958) *The Physical Foundation of Biology*. New York: Pergamon Press.

Ernst, G. W. (1969) Sufficiency conditions for the success of GPS. *Journal of the ACM*, 16: 517–533.

Ernst, G. W. & Newell, A. (1967a) GPS and generality. Pittsburgh: Carnegie Institute of Technology.

Ernst, G. W. & Newell, A. (1967b) Some issues of representation in a general problem solver. *Proceedings of the Spring Joint Computer Conference*, 583–600.

Ernst, G. W. & Newell, A. (1969) *GPS: A Case Study in Generality and Problem Solving*. New York: Academic Press.

Farber, D. J., Griswold, R. E. & Polonsky, I. P. (1964) SNOBOL, a string manipulation language. *Journal of the ACM*, 11: 21–30.

Feigenbaum, E. A. (1961) The simulation of verbal learning behavior. *Proceedings of the Western Joint Computer Conference*, 121–132.

Feigenbaum, E. A. (1968) Artificial intelligence: themes in the second decade. Final supplement to *Proceedings of 1968 International Congress*, International Federation of Information Processing Societies. Edinburgh.

Feigenbaum, E.A. & Feldman, J. (eds.) (1963) *Computers and Thought*. New York: McGraw-Hill.

Fikes, R. (1970) REF:ARF: A system for solving problems stated as procedures. *Artificial Intelligence Journal*, 1: No. 1.

Fine, R. (1948) *Practical Chess Openings*. New York: David McKay Co.

Fine, R. (1952) *Middle Game in Chess*. New York: David McKay Co.

Fine, R. (1967) *The Psychology of the Chess Player*. New York: Dover.

Floyd, R. W. (1961) An algorithm for coding efficient arithmetic operations. *Communications of the ACM*, 4: 42–51.

von Foerster, H. (ed.) (1955) *Transactions of the 10th Macy Conference on Cybernetics*. New York: The Josiah Macy, Jr., Foundation.

Gagné, R. M. & Paradise, N. E. (1961) Abilities and learning sets in knowledge acquisision. *Psychological Monographs*, 75: Whole No. 518.

Gagné, R. N. & Smith, E. C., Jr. (1962) A study of the effects of verbalization on problem solving. *Journal of Experimental Psychology*, 63: 12–18.

Garner, W. R. (1962) *Uncertainty and Structure as Psychological Concepts*. New York: Wiley.

Geldard, F. (1953) *The Human Senses*. New York: Wiley.

Gelernter, H. (1960) Realization of a geometry theorem proving machine. *Proceedings of 1959 International Conference on Information Processing*, 273–282. Paris: UNESCO.

Gelernter, H., Hansen, J. R. & Loveland, D. W. (1960) Empirical exploration of the geometry theorem machine. *Proceedings of the 1960 Western Joint Computer Conference*, 143–147.

Gibson, E. J. (1940) A systematic application of the concepts of generalization and differentiation to verbal learning. *Psychological Review*, 47: 196–229.

Gibson, J. J. (1966) *The Senses Considered as a Perceptual System.* Boston: Houghton Mifflin.

Green, B. F., Wolf, A. K., Chomsky, C. & Laughery, K. (1961) Baseball: an automatic question answerer. *Proceedings of the Western Joint Computer Conference,* 219–224.

Greenblatt, R. B., Eastlake, D. E. & Crocker, S. D. (1967) The Greenblatt Chess Program. *Proceedings of the 1967 Joint Computer Conference,* 30: 801–810.

Gregg, L. W. & Simon, H. A. (1967a) Process models and stochastic theories of simple concept formation. *Journal of Mathematical Psychology,* 4: 246–276.

Gregg, L. W. & Simon, H. A. (1967b) An information-processing explanation of one-trial and incremental learning. *Journal of Verbal Learning and Verbal Behavior,* 6: 780–787.

Gregory, R. L. (1966) *Eye and Brain.* New York: McGraw-Hill.

de Groot, A. D. (1946) *Het Denken van den Schaker.* Amsterdam: N. H. Utig. Mij.

de Groot, A. D. (1965) *Thought and Choice in Chess.* The Hague: Mouton.

de Groot, A. D. (1966) Perception and memory versus thinking, *in* B. Kleinmuntz (ed.) *Problem Solving.* New York: Wiley.

Guilbaud, G. T. (1959) *What Is Cybernetics?* New York: Criterion Books.

Haber, R. N. (ed.) (1969) *Information Processing Approaches to Visual Perception.* New York: Holt, Rinehart & Winston.

Hanson, N. R. (1961) *Patterns of Discovery.* Cambridge: The University Press.

Harris, Z. S. (1951) *Methods in Structural Linguistics.* Chicago: University of Chicago Press.

Hebb, D. O. (1949) *The Organization of Behavior.* New York: Wiley.

Hick, W. E. (1952) On the rate of gain of information. *Quarterly Journal of Experimental Psychology,* 4: 11–26.

Hilgard, E. R. & Bower, G. H. *Theories of Learning* (3rd edition). New York: Appleton-Century-Crofts.

Hovland, C. I. (1938a) Experimental studies of rote learning theory, II. *Journal of Experimental Psychology,* 22: 338–353.

Hovland, C. I. (1938b) Experimental studies of rote learning theory, III. *Journal of Experimental Psychology,* 23: 172–190.

Hovland, C. I. (1940) Experimental studies of rote learning theory, VII. *Journal of Experimental Psychology,* 27: 271–284.

Hovland, C. I. (1949) Experimental studies of rote learning theory, VIII. *Journal of Experimental Psychology,* 39: 714–718.

Hovland, C. I. (1952) A "communicational analysis" of concept learning. *Psychological Review,* 59: 461–472.

Hull, C. L. (1920) Quantitative aspects of the evolution of concepts. *Psychological Monographs,* 28: (Whole No. 123).

Humphrey, G. (1951) *Thinking.* New York: Wiley.

Hunt, E. B. (1962) *Concept Formation.* New York: Wiley.

Hunt, E. B. (1968) Computer simulation: artificial intelligence studies and their relevance to psychology, *in Annual Review of Psychology,* 19: 135–168.

Hunt, E. B. & Hovland, C. I. (1961) Programming a model of human concept formation. *Proceedings of the Western Joint Computer Conference,* 19: 145–155.

John, E. R. (1967) *Mechanisms of Memory.* New York: Academic Press.

Jongman, R. W. (1968) *Het Oog van de Meester.* Amsterdam: van Gorcum and Company.

Kanal, Laveen N. (ed.) (1968) *Pattern Recognition.* Washington, D. C.: Thompson Book Company.

Katona, G. (1940) *Organizing and Memorizing.* New York: Columbia University Press.

Kendler, H. H. (1961) Problems in problem-solving research, *in Current Trends in Psychological Theory: A Bicentennial Program*, 180–207. Pittsburgh: University of Pittsburgh Press.

King, James. (1969) The program verifier. Unpublished doctoral dissertation, Carnegie-Mellon University.

Kister, J., Stein, P., Ulam, S., Walden, W. & Wells, M. (1957) Experiments in chess. *Journal of the ACM*, 4: 174–177.

Kleene, S. C. (1952) *Introduction to Metamathematics.* New York: van Nostrand.

Knuth, D. E. (1968) *The Art of Computer Programming*, Vol. 1, Fundamental Algorithms. Reading, Mass.: Addison-Wesley.

Konig, Denes. (1956) *Theorie der Endlicken und Unendlicken Graphen.* Leipzig: Akademische Verlagsgesellschaft.

Kotok, A. (1962) A chess playing program for the IBM-7090. Unpublished bachelor's thesis, Massachusetts Institute of Technology.

Landauer, T. K. (1962) Rate of implicit speech. *Perceptual and Motor Skills*, 15: 646.

Lasker, E. (1959) *The Adventure of Chess* (second revised edition). New York: Dover.

Lawler, E. L. & Wood, D. E. (1966) Branch-and-bound methods: a survey. *Operations Research*, 14: 699–714.

Lettvin, J. Y., Maturana, H., McCulloch, W. S. & Pitts, W. (1949) What the frog's eye tells the frog's brain. *Proceedings of the IRE*, 47: 1940–1951.

Lindsay, R. K. (1961) Toward the development of machines which comprehend. Unpublished doctoral dissertation, Carnegie Institute of Technology.

Lindsay, R. K. (1963) Inferential memory as the basis of machines which understand natural language, *in* E. A. Feigenbaum & J. Feldman (eds.) *Computers and Thought.* New York: McGraw-Hill.

Locke, W. N. & Booth, A. D. (eds.) (1955) *Machine Translation of Languages.* New York: Wiley.

Lotka, A. J. (1924) *Elements of Physical Biology.* Baltimore: Williams & Wilkens.

Luchins, A. S. (1942) Mechanization in problem solving. *Psychological Monographs*, 54(6), Whole No. 248.

Lyon, D. O. (1914) The relation of length of material to time taken for learning. *Journal of Educational Psychology*, 5: 1–19, 85–91, 155–163.

McCarthy, J. (1956) The inversion of functions defined by Turing machines, in C. E. Shannon & J. McCarthy (eds.) *Automata Studies, Annals of Mathematics Studies*, 34: 177–181. Princeton, N.J.: Princeton University.

McClelland, D. C. (1955) The psychology of mental content reconsidered. *Psychological Review*, 62: 297–320.

Mackworth, N. H. (1965) Visual noise causes tunnel vision. *Psychonomic Science*, 3: 67–68.

Mackworth, N. H. & Mackworth, J. F. (1958) Eye fixations recorded on changing visual scenes by the television eye-marker. *Journal of the Optical Society*, 48: 439–445.

March, J. G. & Simon, H. A. (1958) *Organizations.* New York: Wiley.

Markov, A. A. (1954) *Theory of Algorithms.* Moscow: National Academy of Sciences, U. S. S. R.

Meltzer, B. & Michie, D. (eds.) (1969) *Machine Intelligence 4.* New York: American Elsevier.

Michie, D. (ed.) (1968) *Machine Intelligence 3.* New York: American Elsevier.

Michon, J. A. (1967) The game of JAM—an isomorph of tic-tac-toe. *American Journal of Psychology*, 80: 137–140.

Millenson, J. R. (1967) *Principles of Behavioral Analysis*. New York: Macmillan.

Miller, G. A. (1956) The magical number seven, plus or minus two. *Psychological Review*, 63: 81–97.

Miller, G. A. & Frick, F. C. (1949) Statistical behavioristics and sequences of responses. *Psychological Review*, 56: 311–329.

Miller, G. A., Galanter, E. & Pribram, K. H. (1960) *Plans and the Structure of Behavior*. New York: Holt, Rinehart & Winston.

Minsky, M. (1961) Steps toward artificial intelligence. *Proceedings of the IRE*, 49: 8–29.

Minsky, M. (1967) *Computation: Finite and Infinite Machines*. Englewood Cliffs, N.J.: Prentice-Hall.

Minsky, M. (ed.) (1968) *Semantic Information Processing*. Cambridge, Mass.: Massachusetts Institute of Technology Press.

Minsky, M. & Papert, S. (1969) *Perceptrons*. Cambridge, Mass.: Massachusetts Institute of Technology Press.

Moore, O. K. & Anderson, S. B. (1954a) Modern logic and tasks for experiments on problem solving behavior. *Journal of Psychology*, 38: 151–160.

Moore, O. K. & Anderson, S. B. (1954b) Search behavior in individual and group problem solving. *American Sociological Review*, 19: 702–714.

More, T., Jr. (1957) Deductive logic for automata. Unpublished master's thesis, Massachusetts Institute of Technology.

Moses, J. (1967) Symbolic interpretation. Unpublished doctoral dissertation, Massachusetts Institute of Technology.

Neisser, U. (1963) The imitation of man by machine. *Science*, 139: 193–197.

Neisser, U. (1967) *Cognitive Psychology*. New York: Appleton-Century-Crofts.

von Neumann, J. (1958) *The Computer and the Brain*. New Haven: Yale University Press.

Newell, A. (1955) The chess machine: an example of dealing with a complex task by adaptation. *Proceedings of the Western Joint Computer Conference*, 101–108.

Newell, A. (ed.) (1961) *Information Processing Language V Manual*. Englewood Cliffs, N. J.: Prentice-Hall.

Newell, A. (1962) Some problems of basic organization in problem-solving programs, *in* M. C. Yovits, G. T. Jacobi & G. D. Goldstein (eds.) *Self-Organizing Systems*, 293–423. Washington, D. C.: Spartan Books.

Newell, A. (1963a) Artificial intelligence in engineering. *The Indian and Eastern Engineer*, 104th Anniversary Number, 185–189.

Newell, A. (1963b) Documentation of IPL-V. *Communications of the ACM*, 6: 86–89.

Newell, A. (1963c) A guide to the General Problem Solver Program 2–2. RAND RM-3337, 148p., February.

Newell, A. (1963d) Learning, generality, and problem solving, *Proceedings of the IFIP Congress*, 62: 407–412. Amsterdam: North-Holland Publishing Company.

Newell, A. (1964) The possibility of planning languages in man-computer communication, *in* F. Geldard (ed.) *Communication Processes*, 238–259. New York: Pergamon Press.

Newell, A. (1965) Limitations of the current stock of ideas for problem solving, *in* A. Kent & O. Taulbee (eds.) *Conference on Electronic Information Handling*, 195–208. Washington, D. C.: Spartan Books.

Newell, A. (1966a) Discussion of papers by Dr. Gagné and Dr. Hayes, *in* B. Kleinmuntz (ed.) *Problem Solving: Research, Method, and Theory*, 171–182. New York: Wiley.

Newell, A. (1966b) On the representations of problems. *Computer Science Research Review*, 18–33. Pittsburgh: Carnegie Institute of Technology.

Newell, A. (1967a) Eye movements and problem solving. *Computer Science Research Review*, 29–40. Pittsburgh: Carnegie-Mellon University.

Newell, A. (1967b) The nature of information in living systems, *in* D. M. Ramsey (ed.) *Molecular Coding Problems*, 23–113. New York: New York Academy of Sciences.

Newell, A. (1967c) Studies in problem solving: subject 3 on the cryptarithmetic task: DONALD + GERALD = ROBERT. Pittsburgh: Carnegie-Mellon University.

Newell, A. (1968a) Judgment and its representation: an introduction, *in* B. Kleinmuntz (ed.) *Formal Representation of Human Judgment*, 1–16. New York: Wiley.

Newell, A. (1968b) On the analysis of human problem solving protocols, *in* J. C. Gardin & B. Jaulin, *Calcul et Formalisation dans les Sciences de L'Homme*, 146–185. Paris: Centre National de la Récherche Scientifique.

Newell, A. (1968c) The trip towards flexibility, *in* G. Bugliarello (ed.) *Bio-Engineering—An Engineering View*, 269–285. San Francisco: San Francisco Press.

Newell, A. (1969a) Heuristic programming: ill-structured problems, *in* J. Aronofsky (ed.) *Progress in Operations Research, Vol. III*, 360–414. New York: Wiley.

Newell, A. (1969b) Thoughts on the concept of progress, *in* J. F. Voss (ed.) *Approaches to Thought*, 196–208. Columbus, Ohio: Merrill Publishing Company.

Newell, A. (1970) Remarks on the relationship between artificial intelligence and cognitive psychology, *in* R. B. Banerji & M. D. Mesarovic (eds.) *Theoretical Approaches to Non-Numerical Problem Solving*. Berlin: Springer-Verlag.

Newell, A. & Ernst, G. W. (1965) The search for generality, *in* E. W. Kelenich (ed.) *Proceedings of the IFIP Congress-65*, 17–24. Washington, D. C.: Spartan Books.

Newell, A. & Shaw, J. C. (1957) Programming the logic theory machine. *Proceedings of the Western Joint Computer Conference*, 230–240.

Newell, A., Shaw, J. C. & Simon, H. A. (1957a) Problem solving in humans and computers. *Carnegie Technical*, Vol. 21, No. 4, 34–38.

Newell, A., Shaw, J. C. & Simon, H. A. (1957b) Empirical explorations of the logic theory machine: a case study in heuristics. *Proceedings of the Joint Computer Conference*, 218–230.

Newell, A., Shaw, J. C. & Simon, H. A. (1957c) Preliminary description of the General Problem Solving Program I (GPS I). CIP Working Paper No. 7, December.

Newell, A., Shaw, J. C. & Simon, H. A. (1958a) Note: improvement in the proof of a theorem in the elementary propositional calculus. CIP Working Paper No. 8, 4 p., January.

Newell, A., Shaw, J. C. & Simon, H. A. (1958b) Elements of a theory of human problem solving. *Psychological Review*, 65: 151–166.

Newell, A., Shaw, J. C. & Simon, H. A. (1958c) Chess-playing programs and the problem of complexity. *IBM Journal of Research and Development*, 2: 320–335.

Newell, A., Shaw, J. C. & Simon, H. A. (1959a) Report on the play of chess player I-5 of a book game of Morphy vs. Duke Karl of Brunswick and Count Isouard. CIP Working Paper No. 21, 14 p., April.

Newell, A., Shaw, J. C. & Simon, H. A. (1960a) Report on a general problem-solving program for a computer. *Information Processing: Proceedings of the International Conference on Information Processing*, 256–264. Paris: UNESCO.

Newell, A., Shaw, J. C. & Simon, H. A. (1960b) A variety of intelligent learning in a general problem solver, *in* M. C. Yovits & S. Cameron (eds.) *Self-Organizing Systems: Proceedings of an Interdisciplinary Conference*, 153–189. New York: Pergamon Press.

Newell, A., Shaw, J. C. & Simon, H. A. (1962) The processes of creative thinking, *in* H. E. Gruber, G. Terrell & M. Wertheimer (eds.) *Contemporary Approaches to Creative Thinking*, 63–119. New York: Atherton Press.

Newell, A. & Simon, H. A. (1956a) Current developments in complex information processing, 37 p. Santa Monica: The RAND Corporation.

Newell, A. & Simon, H. A. (1956b) The Logic Theory Machine: a complex information processing system. *IRE Transactions on Information Theory*, Vol. IT-2, No. 3, 61–79.

Newell, A. & Simon, H. A. (1961a) GPS, a program that simulates human thought, *in* H. Billing (ed.) *Lernende Automaten*, 109–124. Munchen: R. Oldenbourg.

Newell, A. & Simon, H. A. (1961b) The simulation of human thought, *in Current Trends in Psychological Theory*, 152–179. Pittsburgh: University of Pittsburgh Press.

Newell, A. & Simon, H. A. (1961c) Computer simulation of human thinking. *Science*, 134: 2011–2017.

Newell, A. & Simon, H. A. (1962) Computer simulation of human thinking and problem solving, *in* M. Greenberger (ed.) *Management and the Computer of the Future*, 94–113. New York: Wiley.

Newell, A. & Simon, H. A. (1963) Computers in psychology, *in* R. D. Luce, R. R. Bush & E. Galanter (eds.) *Handbook of Mathematical Psychology*, Vol. 1, 361–428.

Newell, A. & Simon, H. A. (1964) Problem solving machines. *Science and Technology*, Vol. 3, No. 36, 48–62, December.

Newell, A. & Simon, H. A. (1965a) Simulation of human processing of information. *American Mathematical Monthly*, 72: 111–118.

Newell, A. & Simon, H. A. (1965b) An example of human chess play in the light of chess playing programs, *in* N. Wiener & J. P. Schade (eds.) *Progress in Biocybernetics*, Vol. 2, 19–75. Amsterdam: Elsevier Publishing Company.

Newell, A. & Simon, H. A. (1965c) Programs as theories of higher mental processes, *in* R. W. Stacey & B. Waxman (eds.) *Computers in Biomedical Research*, Vol. 2, 141–172. New York: Academic Press.

Newell, A. & Simon, H. A. (1967) Overview: memory and process in concept formation, *in* B. Kleinmuntz (ed.) *Concepts and the Structure of Memory*, 241–262. New York: Wiley.

Newell, A. & Simon, H. A. (1968) Simulation: individual behavior, *in* D. L. Sills (ed.) *International Encyclopedia of the Social Sciences*, Vol. 14, 262–268. New York: Macmillan and The Free Press.

Newell, A. & Tonge, F. M. (1960) An introduction to Information Processing Language, V. *Communications of the ACM*, 3: 205–211.

Newell, A., Tonge, F. M., Feigenbaum, E. A., Green, B. F., Kelly, H. A. & Mealy, G. (1964) *Information Processing Language V Manual* (2nd edition). Englewood Cliffs, N. J.: Prentice-Hall.

Newman, C. & Uhr, L. (1965) BOGART: a discovery and induction program for games. *Proceedings of the 20th ACM National Conference*, 176–186.

Nilsson, N. (1965) *Learning Machines*. New York: McGraw-Hill.

Noordzij, P. (1967) Registratie van oogbewegingen bij schakers. Doctoraalwerkstuk, Psychology Lab., University van Amsterdam.

Olshavsky, R. (1965) Reaction time measures of information processing behavior. Unpublished master's thesis, Carnegie Institute of Technology.

Paige, J. M. & Simon, H. A. (1966) Cognitive processes in solving algebra word problems, *in* B. Kleinmuntz (ed.) *Problem Solving*, 51–119. New York: Wiley.

Peirce, C. S. (1937) *Collected Papers*, Vol. 5, 145–146. Cambridge, Mass.: Harvard University Press.

Pitrat, Jacques (1966) Réalisation de programmes de démonstration de théorèmes utilisant des méthodes heuristiques. Doctoral thesis: Faculty of Sciences, Université de Paris. (Privately published.)

Pittenger, R. E., Hockett, C. F. & Danehy, J. J. (1960) *The First Five Minutes: A Sample of Microscopic Interview Analysis*. Ithaca, N. Y.: Paul Martineau.

Pitts, W. & McCulloch, W. S. (1943) A logical calculus of the ideas immanent in nervous activity. *Bulletin of Mathematical Biophysics*, 5: 115–137.

Pohl, Ira (1969) Bi-directional and heuristic search in path problems. Unpublished doctoral dissertation, Stanford University.

Polya, G. (1957) *How To Solve It*. Garden City, L. I.: Doubleday-Anchor.

Post, E. L. (1943) Formal reductions of the general combinatorial decision problem. *American Journal of Mathematics*, 65: 197–268.

Quastler, H. (1955) *Information Theory in Psychology*. New York: The Free Press.

Quinlan, J. R. & Hunt, E. B. (1968) A formal deductive problem solving system. *Journal of the ACM*, 15: 625–646.

Reitman, W. R. (1965) *Cognition and Thought*. New York: Wiley.

Resnick, L. B. & Wang, M. C. (1969) Approaches to the validation of learning hierarchies. *Proceedings of the 18th Annual Regional Conference on Testing Problems*. Princeton, N.J.: Educational Testing Service.

Robinson, J. A. (1965) A machine oriented logic based on the resolution principle. *Journal of the ACM*, 12: 23–41.

Rosenbluth, A., Wiener, N. & Bigelow, J. (1943) Behavior, purpose and teleology. *Philosophy of Science*, 10: 18–24.

Rubenfeld, J. S. (1968) Two games by the Rubenfeld Chess Program. *SICART Newsletter*, No. 12, 8–9, October.

Schachter, S. & Singer, J. (1962) Cognitive, social, and physiological determinants of emotional state. *Psychological Review*, 69: 379–399.

Scott, T. T. (1969) A chess game between the MACHAC and the chess program in the University of Lancaster, England. *SICART Newsletter*, No. 16, 9–11, June.

Selfridge, O. F. (1955) Pattern recognition and modern computers. *Proceedings of the 1955 Joint Computer Conference*, 7: 91–93.

Selz, O. (1913) *Uber die Gesetze des Geordneten Denkverlaufs, I*. Stuttgart: Spemann.

Selz, O. (1924) *Die Gesetze der Produktiven und Reproduktiven Geistestätigkeit* (kurzgefasste Darstellung). Bonn.

Sergeant, P. W. (1957) *Morphy's Games of Chess*. New York: Dover.

Shannon, C. E. (1938) A symbolic analysis of relay and switching circuits. *Transactions of the American Institute of Electrical Engineers*, 57: 1–11.

Shannon, C. E. (1950) Programming a computer for playing chess. *Philosophical Magazine*, 41: 256–275.

Shaw, J. C., Newell, A., Simon, H. A. & Ellis, T. O. (1958) A command structure for complex information processing. *Proceedings of the 1958 Western Joint Computer Conference*, 119–128.

Shepard, R. N. (1963) Comments on Professor Underwood's paper, *in* C. N. Cofer & Barbara S. Musgrave (eds.) *Verbal Behavior and Learning*, 48–70. New York: McGraw-Hill.

Shepard, R. N., Hovland, C. I. & Jenkins, H. M. (1961) Learning and memorization of classifications. *Psychological Monographs*, Whole No. 517.

Simon, H. A. (1944) Decision-making and administrative organization. *Public Administration Review*, 4: 16–31.

Simon, H. A. (1947) *Administrative Behavior*. New York: Macmillan.

Simon, H. A. (1955) A behavioral model of rational choice. *Quarterly Journal of Economics*, 69: 99–118.

Simon, H. A. (1956) Rational choice and the structure of the environment. *Psychological Review*, 63: 129–138.

Simon, H. A. (1962) An information-processing theory of intellectual development, *in* W. Kessen & C. Kuhlman (eds.) *Thought in the Young Child. Monographs of the Society for Research in Child Development*, 27: 150–161. Yellow Springs, Ohio: The Antioch Press.

Simon, H. A. (1966a) Thinking by computers, *in* R. G. Colodny (ed.) *Mind and Cosmos: Essays in Contemporary Science and Philosophy*, 3–21. Pittsburgh: University of Pittsburgh Press.

Simon, H. A. (1966b) Scientific discovery and the psychology of problem solving, *in* R. G. Colodny (ed.) *Mind and Cosmos: Essays in Contemporary Science and Philosophy*, 22–40. Pittsburgh: University of Pittsburgh Press.

Simon, H. A. (1967a) Motivational and emotional controls of cognition. *Psychological Review*, 74: 29–39.

Simon, H. A. (1967b) An information-processing explanation of some perceptual phenomena. *British Journal of Psychology*, 58: 1–12.

Simon, H. A. (1969) *The Sciences of the Artificial*. Cambridge, Mass.: The M.I.T. Press.

Simon, H. A. & Barenfeld, M. (1969) Information-processing analysis of perceptual processes in problem solving. *Psychological Review*, 76: 473–483.

Simon, H. A. & Feigenbaum, E. A. (1964) An information-processing theory of some effects of similarity, familiarization, and meaningfulness in verbal learning. *Journal of Verbal Learning and Verbal Behavior*, 3: 385–396.

Simon, H. A. & Kotovsky, K. (1963) Human acquisition of concepts for sequential patterns. *Psychological Review*, 70: 534–546.

Simon, H. A. & Newell, A. (1956) Models: their uses and limitations, *in* L. D. White (ed.) *The State of the Social Sciences*, 66–83. Chicago: University of Chicago Press.

Simon, H. A. & Newell, A. (1958a) Heuristic problem solving: the next advance in operations research. *Operations Research*, 6: 1–10.

Simon, H. A. & Newell, A. (1958b) Reply: heuristic problem solving. *Operations Research*, 6: 449–450.

Simon, H. A. & Newell, A. (1958c) Simulation of cognitive processes: a report on the summer research training institute. Social Science Research Council, *Items*, 17: 37–40.

Simon, H. A. & Newell, A. (1964) Information processing in computer and man. *American Scientist*, 53: 281–300.

Simon, H. A. & Newell, A. (1965) Heuristic problem solving by computer, *in* M. A. Sass & W. D. Wilkinson (eds.) *Computer Augmentation of Human Reasoning*, 25–36. Washington, D. C.: Spartan Books.

Simon, H. A. & Simon, P. A. (1962) Trial and error search in solving difficult problems: evidence from the game of chess. *Behavioral Science*, 7: 425–429.

Simon, H. A. & Sumner, R. K. (1968) Pattern in music, *in* B. Kleinmuntz (ed.) *Formal Representation of Human Judgment*, 219–250. New York: Wiley.

Skinner, B. F. (1953) *Science and Human Behavior*. New York: Macmillan.

Slagle, J. R. & Dixon, J. K. (1969) Experiments with some programs that search game trees. *Journal of the ACM*, 16: 189–207.

Smith, R. C., Jr. (1969) The SCHACH chess program. *SICART Newsletter*, No. 15, 8–12, April.

Soskin, W. F. & John, V. P. (1963) The study of spontaneous talk, *in* R. G. Barber (ed.) *The Stream of Behavior*. New York: Appleton-Century-Crofts.

Sperling, G. (1960) The information available in brief visual presentations. *Psychological Monographs*, 74: (Whole No. 498).

Steffrud, E. (1963) The logic theory machine: a model heuristic program. Santa Monica: THE RAND Corporation. (Mimeo)

Stein, P. & Ulam, S. (1957) Experiments in chess on electronic computing machines. *Computers and Automation*, 6: 14.

Sternberg, S. (1966) High speed scanning in human memory. *Science*, 153: 652–654.

Stone, P. J., Dunphy, D. C., Smith, M. S. & Ogilvie, D. M. (1966) *The General Inquirer*. Cambridge, Mass.: M.I.T. Press.

Strachey, C. S. (1952) Logical or non-mathematical programmes. *Proceedings of the ACM*, 1952.

Taylor, D. W. (1960) Thinking and creativity. *Annals of the New York Academy of Sciences*, 91: 108–127.

Tichomirov, O. K. & Poznyanskaya, E. D. (1966) An investigation of visual search as a means of analyzing heuristics. *Soviet Psychology*, 5: 2–15. [Translated from *Voprosy Psikhologii*, 2(4): 39–53.]

Tiffin, J. (ed.) (1937) Studies in psychology of reading. *Psychological Monographs*, 215.

Tolman, E. C. (1932) *Purposive Behavior in Animals and Men*. Watkins Glen, N. Y.: Century.

Tolman, E. C. & Brunswik, F. (1935) The organism and the causal texture of the environment. *Psychological Review*, 42: 43–77.

Turing, A. M. (1936) On computable numbers, with an application to the Entscheidungsproblem. *Proceedings of the London Mathematics Society* (Series 2), 42: 230–265.

Turing, A. M. (1950) Computing machinery and intelligence. *Mind*, 59: 433–450.

Underwood, B. J. & Schultz, R. W. (1960) *Meaningfulness and Verbal Learning*. Philadelphia: Lippincott.

Uspensky, J. V. & Heaslet, M. A. (1939) *Elementary Number Theory*. New York: McGraw-Hill.

Walter, W. F. (1953) *The Living Brain*. New York: Norton.

Waterman, D. (1970) Generalization learning techniques for automating the learning of heuristics. *Artificial Intelligence*, 1: 121–170.

Waugh, N. & Norman, D. A. (1965) Primary memory. *Psychological Review*, 76: 89–104.

Weizenbaum, J. (1966) ELIZA—a computer program for the study of natural language communication between man and machine. *Journal of the ACM*, 9: 36–45.

Wertheimer, M. (1945) *Productive Thinking*. New York: Harper & Row.

Whitehead, A. N. & Russell, Bertrand (1935) *Principia Mathematica*. Cambridge: The University Press. [Volume I, second edition, reprinted.]

Wiener, N. (1948) *Cybernetics*. New York: Wiley.

Wilkes, M. V., Wheeler, D. J. & Gill, S. (1951) *The Preparation of Programs for an Electronic Digital Computer*. Reading, Mass.: Addison-Wesley.

Williams, D. S. (1969) Computer program organization induced by problem examples. Unpublished doctoral dissertation, Carnegie-Mellon University.

Williams, T. G. (1965) Some studies in game playing with a digital computer. Unpublished doctoral dissertation, Carnegie Institute of Technology.

Winikoff, A. (1967) Eye movements as an aid to protocol analysis of problem solving behavior. Unpublished doctoral dissertation, Carnegie-Mellon University.

Woodworth, R. S. (1938) *Experimental Psychology*. New York: Holt.

Woodworth, R. S. & Schlossberg, H. (1961) *Experimental Psychology*. New York: Holt, Rinehart & Winston.

Yarbus, A. L. (1967) *Eye Movements and Vision*. New York: Plenum Publishing Corporation.

Yngve, V. H. (1958) A programming language for mechanical translation. *Mechanical Translation*, 5: 25–41.

INDEX

AUTHOR INDEX